STANDARD CATALOG OF®
FORD
1903-2002

100 YEARS OF HISTORY, PHOTOS, TECHNICAL DATA AND PRICING

JOHN GUNNELL

Published by

Krause Publications, a division of F+W Media, Inc.
700 East State Street • Iola, WI 54990-0001
715-445-2214 • 888-457-2873
www.krausebooks.com

To order books or other products call toll-free 1-800-258-0929
or visit us online at www.krausebooks.com or www.ShopOldCarsWeekly.com

ISBN-13: 978-1-4402-3036-3
ISBN-10: 1-4402-3036-6

Edited by Old Cars Weekly staff

Printed in United States of America

Ford Motor Company

Henry Ford built his first car in the summer of 1896. Charles Ainsley gave $200 for it and Ford used the money to finance his second car. Several attempts to form a car company followed and in June 16, 1903, the Ford Motor Co. was formed. In October of 1908, the Model T arrived. Henry Ford was finished experimenting. The T lasted almost two decades.

By 1926, after building 15 million Model Ts, even Ford had to admit it was outdated. It was followed by the ubiquitous Model A. From 1927-March 1932, five million As were made. Then, the flathead V-8 arrived, offering 65 hp for $460. This car changed it's styling annually, but the flathead V-8 survived through the '50s. In 1935, it outsold Chevrolet, America's best-selling car. The Ford got four-wheel hydraulic brakes in 1939. A six was introduced in 1941.

On May 26, 1943, Henry's son Edsel died. Henry became president of the Ford. When he died in 1947, Ford started moving into the modern age. New postwar envelope body styling was introduced and Ford remained "the car to have" if you were a performance enthusiast.

A big 1954 change was the introduction of Ford's first overhead valve V-8. Another innovation was the T-Bird. A high-water mark in the horsepower race, for all manufacturers including Ford, was 1957. Ford offered a supercharged version of its 312-cid V-8, plus a 340-hp "NASCAR" version. New for 1958 was the famous "FE" series of 332- and 352-cid V-8s, which grew into the "390" and the awesome "427." The next year was a beauty contest thanks to the 1959 Galaxie — a Fairlane 500 two-door hardtop and with a T-Bird inspired roof.

Through the early '60s, Ford continued on a steady-as-she-goes course, adding the compact Falcon in '60 and mid-size Fairlane in '62. One of the most beautiful cars of the '60s was the '63-1/2 Galaxie 500 fastback. The mid-'64 introduction of the Mustang was historical.

Ford's '65 LTD was a new low-priced car with a luxury image. The big news in '66 was a redesigned Fairlane, now with big-block V-8 power. For 1967, NASCAR allowed mid-size cars to race and Fairlanes took the place of the Galaxies, dominating the big races.

It was the muscle car era and Ford also dominated the streets in the late '60s and early '70s. Then, insurance companies tightened the noose on "Supercar" owners. Experts recognize 1971 as the last year for true high-performance products from Ford until the '80s.

In answer to the growing import threat and new sub-compacts from AMC and Chevy, Ford introduced the Pinto. No automaker offered a more complete line than Ford between 1976 and 1986. Offerings ranged from the sub-compact Pinto through the big Thunderbird. Engines reached all the way up to a 460-cid V-8, which remained available through 1978.

In 1977, the "big 'Bird" was replaced with a modified LTD II. The Torino and Elite soon faded away and the Maverick was about to go too. The Granada became the first American car to offer a standard

four-speed (overdrive) gearbox. The big LTD lasted until 1979.

In the '80s the LTD shrunk and the engines shrunk too. The T-Bird was downsized and the Crown Victoria name reappeared, bringing back memories of the sharpest mid-1950s Ford. Every Ford model endured a loss of sales, but so did most other domestic cars. The front-wheel-drive Escort arrived for 1981 carrying a CHV (hemi) engine. It became America's best-selling car. The Granada was slimmed down. The LTD got a small 255-cid V-8 and a six was standard in the T-Bird. Model year 1982 brought a hot Mustang GT and two-seat EXP.

The massive T-Birds of the '70s seemed forgotten as the 10th generation arrived for 1983. This one was loaded with curves and — before long — an optional turbocharged, fuel-injected four-cylinder engine, a close-ratio five-speed and a "quadra-shock" rear suspension.

Not many new models received as much publicity as the front-wheel-drive Taurus, the leader of the 1986 pack. Then, Ford Motor Co. broke records in 1987 with $4.6 billion in net income. New for 1987 was a four-wheel-drive Tempo and a five-liter Thunderbird Sport model. Ford was now the American car sales leader, ahead of Chevrolet's grand total by 66,000 cars. There seemed to be no stopping Ford and in 1989 in realized a 40,000-car sales increase .

A little-changed T-Bird marked its 35th anniversary in 1990. Most other models were also unaltered. In spring, Ford introduced an all-new '92 Crown Victoria. The '95 Contour "world car" replaced the Tempo. The debut of the 1995 Aspire also occurred early in 1994.

The Taurus SHO sedan was offered with V-8 power for the first time in 1996. An all-new '98 Escort ZX2 was made available in "Cool" or "Hot" versions. They featured unique body panels and frameless door glass. There was no '98 T-Bird.

A new Ford Focus was introduced in 2000. It was a sophisticated compact aimed at the worldwide market. In September, at the Henry Ford Museum & Greenfield Village, Ford celebrated a centennial of Ford racing with a very special event.

In 2002, an all-new two-passenger T-Bird based on the Lincoln LS platform arrived. Ford started taking T-Bird orders on Jan. 8, 2001, the day the car made its regular production debut at the Detroit Auto Show. The 2002 Thunderbird captured Motor Trend magazine's "Car of the Year" award. However, by the end of 2003, the company announced plans to drop the expensive, slow-selling model by 2005 or 2006. In 2005, Ford designers "nailed it" with a beautiful new "retro" Mustang that looked like a throwback to the '60s. Another hit of the same season was the Ford 500, a good-looking family sedan. Unfortunately, it was the pretty, two-seat T-Bird's last year. The Fusion — a new-generation "World Car" arrived in 2006. For enthusiasts, 2007 was the year of the Mustang Shelby Cobra GT 500 model, which did 0-to-60 in 4.9 seconds and the quarter mile in 13.1 at 115 mph.

Table of Contents

1903 Ford

Ford — Model A — Two-Cylinder: Ford Motor Company was incorporated on June 16, 1903. The company's first car was the Model A, a two-seater runabout capable of a maximum speed of 30 mph. This should not be confused with the better-known Model A of the 1930s. Ford used the Model A name twice. With a weight of just 1,250 pounds, the Model A was an early manifestation of Henry Ford's thinking that that would go into the Model T. As was common with most early automobiles, the Model A had a horse-buggy appearance (without the horse of course). The motor was positioned under the single seat. A detachable rear portion of the body — called a "tonneau" — provided seating for two additional passengers who gained access to their seats through a rear door.

VIN:

Serial numbers were mounted on the dashboard, adjacent to the steering column.

Model A

Model No.	Body/ Style No.	Body Type & Seating	Factory Price	Shipping Weight	Production Total
A	----	Runabout-2P	$ 850	1,250 lbs.	Note 1
A	----	Tonneau-2P	$ 950	------	Note 1

Note 1: Total Model A production was either 670 or 1,708 cars, depending upon the source. referred to. Ford officially uses the 670 figure for 1903 models only. The 1,700 seems to relate to combined 1903-1904 production.

Engine:

Model A: Opposed. Two-cylinder. Cast-iron block. B & S: 4 x 4 in. Displacement: 100.4 cu. in. Brake hp: 8. Valve lifters: mechanical. Carburetor: Schebler (early), Holley.

Chassis:

Wheelbase: 72 inches.

Technical:

Model A: Planetary transmission. Speeds: 2F/1R. Floor controls. Chain drive. Differential, band brakes. Wood-spoke wheels.

History: Introduced July 1903. On June 19, 1903, Barney Oldfield drove the Ford 999 racing car to a new one-mile record time of 59.6 seconds. Calendar year production: 1,708. Model-year production: (1903-1904) 1,700. The president of Ford was John S. Gray.

1903 Ford Model A Runabout (OCW)

1904 Ford

Ford — Model A/Model AC/Model C: These Ford models replaced the Model A in late 1904. Both were powered by a larger engine developing 10 hp. Ford claimed the top speed of both cars was 38 mph. The Model AC was essentially a Model A with the new Model C engine. The Model C had its fuel tank positioned under the hood, while that of the AC was located beneath the seat. Both cars had a longer 78-inch wheelbase than the Model A.

Ford — Model B — Four: The Model B was a drastic shift in direction for Henry Ford. With its four-passenger body, polished wood and brass trim, it was an elegant and expensive automobile. Powered by a 318-cid, 24-hp four, it was capable of a top speed of 40 mph. In place of the dry cell batteries carried by earlier Fords, the Model B was equipped with storage batteries. A 15-gallon fuel tank was also fitted. Other

1904 Ford Model B Touring (OCW)

features separating the $2,000 Model B from other Fords was its shaft drive and its rear hub drum brakes.

VIN:

Serial numbers were mounted on the dashboard, adjacent to the steering column.

Model A

Model No.	Body/ Style No.	Body Type & Seating	Factory Price	Shipping Weight	Production Total
A	----	Runabout-2P	$ 850	1,250 lbs.	Note 1
A	----	Tonneau-2P	$ 950	-----	Note 1

Model AC

AC	----	Runabout-2P	$ 850	1,250 lbs.	Note 1
AC	----	Tonneau-2P	$ 950	-----	Note 1

Model C

C	----	Runabout-2P	$ 850	1,250 lbs.	Note 1
C	----	Tonneau-2P	$ 950	-----	Note 1

Model B

B	----	2-dr. Touring-4P	$2,000	1,700 lbs.	Note 1

Note 1: Total production in 1904 was 1,695 cars. Ford reported building a total of 670 model As and 1900 models A and AC altogether. There is no record of Model B production. Other sources show figures that vary from these.

Engines:

Model A: Cylinder layout: opposed. Two. Cast-iron block. B & S: 4 x 4 inches. Displacement: 100.4 cid. Brake hp: 8. Valve lifters: mechanical. Carburetor: Holley.

Model AC/Model C: Two-cylinder. Cast-iron block. B & S: 4-1/4 x 4-1/4 inches. Displacement 120.5 cid. Brake hp: 10. Valve lifters: mechanical. Carburetor: Holley.

Model B: Four-cylinder. Inline. Cast-iron block. B & S: 4-1/4 x 5 inches. Displacement: 283.5 cid. Brake hp; 24. Valve lifters: mechanical.

Carburetor: Holley.

Model A: Wheelbase: 72 in.

Model C/Model AC: Wheelbase: 78 in. Tires: 28 in.

Model B: Wheelbase: 92 in.

Technical:

Model A/AC/C: Planetary transmission. Speeds: 2F/1R. Floor shift controls. Cone clutch. Chain drive. Differential band brakes. Wooden spoke wheels.

Model B: Planetary transmission. Speeds: 2F/1R. Floor shift controls. Cone clutch. Shaft drive. Drum brakes on rear wheels. Wooden spoke wheels.

History:

The Model C and Model AC were introduced September 1904. Calendar-year production: 1,695. Model-year production: (1904-1905) 1,745. The president of Ford was John S. Gray.

1904 Ford Model B touring. [JAC]

1904 Ford Model C Runabout with Tonneau (OCW)

1905 Ford

Ford — Model F — Two-Cylinder: The Ford Models C and B were carried into 1905. The 1905 Model C had light yellow running gear instead of red running gear and wider 3 x 28 wheels. In February 1905, these Fords were joined by the Model F, which was powered by a two-cylinder engine developing approximately 16 hp. The Model F had a wheelbase of 84 inches and was fitted with a green body, cream-colored wheels and cream-colored running gear.

1905 Ford Model C Tonneau Touring (RLC)

Serial numbers were mounted on the dashboard, adjacent to the steering column.

Model C

Model No.	Body/ Style No.	Body Type & Seating	Factory Price	Shipping Weight	Production Total
C	-----	Runabout-2P	$ 800	1,250 lbs.	Note 1
C	-----	Tonneau-2P	$ 950	------	Note 1

Model B

B	----	2-dr. Touring-4P	$2,000	1,700 lbs.	Note 1

Model F

F	-----	2-dr. Touring-4P	$1,000	1,400 lbs.	Note 1
F	-----	2-dr. Coupe-2P	$1,250	------	Note 1

Note 1: Total production for 1905 was 1,599 cars.

Model C: Two-cylinder. Opposed. Cast-iron block. B & S: 4-1/4 x 4-1/2 in. Displacement: 120.5 cid. Brake hp: 10. Valve lifters: mechanical. Carburetor: Holley.
Model B: Four-cylinder. Inline. Cast-iron block. B & S: 4-1/4 x 4 in. Displacement: 283.5 cid. Brake hp: 24. Valve lifters: mechanical. Carburetor: Holley.
Model F: Two-cylinder. Opposed. Cast-iron block. B & S: 4-1/2 x 4 in. Displacement: 127 cid. Brake hp: 16. Valve lifters: mechanical. Carburetors: Holley.

Model C: Wheelbase: 78 in. Tires: 28 in.
Model B: Wheelbase: 92 in. Tires: 32 in.
Model F: Wheelbase: 84 in. Tires: 30 in.

Model C: Planetary transmission. Speeds: 2F/1R. Floor controls. Cone clutch. Chain drive. Differential band brakes. Wooden spoke wheels. Wheel size: 28 in.
Model B: Planetary transmission. Speeds: 2F/1R. Floor controls. Cone clutch. Shaft drive. Drum brakes on two rear wheels. Wood-spoke wheels. Wheel size: 32 in.
Model F: Planetary transmission. Speeds: 2F/1R. Floor controls. Cone clutch. Chain drive. Differential band brakes. Wood-spoke wheels. Wheel size: 30 in.

Top. Windshield. Lights.

Introduced February 1905 (Model F). Calendar-year production: 1,599. Model-year production: (1905-1906) 1,599. The president of Ford was

1905 Ford Model B Tonneau Touring (OCW)

1906 Ford

Ford — Model K — Six: Late in 1905, the Model K Ford debuted. Since Henry Ford was moving close to the final design of the Model T — his "car for the multitudes," it was not surprising that he cared little for the expensive Model K. Along with the Touring model, a Roadster version was offered. It was guaranteed to attain a 60 mph top speed.

Ford — Model N — Four: The $500 Model N, with its front mounted four-cylinder engine, developed over 15 hp. It was capable of going 45 mph. Its styling was highlighted by such features as twin, nickel-plated front lamps and a boattail rear deck. It had an 84-inch wheelbase. Its reputation for reliability represented a solid step forward by Henry Ford and Ford Motor Company in the quest for a low-priced car for the mass market.

Ford — Model F — Two: The Model F was continued into 1906 unchanged.

VIN:

Serial numbers were mounted on the dashboard, adjacent to the steering column.

Model F (Two)

Model No.	Body/ Style No.	Body Type & Seating	Factory Price	Shipping Weight	Production Total
F	-----	2-dr. Touring-4P	$1,100	1,400 lbs.	Note 1

Model K (Six)

| K | ----- | 2-dr. Touring-4P | $2,500 | 2,400 lbs. | Note 1 |
| K | ----- | Runabout-4P | $2,500 | 2,000 lbs. | Note 1 |

Model N (Four)

| N | ----- | Runabout-2P | $ 600 | 800 lbs. | Note 1 |

Note 1: Total production was 2,798 or 8,729, depending on the source. Ford Motor Co. records show both figures.

Engines:

Model F: Two-cylinder. Opposed. Two. Cast-iron block. B & S: 4-1/4 x 4-1/2 in. Displacement: 128 cid. Brake hp: 10. Valve lifters: mechanical. Carburetor: Holley.

Model N: Four-cylinder. Inline. Cast iron block. B & S: 3-3/4 x 3-3/8 in. Displacement: 149 cid. Brake hp: 15-18. Valve lifters: mechanical. Carburetor: Holley.

Model K: Six-cylinder. Inline. Cast-iron block. B & S: 4-1/2 x 4-1/4 in. Displacement: 405 cid. Brake hp: 40. Valve lifters: mechanical. Carburetor: Holley.

Chassis:

Model F: Wheelbase: 84 inches. Tires: 30 in.

Model N: Wheelbase: 84 inches. Tires: 2-1/2 in. wide.

Model K: Wheelbase: 114-120 in.

Technical:

Model F: Transmission: Planetary. Speeds: 2F/1R. Floor shift controls. Cone clutch. Chain drive. Differential band. Wooden spokes. Wheel size: 30 inches.

Model N: Transmission: Planetary. Speeds 2F/1R. Floor controls. Disc clutch. Chain drive.

Model K: Transmission: Planetary. Speeds 2F/1R. Floor shift controls. Disc clutch. Shaft drive.

Options:

Cowl lamps. Bulb horn. Three-inch wheels for Model N ($50).

History:

Henry Ford became president of the Ford Motor Company, following the death of John S. Gray on July 6, 1906. A racing version of the Model K set a new world's 24-hour record of 1,135 miles. It averaged 47.2 mph. The record run took place at Ormond Beach in Florida.

1906 Ford Model N, 4-cyl. runabout (RLC)

1906 Ford Model K Tonneau Touring (RLC)

1907 Ford

Ford — Model N — Four: The Model N was continued unchanged for 1907. As before, it was a handsome automobile with nickel hardware and quarter-circle fenders. Volume production didn't begin until late 1907, when the price rose to $600.

Ford — Model R — Four: The Model R was introduced in February 1907 as a more elaborate version of the Model N. It had footboards in place of the Model N's carriage step. A mechanical lubrication system also replaced the forced-feed oiler of the Model N.

Ford — Model S — Four: The Model S had the same mechanical and appearance features as those of the Model R and also had a single-seat tonneau on the rear.

Ford — Model K — Six: The Model K was unchanged for 1907.

VIN:

Serial numbers were mounted on the dashboard, adjacent to the steering column.

Model N (Four)

Model No.	Body/ Style No.	Body Type & Seating	Factory Price	Shipping Weight	Production Total
N	-----	Runabout-2P	$ 600	1,050 lbs.	-----

Model R (Four)

| R | ----- | Runabout-2P | $ 750 | 1,400 lbs. | Note 1 |

Model S (Four)

| S | ----- | Tonneau-4P | $ 700 | 1,400 lbs. | ------ |
| S | ----- | Roadster-2P | $ 750 | ----- | ------ |

Model K (Six)

| K | ----- | 2-dr. Touring-4P | $2,800 | 2,000 lbs. | ------ |
| K | ----- | Runabout-4P | $2,800 | 2,000 lbs. | ------ |

Note 1: Total production of the Model R was approximately 2,500 cars.

1907 Ford Model K Runabout (OCW)

1907 Ford Model K Touring (OCW)

Engines:

Model N: Four-cylinder. Inline. Cast-iron block. B & S: 3-3/4 x 3-3/8 in. Displacement: 149 cid. Brake hp: 15-18. Valve lifters: mechanical. Carburetor: Holley.

Model R: Four-cylinder. Inline. Cast-iron block. B & S: 3-3/4 x 3-3/8 in. Displacement: 149 cid. Brake hp: 15-18. Valve lifters: mechanical. Carburetor: Holley.

Model S: Four-cylinder. Inline. Cast-iron block. B & S: 3-3/4 x 3-3/8 in. Displacement: 149 cid. Brake hp: 15-18. Valve lifters: mechanical. Carburetor: Holley.

Model K: Six-cylinder. Inline. Cast-iron block. B & S: 4-1/2 x 4-1/4 in. Displacement: 405 cid. Brake hp: 40. Valve lifters: mechanical. Carburetor: Holley.

Chassis:

Model N: Wheelbase: 84 in. Tires: three-inches wide.
Model R: Wheelbase: 84 in. Tires: three-inches wide.
Model S: Wheelbase: 84 in. Tires: three-inches wide.
Model K: Wheelbase: 120 in.

Technical:

Model N: Planetary transmission. Speeds: 2F/1R. Floor controls. Disc clutch. Chain drive.
Model R: Planetary transmission. Speeds: 2F/1R. Floor controls. Disc clutch. Chain drive.
Model S: Planetary transmission. Speeds: 2F/1R. Floor controls. Disc clutch. Chain drive.
Model K: Planetary transmission. Speeds: 2F/1R. Floor controls. Disc clutch. Shaft drive.

History:

Calendar-year production was 6,775 according to some sources and 14,887 according to others. The president of Ford Motor Co. was Henry Ford.

1907 Ford Model S Roadster (OCW)

1908 Ford

Ford — Model N — Four: For the 1908 model year Ford continued to produce the K, N, R, and S models until production of the Model T began in October 1908. The Model N was unchanged. It continued to offer nickel hardware and quarter-circle fenders.

Ford — Model R — Four: The Model R was a more elaborate version of the Model N with footboards and a mechanical lubrication system.

Ford — Model S — Four: The Model S had the same mechanical and appearance features as those of the Model R and also had a single-seat tonneau on the rear.

Ford — Model K — Six: The Model K was unchanged for 1908.

VIN:

Serial numbers were mounted on the dashboard, adjacent to the steering column.

Model N (Four)

Model No.	Body/ Style No.	Body Type & Seating	Factory Price	Shipping Weight	Production Total
N	----	Runabout-2P	$ 600	1,050 lbs.	------
N	----	Landaulette-2P	------	------	------

Model R (Four)

R	----	Runabout-2P	$ 750	1,400 lbs.	------

Model S (Four)

S	----	Tonneau-4P	$ 750	1,400 lbs.	------
S	----	Roadster-2P	$ 700	------	------

Model K (Six)

K	----	2-dr. Touring-4P	$2,800	2,000 lbs.	------
K	----	Runabout-4P	$2,800	2,000 lbs.	------

Note 1: Total production of the Model R was approximately 2,500 cars.

Engines:

Model N: Four-cylinder. Inline. Cast-iron block. B & S: 3-3/4 x 3-3/8 in. Displacement: 149 cid. Brake hp: 15-18. Valve lifters: mechanical. Carburetor: Holley.

Model R: Four-cylinder. Inline. Cast-iron block. B & S: 3-3/4 x 3-3/8 in. Displacement: 149 cid. Brake hp: 15-18. Valve lifters: mechanical. Carburetor: Holley.

Model S: Four-cylinder. Inline. Cast-iron block. B & S: 3-3/4 x 3-3/8 in. Displacement: 149 cid. Brake hp: 15-18. Valve lifters: mechanical. Carburetor: Holley.

Model K: Six-cylinder. Inline. Cast-iron block. B & S: 4-1/2 x 4-1/4 in. Displacement: 405 cid. Brake hp: 40. Valve lifters: mechanical. Carburetor: Holley.

Chassis:

Model N: Wheelbase: 84 in. Tires: three-inches wide.
Model R: Wheelbase: 84 in. Tires: three-inches wide.
Model S: Wheelbase: 84 in. Tires: three-inches wide.
Model K: Wheelbase: 120 in.

Technical:

Model N: Planetary transmission. Speeds: 2F/1R. Floor controls. Disc clutch. Chain drive.

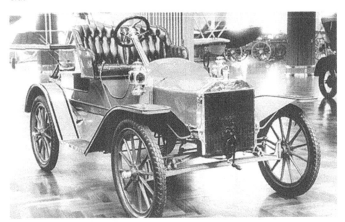

1908 Ford Model S Runabout (RLC)

Model R: Planetary transmission. Speeds: 2F/1R. Floor controls. Disc clutch. Chain drive.

Model S: Planetary transmission. Speeds: 2F/1R. Floor controls. Disc clutch. Chain drive.

Model K: Planetary transmission. Speeds: 2F/1R. Floor controls. Disc clutch. Shaft drive.

History:

Calendar year production was 6,015 according to some sources and 10,202 according to others (including early Model T Fords). The president of Ford Motor Co. was Henry Ford.

1909 Ford

Ford — Early 1909 — Model T: The Model T Ford was introduced in October 1908, and was an entirely new car when compared to Ford's previous models. The engine had four cylinders, cast en bloc with a removable cylinder head, quite unusual for the time. The engine pan was a one-piece steel stamping and had no inspection plate. The chassis featured transverse springs, front and rear, a rear axle housing that was drawn steel rather than a casting. The rear axles were non-tapered, with the hubs being held with a key and a pin and the pin retained by the hub cap. The front axle was a forged "I" beam with spindles that had integral arms. The use of vanadium steel almost throughout made for a stronger, yet lighter, machine that gave the Ford impressive performance for its time. The wheels were 30 in. with 30 x 3 in. tires on the front, and 30 x 3-1/2 in. on the rear. The wheel hub flanges were 5-1/2 in. diameter (compared with 6 in. from 1911 until the end of production in 1927). Windshields and tops were optional equipment on open cars, as were gas headlights, speedometers, robe rails, Prest-O-lite tanks, foot rests, auto chimes, car covers and other accessories that Ford would install at the factory. The radiator was brass, as were any lamps furnished (oil cowl lamps and taillamps were standard equipment). The hood had no louvers and was made of aluminum. The body styles offered were the Touring, the Runabout (a roadster), the Coupe, the Town Car and the Landaulet. The bodies were generally made of wood panels over a wood frame and were offered in red, gray and green. Gray was used primarily on the Runabouts, red on the Touring cars and green on the Town cars and Landaulets. These early cars (first 2,500) were so unique that they are generally considered a separate subject when discussing Model Ts. Essentially, the engines had built-in water pumps and the first 800 cars came with two foot pedals and two control levers (the second lever being for reverse) instead of the usual three pedals and one lever. The front fenders were square tipped, with no "bills."

Ford — Late 1909 — Model T: Beginning about car number 2500, the Model T became more or less standardized. Through most of 1909, the windshields and tops on the open cars remained optional, but more and more were delivered with this equipment, as well as gas headlights, factory installed. By the end of the year, they were standard. Body types and styling continued unchanged. Colors continued as in the early production, except that both green and red Touring cars were produced, along with a mixture of colors in the other models as well. Red was not offered after June 1909. Black was not listed as an available color and only one of the shipping invoices showed black, but early cars extant seem to indicate that black was used. This could be due to oxidation of the top color coat, but black early Fords are an enigma to the Model T student. The one aluminum-paneled touring body, built by Pontiac Body, was discontinued about September 1909. The late 1909 fenders were similar in design to the earlier 1909 fenders, but now had rounded

fronts with small "bills." The engine no longer had the water pump. Instead, it was cooled by thermosyphon action and set the pattern for all later Model T engines.

VIN:

Early 1909: (October 1908 to April 1909) The serial number was between center exhaust ports on side of engine. Starting: 1 (October 1908). Ending: approximately 2500. (The first of the non-water pump engines was 2448, built on April 22, 1909, but there was some mixture of the old and the new in production for a short time.)

Calendar-year engine numbers: 1 to 309, October to December 1908. Car numbers were stamped on a plate on the front seat kick panel and these were the same as the engine numbers. Other numbers stamped on the body sills, etc. were manufacturer's numbers and not an identifying number. [1909] Serial number was behind the timing gear on the lower right side of the engine. Starting: approximately 2501. Ending: approximately 11145. (There is no "break" between the 1909 and 1910 cars, 11146 was the first number assembled in October 1909, the beginning of Ford's fiscal year 1910). 1909 calendar year engine numbers: 310 to 14161 (approximate). Car numbers were stamped on a plate on the front seat kick panel and these were the same as the engine numbers. Other numbers stamped on the body sills, etc. were manufacturer's numbers and not an identifying number.

Model T (Four)

Model No.	Body/ Style No.	Body Type & Seating	Factory Price	Shipping Weight	Production Total
T	------	Touring-5P	$ 850	1,200 lbs.	7,728
T	------	Runabout-5P	$ 825	-----	2,351
T	------	Town Car-4P	$1,000	-----	236
T	------	Landaulet-7P	$ 950	-----	298
T	------	Coupe-2P	$ 950	-----	47

Notes: Prices effective October 1, 1908 (at introduction of the Model T). The production totals are for the fiscal year: Oct. 1, 1908 to Sept. 30, 1909.

Engines:

Early 1909: L-head. Four. Cast iron block. B & S: 3-3/4 x 4 in. Displacement.: 176.7 cid. Compression ratio: 4.5:1 (approximate) Brake hp: 22 at 1600 rpm. NACC hp: 22.5. Main bearings: three. Valve lifters: solid. Carburetor: Kingston five-ball, Buffalo. Torque: 83 at 900 rpm. Used only in first 2,500 Model Ts.

Late 1909: L-head. Four. Cast iron block. B & S: 3-3/4 x 4 in. Displacement.: 176.7 cid. Compression ratio: 4.5:1 (approximate) Brake hp: 22 at 1600 rpm. NACC hp: 22.5. Main bearings: three. Valve lifters: solid. Carburetor: Kingston five-ball, Buffalo. Torque: 83 at 900 rpm.

Chassis:

Model T: Wheelbase: 100 in. Overall length: 11 ft. 2-1/2 in. Front tread: 56 in. Rear tread: 56 in. Tires: (front) 30 x 3 front, (rear) 30 x 3-1/2.

Technical:

Early 1909 Model T: (First 800)] Planetary transmission. Speeds: 2F/1R, two pedal controls and two levers on floor. Multiple-disc clutch (24 discs). Torque tube drive. Straight bevel rear axle. Overall ratio: 3.63:1. Brakes: contracting band in transmission. Hand-operated internal expanding in rear wheels. Foot brake stops driveshaft. Parking brake on two rear wheels. Wheel size: 30 in. Clutch and Brakes [through car 800]: Clutch pedal gives low when pressed to

1909 Ford Model T Touring (HFM)

1909 Ford Model T coupe (HAC)

1909 Ford Model T Tourster (OCW)

floor, high when released, neutral in between. Reverse lever puts clutch in neutral and applies reverse brake band. Second lever is the parking brake. [1909-1927] Planetary transmission. Speeds: 2F/1R. Three pedal controls and one lever on floor. Multiple disc clutch (26 discs 1909-1915), (25 discs 1915-1927). Torque tube drive. Straight bevel rear axle. Overall ratio: 3.63:1. Brakes: Contracting band in transmission. Hand-operated internal expanding in rear wheels. Foot brake stops driveshaft. Parking brake on two rear wheels. Wheel size: 30 in. (21 in. optional in 1925, standard in 1926-1927). Drivetrain options: 4.0:1 optional rear axle ratio beginning in 1919. Clutch and Brakes [after car 800]: Clutch pedal gives low when pressed to floor, high when released, neutral in between. Control lever puts clutch in neutral and applies parking brake. Center foot pedal applies reverse. Third (right-hand) pedal is the service brake, applying transmission brake band. Model T Wheels: Standard wheels are wooden spoke with demountable rims, an option beginning in 1919. In 1925, 21 in. wood spoke demountable rim wheels were an option, these became standard in 1926. Beginning January 1926 optional 21 in. wire wheels became available. These became standard on some closed cars in calendar year 1927. In mid-1925 (1926 models) the transmission brake was made about a half-inch wider, and the rear wheel brakes were enlarged to 11 in. with lined shoes. 1909-1925 were seven in. with cast iron shoes (no lining). Springs were transverse semi-elliptic, front and rear. Model T Steering: 3:1 steering gear ratio by planetary gear at top of steering column until mid-1925 when ratio was changed to 5:1.

Options:

Windshield. Headlamps. Tops. Horns. Prest-O-lite tanks (instead of the carbide tank). Robe rails. Tire chains. Top boots. Foot rests. Spare tire carriers. Speedometers. Bumpers. 60-inch front and rear tread.

1910 Ford

Ford — Model T: The 1910 Fords were unchanged from 1909, except for a number of mechanical modifications in the rear axle and the use of one standard color on all models: dark green. The Landaulet and the Coupe were discontinued in 1910 and a new Tourabout (basically a Touring car using two separate seat sections) was added. All body styles except the Roadster and the Tourabout had two doors with the front compartment being open. Only the Coupe came with doors. The Tourabout was similar to the Touring but had two roadster-like seat sections and no doors. All 1910 Model Ts had windshields.

VIN:

The serial number was behind the timing gear on the lower right side of the engine. Starting: 11146 (approximate). Ending: 31532 (approximate). There is no "break" between the 1910 and 1911 cars. 31533 was the first number assembled in October 1910, the beginning of Ford's fiscal year 1911. The first "1911" car built was a torpedo runabout in which the chassis was assembled October 5, and the final assembly occurred October 26. The first "blue" cars were built during October and are presumed to be "1911" models. 1910 calendar year engine numbers: 14162 (approximate) to 34901. Car numbers were stamped on a plate on the front seat kick panel and these were the same as the engine numbers. Other numbers stamped on the body sills, etc. were manufacturer's numbers and not an identifying number.

1910 Ford Model T Touring (OCW)

1910 Ford Model T Runabout (OCW)

Model T (Four)

Model No.	Body/ Style No.	Body Type & Seating	Factory Price	Shipping Weight	Production Total
T	------	Touring-5P	$ 950	1,200 lbs.	16,890
T	------	Tourabout-5P	$ 950	------	------
T	------	Runabout-5P	$ 900	------	1,486
T	------	Town Car-7P	$1,200	------	377
T	------	Landaulet-7P	$1,100	------	2
T	------	Coupe-2P	$1,050	------	187
T	------	Chassis	-----	------	108

Notes: Prices effective October 1, 1909. Production was for the fiscal year, Oct. 1, 1909, to Sept. 30, 1910.

Combined production of Touring and Tourabouts was 16,890.

Engine:

Model T: L-head. Four. Cast-iron block. B & S: 3-3/4 x 4 in. Displacement.: 176.7 cid. Compression ratio: 4.5:1 (approximate) Brake hp: 22 at 1600 rpm NACC hp: 22.5. Main bearings: three. Valve lifters: solid. Carburetor: Kingston five-ball, Buffalo (early 1910). Torque: 83 at 900 rpm.

Chassis:

Model T: Wheelbase: 100 in. Overall length: 11 ft. 2-1/2 in. Front tread: 56 in. Rear tread: 56 inches. Tires: (front) 30 x 3 front, (rear) 30 x 3-1/2.

Options:

The many options listed for 1909 were not available in 1910. Standard equipment for the open cars now included the windshield, gas headlamps and carbide generator, speedometer and top with side curtains. Interestingly, the more expensive closed cars (Landaulet, Town Car and Coupe) were equipped with horn and oil lamps only. Headlamps and speedometer were $80 extra.

1911 Ford

Ford — Model T: In approximately January 1911, the Model T Ford was completely restyled. New fenders, a new - but similar - radiator, new wheels, new bodies and, during the year a new engine, front axle and rear axle, made the 1911 Ford almost a new beginning. The bodies were now made with steel panels over a wood framework. A

1911 Ford Model T Touring (OCW)

1911 Ford Model T Town Car (HAC)

1911 Ford Model T Touring (OCW)

new standard color of dark blue was used on all models. Body types were the same as offered in 1910. The Tourabout and Landaulet, while listed in the catalogs, were not produced in 1911. The Coupe was phased out and only 45 were built. Two new bodies were offered: the Open Runabout and the Torpedo Runabout. Both of these differed considerably from the other models in that they had curved fenders, a longer hood, a lower seating arrangement, a lower and longer steering column and a gas tank located on the rear deck, behind the seat. The two cars were similar, but not the same. The Open Runabout did not have doors, while the Torpedo Runabout had one door on each side. Near the end of the year - and called a "1912" model - a new Delivery Car was offered. Fender construction was also new, setting a general pattern for the bulk of Model T production until 1926. The new front fenders had larger "bills" than did the 1910 style. Lamps were all brass with gas headlights, and kerosene sidelights and taillights. The rear axle housing was redesigned. The earlier pressed-steel type had gone through a number of modifications in 1909, 1910 and early 1911, but in midyear a new type with a cast-iron center section appeared. The axles were now of taper-end design (perhaps changed before the new housing) and the hub flanges were six inches in diameter. The front axle now used spindles with separate steering arms and the axle ends were modified to accept the new spindles. The front axle remained relatively unchanged in later years.

VIN:

The serial number was behind the timing gear on the lower right side of the engine. Starting: 31533 (approximate). Ending: 70749 (approximate). There is no "break" between the 1911 and 1912 cars. 70750 was the first number assembled in October 1911, the beginning of Ford's fiscal year 1912. 1911 calendar year engine numbers: 34901 to 88900 (approximate). Car numbers were stamped on a plate on the firewall and these might be the same as the engine numbers. Ford now used the engine number to identify all cars. Other numbers stamped on the body sills, etc. were manufacturer's numbers and not an identifying number.

Model T (Four)

Model No.	Body/ Style No.	Body Type & Seating	Factory Price	Shipping Weight	Production Total
T	------	Touring-5P	$ 780	1,200 lbs.	26,405
T	------	Tourabout-4P	$ 725	------	------
T	------	Runabout-2P	$ 680	------	7,845
T	------	Torpedo Runabout-2P	$ 725	------	------
T	------	Open Runabout-2P	$ 680	------	------
T	------	Town Car-7P	$ 960	------	315
T	------	Landaulet-7P	$1,100	------	0
T	------	Coupe-2P	$ 840	------	45
T	------	Chassis	$ 940	------	248

Notes: Prices effective Oct. 1, 1910. Production is for fiscal year, Oct. 1, 1910, to Sept. 30, 1911. Runabouts were not broken out by types in the production figures.

Engine:

Model T: L-head. Four. Cast-iron block. B & S: 3-3/4 x 4 in. Displacement: 176.7 cid. Compression ratio: 4.5:1 (approximate) Brake hp: 22 at 1600 rpm. NACC hp: 22.5. Main bearings: three. Valve lifters: solid. Carburetor: Kingston five-ball, Holley 4500, Holley H-1 4550. Torque: 83 at 900 rpm.

Chassis:

Model T: Wheelbase: 100 in. Overall length: 11 ft. 2-1/2 in. Front tread: 56 in. Rear tread: 56 inches. Tires: (front) 30 x 3 front, (rear) 30 x 3-1/2.

Note: Thermosyphon. Upper main bearings were now babbited. Valve chambers (two) were now enclosed using steel doors held with one stud/nut each. Inspection plate in the crankcase.

Technical:

Model T: Planetary transmission. Speeds: 2F/1R. Three pedal controls and one lever on floor. Multiple disc clutch. Torque tube drive. Straight bevel rear axle. Overall ratio: 3.63:1. Brakes: Contracting band in transmission. Hand-operated internal expanding in rear wheels. Foot brake stops driveshaft. Parking brake on two rear wheels.

1911 Ford Model T Open Runabout (OCW)

All cars were equipped with headlamps, horn, etc. with no options. Ford Motor Co. even said the warranty, would be voided if any accessories were added.

1912 Ford

Ford — Model T: In approximately January 1912, the Model T was again restyled. However, the appearance was similar to the 1911 cars. The touring car was now supplied with "fore doors" that enclosed the front compartment. These were removable and many have been lost over the years. The metal side panels of the touring were now relatively smooth from top to bottom, eliminating the "step" under the seats, which marked the 1911s. The top support straps now fastened to the windshield hinge, rather than to the front of the chassis as they had in prior years. The torpedo runabout was now based on the standard runabout, and the open runabout was discontinued. While retaining the curved rear fenders, the front fenders were now standard. The hood and steering column were also the same as those used on the other 1912 cars. The front compartment was enclosed in a manner similar to the 1911 torpedo. The "1912" style year lasted only about nine months, an all new "1913" car appeared about September. The only color on record for 1912 was dark blue but the existence of black cars of the era seems to indicate that black was available as well.

VIN:

The serial number was behind the timing gear on the lower right-hand side of the engine until about serial number 100000, then it was moved to just behind the water inlet on the left-hand side of the engine. Also, about this time, the location was again changed to the standard position above the water inlet, with some mixture of locations for a time. Starting: 70750 (approximate). Some records show number 69877 built on September 30, 1911. Ending: 157424 (approximate). There is no break between the 1912 and 1913 cars. Number 157425 was the first number assembled on October 1912, the beginning of Ford's 1913 fiscal year. 1912 calendar-year engine numbers: 88901 to 183563. According to Ford records, engines with numbers B1 and B12247 were built at the Detroit plant beginning October 1912 and October 1913, but no records exist as to the exact dates. Car numbers were stamped on a plate on the firewall. Other numbers were stamped on the body sills, etc., were manufacturer's numbers and not an identifying number. Car numbers no longer agreed with the motor numbers and Ford kept no records of them.

Model T (Four)

Model No.	Body/ Style No.	Body Type & Seating	Factory Price	Shipping Weight	Production Total
T	------	Touring-5P	$ 690	1,200 lbs.	50,598
T	------	Torpedo Runabout-2P	$ 590	------	13,376
T	------	Commercial Roadster-4P	$ 590	------	------
T	------	Town Car-7P	$ 900	------	802
T	------	Delivery Car-2P	$ 700	------	1,845
T	------	Coupe-2P	$ 840	------	19
T	------	Chassis	-----	940 lbs.	2,133

Notes: Fiscal year, Oct. 1, 1911, to Sept. 30, 1912. Roadster production figures were combined. The total was 13,376. Coupes and the chassis were not shown in the catalogs.

1912 Ford Model T Open Runabout (OCW)

1912 Ford Model T Touring (OCW)

Engine:

Model T: L-head. Four. Cast-iron block. B & S: 3-3/4 x 4 in. Displacement.: 176.7 cid. Compression ratio: 4.5:1 (approximate). Brake hp: 22 at 1600 rpm. NACC hp: 22.5. Main bearings: three. Valve lifters: solid. Carburetor: Kingston six-ball, Holley H-1 4550. Torque: 83 at 900 rpm.

Note: Thermosyphon. Valve chambers (two) now enclosed using steel doors held with one stud/nut each. Inspection plate in the crankcase. Kingston carburetor used in limited quantities and does not appear in any of the Ford parts lists.

Chassis:

Model T: Wheelbase: 100 in. Overall length: 10 ft. 8 in. Front tread: 56 in. Rear tread: 56 in. Tires: (front) 30 x 3 front, (rear) 30 x 3-1/2.

Technical:

Model T: Planetary transmission. Speeds: 2F/1R. Three pedal controls and one lever on floor. Multiple disc clutch. Torque tube drive. Straight bevel rear axle. Overall ratio: 3.63:1. Brakes: Contracting band in transmission. Hand-operated internal expanding in rear wheels. Foot brake stops driveshaft. Parking brake on two rear wheels.

Options:

The basic equipment included three oil lamps (two side and one tail). Windshield. Headlamps. Tops. Horns. Top boots. Speedometers.

1913 Ford

Ford — Model T: In about September of 1912, Ford introduced the second new body to arrive that calendar year and marketed it as a 1913 Model T. The redesigned Model T set the pattern for the next 12 years. Metal side panels now extended from the firewall to the rear of the car. There was one rear door on the left side of the Touring Car and two doors on the right side. The doors were unique in that they extended clear to the splash apron. There was no metal support between the front and rear sections of the body, which proved to be a problem. The bodies flexed so much that the doors opened during driving. The initial solution to the problem was to add a steel reinforcement across the rear door sills. Later, heavier body sills were used. Still later, Ford used both the steel reinforcements and the heavier sills. The bottom section of the windshield on the open cars now sloped rearwards, while the upper section was vertical and folded forward. The fenders followed the pattern of those used on 1911-1912 Model Ts, except that they no longer had the "bills" at the front. Side, tail and headlamps were still oil fired or gas-fired, but they were now made of painted black steel, except for the tops and rims, which were still made of brass. The rear axle housings were again redesigned so that the center section was larger (fatter) and the axle tubes were flared and riveted to the center section. "Made in USA" now appeared on the radiator under the "Ford" name. The same notation appeared on many other parts as well. This may have been done to differentiate from cars built in Canada Ford of Canada first started manufacturing its own engines and other parts in 1913. According to Ford data, the 1913 cars were painted dark blue, with striping on early models. As in earlier models, black body finish is a possibility, but it is not documented in any Ford literature. Body styles offered were the Touring Car, Runabout and Town Car. The Torpedo Roadster, which had a rear-deck-mounted gas tank, was discontinued. (Ford called the regular Runabout a "Torpedo" for several years after this.) The Delivery Car, which had proved to be a sales disaster, was also dropped.

VIN:

The serial number was above the water inlet on the left side of he engine. Starting: 157425 (approximate) October 1912. Some 1913 cars may have been built earlier. Ending: 248735. (There is no break between the 1913 and 1914 cars. The 1914-style Touring was

1913 Ford Model T Touring (HFM)

introduced about August 1913, which could make the ending number around 320000 for 1913 cars.) 1913 calendar-year engine numbers: 183564 to 408347. According to Ford records, engines with numbers B1 and B12247 were built at the Detroit plant between October 1912 and October 1913, but no records exist as to the exact dates. Numbers stamped on the body sills, etc. were manufacturer's numbers and not an identifying number.

Model T (Four)

Model No.	Body/ Style No.	Body Type & Seating	Factory Price	Shipping Weight	Production Total
T	-----	Touring-5P	$ 600	1,200 lbs.	126,715
T	-----	Runabout-2P	$ 525	------	33,129
T	-----	Town Car-7p	$ 800	------	1,415
T	-----	Delivery Car-2p	$ 625	------	513
T	-----	Coupe-2p	----	------	1
T	-----	Chassis	----	960 lbs.	8,438

Notes: Fiscal year, Oct. 1, 1912, to Sept. 30, 1913. Coupes and the chassis were not shown in the catalogs.

Engine:

Model T: L-head. Four. Cast-iron block. B & S: 3-3/4 x 4 in. Displacement.: 176.7 cid. Compression ratio: 4.0:1. Brake hp: 20 at 1600 rpm. NACC hp: 22.5. Torque: 83 at 900 rpm. Main bearings: three. Valve lifters: solid. Carburetor: Kingston Y (4400), Holley S (4450).

Note: Thermosyphon. Valve chambers (two) now enclosed using steel doors held with one stud/nut each. Inspection plate in the crankcase. Camshaft modified for less power (less overlap in timing). Modified cylinder head for slightly lower compression.

Chassis:

Model T: Wheelbase: 100 in. Overall length: 10 ft. 8 in., chassis and 11 ft. 2-1/2 in., car. Front tread: 56 in. Rear tread: 56 in. Tires: (front) 30 x 3 front, (rear) 30 x 3-1/2. Chassis essentially identical except those after mid-1913 have a longer rear crossmember.

Technical:

Model T: Planetary transmission. Speeds: 2F/1R. Three pedal controls and one lever on floor. Multiple disc clutch. Torque tube drive. Straight bevel rear axle. Overall ratio: 3.63:1. Brakes: Contracting band in transmission. Hand-operated internal expanding in rear wheels. Foot brake stops driveshaft. Parking brake on two rear wheels.

Options:

All cars equipped with headlamps, horn, etc. with no options. Ford even said the warranty would be voided if any accessories were added, although itís doubtful this ever happened.

1914 Ford

Ford — Model T: The 1914 Model Ts looked almost identical to the 1913s, but the doors were now inset into the side panels and the body metal extended across the rear door sills, solving the weakness problem. The windshield, while similar in appearance to the 1913 style, now folded to the rear. The windshield support rods were given a bend to clear the folded section. The fenders were modified and now had embossed reinforcing ribs across the widest part. Later, ribs were added in the apron area of both front and rear fenders. The front fenders had no bill in most 1914 models, but one was added to fenders used late in the year. The front fender iron bracket was secured to the fender with four rivets. Black was now the Ford color, although records in the Ford Archives seem to indicate that Blue was still offered. Interestingly,

1914 Ford Model T Touring (OCW)

1914 Ford Model T Touring

Black was never listed as an available color prior to 1914, in spite of the many seemingly original pre-1914 Black Fords seen today. It is possible that Black was a common color, but there is nothing in the records to prove it. The use of 1913-style black-and-brass lamps continued. The chassis frame was modified and now had a longer rear cross member. This eliminated the use of the forged-metal body brackets used since 1909. A bare chassis was added to the Ford line in 1914. In the fall of the year a Center Door Sedan and a Coupelet (the first "convertible") were introduced, but these were really 1915 models.

VIN:

The serial number was above the water inlet on the left side of the engine. Starting: 348736 (approximate) October 1913. The 1914 cars were built as early as August, which could make the first 1914 cars around serial number 320000. Ending: 670000 (mid-January 1915). The new 1915 Ford was introduced in January at the Highland Park plant, but the 1914 style continued to be built, for a time, at some branches. There is no clear break point in the style years. 1914 calendar-year engine numbers: 408348 to 656063. Numbers stamped on the body sills, etc., were manufacturer's numbers and not an identifying number.

Model T (Four)

Model No.	Body/ Style No.	Body Type & Seating	Factory Price	Shipping Weight	Production Total
T	-----	Touring-5P	$ 550	1,200 lbs.	165,832
T	-----	Runabout-2P	$ 500	------	35,017
T	-----	Town Car-7p	$ 750	------	1,699
T	-----	Chassis	----	960 lbs.	119

Notes: Fiscal year, Oct. 1, 1913, to July 31, 1914.

Engine:

Model T: L-head. Four. Cast-iron block. B & S: 3-3/4 x 4 in. Displacement.: 176.7 cid. Compression ratio: 4.0:1. Brake hp: 20 at 1600 rpm. NACC hp: 22.5. Torque: 83 at 900 rpm. Main bearings: three. Valve lifters: solid. Carburetor: Kingston Y (4400), Holley G (6040 brass body).

Note: Thermosyphon. Valve chambers (two) now enclosed using steel doors held with one stud/nut each. Inspection plate in the crankcase.

Chassis:

Model T: Wheelbase: 100 in. Overall length: 10 ft. 8 in., chassis and 11 ft. 2-1/2 in., car Front tread: 56 in. Rear tread: 56 in. Tires: (front) 30 x 3 front, (rear) 30 x 3-1/2. The chassis was essentially identical except those after mid-1913 have a longer rear crossmember.

Technical:

Model T: Planetary transmission. Speeds: 2F/1R. Three pedal controls and one lever on floor. Multiple disc clutch. Torque tube drive. Straight bevel rear axle. Overall ratio: 3.63:1. Brakes: Contracting band in transmission. Hand-operated internal expanding in rear wheels. Foot brake stops driveshaft. Parking brake on two rear wheels.

Options:

The basic equipment included three oil lamps. (Two side and one tail.) Windshield. Headlamps. Tops. Horns. Top boots. Speedometers.

1915 Ford

Ford — Model T: The 1915-style open Model Ts were introduced at Ford's Highland Park, Michigan plant in January 1915, but the 1914 style continued to be manufactured in some of the branches until as late as April. The bodies were essentially the same as the 1914 bodies, except for the front cowl section. Instead of the exposed wooden firewall, a new metal cowl curved "gracefully" inward to the hood. The hood and radiator were the same as on earlier Model Ts, except for the use of louvers in the hood side panels. The windshield was now upright, with the top section folding towards the rear. Electric headlights were standard. These were of "typical" size and shape and were commonly seen on Model T Fords through the end of production in 1927. Brass headlight rims were used. The sidelights were now of a rounded style and were interchangeable from side to side. The taillight was similar, but had a red lens in the door and a clear lens on the side towards the license plate. The side lamps and taillights were still kerosene-fired. They had brass tops and rims, but were otherwise painted black. The headlights were powered by the engine magneto. The front fenders again had "bills" and were the same as the late-1914 design. While retaining the same style, later the fenders had revised iron brackets held in place with three rivets. The rear fenders were curved to follow the wheel outline. Neither the front or rear fenders were crowned. A bulb-type horn was standard in 1915. It was mounted under the hood. The hood now had louvers, perhaps so that the horn could be heard. Early in the year, Ford began using a magneto-powered horn on some cars it built and, by October 1915, all Model Ts had the new horn. The Sedan model was unique from other Model Ts. The Sedan body was made of aluminum panels and required special rear fenders and splash aprons. The Sedan gas tank was located under the rear seat and proved to be quite unsatisfactory, because of poor fuel flow. The body was redesigned during the year and was then made of steel panels. Also, the gasoline tank was relocated under the driver's seat. The Coupelet had a folding top, but differed from the Runabout in that the doors had windows and the windshield was like that of the Sedan. It also had a larger turtle deck. The rear axle was redesigned for the last time (except for minor modifications). The center section was cast iron and the axle tubes were straight and inserted into it.

VIN:

The serial number was above the water inlet on the left side of the engine. Starting: 670000 approximate (January 1915). The new 1915 Ford was introduced in January at the Highland Park plant, but the 1914 style continued to be built for a time at some branches. There is no clear

1915 Ford Model T Touring (AA)

break point in the style years. Ending: 856513 (July 24, 1915, end of fiscal 1915). 1915 calendar-year engine numbers: 656064 to 1028313. Numbers stamped on the body sills, etc. were manufacturer's numbers and not an identifying number.

Model T (Four)

Model No.	Body/ Style No.	Body Type & Seating	Factory Price	Shipping Weight	Production Total
T	-----	3-dr. Touring-5P	$ 490	1,500 lbs.	244,181
T	-----	2-dr. Runaboout-2P	$ 440	1,380 lbs.	47,116
T	-----	4-dr. Town Car-7P	$ 690	------	-----
T	-----	2-dr. Sedan-5P	$ 975	1,730 lbs.	989
T	-----	2-dr. Coupe-2P	$ 750	1,540 lbs.	2,417
T	-----	Chassis	$ 410	980 lbs.	13,459

Note: Fiscal year, Aug. 1, 1914, to July 31, 1915.

Engine:

Model T: L-head. Four. Cast-iron block. B & S: 3-3/4 x 4 in. Displacement.: 176.7 cid. Compression ratio: 4.0:1. Brake hp: 20 at 1600 rpm. NACC hp: 22.5. Torque: 83 at 900 rpm. Main bearings: three. Valve lifters: solid. Carburetor: Kingston L (6100), Holley G (6040 brass body).

Note: Thermosyphon. Valve chambers (two) now enclosed using steel doors held with one stud/nut each. Inspection plate in the crankcase.

Chassis:

Model T: Wheelbase: 100 in. Overall length: 10 ft. 8 in., chassis and 11 ft. 2-1/2 in., car. Front tread: 56 in. Rear tread: 56 in. Tires: (front) 30 x 3 front, (rear) 30 x 3-1/2. The chassis was essentially identical except those after mid-1913 had a longer rear crossmember.

Technical:

Model T: Planetary transmission. Speeds: 2F/1R. Three pedal controls and one lever on floor. Multiple disc clutch with 26 discs (1909-1915). Torque tube drive. Straight bevel rear axle. Overall ratio: 3.63:1. Brakes: Contracting band in transmission. Hand-operated internal expanding in rear wheels. Foot brake stops driveshaft. Parking brake on two rear wheels.

Options:

The basic equipment included three oil lamps. (Two side and one tail.) Windshield. Headlamps. Tops. Horns. Top boots. Speedometers.

1915 Ford Model T Runabout (OCW)

1915 Ford Model T Center door sedan

1916 Ford

Ford — Model T: The 1916 Fords were merely an extension of the 1915s, except for the deletion of the brass trim on the side lamps and taillights. The hood was now made of steel. All Model Ts were now equipped with the magneto horn. "Portholes" were added to the side of the Coupelet in an effort to allow the driver a better side view. The Sedan body was redesigned to now use standard fenders and splash aprons. There was a new gas tank under the driver's seat. The new body was all steel.

VIN:

The serial number was above the water inlet on the left side of the engine. Starting: 856514 (August 1, 1915). Ending: 1362989 (July 25, 1916, end of fiscal 1916). 1916 calendar-year engine numbers: 1028314 to 1614516. Numbers stamped on the body sills, etc. were manufacturer's numbers and not an identifying number.

Model T (Four)

Model No.	Body/ Style No.	Body Type & Seating	Factory Price	Shipping Weight	Production Total
T	-----	3-dr. Touring-5P	$ 440	1,510 lbs.	363,024
T	-----	2-dr. Runabout-2P	$ 390	1,395 lbs.	98,633
T	-----	4-dr. Town Car-7P	$ 640	------	1,972
T	-----	2-dr. Sedan-5P	$ 740	1,730 lbs.	1,859
T	-----	2-dr. Coupe-2P	$ 590	1,060 lbs.	1,174
T	-----	Chassis	$ 410	980 lbs.	13,459
T	-----	Ambulance (military)	-----	------	20,700

Note: Fiscal year, Aug. 1, 1915, to July 30, 1916. Ambulances built for the military.

Engine:

Model T: L-head. Four. Cast-iron block. B & S: 3-3/4 x 4 in. Displacement: 176.7 cid. Compression ratio: 4.0:1. Brake hp: 20 at 1600 rpm. NACC hp: 22.5. Torque: 83 at 900 rpm. Main bearings: three. Valve lifters: solid. Carburetor: Kingston L (6100), Holley G (6040 brass body).
Note: Thermosyphon. Valve chambers (two) now enclosed using steel doors held with one stud/nut each. Inspection plate in the crankcase.

Chassis:

Model T: Wheelbase: 100 in. Overall length: 10 ft. 8 in., chassis and 11 ft. 2-1/2 in. car. Front tread: 56 in. Rear tread: 56 in. Tires: (front) 30 x 3 front, (rear) 30 x 3-1/2. The chassis was essentially identical except those after mid-1913 had a longer rear crossmember.

Technical:

Model T: Planetary transmission. Speeds: 2F/1R. Three pedal controls and one lever on floor. Multiple disc clutch with 25 discs (1916-on). Torque tube drive. Straight bevel rear axle. Overall ratio: 3.63:1. Brakes: Contracting band in transmission. Hand-operated internal expanding brakes in rear wheels. Foot brake stops driveshaft. Parking brake on two rear wheels.

1916 Ford Model T Coupelet (OCW)

Options:

The basic equipment included three oil lamps. (Two side and one tail.) Windshield. Headlamps. Tops. Horns. Top boots. Speedometers.

1917 Ford

Ford — Model T: The Model T for 1917 looked like an all-new car, but was actually a rather simple evolution from the 1916 version. The brass radiator and the small hood were gone, as were all bits of brass trim. New curved and crowned fenders appeared. There was also a new black radiator shell, a new hood and a new hood former. The body itself was unchanged. Lamps were the same as 1916. During 1917, the Model T continued to get minor modifications, such as a different mounting base for the windshield and new rectangular cross-section top sockets replacing the oval ones used since 1915. Nickel-plating on the steering gear box, hubcaps and radiator filler neck replaced the earlier brass trim. A new engine pan came out in 1917. It had a larger front section to go with a larger fan pulley. The pulley, however, was not enlarged until about 1920. The "convertible" Coupelet was replaced with a "hardtop" Coupelet. While the top could no longer be folded, the side window posts could be removed and stored under the seat. This gave the car a hardtop look. The Town Car was discontinued during the year. Also during 1917, the Ford Model TT truck chassis was introduced.

VIN:

The serial number was above the water inlet on the left side of the engine. Starting: 1362990 (August 1, 1916). Ending: 2113501 (July 28, 1917, end of fiscal year 1917). 1917 calendar-year engine numbers were 1614517 to 2449179. Numbers stamped on the body sills, etc. were manufacturer's numbers and not an identifying number.

Model T (Four)

Model No.	Body/ Style No.	Body Type & Seating	Factory Price	Shipping Weight	Production Total
T	-----	3-dr. Touring-5P	$ 360	1,480 lbs.	583,128
T	-----	2-dr. Runaboout-2P	$ 345	1,385 lbs.	107,240
T	-----	4-dr. Town Car-7P	$ 595	------	2,328
T	-----	2-dr. Sedan-5P	$ 645	1,745 lbs.	7,361
T	-----	2-dr. Coupe-2P	$ 505	1,580 lbs.	7,343
T	-----	Chassis	$ 325	1,060 lbs.	41,165
T	-----	Ambulance (military)	-----	------	1,452

Note: Fiscal year Aug. 1, 1917, to July 30, 1918. Ambulances built for the military.

1916 Ford Model T Coupelet (OCW)

1917 Ford Model T Runabout (HAC)

1917 Ford Model T Touring (OCW)

Engine:

Model T: L-head. Four. Cast-iron block. B & S: 3-3/4 x 4 in. Displacement: 176.7 cid. Compression ratio: 4.0:1. Brake hp: 20 at 1600 rpm. NACC hp: 22.5. Torque: 83 at 900 rpm. Main bearings: three. Valve lifters: solid. Carburetor: Kingston L2 (6100), Holley G (6040 iron body). New cylinder head with slightly lower compression and much larger water jacket.

Note: Thermosyphon. Valve chambers (two) now enclosed using steel doors held with one stud/nut each. Inspection plate in the crankcase.

Chassis:

Model T: Wheelbase: 100 in. Overall length: 10 ft. 8 inches, chassis and 11 ft. 2-1/2 in., car. Front tread: 56 in. Rear tread: 56 in. Tires: (front) 30 x 3 front, (rear) 30 x 3-1/2. Chassis essentially identical except those after mid-1913 have a longer rear crossmember.

Technical:

Model T: Planetary transmission. Speeds: 2F/1R. Three pedal controls and one lever on floor. Multiple disc clutch (25 discs 1915-1927). Torque tube drive. Straight bevel rear axle. Overall ratio: 3.63:1. Brakes: Contracting band in transmission. Hand-operated internal expanding in rear wheels. Foot brake stops driveshaft. Parking brake on two rear wheels.

Options:

The basic equipment included three oil lamps (two side and one tail.) Windshield. Headlamps. Tops. Horns. Top boots. Speedometers.

1918 Ford

Ford — Model T: The Model T for 1918 was a continuation of the 1917 line with only very minor changes.

VIN:

Serial number was above the water inlet on the left side of the engine. Starting: 2113502 (August 1, 1917). Ending: 2756251 (July 27, 1918, end of fiscal year 1918). 1918 calendar-year engine numbers: 2449180 to 2831426. Numbers stamped on the body sills, etc. were manufacturer's numbers and not an identifying number.

Model T (Four)

Model No.	Body/ Style No.	Body Type & Seating	Factory Price	Shipping Weight	Production Total
T	-----	3-dr. Touring-5P	$ 360	1,450 lbs.	432,519
T	-----	2-dr. Runabout-2P	$ 345	1,435 lbs.	73,559
T	-----	4-dr. Town Car-7P	$ 595	------	2,142
T	-----	2-dr. Sedan-5P	$ 645	1,715 lbs.	35,697
T	-----	2-dr. Coupe-2P	$ 505	1,580 lbs.	14,771
T	-----	Chassis	$ 325	1,060 lbs.	37,648
T	-----	Ambulance (military)	------	------	2,163
TT		Truck chassis	$ 600	1,450 lbs.	41,105
T		Delivery car	------	------	399
T		Foreign	-----	------	24,000

Notes: Fiscal year: Aug. 1, 1917 to July 30, 1918. Ambulances built for the military.

Engine:

Model T: L-head. Four. Cast-iron block. B & S: 3-3/4 x 4 in. Displacement: 176.7 cid. Compression ratio: 4.0:1. Brake hp: 20 at 1600 rpm. NACC hp: 22.5. Torque: 83 at 900 rpm. Main bearings: three. Valve lifters: solid. Carburetor: Kingston L2 (6100), Holley G (6040 iron body). New cylinder head with slightly lower compression and much larger water jacket.

1918 Ford Model T Center Door Sedan (HAC)

Note: Thermosyphon. Valve chambers (two) now enclosed using steel doors held with one stud/nut each. Inspection plate in the crankcase.

Chassis:

Model T: Wheelbase: 100 in. Overall length: 10 ft. 8 inches, chassis and 11 ft. 2-1/2 in., car. Front tread: 56 in. Rear tread: 56 in. Tires: (front) 30 x 3 front, (rear) 30 x 3-1/2. Chassis essentially identical except those after mid-1913 have a longer rear crossmember.

Technical:

Model T: Planetary transmission. Speeds: 2F/1R. Three pedal controls and one lever on floor. Multiple disc clutch (25 discs 1915-1927). Torque tube drive. Straight bevel rear axle. Overall ratio: 3.63:1. Brakes: Contracting band in transmission. Hand-operated internal expanding in rear wheels. Foot brake stops driveshaft. Parking brake on two rear wheels.

Options:

The basic equipment included three oil lamps (two side and one tail.) Windshield. Headlamps. Tops. Horns. Top boots. Speedometers.

1919 Ford

Ford — Model T: In 1919, Model T body styling continued unchanged from 1918, but the Ford was finally given a battery and an electric starter. Beginning as standard equipment on the closed cars only, by mid-1919, a starter became an option on open cars, too. This change required a new engine block, a new transmission cover, new flywheel, etc. The general design of these items was unchanged, except for modifications needed to adapt the starter and generator to the engine. Also available as Ford standard equipment for the first time were wheels with demountable rims. These were standard equipment on closed cars and an option on the open models. When demountable wheels were used, all tires were of the same 30 x 3-1/2 size. With the adoption of electrical equipment came an instrument panel for the first time. Factory-installed instrumentation consisted of only an ammeter. Controls located on the instrument panel included the choke knob and an ignition and light switch. A speedometer was a dealer-installed options. The Model T Coupelet body style was redesigned. While looking the same, its door posts were now integral with the doors and the posts were no longer removable. The rear axle was also modified slightly. The oil filler hole was lowered to reduce the amount of oil that could be put in. This reduced a rear axle oil leaking problem. The center

1919 Ford Model T Touring (OCW)

section of the axle was milled to accept a gasket between the two halves. The front radius rod was redesigned and now fastened below the axle, adding strength to the assembly.

1919 Ford Model T Center Door Sedan (OCW)

VIN:

The serial number was above the water inlet on the left-hand side of the engine. Starting: 2756252 (August 1, 1918). Ending: 3277851 (July 30, 1919, end of 1919 fiscal year). 1919 calendar-year engine numbers: 2831427 to 3659971. Numbers stamped on the body sills, etc. were manufacturer's numbers and not an identifying number.

Model T (Four)

Model No.	Body/ Style No.	Body Type & Seating	Factory Price	Shipping Weight	Production Total
T	-----	3-dr. Touring-5P	$ 525	1,500 lbs.	286,935
T	-----	2-dr. Runaboout-2P	$ 500	1,390 lbs.	48,867
T	-----	2-dr. Sedan-5P	$ 875	1,875 lbs.	24,980
T	-----	2-dr. Coupe-2P	$ 750	1,685 lbs.	11,528
T	-----	4-dr. Town Car-7P	----	------	17
T	-----	Chassis	$ 475	1,060 lbs.	47,125
T	-----	Ambulance (military)	------	------	2,227
TT	-----	Truck chassis	$ 550	1,477 lbs.	70,816
TT	-----	Truck chassis (pneumatic tires)	------	------	399
T	-----	Delivery car	------	------	5,847

Notes: Fiscal year: Aug. 1, 1918, to July 30, 1919. Starter optional on open cars at $75. Demountable rims were an additional $25.

Engine:

Model T: L-head. Four. Cast-iron block. B & S: 3-3/4 x 4 in. Displacement: 176.7 cid. Compression ratio: 3.98:1. Brake hp: 20 at 1600 rpm. NACC hp: 22.5. Torque: 83 at 900 rpm. Main bearings: three. Valve lifters: solid. Carburetor: Kingston L4 (6150). Holley NH (6200). New cylinder head with slightly lower compression and much larger water jacket.

Note: Thermosyphon. Valve chambers (two) now enclosed using steel doors held with one stud/nut each. Inspection plate in the crankcase.

Chassis:

Model T: Wheelbase: 100 in. Overall length: 10 ft. 8 in., chassis and 11 ft. 2-1/2 in., car. Front tread: 56 inches. Rear tread: 56 in. Tires: (front) 30 x 3 front, (rear) 30 x 3-1/2. 30 x 3-1/2 all around with demountable rims 1919-1925. Chassis essentially identical except those after mid-1913 had a longer rear crossmember.

Technical:

Model T: Planetary transmission. Speeds: 2F/1R. Three pedal controls and one lever on floor. Multiple disc clutch (25 discs 1915-1927). Torque tube drive. Straight bevel rear axle. Overall ratio: 3.63:1. Brakes: Contracting band in transmission. Hand-operated internal expanding in rear wheels. Foot brake stops driveshaft. Parking brake on two rear wheels.

Options:

All cars equipped with headlamps, horn, etc. Starter ($75). Demountable rims ($25).

Early 1920 Ford

Ford — Model T: The early 1920 Model T Ford was virtually the same car as the 1919 model. In photos, these cars would look identical. An oval-shaped gas tank (located under the driver's seat) replaced the previous round type. This allowed the seat to be lowered.

VIN:

Serial number was above the water inlet on the left side of the engine. Starting: 3277852 (August 1, 1919). Ending: 4233351 (July 31, 1920, end of fiscal year 1920). 1920 calendar-year engine numbers: 3659972 to 4698419. Numbers stamped on the body sills, etc. were manufacturer's numbers and not an identifying number.

Model T (Four)

1919 Ford Model T Runabout (HAC)

Model No.	Body/ Style No.	Body Type & Seating	Factory Price	Shipping Weight	Production Total
T	-----	3-dr. Touring-5P	$ 575	1,500 lbs.	165,929
T	-----	2-dr. Runabout-2P	$ 550	1,390 lbs.	31,889
T	-----	2-dr. Sedan-5P	$ 975	1,875 lbs.	81,616
T	-----	2-dr. Coupe-2P	$ 850	1,760 lbs.	60,215
T	-----	Chassis	$ 525	1,060 lbs.	18,173
TT	-----	Truck chassis	$ 660	1,477 lbs.	135,002
TT	-----	Truck chassis (pneumatic tires)	-----	------	399

Model T (Four) (After in-year price increase)

Model No.	Body/ Style No.	Body Type & Seating	Factory Price	Shipping Weight	Production Total
T	-----	3-dr. Touring-5P	$ 675	1,500 lbs.	367,785
T	-----	2-dr. Runaboout-2P	$ 650	1,540 lbs.	63,514
T	-----	2-dr. Sedan-5P	$ 975	1,875 lbs.	------
T	-----	2-dr. Coupe-2P	$ 850	1,760 lbs.	------
T	-----	Chassis	$ 620	1,210 lbs.	16,919
TT	-----	Truck chassis	$ 640	1,477 lbs.	------

Notes: Fiscal year: Aug. 1, 1919, to July 30, 1920.

Engine:

Model T: L-head. Four. Cast-iron block. B & S: 3-3/4 x 4 in. Displacement: 176.7 cid. Compression ratio: 3.98:1. Brake hp: 20 at 1600 rpm. NACC hp: 22.5. Torque: 83 at 900 rpm. Main bearings:

1919 Ford Model T Coupe (OCW)

three. Valve lifters: solid. Carburetor: Kingston L4 (6150). Holley NH (6200). New cylinder head with slightly lower compression and much larger water jacket.

Note: Thermosyphon. Valve chambers (two) now enclosed using steel doors held with one stud/nut each. Inspection plate in the crankcase.

Chassis:

Model T: Wheelbase: 100 in. Overall length: 10 ft. 8 inches, chassis and 11 ft. 2-1/2 in., car. Front tread: 56 in. Rear tread: 56 in. Tires: (front) 30 x 3 front, (rear) 30 x 3-1/2. 30 x 3-1/2 all around with demountable rims 1919-1925. Chassis after mid-1913 had a longer rear crossmember.

Technical:

Model T: Planetary transmission. Speeds: 2F/1R. Three pedal controls and one lever on floor. Multiple disc clutch (25 discs 1915-1927). Torque tube drive. Straight bevel rear axle. Overall ratio: 3.63:1. Brakes: Contracting band in transmission. Hand-operated internal expanding in rear wheels. Foot brake stops driveshaft. Parking brake on two rear wheels.

Options:

All cars equipped with headlamps, horn, etc. Starter ($75). Demountable rims ($25).

Late 1920 through 1922 Ford

Ford — Model T: Another new Model T Ford body appeared in the open cars in late 1920. It takes an expert to spot differences in the two cars, but they do exist. The most noticeable variation was a new rear quarter panel. It was now an integral part of the side panel and replaced the two-piece assembly used since 1913. Seat backs were given a more comfortable angle and the result was a far more comfortable car. The chassis frame was modified slightly, the running board support brackets were now pressed steel channels instead of the forged brackets with a tie rod used since 1909. Otherwise the basic car was like the previous models. A new pinion bearing spool was used on the rear axle. The earlier type was an iron casting with enclosed mounting studs. The new spool was a forging and used exposed mounting bolts. Body styles offered during this period were the touring, runabout, coupelet and sedan, in addition to the chassis and the truck chassis.

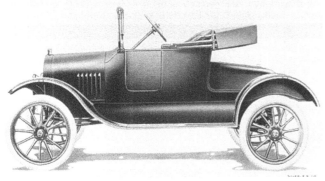

1920 Ford Model T Turtledeck Roadster (RLC)

1921 Ford Model T Turtledeck Roadster (JAC)

VIN:

(1921) Serial number was above the water inlet on the left side of the engine. Starting: 4233352 (August 2, 1920). Ending: 5223135 (July 30, 1921, end of fiscal 1921). 1921 calendar year engine numbers: 4698420 to 5568071. Numbers stamped on the body sills, etc, were manufacturer's numbers and not an identifying number. (1922) Serial number was above the water inlet on the left side of the engine. Starting: 5223136 (August 1, 1921). Ending: 6543606 (September 14, 1922, introduction of first "1923" model). 1922 calendar year engine numbers: 5638072 to 6953071. Numbers stamped on the body sills, etc. were manufacturer's numbers and not an identifying number.

1920-1921 Model T (Four)   (Prices effective Sept. 22, 1920)

Model No.	Body/ Style No.	Body Type & Seating	Factory Price	Shipping Weight	Production Total
T	-----	3-dr. Touring-5P	$ 440	1,500 lbs.	84,970*
T	-----	3-dr. Touring-5P (electric start and demountable rims)	$ 535	1,650 lbs.	647,300
T	-----	2-dr. Runabout-2P	$ 395	1,390 lbs.	25,918*
T	-----	2-dr. Runabout-2P (electric start and demountable rims)	$ 490	1,540 lbs.	171,745
T	-----	2-dr. Sedan-5P (electric start and demountable rims)	$ 795	1,875 lbs.	179,734
T	-----	2-dr. Coupe-2P (electric start and demountable rims)	$ 745	1,760 lbs.	129,159
T	-----	Chassis	$ 360	1,060 lbs.	13,356*
T	-----	Chassis (electric start and demountable rims)	$ 455	1,210 lbs.	23,536
TT	-----	Truck chassis (pneumatic tires)	$ 545	1,477 lbs.	118,583*
T	-----	Canada and foreign production	-----	------	42,860*

*****Note:** Prices Aug. 1, 1920 to Dec. 31, 1921. Ford Motor Co. began calendar year figures in 1921.

1921 Ford Model T Center Door Sedan [JAC]

1921 Ford Model T Touring (OCW)

1921 Model T (Four) (Prices effective June 7, 1921)

T	-----	3-dr. Touring-5P	$ 415	1,500 lbs.	Note 1
T	-----	3-dr. Touring-5P (electric start and demountable rims)	$ 510	1,650 lbs.	Note 1
T	-----	2-dr. Runabout-2P	$ 370	1,390 lbs.	Note 1
T	-----	2-dr. Runabout-2P (electric start and demountable rims)	$ 465	1,540 lbs.	Note 1
T	-----	2-dr. Sedan-5P (electric start and demountable rims)	$ 760	1,875 lbs.	Note 1
T	-----	2-dr. Coupe-2P (electric start and demountable rims)	$ 695	1,760 lbs.	Note 1
T	-----	Chassis	$ 345	1,060 lbs.	Note 1
T	-----	Chassis (electric start and demountable rims)	$ 440	1,210 lbs.	Note 1
TT	-----	Truck chassis (pneumatic tires)	$ 495	1,477 lbs.	Note 1

Note 1 : See chart the top chart for production figures. Ford Motor Co. began calendar year figures in 1921.

1922 Model T (Four) (Prices effective Sept. 2, 1921)

T	-----	3-dr. Touring-5P	$ 355	1,500 lbs.	80,070*
T	-----	3-dr. Touring-5P (electric start and demountable rims)	$ 450	1,650 lbs.	514,333
T	-----	2-dr. Runabout-2P	$ 325	1,390 lbs.	31,923*
T	-----	2-dr. Runabout-2P (electric start and demountable rims)	$ 420	1,540 lbs.	133,433
T	-----	2-dr. Sedan-5P (electric start and demountable rims)	$ 660	1,875 lbs.	146,060
T	-----	2-dr. Coupe-2P (electric start and demountable rims)	$ 595	1,760 lbs.	198,382
T	-----	Chassis	$ 295	1,060 lbs.	15,228*
T	-----	Chassis (electric start and demountable rims)	$ 390	1,210 lbs.	23,313
TT	-----	Truck chassis (pneumatic tires)	$ 445	1,477 lbs.	135,629*

***Note:** Production from Jan. 1, 1922 to Dec. 31, 1922 including foreign production.

1922 Model T (Four) (Prices effective Jan. 16, 1922)

T	-----	3-dr. Touring-5P	$ 348	1,500 lbs.	Note 1
T	-----	3-dr. Touring-5P (electric start and demountable rims)	$ 443	1,650 lbs.	Note 1
T	-----	2-dr. Runabout-2P	$ 319	1,390 lbs.	Note 1
T	-----	2-dr. Runabout-2P (electric start and demountable rims)	$ 414	1,540 lbs.	Note 1
T	-----	2-dr. Sedan-5P (electric start and demountable rims)	$ 645	1,875 lbs.	Note 1
T	-----	2-dr. Coupe-2P (electric start and demountable rims)	$ 580	1,760 lbs.	Note 1
T	-----	Chassis	$ 285	1,060 lbs.	Note 1
T	-----	Chassis (electric start and demountable rims)	$ 380	1,210 lbs.	Note 1
TT	-----	Truck chassis (pneumatic tires)	$ 430	1,477 lbs.	Note 1

Note 1: See the production figures in the first 1922 chart.

1922 Model T (Four) (Prices effective Oct. 17, 1922)

T	-----	3-dr. Touring-5P	$ 298	1,500 lbs.	Note 1
T	-----	3-dr. Touring-5P (electric start and demountable rims)	$ 393	1,650 lbs.	Note 1
T	-----	2-dr. Runabout-2P	$ 269	1,390 lbs.	Note 1
T	-----	2-dr. Runabout-2P (electric start and demountable rims)	$ 364	1,540 lbs.	Note 1
T	-----	2-dr. Sedan-5P (electric start and demountable rims)	$ 595	1,875 lbs.	Note 1
TT	-----	4-dr. Sedan-5P	$ 725	1,950 lbs.	Note 1
T	-----	2-dr. Coupe-2P (electric start and demountable rims)	$ 530	1,760 lbs.	Note 1
T	-----	Chassis	$ 235	1,060 lbs.	Note 1
T	-----	Chassis (electric start and demountable rims)	$ 330	1,210 lbs.	Note 1
TT	-----	Truck chassis	$ 380	1,477 lbs.	Note 1
TT	-----	Truck chassis (electric start and demountable rims)	$ 475	1,577 lbs.	18,410

Note 1: See the production figures in the first 1922 chart.

Engine:

1920 Model T: L-head. Four. Cast-iron block. B & S: 3-3/4 x 4 in. Displacement: 176.7 cid. Compression ratio: 3.98:1. Brake hp: 20 at 1600 rpm. NACC hp: 22.5. Torque: 83 at 900 rpm. Main bearings: three. Valve lifters: solid. Carburetor: Kingston L4 (6150). Holley NH (6200). New cylinder head with slightly lower compression and much larger water jacket.

Note: Thermosyphon. Valve chambers (two) now enclosed using steel doors held with one stud/nut each. Inspection plate in the crankcase. New lightweight connecting rods.

1921 and 1922 Model T: L-head. Four. Cast-iron block. B & S: 3-3/4 x 4 in. Displacement.: 176.7 cid. Compression ratio: 3.98:1. Brake hp: 20 at 1600 rpm. NACC hp: 22.5. Torque: 83 at 900 rpm. Main bearings: three. Valve lifters: solid. Carburetor: Kingston L4 (6150). Holley NH (6200).

Note: Thermosyphon. Single valve chamber covered with one steel door held with two stud/nuts or bolts. Beginning in 1922 (Serial No. 5530000 - April 1922)

Chassis:

Model T: Wheelbase: 100 in. Overall length: 10 ft. 8 in., chassis and 11 ft. 2-1/2 in., car. Front tread: 56 in. Rear tread: 56 in. Tires: (front) 30 x 3 front, (rear) 30 x 3-1/2. 30 x 3-1/2 all around with demountable rims 1919-1925. Chassis after mid-1913 had a longer rear crossmember.

Technical:

Model T: Planetary transmission. Speeds: 2F/1R. Three pedal controls and one lever on floor. Multiple disc clutch (25 discs 1915-1927). Torque tube drive. Straight bevel rear axle. Overall ratio: 3.63:1. Brakes: Contracting band in transmission. Hand-operated internal expanding in rear wheels.

1921 Ford Model T Touring (OCW)

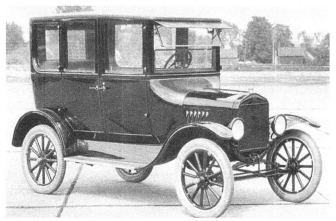

1922 Ford Model T Fordor Sedan (OCW)

1922 Ford Model T Coupe (OCW)

Foot brake stops driveshaft. Parking brake on two rear wheels.

All cars equipped with headlamps, horn, etc. Starter ($75). Demountable

1923 Ford

Ford — Model T: In 1923, open body styles in the Model T lineup were again restyled. They used the same bodies as the 1921-1922 versions, but had a new windshield with a sloping angle and a new "one man" top. These features made the Touring and Runabout look new. The 1923 model was introduced in the fall of 1922 and continued until about June 1923, when another new line of Model Ts appeared. About November 1922, a new Fordor sedan was added to the line. The Fordor body was made of aluminum panels over a wood frame. Instrument panels were now standard on all Model Ts. Cars without and electrical starter had a blank plate where the ammeter would be. The early 1923 cars continued the wooden firewall of all previous Fords. This lasted until early calendar 1923, when the firewall was changed to sheet metal. This took place before the June styling change mentioned above. The starter and generator were standard equipment on all closed cars, as were the demountable wheels. This equipment was optional on the Runabout and Touring car. It was also the last year for the Center Door Sedan and the Coupe with the forward-opening doors.

VIN:

Serial number was above the water inlet on the left side of the engine. Starting: 6543607 (September 22, 1922). Ending: 7927374 (June 30, 1923). 1923 calendar-year engine numbers: 6953072 to 9008371. Numbers stamped on the body sills, etc. were manufacturer's numbers and not an identifying number.

1923 Model T (Four) (Prices effective Oct. 17, 1922)

Model No.	Body/ Style No.	Body Type & Seating	Factory Price	Shipping Weight	Prod. Total
T	—	3 dr. Touring-5P	$ 298	1,500 lbs.	136,441*
T		3 dr. Touring-5P (electric start and demountable rims)	$ 393	1,650 lbs.	792,651
T	—	2 dr. Runabout-2P	$ 269	1,390 lbs.	56,954*
T	---	2 dr. Runabout-2P (electric start and demountable rims)	$ 364	1,540 lbs.	238,638
T	—	2d Sedan-5P (electric start and demountable rims)	$ 595	1,875 lbs.	96,410
T	—	4d Sedan-5P (electric start and demountable rims)	$ 725	1,950 lbs.	144,444
T	—	2d Coupe-2P (electric start and demountable rims)	$ 530	1,760 lbs.	313,273
T	—	Chassis	$ 235	1,060 lbs.	9,443*
		Chassis (electric start and demountable rims)	$ 330	1,210 lbs.	42,874
TT		Truck chassis	$ 380	1,477 lbs.	197,057*
TT		Truck chassis (electric start and demountable rims)	$ 475	1,577 lbs.	64,604

Note: Production totals from Jan. 1, 1923 through Dec. 31, 1923 including foreign production.

1923 Ford Model T Touring Car (OCW)

1923 Model T (Four) (Prices effective Oct. 2, 1923)

T	—	3 dr. Touring-5P	$ 295	1,500 lbs.	Note 1
T		3 dr. Touring-5P (electric start and demountable rims)	$ 380	1,650 lbs.	Note 1
T	—	2 dr. Runabout-2P	$ 265	1,390 lbs.	Note 1
T	---	2 dr. Runabout-2P (electric start and demountable rims)	$ 350	1,540 lbs.	Note 1
T	—	2d Sedan-5P (electric start and demountable rims)	$ 590	1,875 lbs.	Note 1
T	—	4d Sedan-5P (electric start and demountable rims)	$ 685	1,950 lbs.	Note 1
T	—	2d Coupe-2P (electric start and demountable rims)	$ 525	1,760 lbs.	Note 1
T	—	Chassis	$ 230	1,060 lbs.	Note 1
T		Chassis (electric start and demountable rims)	$ 295	1,210 lbs.	Note 1
TT		Truck chassis	$ 370	1,477 lbs.	Note 1
TT		Truck chassis (electric start and demountable rims)	$ 435	1,577 lbs.	Note 1

Note 1: See top 1923 chart for production totals.

1923 Model T (Four) (Prices effective Oct. 2, 1923)

T	—	3 dr. Touring-5P	$ 295	1,500 lbs.	Note 1
T		3 dr. Touring-5P (electric start and demountable rims)	$ 380	1,650 lbs.	Note 1
T	—	2 dr. Runabout-2P	$ 265	1,390 lbs.	Note 1
T	---	2 dr. Runabout-2P (electric start and demountable rims)	$ 350	1,540 lbs.	Note 1
T	—	2d Sedan-5P (electric start and demountable rims)	$ 590	1,875 lbs.	Note 1
T	—	4d Sedan-5P (electric start and demountable rims)	$ 685	1,950 lbs.	Note 1
T	—	2d Coupe-2P (electric start and demountable rims)	$ 525	1,760 lbs.	Note 1
T	—	Chassis	$ 230	1,060 lbs.	Note 1
T		Chassis (electric start and demountable rims)	$ 295	1,210 lbs.	Note 1
TT	----	Truck chassis	$ 370	1,477 lbs.	Note 1
TT	----	Truck chassis (electric start and demountable rims)	$ 455	1,577 lbs.	Note 1
TT	----	Truck with body	$ 490	------	Note 2

Note 1: See top 1923 chart for production totals.
Note 2: This truck was not listed separately from the chassis figures.

Engine:

Model T: L-head. Four. Cast-iron block. B & S: 3-3/4 x 4 in. Displacement: 176.7 cid. Compression ratio: 3.98:1. Brake hp: 20 at 1600 rpm. NACC hp: 22.5. Torque: 83 at 900 rpm. Main bearings: three. Valve lifters: solid. Carburetor: Kingston L4 (6150). Holley NH (6200).

Note: Thermosyphon. Inspection plate in the crankcase. New lightweight connecting rods.

Chassis:

Model T: Wheelbase: 100 in. Overall length: 10 ft. 8 in., chassis and 11 ft. 2-1/2 in., car. Front tread: 56 in. Rear tread: 56 in. Tires: (front) 30 x 3 front, (rear) 30 x 3-1/2. 30 x 3-1/2 all around with demountable rims 1919-1925.

Technical:

Model T: Planetary transmission. Speeds: 2F/1R. Three pedal controls and one lever on floor. Multiple disc clutch (25 discs). Torque tube drive.

1923 Ford Model T Coupe (OCW)

Straight bevel rear axle. Overall ratio: 3.63:1. Brakes: Contracting band in transmission. Hand-operated internal expanding in rear wheels. Foot brake stops driveshaft. Parking brake on two rear wheels.

Options:

The basic equipment included three oil lamps only (two side and one tail). Options listed included: Windshield. Headlamps. Tops. Horns. Prest-o-lite tanks (instead of the carbide tank). Robe rails. Tire chains. Top boots. Foot rests. Spare tire carriers. Speedometers. Bumpers. No prices were given.

1924 Ford

Ford — Model T: In June of 1923, the Model T lineup was restyled again. Cars built after June, but before calendar-year 1924 began, are commonly called "1923" but Ford referred to them as 1924s. The open-body Model Ts continued with the same body, windshield and top as the earlier 1923s, but a new higher radiator and larger hood altered their appearance noticeably. The front fenders were given a lip on the front of the apron to blend in with a new valance under the radiator. This gave the car a more "finished" look. There was a new coupe with an integral rear turtle deck and doors that opened at the rear. A new Tudor Sedan was also introduced. It had doors at the front of the body, instead of at the center. The Fordor Sedan was the same as the earlier one, except for the new hood and front fenders. The lower body panels were now made of steel instead of aluminum.

VIN:

The serial number was above the water inlet on the left side of the engine. Starting: 7927375 (July 2, 1923). Ending: 10266471 (July 31, 1924). 1924 calendar-year engine numbers: 9008372 to 10994033. Numbers stamped on the body sills, etc. were manufacturer's numbers and not an identifying number.

1923 Model T (Four)   (Prices effective Oct. 30, 1923)

Model No.	Body/ Style No.	Body Type & Seating	Factory Price	Shipping Weight	Prod. Total
T	—	3 dr. Touring-5P	$ 295	1,500 lbs.	99,523*
T		3 dr. Touring-5P (electric start and demountable rims)	$ 380	1,650 lbs.	673,579
T	—	2 dr. Runabout-2P	$ 265	1,390 lbs.	43,317*
T	---	2 dr. Runabout-2P (electric start and demountable rims)	$ 350	1,540 lbs.	220,955
T	—	2d Sedan-5P (electric start and demountable rims)	$ 590	1,875 lbs.	223,203
T	—	4d Sedan-5P (electric start and demountable rims)	$ 685	1,950 lbs.	84,733
T	—	2d Coupe-2P (electric start and demountable rims)	$ 525	1,760 lbs.	327,584
T	—	Chassis	$ 230	1,060 lbs.	3,921*
T	---	Chassis (electric start and demountable rims)	$ 295	1,210 lbs.	43,980
TT	----	Truck chassis	$ 370	1,477 lbs.	127,891*
TT	----	Truck chassis (electric start and demountable rims)	$ 435	1,577 lbs.	32,471
TT	----	Truck with body	$ 490	-------	38,840*
TT	----	Truck with body (electric start and demountable rims)	$ 555	-------	5,649

Note: Production totals from Jan. 1, 1924 through Dec. 31, 1924 including foreign production.

1924 Ford Model T Fordor Sedan (OCW)

1923 Model T (Four)   (Prices effective Dec. 2, 1924)

T	—	3 dr. Touring-5P	$ 290	1,500 lbs.	Note 1
T	—	3 dr. Touring-5P (electric start and demountable rims)	$ 375	1,650 lbs.	Note 1
T	—	2 dr. Runabout-2P	$ 260	1,390 lbs.	Note 1
T	---	2 dr. Runabout-2P (electric start and demountable rims)	$ 345	1,540 lbs.	Note 1
T	—	2d Sedan-5P (electric start and demountable rims)	$ 580	1,875 lbs.	Note 1
T	—	4d Sedan-5P (electric start and demountable rims)	$ 660	1,950 lbs.	Note 1
T	—	2d Coupe-2P (electric start and demountable rims)	$ 520	1,760 lbs.	Note 1
T	—	Chassis	$ 225	1,060 lbs.	Note 1
T	---	Chassis (electric start and demountable rims)	$ 290	1,210 lbs.	Note 1
TT	----	Truck chassis	$ 365	1,477 lbs.	Note 1
TT	----	Truck chassis (electric start and demountable rims)	$ 430	1,577 lbs.	Note 1
TT	----	Truck with body	$ 485	-------	Note 1
TT	----	Truck with body (electric start and demountable rims)	$ 550	-------	Note 1

Note 1: See top chart for 1924 production information.

1924 Model T (Four)   (Price effective Oct. 24, 1924)

TT	-----	Stake body truck	$495	-------	Note 2

Note 2: Production figures of this truck were not listed separately. A C truck cab cost $65. The truck rear bed $55 if ordered separately.

Engine:

Model T: L-head. Four. Cast-iron block. B & S: 3-3/4 x 4 in. Displacement: 176.7 cid. Compression ratio: 3.98:1. Brake hp: 20 at 1600 rpm. NACC hp: 22.5. Torque: 83 at 900 rpm. Main bearings: three. Valve lifters: solid. Carburetor: Kingston L4 (6150). Holley NH (6200).

Note: Thermosyphon. Single valve chamber covered with one steel door held with two stud/nuts or bolts.

Chassis:

Model T: Wheelbase: 100 in. Overall length: 10 ft. 8 in., chassis and 11 ft. 2-1/2 in., car. Front tread: 56 in. Rear tread: 56 in. Tires: (front) 30 x 3 front, (rear) 30 x 3-1/2. 30 x 3-1/2 all around with demountable rims 1919-1925. Chassis essentially identical except those after mid-1913 have a longer rear crossmember.

Technical:

Model T: Planetary transmission. Speeds: 2F/1R. Three pedal controls and one lever on floor. Multiple disc clutch (25 discs 1915-1927). Torque tube drive. Straight bevel rear axle. Overall ratio: 3.63:1. Brakes: Contracting band in transmission. Hand-operated internal expanding in rear wheels. Foot brake stops driveshaft. Parking brake on two rear wheels.

Options:

All cars equipped with headlamps, horn, etc. Starter ($75). Demountable rims ($25).

1924 Ford Model T Roadster (OCW)

1924 Ford Model T Coupe (JAC)

1925 Ford

Ford — Model T: The 1924 Model T line continued until about July of 1925 with no major changes except in upholstery material and construction details. About May 1925 the Roadster Pickup and the Closed Cab truck appeared. A new option introduced late in 1925 was 4.40 x 21-in. "balloon" tires mounted on demountable-rim wooden wheels. The wheels came finished in either black or natural.

VIN:

The serial number was above the water inlet on the left side of the engine. Starting: 10266472 (August 1, 1924, start of fiscal 1925). Ending: 12218728 (July 27, 1925, start of "1926" models). 1925 calendar-year engine numbers: 10994034 to 12990076. Numbers stamped on the body sills, etc. were manufacturer's numbers and not an identifying number.

1925 Ford Model T Coupe (OCW)

1925 Ford Model T Touring (OCW)

1925 Model T (Four) (Prices effective Oct. 24, 1924)

Model No.	Body/ Style No.	Body Type & Seating	Factory Price	Shipping Weight	Prod. Total
T	—	3 dr. Touring-5P	$ 290	1,500 lbs.	64,399*
T		3 dr. Touring-5P (electric start and demountable rims)	$ 375	1,650 lbs.	626,813
T	—	2 dr. Runabout-2P	$ 260	1,390 lbs.	34,206*
T	---	2 dr. Runabout-2P (electric start and demountable rims)	$ 345	1,536 lbs.	264,436
T		2d Sedan-5P (electric start and demountable rims)	$ 580	1,875 lbs.	195,001
T		4d Sedan-5P (electric start and demountable rims)	$ 680	1,950 lbs.	81,050
T		2d Coupe-2P (electric start and demountable rims)	$ 520	1,760 lbs.	343,969
T		Chassis	$ 225	1,060 lbs.	6,523*
T	---	Chassis (electric start and demountable rims)	$ 290	1,210 lbs.	53,450
T	----	2-dr. Roadster pickup	$ 281	1,471 lbs.	33,795 +
T	----	2-dr. Roadster pickup	$ 366	1,621 lbs.	------ +
TT	----	Truck chassis	$ 365	1,477 lbs.	186,810*
TT	----	Truck chassis (electric start and demountable rims)	$ 430	1,577 lbs.	32,471
TT	----	Truck with body	$ 490	-------	192,839*
TT	----	Truck with body (electric start and demountable rims)	$ 555	-------	5,649

Note: Production totals from Jan. 1, 1925 through Dec. 31, 1925 including foreign production.

Note +: Roadster pickups were not separated by electric starter or no starter.

1925 Model T (Four)
(Prices effective Mar. 4, 1925 and unchanged Dec. 31, 1925)

T	—	3 dr. Touring-5P	$ 290	1,500 lbs.	Note 1
T		3 dr. Touring-5P (electric start and demountable rims)	$ 375	1,650 lbs.	Note 1
T	—	2 dr. Runabout-2P	$ 260	1,390 lbs.	Note 1
T	---	2 dr. Runabout-2P (electric start and demountable rims)	$ 345	1,540 lbs.	Note 1
T	—	2d Sedan-5P (electric start and demountable rims)	$ 580	1,875 lbs.	Note 1
T	—	4d Sedan-5P (electric start and demountable rims)	$ 660	1,950 lbs.	Note 1
T	—	2d Coupe-2P (electric start and demountable rims)	$ 520	1,760 lbs.	Note 1
T	—	Chassis	$ 225	1,060 lbs.	Note 1
T	---	Chassis (electric start and demountable rims)	$ 290	1,210 lbs.	Note 1
T	----	2-dr. Roadster pickup	$ 281	1,471 lbs.	Notes 1,2
T	----	2-dr. Roadster pickup	$ 366	1,621 lbs.	Notes 1,2
TT	----	Truck chassis	$ 365	1,477 lbs.	Note 1
TT	----	Truck chassis (electric start and demountable rims)	$ 430	1,577 lbs.	Note 1
TT	----	Truck with body	$ 485	-------	Note 1
TT	----	Truck with body (electric start and demountable rims)	$ 550	-------	Note 1

Note 1: See top chart for 1924 production information.

Note 2: Roadster pickups were not separated by electric starter or no starter.

1925 Model T (Four)
(Prices effective Mar. 4, 1925 and unchanged Dec. 31, 1925)

TT	-----	Stake body truck	$495	-------	Note 3

Note 3: Production figures of this truck were not listed separately. The C truck cab cost $65. The truck rear bed $55 if ordered separately.

Engine:

Model T: L-head. Four. Cast-iron block. B & S: 3-3/4 x 4 inches. Displacement: 176.7 cid. Compression ratio: 3.98:1. Brake hp: 20 at 1600 rpm. NACC hp: 22.5. Torque: 83 at 900 rpm. Main bearings: three. Valve lifters: solid. Carburetor: Kingston L4 (6150). Holley NH (6200).

Note: Thermosyphon. Single valve chamber covered with one steel door held with two stud/nuts or bolts.

Chassis:

Model T: Wheelbase: 100 in. Overall length: 10 ft. 8 inches, chassis and 11 ft. 2-1/2 in., car. Front tread: 56 in. Rear tread: 56 in. Tires: (front) 30 x 3 front, (rear) 30 x 3-1/2. 30 x 3-1/2 all around with demountable rims 1919-1925. Chassis essentially identical except those after mid-1913 have a longer rear crossmember.

1925 Ford Model T Tudor Sedan (OCW)

Technical:

Model T: Planetary transmission. Speeds: 2F/1R. Three pedal controls and one lever on floor. Multiple disc clutch (25 discs 1915-1927). Torque tube drive. Straight bevel rear axle. Overall ratio: 3.63:1. Brakes: Contracting band in transmission. Hand-operated internal expanding in rear wheels. Foot brake stops driveshaft. Parking brake on two rear wheels.

Options:

All cars equipped with headlamps, horn, etc. Starter ($75). Demountable rims ($25).

1926 Model T

Ford — Model T: About July 1925, an "Improved Ford" marked the first major restyling of the Model T since 1917. New fenders, new running boards, new bodies (except for the Fordor Sedan), new hoods and even a modified chassis made these Fords unique during the era of the Model T. The Touring Car was given a door on the driver's side for the first time since 1911 on U.S. cars (post-1911 Canadian-built Fords had a driver's side door). The Tudor Sedan and the Coupe were actually all-new designs, though similar in style to the 1925 versions. The Fordor Sedan continued the same basic body introduced in late 1922, except for its new cowl, hood, fenders, etc. The chassis had a new and even longer rear crossmember. With a modification of the springs and front spindles, the entire car was lowered about an inch. While sharing basically the same running gear as earlier models, the 1926-1927 cars had 11-inch rear-wheel brake drums, although they were only operated by the "emergency brake" lever. The foot pedals for low speed and braking were larger and the internal transmission brake was made wider for better life and operation. Initially offered in black, the Coupe and the Tudor were later painted a dark green. The Fordor Sedan came in a dark maroon as its standard color. Open cars continued to be finished in black until mid-1926. When the "126" models were introduced in 1925, the standard wheels on the closed cars were the 30 x 3-1/2-inch demountable type. Open cars had 30 x 3-1/2-inch non-demountable wheels. However, by calendar-year 1926, the 21-inch balloon tires were standard on all models. The gasoline tank was now located in the cowl on all models, except the Fordor Sedan, which continued to have it under the driver's seat.

VIN:

The serial number was above the water inlet on the left side of the engine. Starting: 12218729 (July 27, 1925, start of "1926" models).

1926 Ford Model T Fordor Touring (RLC)

Ending: 14049029 (July 30, 1926, end of fiscal year 1926). 1926 calendar-year engine numbers: 12990077 to 14619254. Numbers stamped on the body sills, etc. were manufacturer's numbers and not an identifying number.

1926 Model T (Four) (Prices effective Jan. 1, 1926)

Model No.	Body/ Style No.	Body Type & Seating	Factory Price	Shipping Weight	Prod. Total
T	—	4 dr. Touring-5P	$ 290	1,633 lbs.*	------
T	—	4 dr. Touring-5P (starter and 21-in. demountable wheels)	$ 375	1,738 lbs.	626,813
T	—	2 dr. Runabout-2P	$ 260	1,550 lbs.*	------
T	---	2 dr. Runabout-2P (electric start and demountable rims)	$ 345	1,655 lbs.	342,575
T	—	2d Sedan-5P (electric start and demountable rims)	$ 580	1,972 lbs.	270,331
T	—	4d Sedan-5P (electric start and demountable rims)	$ 660	2,004 lbs.	102,732
T	—	2d Coupe-2P (electric start and demountable rims)	$ 520	1,860 lbs.	288,342
T	—	Chassis	$ 225	1,167 lbs.*	------
T	---	Chassis (electric start and demountable rims)	$ 290	1,272 lbs.	58,223
T	----	2-dr. Roadster pickup	$ 281	------- *	Note 2
T	----	2-dr. Roadster pickup	$ 366	1,736 lbs.	75,406
TT	----	Truck chassis	$ 365	1,477 lbs.	186,810*
TT	----	Truck chassis (electric start and demountable rims)	$ 430	1,577 lbs.	32,471

Note 1(*): Early models had 30 x 3-1/2-in. non-demountable wheels and no starter. They were 10 lbs. lighter.

Note 2: These pickups were only available by special order by calendar year 1926.

1926 Model T (Four)
(Prices effective June 6, 1926 and unchanged Dec. 31, 1926)

Model No.	Body/ Style No.	Body Type & Seating	Factory Price	Shipping Weight	Prod. Total
T		4 dr. Touring-5P (electric start and demountable rims)	$ 380	1,738 lbs.	Note 1
T	---	2 dr. Runabout-2P (electric start and demountable rims)	$ 360	1,655 lbs.	Note 1
T	—	2d Sedan-5P (electric start and demountable rims)	$ 495	1,972 lbs.	Note 1
T	—	4d Sedan-5P (electric start and demountable rims)	$ 545	2,004 lbs.	Note 1
T	—	2d Coupe-2P (electric start and demountable rims)	$ 485	1,860 lbs.	Note 1
T	---	Chassis (electric start and demountable rims)	$ 300	1,272 lbs.	Note 1
T	----	2-dr. Roadster pickup	$ 381	------	Note 2
TT	----	Truck chassis	$ 325	1,477 lbs.	Note 1
TT	----	Truck chassis (electric start and demountable rims)	$ 375	1,577 lbs.	Note 1

Note 1: See top chart for 1924 production information.

Note 2: Roadster pickups were not separated by electric starter or no starter.

1926 Model T Truck Bodies

Model No.	Body Description	Factory Price	Production Total
TT	Open cab	$ 65	Note 3
TT	Closed cab	$ 85	Note 3
TT	Express body	$ 55	Note 3
TT	Platform body	$ 50	Note 3
TT	Express	$ 110	Note 3

Note 3: Chassis production figures are for U.S. and foreign. Body figures are for U.S. only and are included in the chassis count. Starter production is not listed separately.

Engine:

Model T: L-head. Four. Cast-iron block. B & S: 3-3/4 x 4 in. Displacement: 176.7 cid. Compression ratio: 3.98:1. Brake hp: 20 at 1600 rpm. NACC hp: 22.5. Torque: 83 at 900 rpm. Main bearings: three. Valve lifters: solid. Carburetor: Kingston L4 (6150B). Holley NH (6200C), Holley Vaporizer (6250), Kingston Regenerator.

The transmission housing was now on bolts to the rear of the cylinder. The fan was mounted on the water outlet. Later production used nickel-plated head and water connection bolts.

Chassis:

Model T: Wheelbase: 100 in. Overall length: 10 ft. 8 inches, chassis and 11 ft. 2-1/2 in., car. Front tread: 56 in. Rear tread: 56 in. Tires: (front) 30 x 3-1/2, (rear) 30 x 3-1/2. Chassis essentially identical except those after mid-1913 have a much longer rear cross member. Chassis now lowered about an inch by the use of a different front spindle and

1926 Ford Model T Fordor Sedan (OCW)

1927 Ford Model T Fordor Touring (OCW)

1926 Ford Model T Tudor Sedan (HAC)

spring and a deeper crown in the rear crossmember. In mid-1926, the rear crossmember was made with a flanged edge and the chassis was made of heavier steel.

Technical:

Model T: Planetary transmission. Speeds: 2F/1R. Three pedal controls and one lever on floor. Multiple disc clutch (25 discs 1915-1927). Torque tube drive. Straight bevel rear axle. Overall ratio: 3.63:1. Brakes: Contracting band in transmission. Hand-operated internal expanding in rear wheels. Foot brake stops driveshaft. Parking brake on two rear wheels. In mid-1925 (1926 models) the transmission brake was made about a half-inch wider, and the rear wheel brakes were enlarged to 11 inches with lined shoes. In January 1926 optional 21-inch wire wheels became available, and these became standard on some closed cars in calendar year 1927.

Options:

All cars built after January 1926 are equipped with headlights, horn, starter and 21-inch demountable rims. Windshield wiper (hand operated) (50 cents).* Vacuum-operated windshield wiper ($3.50). Windshield wings for open cars ($6.50 pair). Gipsy curtains for open cars ($3 per pair). Top boot for open cars ($5). Bumpers front and rear ($15). Wire wheels, set of five ($50) and $35) later in 1926. Rearview mirror for open cars (.75).* Dash lamp for open cars (.60).* Stoplight and switch ($2.50). Shock absorbers ($9 per set). Starter and demountable wheels are standard on all cars. Starter is optional on the truck. Pickup body for runabout, $25.

1927 Ford

Ford — Model T: Wire wheels were offered as an option beginning January 1926. In 1926, perhaps as "1927" models (Ford didn't name yearly models consistently), colors were added for the open cars: Gunmetal blue or Phoenix brown. Closed cars were offered in Highland green, Royal maroon, Fawn gray, Moleskin and Drake green. By calendar 1927, any body could be ordered in any standard Ford color. Black could be had on special order on the pickup body, although Commercial green was the standard color. Fenders and running boards were black on all models. By early 1927, many Ford branches were supplying wire wheels as standard equipment on closed cars. Model T production ended in May 1927 although Ford continued building engines through the year, then a few at a time until August 4, 1941.

VIN:

The serial number was above the water inlet on the left side of the engine. Starting: 14049030 (August 2, 1926, start of fiscal 1927). Ending: 15006625 (May 25, 1927, end of Model T Ford car production.)* 1927 calendar year

engine numbers: 14619255 to 15076231.* Numbers stamped on the body sills, etc. were manufacturer's numbers and not an identifying number.

*Most records show 15007032 or 15007033 as the last car but the factory records indicate these numbers were built on May 31, 1927, five days after the car assembly line was stopped. Ford continued building engines through 1927 and at a considerable rate until January 1931 (as many as 12,000 per month after the end of the Model T!). Production averaged about 100 per month in 1931, then dropped to less than 10 and ended, finally, on August 4, 1941, with number 15176888.

1927 Model T (Four)

Model No.	Body/ Style No.	Body Type & Seating	Factory Price	Shipping Weight	Production Total
T		4 dr. Touring-5P (electric start and demountable rims)	$ 380	1,738 lbs.	81,181
T	---	2 dr. Runabout-2P (electric start and demountable rims)	$ 360	1,655 lbs.	95,778
T	—	2 dr. Sedan-5P (electric start and demountable rims)	$ 495	1,972 lbs.	78,105
T	—	4 dr. Sedan-5P (electric start and demountable rims)	$ 545	2,004 lbs.	22,930
T	—	2d Coupe-2P (electric start and demountable rims)	$ 485	1,860 lbs.	69,939
T	---	Chassis (electric start and demountable rims)	$ 300	1,272 lbs.	19,280
T	----	2-dr. Roadster pickup	$ 381	1,736 lbs.	28,143
TT	----	Truck chassis	$ 325	1,477 lbs.	83,202
TT	----	Truck chassis (electric start and demountable rims)	$ 375	1,577 lbs.	------

Notes: Production totals are for Jan.1, 1927 through Dec. 31, 1927. Chassis production figures are for U.S. and foreign. Body figures are for U. S. only and are included in the chassis count. Starter production is not listed separately. Model T production ended May 26, 1927 for automobiles. Trucks continued to be produced for some time.

1927 Model T Truck Bodies

Model No.	Body Description	Factory Price	Production Total
TT	Open cab	$ 65	41, 318 (U.S.)
TT	Closed cab	$ 85	------
TT	Express body	$ 55	------
TT	Platform body	$ 50	------
TT	Express	$ 110	------

Engine:

Model T: L-head. Four. Cast-iron block. B & S: 3-3/4 x 4 in. Displacement: 176.7 cid. Compression ratio: 3.98:1. Brake hp: 20 at 1600 rpm. NACC hp: 22.5. Torque: 83 at 900 rpm. Main bearings: three. Valve lifters: solid. Carburetor: Kingston L4 (6150B). Holley NH (6200C), Holley Vaporizer (6250), Kingston Regenerator.

Transmission housing now bolted to the rear of the cylinder. The fan mounted on the water outlet. Later production used nickel-plated head and water connection bolts.

Chassis:

Model T: Wheelbase: 100 in. Overall length: 10 ft. 8 in., chassis and 11 ft. 2-1/2 in., car. Front tread: 56 in. Rear tread: 56 in. Tires: (front) 30 x 3-1/2, (rear) 30 x 3-1/2. Chassis essentially identical except those after mid-1913 have a much longer rear cross member. Chassis now lowered about an inch by the use of a different front spindle and spring and a deeper crown in the rear crossmember. In mid-1926, the rear

1927 Ford Model T Runabout

1927 Ford Model T Tudor Sedan (OCW)

crossmember was made with a flanged edge and the chassis was made of heavier steel.

Technical:

Model T: Planetary transmission. Speeds: 2F/1R. Three pedal controls and one lever on floor. Multiple disc clutch (25 discs 1915-1927). Torque tube drive. Straight bevel rear axle. Overall ratio: 3.63:1. Brakes: Contracting band in transmission. Hand-operated internal expanding in rear wheels. Foot brake stops driveshaft. Parking brake on two rear wheels. In mid-1925 (1926 models) the transmission brake was made about a half-inch wider, and the rear wheel brakes were enlarged to 11 inches with lined shoes. In January 1926 optional 21-inch wire wheels became available, and these became standard on some closed cars in calendar year 1927.

Options:

All cars built after January 1926 were equipped with headlights, horn, starter and 21-inch demountable rims. Hand-operated windshield wiper (50 cents). Vacuum-operated windshield wiper ($2). Windshield wings for open cars ($2.50). Gipsy curtains for open cars ($1.10 per pair). Top boot for open cars ($4). Bumpers front and rear ($15). Wire wheels, set of five ($35). Rearview mirror for open cars (.75). Dash lamp for open cars (.60). Stoplight and switch ($2.50). Shock absorbers ($9 per set).

1928 Ford

Ford — Model A: Reverting to a Model A designation for the "New Ford" suggested a "new beginning." The A designation also symbolized the impact this new automobile had upon Ford Motor Company. The Model A was a far more complex automobile than the Model T. It had approximately 6,800 different parts, compared to less than 5,000 in a Model T. However, there were still similarities. Both cars had four-cylinder L-head engines. Both cars had semi-elliptic front and rear

springs that were mounted transversely. Beyond these points, the Model A moved far away from the heritage of the Model T. Its engine had a water pump and displaced just over 200 cubic inches. With 40 hp, it was virtually twice as powerful as the Model T engine and provided a 65 mph top speed. Superseding the old magneto ignition was a contemporary battery-and-ignition system. The Model T's planetary transmission gave way to a three-speed sliding-gear unit. Other technical advancements found in the Model A included the use of four-wheel mechanical brakes and Houdaille double-acting hydraulic shock absorbers. The styling of the Model A maintained a link with that of the Model T, but with a 103-1/2 inch wheelbase, 4.50 x 21 tires and a higher belt line, the influence of the Lincoln automobile upon the appearance of the new Ford was unmistakable. Full-crown fenders were used and the bodywork of each of the five original models had the body surrounds outlined in contrasting body colors and pinstriping. The Model A's two-piece front and rear bumpers were similar to those used on the 1927 Model T. Its new radiator shell, with its gentle center vee-dip and moderately curved crossbar for the headlights, made it impossible to confuse the two Fords. The first Model A engine was completed on October 20, 1927, and the following day it was installed in the first Model A assembled. From that day (May 25, 1927) Ford announced it would produce a successor to the Model T. Public interest steadily increased to a level that was finally satisfied on December 2, 1927, when the nationwide introduction of the Model A took place. While many industry observers recognized the passing of the Model T as the end of an era, there was equal appreciation for the extraordinary value the Model A represented and an awareness that it was in all ways more than a worthy successor to the "Tin Lizzie."

VIN:

Serial numbers were located on the top side of the frame near the clutch pedal. Starting: October 20-December 31, 1927 - A1, January 1-December 31, 1928 - A5276. Ending: October 20-December 31, 1927 - A5275, January 1-December 31, 1928 - A810122. Engine numbers were located on boss placed on center of left side of block directly below the cylinder head. A prefix letter A was used and a star is found on either end. Starting: October 20-December 31, 1927 - A1, January 1-December 31, 1928 - A5276. Ending: October 20-December 31, 1927 - A5275, January 1-December 31, 1928 - A810122. Model numbers: 1928 models have a date when the body was manufactured stamped on the upper left side of the firewall.

1928 Model A

Model No.	Body/ Style No.	Body Type & Seating	Factory Price	Shipping Weight	Production Total
A	—	2 dr. Roadster-2/4P	$ 480	2,106 lbs.	Note 1
A	---	4 dr. Phaeton-5P	$ 460	2,140 lbs.	Note 1
A	—	2 dr. Business Coupe-2P	$ 550	2,225 lbs.	Note 1
A	---	2 dr. Coupe-2/4P	$ 550	2,265 lbs.	Note 1
A	—	2 dr. Standard Business Roadster-2P	$ 480	2,050 lbs.	Note 1
A	—	4 dr. Business Coupe-2P	$ 525	------	Note 1
A	—	Tudor-5P	$ 550	2,340 lbs.	Note 1
A	—	Fordor-5P	$ 585	2,386 lbs.	Note 1
A	---	4-dr. Taxi Cab-5PChassis	$ 600	------	Note 1

Note 1: Body style production was a calendar year record. See list at end of 1931 Model A section.

Engine:

Model A: Inline. L-head. Four. Cast-iron block. B & S: 3-7/8 x 4-1/4 in. Displacement: 200.5 cid. Compression ratio: 4.22:1. Brake hp: 40 at 2200 rpm. SAE hp: 24.03. Torque: 128 lb.-ft. at 1000 rpm. Main bearings: three. Valve lifters: mechanical. Carburetor: Zenith or Holley double venturi.

Chassis:

Model A: Wheelbase: 103.5 in. Front tread: 56 in. Rear tread: 56 in. Tires: 4.50 x 21.

1928 Ford Model A Roadster. (BMHV)

Model A: Sliding gear transmission. Speeds: 3F/1R. Floor shift controls. Dry multiple disc clutch. Shaft drive. Three-quarter floating rear axle. Overall ratio: 3.7:1. Mechanical internal expanding brakes on four wheels. Welded wire wheels. Wheel size: 21.

Options:

Single side mount tire. External sun shade. Radiator ornament. Wind vanes. Rearview mirror. Rear luggage rack. Radiator stone guard. Spare tire lock.

1928 Ford Model A Phaeton (JAC)

1928 Ford Model A Town Car w/Joan Crawford (JAC)

1928 Ford Model A Standard Business Roadster (AA)

1928 Ford Model A Business Coupe

1928 Ford Model A Tudor Sedan (RLC)

1928 Ford Model A Fordor Sedan. (JAC)

History:

Introduced December 2, 1927. Innovations: Safety glass installed in all windows. Calendar-year production: 633,594. The president of Ford Motor Co. was Edsel Ford.

1929 Ford

Ford — Model A: The most apparent change made in the 1929 Model A's appearance was the exterior door handles on open models. It also had brighter trim and body paint. With production rapidly increasing, more body styles became available. A Town Car model was introduced on December 13, 1928, followed during 1929 by a wood-bodied station wagon on April 25. Other new styles included a Convertible Cabriolet, several new Fordor Sedans and a Town Sedan. As in 1928, the Model A's base price included many standard equipment features such as a combination tail and stop light, a windshield wiper, front and rear bumpers and a Spartan horn.

VIN:

Serial numbers were located on the top side of frame, near the clutch pedal. Starting: A 810123. Ending: A 2742695. Engine number location: Boss placed on center of left side of block directly below the cylinder head. Starting: A 810123. Ending: A 2724695.

1929 Ford Model A Station Wagon (OCW)

1929 Model A Ford (Four)

Model No.	Body/ Style No.	Body Type & Seating	Factory Price	Shipping Weight	Prod. Total
A	—	2 dr. Roadster-2P	$ 480	2,106 lbs.	Note 1
A	---	4-dr. Station Wagon-5P	$ 650	2,500 lbs.	Note 1
A	—	2-dr. Convertible-2/4P	$ 670	2,339 lbs.	Note 1
A	---	2-dr. Sport Coupe-2/4P	$ 550	2,250 lbs.	Note 1
A	----	2-dr. Roadster-2/4P	$ 450	2,106 lbs.	Note 1
A	----	2-dr. Business Coupe-2P	$ 525	2,216 lbs.	Note 1
A	----	4-dr. Phaeton-5P	$ 460	2,203 lbs.	Note 1
A	----	2-dr. Coupe-2P	$ 550	2,248 lbs.	Note 1
A	----	4-dr. Town Car-5P	$1,400	2,525 lbs.	Note 1
A	----	4-dr. Taxi Cab-5P	$ 800	-------	Note 1

Murray Body Sedans

A	----	4-dr. Sedan-5P	$ 625	2,497 lbs.	Note 1
A	----	4-dr. Town Sedan-5P	$ 695	2,517 lbs.	Note 1

Briggs Body Sedans

A	----	4-dr. Sedan-5P	$ 625	2,497 lbs.	Note 1
A	----	4-dr. Sedan-5P	$ 625	2,419 lbs.	Note 1
A	----	4-dr. Sedan (Long wheelbase)-5P	$ 625	2,500 lbs.	Note 1
A	----	2-dr. Sedan-5P	$ 525	2,348 lbs.	Note 1
A	----	4-dr. Town Sedan-5P	$ 695	2,517 lbs.	Note 1

Note 1: Body style production was recorded only by calendar year. See list at end of 1931 Model A section.

Engine:

Model A: Inline. L-head. Four. Cast-iron block. B & S: 3-7/8 x 4-1/4 in. Displacement: 200.5 cid. Compression ratio: 4.22:1. Brake hp: 40 at 2200 rpm. SAE hp: 24.03. Torque: 128 lb.-ft. at 1000 rpm. Main bearings: three. Valve lifters: mechanical. Carburetor: Zenith or Holley double venturi.

Chassis:

Model A: Wheelbase: 103.5 in. Front tread: 56 in. Rear tread: 56 in. Tires: 4.50 x 21.

Technical:

Model A: Sliding gear transmission. Speeds: 3F/1R. Floor shift controls. Dry multiple disc clutch. Shaft drive. Three-quarter floating rear axle. Overall ratio: 3.7:1. Mechanical internal expanding brakes on four wheels. Welded wire wheels. Wheel size: 21.

Options:

Single side mount tire. External sun shade. Radiator ornament ($3). Wind vanes. Rearview mirror. Rear luggage rack. Radiator stone guard. Spare tire lock.

1929 Ford Model A Rumbleseat Convertible (OCW)

1929 Ford Model A Sport Coupe (AA)

History:

Introduced January 1929. Calendar-year sales: 1,310,147 (registrations). Calendar-year production: 1,507,132. The president of Ford was Edsel Ford. Production of the first million Model A Fords was completed on February 4, 1929. The two-millionth Model A Ford was constructed on July 24, 1929.

1929 Ford Model A Rumbleseat Roadster (HAC)

1929 Ford Model A Standard Business Coupe (HFM)

1928 Ford Model A Phaeton (OCW)

1929 Ford Model A Standard Coupe (HFM)

1929 Ford Model A Town Car with driving compartment open (HFM)

1929 Ford Model A Town Car with driving compartment closed (OCW)

1929 Ford Model A Four-Door Taxi Cab (OCW)

1929 Ford Model A Fordor Sedan by Briggs (OCW)

1929 Ford Model A Fordor Town Sedan by Murray (JAC)

1929 Ford Model A Tudor Sedan (OCW)

1929 Ford Model A Custom Landaulet (OCW)

1929 Ford Model A Sedan Delivery (OCW)

1930 Ford

Ford — Model A: The Model A was given a substantial face-lift for 1930 and it was effective. Larger 4.75 tires on smaller 19-inch wheels resulted in an overall height reduction, which along with wider fenders, a deeper radiator shell and the elimination of the cowl stanchion all were contributors to the Model A's fresh new look. Replacing the older nickel finish for the Ford's exterior bright work was a combination of nickel and stainless steel trim. During the year, a new Victoria body style was introduced, along with a deluxe version of the Phaeton. The Deluxe Roadster and Sport Coupe models included a rumble seat.

VIN:

Serial numbers located on the top side of the frame near the clutch panel. Starting: A 2742696. Ending: A 4237500. Engine numbers were located on a boss on the center of left side of the block, directly below the cylinder head. Starting Engine No: A 2742696. Ending: A 4237500.

1930 Ford Model A (Four)

Model No.	Body/Style No.	Body Type & Seating	Factory Price	Shipping Weight	Production Total
A	35-B	4-dr. Standard Phaeton-5P	$ 440	2,212 lbs.	Note 1
A	40-B	2-dr. Standard Roadster-2P	$ 435	2,155 lbs.	Note 1
A	40-B	2-dr. Deluxe Roadster-2/4P	$ 495	2,230 lbs.	Note 1
A	45-B	2-dr. Standard Coupe-2P	$ 500	2,257 lbs.	Note 1
A	45-B	2-dr. Deluxe Coupe-2/4P	$ 550	2,265 lbs.	Note 1
A	50-B	2-dr. Sport Coupe-2/4P	$ 530	2,283 lbs.	Note 1
A	55-B	Tudor Sedan-5P	$ 490	2,372 lbs.	Note 1
A	68-B	2-dr. Cabriolet-2/4P	$ 645	2,273 lbs.	Note 1
A	150-B	4-dr. Station Wagon-5P	$ 650	2,482 lbs.	Note 1
A	180-A	4-dr. Deluxe Phaeton-5P	$ 645	2,285 lbs.	Note 1
A	190-A	2-dr. Victoria-5P	$ 580	2,375 lbs.	Note 1

Murray Body Sedans

A	155-C	4-dr. Town Sedan-5P	$ 640	2,495 lbs.	Note 1
A	165-C	4-dr. Standard Sedan-5P	$ 580	2,462 lbs.	Note 1

Briggs Body Sedans

A	155-D	4-dr. Town Sedan-5P	$ 650	2,495 lbs.	Note 1
A	165-D	4-dr. Standard Sedan-5P	$ 590	2,462 lbs.	Note 1
A	170-B	4-dr. Two-Window Standard Sedan-5P	$ 590	2,488 lbs.	Note 1
A	170-B	4-dr. Two-Window Sedan-5P	$ 650	2,488 lbs.	Note 1

Note 1: Body style production was recorded only by calendar year. See list at end of 1931 Model A section.

Engine:

Model A: Inline. L-head. Four. Cast-iron block. B & S: 3-7/8 x 4-1/4 in. Displacement: 200.5 cid. Compression ratio: 4.22:1. Brake hp: 40 at 2200 rpm. SAE hp: 24.03. Torque: 128 lbs.-ft. at 1000 rpm. Main bearings: three. Valve lifters: mechanical. Carburetor: Zenith or Holley double venturi.

Chassis:

Model A: Wheelbase: 103.5 in. Front and rear tread: 56 in. Tires: 4.75 x 19.

Technical:

Model A: Sliding gear transmission. Speeds: 3F/1R. Floor shift controls. Dry multiple disc clutch. Shaft drive. Three-quarter floating rear axle. Overall ratio: 3.7:1. Mechanical internal expanding brakes on four wheels. Welded wire wheels. Wheel size: 19 in.

1930 Ford Model A Standard Phaeton (JAC)

Options:

Single side mount ($20). External sun shade. Radiator ornament. Wind vanes. Rearview mirror. Rear luggage rack. Radiator stone guard. Spare tire lock.

1930 Ford Model A Roadster (AA)

1930 Ford Model A Standard Coupe (OCW)

1930 Ford Model A Deluxe Coupe (OCW)

1930 Ford Model A Standard Business Coupe (JAC)

Introduced January 1930. Calendar-year sales: 1,055,097 (registrations). Calendar-year production: 1,155,162. The president of Ford was Edsel Ford. This year Ford Motor Companyís payroll hit $300 million for the year, a record at the time for any U.S. business. In December 1929, Ford announced a $7 per day minimum wage.

1930 Ford Model A Deluxe Phaeton (OCW)

1930 Ford Model A Rumbleseat Sport Coupe (OCW)

1930 Ford Model A Fordor Town Sedan (JAC)

1930 Ford Model A Tudor Sedan (OCW)

1930 Ford Model A Standard Fordor Sedan (OCW)

1930 Ford Model A Rumbleseat Convertible (OCW)

1930 Ford Model A Deluxe Fordor Sedan (OCW)

1930 Ford Model A Station Wagon (OCW)

1930 Ford Model A Deluxe Fordor Two-Window Sedan (OCW)

1930 Ford Model A Budd body Touring Car (OCW)

1931 Ford Model A Deluxe Roadster (OCW)

1931 Ford

Ford — Model A: The final year of Model A production brought revised styling, several new body types and on April 14th, production of the 20-millionth Ford, a Fordor sedan. Heading the list of styling changes was a radiator shell with a relief effect, plus running boards fitted with single-piece slash aprons. In addition to the two-and four-door sedans introduced with a smoother roofline, a revamped Cabriolet was also introduced during 1931. However the star attraction was the Convertible Sedan. It had fixed side window frames over which the top rode up or down on a set of tracks. Standard equipment on the Convertible Sedan included a side-mounted spare tire.

VIN:

Serial numbers were located on the top side of the frame, near the clutch pedal. Starting: A 4237501. Ending: A 4849340. Engine numbers were located on a boss on the center of left side of block, directly below the cylinder head. Starting: A 4327501. Ending: A 4849340.

1931 Model A (Four)

Model No.	Body/ Style No.	Body Type & Seating	Factory Price	Shipping Weight	Production Total
A	—	4-dr. Standard Phaeton-5P	$ 435	2,212 lbs.	Note 1
A	---	2-dr. Standard Roadster-2P	$ 430	2,155 lbs.	Note 1
A	—	2-dr. Deluxe Roadster-2/4P	$ 475	2,230 lbs.	Note 1
A	---	2-dr. Standard Coupe-2P	$ 490	2,257 lbs.	Note 1
A	—	2-dr. Deluxe Coupe-2P	$ 525	2,265 lbs.	Note 1
A	—	2-dr. Sport Coupe-2/4P	$ 500	2,283 lbs.	Note 1
A	—	2-dr. Standard Sedan-5P	$ 490	2,462 lbs.	Note 1
A	----	2-dr. Deluxe Sedan-5P	$525	2,488 lbs.	Note 1
A	----	2-dr. Cabriolet-2/4P	$595	2,273 lbs.	Note 1
A	----	4-dr. Station Wagon-4P	$625	2,505 lbs.	Note 1
A	----	2-dr. Deluxe Phaeton-5P	$580	2,265 lbs.	Note 1
A	----	2-dr. Victoria-5P	$580	2,375 lbs.	Note 1
A	----	2-dr. Convertible Sedan-4P	$640	2,335 lbs.	Note 1

Murray Body Sedans

A	----	4-dr. Sedan-5P	$630	2,495 lbs.	Note 1
A	----	4-dr. Standard Sedan-5P	$590	2,462 lbs.	Note 1

Briggs Body Sedans

A	----	4-dr. Standard Sedan-5P	$590	2,462 lbs.	Note 1
A	----	4-dr. Town Sedan-5P	$630	2,495 lbs.	Note 1
A	----	4-dr. Deluxe Sedan-5P	$630	2,488 lbs.	Note 1
A	----	4-dr. Deluxe Two-Window Sedan-4P	$630	2,499 lbs.	Note 1

Note 1: Body style production was recorded only by calendar year. See list in this section.

Engine:

Model A: Inline. L-head. Four. Cast-iron block. B & S: 3-7/8 x 4-1/4 in. Displacement: 200.5 cid. Compression ratio: 4.22:1. Brake hp: 40 at 2200 rpm. SAE hp: 24.03. Torque: 128 lb.-ft. at 1000 rpm. Main bearings: three. Valve lifters: mechanical. Carburetor: Zenith or Holley double venturi.

Chassis:

Model A: Wheelbase: 103.5 in. Front and rear tread: 56 in. Tires: 4.75

1931 Ford Model A Standard Phaeton

x 19.

Technical:

Model A: Sliding gear transmission. Speeds: 3F/1R. Floor shift controls. Dry multiple disc clutch. Shaft drive. Three-quarter floating rear axle. Overall ratio: 3.77:1. Mechanical internal expanding brakes on four wheels. Welded wire wheels. Wheel size: 19 in.

Options:

Single side mount. External sun shade. Radiator ornament. Wind vanes. Rearview mirror. Rear luggage rack. Radiator stone guard. Spare tire lock.

History:

Introduced January 1931. Calendar-year sales 528,581 (registrations). Calendar-year production: 541,615. The president of Ford was Edsel Ford.

Ford Model A Domestic Production Totals: 1927-1931

	1927	1928	1929	1930	1931	Totals
Standard Phaeton	221	47,255	49,818	16,479	4076	117,849
Deluxe Phaeton	—	—	—	3946	2229	6175
Standard Roadster	269	81,937*	191,529	112,901	5,499	392.135
Deluxe Roadster	----		----	11,318	52,997	64,315
Sport Coupe	734	79,099	134,292	69,167	19,700	302,992
Standard Coupe	629	70,784	178,982	226,027	79,816	556,238
Deluxe Coupe	—	—	—	28,937	23,067	52,004
Business Coupe	—	37,343	37,644	—	—	74,987
Convertible Cabriolet	—	—	16,421	25,868	11,801	54,090
Standard Tudor	1948	208,562	523,922	376,271	148,425	1,259,128
Deluxe Tudor	—	—	—	—	21,984	21,984
Standard Fordor (two-window)	—	82,349	146,097	5279	—	233,725
Deluxe Fordor (two-window)	—	—	—	12,854	3251	16,105
Standard Fordor (three window)	—	—	53 941	41,133	18,127	113,201
Town sedan	—	—	84,970	104,935	55,469	245,374
Convertible Sedan	—	—	—	—	4864	4864
Victoria	—	—	—	6306	33,906	40,212
Town Car	—	89	913	63	—	1065
Station Wagon		5	4954	3510	2848	11,317

1931 Ford Model A Standard Coupe (OCW)

1931 Ford Model A Deluxe Phaeton (OCW)

1931 Ford Model A Deluxe Coupe (OCW)

1931 Ford Model A Victoria (AA)

1931 Ford Model A Rumbleseat Sport Coupe (OCW)

1931 Ford Model A Convertible Sedan (OCW)

1931 Ford Model A Tudor Sedan (OCW)

1931 Ford Model A Fordor Town Sedan (JAC)

1931 Ford Model A Rumbleseat Convertible (OCW)

1931 Ford Model A Standard Fordor Sedan (OCW)

1931 Ford Model A Deluxe Fordor Sedan (OCW)

1931 Ford Model A Taxi (OCW)

1931 Ford Model A Fordor Sedan (20 Millionth)

1931 Ford Model A Station Wagon (OCW)

1932 Ford

Ford — Model B — Four: The new 1932 Ford was extremely handsome. Both the front and rear fenders were fully crowned. The soon-to-be classic radiator shell was slightly veed and carried vertical bars. The new Ford's dash carried all instruments and controls within an engine-turned oval placed in the center of a mahogany colored (early) or walnut (late) grained panel. An anti-theft device was incorporated into the key and ignition switch that was mounted on a bracket attached to the steering column. During the model year, Ford incorporated many changes into the design of its new model. One of the most obvious, intended to improve engine cooling, was a switch from a hood with 20 louvers to one with 25. Somewhat overwhelmed by the public's response to Model 18 V-8, the four-cylinder Ford Model B shared the same body as the V-8, minus V-8 emblems on the headlight tie-bars and with Ford lettering rather than V-8 lettering on its hubcaps. All Fords had single transverse leaf springs front and rear. The locating of the rear spring behind the differential and the use of 18-inch wheels gave the '32 Fords a lower overall height than previous models.

Ford — Model 18 — V-8: Once again Henry Ford made automotive history when, on March 31, 1932, he announced the Ford V-8. This type of engine was not a novelty by that time, but when offered at traditional Ford low prices, this new engine was a true milestone. Henry Ford had this 221-cid unit developed in traditional Ford-style extreme secrecy. A small workforce operating under relatively primitive conditions did the work under Henry Ford's close personal supervision. Its early production life was far from tranquil. Hastily rushed into assembly, many of the 1932 engines experienced piston and bearing failures, plus overheating and block cracking. However, these problems were soon overcome and for the next 21 years this V-8 would be powering Ford automobiles. Positioned in the center of the curved headlight tie-bar was Ford's timeless V-8 logo. Apparently sensitive that most of its competitors had longer wheelbases, Ford measured the distance from the center position of the front spring to the center of the rear and claimed it as the V-8's 112-inch wheelbase. Actually its wheelbase was 106 inches.

VIN:

Serial numbers were located on the top side of the frame, near the clutch pedal. Starting: [Model B] AB 5000001 & up. [Model 18] 18-1. Ending: [Model 18] 18-2031126. Prefix "C" indicates Canadian built. Engine numbers located on boss placed on center of left side of block, directly below the cylinder head [Model B]. Starting: [Model B] AB 5000005 & up. [Model 18] 18-1. Ending: [Model 18] 18-2031126.

Ford Model B (Four)

Model No.	Body/ Style No.	Body Type & Seating	Factory Price	Shipping Weight	Production Total
B	—	2-dr. Deluxe Roadster-2P	$ 410	2,095 lbs.	948
B	---	2-dr. Deluxe Roadster-2/4P	$ 450	2,102 lbs.	3,719
B	—	4-dr. Phaeton-5P	$ 445	2,238 lbs.	593
B	---	4-dr. Deluxe Phaeton-5P	$ 495	2,268 lbs.	281
B	---	2-dr. Coupe-2P	$ 440	2,261 lbs.	20,342
B	---	2-dr. Sport Coupe-2/4P	$ 485	2,286 lbs.	739
B	---	2-dr. Deluxe Coupe-2/4P	$ 425	2,364 lbs.	968
B	---	2-dr. Sedan-5P	$ 450	2,378 lbs.	36,553
B	---	2-dr. Deluxe Sedan-5P	$ 500	2,398 lbs.	4,077
B	---	4-dr. Sedan-5P	$ 540	2,413 lbs.	4,116
B	---	4-dr. Deluxe Sedan-5P	$ 595	2,432 lbs.	2,620
B	---	2-dr. Cabriolet-2/4P	$ 560	2,295 lbs.	427
B	---	2-dr. Victoria-5P	$ 550	2,344 lbs.	521
B	---	2-dr. Convertible Sedan-5P	$ 600	2,349 lbs.	41

1932 Ford Model B Standard 5-Window Coupe (OCW)

Ford Model 18 (V-8)

18	—	2-dr. Deluxe Roadster-2P	$ 460	2,203 lbs.	520
18	---	2-dr. Deluxe Roadster-2/4P	$ 500	2,308 lbs.	6,893
18	—	4-dr. Phaeton-5P	$ 495	2,369 lbs.	483
18	---	4-dr. Deluxe Phaeton-5P	$ 545	2,375 lbs.	923
18	---	2-dr. Coupe-2P	$ 490	2,398 lbs.	28,904
18	---	2-dr. Sport Coupe-2/4P	$ 535	2,405 lbs.	1,982
18	---	2-dr. Deluxe Coupe-2/4P	$ 575	2,493 lbs.	20,506
18	---	2-dr. Sedan-5P	$ 500	2,508 lbs.	57,930
18	---	2-dr. Deluxe Sedan-5P	$ 550	2,518 lbs.	18,836
18	---	4-dr. Sedan-5P	$ 590	2,538 lbs.	9,310
18	---	4-dr. Deluxe Sedan-5P	$ 645	2,568 lbs.	18,880
18	---	2-dr. Cabriolet-2/4P	$ 610	2,398 lbs.	5,499
18	---	2-dr. Victoria-5P	$ 600	2,483 lbs.	7,241
18	---	2-dr. Convertible Sedan-5P	$ 650	2,480 lbs.	842

Engines:

Model B Four: Inline. L-head. Cast-iron block. B & S: 3-7/8 x 4-1/4 in. Displacement: 200.5 cid. Compression ratio: 4.6:1. Brake hp: 50. Taxable hp: 30. Main bearings: three. Valve lifters: mechanical. Carburetor: Zenith or Holley double-venturi.

Model 18 V-8: 90-degree V. L-head. Cast-iron block. B & S: 3-1/16 x 3-3/4 in. Displacement: 221 cid. Compression ratio: 5.5:1. Brake hp: 65 at 3400 rpm. SAE hp: 30. Torque: 130 lbs.-ft. at 1250 rpm. Main bearings: three. Valve lifters: mechanical. Carburetor: Special Ford Detroit Lubricator downdraft, single barrel, 1-1/2-in. throat.

Chassis:

Model 18: Wheelbase: 106 in. Overall length: 165-1/2-in. Height: 68-5/8-in. Front tread: 55.2 in. Rear Tread: 56.7 in. Tires: 5.25 x 18.

Model B: Wheelbase: 106 in. Overall length: 165-1/2-in. Height: 68-5/8-in. Front tread: 55.2 in. Rear Tread: 56.7 in. Tires: 5.25 x 18.

Technical:

Sliding gear transmission. Speeds: 3F/1R. Floor shift controls. Single dry plate, molded asbestos lining clutch. Shaft drive. Three-quarter floating rear axle. Overall ratio: 4.11:1 (early cars - 4.33:1). Mechanical, rod activated brakes on four wheels. Welded wire, drop center rim wheels. Wheel size: 18 in.

1932 Ford Model B Roadster (OCW)

1932 Ford Model B Deluxe Phaeton (OCW)

Options:

Single side mount tires. Dual side mount tires. Clock. Trunk rack. Leather upholstery. Mirror. Twin taillights. Bedford cord upholstery. Cowl lamps, Standard models.

1932 Ford Model B Standard Tudor Sedan (OCW)

1932 Ford Model B Standard Fordor Sedan (OCW)

1932 Ford Model B Station Wagon (OCW)

1932 Ford Model 18 V-8 Roadster (OCW)

Introduced April 2, 1932. The Ford Model 18 marked the first mass production of a low-priced one-piece 90-degree V-8 engine block. Calendar-year sales: 258,927 (registrations). Calendar-year production: 287,285. The president of Ford was Edsel Ford.

1932 Ford Model 18 V-8 Deluxe Roadster (JAC)

1932 Ford Model 18 V-8 Phaeton (OCW)

1932 Ford Model 18 V-8 Deluxe Phaeton (OCW)

1932 Ford Model 18 V-8 Deluxe three-window coupe (AA)

1932 Ford Model 18 V-8 Deluxe Tudor sedan (OCW)

1932 Ford Model 18 V-8 Deluxe Fordor sedan (OCW)

1932 Ford Model 18 V-8 Cabriolet (PH)

1932 Ford Model 18 V-8 Victoria (BMHV)

1933 Ford

Ford — Model 40 — Standard — Four and V-8: In addition to a longer 112-inch wheelbase and an X-member double-drop frame, the 1933 Ford had valanced front and rear fenders, a new radiator design with vertical bars slanted back to match the rear sweep of the windshield and acorn-shaped headlight shells. Curvaceous one-piece bumpers with a center-dip were used at front and rear. Enhancing the Ford's streamlined appearance were the angled side hood louvers. All models, regardless of body color, were delivered with black fenders and 17-inch wire spoke wheels. Accompanying these exterior revisions was a new dash arrangement with a reshaped engine-tuned panel enclosing the gauges placed directly in front of the driver. A similarly shaped glove box was placed on the passenger's side. As before, the V-8 Fords were identical to the four-cylinder models except for the addition of V-8 trim identification. With its teething problems part of the past, the Ford V-8 by virtue of an improved ignition system, better cooling, higher compression ratio and aluminum cylinder heads, developed 75 hp.

Ford — Model 40 — Deluxe — Four/V-8: Deluxe models had two horns, two taillights and shatter-proof glass all around. They also had rustless steel bullet-style headlight buckets.

1933 Ford V-8 Fordor Deluxe Phaeton (OCW)

1933 Ford V-8 Deluxe Cabriolet (OCW)

Serial numbers were located on the top side of the frame near the clutch pedal and also on the left front pillar, the forward portion of left frame member and transmission housing. Starting: (V-8) 18-2031127 & up; (four-cylinder, with prefix "B") 5185849 & up. Engine numbers were located on boss placed on center of left side of block, directly below the cylinder head (four-cylinder); on top of clutch housing (V-8). Starting: (V-8) 18-2031127 & up; (four-cylinder) 5185849 & up.

Ford — Model 40 — Standard (Four)

Model No.	Body/ Style No.	Body Type & Seating	Factory Price	Shipping Weight	Production Total
40	—	2-dr. Roadster-2/4P	$ 425	2,268 lbs.	107
40	---	4-dr. Phaeton-5P	$ 445	2,281 lbs.	457
40	—	2-dr. Three-Window Coupe-2P	$ 440	2,380 lbs.	189
40	---	2-dr. Five-Window Coupe-2P	$ 440	2,220 lbs.	2,148
40	---	2-dr. Sedan-5P	$ 450	2,503 lbs.	2,911
40	---	4-dr. Sedan-5P	$ 510	2,550 lbs.	682

Ford — Model 40 — Deluxe (Four)

40	—	2-dr. Roadster-2/4P	$ 460	2,278 lbs.	101
40	---	2-dr. Cabriolet-2/4P	$ 535	2,306 lbs.	24
40	---	4-dr. Phaeton-5P	$ 495	2,290 lbs.	241
40	---	2-dr. Three-Window Coupe-2P	$ 490	2,220 lbs.	24
40	—	2-dr. Five-Window Coupe-2P	$ 490	2,299 lbs.	28
40	---	2-dr. Victoria-5P	$ 545	2,356 lbs.	25
40	---	2-dr. Sedan-5P	$ 500	2,520 lbs.	85
40	---	4-dr. Sedan-5P	$ 560	2,590 lbs.	179
40	---	4-dr. Station Wagon-5P	$ 590	2,505 lbs.	359

Ford — Model 40 — Standard (V-8)

40	—	2-dr. Roadster-2/4P	$ 475	2,422 lbs.	126
40	---	4-dr. Phaeton-5P	$ 495	2,520 lbs.	232
40	—	2-dr. Three-Window Coupe-2P	$ 490	2,534 lbs.	6,585
40	---	2-dr. Five-Window Coupe-2P	$ 490	2,534 lbs.	31,797
40	---	2-dr. Sedan-5P	$ 500	2,621 lbs.	106,387
40	---	4-dr. Sedan-5P	$ 560	2,675 lbs.	19,602

Ford — Model 40 — Deluxe (V-8)

40	—	2-dr. Roadster-2/4P	$ 510	2,261 lbs.	4,223
40	---	2-dr. Cabriolet-2/4P	$ 585	2,545 lbs.	7,852
40	—	4-dr. Phaeton-5P	$ 545	2,529 lbs.	1,483
40	---	2-dr. Three-Window Coupe-2P	$ 540	2,538 lbs.	15,894
40	—	2-dr. Five-Window Coupe-2P	$ 540	2,538 lbs.	11,244
40	---	2-dr. Victoria-5P	$ 595	2,595 lbs.	4,193
40	---	2-dr. Sedan-5P	$ 550	2,625 lbs.	48,233
40	---	4-dr. Sedan-5P	$ 610	2,684 lbs.	45,443
40	---	4-dr. Station Wagon-5P	$ 640	2,635 lbs.	1,654

Engines:

Model 40 Four: Inline. L-head. Cast-iron block. B & S: 3-7/8 x 4-1/4 in. Displacement: 200.5 cid. Compression ratio: 4.6:1. Brake hp: 50. Taxable hp: 30. Main bearings: three. Valve lifters: mechanical. Carburetor: Zenith or Holley double venturi.

Model 40 V-8: 90 degree V. L-head. Cast-iron block. B & S: 3-1/16 x 3-3/4 in. Displacement: 221 cid. Compression ratio: 6.3:1. Brake hp: 75 at 3800 rpm. Main bearings: three. Valve lifters: mechanical. Carburetor: Detroit Lubricator downdraft, single barrel 1.25-in. throat.

Chassis:

Model 40 V-8: Wheelbase: 112 in. Overall length: 182-9/10 in. Height: 68 in. Front and rear tread: 55-1/5/56-7/10 in. Tires: 5.50 x 17.

Technical:

Sliding gear transmission. Speeds: 3F/1R. Floor shift controls. Single dry plate, woven asbestos lining clutch. Shaft drive. 3/4 floating rear axle. Overall ratio: 4.11:1. Mechanical internal expanding brakes on four wheels. Welded spoke wheels, drop center rims. Wheel Size: 17 in.

Options:

Radio. Heater. Clock. Radio antenna. Greyhound radiator ornament. Trunk. Trunk rack. Twin taillights. Cowl lamps (standard on Deluxe models). Windshield wings. Dual horns (standard on Deluxe models). Whitewall tires. Leather seats. Dual wipers. Steel spare tire cover. Rumble seat (coupes).

History:

Introduced February 9, 1933. Calendar-year sales: 311,113 (registrations). Calendar-year production: 334,969. The president of Ford was Edsel Ford. During 1933 Ford conducted a number of economy runs with the Model 40. Under conditions ranging from the Mojave Desert to the Catskill Mountains the Fords averaged between 18.29 and 22.5 mpg.

1933 Ford V-8 3-Window Deluxe Coupe (OCW)

1933 Ford V-8 Standard 5-Window Coupe (JAC)

1933 Ford V-8 Deluxe 5-Window Coupe (JAC)

1933 Ford V-8 Deluxe Fordor sedan (OCW)

1933 Ford V-8 Station Wagon (OCW)

1933 Ford V-8 Cantrell Station Wagon (OCW)

1933 Ford V-8 Victoria (OCW)

1934 Ford

Ford — Model 40 — Standard — Four and V-8: Visual changes in 1934 Fords were minor. Different V-8 hubcap emblems (now painted rather than chrome-finished and without a painted surround) were used and the side hood louvers were straight instead of curved. Although the same grille form was continued for 1934 there were changes. The 1934 version had fewer vertical bars and its chrome frame was deeper and flatter. The V-8 grille ornament was placed within an inverted 60-degree triangle and carried a vertical divider. Other exterior alterations included smaller headlight and cowl light shells, two (rather than one) hood handles and three (instead of two) body pin stripes. In addition, the fenders were painted in body color on all models. However, black fenders were available as an option. Closed body models featured front door glass that, prior to lowering vertically into the door, moved slightly to the rear. This was usually referred to as "clear vision" ventilation. The dash panel no longer had an engine-turned panel insert. For 1934 this surface was painted.

Ford — Model 40 — Deluxe — Four and V-8: Deluxe models were easily distinguished from their Standard counterparts by their pin striping, cowl lights, twin horns and two taillights. The principal change in the design of the Ford V-8 consisted of a Stromberg carburetor in place of the Detroit Lubricator unit and a reshaped air cleaner. Ford also offered its four-cylinder engine in all models at a price $50 below that of a corresponding V-8 design. This was the final year for this engine's use in a Ford automobile. The four-cylinder engine was designated Model B; but the cars used the same Model 40 designation as V-8 powered models.

VIN:

Serial numbers were on the top side of the frame, near the clutch panel. The number was also on the left front pillar and forward portion of left frame member and the transmission housing. Starting: 18-451478 and up. Engine numbers were on top of the clutch housing. Starting: 18-457478 and up.

Ford Model 40 Standard (Four)

Model No.	Body/ Style No.	Body Type & Seating	Factory Price	Shipping Weight	Production Total
40	—	2-dr. Five Window Coupe-2P	$ 465	2,220 lbs.	20
40	---	2-dr. Sedan-5P	$ 485	2,503 lbs.	185
40	—	4-dr. Sedan-5P	$ 535	2,590 lbs.	405

Ford Model 40 Deluxe (Four)

Model No.	Body/ Style No.	Body Type & Seating	Factory Price	Shipping Weight	Production Total
40	—	2-dr. Roadster-2/4P	$ 475	2,278 lbs.	----
40	---	4-dr. Phaeton-5P	$ 460	2,281 lbs.	377
40	---	4-dr. Phaeton-5P	$ 510	2,290 lbs.	412
40	---	2-dr. Cabriolet-2/4P	$ 540	2,306 lbs.	12
40	---	2-dr. Three-Window Coupe-2/4P	$ 505	2,220 lbs.	7
40	---	2-dr. Five-Window Coupe-2/4P	$ 505	2,299 lbs.	3
40	---	2-dr. Sedan-5P	$ 525	2,520 lbs.	12
40	---	4-dr. Sedan-5P	$ 575	2,590 lbs.	384
40	---	2-dr. Victoria-5P	$ 560	2,356 lbs.	----
40	---	4-dr. Station Wagon-5P	$ 610	2,505 lbs.	95

Ford Model 40 Standard (V-8)

Model No.	Body/ Style No.	Body Type & Seating	Factory Price	Shipping Weight	Production Total
40 V-8	—	2-dr. Five Window Coupe-2P	$ 515	2,534 lbs.	47,623
40 V-8	---	2-dr. Sedan-5P	$ 535	2,621 lbs.	124,870
40 V-8	—	4-dr. Sedan-5P	$ 585	2,675 lbs.	22,394

Ford Model 40 Deluxe (V-8)

Model No.	Body/ Style No.	Body Type & Seating	Factory Price	Shipping Weight	Production Total
40 V-8	—	2-dr. Roadster-2/4P	$ 525	2,461 lbs.	----
40 V-8	---	4-dr. Phaeton-5P	$ 510	2,520 lbs.	373
40 V-8	—	4-dr. Phaeton-5P	$ 550	2,529 lbs.	3,128
40 V-8	---	2-dr. Cabriolet-2/4P	$ 590	2,545 lbs.	14,496
40 V-8	---	2-dr. Three-Window Coupe-2/4P	$ 555	2,538 lbs.	26,348
40 V-8	---	2-dr. Five-Window Coupe-2/4P	$ 555	2,538 lbs.	26,879
40 V-8	---	2-dr. Sedan-5P	$ 575	2,625 lbs.	121,696
40 V-8	---	4-dr. Sedan-5P	$ 625	2,684 lbs.	102,268
40 V-8	---	2-dr. Victoria-5P	$ 610	2,595 lbs.	20,083
40 V-8	---	4-dr. Station Wagon-5P	$ 660	2,635 lbs.	2,905

Engine:

Ford Four: Inline. L-head. Cast-iron block. B & S: 3-7/8 x 4-1/4 in. Displacement: 200.5 cid. Compression ratio: 4.6:1. Brake hp: 50. Taxable hp: 30. Main bearings: three. Valve lifters: mechanical. Carburetor: Zenith or Holley double venturi.

Ford V-8: 90-degree V. L-head. Cast-iron block. B & S: 3-1/16 x 3-3/4 in. Displacement: 221 cid. C.R.: 6.3:1. Brake hp: 85 at 3800 rpm. Torque: 150 lbs.-ft. at 2200 rpm. Main bearings: three. Valve lifters: mechanical. Carburetor: Stromberg EE-1 two-barrel downdraft.

Chassis:

Wheelbase: 112 in. Overall length: 182.9 in. Height: 68 in. Front tread: 55.2. Rear tread: 56.7 in. Tires: 5.50 x 17.

Technical:

Sliding gear transmission. Speeds: 3F/1R. Floor shift controls. Single dry plate, woven asbestos lining. Shaft drive. 3/4 floating rear axle. Overall ratio: 4.11:1. Mechanical internal expanding brakes on four wheels. Welded spoke drop center rims. Wheel size: 17 in.

Options:

Radio (ash tray or glove box door mounted). Heater. Clock. Cigar Lighter. Radio antenna. Seat covers. Spotlight. Cowl lamps (standard on Deluxe models). Trunk. Whitewalls. Greyhound radiator ornament. Special steel spoke wheels. Oversize balloon tires. Bumper guards. Extra horn, black finish (standard on Deluxe models). Dual windshield wiper. Steel tire cover (standard on Deluxe models). Black painted fenders. Two taillights (standard on Deluxe models).

History:

Introduced January 1934. Calendar-year production: 563,921. The president of Ford was Edsel Ford. In April 1934 Clyde Barrow wrote his famous (or infamous) letter to Henry Ford in which he told Ford "what a dandy car you make." At the Ford press preview, held on Dec. 6, 1933, Ford Motor Co. served alcoholic beverages for the first time. Not since 1930 had the Ford Motor Co. reported a profit. That changed in 1934 with a profit of $3,759,311.

1934 Ford V-8 Cabriolet (JAC)

1934 Ford V-8 5-Window Coupe (OCW)

1934 Ford V-8 Deluxe Roadster (OCW)

1934 Ford V-8 5-Window Deluxe Coupe (OCW)

1934 Ford V-8 Fordor Phaeton (OCW)

1934 Ford V-8 Deluxe Tudor Sedan (OCW)

1934 Ford V-8 Fordor Deluxe Phaeton (OCW)

1934 Ford V-8 Victoria (OCW)

1934 Ford V-8 "Bonnie & Clyde" Sedan (OCW)

1934 Ford V-8 Deluxe Fordor Sedan (OCW)

1934 Ford V-8 Station Wagon (AA)

1935 Ford

Ford — Model 48 — Standard — V-8: Few Ford enthusiasts would dispute Ford's claim of "Greater Beauty, Greater Comfort, and Greater Safety" for its 1935 models. The narrower radiator grille lost its sharply veed base and four horizontal bars helped accentuate the 1935 model's new, lower and more streamlined appearance. The fender outlines were now much more rounded and the side hood louvers received three horizontal bright stripes. In profile, the Ford windshield was seen to be more sharply sloped then previously. No longer fitted were the old cowl lamps, since the parking lamps were integral with the headlights. The headlight shells were painted body color. For the first time, Ford offered a built-in trunk for its Tudor and Fordor Sedan models and all Fords had front-hinged doors front and rear. Standard models had painted windshield and grille trim work, single horns and one taillight.

Ford — Model 48 — Deluxe — V-8: Both Standard and Deluxe models shared a painted dash finish, with the Deluxe Fords having a set of horizontal bars running down the center section. External distinctions were obvious. Deluxe models had bright windshield and grille trim work, as well as dual exposed horns and twin taillights. Added to the Ford model lineup was a Convertible Sedan. No longer available was the Victoria.

VIN:

Serial numbers were located on the left side of the frame near the firewall. Starting: 18-1234357. Ending: 18-2207110. Prefix "C" indicates Canadian built. Engine numbers were located on top of the clutch housing. Starting 18-1234357. Ending: 18-2207110.

Ford Model 48 Standard (V-8)

Model No.	Body/ Style No.	Body Type & Seating	Factory Price	Shipping Weight	Production Total
48	—	2-dr. Three-Window Coupe-2P	—	2,647 lbs.	—
48	—	2-dr. Five-Window Coupe-2P	$ 520	2,620 lbs.	78,477
48	—	2-dr. Sedan-5P	$ 510	2,717 lbs.	237,833
48	—	4-dr. Sedan-5P	$ 575	2,760 lbs.	49,176
48	—	4-dr. Station Wagon-5P	$ 670	2,896 lbs.	4,536

Ford Model 48 Deluxe (V-8)

Model No.	Body/ Style No.	Body Type & Seating	Factory Price	Shipping Weight	Production Total
48	—	4-dr. Phaeton-5P	$ 580	2,667 lbs.	6,073
48	—	2-dr. Roadster-2/4P	$ 550	2,597 lbs.	4,896
48	—	2-dr. Cabriolet-2/4P	$ 625	2,687 lbs.	17,000
48	—	4-dr. Convertible Sedan-4P	$ 750	2,827 lbs.	4,234
48	—	2-dr. Three-Window Coupe-2P	$ 570	2,647 lbs.	31,513
48	—	2-dr. Five-Window Coupe-2P	$ 560	2,643 lbs.	33,065
48	—	2-dr. Sedan-5P	$ 595	2,737 lbs.	84,692
48	—	4-dr. Sedan-5P	$ 635	2,767 lbs.	75,807
48	—	2-dr. Trunk Sedan-5P	$ 595	2,772 lbs.	87,336
48	—	4-dr. Trunk Sedan-5P	$ 655	2,787 lbs.	105,157

Engine:

V-8: 90-degree V. L-head. Cast-iron block. B & S: 3-1/16 x 3-3/4 in. Displacement: 221 cid. Compression ratio: 6.3:1. Brake hp: 85 at 3800 rpm. Torque: 144 lb.-ft. at 2200 rpm. Main bearings: three. Valve lifters: mechanical. Carburetor: Stromberg EE-1, two-barrel downdraft.

Chassis:

Wheelbase: 112 in. Overall length: 182-3/4 in. Height: 64-5/8 in. Front tread: 55-1/2. Rear tread: 58-1/4 in. Tires: 6.00 x 16.

Technical:

Sliding gear transmission. Speeds: 3F/1R. Floor shift controls. Single dry plate, woven asbestos lining clutch. Shaft drive. Three-quarter floating rear axle. Overall ratio: 4.33:1. Mechanical, internal expanding brakes on four wheels. Welded spoke, drop center rims on wheels. Wheel size: 16 in.

Options:

Radio. Heater. Clock. Cigar lighter. Radio antenna. Seat covers. Spotlight. Cowl lamps (standard on Deluxe). Trunk. Luggage rack. Whitewall tires. Greyhound radiator ornament. Special steel spoke wheels. Oversize balloon tires. Bumper guards. Extra horns black finish (standard on Deluxe). Dual windshield wipers. Steel tire cover (standard on Deluxe). Black painted fenders. Two taillights (standard on Deluxe). Banjo type steering wheel. Rumbleseat (coupes and roadsters).

1935 Ford V-8 Standard 5-Window Coupe (OCW)

1935 Ford V-8 Standard 5-Window Coupe (OCW)

1935 Ford V-8 Fordor Deluxe Phaeton (OCW)

1935 Ford V-8 Deluxe Rumbleseat Roadster (JAC)

1935 Ford V-8 Convertible Cabriolet (AA)

1935 Ford V-8 Standard Tudor Sedan (OCW)

1935 Ford V-8 Standard Fordor Sedan (OCW)

1935 Ford V-8 Deluxe Convertible Sedan (OCW)

1935 Ford V-8 Deluxe 3-Window Coupe (OCW)

1935 Ford V-8 Deluxe 5-Window Coupe (OCW)

1935 Ford V-8 Deluxe Tudor sedan (OCW)

1935 Ford V-8 Deluxe Fordor Sedan (OCW)

1935 Ford V-8 Brewster Custom Town Car (OCW)

1935 Ford V-8 Deluxe Fordor Touring Sedan (OCW)

History:

Introduced December 1934. Calendar-year registrations: 826,519. Calendar-year production: 942,439. The president of Ford was Edsel Ford. Ford was America's best selling car for 1935. A Ford convertible sedan paced the 1935 Indianapolis 500. Ford produced its two-millionth V-8 engine in June 1935.

1936 Ford

Ford — Model 68 — Standard — V-8: The 1936 Fords retained the same basic body of the 1935 models, but carried a restyled front end and new rear fenders. The grille, which consisted only of vertical bars, extended further around the hood sides. Standard models had a painted grille, painted windshield molding, one horn and one taillight. Standard and Deluxe models this year shared sheet metal and engines.

Ford — Model 68 — Deluxe — V-8: The dual horns of the Deluxe models were placed behind screens set into the fender catwalks. The Convertible Sedan with its "slant-back" body was superseded by a version with a "trunk-back" styling (incorporating a built-in luggage compartment) during the model year. In place of wire wheels, Ford used new pressed-steel artillery-spoke wheels with large 12-inch painted hubcaps and chrome centers carrying a narrow, stylized V-8 logo. The same design was used on the Ford hood ornament. Design changes for 1936 included a larger capacity radiator, better engine cooling via new hood side louvers and front vents and helical-type gears for first and reverse gears. Previously only the second and third gears were of this design. Early 1936 Ford V-8s had domed aluminum pistons, but they were replaced by steel versions during the year. They also had new insert-type main bearings. Deluxe models featured bright work around the grille, headlights and windshield, as well as dual horns and taillights. Deluxe Fords produced late in the model year also had dual windshield wipers, wheel trim rings, a clock and a rearview mirror as standard equipment.

1936 Ford V-8 Deluxe Phaeton (OCW)

VIN:

Serial numbers were located on the left side of the frame near the firewall. Starting: 18-2207111. Ending: 18-3331856. Prefix "C" indicates Canadian built. Engine numbers were located on top of the clutch housing. Starting: 18-2207111. Ending: 18-3331856.

Ford Model 68 Standard (V-8)

Model No.	Body/Style No.	Body Type & Seating	Factory Price	Shipping Weight	Production Total
68	—	2-dr. Five-Window Coupe-2P	$ 510	2,599 lbs.	78,534
68	—	2-dr. Sedan-5P	$ 520	2,659 lbs.	174,770
68	—	2-dr. Trunk Sedan-5P	$ 545	2,718 lbs.	—
68	—	4-dr. Sedan-5P	$ 580	2,699 lbs.	31,505
68	—	4-dr. Trunk Sedan-5P	$ 605	2,771 lbs.	—

Ford Model 68 Deluxe (V-8)

Model No.	Body/Style No.	Body Type & Seating	Factory Price	Shipping Weight	Production Total
68	—	2-dr. Roadster-3P	$ 560	2,561 lbs.	3,862
68	—	4-dr. Phaeton-5P	$ 560	2,561 lbs.	3,862
68	—	2-dr. Cabriolet-5P	$ 625	2,649 lbs.	—
68	—	2-dr. Club Cabriolet-5P	$ 675	2,651 lbs.	4,616
68	ó	2-dr. Five-Window Coupe-2P	$ 510	2,599 lbs.	78,534
68	ó	2-dr. Sedan-5P	$ 520	2,659 lbs.	174,770
68	—	4-dr. Trunk Back Convertible Sedan-5P	$ 780	2,916 lbs.	—
68	—	4-dr. Straight Back Convertible Sedan-5P	$ 760	2,791 lbs.	5,601
68	—	2-dr. Three-Window Coupe-2P	$ 570	2,621 lbs.	21,446
68	—	2-dr. Five-Window Coupe-5P	$ 555	2,641 lbs.	29,938
68	—	2-dr. Sedan-5P	$ 565	2,691 lbs.	20,519
68	—	2-dr. Trunk Sedan-5P	$ 590	2,786 lbs.	125,303
68	—	4-dr. Sedan-5P	$ 625	2,746 lbs.	42,867
68	—	4-dr. Trunk Sedan-5P	$ 650	2,816 lbs.	159,825
68	—	4-dr. Station Wagon-5P	$ 670	3,020 lbs.	7,044

Engine:

Model 68 V-8: 90 degree V. Inline. Cast-iron block. B & S: 3-1/16 x 3-3/4 in. Displacement: 221 cid. Compression ratio: 6.3:1. Brake hp: 85 at 3800 rpm. Taxable hp: 30. Torque: 148 lb.-ft. at 2200 rpm. Main bearings: three. Valve lifters: mechanical. Carburetor: Ford 679510A two-barrel downdraft.

Chassis:

Wheelbase: 112 in. Overall length: 182-3/4 in. Height: 68-5/8 in. Front tread: 55-1/2. Rear tread: 58-1/4 in. Tires: 6.00 x 16.

1936 Ford V-8 Deluxe Roadster (OCW)

1936 Ford V-8 Cabriolet OCW)

1936 Ford V-8 Deluxe Club Cabriolet (OCW)

1936 Ford V-8 Standard Tudor sedan (OCW)

1936 Ford V-8 Trunkback Convertible Sedan (OCW)

1936 Ford V-8 Deluxe Tudor Touring Sedan (OCW)

1936 Ford V-8 Standard five-window Coupe (OCW)

1936 Ford V-8 Standard Fordor sedan (OCW)

1936 Ford V-8 Deluxe five-window coupe (OCW)

1936 Ford V-8 Slantback Convertible Sedan (OCW)

1936 Ford V-8 Deluxe Fordor Touring Sedan (OCW)

Technical:

Sliding gear transmission. Speeds: 3F/1R. Floor shift controls. Single dry plate, molded asbestos lining clutch. Shaft drive. Three-quarter floating rear axle. Overall ratio: 4.33:1. Mechanical, internal expanding brakes on four wheels. Pressed steel wheels, drop center rim. Wheel size: 16 in.

Options:

Radio (five versions from $44.50). Heater ($14). Clock ($9.75). Cigar lighter. Radio antenna. Seat covers. Spotlight. Rumbleseat in Coupe or Roadster ($20). Luggage rack ($7.50). Banjo steering wheel. "Spider" wheel covers ($3.75 early). Wind wings ($10). Combination oil-pressure, gas gauge ($3.75). Dual windshield wipers ($3). Leather upholstery. Electric air horns.

History:

Introduced October 1935. Ford was the overall winner of the 1936 Monte Carlo Rally. Calendar-year registrations: 748,554. Calendar-year production: 791,812. The president of Ford was Edsel Ford.

1936 Ford V-8 Deluxe three-window Coupe (OCW)

1936 Ford V-8 Station Wagon (OCW)

1936 Ford Showroom (OCW)

1937 Ford

Ford — Standard — Model 74 (60-hp) — V-8: The 1937 models were the first Fords to have their headlights mounted in the front fenders and use an all-steel top. The 1937 Ford's styling reflected the strong influence of the Lincoln-Zephyr. The grille with horizontal bars and a center vertical bar cut a sharp vee into the side hood area. As had been the case for many years, the side hood cooling vents reflected the grille's general form. Ford offered Sedans with a "slant-back" or Touring Sedans with a "trunk-back" rear deck. All Ford sedans had access to the trunk area through an external lid. In addition, a new coupe with a rear seat was introduced. All models had a rear-hinged alligator-type hood. Ford introduced a smaller version of its V-8 with a 2-3/5-inch bore and 3-1/5-inch stroke. Its displacement was 136 cid. This 60-hp engine was available only in the Standard Ford bodies, although these were also available with the larger 85-hp V-8 as well. Standard models had painted radiator grilles and windshield frames. A burl mahogany wood grain finish was applied to their interior window trim. Replacing the rod-operated mechanical brake system was a version using a cable linkage.

Ford — Standard — Model 78 (85-hp) — V-8: Standard models with painted radiator grilles and windshield frames were also available in the same body styles with the larger engine. A burl mahogany wood grain finish was applied to their interior window trim. The operation of the 221-cid V-8 was further improved by the use of a higher-capacity water pump, larger insert bearings and cast-alloy steel pistons.

Ford — Deluxe — Model 78 — V-8: Deluxe models had interiors with walnut wood grain window moldings and more exterior trim bright work. There were two matched-tone horns behind the radiator grille, two taillights, two swivel-type interior sun visors, dual windshield wipers and interior lights in coupes and sedans. On the outside, the wheels were dressed up with chrome trim bands. Otherwise, in 1937, the same "speedboat" front end styling was used on all Fords. The hood was hinged at the cowl and opened from the front, a modern feature for 1937. The battery was located on the firewall, below the hood. The V-type slanting windshield used in closed cars could be opened slightly for ventilation.

VIN:

Serial numbers were located on the left side of the frame near the firewall. Starting: (Model 74) 54-6602. (Model 78) 18-3331857. Ending: (Model 74) 54-358334. (Model 78) 18-4186446. Prefix "C" indicates Canadian built. Engine numbers located on top of clutch housing. Starting: (Model 74) 54-6602, (Model 78) 18-3331857. Ending: (Model 74) 54-358334, (Model 78) 18-4186446.

Ford Standard — Model 74 — V-8 (60 hp)

Model No.	Body/ Style No.	Body Type & Seating	Factory Price	Shipping Weight	Production Total
74	—	2-dr. Five-Window Cpe-2P	$ 529	2,275 lbs.	—
74	—	2-dr. Sedan-5P	$ 579	2,405 lbs.	—
74	—	2-dr. Trunk Sedan-5P	$ 604	2,415 lbs.	—
74	—	4-dr. Sedan-5P	$ 639	2,435 lbs.	—
74	—	4-dr. Trunk Sedan-5P	$ 664	2,445 lbs.	—

Ford Standard — Model 78 — V-8 (85 hp)

Model No.	Body/ Style No.	Body Type & Seating	Factory Price	Shipping Weight	Production Total
78	—	2-dr. Five-Window Coupe-2P	$ 586	2,496 lbs.	90,347
78	6	2-dr. Sedan-5P	$ 611	2,616 lbs.	308,446
78	—	2-dr. Trunk Sedan-5P	$ 636	2,648 lbs.	—
78	—	4-dr. Sedan-5P	$ 671	2,649 lbs.	49,062
78	—	4-dr. Trunk Sedan-5P	$ 696	2,666 lbs.	45,531

Ford Deluxe — Model 78 — V-8 (85 hp)

Model No.	Body/ Style No.	Body Type & Seating	Factory Price	Shipping Weight	Production Total
78	—	2-dr. Roadster-2P	$ 694	2,576 lbs.	1,250
78	—	4-dr. Phaeton-5P	$ 749	2,691 lbs.	3,723
78	—	2-dr. Cabriolet-4P	$ 719	2,616 lbs.	10,184
78	—	2-dr. Club Cabriolet-5P	$ 759	2,636 lbs.	8,001
78	—	4-dr. Trunk Sedan-5P	$ 696	2,666 lbs.	45,531
78	—	4-dr. Convertible Sedan-5P	$ 859	2,861 lbs.	4,378
78	—	2-dr. Five-Window Coupe-2P	$ 659	2,506 lbs.	26,738
78	—	2-dr. Five-Window Club Coupe-5P	$ 719	2,616 lbs.	16,992
78	—	2 dr, Sedan-5P	$ 674	2,656 lbs.	33,683
78	—	2-dr. Trunk Sedan-5P	$ 699	2,679 lbs.	—
78	—	4-dr. Sedan-5P	$ 734	2,671 lbs.	22,885
78	—	4-dr. Trunk Sedan-5P	$ 759	2,696 lbs.	98,687
78	—	4-dr. Station Wagon-5P	$ 755	2,991 lbs.	9,304

Engines:

Model 74 60-hp V-8: 90-degree V. Inline. Cast-iron block. B & S: 2-3/5 x 3-1/5 in. Displacement: 136 cid. Compression ratio: 6.6:1. Brake hp 60 at 3600 rpm Taxable hp: 21.6. Torque: 94 lb.-ft. at 2500 rpm. Main bearings: three. Valve lifters: mechanical. Carburetor: Stromberg 922A-9510A two-barrel downdraft.

1937 Ford V-8 Model 74 Standard Tudor Sedan (OCW)

1937 Ford V-8 Model 74 Deluxe five-window Coupe (OCW)

1937 Ford V-8 Model 78 Standard Tudor Sedan (OCW)

1937 Ford V-8 Model 78 Standard Tudor Touring Sedan (OCW)

1937 Ford V-8 Model 78 Standard Fordor Touring Sedan (OCW)

1937 Ford V-8 Model 78 Deluxe Cabriolet (OCW)

Model 78 85-hp V-8: 90-degree V. Inline. Cast-iron block. B & S: 3-1/16 x 3-3/4 in. Displacement: 221 cid. Compression ratio: 6.3:1. Brake hp: 85 at 3800 rpm Taxable hp: 30.01. Torque: 153 lb.-ft. at 2200 rpm. Main bearings: three. Valve lifters: mechanical. Carburetor: Stromberg 67-9510A two-barrel downdraft.

Chassis:

Model 74: Wheelbase: 112 in. Overall length: 179-1/2 in. Height: 68-5/8 in. Front tread: 55-1/2 in. Rear tread: 58-1/4 in. Tires: 5.50 x 16.
Model 78: Wheelbase: 112 in. Overall length: 179-1/2 in. Height: 68-5/8 in. Front tread: 55-1/2 in. Rear tread: 58-1/4 in. Tires: 5.50 x 16.

Technical:

Sliding gear transmission. Speeds: 3F/1R. Floor shift controls. Single dry plate, molded asbestos lining clutch. Shaft drive. Three-quarter floating rear axle. Overall ratio: 4.33:1. Mechanical, internal expanding brakes on four wheels. Pressed steel, drop center rim wheels. Wheel size: 16 in.

1937 Ford V-8 Model 78 Deluxe Club Cabriolet (OCW)

1937 Ford V-8 Model 78 Deluxe five-window Coupe (AA)

1937 Ford V-8 Model 78 Deluxe five-window Coupe rearview (OCW)

1937 Ford V-8 Model 78 Deluxe Convertible Sedan (OCW)

Fender skirts. Radio. Heater. Clock (mirror clock and glove box clock). Cigar lighter. Radio antenna. Seat covers. Side view mirror. Dual wipers. Sport light. Dual taillights (standard on Deluxe). Fog lamps. Locking gas cap. Glove box lock. Defroster. Draft deflectors. Vanity mirror. Wheel trim bands. Deluxe hubcaps. White sidewall tires. Center bumper guard. Deluxe steering wheel. Sliding glass panels on station wagon ($20).

1937 Ford V-8 Model 78 Deluxe Tudor Sedan (AA)

1937 Ford V-8 Model 78 Deluxe Tudor Touring Sedan (OCW)

1937 Ford V-8 Model 78 Deluxe Fordor Sedan (OCW)

1937 Ford V-8 Model 78 Deluxe Fordor Touring Sedan (OCW)

1937 Ford V-8 Model 78 Deluxe Station Wagon (JAC)

The 1937 Fords were introduced in November 1936. First year for 60 hp V-8. It was the first year for rear fender skirts. Calendar-year sales: 765,933 (registrations). Calendar-year production: 848,608. The president of Ford Motor Co. was Edsel Ford.

1938 Ford

Ford — Standard — Model 81A (85-hp) — V-8: The Standard Fords were also available with the 221-cid V-8. With this engine they were designated part of the Standard Model 81A line.

Ford — Deluxe — Model 81A (85-hp) — V-8: The Deluxe Ford body had a decidedly rounded V-type nose with horizontal grille bars on either side and V-8 insignia mounted in the clear spaces between the grille bars and the horizontal hood louvers. Interior alterations consisted of a new instrument panel with a centrally located radio speaker grille and recessed control knobs. As before, the windshield opening knob was centered high on the dash. The Deluxe model's "banjo" steering wheel had flexible, multiple steel spokes.

Serial numbers were located on the left-hand frame side member near the firewall. Starting: 81A - 18-4186447, 82A - 54-358335 & up. Ending: 81A - 18-4661100. Engine numbers were located on top of the clutch housing. Starting: 81A - 18-4186447, 82A - 54-358335 and up. Ending: 81A - 18-4661100.

Ford Standard Model 82A V-8 (60 hp)

Model No.	Body/ Style No.	Body Type & Seating	Factory Price	Shipping Weight	Production Total
82A	—	2-dr. Five-Window Coupe-2P	$ 595	2,354 lbs.	—
82A	—	2-dr. Sedan-5P	$ 640	2,455 lbs.	—
82A	—	4-dr. Sedan-5P	$ 685	2,481 lbs.	—

Ford Standard Model 81A V-8 (85 HP)

81A	—	2-dr. Five-Window Coupe-2P	$ 625	2,575 lbs.	34,059
81A	—	2-dr. Sedan-5P	$ 665	2,674 lbs.	106,117
81A	—	4-dr. Sedan-5P	$ 710	2,697 lbs.	30,287

Ford Deluxe Model 81A V-8 (85 HP)

81A	-	4-dr. Station Wagon-5P	$ 825	2,981 lbs.	6,944
81A	-	4-dr. Phaeton-5P	$ 820	2,748 lbs.	1,169
81A	-	2-dr. Club Cabriolet-5P	$ 800	2,719 lbs.	6,080
81A	---	2-dr. Cabriolet-3P	$ 770	2,679 lbs.	4,702
81A	---	4-dr. Convertible Sedan-5P	$ 900	2,683 lbs.	2,703
81A	---	2-dr. Five-Window Coupe-3P	$ 685	2,606 lbs.	22,225
81A	---	2-dr. Five-Window Club Coupe-5P	$ 745	2,688 lbs.	7,171
81A	---	2-dr. Sedan-5P	$ 725	2,742 lbs.	101,647
81A	---	4-dr. Sedan-5P	$ 770	2,773 lbs.	92,020

60-hp V-8: 90-degree V. Inline. Cast-iron block. B & S: 2-3/5 x 3-1/5 in. Displacement: 136 cid. Compression ratio: 6.6:1. Brake hp 60 at 3500 rpm Taxable hp: 21.6. Torque: 94 lbs.-ft. at 2500 rpm. Main bearings: three. Valve lifters: mechanical. Carburetor: Chandler-Groves and Stromberg 9221-95101, two-barrel downdraft.

85-hp V-8: 90-degree V. Inline. Cast-iron block. B & S: 3-1/16 x 3-3/4 in. Displacement: 221 cid. Compression ratio: 6.3:1. Brake hp: 85 at 3800 rpm Taxable hp: 30. Torque: 146 lbs.-ft. at 2000 rpm. Main bearings: three. Valve lifters: mechanical. Carburetor: Chandler-Groves and Stromberg 21A-9510A, two-barrel downdraft.

Model 82A: Wheelbase: 112 in. Overall length: 179-1/2 in. Height: 68-5/8 in. Front tread: 55-1/2 in. Rear tread: 58-1/4 in. Tires: 5.50 x 16.

1938 Ford V-8 Model 82A Standard Fordor Sedan (OCW)

Model 81A: Wheelbase: 112 in. Overall length: 179-1/2 in. Height: 68-5/8 in. Front tread: 55-1/2 in. Rear tread: 58-1/4 in. Tires: 6.00 x 16.

Technical:

Sliding gear transmission. Speeds: 3F/1R. Floor shift controls. Single dry plate, molded asbestos lining clutch. Shaft drive. Three-quarter floating rear axle. Overall ratio: 4.33:1. Mechanical, internal expanding brakes on four wheels. Pressed steel, drop center rim wheels. Wheel size: 16 in.

Options:

Fender skirts. Bumper guards. Radio. Heater. Clock (mirror and glove box types). Cigar lighter. Seat covers. Side view mirror. Dual wipers. Sport light. Dual taillights (standard on Deluxe). Fog lights. Locking gas cap. Glove box lock. Defroster. Draft deflectors. Vanity mirror. Wheel trim bands. Deluxe hubcaps (standard on Deluxe). White sidewall tires. Deluxe steering wheel (standard on Deluxe). License plate frame.

1938 Ford V-8 Model 82A Standard five-window Coupe (HAC)

1938 Ford V-8 Model 82A Standard Tudor Sedan (OCW)

1938 Ford V-8 Model 81A Standard Fordor Sedan (OCW)

1938 Ford V-8 Model 81A Deluxe Station Wagon (AA)

History:

Introduced November 1937. Ford secured its second victory in the Monte Carlo Rally. Calendar-year registrations: 363,688. Calendar-year production: 410,048. The president of Ford Motor Co. was Edsel Ford.

1938 Ford V-8 Model 81A Deluxe Cabriolet (OCW)

1938 Ford V-8 Model 81A Deluxe Fordor Sedan (OCW)

1938 Ford V-8 Model 81A Deluxe five-window Coupe (OCW)

1939 Ford

Ford — Standard — Model 922A (60-hp) — V-8: Only four body styles were offered in the Standard series. Standard models carried the general "speedboat" front end styling of the 1938 Ford Deluxe. They had a sharply veed grille with horizontal bars, headlights mounted inboard of the fenders and small side hood louvers. Standard models were not equipped with a banjo-style steering wheel, glove box lock or clock as standard equipment. The smaller 60-hp flathead V-8 was offered only in Standard bodies. A significant 1939 technical development was the adoption by Ford of Lockheed hydraulic brakes.

Ford — Standard — Model 91A (85-hp) — V-8: The Standard Ford models were also available with the larger 85-hp V-8.

Ford — Deluxe — Model 91A (85-hp) — V-8: Deluxe models had a much more modern appearance. Their teardrop-shaped headlights blended smoothly into the leading edges of the front fenders. The radiator grille was set lower in the hood than before. Simple chrome trim replaced the hood louvers and a smoother body profile was featured. Deluxe models had a banjo steering wheel, a locking glove box and a clock as standard equipment.

1939 Ford V-8 Model 922A Standard five-window Coupe (OCW)

1939 Ford V-8 Model 922A Standard Tudor Sedan (OCW)

VIN:

Serial numbers were located on the left side member near the firewall. Starting No.: Model 91A - 18-4661001. Model 922A - 54506501 and up. Ending: 91A - 18-210700. Engine No. location was on top of the clutch housing. Starting: Model 91A - 18-4661001. Model 922A - 54-506501 and up. Ending: Model 91A - 18-5210700.

Ford Standard Model 922A V-8 (60 hp)

Model No.	Body Type & Seating	Factory Price	Shipping Weight	Production Total
922A	2-dr. Five-Window Coupe-2P	$ 599	2,463 lbs.	—
922A	2-dr. Sedan-5P	$ 640	2,608 lbs.	—
922A	4-dr. Sedan-5P	$ 686	2,623 lbs.	—

Ford Standard Model 91A V-8 (85 hp)

91A	2-dr. Five-Window Coupe-2P	$ 640	2,710 lbs.	38,197
91A	2-dr. Sedan-5P	$ 681	2,830 lbs.	124,866
91A	4-dr. Sedan-5P	$ 727	2,850 lbs.	—
91A	4-dr. Station Wagom-5P	$ 840	3,080 lbs.	3,277

Ford Deluxe Model 91A V-8 (85 hp)

91A	2-dr. Convertible-3P	$ 770	2,679 lbs.	4,702
91A	4-dr. Convertible Sedan-5P	$ 900	2,863 lbs.	2,703
91A	2-dr. Five-Window Coupe-2P	$ 685	2,606 lbs.	22,225
91A	2-dr. Sedan-5P	$ 725	2,742 lbs.	101,647
91A	4-dr. Sedan-5P	$ 770	2,773 lbs.	92,020
91A	4-dr. Station Wagom-5P	$ 825	2,981 lbs.	6,944

Engine:

60-hp V-8: 90-degree V. Cast-iron block. B & S: 2-3/5 x 3-1/5 in. Displacement: 136 cid. Compression ratio: 6.6:1. Brake hp 60 at 3500 rpm Taxable hp: 21.6. Torque: 94 lbs.-ft. at 2500 rpm. Main bearings: three. Valve lifters: mechanical. Carburetor: Stromberg 922A-9510A two-barrel downdraft.

85-hp V-8: 90-degree V. Cast-iron block. B & S: 3-1/16 x 3-3/4 in. Displacement: 221 cid. Compression ratio: 6.3:1. Brake hp: 85 at 3800 rpm Taxable hp: 30. Torque: 146 lbs.-ft. at 2000 rpm. Main bearings: three. Valve lifters: mechanical. Carburetor: Chandler-Groves and Stromberg 21A-951A two-barrel downdraft.

Chassis:

Model 922A: Wheelbase: 112 in. Overall length: 179-1/2 in. Height: 68-5/8 in. Front tread: 55-1/2 in. Rear tread: 58-1/4 in. Tires: 5.50 x 16.

Model 91A: Wheelbase: 112 in. Overall length: 179-1/2 in. Height: 68-5/8 in. Front tread: 55-1/2 in. Rear tread: 58-1/4 in. Tires: 6.00 x 16.

Technical:

Sliding gear transmission. Speeds: 3F/1R. Floor shift controls. Single dry plate, molded asbestos lining clutch. Shaft drive. Three-quarter floating rear axle. Overall ratio: 4.33:1. Lockheed hydraulic brakes on four wheels. Pressed steel, drop center rim wheels. Wheel size: 16 in.

Options:

Bumper guards. Radio. Heater. Clock (standard on Deluxe). Seat covers. Side view mirror. Sport light. Fog lamps. Locking gas cap. Draft deflectors. Vanity mirror. Wheel dress up rings (standard on Deluxe). Deluxe hubcaps for Standard. White sidewall tires. License plate frames. Fender skirts.

History:

Introduced November 4, 1938. Lockheed hydraulic brakes. Calendar-year registrations: 481,496. Calendar-year production: 532,152. The president of Ford Motor Co. was Edsel Ford.

1939 Ford V-8 Model 91A Standard five-window Coupe (OCW)

1939 Ford V-8 Model 91A Standard Tudor Sedan (OCW)

1939 Ford V-8 Model 91A Standard Fordor Sedan (OCW)

1939 Ford V-8 Model 91A Standard Station Wagon (OCW)

1939 Ford V-8 Model 91A Deluxe Convertible (OCW)

1939 Ford V-8 Model 91A Deluxe Convertible Sedan (OCW)

1939 Ford V-8 Model 91A Deluxe five-window Coupe (OCW)

1939 Ford V-8 Model 91A Deluxe Tudor Sedan (OCW)

1939 Ford V-8 Model 91A Deluxe Station Wagon (OCW)

1939 Ford V-8 Model 91A Deluxe Fordor Sedan (OCW)

1940 Ford

Ford — Model 02A — Standard (60-hp) — V-8: Standard Fords had a grille and hood similar to those of the 1939 Deluxe models. Their headlight shells were finished in the body color and the integral parking lamp lacked the ribbed surround used on Deluxe models. The vertical grille bars were also painted to match the body color. Deluxe hubcaps had a series of concentric rings surrounding a blue V-8. The Standard dash and steering wheel had a Briarwood Brown finish and the instrument panel had a larger speedometer face. Standard models had front vent windows. This was the final year for availability of the 60-hp V-8 as an option in Standard models only.

Ford — Model 01A — Standard (85-hp) — V-8: As in the past few years, cars with the Standard Ford body were also offered with the larger 85-hp V-8.

Ford — Model 01A — Deluxe (85-HP) — V-8: The 1940 Ford Deluxe body featured extremely handsome styling by Eugene Gregorie. All Fords, including Deluxe models, were fitted with sealed beam headlights and a steering column-mounted shift lever. Deluxe models were distinguished by their chrome headlight trim rings with the parking light cast into its upper surface. The bright Deluxe grille combined a center section with horizontal bars and secondary side grids whose horizontal bars were subdivided into three sections by thicker molding. Hubcaps for these top-level Fords featured bright red "Ford Deluxe" lettering and trim rings finished in the body color. The Deluxe instrument panel was given a maroon-and-sand two-tone finish that matched that of the steering wheel. Only the 85-hp V-8 was available in Deluxe models.

VIN:

Serial numbers were located on the left frame side member near the firewall. Starting: [Model 01A] 18-5210701, [Model 022A] 54-506501 and up. Ending: [Model 01A] 18-5896294. Engine numbers were located on the top of the clutch housing. Starting: [Model 01A] 18-5210701, [Model 022A] 54-506401 and up. Ending: [Model 01A] 18-5896294.

Ford Standard Model 02A V-8 (60 HP)

Model No.	Body/ Style No.	Body Type & Seating	Factory Price	Shipping Weight	Production Total
02A	—	2-dr. Five-Window Coupe-2P	$ 619	2,519 lbs.	—
02A	—	2-dr. Business Coupe-2P	$ 640	2,549 lbs.	—
02A	—	2-dr. Sedan-5P	$ 660	2,669 lbs.	—
02A	—	4-dr. Sedan-5P	$ 706	2,696 lbs.	—

Ford Standard Model 01A V-8 (85 HP)

02A	—	2-dr. Five-Window Coupe-2P	$ 660	2,763 lbs.	33,693
02A	—	2-dr. Business Coupe-2P	$ 681	2,801 lbs.	16,785
02A	—	2-dr. Sedan-5P	$ 701	2,909 lbs.	150,933
02A	—	4-dr. Sedan-5P	$ 747	2,936 lbs.	25,545
02A	—	4-dr. Station Wagon-5P	$ 875	3,249 lbs.	4,469

Ford Deluxe Model 01A V-8 (85 hp)

01A	—	2-dr. Five-Window Coupe-2P	$ 722	2,791 lbs.	27,919
01A	—	2-dr. Business Coupe-2P	$ 742	2,831 lbs.	20,183
01A	—	2-dr. Convertible-5P	$ 849	2,956 lbs.	23,704
01A	—	2-dr. Sedan-5P	$ 765	2,927 lbs.	171,368
01A	—	4-dr. Sedan-5P	$ 747	2,936 lbs.	25,545
01A	—	4-dr. Station Wagon-5P	$ 810	2,966 lbs.	91,756
01A	—	4-dr. Station Wagon-5P	$ 950	3,262 lbs.	8,730

Engine:

60-hp V-8: 90-degree V. Cast-iron block. B & S: 2-3/5 x 3-1/5 in. Displacement: 136 cid. Compression ratio: 6.6:1. Brake hp 60 at 3500 rpm Taxable hp: 21.6. Torque: 94 lbs.-ft. at 2500 rpm. Main bearings: three. Valve lifters: mechanical. Carburetor: Chandler-Groves 922A-9510A two-barrel downdraft.

1940 Ford V-8 Model 02A Standard five-window Coupe (OCW)

1940 Ford V-8 Model 01A Standard Tudor Sedan (OCW)

1940 Ford V-8 Model 01A Standard Station Wagon (OCW)

1940 Ford V-8 Model 01A Deluxe five-window Coupe (OCW)

1940 Ford V-8 Model 01A Deluxe Station Wagon (OCW)

1940 Ford V-8 Model 01A Deluxe Fordor Sedan (OCW)

90-hp V-8: 90-degree V. Cast-iron block. B & S: 3-1/16 x 3-3/4 in. Displacement: 221 cid. Compression ratio: 6.15:1. Brake hp: 85 at 3800 rpm Taxable hp: 30. Torque: 155 lbs.-ft. at 2200 rpm. Main bearings: three. Valve lifters: mechanical. Carburetor: Chandler-Groves 21A-9510A, two-barrel downdraft.

Chassis:

Model 02A: Wheelbase: 112 in. Overall length: 188-1/4 in. Height: 68 in. Front tread: 55-3/4 in. Rear tread: 58-1/4 in. Tires: 5.50 x 16.

Model 01A: Wheelbase: 112 in. Overall length: 188-1/4 in. Height: 68 in. Front tread: 55-3/4 in. Rear tread: 58-1/4 in. Tires: 6.00 x 16.

Technical:

Sliding gear transmission. Speeds: 3F/1R. Floor shift controls. Single dry plate, molded asbestos lining clutch. Shaft drive. Three-quarter floating rear axle. Overall ratio: 4.33:1. Lockheed hydraulic brakes on four wheel. Pressed steel, drop center rim wheels. Wheel size: 16 in.

Options:

Fender skirts. Bumper guards. Radio. Heater. Cigar lighter. Radio antenna. Seat covers. Side view mirror. Right-hand side view mirror. Spotlight. Fog lamps. Locking gas cap. Defroster. Vanity mirror. Deluxe wheel rings (standard on Deluxe). Deluxe hubcaps (standard on Deluxe). White sidewall tires. Gravel deflectors. License plate frame. Two-tone paint.

History:

Introduced in October 1940. Calendar-year sales: 542,755 (registrations). Calendar-year production: 599,175. The president of Ford Motor Co. was Edsel Ford.

1941 Ford

Ford — Special — Series 1GA/11A — Six and V-8: The 1941 Fords had fresh styling and a revamped chassis and were easily recognizable as new models. All versions were mounted on a two-inch-longer wheelbase. The use of a wider body substantially increased the Ford's interior dimensions. Emphasizing the rounder, more curved body form was a new three-piece grille that consisted of a neo-traditional vertical center section with two auxiliary units set low on either side. Running boards were continued, but due to the body's greater width, they were far less noticeable than on earlier Fords. Further accentuating the lower-and-wider nature of the '41 Ford was the position of the headlights, which were set further apart in the fenders. Base cars this year were called "Specials" rather than "Standards." The three Special models were offered only in a Harbor Gray finish. The windshield divider was painted black. The center grille section was, however, chromed. Specials came equipped with a single taillight, only one horn, one windshield wiper and one sun visor. Lacking from their interior were such appointments as armrests, a dome light, a cigarette lighter and a glove box lock. On Monday, June 2, 1941 the following announcement was printed in *Time* magazine: "Last week, for the first time since 1908, auto dealers had for sale a six-cylinder Ford. Expected for months (*Time*, September 9, 1941), the six was not a new car, but a new engine in the V-8 body. It was priced at the old price of the V-8, which was simultaneously raised $15. No official specifications were released, but dealers described the six as a cheaper, more economical (than the V-8), 90-hp L-head engine with three-point suspension." Since the six-cylinder engine arrived so late, some sources say it was available only in Specials. *The Official Blue Book New & Used Car Guide* effective May-June, 1942 indicates that the six was available in all Ford bodies. We also found a Ford ad in the *Motor* show annual for 1941 that incorrectly makes it appear that the six was first announced for 1942 models.

Ford — Deluxe — Series 1GA/11A — Six and V-8: Deluxe series Fords instrument panels were finished in an Ebony grain pattern. Among their standard features were a glove box lock, dual windshield wipers and two interior sun visors. The wheels of these cars were all painted Black. Only the center grille portion was chromed on Deluxe models. Initially, Deluxe Fords were available only with Ford's improved 90-hp V-8 Among its design features were four main bearings, a vibration damper, forged connecting rods, molybdenum-chrome alloy steel valve seat inserts and solid valve lifters. The six-cylinder engine was announced in June and its availability required new hood trim. Prior to the six's introduction the hood molding was a plain trim piece with horizontal liner. With the availability of two engines it now carried either a "6" or a "V-8" logo against the blue background.

Ford — Super Deluxe — Series 1GA/11A — Six and V-8: Super Deluxe Fords were easily identified by the bright trim on the edges of their running boards and their chrome grille sections. Super Deluxe bumpers had ridges along their bottom edge. A March 1941 revision added bright trim to the front and rear fenders, the windshield, the side windows and the rear window. A Super Deluxe script was placed in an inboard position on the left front fender. Bright rear taillight surrounds were installed on Super Deluxe models. In addition, standard features of the Super Deluxe models included a trunk light, a glove box-mounted clock, bright wheel trim rings, twin interior sun visors, dual wipers, a unique license plate guard and plastic Kelobra-grain dashboard trim. The Super Deluxe wheels had either Vermillion or Silver Gray striping. Seven body styles were offered in Super Deluxe form. Initially, all Super Deluxes came with a V-8 engine, but the six-cylinder engine was available after June of 1941.

VIN:

Serial numbers were located on the left frame member, directly behind the front engine mount. Starting: (six-cylinder), (V-8) 18-5986295. Ending: (six-cylinder): IGA-34800, (V-8) 18-6769035. Prefix "C" indicates Canadian built. Engine numbers were located on the top of the clutch housing. Starting: (six-cylinder) IGA-1, (V-8) 18-5986295. Ending: (six-cylinder) IGA-34800, (V-8) 18-6769035.

1941 Ford Six Model 1GA Special Coupe (OCW)

1941 Ford Six Model 1GA Deluxe Tudor Sedan (OCW)

Ford Special Model 1GA (Six)

Model No.	Body/ Style No.	Body Type & Seating	Factory Price	Shipping Weight	Production Total
1GA	---	2-dr. Coupe-2P	$ 684	2,870 lbs.	---
1GA	---	2-dr. Sedan-5P	$ 720	2,975 lbs.	---
1GA	---	4-dr. Sedan-5P	$ 761	3,020 lbs.	---

Ford Deluxe Model 1GA (Six)

1GA	---	2-dr. Five-Window Coupe-2P	$ 715	2,947 lbs.	---
1GA	---	2-dr. Auxiliary Seat Coupe-2/4P	$ 746	2,970 lbs.	---
1GA	---	2-dr. Sedan-5P	$ 756	3,065 lbs.	---
1GA	---	4-dr. Sedan-5P	$ 797	3,100 lbs.	---
1GA	---	4-dr. Station Wagon-5P	$ 946	3,305 lbs.	---

Ford Super Deluxe Model 1GA (Six)

1GA	---	2-dr. Five-Window Coupe-2P	$ 722	2,791 lbs.	---
1GA	---	2-dr. Auxiliary Seat Coupe-2/4P	$ 742	2,831 lbs.	---
1GA	---	2-dr. Sedan Coupe-5P	$ 742	2,831 lbs.	---
1GA	---	2-dr. Convertible-5P	$ 849	2,956 lbs.	---
1GA	---	2-dr. Sedan-5P	$ 765	2,927 lbs.	---
1GA	---	4-dr. Sedan-5P	$ 747	2,936 lbs.	---
1GA	---	4-dr. Station Wagon-5P	$ 810	2,966 lbs.	---

Ford Special Model 11A (V-8)

11A	---	2-dr. Coupe-2P	$ 706	2,878 lbs.	9,823
11A	---	2-dr. Sedan-5P	$ 735	2,983 lbs.	27,189
11A	---	4-dr. Sedan-5P	$ 775	3,033 lbs.	3,838

Ford Deluxe Model 11A (V-8)

11A	---	2-dr. Five-Window Coupe-2P	$ 730	2,953 lbs.	33,598
11A	---	2-dr. Auxiliary Seat Coupe-2/4P	$ 750	2,981 lbs.	12,844
11A	---	2-dr. Sedan-5P	$ 775	3,095 lbs.	177,018
11A	---	4-dr. Sedan-5P	$ 815	3,121 lbs.	25,928
11A	---	4-dr. Station Wagon-5P	$ 965	3,412 lbs.	6,116

Ford Super Deluxe Model 11A (V-8)

11A	---	2-dr. Five-Window Coupe-2P	$ 775	2,969 lbs.	22,878
11A	---	2-dr. Auxiliary Seat Coupe-2/4P	$ 800	3,001 lbs.	10,796
11A	---	2-dr. Sedan Coupe-5P	$ 850	3,052 lbs.	45,977
11A	---	2-dr. Convertible-5P	$ 950	3,187 lbs.	30,240
11A	---	2-dr. Sedan-5P	$ 820	3,110 lbs.	185,788
11A	---	4-dr. Sedan-5P	$ 860	3,146 lbs.	88,053
11A	---	4-dr. Station Wagon-5P	$1,015	3,419 lbs.	9,845

Note: Production totals are combined six-cylinder/V-8 production for series and body style.

Engine:

Ford Six: L-head. Cast-iron block. B & S: 3-3/10 x 4-2/5 in. Displacement: 225.8 cid. Compression ratio: 6.7:1. Brake hp: 90 at 3300 rpm. Taxable hp: 30. Torque: 180 lbs.-ft. at 2000 rpm. Main bearings: four. Valve lifters: mechanical. Carburetor: Ford 1GA-9510A one-barrel.

Ford V-8: 90-degree V. Cast-iron block. B & S: 3-1/16 x 3-3/4 in. Displacement: 221 cid. Compression ratio: 6.15:1. Brake hp: 90 at 3800 rpm Taxable hp: 30. Torque: 156 lbs.-ft. at 2200 rpm. Main bearings: three. Valve lifters: mechanical. Carburetor: Ford 21A-9510A two-barrel downdraft.

Chassis:

All: Wheelbase: 114 in. Overall length: 194.3 in. Height: 68.15 in. Front tread: 55-3/4 in. Rear tread: 58-1/4 in. Tires: 6.00 x 16.

1941 Ford Six Model 1GA Deluxe Station Wagon (OCW)

Sliding gear transmission. Speeds: 3F/1R. Floor shift controls. Single dry plate, molded asbestos lining clutch. Shaft drive. Three-quarter floating rear axle. Overall ratio: 3.78:1. Hydraulic brakes on four wheels. Pressed steel, drop center rim wheels. Wheel size: 16 in.

Options:

Fender skirts ($12.50). Radio. Hot air heater ($23). Hot water heater ($20). Clock. Seat covers. Side view mirror. Passenger side mirror. Spotlight. Locking gas cap. Glove compartment lock. Defroster. Vanity mirror. Radio foot control. Wheel trim rings. Deluxe hubcaps. White sidewall tires. Front center bumper guards - front ($3.50). Front center bumper guards - rear ($2.50). Gravel deflector ($1.50).

1941 Ford V-8 Model 11A Deluxe five-window Coupe (OCW)

1941 Ford Six Model 1GA Super Deluxe Convertible (OCW)

1941 Ford V-8 Model 11A Deluxe Tudor Sedan (OCW)

1941 Ford Six Model 1GA Super Deluxe Tudor Sedan (OCW)

1941 Ford V-8 Model 11A Super Deluxe five-window Coupe (AA)

1941 Ford Six Model 1GA Super Deluxe Fordor Sedan (OCW)

1941 Ford V-8 Model 11A Super Deluxe Convertible (OCW)

1941 Ford V-8 Model 11A Special Coupe (OCW)

1941 Ford V-8 Model 11A Super Deluxe Tudor Sedan (OCW)

Introduced September 1941. Calendar-year sales: 602,013 (registrations). Calendar-year production: 600,814. The president of Ford was Edsel Ford. On April 29, 1941, the 29-millionth Ford was constructed.

1941 Ford V-8 Model 11A Super Deluxe Fordor Sedan (OCW)

1941 Ford V-8 Model 11A Super Deluxe Station Wagon (OCW)

1941 Ford V-8 Airport Limousine (OCW)

1942 Ford

Ford — Special Economy Six — Series 2GA — Six: The 1942 Fords were redesigned with fully-concealed running boards plus new front fenders and hood sheet metal. The headlights were flush with the fronts of the fenders and horizontal parking lights were located in the sheet metal above the grille. A new grille design featured a narrow center section in conjunction with side grilles considerably larger and more squared off than previous ones. There were three Special Economy 6 models: a single-cushion Coupe, a Tudor sedan and a Fordor sedan. These cars were offered only with Black finish. This year the lowest-priced Fords also came only with six-cylinder engines. They lacked bumper guards. Black wheel covers were standard and like those on all 1942 models, carried blue Ford script. Common to all 1942 Fords was a revised frame design that was lower by one inch than the 1941 version. All Fords also had lower and wider leaf springs, a two-inch wider tread and dual lateral stabilizer bars. The transition to a wartime economy brought many material substitutes in the 1942 models. Among the more obvious was the use of plastic interior components and the replacement of nickel by molybdenum in valves, gears and shafts. The final 1942 model Fords were produced on February 10, 1942. The new Ford looked larger and more massive. Riding comfort was improved slightly due to the use of longer springs. Larger brake pistons split the braking power 60-40 front and rear, instead of the previous 55-45. The redesigned frame was more rigid. New rubber rear engine mounts were adopted.

Ford — Deluxe — Series 2GA/21A — Six and V-8: The 1942 Ford Deluxe models were equipped with the bumpers used on the 1941 Super Deluxe models. The grille frame was painted in body color.

1942 Ford Six Model 2GA Super Deluxe Tudor Sedan (OCW)

Unique to the Deluxe Ford was its center grille panel with "Deluxe" spelled out vertically, in bright letters, against a blue background. The wheel covers were painted to match body color. The Deluxe instrument panel was finished in Crackle Mahogany grain.

Ford — Super Deluxe — Series 2GA/21A — Six and V-8: The Super Deluxe grille had its bright work accentuated by blue-painted grooves. Used only on these top-of-the-line Fords were front and rear bumpers with ridges along their upper surface. A Super Deluxe script was now positioned just below the left headlight. The taillights on all models were now horizontally positioned, but only those on the Super Deluxe had bright trim plates. Also unique to Super Deluxe Fords was bright trim surrounds for the windshield, rear window and side windows. The wheel covers were painted to match body color and carried three stripes. Wheel trim rings were standard equipment. Interior features included an electric clock, a left-hand front door armrest, a steering wheel with a full-circle horn ring and crank-operated front vent windows. The instrument panel was finished in Sequoia grain. Assist cords were installed on Sedan and Sedan Coupe models.

Serial numbers were located on the left frame member directly behind the front engine mount. Starting: (six-cylinder) IGA-34801, V-8 18-6769036. Ending: (six-cylinder) IGA-227,523, V-8 18-6925878. Prefix "C" indicates Canadian built. Engine numbers were located on top of clutch housing. Starting: (six-cylinder) IGA-34801, V-8 18-6769036. Ending: (six-cylinder) — IGA-227523, V-8 — 18-6925898.

Ford Special Model 1GA (Six)

Model No.	Body/ Style No.	Body Type and Seating	Factory Price	Shipping Weight	Production Total
2GA	77C	2-dr. Coupe-3P	$780	2,910 lbs.	1,606
2GA	70C	2-dr. Sedan-6P	$815	3,053 lbs.	3,187
2GA	73C	4-dr. Sedan-6P	$850	3,093 lbs.	27,189

1942 Ford Six Model 2GA Super Deluxe Station Wagon (OCW)

Ford Deluxe Model 2GA (Six)

2GA	77A	2-dr. Five-Window Coupe-3P	$ 805	2,958 lbs.	-----
2GA	72A	2-dr. Sedan Coupe-6P	$ 865	3,045 lbs.	-----
2GA	70A	2-dr. Sedan-6P	$ 840	3,122 lbs.	-----
2GA	73A	4-dr. Sedan-6P	$ 875	3,141 lbs.	-----
2GA	79A	4-dr. Station Wagon-8P	$1,035	3,400 lbs.	-----

Ford Super Deluxe Model 2GA (Six)

2GA	77B	2-dr. Five-Window Coupe-3P	$ 850	3,030 lbs.	-----
2GA	72B	2-dr. Sedan Coupe-6P	$ 910	3,109 lbs.	-----
2GA	76	2-dr. Convertible-5P	$1,080	3,218 lbs.	-----
2GA	70B	2-dr. Sedan-6P	$ 885	3,136 lbs.	-----
2GA	73B	4-dr. Sedan-6P	$ 920	3,179 lbs.	-----
2GA	79B	4-dr. Station Wagon-8P	$1,115	3,453 lbs.	-----

Ford Deluxe Model 2GA (V-8)

21A	77A	2-dr. Five-Window Coupe-3P	$ 815	2,978 lbs.	5,936
21A	72A	2-dr. Sedan Coupe-6P	$ 875	3,065 lbs.	5,419
21A	70A	2-dr. Sedan-6P	$ 850	3,141 lbs.	27,302
21A	73A	4-dr. Sedan-6P	$ 885	3,161 lbs.	5,127
21A	79A	4-dr. Station Wagon-8P	$1,090	3,460 lbs.	567

Ford Super Deluxe Model 21A (V-8)

21A	77B	2-dr. Five-Window Coupe-3P	$ 860	3,050 lbs.	5,411
21A	72B	2-dr. Sedan Coupe-6P	$ 920	3,120 lbs.	13,543
21A	76	2-dr. Convertible-5P	$1,090	3,238 lbs.	2,920
21A	70B	2-dr. Sedan-6P	$ 895	3,159 lbs.	37,199
21A	73B	4-dr. Sedan-6P	$ 930	3,200 lbs.	24,846
21A	79B	4-dr. Station Wagon-8P	$1,125	3,468 lbs.	5,483

Engines:

Ford Six: L-head. Cast-iron block. B & S: 3-3/10 x 4-2/5 in. Displacement: 225.8 cid. Compression ratio: 6.7:1. Brake hp: 90 at 3300 rpm. Taxable hp: 30. Torque: 180 lbs.-ft. at 2000 rpm. Main bearings: four. Valve lifters: mechanical. Carburetor: Ford 1GA-9510A one-barrel.

Ford V-8: 90-degree V. Cast-iron block. B & S: 3-1/16 x 3-3/4 in. Displacement: 221 cid. Compression ratio: 6.2:1. Brake hp: 96 at 3800 rpm Taxable hp: 30. Torque: 156 lbs.-ft. at 2200 rpm. Main bearings: three. Valve lifters: mechanical. Carburetor: Ford 21A-9510A two-barrel downdraft.

Chassis:

All: Wheelbase: 114 in. Overall length: 194.4 in. Height: 68.15 in. Front Tread: 58 in. Rear Tread: 60 in. Tires: 6.00 x 16.

Technical:

Sliding gear transmission. Speeds: 3F/1R. Floor shift controls. Single dry plate, molded asbestos lining clutch. Shaft drive. Three-quarter floating rear axle. Overall ratio: 3.78:1. Hydraulic brakes on four wheels. Pressed steel, drop center rim wheels. Wheel size: 16 in.

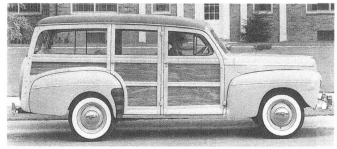

1942 Ford V-8 Model 21A Deluxe Station Wagon (OCW)

1942 Ford V-8 Model 21A Super Deluxe five-window Coupe (PH)

Options:

Fender skirts. Center bumper guards. Radio ($39). Hot air heater ($23). Hot water heater ($20). Clock. Side view mirror. Passenger side mirror. Sport light. Locking gas cap. Fog lights. Seat covers. Defroster. Visor-vanity mirror. Radio foot control. Wheel trim rings. White sidewall tires ($15). Bumper end guards ($2.75 a pair). Oil filter ($6.14). License plate frames.

History:

Introduced September 12, 1941. Calendar-year production 43,407. Model-year production: 160,211. The president of Ford Motor Co. was Edsel Ford.

1942 Ford V-8 Model 21A Super Deluxe Sedan Coupe (OCW)

1942 Ford V-8 Model 21A Super Deluxe Tudor Sedan (OCW)

1942 Ford V-8 Model 21A Super Deluxe Fordor Sedan (OCW)

1946 Ford

Ford — Deluxe — Series 6GA/69A — Six and V-8: All 1946 Fords were, in essence, restyled 1942 models utilizing the same drive train as the prewar models. The grille was restyled with horizontal bars on the outside of the rectangular opening, instead of the flush-mounted grille of the 1942 model. The remainder of the body was virtually the same as the prewar model. The Deluxe series was the base trim level for 1946 and included rubber moldings around all window openings, a horn button instead of a ring, one sun visor and armrests only on the driver's door.

Ford — Super Deluxe — Series 6GA/69A — Six and V-8: The Super Deluxe series was the top trim level for 1946 and included chrome moldings around all windows, a horn ring, two sun visors, armrests on all doors, passenger assist straps on the interior "B" pillars for easier rear seat egress, horizontal chrome trim on the body and leather interior on the convertible models.

1946 Ford Six Model 6GA Deluxe Tudor Sedan (OCW)

1946 Ford Six Model 6GA Deluxe Fordor Sedan (OCW)

1946 Ford Six Model 6GA Super Deluxe Sedan Coupe (OCW)

1946 Ford Six Model 6GA Super Deluxe Tudor Sedan (OCW)

1946 Ford Six Model 6GA Super Deluxe Fordor Sedan (OCW)

1946 Ford Six Model 6GA Super Deluxe Station Wagon (OCW)

1946 Ford V-8 Model 69A Super Deluxe Convertible (OCW)

VIN:

Deluxe six-cylinder models began with the designation, "6GA," with production numbers beginning at 1GA-227524 and going to 1GA-326417. Deluxe V-8-powered models began with the designation, "69A", with production numbers beginning at 99A-650280 and going to 99A-1412707. Super Deluxe six-cylinder models began with the same "6GA" designation and used the same production numbers as the Deluxe models. Super Deluxe V-8 models began with the same "69A" designation and used the same production numbers as the Deluxe models.

Ford — Deluxe — Series 6GA (Six)

Model No.	Body/ Style No.	Body Type & Seating	Factory Price	Shipping Weight	Production Total
6GA	77A	2-dr. Coupe-3P	$1,074	3,007 lbs.	------
6GA	70A	2-dr. Sedan-6P	$1,136	3,157 lbs.	------
6GA	73A	4-dr. Sedan-6P	$1,198	3,167 lbs.	------

Ford —Deluxe — Series 69A (V-8)

6GA	77A	2-dr. Coupe-3P	$1,123	3,040 lbs.	10,760
6GA	70A	2-dr. Sedan-6P	$1,165	3,190 lbs.	74,954
6GA	73A	4-dr. Sedan-6P	$1,248	3,220 lbs.	9,246

Ford — Super Deluxe — Series 6GA (Six)

6GA	77B	2-dr. Coupe-3P	$1,148	3,007 lbs.	------
6GA	72B	2-dr. Sedan Coupe-6P	$1,257	3,107 lbs.	------
6GA	70B	2-dr. Sedan-6P	$1,211	3,157 lbs.	------
6GA	73B	4-dr. Sedan-6P	$1,273	3,207 lbs.	------
6GA	79B	4-dr. Station Wagon-8P	$1,504	3,457 lbs.	------

Ford — Super Deluxe — Series 6GA (V-8)

6GA	77B	2-dr. Coupe-3P	$1,197	3,040 lbs.	12,249
6GA	72B	2-dr. Sedan Coupe-6P	$1,307	3,140 lbs.	70,826
6GA	76	2-dr. Convertible-6P	$1,488	3,240 lbs.	16,359
6GA	71	2-dr. Sportsman-6P	$1,982	3,340 lbs.	723
6GA	70B	2-dr. Sedan-6P	$1,260	3,190 lbs.	163,370
6GA	73B	4-dr. Sedan-6P	$1,322	3,240 lbs.	92,056
6GA	79B	4-dr. Station Wagon-8P	$1,553	3,490 lbs.	16,960

Note 1: Production totals are combined six-cylinder and V-8 production for series and body style.

Engines:

Ford Six: L-head. Cast-iron block. B & S: 3-3/10 x 4-2/5 in. Displacement: 225.8 cid. Compression ratio: 6.8:1. Brake hp: 90 at 3300 rpm. Taxable hp: 30. Torque: 180 lbs.-ft. at 2000 rpm. Main bearings: four. Valve lifters: mechanical. Carburetor: Holley single-barrel Model 847F.

1946 Ford V-8 Model 69A Super Deluxe Sportsman Convertible (OCW)

1946 Ford V-8 Model 69A Super Deluxe Tudor Sedan (OCW)

1946 Ford V-8 Model 69A Super Deluxe Fordor Sedan (OCW)

1946 Ford V-8 Model 69A Super Deluxe Station Wagon (OCW)

Ford V-8: L-head. Cast-iron block. B & S: 3.19 x 3.75 in. Displacement: 239 cid. Compression ratio: 6.75:1. Brake hp: 100 at 3800 rpm. Torque: 180 at 2000 rpm. Taxable hp: 32.5. Three main bearings. Solid valve lifters. Crankcase capacity: 5 qt. (add 1 qt. with new oil filter). Cooling system capacity: 22 qt. Carburetor: Holley (Chandler-Groves) Ford No. 59A-9510-A two-barrel downdraft.

Chassis:

Wheelbase: 114 inches. Overall length: 196.2 inches. Tires: 6.00 x 16.

Technical:

Sliding gear transmission. Speeds: 3F/1R. Floor shift controls. Single dry plate, molded asbestos lining clutch. Shaft drive. Three-quarter floating rear axle. Hydraulic brakes on four wheels. Pressed steel, drop center rim wheels. Wheel size: 16 in.

Options:

Fender skirts. Center bumper guards. Radio. Hot air heater. Hot water heater. Clock. Side view mirror. Passenger side mirror. Sport light. Locking gas cap. Fog lights. Seat covers. Defroster. Visor-vanity mirror. Radio foot control. Wheel trim rings. White sidewall tires. Bumper end guards. Oil filter. License plate frames.

History:

The "new" postwar Fords were introduced in dealer showrooms on Oct. 22, 1945.

1947 Ford

Ford — Deluxe — Series 7GA/79A (Six and V-8): The 1947 Fords were slightly changed from the previous year. For example, the red tracer paint on the grille was dropped, a hood-mounted emblem was seen up front and relocated circular parking lights looked attractive. The Deluxe series was the base trim level and included rubber moldings around all window openings, a horn button instead of a ring, one sun visor and armrests only on the driver's door.

Ford — Super Deluxe — Series 7GA/79A (Six and V-8): The Super Deluxe series was the top trim level for 1947 and included chrome moldings around all windows, a horn ring, two sun visors, armrests on all doors, passenger assist straps on the interior "B" pillars for easier rear seat egress, horizontal chrome trim on body and leather interior on the convertible models.

VIN:

Began with the designation "7GA." Production numbers were 71GA-326418 to 71GA-414366, also (beginning 10/3/47) 77HA-0512 to 77HA-9038. Deluxe V-8 models began with the designation, "79A," with the production numbers beginning at 799A-1412708 and going to 799A-2071231. Super Deluxe V-8 models began with the same "79A" designation and used the same production numbers as the Deluxe models.

Ford — Deluxe — Series 7GA (Six)

Model No.	Body/ Style No.	Body Type & Seating	Factory Price	Shipping Weight	Factory Price
7GA	77A	2-dr. Coupe-3P	$1,154	3,033 lbs.	-------
7GA	70A	2-dr. Sedan-6P	$1,212	3,183 lbs.	-------
7GA	73A	4-dr. Sedan-6P	$1,270	3,213 lbs.	-------

Ford — Deluxe — Series 79A (V-8)

Model No.	Body/ Style No.	Body Type & Seating	Factory Price	Shipping Weight	Factory Price
79A	77A	2-dr. Coupe-3P	$1,230	3,066 lbs.	10,872
79A	70A	2-dr. Sedan-6P	$1,268	3,216 lbs.	44,523
79A	73A	4-dr. Sedan-6P	$1,346	3,246 lbs.	44,563

Ford — Super Deluxe — Series 7GA (Six)

Model No.	Body/ Style No.	Body Type & Seating	Factory Price	Shipping Weight	Factory Price
7GA	77B	2-dr. Coupe-3P	$1,251	3,033 lbs.	-----
7GA	72B	2-dr. Sedan Coupe-6P	$1,330	3,133 lbs.	-----
7GA	70B	2-dr. Sedan-6P	$1,309	3,183 lbs.	-----
7GA	73B	4-dr. Sedan-6P	$1,372	3,233 lbs.	-----
7GA	79B	4-dr. Station Wagon-8P	$1,893	3,487 lbs.	-----

Ford — Super Deluxe — Series 7GA (V-8)

Model No.	Body/ Style No.	Body Type & Seating	Factory Price	Shipping Weight	Factory Price
7GA	77B	2-dr. Coupe-3P	$1,330	3,066 lbs.	10,872
7GA	72B	2-dr. Sedan Coupe-6P	$1,409	3,166 lbs.	80,830
7GA	76	2-dr. Convertible-6P	$1,740	3,266 lbs.	22,159
7GA	71	2-dr. Sportsman-6P	$2,282	3,366 lbs.	2,274
7GA	70B	2-dr. Sedan-6P	$1,382	3,216 lbs.	132,126
7GA	73B	4-dr. Sedan-6P	$1,440	3,266 lbs.	116,744
7GA	79B	4-dr. Station Wagon-8P	$1,972	3,520 lbs.	16,104

Note 1: Production totals are combined six-cylinder/V-8 production for series and body style.

1947 Ford Six Model 7GA Super Deluxe Tudor Sedan (OCW)

1947 Ford Six Model 7GA Deluxe Coupe (PH)

1947 Ford Six Model 7GA Super Deluxe Station Wagon (OCW)

1947 Ford V-8 Model 79A Super Deluxe Sportsman Convertible (OCW)

1947 Ford V-8 Model 79A Super Deluxe Convertible (OCW)

Engines:

Ford Six: L-head. Cast-iron block. B & S: 3-3/10 x 4-2/5 in. Displacement: 225.8 cid. Compression ratio: 6.8:1. Brake hp: 90 at 3300 rpm. Taxable hp: 30. Torque: 180 lbs.-ft. at 2000 rpm. Main bearings: four. Valve lifters: mechanical. Carburetor: Holley single-barrel Model 847F.

Ford V-8: L-head. Cast-iron block. B & S: 3.19 x 3.75 in. Displacement: 239 cid. Compression ratio: 6.75:1. Brake hp: 100 at 3800 rpm. Torque: 180 lbs.-ft. at 2000 rpm. Taxable hp: 32.5. Three main bearings. Solid valve lifters. Crankcase capacity: 5 qt. (add 1 qt. with new oil filter). Cooling system capacity: 22 qt. Carburetor: Holley two-barrel Model 94. Three main bearings.

Chassis:

Wheelbase: 114 in. Overall length: 198.2 in. Tires: 6.00 x 16.

Technical:

Sliding gear transmission. Speeds: 3F/1R. Floor shift controls. Single dry plate, molded asbestos lining clutch. Shaft drive. Three-quarter floating rear axle. Hydraulic brakes on four wheels. Pressed steel, drop center rim wheels. Wheel size: 16 in.

Options:

Fender skirts. Center bumper guards. Radio. Hot air heater. Hot water heater. Clock. Side view mirror. Passenger side mirror. Sport light. Locking gas cap. Fog lights. Seat covers. Defroster. Visor-vanity mirror. Radio foot control. Wheel trim rings. White sidewall tires. Bumper end guards. Oil filter. License plate frames.

History:

The man who put America on wheels, Henry Ford, founder of Ford Motor Co., died at the age of 83 on April 7, 1947.

1948 Ford

Ford — Deluxe — Series 87HA/89A (Six and V-8): The 1948 Fords continued to share the 1946 and 1947 bodies with only slight trim changes. The Deluxe series was the base trim level for 1948 and included rubber moldings around window openings, a horn button instead of horn ring, one sun visor and one armrest only on the driver's door.

Ford — Super Deluxe — Series 87HA/89A (Six and V-8): The Super Deluxe series was the top trim level for 1948 and included chrome moldings around the windows, horn ring, two sun visors, armrests on all doors, passenger assist straps on the interior "B" pillar for easier rear seat egress, horizontal chrome trim on the body and leather interior on the convertible models.

VIN:

Deluxe six-cylinder models began with the designation, "87HA," with production numbers beginning at 87HA-0536 and going to 87HA-73901. Super Deluxe V-8-powered models began with the same "89A" designation and used the same production numbers as the Deluxe models.

Ford — Deluxe — Series 87HA (Six)

Model No.	Body/Style No.	Body Type & Seating	Factory Price	Shipping Weight	Production Total
87HA	77A	2-dr. Coupe-3P	$1,154	3,033 lbs.	------
87HA	70A	2 dr. Sedan-6P	$1,212	3,183 lbs.	------
87HA	73A	4-dr. Sedan-6P	$1,270	3,213 lbs.	------

Ford — Deluxe — Series 89A (V-8)

Model No.	Body/Style No.	Body Type & Seating	Factory Price	Shipping Weight	Production Total
89A	77A	2-dr. Coupe-3P	$1,230	3,066 lbs.	5,048
89A	70A	2 dr. Sedan-6P	$1,268	3,216 lbs.	23,356
89A	73A	4-dr. Sedan-6P	$1,346	3,246 lbs.	------

Ford — Super Deluxe — Series 87HA (Six)

Model No.	Body/Style No.	Body Type & Seating	Factory Price	Shipping Weight	Production Total
87HA	77B	2-dr. Coupe-3P	$1,251	3,033 lbs.	------
87HA	72B	2-dr. Sedan Coupe-6P	$1,330	3,133 lbs.	------
87HA	70B	2 dr. Sedan-6P	$1,309	3,183 lbs.	------
87HA	73B	4-dr. Sedan-6P	$1,372	3,233 lbs.	------
87HA	79B	4-dr. Station Wagon-8P	$1,893	3,487 lbs.	------

Ford — Super Deluxe — Series 89A (V-8):

Model No.	Body/Style No.	Body Type & Seating	Factory Price	Shipping Weight	Production Total
89A	77B	2-dr. Coupe-3P	$1,330	3,066 lbs.	------
89A	72B	2-dr. Sedan Coupe-6P	$1,409	3,166 lbs.	44,828
89A	76	2-dr. Convertible-6P	$1,740	3,266 lbs.	12,033
89A	71	2-dr. Sportsman-6P	$2,282	3,366 lbs.	28
89A	70B	2 dr. Sedan-6P	$1,382	3,316 lbs.	82,161
89A	73B	4-dr. Sedan-6P	$1,440	3,266 lbs.	71,358
89A	79B	4-dr. Station Wagon-8P	$1,972	3,520 lbs.	8,912

Note 1: Production totals are combined six and V-8 production for the series and body style.

1948 Ford Six Model 87HA Super Deluxe Coupe (OCW)

Engines:

Ford Six: L-head. Cast-iron block. B & S: 3-3/10 x 4-2/5 in. Displacement: 225.8 cid. Compression ratio: 6.8:1. Brake hp: 95 at 3300 rpm. Taxable hp: 30. Torque: 180 lbs.-ft. at 2000 rpm. Main bearings: four. Valve lifters: mechanical. Carburetor: Holley single-barrel Model 847F.

V-8: L-head. Cast-iron block. B & S: 3.19 x 3.75 in. Displacement: 239 cid. Compression ratio: 6.75:1. Brake hp: 100 at 3800 rpm. Torque: 180 at 2000 rpm. Taxable hp: 32.5. Three main bearings. Solid valve lifters. Crankcase capacity: 5 qt. (add 1 qt. with new oil filter). Cooling system capacity: 22 qt. Carburetor: Holley two-barrel Model 94. Three main bearings.

Chassis:

Wheelbase: 114 in. Overall length: 198.2 in. Tires: 6.00 x 16.

Technical:

Sliding gear transmission. Speeds: 3F/1R. Floor shift controls. Single dry plate, molded asbestos lining clutch. Shaft drive. Three-quarter floating rear axle. Hydraulic brakes on four wheels. Pressed steel, drop center rim wheels. Wheel size: 16 in.

Options:

Fender skirts. Center bumper guards. Radio. Hot air heater. Hot water heater. Clock. Side view mirror. Passenger side mirror. Sport light. Locking gas cap. Fog lights. Seat covers. Defroster. Visor-vanity mirror. Radio foot control. Wheel trim rings. White sidewall tires. Bumper end guards. Oil filter. License plate frames.

History:

The actual production run of 1948 Fords, basically retitled 1947 models, ended early, in mid-spring, so retooling could take place for the all-new 1949 Fords. The 1949 Fords were also introduced early, in June 1948.

1948 Ford V-8 Model 89A Super Deluxe Convertible (OCW)

1948 Ford V-8 Model 89A Super Deluxe Sportsman Convertible (OCW)

1948 Ford V-8 Model 89A Super Deluxe Fordor Sedan (AA)

1948 Ford Six Model 87HA Deluxe Fordor Sedan (OCW)

1948 Ford V-8 Model 89A Super Deluxe Tudor Sedan (OCW)

1948 Ford V-8 Model 89A Deluxe Station Wagon (OCW)

1948 Ford V-8 Model 89A Deluxe Fordor Sedan (OCW)

1948 Ford V-8 Model 89A Super Deluxe Station Wagon (OCW)

1949 Ford

Ford — Series 98HA / Series 98BA (Six and V-8): The 1949 model represented the first totally new automobile produced by Ford since 1941. The chassis was of the wishbone type, with longitudinal rear springs replacing the transverse springs used on earlier models. Styling featured a heavy chrome molding curving from the top of the grille down to the gravel deflector, with "FORD" in large block letters mounted above the grille molding. There was a horizontal chrome bar in the center of the grille, extending the full width of the opening, with parking lamps mounted on the ends of the bar. In the center of the bar was a large spinner with either a "6" or "8" designation indicating the type of engine. The body was slab-sided, eliminating the rear fender bulge altogether. A chrome strip near the bottom of the body extended from the front fender openings back to the gas cap. Models for 1949 included the base Ford series and the top line Custom series. The Ford series was the base trim level for 1949 and featured rubber window moldings, a horn button instead of horn ring, one sun visor and an armrest only on the driver's door.

Custom — Series 98A / Series 98BA (Six and V-8): The Custom series was the top trim level for 1949 and included chrome window moldings, a horn ring, two sun visors, passenger assist straps on the interior B pillars for easier rear seat egress and horizontal chrome trim along the lower half of the body.

VIN:

The vehicle identification number was stamped on a plate attached to the front face of the cowl. It was also on the right frame side rail just to the rear of the upper front suspension arm. Ford six-cylinder models began with the designation, "98HA," with production numbers beginning at 98HA-101 and going to 98HA-173310. Custom six-cylinder models began with the same "98HA" designation and used the same production numbers as the Ford series. Ford V-8 models began with the designation, "98BA," with production numbers beginning at 98BA-101 and going to 98BA-948236. Custom V-8 models began with the same "98HA" designation and used the same production numbers as the Ford series.

Ford (Six)

Model No.	Body/ Style No.	Body Type & Seating	Factory Price	Shipping Weight	Production Total
98HA	73A	4-dr. Sedan-6P	$1,472	2,990 lbs.	Note 1
98HA	70A	2-dr. Sedan-6P	$1,425	2,945 lbs.	Note 1
98HA	72A	2-dr. Club Coupe-6P	$1,415	2,925 lbs.	Note 1
98HA	72C	2-dr. Business Coupe-3P	$1,333	2,871 lbs.	Note 1

Ford (V-8)

Model No.	Body/ Style No.	Body Type & Seating	Factory Price	Shipping Weight	Production Total
98HA	73A	4-dr. Sedan-6P	$1,546	3,030 lbs.	44,563
98HA	70A	2-dr. Sedan-6P	$1,499	2,965 lbs.	126,770
98HA	72A	2-dr. Club Coupe-6P	$1,523	2,965 lbs.	4,170
98HA	72C	2-dr. Business Coupe-3P	$1,420	2,911 lbs.	28,946

Custom (Six)

Model No.	Body/ Style No.	Body Type & Seating	Factory Price	Shipping Weight	Production Total
98HA	73B	4-dr. Sedan-6P	$1,559	2,993 lbs.	Note 1
98HA	70B	2-dr. Sedan-6P	$1,511	2,948 lbs.	Note 1
98HA	72B	2-dr. Club Coupe-6P	$1,511	2,928 lbs.	Note 1
98HA	76	2-dr. Convertible-6P	$1,886	3,234 lbs.	Note 1
98HA	79	4-dr. Station Wagon-8P	$2,119	3,523 lbs.	Note 1

Custom (V-8)

Model No.	Body/ Style No.	Body Type & Seating	Factory Price	Shipping Weight	Production Total
98BA	73B	4-dr. Sedan-6P	$1,637	3,093 lbs.	248,176
98BA	70B	2-dr. Sedan-6P	$1,590	3,031 lbs.	433,315
98BA	72B	2-dr. Club Coupe-6P	$1,595	3,003 lbs.	150,254
98BA	76	2-dr. Convertible-6P	$1,948	3,263 lbs.	51,133
98BA	79	2-dr. Station Wagon-6P	$2,107	3,531 lbs.	31,412

Note 1: Production of six and V-8 models of each body style was a combined total.

Engines:

Ford Six: L-head. Cast-iron block. Displacement: 226 cid. B & S: 3.30 x 4.40 in. Compression ratio: 6.6:1. Brake hp: 95 at 3300 rpm. Carburetor: Holley one-barrel Model 847F5S. Four main bearings. Code H.

Custom Six: L-head. Cast-iron block. Displacement: 226 cid. B & S: 3.30 x 4.40 in. Compression ratio: 6.6:1. Brake hp: 95 at 3300 rpm. Carburetor: Holley one-barrel Model 847FS. Four main bearings. Code H.

Ford V-8: L-head. Cast-iron block. Displacement: 239 cid. B & S: 3.19 x 3.75 in. Compression ratio: 6.8:1. Brake hp: 100 at 3600 rpm. Carburetor: Holley two-barrel Model AA-1. Three main bearings. Code B.

Custom V-8: L-head. Cast-iron block. Displacement: 239 cid. B & S: 3.19 x 3.75 inches. Compression ratio: 6.8:1. Brake hp: 100 at 3600 rpm. Carburetor: Holley two-barrel Model AA-1. Three main bearings. Code B.

Chassis:

Ford: Wheelbase: 114 in. Overall length: 196.8 in., car and 208 in., station wagon. Overall width: 72.8 in. Tires: 6.00 x 16, standard, 7.10 x 15, station wagon and 6.70 x 15, optional.

Custom: Wheelbase: 114 in. Overall length: 196.8 in., car and 208 in., station wagon. Overall width: 72.8 in. Tires: 6.00 x 16, standard, 7.10 x 15, station wagon and 6.70 x 15, optional.

Technical:

Ford: The standard Ford transmission was a three-speed manual type with semi-centrifugal-type clutch; three-speed helical gear set and synchronizers for second and third gears. A three-speed manual gearbox with automatic overdrive was optional. The automatic overdrive function cut in at 27 mph and out at 21 mph. Approximate drive ratio was 0.70:1. Rear axle gear ratios with standard transmission: (passenger car) 3.73:1; (station wagon) 3.92:1. Rear axle gear ratio with automatic overdrive: (passenger car) 4.10:1; (station wagon) 4.27:1.

Custom: The standard Ford transmission was a three-speed manual type with semi-centrifugal-type clutch; three-speed helical gear set and synchronizers for second and third gears. A three-speed manual gearbox with automatic overdrive was optional. The automatic overdrive function cut in at 27 mph and out at 21 mph. Approximate drive ratio was 0.70:1. Rear axle gear ratios with standard transmission: (passenger car) 3.73:1; (station wagon) 3.92:1. Rear axle gear ratio with automatic overdrive: (passenger car) 4.10:1; (station wagon) 4.27:1.

Options:

White sidewall tires. Fender skirts. Turn signal indicators. Outside rearview mirror. Full wheel discs. Wheel trim rings.

History:

The 1949 Fords were introduced at the Waldorf-Astoria Hotel in New York City on June 10, 1948, beating General Motors and Chrysler to the punch in the garnering of new-model publicity. Ford also surpassed the million mark in production in 1949 with 1,118,740 units built in the calendar year.

1949 Ford four-door Police Sedan (OCW)

1949 Ford two-door Sedan (OCW)

1950 Ford Custom four-door Sedan (OCW)

1949 Ford Custom two-door Sedan (AA)

1949 Ford two-door Club Coupe (OCW)

1949 Ford Custom two-door Convertible (OCW)

1949 Ford Custom two-door Station Wagon (OCW)

1950 Ford

Deluxe — Series OHA / Series OBA (Six and V-8): That wonderful year 1950. At first glance, the 1950 Ford seemed identical to the 1949 model, but it was said to include "50 improvements for '50." Obvious changes were very modest. Once again a heavy chrome molding curved from the top of the "Air Foil" grille down to the gravel deflector. Instead of the Ford name, a shield-shaped badge now sat above the center of the grille. The horizontal center bar again extended the full width of the opening. In the center was a large spinner with either a "'6" or "8" designation. The center grille bar now wrapped around the body corners. Horizontally ribbed plates, which housed the rectangular parking lights, were now seen between that bar and the bumper. A chrome strip extended from behind the front wheel openings to just above and behind the rear wheel opening. The gas filler cap was now hidden behind a lift-up door on the upper left-hand rear fender. A new finned "knight's helmet" hood ornament was seen. Other changes a three-bladed cooling fan and push-button handles on exterior doors. When a fancy steering wheel was fitted, it included a flat-topped horn ring. The 1950 Fords had similar dimensions to 1949 models. Important selling features for 1950 Fords included an Equa-Flo cooling system, full-pressure engine lubrication, "Deep-Breath" intake manifolding, "Power-Dome" combustion chambers, the use of four-ring pistons, Equa-Poise

engine mountings, a Loadomatic ignition system, a Soft-Action clutch and Black-Light dashboard dials. Dual downdraft carburetion was featured on V-8 models. Ford also promoted Mid-Ship Ride, Lifeguard body construction, Hydra-Coil springs, Magic-Action brakes and Fender-Guard bumpers. Inside, Ford's offered more hip room and more shoulder room than any other car in their price class. The "Jewel Box" interior featured non-sagging front seat springs and special foam rubber seat cushions that were claimed to be more comfortable than ever before. The seats themselves were described as being "Sofa-Wide." Interior fabrics came in a choice of broadcloth or mohair. "You travel first class without extra fare in the Big Ford," said one advertisement. Another ad described this particular model as "A "personal" car with all Ford quality features! Mid Ship Ride! Lifeguard Body! 35% easier-acting King-Size Brakes! And a Deep Deck Locker that holds all the bags and baggage!" The Deluxe series was the base trim level for 1950 Fords and cars in this line had a black rubber windshield gasket, black rubber window moldings, a horn button instead of horn ring, one sun visor and an armrest on the driver's door only. There was no chrome trim around the side windows or windshield. A single chrome body strip without nameplate decorated the body sides. The Deluxe model lineup consisted of the Business Coupe and two- and four-door sedans. (Ford actually described the latter models as the "Tudor" and "Fordor" sedans). A choice of an in-line six-cylinder or flathead V-8 engine was offered.

Custom Deluxe — Series OHA / Series OBA (Six and V-8): The Custom Deluxe series was Ford's top trim level and the cars in this line included chrome window moldings, a chrome horn ring, twin sun visors, armrests on all doors and passenger assist straps on the interior "B" pillars (for easier rear seat egress). The word "Custom" was spelled out in capital letters on the spear-tip-shaped nameplates on the front fenders. Four body styles were offered in the Custom Deluxe six-cylinder lineup. These were the Club Coupe, the Tudor Sedan, the Fordor sedan and the wood-bodied station wagon, which took on the Country Squire name as a running change. Station wagons, required larger-than-usual 7.10 x 15 tires to support the heavier weight of their wood body. The "Country Squire" station wagons included a stowaway center seat, a

1950 Ford Deluxe two-door Sedan (OCW)

1950 Ford Deluxe two-door Business Coupe (OCW)

1950 Ford Deluxe two-door Business Coupe (OCW)

flat-deck loading platform and a rear seat that was easily removable without the use of tools. With the "Level-Loading" tailgate lowered, there was 38.8 square feet of flat deck to handle half a ton of freight with ease. Also available only with a V-8 engine were the Crestliner and the convertible. The 1950 Crestliner was a rare Ford. The Crestliner was released on Sunday, July 9, 1950 as Ford's answer to the popular General Motors hardtops. The distinctive new two-tone Sports Sedan had a black basket weave vinyl top and a striking "Airfoil" paint treatment. It came in Sportsman's Green with a black top and black airfoil side panels or in Coronation Red with a black top and side panels. Ford said the Crestliner's interior trim resembled that of European sports cars. The "Crestliner" name appeared in gold die-cast emblems on each front fender. Completely new full wheel disks with the circular depressions painted black were standard, as were fender skirts and twin side view mirrors. A protective and decorative molding of polished stainless steel extended along the bottom edge of the car. Inside the Crestliner had a two-tone instrument panel with special finish and trim treatments, a 4-spoke airplane type steering wheel and special upholstery and carpeting. The Custom Deluxe convertible was not as rare as the Crestliner. but had special top-down appeal. Said one Ford advertisement, "When the moon looks cool as sherbet, it doesn't take a share of Fort Knox to enjoy it . . . it merely takes a Ford convertible. For no car, yes, <u>no</u> car, has a happier way with your heartstrings for so little money."

VIN:

The vehicle identification number was stamped on a plate attached to the front face of the cowl. It was also on the right frame side rail just to the rear of the upper front suspension arm. The first symbol indicated the engine: H=226-cid six-cylinder, B=239-cid V-8 and P=239-cid police V-8. The second symbol indicated the model year: 0=1950. The third and fourth symbols indicated the assembly plant: AT=Atlanta, Georgia, BF=Buffalo, N.Y., CS=Chester, Pennsylvania, CH=Chicago, Illinois, DL=Dallas, Texas, HM=Highland Park, Michigan, DA=Dearborn, Michigan, LU=Louisville, Kentucky, EG=Edgewater, N.J., KC=Kansas City, Kansas, LB=Long Beach, California, MP=Memphis, Tennessee, NR=Norfolk, Virginia, RH=Richmond, Virginia, SR=Somerville, Massachusetts and SP=Twin Cities, St. Paul, Minnesota. The last six symbols are the sequential production number starting at 100001 and up in each factory.

Deluxe (Six)

Model No.	Body/ Style No.	Body Type & Seating	Factory Price	Shipping Weight	Production Total
OHA	D73	4-dr. Sedan-6P	$1,472	3,050 lbs.	Note 1
OHA	D70	2-dr. Sedan-6P	$1,424	2,988 lbs.	Note 1
OHA	D72C	2 dr. Business Coupe-3P	$1,333	2,933 lbs.	Note 1

Deluxe (V-8)

Model No.	Body/ Style No.	Body Type & Seating	Factory Price	Shipping Weight	Production Total
OBA	D73	4-dr. Sedan-6P	$1,545	3,078 lbs.	77,888
OBA	D70	2-dr. Sedan-6P	$1,498	3,026 lbs.	275,360
OBA	D72C	2 dr. Business Coupe-3P	$1,419	2,965 lbs.	35,120

Custom Deluxe (Six)

OHA	C73	4-dr. Sedan-6P	$1,558	3,062 lbs.	Note 1
OHA	C70	2-dr. Sedan-6P	$1,511	2,999 lbs.	Note 1
OHA	C72	2 dr. Club Coupe-6P	$1,511	2,959 lbs.	Note 1
OHA	C79	4-dr. Station Wagon-8P	$2,028	3,491 lbs.	Note 1

Custom Deluxe (V-8)

OBA	C73	4-dr. Sedan-6P	$1,637	3,093 lbs.	247,181
OBA	C70	2-dr. Sedan-6P	$1,590	3,031 lbs.	396,060
OBA	C70C	2-dr. Crestliner-6P	$1,711	3,050 lbs.	8,703
OBA	C72	2 dr. Club Coupe-6P	$1,595	3,003 lbs.	85,111
OBA	C76	2-dr. Convertible-6P	$1,948	3,263 lbs.	50,299
OHA	C79	2-dr. Station Wagon-6P	$2,107	3,531 lbs.	29,017

Note 1: Production of six-cylinder and V-8 models of each body style is a combined total.

Engines:

Custom Six: L-head. Cast-iron block. Displacement: 226 cid. B & S: 3.30 x 4.40 in. Compression ratio: 6.8:1. Brake hp: 95 at 3300 rpm. Carburetor: Holley one-barrel Model 847F5. Four main bearings. Code H.

Custom Deluxe Six: L-head. Cast-iron block. Displacement: 226 cid. B & S: 3.30 x 4.40 in. Compression ratio: 6.8:1. Brake hp: 95 at 3300 rpm. Carburetor: Holley one-barrel Model 847F5. Four main bearings. Code H.

Custom Eight: L-head V-8. Cast-iron block. Displacement: 239 cid. Bore and stroke: 3.19 x 3.75 in. Compression ratio: 6.8:1. Brake hp: 100 at 3600 rpm. Carburetor: Holley two-barrel Model AA-1. Three main bearings. Code B.

Custom Deluxe Eight: L-head V-8. Cast-iron block. Displacement: 239 cid. Bore and stroke: 3.19 x 3.75 in. Compression ratio: 6.8:1. Brake hp: 100 at 3600 rpm. Carburetor: Holley two-barrel Model AA-1. Three main bearings. Code B.

Chassis:

Custom: Wheelbase: 114 in. Overall length: 196.6 in., car and 206 in., station wagon. Overall width: 72.8 in. Tires: 6.00 x 16, standard, 7.10 x 15, station wagon and 6.70 x 15, optional.

Custom Deluxe: Wheelbase: 114 in. Overall length: 196.6 in., car and 206 in., station wagon. Overall width: 72.8 in. Tires: 6.00 x 16, standard, 7.10 x 15, station wagon and 6.70 x 15, optional.

Technical:

Custom: The standard Ford transmission was a three-speed manual type with semi-centrifugal-type clutch; three-speed helical gear set and synchronizers for second and third gears. A three-speed manual gearbox with automatic overdrive was optional. The rear axle gear ratios with standard transmission were: 3.73:1, car and 3.92:1, station

1950 Ford Custom Deluxe four-door Sedan (AA)

1950 Ford Custom Deluxe Crestliner two-door Sedan (PH)

1950 Ford Custom Deluxe two-door Sedan (OCW)

1950 Ford Custom Deluxe Crestliner two-door Sedan (OCW)

wagon. The rear axle gear ratio with automatic overdrive was: 4.10:1, car and 4.17:1, station wagon.

Custom Deluxe: The standard Ford transmission was a three-speed manual type with semi-centrifugal-type clutch; three-speed helical gear set and synchronizers for second and third gears. A three-speed manual gearbox with automatic overdrive was optional. The rear axle gear ratios with standard transmission were: 3.73:1, car and 3.92:1, station wagon. The rear axle gear ratios with automatic overdrive were: 4.10:1, car and 4.17:1, station wagon.

Options:

White sidewall tires. Fender skirts. Turn signal indicators. Outside rearview mirror. Full wheel discs. Wheel trim rings.

History:

Calendar-year production: 1,187,120 cars. The 1950 Fords were introduced in November of 1949 and the model year closed in November 1950. They had estimated model-year production of 1,209,548 cars. Of these, 897,463 were V-8s and 289,659 were sixes. Calendar-year

1950 Ford Custom Deluxe two-door **Club Coupe** (AA)

1950 Ford Custom Deluxe two-door **Station Wagon** (OCW)

1950 Ford Custom Deluxe two-door **Convertible** (OCW)

1950 Ford **"Fashion Car" Interior** (OCW)

output was 1,187,120 units, representing 17.79 percent of total industry production. For the second year in a row, the Ford was named "Fashion Car of the Year" by New York's famed Fashion Academy.

1951 Ford

Deluxe — Series 1HA / Series 1BA — Six and V-8: According to the March 26, 1951 issue of *Quick* magazine, "The productive genius of the Ford Motor Co. solved a year-old dilemma." The problem was how to keep children from "liberating" the red-white-and-blue golden lion crests from the hoods of 1950 Fords. It seems that the kids liked to put these on beanies, belts and bikes. Ford's solution was to tell the kids they could write to Ford to get a miniature crest for free. Considering the Ford emblems' popularity among potential future customers, it's no wonder the crest remained on the hood in 1951. Other styling changes were again minor. The new grille featured dual "spinners" that were positioned at the outer edges of the center grille bar. The new front parking lights were round rather than rectangular. The hood ornament looked like an abstract bird, instead of a knight's helmet. At the rear of the car, Ford's "Tell Tale" rear lamps were decorated with jet-style chrome spears that tapered towards the front as they ran down the slab-sided body. Series or model names appeared on a front fender trim plate that looked more like a fin than a spear tip. Squire name in script on the upper front corner of the front doors. The woodie was promoted as a "Double Duty Dandy." Cars with V-8 engines under the hood also had a V-8 emblem on the front fender. Ford offered the coupe, Tudor sedan and Fordor sedan in the Deluxe Six series. These body styles also came as Deluxe Eights. For some reason the coupe cost $87 more with a V-8, while the two- and four-door sedans cost only $75 more with a V-8. Chances are, the Deluxe six coupe was used as a "loss leader" to feature in print ads to get buyers into the showroom. This might explain the larger discount for a six-cylinder version. The "Mileage Maker" in-line six was the same one used in 1950. The optional "Strato-Star" flathead V-8 was also unchanged. Ford engines featured a waterproof ignition system, Loadomatic distributors, and an Equa-Flow cooling system with a Silent-Spin fan, Forced-Feed lubrication, a "Full-Flo" fuel pump, Power-Dome combustion and "Rota-Quiet" valves. A three-speed manual gearbox was standard and overdrive was optional. Ford described its popular overdrive as an automatic fourth gear that reduced engine wear and cut fuel costs up to 15 percent. A fully-automatic transmission was offered for the very first time in 1951, but only in cars with V-8 engines. Ford advertised that the new Ford-O-Matic transmission provided "the magic of liquid-smooth, effortless automatic drive." This unit consisted of a torque converter with a three-speed automatic planetary gear. The five-position Semaphore Drive Selector with an illuminated dial was positioned on the steering column. "The Ford-O-Matic Ford brings you automatic driving at its finest and flexible best," said Ford. "You get flashing getaway . . . instant acceleration . . . plenty of zip for passing and hill climbing . . . and all with real economy." Automatic Ride Control was the name of a new and heavily-advertised Ford feature for 1951. The ad copywriters described it as a "three-way partnership" between the Hydra-Coil front springs, the variable-rate rear leaf springs and the viscous-control

1951 Ford Deluxe two-door **Sedan** (AA)

1951 Ford Deluxe four-door **Sedan** (OCW)

telescopic shock absorbers. This system was designed to maintain a level ride and eliminate pitch, jounce and roll. It was advertised as "a new and unique springing system that automatically adjusts spring reaction to road conditions." Ford interiors were highlighted by a new Safety-Glow control panel with knobs and dials that were easy to reach and easy to read. Ignition-key starting was new this year. "Just turn the ignition key to the right - your engine starts. No reaching for a button - no stretching for a starter pedal," Ford explained. The "Chanalited" instrument cluster had all of the gauges located within the speedometer scale for easy readability. The speed indicator incorporated a ring at its end that circled the traveling speed in red and glowed at night. All controls had "Glow-Cup" lighting for night-driving convenience. "Automatic Posture Control" was Ford's trade name for a design in which the entire seat was angled for maximum comfort. Cushioning was by foam rubber over non-sag springs. The seats featured long-wearing Fordcraft fabrics and new harmonized appointments, while "Colorblend" carpeting covered the floor. A "Magic-Air" weather-control system was optional.

Custom Deluxe — Series 1HA / Series 1BA — Six and V-8: Ford offered the Club Coupe, Tudor Sedan, Fordor Sedan and station wagon in the Custom Deluxe Six series and the first two had a chrome body side molding for identification. The wood-paneled wagons did not have room for moldings, but now carried the name "Country Squire" on its front fender. These three body styles came as Custom Deluxe eights as well. The Crestliner Tudor, the convertible and the Victoria hardtop came only with the V-8 engine. The Crestliner, first introduced in 1950, was a special two-door sedan with a vinyl top, extra chrome, a special steering wheel, special two-tone paint and full wheel covers. A special trim plate carried the name Victoria on the hardtop model. It was Ford's first true pillarless hardtop and was aptly described as "the Belle of the Boulevard!" "The car that gives you the smart styling of a convertible with the snugness of a sedan," is how ad copywriters described this convertible-looking model. It featured "Luxury Lounge" interiors that were color-keyed to the finish of the car, which was usually two-toned.

1951 Ford Custom Deluxe four-door Sedan (PH)

1951 Ford Custom Deluxe two-door Sedan (PH)

VIN:

The vehicle identification number was stamped on a plate attached to the front face of the cowl. It was also on the right frame side rail just to the rear of the upper front suspension arm. The first symbol indicated the engine: H=226-cid six-cylinder, B=239-cid V-8 and P=239-cid police V-8. The second symbol indicated the model year: 1=1951. The third and fourth symbols indicated the assembly plant: AT=Atlanta, Georgia, BF=Buffalo, N.Y., CS=Chester, Pennsylvania, CH=Chicago, Illinois, DL=Dallas, Texas, HM=Highland Park, Michigan, DA=Dearborn, Michigan, LU=Louisville, Kentucky, EG=Edgewater, N.J., KC=Kansas City, Kansas, LB=Long Beach, California, MP=Memphis, Tennessee, NR=Norfolk, Virginia, RH=Richmond, Virginia, SR=Somerville, Massachusetts and SP=Twin Cities, St. Paul, Minnesota. The last six symbols are the sequential production number starting at 100001 and up in each factory.

Deluxe (Six)

Model No.	Body/ Style No.	Body Type & Seating	Factory Price	Shipping Weight	Production Total
1HA	73	4-dr. Sedan-6P	$1,466	3,089 lbs.	Note 1
1HA	70	2-dr. Sedan-6P	$1,417	3,023 lbs.	Note 1
1HA	72C	2-dr. Business Coupe-3P	$1,324	2,960 lbs.	Note 1

Deluxe (V-8)

Model No.	Body/ Style No.	Body Type & Seating	Factory Price	Shipping Weight	Production Total
1BA	73	4-dr. Sedan-6P	$1,540	3,114 lbs.	54,265
1BA	70	2-dr. Sedan-6P	$1,492	3,062 lbs.	146,010
1BA	72C	2-dr. Business Coupe-3P	$1,411	2,997 lbs.	20,343

Custom Deluxe (Six)

Model No.	Body/ Style No.	Body Type & Seating	Factory Price	Shipping Weight	Production Total
1HA	73	4-dr. Sedan-6P	$1,553	3,089 lbs.	Note 1
1HA	70	2-dr. Sedan-6P	$1,505	3,023 lbs.	Note 1
1HA	72C	2-dr. Club Coupe-6P	$1,505	2,995 lbs.	Note 1
1HA	79	2-dr. Country Squire-8P	------	------	Note 1
1HA	79	2-dr. Station Wagon-6P	$2,029	3,510 lbs.	Note 1

Custom Deluxe (V-8)

Model No.	Body/ Style No.	Body Type & Seating	Factory Price	Shipping Weight	Production Total
1BA	73B	4-dr. Sedan-6P	$1,633	3,114 lbs.	232,691
1BA	70B	2-dr. Sedan-6P	$1,585	3,062 lbs.	317,869
1BA	70C	2-dr. Crestliner-6P	$1,595	3,085 lbs.	8,703
1BA	72C	2-dr. Club Coupe-6P	$1,590	3,034 lbs.	53,263
1BA	60	2-dr. Victoria Hardtop-6P	$1,925	3,188 lbs.	110,286
1BA	76	2-dr. Convertible-6P	$1,949	3,268 lbs.	40,934
1BA	79	2-dr. Country Squire-8P	------	------	-----
1BA	79	2-dr. Station Wagon-6P	$2,110	3,550 lbs.	29,617

Note 1: Production of six-cylinder and V-8 models of each body style is a combined total.

Engines:

Custom Six: L-head. Cast-iron block. Displacement: 226 cid. B & S: 3.30 x 4.40 in. Compression ratio: 6.8:1. Brake hp: 95 at 3600 rpm. Carburetor: Holley one-barrel Model 847F5. Four main bearings. Code H.

Custom Deluxe Six: L-head. Cast-iron block. Displacement: 226 cid. B & S: 3.30 x 4.40 in. Compression ratio: 6.8:1. Brake hp: 95 at 3600 rpm. Carburetor: Holley one-barrel Model 847F5. Four main bearings. Code H.

Custom Eight: L-head V-8. Cast-iron block. Displacement: 239 cid. B & S: 3.19 x 3.75 in. Compression ratio: 6.8:1. Brake hp: 100 at 3600 rpm. Carburetor: Holley two-barrel Model AA-1. Three main bearings. Code B.

Custom Deluxe Eight: L-head V-8. Cast-iron block. Displacement: 239 cid. B & S: 3.19 x 3.75 in. Compression ratio: 6.8:1. Brake hp: 100 at 3600 rpm. Carburetor: Holley two-barrel Model AA-1. Three main bearings. Code B.

Chassis:

Custom: Wheelbase: 114 in. Overall length: 196.4 in., car and 208 in., station wagon. Overall width: 72.9 in. Tires: 6.00 x 16, standard, 7.10 x 15, station wagon and 6.70 x 15, optional.

Custom Deluxe: Wheelbase: 114 in. Overall length: 196.4 in., car and 208 in., station wagon. Overall width: 72.9 in. Tires: 6.00 x 16, standard, 7.10 x 15, station wagon and 6.70 x 15, optional.

Technical:

Custom: The standard Ford transmission was a three-speed manual type with semi-centrifugal-type clutch; three-speed helical gear set and synchronizers for second and third gears. A three-speed manual gearbox with automatic overdrive was optional at $92 extra. Two-speed Ford-O-Matic transmission was optional at $159 extra. Rear axle gear ratios with standard transmissions were: 3.73:1, cars and 4.10:1, optional. The rear axle gear ratio with automatic overdrive was 4.10:1. The rear axle gear ratio with Ford-O-Matic automatic transmission was 3.31:1.

Custom Deluxe: The standard Ford transmission was a three-speed manual type with semi-centrifugal-type clutch and three-speed helical gear set and synchronizers for second and third gears. A three-speed manual gearbox with automatic overdrive was optional at $92 extra. Two-speed Ford-O-Matic transmission was optional at $159 extra. The rear axle gear ratios with standard transmission were 3.73:1, car and 4.10:1, optional. The rear axle gear ratio with automatic overdrive was 4.10:1. The rear axle gear ratio with Ford-O-Matic automatic transmission was 3.31:1.

Options:

White sidewall tires. Fender skirts. Turn signal indicators. Outside rearview mirror. Full wheel discs. Wheel trim rings. Ford-O-Matic transmission.

1951 Ford Custom Deluxe two-door Victoria Hardtop (AA)

1951 Ford Custom Deluxe Crestliner two-door Sedan (OCW)

1951 Ford Custom Deluxe Crestliner two-door Sedan (OCW)

1951 Ford Custom Deluxe two-door Club Coupe (AA)

1951 Ford Custom Deluxe two-door Convertible (OCW)

1951 Ford Custom Deluxe two-door Station Wagon (OCW)

1951 Ford Custom Deluxe two-door Country Squire (OCW)

History:

Henry Ford II was president of Ford Motor Company and Earnest R. Breech was executive vice president. C. L. Waterhouse was styling manager. L.O. Crusoe was general manager of Ford Division and L.W. Smead was general sales manager. Although the image of the "shoe box" Ford didn't change much in 1951, Ford general manager L. D. Crusoe was focused on the goal of making Ford the top-selling car brand in America. In addition to offering free replicas of the company's crest to youngsters who might buy Fords tomorrow, he was carefully plotting the course to better future sales with the introduction of modern features like automatic transmission and hardtop styling. Unfortunately, the United States government threw up roadblocks in 1951 by instituting production controls due to the Korean crisis. They held Ford's output to 24 percent below the 1950 figure. Model-year production was 1,013,391 vehicles, which included 753,265 cars with V-8 engines and 147,495 sixes. Calendar-year output was 900,770, giving Ford second place on the sales charts, but only 16.87 percent market share, down from 17.79 the previous year. This year, the sales were lost to Chrysler, which gained market share for all of its divisions. The only GM branch to gain market share in the calendar year was Cadillac. This was a sure sign that the big overhead valve V-8s offered by MoPar and Cadillac had sales appeal. Certainly, Ford was watching this trend as its sights were set in the direction of introducing a new V-8 in the not-too-distant future. In 1951, Ford started new operations at an engine plant in Cleveland, Ohio and a stamping plant in Buffalo, N.Y. The company made aircraft engines, bazooka rockets and medium tanks for the war effort.

1952 Ford

Mainline — Series A2 / Series B2 — Six and V-8: The new Fords introduced to the public on February 1, 1952 were wider, longer, roomier, stronger and more powerful than ever before. Highlighting new-model introductions was the first totally new body for Ford since 1949. The cars were arranged in three different, renamed product lines with each series - Mainline, Customline and Crestline - offering different combinations of body styles, trim and engines. Some body types and all Crestlines were available only with the V-8 engine. Styling-wise, the 1952 Fords featured a new Curva-Lite Safety-View one-piece curved windshield with no center bar, a 48 percent larger full-width rear window, Search-Mount headlights with protruding round parking lights directly below behind "triple spinner" bars, a round three-bladed spinner in the center of the grille bar, a simulated air scoop on the rear quarter panels, a redesigned instrument panel and "Power-Pivot" suspended clutch and brake pedals. This year the gas filler pipe and neck were concealed behind a hinged rear license plate. The Mainline series was the base trim level for 1952. Cars in this line had rubber window moldings, a horn button instead of horn ring, one sun visor and an armrest only on the driver's door. There were four body types in this range: Business Coupe, Tudor Sedan, Fordor Sedan and new all-steel two-door Ranch Wagon. All were available with both engines. The six-cylinder engine was the new overhead-valve "Mileage Maker" Six. Some said this six performed better than the old 239-cid Strato-Star flathead V-8, which was boosted to 110-hp. Of course, any V-8-powered Ford could be "improved" with aftermarket goodies, while there was not nearly as much "hop-up" equipment available for the in-line six. Automatic Power Pilot was the name given to Ford's completely integrated carburetion-ignition-combustion system. It featured a downdraft carburetor that automatically switched to economy jets for idling and a Loadomatic ignition distributor that automatically controlled spark advance. Ford's standard transmission was a three-speed manual-type of the usual design. Three-speed manual with automatic overdrive was a optional. Ford-O-Matic transmission was an option. It featured a torque converter transmission with automatic planetary gear train, a single stage three-element hydraulic torque converter, hydraulic-mechanical automatic controls (with no electrical or vacuum connections), forced-air cooling and power flow through the fluid member at all times. Cars with the automatic transmission had a Ford-O-Matic nameplate on the trunk lid. Others said "Overdrive" in the same spot. A completely new line of custom accessories was brought out by the Ford Motor Company to match 1952 styling.

Customline — Series A2 / Series B2 — Six and V-8: The Customline series was the intermediate trim level for 1952 and included chrome window moldings, a chrome horn ring, two sun visors, armrests on all doors, passenger assist straps on the interior "B" pillars (for easier rear seat egress), a horizontal chrome strip on the front fenders and a chrome opening on the rear quarter panel scoop. Three sixes were offered in Customline trim: the Club Coupe, the Tudor and the Fordor. These were available with a V-8 for $70 more. A four-door Country Sedan station wagon was also offered in the Customline V-8 series.

Crestline — Series B2 — V-8: Crestline was the name of the top-trim-level series for 1952. Crestline models included the Victoria hardtop, the Sunliner convertible and the Country Squire. The latter was now a four-door all-metal station wagon that came with woodgrain side trim appliqués. All three "name" cars were offered only with V-8 engines. This series included all features of the Customline models, plus full wheel covers and additional chrome trim along the bottom of the side windows. The Sunliner included a push-button-operated power soft top. The top-of-the-line Country Squire station wagon was the year's rarest Ford product.

VIN:

The vehicle identification number was stamped on a plate attached to the right front body pillar below the upper hinge opening. It was also stamped on the right frame reinforcement and on the top of the rear frame X-member near the right-hand end. It was also stamped on the top of the second cross member (except on convertibles). The first symbol indicated the engine: A=215-cid six-cylinder, B=239-cid V-8 and P=239-cid police V-8. The second symbol indicated the model year: 2=1952. The third and fourth symbols indicated the assembly plant: AT=Atlanta, Georgia, BF=Buffalo, N.Y., CS=Chester, Pennsylvania, CH=Chicago, Illinois, DL=Dallas, Texas, DA=Dearborn, Michigan, LU=Louisville, Kentucky, EG=Edgewater, N.J., KC=Kansas City, Kansas, LB=Long Beach, California, MP=Memphis, Tennessee, NR=Norfolk, Virginia, RH=Richmond, Virginia, SR=Somerville, Massachusetts and SP=Twin Cities, St. Paul, Minnesota. The last six symbols are the sequential production number starting at 100001 and up in each factory.

1952 Ford Mainline two-door Sedan (OCW)

1952 Ford Mainline two-door Station Wagon (AA)

Mainline (Six)

Model No.	Body/Style No.	Body Type & Seating	Factory Price	Shipping Weight	Production Total
A2	73A	4-dr. Sedan-6P	$1,530	3,173 lbs.	Note 1
A2	70A	2-dr. Sedan-6P	$1,485	3,070 lbs.	Note 1
A2	72C	2-dr. Business Coupe-3P	$1,389	2,984 lbs.	Note 1
A2	59A	2-dr. Station Wagon-6P	$1,832	3,377 lbs.	Note 1

Mainline (V-8)

Model No.	Body/Style No.	Body Type & Seating	Factory Price	Shipping Weight	Production Total
A2	73A	4-dr. Sedan-6P	$1,600	3,207 lbs.	41,277
A2	70A	2-dr. Sedan-6P	$1,555	3,151 lbs.	79,931
A2	72C	2-dr. Business Coupe-3P	$1,459	3,085 lbs.	10,137
A2	59A	2-dr. Station Wagon-6P	$1,902	3,406 lbs.	32,566

Customline (Six)

Model No.	Body/Style No.	Body Type & Seating	Factory Price	Shipping Weight	Production Total
A2	73B	4-dr. Sedan-6P	$1,615	3,173 lbs.	Note 1
A2	70B	2-dr. Sedan-6P	$1,570	3,070 lbs.	Note 1
A2	72B	2-dr. Club Coupe-6P	$1,579	3,079 lbs.	Note 1

Customline (V-8)

Model No.	Body/Style No.	Body Type & Seating	Factory Price	Shipping Weight	Production Total
B2	73B	4-dr. Sedan-6P	$1,685	3,207 lbs.	188,303
B2	70B	2-dr. Sedan-6P	$1,640	3,151 lbs.	175,762
B2	72B	2-dr. Club Coupe-6P	$1,649	3,153 lbs.	26,550
B2	79C	2-dr. Station Wagon-6P	$2,060	3,617 lbs.	11,927

Crestline (V-8)

Model No.	Body/Style No.	Body Type & Seating	Factory Price	Shipping Weight	Production Total
B2	60B	2-dr. Victoria Hardtop-6P	$1,925	3,274 lbs.	77,320
B2	76B	2-dr. Convertible-6P	$2,027	3,339 lbs.	22,534
B2	79B	2-dr. Country Squire-8P	$2,186	3,640 lbs.	5,426

Note 1: Production of six-cylinder and V-8 models of each body style is a combined total.

Engines:

Mainline Six: Overhead valve. Cast-iron block. Displacement: 215.3 cid. B & S: 3.56 x 3.60 in. Compression ratio: 7.0:1. Brake hp: 101 at 3500 rpm. Carburetor: Holley one-barrel Model 847F5. Four main bearings. Code A.

Customline Six: Overhead valve. Cast-iron block. Displacement: 215.3 cid. B & S: 3.56 x 3.60 in. Compression ratio: 7.0:1. Brake hp: 101 at 3500 rpm. Carburetor: Holley one-barrel Model 847F5. Four main bearings. Code A.

Mainline Eight: L-head V-8. Cast-iron block. Displacement: 239 cid. B & S: 3.19 x 3.75 in. Compression ratio: 7.2:1. Brake hp: 110 at 3800 rpm. Carburetor: Ford two-barrel Model 8BA. Three main bearings. Code B.

1952 Ford Mainline four-door Sedan (OCW)

1952 Ford Mainline two-door Business Coupe (OCW)

1952 Ford Customline four-door Sedan (OCW)

1952 Ford Customline two-door Sedan (OCW)

Customline Eight: L-head V-8. Cast-iron block. Displacement: 239 cid. B & S: 3.19 x 3.75 in. Compression ratio: 7.2:1. Brake hp: 110 at 3800 rpm. Carburetor: Ford two-barrel Model 8BA. Three main bearings. Code B.

Crestline Eight: L-head V-8. Cast-iron block. Displacement: 239 cid. B & S: 3.19 x 3.75 in. Compression ratio: 7.2:1. Brake hp: 110 at 3800 rpm. Carburetor: Ford two-barrel Model 8BA. Three main bearings. Code B.

Chassis:

Mainline: Wheelbase: 115 in. Overall length: 197.8 in. Overall width: 73.2 in. Tires: 6.00 x 16, standard and 6.70 x 15, optional.

Customline: Wheelbase: 115 in. Overall length: 197.8 in. Overall width: 73.2 in. Tires: 6.00 x 16, standard and 6.70 x 15, optional.

Crestline: Wheelbase: 115 in. Overall length: 197.8 in. Overall width: 73.2 in. Tires: 6.00 x 16, standard and 6.70 x 15. optional.

Technical:

Mainline, Customline and Crestline: The standard transmission was a three-speed manual-type of the usual design. Three-speed manual with automatic overdrive was a $102 option. Ford-O-Matic transmission was a $170 option. Ford-O-Matic featured a torque converter transmission with automatic planetary gear train, single stage three-element hydraulic torque converter, hydraulic mechanical automatic controls with no electrical or vacuum connections, forced air cooling, and power flow through the fluid member at all times. There rear axle gear ratios were: 3.90:1, manual transmission, 4.10:1, overdrive, 3.15:1, optional overdrive, 3.31:1 with Ford-O-Matic and 3.54:1, an option with Ford-O-Matic.

Options:

A completely new line of custom accessories was brought out by the Ford Motor Co. to match 1952 styling. Several interesting additions on the list were a speed governor, turn indicators, illuminated vanity mirror, engine compartment light, five-tube Deluxe radio, seven-tube Custom radio, spring wound clock, electric clock, color-keyed rubber floor mats, wheel discs, wheel trim rings, rear fender skirts, rocker panel trim strips, hand brake signal lamp and Magic Air heater and defroster.

History:

The 1952 Fords were introduced to the public on Feb. 1, 1952. L.D. Crusoe managed to grow Ford Division in 1952, opening nine new parts depots nationwide and starting work on three more new facilities in the East and Midwest. But government restrictions, along with a steel strike and other disputes, held model-year production to 671,725 units. For the calendar-year, Ford built 777,531 cars or 17.93 percent of the industry total. Over 32 percent of cars built this year had Ford-O-Matic gear shifting and over 20 percent of the cars built with manual transmissions had the overdrive option. Ford also led the industry in station wagon production with 32 percent of total industry output for this body style. The Federal-Aid Highway Act of 1952 authorized $25 million for the

interstate highway system on a 50-50 matching basis. These were the first funds authorized specifically for interstate road construction and Ford Motor Company ran a series "American Road" advertisements to support the initiative. The ads touched on the history of American roads from single-file Indian paths, to "Good Roads" movements to modern cloverleaf highways. "We need more of those superb new turnpikes, expressways and superhighways with their overpasses and underpasses, and glittering silver-steel bridges that soar across rivers of the land," one ad suggested. It also pointed out that Ford had put 35 million cars on those roads over the years.

1952 Ford Customline two-door Club Coupe (OCW)

1952 Ford Customline four-door Country Sedan (OCW)

1952 Ford Crestline two-door Victoria Hardtop (OCW)

1952 Ford Crestline two-door Victoria Hardtop (OCW)

1952 Ford Sunliner two-door Convertible (OCW)

1952 Ford Crestline four-door Country Squire (OCW)

1952 Ford interior (OCW)

1953 Ford

Mainline — Series A3 / Series B3 — Six and V-8: Ford held dealer introductions for its 1953 "Golden Jubilee" models on December 12, 1952. The new cars utilized 1952 bodies with moderate trim updating. However, they were said to offer "41 Worth More Features." Selling features for the year included double-seal Magic-Action brakes, push-button door handles, a self-lifting deck lid, "Hull-Tight" body construction, Silent-Doorman two-stage front door checks, Center-Fill fueling, a flight-style control panel, a K-bar frame, high alloy exhaust valves, aluminum pistons and a Safety-Sequence drive selector in cars with Ford-O-Matic transmission. The 1953 grille incorporated a larger horizontal bar with three vertical stripes on either side of a large spinner. The length of this bar was increased and it now wrapped around the front edges of the fenders. The parking lights were horizontal rectangles instead of circles. The Ford crest appeared in the center of the steering wheel hub and contained the words, "50th Anniversary 1903-1953." Ford's Mainline series was the base trim level for 1953 and cars in this line included rubber windshield and rear window moldings, fixed rear vent windows, a horn button instead of a horn ring, one sun visor and an armrest on the driver's door only. Mainline models had no chrome sweep spears on the front and rear fenders. Partial chrome gravel deflectors accented the bulges on the rear quarter panels, just ahead of the rear wheel openings. The Mainline name appeared on the front fenders. The two-door Ranch Wagon, which was part of this series, had no wood-look exterior panels. Body style offerings were identical to those offered in 1952. V-8 power for was $70 additional. Engine choices in 1953 looked identical to those of the previous season. Three-speed manual transmission was again standard. Overdrive was a $108 option. The automatic overdrive function cut in at 27 mph and cut out at 21 mph. Ford-O-Matic automatic transmission was optional. Ford's Automatic Ride Control suspension design was improved for 1953. The new "balanced" system integrated a rubber-cushioned front suspension with variable-rate rear leaf springs and diagonally-mounted telescopic shock absorbers to minimize side-sway on turns. The front tread width was two inches wider than the rear tread width to give better "footing" for easier handling.

1953 Ford Mainline four-door Sedan (OCW)

Customline — Series A3 / Series B3 — Six and V-8: The Customline series was the intermediate trim level for 1953 and included chrome windshield and rear window moldings, a chrome horn half-ring, two sun visors, armrests on all doors and passenger assist straps on interior "B" pillars for easier rear seat egress. A horizontal chrome strip decorated the front fenders just above the wheel opening. Chrome gravel deflectors capped the entire front height of the rear quarter panel scoops. There was another horizontal chrome strip running from the scoop opening, above the rear wheel opening, to the back of the body. The Customline name was on a spear tip at the leading edge of the front fender molding. If a V-8 was installed, an appropriate emblem was placed behind the spear tip. The Country Sedan wagon in this line had four doors, but no exterior woodgrained paneling. Body style offering were again as in 1952.

Crestline — Series B3 — V-8: The Crestline series was the top trim level for 1953 and was again offered only with V-8 engines. This series included all trim in the Customline series, plus wheel covers and additional chrome trim along the bottom of the side windows. The Victoria hardtop, the Sunliner convertible and the Country Squire wood-trimmed wagon were in this series.

VIN:

The vehicle identification number was stamped on a plate attached to the left front body pillar. It was also stamped on the right front frame cross member reinforcement. The first symbol indicated the engine: A=215-cid six-cylinder, B=239-cid V-8 and P=239-cid police V-8. The second symbol indicated the model year: 3=1953. The third symbol indicated the assembly plant: A=Atlanta, Georgia, B=Buffalo, N.Y., C=Chester, Pennsylvania, D=Dallas, Texas, E=Edgewater, N.J., F=Dearborn, Michigan, G=Chicago, Illinois, H=Highland Park, Michigan, K=Kansas City, Kansas, L=Long Beach, California, M=Memphis, Tennessee, N=Norfolk, Virginia, P=Twin Cities, St. Paul, Minnesota, R=Richmond, Virginia, S=Somerville, Massachusetts and U=Louisville, Kentucky. The fourth symbol indicated the body style: C=Convertible, W=Ranch Wagon, X=Country Sedan, Y=Country Squire, V=Victoria, G=All other styles. The last six symbols are the sequential production number starting at 100001 and up in each factory.

Mainline (Six)

Model No.	Body/ Style No.	Body Type & Seating	Factory Price	Shipping Weight	Production Total
A3	73B	4-dr. Sedan-6P	$1,783	3,115 lbs.	Note 1
A3	70A	2-dr. Sedan-6P	$1,734	3,067 lbs.	Note 1
A3	72B	2-dr. Club Coupe-6P	$1,743	3,046 lbs.	Note 1

Mainline (V-8)

Model No.	Body/ Style No.	Body Type & Seating	Factory Price	Shipping Weight	Production Total
B3	73A	4-dr. Sedan-6P	$1,766	3,181 lbs.	66,463
B3	70A	2-dr. Sedan-6P	$1,717	3,136 lbs.	132,995
B3	72C	2-dr. Business Coupe-3P	$1,614	3,068 lbs.	16,280
B3	59A	2-dr. Station Wagon-6P	$2,095	3,408 lbs.	66,976

Customline (Six)

Model No.	Body/ Style No.	Body Type & Seating	Factory Price	Shipping Weight	Production Total
A3	73B	4-dr. Sedan-6P	$1,783	3,115 lbs.	Note 1
A3	70B	2-dr. Sedan-6P	$1,734	3,087 lbs.	Note 1
A3	72B	2-dr. Club Coupe-6P	$1,743	3,046 lbs.	Note 1

Customline (V-8)

Model No.	Body/ Style No.	Body Type & Seating	Factory Price	Shipping Weight	Production Total
B3	73B	4-dr. Sedan-6P	$1,783	3,193 lbs.	374,487
B3	70B	2-dr. Sedan-6P	$1,734	3,133 lbs.	305,433
B3	72B	2-dr. Club Coupe-6P	$1,743	3,121 lbs.	43,999
B3	79B	2-dr. Station Wagon-6P	$2,267	3,539 lbs.	37,743

Crestline (V-8)

Model No.	Body/ Style No.	Body Type & Seating	Factory Price	Shipping Weight	Production Total
B3	60B	2-dr. Victoria Hardtop-6P	$2,120	3,250 lbs.	128,302
B3	76B	2-dr. Convertible-6P	$2,230	3,334 lbs.	40,861
B3	79C	2-dr. Country Squire-6P	$2,403	3,609 lbs.	11,001

Note 1: Production of six-cylinder and V-8 models of each body style is a combined total.

1953 Ford Mainline two-door Sedan (OCW)

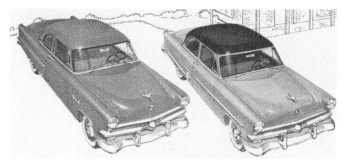

1953 Ford Mainline two-door Business Coupe and Sedan (OCW)

1953 Ford Customline four-door Sedan (AA)

1953 Ford Mainline two-door Station Wagon (OCW)

1953 Ford Customline two-door Sedan (OCW)

Engines:

Mainline Six: Overhead valve. Cast-iron block. Displacement: 215.3 cid. B & S: 3.56 x 3.60 in. Compression ratio: 7.0:1. Brake hp: 101 at 3500 rpm. Carburetor: Holley one-barrel Model 1904F. Four main bearings. Code A.

Customline Six: Overhead valve. Cast-iron block. Displacement: 215.3 cid. B & S: 3.56 x 3.60 in. Compression ratio: 7.0:1. Brake hp: 101 at 3500 rpm. Carburetor: Holley one-barrel Model 1904F. Four main bearings. Code A.

Mainline Eight: L-head V-8. Cast-iron block. Displacement: 239 cid. B & S: 3.19 x 3.75 in. Compression ratio: 7.2:1. Brake hp: 110 at 3800 rpm. Carburetor: Ford two-barrel Model 2100. Three main bearings. Code B.

Customline Eight: L-head V-8. Cast-iron block. Displacement: 239 cid. B & S: 3.19 x 3.75 in. Compression ratio: 7.2:1. Brake hp: 110 at 3800 rpm. Carburetor: Ford two-barrel Model 2100. Three main bearings. Code B.

Crestline Eight: L-head V-8. Cast-iron block. Displacement: 239 cid. B & S: 3.19 x 3.75 in. Compression ratio: 7.2:1. Brake hp: 110 at 3800 rpm. Carburetor: Ford two-barrel Model 2100. Three main bearings. Code B.

Chassis:

Mainline: Wheelbase: 115 in. Overall length: 197.8 in. Overall width: 74.3 in. Tires: 6.70 x 15, standard and 7.10 x 15, station wagon.

Customline: Wheelbase: 115 in. Overall length: 197.8 in. Overall width: 74.3 in. Tires: 6.70 x 15, standard and 7.10 x 15, station wagon.

Crestline: Wheelbase: 115 in. Overall length: 197.8 in. Overall width: 74.3 in. Tires: 6.70 x 15, standard and 7.10 x 15, station wagon.

Technical:

Mainline, Customline and Crestline: Three-speed manual transmission was standard. This unit featured a semi-centrifugal-type clutch, three-speed helical gears with synchronizers for second and third gears. Three-speed manual transmission with automatic overdrive was a $108 option. Specifications were the same above with automatic overdrive function cutting in at 27 mph, cutting out at 21 mph. Approximate drive ratio was: 0.70:1. Manual control was provided below the instrument panel. Ford-O-Matic automatic transmission was a $184 option. This was a torque converter-type transmission with automatic planetary gear train, single stage, three-element hydraulic torque converter, hydraulic-mechanical automatic controls and no electrical or vacuum connections. Power was transmitted through the fluid member at all times.

Options:

Power steering ($125). Power brakes ($35). Ford-O-Matic transmission ($184). Overdrive ($108). Six-tube Deluxe radio ($88). Eight-tube Custom radio ($100). Recirculation-type heater ($44). Deluxe heater ($71). Electric clock ($15). Directional signals ($15). Windshield washer ($10). Tinted glass ($23). White sidewall tires ($27).

History:

Introduction of 1953 models took place December 12, 1953. On a model year basis 1,240,000 cars were built, of which 876,300 were estimated to be V-8-powered units. Ford opened a new Technical Service Laboratory at Livonia, Michigan this year. A specially trimmed Sunliner convertible paced the 1953 Indianapolis 500-Mile Race. Master Guide power steering was introduced June 16, 1953. A 1953 Ford Mainliner four-door sedan averaged 27.03 mpg in the Mobilgas Economy Run from Los Angeles to Sun Valley. Business wise, 1953 had a "split personality" at Ford Division. During the first part of the year, auto production was hampered by government limitations, strikes and disputes with parts suppliers. This changed to six-day weeks and overtime during the second half of the year, as Ford's output exploded to a level 52 percent ahead of 1952. By the time the dust cleared, model-year production stood at 1,240,000 cars of which 876,300 were estimated to be V-8-powered units. Six-cylinder model production nearly doubled to 307,887. Calendar-year production climbed steeply to 1,184,187 units or 19.30 percent of industry, although Chevrolet gained nearly four full points of market share compared to just over one point for Ford. Ford-O-Matic transmission grew so popular in 1953 that production schedules had to be expanded. However, due to a 10-week supplier strike at Borg-Warner, which made the Ford automatic, 85 percent of the cars made in June were equipped with stick shift. Nevertheless, 346,939 cars got the automatic. The power steering option released in June was popular enough to go into eight percent of all 1953 Fords made by the end of the year. Ford also upped its production of station wagons to 38 percent of total industry output and made more convertibles (39,945 in the calendar year) than any other automaker. The anniversary year brought several milestones. In May, a specially-trimmed 1953 Ford Sunliner convertible paced the Indianapolis 500-Mile Race. Ford also opened a new Technical Service Laboratory, at Livonia, Michigan, during the year.

1953 Ford Customline four-door Country Sedan (CCC)

1953 Ford Customline two-door Club Coupe (OCW)

1953 Ford Crestline two-door Victoria Hardtop (OCW)

1953 Ford Sunliner two-door Convertible (OCW)

1953 Ford Crestline four-door Country Squire (OCW)

1953 Ford grille detail (OCW)

1953 Ford taillight detail (OCW)

1953 Ford Crestline Victoria interior (OCW)

1954 Ford

Mainline — Series A4 / Series U4 — Six and V-8: Contemporary style was reflected in the '54 Ford's appearance. "Ford brings you tomorrow's clean uncluttered look today," said an advertisement. In truth, this was an easy accomplishment, since barely any changes were made from the cars' 1952 and 1953 styling. The same basic body was used. The modestly-updated grille incorporated a large horizontal bar with large slots on either side of a centrally located spinner. Round parking lights were located in smaller spinners at either end of the horizontal bar. Making news was the availability of a new V-8 engine (promoted as the Ford "Y-8") with *overhead* valves. It was now optional in *all* models. This new engine was rated for nearly 25 percent more power than the 1953 flathead. Ford added many new convenience items to its optional equipment list in 1954. Among them were power windows, four-way power seats and power brakes. Ball joints replaced king pins in the front suspension. Mainline, Customline and Crestline car-lines were offered again and all body styles in all three trim levels were available with either engine. This added up to 14 body style and trim combinations times two engines for a total of 28 basic Ford models. Selling features promoted by Ford salesmen of the day were primarily the same ones offered in 1953 and included center-fill fueling, hull-tight body, two-stage door checks, non-sag seats, a K-bar frame, variable-rate rear leaf springs, full-displacement tubular shock absorbers, tailored-to-weight coil front springs, a semi-floating rear axle and hypoid gears. The Mainline series was the base trim level for 1954 and included a Business Coupe, a Tudor Sedan, a Fordor Sedan and a two-door Ranch Wagon with six-passenger seating. These cars had rubber window moldings, a horn button instead of horn ring, a single sun visor and an armrest on the driver's door only. The Mainline name appeared in chrome script on the front fender of the passenger cars, just ahead of the door break line. Station wagons had a Ranch Wagon script plate instead. Small gravel shields were seen on the rear fender "pontoons," just ahead of the rear wheel openings. Naturally, V-8-powered cars had "Y-8" badges just ahead of the front wheel openings. The overhead-valve in-line six was bored out to 223 cid. The new overhead-valve V-8 (or "Y-8") retained the old 239-cubic-inch displacement figure. Transmission options were as in the past.

Customline — Series A4 / Series U4 — Six and V-8: The Customline series was the intermediate trim level for 1954. The Customline Six series offered a Club Coupe, a Tudor Sedan, a Fordor Sedan, a two-door Ranch Wagon with six-passenger seating and a four-door Country Sedan eight-passenger wagon. These cars had chrome window moldings, a chrome half-horn ring, two sun visors, armrests on all doors and passenger assist straps on the interior "B" pillars. On the passenger cars, the Customline name appeared in chrome script on the upper front "corner" of the rear fender pontoon. Two-door Customline wagons had a Ranch Wagon script in the same location and their four-door counterparts had a Country Sedan script there. A sweep spear molding ran from the front to the rear of the car at just-below-headlight level. This trim dipped down in a scalloped V-shape around the upper front corner of the rear fender pontoon. The same small gravel shields used on Mainlines were placed just ahead of the rear wheel openings.

Crestline — Series A4 / Series U4 — Six and V-8: The Crestline series was the top trim level for 1954. This car-line included the exciting new Skyliner hardtop. This model had a tinted, transparent roof panel above the driver's seat. There was also a Fordor sedan, a Victoria two-door hardtop, a Sunliner convertible and the four-door Country Squire eight-passenger wagon with simulated wood-grained trim. The Crestline models were offered with a six-cylinder engine for the first time since the series began in 1950. This series included all of the Customline trim features, plus three chrome hash marks behind the gravel shields, chrome "A" pillar moldings, additional chrome trim along the bottom of the side windows and full wheel covers. The Crestline name appeared on the rear fender pontoon of all models except the wagon, which had Country Squire scripted on the front door instead. On the Victoria, Skyliner and Sunliner models, the model name was engraved in the chrome windowsills along with multiple hash marks. All hardtops had special rear roof pillar trim plates (gold-colored on Skyliners) with medallions.

VIN:

The vehicle identification number was stamped on a plate attached to the left front body pillar below the hinge opening. The first symbol indicated the engine: A=223-cid six-cylinder, U=239-cid V-8 and P=239-cid police V-8. The second symbol indicated the model year: 4=1954. The third symbol indicated the assembly plant: A=Atlanta, Georgia, B=Buffalo, N.Y., C=Chester, Pennsylvania, D=Dallas, Texas, E=Edgewater, N.J., F=Dearborn, Michigan, G=Chicago, Illinois, H=Highland Park, Michigan, K=Kansas City, Kansas, L=Long Beach, California, M=Memphis, Tennessee, N=Norfolk, Virginia, P=Twin Cities, St. Paul, Minnesota, R=Richmond, Virginia, S=Somerville, Massachusetts and U=Louisville, Kentucky. The fourth symbol indicated the body style: C=Sunliner Convertible, F=Skyliner Glasstop, R=Customline Ranch Wagon, W=Mainline Ranch Wagon, T=Crestline Fordor, X=Country Sedan, Y=Country Squire, V=Victoria, G=All other styles. The last six symbols are the sequential production number starting at 100001 and up in each factory.

Mainline (Six)

Model No.	Body/ Style No.	Body Type & Seating	Factory Price	Shipping Weight	Production Total
A4	73A	4-dr. Sedan-6P	$1,701	3,142 lbs.	Note 1
A4	70A	2-dr. Sedan-6P	$1,651	3,086 lbs.	Note 1
A4	72C	2-dr. Business Coupe-3P	$1,548	3,021 lbs.	Note 1
A4	59A	2-dr. Station Wagon-6P	$2,029	3,228 lbs.	Note 1

Mainline (V-8)

U4	73A	4-dr. Sedan-6P	$1,777	3,263 lbs.	55,371
U4	70A	2-dr. Sedan-6P	$1,728	3,207 lbs.	123,329
U4	72C	2-dr. Business Coupe-3P	$1,625	3,142 lbs.	10,665
U4	59A	2-dr. Station Wagon-6P	$2,106	3,459 lbs.	44,315

Customline (Six)

A4	73B	4-dr. Sedan-6P	$1,793	3,155 lbs.	Note 1
A4	70B	2-dr. Sedan-6P	$1,744	3,099 lbs.	Note 1
A4	72B	2-dr. Club Coupe-6P	$1,753	3,080 lbs.	Note 1
A4	59B	2-dr. Station Wagon-6P	$2,122	3,344 lbs.	Note 1
A4	79B	4-dr. Station Wagon-6P	$2,202	3,513 lbs.	Note 1

Customline (V-8)

U4	73B	4-dr. Sedan-6P	$1,870	3,276 lbs.	262,499
U4	70B	2-dr. Sedan-6P	$1,820	3,220 lbs.	293,375
U4	72B	2-dr. Club Coupe-6P	$1,830	3,201 lbs.	33,051
U4	59B	2-dr. Station Wagon-6P	$2,198	3,465 lbs.	36,086
U4	79B	4-dr. Station Wagon-6P	$2,279	3,634 lbs.	43,384

Crestline (Six)

A4	73C	4-dr. Sedan-6P	$1,898	3,159 lbs.	Note 1
A4	60B	2-dr. Victoria Hardtop-6P	$2,055	3,184 lbs.	Note 1
A4	60F	2-dr. Skyliner-6P	$2,164	3,204 lbs.	Note 1
A4	76B	2-dr. Convertible-6P	$2,164	3,231 lbs.	Note 1
A4	79C	2-dr. Country Squire-8P	$2,339	3,563 lbs.	Note 1

Crestline (V-8)

U4	73C	4-dr. Sedan-6P	$1,975	3,280 lbs.	99,677
U4	60B	2-dr. Victoria Hardtop-6P	$2,131	3,305 lbs.	95,464
U4	60F	2-dr. Skyliner-6P	$2,241	3,325 lbs.	13,144
U4	76B	2-dr. Convertible-6P	$2,241	3,352 lbs.	33,685
U4	79C	2-dr. Country Squire-8P	$2,415	3,684 lbs.	12,797

Note 1: Production of six-cylinder and V-8 models of each body style is a combined total.

1954 Ford Mainline two-door Business Coupe (AA)

1954 Ford Mainline two-door Sedan (OCW)

Engines:

Mainline Six: Overhead valve. Cast-iron block. Displacement: 223 cid. B & S: 3.62 x 3.60 in. Compression ratio: 7.2:1. Brake hp: 115 at 3900 rpm. Carburetor: Holley one-barrel Model 1904F. Four main bearings. Code A.

Customline Six: Overhead valve. Cast-iron block. Displacement: 223 cid. B & S: 3.62 x 3.60 in. Compression ratio: 7.2:1. Brake hp: 115 at 3900 rpm. Carburetor: Holley one-barrel Model 1904F. Four main bearings. Code A.

Crestline Six: Overhead valve. Cast-iron block. Displacement: 223 cid. B & S: 3.62 x 3.60 in. Compression ratio: 7.2:1. Brake hp: 115 at 3900 rpm. Carburetor: Holley one-barrel Model 1904F. Four main bearings. Code A.

Mainline Eight: Overhead valve V-8. Cast-iron block. Displacement: 239 cid. B & S: 3.50 x 3.10 in. Compression ratio: 7.2:1. Brake hp: 115 at 3900 rpm. Carburetor: Holley two-barrel Model AA. Four main bearings. Code U.

Customline Eight: Overhead valve V-8. Cast-iron block. Displacement: 239 cid. B & S: 3.50 x 3.10 in. Compression ratio: 7.2:1. Brake hp: 115 at 3900 rpm. Carburetor: Holley two-barrel Model AA. Four main bearings. Code U.

Crestline Eight: Overhead valve V-8. Cast-iron block. Displacement: 239 cid. B & S: 3.50 x 3.10 in. Compression ratio: 7.2:1. Brake hp: 115 at 3900 rpm. Carburetor: Holley two-barrel Model AA. Four main bearings. Code U.

1954 Ford Mainline two-door Station Wagon (OCW)

1954 Ford Customline four-door Sedan (AA)

1954 Ford Customline two-door Sedan (OCW)

Chassis:

Mainline, Customline and Crestline: Wheelbase: 115 in. Overall length: 198.3 in. Overall width: 73.5 in. Tires: 6.70 x 15, standard and 7.10 x 15, station wagon.

Technical:

Mainline, Customline and Crestline: Three-speed manual transmission was standard equipment. It featured a semi-centrifugal-type clutch, three-speed helical gears and synchronizers for second and third gears. Three-speed with automatic overdrive was optional. Specifications were the same as above with automatic overdrive function cutting in at 27 mph, cutting out at 21 mph. Approximate drive ratio: 0.70:1. Manual control was mounted below the instrument panel. Ford-O-Matic automatic transmission was optional. This was a torque converter-type transmission with automatic planetary gear train, single stage, three-element hydraulic torque converter, hydraulic-mechanical automatic controls with no electrical or vacuum connections and power flow through the fluid member at all times. Rear axle gear ratios: 3.90:1, standard, 4.10:1, with overdrive and 3.31:1 with Ford-O-Matic.

Options:

Automatic overdrive ($110). Ford-O-Matic transmission ($184). Power steering ($134). Power brakes ($41). Radio ($88 to $99). Heater and defroster ($44 to $71). Power windows ($102). Power seat ($64). White sidewall tires ($27 exchange). Note: Power windows were available on Customline and Crestline only.

1954 Ford Customline two-door Club Coupe (OCW)

1954 Ford Customline two-door Ranch Wagon (OCW)

1954 Ford Customline four-door Country Sedan (AA)

1954 Ford Crestline four-door Sedan (PH)

History:

Of the total 1,165,942 Fords built in the 1954 calendar year, industry sources estimate that 863,096 had V-8 engines installed. The 1,000,000th car of the 1954 production run was turned out August 24, 1954. Production of cars built to 1955 specifications began October 25, 1954. Public presentation of the 1954 Ford line was made on January 6, 1954. Of the total 1,165,942 Fords built in the 1954 model year, industry sources estimate that 863,096 had V-8 engines installed. the 1,000,000th Ford of the 1954 production run was turned out August 24, 1954 and in December, Ford announced that it had recorded its best year since 1925.

1954 Ford Crestline two-door Victoria Hardtop (right)

1954 Ford Crestline Skyliner two-door Victoria Hardtop (OCW)

1954 Ford Sunliner two-door Convertible (OCW)

1954 Ford Crestline four-door Country Squire (OCW)

1954 Ford instrument panel detail (OCW)

1954 Ford V-8 engine compartment detail (OCW)

1955 Ford

Mainline — Series A5 / Series U5 — Six and V-8: That wonderful year 1955 brought us 12 months filled with changes. In Great Britain, Anthony Eden took over as Prime Minister after Winston Churchill stepped down. Nikolai Bulganin replaced Georgi Malenkov as premier of the Soviet Union. In Argentina, dictator Juan Peron got the boot after 10 years as President (although he'd return in the 1970s). Ford's 1952 through 1954 styling also got the boot in 1955, but the really big change in Dearborn was a total redesign of the entire Ford line. The new full-size Fords were longer, lower and wider. The cars had a new concave cellular grille, new side trim treatments, a wraparound windshield, Thunderbird Bird-like rear fenders and new series names. Station wagons were now grouped in a separate series. Mainline was the base trim level and included rubber window moldings, a horn button instead of chrome horn ring, one sun visor and an armrest only on the driver's door. These car had a Ford crest on the hood, no series nameplates, no side trim moldings and untrimmed body-color headlight "doors." Just three body styles comprised the Mainline Six offerings. All three models could be had with Ford's famous "Y-block" V-8 for an extra $100. In this case, "Y-8" emblems were placed just ahead of the front wheel openings.

Customline — Series A5 / Series U5 — Six and V-8: The Customline was the intermediate trim level for 1955 and the cars in it included chrome window moldings, a chrome horn half-ring, two sun visors and armrests on all doors. A horizontal chrome strip ran the length of the body from below the headlights to the center of the taillights. A Customline script decorated the front fenders. Only "Tudor" and "Fordor" (in Ford's nomenclature) Sedans remained in the Customline Six series. Both came with a V-8 for $100 more.

Fairlane — Series A5 / Series U5 — Six and V-8: The Fairlane series was the top trim level for 1955 and included chrome window and "A" pillar moldings (hardtops and Sunliner), chrome eyebrows on the headlights and a chrome side sweep molding that dipped on the front doors. The Fairlane name appeared on the hood, below the Ford crest. There were six Fairlane Six models the two-door sedan (called Club Sedan), the four-door sedan (called Town Sedan), the two-door hardtop (called a Victoria), the Crown Victoria (a two-door hardtop with a tiara-style roof band), the Crown Victoria Skyliner (a hardtop with a transparent forward roof section) and the convertible (called the Sunliner). All could be had with the V-8 for an extra C-Note. The Town Sedan and Club Sedan had rear fender tip scripts. The others had the model name on the door, just behind the dip in the chrome molding.

Station Wagon — Series A5 / Series U5 — Six and V-8: The two-door Ranch Wagon was the base station wagon for six passengers. The Custom Ranch Wagon carried Customline body side moldings. Both of these cars had "Ranch Wagon" scripts on the front fenders. Six- and eight-passenger Country Sedans were offered. The six-passenger had Customline trim with "Country Sedan" on the front fenders, while the eight-passenger had dipping Fairlane sedan trim with "Country Sedan" on the rear fenders. The Country Squire was the top station wagon. It was trimmed on the outside with mahogany-grain panels and blonde fiberglass moldings. The model name was seen on the rear fenders. All five wagons were available with the six-cylinder engine at prices between $2,043 and $2,991 and a V-8 was $100 additional. See how easy things were back in the "Good Old Days?"

VIN:

The vehicle identification number was stamped on a plate attached to the left front body pillar below the hinge opening. The first symbol indicated the engine: A=223-cid six-cylinder, M=272-cid four-barrel V-8, U=272-cid two-barrel V-8 and P=292-cid police V-8. The second symbol indicated the model year: 5=1955. The third symbol indicated the assembly plant: A=Atlanta, Georgia, B=Buffalo, N.Y., C=Chester, Pennsylvania, D=Dallas, Texas, E=Edgewater, N.J., F=Dearborn, Michigan, G=Chicago, Illinois, K=Kansas City, Kansas, L=Long Beach,

California, M=Memphis, Tennessee, N≈Norfolk, Virginia, P=Twin Cities, St. Paul, Minnesota, R=San Jose, California, S=Somerville, Massachusetts and U=Louisville, Kentucky. The fourth symbol indicated the body style: C=Sunliner Convertible, F=Skyliner Glasstop, R=Ranch Wagon, T=Fairlane Tudor/Fordor, V=Victoria Tudor, X=Country Sedan, Y=Country Squire, G=All other styles, W=Special body solid top. The last six symbols were the sequential production number starting at 100001 and up in each factory.

Mainline (Six)

Model No.	Body/ Style No.	Body Type & Seating	Factory Price	Shipping Weight	Production Total
A5	73A	4-dr. Sedan-6P	$1,824	3,106 lbs.	24,132
A5	70A	2-dr. Sedan-6P	$1,778	3,064 lbs.	45,331
A5	70D	2-dr. Business Coupe-3P	$1,677	3,026 lbs.	6,567

Mainline (V-8)

Model No.	Body/ Style No.	Body Type & Seating	Factory Price	Shipping Weight	Production Total
U5	73A	4-dr. Sedan-6P	$1,924	3,216 lbs.	13,583
U5	70A	2-dr. Sedan-6P	$1,878	3,174 lbs.	32,999
U5	70D	2-dr. Business Coupe-3P	$1,777	3,136 lbs.	3,587

Customline (Six)

Model No.	Body/ Style No.	Body Type & Seating	Factory Price	Shipping Weight	Production Total
A5	73B	4-dr. Sedan-6P	$1,916	3,126 lbs.	42,100
A5	70B	2-dr. Sedan-6P	$1,872	3,084 lbs.	55,012

Customline (V-8)

Model No.	Body/ Style No.	Body Type & Seating	Factory Price	Shipping Weight	Production Total
U5	73B	4-dr. Sedan-6P	$2,016	3,236 lbs.	187,089
U5	70B	2-dr. Sedan-6P	$1,972	3,194 lbs.	190,133

Fairlane (Six)

Model No.	Body/ Style No.	Body Type & Seating	Factory Price	Shipping Weight	Production Total
A5	73C	4-dr. Town Sedan-6P	$2,031	3,134 lbs.	3,520
A5	70C	2-dr. Club Sedan-6P	$1,985	3,088 lbs.	1,784
A5	60B	2-dr. Victoria Hardtop-6P	$2,166	3,184 lbs.	556
A5	60F	2-dr. Crown Victoria-6P	$2,273	3,246 lbs.	50
A5	76B	2-dr. Skyliner-6P	$2,343	3,254 lbs.	35
A5	79C	2-dr. Convertible-6P	$2,295	3,248 lbs.	188

Fairlane (V-8)

Model No.	Body/ Style No.	Body Type & Seating	Factory Price	Shipping Weight	Production Total
U5	73C	4-dr. Town Sedan-6P	$2,131	3,268 lbs.	254,680
U5	70C	2-dr. Club Sedan-6P	$2,085	3,222 lbs.	178,086
U5	60B	2-dr. Victoria Hardtop-6P	$2,266	3,318 lbs.	95,439
U5	60F	2-dr. Crown Victoria-6P	$2,373	3,380 lbs.	34,779
U5	76B	2-dr. Skyliner-6P	$2,443	3,388 lbs.	20,000
U5	79C	2-dr. Convertible-6P	$2,395	3,382 lbs.	50,582

Station Wagon (Six)

Model No.	Body/ Style No.	Body Type & Seating	Factory Price	Shipping Weight	Production Total
A5	59A	2-dr. Ranch Wagon-6P	$2,114	3,309 lbs.	14,002
A5	59B	2-dr. Custom Ranch Wagon-6P	$2,180	3,327 lbs.	5,737
A5	79D	4-dr. Country Sedan-6P	$2,227	3,393 lbs.	3,929
A5	79B	4-dr. Country Sedan-8P	$2,358	3,469 lbs.	3,450
A5	79C	4-dr. Country Squire-8P	$2,463	3,471 lbs.	112

Station Wagon (V-8)

Model No.	Body/ Style No.	Body Type & Seating	Factory Price	Shipping Weight	Production Total
U5	59A	2-dr. Ranch Wagon-6P	$2,214	3,443 lbs.	26,614
U5	59B	2-dr. Custom Ranch Wagon-6P	$2,280	3,461 lbs.	39,231
U5	79D	4-dr. Country Sedan-6P	$2,327	3,527 lbs.	51,192
U5	79B	4-dr. Country Sedan-8P	$2,458	3,603 lbs.	47,320
U5	79C	4-dr. Country Squire-8P	$2,563	3,605 lbs.	18,745

Engines:

Base Six: (All) Overhead valve. Cast-iron block. Displacement: 223 cid. B & S: 3.62 x 3.60 in. Compression ratio: 7.5:1. Brake hp: 120 at 4000 rpm. Carburetor: Holley single-barrel. Four main bearings. Code A.

Base V-8: (All) Overhead valve. Cast-iron block. B & S: 3.62 x 3.30 in. Displacement: 272 cid. Compression ratio: 7.60:1. Brake hp: 162 at 4400

1955 Ford Mainline four-door Sedan (OCW)

rpm. Taxable hp: 42.0. Torque: 258 at 2200 rpm. Five main bearings. Solid valve lifters. Crankcase capacity: 5 qt. (add 1 qt. with new oil filter). Cooling system capacity: 19 qt. Carburetor: Holley two-barrel. Code U.

Optional Power-Pack V-8 (All): Overhead valve. Cast-iron block. B & S: 3.62 x 3.30 in. Displacement: 272 cid. Compression ratio: 7.60:1. Brake hp: 182 at 4400 rpm. Taxable hp: 42.0. Torque: 268 at 2600 rpm. Five main bearings. Solid valve lifters. Crankcase capacity: 5 qt. (add 1 qt. with new oil filter). Cooling system capacity: 19 qt. Carburetor: Holley four-barrel. Code M.

Optional Thunderbird V-8 (Manual Transmission): Overhead valve. Cast-iron block. B & S: 3.75 x 3.30 in. Displacement: 292 cid. Compression ratio: 8.1:1. Brake hp: 193 at 4400 rpm. (Taxable hp: 45. Torque: 280 at 2600 rpm. Five main bearings. Solid valve lifters. Crankcase capacity: 5 qt. (add 1 qt. with new oil filter). Cooling system capacity: 19 qt. Carburetor: Holley four-barrel. Code P.

Optional Thunderbird V-8 (Ford-O-Matic Transmission): Overhead valve. Cast-iron block. B & S: 3.75 x 3.30 in. Displacement: 292 cid. Compression ratio: 8.50:1. Brake hp: 198 at 4400 rpm. Taxable hp: 45. Torque: 286 at 2500 rpm. Five main bearings. Solid valve lifters. Crankcase capacity: 5 qt. (add 1 qt. with new oil filter). Cooling system capacity: 19 qt. Carburetor: Holley four-barrel. Code P.

Chassis:

Mainline, Customline and Fairlane: Wheelbase: 115.5 in. Overall length: 198.5 in. Overall width: 75.9 in. Tires: 6.70 x 15 tubeless. Front tread: 58 in. Rear tread: 56 in.

1955 Ford Mainline two-door Business Coupe (OCW)

1955 Ford Customline four-door Sedan (OCW)

1955 Ford Customline two-door Sedan (AA)

1955 Ford Fairlane four-door Sedan (OCW)

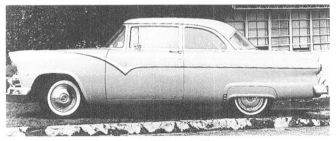

1955 Ford Fairlane two-door Club Sedan (OCW)

1955 Ford Mainline two-door Sedan (OCW)

1955 Ford Fairlane two-door Victoria Hardtop (OCW)

1955 Ford Fairlane two-door Crown Victoria Hardtop (PH)

1955 Ford Fairlane two-door Crown Victoria Hardtop (PH)

1955 Ford Sunliner two-door Convertible (OCW)

Station Wagon: Wheelbase: 115.5 in. Overall length: 197.6 in. Overall width: 75.9 in. Tires: 7.10 x 15 tubeless. Front tread: 58 in. Rear tread: 56 in.

Mainline, Customline and Fairlane: Three-speed manual was standard equipment. It featured a semi-centrifugal-type clutch, three-speed helical gears and synchronizers for second and third gears. Three-speed with automatic overdrive was optional. Specifications were the same as above with automatic overdrive function cutting in at 27 mph and cutting out at 21 mph. The approximate drive ratio was 0.70:1. Manual control below instrument panel.

Station Wagon: Three-speed manual was standard equipment. It featured a semi-centrifugal-type clutch, three-speed helical gears and synchronizers for second and third gears. Three-speed with automatic overdrive was optional. Specifications were the same as above with automatic overdrive function cutting in at 27 mph and cutting out at 21 mph. Approximate drive ratio: 0.70:1. Manual control below instrument panel.

Overdrive transmission ($110). Ford-O-Matic automatic transmission ($178). Radio ($99). Heater ($71). Power brakes ($32). Power seat ($64). Power windows ($102). White sidewall tires ($27 exchange). Power steering ($91). Other standard factory and dealer-installed-type options and accessories.

The 1955 Ford was introduced to the public November 12, 1954. Of the total 1,435,002 cars built from October 1954 to September 1955, the majority were V-8s. During the 1955 calendar year, 1,546,762 Ford V-8s and 217,762 sixes were manufactured. Also on a calendar year basis, 230,000 Fords had power steering, 31,800 had power brakes, 22,575 (of all FoMoCo products) had air conditioning, 197,215 cars had overdrive and 1,014,500 cars had automatic transmissions. The 1955 run was the second best in Ford Motor Co. history, behind 1923 when Model Ts dominated the industry. A new factory in Mahwah, N.J., opened this year, to replace one in Edgewater, N.J. A new factory in San Jose, California, replaced a one-third-as-big West Coast plant in Richmond, California. A new factory was also opened in Louisville, Kentucky, replacing a smaller facility in the same city. Robert S. McNamara was vice-president and

1955 Ford two-door Ranch Wagon (OCW)

1955 Ford four-door Country Sedan 8P (OCW)

1955 Ford four-door Country Sedan 6P (OCW)

1955 Ford four-door Country Squire (OCW)

1955 Ford Sunliner trim detail (OCW)

general manager of Ford Division. Ford Motor Company engineering had an experimental turbine-powered vehicle this year. It featured a modified 1955 body shell with an altered grille and exhaust system. This car was actually built in 1954 and had a "4" designation in the prefix code to the assigned serial number, which was from the 1954 production serial number series. The car was scrapped after testing was completed.

1956 Ford

Mainline — Series A6 / Series U6 — Six and V-8: In 1956, Ford re-used its 1955-style body shell. Wheelbase, length, width and height were unchanged. A 12-volt electrical system was adapted for the first time. A wider grille had oblong parking lights at its outer ends. All body side decorations were revamped and the Mainline models finally got body side moldings. Newly-designed taillights featured large, round red lenses with protruding ribbed-chrome center rings. The hood ornament looked like a chrome rocket in a soft tortilla shell. Safety was a popular theme in 1956 and the new Fords featured a completely redesigned instrument panel. A "Lifeguard Safety Package" with dashboard padding, padded sun visors and other ingredients was optional. The steering wheel featured a 2-1/2-inch recessed hub designed to lessen injury to the driver in the event of an accident. Seat belts were also offered for the first time. The Mainline series was the base trim level for 1956. Mainline models built early in the year had rubber window moldings, a horn button instead of horn ring, one sun visor and an armrest on the driver's door only. Later models had bright metal windshield and window molding and a unique molding treatment along the body side. This consisted of two parallel moldings running forward from the taillights, with the longer upper molding curving downwards to a spear tip plate below the rear side window. The lower molding stopped about a foot back and an upward-curving molding connected it with the upper molding near the spear tip. The area between the moldings could be finished in a contrasting color, sometimes matching the roof color. The trunk carried a Ford crest with horizontal chrome bars jutting from either side. Mainline Six models were the same as in 1955. A V-8 was $100 extra in any Mainline model. Ford offered a total of eight engines throughout the model lineup this year. The 223-cid overhead-valve six had another compression ratio boost, which gave it 17 more horsepower. When it came to V-8s, big Fords with manual transmission started with a 272-cid job with a two-barrel carburetor. With Ford-O-Matic, the rating went up. A 292-cid V-8 with a Holley four-barrel was optional. The base Thunderbird V-8 was a dual-exhaust version of the 292. Performance buffs could order a 312-cid Thunderbird Special V-8 with manual transmission or overdrive. By

1956 Ford Mainline two-door Sedan (OCW)

bumping compression up to 9.0:1, Ford made the Thunderbird Special V-8 with Ford-O-Matic transmission attachment even hotter. With two Holley four-barrel carburetors the Thunderbird Special V-8 was top dog except for some rare cars with superchargers.

Customline — Series A6 / Series U6 — Six and V-8: The Customline series was the intermediate trim level and included chrome window moldings, a horn ring, two sun visors, armrests on all doors and passenger assist straps on two-door interior "B" pillars. A constant-width body side molding started on the sides of the front fenders, just behind the headlight hoods, and curved slightly downward, extending past the "Customline" nameplates on the rear doors (or rear quarter panels of four-door models). The rear sections ran from the nameplate to a point just above the taillights. Where the two moldings met there was a "tree branch" effect. Trunk lid identification again consisted of a Ford crest with horizontal chrome bars on either side of the crest. The Tudor Sedan, the Fordor Sedan and a new Victoria Tudor formed the Customline Six series. The $100-more-expensive Customline V-8 models came in the same body styles.

Fairlane — Series A6 / Series U6 — Six and V-8: The Fairlane series was the top trim level for 1956 and included chrome window moldings and chrome "A" pillar moldings on Sunliner convertibles. Fairlane nameplates and crests appeared on the hood and the rear deck lid. Body style nameplates were placed on the front doors. A wide, flared body side molding started on top of the headlight hoods, curved down to dips on the front doors and extended to the rear taillights. Sections to the rear of the "dips" had triple horizontal scoring with eight vertical intersects near the rear. This gave the side trim on the body an "external exhaust pipe" look. The trunk emblem was a black trapezoid with a V-shaped molding on V-8-powered cars. There were seven Fairlane models with a new four-door Victoria hardtop added to the same six body styles offered in 1955. You had to add $100 to get a V-8 engine.

Station Wagon — Series A6 / Series U6 — Six and V-8: Station wagons continued as their own series for 1956. The Ranch Wagon was the base trim level two-door station wagon, while Country Sedans were the intermediate trim level and Country Squires were the top trim level with simulated wood grain exterior paneling. The level of equipment paralleled the Mainline, Customline and Fairlane series of passenger cars. You could get a six-cylinder Ranch Wagon for as little as $2,185 or cough up as much as $2,633 for the V-8 powered "woodie." The all-new Parklane two-door Sport Wagon was not a hardtop like some other non-Ford '56 wagons, but it was decorated with Fairlane side moldings and large chrome trim plates around the front door windows to give it a snazzy, competitive look.

The vehicle identification number was stamped on a plate attached to the left front body pillar below the hinge opening. The first symbol indicated the engine: A=223-cid six-cylinder, M=292-cid four-barrel V-8, P=312-cid four-barrel V-8 and U=272-cid two-barrel V-8. The second symbol indicated the model year: 6=1956. The third symbol indicated the assembly plant: A=Atlanta, Georgia, B=Buffalo, N.Y., C=Chester, Pennsylvania, D=Dallas, Texas, E=Edgewater, N.J., F=Dearborn, Michigan, G=Chicago, Illinois, K=Kansas City, Kansas, L=Long Beach, California, M=Memphis, Tennessee, N=Norfolk, Virginia, P=Twin Cities, St. Paul, Minnesota, R=San Jose, California, S=Somerville, Massachusetts and U=Louisville, Kentucky. The fourth symbol indicated the body style: C=Sunliner Convertible, F=Skyliner Glasstop, R=Ranch Wagon, T=Fairlane Tudor/Fordor, V=Victoria Tudor, X=Country Sedan, Y=Country Squire, G=All other styles, W=Special body solid top. The last six symbols are the sequential production number starting at 100001 and up in each factory.

Mainline (Six)

Model No.	Body/Style No.	Body Type & Seating	Factory Price	Shipping Weight	Production Total
A6	73A	4-dr. Sedan-6P	$1,938	3,127 lbs.	23,403
A6	70A	2-dr. Sedan-6P	$1,892	3,087 lbs.	52,078
A6	70D	2-dr. Business Coupe-3P	$1,791	3,032 lbs.	6,160

Mainline (V-8)

U6	73A	4-dr. Sedan-6P	$1,995	3,238 lbs.	32,081
U6	70A	2-dr. Sedan-6P	$1,992	3,198 lbs.	54,895
U6	70D	2-dr. Business Coupe-3P	$1,891	3,143 lbs.	1,860

Customline (Six)

A6	73B	4-dr. Sedan-6P	$2,043	3,147 lbs.	25,092
A6	70B	2-dr. Sedan-6P	$1,996	3,107 lbs.	29,127
A6	60B	2-dr. Victoria Hardtop-6P	$2,136	3,170 lbs.	1,791

Customline (V-8)

U6	73B	4-dr. Sedan-6P	$2,143	3,258 lbs.	145,603
U6	70B	2-dr. Sedan-6P	$2,096	3,218 lbs.	135,701
U6	60B	2-dr. Victoria Hardtop-6P	$2,236	3,313 lbs.	31,339

Fairlane (Six)

A6	73C	4-dr. Town Sedan-6P	$2,136	3,147 lbs.	3,638
A6	70C	2-dr. Club Sedan-6P	$2,090	3,147 lbs.	1,328
A6	64C	2-dr. Victoria Hardtop-6P	$2,237	3,202 lbs.	727
A6	57A	4-dr. Victoria Hardtop-6P	$2,291	3,297 lbs.	193
A6	64A	2-dr. Crown Victoria-6P	$2,380	3,217 lbs.	103
A6	64B	2-dr. Skyliner-6P	$2,407	3,227 lbs.	Note 1
A6	76B	2-dr. Convertible-6P	$2,402	3,312 lbs.	275

Fairlane (V-8)

U6	73C	4-dr. Town Sedan-6P	$2,190	3,250 lbs.	221,234
U6	70C	2-dr. Club Sedan-6P	$2,014	3,222 lbs.	141,301
U6	64C	2-dr. Victoria Hardtop-6P	$2,337	3,345 lbs.	177,008
U6	57A	4-dr. Victoria Hardtop-6P	$2,391	3,440 lbs.	31,918
U6	64A	2-dr. Crown Victoria-6P	$2,490	3,360 lbs.	9,709
U6	64B	2-dr. Skyliner-6P	$2,507	3,370 lbs.	Note 1
U6	76B	2-dr. Convertible-6P	$2,502	3,455 lbs.	57,872

Station Wagon (Six)

A6	59A	2-dr. Ranch Wagon-6P	$2,227	3,330 lbs.	16,267
A6	59B	2-dr. Custom Ranch Wagon-6P	$2,293	3,345 lbs.	4,272
A6	79D	4-dr. Country Sedan-6P	$2,239	3,420 lbs.	4,770
A6	79B	4-dr. Country Sedan-8P	$2,471	3,485 lbs.	2,248
A6	59C	2-dr. Parklane-6P	$2,471	3,360 lbs.	140
A6	79C	2-dr. Country Squire-8P	$2,576	3,495 lbs.	93

Station Wagon (V-8)

U6	59A	2-dr. Ranch Wagon-6P	$2,327	3,473 lbs.	32,081
U6	59B	2-dr. Custom Ranch Wagon-6P	$2,392	3,488 lbs.	38,045
U6	79D	4-dr. Country Sedan-6P	$2,439	3,563 lbs.	80,604
U6	79B	4-dr. Country Sedan-8P	$2,571	3,628 lbs.	58,008
U6	79C	2-dr. Parklane-6P	$2,571	3,503 lbs.	15,046
U6	79C	2-dr. Country Squire-8P	$2,633	3,638 lbs.	23,128

Note 1: Sources did not separate Crown Victoria Skyliner production. It's likely that the Crown Victoria production numbers above include the 603 Crown Victoria Skyliner Hardtops built. The total of 603 is for sixes and V-8s combined.

Base Six: (All): Overhead valve. Cast-iron block. Displacement: 223 cid. B & S: 3.62 x 3.60 in. Compression ratio: 7.5:1. Brake hp: 120 at 4000 rpm. Carburetor: Holley single-barrel. Four main bearings. Code A.

Model U V-8 (Manual transmission): Overhead valve. Cast-iron block. B & S: 3.62 x 3.30 in. Displacement: 272 cid. Compression ratio: 8.40:1. Brake hp: 173 at 4400 rpm. Taxable hp: 42.0. Torque: 260 lbs.-ft. at 2400 rpm. Taxable hp: 42. Five main bearings. Solid valve lifters. Crankcase capacity: 5 qt. (add 1 qt. with new oil filter). Cooling system capacity: 19 qt. Carburetor: Two-barrel. Code U.

1956 Ford Customline four-door Sedan (AA)

1956 Ford Mainline two-door Business Coupe (OCW)

Model U V-8 (Ford-O-Matic): Overhead valve. Cast-iron block. B & S: 3.62 x 3.30 in. Displacement: 272 cid. Compression ratio: 8.40:1. Brake hp: 176 at 4400 rpm. Taxable hp: 42.0. Five main bearings. Solid valve lifters. Crankcase capacity: 5 qt. (add 1 qt. with new oil filter). Cooling system capacity: 19 qt. Carburetor: Two-barrel. Code U.

Model M Fairlane V-8: Overhead valve. Cast-iron block. B & S: 3.75 x 3.30 in. Displacement: 292 cid. Compression ratio: 8.40:1. Brake hp: 200 at 4600 rpm. Taxable hp: 45. Torque: 285 lbs.-ft. at 2600 rpm. Taxable hp: 45.0. Five main bearings. Solid valve lifters. Crankcase capacity: 5 qt. (add 1 qt. with new oil filter). Cooling system capacity: 19 qt. Carburetor: Holley 4000 four-barrel. Code M.

Thunderbird V-8: Overhead valve. Cast-iron block. B & S: 3.75 x 3.30 in. Displacement: 292 cid. Compression ratio: 8.40:1. Brake hp: 202 at 4600 rpm. Taxable hp: 45. Torque: 289 lbs.-ft. at 2600 rpm. Taxable hp: 45.0. Five main bearings. Solid valve lifters. Crankcase capacity: 5 qt. (add 1 qt. with new oil filter). Cooling system capacity: 19 qt. Carburetor: Holley 4000 four-barrel. Code M.

Thunderbird V-8: (Manual transmission or overdrive.) Overhead valve. Cast-iron block. B & S: 3.60 x 3.44 in. Displacement: 312 cid. Compression ratio: 8.4:1. Brake hp: 215 at 4600 rpm. Taxable hp: 45. Torque: 317 lbs.-ft. at 2600 rpm. Five main bearings. Crankcase capacity: 5 qt. (add 1 qt. with new oil filter). Cooling system capacity: 19 qt. Carburetor: Holley 4000 four-barrel. Code P.

Thunderbird Special V-8: (With Ford-O-Matic.) Overhead valve. Cast-iron block. B & S: 3.60 x 3.44 in. Displacement: 312 cid. Compression ratio: 9.0:1. Brake hp: 225 at 4600 rpm. Taxable hp: 45. Torque: 324 lbs.-ft. at 2600 rpm. Five main bearings. Crankcase capacity: 5 qt. (add

1 qt. with new oil filter). Cooling system capacity: 19 qt. Carburetor: Holley 4000 four-barrel. Code L.

Thunderbird Special V-8: (With dual four-barrel carburetion.) Overhead valve. Cast-iron block. B & S: 3.60 x 3.44 in. Displacement: 312 cid. Compression ratio: 9.5:1. Brake hp: 260 at unknown rpm. Taxable hp: 45. Torque: unknown. Five main bearings. Crankcase capacity: 5 qt. (add 1 qt. with new oil filter). Cooling system capacity: 19 qt. Carburetor: Two Holley four-barrel. Code P.

Mainline: Wheelbase: 115.5 in. Overall length: 198.5 in. Overall width: 75.9 in. Tires: 6.70 x 15 tubeless. Front tread: 58 in. Rear tread: 56 in.

Customline: Wheelbase: 115.5 in. Overall length: 198.5 in. Overall width: 75.9 in. Tires: 6.70 x 15 tubeless. Front tread: 58 in. Rear tread: 56 in.

Fairlane: Wheelbase: 115.5 in. Overall length: 198.5 in. Overall width: 75.9 in. Tires: 6.70 x 15 tubeless. Front tread: 58 in. Rear tread: 56 in.

Station Wagon: Wheelbase: 115.5 in. Overall length: 197.6 in. Overall width: 75.9 in. Tires: 7.10 x 15 tubeless. Front tread: 58 in. Rear tread: 56 in.

Mainline, Customline, Fairlane and Station Wagon: Three-speed manual transmission with a semi-centrifugal-type clutch, three-speed helical gears and synchronizers for second and third gears standard equipment. Three-speed with automatic overdrive was optional (specifications same as above with automatic overdrive function cutting in at 27 mph, cutting out at 21 mph. Approximate drive ratio: 0.70:1. Manual control below instrument panel.) Ford-O-Matic automatic transmission was optional. This was a torque converter transmission with automatic planetary gear train; single stage, three-element hydraulic torque converter; hydro-mechanical automatic controls with no electric or vacuum connections and power flow through fluid member at all times. Six-cylinder rear axle ratios: (Ford-O-Matic) 3.22:1; (manual transmission) 3.89:1 and (overdrive) 3.89:1. V-8 rear axle ratios: (Ford-O-Matic) 3.22:1; (manual transmission) 3.78:1 and (overdrive) 3.89:1.

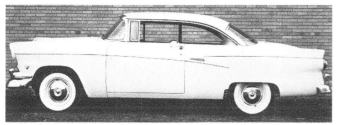

1956 Ford Customline two-door Victoria (PH)

1956 Ford Customline two-door Victoria (OCW)

1956 Ford Fairlane four-door Town Sedan (OCW)

1956 Ford Fairlane two-door Club Sedan (OCW)

1956 Ford Fairlane four-door Town Victoria Hardtop (OCW)

1956 Ford Fairlane two-door Club Victoria Hardtop (OCW)

1956 Ford Fairlane two-door Crown Victoria Skyliner Hardtop (OCW)

Automatic overdrive transmission ($110 to $148). Ford-O-Matic transmission ($178 to $215). Power steering for Mainline models ($91). Power steering for other models ($51 to $64). Power seat ($60). Radio ($100). Heater ($85). Power brakes ($32). Thunderbird V-8 for Fairlane ($123). Power brakes ($40). Windshield washers ($10). Wire wheel covers ($35). Power windows ($70). Chrome engine dress-up kit ($25). Rear fender shields. Full wheel discs. White sidewall tires. Continental tire kit. Tinted windshield. Tinted glass. Life-Guard safety equipment. Two-tone paint finish. Front and rear bumper guards. Grille guard package. Rear guard package. Rear mount radio antenna.

History:

Production of 1956 Fords started September 6, 1955. The Parklane station wagon was a Deluxe Fairlane trim level two-door Ranch Wagon. The Crown Victoria Skyliner featured a plexiglass, tinted transparent forward roof, the last year for this type construction. The Sunliner was a two-door convertible. The new Y-block Thunderbird V-8 came with double twin-jet carburetion; integrated automatic choke; dual exhaust; turbo-wedge-shaped combustion chambers and automatic Power Pilot. A 12-volt electrical system and 18-mm anti-fouling spark plugs were adopted this season. Model year sales peaked at 1,392,847 units. Calendar year production hit 1,373,542 vehicles. (Both figures include Thunderbird sales and production). A brand new NBC Television program called "The Ford Show" bowed to the public on October 4, 1956. Many people think the Ford Motor Company-sponsored show was named for its star - Tennessee Ernie Ford. The entertainer had been a big hit in 1955 and 1956 in his own "Tennessee Ernie Ford Show" that aired during daytime hours. The new prime-time evening show increased Ernie's popularity immensely, while selling lots of Fords and Thunderbirds at the same time. Eventually, "The Ford Show" would become the top half-hour variety program in the United States. Ford's trademark closing number was almost always a hymn, gospel or spiritual song. The advertising gurus had flinched when this was proposed, but it turned out to be the winning touch that made the show a big success.

1956 Ford Fairlane two-door Crown Victoria Hardtop (OCW)

1956 Ford Sunliner two-door Convertible (OCW)

1956 Ford two-door Ranch Wagon (OCW)

1956 Ford two-door Custom Ranch Wagon (OCW)

1956 Ford four-door Country Sedan 6P (OCW)

1956 Ford four-door Country Sedan 8P (OCW)

1956 Ford two-door Parklane Sport wagon (OCW)

1956 Ford two-door Parklane Sport wagon (OCW)

1956 Ford four-door Country Squire (OCW)

1957 Ford

Custom — Series A7 / Series U7 — Six and V-8: The 1957 Fords were completely restyled and had several new series designations. They bore only a slight resemblance to 1956 models. Custom models were three inches longer overall and had a one-half-inch longer wheelbase. All models had 14-inch wheels for the first time. The smaller-diameter wheels also contributed to their low-slung lines. Other design changes included a rear-opening hood, streamlined wheel openings and a wraparound windshield with posts that sloped rearward at the bottom. All Fords also sported tail fins, which the automaker described as "high-canted fenders." The big news was the Skyliner model. This car was the world's only true hardtop convertible - or retractable hardtop, depending on how you look at it. A push-button automatic folding mechanism retracted the car's roof into the trunk. Fords in the base Custom car-line had no series nameplates on their fenders. The body side moldings extended from the center side window pillar to the taillights, with a pointed dip on the rear door or fender. Body style offerings consisted of three sedans called the Business Tudor, the Tudor and the Fordor. V-8 versions of each style were $100 additional. This year's base engine was the 223-cid inline six-cylinder. The base V-8 was a 272-cid 190-hp two-barrel version. A 292-cid four-barrel Thunderbird V-8 was optional. Other choices included the 312-cid Thunderbird Special V-8 that came in a 245-hp single four-barrel version, a 270-hp dual four-barrel version, a 285-hp racing version and a 300-hp version (340-hp in NASCAR tune) with a McCulloch/Paxton centrifugal supercharger.

Custom 300 — Series A7 / Series U7 — Six and V-8: The Custom 300 was a new, upper trim level in the short-wheelbase Custom series. Two body styles were available, the Tudor and the Fordor. They had added bright work such as chrome window moldings and a chrome horn ring. Inside there were two sun visors and armrests on all doors. The word F-O-R-D was spelled out in block letters above the grille and a small Ford crest appeared on the trunk lid. There were no series nameplates on the sides of the body. A full-length side molding came with an optional gold aluminum insert that made the smaller, less-expensive Custom 300 look somewhat like a Fairlane 500. The difference was that the rear portion of the molding behind the door dip ran straight to the taillights instead of accenting the tops of the tail fins. This trim lured the author's father into buying a Custom 300 instead of a Fairlane 500, since he felt there wasn't enough difference in the two to justify the Fairlane's higher price. Ford's trim upgrade obviously appealed to buyers of the less-expensive cars. For $100 extra, you could turn your Custom 300 Six into an Eight. (Dad did at least get the V-8!)

Fairlane — Series A7 / Series U7 — Six and V-8: Fairlane was the base trim level for the longer wheelbase Ford series. There were four body styles in this car-line and each was available as a six, at the base price, or as a V-8 for $100 additional. The models available were the two-door Club Sedan, the four-door Town Sedan, the Club Victoria (two-door hardtop) and the Town Victoria (four-door hardtop). These cars had bright Fairlane nameplates on their rear fenders, extra chrome around the roof "C" pillar and bullet-shaped accent panels on the rear fenders - and rear doors of four-door models. The Fairlane name appeared in script on the side of the fenders, above the grille and on the trunk lid. A large, V-shaped Fairlane crest appeared on the trunk lid whenever V-8 engines were added.

Fairlane 500 — Series A7 / Series U7 — Six and V-8: Fairlane 500 was the top trim level in the Fairlane series and included all the trim used on the Fairlane models plus slightly more chrome on the "C" pillars and different side trim. The side trim was a modified version of the Fairlane sweep, which included a gold anodized insert between two chrome strips. It began on the sides of the front fenders, dipping near the back of the front doors, merging into a strip and following the crest of the fins to the rear of the body. Five Fairlane 500s could be had with a six-cylinder engine: Club Sedan, Town Sedan, Club Victoria, Town Victoria and Sunliner convertible. All of these were available with V-8 power for $100 more. A sixth V-8-only model was also offered. This was the Skyliner convertible (retractable hardtop).

Station Wagon — Series A7 / Series U7 — Six and V-8: The Ranch Wagon was the base trim level two-door station wagon for 1957. Country Sedans were the intermediate level with four-door styling. Country Squires were the top trim level, also with four-door styling. The level of equipment paralleled Custom, Custom 300 and Fairlane 500 models of passenger cars.

VIN:

The vehicle identification number was stamped on a plate attached to the left front body pillar below the hinge opening. The first symbol indicated the engine: A=223-cid six-cylinder, B=272-cid V-8, C=292-cid V-8, D=312-cid four-barrel V-8, E=312-cid 2 x four-barrel V-8 and F=312-cid Supercharged V-8. The second symbol indicated the model year: 7=1957. The third symbol indicated the assembly plant: A=Atlanta, Georgia, B=Buffalo, N.Y., C=Chester, Pennsylvania, D=Dallas, Texas, E=Mahwah, N.J., F=Dearborn, Michigan, G=Chicago, Illinois, K=Kansas City, Kansas, L=Long Beach, California, M=Memphis, Tennessee, N=Norfolk, Virginia, P=Twin Cities, St. Paul, Minnesota, R=San Jose, California, S=Somerville, Massachusetts and U=Louisville, Kentucky. The fourth symbol indicated the body style: C=Fairlane 500 Sunliner Convertible, G=Custom and Custom 300 sedans, R=Custom 300 and Ranch Wagon, T=Fairlane Tudor/Fordor, V=Fairlane 500 Victoria Tudor/Fordor, W=Fairlane 500 Skyliner Retractable Hardtop, X=Country Sedan and Y=Country Squire. The last six symbols are the sequential production number starting at 100001 and up in each factory.

1957 Ford Custom two-door Business Sedan (OCW)

1957 Ford Custom 300 four-door Sedan (OCW)

1957 Ford Custom 300 two-door Sedan (AA)

1957 Ford Fairlane four-door Town Sedan (AA)

1957 Ford Custom four-door Sedan (OCW)

1957 Ford Custom two-door Sedan (OCW)

Custom (Six)

Model No.	Body/ Style No.	Body Type & Seating	Factory Price	Shipping Weight	Production Total
A7	73A	4-dr. Sedan-6P	$2,112	3,193 lbs.	37,719
A7	70A	2 dr. Sedan-6P	$2,061	3,150 lbs.	74,477
A7	70A	2-dr. Business Sedan-3P	$1,949	3,141 lbs.	5,242

Custom (V-8)

Model No.	Body/ Style No.	Body Type & Seating	Factory Price	Shipping Weight	Production Total
U7	73A	4-dr. Sedan-6P	$2,212	3,315 lbs.	31,205
U7	70A	2 dr. Sedan-6P	$2,161	3,272 lbs.	42,486
U7	70D	2-dr. Business Sedan-3P	$2,049	3,263 lbs.	1,646

Custom 300 (Six)

Model No.	Body/ Style No.	Body Type & Seating	Factory Price	Shipping Weight	Production Total
A7	73B	4-dr. Sedan-6P	$2,227	3,208 lbs.	33,585
A7	70B	2 dr. Sedan-6P	$2,175	3,163 lbs.	34,242

Custom 300 (V-8)

Model No.	Body/ Style No.	Body Type & Seating	Factory Price	Shipping Weight	Production Total
U7	73B	4-dr. Sedan-6P	$2,327	3,330 lbs.	161,291
U7	70B	2-dr. Sedan-6P	$2,275	3,285 lbs.	126,118

Fairlane (Six)

Model No.	Body/ Style No.	Body Type & Seating	Factory Price	Shipping Weight	Production Total
A7	58A	4-dr. Town Sedan-6P	$2,356	3,315 lbs.	2,304
A7	64A	2-dr. Club Sedan-6P	$2,305	3,270 lbs.	2,199
A7	63B	2-dr. Victoria Hardtop-6p	$2,363	3,305 lbs.	260
A7	57B	4-dr. Victoria Hardtop-6P	$2,427	3,350 lbs.	1,139

Fairlane (V-8)

Model No.	Body/ Style No.	Body Type & Seating	Factory Price	Shipping Weight	Production Total
U7	58A	4-dr. Town Sedan-6P	$2,456	3,437 lbs.	49,756
U7	64A	2-dr. Club Sedan-6P	$2,405	3,392 lbs.	37,644
U7	63B	2-dr. Victoria Hardtop-6p	$2,463	3,427 lbs.	43,867
U7	57B	4-dr. Victoria Hardtop-6P	$2,527	3,472 lbs.	11,556

Fairlane 500 (Six)

Model No.	Body/ Style No.	Body Type & Seating	Factory Price	Shipping Weight	Production Total
A7	58B	4-dr. Town Sedan-6P	$2,403	3,330 lbs.	4,076
A7	64B	2-dr. Club Sedan-6P	$2,351	3,285 lbs.	2,217
A7	63A	2-dr. Victoria Hardtop-6p	$2,389	3,320 lbs.	2,389
A7	57A	4-dr. Victoria Hardtop-6P	$2,474	3,365 lbs.	932
A7	76B	2-dr. Convertible-6P	$2,575	3,475 lbs.	832

Fairlane 500 (V-8)

Model No.	Body/ Style No.	Body Type & Seating	Factory Price	Shipping Weight	Production Total
U7	58B	4-dr. Town Sedan-6P	$2,503	3,452 lbs.	189,086
U7	64B	2-dr. Club Sedan-6P	$2,451	3,407 lbs.	91,536
U7	63A	2-dr. Victoria Hardtop-6P	$2,509	3,442 lbs.	180,813
U7	57A	4-dr. Victoria Hardtop-6P	$2,574	3,487 lbs.	67,618
U7	51A	2-dr. Retractable-6P	$3,012	3,916 lbs.	20,766
U7	76B	2-dr. Convertible-6P	$2,675	3,597 lbs.	76,896

Station Wagon (Six)

Model No.	Body/ Style No.	Body Type & Seating	Factory Price	Shipping Weight	Production Total
A7	59A	2-dr. Ranch Wagon-6P	$2,371	3,394 lbs.	23,924
A7	59B	2-dr. Del Rio Wagon-6P	$2,467	3,401 lbs.	4,981
A7	79D	4-dr. Country Sedan-6P	$2,521	3,464 lbs.	9,007
A7	79B	4-dr. Country Sedan-8P	$2,626	3,553 lbs.	3,830
A7	79E	2-dr. Country Squire-8P	$2,754	3,567 lbs.	245

Station Wagon (V-8)

Model No.	Body/ Style No.	Body Type & Seating	Factory Price	Shipping Weight	Production Total
U7	59A	2-dr. Ranch Wagon-6P	$2,471	3,516 lbs.	36,562
U7	59B	2-dr. Del Rio Wagon-6P	$2,567	3,523 lbs.	41,124
U7	79D	4-dr. Country Sedan-6P	$2,621	3,586 lbs.	128,244
U7	79B	4-dr. Country Sedan-8P	$2,726	3,675 lbs.	45,808
U7	79E	2-dr. Country Squire-8P	$2,854	3,689 lbs.	27,445

Engines:

Base Six: Overhead valve. Cast-iron block. Displacement: 223 cid. B & S: 3.62 x 3.60 in. Compression ratio: 8.6:1. Brake hp: 144 at 4200 rpm. Carburetor: Holley one-barrel. Four main bearings. Code A.

Optional V-8 with manual transmission: Overhead valve. Cast-iron block. B & S: 3.62 x 3.30 in. Displacement: 272 cid. Compression ratio:

1957 Ford Fairlane two-door Club Victoria Hardtop (OCW)

8.40:1. Brake hp: 173 at 4400 rpm. Taxable hp: 42.0. Torque: 260 lbs.-ft. at 2400 rpm. Taxable hp: 42. Five main bearings. Solid valve lifters. Crankcase capacity: 5 qt. (add 1 qt. with new oil filter). Cooling system capacity: 19 qt. Carburetor: Two-barrel. Code U.

Optional V-8 with Ford-O-Matic transmission: Overhead valve. Cast-iron block. B & S: 3.62 x 3.30 in. Displacement: 272 cid. Compression ratio: 8.40:1. Brake hp: 176 at 4400 rpm. Taxable hp: 42.0. Five main bearings. Solid valve lifters. Crankcase capacity: 5 qt. (add 1 qt. with new oil filter). Cooling system capacity: 19 qt. Carburetor: Two-barrel. Code U.

Optional Fairlane V-8: Overhead valve. Cast-iron block. B & S: 3.75 x 3.30 in. Displacement: 292 cid. Compression ratio: 8.40:1. Brake hp: 200 at 4600 rpm. Taxable hp: 45. Torque: 285 lbs.-ft. at 2600 rpm. Taxable hp: 45.0. Five main bearings. Solid valve lifters. Crankcase capacity: 5 qt. (add 1 qt. with new oil filter). Cooling system capacity: 19 qt. Carburetor: Holley 4000 four-barrel. Code M.

1957 Ford Fairlane two-door Club Sedan (OCW)

1957 Ford Fairlane 500 four-door Town Sedan (PH)

1957 Ford Fairlane 500 Club Victoria two-door hardtop (OCW)

1957 Ford Sunliner two-door Convertible (OCW)

1957 Ford Skyliner two-door Retractable (OCW)

Optional Thunderbird V-8: Overhead valve. Cast-iron block. B & S: 3.75 x 3.30 in. Displacement: 292 cid. Compression ratio: 8.40:1. Brake hp: 202 at 4600 rpm. Taxable hp: 45. Torque: 289 lbs.-ft. at 2600 rpm. Taxable hp: 45.0. Five main bearings. Solid valve lifters. Crankcase capacity: 5 qt. (add 1 qt. with new oil filter). Cooling system capacity: 19 qt. Carburetor: Holley 4000 four-barrel. Code M.

Optional Thunderbird Special V-8 (Manual or overdrive transmission): Overhead valve. Cast-iron block. B & S: 3.60 x 3.44 in. Displacement: 312 cid. Compression ratio: 8.4:1. Brake hp: 215 at 4600 rpm. Taxable hp: 45. Torque: 317 lbs.-ft. at 2600 rpm. Five main bearings. Crankcase capacity: 5 qt. (add 1 qt. with new oil filter). Cooling system capacity: 19 qt. Carburetor: Holley 4000 four-barrel. Code P.

Optional Thunderbird Special V-8 (Ford-O-Matic transmission): Overhead valve. Cast-iron block. B & S: 3.60 x 3.44 in. Displacement: 312 cid. Compression ratio: 9.0:1. Brake hp: 225 at 4600 rpm. Taxable hp: 45. Torque: 324 lbs.-ft. at 2600 rpm. Five main bearings. Crankcase

capacity: 5 qt. (add 1 qt. with new oil filter). Cooling system capacity: 19 qt. Carburetor: Holley 4000 four-barrel. Code L.

Optional Thunderbird Special V-8 (with dual four-barrel carburetors): Overhead valve. Cast-iron block. B & S: 3.60 x 3.44 in. Displacement: 312 cid. Compression ratio: 9.5:1. Brake hp: 260 at unknown rpm. Taxable hp: 45. Torque: unknown. Five main bearings. Crankcase capacity: 5 qt. (add 1 qt. with new oil filter). Cooling system capacity: 19 qt. Carburetor: Two Holley four-barrel. Code P.

Technical:

Custom, Custom 300, Fairlane, Fairlane 500 and Station Wagon: Three-speed manual transmission (with semi-centrifugal-type clutch, three-speed helical gears and synchronizers for second and third gears) standard. Three-speed with automatic overdrive was optional. Specifications were the same as above with automatic overdrive function cutting in at 27 mph,

1957 Ford Fairlane 500 two-door Club Sedan (OCW)

1957 Ford Fairlane 500 two-door Club Sedan (OCW)

1957 Ford Fairlane 500 Town Victoria four-door hardtop (OCW)

1957 Ford two-door Del Rio Ranch Wagon (OCW)

1957 Ford four-door Country Sedan 6P (OCW)

1957 Ford four-door Country Sedan 8P (PH)

1957 Ford four-door Country Squire (OCW)

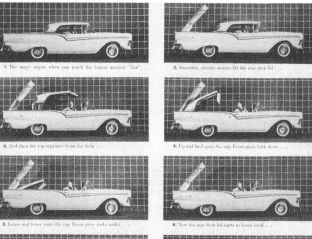

1957 Ford Skyliner (OCW)

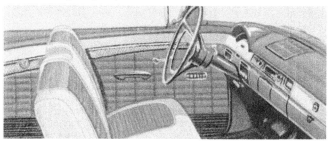

1957 Ford Fairlane 500 interior detail (OCW)

cutting out at 21 mph. Approximate drive ratio: 0.70:1. Manual control below instrument panel. Ford-O-Matic automatic transmission was optional. This was a torque converter transmission with automatic planetary gear train single-stage, three-element hydraulic torque converter hydro-mechanical automatic controls with no electric or vacuum connections and power flow through fluid member at all times. Six-cylinder rear axle ratios: (Ford-O-Matic) 3.22:1 (manual transmission) 3.89:1 and (automatic overdrive) 4.11:1. V-8 rear axle ratios: (Ford-O-Matic) 3.10:1 (manual transmission) 3.56:1 and (automatic overdrive) 3.70:1.

292-cid V-8 ($439). Ford-O-Matic ($188). Automatic overdrive ($108). Power steering ($68). Radio ($100). Heater and defroster ($85). Power brakes ($38). Fairlane/station wagon 312-cid V-8 engine option ($43). Rear fender shields (skirts). Two-tone paint. Back-up lamps. Large wheel covers (standard on Fairlane 500). White sidewall tires. Continental tire extension kit. Outside rearview mirror. Lifeguard safety equipment package. Oversized tires. Radio antenna. Non-glare mirror.

History:

The introduction of 1957 Fords and Thunderbirds took place in October 1956. The Fairlane 500 Skyliner with retractable hardtop was introduced as a midyear addition to the line. Overdrive or Ford-O-Matic transmission could now be ordered for any car with any engine. Model-year production was 1,655,068 vehicles. Calendar-year sales amounted to 1,522,406 Fords and Thunderbirds. Ford out-produced Chevrolet this season, to become America's number one automaker of 1957 on a model-year-production basis. The name Del Rio was used for a deluxe two-door Ranch Wagon that came with Fairlane level trim.

1958 Ford

Custom 300 — Series A8 / Series U8 — (Six and V-8): The 1958 Fords utilized the same basic body used in 1957 with many new styling ideas. A simulated air scoop hood and honeycomb grille were borrowed from the Thunderbird. Dual headlights and a sculptured rear deck lid created a more futuristic image. Cruise-O-Matic three-speed automatic transmission was offered for the first time, along with 332-cid and 352-cid V-8s. Also new was the one-year-only Ford-Aire air-suspension system for Fairlanes. Custom 300s included chrome window moldings, a horn button instead of a horn ring, one sun visor, an armrest on the driver's door only and a single chrome strip on the body side. This molding began on the side of the front fender, continued horizontally to the back of the front door, then turned down and joined a horizontal chrome strip that continued to the back of the body. A top-of-the-line Styletone trim option duplicated this side trim, except the lower horizontal strip was a double strip with a gold anodized insert. A mid-level Special trim option was also available with a small horizontal chrome strip that turned upward just behind the door. Model offerings were the same as 1957 with prices up $70 to $90. This year adding a V-8 cost $137. The 223-cid six-cylinder engine gained one horsepower. The base Ford V-8 was the 272 with a Holley two-barrel. A new 332-cid Interceptor V-8 came with a two-barrel or four-barrel carburetor. There was also a high-horsepower Interceptor Special V-8 with a single four-barrel carburetor and 10.2:1 compression ratio.

Fairlane — Series A8 / Series U8 — (Six and V-8): The Fairlane model was the entry-level long-wheelbase Ford. It included chrome window moldings (with slightly less chrome around the "C" pillar than Fairlane 500 models) and different side stripe treatments. The initial version had two strips. The lower molding began at the rear of the front wheel opening, then went straight to the back of the front door. From there it began to gradually curve upward. The upper strip began at the front of the fender and went straight back, to the back of the front door. It then began to curve gradually downward, merging with the lower strip directly over the rear wheel opening. A Fairlane script appeared on the rear fenders and directly above the grille opening. Starting at midyear an additional sweep spear of anodized aluminum trim was centered in the panel between the moldings and three "port hole" style trim pieces were added at the rear. The 1957 body styles were carried over. New (and offered only in 1958) was the Ford-Aire suspension system for use in Fairlane series cars and station wagons.

Fairlane 500 — Series A8 / Series U8 — (Six and V-8): The Fairlane 500 models had the top trim level in the Fairlane series. They included all the trim used in the Fairlane models plus slightly more chrome on the "C" pillars and different side trim. The side trim was a double runner chrome strip with a gold anodized insert. The top chrome strip began on the side of the front fender, sloped slightly, and terminated at the top of the rear bumper. The lower molding split from the upper strip where the front door began, dropped in a modified Fairlane sweep and merged with the upper strip at the rear bumper. A Fairlane script appeared

above the grille and on the trunk lid, while the Fairlane 500 script appeared on the rear fenders, above the chrome side trim. This series also had the same styles as last year with similar price differentials.

Station Wagon — Series A8 / Series U8 — (Six and V-8): The Ranch Wagon was the base trim level two-door and four-door station wagons for 1958. The two-door Del Rio wagon also re-appeared. Country Sedans were intermediate level station wagons and Country Squires were the top trim level. You could buy a cheap six-cylinder Ford wagon for under $2,400 or move up a full 12 notches to the V-8-powered Country Squire with a list price approaching $3,000. Ford sure packed a lot of station wagon models into a $600 price spread.

Ford's coding system for serial numbers can be broken down, as follows: The first symbol designates the engine type: (A) 223-cid six-cylinder, (B) 332-cid V-8, (C) 292-cid V-8, (G) 332-cid V-8, (H) 352-cid V-8. The second symbol designates the model year: "8" for 1958. The third symbol designates the final assembly plant, as follows: A = Atlanta, B = Buffalo, C = Chester, D = Dallas, G = Chicago, F= Dearborn, E = Mahwah, K = Kansas City, L = Long Beach, M = Memphis, N = Norfolk, R = San Jose, U = Louisville, P = Twin City (St. Paul). The fourth symbol designates body type, as follows: C = Fairlane 500 convertible,

1958 Ford Custom 300 two-door Sedan (OCW)

1958 Ford Fairlane four-door Town Sedan (OCW)

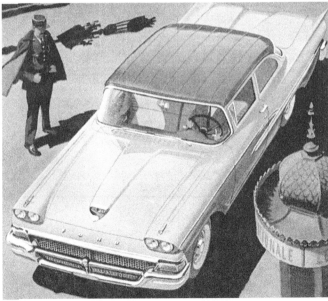

1958 Ford Fairlane 500 two-door Club Sedan (OCW)

G = Custom 300 (two-door and four-door), R = Custom 300 Ranch Wagon, Del Rio, T = Fairlane/Fairlane 500 (two-door and four-door), V = Fairlane/Fairlane 500/Victoria (two-door and four-door), W = Retractable hardtop, X = Country Sedan, Y = Country Squire. The fifth through tenth digits indicate the number of the unit built at each assembly plant, beginning with 100001. Custom 300 six-cylinder models began with the designation "A8" followed by assembly plant code, body type code, and, finally, the unit's production number, according to the final assembly location. Each plant began at 100001 and went up.

Custom 300 (Six)

Model No.	Body/ Style No.	Body Type & Seating	Factory Price	Shipping Weight	Production Total
A8	73A	4-dr. Sedan-6P	$2,180	3,222 lbs.	71,306
A8	70A	2-dr. Sedan-6P	$2,126	3,194 lbs.	102,375
A8	70D	2-dr. Business Sedan-3P	$2,038	3,171 lbs.	3,291

Custom 300 (V-8)

Model No.	Body/ Style No.	Body Type & Seating	Factory Price	Shipping Weight	Production Total
A8	73A	4-dr. Sedan-6P	$2,317	3,334 lbs.	92,062
A8	70A	2-dr. Sedan-6P	$2,263	3,306 lbs.	71,066
A8	70D	2-dr. Business Sedan-3P	$2,175	3,283 lbs.	771

Fairlane (Six)

Model No.	Body/ Style No.	Body Type & Seating	Factory Price	Shipping Weight	Production Total
A8	58A	4-dr. Town Sedan-6P	$2,346	3,371 lbs.	8,448
A8	64A	2-dr. Club Sedan-6P	$2,292	3,319 lbs.	9,005
A8	63B	2-dr. Victoria Hardtop-6P	$2,425	3,317 lbs.	1,294
A8	57B	4-dr. Victoria Hardtop-6P	$2,490	3,394 lbs.	215

Fairlane (V-8)

Model No.	Body/ Style No.	Body Type & Seating	Factory Price	Shipping Weight	Production Total
U8	58A	4-dr. Town Sedan-6P	$2,454	3,483 lbs.	49,042
U8	64A	2-dr. Club Sedan-6P	$2,400	3,431 lbs.	29,361
U8	63B	2-dr. Victoria Hardtop-6P	$2,549	3,429 lbs.	15,122
U8	57B	4-dr. Victoria Hardtop-6P	$2,612	3,506 lbs.	5,653

Fairlane 500 (Six)

Model No.	Body/ Style No.	Body Type & Seating	Factory Price	Shipping Weight	Production Total
A8	58A	4-dr. Town Sedan-6P	$2,499	3,379 lbs.	3,694
A8	64B	2-dr. Club Sedan-6P	$2,445	3,307 lbs.	1,311
A8	63A	2-dr. Victoria Hardtop-6P	$2,506	3,317 lbs.	1,766
A8	57A	4-dr. Victoria Hardtop-6P	$2,570	3,414 lbs.	758
A8	76B	2-dr. Convertible-6P	$2,721	3,483 lbs.	581

Fairlane 500 (V-8)

Model No.	Body/ Style No.	Body Type & Seating	Factory Price	Shipping Weight	Production Total
U8	58A	4-dr. Town Sedan-6P	$2,605	3,526 lbs.	102,004
U8	64B	2-dr. Club Sedan-6P	$2,551	3,454 lbs.	32,730
U8	63A	2-dr. Victoria Hardtop-6P	$2,612	3,464 lbs.	78,673
U8	57A	4-dr. Victoria Hardtop-6P	$2,676	3,561 lbs.	35,751
U8	51A	2-dr. Retractable-6P	$3,234	4,069 lbs.	14,713
U8	76B	2-dr. Convertible-6P	$2,845	3,630 lbs.	34,448

Station Wagon (Six)

Model No.	Body/ Style No.	Body Type & Seating	Factory Price	Shipping Weight	Production Total
A8	59A	2-dr. Ranch Wagon-6P	$2,468	3,483 lbs.	19,004
A8	79A	4-dr. Ranch Wagon-6P	$2,522	3,540 lbs.	13,816
A8	59B	2-dr. Del Rio Wagon-6P	$2,574	3,488 lbs.	1,570
A8	79D	4-dr. Country Sedan-6P	$2,628	3,545 lbs.	4,964
A8	79C	4-dr. Country Sedan-8P	$2,735	3,613 lbs.	2,420
A8	79E	4-dr. Country Squire-8P	$2,865	3,650 lbs.	230

Station Wagon (V-8)

Model No.	Body/ Style No.	Body Type & Seating	Factory Price	Shipping Weight	Production Total
U8	59A	2-dr. Ranch Wagon-6P	$2,575	3,620 lbs.	14,997
U8	79A	4-dr. Ranch Wagon-6P	$2,629	3,677 lbs.	19,038
U8	59B	2-dr. Del Rio Wagon-6P	$2,681	3,625 lbs.	11,117
U8	79D	4-dr. Country Sedan-6P	$2,735	3,682 lbs.	63,808
U8	79C	4-dr. Country Sedan-8P	$2,842	3,750 lbs.	18,282
U8	79E	4-dr. Country Squire-8P	$2,972	3,787 lbs.	14,790

Engines:

Base Six: Overhead valve. Cast-iron block. Displacement: 223 cid. B & S: 3.62 x 3.60 in. Compression ratio: 6.6:1. Brake hp: 145 at 4200 rpm. Carburetor: Holley one-barrel. Four main bearings. Code A.

Base V-8: Overhead valve. Cast-iron block. B & S: 3.75 x 3.30 in. Displacement: 292 cid. Compression ratio: 9.10:1. Brake hp: 205 at 4500 rpm. Taxable hp: 45.0. Torque: 295 lbs.-ft. at 2400 rpm. Five main bearings. Solid valve lifters. Crankcase capacity: 5 qt. (add 1 qt. with new oil filter). Cooling system capacity: 19 qt. Carburetor: Holley four-barrel Model R-1281-3A with standard or R-1282-3A with automatic transmission. Code C.

Interceptor V-8: Overhead valve. Cast-iron block. B & S: 4.00 x 3.30 in. Displacement: 332 cid. Compression ratio: 9.50:1. Brake hp: 240 at 4600 rpm. Taxable hp: 51.2. Torque: 360 lbs.-ft. at 2800 rpm. Five main bearings. Valve lifters: hydraulic. Crankcase capacity: 5 qt. (add 1 qt. with new oil filter). Cooling system capacity: 19 qt. Dual exhaust. Carburetor: Holley four-barrel Model R-1406-A with standard transmission or R-1552-A with automatic transmission. Code G.

Interceptor V-8: Overhead valve. Cast-iron block. B & S: 4.00 x 3.30 in. Displacement: 332 cid. Compression ratio: 9.60:1. Brake hp: 265 at 4600 rpm. Taxable hp: 51.2. Torque: 360 lbs.-ft. at 2800 rpm. Five main bearings. Solid valve lifters. Crankcase capacity: 5 qt. (add 1 qt. with new oil filter). Cooling system capacity: 19 qt. Dual exhaust. Carburetor: Holley two-barrel Model R-1406-A with standard transmission or R-1552-A with automatic transmission. Code G.

Thunderbird V-8: Overhead valve. Cast-iron block. B & S: 4.00 x 3.50 in. Displacement: 352 cid. Compression ratio: 10.2:1. Brake hp: 300 at 4600 rpm. Taxable hp: 51.2. Torque: 395 lbs.-ft. at 2800 rpm. Five main bearings. Valve lifters: (early) solid, (late) hydraulic. Crankcase capacity: 5 qt. (add 1 qt. with new oil filter). Cooling system capacity: 19.5 qt. Dual exhaust. Carburetor: Ford-Holley Model B8A-9510-E four-barrel or Carter nos. 2640S-SA-SC four-barrel. Code H.

Police Special V-8: Overhead valve. Cast-iron block. B & S: 4.05 x 3.50 in. Displacement: 361 cid. Compression ratio: 10.50:1. Brake hp:

1958 Ford Fairlane 500 four-door Town Sedan (OCW)

1958 Ford Fairlane 500 Town Victoria four-door hardtop (OCW)

1958 Ford Fairlane 500 Club Victoria two-door hardtop (OCW)

1958 Ford Sunliner two-door Convertible (OCW)

303 at 4600 rpm. Taxable hp: 52.49. Torque: 400 lbs.-ft. at 2800 rpm. Five main bearings. Solid valve lifters. Crankcase capacity: 5 qt. (add 1 qt. with new oil filter). Cooling system capacity (Add 1 qt. for heater): 18.5 qt. Carburetor: (Manual transmission) Holley R-1482-A four-barrel, (Automatic transmission) Holley R-1483-A four-barrel. Engine code: W.

Chassis:

Custom 300: Wheelbase: 116 in. Overall length: 202 in. Overall width: 78 in. Tires: 7.50 x 14.

Fairlane: Wheelbase: 118 in. Overall length: 207 in. Overall width: 78 in. Tires: 7.50 x 14.

Fairlane 500: Wheelbase: 118 in. Overall length: 211 in., Skyliner retractable and 207 in., other Fairlane models. Overall width: 78 in. Tires: 8.00 x 14, Skyliner retractable and 7.50 x 14, other Fairlane 500 models.

Station Wagon: Wheelbase: 116 in. Overall length: 202.7 in. Overall width: 78 in. Tires: 7.50 x 14 and 8.00 x 14, nine-passenger station wagons.

Technical:

Custom 300, Fairlane, Fairlane 500 and Station Wagon: Three-speed manual transmission was standard equipment. It featured semi-centrifugal-type clutch, three-speed helical gears, with synchronizers for second and third gears. Three-speed with automatic overdrive was optional. Specifications were the same as above with automatic overdrive function cutting in at 27 mph, cutting out at 21 mph. Approximate drive ratio: 0.70:1. Manual control below instrument panel. Ford-O-Matic automatic transmission was optional. This was a torque converter transmission with automatic planetary gear train, single-stage, three-element hydraulic torque converter, hydro-mechanical automatic controls with no electrical or vacuum connections and power flow through fluid member at all times. Cruise-O-Matic automatic transmission was also optional. This unit was the same as Ford-O-Matic, except for having three-speeds forward. It was a high-performance automatic transmission with two selective drive ranges for smooth 1-2-3 full-power stabs, or 2-3 gradual acceleration and axle ratio of 2.69:1 for fuel economy. Six-cylinder rear axle ratios: (Ford-O-Matic) 3.22:1, (manual transmission) 3.89:1 and (automatic overdrive) 4.11:1. V-8 rear axle ratios: (Cruise-O-Matic) 2.69:1, (Ford-O-Matic) 3.10:1, (manual transmission) 3.56:1 and (automatic overdrive) 3.70:1.

Options:

Ford-O-Matic ($180). Cruise-O-Matic ($197). Ford-Aire suspension ($156). Overdrive ($108). Power brakes ($37). Power steering ($69). Front power windows ($50), on Custom 300 'business' two-door ($64). Front and rear power windows ($101). Manual four-way adjustable seat ($17). Four-way power adjustable seat ($64). Six-tube radio and antenna ($77). Nine-tube Signal-Seeking radio and antenna ($99). White sidewall tires, four-ply size 7.50 x 14 ($33). White sidewall tires, four-ply, size 6.00 x 14 ($50). Wheel covers ($19 and standard on Fairlane 500). Styletone two-tone paint ($22). Tinted glass ($20). Back-up lights ($10). Custom 300 Deluxe interior trim ($24). Electric clock ($15 and standard on Fairlane 500). Windshield washer ($12). Positive action windshield wiper ($11). Lifeguard safety package with padded

1958 Ford Skyliner two-door Retractable (OCW)

1958 Ford four-door Country Sedan 6P (OCW)

instrument panel and sun visors ($19). Lifeguard safety package, as above, plus two front seat belts ($33). Polar Air Conditioner, includes tinted glass ($271). Select Air Conditioner, includes tinted glass ($395). Interceptor 265-hp V-8 in Custom 300 ($196), in Fairlane ($163). Interceptor Special 300-hp V-8 in Fairlane 500 ($159), in station wagon ($150). Note: Interceptor engine prices are in place of base six-cylinder prices. Automatic overdrive ($108). Heater and defroster ($80). Heater and defroster in Fairlanes and station wagons ($85).

History:

Dealer introductions for 1958 Fords were held November 7, 1957. Dealer introductions for 1958 Thunderbirds were held February 13, 1958. Production at three factories — Memphis, Buffalo and Somerville — was phased out this season. In June 1958, a new plant, having capacity equal to all three aforementioned factories, was opened at Loraine, Ohio. On a model year basis, 74.4 percent of all Fords built in the 1958 run had V-8 power. Sixty-eight percent of these cars had automatic transmission. Model year production of Fords and Thunderbirds totaled 967,945 cars. Calendar -ear sales of Fords and Thunderbirds peaked at 1,038,560 units.

1958 Ford four-door Country Sedan 8P (PH)

1958 Ford Instrument Panel (OCW)

1958 Ford Del Rio Ranch wagon (OCW)

1958 Ford Country Squire (OCW)

1959 Ford

Custom 300 — Series A9 / Series U9 — (Six and V-8): The 1958 Brussels World's Fair drew 42 million visitors to Hetsel Park, in Brussels, Belgium, to celebrate the theme, "For a more human world." The six-month-long extravaganza involved 4,645 expositors from 51 different nations. Ford Motor Company was one of the participants from the United States and used the fair to launch its redesigned 1959 models. The "Altogether New" '59 Fords were awarded a Gold Medal, at the Fair, by the Comité Francais de L'Elégance, which honored the cars' distinctiveness of style and beautiful proportions. Even now, many Ford enthusiasts and collectors consider the 1959 Fords to be the most beautifully styled Fords ever built. With elegance and understated class, the cars showed remarkably good taste. At a time when other automakers were designing cars that looked capable of interstellar travel or supersonic speeds, Ford exercised great restraint. The designers swept the rear fender feature lines to the back of the car, formed a housing for the back-up lights and curved the lower portion around an oversized taillight for a startling effect. At the front end, a new full-width grille featured an insert with a pattern of "floating" stylized stars. The parking lights were recessed into the bumper. The flat-top front fenders hooded dual headlights. They had a sculptured effect along the sides of the front fender and doors and rolled over the side trim. An exceptionally flat hood characterized these long, low cars. Bright new colors were offered. The Custom 300 series was the base trim level for 1959. These cars wore no series nameplates, but had a Ford crest medallion on the rear deck lid. "Tee Ball" front fender ornaments were optional, as were four "Flying Dart" rear quarter panel ornaments. The side trim consisted of a single molding running back along the front fender/door feature line, then curving upwards the top of the tail fin which it trimmed straight back to the rear of the car. The Business Tudor, Tudor and Fordor were offered as Custom 300 Sixes. All three were available as Custom 300 V-8 models for $110 additional. This year, the big Fords were available with a choice of four engines, starting with the Mileage Maker Six. The 292-cid Thunderbird V-8 had a two-barrel carburetor. Next came the 332-cid Thunderbird Special V-8, also with a two-barrel carb and a higher 8.9:1 compression ratio. The top option was the 352-cid 300-hp Thunderbird Special with a four-barrel Holley carburetor and even higher compression ratio. Selling features highlighted for '59 included Ford's rugged "Lifeguard" design with a husky frame that spread out a full foot wider around the passenger compartment for greater side-impact protection. Automatic Ride Control teamed a new front suspension with Tyrex tires and the variable-rate rear suspension for a smoother, better-controlled ride. A lighter, simplified version of Ford-O-Matic Drive promised satin-smooth shifting and greater durability.

Fairlane — Series A9 / Series U9 — (Six and V-8): The Fairlane model was the intermediate trim level for 1959 and included the following

1959 Ford Custom 300 four-door Sedan (OCW)

1959 Ford Custom 300 two-door Sedan (OCW)

1959 Ford Custom 300 two-door Business Coupe (OCW)

features that were not standard on Custom 300s: chrome window moldings, a chrome horn ring, two sun visors and armrests on all doors. The Fairlane name appeared on the rear fenders. On these cars, there was a second molding on the front fender and door that flared slightly outwards as it ran rearwards. It ran farther back than the upper molding and a curved piece joined the two. This piece created a bullet-shaped pattern at the front of the rear fender "tube." Painted finish within the two front fender/door moldings was standard and an aluminum insert was optional. The rear deck lid had a bright metal "V" with a gold aluminum insert in the area below the Fairlane name only. Fairlanes included the Tudor Special sedan and Fordor Special sedan.

Fairlane 500 — Series A9 / Series U9 — (Six and V-8): Early in the 1959 model year, Ford's top-of-the-line car was the Fairlane 500. It included all Fairlane trim as well as the aluminum insert between the front moldings. The "Fairlane 500" name appeared at the extreme rear end of the rear fender tubes. In addition, a large, finely-ribbed aluminum panel surrounded the rear wheel opening and ran to the rear bumper. Optional stainless steel fender skirts could be ordered to expand the large expanse of bright metal trim. The rear deck lid was trimmed with a huge chrome V molding that ran from tail fin to tail fin and had the Fairlane 500 name above the center of the "vee." Five Fairlane 500 Sixes were available: the Tudor Special sedan, the Fordor Special sedan, the Tudor Victoria hardtop, the Fordor Victoria hardtop and the Sunliner convertible. The V-8 series offered all of these models for $110 additional, plus the Skyliner retractable hardtop.

Galaxie — Series A9 / Series U9 — (Six and V-8): Shortly after Ford made its new model introductions on Oct. 17, 1958, the Galaxie lineup was introduced. This was a trimmed as a Fairlane 500 sub-series, as it carried the Fairlane 500 name on the deck lid, but the Galaxie name on the rear fender tubes. Like the Fairlane 500 line, the Galaxie series had five six-cylinder cars and six V-8s including the Skyliner. However, some models had different names. The two-door sedan was called the Tudor Club Sedan. The four-door sedan was called the Fordor Town Sedan. The hardtop coupe was called the Club Victoria and the four-door hardtop was called the Town Victoria. The Sunliner and Skyliner names were retained. The difference between the Galaxie and the Fairlane 500 was the styling of the top. Galaxies used the standard top with a Thunderbird style "C" pillar. This combination created one of the best looking cars ever to come out of Dearborn. Galaxies were priced $48 higher than comparable Fairlane 500 models.

Station Wagon — Series A9 / Series U9 — (Six and V-8): The Ranch Wagons were the base trim level two-door and four-door station wagons for 1959. The Del Rio Ranch Wagon was a slightly fancier version of the two-door wagon. It was essentially the two-door Ranch wagon with Country Sedan trim. Country Sedans were the intermediate trim level, comparable to Fairlanes. Country Squires were the top trim level. Their level of equipment paralleled Fairlane 500 and Galaxie models. Again, the 12 wagons were sold with a relatively narrow $500 price spread between the low- and high-end models.

VIN:

Ford's coding system for serial numbers can be broken down, as follows: The first symbol designates the engine type: (A) 223-cid six-cylinder, (B) 332-cid V-8, (C) 292-cid V-8, (H) 352-cid V-8, (J) 430-cid V-8. The second symbol designates the model year: "9" for 1959. The third symbol designates the final assembly plant, as follows: A = Atlanta, C = Chester, D = Dallas, G = Chicago, F= Dearborn, E = Mawhah, H = Loraine, K = Kansas City, L = Long Beach, N = Norfolk, R = San Jose, U = Louisville, P = Twin City (St. Paul). The fourth symbol designates body type, as follows: C = Convertible, G = Custom 300 (two-door and four-door), R = Ranch Wagon, Country Sedan, S = Fairlane 500, Galaxie (two-door and four-door), T = Fairlane (two-door and four-door), V = Fairlane 500 (two-door and four-door), W = Retractable hardtop, Y = Country Squire. The fifth through tenth digits indicate the number of the unit built at each assembly plant, beginning with 100001. Custom 300 six-cylinder models began with the designation "A9" followed by assembly plant code, body type code, and, finally, the unit's production number, according to the final assembly location. Each plant began at 100001 and went up.

Custom 300 (Six)

Model No.	Body/ Style No.	Body Type & Seating	Factory Price	Shipping Weight	Production Total
A9	58E	4-dr. Sedan-6P	$2,180	3,385 lbs.	107,061
A9	64F	2-dr. Sedan-6P	$2,294	3,310 lbs.	120,412
A9	64G	2-dr. Business Tudor-3P	$2,207	3,203 lbs.	3,257

Custom 300 (V-8)

U9	58E	4-dr. Sedan-6P	$2,466	3,486 lbs.	142,492
U9	64F	2-dr. Sedan-6P	$2,412	3,411 lbs.	108,161
U9	64G	2-dr. Business Tudor-3P	$2,325	3,384 lbs.	827

Fairlane (Six)

A9	58A	4-dr. Town Sedan-6P	$2,486	3,415 lbs.	10,564
A9	64A	2-dr. Club Sedan-6P	$2,432	3,332 lbs.	8,197

Fairlane (V-8)

U9	58A	4-dr. Town Sedan-6P	$2,604	3,516 lbs.	54,099
U9	64A	2-dr. Club Sedan-6P	$2,550	3,433 lbs.	26,929

Fairlane 500 (Six)

A9	58B	4-dr. Town Sedan-6P	$2,605	3,417 lbs.	2,118
A9	64B	2-dr. Club Sedan-6P	$2,551	3,338 lbs.	804
A9	63A	2-dr. Victoria Hardtop-6P	$2,612	3,365 lbs.	717
A9	57A	4-dr. Victoria Hardtop-6P	$2,677	3,451 lbs.	414

Fairlane 500 (V-8)

U9	58B	4-dr. Town Sedan-6P	$2,723	3,518 lbs.	33,552
U9	64B	2-dr. Club Sedan-6P	$2,669	3,439 lbs.	9,337
U9	63A	2-dr. Victoria Hardtop-6P	$2,730	3,466 lbs.	23,175
U9	57A	4-dr. Victoria Hardtop-6P	$2,795	3,552 lbs.	8,894

Galaxie (Six)

A9	54A	4-dr. Town Sedan-6P	$2,657	3,405 lbs.	8,314
A9	64H	2-dr. Club Sedan-6P	$2,603	3,338 lbs.	5,609
A9	65A	2-dr. Victoria Hardtop-6P	$2,664	3,377 lbs.	4,312
A9	75A	4-dr. Victoria Hardtop-6P	$2,729	3,494 lbs.	1,216
A9	76B	2-dr. Sunliner-6P	$2,914	3,527 lbs.	1,385

Galaxie (V-8)

U9	54A	4-dr. Town Sedan-6P	$2,775	3,506 lbs.	174,794
U9	64H	2-dr. Club Sedan-6P	$2,721	3,439 lbs.	47,239
U9	65A	2-dr. Victoria Hardtop-6P	$2,782	3,478 lbs.	117,557
U9	75A	4-dr. Victoria Hardtop-6P	$2,847	3,595 lbs.	46,512
U9	76B	2-dr. Sunliner-6P	$3,032	3,628 lbs.	44,483
U9	51A	2-dr. Skyliner-6P	$3,421	4,064 lbs.	12,915

Station Wagon (Six)

A9	59C	2-dr. Ranch Wagon-6P	$2,642	3,590 lbs.	21,540
A9	71H	4-dr. Ranch Wagon-6P	$2,709	3,685 lbs.	25,359
A9	59D	2-dr. Del Rio Wagon-6P	$2,753	3,613 lbs.	1,430
A9	71F	4-dr. Country Sedan-6P	$2,820	3,718 lbs.	6,831
A9	71E	4-dr. Country Sedan-8P	$2,904	3,767 lbs.	3,339
A9	71G	4-dr. Country Squire-8P	$3,033	3,758 lbs.	545

Station Wagon (V-8)

U9	59C	2-dr. Ranch Wagon-6P	$2,760	3,691 lbs.	24,049
U9	71H	4-dr. Ranch Wagon-6P	$2,827	3,786 lbs.	41,979
U9	59D	2-dr. Del Rio Wagon-6P	$2,871	3,714 lbs.	7,233
U9	71F	4-dr. Country Sedan-6P	$2,938	3,819 lbs.	87,770
U9	71E	4-dr. Country Sedan-8P	$3,032	3,868 lbs.	25,472
U9	71G	4-dr. Country Squire-8P	$3,151	3,859 lbs.	23,791

Engines:

Base Six: Overhead valve. Cast-iron block. Displacement: 223 cid. B & S: 3.62 x 3.60 in. Compression ratio: 8.6:1. Brake hp: 145 at 4000 rpm. Carburetor: Holley one-barrel. Four main bearings. Code A.

Base V-8: Overhead valve. Cast-iron block. B & S: 3.75 x 3.30 in. Displacement: 292 cid. Compression ratio: 8.80:1. Brake hp: 200 at 4400 rpm. Taxable hp: 45.0. Torque: 285 lbs.-ft. at 2200 rpm. Five main bearings. Solid valve lifters. Crankcase capacity: 5 qt. (add 1 qt. with new oil filter). Cooling system capacity: 19 qt. Carburetor: Ford two-barrel Model 5752306 and 5752307. Code C.

332 Special V-8: Overhead valve. Cast-iron block. B & S: 4.00 x 3.30 in. Displacement: 332 cid. Compression ratio: 8.90:1. Brake hp: 225 at 4400 rpm. Taxable hp: 51.2. Torque: 325 lbs.-ft. at 2200 rpm. Five main bearings. Hydraulic valve lifters. Crankcase capacity: 5 qt. (add 1 qt. with new oil filter). Cooling system capacity: 19 qt. Carburetor: Holley two-barrel Model R-1843A with standard transmission, R-1844A with automatic transmission or R-1929-AAS as a field service unit. Code B.

Thunderbird 352 Special V-8: Overhead valve. Cast-iron block. B & S: 4.00 x 3.50 in. Displacement: 352 cid. Compression ratio: 10.2:1. Brake hp: 300 at 4600 rpm. Taxable hp: 51.2. Torque: 395 lbs.-ft. at 2800 rpm. Five main bearings. Hydraulic valve lifters. Crankcase capacity: 5 qt. (add 1 qt. with new oil filter). Cooling system capacity: 19.5 qt. Dual exhaust. Carburetor: Ford four-barrel Model 5752304 and 5752305 or Holley four-barrel. Code H.

Thunderbird 430 Special V-8 (Cruise-O-Matic only): Overhead valve. Cast-iron block. B & S: 4.30 x 3.70 in. Displacement: 430 cid.

Compression ratio: 10.0:1. Brake hp: 350 at 4600 rpm. Taxable hp: 51.2. Torque: 490 lbs.-ft. at 2800 rpm. Five main bearings. Hydraulic valve lifters. Crankcase capacity: 5 qt. (add 1 qt. with new oil filter). Cooling system capacity: 19.5 qt. Dual exhaust. Carburetor: Holley four-barrel Model 4160-C. Code J.

Chassis:

Custom 300: Wheelbase: 118 in. Overall length: 208 in. Overall width: 76.6 in. Tires: 7.50 x 14 four-ply tubeless.

Fairlane. Fairlane 500, Galaxie: Wheelbase: 118 in. Overall length: 208 in. and 208.1 in., Skyliner. Overall width: 76.6 in. Tires: 7.50 x 14 four-ply tubeless and 6.00 x 14 four-ply tubeless, Skyliner and Sunliner with automatic transmission.

Station Wagon: Wheelbase: 118 in. Overall length: 208 in. Overall width: 76.6 in. Tires: 7.50 x 14 four-ply tubeless and 6.00 x 14 four-ply tubeless, nine-passenger station wagon.

Technical:

Custom 300: Three-speed manual transmission was standard. It featured a semi-centrifugal-type clutch, three-speed helical gears and synchronizers for second and third gears. Three-speed with automatic overdrive was optional. Specifications were the same as above with automatic overdrive function cutting in at 27 mph, cutting out at 21 mph. Approximate drive ratio: 0.70:1. Manual control below instrument panel. Ford-O-Matic transmission was also optional. This was a torque converter transmission with automatic planetary gear train, single-stage, three-element hydraulic torque converter, hydro-mechanical

1959 Ford Fairlane 500 Town Victoria four-door hardtop (OCW)

1959 Ford Fairlane 500 Club Victoria two-door hardtop (OCW)

1959 Ford Galaxie Club Victoria two-door hardtop (OCW)

1959 Ford Galaxie Sunliner two-door Convertible (OCW)

controls with no electric or vacuum connections and power flow through fluid member at all times. Six-cylinder rear axle gear ratios: (Ford-O-Matic) 3.56:1, (manual transmission) 3.56:1, (optional with automatic overdrive) 3.56:1. V-8 rear axle gear ratios: (Ford-O-Matic with 292-cid V-8) 3.10:1, (Ford-O-Matic with 332/352-cid V-8) 2.91:1, (Cruise-O-Matic with 292-cid V-8) 3.10:1, (Cruise-O-Matic with 332-cid V-8) 2.91:1, Cruise-O-Matic with 352-cid V-8) 2.69:1, (manual transmission) 3.56:1. Equa-Lock rear axle gear ratios: 3.70:1 or 3.10:1.

Fairlane, Fairlane 500, Galaxie: Three-speed manual transmission was standard. It featured a semi-centrifugal-type clutch, three-speed helical gears and synchronizers for second and third gears. Three-speed with automatic overdrive was optional. Specifications were the same as above with automatic overdrive function cutting in at 27 mph, cutting out at 21 mph. Approximate drive ratio: 0.70:1. Manual control below instrument panel. Ford-O-Matic transmission was also optional. This was a torque converter transmission with automatic planetary gear train, single-stage, three-element hydraulic torque converter, hydro-mechanical controls with no electric or vacuum connections and power flow through fluid member at all times. Six-cylinder rear axle gear ratios: (Ford-O-Matic) 3.56:1, (manual transmission) 3.56:1, (optional with automatic overdrive) 3.56:1. V-8 rear axle gear ratios: (Ford-O-Matic with 292-cid V-8) 3.10:1, (Ford-O-Matic with 332/352-cid V-8) 2.91:1, (Cruise-O-Matic with 292-cid V-8) 3.10:1, (Cruise-O-Matic with 332-cid V-8) 2.91:1, (Cruise-O-Matic with 352-cid V-8) 2.69:1, (manual transmission) 3.56:1. Equa-Lock rear axle gear ratios: 3.70:1 or 3.10:1.

Station Wagon: Three-speed manual transmission was standard. It featured a semi-centrifugal-type clutch, three-speed helical gears and synchronizers for second and third gears. Three-speed with automatic overdrive was optional. Specifications were the same as above with automatic overdrive function cutting in at 27 mph, cutting out at 21 mph. Approximate drive ratio: 0.70:1. Manual control below instrument panel. Ford-O-Matic transmission was also optional. This was a torque converter transmission with automatic planetary gear train, single-stage, three-element hydraulic torque converter, hydro-mechanical controls with no electric or vacuum connections and power flow through fluid member at all times. Six-cylinder rear axle gear ratios: (Ford-O-Matic) 3.56:1, (manual transmission) 3.56:1, (optional with automatic overdrive) 3.56:1. V-8 rear axle gear ratios: (Ford-O-Matic with 292-cid V-8) 3.10:1, (Ford-O-Matic with 332/352-cid V-8) 2.91:1, (Cruise-O-Matic with 292-cid V-8) 3.10:1, (Cruise-O-Matic with 332-cid V-8) 2.91:1, (Cruise-O-Matic with 352-cid V-8) 2.69:1, (manual transmission) 3.56:1. Equa-Lock rear axle gear ratios: 3.70:1 or 3.10:1.

Ford-O-Matic ($190). Cruise-O-Matic ($231). Automatic overdrive ($108). Power brakes ($43). Power steering ($75). Front and rear power window lifts ($102). Four-Way power seat ($64). Radio and push-button antenna ($59). Signal-seeking radio and antenna ($83). Fresh Air heater and defroster ($75). Recirculating heater and defroster ($48). White sidewall tires, four-ply, 7.50 x 14 ($33), 8.00 x 14 ($50). Wheel covers as option ($17). Styletone two-tone paint ($26). Tinted glass ($26). Back-up lights ($10). Custom 300 and Ranch Wagon Deluxe ornamentation package ($32). Electric clock ($15). Windshield washer ($14). Two-speed windshield wipers ($7). Lifeguard safety package including padded instrument panel and sun visor ($19), plus pair of front seat safety belts ($21). Polar Air Conditioner, with tinted glass ($271). Select Aire Conditioner, with tinted glass ($404). Heavy-duty 70-amp battery ($6). Equa-Lock differential ($39). Four-way manual seat ($17). Fairlane side molding ($11). Fairlane 500 rocker panel molding ($11). Thunderbird Special 332 cid/225 hp V-8 ($141 over base six). Thunderbird Special 352 cid/300 hp V-8 ($167 over base six). Standard 292-cid two-barrel V-8, all except Skyliner ($118).

History:

Model-year production of Fords and Thunderbird was 1,462,140 units, which was not enough to top Chevrolet's 1,481,071. Fords were 25 percent of the industry's output. Calendar-year output was 1,352,112

1959 Ford Galaxie two-door **Skyliner Retractable** (OCW)

1959 Ford two-door **Ranch Wagon** (OCW)

1959 Ford four-door **Ranch Wagon** (OCW)

1959 Ford four-door **Country Sedan 9P** (OCW)

1959 Ford four-door **Country Sedan 6P** (OCW)

1959 Ford Fairlane 500 **Sunliner two-door Convertible** (OCW)

1959 Ford Fairlane 500 two-door **Skyliner Retractable** (OCW)

1959 Ford four-door Country Squire (OCW)

Fords, 100,757 Falcons, and 75,723 Thunderbirds and that was higher than the calendar-year total of Chevys, Corvettes and Corvairs. As you can see, the calendar-year numbers include 1960 cars built in the fall of 1959. In March 1958, Ford reported it had *reduced* the cost of making an automobile by $94 per unit between 1954 and 1958. On a model year basis, 78.1 percent of all 1959 Fords had V-8 power and 71.7 percent featured automatic transmission.

1960 Ford

Falcon — Series S — (Six): The Falcon was Ford's contribution to the compact-car field. While being nearly three feet shorter overall than the full-size Fords, the Falcon offered an interior spacious enough for occupants more than six-feet tall. The compact station wagon offered more than enough cargo space for the majority of buyers. Falcon styling was simple and ultra-conservative. The body was slab-sided, with just a slightly recessed feature line. Two single headlights were mounted inside the grille opening and the grille itself was an aluminum stamping consisting of horizontal and vertical bars. The name Ford appeared on the hood, in front of the power bulge-type simulated scoop. At the rear, the word Falcon, in block letters, appeared between the two round taillights. Standard Falcon equipment included turn signals, a left-hand sun visor and five black tubeless tires.

Falcon Deluxe — Series S — (Six) A Deluxe trim package was a popular $65.80 option for the Falcon.

Fairlane — Series V — (Six and V-8): Fords were totally redesigned from the ground up for 1960. They shared nothing with the previous models except engines and drivelines. While 1960 styling was considered controversial by many, it remains one of the smoothest designs ever to come from the Dearborn drawing boards. The new models were longer, lower and wider than their predecessors and were restrained, especially when compared to some of their contemporaries. All 1960 Fords featured a single chrome strip from the top of the front bumper, sweeping up to the top of the front fender, then back, horizontally along the beltline, to the back of the car. There it turned inward and capped the small horizontal fin. Large semi-circular taillights were housed in an aluminum escutcheon panel below the fins and directly above a large chrome bumper. At the front end, a large, recessed mesh grille housed the dual headlights. In 1960, the Fairlane name was used on the lower-priced full-size models. The Fairlane series contained the word Ford spaced along the recessed section of the full-width hood and

1960 Ford Falcon two-door Sedan (PH)

1960 Ford Falcon four-door Sedan (PH)

used four cast stripes along the rear quarter panel for trim. The Fairlane series was the base trim level for 1960 and included a Fairlane script on the sides of the front fenders. There were chrome moldings around the windshield and rear windows, two sun visors, armrests on all doors and no extra chrome side trim. Standard Fairlane equipment included electric windshield wipers, an oil-bath air cleaner, an oil filter, dual sun visors, a cigarette lighter and five black tubeless tires.

Fairlane 500 — Series V — (Six and V-8): The Fairlane 500 was the intermediate trim level and included all the Fairlane trim plus five "delta wing" chrome stripes on the rear fenders (only on two-door Club Sedans) and the Fairlane crest on the hood. Standard Fairlane 500 equipment included electric windshield wipers, an oil-bath air cleaner, an oil filter, dual sun visors, a cigarette lighter and five black tubeless tires

Galaxie — Series V — (Six and V-8): The Galaxie and Galaxie Special series were the top trim levels for 1960. They included chrome "A" pillar moldings and chrome window moldings. A single chrome strip began near the center of the front door and continued back to the taillights on the side. There was also ribbed aluminum stone shields behind the rear wheels, a Galaxie script on the front fenders, a Galaxie script on the trunk lid and a Ford crest on the hood. Standard Galaxie equipment included electric windshield wipers, an oil-bath air cleaner, an oil filter, dual sun visors, a cigarette lighter, five black tubeless tires, back-up lights and an electric clock.

Galaxie Special — Series V — (Six and V-8): The Galaxie Special series included the Starliner and Sunliner with all the high-level trim, except that the Galaxie script on the trunk lid was replaced with either the Sunliner or Starliner script. Standard Galaxie Special equipment included electric windshield wipers, an oil-bath air cleaner, an oil filter, dual sun visors, a cigarette lighter, five black tubeless tires, back-up lights and an electric clock.

Station Wagon — Series V — (Six and V-8): The Ranch Wagon was the base trim level station wagon. Country Sedans were the intermediate level of station wagons with more trim and equipment. Country Squires were the top trim level. The level of equipment paralleled Fairlane, Fairlane 500 and Galaxie models of passenger cars.

VIN (Falcon):

The VIN for Falcons was die-stamped into the surface of the left-hand brace between the top of the firewall and the left front wheel housing. The first symbol indicates year: 0 = 1960. The second symbol identifies assembly plant, as follows: A=Atlanta, Georgia, C=Chester, Pennsylvania, D=Dallas, Texas, E=Mahwah, New Jersey, F=Dearborn, Michigan, G=Chicago, Illinois, H=Loraine, Ohio, J=Los Angeles, California, K=Kansas City, Kansas, N = Norfolk, Virginia, P=Twin Cities, Minnesota, R=San Jose, S=Pilot Plant, T=Metuchen, New Jersey, U=Louisville, Kentucky, Y=Wixom, Michigan. The third and fourth symbols identify body series (see second column of tables). The fifth symbol identifies engine code, as follows: S=144-cid six-cylinder, D=144-cid low-compression six-cylinder. The last six digits are the unit's production number, beginning at 100001 and going up, at each of the assembly plants.

VIN (Ford):

The VIN for full-size Fords was die-stamped into the top right-hand of the frame ahead of the front suspension member. The first symbol indicates year: 0 = 1960. The second symbol identifies assembly plant, as follows: A=Atlanta, Georgia, C=Chester, Pennsylvania, D=Dallas, Texas, E=Mahwah, New Jersey, F=Dearborn, Michigan, G=Chicago, Illinois, H=Loraine, Ohio, J=Los Angeles, California, K=Kansas City, Kansas, N = Norfolk, Virginia, P=Twin Cities, Minnesota, R=San Jose, S=Pilot Plant, T=Metuchen, New Jersey, U=Louisville, Kentucky, Y=Wixom, Michigan. The third and fourth symbols identify body series (see second column of tables). The fifth symbol identifies engine code, as follows: V=223-cid six-cylinder, W=292-cid V-8, X=352-cid V-8 with two-barrel carburetor, Y=352-cid V-8 with four-barrel carburetor, T=292-cid export V-8 and G=352-cid export V-8. The last six digits are the unit's production number, beginning at 100001 and going up, at each of the assembly plants.

1960 Ford Falcon two-door Station Wagon (PH)

Falcon Standard (Six)

Model No.	Body/Style No.	Body Type & Seating	Factory Price	Shipping Weight	Production Total
S	58A	4-dr. Sedan-6P	$2,042	2,317 lbs.	45,164
S	64A	2-dr. Sedan-6P	$1,980	2,282 lbs.	73,325
S	71A	2-dr. Station Wagon-6P	$2,355	2,275 lbs.	16,272
S	59A	2-dr. Station Wagon-6P	$2,293	2,540 lbs.	14,299

Falcon Deluxe (Six)

S	58A	4-dr. Sedan-6P	$2,108	2,317 lbs.	122,732
S	64A	2-dr. Sedan-6P	$2,046	2,282 lbs.	120,149
S	71A	2-dr. Station Wagon-6P	$2,421	2,275 lbs.	30,486
S	59A	2-dr. Station Wagon-6P	$2,245	2,540 lbs.	13,253

Fairlane (Six)

B0	32	4-dr. Sedan-6P	$2,386	3,606 lbs.	68,607
B0	31	2-dr. Sedan-6P	$2,332	3,606 lbs.	69,086
B0	32	2-dr. Business Tudor-3P	$2,245	3,507 lbs.	1,458

Fairlane (V-8)

V0	32	4-dr. Sedan-6P	$2,499	3,706 lbs.	41,294
V0	31	2-dr. Sedan-6P	$2,445	3,632 lbs.	24,173
V0	32	2-dr. Business Tudor-3P	$2,358	3,607 lbs.	275

Fairlane 500 (Six)

B0	42	4-dr. Town Sedan-6P	$2,463	3,610 lbs.	45,626
B0	41	2-dr. Club Sedan-6P	$2,409	3,536 lbs.	43,962

Fairlane 500 (V-8)

V0	42	4-dr. Town Sedan-6P	$2,576	3,710 lbs.	107,608
V0	41	2-dr. Club Sedan-6P	$2,522	3,636 lbs.	47,079

Galaxie (Six)

B0	52	4-dr. Town Sedan-6P	$2,678	3,634 lbs.	6,783
B0	51	2-dr. Club Sedan-6P	$2,624	3,553 lbs.	6,009
B0	54	4-dr. Victoria-6P	$2,750	3,642 lbs.	1,462

Galaxie (V-8)

V0	52	4-dr. Town Sedan-6P	$2,791	3,734 lbs.	98,001
V0	51	2-dr. Club Sedan-6P	$2,737	3,653 lbs.	25,767
V0	54	4-dr. Victoria-6P	$2,863	3,742 lbs.	37,753

Galaxie Special (Six)

B0	53	2-dr. Victoria-6P	$2,685	2,672 lbs.	2,672
B0	55	2-dr. Sunliner-6P	$2,935	2,689 lbs.	2,689

Galaxie Special (V-8)

V0	53	2-dr. Victoria-6P	$2,798	3,667 lbs.	65,969
V0	55	2-dr. Sunliner-6P	$3,048	3,841 lbs.	42,073

Station Wagon (Six)

B0	61	2-dr. Ranch Wagon-6P	$2,661	3,831 lbs.	18,287
B0	62	4-dr. Ranch Wagon-6P	$2,731	3,948 lbs.	21,154
B0	64	4-dr. Country Sedan-6P	$2,827	3,962 lbs.	5,081
B0	66	4-dr. Country Sedan-8P	$2,912	4,008 lbs.	3,409
B0	68	4-dr. Country Squire-8P	$3,042	4,022 lbs.	577

Station Wagon (Six)

V0	61	2-dr. Ranch Wagon-6P	$2,774	3,931 lbs.	8,849
V0	62	4-dr. Ranch Wagon-6P	$2,844	4,048 lbs.	22,718
V0	64	4-dr. Country Sedan-6P	$2,940	4,062 lbs.	54,221
V0	66	4-dr. Country Sedan-8P	$3,025	4,108 lbs.	15,868
V0	68	4-dr. Country Squire-8P	$3,155	4,122 lbs.	21,660

Engines:

Falcon Six: Overhead valve. Cast-iron block. Displacement: 144 cid. B & S: 3.50 x 2.50 in. Compression ratio: 8.7:1. Brake hp: 85 at 4200 rpm. Carburetor: Holley one-barrel. Four main bearings. Code S, (D on export models).

Ford Six: Overhead valve. Cast-iron block. Displacement: 223 cid. B & S: 3.62 x 3.60 in. Compression ratio: 8.4:1. Brake hp: 145 at 4000 rpm. Carburetor: Holley single barrel. Four main bearings. Code V.

Base V-8: Overhead valve. Cast-iron block. B & S: 3.75 x 3.30 in. Displacement: 292 cid. Compression ratio: 8.80:1. Brake hp: 185 at 4200 rpm. Taxable hp: 45.0. Torque: 292 at 2200 rpm. Five main bearings. Solid valve lifters. Crankcase capacity: 5 qt. (add 1 qt. with new oil filter). Cooling system capacity: 19 qt. Carburetor: Ford-Holley two-barrel Model COAE-9510-M with standard transmission or COAE-9510-H with automatic transmission. Code W.

Interceptor V-8: Overhead valve. Cast-iron block. B & S: 4.00 x 3.50 in. Displacement: 352 cid. Compression ratio: 8.90:1. Brake hp: 235 at 4400 rpm. Taxable hp: 51.2. Torque: 350 lbs.-ft. at 2400 rpm. Five main bearings. Hydraulic valve lifters. Crankcase capacity: 5 qt. (add 1 qt. with new oil filter). Cooling system capacity: 19.5 qt. Dual exhaust. Carburetor: Ford-Holley two-barrel Model COAE-9510-R with standard transmission or COAE-9510-S with automatic transmission. Code X (Export code G).

Interceptor Special V-8: Overhead valve. Cast-iron block. B & S: 4.00 x 3.50 in. Displacement: 352 cid. Compression ratio: 9.60:1. Brake hp: 300 at 4600 rpm. Taxable hp: 51.2. Torque: 381 lbs.-ft. at 2800 rpm. Five main bearings. Hydraulic valve lifters. Crankcase capacity: 5 qt. (add 1 qt. with new oil filter). Cooling system capacity: 19.5 qt. Dual exhaust. Carburetor: Ford-Holley four-barrel Model COAE-9510-J with standard transmission or COAE-9510-K with automatic transmission. Code Y.

Note: This engine was not mentioned in early 1960 Ford literature. It had an aluminum intake and a Holley carburetor. This engine was not available in cars with power steering or power brakes.

Interceptor Special V-8: Overhead valve. Cast-iron block. B & S: 4.00 x 3.50 in. Displacement: 352 cid. Compression ratio: 10.60:1. Brake hp: 360. Taxable hp: 51.2. Five main bearings. Hydraulic valve lifters. Crankcase capacity: 5 qt. (add 1 qt. with new oil filter). Cooling system capacity: 19.5 qt. Dual exhaust with special header-type exhaust manifolds. Aluminum intake manifold. Dual point distributor. Carburetor: Holley four-barrel. Code Y.

Chassis:

Falcon: Wheelbase: 109.5 in. Overall length: 181.2 in., car and 189 in., station wagon. Overall width: 70 in. Overall height: 54.5 in. Tires: 6.00 x 13, car and 6.50 x 13, station wagon.

Ford: Wheelbase: 119 in. Overall length: 213.7 in. Overall width: 81.5 in. Overall height: 55 in. Tires: 7.50 x 14, most cars and 8.00 x 14, convertible and station wagon.

Options:

Falcon: Heavy-duty battery ($7.60). Deluxe trim package ($65.80). Fresh Air heater/defroster ($67.80). Two-tone paint ($16.80). Manual radio and antenna ($54.05). Safety equipment: padded dash and visors ($19.20). Front seat safety belts ($20.60). Whitewall tires ($28.70). Automatic transmission ($159.40). Wheel covers ($16). Windshield washer ($13.70). Electric windshield wiper ($9.65).

Ford: Standard 185-hp V-8 engine ($113.00). Two-barrel 235-hp V-8 ($147.80). Four-barrel 300-hp V-8 ($177.40). Polar Air conditioning, including tinted glass and V-8 ($270.90). Select Air conditioning, including tinted glass and V-8 ($403.80). Back-up lights ($10.70). Heavy-duty 70-amp battery ($7.60). Equa-Lock differential ($14.60). Fresh Air heater/defroster ($75.10). Recirculating heater/defroster ($46.90). Four-way manual seat ($17.00). Rocker panel molding ($14.20). Padded dash and visors ($24.30). Two-tone paint ($19.40). Power brakes ($43.20). Power seat ($63.80). Power steering ($76.50). Front and rear power windows ($102.10). Push-button radio and antenna ($58.50). Front seat belts ($20.60). Tinted glass ($43.00). Cruise-O-Matic ($211.10). Ford-O-Matic with six-cylinder ($179.80). Ford-O-Matic with V-8 ($189.60). Overdrive ($108.40). Wheel covers ($16.60). Windshield washer ($13.70). Two-speed windshield wipers ($9.70). Five 7.50 x 14 black sidewall tires standard all models except convertible, wagons and all models equipped

1960 Ford Falcon four-door Station Wagon (OCW)

1960 Ford Falcon four-door Sedan (PH)

with 235- or 300-hp V-8s (no charge) . Five 7.50 x 14 white sidewall tires for all models using standard 7.50 x 14 black sidewall tires ($32.60 additional). Five 8.00 x 14 black sidewall tires standard on convertibles, wagons and cars with 235-hp or 300-hp V-8 (no charge). Five 8.00 x 14 white sidewall tires on convertibles or wagons or 235- and 300-hp cars having 8.00 x 14 black sidewall tires as standard equipment ($35.70 extra). Five 8.00 x 14 white sidewall tires on other Fords ($49.00).

History:

All three lines of 1960 Fords were introduced to the public on October 8, 1959. Falcon station wagons were added to the new compact series in March 1960. Although Ford did not provide production breakouts by engine type, trade publications recorded that 67.5 percent of all Fords (excluding Thunderbirds and Falcons) had V-8 engines installed. All Falcons were sixes. Automatic transmissions were installed in 67.1 percent of all Fords, 44.5 percent of all Falcons and 97.9 percent of all Thunderbirds built during the model run. Ford's share of the overall automobile market dropped to 22.55 percent this year, compared

1960 Ford Fairlane 500 four-door Town Sedan (OCW)

1960 Ford Galaxie four-door Town Sedan (OCW)

1960 Ford Galaxie Town Victoria four-door hardtop(OCW)

1960 Ford Galaxie Special Starliner two-door hardtop (OCW)

1960 Ford Galaxie Special Sunliner two-door Convertible (PH)

to 27.33 percent in 1959. Model year production peaked at 911,034 Fords and 435,676 Falcons. Model year series production was as follows: (Custom 300) 900, (Fairlane) 204,700, (Fairlane 500) 244,300, (Galaxie) 289,200, (station wagon) 171,800. Just 297,400 six-cylinder Fords were produced for the model year.

1960 Ford Sunliner (OCW)

1960 Ford four-door Country Squire (PH)

1961 Ford

Falcon — Series S/U — (Six): The Falcon continued unchanged from 1961, with the exception of a new convex grille. A new 170-cid six-cylinder engine was added to the lineup and the Futura two-door sedan was added to give a sporty flair to the compact car line. The Futura used the same body shell as the Falcon Tudor Sedan, but it was equipped with a bucket seat interior and a center console. Standard Falcon equipment included turn signals, a left-hand sun visor and five 6.00 x 13 black sidewall tubeless tires. Station wagons used 6.50 x 13 tires.

Fairlane — Series V — (Six and V-8): Model-year 1961 saw the third major restyling of the full-size Ford line in as many years. From the beltline down, the 1961 Fords were completely new. The upper body structure was retained from the 1960 lineup. A full-width concave grille with a horizontal dividing bar highlighted front end styling. The Ford name, in block letters, replaced the crest used in previous years on Fairlane models and the series designation appeared on the front fenders, behind the headlights. The horizontal full-length fin, used in 1960, was replaced with a smaller canted fin, nearly identical in size and shape to the fin used on 1957 and 1958 Custom series cars. Large, round taillights were used once again. A horizontal chrome strip, similar to one used on 1960 models, was used once again. The year 1961 saw the beginning of the great horsepower race of the 1960s, and Ford cracked the magic 400-hp barrier with a new 390-cid V-8. The Fairlane series was the base trim level for 1961 and included chrome moldings around the windshield and rear window, two sun visors, a horn button instead of horn ring, an armrest on all doors and no extra side chrome. Standard equipment included electric windshield wipers, an oil-bath air cleaner, an oil filter, dual sun visors, a cigarette lighter and five tubeless black sidewall tires.

Fairlane 500 — Series V — (Six and V-8): The Fairlane 500 was the intermediate trim level and included all the Fairlane trim plus a chrome horn ring and a single horizontal chrome strip running from the back of

1961 Ford Falcon two-door Sedan (OCW)

the front wheel well to the rear bumper. Standard equipment included electric windshield wipers, an oil-bath air cleaner, an oil filter, dual sun visors, a cigarette lighter and five tubeless black sidewall tires.

Galaxie — (Six and V-8): The Galaxie series was the top trim level for 1961 and included chrome "A" pillar moldings, chrome window moldings, horizontal chrome strip on the side of the body, ribbed aluminum stone shield behind the rear wheel opening, a stamped aluminum escutcheon panel between the taillights (duplicating the pattern of the grille) and either Galaxie, Starliner or Sunliner script on the trunk lid. Standard equipment included electric windshield wipers, an oil-bath air cleaner, an oil filter, dual sun visors, a cigarette lighter, back-up lights, an electric clock and five tubeless black sidewall tires.

Station Wagon — (Six and V-8): The Ranch Wagon was the base trim level station wagon, Country Sedans were the intermediate level and Country Squires were the top trim level. The level of equipment paralleled Fairlane, Fairlane 500 and Galaxie models of passenger cars. Standard equipment on all wagons included electric windshield wipers, an oil-bath air cleaner, an oil filter, dual sun visors, a cigarette lighter and five tubeless black sidewall tires. The Country Squire also had back-up lights and an electric clock. Nine-passenger station wagons also had a power tailgate window.

VIN (Falcon):

The VIN for Falcons was die-stamped into the surface of the left-hand brace between the top of the firewall and the left front wheel housing. The first symbol indicates year: 1=1961. The second symbol identifies assembly plant, as follows: A=Atlanta, Georgia, C=Chester, Pennsylvania, D=Dallas, Texas, E=Mahwah, New Jersey, F=Dearborn, Michigan, G=Chicago, Illinois, H=Lorain, Ohio, J=Los Angeles, California, K=Kansas City, Kansas, N=Norfolk, Virginia, P=Twin Cities, Minnesota, R=San Jose, S=Pilot Plant, T=Metuchen, New Jersey, U=Louisville, Kentucky, Y=Wixom, Michigan. The third and fourth symbols identify body series (see second column of tables). The fifth symbol identifies engine code, as follows: S=144-cid six-cylinder, D=144-cid low-compression six-cylinder, U=170-cid six-cylinder. The last six digits are the unit's production number, beginning at 100001 and going up, at each of the assembly plants. Falcons not built at all Ford plants.

VIN (Ford):

The VIN for full-size Fords was die-stamped into the top right-hand of the frame ahead of the front suspension member. The first symbol indicates year: 1=1961. The second symbol identifies assembly plant, as follows: A=Atlanta, Georgia, C=Chester, Pennsylvania, D=Dallas, Texas, E=Mahwah, New Jersey, F=Dearborn, Michigan, G=Chicago, Illinois, H=Lorain, Ohio, J=Los Angeles, California, K=Kansas City, Kansas, N = Norfolk, Virginia, P=Twin Cities, Minnesota, R=San Jose, S=Pilot Plant, T=Metuchen, New Jersey, U=Louisville, Kentucky, Y=Wixom, Michigan. The third and fourth symbols identify body series (see second column of tables). The fifth symbol identifies engine code, as follows: V=223-cid six-cylinder, W=292-cid V-8, X=352-cid V-8 with two-barrel carburetor, Z=390-cid V-8 with four-barrel carburetor, R=390-cid V-8 low-compression, E=170-cid low-compression six-cylinder, Z=390-cid four-barrel high-horsepower V-8, Z=390-cid dual four-barrel carburetor high-horsepower V-8, Z=390-cid four-barrel police V-8. The last six digits are the unit's production number, beginning at 100001 and going up, at each of the assembly plants. Full-size Fords not built at all Ford plants.

1961 Ford Falcon Futura two-door Sedan (OCW)

1961 Ford Falcon four-door Sedan (PH)

Falcon Standard (Six)

Model No.	Body/ Style No.	Body Type & Seating	Factory Price	Shipping Weight	Production Total
S/U	12	4-dr. Sedan-6P	$2,047	2,289 lbs.	55,437
S/U	11	2-dr. Sedan-6P	$1,985	2,254 lbs.	74,292
S/U	22	4-dr. Station Wagon-6P	$2,341	2,558 lbs.	24,445
S/U	21	2-dr. Station Wagon-6P	$2,298	2,525 lbs.	13,940

Falcon Deluxe (Six)

S/U	12	4-dr. Sedan-6P	$2,125	2,289 lbs.	104,324
S/U	11	2-dr. Sedan-6P	$2,063	2,254 lbs.	75,740
S/U	22	4-dr. Station Wagon-6P	$2,419	2,558 lbs.	63,488
S/U	21	2-dr. Station Wagon-6P	$2,376	2,525 lbs.	18,105

Falcon Futura (Six)

S/U	17	2-dr. Futura Sedan-6P	$2,233	2,322 lbs.	44,470

Fairlane (Six)

B0	32	4-dr. Sedan-6P	$2,390	3,585 lbs.	57,282
B0	31	2-dr. Sedan-6P	$2,336	3,487 lbs.	46,471

Fairlane (V-8)

V0	32	4-dr. Sedan-6P	$2,506	3,683 lbs.	39,425
V0	31	2-dr. Sedan-6P	$2,452	3,585 lbs.	20,329

Fairlane 500 (Six)

B0	42	4-dr. Town Sedan-6P	$2,505	3,593 lbs.	25,911
B0	41	2-dr. Club Sedan-6P	$2,451	3,502 lbs.	16,665

Fairlane 500 (V-8)

V0	42	4-dr. Town Sedan-6P	$2,621	3,961 lbs.	72,738
V0	41	2-dr. Club Sedan-6P	$2,567	3,600 lbs.	25,733

Galaxie (Six)

B0	52	4-dr. Town Sedan-6P	$2,665	3,570 lbs.	11,904
B0	51	2-dr. Club Sedan-6P	$2,611	3,488 lbs.	5,716
B0	54	4-dr. Victoria-6P	$2,737	3,588 lbs.	1,466
B0	57	2-dr. Victoria-6P	$2,672	3,545 lbs.	4,279
B0	53	2-dr. Starliner-6P	$2,672	3,517 lbs.	941
B0	55	2-dr. Sunliner-6P	$2,922	3,694 lbs.	2,764

Galaxie (V-8)

V0	52	4-dr. Town Sedan-6P	$2,781	3,668 lbs.	129,366
V0	51	2-dr. Club Sedan-6P	$2,727	3,586 lbs.	21,997
V0	54	4-dr. Victoria-6P	$2,853	3,686 lbs.	28,846
V0	57	2-dr. Victoria-6P	$2,788	3,643 lbs.	71,038
V0	53	2-dr. Starliner-6P	$2,788	3,615 lbs.	28,728
V0	55	2-dr. Sunliner-6P	$3,038	3,792 lbs.	41,810

Station Wagon (Six)

B0	61	2-dr. Ranch Wagon-6P	$2,661	3,914 lbs.	4,785
B0	62	4-dr. Ranch Wagon-6P	$2,731	3,911 lbs.	13,310
B0	64	4-dr. Country Sedan-6P	$2,827	3,934 lbs.	3,610
B0	66	4-dr. Country Sedan-8P	$2,931	3,962 lbs.	2,848
B0	67	4-dr. Country Squire-6P	$3,016	3,938 lbs.	521
B0	68	4-dr. Country Squire-9P	$3,086	3,966 lbs.	302

Station Wagon (V-8)

V0	61	2-dr. Ranch Wagon-6P	$2,777	3,816 lbs.	7,257
V0	62	4-dr. Ranch Wagon-6P	$2,847	4,009 lbs.	16,982
V0	64	4-dr. Country Sedan-6P	$2,943	4,032 lbs.	42,701
V0	66	4-dr. Country Sedan-8P	$3,047	4,060 lbs.	13,508
V0	67	4-dr. Country Squire-6P	$3,132	4,036 lbs.	16,440
V0	68	4-dr. Country Squire-9P	$3,202	4,064 lbs.	14,355

1961 Ford Fairlane four-door Sedan (OCW)

1961 Ford Falcon Futura two-door Sedan interior detail (OCW)

1961 Ford Galaxie two-door Club Sedan (OCW)

Engines:

Falcon Six: Overhead valve. Cast-iron block. Displacement: 144 cid. B & S: 3.50 x 2.50 in. Compression ratio: 6.7:1. Brake hp: 65 at 4200 rpm. Carburetor: Holley one-barrel. Four main bearings. Code S (Code D, export models).

Falcon Six: Overhead valve. Cast-iron block. Displacement: 170 cid. B & S: 3.50 x 2.94 in. Compression ratio: 8.7:1. Brake hp: 101 at 4400 rpm. Carburetor: Holley one-barrel. Four main bearings. Code U.

Ford Six: Overhead valve. Cast-iron block. Displacement: 223 cid. B & S: 3.62 x 3.60 in. Compression ratio: 6.4:1. Brake hp: 135 at 4000 rpm. Carburetor: Holley one-barrel. Four main bearings. Code V.

Base V-8: Overhead valve. Cast-iron block. B & S: 3.75 x 3.30 in. Displacement: 292 cid. Compression ratio: 8.80:1. Brake hp: 175 at 4200 rpm. Taxable hp: 45.0. Torque: 279 lbs.-ft. at 2200 rpm. Five main bearings. Solid valve lifters. Crankcase capacity: 5 qt. (add 1 qt. with new oil filter). Cooling system capacity: 19 qt. Carburetor: (with PCV) Ford two-barrel Model CIAE-9510-AA with standard transmission or CIAE-9510-AB with automatic transmission, (without PCV) Ford two-barrel Model CIAE-9510-Y with standard transmission or CIAE-9510-Z with automatic transmission. Code W (Code T, export models).

Interceptor V-8: Overhead valve. Cast-iron block. B & S: 4.00 x 3.50 in. Displacement: 352 cid. Compression ratio: 8.90:1. Brake hp: 220 at 4400 rpm. Taxable hp: 51.2. Torque: 336 lbs.-ft. at 2400 rpm. Five main bearings. Hydraulic valve lifters. Crankcase capacity: 5 qt. (add 1 qt. with new oil filter). Cooling system capacity: 19.5 qt. Carburetor: (with PCV) Ford two-barrel Model CIAE-9510-AE with standard transmission or CIAE-9510-AF with automatic transmission, (without PCV) Ford two-barrel Model CIAE-9510-AC with standard transmission or CIAE-9510-AD with automatic transmission. Code X (Code G, export models).

Thunderbird V-8: Overhead valve. Cast-iron block. B & S: 4.05 x 3.78 in. Displacement: 390 cid. Compression ratio: 9.60:1. Brake hp: 300 at 4600 rpm. Taxable hp: 52.49. Torque: 427 lbs.-ft. at 2800 rpm. Five main bearings. Hydraulic valve lifters. Crankcase capacity: 5 qt. (add 1 qt. with new oil filter). Cooling system capacity: 19 qt. Carburetor: Ford four-barrel Model CIAE-9510-AG with standard transmission or CIAE-9510-AH with automatic transmission. Code Z.

Interceptor 390 V-8: Overhead valve. Cast-iron block. Displacement: 390 cid. B & S: 4.05 x 3.78 in. Compression ratio: 9.60:1. Brake hp: 330 at 5000 rpm. Torque: 427 lbs.-ft. at 3200 rpm. Five main bearings. Hydraulic valve lifters. Carburetor: (with PCV) Ford four-barrel Model C2AE-9510-AJ with standard transmission or C2AE-9510-AK with automatic transmission, (without PCV) Ford two-barrel Model C2AE-9510-AG with standard transmission or C2AE-9510-AR with automatic transmission. Cooling system capacity: 20.5 qt. with heater. Crankcase capacity: 5 qt. (add 1 qt. with new oil filter). Dual exhausts. Code Z or Code P (Police).

Thunderbird Special V-8: Overhead valve. Cast-iron block. B & S: 4.05 x 3.78 in. Displacement: 390 cid. Compression ratio: 10.60:1. Brake hp: 375 at 6000 rpm. Taxable hp: 52.49. Torque: 427 lbs.-ft. at 3400 rpm. Five main bearings. Solid valve lifters. Crankcase capacity: 5 qt. (add 1 qt. with new oil filter). Cooling system capacity: 19 qt. Carburetor: Ford four-barrel Model CIAE-9510-AG with standard transmission or CIAE-9510-AH with automatic transmission. Code Q (Early versions may use code Z and export models used code R).

Note: Some cars were delivered with the intake manifold and carburetors in the trunk.

Thunderbird 6V V-8: Overhead valve. Cast-iron block. B & S: 4.05 x 3.78 in. Displacement: 390 cid. Compression ratio: 10.60:1. Brake hp: 401 at 6000 rpm. Taxable hp: 52.49. Torque: 430 lbs.-ft. at 3500 rpm. Five main bearings. Solid valve lifters. Crankcase capacity: 5 qt. (add 1 qt. with new oil filter). Cooling system capacity: 19 qt. Carburetor: Three two-barrel carburetors. Code Q (Early versions may use code Z).

Chassis:

Falcon: Wheelbase: 109.5 in. Overall length: 181.2 in., car and 189 in., station wagon. Front tread: 55 in. Rear tread: 54.5 in. Tires: 6.00 x 13 and 6.50 x 13, station wagon.

Ford: Wheelbase: 119 in. Overall length: 209.9 in. Front tread: 61 in. Rear tread: 60 in. Tires: 7.50 x 14 and 8.00 x 14, station wagon.

Options:

Falcon: Back-up lights ($10.70). Heavy-duty battery ($7.60). Crankcase vent system ($5.70). Deluxe trim package ($78.30). Engine, 170 cid/101 hp ($37.40). Fresh Air heater/defroster ($73.40). Station wagon luggage rack ($35.10). Two-tone paint ($19.40). Manual radio and antenna ($54.05). Safety equipment, including padded dash and visors ($21.89). Front seat belts ($20.60). Electric tailgate windows for station wagons ($29.75). Automatic transmission ($163.10). Wheel covers ($16). Windshield washer ($13.70). Electric windshield wiper ($9.65). Five 6.00 x13 white sidewall tires for sedans ($29.90). Five 6.50 x13 black sidewall tires for sedans ($10.20). Five 6.50 x13 white sidewall tires for sedans ($43.30). Five 6.50 x13 white sidewall tires for wagons ($33). Five 6.50 x13 black sidewall 6-ply tires for wagons ($27.80). Five 6.50 x13 white sidewall 6-ply tires for wagons ($60.90).

Ford: Standard 175-hp V-8 engine ($116.00). Two-barrel, 220-hp V-8 ($148.20). Four-barrel, 300-hp V-8 ($196.70). Polar Air conditioner, including tinted glass ($270.90). Select Aire air conditioner, including tinted glass ($436.00). Back-up lights ($10.70). Heavy-duty, 70-amp battery ($7.60). Crankcase vent system ($5.70). Equa-Lock differential ($38.60). Electric clock ($14.60). Magic-Aire heater/defroster ($75.10). Recirculating heater/defroster ($46.90). Four-way manual seat ($17.00). Rocker panel molding ($16.10). Padded dash and visors ($24.30). Two-tone paint ($22). Power brakes ($43.20). Power seat ($63.80). Power steering ($81.70). Power tailgate window ($32.30). Front and rear power windows ($10210). Push-button radio and antenna ($58.50). Front seat belts ($20.60). Tinted glass ($43.00). Cruise-O-Matic transmission ($212.30). Ford-O-Matic transmission with six-cylinder engine ($179.80). Ford-O-Matic transmission with V-8 engine ($189.60). Overdrive transmission ($108.40). Wheel covers ($18.60). Windshield washer ($13.70). Two-speed windshield wipers ($11.60). Five 7.50 x 14 black sidewall tires standard on all models except wagons and cars equipped

1961 Ford Galaxie four-door Town Sedan (OCW)

1961 Ford Galaxie Club Victoria two-door hardtop (OCW)

1961 Ford Galaxie Special Starliner two-door hardtop (OCW)

with 220- or 300-hp V-8s and air conditioning (no charge). Five 7.50 x 14 white sidewall tires standard on all models equipped with standard 7.50 x 14 tires ($33.90). Five 8.00 x 14 black sidewall tires standard on wagons and cars equipped with 220- or 300-hp V-8s and air conditioning (no charge). Five 8.00 x 14 black sidewall tires standard on other full-size Fords ($15.50). Five 8.00 x 14 white sidewall tires standard on wagons and cars equipped with 220- or 300-hp V-8s and air conditioning ($37). Five 8.00 x 14 white sidewall tires on other full-size Fords ($52.40 extra). Five 8.00 x 14 black sidewall 6-ply tires on wagons ($44.50). Five 8.00 x 14 white sidewall 6-ply tires on wagons ($81.40).

History:

Lee A. Iacocca was in his second season at the Ford helm this year. Calendar year output totaled 1,362,186 cars. Market penetration was up to 24 percent as model year production peaked at 163,600 Fairlanes, 141,500 Fairlane 500s, 349,700 Galaxies, 136,600 station wagons, 73,000 Thunderbirds, 129,700 standard Falcons, 224,500 Deluxe Falcons and 135,100 Falcon station wagons. Dealer introduction dates were September 29, 1960, for Fords and Falcons, November 12, 1960, for Thunderbirds. The full-size line production totals included 201,700 six-cylinder cars, while all Falcons were sixes and all Thunderbirds V-8s.

1961 Ford Galaxie Special Sunliner two-door Convertible (OCW)

1961 Ford four-door Country Squire (OCW)

1962 Ford

Falcon (Six): The Falcon line continued unchanged from the previous year except for the addition of an updated grille. The convex grille bars carried a vertical pattern. A new Galaxie-style top configuration was seen. Standard equipment included turn signals, dual sun visors, front arm rests, an oil filter, a fresh air heater and defroster and five 6.00 x 13 black tubeless tires. Station wagons had 6.50 x 13 4-ply tires.

Falcon Deluxe (Six): There were two separate Falcon lines this year: standard and deluxe series. The latter replaced the Deluxe trim package, which was optional on all 1960 and 1961 Falcons. The Deluxe trim package included all-vinyl trim and aluminum trim panels behind the rear wheel openings. In addition to the equipment on other models, the sporty new Futura two-door sedan included carpets, a cigarette

1962 Ford Falcon Futura Sport Coupe (PH)

lighter, automatic door light switches, chrome door and window frames, a special steering wheel, wheel covers, bucket seats with a console storage department, special interior upholstery and trim and foam-padded rear seats. The new wood-grained Squire station wagon also had a power tailgate window.

Fairlane — (Six and V-8): The big news for 1962 was the introduction of the intermediate-size Fairlane. The new model was nearly 12 inches shorter than the full-size Galaxie, yet was nearly eight inches longer than the compact Falcon. At the time of their introduction, the Fairlanes were compared to the 1949-1950 Fords in length and width. They were nearly identical to the old "shoe box" models, but were considerably lower. No one would ever guess the Fairlane was anything but a Ford. It featured Ford's characteristic round taillights and high-canted fenders, plus a grille that was nearly identical to the Galaxie's. The styling was somewhat similar to that of 1961 full-size Fords, so there was no doubt of the Fairlane's heritage. The Fairlane lineup started with base Fairlane models. The Fairlane introduced the famous 221 series small-block Ford V-8 that used a new thin-wall casting technique that allowed Ford to produce the lightest complete V-8 engine of its time.

Fairlane 500 — (Six and V-8): The Fairlane 500 models were the top trim level and included chrome window moldings, a chrome horn ring, armrests on all doors, simulated chrome inserts on the door upholstery, a two-piece chrome Fairlane sweep with a ribbed aluminum insert and two sun visors. The Sport Coupe two-door sedan, introduced at midyear, included bucket seats and special identification.

Mainliner (Six and V-8): Ford continued its policy of making major annual styling changes in least one car line. The full-size 1962 Fords were restyled and the end result was recognized as one of the cleanest designs to come from Dearborn. Except for one horizontal feature line at the beltline, the body was slab-sided. The model designation was carried in script along the rear fender. Ford continued the tradition of large round taillights throughout the entire line. The model designation was spelled out, in block letters, across the trunk lid. At the front end, a full-width grille carried a horizontal grid pattern and was capped on each end by the dual headlights. The Ford crest was centered at the front of the hood throughout the full-size line. Standard equipment on the low-cost Mainliner models, which were available for fleet sales only, included an oil bath air cleaner, an oil filter, dual sun visors, a cigarette lighter, a foam-padded front seat, a trunk light and five tubeless black sidewall tires. The Mainliner four-door sedan had no ash tray in back of the front seat.

Galaxie (Six and V-8): The taillights on Galaxies were separated by a stamped aluminum escutcheon panel. Standard equipment on the Galaxie models included an oil bath air cleaner, an oil filter, dual sun visors, a cigarette lighter, a foam-padded front seat, a trunk light, carpets and five tubeless black sidewall tires. The Galaxies also had richer upholstery than the Mainliner models.

Galaxie 500 (Six and V-8): Galaxie 500s had all of the same features as regular Galaxies, plus chrome A-pillar moldings, chrome window moldings, a color-keyed horizontal strip at the belt line, chrome rocker panel moldings, chrome quarter panel moldings, chrome strips with a Ford crest at the base of the S-pillar (on the top), back-up lights, special upholstery, special exterior trim, and an electric clock.

Galaxie 500/XL (V-8): Introduced as a midyear addition to the line, the sporty Galaxie 500/XL models included bucket seats with a Thunderbird-styled console in between them and Galaxie 500/XL rear fender nameplates. The hardtop also had special oval badges on the roof sail panels replacing the regular Galaxie 500 crest emblems. Interior trim was also somewhat richer. A new option offered this year was an optional "Starlift" removable convertible top.

Station Wagon (Six and V-8): Ranch wagons compared to Mainliners in their level of equipment and trim, Country Sedans compared to Galaxies in the level of equipment and trim and Country Squires compared to Galaxie 500s in their general level of equipment and trim. Country Squires also had wood-grained exterior paneling and the Country Squire 9-passenger model had a power tailgate window.

1961 Ford Falcon four-door Sedan (OCW)

1962 Ford Galaxie 500 rear view

1962 Ford Falcon Deluxe four-door Sedan (OCW)

VIN (Falcon):

The VIN for Falcons was die-stamped into the surface of the left-hand brace between the top of the firewall and the left front wheel housing. The first symbol indicates year: 2=1962. The second symbol identifies assembly plant, as follows: A=Atlanta, Georgia, D=Dallas, Texas, E=Mahwah, New Jersey, F=Dearborn, Michigan, G=Chicago, Illinois, H=Lorain, Ohio, J=Los Angeles, California, K=Kansas City, Kansas, N=Norfolk, Virginia, P=Twin Cities, Minnesota, R=San Jose, California, S=Pilot Plant, T=Metuchen, New Jersey, U=Louisville, Kentucky, W=Wayne, Michigan, Y=Wixom, Michigan, Z=St. Louis, Mo. The third and fourth symbols identify body series code: 11=two-door, 12=four-door, 17=Tudor Futura, 21=two-door station wagon, 22=four-door station wagon, 26=four-door Squire station wagon. The fifth symbol identifies engine code, as follows: E=170-cid six-cylinder, S=144-cid six-cylinder, D=144-cid low-compression six-cylinder, U=170-cid six-cylinder. The last six digits are the unit's production number, beginning at 100001 and going up, at each of the assembly plants. Falcons not built at all Ford plants.

VIN (Fairlane):

The VIN for Fairlanes was die-stamped into the side of the left-hand front inner fender apron near the top. The first symbol indicates year: 2=1962. The second symbol identifies assembly plant, as follows: A=Atlanta, Georgia, D=Dallas, Texas, E=Mahwah, New Jersey, F=Dearborn, Michigan, G=Chicago, Illinois, H=Lorain, Ohio, J=Los Angeles, California, K=Kansas City, Kansas, N=Norfolk, Virginia, P=Twin Cities, Minnesota, R=San Jose, California, S=Pilot Plant, T=Metuchen, New Jersey, U=Louisville, Kentucky, W=Wayne, Michigan, Y=Wixom, Michigan, Z=St. Louis, Mo. The third and fourth symbols identify body series code: 31=Fairlane two-door Club Sedan, 32=Fairlane four-door Town Sedan, 41=Fairlane 500 two-door Club Sedan, 42=Fairlane 500 four-door Town sedan, 47=Fairlane 500 two-door Sport Coupe. The fifth symbol identifies engine code, as follows: U=170-cid six-cylinder, C=221-cid low-compression export V-8, E=170-cid low-compression export six-cylinder, L=221-cid V-8, F=260-cid V-8. The last six digits are the unit's production number, beginning at 100001 and going up, at each of the assembly plants. Fairlanes not built at all Ford plants.

VIN (Ford):

The VIN for full-size Fords was die-stamped into the top right-hand side rail of the frame ahead of the front suspension member. The first symbol indicates year: 2=1962. The second symbol identifies assembly plant, as follows: A=Atlanta, Georgia, D=Dallas, Texas, E=Mahwah, New Jersey, F=Dearborn, Michigan, G=Chicago, Illinois, H=Lorain, Ohio, J=Los Angeles, California, K=Kansas City, Kansas, N=Norfolk, Virginia, P=Twin Cities, Minnesota, R=San Jose, California, S=Pilot Plant, T=Metuchen, New Jersey, U=Louisville, Kentucky, W=Wayne, Michigan, Y=Wixom, Michigan, Z=St. Louis, Mo. The third and fourth symbols identify body series SG316=Ford Mainliner two-door sedan, SG326=Ford Mainliner four-door sedan, 51=Galaxie two-door Club Sedan, 52=Galaxie four-door Town Sedan, 61=Galaxie 500 two-door

Club Sedan, 62=Galaxie 500 four-door Town sedan, 63=Galaxie 500 two-door Victoria Hardtop, 64=Galaxie 500 four-door Victoria Hardtop, 65=Galaxie 500 Sunliner convertible, 83=Galaxie 500/XL two-door Victoria Hardtop, 85=Galaxie 500/XL Sunliner convertible, 71=two-door Ranch Wagon station wagon, 72=four-door Country Sedan six-passenger station wagon, 74=four-door Country Sedan nine-passenger station wagon, 76=four-door Country Squire six-passenger station wagon, 78=four-door Country Squire nine-passenger station wagon. The fifth symbol identifies engine code, as follows: V=223-cid six-cylinder, W=292-cid two-barrel V-8, X=352-cid two-barrel V-8, Z=390-cid four-barrel V-8, T=292-cid low-compression export two-barrel V-8, R=390-cid low-compression export four-barrel V-8, M=390-cid high-performance V-8 with three two-barrel carburetors, Q=390-cid four-barrel high-performance V-8, P=390-cid four-barrel Police V-8, B=406-cid four-barrel V-8 and G=406-cid low-compression six-cylinder high-performance V-8 with three two-barrel carburetors. The last six digits are the unit's production number, beginning at 100001 and going up, at each of the assembly plants. Full-size Fords not built at all Ford plants.

Falcon Standard (Six)

Model No.	Body/ Style No.	Body Type & Seating	Factory Price	Shipping Weight	Production Total
58A	12	4-dr. Sedan-6P	$2,047	2,279 lbs.	54,804
64A	11	2-dr. Sedan-6P	$1,985	2,243 lbs.	64,266
71A	22	4-dr. Station Wagon-6P	$2,341	2,575 lbs.	23,590
59A	21	2-dr. Station Wagon-6P	$2,298	2,539 lbs.	12,232

Falcon Deluxe (Six)

58B	12	4-dr. Sedan-6P	$2,133	2,285 lbs.	71,237
64B	11	2-dr. Sedan-6P	$2,071	2,249 lbs.	47,825
71B	22	4-dr. Station Wagon-6P	$2,427	2,581 lbs.	43,229
59B	21	2-dr. Station Wagon-6P	$2,384	2,545 lbs.	7,793

Falcon Futura (Six)

64C	17	2-dr. Coupe-6P	$2,232	2,328 lbs.	31,559
62C	17	2-dr. Sport Coupe-6P	$2,273	2,232 lbs.	17,011
71C	26	2-dr. Squire Wagon-6P	$2,603	2,591 lbs.	22,583

Fairlane (Six)

54A	32	4-dr. Sedan-6P	$2,216	2,791 lbs.	27,996
62A	31	2-dr. Sedan-6P	$2,154	2,757 lbs.	23,511

Fairlane (V-8)

54A	32	4-dr. Sedan-6P	$2,319	2,949 lbs.	18,346
62A	31	2-dr. Sedan-6P	$2,257	2,915 lbs.	10,753

Fairlane 500 (Six)

54B	42	4-dr. Town Sedan-6P	$2,304	2,808 lbs.	31,113
62B	41	2-dr. Club Sedan-6P	$2,242	2,774 lbs.	26,533
62C	41	2-dr. Sport Coupe-6P	$2,403	2,842 lbs.	1,659

Fairlane 500 (V-8)

54B	42	4-dr. Town Sedan-6P	$2,407	2,966 lbs.	98,145
62B	41	2-dr. Club Sedan-6P	$2,345	2,932 lbs.	42,091
62C	41	2-dr. Sport Coupe-6P	$2,506	3,002 lbs.	17,969

Mainliner and Galaxie (Six)

54B	52	4-dr. Town Sedan-6P	$2,507	3,581 lbs.	37,994
62B	51	2-dr. Club Sedan-6P	$2,453	3,486 lbs.	26,114

Mainliner and Galaxie (V-8)

54B	52	4-dr. Town Sedan-6P	$2,616	3,692 lbs.	77,600
62B	51	2-dr. Club Sedan-6P	$2,562	3,597 lbs.	28,816

Note: Production includes Mainliner models available for fleet sales only.

Galaxie 500 (Six)

54A	62	4-dr. Town Sedan-6P	$2,667	3,594 lbs.	8,917
62A	61	2-dr. Club Sedan-6P	$2,613	3,484 lbs.	3,510
75A	64	4-dr. Victoria-6P	$2,739	3,585 lbs.	952
65A	63	2-dr. Victoria-6P	$2,674	3,513 lbs.	3,151
76A	65	2-dr. Sunliner-6P	$2,924	3,675 lbs.	2,616

Galaxie 500 (V-8)

54A	62	4-dr. Town Sedan-6P	$2,776	3,705 lbs.	11,904
62A	61	2-dr. Club Sedan-6P	$2,722	3,595 lbs.	165,278
75A	64	4-dr. Victoria-6P	$2,848	3,696 lbs.	29,826
65A	63	2-dr. Victoria-6P	$2,783	3,624 lbs.	84,411
76A	65	2-dr. Sunliner-6P	$3,033	3,786 lbs.	40,030

Galaxie 500/XL (V-8)

65B	64	2-dr. Victoria-6P	$3,056	3,672 lbs.	28,412
76B	65	2-dr. Sunliner-6P	$3,306	3,831 lbs.	13,183

Station Wagon (Six)

71D	71	4-dr. Ranch Wagon-6P	$2,733	3,913 lbs.	13,171
71C	72	4-dr. Country Sedan-6P	$2,829	3,936 lbs.	2,603
71B	74	4-dr. Country Sedan-8P	$2,933	3,954 lbs.	1,774
71A	76	4-dr. Country Squire-6P	$3,018	3,950 lbs.	411
71E	78	4-dr. Country Squire-9P	$3,088	3,967 lbs.	281

Station Wagon (V-8)

71D	71	4-dr. Ranch Wagon-6P	$2,842	4,024 lbs.	20,503
71C	72	4-dr. Country Sedan-6P	$2,938	4,065 lbs.	45,032
71B	74	4-dr. Country Sedan-8P	$3,042	4,067 lbs.	14,788
71A	76	4-dr. Country Squire-6P	$3,127	4,078 lbs.	15,703
71E	78	4-dr. Country Squire-9P	$3,197	4,061 lbs.	15,385

Engines:

Falcon Six: Overhead valve. Cast-iron block. Displacement: 144 cid. B & S: 3.50 x 2.50 in. Compression ratio: 6.7:1. Brake hp: 65 at 4200 rpm. Carburetor: Holley one-barrel. Seven main bearings. Code S.

Falcon Six: Overhead valve. Cast-iron block. Displacement: 170 cid. B & S: 3.50 x 2.94 in. Compression ratio: 8.7:1. Brake hp: 101 at 4400 rpm. Carburetor: Holley one-barrel. Seven main bearings. Code U.

Ford Six: Overhead valve. Cast-iron block. Displacement: 223 cid. B & S: 3.62 x 3.60 in. Compression ratio: 8.4:1. Brake hp: 138 at 4200 rpm. Carburetor: Holley one-barrel. Four main bearings. Code V.

Base Fairlane V-8: Overhead valve. Cast-iron block. Displacement: 221 cid. B & S: 3.50 x 2.87 in. Compression ratio: 8.70:1. Brake hp: 145 at 4400 rpm. Torque: 216 lbs.-ft. at 2200 rpm. Five main bearings. Hydraulic valve lifters. Carburetor: Ford two-barrel Model C20E-9510-N with standard transmission or C20E-9510-T with automatic transmission. Cooling system capacity: 14.5 qt. with heater. Crankcase capacity: 4 qt. (add 1 qt. with new oil filter). Code L.

Challenger 260 Fairlane V-8 (mid-year): Overhead valve. Cast-iron block. Displacement: 260 cid. B & S: 3.80 x 2.87 in. Compression ratio: 8.70:1. Brake hp: 164 at 4400 rpm. Torque: 258 lbs.-ft. at 2200 rpm. Five main bearings. Hydraulic valve lifters. Carburetor: Ford two-barrel Model C20F-9510-A. Cooling system capacity: 14.5 qt. with heater. Crankcase capacity: 4 qt. (add 1 qt. with new oil filter). Code F.

Base Ford V-8: Overhead valve. Cast-iron block. Displacement: 292 cid. B & S: 3.75 x 3.30 in. Compression ratio: 8.80:1. Brake hp: 170 at 4200 rpm. Torque: 279 lbs.-ft. at 2200 rpm. Five main bearings. Solid valve lifters. Carburetor: (with PCV) Ford two-barrel Model C2AE-9510-AA with standard transmission or C2AE-9510-AB with automatic transmission, (without PCV) Ford two-barrel Model C2AE-9510-Y with standard transmission or C2AE-9510-Z with automatic transmission.

1962 Ford Falcon Deluxe two-door Sedan (OCW)

1962 Ford Falcon Sports Futura two-door Coupe (OCW)

1962 Ford Falcon Sports Futura interior detail (OCW)

1962 Ford Falcon four-door Squire Station Wagon (OCW)

Cooling system capacity: 16 qt. with heater. Crankcase capacity: 5 qt. (add 1 qt. with new oil filter). Code W.

Interceptor 352 V-8: Overhead valve. Cast-iron block. Displacement: 352 cid. B & S: 4.00 x 3.50 in. Compression ratio: 8.90:1. Brake hp: 220 at 4300 rpm. Torque: 336 lbs.-ft. at 2600 rpm. Five main bearings. Hydraulic valve lifters. Carburetor: (with PCV) Ford two-barrel Model C2AE-9510-AE with standard transmission or C2AE-9510-AF with automatic transmission, (without PCV) Ford two-barrel Model C2AE-9510-AC with standard transmission or C2AE-9510-AD with automatic transmission. Cooling system capacity: 20.5 qt. with heater. Crankcase capacity: 5 qt. (add 1 qt. with new oil filter). Code X.

Interceptor 390 V-8: Overhead valve. Cast-iron block. Displacement: 390 cid. B & S: 4.05 x 3.78 in. Compression ratio: 9.60:1. Brake hp: 300 at 4600 rpm. Torque: 427 lbs.-ft. at 2800 rpm. Hydraulic valve lifters. Carburetor: (with PCV) Ford four-barrel Model C2AE-9510-AJ with standard transmission or C2AE-9510-AK with automatic transmission. Cooling system capacity: 20.5 qt. with heater. Crankcase capacity: 5 qt. (add 1 qt. with new oil filter). Dual exhaust. Code Z.

Interceptor 390 V-8: Overhead valve. Cast-iron block. Displacement: 390 cid. B & S: 4.05 x 3.78 in. Compression ratio: 9.60:1. Brake hp: 330 at 5000 rpm. Torque: 427 lbs.-ft. at 3200 rpm. Five main bearings. Solid valve lifters. Carburetor: (with PCV) Ford four-barrel Model C2AE-9510-AJ with standard transmission or C2AE-9510-AK with automatic transmission, (without PCV) Ford two-barrel Model C2AE-9510-AG with standard transmission or C2AE-9510-AR with automatic transmission. Cooling system capacity: 20.5 qt. with heater. Crankcase capacity: 5 qt. (add 1 qt. with new oil filter). Dual exhausts. Code P.

390-375 Optional Ford V-8: Overhead valve. Cast-iron block. Displacement: 390 cid. B & S: 4.05 x 3.78 in. Compression ratio: 10.60:1. Brake hp: 375 at 6000 rpm. Torque: 427 lbs.-ft. at 3400 rpm. Five main bearings. Solid valve lifters. Carburetor: Holley Model R-3228A four-barrel. Cooling system capacity: 20.5 qt. with heater. Crankcase capacity: 5 qt. (add 1 qt. with new oil filter). Dual exhausts Code Q.

Thunderbird 406 V-8: Overhead valve. Cast-iron block. Displacement: 406 cid. B & S: 4.13 x 3.78 in. Compression ratio: 11.40:1. Brake hp: 385 at 5800 rpm. Torque: 444 lbs.-ft. at 3400 rpm. Five main bearings. Solid valve lifters. Carburetor: Ford four-barrel Model CIAE-9510-AG with standard transmission or CIAE-9510-AH with automatic transmission. Cooling system capacity: 20.5 qt. with heater. Crankcase capacity: 5 qt. (add 1 qt. with new oil filter). Dual exhausts. Code B.

390-401 Optional Ford V-8: Overhead valve. Cast-iron block. Displacement: 390 cid. B & S: 4.05 x 3.78 in. Compression ratio: 10.60:1. Brake hp: 401 at 6000 rpm. Torque: 430 lbs.-ft. at 3500 rpm. Five main bearings. Solid valve lifters. Carburetor: Holley three two barrels. Cooling system capacity: 20.5 qt. with heater. Crankcase capacity: 5 qt. (add 1 qt. with new oil filter). Dual exhausts. Code M.

Thunderbird Special 406 V-8: Overhead valve. Cast-iron block. Displacement: 406 cid. B & S: 4.13 x 3.78 in. Compression ratio: 11.40:1. Brake hp: 405 at 5800 rpm. Torque: 448 lbs.-ft. at 3500 rpm. Five main bearings. Solid valve lifters. Carburetor: Holley three two-barrel. Cooling system capacity: 20.5 qt. with heater. Crankcase capacity: 5 qt. (add 1 qt. with new oil filter). Dual exhausts. Code G.

Falcon: Wheelbase: 109.5 in. Overall length: 181.1 in. and 189 in., station wagon. Tires: 6.00 x 13, car and 6.50 x 13, station wagon.

Fairlane: Wheelbase: 115.5 in. Overall length: 197.6 in. Tires: 6.50 x 13, Fairlane six, 7.00 x 14, Fairlane V-8 and 7.00 x 13, Fairlane 260 V-8.

Ford: Wheelbase: 119 in. Overall length: 209.3 in. Tires: 7.50 x 14, car and 8.00 x 14, station wagon.

Options:

Falcon and Fairlane: Back-up lights ($11). Heavy-duty battery ($8). Squire bucket seats and console ($120). Crankcase ventilation system ($6). Deluxe trim package ($87). Engine, 170 cid/101 hp ($38). Tinted glass ($27). Windshield tinted glass ($13). Station wagon luggage rack ($39). Two-tone paint ($19). Push-button radio and antenna ($59). Safety equipment, including padded dash and front visors ($22). Seat safety belts ($21). Electric tailgate windows ($30). Automatic transmission ($163). Vinyl trim for sedan (Deluxe trim package required) ($25). Wheel covers ($16). Windshield washer ($14). Electric windshield wiper ($10).

1962 Ford Fairlane two-door Sedan (OCW)

1962 Ford Fairlane 500 four-door Town Sedan (OCW)

1962 Ford Fairlane 500 four-door Town Sedan (OCW)

1962 Ford Fairlane 500 two-door Sports Coupe (OCW)

1962 Ford Galaxie two-door Club Sedan (OCW)

Ford: Polar Air conditioning with V-8 ($271). Select Aire air conditioning with V-8 ($361). Back-up lights, standard Galaxie 500 ($11). Heavy-duty battery, 70-amp ($8). Crankcase ventilation system ($6). Equa-Lock differential ($39). Electric clock, standard Galaxy 500 ($15). Re-circulating heater and defroster ($28 deduct option). Chrome luggage rack ($39). Four-way manual seat ($17). Rocker panel molding ($16). Padded dash and visors ($24). Two-tone paint ($22). Power brakes ($43). Power seat ($64). Power steering ($82). Power tailgate window ($32). Front and rear power windows ($102). Push-button radio and antenna ($59). Front seat belts ($21). Tinted glass ($40). Tinted windshield ($22). Cruise-O-Matic transmission ($212). Ford-O-Matic with six-cylinder ($180). Ford-O-Matic with V-8 ($190). Overdrive transmission ($108). Four-speed manual transmission, 375-hp or 401-hp V-8 required ($188). Vinyl trim, Galaxie 500 except convertible ($26). Deluxe wheel covers ($26). Wheel covers ($19). Windshield washer and wipers, two-speed ($20).

History:

The 1962 Falcon was introduced September 29, 1961. The 1962 Galaxie and station wagon lines appeared the same day. The Fairlane series did not debut until November 16, 1961. Ford announced the introduction of the first transistorized ignition system, for production cars, in March 1962. A total of 30,216 Fairlanes had the 260-cid V-8 installed. A total of 722,647 Galaxies, 386,192 Fairlanes, 381,559 Falcons and 75,536 Thunderbirds were built this year, second only to the record production season 1955. Midyear models included the Galaxie 500/XL hardtop and convertible, the Fairlane 500 Sport Sedan and the Falcon Sport Futura. Lee A. Iacocca was vice-president and general manager of the Ford Division again this year. In a historic move, Ford built 10 Galaxie "factory lightweight" drag racing cars late in model year 1962. This year saw a continuation of the great 1960's horsepower race and to do combat with the General Motors and Chrysler offerings, Ford introduced the famous 406 cid/405 hp V-8. The re-sizing of the Fairlane also brought the introduction of a completely new line of small V-8 engines. At 221 cid, the new base V-8 was the same displacement as the first Ford flathead V-8. It was of thin wall casting design and was the first in a series of lightweight V-8s.

1962 Ford Galaxie 500 two-door Club Sedan (OCW)

1962 Ford Galaxie 500 four-door Town Sedan (OCW)

1962 Ford Galaxie 500 Club Victoria two-door hardtop (OCW)

1962 Ford Galaxie 500 Sunliner two-door Convertible (OCW)

1962 Ford Galaxie 500/XL Club Victoria two-door hardtop (OCW)

1962 Ford Galaxie 500/XL Sunliner two-door convertible (OCW)

1963 Ford

Falcon — Series 06 — (Six and V-8): The Falcon line continued to use the body shell introduced in 1960. A new convex grille featured a full-width horizontal center bar with three full-width horizontal bars above it and four below it. These were intersected by five vertical bars spaced fairly widely apart. This created a grid-work of narrow horizontal openings. The standard models had no body side moldings. The front fenders carried a black oval with a Falcon emblem in it and the "Falcon" name in chrome script just behind the emblems. There was a chrome piece on the front of the simulated hood air scoop and a ribbed chrome piece at the base of the roof pillar. Small "doggie dish" hubcaps were included. The slightly-revised taillight lenses had additional chrome around the inside of the lens. The standard series include two- and four-door sedans. Standard equipment included a six-cylinder 85-hp engine with self-adjusting valves, a three-speed manual transmission, self-adjusting brakes, a full-flow oil filter, a 36,000-mile fuel filter, a fully-aluminized muffler, galvanized main underbody members, a bright-metal windshield molding, a bright-metal rear window molding, parallel-action single-speed electric windshield wipers, two horns, two sun visors, two front arm rests, two coat hooks, a foam-cushioned front seat, a front ash tray, a white vinyl headlining, gold ladder-pattern cloth-and-vinyl seat trim, a color-keyed 3-spoke steering wheel, front seat belt anchors, turn signals with new "safety Amber" lenses and center-fill fueling. A heater was installed during production unless otherwise specified. If deleted, an appropriate price reduction was made. In addition to the above, the following Deluxe Trim items were available for Standard Falcon models at slight additional cost: Bright body side moldings, fender-top ornaments, a choice of red or blue cloth-and-vinyl interior trim, rear arm rests, an ash tray, a cigarette lighter, a chrome horn ring and an automatic dome light. Also introduced at midyear, for all Falcons, was an optional V-8 engine.

1963 Ford Falcon Futura four-door Sedan (OCW)

1963 Ford Falcon Sports Futura two-door Sedan (OCW)

Falcon Futura — Series 10 — (Six and V-8): Ford said that Falcon Futura models had the bold, modern beauty of their Thunderbird cousins. A new body style was a convertible. Standard features included all the equipment that Standard Falcons came with the following additions or replacements: bright-metal side window frames, side body moldings with front fender spear tips and complementary color inserts, fender-top ornaments, "Futura" in block letters and a molding on the rear body panel, a choice of five different "Bar-Line" pattern pleated cloth-and-vinyl interior trims, a chrome-backed rearview mirror, color-keyed carpeting front and rear, a cigarette lighter, rear arm rests, a rear ash tray, a chrome horn ring, an automatic dome light, a Futura molding across the instrument panel, bright inserts in the dashboard control knobs, Futura full wheel covers and a Futura chrome script on the sides of the rear fenders above the body side moldings. Hardtop and convertible models were additions to the lineup. Standard equipment in the convertible included the Falcon 170 Special six with 101 hp, a choice of five pleated all-vinyl interior trims, foam-padded front and rear seat cushions, an electric-hydraulic power-operated convertible top, vinyl 3-ply top material in white, blue or black, added underbody torque boxes, Safety-Yoke door locks, Futura front arm rests, front and rear ash trays and a chrome-backed "floating" windshield mirror.

Falcon Futura Sports — (Six and V-8): This Falcon Futura sub-series contained all of the sporty models, some of which were midyear additions to the lineup. The Futura Sports Sedan, which appeared in the introductory sales catalog, was a two-door sedan that included all regular standard equipment plus foam-cushioned black vinyl bucket front seats, a console, foam-cushioned black bucket-style rear seats, a choice of five pleated all-vinyl interior trims, a unique white whipcord vinyl headlining and special Sports Sedan armrests and ash trays front and rear. A new option for this car was a vinyl roof that came in black or white. In addition to all the features of the Futura convertible, the Futura Sports convertible included bucket front seats, a console and bucket-style rear seat cushions.

Falcon Sprint — (V-8): The Sprint hardtop and Sprint convertible were midyear additions to the lineup. They were created in honor of the Falcon's winning performance in the Monte Carlo Rally. The Sprint models had all the features of the Falcon Futura Sports hardtop and convertible, plus a standard V-8 engine, a tachometer and a special steering wheel.

Falcon Station Wagon — Series 20 — (Six and V-8): Both two- and four-door station wagons were introduced to the Falcon lineup this year. They came in Standard, Futura and Futura Sport trim levels. The Futura versions carried Squire identification and wood-grained exterior trim. The Futura Squire Sport had bucket seats. The sales catalog listed specific station wagon features, which were comparable to the features of the Standard, Futura and Futura Sport trim levels with certain alterations distinct to station wagons.

Fairlane — Series 30 — (Six and V-8): All-new front end styling for the Fairlane was characterized by a concave grille with a cross-hatched insert with chrome ovals in each small opening for a very ornate look. The model lineup was expanded for some series, but the basic series still consisted of two- and four-door sedans. These cars featured the Fairlane name in chrome script on the roof pillar, a ribbed chrome piece

1963 Ford Falcon two-door Sedan (OCW)

1963 Ford Falcon Futura two-door Sedan (OCW)

below the script, a chrome belt line molding with a half spear tip. A ribbed rear beauty panel with crest in the middle, chrome-circled round taillights and "doggie dish" hubcaps with the Ford name embossed in them. Standard features included a choice of "Square-Puff" cloth-and-vinyl upholstery in blue, gold or red, a choice of 11 Diamond Lustre Enamel exterior colors, a bright-metal windshield molding, a white vinyl headlining, a color-keyed 3-spoke steering wheel, dual sun visors, dual coat hooks, front arm rests, a front ash tray, a locking glove box, front seat belt anchors, Safety-Yoke door locks, a foam-cushioned front seat, turn signals with new amber safety lenses in the front bumper, parallel-action single-speed electric wipers, an illuminated trunk (with taillights on), a 101-hp Fairlane Six engine, a three-speed manual transmission, self-adjusting brakes, Zinclad rocker panels and main underbody members, a 6,000-mile full-flow oil filter, a fully-aluminized muffler and a 36,000-mile replaceable fuel filter element.

Fairlane 500 — Series 40 — (Six and V-8): The Fairlane 500 models were the top trim level and included all Fairlane features with the

1963 Ford Falcon Futura two-door Convertible (AA)

1963 Ford Falcon Sprint two-door Hardtop (PH)

1962 Ford Falcon Sprint two-door Convertible (OCW)

1962 Ford Falcon four-door Station Wagon (OCW)

1963 Ford Falcon Deluxe two-door Station Wagon (OCW)

following variations: a choice of "Wheel-Pattern" pleated cloth-and-vinyl interior trims in blue, turquoise, beige, gold or red, a choice of 12 Diamond Lustre enamel exterior colors, bright-metal side window moldings, Fairlane 500 scripts on the roof sail panels, fin-shaped body side moldings with color-keyed inserts, front fender top trim pieces, full wheel covers of a specific design, front and rear arm rests, front and rear ash trays, a cigarette lighter, an automatic dome light, a chrome horn ring and color-keyed wall-to-wall carpeting. The Fairlane 500 hardtop also included a "floating" inside rearview mirror. The Fairlane 500 Sports Coupe also included a choice of all-vinyl interior trims in blue, black, red, chestnut or gold, a choice of 13 Diamond Lustre enamel exterior colors, foam-cushioned front bucket seats with a center console, a unique white whipcord vinyl headlining and a bucket-style rear seat. On hardtops the Fairlane 500 script was moved from the roof sail panels to the side of the cowl below the fin-shaped moldings. The sail panels also had T-bird like red, white and blue emblems. The Fairlane 500 Sports coupe had the same wheel covers as other Fairlane 500s. The Fairlane 500 hardtop had three slashes inside the moldings on the front fenders and full wheel covers with tri-bar "spinner" type centers.

Fairlane Station Wagon — (Six and V-8): The Fairlane station wagons came in three four-door models: Ranch Wagon, Custom Ranch Wagon and Squire. Standard Ranch Wagon equipment started with all of the Fairlane sedan features and then included these variations: a choice of "Preline Pattern" vinyl-and-vinyl interior trims in blue and beige, a choice of 11 Diamond Lustre enamel exterior colors, front and rear foam-cushioned seats, a color-keyed cargo area inlay, a roll-down tailgate window with painted molding and a folding second seat. The Custom Ranch Wagon included all Fairlane 500 sedan equipment , a choice of beige pleated "Wheel-Pattern" cloth-and-vinyl interior all-vinyl pleated trim in red, blue or beige, color-keyed vinyl-coated rubber floor coverings, a stowage compartment lock and a bright-metal tailgate molding. The Fairlane Squire also included a choice of beige pleated "Wheel-Pattern" cloth-and-vinyl or pleated all-vinyl interior trims in red, blue or beige, distinctive limed oak fiberglass moldings enclosing walnut-

1963 Ford Falcon four-door Squire Station Wagon (OCW)

1963-1/2 Ford Falcon (OCW)

1963 Ford Fairlane two-door Sedan (OCW)

1963 Ford Fairlane 500 four-door Sedan (OCW)

colored steel panels on the body sides and rear, color-keyed carpeting on the passenger floor and a power-operated tailgate window.

Ford 300 — Series 50 — (Six and V-8): Ford styling for '63 was influenced by the Thunderbird. Changes included a flatter roof line and recessed rear window on some models. Up to 36 power combinations were available in big Fords. The four-door sedan had no ash tray in back of the front seat. Crank-operated vent windows, a compliance-link front suspension and Swing-Away steering columns were new features or options this year. The all-new Ford 300 was the newest and lowest-priced of the big Fords. It was offered in two- and four-door sedan models that incorporated the roominess, comfort and convenience of Twice-A-Year Maintenance and all of Ford's service-saving features. The all-new Ford 300 was built to the same high-quality standards as Galaxie models. Buyers of these cars had a choice of three attractive cloth-and-vinyl interior trims in blue, gold or red. Galaxie options and power accessories were available.

Galaxie — Series 50 — (Six and V-8): Galaxie models also came only in two- and four-door sedan models. They had a chrome molding running from the front door to the top of the rear bumper end. Ahead of this was chrome Galaxie script. There were also chrome F-O-R-D block letters on the lip of the hood, chrome fender-top ornaments, red, white and blue crest emblems on the roof sail panels, ribbed chrome pieces at the base of the sail panels and "doggie dish" style hubcaps. Standard equipment included a choice of "Puff-Stripe" cloth-and-vinyl interior trim in blue, beige, gold, turquoise and red, a choice of 11 Diamond Lustre enamel exterior colors, a bright metal windshield molding, a bright metal rear window molding, bright-metal drip rails moldings, Galaxie body trim and side moldings, fender-top ornaments, color-keyed wall-to-wall carpeting, a white vinyl headlining, a color-keyed Lifeguard steering wheel with chrome horn ring, dual sun visors, dual coat hooks, a cigarette lighter, arm rests, front and rear ash trays, an illuminated front ash tray, a locking glove box, a locking luggage compartment, an automatic dome light, front seat belt anchors, Safety-Yoke door locks, a foam-cushioned front seat, crank-adjusted vent windows, turn signals with new safety amber lenses in the front bumper, parallel-action single-speed electric windshield wipers, a step-on parking brake, a 138-hp Mileage Maker Six engine, a Synchro-Smooth Drive three-speed manual transmission, self-adjusting brakes, a full-flow oil filter, a 36,000-mile fuel filter, a fully-aluminized muffler and center-fill fueling.

Galaxie 500 — (Six and V-8): Galaxie 500s had all of the same features as regular Galaxies, plus additional luxury items that varied by body style. The two-and four-door sedans had these extras: a choice of "Gleam" cloth-and vinyl interior trims in blue, beige, chestnut, turquoise, gold, red and black, a choice of 13 Diamond Lustre enamel exterior colors, chrome-like Mylar accents on the seats, doors and side panels, pleated seat fabrics, pleated door panels, pleated side trim panel, deluxe arm rests, front and

1963 Ford Fairlane 500 two-door Hardtop (OCW)

1963 Ford Fairlane four-door Ranch Wagon (OCW)

1963 Ford Fairlane Custom four-door Ranch Wagon (OCW)

rear ash trays, a chrome-backed inside rearview mirror, bright-metal seat side shields, a self-regulating electric clock and back-up lights centered in the taillights. Special exterior body trim included seven has marks on the body sides ahead of the taillights, G-A-L-A-X-I-E block letters on the trunk lip, wider ribbed chrome decorations at the base of the roof side panels, Galaxie 500 scripts and gold badges behind the front wheel openings, full wheel covers with red, white and blue plastic center inserts, double body side moldings (full-length upper and three-quarter lower moldings joined at the rear), and a grille-like rear body trim panel with a crest in its center. The two-and four-door hardtops had these extras: a choice of "Gleam" cloth-and vinyl interior trims in blue, beige, chestnut, turquoise, gold, red and black, a choice of 13 Diamond Lustre enamel exterior colors, chrome-like Mylar accents on the seats, doors and side panels, pleated seat fabrics, pleated door panels, pleated side trim panel, deluxe arm rests, front and rear ash trays, a chrome-backed inside rearview mirror, bright-metal seat side shields, a self-regulating electric clock and back-up lights centered in the taillights. Special exterior body trim included seven has marks on the body sides ahead of the taillights, G-A-L-A-X-I-E block letters on the trunk lip, wider ribbed chrome decorations at the base of the roof side panels, Galaxie 500 scripts and gold badges behind the front wheel openings, full wheel covers with red, white and blue plastic center inserts, double body side moldings (full-length upper and three-quarter lower moldings joined at the rear), and a grille-like rear body trim panel with a crest in its center. The Galaxie 500 convertible had these extras: a choice of pleated all-vinyl interior trims in blue, beige, chestnut, turquoise, gold, red and black, a choice of 13 Diamond Lustre enamel exterior colors, a 3-ply vinyl power-operated top in a choice of white, black or blue, an anti-ballooning top design, a zip-out clear vinyl rear window, a color-keyed and contoured top boot, automatic courtesy lights under the dashboard and a "floating" rearview mirror bonded to the windshield.

Galaxie 500/XL — (V-8): The lively-in-looks Galaxie 500/XL now came in four variations, two-door formal-roof hardtop, two-door fastback hardtop, four-door hardtop and convertible. Standard equipment on the hardtops included everything on Galaxies and Galaxie 500s with the following variations: a choice of all-vinyl interior trims in blue, beige, chestnut, turquoise, gold, red and black, a choice of 13 Diamond Lustre enamel exterior colors, individually-adjusted 100-percent foam-cushioned front bucket seats, a full-length Command Console, an individually-contoured 100-percent full-foam bucket-style rear seat, chrome-like Mylar accents on the seats, doors and side panels, color-keyed wall-to-wall carpeting, a color-keyed instrument panel with full chrome controls, super deluxe front and rear arm rests and ash trays, bright-metal seat side shields and door-lock buttons, bright-metal-accented accelerator and brake pedals, automatic courtesy safety lights in both lower door panels, a 164-hp Galaxie V-8 engine, two-speed Ford-O-Matic Drive transmission with a console-mounted "Sports Stick" and full wheel covers with simulated knock-off spinners. Standard equipment on the Galaxie 500/XL convertible included everything on the Galaxie 500 ragtop, plus a choice of pleated all-vinyl interior trims in blue, Rose Beige, chestnut, turquoise, gold, red or black, a choice of 13 Diamond Lustre enamel exterior colors, individually-adjusted 100-percent foam-cushioned front bucket seats, a full-length Command Console, an individually-contoured 100-percent full-foam bucket-style rear seat, a 3-ply vinyl power-operated top in a choice of white, black or blue, a color-keyed contour-padded top boot with concealed fasteners, color-keyed wall-to-wall carpeting, automatic courtesy safety lights in both lower door panels, a 164-hp Galaxie V-8 engine, two-speed Ford-O-Matic Drive transmission with a console-mounted "Sports Stick" and full wheel covers with simulated knock-off spinners.

1963 Ford Fairlane 500 four-door Ranch Wagon (OCW)

1963 Ford Fairlane Custom four-door Squire Wagon (OCW)

Galaxie Station Wagon — (Six and V-8): Country Sedans compared to Galaxies in the level of equipment and trim and Country Squires compared to Galaxie 500s in their general level of equipment and trim. Country Squires also had wood-grained exterior paneling and the Country Squire 9-passenger model had a power tailgate window.

VIN Falcon:

The VIN for Falcons was die-stamped into the surface of the left-hand brace between the top of the firewall and the left front wheel housing. The first symbol indicates year: 3=1963. The second symbol identifies assembly plant, as follows: A=Atlanta, Georgia, D=Dallas, Texas, E=Mawhah, New Jersey, F=Dearborn, Michigan, G=Chicago, Illinois, H=Lorain, Ohio, J=Los Angeles, California, K=Kansas City, Kansas, N=Norfolk, Virginia, P=Twin Cities, Minnesota, R=San Jose, California, S=Pilot Plant, T=Metuchen, New Jersey, U=Louisville, Kentucky, W=Wayne, Michigan, Y=Wixom, Michigan, Z=St. Louis, Mo. The third and fourth symbols identify body series code: 01=two-door, 02=four-door, 15=convertible, 16=four-door sedan, 17=two-door hardtop, 19=two-door sedan, 21=two-door station wagon, 22=four-door station wagon, 23=two-door Deluxe station wagon, 24=four-door Deluxe station wagon, 26=four-door Squire station wagon. The fifth symbol identifies engine code, as follows: S=144-cid six-cylinder, 2=144-cid six-cylinder, U=170-cid six-cylinder, 4=170-cid six-cylinder, F=260-cid V-8, 8=260-cid V-8 low-compression. The last six digits are the unit's production number, beginning at 100001 and going up, at each of the assembly plants. Falcons not built at all Ford plants.

VIN Fairlane:

The VIN for Fairlanes was die-stamped into the side of the left-hand front inner fender apron near the top. The first symbol indicates year: 3=1962. The second symbol identifies assembly plant, as follows: A=Atlanta, Georgia, D=Dallas, Texas, E=Mawhah, New Jersey, F=Dearborn, Michigan, G=Chicago, Illinois, H=Lorain, Ohio, J=Los Angeles, California, K=Kansas City, Kansas, N=Norfolk, Virginia, P=Twin Cities, Minnesota, R=San Jose, California, S=Pilot Plant, T=Metuchen, New Jersey, U=Louisville, Kentucky, W=Wayne, Michigan, Y=Wixom, Michigan, Z=St. Louis, Mo. The third and fourth symbols identify body series code: 31=Fairlane two-door Club Sedan, 32=Fairlane four-door Town Sedan, 41=Fairlane 500 two-door Club Sedan, 42=Fairlane 500 four-door Town sedan, 43=Fairlane 500 two-door hardtop, 47=Fairlane 500 two-door Sport Coupe. The fifth symbol identifies engine code, as follows: U=170-cid six-cylinder, R=170-cid six-cylinder, T=200-cid six-cylinder, L=221-cid V-8, 3=221-cid V-8, F=260-cid V-8, 8=260-cid V-8 and K=289-cid V-8. The last six digits are the unit's production number, beginning at 100001 and going up, at each of the assembly plants. Fairlanes not built at all Ford plants.

VIN Ford:

The VIN for full-size Fords was die-stamped into the top right-hand side rail of the frame ahead of the front suspension member. The first symbol indicates year: 3=1963. The second symbol identifies assembly plant, as follows: A=Atlanta, Georgia, D=Dallas, Texas, E=Mawhah, New Jersey, F=Dearborn, Michigan, G=Chicago, Illinois, H=Lorain, Ohio, J=Los Angeles, California, K=Kansas City, Kansas, N=Norfolk, Virginia, P=Twin Cities, Minnesota, R=San Jose, California, S=Pilot Plant, T=Metuchen, New Jersey, U=Louisville, Kentucky, W=Wayne, Michigan, Y=Wixom, Michigan, Z=St. Louis, Mo. The third and fourth symbols identify body series 51=Galaxie two-door Club Sedan, 52=Galaxie four-door Town Sedan, 53=Ford 300 two-door sedan, 54=Ford 300 four-door sedan, 61=Galaxie 500 two-door Club Sedan, 62=Galaxie 500 four-door Town sedan, 63=Galaxie 500 two-door Victoria Hardtop, 64=Galaxie 500 four-door Victoria Hardtop, 65=Galaxie 500 Sunliner convertible, 66=Galaxie 500 fastback, 67=Galaxie 500/XL two-door hardtop, 60=Galaxie 500/XL four-door hardtop, 68=Galaxie 500/XL fastback, 69=Galaxie 500/XL two-door convertible, 38=four-door six-passenger station wagon, 48=four-door Custom six-passenger station wagon, 49=four-door Country Squire station wagon, 72=four-door station wagon, 74=four-door station wagon, 76=four-door station wagon

1963 Ford Galaxie two-door Sedan (PH)

and 78=four-door station wagon. The fifth symbol identifies engine code, as follows: V=223-cid six-cylinder, 5=223-cid six-cylinder, E=223-cid six-cylinder, F=260-cid V-8, 8=260-cid V-8, C=289-cid two-barrel V-8, X=352-cid two-barrel V-8, Z=390-cid four-barrel V-8, 9=390-cid V-8, P=390-cid V-8, B=406-cid V-8, G=406-cid V-8, Q=427-cid V-8, R=427-cid V-8. The last six digits are the unit's production number, beginning at 100001 and going up, at each of the assembly plants. Full-size Fords not built at all Ford plants.

Falcon Standard (Six)

Model No.	Body/Style No.	Body Type & Seating	Factory Price	Shipping Weight	Production Total
62A	01	2-dr. Sedan-6P	$1,985	2,305 lbs.	68,429
54A	02	4-dr. Sedan-6P	$2,047	2,345 lbs.	59,983

Falcon Standard (V-8)

Model No.	Body/Style No.	Body Type & Seating	Factory Price	Shipping Weight	Production Total
62A	01	2-dr. Sedan-6P	$2,147	2,625 lbs.	2,201
54A	02	4-dr. Sedan-6P	$2,209	2,665 lbs.	2,382

Falcon Futura (Six)

Model No.	Body/Style No.	Body Type & Seating	Factory Price	Shipping Weight	Production Total
62B	19	2-dr. Sedan-6P	$2,116	2,315 lbs.	15,298
54B	16	4-dr. Sedan-6P	$2,165	2,350 lbs.	28,929
63B	17	2-dr. Hardtop-6P	$2,198	2,455 lbs.	11,124
76A	15	2-dr. Convertible-6P	$2,470	2,655 lbs.	16,091

Falcon Futura (V-8)

Model No.	Body/Style No.	Body Type & Seating	Factory Price	Shipping Weight	Production Total
62B	19	2-dr. Sedan-6P	$2,278	2,635 lbs.	1,376
54B	16	4-dr. Sedan-6P	$2,327	2,670 lbs.	2,807
63B	17	2-dr. Hardtop-6P	$2,360	2,722 lbs.	6,400
76A	15	2-dr. Convertible-6P	$2,595	2,913 lbs.	2,851

Falcon Futura Sport (Six)

Model No.	Body/Style No.	Body Type & Seating	Factory Price	Shipping Weight	Production Total
62C	19	2-dr. Sport Coupe-6P	$2,237	2,350 lbs.	9,794
63C	17	4-dr. Sport Hardtop-6P	$2,319	2,490 lbs.	7,449
76B	15	2-dr. Sport Convertible-6P	$2,591	2,690 lbs.	10,690

Falcon Futura Sport (V-8)

Model No.	Body/Style No.	Body Type & Seating	Factory Price	Shipping Weight	Production Total
62C	19	2-dr. Sport Coupe-6P	$2,399	2,670 lbs.	550
63C	17	4-dr. Sport Hardtop-6P	$2,481	2,757 lbs.	3,523
76B	15	2-dr. Sport Convertible-6P	$2,716	2,948 lbs.	1,560

Falcon Futura Sprint (V-8)

Model No.	Body/Style No.	Body Type & Seating	Factory Price	Shipping Weight	Production Total
63D	17	2-dr. Sprint Hardtop-6P	$2,603	2,829 lbs.	10,479
76C	15	2-dr. Sprint Convertible-6P	$2,837	3,029 lbs.	4,602

Falcon Station Wagon (Six)

Model No.	Body/Style No.	Body Type & Seating	Factory Price	Shipping Weight	Production Total
59A	21	2-dr. Station Wagon-6P	$2,298	2,590 lbs.	7,024
71A	22	4-dr. Station Wagon-6P	$2,341	2,625 lbs.	17,595

Falcon Station Wagon (V-8)

Model No.	Body/Style No.	Body Type & Seating	Factory Price	Shipping Weight	Production Total
59A	21	2-dr. Station Wagon-6P	$2,460	2,903 lbs.	298
71A	22	4-dr. Station Wagon-6P	$2,503	2,938 lbs.	889

Futura Station Wagon (Six)

Model No.	Body/Style No.	Body Type & Seating	Factory Price	Shipping Weight	Production Total
59B	23	2-dr. Station Wagon-6P	$2,384	2,605 lbs.	3,980
71B	24	4-dr. Station Wagon-6P	$2,427	2,645 lbs.	21,177

Futura Station Wagon (V-8)

Model No.	Body/Style No.	Body Type & Seating	Factory Price	Shipping Weight	Production Total
59B	23	2-dr. Station Wagon-6P	$2,546	2,918 lbs.	289
71B	24	4-dr. Station Wagon-6P	$2,589	2,958 lbs.	2,300

Futura Squire Station Wagon (Six)

Model No.	Body/Style No.	Body Type & Seating	Factory Price	Shipping Weight	Production Total
71C	26	4-dr. Station Wagon-6P	$2,603	2,645 lbs.	6,068

Futura Squire Station Wagon (V-8)

Model No.	Body/Style No.	Body Type & Seating	Factory Price	Shipping Weight	Production Total
71C	26	4-dr. Station Wagon-6P	$2,765	2,958 lbs.	740

Futura Squire Sport (Bucket Seat) Wagon (Six)

Model No.	Body/Style No.	Body Type & Seating	Factory Price	Shipping Weight	Production Total
71D	26	4-dr. Station Wagon-6P	$2,724	2,680 lbs.	1,299

Futura Squire Sport (Bucket Seat) Wagon (V-8)

Model No.	Body/Style No.	Body Type & Seating	Factory Price	Shipping Weight	Production Total
71D	26	4-dr. Station Wagon-9P	$2,886	2,993 lbs.	162

Fairlane (Six)

Model No.	Body/Style No.	Body Type & Seating	Factory Price	Shipping Weight	Production Total
62A	31	2-dr. Sedan-6P	$2,154	2,815 lbs.	20,347
54A	32	4-dr. Sedan-6P	$2,216	2,855 lbs.	24,727

Fairlane (V-8)

Model No.	Body/Style No.	Body Type & Seating	Factory Price	Shipping Weight	Production Total
62A	31	2-dr. Sedan-6P	$2,257	2,947 lbs.	8,637
54A	32	4-dr. Sedan-6P	$2,319	2,987 lbs.	19,727

Fairlane 500 (Six)

62B	41	2-dr. Sedan-6P	$2,242	2,830 lbs.	11,494
54B	42	4-dr. Sedan-6P	$2,304	2,870 lbs.	20,915
65A	43	2-dr. Hardtop-6P	$2,324	2,850 lbs.	4,610

Fairlane 500 (V-8)

62B	41	2-dr. Sedan-6P	$2,345	2,962 lbs.	23,270
54B	42	4-dr. Sedan-6P	$2,407	3,002 lbs.	83,260
65A	43	2-dr. Hardtop-6P	$2,427	2,982 lbs.	37,031

Fairlane 500 Sport (Six)

65B	47	2-dr. Hardtop-6P	$2,504	2,870 lbs.	1,351

Fairlane 500 Sport (V-8)

65B	47	2-dr. Hardtop-6P	$2,607	3,002 lbs.	26,917

Fairlane Ranch Wagon (Six)

71D	38	4-dr. Station Wagon-6P	$2,525	3,195 lbs.	5,972
71D	38	4-dr. Station Wagon-9P	$2,575	3,210 lbs.	1,180

Fairlane Ranch Wagon (V-8)

71D	38	4-dr. Station Wagon-6P	$2,628	3,327 lbs.	12,691
71D	38	4-dr. Station Wagon-9P	$2,678	3,342 lbs.	4,163

Fairlane Custom Ranch Wagon (Six)

71B	48	4-dr. Station Wagon-6P	$2,613	3,210 lbs.	1,313
71B	48	4-dr. Station Wagon-9P	$2,663	3,225 lbs.	897

Fairlane Custom Ranch Wagon (V-8)

71B	48	4-dr. Station Wagon-6P	$2,716	3,342 lbs.	13,838
71B	48	4-dr. Station Wagon-9P	$2,766	3,357 lbs.	13,564

Fairlane Squire Wagon (Six)

71E	36	4-dr. Station Wagon-6P	$2,781	3,220 lbs.	197
71G	36	4-dr. Station Wagon-9P	$2,831	3,235 lbs.	133

Fairlane Squire Wagon (V-8)

71E	36	4-dr. Station Wagon-6P	$2,884	3,352 lbs.	3,872
71G	36	4-dr. Station Wagon-9P	$2,934	3,367 lbs.	3,781

Ford 300 (Six)

62E	53	2-dr. Sedan-6P	$2,324	3,565 lbs.	13,465
54E	54	4-dr. Sedan-6P	$2,378	3,645 lbs.	19,669

Ford 300 (V-8)

62E	53	2-dr. Sedan-6P	$2,433	3,560 lbs.	12,545
54E	54	4-dr. Sedan-6P	$2,487	3,640 lbs.	24,473

Galaxie (Six)

62B	51	2-dr. Sedan-6P	$2,453	3,575 lbs.	9,677
54B	52	4-dr. Sedan-6P	$2,507	3,665 lbs.	15,977

Galaxie (V-8)

62B	51	2-dr. Sedan-6P	$2,562	3,580 lbs.	20,658
54B	52	4-dr. Sedan-6P	$2,616	3,660 lbs.	66,442

Galaxie 500 (Six)

62A	61	2-dr. Sedan-6P	$2,613	3,605 lbs.	2,023
54A	62	4-dr. Sedan-6P	$2,667	3,685 lbs.	6,603
65A	63	2-dr. Fastback-6P	$2,674	3,620 lbs.	2,561
65A	63	2-dr. Hardtop-6P	$2,674	3,620 lbs.	1,245
75A	64	4-dr. Hardtop-6P	$2,739	3,700 lbs.	620
76A	65	2-dr. Convertible-6P	$2,924	3,775 lbs.	1,512

Galaxie 500 (V-8)

62A	61	2-dr. Sedan-6P	$2,722	3,600 lbs.	19,114
54A	62	4-dr. Sedan-6P	$2,776	3,680 lbs.	199,119
65A	63	2-dr. Fastback-6P	$2,783	3,615 lbs.	97,939
65A	63	2-dr. Hardtop-6P	$2,783	3,615 lbs.	48,488
75A	64	4-dr. Hardtop-6P	$2,848	3,695 lbs.	25,938
76A	65	2-dr. Convertible-6P	$3,033	3,770 lbs.	35,364

Galaxie 500/XL (V-8)

65A	63	2-dr. Fastback-6P	$3,268	3,670 lbs.	33,870
65A	63	2-dr. Hardtop-6P	$3,268	3,670 lbs.	29,713
75A	64	4-dr. Hardtop-6P	$3,333	3,750 lbs.	12,596
76A	65	2-dr. Convertible-6P	$3,518	3,820 lbs.	18,551

Station Wagon (Six)

71C	72	4-dr. Country Sedan-6P	$2,829	3,990 lbs.	4,704
71B	74	4-dr. Country Sedan-8P	$2,933	4,005 lbs.	1,675
71A	76	4-dr. Country Squire-6P	$3,018	4,005 lbs.	301
71E	78	4-dr. Country Squire-8P	$3,088	4,015 lbs.	171

Station Wagon (V-8)

71C	72	4-dr. Country Sedan-6P	$2,938	3,985 lbs.	60,250
71B	74	4-dr. Country Sedan-8P	$3,042	4,000 lbs.	20,575
71A	76	4-dr. Country Squire-6P	$3,127	4,000 lbs.	20,058
71E	78	4-dr. Country Squire-8P	$3,197	4,010 lbs.	19,396

Engines:

Falcon Six: Overhead valve. Cast-iron block. Displacement: 144 cid. B & S: 3.50 x 2.50 in. Compression ratio: 6.7:1. Brake hp: 65 at 4200 rpm. Carburetor: Holley one-barrel. Seven main bearings. Code S.

Falcon Six: Overhead valve. Cast-iron block. Displacement: 170 cid. B & S: 3.50 x 2.94 in. Compression ratio: 8.7:1. Brake hp: 101 at 4400 rpm. Carburetor: Holley one-barrel. Seven main bearings. Code U.

Ford Six: Overhead valve. Cast-iron block. Displacement: 223 cid. B & S: 3.62 x 3.60 in. Compression ratio: 8.4:1. Brake hp: 138 at 4200 rpm. Carburetor: Holley one-barrel. Four main bearings. Code V.

Base Fairlane V-8: Overhead valve. Cast-iron block. Displacement: 221 cid. B & S: 3.50 x 2.87 in. Compression ratio: 8.70:1. Brake hp: 145 at 4400 rpm. Torque: 216 lbs.-ft. at 2200 rpm. Five main bearings. Hydraulic valve lifters. Carburetor: Ford two-barrel C30F-9510-C. Cooling system capacity: 14.5 qt. with heater. Crankcase capacity: 4 qt. (add 1 qt. with new oil filter). Code L. (Export Code 3)

Challenger 260 V-8 (Optional Fairlane and Ford): Overhead valve. Cast-iron block. Displacement: 260 cid. B & S: 3.80 x 2.87 in. Compression ratio: 8.70:1. Brake hp: 164 at 4400 rpm. Torque: 258 lbs.-ft. at 2200 rpm. Five main bearings. Hydraulic valve lifters. Carburetor: Ford two-barrel C30F-9510-E. Cooling system capacity: 14.5 qt. with heater. Crankcase capacity: 4 qt. (add 1 qt. with new oil filter). Code F. (Export code 6).

High-Performance Challenger 289 V-8 (1963-1/2 Fairlane): Overhead valve. Cast-iron block. Displacement: 289 cid. B & S: 4.00 x 2.87 in. Compression ratio: 9.00:1. Brake hp: 195 at 4400 rpm. Torque: 282 lbs.-ft. at 2200 rpm. Five main bearings. Hydraulic valve lifters. Carburetor: Ford two-barrel C30F-9510. Cooling system capacity: 14.5 qt. with heater. Crankcase capacity: 4 qt. (add 1 qt. with new oil filter). Code C.

Interceptor V-8 (Standard in Galaxie 500/XL): Overhead valve. Cast-iron block. Displacement: 352 cid. B & S: 4.00 x 3.50 in. Compression ratio: 8.90:1. Brake hp: 220 at 4300 rpm. Torque: 336 lbs.-ft. at 2600 rpm. Five main bearings. Hydraulic valve lifters. Carburetor: Two-barrel. Cooling system capacity: 20.5 qt. with heater. Crankcase capacity: 5 qt. (add 1 qt. with new oil filter). Code X.

High-Performance C289 V-8 (1963-1/2 Fairlane): Overhead valve. Cast-iron block. Displacement: 289 cid. B & S: 4.00 x 2.87 in. Compression ratio: 10.50:1. Brake hp: 271 at 6000 rpm. Torque: 312 lbs.-ft. at 3400 rpm. Five main bearings. Solid valve lifters. Carburetor: Four-barrel. Cooling system capacity: 14.5 qt. with heater. Crankcase capacity: 4 qt. (add 1 qt. with new oil filter). Code K.

Interceptor 390 V-8: Overhead valve. Cast-iron block. Displacement: 390 cid. B & S: 4.05 x 3.78 in. Compression ratio: 9.60:1. Brake hp: 300 at 4600 rpm. Torque: 427 lbs.-ft. at 2800 rpm. Five main bearings. Hydraulic valve lifters. Carburetor: Ford four-barrel C2AF-9510. Cooling system capacity: 20.5 qt. with heater. Crankcase capacity: 5 qt. (add 1 qt. with new oil filter). Dual exhausts. Code Z.

Interceptor 390 V-8: Overhead valve. Cast-iron block. Displacement: 390 cid. B & S: 4.05 x 3.78 in. Compression ratio: 9.60:1. Brake hp: 330 at 5000 rpm. Torque: 427 lbs.-ft. at 3200 rpm. Five main bearings. Solid valve lifters. Carburetor: Ford four-barrel. Cooling system capacity: 20.5 qt. with heater. Crankcase capacity: 5 qt. (add 1 qt. with new oil filter). Dual exhausts. Code P. (Export code 9)

Thunderbird 406 V-8: Overhead valve. Cast-iron block. Displacement: 406 cid. B & S: 4.13 x 3.78 in. Compression ratio: 11.40:1. Brake hp: 385 at 5800 rpm. Torque: 444 lbs.-ft. at 3400 rpm. Five main bearings. Solid valve lifters. Carburetor: Holley four-barrel. Cooling system capacity: 20.5 qt. with heater. Crankcase capacity: 5 qt. (add 1 qt. with new oil filter). Dual exhausts. Code B.

Thunderbird Special 406 V-8: Overhead valve. Cast-iron block. Displacement: 406 cid. B & S: 4.13 x 3.78 in. Compression ratio: 11.40:1. Brake hp: 405 at 5800 rpm. Torque: 448 lbs.-ft. at 3500 rpm. Five main bearings. Solid valve lifters. Carburetor: Holley three two-barrel. Cooling system capacity: 20.5 qt. with heater. Crankcase capacity: 5 qt. (add 1 qt. with new oil filter). Dual exhausts. Code G.

Note: Export engines have lower compression and less horsepower.

Chassis:

Falcon: Wheelbase: 109.5 in. Overall length: 181.1 in. Tires: 6.00 x 13 four-ply tubeless blackwall (6.50 x 13 four-ply tubeless on station wagons and convertibles).

Fairlane: Wheelbase: 115.5 in. Overall length: 197.6 in. (201.8 in. on station wagons). Tires: 6.50 x 13 four-ply blackwall tubeless (7.00 x 14 four-ply blackwall tubeless on station wagons).

Ford: Wheelbase: 119 in. Overall length: 209.0 in. Tires: 7.50 x 14 four-ply tubeless blackwalls (8.00 x 14 four-ply tubeless blackwalls on station wagons).

Options:

Falcon: Air conditioner ($231.70). Back-up lights ($10.70). Heavy-duty battery ($7.60). Bucket seats and console in Squire station wagon ($120.40). Convenience package ($37.80). 170-cid 101-hp six-cylinder engine ($37.40, but standard in convertible). Tinted glass ($27). Tinted windshield ($12.95). Heater and defroster delete ($73.40 credit). Chrome luggage rack for station wagon ($45.40). Rocker panel molding ($16.10). Two-tone paint ($19.40). Push-button radio and antenna ($58.50). Padded dashboard in convertible ($17.30). Padded dashboard and sun visors, except convertible ($21.80). Safety belts ($16.80). Electric tailgate window in station wagons ($29.75, but standard in Falcon Squire). Five 6.00 x 13 4-ply white sidewall tires on sedans ($29.90). Five 6.50 x 13 4-ply black sidewall tires on sedans ($10.40). Five 6.50 x 13 4-ply white sidewall tires on sedans ($43.50). Five 6.50 x 13 4-ply white sidewall tires on convertibles and station wagons ($33). Five 6.50 x 13 6-ply black sidewall tires on convertibles and station wagons ($28). Five 6.50 x 13 6-ply white sidewall tires on convertibles and station wagons ($61.10). Automatic transmission ($163.10). Four-speed manual transmission ($90.10). Vinyl roof on Futura Sports Sedan ($75.80). Vinyl trim in Futura Sports Sedan ($25). Wheel covers ($16.00, but standard on Futuras). Wire design wheel covers, except Futura ($45.10). Wire design wheel covers on Futuras ($27.40). Two-speed electric wiper washers ($20.10).

Ford and Fairlane: Air conditioner ($231.70 and requires 7.00 tires on Fairlanes). Select Aire air conditioner ($360.90, but standard in Galaxie 500, 500/XL and Squires). Back-up lights ($10.70). Heavy-duty battery ($7.60). Equa-Lock differential ($42.50). Electric clock in Ford 300, Galaxie and Country Sedan wagon ($14.60). Chrome luggage rack for station wagon ($45.40). Rocker panel molding ($16.10). Padded dashboard in convertible ($18.60). Padded dashboard and sun visors, except convertible ($24.30). Tu-Tone paint ($22). Power brakes ($43.20). Full-width power front seat ($63.80, but not available in Fairlane series). Power driver seat only in Galaxie 500/XL ($92.10). Power steering ($81.70). Power tailgate window in Country Sedan six-passenger, Ranch Wagon and Custom Ranch Wagon ($32.30). Front and rear power windows ($102.10). Radio and antenna ($58.50). AM/FM radio and antenna in Fords ($129.30). Safety belts ($16.80). Front bucket seats with console in Fairlane Squire ($120.50). Front bucket seats with console in Galaxie Squire ($141.60). Movable steering column in Ford 300 and all Galaxies ($50 and requires power steering and automatic transmission). Tinted glass ($40.30). Tinted windshield ($21.55). Cruise-O-Matic transmission ($212.30). Ford-O-Matic transmission with six-cylinder ($179.80). Ford-O-Matic transmission with V-8 ($189.60). Overdrive ($108.40). Four-speed manual transmission in all except Galaxie 500/XL ($188 and required V-8 engine with Fairlanes). Four-speed manual transmission in Galaxie 500/XL ($34.80 credit). Vinyl trim in Fairlane 500 and Galaxie 500 ($25.00 and standard in Fairlane Sport Coupe and Galaxie 500/XL). Vinyl trim in Ford 300, Galaxie and Country Sedan ($32.20). Wire design wheel covers, except Fairlane 500 Sports

Coupe and Galaxie 500/XL ($45.10). Wire design wheel covers on Fairlane 500 Sports Coupe and Galaxie 500/XL ($27.40). Deluxe wheel covers ($18.60, but standard on Fairlane Sports Coupe and Galaxie 500/XL). Two-speed electric wiper washers ($20.10).

Tires:

Fairlane: Five 6.50 x 13 4-ply black sidewall tires on six-cylinder sedans and hardtops without air conditioning (standard). Five 7.00 x 13 4-ply black sidewall tires on six-cylinder sedans and hardtops with air conditioning (standard). Five 7.00 x 13 4-ply black sidewall tires on V-8 sedans and hardtops with or without air conditioning (standard). Five 7.00 x 14 4-ply black sidewall tires on station wagons (standard). Ford: Various tire options based on 7.00 x 14, 7.50 x 14, 8.00 x 14, 6.70 x 15 and 7.10 x 15 in 4-ply, 6-ply and Nylon models priced in relation to standard equipment.

History:

The Fairlane 500 Sport Coupe was a two-door pillarless hardtop. The Falcon Sprint was a compact, high-performance V-8-powered Falcon. The Galaxie Fastback was a full-size two-door hardtop with more gently sloping roofline than conventional hardtop, to produce less wind resistance. Ford built 50 Galaxie "factory lightweight" race cars this year. A team of specially prepared 1963 Falcon Sprint hardtops terrorized the European rally circuit, with some very non-Falcon-like performance.

1963 Ford Galaxie 500 Formal two-door hardtop(OCW)

1963 Ford Galaxie 500/XL two-door fastback (PH)

1963 Ford Galaxie 500/XL two-door convertible (AA)

1963 Ford Galaxie two-door Country Sedan 9P (OCW)

1963 Ford Galaxie 500 Sunliner two-door Convertible (OCW)

1963 Ford four-door Country Squire Wagon (OCW)

1963 Ford Galaxie 500 four-door Sedan (OCW)

1964 Ford

Falcon — (Six and V-8): The 1964 Falcons reflected the 'Total Performance' image in their new styling. A more aggressive, angled grille led a completely restyled body. As in 1963, the base trim level was the standard series, and the top trim level was the Futura. The highly sculptured body sides gave the 1964 Falcons a racy appearance and added rigidity to the sheet metal. A convex feature line began on the front fenders, but sloped slightly and increased in width gradually, until it met the taillights. The word "Ford" was spelled out across the hood in block letters and "Falcon" was spelled out in block letters between the taillights. The new grille featured a rectangular design that was angularly recessed and complemented the side profile. As in past years, the Falcons continued to use single headlamps. Standard equipment included a six-cylinder 85-hp engine with self-adjusting valves, a three-speed manual transmission, self-adjusting brakes, a full-flow oil filter, a 36,000-mile fuel filter, a fully-aluminized muffler, galvanized main underbody members, a bright-metal windshield molding, a bright-metal rear window molding, parallel-action single-speed electric windshield wipers, two horns, two sun visors, two front arm rests, two coat hooks, a foam-cushioned front seat, a front ash tray, a white vinyl headlining, gold ladder-pattern cloth-and-vinyl seat trim, a color-keyed 3-spoke steering wheel, front seat belt anchors, and turn signals. A heater was installed during production unless otherwise specified. If deleted, an appropriate price reduction was made. In addition to the above, the following Deluxe Trim items were available for Standard Falcon models at slight additional cost: Bright body side moldings, upgraded cloth-and-vinyl interior trim, rear arm rests, an ash tray, a cigarette lighter, a chrome horn ring and an automatic dome light.

Falcon Futura — (Six and V-8): The Futura series was the top trim level for 1964 Standard features included all the equipment that Standard Falcons came with the following additions or replacements: bright-metal side window frames, two horizontal sloping chrome strips on the body side, four cast "hash marks" on the rear fender in front of the taillights a chrome hood ornament, "Futura" on the front fenders, a choice of five different "Bar-Line" pattern pleated cloth-and-vinyl interior trims, a chrome-backed rearview mirror, color-keyed carpeting front and rear, a cigarette lighter, rear arm rests, a rear ash tray, a chrome horn ring, an automatic dome light, a Futura molding across the instrument panel, bright inserts in the dashboard control knobs, Futura full wheel covers and a Futura chrome script on the sides of the rear fenders above the body side moldings. Hardtop and convertible models were additions to the lineup. Standard equipment in the convertible included the Falcon 170 Special six with 101 hp, a choice of five pleated all-vinyl interior trims, foam-padded front and rear seat cushions, an electric-hydraulic power-operated convertible top, vinyl 3-ply top material in white, blue or black, added underbody torque boxes, Safety-Yoke door locks, Futura front arm rests, front and rear ash trays and a chrome-backed "floating" windshield mirror.

Falcon Futura Sprint — (Six and V-8): This Falcon Futura Sprint sub-series contained two sporty models this year. The Sprint versions of the Futura hardtop and convertible also featured a V-8 engine, bucket seats and wire wheel covers.

1964 Ford Falcon Sprint two-door Hardtop (OCW)

1964 Ford Falcon Sprint two-door Convertible (OCW)

Falcon Station Wagon — (Six and V-8): Both two- and four-door station wagons were again available in the Falcon lineup this year. The Standard wagon came in both body styles. The Deluxe station wagon came only in the four-door model with 78.5 cubic feet of cargo space. Deluxe and Squire versions that were more or less comparable to Falcon, Futura and Sprint variations. The Squire included wood-grained exterior trim. The Deluxe and Squire wagons used a larger six-cylinder engine and the Squire also had a power tailgate window and carpeted floors.

Fairlane — (Six and V-8): The 1964 Fairlane styling featured new sheet metal for the body sides and rear, which seemed to add to the Fairlane's "Total Performance" image. The rear fenders featured a smoother top than in 1963, with a complete absence of fins. The sides were sculptured into a convex shape, which flowed forward from the sides of the taillights and terminated in a chrome scoop. The grille carried the familiar horizontal grid with thin vertical dividers. Standard features included a choice of cloth-and-vinyl upholstery, a choice of Diamond Lustre Enamel exterior colors, a bright-metal windshield molding, a white vinyl headlining, a color-keyed 3-spoke steering wheel, dual sun visors, dual coat hooks, front arm rests, a front ash tray, a locking glove box, front seat belt anchors, Safety-Yoke door locks, a foam-cushioned front seat, turn signals with new amber safety lenses in the front bumper, parallel-action single-speed electric wipers, an illuminated trunk (with taillights on), a 101-hp Fairlane Six engine, a three-speed manual transmission, self-adjusting brakes, Zinclad rocker panels and main underbody members, a 6,000-mile full-flow oil filter, a fully-aluminized muffler and a 36,000-mile replaceable fuel filter element.

Fairlane 500 — (Six and V-8): The Fairlane 500 models were the top trim level and included all Fairlane features with the following variations: a choice of "Wheel-Pattern" pleated cloth-and-vinyl interior trims in blue, turquoise, beige, gold or red, a choice of 12 Diamond Lustre enamel exterior colors, bright-metal side window moldings, Fairlane 500 scripts on the roof sail panels, twin-spear body side moldings running the full length of the body with red, black or white accents between the spears, front fender top trim pieces, full wheel covers of a specific design, front and rear arm rests on all doors, front and rear ash trays, a cigarette lighter, an automatic dome light, a chrome horn ring and color-keyed wall-to-wall carpeting. The Fairlane 500 hardtop also included a "floating" inside rearview mirror. The Fairlane 500 Sports Coupe also included a choice of leather-like all-vinyl interior trims, additional Diamond Lustre enamel exterior colors, foam-cushioned front bucket seats with a center console and

1964 Ford Falcon two-door Sedan (OCW)

1964 Ford Falcon Futura four-door Sedan (OCW)

1964 Ford Falcon Sports Futura two-door Hardtop (OCW)

1962 Ford Falcon four-door Station Wagon (OCW)

1964 Ford Falcon four-door Squire Station Wagon (PH)

1964 Ford Fairlane 500 two-door Sedan

1964 Ford Fairlane 500 two-door Hardtop (OCW)

1964 Ford Fairlane 500 two-door Sports Coupe (OCW)

1964 Ford Fairlane 500 two-door Sports Coupe (OCW)

a upgraded headliner. On Fairlane 500s the model identifying script was on the sides of the cowl above the body. The sail panels also had T-bird like ribbed trim panels and emblems.

Fairlane Station Wagon — (Six and V-8): The Fairlane station wagons came in two four-door models: Ranch Wagon and Custom Ranch Wagon. Standard Ranch Wagon equipment started with all of the Fairlane sedan features and then included these variations: a choice of special vinyl-and-vinyl interior trims, a choice of additional Diamond Lustre enamel exterior colors, front and rear foam-cushioned seats, a color-keyed cargo area inlay, a roll-down tailgate window with painted molding and a folding second seat. The Custom Ranch Wagon included all Fairlane 500 sedan equipment, a choice upgraded cloth-and-vinyl trim, color-keyed vinyl-coated rubber floor coverings, a stowage compartment lock and a bright-metal tailgate molding.

Ford Custom — (Six and V-8): Full-size Fords were completely revamped for 1964. They were recognizable as Ford products only because of their traditional large, round taillights. The grille carried a horizontal grid highlighted with three vertical ribs. The Ford name, in block letters, was seen on all models, but side trim differed considerably. A sheet metal feature line began on the front fender at beltline level. It continued horizontally, to the rear of the car, and dipped down. A lower sheet metal feature line began behind the front wheels and continued, horizontally, toward the rear of the car. There it swept upward and merged with the upper feature line. All models using optional large displacement V-8s earned the engine designation symbol on the lower front fender. Ford said the base-level Custom series cars could fool a buyer because they looked expensive, but weren't. Two- and four-door sedans were available. The four-door sedan had no ash tray in back of the front seat. Crank-operated vent windows, a compliance-link front suspension and Swing-Away steering columns were new features or options this year. Doggie-dish hubcaps were provided. Buyers of these cars had a choice of attractive cloth-and-vinyl interiors. Galaxie options and power accessories were available.

Custom 500 — (Six and V-8): The Custom 500 was the upper trim level of the base-line Custom series and included chrome windshield and rear window moldings, nylon carpeting (instead of the rubber mats used in the Custom models), armrests with ashtrays on all doors, two sun visors and all trim used in the Custom models, plus a single horizontal chrome strip on the exterior body side on the front fender and door and "hash mark" front fender trim plates.

Galaxie 500 — (Six and V-8): The Galaxie 500 was the base Galaxie trim level for 1964 and included all Custom trim, plus chrome fender top ornamentation, chrome window frames, the Ford crest on the roof 'C' pillar and a full-length chrome strip (which split at the rear of the front doors and widened forward of that point with an aluminum insert added). A 'Galaxie 500' script, was included in the aluminum insert, near the front inside a sculptured indentation. A stamped aluminum insert also highlighted the rear end treatment and included 'Galaxie 500' in script on the right side of the insert. Two-tone vinyl trim was used on the side of the doors and on the seats. The front floor hump was a third smaller than in 1963, while headroom was increased. Galaxie 500s had all of the same all Custom 500 features, plus additional luxury items that varied by body style. The two-and four-door sedans had these extras: a choice of cloth-and vinyl interior trims in, a choice of additional Diamond Lustre enamel exterior colors, chrome-like Mylar accents on the seats, doors and side panels, pleated seat fabrics, two-tone door panels, deluxe arm

rests, front and rear ash trays, a chrome-backed inside rearview mirror, bright-metal seat side shields, a self-regulating electric clock and back-up lights centered in the taillights. The two-and four-door hardtops also had cloth-and vinyl interior options, Diamond Lustre enamel exterior finish, chrome-like Mylar accents on the seats, doors and side panels, two-tone door panels, deluxe arm rests, front and rear ash trays, a chrome-backed inside rearview mirror, bright-metal seat side shields, a self-regulating electric clock and back-up lights centered in the taillights. The Galaxie 500 Sunliner convertible had all-vinyl interior trims, a choice of Diamond Lustre enamel exterior colors, a 3-ply vinyl power-operated top, an anti-ballooning top design, a zip-out clear vinyl rear window, a color-keyed and contoured top boot, automatic courtesy lights under the dashboard and a "floating" rearview mirror bonded to the windshield.

Galaxie 500/XL — (V-8): The Galaxie 500/XL series now included just three models, two- and four-door hardtops and convertible. These cars included all the trim features of the Galaxie models plus shell-type bucket seats, a console, a floor-mounted transmission shifter, polished door trim panels, dual-lens courtesy/warning lights in the doors, rear reading lights in hardtops and Galaxie 500/XL badges on the body exterior. A 289-cid 195-hp V-8 was standard in all Galaxie 500/XLs.

Galaxie Station Wagon — (Six and V-8): All 1964 full-size Ford station wagons were four-door models. The Country Sedans were the base trim level station wagons for 1964, with the Country Squires being the top trim level. Both were offered in two- and four-door body styles. The trim paralleled the Galaxie 500 and Galaxie 500XL models of passenger cars. Country Squires also had wood-grained exterior paneling and a power tailgate window.

VIN (Falcon):

The VIN for Falcons was die-stamped into the top of the left-hand front inner fender apron. The first symbol indicates year: 4=1964. The second symbol identifies assembly plant, as follows: A=Atlanta, Georgia, D=Dallas, Texas, E=Mahwah, New Jersey, F=Dearborn, Michigan, G=Chicago, Illinois, H=Lorain, Ohio, J=Los Angeles, California, K=Kansas City, Kansas, N=Norfolk, Virginia, P=Twin Cities, Minnesota, R=San Jose, California, S=Pilot Plant, T=Metuchen, New Jersey, U=Louisville, Kentucky, W=Wayne, Michigan, Y=Wixom, Michigan, Z=St. Louis, Mo. The third and fourth symbols identify body series code: 01=two-door sedan, 02=four-door sedan, 11=two-door hardtop with bucket seats, 12=two-door convertible with bucket seats, 13=Sprint two-door hardtop, 14=Sprint two-door convertible, 15=two-door bench-seat convertible, 16=four-door bench-seat sedan, 17=four-door bench-seat hardtop, 19=two-door bench-seat sedan, 21=two-door station wagon, 22=four-door station wagon, 24=four-door Deluxe station wagon, 26=four-door Squire station wagon. The fifth symbol identifies engine code, as follows: S=144-cid six-cylinder, U=170-cid six-cylinder, 4=170-cid six-cylinder, T=200-cid six-cylinder, F=260-cid V-8, G=260-cid V-8 low-compression and K=289-cid V-8. The last six digits are the unit's production number, beginning at 100001 and going up, at each of the assembly plants. Falcons not built at all Ford plants.

VIN (Fairlane):

The VIN for Fairlanes was die-stamped into the side of the left-hand front inner fender apron near the top. The first symbol indicates year: 4=1964. The second symbol identifies assembly plant, as follows: A=Atlanta, Georgia, D=Dallas, Texas, E=Mahwah, New Jersey, F=Dearborn, Michigan, G=Chicago, Illinois, H=Lorain, Ohio, J=Los Angeles, California, K=Kansas City, Kansas, N=Norfolk, Virginia, P=Twin Cities, Minnesota, R=San Jose, California, S=Pilot Plant, T=Metuchen, New Jersey, U=Louisville, Kentucky, W=Wayne, Michigan, Y=Wixom, Michigan, Z=St. Louis, Mo. The third and fourth symbols identify body series code: 31=Fairlane two-door sedan, 32=Fairlane four-door sedan, 41=Fairlane 500 two-door sedan, 42=Fairlane 500 four-door sedan, 43=Fairlane 500 two-door hardtop, 47=Fairlane 500 two-door Sport Coupe, 38=Fairlane four-door six-passenger station wagon, 48=Fairlane Custom four-door six-passenger station wagon. The fifth symbol identifies engine code, as follows: U=170-cid six-cylinder, 4=170-cid low-compression export six-cylinder, T=200-cid six-cylinder, F=260-cid V-8, 6=260-cid low-compression export V-8, C=289-cid two-barrel V-8, 3=289-cid low-compression export two-barrel V-8, K=289-cid four-barrel V-8 and R=427-cid dual four-barrel V-8. The last six digits are the unit's production number, beginning at 100001 and going up, at each of the assembly plants. Fairlanes not built at all Ford plants.

VIN (Ford):

The VIN for full-size Fords was die-stamped into the top right-hand side rail of the frame ahead of the front suspension member. The first symbol indicates year: 4=1964. The second symbol identifies assembly plant, as follows: A=Atlanta, Georgia, D=Dallas, Texas, E=Mahwah, New Jersey, F=Dearborn, Michigan, G=Chicago, Illinois, H=Lorain, Ohio, J=Los Angeles, California, K=Kansas City, Kansas, N=Norfolk, Virginia, P=Twin Cities, Minnesota, R=San Jose, California, S=Pilot Plant, T=Metuchen, New Jersey, U=Louisville, Kentucky, W=Wayne, Michigan, Y=Wixom, Michigan, Z=St. Louis, Mo. The third and fourth symbols identify body series 51=Custom 500 two-door sedan, 52=Custom 500 four-door sedan, 53=Custrom two-door sedan, 54=Custom four-door sedan, 61=Galaxie 500 two-door sedan, 62=Galaxie 500 four-door sedan, 64=Galaxie 500 four-door Victoria Hardtop, 65=Galaxie 500 Sunliner convertible, 66=Galaxie 500 fastback, 60=Galaxie 500/XL four-door hardtop, 68=Galaxie 500/XL fastback, 69=Galaxie 500/XL two-door convertible, 72=four-door six-passenger Country Sedan station wagon, 74=four-door nine-passenger Country Sedan station wagon, 76=four-door Country Squire six-passenger station wagon and 78=four-door Country Squire nine-passenger station wagon. The fifth symbol identifies engine code, as follows: V=223-cid six-cylinder, 5=223-cid Export six-cylinder, B=223-cid Police six, E=223-cid Taxi six-cylinder, C=289-cid two-barrel V-8,

3=289-cid low-compression export two-barrel V-8, X=352-cid two-barrel V-8, Z=390-cid four-barrel V-8, 9=390-cid V-8, P=390-cid V-8, Q=427-cid V-8, R=427-cid V-8. The last six digits are the unit's production number, beginning at 100001 and going up, at each of the assembly plants. Full-size Fords not built at all Ford plants.

Falcon Standard (Six)

Model No.	Body/ Style No.	Body Style and Seating	Factory Price	Shipping Weight	Production Total
62A	01	2-dr. Sedan-6P	$1,996	2,358 lbs.	61,624
54A	02	4-dr. Sedan-6P	$2,058	2,393 lbs.	50,930

Falcon Standard (V-8)

Model No.	Body/ Style No.	Body Style and Seating	Factory Price	Shipping Weight	Production Total
62A	01	2-dr. Sedan-6P	$2,165	2,713 lbs.	3,228
54A	02	4-dr. Sedan-6P	$2,227	2,748 lbs.	4,224

Falcon Futura (Six)

Model No.	Body/ Style No.	Body Style and Seating	Factory Price	Shipping Weight	Production Total
62B	19	2-dr. Sedan-6P	$2,127	2,367 lbs.	14,682
54B	16	4-dr. Sedan-6P	$2,176	2,402 lbs.	32,097
63B	17	2-dr. Hardtop-6P	$2,209	2,505 lbs.	18,095
76A	15	2-dr. Convertible-6P	$2,481	2,700 lbs.	9.108

Falcon Futura (V-8)

Model No.	Body/ Style No.	Body Style and Seating	Factory Price	Shipping Weight	Production Total
62B	19	2-dr. Sedan-6P	$2,296	2,722 lbs.	2,151
54B	16	4-dr. Sedan-6P	$2,345	2,757 lbs.	5,935
63B	17	2-dr. Hardtop-6P	$2,378	2,809 lbs.	14,513
76A	15	2-dr. Convertible-6P	$2,634	2,982 lbs.	4,112

Falcon Futura Sport (Six)

Model No.	Body/ Style No.	Body Style and Seating	Factory Price	Shipping Weight	Production Total
63C	11	2-dr. Sport Hardtop-6P	$2,325	2,533 lbs.	4,492
76B	12	4-dr. Sport Convertible-6P	$2,591	2,690 lbs.	10,690

Falcon Futura Sport (V-8)

Model No.	Body/ Style No.	Body Style and Seating	Factory Price	Shipping Weight	Production Total
63C	11	2-dr. Sport Hardtop-6P	$2,494	2,837 lbs.	4,115
76B	12	4-dr. Sport Convertible-6P	$2,750	3,010 lbs.	1,256

Falcon Futura Sprint (V-8)

Model No.	Body/ Style No.	Body Style and Seating	Factory Price	Shipping Weight	Production Total
63D/E	13	2-dr. Sprint Hardtop-6P	$2,436	2,803 lbs.	13,830
76D/E	14	4-dr. Sprint Convertible-6P	$2,671	2,976 lbs.	4,278

D=Bucket seats, E=Bench seats

Falcon Station Wagon (Six)

Model No.	Body/ Style No.	Body Style and Seating	Factory Price	Shipping Weight	Production Total
59A	21	2-dr. Station Wagon-6P	$2,326	2,620 lbs.	5,404
71A	22	4-dr. Station Wagon-6P	$2,360	2,655 lbs.	16,007

Falcon Station Wagon (V-8)

Model No.	Body/ Style No.	Body Style and Seating	Factory Price	Shipping Weight	Production Total
59A	21	2-dr. Station Wagon-6P	$2,479	2,975 lbs.	630
71A	22	4-dr. Station Wagon-6P	$2,513	3,010 lbs.	1,772

Deluxe Ranch Wagon (Six)

Model No.	Body/ Style No.	Body Style and Seating	Factory Price	Shipping Weight	Production Total
71B	24	4-dr. Station Wagon-6P	$2,446	2,673 lbs.	15,738

Deluxe Ranch Wagon (V-8)

Model No.	Body/ Style No.	Body Style and Seating	Factory Price	Shipping Weight	Production Total
71B	24	4-dr. Station Wagon-6P	$2,599	3,028 lbs.	4,959

Futura Squire Station Wagon (Six)

Model No.	Body/ Style No.	Body Style and Seating	Factory Price	Shipping Weight	Production Total
71C	26	4-dr. Station Wagon-6P	$2,622	2,675 lbs.	4,304

Futura Squire Station Wagon (V-8)

Model No.	Body/ Style No.	Body Style and Seating	Factory Price	Shipping Weight	Production Total
71C	26	4-dr. Station Wagon-6P	$2,775	3,030 lbs.	2,462

Fairlane (Six)

Model No.	Body/ Style No.	Body Style and Seating	Factory Price	Shipping Weight	Production Total
62A	31	2-dr. Sedan-6P	$2,194	2,805 lbs.	14,777
54A	32	4-dr. Sedan-6P	$2,235	2,857 lbs.	22,233

Fairlane (V-8)

Model No.	Body/ Style No.	Body Style and Seating	Factory Price	Shipping Weight	Production Total
62A	31	2-dr. Sedan-6P	$2,294	2,997 lbs.	5,644
54A	32	4-dr. Sedan-6P	$2,335	3,049 lbs.	14,460

Fairlane 500 (Six)

Model No.	Body/ Style No.	Body Style and Seating	Factory Price	Shipping Weight	Production Total
62B	41	2-dr. Sedan-6P	$2,276	2,820 lbs.	8,760
54B	42	4-dr. Sedan-6P	$2,317	2,872 lbs.	18,791
65A	43	2-dr. Hardtop-6P	$2,341	2,880 lbs.	4,467

Fairlane 500 (V-8)

Model No.	Body/ Style No.	Body Style and Seating	Factory Price	Shipping Weight	Production Total
62B	41	2-dr. Sedan-6P	$2,376	3,012 lbs.	14,687
54B	42	4-dr. Sedan-6P	$2,417	3,064 lbs.	68,128
65A	43	2-dr. Hardtop-6P	$2,441	3,072 lbs.	22,296

Fairlane 500 Sport (Six)

Model No.	Body/ Style No.	Body Style and Seating	Factory Price	Shipping Weight	Production Total
65B	47	2-dr. Hardtop-6P	$2,502	2,904 lbs.	946

1964 Ford Fairlane four-door Custom Ranch Wagon (OCW)

Fairlane 500 Sport (V-8)

65B	47	2-dr. Hardtop-6P	$2,602	3,096 lbs.	20,485

Fairlane Ranch Wagon (Six)

71D	38	4-dr. Station Wagon-6P	$2,531	3,207 lbs.	7,324

Fairlane Ranch Wagon (V-8)

71D	38	4-dr. Station Wagon-6P	$2,631	3,399 lbs.	13,656

Fairlane Custom Ranch Wagon (Six)

71B	48	4-dr. Station Wagon-6P	$2,612	3,237 lbs.	2,666

Fairlane Custom Ranch Wagon (V-8)

71B	48	4-dr. Station Wagon-6P	$2,712	3,429 lbs.	22,296

Ford Custom (Six)

62E	53	2-dr. Sedan-6P	$2,361	3,538 lbs.	22,214
54E	54	4-dr. Sedan-6P	$2,415	3,628 lbs.	22,661

Ford Custom (V-8)

62E	53	2-dr. Sedan-6P	$2,470	3,549 lbs.	19,145
54E	54	4-dr. Sedan-6P	$2,524	3,639 lbs.	35,303

Custom 500 (Six)

62B	51	2-dr. Sedan-6P	$2,464	3,571 lbs.	5,785
54B	52	4-dr. Sedan-6P	$2,518	3,671 lbs.	10,256

Custom 500 (V-8)

62B	51	2-dr. Sedan-6P	$2,573	3,582 lbs.	14,834
54B	52	4-dr. Sedan-6P	$2,627	3,682 lbs.	58,572

Galaxie 500 (Six)

62A	61	2-dr. Sedan-6P	$2,624	3,586 lbs.	1,029
54A	62	4-dr. Sedan-6P	$2,678	3,686 lbs.	5,133
63B	63	2-dr. Fastback-6P	$2,685	3,597 lbs.	5,035
57B	64	4-dr. Hardtop-6P	$2,750	3,698 lbs.	710
76A	65	2-dr. Convertible-6P	$2,947	3,798 lbs.	1,034

Galaxie 500 (V-8)

62A	61	2-dr. Sedan-6P	$2,733	3,697 lbs.	12,012
54A	62	4-dr. Sedan-6P	$2,787	3,697 lbs.	193,672
63B	63	2-dr. Fastback-6P	$2,794	3,608 lbs.	201,963
57B	64	4-dr. Hardtop-6P	$2,859	3,709 lbs.	48,532
76A	65	2-dr. Convertible-6P	$3,056	3,779 lbs.	36,277

Galaxie 500/XL (V-8)

63C	63	2-dr. Fastback-6P	$3,233	3,633 lbs.	58,306
57C	64	4-dr. Hardtop-6P	$3,298	3,734 lbs.	14,661
76A	65	2-dr. Convertible-6P	$3,495	3,801 lbs.	15,169

Station Wagon (Six)

71C	72	4-dr. Country Sedan-6P	$2,840	3,990 lbs.	3,813
71B	74	4-dr. Country Sedan-8P	$2,944	4,002 lbs.	1,030
71E	76	4-dr. Country Squire-6P	$3,029	4,004 lbs.	234
71A	78	4-dr. Country Squire-8P	$3,099	4,016 lbs.	121

Station Wagon (V-8)

71C	72	4-dr. Country Sedan-6P	$2,949	4,001 lbs.	64,765
71B	74	4-dr. Country Sedan-8P	$3,053	4,013 lbs.	24,631
71E	76	4-dr. Country Squire-6P	$3,138	4,015 lbs.	23,336
71A	78	4-dr. Country Squire-8P	$3,208	4,027 lbs.	22,999

Engines:

Falcon Six: Overhead valve. Cast-iron block. Displacement: 144 cid. B & S: 3.50 x 2.50 in. Compression ratio: 6.7:1. Brake hp: 65 at 4200 rpm. Carburetor: Holley one-barrel. Seven main bearings. Code S.

Falcon Six: Overhead valve. Cast-iron block. Displacement: 170 cid. B & S: 3.50 x 2.94 in. Compression ratio: 8.7:1. Brake hp: 101 at 4400 rpm. Carburetor: Holley one-barrel. Seven main bearings. Code U.

Ford Six: Overhead valve. Cast-iron block. Displacement: 223 cid. B & S: 3.62 x 3.60 in. Compression ratio: 8.4:1. Brake hp: 138 at 4200 rpm. Carburetor: Holley one-barrel. Four main bearings. Code V.

Challenger 260 V-8 (Optional in Fairlane and Ford): Overhead valve. Cast-iron block. Displacement: 260 cid. B & S: 3.80 x 2.87 in. Compression ratio: 8.8:1. Brake hp: 164 at 4400 rpm. Torque: 258 lbs.-ft. at 2200 rpm. Five main bearings. Hydraulic valve lifters. Carburetor: Two-barrel. Cooling system capacity: 15.5 qt. with heater. Crankcase capacity: 4 qt. (add 1 qt. with new oil filter). Code F.

Challenger 289 V-8: Overhead valve. Cast-iron block. Displacement:

289 cid. B & S: 4.00 x 2.87 in. Compression ratio: 9.00:1. Brake hp: 195 at 4400 rpm. Torque: 282 lbs.-ft. at 2200 rpm. Five main bearings. Hydraulic valve lifters. Carburetor: Ford two-barrel C30F-9510. Cooling system capacity: 16 qt. with heater. Crankcase capacity: 4 qt. (add 1 qt. with new oil filter). Code C.

Challenger 289 V-8 Four Barrel: Overhead valve. Cast-iron block. Displacement: 289 cid. B & S: 4.00 x 2.87 in. Compression ratio: 9.0:1. Brake hp: 210 at 4400 rpm. Torque: 300 lbs.-ft. at 2800 rpm. Five main bearings. Hydraulic valve lifters. Carburetor: Four-barrel. Cooling system capacity: 16 qt. with heater. Crankcase capacity: 4 qt. (add 1 qt. with new oil filter). Code C.

Interceptor V-8 (Base Galaxie 500/XL V-8 and optional in other Fords): Overhead valve. Cast-iron block. Displacement: 352 cid. B & S: 4.00 x 3.50 in. Compression ratio: 9.30:1. Brake hp: 250 at 4400 rpm. Torque: 352 at 2800 rpm. Five main bearings. Hydraulic valve lifters. Carburetor: Four-barrel. Cooling system capacity: 20 qt. with heater. Crankcase capacity: 5 qt. (add 1 qt. with new oil filter). Code X.

High-Performance Challenger 289 V-8: Overhead valve. Cast-iron block. Displacement: 289 cid. B & S: 4.00 x 2.87 in. Compression ratio: 10.50:1. Brake hp: 271 at 6000 rpm. Torque: 312 lbs.-ft. at 3400 rpm. Five main bearings. Solid valve lifters. Carburetor: Four-barrel. Cooling system capacity: 16 qt. with heater. Crankcase capacity: 4 qt. (add 1 qt. with new oil filter). Code K.

Thunderbird 390 V-8 (Optional in Fords): Overhead valve. Cast-iron block. Displacement: 390 cid. B & S: 4.05 x 3.78 in. Compression ratio: 10.0:1. Brake hp: 300 at 4600 rpm. Torque: 427 lbs.-ft. at 2800 rpm. Five main bearings. Hydraulic valve lifters. Carburetor: Four-barrel. Cooling system capacity: 20 qt. with heater. Crankcase capacity: 5 qt. (add 1 qt. with new oil filter). Dual exhausts. Code Z.

Thunderbird Police Special 390 V-8: Overhead valve. Cast-iron block. Displacement: 390 cid. B & S: 4.05 x 3.78 in. Compression ratio: 10.0:1. Brake hp: 330 at 5000 rpm. Torque: 427 lbs.-ft. at 3200 rpm. Five main bearings. Solid valve lifters. Carburetor: Ford four-barrel. Cooling system capacity: 20 qt. with heater. Crankcase capacity: 5 qt. (add 1 qt. with new oil filter). Dual exhausts. Code P.

Thunderbird High-Performance V-8: Overhead valve. Cast-iron block. Displacement: 427 cid. B & S: 4.23 x 3.78 in. Compression ratio: 11.50:1. Brake hp: 410 at 5600 rpm. Torque: 476 lbs.-ft. at 3400 rpm. Five main bearings. Solid valve lifters. Carburetor: Holley four-barrel. Cooling system capacity: 20 qt. with heater. Crankcase capacity: 5 qt. (add 1 qt. with new oil filter). Dual exhausts. Code Q.

Thunderbird Super High Performance V-8: Overhead valve. Cast-iron block. Displacement: 427 cid. B & S: 4.23 x 3.78 in. Compression ratio: 11.50:1. Brake hp: 425 at 6000 rpm. Torque: 480 lbs.-ft. at 3700 rpm. Five main bearings. Solid valve lifters. Carburetor: Two Holley four-barrel. Cooling system capacity: 20 qt. with heater. Crankcase capacity: 5 qt. (add 1 qt. with new oil filter). Dual exhausts. Code R.

Chassis:

Falcon: Wheelbase: 109.5 in. Overall length: 181.1 in., cars and 189 in., wagons. Tires: 6.00 x 13 four-ply tubeless blackwall and 6.50 x 13 four-ply tubeless on station wagons and convertibles.

Fairlane: Wheelbase: 115.5 in. Overall length: 197.6 in. and 201.8 in., station wagons. Tires: 6.50 x 13 four-ply blackwall tubeless and 7.00 x 14 four-ply blackwall tubeless on station wagons.

1964 Ford Custom four-door Sedan

1964 Ford Custom 500 two-door Sedan (OCW)

Ford: Wheelbase: 119 in. Overall length: 209.0 in. Tires: 7.50 x 14 four-ply tubeless blackwalls and 8.00 x 14 four-ply tubeless blackwalls on station wagons.

Options:

Falcon: 170-cid six-cylinder engine ($17). The 260-cid V-8 engine ($170). Ford-O-Matic automatic transmission ($177). Four-speed manual transmission ($92 with six-cylinder, $188 with V-8). AM radio ($58). Two-tone paint ($19). White sidewall tires ($30). Back-up lights ($10). Deluxe trim package for standard sedans ($43). Popular Falcon station wagon options included all those for sedans, plus power tailgate window ($30).

Fairlane: 260-cid V-8 engine ($100). The 289-cid V-8 engine ($145). 390-cid V-8. 427-cid V-8. Ford-O-Matic automatic transmission ($189). Cruise-O-Matic automatic transmission ($189). Four-speed manual transmissions with V-8 engines ($188). AM radio ($58). Power steering ($86). Power tailgate window on station wagons ($32). Luggage rack on station wagons ($45). Two-tone paint ($22). White sidewall tires ($33). Wheel covers ($18). Vinyl roof on two-door hardtops ($75).

Ford: Popular Custom and Galaxie series options included 289-cid V-8 engine ($109). 390-cid V-8 engine ($246). Cruise-O-Matic automatic transmission ($189 or $212). Four-speed manual transmission ($188). Power steering ($86). Power brakes ($43). Power windows ($102). Tinted windshield ($21). AM radio ($58). Vinyl roof on two-door Victorias ($75). Wheel covers ($45). White sidewall tires ($33). Popular station wagon options included the 390-cid V-8 engine ($246). Cruise-O-Matic automatic transmission ($212). Power steering ($86). Power brakes ($43). Power tailgate window ($32). Luggage rack ($45). White sidewall tires ($33). Electric clock ($14). Radio ($58 for AM, $129 for AM/FM).

1964 Ford Galaxie 500 four-door Sedan (OCW)

1964 Ford Galaxie 500 four-door sedan (OCW)

1964 Ford Galaxie 500 four-door hardtop (OCW)

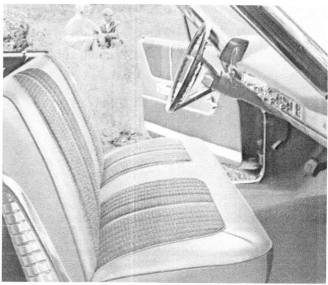
1964 Ford Galaxie 500 four-door hardtop interior (OCW)

1964 Ford Galaxie 500/XL Convertible shell bucket seat interior (OCW)

1964 Ford Galaxie 500/XL two-door fastback (PH)

1964 Ford Galaxie 500/XL two-door convertible (OCW)

1964 Ford Galaxie 500/XL four-door hardtop (OCW)

1964 Ford four-door Country Sedan 6P (OCW)

1964 Ford four-door Country Squire Wagon (OCW)

History:

The full-size Fords, Fairlanes and Falcons were introduced September 27, 1963, and the Mustang appeared in dealer showrooms on April 17, 1964. Model-year production peaked at 1,015,697 units. Calendar-year production of 1,787,535 cars was recorded. The entire lineup of 1964 Fords received *Motor Trend* magazine's "Car of the Year" award. Lee A. Iacocca was the chief executive officer of the company this year. Ford introduced the famous Fairlane Thunderbolt drag cars and also the single-overhead cam hemi-engine that Ford tried to use for NASCAR racing. It was disallowed due to insufficient number produced for homologation.

1965 Ford

Falcon — (Six and V-8): Falcons were the base trim level for 1965. While continuing to use the 1964 body shell, trim changes made the 1965 Falcon look considerably different than the previous year. The grille was a thin horizontal bar design, which was divided into two sections by a wider vertical bar at the center. A vertical, three-colored crest was used on the center divider. The round taillights utilized chrome "cross-hairs" for accent, and the optional back-up lights were mounted in the center of the lens. A new Falcon emblem with black, paint-filled Falcon letters was attached to the front fender behind the wheel opening. Standard equipment included chrome windshield and rear window moldings, two horns, two sun visors, armrests on the front doors only, a horn button (instead of a chrome horn ring), a heater and defroster, directional signals, an alternator and five black sidewall tuneless tires.

Falcon Futura — (Six and V-8): The Futura series was the top Falcon trim level for 1965. Futura models included all standard Falcon features and also added armrests front and rear, front and rear ashtrays, dual horns, Futura wheel covers, a chrome hood ornament, a Futura symbol on the front fender behind the wheel well, chrome windshield moldings, chrome rear window moldings, chrome side window moldings, a full-length, spear-type chrome body side molding with either red, white or black painted insert, foam rubber seat cushions and a deluxe steering wheel with a chrome horn ring.

Falcon Station Wagon — (Six and V-8): Both two- and four-door station wagons were again available in the Falcon lineup this year. The Standard wagon came in both body styles. The more deluxe Futura station wagon came only in the four-door model. The Squire included wood-grained exterior trim. The Deluxe and Squire wagons used a more powerful 120-hp six-cylinder engine and the Squire also had a power tailgate window and carpeted floors.

Fairlane — (Six and V-8): The Fairlane was the base trim level for Ford's mid-sized line. The 1965 Fairlane featured new sheet metal below the beltline. This gave it new front, rear and side appearances. The overall length and width were increased. This resulted in the first total restyling of the Fairlane line since its introduction in 1962. The new front end featured a wide horizontal grille and horizontal dual headlights. The hood incorporated a small peak in the center that swept forward over the leading edge and met a similar accent line in the grille. The overall profile was changed and had a higher fender line that traveled farther back and created a more massive look. For the first time since its

introduction, the Fairlane's taillights were rectangular instead of circular. They were accented with chrome 'cross-hair' accents across the face of the lens. When ordered, optional back-up lights were mounted in the center of the taillight lens. Standard equipment included chrome windshield moldings, chrome rear window moldings, a deluxe steering wheel with a chrome horn ring, front and rear armrests, a cigarette lighter, a fresh air heater and defroster, seat belts, vinyl coated rubber floor mats, the Fairlane name in block letters at the front of the front fenders, five black sidewall tubeless tires and a 200-cid 120-hp six-cylinder engine.

Fairlane 500 — (Six and V-8): The Fairlane 500 models were the top-level cars in Ford's mid-size or intermediate line and had richer appointments and trim than regular Fairlanes. "F-O-R-D" appeared, in block letters, across the rear escutcheon panel, with two chrome strips between the taillights and a Ford crest in the center of the panel. In addition to the features used on base models, the Fairlane 500s had chrome window moldings, a deluxe steering wheel with a chrome horn ring, and front and rear armrests, special interior upholstery and trim, a Ford crest on the roof "C" pillar, a chrome hood ornament, a single horizontal chrome strip with an aluminum insert and carpeting. The Sports Coupe version of the two-door hardtop also had front bucket seats and special full wheel covers.

Fairlane Station Wagon — (Six and V-8): The Fairlane station wagons came in two four-door models: Fairlane and Fairlane 500. Fairlane Wagon equipment started with all of the Fairlane sedan features and then included these variations: a choice of special vinyl-and-vinyl interior trims, a choice of additional Diamond Lustre enamel exterior colors, front and rear foam-cushioned seats, a color-keyed cargo area inlay, a roll-down tailgate window and a folding second seat. The Custom Ranch Wagon included all Fairlane 500 sedan equipment, a choice upgraded cloth-and-vinyl trim, color-keyed vinyl-coated rubber floor coverings, a stowage compartment lock and a bright-metal tailgate molding.

Custom — (Six and V-8): The new "Total Performance" Ford lineup represented the widest choice of models in Ford Division's history. The 1965 full-size Fords were billed as the 'Newest since 1949.' Luxury and comfort were featured with the big Fords, which used rear coil springs for the first time and featured new interior styling. 'Silent Flow' ventilation systems were standard on four-door hardtops. Completely restyled once again, the full-size Fords possessed incredibly clean styling with sharp, square lines and almost no curves. The new grille featured thin horizontal bars that followed the leading edge contour of the hood and were framed by the new vertical dual headlights. From the side, a single, horizontal feature line divided the less prominent beltline and lower body lines. As in 1964, all full-size Fords carried the engine designation symbol on the front fender behind the front wheel, for the larger, optional V-8 engines. The Custom series was the base trim level full-size Ford for 1965 and included chrome windshield and rear window moldings, two sun visors, a chrome horn ring, armrests on all doors, a MagicAire heater and defroster, the "Custom" name on the front fender, five black sidewall tubeless tires and a 240-cid six-cylinder engine. The taillights were circular lenses in a rectangular housing. The Ford name appeared in block letters across the front of the hood and on the vertical section of the trunk lid.

1965 Ford Falcon Futura two-door Convertible

1965 Ford Falcon Sports Futura two-door Hardtop (PH)

1965 Ford Falcon four-door Squire Station Wagon (PH)

Custom 500 — (Six and V-8): The Custom 500 was the upper trim level of the base-line Custom series and included all Custom features plus chrome windshield and rear window moldings, nylon carpeting instead of the rubber mats used in the Custom models, armrests, with ashtrays, on all doors, two sun visors and all the trim used in the Custom models, plus a short horizontal chrome strip along the front fender and front door.

Galaxie 500 — (Six and V-8): The Galaxie 500 was the intermediate trim level for 1965 and included all the Custom 500 features, plus a chrome hood ornament, Ford crest in the center of the trunk lid, chrome window frames, the Ford crest on the roof "C" pillar, "Galaxie 500" in block letters at the front of the front fenders, chrome rocker panel trim, hexagonal taillights with chrome 'cross-hairs' trim, back-up lights, an electric clock and special interior upholstery and trim. Two-tone vinyl trim was used on the insides of the doors and on the seats.

Galaxie 500/XL — (V-8): Galaxie 500/XL was the sport trim version of the Galaxie 500 two-door hardtop and two-door convertible. The Galaxie 500/XL models included all Galaxie 500 trim, plus bucket seats, a floor-mounted gearshift lever, polished door trim panels with carpeting on the lower portion of the doors, dual-lens courtesy/warning lights in the door panels, rear reading lights in hardtops, Galaxie 500/XL badges on the body exterior and deluxe wheel covers. The 289-cid 200-hp V-8 and Cruise-O-Matic automatic transmission were standard in both Galaxie 500/XL models.

Galaxie 500 LTD — (V-8): The Galaxie 500 LTD was the new top trim level for 1965. It also offered the two-door hardtop, plus a four-door hardtop. The Galaxie 500 LTDs included all the Galaxie 500/XL trim, plus a 289-cid 200-hp V-8, Cruise-O-Matic automatic transmission, thickly padded seats with 'pinseal' upholstery, simulated walnut appliques on the lower edge of the instrument panel, a Gabardine finish headlining, Gabardine finish sun visors, front and rear door courtesy/warning lights, courtesy lights in the rear roof pillars on the interior, courtesy lights under the instrument panel, a glove box light, an ash tray light and a self regulating clock.

Galaxie Station Wagon — (Six and V-8): The Ranch Wagon was once again the base trim level station wagon for 1965, with the Country Sedans being the intermediate level and the Country Squires being the top trim level. The trim paralleled the Custom 500, Galaxie 500 and Galaxie 500 LTD models of passenger cars.

VIN (Falcon):

The VIN for Falcons was die-stamped into the top of the left-hand front inner fender apron. The first symbol indicates year: 5=1965. The second symbol identifies assembly plant, as follows: A=Atlanta, Georgia, B=Oakville, Ontario, Canada, D=Dallas, Texas, E=Mahwah, New Jersey, F=Dearborn, Michigan, G=Chicago, Illinois, H=Lorain, Ohio, J=Los Angeles, California, K=Kansas City, Kansas, L=Long Beach, California, N=Norfolk, Virginia, P=Twin Cities, Minnesota, R=San Jose, California, S=Pilot Plant, T=Metuchen, New Jersey, U=Louisville, Kentucky, W=Wayne, Michigan, Y=Wixom, Michigan, Z=St. Louis, Mo. The third and fourth symbols identify body series code: 01=two-door sedan, 02=four-door sedan, 11=two-door hardtop with bucket seats, 12=two-door convertible with bucket seats, 15=two-door bench-seat convertible, 16=four-door bench-seat sedan, 27=deluxe, 19=two-door bench-seat sedan, 21=two-door station wagon, 22=four-door station wagon, 24=four-door Deluxe station wagon, 26=four-door Squire station wagon. The fifth symbol identifies engine code, as follows: U=170-cid six-cylinder, 4=170-cid export six-cylinder, T=200-cid six-cylinder, 2=200-

cid export six-cylinder, C=289-cid two-barrel V-8, 3=289-cid export two-barrel V-8 and A=289-cid four-barrel V-8. The last six digits are the unit's production number, beginning at 100001 and going up, at each of the assembly plants. Falcons not built at all Ford plants.

VIN (Fairlane):

The VIN for Fairlanes was die-stamped into the side of the left-hand front inner fender apron near the top. The first symbol indicates year: 5=1965. The second symbol identifies assembly plant, as follows: A=Atlanta, Georgia, B=Oakville, Ontario, Canada, D=Dallas, Texas, E=Mahwah, New Jersey, F=Dearborn, Michigan, G=Chicago, Illinois, H=Lorain, Ohio, J=Los Angeles, California, K=Kansas City, Kansas, L=Long Beach, California, N=Norfolk, Virginia, P=Twin Cities, Minnesota, R=San Jose, California, S=Pilot Plant, T=Metuchen, New Jersey, U=Louisville, Kentucky, W=Wayne, Michigan, Y=Wixom, Michigan, Z=St. Louis, Mo. The third and fourth symbols identify body series code: 31=Fairlane two-door sedan, 32=Fairlane four-door sedan, 41=Fairlane 500 two-door sedan, 42=Fairlane 500 four-door sedan, 43=Fairlane 500 two-door hardtop, 47=Fairlane 500 two-door Sport Coupe, 38=Fairlane four-door six-passenger station wagon, 48=Fairlane Custom four-door six-passenger station wagon. The fifth symbol identifies engine code, as follows: T=200-cid six-cylinder, 2=200-cid export six-cylinder, C=289-cid two-barrel V-8, 3=289-cid export two-barrel V-8 and A=289-cid four-barrel V-8 and K=289-cid four-barrel V-8. The last six digits are the unit's production number, beginning at 100001 and going up, at each of the assembly plants. Fairlanes not built at all Ford plants.

VIN (Ford):

The VIN for full-size Fords was die-stamped into the top right-hand side rail of the frame ahead of the front suspension member. The first symbol indicates year: 5=1965. The second symbol identifies assembly plant, as follows: A=Atlanta, Georgia, B=Oakville, Ontario, Canada, D=Dallas, Texas, E=Mahwah, New Jersey, F=Dearborn, Michigan, G=Chicago, Illinois, H=Lorain, Ohio, J=Los Angeles, California, K=Kansas City, Kansas, L=Long Beach, California, N=Norfolk, Virginia, P=Twin Cities, Minnesota, R=San Jose, California, S=Pilot Plant, T=Metuchen, New Jersey, U=Louisville, Kentucky, W=Wayne, Michigan, Y=Wixom, Michigan, Z=St. Louis, Mo. The third and fourth symbols identify body series 51=Custom 500 two-door sedan, 52=Custom 500 four-door sedan, 53=Custom two-door sedan, 54=Custom four-door sedan, 62=Galaxie 500 four-door sedan, 64=Galaxie 500 four-door Victoria Hardtop, 65=Galaxie 500 Sunliner convertible, 66=Galaxie 500 fastback, 60=Galaxie 500 LTD four-door hardtop, 67=Galaxie 500 LTD fastback, 68=Galaxie 500/XL fastback, 69=Galaxie 500/XL two-door convertible, 72=four-door six-passenger Country Sedan station wagon, 74=four-door nine-passenger Country Sedan station wagon, 76=four-door Country Squire six-passenger station wagon and 78=four-door Country Squire nine-passenger station wagon. The fifth symbol identifies engine code, as follows: V=223-cid six-cylinder, 5=223-cid Export six-cylinder, B=223-cid Police six, E=223-cid Taxi six-cylinder, C=289-cid two-barrel V-8, 3=289-cid low-compression export two-barrel V-8, X=352-cid two-barrel V-8, Z=390-cid four-barrel V-8, 9=390-cid V-8, P=390-cid V-8, R=427-cid V-8. Racing engines: L=427-cid four-barrel V-8 and M=427-cid dual four-barrel V-8. The last six digits are the unit's production number, beginning at 100001 and going up, at each of the assembly plants. Full-size Fords not built at all Ford plants.

1965 Ford Custom two-door sedan (OCW)

1965 Ford Fairlane 500 two-door Sports Coupe (OCW)

1965 Ford Fairlane 500 four-door station wagon (PH)

1965 Ford Galaxie 500 four-door sedan (OCW)

Falcon Standard (Six)

Model No.	Body/Style No.	Body Style and Seating	Factory Price	Shipping Weight	Production Total
62A	01	2-dr. Sedan-6P	$1,997	2,370 lbs.	46,504
54A	02	4-dr. Sedan-6P	$2,038	2,410 lbs.	38,852

Falcon Standard (V-8)

62A	01	2-dr. Sedan-6P	$2,127	2,726 lbs.	3,178
54A	02	4-dr. Sedan-6P	$2,188	2,766 lbs.	5,184

Falcon Futura (Six)

62B	19	2-dr. Sedan-6P	$2,099	2,373 lbs.	9,862
54B	16	4-dr. Sedan-6P	$2,146	2,415 lbs.	28,640
63*	17	2-dr. Hardtop-6P	$2,179	2,395 lbs.	13,723
76*	15	2-dr. Convertible-6P	$2,428	2,675 lbs.	3,944

Falcon Futura (V-8)

62B	19	2-dr. Sedan-6P	$2,248	2,731 lbs.	1,808
54B	16	4-dr. Sedan-6P	$2,295	2,771 lbs.	5,345
63*	17	2-dr. Hardtop-6P	$2,329	2,696 lbs.	14,837
76*	15	2-dr. Convertible-6P	$2,578	2,972 lbs.	3,223

*Suffixes: A=Bench Seat, B=Bucket Seat With Console, H=Bucket Seat Less Console

Falcon Station Wagon (Six)

59A	21	2-dr. Station Wagon-6P	$2,284	2,640 lbs.	4,396
71A	22	4-dr. Station Wagon-6P	$2,317	2,680 lbs.	13,111

Falcon Station Wagon (V-8)

59A	21	2-dr. Station Wagon-6P	$2,433	2,966 lbs.	495
71A	22	4-dr. Station Wagon-6P	$2,467	3,006 lbs.	1,800

Falcon Futura Ranch Wagon (Six)

71B	24	4-dr. Station Wagon-6P	$2,453	2,670 lbs.	9,325

Falcon Futura Ranch Wagon (V-8)

71B	24	4-dr. Station Wagon-6P	$2,558	2,996 lbs.	2,671

Futura Squire Station Wagon (Six)

71C	26	4-dr. Station Wagon-6P	$2,608	2,695 lbs.	3,661

Futura Squire Station Wagon (V-8)

71C	26	4-dr. Station Wagon-6P	$2,714	3,018 lbs.	3,042

Fairlane (Six)

62A	31	2-dr. Sedan-6P	$2,194	2,805 lbs.	14,777
54A	32	4-dr. Sedan-6P	$2,235	2,857 lbs.	22,233

Fairlane (V-8)

62A	31	2-dr. Sedan-6P	$2,294	2,997 lbs.	5,644
54A	32	4-dr. Sedan-6P	$2,335	3,049 lbs.	14,460

Fairlane 500 (Six)

62B	41	2-dr. Sedan-6P	$2,276	2,820 lbs.	8,760
54B	42	4-dr. Sedan-6P	$2,317	2,872 lbs.	18,791
65A	43	2-dr. Hardtop-6P	$2,341	2,880 lbs.	4,467

Fairlane 500 (V-8)

62B	41	2-dr. Sedan-6P	$2,376	3,012 lbs.	14,687
54B	42	4-dr. Sedan-6P	$2,417	3,064 lbs.	68,128
65A	43	2-dr. Hardtop-6P	$2,441	3,072 lbs.	22,296

Fairlane 500 Sport (Six)

65B	47	2-dr. Hardtop-6P	$2,502	2,904 lbs.	946

Fairlane 500 Sport (V-8)

65B	47	2-dr. Hardtop-6P	$2,602	3,096 lbs.	20,485

Fairlane Ranch Wagon (Six)

71D	38	4-dr. Station Wagon-6P	$2,531	3,207 lbs.	7,324

Fairlane Ranch Wagon (V-8)

71D	38	4-dr. Station Wagon-6P	$2,631	3,399 lbs.	13,656

Fairlane Custom Ranch Wagon (Six)

71B	48	4-dr. Station Wagon-6P	$2,612	3,237 lbs.	2,666

Fairlane Custom Ranch Wagon (V-8)

71B	48	4-dr. Station Wagon-6P	$2,712	3,429 lbs.	22,296

Ford Custom (Six)

62E	53	2-dr. Sedan-6P	$2,313	3,275 lbs.	28,094
54E	54	4-dr. Sedan-6P	$2,366	3,378 lbs.	44,278

Ford Custom (V-8)

62E	53	2-dr. Sedan-6P	$2,420	3,319 lbs.	20,940
54E	54	4-dr. Sedan-6P	$2,472	3,422 lbs.	52,115

Custom 500 (Six)

62B	51	2-dr. Sedan-6P	$2,414	3,323 lbs.	6,238
54B	52	4-dr. Sedan-6P	$2,467	3,382 lbs.	13,157

Custom 500 (V-8)

62B	51	2-dr. Sedan-6P	$2,520	3,367 lbs.	13,365
54B	52	4-dr. Sedan-6P	$2,573	3,426 lbs.	58,570

Galaxie 500 (Six)

54A	62	4-dr. Sedan-6P	$2,623	3,393 lbs.	8,417
63B	66	2-dr. Fastback-6P	$2,630	3,351 lbs.	7,099
57B	64	4-dr. Hardtop-6P	$2,708	3,477 lbs.	833
76B	65	2-dr. Convertible-6P	$2,889	3,590 lbs.	1,034

Galaxie 500 (V-8)

54A	62	4-dr. Sedan-6P	$2,730	3,437 lbs.	172,766
63B	66	2-dr. Fastback-6P	$2,737	3,395 lbs.	150,185
57B	64	4-dr. Hardtop-6P	$2,815	3,521 lbs.	49,149
76B	65	2-dr. Convertible-6P	$2,996	3,635 lbs.	30,896

Galaxie 500/XL (V-8)

63C	68	2-dr. Fastback-6P	$3,167	3,556 lbs.	28,141
76B	69	2-dr. Convertible-6P	$3,426	3,704 lbs.	9,849

Galaxie 500 LTD (V-8)

63F	67	2-dr. Fastback-6P	$3,167	3,633 lbs.	58,306
57F	60	4-dr. Hardtop-6P	$3,245	3,611 lbs.	68,038

Ranch Wagon (Six)

71D	71	4-dr. Station Wagon-6P	$2,707	3,819 lbs.	7,889

Custom Ranch Wagon (Six)

71C	72	4-dr. Station Wagon-6P	$2,797	3,849 lbs.	2,661
71B	74	4-dr. Station Wagon-9P	$2,899	3,895 lbs.	1,512

Country Squire Station Wagon (Six)

71E	76	4-dr. Station Wagon-6P	$3,041	3,906 lbs.	245
71A	78	4-dr. Station Wagon-9P	$3,109	3,920 lbs.	179

Ranch Wagon (V-8)

71D	72	4-dr. Station Wagon-6P	$2,813	3,863 lbs.	22,928

Custom Ranch Wagon (V-8)

71C	72	4-dr. Station Wagon-6P	$2,904	3,893 lbs.	57,232
71B	74	4-dr. Station Wagon-9P	$3,005	3,939 lbs.	30,832

Country Squire Station Wagon (V-8)

71E	76	4-dr. Station Wagon-6P	$3,147	3,950 lbs.	24,063
71A	78	4-dr. Station Wagon-9P	$3,216	3,964 lbs.	30,323

Engines:

Falcon Six: Overhead valve. Cast-iron block. Displacement: 144 cid. B & S: 3.50 x 2.50 in. Compression ratio: 6.7:1. Brake hp: 65 at 4200 rpm. Carburetor: Holley one-barrel. Seven main bearings. Code S.

Falcon Six: Overhead valve. Cast-iron block. Displacement: 170 cid. B & S: 3.50 x 2.94 in. Compression ratio: 8.7:1. Brake hp: 101 at 4400 rpm. Carburetor: Holley one-barrel. Seven main bearings. Code U.

Ford Six: Overhead valve. Cast-iron block. Displacement: 223 cid. B & S: 3.62 x 3.60 in. Compression ratio: 8.4:1. Brake hp: 138 at 4200 rpm. Carburetor: Holley one-barrel. Four main bearings. Code V.

Challenger 289 V-8: Overhead valve. Cast-iron block. Displacement: 289 cid. B & S: 4.00 x 2.87 in. Compression ratio: 9.30:1. Brake hp: 200 at 4400 rpm. Torque: 282 lbs.-ft. at 2400 rpm. Five main bearings. Hydraulic valve lifters. Carburetor: Two-barrel. Cooling system capacity: 16 qt. with heater. Crankcase capacity: 4 qt. (add 1 qt. with new oil filter). Code C.

Challenger 289 Four-Barrel V-8: Overhead valve. Cast-iron block. Displacement: 289 cid. B & S: 4.00 x 2.87 in. Compression ratio: 10.0:1. Brake hp: 225 at 4800 rpm. Torque: 305 lbs.-ft. at 3200 rpm. Five main bearings. Hydraulic valve lifters. Carburetor: Four-barrel. Cooling system capacity: 16 qt. with heater. Crankcase capacity: 4 qt. with new oil filter). Code A.

Interceptor V-8 (Base Galaxie 500/XL V-8 and optional in other full-size Fords): Overhead valve. Cast- iron block. Displacement: 352 cid. B & S: 4.00 x 3.50 in. Compression ratio: 9.30:1. Brake hp: 250 at 4400 rpm. Torque: 352 lbs.-ft. at 2800 rpm. Five main bearings. Hydraulic valve lifters. Carburetor: Four-barrel. Cooling system capacity: 20.5 qt. with heater. Crankcase capacity: 5 qt. (add 1 qt. with new oil filter). Code X.

Challenger 289 High-Performance Four-Barrel V-8: Overhead valve. Cast-iron block. Displacement: 289 cid. B & S: 4.00 x 2.87 in. Compression ratio: 10.5:1. Brake hp: 271 at 6000 rpm. Torque: 312 lbs.-ft. at 3400 rpm. Five main bearings. Solid valve lifters. Carburetor: Four-barrel. Cooling system capacity: 16 qt. with heater. Crankcase capacity: 4 qt. (add 1 qt. with new oil filter). Code K.

Thunderbird 390 V-8 (Optional in full-size Ford): Overhead valve. Cast-iron block. Displacement: 390 cid. B & S: 4.05 x 3.78 in. Compression ratio: 10.0:1. Brake hp: 300 at 4600 rpm. Torque: 427 lbs.-ft. at 2800 rpm. Five main bearings. Hydraulic valve lifters. Carburetor: Four-barrel. Cooling system capacity: 20.5 qt. with heater. Crankcase capacity: 5 qt. (add 1 qt. with new oil filter). Dual exhausts. Code Z.

Thunderbird Interceptor Special 390 V-8: Overhead valve. Cast-iron block. Displacement: 390 cid. B & S: 4.05 x 3.78 in. Compression ratio: 10.0:1. Brake hp: 330 at 5000 rpm. Torque: 427 lbs.-ft. at 3200 rpm. Five main bearings. Solid valve lifters. Carburetor: Ford four-barrel. Cooling system capacity: 20.5 qt. with heater. Crankcase capacity: 5 qt. (add 1 qt. with new oil filter). Dual exhausts. Code P.

Thunderbird Super-High-Performance V-8: Overhead valve. Cast-iron block. Displacement: 427 cid. B & S: 4.23 x 3.78 in. Compression ratio: 11.50:1. Brake hp: 425 at 6000 rpm. Torque: 480 lbs.-ft. at 3700 rpm. Five main bearings. Solid valve lifters. Carburetor: Two Holley four-barrel. Cooling system capacity: 20.5 qt. with heater. Crankcase capacity: 5 qt. (add 1 qt. with new oil filter). Dual exhausts. Code R.

"SOHC 427" 4V V-8: Overhead valve. Cast-iron block. Hemispherical combustion chambers with overhead valves and overhead camshafts for each engine bank. Displacement: 427 cid. B & S: 4.23 x 3.78 in. Compression ratio: 12.10:1. Brake hp: 616 at 7000 rpm. Five main bearings. Carburetor: Holley four-barrel. Cooling system capacity: 20.5 qt. with heater. Crankcase capacity: 5 qt. (add 1 qt. with new oil filter). Dual exhausts. Code L ($2,500). (This engine was not installed in any Ford production vehicles.)

"SOHC 427" 4V V-8: Overhead valve. Cast-iron block. Hemispherical combustion chambers with overhead valves and overhead camshafts for each engine bank. Displacement: 427 cid. B & S: 4.23 x 3.78 in. Compression ratio: 12.10:1. Brake hp: 657 at 7500 rpm. Five main bearings. Hydraulic valve lifters. Carburetor: Two Holley four-barrel. Cooling system capacity: 20.5 qt. with heater. Crankcase capacity: 5 qt. (add 1 qt. with new oil filter). Dual exhausts. Code M. (This engine was not installed in any Ford production vehicles.)

Chassis:

Falcon: Wheelbase: 109.5 in. Overall length: 181.6 in. and 190 in. on station wagons. Tires: 6.50 x 13 and 7.00 x 13 on station wagons. All tires were four-ply tubeless blackwalls.

Fairlane: Wheelbase: 116 in. Overall length: 198.4 in. and 203.2 in. on station wagons. Tires: 6.94 x 14 four-ply tubeless blackwalls and 7.35 x 14 four-ply tubeless on station wagons.

Ford: Wheelbase: 119 in. Overall length: 210 in. Tires: 7.35 x 15 four-ply tubeless blackwalls and 8.15 x 15 four-ply tubeless blackwalls on station wagons.

Options:

Falcon: 200-cid six-cylinder engine ($45), or 289-cid V-8 engine ($153). Cruise-O-Matic automatic transmission ($182 or $172 with six-cylinder). Front bucket seats ($69). AM radio ($58). Two-tone paint ($19). White sidewall tires ($30). Sprint package ($222 and $273 on convertibles). Popular Falcon station wagon options included all those of the sedans plus the following: Power tailgate window ($30). Luggage rack ($45).

Fairlane: 289-cid V-8 engine ($108), or high-performance 289-cid V-8 ($430). Cruise-O-Matic automatic. transmission ($190), four-speed manual transmission ($188). AM radio ($58). Power steering ($86). Power tailgate window on station wagons ($32). Luggage rack on station wagons ($45). Two-tone paint ($22). White sidewall tires ($34). Wheel covers ($22). Vinyl roof on two-door hardtops ($76).

Ford: Popular Custom and Custom 500 model options included the 289-cid V-8 engine ($109). Cruise-O-Matic automatic transmission ($189). Power steering ($97). AM radio ($58). Wheel covers ($25). White sidewall tires ($34). Popular Galaxie 500 and Galaxie 500XL options included the 390-cid V-8 engine ($246). Cruise-O-Matic automatic transmission ($190), four-speed manual transmission ($188 - no charge on XLs). Power steering ($97). Power brakes ($43). Power windows ($102). Tinted windshield ($40). Air conditioning ($36). AM radio ($58). Vinyl roof ($76). Wheel covers ($26). White sidewall tires ($34). Popular LTD options included the 390-cid V-8 engine ($137). Power steering ($97). Power brakes ($43). Power windows ($102). Tinted windshield ($40). Air conditioning ($364). AM radio ($72). AM/FM radio ($142). Vinyl roof ($76). White sidewall tires ($34). Popular station wagon options included the 390-cid V-8 engine ($246). Cruise-O-Matic automatic transmission ($190). Power steering ($97). Power brakes ($43). Tinted windows ($40). Power tailgate window ($32). Luggage rack ($45). AM radio ($58). White sidewall tires ($34). Wheel covers ($25). A Borg-Warner T-10 four-speed transmission was replaced, for 1965, with the Ford produced T&C 'top-loader' four-speed.

History:

Model names were dropped for 1965, in favor of designating the car by its actual body style, i.e., "Club Victoria" became "two-door hardtop," and "Sunliner" became "two-door convertible," etc. The 427-cid single-overhead cam engine was installed in the Fairlane Thunderbolt drag cars.

1965 Ford Galaxie 500/XL two-door convertible (OCW)

1965 Ford Galaxie 500 LTD four-door hardtop (PH)

1965 Ford four-door Country Squire Wagon (OCW)

1965 Ford Galaxie 500 two-door hardtop (OCW)

1965 Ford Galaxie 500/XL two-door fastback (PH)

1966 Ford

Falcon — (Six and V-8): The Falcon series received a total restyling for 1966. It had a longer hood, a shorter trunk and rounder lines than in 1965. The two-door hardtops were discontinued for 1966, with the Futura Sports Coupe carrying the sporty image for the year. A Falcon script was located on the front fender behind the front wheel opening. F-O-R-D was spelled out, in block letters, across the front of the hood. F-A-L-C-O-N was spelled out, in block letters, across the vertical section of the trunk lid. Falcon was the base trim level of the compact Falcon line for 1966 and included chrome windshield moldings, chrome rear window moldings, chrome rain gutter moldings, twin horns, dual sun visors, armrests on the front doors only and a standard steering wheel with horn button.

Falcon Futura — (Six and V-8): The Futura series was the top trim level for 1966 and included all the standard Falcon features, plus a cigarette lighter, rear armrests, rear ashtrays, a deluxe steering wheel with a chrome horn ring, nylon carpeting, special Futura moldings, Futura trim, Futura emblems, Futura nameplates and chrome side window frames. In addition, the Falcon Futura Sports Coupe was a sporty version of the two-door sedan that featured the 200-cid 120-hp six-cylinder engine, front bucket seats, special Sports Coupe nameplates and special wheel covers. The Futura convertible also included front bucket seats.

Falcon Station Wagon — (Six and V-8): Only four-door station wagons were available in the Falcon lineup this year. The Standard wagon came in both body styles. The more Deluxe station wagon had richer trim.

Fairlane — (Six and V-8): A major restyling was done to the Fairlane, which included 13 different models. They were longer, lower and wider and featured new front and rear suspensions. The full-width grille featured a horizontal grid with a large divider bar and the Fairlane crest in the center of the grille. The headlights were vertically stacked and angled back at the bottom, for a more aggressive look. A full-length horizontal

1966 Ford Falcon two-door Sedan (OCW)

1966 Ford Falcon standard cloth-and-vinyl interior (OCW)

1966 Ford Falcon Futura two-door Sedan

1966 Ford Falcon Futura four-door Sedan (OCW)

1966 Ford Falcon Futura two-door Sports Coupe (OCW)

feature line was used for emphasis and the model designation, in block letters, was located on the rear fender. The taillights were rectangular and featured a chrome ring around the outside and around the centrally located back-up lights. The Fairlane was the base trim level for 1966 and included chrome windshield moldings, chrome rear window moldings, chrome rain gutter moldings, a deluxe steering wheel with a chrome horn ring, front and rear armrests, a cigarette lighter and vinyl-coated rubber floor mats. Engine choices ranged from the 200-cid 120-hp six-cylinder engine up to the mighty 390-cid 335-hp GT V-8 engine. For the first time, three convertibles were added to the lineup of hardtops and sedans.

Fairlane 500 — (Six and V-8) The Fairlane 500 was the intermediate trim level for 1966 and included all the Fairlane trim plus polished aluminum rocker panel moldings, a Fairlane crest in the center of the grille, color-keyed carpets (front and rear) and Fairlane 500 identification, in block letters, on the rear fenders. A Fairlane crest and Fairlane script also appeared on the right-hand vertical section of the trunk lid.

Fairlane 500/XL — (Six and V-8): The Fairlane 500/XL was the sporty version of the Fairlane 500 series and included all the Fairlane 500 features, plus bucket seats, a console, special name plaques, special exterior trim, deluxe wheel covers, red safety lights and white courtesy lights in the door armrests.

Fairlane 500 GT — (V-8): The Fairlane 500/XL was the sporty version of the Fairlane 500 series and included all the Fairlane 500 features, plus bucket seats, a console, special name plaques, special exterior trim, deluxe wheel covers, red safety lights and white courtesy lights in the door armrests.

Fairlane Station Wagon — (Six and V-8): The Fairlane station wagons came in a two-door Ranch Wagon, a four-door Custom Ranch Wagon and four-door Squire models. These were comparable to Fairlane, Fairlane 500 and Fairlane 500/XL cars. Fairlane Wagon equipment started with all of the Fairlane sedan features and then included these variations: a choice of special vinyl-and-vinyl interior trims, a choice of additional Diamond Lustre enamel exterior colors, front and rear foam-cushioned seats, a color-keyed cargo area inlay, a roll-down tailgate window and a folding second seat. The Custom Ranch Wagon included all Fairlane 500 sedan equipment, a choice upgraded cloth-and-vinyl trim, color-keyed vinyl-coated rubber floor coverings, a stowage compartment lock and a bright-metal tailgate molding. The Squire was even richer in trim and appointments than the Custom Ranch Wagon and it had wood trim.

Ford Custom — (Six and V-8): While 1965 and 1966 full-size Fords bear a resemblance to each other, they are quite different cars. The hood is the only interchangeable exterior body component. The 1966 models feature more rounded lines than the previous year's models, even though the feature lines are in the same location. The Custom series is the base trim level and includes chrome windshield moldings, chrome rear window moldings, two sun visors, a deluxe steering wheel with chrome horn ring, armrests on all doors and the Custom name, in script, on the rear fenders. The taillights had square lenses, with centrally-mounted back-up lights surrounded by a chrome bezel. The Ford name appeared, in block letters, across the front of the hood and across the vertical section of the trunk lid.

1966 Ford Falcon Futura Sports all-vinyl interior (OCW)

1966 Ford Falcon four-door Station Wagon (OCW)

Custom 500 — (Six and V-8): The Custom 500 was the upper trim level of the base line Custom series and included all trim used in the Custom models plus, chrome windshield moldings, chrome rear window moldings, nylon carpeting, armrests with ashtrays on all doors, two sun visors and. There was also a horizontal chrome strip along the side feature line and the designation "500" in a die-cast block, with black-painted background, in front of the Custom script. A small Ford crest was located in the chrome side strip, on the front of the front fenders.

Galaxie 500 — (Six and V-8): The Galaxie 500 was the intermediate trim level for 1966 and included all the Custom trim, plus a chrome hood ornament, the Ford crest in the feature line on the front fender and stamped aluminum rocker panel moldings. A stamped aluminum insert decorated the space between the two chrome strips on the vertical section of the trunk lid and the word F-O-R-D was spelled out in block letters, spaced evenly across it. Two-tone vinyl trim was used on the seats and on the inside of the doors. Simulated wood appliques were used on the instrument panel trim pieces.

Galaxie 500/XL — (V-8): Galaxie 500/XL was the sport trim version of the Galaxie 500 two-door hardtop and two-door convertible and included all Galaxie 500 trim, plus bucket front seats, a floor-mounted shift lever, polished door trim with carpeting on the lower position of the doors, dual-lens courtesy/warning lights in the door panels, rear reading lights (in hardtops) and Galaxie 500/XL badges on the body exterior. The 289-cid 200-hp V-8 and Cruise-O-Matic automatic transmission were standard in both 500/XL body styles.

Galaxie 500/XL 7-Litre — (V-8): The "7-Litre" was a high-performance version of the Galaxie 500/XL and was equipped with the 428-cid 345-hp V-8 engine as standard equipment. It also came with Cruise-O-Matic automatic transmission. A four-speed manual transmission was available as a no-cost option for those who chose to be even more sporting. Along with the 428-cid engine, standard equipment also included a simulated English walnut Sport steering wheel, front bucket seats, a floor-mounted gearshift, low-restriction dual exhaust and a non-silenced air cleaner system. Also standard were power disc brakes.

Galaxie 500 LTD (V-8): The Galaxie 500 LTD was the top trim level for 1966 and included all the Galaxie 500 trim, plus the 289-cid 200-hp V-8 engine, Cruise-O-Matic automatic transmission, thickly padded seats with "pinseal" upholstery, simulated walnut appliqués on the lower edge of the instrument panel, simulated walnut appliqués in the door inserts, a Gabardine finish headliner, Gabardine finish sun visors, front and rear door courtesy/warning lights, courtesy lights on the rear interior roof pillars, courtesy lights under the instrument panel, a glove box light, ashtray lights and a self-regulating clock.

1966 Ford Falcon Futura four-door Station Wagon (OCW)

1966 Ford Fairlane four-door sedan

Galaxie Station Wagon (Six and V-8): The Ranch Wagon was the base trim level station wagon for 1966. The Country Sedans were the intermediate level and the Country Squires were the top trim level. The trim paralleled the Custom 500, Galaxie 500 and Galaxie 500 LTD models of passenger cars.

VIN (Falcon):

The VIN for Falcons was die-stamped into the inner fender panel and radiator support at the left side under the hood. The first symbol indicates year: 6=1966. The second symbol identifies assembly plant, as follows: A=Atlanta, Georgia, B=Oakville, Ontario, Canada, C=Ontario, Canada, D=Dallas, Texas, E=Mahwah, New Jersey, F=Dearborn, Michigan, G=Chicago, Illinois, H=Lorain, Ohio, J=Los Angeles, California, K=Kansas City, Kansas, L=Long Beach, California, N=Norfolk, Virginia, P=Twin Cities, Minnesota, R=San Jose, California, S=Pilot Plant, T=Metuchen, New Jersey, U=Louisville, Kentucky, W=Wayne, Michigan, Y=Wixom, Michigan, Z=St. Louis, Mo. The third and fourth symbols identify body series code: 01=two-door sedan, 02=four-door sedan, 11=two-door hardtop with bucket seats, 12=two-door convertible with bucket seats, 14=two-door bucket seat Sport Coupe, 22=four-door station wagon, 24=four-door Deluxe station wagon. The fifth symbol identifies engine code, as follows: U=170-cid six-cylinder, 4=170-cid export six-cylinder, T=200-cid six-cylinder, 2=200-cid export six-cylinder, C=289-cid two-barrel V-8 and 3=289-cid export two-barrel V-8. The last six digits are the unit's production number, beginning at 100001 and going up, at each of the assembly plants. Falcons not built at all Ford plants.

VIN (Fairlane):

The VIN for Fairlanes was die-stamped into the inner fender panel and radiator support at the left side under the hood. The first symbol indicates year: 6=1966. The second symbol identifies assembly plant, as follows: A=Atlanta, Georgia, B=Oakville, Ontario, Canada, C=Ontario, Canada, D=Dallas, Texas, E=Mahwah, New Jersey, F=Dearborn, Michigan, G=Chicago, Illinois, H=Lorain, Ohio, J=Los Angeles, California, K=Kansas City, Kansas, L=Long Beach, California, N=Norfolk, Virginia, P=Twin Cities, Minnesota, R=San Jose, California, S=Pilot Plant, T=Metuchen, New Jersey, U=Louisville, Kentucky, W=Wayne, Michigan, Y=Wixom, Michigan, Z=St. Louis, Mo. The third and fourth symbols identify body series code: 31=Fairlane two-door sedan, 32=Fairlane four-door sedan, 40=Fairlane 500 GT bucket seat two-door hardtop, 44=Fairlane 500 GT bucket seat two-door convertible, 41=Fairlane 500 two-door sedan, 42=Fairlane 500 four-door sedan, 43=Fairlane 500 two-door hardtop, 45=Fairlane 500 two-door convertible, 46=Fairlane 500/XL bucket seat two-door convertible, 47=Fairlane 500/XL two-door bucket-seat hardtop, 38=Fairlane four-door six-passenger station wagon, 48=Fairlane Custom four-door six-passenger station wagon, 49=Fairlane 500 four-door Squire station wagon. The fifth symbol identifies engine code, as follows: T=200-cid six-cylinder, 2=200-cid export six-cylinder, C=289-cid two-barrel V-8, 3=289-cid export two-barrel V-8, Y=390-cid two-barrel V-8, H=390-cid two-barrel V-8 and S=390-cid four-barrel V-8. The last six digits are the unit's production number, beginning at 100001 and going up, at each of the assembly plants. Fairlanes not built at all Ford plants.

VIN (Ford):

The VIN for full-size Fords was die-stamped into an extension tab on the top of the cowl on the right-hand side of the car under the hood. The first symbol indicates year: 6=1966. The second symbol identifies assembly plant, as follows: A=Atlanta, Georgia, B=Oakville, Ontario,

1966 Ford Fairlane 500 two-door Sedan

1966 Ford Fairlane 500 trunk space (OCW)

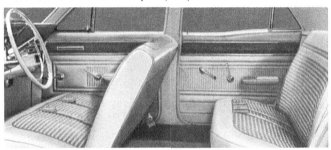

1966 Ford Fairlane 500 all-vinyl interior (OCW)

1966 Ford Fairlane 500 four-door Sedan (OCW)

1966 Ford Fairlane 500 two-door Hardtop (OCW)

Canada, C=Ontario, Canada, D=Dallas, Texas, E=Mahwah, New Jersey, F=Dearborn, Michigan, G=Chicago, Illinois, H=Lorain, Ohio, J=Los Angeles, California, K=Kansas City, Kansas, L=Long Beach, California, N=Norfolk, Virginia, P=Twin Cities, Minnesota, R=San Jose, California, S=Pilot Plant, T=Metuchen, New Jersey, U=Louisville, Kentucky, W=Wayne, Michigan, Y=Wixom, Michigan, Z=St. Louis, Mo. The third and fourth symbols identify body series 51=Custom 500 two-door sedan, 52=Custom 500 four-door sedan, 53=Custom two-door sedan, 54=Custom four-door sedan, 61=Galaxie 7-Litre two-door fastback, 62=Galaxie 500 four-door sedan, 63=Galaxie 7-Litre two-door convertible, 64=Galaxie 500 four-door Victoria Hardtop, 65=Galaxie 500 Sunliner convertible, 66=Galaxie 500 fastback, 60=Galaxie 500 LTD four-door hardtop, 67=Galaxie 500 LTD fastback, 68=Galaxie 500/XL fastback, 69=Galaxie 500/XL two-door convertible, 71=four-door six-passenger Ranch Wagon, 72=four-door six-passenger Country Sedan station wagon, 74=four-door nine-passenger Country Sedan station wagon, 76=four-door Country Squire six-passenger station wagon and 78=four-door Country Squire nine-passenger station wagon. The fifth symbol identifies engine code, as follows: V=223-cid six-cylinder, 5=223-cid Export six-cylinder, B=223-cid Police six, E=223-cid Taxi six-cylinder, C=289-cid two-barrel V-8, 3=289-cid low-compression export two-barrel V-8, X=352-cid two-barrel V-8, H=390-cid two-barrel V-8, Z=390-cid four-barrel V-8, Q=428-cid four-barrel V-8, 8=428-cid four-barrel V-8, P=428-cid four-barrel V-8, W=427-cid four-barrel V-8 and 4=427-cid four-barrel V-8. The last six digits are the unit's production number, beginning at 100001 and going up, at each of the assembly plants. Full-size Fords not built at all Ford plants.

Falcon Standard (Six)

Model No.	Body/ Style No.	Body Style and Seating	Factory Price	Shipping Weight	Production Total
62A	01	2-dr. Sedan-6P	$2,060	2,519 lbs.	32,088
54A	02	4-dr. Sedan-6P	$2,114	2,559 lbs.	26,105

Falcon Standard (V-8)

62A	01	2-dr. Sedan-6P	$2,127	2,726 lbs.	3,178
54A	02	4-dr. Sedan-6P	$2,188	2,766 lbs.	5,184

Falcon Futura (Six)

62A	11	2-dr. Sedan-6P	$2,183	2,527 lbs.	14,604
54A	12	4-dr. Sedan-6P	$2,237	2,567 lbs.	25,033
62C	13	2-dr. Sport Coupe-6P	$2,328	2,597 lbs.	8,898

Falcon Futura (V-8)

62B	11	2-dr. Sedan-6P	$2,315	2,813 lbs.	3,692
54B	12	4-dr. Sedan-6P	$2,369	2,853 lbs.	4,201
62C	13	2-dr. Sport Coupe-6P	$2,434	2,883 lbs.	8,103

Falcon Station Wagon (Six)

71A	22	4-dr. Station Wagon-6P	$2,442	3,037 lbs.	10,484

Falcon Station Wagon (V-8)

71A	22	4-dr. Station Wagon-6P	$2,548	3,236 lbs.	1,999

Falcon Deluxe Station Wagon (Six)

71B	24	4-dr. Station Wagon-6P	$2,553	3,045 lbs.	7,038

Falcon Deluxe Station Wagon (V-8)

71B	24	4-dr. Station Wagon-6P	$2,659	3,244 lbs.	3,938

Fairlane (Six)

62A	31	2-dr. Sedan-6P	$2,240	2,747 lbs.	8,440
54A	32	4-dr. Sedan-6P	$2,280	2,792 lbs.	11,731

Fairlane (V-8)

62A	31	2-dr. Sedan-6P	$2,345	2,916 lbs.	4,258
54A	32	4-dr. Sedan-6P	$2,386	2,961 lbs.	11,774

Fairlane 500 (Six)

62B	41	2-dr. Sedan-6P	$2,317	2,754 lbs.	4,617
54B	42	4-dr. Sedan-6P	$2,357	2,798 lbs.	12,017
63B	43	2-dr. Hardtop-6P	$2,378	2,856 lbs.	7,300
76B	45	2-dr. Convertible-6P	$2,608	3,084 lbs.	1,033

Fairlane 500 (V-8)

62B	41	2-dr. Sedan-6P	$2,423	2,923 lbs.	8,949
54B	42	4-dr. Sedan-6P	$2,463	2,967 lbs.	53,454
63B	43	2-dr. Hardtop-6P	$2,484	3,025 lbs.	65,343
76B	45	2-dr. Convertible-6P	$2,709	3,253 lbs.	8,039

Fairlane 500/XL (Six)

63B	47	2-dr. Hardtop-6P	$2,543	2,884 lbs.	629
76B	46	2-dr. Convertible-6P	$2,768	3,099 lbs.	155

Fairlane 500/XL (V-8)

63C	47	2-dr. Hardtop-6P	$2,649	3,053 lbs.	21,315
76C	46	2-dr. Convertible-6P	$2,709	3,253 lbs.	4,305

Fairlane GT (V-8)

63D	40	2-dr. Hardtop-6P	$2,843	3,335 lbs.	33,015
76D	44	2-dr. Convertible-6P	$3,068	3,500 lbs.	4,327

Fairlane Ranch Wagon (Six)

71D	38	4-dr. Station Wagon-6P	$2,589	3,182 lbs.	3,623

Fairlane Ranch Wagon (V-8)

71D	38	4-dr. Station Wagon-6P	$2,694	3,351 lbs.	8,530

Fairlane Custom Ranch Wagon (Six)

71B	48	4-dr. Station Wagon-6P	$2,665	3,192 lbs.	1,613

Fairlane Custom Ranch Wagon (V-8)

71B	48	4-dr. Station Wagon-6P	$2,770	3,361 lbs.	17,904

Fairlane Squire Wagon (Six)

71E	48	4-dr. Station Wagon-6P	$2,796	3,200 lbs.	771

Fairlane Squire Wagon (V-8)

71E	48	4-dr. Station Wagon-6P	$2,901	3,369 lbs.	10,787

Ford Custom (Six)

62E	53	2-dr. Sedan-6P	$2,380	3,333 lbs.	12,951
54E	54	4-dr. Sedan-6P	$2,432	3,433 lbs.	22,622

Ford Custom (V-8)

62E	53	2-dr. Sedan-6P	$2,487	3,377 lbs.	11,470
54E	54	4-dr. Sedan-6P	$2,539	3,477 lbs.	32,095

Custom 500 (Six)

62B	51	2-dr. Sedan-6P	$2,481	3,375 lbs.	11,882
54B	52	4-dr. Sedan-6P	$2,533	3,444 lbs.	27,164

Custom 500 (V-8)

62B	51	2-dr. Sedan-6P	$2,588	3,419 lbs.	12,454
54B	52	4-dr. Sedan-6P	$2,639	3,488 lbs.	69,771

Galaxie 500 (Six)

54A	62	4-dr. Sedan-6P	$2,677	3,456 lbs.	6,787
63B	66	4-dr. Fastback-6P	$2,685	3,437 lbs.	9,441
57B	64	4-dr. Hardtop-6P	$2,762	3,526 lbs.	727
76A	65	2-dr. Convertible-6P	$2,934	3,633 lbs.	791

Galaxie 500 (V-8)

54A	62	4-dr. Sedan-6P	$2,784	3,500 lbs.	156,769
63B	66	4-dr. Fastback-6P	$2,791	3,481 lbs.	176,790
57B	64	4-dr. Hardtop-6P	$2,869	3,570 lbs.	51,679
76A	65	2-dr. Convertible-6P	$3,041	3,677 lbs.	24,550

Galaxie 500/XL (V-8)

63B	68	2-dr. Fastback-6P	$3,231	3,616 lbs.	22,247
76B	69	2-dr. Convertible-6P	$3,480	3,761 lbs.	5,106

Galaxie 500 LTD (V-8)

63F	67	2-dr. Fastback-6P	$3,201	3,601 lbs.	30,810
57F	60	4-dr. Hardtop-6P	$3,278	3,649 lbs.	66,255

Galaxie 7-Litre (V-8)

63D	67	2-dr. Fastback-6P	$3,621	3,914 lbs.	8,705
76D	60	2-dr. Convertible-6P	$3,872	4,059 lbs.	2,368

Ranch Wagon (Six)

71D	71	4-dr. Station Wagon-6P	$2,793	3,919 lbs.	6,216

Ranch Wagon (V-8)

71D	72	4-dr. Station Wagon-6P	$2,900	3,963 lbs.	27,090

Custom Ranch Wagon (Six)

71C	72	4-dr. Station Wagon-6P	$2,882	3,934 lbs.	1,314
71B	74	4-dr. Station Wagon-9P	$2,999	3,975 lbs.	1,192

Custom Ranch Wagon (V-8)

71C	72	4-dr. Station Wagon-6P	$2,989	3,978 lbs.	50,966
71B	74	4-dr. Station Wagon-9P	$3,105	4,019 lbs.	34,316

Country Squire Station Wagon (Six)

71E	76	4-dr. Station Wagon-6P	$3,182	4,004 lbs.	159
71A	78	4-dr. Station Wagon-9P	$3,265	4,018 lbs.	150

Country Squire Station Wagon (V-8)

71E	76	4-dr. Station Wagon-6P	$3,289	4,048 lbs.	26,184
71A	78	4-dr. Station Wagon-9P	$3,372	4,062 lbs.	40,378

Engines:

Falcon and Fairlane Six: Overhead valve. Cast-iron block. Displacement: 170 cid. B & S: 3.50 x 2.94 in. Compression ratio: 9.1:1. Brake hp: 105 at 4400 rpm. Carburetor: Holley one-barrel. Seven main bearings. Code 4.

1966 Ford Fairlane 500 two-door convertible (OCW)

1966 Ford Fairlane four-door Ranch Wagon (OCW)

1966 Ford Fairlane 500 four-door station wagon (OCW)

Falcon and Fairlane Six: Overhead valve. Cast-iron block. Displacement: 200 cid. B & S: 3.68 x 3.13 in. Compression ratio: 9.2:1. Brake hp: 120 at 4400 rpm. Carburetor: Holley one-barrel. Seven main bearings. Code U.

Ford Six: Overhead valve. Cast-iron block. Displacement: 240 cid. B & S: 4.00 x 3.18 in. Compression ratio: 9.2:1. Brake hp: 150 at 4000 rpm. Carburetor: Holley one-barrel. Seven main bearings. Code V (Police code B and taxi code E).

Challenger 289 V-8: Overhead valve. Cast-iron block. Displacement: 289 cid. B & S: 4.00 x 2.87 in. Compression ratio: 9.30:1. Brake hp: 200 at 4400 rpm. Torque: 282 lbs.-ft. at 2400 rpm. Five main bearings. Hydraulic valve lifters. Carburetor: Two-barrel. Cooling system capacity: 15 qt. with heater. Crankcase capacity: 4 qt. (add 1 qt. with new oil filter). Code C.

Challenger 289 Four-Barrel V-8: Overhead valve. Cast-iron block. Displacement: 289 cid. B & S: 4.00 x 2.87 in. Compression ratio: 10.0:1. Brake hp: 225 at 4800 rpm. Torque: 305 lbs.-ft. at 3200 rpm. Five main bearings. Hydraulic valve lifters. Carburetor: Four-barrel. Cooling system capacity: 15 qt. with heater. Crankcase capacity: 4 qt. (add 1 qt. with new oil filter). Code A.

Interceptor V-8 (Base Galaxie 500XL V-8 and optional in other full-size Fords): Overhead valve. Cast-iron block. Displacement: 352 cid. B & S: 4.00 x 3.50 in. Compression ratio: 9.30:1. Brake hp: 250 at 4400 rpm. Torque: 352 lbs.-ft. at 2800 rpm. Five main bearings. Hydraulic valve lifters. Carburetor: Four-barrel. Cooling system capacity: 20.5 qt. with heater. Crankcase capacity: 5 qt. (add 1 qt. with new oil filter). Code X.

Challenger 289 High-Performance Four-Barrel V-8: Overhead valve. Cast-iron block. Displacement: 289 cid. Bore and stroke: 4.00 x 2.87 inches. Compression ratio: 10.5:1. Brake hp: 271 at 6000 rpm. Torque: 312 at 3400 rpm. Five main bearings. Hydraulic valve lifters. Carburetor: Four-barrel. Cooling system capacity: 15 qt. with heater. Crankcase capacity: 4 qt. (add 1 qt. with new oil filter). Code K.

Thunderbird 390 Two-Barrel V-8 (Optional in full-size Fords): Overhead valve. Cast-iron block. Displacement: 390 cid. B & S: 4.05 x 3.78 in. Compression ratio: 9.5:1. Brake hp: 275 at 4400 rpm. Torque: 405 at 2600 rpm. Five main bearings. Solid valve lifters. Carburetor: Two-barrel. Cooling system capacity: 20.5 qt. with heater. Crankcase capacity: 4 qt. (add 1 qt. with new oil filter). Code Y.

Thunderbird 390 Four-Barrel V-8 (Optional in full-size Fords): Overhead valve. Cast-iron block. Displacement: 390 cid. B & S: 4.05 x 3.78 in. Compression ratio: 10.5:1. Brake hp: 315 at 4600 rpm. Torque: 427 lbs.-ft. at 2800 rpm. Five main bearings. Hydraulic valve lifters. Carburetor: Four-barrel. Cooling system capacity: 20.5 qt. with heater. Crankcase capacity: 4 qt. (add 1 qt. with new oil filter). Dual exhausts. Code Z.

1966 Ford Fairlane 500 four-door Squire station wagon (OCW)

1966 Ford Fairlane 500 two-door convertible (OCW)

1966 Ford Fairlane 500/XL two-door convertible (OCW)

1966 Ford Fairlane 500/XL two-door convertible seats (OCW)

1966 Ford Fairlane 500/XL two-door hardtop (OCW)

1966 Ford Fairlane 500 GTA two-door hardtop (OCW)

Optional Fairlane GT 390 V-8: Overhead valve. Cast-iron block. Displacement: 390 cid. B & S: 4.05 x 3.78 in. Compression ratio: 11.0:1. Brake hp: 335 at 4800 rpm. Torque: 427 lbs.-ft. at 3200 rpm. Five main bearings. Hydraulic valve lifters. Carburetor: Holley four-barrel. Cooling system capacity: 20.5 qt. with heater. Crankcase capacity: 4 qt. (add 1 qt. with new oil filter). Dual exhaust. Code S.

Thunderbird Special V-8: Overhead valve. Cast-iron block. Displacement: 428 cid. B & S: 4.13 x 3.98 in. Compression ratio: 10.50:1. Brake hp: 345 at 4600 rpm. Torque: 462 lbs.-ft. at 2800 rpm. Five main bearings. Hydraulic valve lifters. Carburetor: Four-barrel. Cooling system capacity: 20.5 qt. with heater. Crankcase capacity: 4 qt. (add 1 qt. with new oil filter). Dual exhausts Code Q.

Police Interceptor V-8: Overhead valve. Cast-iron block. Displacement: 428 cid. B & S: 4.13 x 3.98 in. Compression ratio: 10.50:1. Brake hp: 360 at 5400 rpm. Torque: 459 lbs.-ft. at 3200 rpm. Five main bearings. Solid valve lifters. Carburetor: Four-barrel. Cooling system capacity: 20.5 qt. with heater. Crankcase capacity: 4 qt. (add 1 qt. with new oil filter). Dual exhausts. Code P.

Thunderbird High Performance V-8: Overhead valve. Cast-iron block. Displacement: 427 cid. B & S: 4.23 x 3.78 in. Compression ratio: 11.00:1. Brake hp: 410 at 5600 rpm. Torque: 476 lbs.-ft. at 3400 rpm. Five main bearings. Solid valve lifters. Carburetor: Holley four-barrel. Cooling system capacity: 20.5 qt. with heater. Crankcase capacity: 5 qt. (add 1 qt. with new oil filter). Dual exhausts. Code W.

Thunderbird Super-High-Performance V-8: Overhead valve. Cast-iron block. Displacement: 427 cid. B & S: 4.23 x 3.78 in. Compression ratio: 11.50:1. Brake hp: 425 at 6000 rpm. Torque: 480 lbs.-ft. at 3700 rpm. Five main bearings. Hydraulic valve lifters. Carburetor: Two Holley four-barrel. Cooling system capacity: 20.5 qt. with heater. Crankcase capacity: 5 qt. (add 1 qt. with new oil filter). Dual exhausts. Code R.

"SOHC 427" 4V V-8: Overhead valve. Cast-iron block. Hemispherical combustion chambers with overhead valves and overhead camshafts for each engine bank. Displacement: 427 cid. B & S: 4.23 x 3.78 inches. Compression ratio: 12.10:1. Brake hp: 616 at 7000 rpm. Five main bearings. Carburetor: Holley four-barrel. Cooling system capacity: 20.5 qt. with heater. Crankcase capacity: 5 qt. (add 1 qt. with new oil filter). Dual exhaust. Code L. (This engine was available only "over the counter" for $2,500.)

"SOHC 427" 4V V-8: Overhead valve. Cast-iron block. Hemispherical combustion chambers with overhead valves and overhead camshafts for each engine bank. Displacement: 427 cid. B & S: 4.23 x 3.78 in.

Compression ratio: 12.10:1. Brake hp: 657 at 7500 rpm. Five main bearings. Hydraulic valve lifters. Carburetor: Two Holley four-barrel. Cooling system capacity: 20.5 qt. with heater. Crankcase capacity: 5 qt. (add 1 qt. with new oil filter). Dual exhausts. Code M.

Chassis:

Falcon: Wheelbase: 110.9 in and 113 in., station wagons. Overall length: 184.3 in. and 198.7 in., station wagons. Tires: 6.50 x 13 four-ply tubeless blackwall and 7.75 x 14 four-ply tubeless blackwall on station wagons.

Fairlane: Wheelbase: 116 in. and 113 in. on station wagons. Overall length: 197 in. and 199.8 in. on station wagons. Tires: 6.95 x 14 four-ply tubeless blackwall and 7.75 x 14 four-ply tubeless blackwall on station wagons.

Ford: Wheelbase: 119 in. Overall length: 210 in. and 210.9 in. on station wagons. Tires: 7.35 x 15 four-ply tubeless blackwall and 8.45 x 15 four-ply tubeless blackwall on station wagons.

Options:

Falcon: 200-cid six-cylinder engine ($26). The 289-cid V-8 engine ($131). Cruise-O-Matic automatic transmission ($167 with six-cylinder engine, $156 with 289-cid V-8). Power Steering ($84). Power tailgate on station wagons ($44). AM radio ($57). Vinyl roof on two-door models ($74). Wheel covers ($21). White sidewall tires ($32).

Fairlane: 289-cid V-8 engine ($105 and not available on GT). 390-cid V-8 engine ($206 and standard on GT). Cruise-O-Matic automatic transmission ($184 with 289-cid V-8, $214 with 390-cid V-8). Four-speed manual transmission ($183). AM radio ($57). Power steering ($84). Power tailgate window on station wagons ($31). Luggage rack on station wagons ($44). Two-tone paint ($21). White sidewall tires ($33). Wheel covers ($21). Vinyl roof on two-door hardtops ($76).

Ford: Popular Custom and Custom 500 options included the 289-cid V-8 engine ($106). Cruise-O-Matic automatic transmission ($184). Power steering ($94). AM radio ($57). Wheel covers ($22). White sidewall tires ($33). Popular Galaxie 500/Galaxie 500XL/Galaxie 500 7-Litre/Galaxie 500 LTD options included the 390-cid V-8 engine ($101 for two-barrel engine, $153 for four-barrel engine and not available in 7-Litre models). Power steering ($94). Power brakes ($42). Power windows ($99). Tinted windshield ($21). Air conditioning ($353). AM radio ($57). AM/FM radio ($133). Vinyl roof on two-door hardtops ($74), on four-door hardtops ($83). White sidewall tires ($33). Popular station wagon options included all those in the Galaxie 500 models plus power tailgate window ($31). Luggage rack ($44). Third passenger seat ($29).

The full-size Fords were introduced October 1, 1965, and all the Ford lines appeared in dealer showrooms the same day. Model-year production peaked at 2,093,832 units. Calendar-year sales of 2,038,415 cars were recorded. Donald N. Frey was the chief executive officer of the company this year. On a calendar-year sales basis, Ford was the number two maker in America this year and held a 23.71 percent share of total market. Only 237 Ford Motor Co. products, of all types, had 427-cid V-8s installed during the 1966 calendar year. A positive note was the performance of the Ford GT-40 in the European Grand Prix racing circuit. A trio of these cars, running at Le Mans, finished first, second and third. It was the first time American entries had ever captured the championship honors in the prestigious race.

1966 Ford Fairlane 500 GT two-door convertible (OCW)

1966 Ford Custom two-door sedan (OCW)

1966 Ford Custom 500 four-door Sedan

1966 Ford Galaxie 500 four-door Sedan (OCW)

1966 Ford Galaxie 500 two-door fastback (OCW)

1966 Ford Galaxie 500 four-door hardtop (OCW)

1966 Ford Galaxie 500 Sunliner two-door Convertible (OCW)

1966 Ford Galaxie 500/XL bucket seat interior (OCW)

1966 Ford Galaxie 500 LTD four-door interior (OCW)

1966 Ford Galaxie 500/XL two-door convertible (OCW)

1966 Ford Galaxie 500/XL two-door fastback (OCW)

1966 Ford Galaxie 500 LTD four-door hardtop (OCW)

1966 Ford Galaxie 500 7-Litre two-door hardtop (OCW)

1966 Ford Galaxie 500 7-Litre two-door convertible (OCW)

1966 Ford four-door Ranch Wagon (OCW)

1966 Ford four-door Country Sedan 6P (OCW)

1966 Ford four-door Country Squire Wagon (OCW)

1967 Ford

Falcon — (Six and V-8): The 1967 Ford Falcons were updated but not totally restyled. The most noticeable change in the two years, was the scoop-like indentations behind the front wheel openings, on the front fenders. The grille was nearly identical, with a horizontal and vertical dividing bar being the only difference. Falcon was the base trim level of the compact Falcon line for 1967 and included a 105-hp six-cylinder engine, a heater and defroster, directionals with a lane-change signal, a padded instrument panel, padded sun visors, front and rear seat belts with retractors, an outside rearview mirror, and inside day/night mirror, a dual braking system with a warning light, back-up lights, four-way emergency flashers, two-speed windshield wipers and washers, foam-padded seat cushions and front arm rests. The Falcon also had a chrome windshield molding, a chrome rear window molding, chrome rain gutter moldings, armrests on the front doors only and a horn button. The Falcon name, in script, was located on the rear fender, just ahead of the taillights and, in block letters, across the vertical section of the trunk lid.

Falcon Futura — (Six and V-8): The Futura series was the top trim level for 1967 and included all the standard Falcon features, plus a cigarette lighter, rear armrests, rear ashtrays, a deluxe steering wheel with a chrome horn ring, nylon carpeting, special Futura moldings, Futura trim, Futura emblems, Futura nameplates and chrome side window frames. In addition, the Falcon Futura Sports Coupe was a sporty version of the two-door sedan that featured the 200-cid 120-hp six-cylinder engine, front bucket seats, special Sports Coupe nameplates and special wheel covers. The Futura convertible also included front bucket seats.

Falcon Station Wagon — (Six and V-8): Only four-door station wagons were available in the Falcon lineup this year. The Standard wagon came in both body styles. The standard equipment list was similar to that of the base Falcon. The more Deluxe station wagon had richer trim. Futura wagons also had all-vinyl interior trim

Fairlane — (Six and V-8): The Fairlane was the base trim level for 1967 and included the Fairlane name, in block letters, at the front end. The Fairlane continued to use the body introduced in 1966 with minor trim changes. The new grille was a single aluminum stamping instead of the two grilles used in the previous model and the taillights were divided horizontally by the back-up light, instead of vertically as in 1966. Standard Fairlane equipment included all federally-mandated Ford safety features plus vinyl-covered rubber floor mats, foam-padded cushions, courtesy lights, a heater and defroster, a cigarette lighter, ashtrays, a 200-cid six-cylinder engine and a choice of three cloth-and-vinyl interiors.

Fairlane 500 — (Six and V-8): The Fairlane 500 was the intermediate trim level for 1967 and included all the Fairlane trim plus simulated wood door paneling, carpets and an electric clock. The two-door hardtop and the convertible had a "floating" inside day/night mirror. Sedans and hardtops had a choice of four cloth-and-vinyl interiors, while convertibles have a choice of six all-vinyl trims.

Fairlane 500/XL — (Six and V-8): The Fairlane 500/XL included all features found on Fairlane 500s plus adjustable front bucket seats, a center console, courtesy lights, wheel covers and a choice of seven all-vinyl trims.

1967 Ford Falcon two-door Sports Coupe (OCW)

1967 Ford Falcon four-door Futura station wagon (OCW)

Fairlane GT — (V-8): The Fairlane GT included the Fairlane 500/XL features, plus power disc brakes, Wide-Oval sports white tires, GT simulated hood power domes with integral turn indicators, GT stripes, GT fender plaques, a GT black-out grille, deluxe wheel covers, a 289-cid V-8. A left-hand outside rearview mirror and deluxe seat belts .

Fairlane Station Wagon — (Six and V-8): The Fairlane station wagons came in a four-door Fairlane Wagon, a four-door Fairlane 500 Wagon and a four-door Squire model. Fairlane Wagon equipment started with all of the Fairlane sedan features and then included these variations: the Ford Magic Doorgate, foam seat cushions, a heater-and-defroster, a cigar lighter, ash trays, courtesy lighting and a choice of three all-vinyl trims. The Fairlane 500 wagon also had carpeting, an electric clock, a locking stowage compartment and a choice of four pleated all-vinyl trims. The Squire wagon also had simulated wood body trim and as power door gate window.

Ford Custom — (Six and V-8): As in the previous 10 years, Ford continued to restyle at least one of the model lines. The 1967 full-size Fords were completely restyled from the previous year, sharing only drive trains with the 1966 models. The new models were more rounded, with rounder tops and fenders. At the front end, stacked quad headlights were used once again, but the grille was all new. It was a double-stamped aluminum piece featuring horizontal bars divided by five vertical bars. The center portion of the grille projected forward and this point was duplicated in the forward edge of the hood and in the bumper configuration. The body side feature lines were in the same location as the 1966 models, but were somewhat less pronounced. The taillights were vertically situated rectangular units with chrome moldings and chrome cross-hairs surrounding the standard equipment back-up lights. All 1967 Fords are easily recognizable by the energy-absorbing steering wheels used in every model. A large, deeply-padded hub predominated the wheel. Also, all 1967 Fords were equipped with a dual brake master cylinder for the first time. The Custom series was the base trim level Ford for 1967 and included chrome windshield and rear window moldings, a chrome horn ring, nylon carpeting, the Custom name in script on the front fenders and the Ford name, in block letters, spaced across the front of the hood and across the vertical section of the trunk lid. Standard features included a heater and defroster, front and rear seat belts with a reminder light, front seat belt retractors, a non-glare day/night inside rearview mirror, two-speed windshield wipers and washers, back-up lights, Safety-Yoke door latches, emergency flashers, a lane-changing signal, foam seat cushions, courtesy lighting, a cigarette lighter, ash trays, a 240-cid six-cylinder engine, a remote-control outside rearview mirror, a padded dashboard, padded windshield pillars, padded sun visors and three cloth-and-vinyl interior trims.

Custom 500 — (Six and V-8): The Custom 500 was the upper trim level of the base line Custom series and included all the Custom trim plus special Custom 500 exterior trim and choice of four different interior upholstery choices.

Galaxie 500 — (Six and V-8): The Galaxie 500 was the intermediate trim level for 1967 and included all the Custom series trim plus stamped aluminum lower body side moldings, chrome side window moldings, simulated woodgrain appliques on the instrument panel and inner door panels, an electric clock, a trunk light, a glove box light, bright seat side shields and a stamped aluminum trim panel on the vertical section of the trunk lid. The name, Galaxie 500, in block letters, was located on the rear fenders and the Ford crest was located on the trunk lid above the aluminum trim panel. The Galaxie 500 convertible also had a 5-ply

1967 Ford Fairlane 500 four-door Sedan (OCW)

1967 Ford Fairlane 500 four-door Sedan (OCW)

1967 Ford Fairlane 500 four-door Squire station wagon (OCW)

1967 Ford Fairlane 500XL two-door hardtop (OCW)

vinyl power-operated top and a choice of seven all-vinyl interior trims. Hardtops had the same choice of seven all-vinyl interior trims.

Galaxie 500/XL — (V-8): The Galaxie 500XL was the sport trim version of the two-door fastback and two-door convertible and included the 289-cid/200-hp V-8 engine and SelectShift Cruise-O-Matic automatic transmission with a T-bar selector as standard equipment. Also, the model line included individually-adjustable bucket seats, a front Command console with door-ajar warning, bright brake and accelerator pedal trim, courtesy door lights, deluxe wheel covers, a die-cast grille, all Galaxie 500 trim, special ornamentation, automatic courtesy and warning lights in the door panels and chrome trim on the foot pedals. Seven all-vinyl interior trims were available. A four-speed manual gearbox was a no-cost option.

LTD — (V-8): The LTD was the top trim level full-size Ford for 1967 and was considered its own series for the first time since introduced in 1965. LTDs included all the Galaxie 500 trim plus the 289-cid/200-hp V-8 engine and SelectShift Cruise-O-Matic automatic transmission as standard equipment. Other regular features were a Comfort Stream flow-through ventilation system, distinctive LTD trim and ornamentation, special wheel covers, simulated walnut on the instrument panel and door panels, automatic courtesy and warning lights in the doors, deep-foam cushioning in the seating surfaces, pull-down armrests front and rear, color-keyed steering wheel and vinyl top on two-door hardtops. There was a choice of seven all-vinyl trims. A four-speed manual gearbox was a no-cost option.

Galaxie Station Wagon — (Six and V-8): The Ranch Wagon was the base trim level station wagon for 1967, with the Country Sedans being the intermediate level and the Country Squires being the top trim level. The trim paralleled the Custom 500, Galaxie 500 and LTD models of passenger cars. Standard equipment included all standard Ford safety items, a Magic Doorgate, carpeting, foam seats, courtesy lighting, a cigarette lighter, ash trays, a heater and defroster, and a choice of three all-vinyl trims. The Country Sedan also had bright metal exterior trim and a choice of four interiors. The Squire had simulated wood body trim, a power rear window, an electric clock and a choice of six trim options. The Model 72 and Model 74 station wagons also dual facing rear seats, rear bumper steps, a power rear window and power brakes.

VIN (Falcon):

The VIN for Falcons was die-stamped on the top surface of the radiator and the front fender apron support. The first symbol indicates year: 7=1967. The second symbol identifies assembly plant, as follows: A=Atlanta, Georgia, B=Oakville, Ontario, Canada, C=Ontario, Canada, D=Dallas, Texas, E=Mahwah, New Jersey, F=Dearborn, Michigan, G=Chicago, Illinois, H=Lorain, Ohio, J=Los Angeles, California, K=Kansas City, Kansas, N=Norfolk, Virginia, P=Twin Cities, Minnesota, R=San Jose, California, S=Pilot Plant, T=Metuchen, New Jersey, U=Louisville, Kentucky, W=Wayne, Michigan, Y=Wixom, Michigan, Z=St. Louis, Mo. The third and fourth symbols identify body series code: 10=Falcon two-door Club Coupe, 11=Falcon four-door bench seat sedan, 20=Futura two-door Club Coupe with bench seat, 21=Futura four-door sedan with bench seat, 22=Futura two-door hardtop with bucket seats, 12=four-door station wagon, 23=four-door Deluxe station wagon. The fifth symbol identifies engine code, as follows: U=170-cid six-cylinder one-barrel, T=200-cid six-cylinder one-barrel, 2=200-cid export six-cylinder one-barrel, C=289-cid V-8 two-barrel, 3=289-cid export V-8 two-barrel and A=289-cid V-8 four-barrel. The last six digits are the unit's production number, beginning at 100001 and going up, at each of the assembly plants. Falcons were not built at all Ford plants.

VIN (Fairlane):

The VIN for Fairlanes was die-stamped on the top surface of the radiator and the front fender apron support. The first symbol indicates year: 7=1967. The second symbol identifies assembly plant, as follows: A=Atlanta, Georgia, B=Oakville, Ontario, Canada, C=Ontario, Canada, D=Dallas, Texas, E=Mahwah, New Jersey, F=Dearborn, Michigan, G=Chicago, Illinois, H=Lorain, Ohio, J=Los Angeles, California, K=Kansas City, Kansas, N=Norfolk, Virginia, P=Twin Cities, Minnesota, R=San Jose, California, S=Pilot Plant, T=Metuchen, New Jersey, U=Louisville, Kentucky, W=Wayne, Michigan, Y=Wixom, Michigan, Z=St. Louis, Mo. The third and fourth symbols identify body series code: 30=Fairlane two-door sedan, 31=Fairlane four-door sedan, 33=Fairlane 500 two-door sedan with bench seats, 34=Fairlane 500 four-door sedan with bench seats, 35=Fairlane 500 two-door hardtop with bench seats, 36=Fairlane 500 convertible with bench seats, 40=Fairlane 500 XL bucket seat two-door hardtop, 41=Fairlane 500 XL bucket seat two-door convertible, 42=Fairlane 500 GT bucket seat two-door hardtop, 43=Fairlane 500 GT bucket seat two-door convertible, 32=Fairlane four-door six-passenger station wagon, 37=Fairlane 500 four-door six-passenger station wagon, 38=Fairlane 500 four-door Squire station wagon. The fifth symbol identifies engine code, as follows: T=200-cid six-cylinder one-barrel, 2=200-cid export six-cylinder one-barrel, C=289-cid V-8 two-barrel, 3=289-cid export V-8 two-barrel, A=289-cid V-8 four-barrel, K=289-cid four-barrel hi-performance V-8, S=390-cid V-8 four-barrel. The last six digits are the unit's production number, beginning at 100001 and going up, at each of the assembly plants. Fairlanes were not built at all Ford plants.

VIN (Ford):

The VIN for Fords was die-stamped on the top surface of the radiator and the front fender apron support. The first symbol indicates year: 7=1967. The second symbol identifies assembly plant, as follows: A=Atlanta, Georgia, B=Oakville, Ontario, Canada, C=Ontario, Canada, D=Dallas, Texas, E=Mahwah, New Jersey, F=Dearborn, Michigan, G=Chicago, Illinois, H=Lorain, Ohio, J=Los Angeles, California, K=Kansas City, Kansas, N=Norfolk, Virginia, P=Twin Cities, Minnesota, R=San Jose, California, S=Pilot Plant, T=Metuchen, New Jersey, U=Louisville, Kentucky, W=Wayne, Michigan, Y=Wixom, Michigan, Z=St. Louis, Mo. The third and fourth symbols identify body series 50=Custom 500 two-door sedan with bench seat, 51=Custom 500 four-door sedan with bench seat, 52=Custom two-door sedan with bench seat, 53=Custom four-door sedan with bench seat, 54=Galaxie 500 four-door sedan with bench seat, 56=Galaxie 500 four-door hardtop with bench seat, 57=Galaxie 500 two-door with bench seat, 55=Galaxie 500 two-door fastback with bench seat, 58=Galaxie 500/XL two-door hardtop with bucket seats, 59=Galaxie 500/XL two-door convertible with bucket seats, 66=LTD four-door hardtop with bench seat, 62=LTD two-door hardtop with bucket seats and formal roof, 64=LTD four-door sedan, 63=LTD two-door convertible with bucket seats and formal roof, 61=LTD two-door hardtop with bench seat, 3=LTD two-door convertible with bench seat, 70=four-door six-passenger Ranch Wagon, 71=four-door six-passenger Country Sedan station wagon, 72=four-door 10-passenger Country Sedan station wagon, 73=four-door Country Squire six-passenger station wagon and 74=four-door Country Squire 10-passenger station wagon. The fifth symbol identifies engine code, as follows: V=223-cid six-cylinder, 5=223-cid Export six-cylinder, B=223-

cid Police six, E=223-cid Taxi six-cylinder, C=289-cid two-barrel V-8, 3=289-cid low-compression export two-barrel V-8, Y=390-cid two-barrel V-8, H=390-cid two-barrel V-8, Z=390-cid four-barrel V-8, Q=428-cid four-barrel V-8, 8=428-cid four-barrel V-8, 8=428-cid four-barrel V-8, P=428-cid four-barrel V-8, W=427-cid four-barrel V-8 and R=427-cid dual four-barrel V-8. The last six digits are the unit's production number, beginning at 100001 and going up, at each of the assembly plants. Full-size Fords not built at all Ford plants.

Falcon Standard (Six)

Model No.	Body/Style No.	Body Style and Seating	Factory Price	Shipping Weight	Production Total
62A	11	2-dr. Sedan-6P	$2,118	2,520 lbs.	15,352
54A	12	4-dr. Sedan-6P	$2,167	2,551 lbs.	26,105

Falcon Standard (V-8)

62A	11	2-dr. Sedan-6P	$2,249	2,806 lbs.	730
54A	12	4-dr. Sedan-6P	$2,299	2,837 lbs.	1,073

Falcon Futura (Six)

62B	11	2-dr. Sedan-6P	$2,280	2,528 lbs.	4,414
54B	12	4-dr. Sedan-6P	$2,322	2,559 lbs.	7,949
62C	13	2-dr. Sport Coupe-6P	$2,256	2,556 lbs.	2,256

Falcon Futura (V-8)

62B	11	2-dr. Sedan-6P	$2,386	2,814 lbs.	1,872
54B	12	4-dr. Sedan-6P	$2,428	2,845 lbs.	3,305
62C	13	2-dr. Sport Coupe-6P	$2,543	2,842 lbs.	4,797

Falcon Station Wagon (Six)

71A	22	4-dr. Station Wagon-6P	$2,497	3,030 lbs.	3,889

Falcon Station Wagon (V-8)

71A	22	4-dr. Station Wagon-6P	$2,603	3,229 lbs.	1,714

Falcon Deluxe Station Wagon (Six)

71B	24	4-dr. Station Wagon-6P	$2,609	3,062 lbs.	1,691

Falcon Deluxe Station Wagon (V-8)

71B	24	4-dr. Station Wagon-6P	$2,714	3,261 lbs.	2,861

Fairlane (Six)

62A	31	2-dr. Sedan-6P	$2,297	2,747 lbs.	6,948
54A	32	4-dr. Sedan-6P	$2,339	2,782 lbs.	9,461

Fairlane (V-8)

62A	31	2-dr. Sedan-6P	$2,402	2,916 lbs.	3,680
54A	32	4-dr. Sedan-6P	$2,445	2,951 lbs.	10,279

Fairlane 500 (Six)

62B	41	2-dr. Sedan-6P	$2,377	2,755 lbs.	2,934
54B	42	4-dr. Sedan-6P	$2,417	2,802 lbs.	7,149
63B	43	2-dr. Hardtop-6P	$2,439	2,842 lbs.	4,879
76B	45	2-dr. Convertible-6P	$2,664	3,159 lbs.	454

Fairlane 500 (V-8)

62B	41	2-dr. Sedan-6P	$2,482	2,924 lbs.	5,539
54B	42	4-dr. Sedan-6P	$2,522	2,971 lbs.	44,403
63B	43	2-dr. Hardtop-6P	$2,545	3,011 lbs.	65,256
76B	45	2-dr. Convertible-6P	$2,770	3,328 lbs.	4,974

Fairlane 500/XL (Six)

63C	47	2-dr. Hardtop-6P	$2,619	2,870 lbs.	330
76C	46	2-dr. Convertible-6P	$2,843	3,187 lbs.	49

Fairlane 500/XL (V-8)

63C	47	2-dr. Hardtop-6P	$2,724	3,039 lbs.	14,541
76C	46	2-dr. Convertible-6P	$3,064	3,356 lbs.	1,894

Fairlane GT (V-8)

63D	40	2-dr. Hardtop-6P	$2,839	3,301 lbs.	18,670
76D	44	2-dr. Convertible-6P	$3,064	3,607 lbs.	2,117

Fairlane Station Wagon (Six)

71D	38	4-dr. Station Wagon-6P	$2,643	3,198 lbs.	3,057

Fairlane Station Wagon (V-8)

71D	38	4-dr. Station Wagon-6P	$2,748	3,367 lbs.	7,824

Fairlane Squire Wagon (Six)

71E	48	4-dr. Station Wagon-6P	$2,902	3,217 lbs.	425

1967 Ford Fairlane 500XL GTA two-door hardtop (OCW)

1967 Ford Fairlane 500XL GTA two-door convertible (OCW)

Fairlane Squire Wagon (V-8)

71E	48	4-dr. Station Wagon-6P	$3,007	3,386 lbs.	7,923

Ford Custom (Six)

62E	53	2-dr. Sedan-6P	$2,441	3,411 lbs.	7,982
54E	54	4-dr. Sedan-6P	$2,496	3,469 lbs.	13,284

Ford Custom (V-8)

62E	53	2-dr. Sedan-6P	$2,548	3,449 lbs.	10,125
54E	54	4-dr. Sedan-6P	$2,602	3,507 lbs.	28,133

Custom 500 (Six)

62B	51	2-dr. Sedan-6P	$2,553	3,413 lbs.	5,070
54B	52	4-dr. Sedan-6P	$2,595	3,471 lbs.	9,033

Custom 500 (V-8)

62B	51	2-dr. Sedan-6P	$2,659	3,451 lbs.	13,076
54B	52	4-dr. Sedan-6P	$2,701	3,509 lbs.	74,227

Galaxie 500 (Six)

54A	62	4-dr. Sedan-6P	$2,732	3,481 lbs.	2,038
63B	66	2-dr. Fastback-6P	$2,755	3,484 lbs.	2,814
57B	64	4-dr. Hardtop-6P	$2,808	3,552 lbs.	295
76A	65	2-dr. Convertible-6P	$3,003	3,666 lbs.	209

Galaxie 500 (V-8)

54A	62	4-dr. Sedan-6P	$2,838	3,519 lbs.	128,025
63B	66	2-dr. Fastback-6P	$2,861	3,522 lbs.	194,574
57B	64	4-dr. Hardtop-6P	$2,914	3,590 lbs.	56,792
76A	65	2-dr. Convertible-6P	$3,110	3,704 lbs.	18,859

Galaxie 500/XL (V-8)

63C	68	2-dr. Fastback-6P	$3,243	3,594 lbs.	18,174
76B	69	2-dr. Convertible-6P	$3,493	3,794 lbs.	5,161

LTD (V-8)

54B	62	4-dr. Sedan-6P	$3,298	3,562 lbs.	12,491
63F	67	2-dr. Fastback-6P	$3,362	3,632 lbs.	46,036
57F	60	4-dr. Hardtop-6P	$3,369	3,676 lbs.	51,978

Ranch Wagon (Six)

71D	71	4-dr. Station Wagon-6P	$2,836	3,911 lbs.	2,681

Ranch Wagon (V-8)

71D	72	4-dr. Station Wagon-6P	$2,943	3,949 lbs.	21,251

Custom Ranch Wagon (Six)

71C	72	4-dr. Station Wagon-6P	$2,935	3,924 lbs.	523
71B	74	4-dr. Station Wagon-9P	$3,061	4,004 lbs.	445

Custom Ranch Wagon (V-8)

71C	72	4-dr. Station Wagon-6P	$3,042	3,962 lbs.	50,295
71B	74	4-dr. Station Wagon-9P	$3,168	4,042 lbs.	33,932

Country Squire Station Wagon (Six)

71E	76	4-dr. Station Wagon-6P	$3,234	3,971 lbs.	74
71A	78	4-dr. Station Wagon-9P	$3,359	4,011 lbs.	61

Country Squire Station Wagon (V-8)

71E	76	4-dr. Station Wagon-6P	$3,340	4,009 lbs.	25,526
71A	78	4-dr. Station Wagon-9P	$3,466	4,049 lbs.	43,963

Engines:

Falcon and Fairlane Six: Overhead valve. Cast-iron block. Displacement: 170 cid. B & S: 3.50 x 2.94 in. Compression ratio: 9.1:1. Brake hp: 105 at 4400 rpm. Carburetor: Holley one-barrel. Seven main bearings. Code 4.

1967 Ford Galaxie 500XL two-door fastback hardtop (OCW)

Falcon and Fairlane Six: Overhead valve. Cast-iron block. Displacement: 200 cid. B & S: 3.68 x 3.13 in. Compression ratio: 9.2:1. Brake hp: 120 at 4400 rpm. Carburetor: Holley one-barrel. Seven main bearings. Code U.

Ford Six: Overhead valve. Cast-iron block. Displacement: 240 cid. B & S: 4.00 x 3.18 in. Compression ratio: 9.2:1. Brake hp: 150 at 4000 rpm. Carburetor: Holley one-barrel. Seven main bearings. Code V (Police code B and taxi code E).

Challenger 289 V-8: Overhead valve. Cast-iron block. Displacement: 289 cid. B & S: 4.00 x 2.87 in. Compression ratio: 9.30:1. Brake hp: 200 at 4400 rpm. Torque: 282 lbs.-ft. at 2400 rpm. Five main bearings. Hydraulic valve lifters. Carburetor: Two-barrel. Cooling system capacity: 15 qt. with heater. Crankcase capacity: 4 qt. (add 1 qt. with new oil filter). Code C.

Challenger 289 Four-Barrel V-8: Overhead valve. Cast-iron block. Displacement: 289 cid. B & S: 4.00 x 2.87 in. Compression ratio: 10.0:1. Brake hp: 225 at 4800 rpm. Torque: 305 lbs.-ft. at 3200 rpm. Five main bearings. Hydraulic valve lifters. Carburetor: Four-barrel. Cooling system capacity: 15 qt. with heater. Crankcase capacity: 4 qt. (add 1 qt. with new oil filter). Code A.

Challenger 289 Four-Barrel V-8: Overhead valve. Cast-iron block. Displacement: 289 cid. B & S: 4.00 x 2.87 in. Compression ratio: 10.5:1. Brake hp: 271 at 6000 rpm. Torque: 312 lbs.-ft. at 3400 rpm. Five main bearings. Solid valve lifters. Carburetor: Four-barrel. Cooling system capacity: 15 qt. with heater. Crankcase capacity: 4 qt. (add 1 qt. with new oil filter). Code K.

Thunderbird 390 V-8 (Optional in full-size Fords): Overhead valve. Cast-iron block. Displacement: 390 cid. B & S: 4.05 x 3.78 in. Compression ratio: 9.5:1. Brake hp: 275 at 4400 rpm. Torque: 405 lbs.-ft. at 2600 rpm. Five main bearings. Hydraulic valve lifters. Carburetor: Two-barrel. Cooling system capacity: 20.5 qt. with heater. Crankcase capacity: 4 qt. (add 1 qt. with new oil filter). Code Y.

Thunderbird 390 Four-Barrel V-8 (Optional in full-size Fords): Overhead valve. Cast-iron block. Displacement: 390 cid. B & S: 4.05 x 3.78 in. Compression ratio: 10.5:1. Brake hp: 315 at 4600 rpm. Torque: 427 lbs-ft. at 2800 rpm. Five main bearings. Hydraulic valve lifters. Carburetor: Four-barrel. Cooling system capacity: 20.5 qt. with heater. Crankcase capacity: 4 qt. (add 1 qt. with new oil filter). Dual exhausts. Code Z.

Optional Fairlane GT 390 V-8: Overhead valve. Cast-iron block. Displacement: 390 cid. B & S: 4.05 x 3.78 in. Compression ratio: 11.0:1. Brake hp: 335 at 4800 rpm. Torque: 427 lbs.-ft. at 3200 rpm. Five main bearings. Hydraulic valve lifters. Carburetor: Holley four-barrel. Cooling system capacity: 20.5 qt. with heater. Crankcase capacity: 4 qt. (add 1 qt. with new oil filter). Dual exhausts. Code S.

Thunderbird Special V-8: Overhead valve. Cast-iron block. Displacement: 428 cid. B & S: 4.13 x 3.98 in. Compression ratio: 10.50:1. Brake hp: 345 at 4600 rpm. Torque: 462 lbs.-ft. at 2800 rpm. Five main bearings. Hydraulic valve lifters. Carburetor: Four-barrel. Cooling system capacity: 20.5 qt. with heater. Crankcase capacity: 4 qt. (add 1 qt. with new oil filter). Dual exhausts. Code Q.

Police Interceptor V-8: Overhead valve. Cast-iron block. Displacement: 428 cid. B & S: 4.13 x 3.98 in. Compression ratio: 10.50:1. Brake hp: 360 at 5400 rpm. Torque: 459 lbs.-ft. at 3200 rpm. Five main bearings. Solid valve lifters. Carburetor: Holley four-barrel. Cooling system capacity: 20.5 qt. with heater. Crankcase capacity: 4 qt. (add 1 qt. with new oil filter). Dual exhausts. Code P.

Thunderbird High-Performance V-8: Overhead valve. Cast-iron block. Displacement: 427 cid. B & S: 4.23 x 3.78 in. Compression ratio: 11.00:1. Brake hp: 410 at 5600 rpm. Torque: 476 lbs.-ft. at 3400 rpm. Five main bearings. Solid valve lifters. Carburetor: Holley four-barrel. Cooling system capacity: 19.5 qt. with heater. Crankcase capacity: 5 qt. (add 1 qt. with new oil filter). Dual exhausts. Code W.

Thunderbird Super-High-Performance V-8: Overhead valve. Cast-iron block. Displacement: 427 cid. B & S: 4.23 x 3.78 in. Compression ratio: 11.50:1. Brake hp: 425 at 6000 rpm. Torque: 480 lbs.-ft. at 3700 rpm. Five main bearings. Solid valve lifters. Carburetor: Two Holley four-barrel. Cooling system capacity: 19.5 qt. with heater. Crankcase capacity: 5 qt. (add 1 qt. with new oil filter). Dual exhausts. Code R.

"SOHC 427" 4V V-8: Overhead valve. Cast-iron block. Hemispherical combustion chambers with overhead valves and overhead camshafts for each engine bank. Displacement: 427 cid. B & S: 4.23 x 3.78 in. Compression ratio: 12.10:1. Brake hp: 616 at 7000 rpm. Five main bearings. Carburetor: Holley four-barrel. Cooling system capacity: 20.5 qt. with heater. Crankcase capacity: 5 qt. (add 1 qt. with new oil filter). Dual exhausts. Code L. (This engine was available only "over the counter" for $2,500.)

"SOHC 427" 4V V-8: Overhead valve. Cast-iron block. Hemispherical combustion chambers with overhead valves and overhead camshafts for each engine bank. Displacement: 427 cid. B & S: 4.23 x 3.78 in.

1967 Ford Galaxie 500XL two-door convertible (OCW)

Compression ratio: 12.10:1. Brake hp: 657 at 7500 rpm. Five main bearings. Hydraulic valve lifters. Carburetor: Two Holley four-barrel. Cooling system capacity: 20.5 qt. with heater. Crankcase capacity: 5 qt. (add 1 qt. with new oil filter). Dual exhausts. Code M.

Note: A tunnel-port 427 was available as an over-the-counter kit. It included a special tunnel-port intake manifold and special cylinder heads.

Chassis:

Falcon: Wheelbase: 110.9 in. and 113 in., station wagons. Overall length: 184.3 in. and 197 in., station wagons. Tires: 6.50 x 13 four-ply tubeless blackwall, 7.35 x 14 four-ply tubeless blackwall, Sport Coupe and 7.75 x 14 four-ply tubeless blackwall, station wagons.

Fairlane: Wheelbase: 116 in. and 113 in., station wagons. Overall length: 197 in. and 199.8 in., station wagons. Tires: 6.95 x 14 four-ply tubeless blackwall and 7.15 x 14 four-ply tubeless blackwall, hardtops and station wagons.

Ford: Wheelbase: 119 in. Overall length: 213 in. and 213.9 in., station wagons. Tires: 7.75 x 15 four-ply tubeless blackwall, sedans, 8.15 x 15 four-ply tubeless blackwall, hardtops and 8.45 x 15 four-ply tubeless blackwall, station wagons.

Options:

Falcon: SelectAire air conditioner with V-8 and radio required and tinted glass ($356.09). 42-amp alternator ($10.42). 55-amp alternator ($29.56). High-ratio axle ($2.63). Heavy-duty 55-amp battery ($7.44). Bright window frames on Futura station wagon ($25.91). Courtesy light group including ash tray light, glove box light, trunk or cargo area light and rear door courtesy lamp switches ($14.49, standard on Falcon Sport Coupe). Limited-slip differential ($37.20). Dual-Action tailgate, station wagon only ($45.39). Closed crankcase emission system, exhaust ECS required ($5.19). Exhaust emission control system, not available with 170-cid six teamed with air conditioning ($45.45). Accent stripes and quarter panel peak moldings in standard models ($19.06). Extra-cooling package for Falcon six ($7.44, not available with air conditioning). Extra-cooling package for Falcon V-8 ($10.47, not available with air conditioning). Windshield with tinted band ($30.73). Tinted windshield glass ($21.09). Magic-Aire heater delete, except with air conditioning ($71.85 credit). Chrome luggage rack ($44.44). Outside remote-control mirror ($9.58, standard on Sport Coupe). Right-hand rearview mirror on station wagon ($6.95). Two-tone paint, except station wagon ($18.99). Power brakes ($42.29). Power disc brakes, with V-8s ($97.21). Power steering ($84.47). Power tailgate window ($31.62). Protection group including color-keyed front and rear floor mats, license plate frames and door edge guards on two-door models ($25.28). Protection group including color-keyed front and rear floor mats, license plate frames and door edge guards on two-door models ($29.17). Push-button radio and antenna ($57.44). Deluxe seat belts with warning lights ($10.42 and standard in Sport Coupe). Front shoulder harness ($27.27). Stereosonic tape system ($128.49, but not available with air conditioning teamed with four-speed manual transmission). Heavy-duty suspension on station wagons ($23.38). Cruise-O-Matic Select-Shift automatic transmission with six-cylinder engine ($168.47). Cruise-O-Matic Select-Shift automatic transmission with V-8 engine ($186.80). Four-speed manual transmission with V-8 ($184.02, except not in station wagons). Three-speed manual transmission with 200-cid six-cylinder engine ($32.44, but standard in station wagons). Vinyl roof for Futura models ($74.19). Vinyl trim for Futura models ($24.47, but standard in Sport Coupe and station wagons). Full wheel covers ($21.34, but standard in Sports Coupe). Standard tire equipment was five 6.95 x 14 4-ply-rated black sidewall tires on all models except Sport Coupe and station wagons. Added charge for 6.95 x 14 4-ply-rated whitewalls was $32.47. Added charge for 7.35 x 14 4-ply-rated blackwalls was $14.23. Added charge for 7.35 x 14 4-ply-rated whitewalls was $50.48. Standard tire equipment on Sports Coupe was 7.35 x 14 4-ply-rated blackwall. Added charge for whitewalls was $36.35. Standard tire equipment was five 7.7 x 14 4-ply-rated black sidewall tires on all station wagons. Added charge for 7.75 x 14 4-ply-rated whitewalls was $36.34. Added charge for 7.75 x 14 8-ply-rated blackwalls was $33.45 Added charge for 7.75 x 14 8-ply-rated whitewalls was $69.67. Five 7.35 x 14 (185R) radial tires in blackwall and whitewall styles were a limited-production option, but prices were not available when source information was published.

1967 Ford LTD two-door fastback hardtop (OCW)

Ford and Fairlane: Single body side accent stripe on hardtops and convertibles except Fairlanes ($13.90). Body side accent stripe on Fairlane 500, Fairlane 500/XL and Fairlane GT, except station wagons ($13.90). SelectAire air conditioner with V-8 and radio required and tinted glass recommended ($356.09). 42-amp alternator ($10.42, but not available with air conditioner). 55-amp alternator ($21.09, standard with air conditioner, but not available on six with power steering). High-ratio axle ($2.63). Heavy-duty battery ($7.44, but standard with 427- and 428-cid engines). Center console for GT models ($47.92). Limited-slip differential ($41.60 on all except Fairlane but not optional with 427-cid V-8s). Limited-slip differential on Fairlanes ($37.20). Closed crankcase emission system, exhaust ECS required ($5.19). Exhaust emission control system, all models where mandatory ($45.45). Electric clock ($15.59, but standard in Fairlane, Fairlane XL, Fairlane GT, Ford LTD and Ford Squire). 390-cid 320-hp four-barrel V-8 over 289-cid 200-hp V-8 in Fairlane ($158.08 and extra-cost transmission require). 390-cid 270-hp two-barrel V-8 in all ($78.25). 390-cid 31`5-hp four-barrel V-8 in all except Fairlane ($158.08 and extra-cost transmission required). 428-cid 345-hp four-barrel V-8 in all except Fairlane and standard with 7-Litre package ($975.09). 427-cid 410-hp four-barrel V-8 including transistorized ignition, heavy-duty battery, heavy-duty suspension, extra-cooling package, four-speed manual transmission, 8.15 x 15 black nylon tires in all except Fairlane and cars with 7-Litre package ($975.09, not available in station wagons and 4-ply tires required at extra cost). 427-cid 410-hp four-barrel V-8 with 7-Litre Sports package only ($647.51). 427-cid 425-hp dual four-barrel V-8 in all except Fairlane and cars with 7-Litre Sports package ($975.09). 427-cid 425-hp dual four-barrel V-8 with 7-Litre Sports package only ($647.51). Tinted glass in Fairlanes ($30.73). Tinted glass in all except Fairlane ($39.45). Tinted windshield ($21.09). Manually-adjustable load-leveling system for Fords ($42.19). Automatic load-leveling system for Fords ($84.78). Chrome luggage rack for station wagons ($44.44). Adjustable luggage rack for station wagons, except Fairlane ($63.08). Luxury trim package including electric clock, Comfort Stream ventilation and console control panel for Ford XL models ($167.11). Right-hand outside rearview mirror for all station wagons ($6.95). Remote-control left-hand outside rearview mirror ($9.58, but standard on GT). Magic-Aire heater delete, not available with air conditioning, Comfort Stream ventilation option or LTD model ($73.51 credit). Tutone paint for Fairlane and Fairlane 500 two- and four-door sedans and all Fords except convertible or Country Squire ($21.54). Power brakes for all cars except those with 427-cid V-8 ($42.49, but standard in station wagons with dual facing rear seats). Full-width six-way power seat for cars without four-speed manual transmission ($94.75, but not available in Fairlane). Six-way power driver's bucket seat ($84.25, but not available in Fairlane). Driver-only six-way power LTD Twin Comfort Lounge seat, except Fairlane ($84.25). Driver-and-passenger six-way power LTD Twin Comfort Lounge seat, except Fairlanes ($168.40). Power disc brakes, except in station wagons with dual facing rear seats ($97.21). Power disc brakes in station wagons with dual facing rear seats ($54.87). Power steering in Fairlane ($84.47). Power steering in Fords ($94.95). Power tailgate window in Fairlane wagons and Ford Ranch Wagon and Country Sedan ($54.87). Power top on Fairlane convertible ($52.95). Power windows on Galaxie, Galaxie 500, Galaxie 500XL, LTD, Country Squire and Country Sedan with deluxe trim ($99.94). Front push-button power radio antenna for Fairlane ($57.46). Front push-button power radio antenna for Ford, rear speaker required on Galaxie XL and LTD without stereosonic ($57.51). Front power antenna for AM/FM radio in Fords ($133.65 with rear speaker required in Galaxie XL and LTD without stereo). Rear right radio antenna, except Fairlanes and station wagons ($9.50). Rear speaker, except Fairlanes or wagons ($13.22). Deluxe seat belts with warning light ($10.42 and standard on GT). Reclining passenger seat with headrest for Ford Galaxie 500/XL ($44.15). Third facing rear seat for Fairlane station wagons ($29.27). Comfort Lounge seat for Ford LTD models ($116.59). Front shoulder harness ($27.27). Automatic speed control for Fords with V-8s and Cruise-O-Matic ($71.30). Deluxe woodgrain steering wheel for Fairlane ($31.52). Stereosonic tape system for Ford, AM radio required ($128.49). Stereosonic tape for Fairlanes, except cars with four-speed transmission and air conditioning combined ($128.49). Heavy-duty suspension for Fairlane six ($9.58). Heavy-duty suspension for Fairlane V-8 ($13.02, but standard with GT or 390-cid four-barrel V-8). Extra heavy-duty suspension on Ford station wagons ($7.27). Soft Ride suspension on Fords ($23.28, but standard in station wagons with 427-cid V-8). High-speed handling

1967 Ford four-door Country Squire Wagon (OCW)

suspension in Fords, except station wagons ($30.64, but standard in 7 Litre). Tachometer in Fairlanes ($47.92). Cruise-O-Matic transmission with six ($188.18). Cruise-O-Matic transmission with 289-cid V-8 ($197.89, but standard in Galaxie XL and LTD). Cruise-O-Matic transmission with 390-cid/428-cid V-8, in Galaxie XL or LTD only ($34.63). Cruise-O-Matic transmission with 390-cid/428-cid V-8, except in Galaxie XL or LTD ($220.17). Heavy-duty three-speed manual transmission, required with 390-cid four-barrel V-8 ($47.92). Four-speed manual transmission in Fairlane V-8 and other cars with big-block V-8s except Galaxie XL and LTD ($184.62, but not available in station wagons.) Overdrive in Fairlane with 289-cid two-barrel V-8 and other models with 240-cid and 289-cid engines ($116.59). Vinyl roof on four-door sedan and four-door hardtop, except Fairlane ($83.41, but standard on LTDs). Vinyl trim in Galaxie 500 and Fairlane 500 hardtops and sedans ($24.47, but standard in all station wagons). Luxury vinyl trim in LTDs ($24.47). Comfort Stream ventilation system except in Fairlane or with air conditioning ($40.02, but standard in Ford XL and LTD with luxury trim). Deluxe wheel covers on all Fairlanes except XL and Squire ($40.76). Deluxe wheel covers on Fairlane XL and Squire ($19.48). Full wheel covers on all except Galaxie 500/XL, Ford XL, LTD and Squire ($21.34). Styled steel wheel covers, on all Fairlanes except XL, Ford XL and with exterior décor group ($35.70). Styled steel 14-inch wheels on all Fairlanes except XL, GT and Squire ($115.11). Styled steel 14-inch wheels on Fairlane XL and Squire ($93.84). Styled steel 14-inch wheels on Fairlane GT ($74.36). Exterior décor group including bright window frames and full wheel covers for Ford Custom, Custom 500 and Ranch Wagon with whitewall tires ($51.82). Protection Group including front and rear floor mats, license plate frames and door edge guards for two-door models ($25.28); for four-door models ($29.17). Courtesy light group including glove box light, ash tray light, trunk light or cargo area light and rear door courtesy switches for Galaxie 500 two-door hardtop and convertible, Ford XL and LTD with parking brake signal and swivel dome lamp switch ($5.09); for all other models except Fairlane ($22.54); for Fairlane with map light ($14.49). Deluxe trim group including Squire-type trim and electric clock for Country Sedans ($108.58). Extra-cooling package for Fairlanes except GT with the 390-cid V-8 ($25.25); for Fairlane GT ($13.58, but standard with air conditioning and the 427-cid engine). Extra-cooling package for all six-cylinder ($9.10); for Fairlane with 289-cid V-8 and Ford V-8 ($10.47). Trailer towing package for Fords except 7-Litre and station wagons, requires 390-cid V-8 with Cruise-O-Matic or 428-cid V-8 ($30.93). Convenience Control Panel includes speed-actuated power door locks, door ajar light, low fuel light, parking brake light and seat belt warning lights on Ford XL ($51.82); on two-door models except Fairlanes and XL ($64.77); on four-door models except Fairlanes ($84.25). 7-Litre Sports Package includes 428-cid V-8, Select Shift Cruise-O-Matic, power disc brakes, extra-heavy-duty suspension, deluxe woodgrain steering wheel, 3.25:1 rear axle ratio, G70-15 whitewall Wide-Oval tires and four-speed manual transmission as a no-cost option ($515.86). Five 7.35 x 14 4-ply-rated Rayon blackwall tires were standard on all convertibles except GTs and all sedans, coupes and hardtops except GTs and 7.35 x 14 4-ply-rated whitewalls were $34.45 additional; 7.75 x 14 4-ply-rated blackwalls were $13.83 additional; 7.75 x 14 4-ply-rated whitewalls were $48.35 additional and F70-14 whitewall Wide-Oval tires were $83.12 additional. Five 7.75 x 14 4-ply-rated Rayon blackwall tires were standard on all station wagons with the 200-cid six or 289-cid V-8 and all convertibles, except GTs, with the 390-cid V-8 and 7.75 x 14 4-ply-rated whitewalls were $34.52 additional; 7.75 x 14 8-ply-rated blackwalls were $33.45 additional on station wagons only; 7.75 x 14 8-ply-rated whitewalls were $68.00 additional on station wagons only and F70-14 whitewall Wide-Oval tires were $82.98 additional on all except station wagons. On all station wagons with the 390-cid V-8 7.75 x 14 8-ply-rated whitewall tires were available for $34.55 extra. Five 7.75 x 14 4-ply-rated Rayon blackwall tires were standard on all Ford Custom, Custom 500 and Galaxie 500 four-door sedans with the standard six or V-8 and 7.75 x 14 4-ply-rated whitewalls were $35.47 additional; 8.15 x 14 4-ply-rated blackwalls were $15.49 additional; 8.15 x 14 4-ply-rated whitewalls were $51,77 additional; 8.45 x 14 4-ply-rated blackwalls were $31.08 additional and 8.45 x 14 4-ply-rated whitewalls were $67.48 additional. Five 7.75 x 14 4-ply-rated Rayon blackwall tires were standard on all Ford Custom, Custom 500 and Galaxie 500 four-door sedans with

1967 Ford LTD four-door formal hardtop (OCW)

the standard six or V-8 and 8.15 x 15 or 205 R15 blackwall or whitewall radials were additional; 8.45 x 15 or 215 R15 blackwall or whitewall radials were additional. (The prices for radial tire options were mot available at the time our source material was published.) Five 8.15 x 15 4-ply-rated Rayon blackwall tires were standard on all Ford Custom, Custom 500 and Galaxie 500 four-door sedans with 390-cid or 428-cid V-8s and 8.15 x 15 4-ply-rated whitewalls were $36.37 additional; 8.45 x 15 4-ply-rated blackwalls were $15.59 additional and 8.45 x 14 4-ply-rated whitewalls were $51.99 additional. Five 7.75 x 14 4-ply-rated Rayon blackwall tires were standard on all Ford Custom, Custom 500 and Galaxie 500 four-door sedans with the standard six or V-8 and 8.15 x 15 or 205 R15 blackwall or whitewall radials were additional; 8.45 x 15 or 215 R15 blackwall or whitewall radials were additional. Note: The prices for radial tire options were mot available at the time our source material was published. Five 8.15 x 15 4-ply-rated Rayon blackwall tires were standard on all Fords with 427-cid V-8s and 8.15 x 15 4-ply-rated Nylon blackwalls were $46.53 additional; 8.15 x 15 4-ply-rated Nylon whitewalls were $82.83 additional; 8.45 x 15 4-ply-rated Nylon blackwalls were $62.22 additional and 8.45 x 14 4-ply-rated Nylon whitewalls were $98.52 additional. On Ford station wagons that came standard with five 8.45 x 15 4-ply-rated Rayon blackwall tires comparable whitewalls were $36.40. These wagons were also available with 215 R15 radial-ply tires in either black sidewall or white sidewall styles. (The prices for radial tire options were mot available at the time our source material was published.)

History:

The 1967 Fords were introduced Sept. 30, 1966. The grand total of assemblies for the 1967 model year was 1,742,311 units. This included 877,128 Fords, 233,688 Fairlanes and 76,500 Falcons. Calendar-year production for all the above lines peaked at 240,712 units. As far as sales and production it was a good year for America's number two automaker. However, vice-president and general manager M.S. McLaughlin did have other things to deal with, such as a 57-day United Auto Worker's strike. It was the longest lasting labor dispute in Ford history and culminated in a three-year contract agreement that included unprecedented wage and benefits packages.

1968 Ford

Falcon — (Six and V-8): The 1968 Falcons again used the same body shell as the previous two years, with only minor trim changes. The most noticeable change in the Falcon was that the taillights were square, instead of the round type used on the car since its introduction in 1960. The grille was a stamped aluminum piece, with a rectangular mesh pattern. The grille was divided by the Falcon crest in the center. The simulated exhaust port, used on the front fender of the 1967 Falcons, was not continued into the year 1968. Standard equipment included a chrome windshield molding, a chrome rear window molding, rain gutter moldings, armrests on the front doors only, a steering wheel horn button, a 170-cid 100-hp six-cylinder engine, a heater and defroster and 6.95 x 14 four-ply tires. The Falcon name, in script, appeared on the rear fenders, just ahead of the taillights and in block letters, across the vertical section of the trunk lid.

Falcon Futura — (Six and V-8): The Futura series was the top trim level for 1968 and included all the standard Falcon features, plus the 200-cid 120-hp six-cylinder engine, a cigarette lighter, front and rear door armrests, front and rear door ashtrays, a deluxe steering wheel with a chrome horn ring, nylon carpeting, special Futura moldings, Futura trim, Futura emblems, Futura nameplates and chrome side window frames. In addition, the Falcon Futura Sports Coupe was a sporty version of the two-door sedan that featured front bucket seats, special Sports Coupe nameplates, a map light, an ash tray, a glove box light, a trunk light, side accent stripes, a driver's side remote-control outside rearview mirror, deluxe seat belts, 7.35 x 14 tires and special wheel covers. The Futura convertible also included front bucket seats.

1968 Ford Falcon Futura two-door Sports Coupe (OCW)

1968 Ford Falcon Futura four-door Sports Coupe (OCW)

Falcon Station Wagon — (Six and V-8): Only four-door station wagons were available in the Falcon lineup this year. The Standard wagon came in both body styles. The standard equipment list was similar to that of the base Falcon. The more Deluxe station wagon had richer trim. Futura wagons also had all-vinyl interior trim. A 200-cid 115-hp six-cylinder engine was used in station wagons, which also had 7.75 x 14 four-ply tires and vinyl seat trim.

Fairlane — (Six and V-8): The Fairlane line was the one chosen for major restyling for the new year. It was undoubtedly one of the nicest looking Fairlanes ever to come out of Detroit. It had a full-width grille, containing horizontally mounted quad headlights, and smooth sides with a single horizontal feature line running front to rear. The taillights were vertically situated rectangular units with a centrally located back-up light. The word Ford was spaced evenly across the trunk lid in block letters. Fairlane was Ford's base trim level for 1968 mid-size models and included a 200-cid 115-hp six-cylinder engine or a 302-cid 210-hp V-8, chrome windshield moldings, chrome rear window moldings; chrome rain gutters, chrome side window frames; a chrome horn ring; front and rear armrests; a cigarette lighter; vinyl-coated rubber floor mats, 7.35 x 14 4-ply-rated tires and the Fairlane name, in script, on the side of the rear fender. The Ford name was spelled out, in block letters, across the front of the hood and across the vertical section of the trunk lid. The top-line Fairlane models for 1968 were called Torinos and Torino GTs, with the Fairlane 500 being demoted to intermediate trim level.

Fairlane 500 — (Six and V-8): The Fairlane 500 was the intermediate trim level for 1968 and included all the Fairlane features, plus special Fairlane 500 trim and moldings, color-keyed carpeting front and rear and a choice of four nylon and vinyl upholsteries. Also included was an aluminum dividing bar, in the center of the vertical portion of the trunk lid, and a horizontal dividing bar, in the center of the grille. The Fairlane 500 name, in script, appeared on the rear fender, just ahead of the taillights.

Fairlane Torino — (Six and V-8): The Fairlane Torino included all features found on Fairlane 500s, plus wheel covers, an electric clock and 7.35 x 14 four-ply-rated black sidewall tires.

Fairlane Torino GT — (V-8): The Fairlane Torino GT included all Fairlane Torino features, plus a vinyl-trimmed bench seat, a GT Handling suspension, Argent Silver styled wheels, chrome wheel trim rings, an electric clock, F70 x 14 Wide-Oval white sidewall tires, GT stripes, a gray-finished grille, GT nameplates and a 302-cid V-8. Power brakes were also a required add-on if the 390-cid four-barrel V-8 was ordered.

Fairlane /Torino Station Wagon — (Six and V-8): The Fairlane station wagons came in a four-door Fairlane Wagon, a four-door Fairlane 500 Wagon and a four-door Fairlane Torino Squire model. Fairlane Wagon equipment started with all of the Fairlane sedan features and then included these variations: the Ford Magic Doorgate, foam seat cushions, a heater-and-defroster, a cigar lighter, ash trays, courtesy lighting and a choice of three all-vinyl trims. The Fairlane 500 wagon also had carpeting, an electric clock, a locking stowage compartment and a choice of four pleated all-vinyl trims. The Fairlane Torino Squire wagon also had simulated wood body trim and as power door gate window.

Ford Custom — (Six and V-8): The 1968 "big" Fords were basically 1967 body shells with updated front ends. The two years look completely different, to be sure, but there is little that changed behind the windshield. The new grille work was less protruding than the 1967 version and offered hidden headlights on the upper lines. It was a honeycomb grille with a single, centrally located vertical dividing bar.

The Ford name, in block letters, and the Ford crest, in a small emblem on the driver's side headlight door, appeared. The rooflines were a little more formal than the previous year and the taillights, although retaining the same shape, were divided horizontally (rather than vertically) by the back-up lights. The large, padded hub used on the steering wheels of all 1967 Fords, was replaced by a more conventional pad covering the entire center spoke. More federally-mandated safety regulations appeared in the form of front and rear fender marker lights. Power-wise, the mighty 427-cid V-8 engine was detuned to 390 hp by limiting carburetion to a single four-barrel and replacing the wild solid-lifter camshaft with a more timid hydraulic rider cam. At midyear, the 427 was discontinued and replaced by the equally famous and powerful Cobra Jet 428 and Super Cobra Jet 428 V-8s. These engines dominated the Super Stock classes at the drag races in 1968, when installed in the light Mustang bodies. The Custom series was the base trim level Ford for 1968 and included chrome windshield moldings, chrome rear window moldings, a chrome horn ring, nylon carpeting, a heater and defroster, body side moldings, the Custom name in script on the rear fenders, the 240-cid six or 302-cid V-8 and 7.75 X 15 four-ply-rated tires. The Ford name, in block letters, appeared across the front of the hood.

Custom 500 — (Six and V-8): The Custom 500 was the upper trim level of the base line Custom series and included all the Custom trim plus special Custom 500 exterior trim and choice of several richer interior upholstery combinations.

Galaxie 500 — (Six and V-8): The Galaxie 500 was the intermediate trim level for 1968 and included all the Custom series trim plus stamped aluminum lower body side moldings, chrome side window moldings, simulated woodgrain appliques on the instrument panel and inner door panels, an electric clock, a trunk light, a glove box light, bright seat side shields and a stamped aluminum trim panel on the vertical section of the trunk lid. The name, Galaxie 500, in block letters, was located on the rear fenders and the Ford crest was located on the trunk lid above the aluminum trim panel. The Galaxie 500 convertible also had a 5-ply vinyl power-operated top and all-vinyl interior trims. The four-door hardtop came with larger 8.15 x 14 four-ply-rated tires.

Ford XL — (V-8): The Ford XL (the Galaxie 500/XL description was dropped) included sport trim versions of the two-door fastback and two-door convertible. New this year was a standard 150-hp six instead of a standard V-8. The 302-cid 210-hp V-8 was available as the base V-8. Other standard features of the Ford XL models included a vinyl bench seat, full wheel covers and an electric clock.

LTD — (V-8): The LTD was the top trim level full-size Ford for 1968. LTDs included all the Ford XL trim plus the 302-cid/210-hp V-8, 8.15 x 15 four-ply-rated black sidewall tires engine, full wheel covers, dual accent striping and an electric clock.

Ford Station Wagon — (Six and V-8): The Ranch Wagon was the base trim level station wagon for 1968 and had the features of the Ford Custom models, plus larger 8.45 x 15 four-ply-rated tires. Also available with Custom 500 level trimmings were the 6- and 9-passenger Ranch Wagons, the latter with dual facing rear seats. They also had the larger-size tires. Clones of those two models with fancier all-vinyl trim were included in the Galaxie 500 line. The two seating variations also came in the LTD series with Country Squire nameplates and trim. The 302-cid 210-hp V-8 was standard equipment in Country Squire wagons.

VIN (Ford):

The VIN for Fords was die-stamped on the top surface of the radiator and the front fender apron support. The first symbol indicates year: 8=1968. The second symbol identifies assembly plant, as follows: A=Atlanta, Georgia, B=Oakville, Ontario, Canada, C=Ontario, Canada, D=Dallas, Texas, E=Mahwah, New Jersey, F=Dearborn, Michigan, G=Chicago, Illinois, H=Lorain, Ohio, J=Los Angeles, California, K=Kansas City, Kansas, N=Norfolk, Virginia, P=Twin Cities, Minnesota, R=San Jose, California, S=Pilot Plant, T=Metuchen, New Jersey, U=Louisville, Kentucky, W=Wayne, Michigan, Y=Wixom, Michigan, Z=St. Louis, Mo. The third and fourth symbols identify body series 50=Custom two-door

1968 Ford Falcon four-door Futura station wagon (OCW)

sedan with bench seat, 51=Custom four-door sedan with bench seat, 52=Custom 500 two-door sedan with bench seat, 53=Custom 500 four-door sedan with bench seat, 54=Galaxie 500 four-door sedan with bench seat, 56=Galaxie 500 four-door hardtop with bench seat, 57=Galaxie 500 two-door with bench seat, 55=Galaxie 500 two-door fastback with bench seat, 58=Galaxie 500/XL two-door hardtop with bucket seats, 60=Ford XL four-door hardtop, 61=Ford XL two-door convertible, 66=LTD four-door hardtop with bench seat, 62=LTD two-door hardtop with bucket seats and formal roof, 64=LTD four-door sedan, 70=four-door six-passenger Ranch Wagon, 71=four-door six-passenger Country Sedan station wagon, 72=four-door 10-passenger Country Sedan station wagon, 73=four-door Country Squire six-passenger station wagon and 74=four-door Country Squire 10-passenger station wagon, 75=Country Squire six-passenger station wagon, 76=Country Squire 10-passenger station wagon, 30=Fairlane two-door hardtop with bench seat, 31=Fairlane four-door sedan with bench seat and formal roof, 33=Fairlane 500 two-door hardtop with bench seat and formal roof, 34=Fairlane 500 four-door sedan with bench seat, 35=Fairlane 500 two-door hardtop with bucket seats, 36=Fairlane 500 two-door convertible with bench seats, 33=Fairlane 500 two-door hardtop with bucket seats and formal roof, 35=Fairlane 500 two-door hardtop with bench seat, 36=Fair 500 convertible with bucket seats, 40=Torino two-door hardtop with bench seat and formal roof, 41=Torino four-door sedan with bench seat, 42=Torino GT two-door hardtop with bucket seats, 44=Torino GT with bucket seats and formal roof, 43=Torino GT convertible with bucket seats, 32=Fairlane four-door station wagon with bench seats, 37=Fairlane 500 four-door station wagon with bench seat, 38=Torino Squire four-door station wagon with bench seat, 10=Standard Falcon two-door club coupe with bench seat, 11-Standard Falcon four-door sedan with bench seat, 20-Falcon Futura two-door club coupe with bench seat, 21=Falcon Futura four-door sedan with bench seat, 22=Falcon Sport Coupe with bucket seats, 12=Falcon four-door station Wagon and 23=Falcon Deluxe four-door station wagon. The fifth symbol identifies engine code, as follows: B=240-cid six-cylinder police engine, C=289-cid two-barrel V-8, E=240-cid six-cylinder taxi engine, F=302-cid two-barrel V-8, J=302-cid four-barrel V-8, N=429-cid four-barrel V-8, P=428-cid four-barrel police V-8, Q-428-cid four-barrel V-8, R=428-cid dual four-barrel Cobra-Jet V-8, S=390-cid four-barrel GT V-8, T=200-cid one-barrel six-cylinder, U=170-cid one-barrel six, V=240-cid six-cylinder, W=427-cid four-barrel V-8, X=390-cid two-barrel premium-fuel V-8, Y=390-cid two-barrel V-8, Z=390-cid four-barrel V-8, 2=200-cid low-compression one-barrel six, 5=240-cid low-compression export six-cylinder, 6=302-cid two-barrel low-compression V-8, 8=428-cid four-barrel low-compression V-8. The last six digits are the unit's production number, beginning at 100001 and going up, at each of the assembly plants. Full-size Fords not built at all Ford plants.

Falcon Standard (Six)

Model No.	Body/Style No.	Body Style and Seating	Factory Price	Shipping Weight	Production Total
62A	11	2-dr. Sedan-6P	$2,252	2,680 lbs.	7,788
54A	12	4-dr. Sedan-6P	$2,301	2,714 lbs.	7,567

Falcon Standard (V-8)

| 62A | 11 | 2-dr. Sedan-6P | $2,383 | 2,878 lbs. | 466 |
| 54A | 12 | 4-dr. Sedan-6P | $2,433 | 2,912 lbs. | 635 |

Falcon Futura (Six)

62B	11	2-dr. Sedan-6P	$2,419	2,685 lbs.	1,310
54B	12	4-dr. Sedan-6P	$2,456	2,719 lbs.	2,616
62C	13	2-dr. Sport Coupe-6P	$2,541	2,713 lbs.	787

Falcon Futura (V-8)

62A	11	2-dr. Sedan-6P	$2,521	2,685 lbs.	659
54A	12	4-dr. Sedan-6P	$2,562	2,719 lbs.	1,503
62C	13	2-dr. Sport Coupe-6P	$2,647	2,713 lbs.	1,276

Falcon Station Wagon (Six)

| 71A | 22 | 4-dr. Station Wagon-6P | $2,617 | 3,123 lbs. | 2,040 |

1968 Ford Fairlane Torino four-door sedan (OCW)

Falcon Station Wagon (V-8)

| 71A | 22 | 4-dr. Station Wagon-6P | $2,722 | 3,277 lbs. | 1,385 |

Falcon Deluxe Station Wagon (Six)

| 71B | 24 | 4-dr. Station Wagon-6P | $2,728 | 3,123 lbs. | 775 |

Falcon Deluxe Station Wagon (V-8)

| 71B | 24 | 4-dr. Station Wagon-6P | $2,833 | 3,277 lbs. | 1,606 |

Fairlane (Six)

| 65A | 31 | 2-dr. Hardtop-6P | $2,456 | 3,125 lbs. | 15,753 |
| 54A | 32 | 4-dr. Sedan-6P | $2,464 | 3,083 lbs. | 8,828 |

Fairlane (V-8)

| 65A | 31 | 2-dr. Hardtop-6P | $2,544 | 3,317 lbs. | 28,930 |
| 54A | 32 | 4-dr. Sedan-6P | $2,551 | 3,275 lbs. | 9,318 |

Fairlane 500 (Bench Seats) (Six)

65B	33	2-dr. Formal Hardtop-6P	$2,591	2,983 lbs.	2,723
54B	34	4-dr. Sedan-6P	$2,543	2,927 lbs.	5,142
63B	35	2-dr. Fastback-6P	$2,566	2,969 lbs.	1,269
76B	36	2-dr. Convertible-6P	$2,822	3,129 lbs.	215

Fairlane 500 (Bucket Seats) (Six)

65B	33	2-dr. Formal Hardtop-6P	$2,701	2,983 lbs.	100
63B	35	2-dr. Fastback-6P	$2,676	2,969 lbs.	80
76B	36	2-dr. Convertible-6P	$2,932	3,129 lbs.	11

Fairlane 500 (Bench Seats) (V-8)

65B	33	2-dr. Formal Hardtop-6P	$2,679	3,175 lbs.	28,738
54B	34	4-dr. Sedan-6P	$2,611	3,119 lbs.	37,788
63B	35	2-dr. Fastback-6P	$2,653	3,161 lbs.	27,899
76B	36	2-dr. Convertible-6P	$2,910	3,321 lbs.	3,207

Fairlane 500 (Bucket Seats) (V-8)

65B	33	2-dr. Formal Hardtop-6P	$2,789	3,175 lbs.	1,721
63B	35	2-dr. Fastback-6P	$2,763	3,161 lbs.	3,204
76B	36	2-dr. Convertible-6P	$3,020	3,321 lbs.	328

Fairlane/Torino (Six)

| 54C | 34 | 4-dr. Sedan-6P | $2,688 | 2,965 lbs. | 502 |
| 65C | 47 | 2-dr. Hardtop-6P | $2,710 | 3,001 lbs. | 773 |

Fairlane/Torino (V-8)

| 54C | 34 | 4-dr. Sedan-6P | $2,776 | 3,157 lbs. | 17,460 |
| 65C | 47 | 2-dr. Hardtop-6P | $2,798 | 3,193 lbs. | 35,191 |

Fairlane/Torino GT (V-8)

63D	40	2-dr. Fastback-6P	$2,747	3,194 lbs.	23,939
65D	40	2-dr. Formal Hardtop-6P	$2,772	3,208 lbs.	74,135
76D	44	2-dr. Convertible-6P	$3,001	3,352 lbs.	5,310

Fairlane Station Wagon (Six)

| 71D | 38 | 4-dr. Station Wagon-6P | $2,770 | 3,422 lbs. | 573 |

Fairlane Station Wagon (V-8)

| 71D | 38 | 4-dr. Station Wagon-6P | $2,858 | 3,614 lbs. | 14,227 |

Fairlane 500 Station Wagon (Six)

| 71B | 48 | 4-dr. Station Wagon-6P | $2,881 | 3,288 lbs. | 2,496 |

Fairlane 500 Station Wagon (V-8)

| 71B | 48 | 4-dr. Station Wagon-6P | $2,968 | 3,480 lbs. | 7,694 |

Fairlane/Torino Station Wagon (Six)

| 71D | 48 | 4-dr. Station Wagon-6P | $3,032 | 3,336 lbs. | 325 |

Fairlane/Torino Station Wagon (V-8)

| 71D | 48 | 4-dr. Station Wagon-6P | $3,119 | 3,528 lbs. | 14,448 |

Ford Custom (Six)

| 62E | 53 | 2-dr. Hardtop-6P | $2,584 | 3,444 lbs. | 6,355 |
| 54E | 54 | 4-dr. Sedan-6P | $2,642 | 3,471 lbs. | 11,055 |

Ford Custom (V-8)

| 62E | 53 | 2-dr. Hardtop-6P | $2,662 | 3,491 lbs. | 9,272 |
| 54E | 54 | 4-dr. Sedan-6P | $2,749 | 3,518 lbs. | 27,356 |

Custom 500 (Six)

| 62B | 51 | 2-dr. Hardtop-6P | $2,699 | 3,433 lbs. | 1,497 |
| 54B | 52 | 4-dr. Sedan-6P | $2,741 | 3,484 lbs. | 3,353 |

Custom 500 (V-8)

| 62B | 51 | 2-dr. Hardtop-6P | $2,806 | 3,480 lbs. | 6,557 |
| 54B | 52 | 4-dr. Sedan-6P | $2,848 | 3,531 lbs. | 41,493 |

Galaxie 500 (Six)

54A	62	4-dr. Sedan-6P	$2,864	3,489 lbs.	1,108
63B	66	2-dr. Fastback-6P	$2,881	3,507 lbs.	770
65C	66	2-dr. Formal Hardtop-6P	$2,916	3,513 lbs.	592
57B	64	4-dr. Hardtop-6P	$2,936	3,535 lbs.	146
76A	65	2-dr. Convertible-6P	$3,108	3,652 lbs.	72

Galaxie 500 (V-8)

54A	62	4-dr. Sedan-6P	$2,971	3,536 lbs.	109,137
63B	66	2-dr. Fastback-6P	$2,988	3,554 lbs.	76,133
65C	66	2-dr. Formal Hardtop-6P	$3,022	3,560 lbs.	62,139
57B	64	4-dr. Hardtop-6P	$3,043	3,582 lbs.	52,250
76A	65	2-dr. Convertible-6P	$3,215	3,699 lbs.	11,760

Ford XL (Six)

| 63C | 68 | 2-dr. Fastback-6P | $2,985 | 3,581 lbs. | 132 |
| 76B | 69 | 2-dr. Convertible-6P | $3,214 | 3,718 lbs. | 8 |

Ford XL (V-8)

| 63C | 68 | 2-dr. Fastback-6P | $3,092 | 3,608 lbs. | 45,984 |
| 76B | 69 | 2-dr. Convertible-6P | $3,321 | 3,765 lbs. | 6,058 |

Ford LTD (V-8)

54C	62	4-dr. Sedan-6P	$3,135	3,596 lbs.	21,388
65A	67	2-dr. Fastback-6P	$3,153	3,679 lbs.	50,104
57F	60	4-dr. Hardtop-6P	$3,206	3,642 lbs.	56,924

Ranch Wagon (Six)

| 71D | 71 | 4-dr. Station Wagon-6P | $3,000 | 3,898 lbs. | 1,529 |

Ranch Wagon (V-8)

| 71D | 72 | 4-dr. Station Wagon-6P | $3,107 | 3,945 lbs. | 14,250 |

Custom Ranch Wagon (Six)

| 71H | 72 | 4-dr. Station Wagon-6P | $3,063 | 3,908 lbs. | 280 |
| 71J | 74 | 4-dr. Station Wagon-9P | $3,176 | 3,954 lbs. | 193 |

Custom Ranch Wagon (V-8)

| 71H | 72 | 4-dr. Station Wagon-6P | $3,170 | 3,955 lbs. | 15,850 |
| 71J | 74 | 4-dr. Station Wagon-9P | $3,283 | 4,001 lbs. | 11,745 |

Country Sedan (Six)

| 71B | 76 | 4-dr. Station Wagon-6P | $3,181 | 3,917 lbs. | 138 |
| 71C | 78 | 4-dr. Station Wagon-9P | $3,295 | 3,974 lbs. | 83 |

Country Sedan (V-8)

| 71B | 76 | 4-dr. Station Wagon-6P | $3,288 | 3,964 lbs. | 35,895 |
| 71C | 78 | 4-dr. Station Wagon-9P | $3,402 | 4,021 lbs. | 26,885 |

LTD Country Squire (V-8)

| 71E | 76 | 4-dr. Station Wagon-6P | $3,539 | 4,013 lbs. | 29,923 |
| 71A | 78 | 4-dr. Station Wagon-9P | $3,619 | 4,059 lbs. | 52,256 |

Engines:

Falcon (Six): Overhead valve. Cast-iron block. Displacement: 170 cid. B & S: 3.50 x 2.94 in. Compression ratio: 8.7:1. Brake hp: 100 at 4000 rpm. Torque: 158 lbs.-ft. at 2400 rpm. Carburetor: Holley one-barrel. Seven main bearings. Code U.

Falcon, Fairlane and Torino Six: Overhead valve. Cast-iron block. Displacement: 200 cid. B & S: 3.68 x 3.13 in. Compression ratio: 8.8:1. Brake hp: 115 at 3800 rpm. Torque: 190 lbs.-ft. at 2200 rpm. Carburetor: Holley one-barrel. Seven main bearings. Code T.

Ford, Fairlane and Torino Six: Overhead valve. Cast-iron block. Displacement: 240 cid. B & S: 4.00 x 3.18 in. Compression ratio: 9.20:1. Brake hp: 150 at 4000 rpm. Torque: 234 lbs.-ft. at 2200 rpm. Carburetor: Holley one-barrel. Seven main bearings. Code V (Police code B and taxi code E).

Ford, Fairlane and Torino Six: Overhead valve. Cast-iron block. Displacement: 250 cid. B & S: 3.68 x 3.91 in. Compression ratio: 8.50:1. Brake hp: 155 at 4000 rpm. Torque: 240 lbs.-ft. at 1600 rpm. Carburetor: Holley one-barrel. Seven main bearings. Code 5.

Challenger 289 V-8: Overhead valve. Cast-iron block. Displacement: 289 cid. B & S: 4.00 x 2.87 in. Compression ratio: 8.70:1. Brake hp: 195 at 4600 rpm. Torque: 288 lbs.-ft. at 2600 rpm. Hydraulic valve lifters. Carburetor: Two-barrel. Cooling system capacity:

1968 Ford Fairlane Torino two-door hardtop (PH)

1968 Ford Fairlane Torino four-door Squire station wagon (OCW)

15 qt. with heater. Crankcase capacity: 4 qt. (add 1 qt. with new oil filter). Code C.

302 Two-Barrel V-8: Overhead valve. Cast-iron block. Displacement: 302 cid. B & S: 4.00 x 3.00 in. Compression ratio: 9.00:1. Brake hp: 210 at 4400 rpm. Torque: 300 lbs.-ft. at 2600 rpm. Five main bearings. Hydraulic valve lifters. Carburetor: Two-barrel. Cooling system capacity: 15 qt. with heater. Crankcase capacity: Mid-size and Mustang 4 qt. and (full-Size and Thunderbird) 5 qt. (add 1 qt. with new oil filter). Code F and Export code 6.

302 Four-Barrel V-8: Overhead valve. Cast-iron block. Displacement: 302 cid. B & S: 4.00 x 3.00 in. Compression ratio: 10.00:1. Brake hp: 230 at 4800 rpm. Torque: 310 lbs.-ft. at 2800 rpm. Five main bearings. Hydraulic valve lifters. Carburetor: Two-barrel. Cooling system capacity: 15 qt. with heater. Crankcase capacity: (Mid-size and Mustang) 4 qt. and full-size and Thunderbird 5 qt. (add 1 qt. with new oil filter). Code J.

390 Four-Barrel V-8 (Optional in Ford): Overhead valve. Cast-iron block. Displacement: 390 cid. B & S: 4.05 x 3.78 in. Compression ratio: 9.5:1. Brake hp: 265 at 4400 rpm. Torque: 390 lbs.-ft. at 2600 rpm. Five main bearings. Hydraulic valve lifters. Carburetor: Two-barrel. Cooling system capacity: 20.5 qt. with heater. Crankcase capacity: 5 qt. (add 1 qt. with new oil filter). Code Y.

390 Four-Barrel V-8 (Optional in Ford): Overhead valve. Cast-iron block. Displacement: 390 cid. B & S: 4.05 x 3.78 in. Compression ratio: 10.5:1. Brake hp: 280 at 4400 rpm. Torque: 403 lbs.-ft. at 2600 rpm. Five main bearings. Hydraulic valve lifters. Carburetor: Two-barrel. Cooling system capacity: (Mid-size and Mustang) 4 qt. and full-size and Thunderbird, 5 qt. (add 1 qt. with new oil filter). Dual exhausts. Code X.

390 Four-Barrel V-8 (Optional in Ford): Overhead valve. Cast-iron block. Displacement: 390 cid. B & S: 4.05 x 3.78 in. Compression ratio: 10.5:1. Brake hp: 315 at 4600 rpm. Torque: 427 lbs.-ft. at 2800 rpm. Five main bearings. Hydraulic valve lifters. Carburetor: Four-barrel. Cooling system capacity: 20.5 qt. with heater. Crankcase capacity: (Mid-size and Mustang) 4 qt. and (full-size and Thunderbird), 5 qt. (add 1 qt. with new oil filter). Dual exhausts. Code Z.

Fairlane GT 390 V-8: Overhead valve. Cast-iron block. Displacement: 390 cid. B & S: 4.05 x 3.78 in. Compression ratio: 10.5:1. Brake hp: 325 at 4800 rpm. Torque: 427 lbs.-ft. at 3200 rpm. Five main bearings. Hydraulic valve lifters. Carburetor: Holley four-barrel. Cooling system capacity: 20.5 qt. with heater. Crankcase capacity: (Mid-size and Mustang) 4 qt. and (Full-Size and Thunderbird) 5 qt. (add 1 qt. with new oil filter). Dual exhausts. Code S. (Some literature listed this engine with a 335-hp rating.)

Cobra Jet 428 V-8: Overhead valve. Cast-iron block. Displacement: 428 cid. B & S: 4.13 x 3.98 in. Compression ratio: 10.70:1. Brake hp: 335 at 5600 rpm. Torque: 445 lbs.-ft. at 3400 rpm. Five main bearings. Hydraulic valve lifters. Carburetor: Holley four-barrel. Cooling system capacity: 20 qt. with heater. Crankcase capacity: 5 qt. (add 1 qt. with new oil filter). Dual exhausts. Code Q or R.

Thunderbird 428 V-8: Overhead valve. Cast-iron block. Displacement: 428 cid. B & S: 4.13 x 3.98 in. Compression ratio: 10.50:1. Brake hp: 340 at 5400 rpm. Torque: 462 lbs.-ft. at 2800 rpm. Five main bearings. Hydraulic valve lifters. Carburetor: Holley four-barrel. Cooling system capacity: 20 qt. with heater. Crankcase capacity: 5 qt. (add 1 qt. with new oil filter). Dual exhausts. Code Q.

1968 Ford Fairlane Torino GT two-door convertible (OCW)

1968 Ford Fairlane Torino GT two-door fastback (OCW)

1968 Ford Galaxie 500 two-door hardtop (OCW)

1968 Ford Galaxie 500 two-door convertible (OCW)

Cobra Jet 428 V-8: Overhead valve. Cast-iron block. Displacement: 428 cid. B & S: 4.13 x 3.98 in. Compression ratio: 10.50:1. Brake hp: 360 at 5400 rpm. Torque: 460 lbs.-ft. at 3200 rpm. Five main bearings. Solid valve lifters. Carburetor: Holley four-barrel. Cooling system capacity: 20 qt. with heater. Crankcase capacity: 5 qt. (add 1 qt. with new oil filter). Dual exhausts. Code P.

Thunder Jet 429 V-8: Overhead valve. Cast-iron block. Displacement: 429 cid. B & S: 4.36 x 3.59 in. Compression ratio: 10.50:1. Brake hp: 360 at 4600 rpm. Torque: 480 lbs.-ft.at 2800 rpm. Five main bearings. Hydraulic valve lifters. Carburetor: Motorcraft four-barrel. Cooling system capacity: 18.6 qt. with heater (T-bird 19.4 qt.). Crankcase capacity: 5 qt. (add 1 qt. with new oil filter). Dual exhausts. Code N.

Thunderbird High Performance V-8: Overhead valve. Cast-iron block. Displacement: 427 cid. B & S: 4.23 x 3.78 in. Compression ratio: 10.90:1. Brake hp: 390 at 4600 rpm. Torque: 460 lbs.-ft. at 3200 rpm. Five main bearings. Hydraulic valve lifters. Carburetor: Holley four-barrel. Cooling system capacity: 20 qt. with heater. Crankcase capacity: 4 qt. (add 1 qt. with new oil filter). Dual exhausts. Code W.

Chassis:

Falcon: Wheelbase: 110.9 in. and 113 in., station wagons. Overall length: 184.3 in. and 198.7 in., station wagons. Tires: 6.95 x 14 four-ply tubeless blackwall and 7.75 x 14 four-ply tubeless blackwall, station wagons.

Fairlane and Torino: Wheelbase: 116 in. and 113 in., station wagons. Overall length: 201 in. and 203.9 in., station wagons. Tires: 7.35 x 14 tubeless blackwall, 7.75 x 14 tubeless blackwall, station wagons and F870-14, GT.

Ford: Wheelbase: 119 in.. Overall length: 213.3 in. and 213.9 in., station wagons. Tires: 7.75 x 15 four-ply tubeless blackwall, 8.15 x 15 four-ply tubeless blackwall, hardtops and 8.45 x 15 four-ply tubeless blackwall, station wagons.

Options:

Falcon: SelectAire air conditioner with V-8 and radio required and tinted glass recommended ($56.09). Rear air deflector for station wagon ($19.48 and luggage rack required). High ratio axle ratio ($6.53). Heavy-duty battery ($7.44). Rear window defogger ($21.27 for all models except wagons). Limited-slip differential ($41.60). Station wagon dual-action tailgate ($45.39). 200-cid 115-hp six ($25.91). 289-cid 195-hp two-barrel V-8 ($131.54). 289-cid 195-hp two-barrel V-8 ($105.63). 302-cid 230-hp four-barrel V-8 ($197.68). 302-cid 230-hp four-barrel V-8 ($171.77). Complete tinted glass ($30.73). Adjustable front head rests ($42.02). Chrome luggage rack for station wagon ($44.44). Remote-control outside rearview mirror ($9.58). Two-tone paint, except station wagons ($24.28). Power disc brakes with all models except six-cylinder sedans and Sport Coupes ($64.77). Power steering ($84.47). Power tailgate window for station wagon ($31.62). AM radio ($61.40) AM/FM stereo radio ($181.36). Dual rear radio speakers, except station wagon ($25.91) Front shoulder belt ($23.38). Rear shoulder belt ($23.38) Deluxe seat with warning light ($12.95). Deluxe seat with warning light and front or rear shoulder belts ($15.59). Deluxe seat with warning light and front and rear shoulder belts ($18.22). Heavy-duty suspension for station wagons only ($23.38). Select-Shift Cruise-O-Matic transmission with six-cylinder ($171.39). Select-Shift Cruise-O-Matic transmission with V-8 ($189.66). Four-speed manual ($184.02). Vinyl roof on two-door models ($74.19). Vinyl interior trim in Futura ($16.85, standard in station wagons and Falcon Sport Coupe). Full wheel covers ($21.34, standard on Sport Coupe model). Deluxe or Sport wheel covers, Sport Coupe ($12.95). Deluxe or Sport wheel covers on models other than Sport Coupe ($34.29). 6.95 x 14 4-ply-rated white sidewall tires on cars with five standard 6.95 x 14 4-ply-rated Rayon black sidewall tires except station wagons ($32.47). 7.35 x 14 4-ply-rated black sidewall tires on cars with five standard 6.95 x 14 4-ply-rated Rayon black sidewall tires except station wagons ($52.73). 7.35 x 14 4-ply-rated white sidewall tires on cars with five standard 6.95 x 14 4-ply-rated Rayon black sidewall tires except station wagons ($85.21). 7.75 x 14 4-ply-rated white sidewall tires on station wagons with five standard 7.75 x 14 4-ply-rated Rayon black sidewall tires ($32.52). 7.75 x 14 8-ply-rated black sidewall tires on station wagons with five standard 7.75 x 14 4-ply-rated Rayon black sidewall tires ($33.45). 7.75 x 14 8-ply-rated white sidewall tires on station wagons with five standard 7.75 x 14 4-ply-rated Rayon black sidewall tires ($65.80). Convenience group including seat belt light, door-ajar light, parking brake light and low-fuel light ($32.44). Protection group including front and rear color-keyed floor mats, license plate frames, door edge moldings and glove box lock on two-door models ($25.28). Protection group including front and rear color-keyed floor mats, license plate frames, door edge moldings and glove box lock on four-door models ($29.17). Visibility group including ash tray light, glove box light, trunk or cargo area light, map light, remote-control outside rearview mirror and rear door courtesy light switches ($24.01).

Ford and Fairlane: Single body side accent stripe on Galaxie 500 and Country Sedans ($13.90, not available with body side molding). Body side accent stripe on Fairlane, except Torino and wagons ($13.90, not available with C stripe). SelectAire air conditioner in Fairlane with V-8 other than 427-cid, radio required ($360.30). SelectAire air conditioner in all except Fairlane ($368.72). Rear air deflector for Fairlane station wagons, luggage rack required ($19.48). Heavy-duty alternator ($21.09). Heavy-duty dual-belt alternator for Fords ($21.09, but standard with air conditioner). High-ratio axle ($6.53). Heavy-duty battery ($7.44, but standard with 427- and 428-cid engines). Center console for Fairlanes, bucket seats required ($50,66). Rear window defogger, for all models except convertibles or station wagons ($21.27). Limited-slip differential ($41.60, but not optional with 427-cid V-8s). Electric clock ($15.59, but standard in Torino, Torino GT, LTD, XL and Squire). 390-cid 265-hp two-barrel V-8 for all Fords and Fairlanes ($78.25 over the cost of the base V-8). 390-cid 315-hp in Ford/325-hp in Fairlane four-barrel V-8 over base V-8 ($158.08 and extra-cost transmission required). 428-cid 340-hp four-barrel V-8 in all except Fairlane ($244.77). 427-cid 390-hp four-barrel V-8 for Fairlane two-door hardtops and all Fords includes transistorized ignition, heavy-duty battery, heavy-duty suspension, extra-cooling package, four-speed manual transmission ($622.97, not available in Fairlanes with Select Aire, 55-amp alternator, heavy-duty suspension and 4-ply tires required at extra cost). Tinted glass in Fairlanes ($34.97). Tinted glass in all except Fairlane ($42.12). Adjustable front headrests ($42.02). Automatic load-leveling system for Ford V-8s ($89.94). Chrome luggage rack for station wagons ($46.55). Chrome luggage rack for station wagons ($46.55). Adjustable luggage rack for station wagons, except Fairlane ($63.08). Right-hand outside rearview mirror for all except Fairlane ($4,42). Right-hand manual outside rearview mirror, remote style, for all except Fairlanes ($6.95). Remote-control left-hand outside rearview mirror ($9.58, but standard with visibility group). Body side moldings for all full-size Ford and base Fairlane, but not available with Accent ($20.75 and standard on Custom 500 and Squire). Bright window frames for Fairlane 500 four-door sedan ($20.75).Bright window frames for Fairlane 500 four-door wagon ($25.91). TuTone paint for Fairlane and all Fords except convertible and Squire ($26.85). Power disc brakes for all models, required with Fairlane 390 or Ford 427 ($64.77, but standard with GT equipment group). Vacuum

1968 Ford Galaxie XL two-door fastback (PH)

1968 Ford LTD two-door hardtop (PH)

1968 Ford LTD four-door hardtop (PH)

1968 Ford four-door Country Squire Wagon (PH)

door locks for two-doors except base Fairlane ($45.39). Vacuum door locks for four-doors except Fairlane ($68.67). Full-width six-way seats in all except Fairlane ($94.75, but not with four-speed manual transmission). Driver's 6-way seat in all with XL bucket seats and console, except Fairlane ($84.25). Comfort Lounge driver seats in LTD hardtops with Brougham trim ($84.25, but not with four-speed manual transmission). Power steering ($94.95). Power tailgate window in station wagons ($31.62, but standard in Squire and other station wagons with dual facing rear seats). Power windows in all except Custom and Custom 500 ($99.94). AM radio ($61.40). AM/FM radio with two speakers ($181.36). Right rear quarter mounted radio speaker for all Fords except station wagons ($12.95). Dual rear radio speakers for Fairlanes ($25.91, but not available on convertible and station wagon). Dual rear radio speakers for all except Fairlanes with AM/FM radio or tape player ($25.91). Single rear radio speakers for all except Fairlanes with AM radio ($13.22). Stereosonic tape system with two front speakers for all except Fairlane, AM radio required ($133.86, but not available with AM/FM radio). Reflective stripes and paint for Torino GT and XL models ($12.95, but not available with GT equipment group). Front bucket seats for Fairlane 500 hardtops, Fairlane 500 convertible and Torino GT ($110.16). Front bucket seats with console in Ford XL only ($90.68). Rear-facing third seat in Fairlane station wagons, including seat belts ($53.18). Twin Comfort Lounge seat in LTD hardtops with Brougham trim ($77.73). Front shoulder belts ($23.38). Rear shoulder belts in all except convertible ($23.38). Deluxe seat belts with warning light ($12.95). Seat belts with front or rear shoulder belts ($15.59). Seat belts with front and rear shoulder belts ($18.22). Fingertip speed control in cars with V-8 and Cruise-O-Matic transmission, except Fairlanes ($73.83, but not available with 427-cid V-8). Tilt steering wheel for all except Fairlane with power steering plus automatic or four-speed manual transmission ($42.76). Heavy-duty suspension including heavy-duty front and rear springs, heavy-duty front and rear shock absorbers and heavy-duty stabilizer bar for all V-8-powered Fairlanes except 427s ($13.02). Heavy-duty suspension including heavy-duty front and rear springs, heavy-duty front and rear shock absorbers and heavy-duty stabilizer bar for all Fords ($23.38, but standard with 427 V-8). Maximum handling suspension for all V-8-powered Fords except station wagon ($30.64, but standard with GT equipment). 6000-rpm tachometer in Fairlane V-8 ($47.92). Console-mounted 8000-rpm tachometer in all except Fairlane with XL bucket seats and console only ($47.92). Select Shift Cruise-O-Matic transmission in six-cylinder models ($191.13). Select Shift Cruise-O-Matic transmission in models with 302-cid two-barrel V-8 ($200.85). Select Shift Cruise-O-Matic transmission in models with 390-cid two-barrel V-8 ($223.03). Select Shift Cruise-O-Matic transmission in models with 390-, 427- or 428-cid four-barrel V-8s ($233.17). Heavy-duty three-speed manual transmission for all ($79.20 and required on 390-cid V-8 with three-speed transmission). Four-speed manual transmission for Fairlane V-8 without 427 and all other models, except station wagons, with 390- or 428-cid four-barrel V-8 ($184.02). Vinyl roof on two-door Ford hardtops and all Fairlanes except fastbacks or station wagons ($84.99). Vinyl roof on four-door Ford hardtops and LTD four-door sedan ($94.05). Knitted vinyl trim on Fairlane 500 station wagon ($24.53). Vinyl trim in Galaxie 500 and Fairlane 500 models except convertible or station wagon ($16.85, but standard on Galaxie 500 convertible and station wagon). Comfort Stream ventilation system on Fairlanes without air conditioning ($15.59). Comfort Stream ventilation system on all except Fairlane ($40.02, but not available with air conditioning). Full wheel covers on all except GTs ($21.34, but standard on Torino, XL, LTD, Squire and cars with Décor Group option). Deluxe full wheel covers on XL, LTD, Squire and models with Décor Group option ($56.88, but not available with GT equipment). Deluxe wheel covers for all other Fords

($78.35). Deluxe or Sport wheel covers for Torinos ($12.95). Deluxe or Sport wheel covers for Fairlanes other than Torinos ($34.99). Argent styled wheels for Torinos ($17.59, but standard on Torino GT). Argent styled wheels for Fairlanes other than Torinos and GTs ($38.86). Chrome styled wheels for Torinos ($95.31). Chrome styled wheels for Torino GT ($77.73). Chrome styled wheels for Fairlane passenger cars other than Torino/Torino GT ($116.59). Chrome styled wheels for Ford XL, LTD, Squire and cars with Décor group ($35.70). Brougham trim group including luxury seat trim, luxury door trim, front courtesy lights, cut-pile carpet, rear center armrest, bright seat side shields, wood grain ornamentation and deluxe luggage compartment trim for LTD models except Squire ($112.69). Convenience group including door ajar light, low fuel light, parking brake light and seat belt warning light for Torino, GT and Fords except XL convertible ($32.44). Convenience group including door ajar light, low fuel light, parking brake light, seat belt warning light and electric clock for Fairlane, except Torino and Torino GT ($47.92). Exterior décor group including bright window frames and full wheel covers for Ford Custom, Custom 500 and Ranch Wagon with whitewall tires ($51.82). Extra-cooling package including viscous-drive fan or flex-blade fan, fan shroud and extra-cooling radiator in Fairlane with 302-cid two-barrel V-8 ($12.95, but standard in Fairlanes with air conditioning). Extra-cooling package including viscous-drive fan or flex-blade fan, fan shroud and extra-cooling radiator in Fairlane with 390-cid V-8 except Torino GT ($25.25, but standard in Fairlanes with air conditioning). Extra-cooling package including viscous-drive fan or flex-blade fan, fan shroud and extra-cooling radiator in Torino GT with 390-cid V-8 ($13,58, but standard with air conditioning). Extra-cooling package including viscous-drive fan or flex-blade fan, fan shroud and extra-cooling radiator in six-cylinder or V-8 Fords ($12.95, but not available with air conditioning). GT Equipment Group including power disc brakes, Maximum Handling suspension, high-ratio rear axle, simulated mag wheel covers, non-reflective GT tape stripes, GT ornamentation and G70 x 15 Wide-Oval white sidewall tires for XL models with 390- or 428-cid engines ($204.64). GT Handling Suspension including extra-heavy-duty rear springs, heavy-duty front and rear shock absorbers and heavy-duty front and rear stabilizer bars for Fairlane hardtops and convertibles with 427-cid four-barrel V-8 and Torino GT ($30.64). Protection Group including front and rear floor mats, license plate frames and door edge guards for two-door models ($25.28); for four-door models ($29.17). Trailer towing package for Fords except 7-Litre and station wagons, requires 390-cid V-8 with Cruise-O-Matic and 428-cid V-8 ($30.93). Visibility group including ashtray light, glove box light, trunk or cargo area lights, rear door courtesy switches, remote-control mirror and map light for Fairlanes ($24.01). Visibility group including brake-on light and remote-control mirror for Galaxie 500 two-door hardtops and convertible, XL and LTDs ($14.64). Visibility group for all other models including ashtray light, glove box light, trunk or cargo area lights, rear door courtesy switches, remote-control mirror, map light, brake-on light and remote-control mirror ($24.01). Tires for all Fairlane sedans, hardtops and convertibles, except Torino GTs, with 200-cid six or 302-cid two-barrel V-8 using five 7.35 x 14 four-ply blackwall rayon tires as standard equipment: 7.35 x 14 four-ply whitewall ($34.35); F70 x 14 Wide Oval whitewall ($64.43); 7.35 x 14 or 185 R14 radial blackwalls ($38.53); 7.35 x 14 or 185 R14 radial whitewalls ($73.64); F70 x 14 Wide Oval whitewall radials ($103.44 and GT suspension required). Tires for all Fairlane sedans, hardtops and convertibles, except Torino GTs, with 390-cid V-8s or wagons with 390-cid six or 302-cid two-barrel V-8 using five 7.35 x 14 four-ply blackwall rayon tires as standard equipment: 7.75 x 14 four-ply whitewall ($34.52); 7.75 x 14 eight-ply blackwall ($33.45 on wagons only); 7.75 x 14 eight-ply whitewall ($68.00 on wagons only); F70 x 14 Wide Oval whitewall ($50.13, not available on wagons); F70 x 14 Wide Oval whitewall radials

($89.14, not available on wagons, GT Handling suspension required). Extra charge for 7.75 x 14 eight-ply-rated whitewalls on station wagons with 390-cid V-8 having 7.75 x 14 eight-ply-rated blackwall rayon tires as standard equipment ($34.55). Extra charge for FR70 x 14 eight-ply-rated whitewall nylon Wide-Oval tires on GT models without 427-cid V-8 with standard F70 x 14 whitewall Wide-Oval tires ($39.11). Tires for all Fords except Galaxie 500 four-door hardtop, LTD and station wagons with 240-cid six or 302-cid V-8 using five 7.75 x 15 four-ply blackwall rayon tires as standard equipment: 7.75 x 14 four-ply whitewall ($35.47); 8.15 x 15 four-ply blackwall ($15.49); 8.15 x 15 four-ply whitewall ($51.77); 8.45 x 15 four-ply blackwall ($31.08); G70 x 15 Wide Oval nylon whitewall ($85.09); 8.15 x 15 or 205 R15 radial blackwalls ($54.02); 8.15 x 15 or 205 R15 radial whitewalls ($90.41); 8.45 x 15 or 215 R15 radial blackwalls ($69.60); 8.45 x 15 or 215 R15 radial whitewalls ($106.00); 8.45 x 15 four-ply-rated whitewalls ($67.48). Tires for Fords, except station wagons, with 302-cid two-barrel V-8, 390-cid V-8 or 428-cid V-8 using five 8.15 x 15 four-ply blackwall rayon tires as standard equipment, plus convertibles with air conditioning and Galaxie 500 four-door hardtop with 240-cid six or 302-cid V-8 using same tires: 8.15 x 15 four-ply whitewall ($36.37); 8.45 x 15 four-ply blackwall ($15.59); 8.45 x 15 four-ply whitewall ($51.89); G70 x 15 Wide Oval nylon whitewall ($69.82); 8.15 x 15 or 205 R15 radial blackwalls ($38.75); 8.15 x 15 or 205 R15 radial whitewalls ($75.14); 8.45 x 15 or 215 R15 radial blackwalls ($54.34); 8.45 x 15 or 215 R15 radial whitewalls ($90.83). Tire options for Ford models having five 8.45 x 15 four-ply-rated blackwall rayon tires as standard equipment and all wagons and LTD hardtops with 390- or 428-cid V-8s with air conditioning: extra charge for 8.45 x 15 whitewalls ($36.40); 8.45 x 15 or 215 R15 blackwall radials ($39.00); 8.45 x 15 or 215 R15 whitewall radial ($75.39).

History:

Ford products captured over 20 checkered flags in NASCAR stock car racing during 1968, with Ford driver David Pearson taking the overall championship. In USAC competition, Ford pilot A.J. Foyt was the top driver of the year. Benny Parsons and Cale Yarborough also made Ford racing history this year, driving Fairlanes and Torinos in ARCA contests. A specially-trimmed Torino convertible paced the 52nd Indianapolis 500-Mile race. The new Fords were introduced to the public on Sept. 22, 1967. In Europe, Ford GT-40s competed in the international class races, attempting to repeat the success of 1966, when similar machines finished first, second and third at Le Mans. Early in 1968, Semon E. "Bunkie" Knudsen became the chief executive officer of Ford Motor Co. Knudsen had held a similar position with Pontiac and Chevrolet during some of the most exciting years in automotive history.

1969 Ford

Falcon — 6 and V-8: The Falcons were the base trim level for 1969 and included chrome windshield, rear window and rain gutter molding. Armrests were on the front doors only and a horn button was used instead of the chrome ring found on the more trimmed Futuras. The Falcon name, in script, appeared on the rear fenders and on the vertical section of the trunk lid on the passenger side. Falcons continued to use the same body style as in the previous three years, with no major changes in either sheet metal or trim. An optional V-8, new safety steering wheel and redesigned side marker lamps were the most noticeable revisions from the past. A full-width anodized aluminum grille helped impart a "big car" appearance.

Futura — 6 and V-8: The Futura series was the top trim level for the 1969 Falcons and included all the standard Falcon features plus a cigarette lighter, armrests and ash trays on all doors, a chrome horn ring, nylon carpeting, special Futura moldings, trim, emblems and nameplates and chrome side window frames. The Futura Sports Coupe offered front bucket seats, special nameplates, a map light, glove box and trunk lights plus 7.35 x 14 tires, a side chrome accent stripe, polished aluminum rocker panel moldings and wheel well trim, a remote-control outside driver's mirror and deluxe seat belts.

Maverick — 6: The Maverick was introduced during the 1969 model year on April 17, 1969 as a 1970 model. It used a Falcon chassis and 170-cid

1969 Galaxie 500XL fastback hardtop

1969 Custom 500 four-door sedan

1969 Galaxie 500 convertible

six-cylinder engine to power the only body style available, a two-door sedan. Mavericks featured a sloped hatchback style and boasted about their 10.4 cubic-feet of trunk space. Ford Motor Co. positioned the Maverick as a car that attempted to fill a gap between compacts and imports. Priced at $1,995, Ford said it was "the car of the '70s at 1960s prices." The company also mentioned the car's long service intervals including 6,000 miles between oil changes and 108,000 miles of service intervals over nine years in the owner's manual. Ford advertising said the Maverick "pinches pennies, not people." To emphasize the original nature of the car, the first year color choices included names like Original Cinnamon, Hulla Blue, Freudian Gilt, Thanks Vermillion and Anti-Establish Mint. The Maverick came with Tartan plaid cloth and vinyl seat trim, a fully-padded two-spoke steering wheel with a half horn ring, door-activated courtesy light, a three-speed blower with heater, lighted controls, suspended accelerator, clutch and brake pedals, curved side glass without window vents, coat hooks, cowl induction, flip-type rear quarter windows, a full-width storage tray, a luggage compartment mat and a center fuel filler door. Mavericks would go on to be made in both Mexico and Brazil. There even were Shelby Maverick versions made by Shelby of Mexico.

Fairlane — 6 and V-8: The Fairlane was the base trim level for 1969 and included a chrome windshield and rear window moldings, chrome rain gutters and side window frames, a chrome horn ring, front and rear armrests, vinyl-coated rubber floor mats and the Fairlane name, in script, on the passenger side of the escutcheon panel. The Ford name was spelled out in block letters across the front of the hood and on the vertical section of the trunk lid. Performance was the key word in the Fairlane lineup for 1969. Visually all models, except four-door sedans, looked fast. And most of them were. When equipped with the Cobra Jet 428, the Fairlanes were awesome as well as beautiful. They shared the same body as the 1968 models, with only minor trim updating. The taillights were revised slightly and were squarer than in 1968. The grille was revised slightly, with a more prominent center dividing bar for 1969. At midyear, the Torino Talladega Special was released in extremely limited quantities, just enough to qualify the body style for use in NASCAR racing. The Talladega front end was extended several inches and used a flat grille, mounted at the front of the opening, rather than several inches back, as on standard models. Also, the rear bumper from a standard Fairlane was used up front, because it was more aerodynamic than the original front bumper. All Torino Talladega Specials were equipped with the Cobra Jet 428 engine and offered a choice of either Select Shift Cruise-O-Matic automatic transmission, or the bulletproof "top-loader" four-speed manual gearbox. The Fairlane 500 was the intermediate trim level for 1969 and included all Fairlane trim plus special 500 trim and moldings, color-keyed carpeting in the front and rear plus a choice of four nylon and vinyl upholsteries. Also included was an aluminum trim panel in the center of the rear escutcheon panel, between the taillights. The Fairlane 500 name, in script, appeared on the rear fender, just in front of the taillights.

Torino — 6 and V-8: The Fairlane Torino was the top trim level for 1969 and included all the Fairlane 500 trim plus a polished aluminum rocker panel molding, special emblems and trim inside and out and a Torino crest on the "C" pillars on the two-door hardtop and four-door sedan versions. The Fairlane Torino GT was the sporty version of the Fairlane 500 series and included all the Fairlane 500 features plus the 302-cid, 220 hp V-8, bucket seats and console, special name plaques and exterior trim, styled steel wheels, lower body striping on two-door hardtop and two-door convertible versions and a body stripe "C" on the two-door fastback Sportsroof version. A high-performance version, the Torino Cobra, was also offered. It included the 428-cid, 335-hp V-8, four-speed manual transmission and F70-14 wide oval tires as standard equipment.

1969 Galaxie 500XL GT convertible

1969 LTD Formal two-door hardtop

1969 LTD Country Squire station wagon

1969 Fairlane 500 convertible

Custom and Custom 500 — 6 and V-8: The 1969 full-size Fords were totally restyled and shared nothing with the previous year's offering. The lines of the new models were even rounder than previous editions. They looked more luxurious and luxury was highly promoted. Velour interiors and vinyl tops were the order of the day in the LTD lineup. All full-size Fords shared the same body lines, with the LTD receiving its own front end treatment, segregating it from Customs and Galaxies. The Custom series was the base trim level and included chrome windshield and rear window moldings, a chrome horn ring, nylon carpeting, the Custom name, in script, on the rear fender just in front of the rear marker light, the Ford name in block letters across the rear escutcheon panel and a single horizontal chrome strip along the center of the body. The Custom 500 was the upper trim level of the base Custom series and included all the Custom trim plus special Custom 500 exterior trim and choices of four different upholsteries on the interior..

Galaxie 500 and Galaxie 500XL — 6 and V-8: The Galaxie 500 was the intermediate trim level for 1969 and included all the Custom series trim plus stamped aluminum lower body moldings and pleated interior trim. The Galaxie 500XL was the sport trim version of the Galaxie 500. It came in the two-door fastback coupe style Ford Motor Co. called the "Sportsroof" plus a convertible version. Standard equipment included bucket seats, wheel covers, die-cast grille, retractable headlights, pleated, all-vinyl interior trim and five vertical "hash marks" on the forward portion part of the front fenders. The 500XL also carried all of the standard Galaxie 500 trim.

LTD — (V-8): The LTD was the top level 1969 full-size Ford and included all the Galaxie 500 trim plus the 302-cid, 220-hp V-8, Select Shift Cruise-O-Matic automatic transmission, an electric clock, bright exterior moldings and dual accent paint stripes. The LTD station wagons also had simulated wood grain appliqués on their bodies. All LTDs also came with retractable headlights and die-cast grilles.

VIN: Falcon, Maverick, Fairlane and Ford:

The serial number code was broken down in this manner. The first symbol indicated the year: 9 = 1969. The second symbol identified the assembly plant: A = Atlanta, Georgia; B = Oakville, Ontario, Canada, E = Mahwah, New Jersey, F = Dearborn, Michigan, G =Chicago, Illinois, H = Loraine, Ohio, J = Los Angeles, California, K = Kansas City, Missouri, N = Norfolk, Virginia, P = Twin Cities (Minneapolis and St. Paul), Minnesota, R = San Jose, California, S = Allen Park Pilot Plant, T = Metuchen, New Jersey, U = Louisville, Kentucky, W = Wayne, Michigan, X = St. Thomas, Ontario, Canada, Y = Wixom. Michigan and Z = St. Louis, Missouri. The third and fourth symbols identified the body type and series: 91 = Maverick. The fifth symbol identified the engine code: F = 302-cid V-8; G = 302-cid Boss V-8 with four-barrel carb; H = 351-cid V-8; K = 429-cid V-8; L = 250-cid six-cylinder; M = 351-cid V-8 with four-barrel carb; N = 429-cid V-8 with four-barrel carb; Q = 428-cid V-8 with four-barrel carb; R = 428-cid Super Cobra Jet V-8 with four-barrel carb; S = 390-cid V-8 with four-barrel carb; T = 200-cid six-cylinder; U = 170-cid six-cylinder; V = 240-cid six-cylinder; Y = 390-cid V-8; Z = 429-cid Boss V-8 with four-barrel carb. The last six digits were the unit's production number, beginning at 100001.

The 1969 Ford data plate could be read as follows. After the vehicle ID number was the body type: 62A = two-door sedan. The next space was for color coding: M=White. In the second row was the trim code: 1Y = Light Nugget vinyl. The next space in row two was the axle ratio code: 5 = 2.83:1. Space three in row two was the transmission code: W = C4 automatic. The final space designated the district or special equipment

code. Ford Motor Co. used 44 of these codes in 1969 including 37 U. S. districts, one for Ford of Canada (83) and six other codes such as 83 = government and 84 = home office.

Falcon (6)

Model No.	Body/ Style No.	Body Type & Seating	Factory Price	Shipping Weight	Production Total
----	54A	4-dr. Sedan-6P	$2,316	2,735 lbs.	----
----	62A	2-dr. Sedan-4P	$2,226	2,700 lbs.	----
----	71A	4-dr. Station Wagon-6P	$2,643	3,110 lbs.	----

Falcon (V-8)

----	54A	4-dr. Sedan-6P	$2,431	2,735 lbs.	22,719
----	62A	2-dr. Sedan-4P	$2,381	2,700 lbs.	29,263
----	71A	4-dr. Station Wagon-6P	$2,733	3,110 lbs.	11,568

Note: Total Falcon output was 63,550 units in 1969. Ford did not indicate the numbers of sixes or V-8s made. All production figures were the total of each body style with both engines.

Futura (6)

----	54B	4-dr. Sedan-6P	$2,481	2,748 lbs.	----
----	62B	2-dr. Sedan-4P	$2,444	2,715 lbs.	----
----	62C	2-dr. Sport Coupe	$2,581	2,738 lbs.	----
----	71B	4-dr. Station Wagon-6P	$2,754	3,120 lbs.	----

Futura (V-8)

----	54B	4-dr. Sedan-6P	$2,571	2,748 lbs.	11,850
----	62B	2-dr. Sedan-4P	$2,534	2,715 lbs.	6,482
----	62C	2-dr. Sport Coupe	$2,671	2,738 lbs.	5,931
----	71B	4-dr. Station Wagon-6P	$2,844	3,120 lbs.	7,203

Note: Total series output was 31,466 units. Ford did not indicate the number of sixes or V-8s produced. All production figures were the totals for each body style.

Maverick (6)

----	91	2-dr. Sedan-6P	$1,995	2,411 lbs.	127,833

Fairlane (6)

----	54A	4-dr. Sedan-6P	$2,471	3,010 lbs.	27,296
----	65A	2-dr. Hardtop Coupe-6P	$2,482	3,025 lbs.	85,630
----	71B	4-dr. Station Wagon-6P	$2,824	3,387 lbs.	10,882

Fairlane (V-8)

----	54A	4-dr. Sedan-6P	$2,561	3,120 lbs.	27,296
----	65A	2-dr. Hardtop Coupe-6P	$2,572	3,133 lbs.	85,630
----	71B	4-dr. Station Wagon-6P	$2,914	3,387 lbs.	10,882

Note: Total series output was 123,808 units. Ford did not indicate the number of models produced with sixes and V-8s. All production figures were the total production of each body style with both engines.

Fairlane 500 (6)

----	54B	4-dr. Sedan-6P	$2,551	3,029 lbs.	40,888
----	65B	2-dr. Formal Hardtop Coupe-6P	$2,609	3,036 lbs.	28,179
----	63B	4-dr. Fastback Coupe-6P	$2,584	3,083 lbs.	29,849
----	76B	2-dr. Convertible-6P	$2,834	3,220 lbs.	2,264
----	71B	4-dr. Station Wagon-6P	$2,934	3,415 lbs.	12,869

Fairlane 500 (V-8)

----	54B	4-dr. Sedan-6P	$2,641	3,135 lbs.	40,888
----	65B	2-dr. Formal Hardtop Coupe-6P	$2,699	3,143 lbs.	28,179
----	63B	4-dr. Fastback Coupe-6P	$2,674	3,190 lbs.	29,849
----	76B	2-dr. Convertible-6P	$2,924	3,336 lbs.	2,264
----	71B	4-dr. Station Wagon-6P	$3,024	3,523 lbs.	12,869

Note: Total series output was 114,049 units including 3,379 Formal Hardtop coupes, 7,345 Sportsroof fastback coupes and 219 convertibles, all produced with bucket seats. Ford did not indicate the number of sixes or V-8s produced, only total production figures for each body style.

Fairlane Torino (6)

----	54C	4-dr. Sedan-6P	$2,716	3,075 lbs.	11,971
----	65C	2-dr. Fastback Coupe-6P	$2,737	3,090 lbs.	20,789
----	71E	4-dr. Squire Station Wagon-6P	$3,090	3,450 lbs.	14,472

Fairlane Torino (V-8)

----	54C	4-dr. Sedan-6P	$2,806	3,180 lbs.	11,971
----	65C	2-dr. Fastback Coupe-6P	$2,827	3,195 lbs.	20,789
----	71E	4-dr. Squire Station Wagon-6P	$3,180	3,556 lbs.	14,472

Note: Total series output was 47,232 units. Ford did not indicate the number of models produced with sixes or V-8s. All production figures were totals for each body style.

Fairlane Torino GT (V-8)

----	65D	2-dr. Formal Hardtop Coupe-5P	$2,848	3,173 lbs.	17,951
----	63D	2-dr. Fastback Coupe-5P	$2,823	3,220 lbs.	61,319
----	76D	2-dr. Convertible-5P	$3,073	3,356 lbs.	2,552

Fairlane Torino GT Cobra (V-8)

----	65A	2-dr. Hardtop Coupe-5P	$3,208	3,490 lbs.	------
----	63B	2-dr. Fastback Coupe-5P	$3,183	3,537 lbs.	------

Note: Total series output was 81,822 units, including the unrecorded numbers of Cobra models. Ford did not indicate the number of each model produced. Totals are production numbers of each body style with both sixes and V-8s.

Custom (6)

----	54E	4-dr. Sedan-6P	$2,674	3,608 lbs.	45,653
----	62E	2-dr. Sedan-6P	$2,632	3,585 lbs.	15,439
----	71D	4-dr. Ranch Wagon-6P	$3,074	4,069 lbs.	17,489

Custom (V-8)

----	54E	4-dr. Sedan-6P	$2,779	3,648 lbs.	45,653
----	62E	2-dr. Sedan-6P	$2,737	3,625 lbs.	15,439
----	71D	4-dr. Ranch Wagon-6P	$3,179	4,109 lbs.	17,489

Note: Total series output was 78,581 units. Ford did not indicate the number of each model with sixes or V-8s. All production figures were total figures for each body style with both engines.

Custom 500 (6)

----	54B	4-dr. Sedan-6P	$2,773	3,620 lbs.	45,761
----	62B	2-dr. Sedan-6P	$2,731	3,570 lbs.	7,585
----	71H	4-dr. Ranch Wagon-6P	$3,138	4,082 lbs.	16,432
----	71J	4-dr. Ranch Wagon-10P	$3,251	4,132 lbs.	11,563

1969 Fairlane Torino four-door sedan

1969 Fairlane Torino Formal two-door hardtop

Custom 500 (V-8)

----	54B	4-dr. Sedan-6P	$2,878	3,660 lbs.	45,761
----	62B	2-dr. Sedan-6P	$2,836	3,610 lbs.	7,585
----	71H	4-dr. Ranch Wagon-6P	$3,243	4,122 lbs.	16,432
----	71J	4-dr. Ranch Wagon-10P	$3,556	4,172 lbs.	11,563

Note: Total series output was 81,341 units. Ford did not indicate the models produced with sixes or V-8s. All production figures were totals for each body style with both engines.

Galaxie 500 (6)

----	54A	4-dr. Sedan-6P	$2,897	3,670 lbs.	104,606
----	64B	2-dr. Fastback Coupe-6P	$2,913	3,680 lbs.	63,921
----	65C	2-dr. Formal Hardtop Coupe-6P	$2,965	3,635 lbs.	71,920
----	57B	4-dr. Hardtop Sedan-6P	$2,966	3,705 lbs.	64,031
----	76A	2-dr. Convertible-6P	$3,142	3,840 lbs.	6,910
----	71B	4-dr. Country Sedan-6P	$3,257	4,067 lbs.	36,287
----	71C	4-dr. Country Sedan-10P	$3,373	3,092 lbs.	11,563

Galaxie 500 (V-8)

----	54A	4-dr. Sedan-6P	$3,002	3,710 lbs.	104,606
----	63B	2-dr. Fastback Coupe-6P	$3,018	3,720 lbs.	63,921
----	65C	2-dr. Formal Hardtop Coupe-6P	$3,070	3,675 lbs.	71,920
----	57B	4-dr. Hardtop Sedan-6P	$3,071	3,745 lbs.	64,031
----	76A	2-dr. Convertible-6P	$3,247	3,880 lbs.	6,910
----	71B	4-dr. Country Sedan-6P	$3,362	4,107 lbs.	36,287
----	71C	4-dr. Country Sedan-10P	$3,487	4,132 lbs.	11,563

Note: Total series output was 359,238 units. Ford didn't indicate the models produced with sixes or V-8s. All production figures were total production of each body style with both engines.

Galaxie 500XL (V-8)

----	63C	2-dr. Fastback Coupe-5P	$3,052	3,785 lbs.	54,557
----	76B	2-dr. Convertible-5P	$3,280	3,935 lbs.	7,402

Note: Total series output was 61,959 units. Ford did not indicate the number of model produced with sixes or V-8s. All production figures were the totals with both engines.

LTD (V-8)

----	54C	4-dr. Sedan-6P	$3,192	3,745 lbs.	63,709
----	57F	4-dr. Sedan-6P	$3,261	3,840 lbs.	113,168
----	65A	2-dr. Formal Hardtop Coupe-6P	$3,234	3,745 lbs.	111,565
----	71E	4-dr. Country Sedan-6P	$3,644	4,202 lbs.	46,445
----	71A	4-dr. Country Sedan-10P	$3,721	4,227 lbs.	82,790

Note: Total series output was 417,677 units.

Engines:

Falcon and Maverick Base Six: Overhead valve. Cast-iron block. Displacement: 170 cid. B & S: 3.50 x 2.94 in. Compression ratio: 8.7:1. Brake hp: 100 at 4000 rpm. Carburetor: Holley one-barrel. Seven main bearings. Code U.

Fairlane Base Six (Falcon and Maverick Optional): Overhead valve. Cast-iron block. Displacement: 200 cid. B & S: 3.68 x 3.13 in. Compression ratio: 8.8:1. Brake hp: 115 at 3800 rpm. Carburetor: Motorcraft one-barrel. Seven main bearings. Code T.

Ford Base Six: Overhead valve. Cast-iron block. Displacement: 240 cid. B & S: 4.00 x 3.18 in. Compression ratio: 9.2:1. Brake hp: 150 at 4000 rpm. Carburetor: Motorcraft one-barrel. Seven main bearings. Code V. (Police code B and taxi code E.)

Ford Optional Six: Overhead valve. Cast-iron block. Displacement: 250 cid. B & S: 3.68 x 3.91 in. Compression ratio: 9.0:1. Brake hp: 155 at 4000 rpm. Carburetor: Motorcraft one-barrel. Seven main bearings. Code L.

Torino GT Base 302 V-8: Overhead valve. Cast-iron block. Displacement: 302 cid. B & S: 4.00 x 3.00 in. Compression ratio: 9.5:1. Brake hp: 220 at 4600 rpm. Carburetor: Motorcraft two-barrel. Five main bearings. Code F. (Police and taxi code D).

1969 Fairlane Torino GT Cobra two-door hardtop

1969 Torino GT two-door convertible

1969 Torino GT two-door hardtop, Sportsroof

1969 Torino GT Talladega Special two-door, Sportsroof

Boss 302 V-8: Overhead valve. Cast-iron block. Displacement: 302 cid. B & S: 4.00 x 3.00 in. Compression ratio: 10.5:1. Brake hp: 290 at 5600 rpm. Carburetor: Holley four-barrel. Five main bearings. Code G.

Falcon, Fairlane and Torino Optional 351 V-8: Overhead valve. Cast-iron block. Displacement: 351 cid. B & S: 4.00 x 3.50 in. Compression ratio: 9.5:1. Brake hp: 250 at 4600 rpm. Carburetor: Motorcraft two-barrel. Five main bearings. Code H.

351 Four-Barrel V-8: Overhead valve. Cast-iron block. Displacement: 351 cid. B & S: 4.00 x 3.50 in. Compression ratio: 10.7:1. Brake hp: 290 at 4800 rpm. Carburetor: Motorcraft four-barrel. Five main bearings. Code M.

Ford Optional Interceptor V-8: Overhead valve. Cast-iron block. Displacement: 390 cid. B & S: 4.05 x 3.78 in. Compression ratio: 9.5:1. Brake hp: 265 at 4400 rpm. Carburetor: Motorcraft two-barrel. Five main bearings. Code Y.

Ford Optional 390 V-8: Overhead valve. Cast-iron block. Displacement: 390 cid. B & S: 4.05 x 3.78 in. Compression ratio: 10.5:1. Brake hp: 320 at 4600 rpm. Carburetor: Holley four-barrel. Five main bearings. Code S.

Cobra GT Optional Cobra Jet 428 V-8: Overhead valve. Cast-iron block. Displacement: 428 cid. B & S: 4.13 x 3.98 in. Compression ratio: 10.6:1. Brake hp: 335 at 5200 rpm. Carburetor: Holley four-barrel. Five main bearings. Code Q.

Cobra GT Optional Super Cobra Jet 428 V-8: Overhead valve. Cast-iron block. Displacement: 428 cid. B & S: 4.13 x 3.98 in. Compression ratio: 10.5:1. Brake hp: 360 at 5400 rpm. Carburetor: Holley four-barrel. Five main bearings. C Code P.

Ford Optional Thunder Jet 429 V-8: Overhead valve. Cast-iron block. Displacement: 429 cid. B & S: 4.36 x 3.59 in. Compression ratio: 10.5:1. Brake hp: 320 at 4500 rpm. Carburetor: Motorcraft two-barrel. Five main bearings. Code K.

Ford Optional Thunder Jet 429 Four Barrel V-8: Overhead valve. Cast-iron block. Displacement: 429 cid. B & S: 4.36 x 3.59 in. Compression ratio: 10.5:1. Brake hp: 360 at 4600 rpm. Carburetor: Motorcraft four-barrel. Five main bearings. Code N.

Boss 429 V-8: Overhead valve. Cast-iron block. Displacement: 429 cid. B & S: 4.36 x 3.59 in. Compression ratio: 11.3:1. Brake hp: 375 at 5600 rpm. Carburetor: Holley four-barrel. Five main bearings. Code Z.

Chassis:

Falcon: Wheelbase: 113 in., station wagons and 110.9 in., other models Overall length: 184.3 in. and 198.7 in., station wagons. Tires: 7.75 x 14 four-ply tubeless blackwall, station wagon; 7.35 x 14 four-ply tubeless blackwall, Sports Coupe and 6.95 x 14 four-ply tubeless blackwall, other models.

1969 Falcon Futura two-door Sports Coupe

1969 Falcon four-door sedan

1969 Falcon Futura station wagon

Maverick: Wheelbase: 103 inches. Overall length: 179.4 inches. Tires: 6.00 x 13 four-ply tubeless blackwall.

Fairlane: Wheelbase: 116.0 in. and 113 in., station wagons. Overall length: 201 in. and 203.9 in., station wagons. Tires: 7.35 x 14 four-ply tubeless blackwall, 7.50 x 14 four-ply blackwall, convertibles and F70-14, Cobra.

Ford: Wheelbase: 121 in. Overall length: 213.9 in. and 216.9 in., station wagons. Tires: 8.25 x 15 four-ply tubeless blackwall and 9.00 x 15 four-ply tubeless blackwall, station wagons.

Options:

Falcon: 200-cid six-cylinder engine ($26). 302-cid V-8 engine ($79). Cruise-O-Matic automatic transmission ($175). Power steering ($89). Power tailgate window, station wagons ($35). Tinted windshield ($32). AM radio ($61). Wheel covers ($21).

Maverick: 200-cid six-cylinder engine. Selectaire air conditioning. Tinted glass. Day/night rearview mirror. Cruise-O-Matic automatic transmission ($175). AM radio ($61). White sidewall tires ($34). Accent seat trim. Grabber group package.

Fairlane and Torino: 302-cid, 220-hp V-8, standard on Torino GT. 351-cid V-8 engine ($84). Cruise-O-Matic automatic transmission ($222). Four-speed manual transmission ($194, standard on Cobra). AM radio ($61). Power steering ($100). Power tailgate window on station wagons ($35). Luggage rack on station wagons ($47). Two-tone paint ($27). White sidewall tires ($34). Vinyl roof on two-door hardtops and four-door sedans ($90).

Ford: 390-cid, 265-hp V-8 engine ($58). 429-cid, 320-hp V-8 ($163). 429-cid, 360-hp V-8 ($237). Cruise-O-Matic automatic transmission ($222). Power steering ($100). Power front disc brakes ($65). Tinted windshield ($45). Air conditioning ($369). AM radio ($61). AM/FM stereo radio ($181). Vinyl roof ($100). White sidewall tires ($33).

History:

The 1969 Ford lines were publicly introduced on Sept. 27, 1968. Calendar year production for America's number two automaker hit the 1,743,442 unit level this year. A total of 1,880,384 Fords were registered as new cars during calendar year 1969. Semon E. (Bunkie) Knudsen remained as president of the company and continued to actively pursue a strong

1969 Torino Squire station wagon

high-performance image. Stock car driver Richard Petty was enticed to drive for Ford in 1969, after a long and successful association with Plymouth. He captured the checkered flag in the Riverside 500 Grand National Race. David Pearson, also driving Fords, won the NASCAR championship with 26 Grand National victories. They drove streamlined Torino Talladega Specials that sold for $3,680. A total of 754 were built during January and February of 1969. It was the next to last season for the compact Falcon, which could not be modified to meet federal safety regulations at reasonable cost. Ford called its fastback cars "Sportsroof" models and used the name "Squire" on its fanciest station wagons. The Maverick was designed to be direct competition for the Volkswagen and was intended to influence those who liked a small and economical car. With a base price of $1,995 it was the only Ford under $2,000.

1970 Ford

Maverick — 6: The Maverick was introduced on April 17, 1969 as a 1970 model. Ford Motor Co. chose the date, as close as possible to the introductory date of the Mustang, with the skyrocketing success of that midyear Ford's sales beginning in April 1964. Maverick didn't set Mustang type sales records but it was a sales success and was back for the full 1970 model year. It used a Falcon chassis and 170-cid six-cylinder engine and came only as a two-door sedan. Essentially, it replaced the economy minded Falcon, in its last year and this time as a Fairlane sub series. The Maverick Grabber package was enhanced in 1970 with plenty of options including distinctive black hood and body stripes, a three-spoke wooden steering wheel and C78 x 14 tires. Five Grabber colors also were introduced in 1970: Brite Yellow, Grabber Yellow, Vermillion, Grabber Green and Grabber Blue. In December 1970, the 302 V-8 was offered as an option for the Maverick series in addition to the 250-cid six cylinder engine.

Fairlane — 6 and V-8: The base trim level of the intermediate Fairlane series was simply called the Fairlane and included a chrome windshield, rear window and rain gutter moldings plus front and rear door armrests and nylon carpeting. The Fairlane 500 had that name in script, on the rear fenders above the side marker lights, two chrome "hash marks" on the front fenders, behind the front wheel opening and the Ford name, in block letters, on the driver's side of the hood and across the escutcheon panel. The Fairlane series was completely restyled, with a sleek body shell and rounded fender contours. The midyear 1969 introduction of the 1970 Maverick drew attention was from the aging Falcon series and its sales plummeted. For the first half of 1970, the 1969 Falcon Futura was again offered as a 1970 series in two-door and four-door sedan versions as well as a station wagon. At mid model year, the revised Falcon, sans the Futura name completely, was repositioned as the lowest-price Fairlane model. It was available only as a two-door sedan, although all the high-performance engine options were offered in it. The Falcon continued to be produced by Ford Motor Co. as a popular series in such overseas markets as South America and Australia.

Torino — 6 and V-8: The Torino was now considered to be a separate series from the Fairlane and offered an intermediate trim level. Yet it still was based on the Fairlane and included all the Fairlane 500 trim plus a single horizontal chrome strip along the body side. The Torino name appeared, in script, on the driver's side of the hood and in block letters on the side of the front fenders, behind the front wheel opening.

1970 Galaxie 500 four-door sedan

Torino Brougham — V-8: The Torino Brougham was the top trim level of the 1970 Torino series and included all the Torino trim plus polished aluminum wheel well and rocker panel moldings, retractable headlights, wheel covers and the 302-cid, 220-hp V-8. The station wagon version included all of the above features plus simulated wood grain appliqués and power front disc brakes.

Torino GT and Cobra — V-8: The Torino GT was the sport version of the Torino series and included all the Torino trim plus hood scoop, trim rings with hubcaps, courtesy lights, carpeting, padded seats, GT emblems, the 302-cid, 220-hp V-8 engine and E70-14 fiberglass-belted white sidewall tires. There were F70-14 tires on convertible versions. The Torino Cobra was the high-performance version of the Torino series and included all of the Torino trim plus the 429-cid, 360-hp V-8, a four-speed manual transmission, competition suspension, seven-inch wide wheels with hubcaps, black center hood, hood locking pins, bright exterior moldings, courtesy lights, Cobra emblems and F70-14 fiberglass-belted black sidewall tires with raised white letters. The Cobra package included a functional hood scoop and rear window louvers.

Custom — 6 and V-8: The full-size Fords were only slightly restyled for 1970, with a revamped rear end treatment. The taillights of the new model were positioned lower in the body and the grille was updated. The Custom series was the base trim level and included chrome windshield and rear window moldings, nylon carpeting, the script Custom name on the rear fenders and the Ford name, in block letters, across the front of the hood and in the rear escutcheon panel. The Custom 500 models offered Custom trim plus a horizontal chrome strip along the mid-section of the body and a brushed aluminum trim strip at the front of the hood.

Galaxie 500 — 6 and V-8: The Galaxie 500 was the intermediate trim level for 1970 and included all the Custom trim plus a pleated vinyl interior, chrome side window and rain gutter moldings and polished aluminum wheel opening moldings.

XL — V-8: The Ford XL was the sport trim version of the full-size two-door convertible and two-door fastback models and included the Galaxie 500's features plus the 302-cid V-8, bucket seats, special wheel covers, LTD-style die-cast grille, retractable headlights, pleated, all-vinyl interior trim and the XL designation, in block letters and in the center of the front of the hood.

LTD — V-8: The LTD was the top trim level full-size Ford for 1970 and included all the Galaxie 500 trim plus the 351-cid, 250-hp V-8 engine, Cruise-O-Matic automatic transmission, electric clock, bright exterior moldings and dual accent paint stripes. The LTD station wagon models, essentially Country Squires also included simulated wood grain appliqués on the body. All LTDs also included retractable headlights and a die-cast grille. The absolute top trim level for 1970 was the LTD Brougham two- and four-door hardtops and four-door sedan. These were LTDs with more lavish interiors than the regular LTD offered. Exterior trim remained the same as the standard LTD.

VIN: Falcon, Fairlane, Ford, Maverick and Torino

The serial number code was broken down in the following manner. First symbol indicated the year: 0 = 1970. The second symbol identified assembly plant, as follows: A = Atlanta, Georgia, B = Oakville, Ontario, Canada, E = Mahwah, New Jersey, F = Dearborn, Michigan, G = Chicago, Illinois, H = Loraine, Ohio, J = Los Angeles, California, K = Kansas City, Missouri, N = Norfolk, Virginia, P = Twin Cities (Minneapolis and St. Paul, Minnesota), R = San Jose, California, S = Allen Park Pilot Plant, T = Metuchen, New Jersey, U = Louisville, Kentucky, W = Wayne, Michigan, X = St. Thomas, Ontario, Canada, Y = Wixom, Michigan and Z = St.

1970 XL convertible

1970 XL Sportsroof two-door hardtop

Louis, Missouri. The third and fourth symbols identified the body series. The fifth symbol identified engine code, as follows: C = 429-cid V-8, F = 302-cid V-8, G = 302-cid Boss V-8 with four barrel carb, H = 351-cid V-8, J = 429-cid V-8, K = 429-cid V-8, L = 250-cid six-cylinder, M = 351-cid V-8 with four-barrel carb, N = 429-cid V-8 with four-barrel carb, R = 428-cid Super Cobra Jet V-8 with four-barrel carb, S = 390-cid V-8 with four-barrel carb, T = 200-cid six-cylinder, U = 170-cid six-cylinder, V = 240-cid six-cylinder, X = 390-cid V-8; Y = 390-cid V-8 and Z = 429-cid Boss V-8 with four-barrel carb. The last six digits were the unit's production number, beginning at 100001 and up at each of the assembly plants.

Maverick (6)

Model No.	Body/ Style No.	Body Type & Seating	Factory Price	Shipping Weight	Production Total
----	91	2-dr. Sedan-6P	$1,995	2,411 lbs.	451,081

Note: Total series output was 451,081 units.

Falcon Sub-Series (6)

	54A	4-dr. Sedan-6P	$2,500	3,116 lbs.	Note 1
----	62A	2-dr. Sedan-6P	$2,460	3,100 lbs.	Note 1
----	71D	4-dr. Station Wagon-6P	$2,767	3,155 lbs.	Note 1

Fairlane 500 (6)

	54B	4-dr. Sedan-6P	$2,627	3,116 lbs.	Note 1
----	65B	2-dr. Hardtop -6P	$2,660	3,128 lbs.	Note 1
----	71B	4-dr. Station Wagon-6P	$2,957	3,508 lbs.	Note 1

Fairlane 500 (V-8)

	54A	4-dr. Sedan-6P	$2,528	3,216 lbs.	30,443
----	62A	2-dr. Sedan-6P	$2,479	3,200 lbs.	26,071
----	71D	4-dr. Station Wagon-6P	$2,856	3,255 lbs.	10,539
----	54B	4-dr. Sedan-6P	$2,716	3,216 lbs.	25,780
----	65B	2-dr. Hardtop-6P	$2,750	3,228 lbs.	70,636
----	71B	4-dr. Station Wagon-6P	$3,047	3,608 lbs.	13,613

Note 1: Fairlane series production was 177,091 units. Ford did not indicate the number of sixes or V-8s produced so the production figures are totals for each body style with both engines.

Torino (6)

	54C	4-dr. Sedan-6P	$2,689	3,158 lbs.	Note 1
----	57C	4-dr. Hardtop-6P	$2,795	3,189 lbs.	Note 1
----	65C	2-dr. Hardtop-6P	$2,722	3,173 lbs.	Note 1
----	63C	2-dr. Fastback-6P	$2,810	3,211 lbs.	Note 1
----	71C	4-dr. Station Wagon-6P	$3,074	3,553 lbs.	Note 1

Torino (V-8)

	54C	4-dr. Sedan-6P	$2,778	3,258 lbs.	30,117
----	57C	4-dr. Hardtop-6P	$2,885	3,289 lbs.	14,312
----	65C	2-dr. Hardtop-6P	$2,812	3,273 lbs.	49,826
----	63C	2-dr. Fastback-6P	$2,899	3,311 lbs.	12,490
----	71C	4-dr. Station Wagon-6P	$3,164	3,653 lbs.	10.613

Note 1: Total Torino series output was 117,358 units. Ford did not indicate the number of sixes or V-8s produced so the production figures are totals for each body style with both engines.

Torino Brougham (V-8)

	57E	4-dr. Hardtop-6P	$3,078	3,309 lbs.	14,543
----	65E	2-dr. Hardtop-6P	$3,006	3,293 lbs.	16,911
----	71E	4-dr. Squire Station Wagon-6P	$3,379	3,673 lbs.	13,166

Note: Total series output was 44,620 units.

Torino GT (V-8)

	63F	2-dr. Fastback-5P	$3,105	3,366 lbs.	56,819
----	76F	2-dr. Convertible-5P	$3,212	3,490 lbs.	3,939

Torino GT Cobra (V-8)

	63H	2-dr. Fastback-5P	$3,270	3,774 lbs.	7,675

Note: Total series output was 68,433 units.

1970 LTD Brougham two-door hardtop

Custom (6)

	54E	4-dr. Sedan-6P	$2,771	3,527 lbs.	Note 1
----	54B	4-dr. Sedan-6P	$2,872	3,567 lbs.	Note 1

Custom (V-8)

	54E	4-dr. Sedan-6P	$2,850	3,563 lbs.	42,849
----	71D	4-dr. Ranch Wagon-6P	$3,305	4,079 lbs.	15,086
----	54B	4-dr. Sedan-6P	$2,951	3,603 lbs.	41,261
----	71H	4-dr. Ranch Wagon-6P	$3,368	4,049 lbs.	15,304
----	71J	4-dr. Ranch Wagon-10P	$3,481	4,137 lbs.	9,943

Note: Total Custom series output was 124,443 units. Ford did not indicate the number of sixes or V-8s produced so the production figures are totals for each body style with both engines.

Galaxie 500 (6)

	54A	4-dr. Sedan-6P	$3,026	3,540 lbs.	Note 1
----	57B	4-dr. Hardtop-6P	$3,096	3,611 lbs.	Note 1
----	65C	2-dr. Formal Hardtop Coupe-6P	$3,094	3,550 lbs.	Note 1
----	63B	2-dr. Fastback-6P	$3,043	3,549 lbs.	Note 1

Galaxie 500 (V-8)

	54A	4-dr. Sedan-6P	$3,137	3,661 lbs.	101,784
----	57B	4-dr. Hardtop-6P	$3,208	3,732 lbs.	53,817
----	65C	2-dr. Formal Hardtop Coupe-6P	$3,205	3,671 lbs.	57,059
----	63B	2-dr. Fastback-6P	$3,154	3,670 lbs.	50,825
----	71B	4-dr. Country Sedan-6P	$3,488	4,089 lbs.	32,209
----	71C	4-dr. Country Sedan-10P	$3,600	4,112 lbs.	22,645

Note: Total Galaxie series output was 318,339 units. Ford did not indicate the number of sixes or V-8s produced so the production figures are totals for each body style with both engines.

XL (V-8)

	63C	2-dr. Fastback-5P	$3,293	3,750 lbs.	27,251
----	76B	2-dr. Convertible-5P	$3,501	3,983 lbs.	6,348

Note: Total XL series output was 33,599 units.

LTD (V-8)

	54C	4-dr. Sedan-6P	$3,307	3,701 lbs.	78,306
----	57F	4-dr. Hardtop-6P	$3,385	3,771 lbs.	90,390
----	65A	2-dr. Hardtop-6P	$3,356	3,727 lbs.	96,324
----	71E	4-dr. Country Squire Wagon-6P	$3,832	4,139 lbs.	39,837
----	71A	4-dr. Country Squire Wagon-10P	$3,909	4,185 lbs.	69,077

LTD Brougham (V-8)

	54	4-dr. Sedan-6P	$3,502	3,829 lbs.	Note 1
----	57	4-dr. Hardtop-6P	$3,579	4,029 lbs.	Note 1
----	65	2-dr. Hardtop-6P	$3,537	3,855 lbs.	Note 1

Note: Total series output was 373,934 units. Production was not broken down by LTD and LTD Brougham models.

Engines:

Maverick Base Six: Overhead valve. Cast-iron block. Displacement: 170 cid. B & S: 3.50 x 2.94 in. Compression ratio: 9.0:1. Brake hp: 105 at 4400 rpm. Carburetor: Holley one-barrel. Seven main bearings. Code U.

Maverick Optional Six: Overhead valve. Cast-iron block. Displacement: 200 cid. B & S: 3.68 x 3.13 in. Compression ratio: 8.0:1. Brake hp: 120 at 4400 rpm. Carburetor: Motorcraft one-barrel. Seven main bearings. Code T.

Ford Base Six: Overhead valve. Cast-iron block. Displacement: 240 cid. B & S: 4.00 x 3.18 in. Compression ratio: 9.2:1. Brake hp: 150 at 4000 rpm. Carburetor: Motorcraft one-barrel. Seven main bearings. Code V.

Ford and Maverick Optional Six: Overhead valve. Cast-iron block. Displacement: 250 cid. B & S: 3.68 x 3.91 in. Compression ratio: 9.0:1. Brake hp: 155 at 4400 rpm. Carburetor: Motorcraft one-barrel. Seven main bearings. Code L.

Torino GT Base 302 V-8: Overhead valve. Cast-iron block. Displacement: 302 cid. B & S: 4.00 x 3.00 in. Compression ratio: 9.5:1. Brake hp: 220 at 4600 rpm. Carburetor: Motorcraft two-barrel. Five main bearings. Code F.

Boss 302 V-8: Overhead valve. Cast-iron block. Displacement: 302 cid. Compression ratio: 10.6:1. Brake hp: 290 at 5800 rpm. Carburetor: Holley four-barrel. Five main bearings. Code G.

Falcon, Fairlane and Torino Optional 351 V-8: Overhead valve. Cast-iron block. Displacement: 351 cid. B & S: 4.00 x 3.50 in. Compression ratio: 9.5:1. Brake hp: 250 at 4600 rpm. Carburetor: Motorcraft two-barrel. Five main bearings. Code H.

1970 LTD four-door hardtop

1970 LTD two-door hardtop

1970 Country Squire station wagon

351 Four-Barrel V-8: Overhead valve. Cast-iron block. Displacement: 351 cid. B & S: 4.00 x 3.50 in. Compression ratio: 11.0:1. Brake hp: 300 at 5400 rpm. Carburetor: Motorcraft four-barrel. Five main bearings. Code M.

Ford Optional 390 V-8: Overhead valve. Cast-iron block. Displacement: 390 cid. B & S: 4.05 x 3.78 in. Compression ratio: 9.5:1. Brake hp: 270 at 4400 rpm. Carburetor: Motorcraft two-barrel. Five main bearings. Code X.

Cobra GT Optional Cobra Jet 428 V-8: Overhead valve. Cast-iron block. Displacement: 428 cid. B & S: 4.13 x 3.98 in. Compression ratio: 10.6:1. Brake hp: 335 at 5200 rpm. Carburetor: Holley four-barrel. Five main bearings.

Cobra GT Optional Super Cobra Jet 428 V-8: Overhead valve. Cast-iron block. Displacement: 428 cid. B & S: 4.13 x 3.98 in. Compression ratio: 10.5:1. Brake hp: 360 at 5400 rpm. Carburetor: Holley four-barrel. Five main bearings. Code R.

Ford Optional Thunder-Jet 429 V-8: Overhead valve. Cast-iron block. Displacement: 429 cid. B & S: 4.36 x 3.59 in. Compression ratio: 10.5:1. Brake hp: 320 at 4400 rpm. Carburetor: Motorcraft two-barrel. Five main bearings. Code K.

Ford Optional Thunder-Jet 429 Four-Barrel V-8: Overhead valve. Cast-iron block. Displacement: 429 cid. B & S: 4.36 x 3.59 in. Compression ratio: 10.5:1. Brake hp: 360 at 4600 rpm. Carburetor: Motorcraft four-barrel. Five main bearings. Code N.

Ford Optional Police Interceptor 429 V-8: Overhead valve. Cast-iron block. Displacement: 429 cid. B & S: 4.36 x 3.59 in. Compression ratio: 11.3:1. Brake hp: 370 at 5400 rpm. Carburetor: Holley four-barrel. Five main bearings.

Boss 429 V-8: Overhead valve. Cast-iron block. Displacement: 429 cid. B & S: 4.36 x 3.59 in. Compression ratio: 11.3:1. Brake hp: 375 at 5600 rpm. Carburetor: Holley four-barrel. Five main bearings. Code Z.

Note: The Ram Air Boss 429-cid V-8 had the same specifications as the Boss 429.

Chassis:

Falcon: Wheelbase: 110.9 in. and 113 in., station wagons. Overall length: 184.3 in. and 198.7 in., station wagons. Tires: 6.95 x 14 four-ply tubeless blackwall and 7.75 x 14 four-ply tubeless blackwall, station wagons.

Maverick: Wheelbase: 103 in. Overall length: 179.4 in. Tires: 6.00 x 13 four-ply tubeless blackwall.

Fairlane/Torino: Wheelbase: 117.0 in. and 114 in., station wagons. Overall length: 206.2 in. and 209 in., station wagons. Tires: E78 x 14, G78 x 14, station wagons and F70 x 14, convertibles. The GT used E70 x 14 tires.

Ford: Wheelbase: 121 in. Overall length: 213.9 in. and 216.9 in., station wagons. Tires: F78 x 15 four-ply blackwall, G78 x 15 four-ply tubeless blackwall, Custom and Custom 500 V-8 and H78 x 15 four-ply tubeless blackwall, Galaxie 500 and LTD.

Options:

Maverick: 200-cid six-cylinder engine. 250-cid six cylinder engine. 302-cid V-8 [after December 1970]. Selectaire air conditioning. Tinted glass. Day/night rearview mirror. Cruise-O-Matic automatic transmission ($175). AM radio ($61). White sidewall tires ($34). Accent seat trim. Grabber package with 200-cid six, three-speed manual transmission, black grille and black hood and side body stripes, 14-inch wheels with trim rings, deck-lid spoiler, dual racing mirrors, C78 x 14 tires, three-spoke wood trim steering wheel and black vinyl interior trim.

Fairlane and Torino: Power steering ($100). Air conditioning ($389). Cruise-O-Matic automatic transmission ($201 to $222). Four-speed manual transmission ($194). AM radio ($61). Station wagon power tailgate window ($35). Station wagon rooftop luggage rack ($46). White sidewall tires ($34). Vinyl roof on two- and four-door hardtops and sedan ($95). 250-hp 351-cid V-8 engine ($45).

Ford: Power disc brakes ($65). Power steering ($105). Air conditioning ($389). Cruise-O-Matic automatic transmission ($201 to $222). Tinted windshield ($45). AM radio ($61). AM/FM radio ($240). Vinyl roof ($105). White sidewall tires ($34). Custom 390-cid, 265-hp V-8 ($131). Galaxie 500/XL/LTD 390-cid, 265-hp V-8 ($86). Custom 429-cid, 320-hp V-8 ($213). Galaxie 500/XL/LTD 429-cid, 320-hp V-8 ($168). LTD Luxury trim package ($104).

1970-1/2 Falcon two-door sedan

1970 Falcon Futura two-door sedan

1970 Falcon Futura sedan

1970 Falcon Futura station wagon

The full-size Fords were introduced in September 1969. The Falcon and Torino appeared in dealer showrooms at midyear. Model year production peaked at 1,326,533 units and a calendar year production of 1,647,918 cars was recorded. The new reverse-curve Torino rear window design was influenced by Ford's involvement in racing. These cars competed with the aerodynamic Dodge Daytona and Plymouth Superbird. Only six checkered flags were taken by FoMoCo stock car drivers. The DeTomaso Pantera, an Italian-built specialty sports car powered by a 351-cid, 310-hp Ford "Cleveland" V-8 debuted in 1970. Early in the 1970 model year, the Falcon compact was marketed in three styles: two- and four-door sedans and station wagons. It was replaced by the Fairlane-based 1970-1/2 Falcon later in the 1970 model year.

1970 Torino Brougham four-door hardtop

1970 Fairlane 500 two-door hardtop

1970 Torino GT Sportsroof two-door hardtop

1970 Torino two-door hardtop

1970 Torino GT convertible

1970-1/2 Torino Sportsroof two-door hardtop

1970 Torino GT Cobra Sportsroof two-door hardtop

1970 Torino Brougham two-door hardtop

1970 Torino Brougham Squire station wagon

1970-1/2 Maverick Grabber

1970 Maverick

1971 Ford

Pinto — Four: The Pinto was Ford's new sub-compact offering, built to serve the ever-growing small car market and compete with imports and domestic sub-compacts such as Chevrolet's Vega and the American Motor's Gremlin. It came only as a two-door sedan at first. Standard equipment included ventless door windows, high back slim line bucket seats, all-vinyl upholstery, two-pod instrument cluster, glove box, interior dome light, floor-mounted transmission controls, rack and pinion steering, hot water heater, Direct-Aire ventilation system and 6.00 x 13 rayon blackwall tires. In mid-season, a three-door Pinto Runabout was added. Its standard equipment was the same as the above with a fold-down rear seat, load floor color-keyed carpeting and passenger compartment color-keyed carpeting. Pintos were available with either a British-built 1600cc overhead valve four-cylinder engine, or a second, more powerful and more popular German-built 2000cc four-cylinder engine. Both engines used a four-speed manual transmission, but only the larger engine was available with the three-speed Cruise-O-Matic transmission. While good fuel economy was the main objective of the new Pinto, those equipped with the larger engine and four-speed manual transmission provided quite brisk performance by any standards.

Maverick 6 and V-8: The 1971 Maverick added a four-door sedan to the model choices and the Grabber, which had been an option package, now became another version of the two-door sedan. Also the 210-hp, 302-cid V-8 engine was available for the first time. The 302 proved to be a brisk performer in the small bodied Maverick and the perfect combination with the Grabber two-door sedan. The Maverick continued its list of standard features from the 1970 model including the economy-minded 170-cid six cylinder engine and three-speed transmission as standard equipment. The Grabber edition included a simulated hood scoop, grille-mounted road lamps, trim rings and hub caps, special stripes on the sides plus fender decals, blackout paint on the hood, grille and lower back panel plus color-keyed dual racing mirrors with the left side a remote-controlled mirror. The Grabber also offered bright window frames and a deluxe steering wheel.

Torino and Torino 500 — 6 and V-8: The 1971 Torinos were merely 1970 bodies with updated trim and a slightly revised grille. Standard equipment on the base Torino series included a chrome-trimmed windshield, rear window and rain gutter moldings, front and rear armrests and the Torino name, in block letters, on the rear fenders. The Torino 500 series had all the base Torino trim plus color-keyed carpeting, cloth and vinyl interior trim, an Argent-painted egg crate grille and polished aluminum wheel well and rocker panel moldings.

Torino Brougham, Torino GT and Torino Cobra — V-8: The Torino Brougham was the top trim level Torino for 1971 and included all the Torino 500 equipment plus wheel covers, chrome exterior moldings, soundproofing, Brougham ornamentation, cloth interior trims in four colors and a 210-hp, 302-cid V-8. The Squire wagon also included power front disc brakes, simulated wood grain paneling on the body and G78-14 belted black sidewall tires. The Torino GT was the sporty version of the Brougham series and included all the basic Brougham trim plus color-keyed outside racing mirrors with a remote-controlled left-hand mirror. GT identification was on the grille and rocker panels and it also included simulated hood scoop, hubcaps with trim rings, chrome-trimmed foot pedals, a full-width taillight and E70-14 white sidewall Wide-Oval tires. The convertible also had a power top. The Torino Cobra was the high-performance version of the Brougham series and included all the Brougham trim plus the 285-hp, 351-cid "Cleveland" V-8, four-speed manual transmission with a Hurst shifter, special Cobra identification, heavy-duty suspension, seven-inch wide, Argent-painted wheels with chrome hubcaps, a black grille and lower escutcheon panel, a black-finished hood with non-reflective paint, polished aluminum wheel well moldings, F70-14 white sidewall Wide-Oval tires and a 55-amp heavy-duty battery. The cars also had dual exhausts and pleated vinyl seat trim.

Custom — 6 and V-8: The full-size Fords received a total restyling. The grille was a full-width horizontal unit, with a larger, vertical center section that protruded forward. The hood peaked at the center section of the grille and became wider toward the windshield. The Custom series was the base trim level full-size 1971 Ford and included a chrome-trimmed windshield and rear window moldings, nylon carpeting and the Custom name, in block letters, on the rear fenders and rear escutcheon panel. The Custom 500 models included the Custom trim plus polished aluminum wheel well moldings, argent and chrome appliqués on the instrument panel plus rear deck moldings and Custom 500 ornamentation. The Custom and Custom 500 models were available with either the 140-hp, 240 cid six-cylinder or the 210-hp, 302-cid V-8 as standard equipment.

Galaxie 500 — 6 and V-8: The Galaxie 500 was the intermediate trim level full-size 1971 Ford and included all the Custom trim plus wood grain appliqués on the interior doors and instrument panel black-painted inserts, polished aluminum wheel well moldings, chrome window frames, deck and rear quarter extension moldings, additional Galaxie 500 ornamentation, the 351-cid, 240-hp V-8 and F78-15 belted black sidewall tires. The Country Sedan used H78-15 tires.

LTD — V-8: A more formal roof line was used in the LTD series and the interiors were completely restyled, with the emphasis on a luxury appearance. The taillights were rectangular and were located at either end of the rear escutcheon panel. The LTDs featured an additional red plastic center reflector that gave the illusion of a full-width taillight. The LTD included all the Galaxie 500 trim plus power front disc brakes, an electric clock, luxury seat trim on all but convertibles, a left-hand outside rearview mirror, nylon carpeting, a power top on convertibles and G78-15 belted tires. The LTD Country Squire station wagons also included wheel covers, a power tailgate window, simulated wood grain appliqués on the body, pleated vinyl trim and H78-15 belted black sidewall tires. The LTD Brougham series included the LTD trim plus wheel covers, Brougham seat trim, a deluxe steering wheel, a front door courtesy light, cut-pile carpeting, a front seat center armrest and polished seat side shields, rear door courtesy light switches, LTD "C" pillar ornamentation and high back bucket seats on the two-door hardtop.

VIN:

The 1971 Ford serial number code was broken down as follows: The first symbol indicated the year: 1 = 1971. The second symbol identified the assembly plant: A = Atlanta, Georgia; B = Oakville, Ontario, Canada, E = Mahwah, New Jersey, F = Dearborn, Michigan, G = Chicago, Illinois, H = Lorain, Ohio, J = Los Angeles, California, K = Kansas City, Missouri; N = Norfolk, Virginia, P = Twin Cities (Minneapolis and St. Paul, Minnesota), R = San Jose, California, S = Allen Park Pilot Plant, T = Metuchen, New Jersey, U = Louisville, Kentucky, W = Wayne, Michigan, X = St. Thomas, Ontario, Canada, Y = Wixom, Michigan and Z = St. Louis, Missouri. The third and fourth symbols identified the body series: 64B=Pinto Runabout. The fifth symbol identified the engine codes: C = 429-cid V-8, D = 302-cid high-output V-8, F = 302-cid V-8, G = 302-cid Boss V-8 with four-barrel

1971 Galaxie 500 four-door hardtop

1971 LTD Country Squire station wagon

1971 LTD Brougham two-door hardtop

1971 LTD Brougham four-door hardtop

1971 LTD two-door hardtop

carb, H = 351-cid V-8, J = 429-cid V-8, K = 429-cid V-8, L = 250-cid six-cylinder, M = 351-cid V-8 with four-barrel carb, N = 429-cid V-8 with four-barrel carb, P = 429-cid V-8, Q = 351-cid V-8, R = 351-cid Boss V-8, S = 400-cid V-8, T = 200-cid six-cylinder, U = 170-cid six-cylinder, V = 240-cid six-cylinder, W = 98-cid four-cylinder, X = 122-cid four-cylinder and Y = 390-cid V-8. The last six digits were the unit's production number, beginning at 100001 and up.

Pinto (Four)

Model No.	Body/ Style No.	Body Type & Seating	Factory Price	Shipping Weight	Production Total
---	62B	2-dr. Sedan-4P	$1,919	1,949 lbs.	288,606
---	64BD	2-dr. Runabout-4P	$2,062	1,994 lbs.	63,796

Note: Total series output was 352,402 units.

Maverick (6)

---	54A	4-dr. Sedan-6P	$2,235	2,610 lbs.	Note
---	62B	2-dr. Runabout-6P	$2,175	2,478 lbs.	Note
---	62D	2-dr. Grabber-6P	$2,354	2,570 lbs.	Note

Maverick (V-8)

---	54A	4-dr. Sedan-6P	$2,404	2,803 lbs.	73,208
---	62B	2-dr. Runabout-6P	$2,344	2,671 lbs.	159,726
---	62D	2-dr. Grabber-6P	$2,523	2,763 lbs.	38,963

Note: Total series output was 271,697 units.

Torino (6)

---	54A	4-dr. Sedan-6P	$2,672	3,141 lbs.	----
---	62A	2-dr. Hardtop-6P	$2,706	3,151 lbs.	----
---	71D	2-dr. Station Wagon-6P	$3,023	3,498 lbs.	----

Torino (V-8)

---	54A	4-dr. Sedan-6P	$2,767	3,220 lbs.	29,501
---	62A	2-dr. Hardtop-6P	$2,801	3,230 lbs.	37,518
---	71D	2-dr. Station Wagon-6P	$2,950	3,577 lbs.	21,570

Note: Total series output was 261,349 units.

Torino Brougham (V-8)

---	57E	4-dr. Brougham Hardtop-6P	$3,248	3,345 lbs.	4,408
---	65E	2-dr. Brougham Hardtop-6P	$3,175	3,390 lbs.	8,593
---	71E	2-dr. Squire Station Wagon-6P	$3,560	3,663 lbs.	15,805

Torino GT and Torino Cobra (V-8)

---	63F	2-dr. GT Sport Coupe-5P	$3,150	3,346 lbs.	31,641
---	76F	2-dr. GT Convertible-5P	$3,408	3,486 lbs.	1,613
---	63E	2-dr. Cobra Hardtop-5P	$3,295	3,594 lbs.	3,054

Note: Total series output was 65,114 units.

Custom (6)

| --- | 54B | 4-dr. Sedan-6P | $3,288 | 3,683 lbs. | Note 1 |

Custom (V-8)

| --- | 54B | 4-dr. Sedan-6P | $3,363 | 3,724 lbs. | 41,062 |
| --- | 71B | 4-dr. Ranch Wagon-6P | $3,890 | 4,190 lbs. | 16,696 |

Custom 500 (6)

| --- | 54D | 4-dr. Sedan-6P | $3,426 | 3,688 lbs. | Note 1 |

Custom 500 (V-8)

| --- | 54D | 4-dr. Sedan-6P | $3,501 | 3,729 lbs. | 33,765 |
| --- | 71D | 4-dr. Ranch Wagon-6P | $3,982 | 4,215 lbs. | 25,957 |

Note 1: Total Custom and Custom 500 series output was 117,480 units. Six and V-8 production figures were not broken out by Ford.

Galaxie 500 (6)

---	54F	4-dr. Sedan-6P	$3,246	3,668 lbs.	Note 1
---	57F	4-dr. Hardtop-6P	$3,665	3,723 lbs.	Note 1
---	65F	2-dr. Hardtop-6P	$3,628	3,668 lbs.	Note 1

Galaxie 500 (V-8)

---	54F	4-dr. Sedan-6P	$3,367	3,826 lbs.	98,130
---	57F	4-dr. Hardtop-6P	$3,786	3,881 lbs.	46,595
---	65F	2-dr. Hardtop-6P	$3,749	3,826 lbs.	117,139
---	71F	4-dr. Country Sedan-6P	$4,074	4,241 lbs.	60,487
---	71D	4-dr. Country Sedan-10P	$4,188	4,291 lbs.	-----

Note: Total series output was 322,351 units. Production figures for the 10-passenger Country Sedan were not available. Six and V-8 production figures were not broken out by Ford.

LTD (V-8)

---	53H	4-dr. Sedan-6P	$3,931	3,913 lbs.	92,260
---	57H	4-dr. Hardtop-6P	$3,969	3,908 lbs.	48,166
---	65H	2-dr. Formal Hardtop-6P	$3,923	3,853 lbs.	103,896
---	76H	2-dr. Convertible-6P	$4,094	4,091 lbs.	5,750
---	71H	4-dr. Country Squire-6P	$4,308	4,308 lbs.	130,644
---	71H	4-dr. Country Squire-10P	$4,496	4,358 lbs.	------

LTD Brougham (V-8)

---	53K	4-dr. Sedan-6P	$4,094	3,949 lbs.	26,186
---	57K	4-dr. Hardtop-6P	$4,140	3,944 lbs.	27,820
---	65K	2-dr. Hardtop-6P	$4,097	3,883 lbs.	43,303

Note: Total series output was 478,025 units. Production figures for the 10-passenger Country Sedan were not available.

Engines:

Pinto Four: Overhead cam. Cast-iron block. Displacement: 98 cid. B & S: 3.19 x 3.06 in. Compression ratio: 8.4:1. Brake hp: 75 at 5000 rpm. Carburetor: one-barrel. Five main bearings. Code W.

Pinto Alternate Four: Overhead cam. Cast-iron block. Displacement: 122 cid. B & S: 3.58 x 3.03 in. Compression ratio: 9.0:1. Brake hp: 100 at 5600 rpm. Carburetor: Ford/Weber two-barrel. Five main bearings. Code X.

Maverick Base Six: Overhead valve. Cast-iron block. Displacement: 170 cid. B & S: 3.50 x 2.94 in. Compression ratio: 8.7:1. Brake hp: 100 at 4200 rpm. Carburetor: Motorcraft one-barrel. Seven main bearings. Code U.

Maverick Optional Six: Overhead valve. Cast-iron block. Displacement: 200 cid. B & S: 3.68 x 3.13 in. Compression ratio: 8.7:1. Brake hp: 115 at 4000 rpm. Carburetor: Motorcraft one-barrel. Seven main bearings. Code T.

Ford Base Six: Overhead valve. Cast-iron block. Displacement: 240 cid. B & S: 4.00 x 3.18 in. Compression ratio: 8.9:1. Brake hp: 140 at 4000 rpm. Carburetor: Motorcraft one-barrel. Seven main bearings. Code V.

Ford and Maverick Optional Six: Overhead valve. Cast-iron block. Displacement: 250 cid. B & S: 3.68 x 3.91 inches. Compression ratio: 9.0:1. Brake hp: 145 at 4000 rpm. Carburetor: Motorcraft one-barrel. Seven main bearings. Code L.

Torino GT Base 302 V-8: Overhead valve. Cast-iron block. Displacement: 302 cid. B & S: 4.00 x 3.00 in. Compression ratio: 9.0:1. Brake hp: 210 at 4600 rpm. Carburetor: Motorcraft two-barrel. Five main bearings. Code F.

1971 Torino 500 four-door hardtop

1971 Torino Brougham four-door hardtop

1971 Torino GT Sportsroof two-door hardtop

1971 Torino Brougham Squire station wagon

1971 Torino Cobra two-door hardtop

1971 Maverick four-door sedan

Fairlane and Torino Optional 351 "Cleveland" two-barrel V-8: Overhead valve. Cast-iron block. Displacement: 351 cid. B & S: 4.00 x 3.50 in. Compression ratio: 9.0:1. Brake hp: 240 at 4600 rpm. Carburetor: Motorcraft two-barrel. Five main bearings. Code H.

351 "Cleveland" four-barrel V-8: Overhead valve. Cast-iron block. Displacement: 351 cid. B & S: 4.00 x 3.50 in. Compression ratio: 10.7:1. Brake hp: 285 at 5400 rpm. Carburetor: Holley four-barrel. Five main bearings. Code M.

Boss 351 V-8: Overhead valve. Cast-iron block. Displacement: 351 cid. B & S: 4.00 x 3.50 in. Compression ratio: 11.1:1. Brake hp: 330 at 5400 rpm. Carburetor: Holley four-barrel. Five main bearings. Code R.

Ford Optional 390 V-8: Overhead valve. Cast-iron block. Displacement: 390 cid. B & S: 4.05 x 3.78 in. Compression ratio: 8.6:1. Brake hp: 225 at 4400 rpm. Carburetor: Motorcraft two-barrel. Five main bearings. Code Y.

Ford Optional 400 "Cleveland" V-8: Overhead valve. Cast-iron block. Displacement: 400 cid. B & S: 4.00 x 4.00 in. Compression ratio: 9.0:1. Brake hp: 260 at 4400 rpm. Carburetor: Motorcraft two-barrel. Five main bearings. Code S.

Ford Thunder Jet 429 four-barrel V-8: Overhead valve. Cast-iron block. Displacement: 429 cid. B & S: 4.36 x 3.59 in. Compression ratio: 10.5:1. Brake hp: 360 at 4600 rpm. Carburetor: Motorcraft four-barrel. Five main bearings. Code N.

Ford Cobra Jet 429 V-8: Overhead valve. Cast-iron block. Displacement: 429 cid. B & S: 4.36 x 3.59 in. Compression ratio: 11.3:1. Brake hp: 370 at 5400 rpm. Carburetor: Holley four-barrel. Five main bearings. Code C.

Super Cobra Jet 429 V-8: Overhead valve. Cast-iron block. Displacement: 429 cid. B & S: 4.36 x 3.59 in. Compression ratio: 11.3:1. Brake hp: 375 at 5600 rpm. Carburetor: Holley four-barrel with Ram-Air induction. Five main bearings. Code J.

Chassis:

Pinto: Wheelbase: 94 in. Overall length: 163 in. Tires: 6.00 x 13 belted black sidewall.

Maverick: Wheelbase: 103 in. Overall length: 179.4 in. Tires: 6.45 x 14 and 6.50 x 14 on V-8s.

Torino: Wheelbase: 117 in. and 114 in. on station wagons. Overall length: 206.2 inches and 209 in. on station wagons. Tires: E78-14 belted blackwall.

Ford: Wheelbase: 121 in. Overall length: 216.2 in. and 219.2 in. on station wagons. Tires: F78-15 belted black sidewall, G78-15 on Galaxie 500s and LTDs and H78-15 on station wagons.

Options:

Pinto: 122-cid, 100-hp four-cylinder overhead cam engine ($50). Cruise-O-Matic automatic transmission ($175). AM radio ($61). Chrome window moldings ($60). White sidewall tires ($33).

Maverick: 200-cid, 115-hp six ($39). 250-cid, 145-hp six ($79). 302-cid, 210-hp V-8. Cruise-O-Matic automatic transmission ($183). AM radio ($61). Power steering ($95). White sidewall tires ($34). Rear window defroster. Tinted glass. Vinyl roof. Deluxe seat belts. Heavy duty suspension. Heavy duty battery. Consolette with storage. Consolette with storage plus an electric clock. Protection group with black vinyl body moldings and front and rear bumper guards.

Torino: 351-cid, 240-hp V-8 ($45). 351-cid, 285-hp V-8 ($93). 429-cid, 370-hp Cobra Jet V-8, Cobra ($279) and in other Torinos ($372). Cruise-O-Matic automatic transmission, Torino ($217) and Cobra ($238). Four-speed manual transmission ($250). AM radio ($66). Power steering ($115). Power tailgate window on station wagons ($35). Luggage rack on station wagon ($52). Vinyl roof ($95). White sidewall tires ($34).

Ford: 400-cid, 260-hp V-8. 390-cid, 255-hp V-8 ($98). 429-cid, 320-hp V-8 ($168). 429-cid, 360-hp V-8 ($268). Cruise-O-Matic automatic transmission, price varies with engine choice ($217 to $238). Power steering ($115). Power front disc brakes ($52). Tinted windshield ($54). Air conditioning ($420). Cruise control ($84). AM radio ($66). AM/FM radio ($240). Vinyl roof on passenger cars ($113) and $142, station wagons ($142). White sidewall tires ($34).

History:

The 1971 Fords were introduced on Sept. 18, 1970. Model year production peaked at 1,910,924 units. Calendar year production of 2,176,425 cars was recorded. (Note: The model year figure includes only Fords, Torinos, Mavericks, Pintos and Thunderbirds while the calendar year figure covers all passenger car and station wagon models.) The more expensive full-size Ford four-door sedans were advertised as "pillared hardtops" in 1971. Fords captured only three NASCAR races as the performance era wound to its close. Lee Iacocca became the president of Ford Motor Co. The "FE" series big-block V-8 was dropped and the Fairlane name ceased to exist with the end of the 1970 model year. The big-block, 390-cid and 428-cid V-8s were gradually phased-out during the 1971 production run. They were replaced by a new 400-cid "Cleveland" V-8 and the 429-cid V-8.

1971 Maverick four-door sedan

1971 Maverick Grabber two-door sedan

1971 Pinto two-door hatchback

1972 Ford

Pinto — Four: The Pintos were unchanged from the 1971 models. The big news was the addition of a two-door station wagon. The Runabout received a larger rear window. Once again in 1972, the Pinto standard equipment included vent less door windows, high back slim line bucket seats, all-vinyl upholstery, two-pod instrument cluster, glove box, interior dome light, floor-mounted transmission controls, rack and pinion steering, hot water heater, Direct-Aire ventilation system and 6.00 x 13 rayon blackwall tires. Pintos were available with either a standard British-built 1600cc (98 cid) 54-hp overhead valve four-cylinder engine, or a second, more powerful and more popular German-built 2000cc (122 cid) 86 hp four-cylinder engine. Both engines used a four-speed manual transmission, but only the larger engine was available with the three-speed Cruise-O-Matic transmission. While good fuel economy was the main objective of the new Pinto, those equipped with the larger engine and four-speed manual transmission provided quite brisk performance by any standards.

Maverick 6 and V-8: Back again for 1972 was the Maverick in standard two-door and four-door versions along with the two-door Grabber version. The basic Mavericks came with the 170-cid six and three-speed manual transmission plus 6.45 x 14 blackwall tires. Other standard features in 1972 included cowl intake ventilation, center rear fuel filler, curved vent less side glass with flip-style rear windows on the two-door, full-width seats in cloth and vinyl trim, color-keyed floor mats, door-operated courtesy lights, a two-spoke steering wheel and a three-speed blower and blend-air heater. Again in 1972, the Grabber edition was available with simulated hood scoops, grille-mounted road lamps, trim rings and hub caps, black or two-color hood stripes and body stripes with the Grabber logo, dual racing mirrors with the left side a remote-controlled mirror, full-width seats in Ruffino vinyl or Manston cloth, a deck lid spoiler and

1972 Galaxie 500 four-door hardtop

1972 LTD Country Squire station wagon

1972 LTD convertible

quarter panel extension moldings, blackout paint on the grille, headlamp surrounds and stone deflector. The Grabber also offered bright window frames and a deluxe steering wheel. Once again, Maverick buyers could opt for the 200 or 250-cid six or the 302-cid V-8.

Torino — 6 and V-8: Two basic lines of intermediate-size Ford Torinos remained. Both the base Torino models and the top-line Gran Torinos were restyled from end-to-end. The Torino models featured a chrome-trimmed windshield, rear window and rain gutter moldings, highback bench seats, all-vinyl seat and door trim, floor mats, hubcaps with trim rings, a 250-cid six-cylinder engine and a three-speed manual transmission. The Torino station wagon also included power front disc brakes and a three-way tailgate. The Gran Torino was the top trim level for 1972 and included all the Torino trim plus manual front disc brakes, cloth and vinyl trim on seats and interior door panels, carpeting, lower body, wheel well and deck lid moldings, dual-note horn, trunk mat, deluxe steering wheel and chrome trim on the foot pedals. The Gran Torino Squire station wagon also included the 302-cid, 140-hp V-8, deluxe pleated vinyl interior trim, wheel covers and wood grain appliqués on the body, tailgate and instrument panel. The Gran Torino Sport was the rakish version of the Gran Torino line and included all the Gran Torino features plus the 302-cid, 140-hp V-8 engine, pleated all-vinyl trim, hood scoops, color-keyed dual racing mirrors and a unique grille. The Torino's "Coke bottle" shape was even more pronounced for 1972. There were rounded front fender profiles, and a rear fender that swept up toward the roof "C" pillar, then tapered toward the rear of the car. Behind the car was a massive rear bumper that housed rectangular taillights at each end. The grille was slightly reminiscent of the Cobra with its large oval between the quad headlights. Automotive writer Tom McCahill observed that the 1972 Torinos looked like "land-locked tunas sucking air." The top profile of the four-door sedans was rounder than in previous years, and the two-door fastback "Sportsroof" featured an extremely low roofline.

Ford Custom and Custom 500 — 6 and V-8: The 1972 full-size Fords received only minor trim updating with a slightly restyled grille set within the same grille opening. There was a slightly more protective front bumper. The rest of the body styling remained unchanged. The Custom was the base trim level for 1971 and included a chrome-trimmed windshield and rear window moldings; nylon carpeting, an ignition key warning buzzer, a 351-cid V-8 and Cruise-O-Matic automatic transmission. Six-cylinder versions were available for fleet and taxi use as well. Power steering and F78-15 belted black sidewall tires were also standard. The Custom 500 versions included all the Custom trim plus lower back panel and wheel lip moldings, and cloth and vinyl seating surfaces. Station wagons also included H78-15 belted black sidewall tires and power tailgate window.

Galaxie 500 — 6 and V-8: The Galaxie 500 was the intermediate trim level full-size Ford for 1972 and included all the Custom 500 trim plus wheel lip and deck lid moldings, rocker panel moldings and wood grain appliqués on the instrument panel.

Ford LTD — V-8: The LTD was the top trim level full-size Ford for 1972 and included all the Galaxie 500 trim plus power front disc brakes, electric clock, luxury seat trim except convertibles, rear bumper guards, wood grain accents on interior door panels, front door courtesy lights, chrome trim on foot pedals, chrome armrest bases, F78-15 belted black sidewall tires on two-door hardtops and G78-15 tires on all others, except station wagons. Country Squire station wagons also included full wheel covers and reflective rear wood grain paneling, in addition to the wood grain paneling on the body. LTD Brougham included all the standard LTD features plus full wheel covers, rocker panel moldings, unique Brougham seat and door trim, highback, flight-bench seats with center armrest, cut-pile carpeting, rear door courtesy light switches, front end rear dual armrests and G78-15 belted black sidewall tires.

VIN:

The 1972 Ford serial number code was broken down as follows: The first symbol indicated the year: 2 = 1972. The second symbol identified the assembly plant: A = Atlanta, Georgia; B = Oakville, Ontario, Canada, E = Mahwah, New Jersey, F = Dearborn, Michigan, G = Chicago, Illinois, H = Lorain, Ohio, J = Los Angeles, California, K = Kansas City, Missouri; N = Norfolk, Virginia, P = Twin Cities (Minneapolis and St. Paul, Minnesota), R = San Jose, California, S = Allen Park Pilot Plant, T = Metuchen, New Jersey, U = Louisville, Kentucky, W = Wayne, Michigan, X = St. Thomas, Ontario, Canada, Y = Wixom, Michigan and Z = St. Louis, Missouri. The third and fourth symbols identified the body series: 62D=Maverick Grabber two-door. The fifth symbol identified the engine codes: A=460 V-8, F = 302-cid V-8, H = 351-cid V-8, L = 250-cid six-cylinder, N = 429-cid V-8 with four-barrel carb, Q = 351-cid V-8, R = 351-cid Boss V-8, S = 400-cid V-8, T = 200-cid six-cylinder, U = 170-cid six-cylinder, V = 240-cid six-cylinder, W = 98-cid four-cylinder and X = 122-cid four-cylinder. The last six digits were the unit's production number, beginning at 100001 and up.

Pinto (Four)

Model No.	Body/ Style No.	Body Type & Seating	Factory Price	Shipping Weight	Production Total
---	62B	2-dr. Sedan-4P	$1,960	1,968 lbs.	181,002
---	64B	2-dr. Runabout-4P	$2,078	2,012 lbs.	197,920
---	73B	2-dr. Station Wagon-4P	$2,265	2,293 lbs.	101,483

Note: Total series output was 480,405 units.

Maverick (6)

	54A	4-dr. Sedan-6P	$2,245	2,833 lbs.	Note
---	62A	2-dr. Runabout-6P	$2,190	2,538 lbs.	Note
---	62D	2-dr. Grabber-6P	$2,359	2,493 lbs.	Note

Maverick (V-8)

	54A	4-dr. Sedan-6P	$2,406	2,826 lbs.	73,686
---	62A	2-dr. Runabout-6P	$2,350	2,731 lbs.	145,931
---	62D	2-dr. Grabber-6P	$2,519	2,786 lbs.	35,347

Note: Total series output was 254,964 units.

Torino (6)

	53B	4-dr. Hardtop-6P	$2,641	3,469 lbs.	Note
---	65B	2-dr. Hardtop-6P	$2,673	3,369 lbs.	Note
---	71B	4-dr. Station Wagon-6P	$2,955	3,879 lbs.	Note
---	53D	4-dr. Sedan-6P	$2,856	3,476 lbs.	Note

Torino (V-8)

	53B	4-dr. Hardtop-6P	$2,731	3,548 lbs.	33,486
---	65B	2-dr. Hardtop-6P	$2,762	3,448 lbs.	33,530
---	71B	4-dr. Station Wagon-6P	$3,045	3,958 lbs.	22,204
---	53D	4-dr. Sedan-6P	$2,947	3,555 lbs.	102,300

1972 LTD Brougham two-door hardtop

Gran Torino (6)

	65D	2-dr. Hardtop-6P	$2,878	3,395 lbs.	Note 1
---	71D	4-dr. Station Wagon-6P	$3,096	3,881 lbs.	Note 1

Gran Torino (V-8)

	65D	2-dr. Hardtop-6P	$2,967	3,474 lbs.	132,284
---	71D	4-dr. Station Wagon-6P	$3,186	3,960 lbs.	45,212
---	63R	2-dr. Fastback-6P	$3,094	3,496 lbs.	60,794
---	65R	2-dr. Sport Hardtop-6P	$3,094	3,474 lbs.	31,239
---	71K	4-dr. Squire Station Wagon-6P	$3,486	4,042 lbs.	35,595

Note: Total series output was 496,645 units. Six and V-8 production was not documented by Ford Motor Co.

Custom (6 and V-8)

	54B	4-dr. Sedan-6P	$3,288	3,759 lbs.	33,014
---	71B	4-dr. Ranch Wagon-6P	$3,806	4,317 lbs.	13,064

Custom 500 (6 and V-8)

	54D	4-dr. Sedan-6P	$3,418	3,764 lbs.	24,870
---	71D	4-dr. Ranch Wagon-6P	$3,895	4,327 lbs.	16,834

Note: Total series output was 87,782 units. Six and 10-passenger station wagon production was not broken out.

Galaxie 500 (6 and V-8)

	54F	4-dr. Sedan-6P	$3,685	3,826 lbs.	104,167
---	57F	4-dr. Hardtop-6P	$3,720	3,881 lbs.	28,939
---	65F	2-dr. Hardtop-6P	$3,752	3,826 lbs.	80,855
---	71F	4-dr. Country Sedan-6P	$4,028	4,308 lbs.	55,238

Note: Total series output was 269,199 units. Six and 10-passenger station wagon production was not broken out

LTD (V-8)

	53H	4-dr. Sedan-6P	$3,906	3,913 lbs.	104,167
---	57H	4-dr. Hardtop-6P	$3,941	3,908 lbs.	33,742
---	65H	2-dr. Hardtop-6P	$3,898	3,853 lbs.	101,048
---	76H	2-dr. Convertible-6P	$4,073	4,091 lbs.	4,234
---	71H	4-dr. Country Squire-6P	$4,318	4,308 lbs.	121,419

LTD Brougham (V-8)

	53K	4-dr. Sedan-6P	$4,047	3,949 lbs.	36,909
---	57K	4-dr. Hardtop-6P	$4,090	3,944 lbs.	23,364
---	65K	2-dr. Hardtop-6P	$4,050	3,883 lbs.	50,409

Note: Total series output was 475,292 units. Station wagon production was not broken out between six- and 10-passenger models.

Engines:

Pinto Base Four: Overhead cam. Cast-iron block. Displacement: 98 cid. B & S: 3.19 x 3.06 in. Compression ratio: 8.0:1. Net hp: 54 at 4600 rpm. Carburetor: Motorcraft one-barrel. Five main bearings. Code W.

Pinto Optional Four: Overhead cam. Cast-iron block. Displacement: 122 cid. B & S: 3.58 x 3.03 in. Compression ratio: 8.2:1. Net hp: 86 at 5400 rpm. Carburetor: Ford/Weber two-barrel. Five main bearings. Code X.

Maverick Base Six: Overhead valve. Cast-iron block. Displacement: 170 cid. B & S: 3.50 x 2.94 in. Compression ratio: 8.3:1. Net hp: 82 at 4400 rpm. Carburetor: Motorcraft one-barrel. Seven main bearings. Code U.

1972 LTD two-door hardtop with moon roof

Ford Base Six: Overhead valve. Cast-iron block. Displacement: 240 cid. B & S: 4.00 x 3.18 in. Compression ratio: 8.5:1. Net hp: 103 at 3800 rpm. Carburetor: Motorcraft one-barrel. Seven main bearings. Code V.

Torino Base and Maverick Optional Six: Overhead valve. Displacement: 250 cid. B & S: 3.68 x 3.91 in. Compression ratio: 8.0:1. Net hp: 98 at 3400 rpm. Carburetor: Motorcraft one-barrel. Seven main bearings. Code L.

Torino and Gran Torino Base 302 V-8: Overhead valve. Cast-iron block. Displacement: 302 cid. B & S: 4.00 x 3.00 in. Compression ratio: 8.5:1. Net hp: 140 at 4000 rpm. Carburetor: Motorcraft two-barrel. Five main bearings. Code F.

351 "Windsor" V-8: Overhead valve. Cast-iron block. Displacement: 351 cid. B & S: 4.00 x 3.50 in. Compression ratio: 8.3:1. Net hp: 153 at 3800 rpm. Carburetor: Motorcraft two-barrel. Five main bearings.

Torino and Gran Torino Optional V-8, 351 "Cleveland" two-barrel: Overhead valve. Cast iron block. Displacement: 351 cid. B & S: 4.00 x 3.50 in. Compression ratio: 8.6:1. Net hp: 163 at 3800 rpm. Carburetor: Motorcraft two-barrel. Five main bearings. Code H.

Torino and Gran Torino Optional V-8, 351 "Cleveland" four-barrel: Overhead valve. Cast-iron block. Displacement: 351 cid. B & S: 4.00 x 3.50 in. Compression ratio: 8.6:1. Net hp: 248 at 5400 rpm. Carburetor: Holley four-barrel. Five main bearings.

351 HO "Cleveland" V-8: Overhead valve. Cast-iron block. Displacement: 351 cid. B & S: 4.00 x 3.50 in. Compression ratio: 8.6:1. Net hp: 266 at 5400 rpm. Carburetor: Holley four-barrel. Five main bearings. Code Q.

Ford Optional 400 "Cleveland" V-8: Overhead valve. Cast-iron block. Displacement: 400 cid. B & S: 4.00 x 4.00 in. Compression ratio: 8.5:1. Net hp: 172 at 4000 rpm. Carburetor: Motorcraft two-barrel. Five main bearings. Code S.

Ford Optional Thunderbird 429 V-8: Overhead valve. Cast-iron block. Displacement: 429 cid. B & S: 4.36 x 3.59 in. Compression ratio: 8.5:1. Net hp: 212 at 4400 rpm. Carburetor: Motorcraft four-barrel. Five main bearings. Code N.

Thunderbird 460 V-8: Overhead valve. Cast-iron block. Displacement: 460 cid. B & S: 4.36 x 3.85 in. Compression ratio: 8.5:1. Net hp: 224 at 4400 rpm. Carburetor: Motorcraft four-barrel. Five main bearings. Code A.

1972 Torino two-door hardtop

1972 Gran Torino Sport fastback

1972 Gran Torino Squire station wagon

Chassis:

Pinto: Wheelbase: 94 in. Overall length: 163 in. Tires: 6.00 x 13 rayon black sidewall. A78-13, A70-13 and 175-R13 tires were optional.

Maverick: Wheelbase: 103 in. Overall length: 179.4 in. Tires: C78-14 tubeless blackwall, V-8 and 6.45 x 14 tubeless blackwall, six.

Torino and Gran Torino: Wheelbase: 118 in., four-door sedan and 114 in., other models. Overall length: 203.7 in., two-door, 207.3 in., four-door and 211.6 in., station wagon. Tires: E78-14. Torino two-door, F78-14, Gran Torino and Torino four-door and H78-14, station wagons. E70-14, Gran Torino Sport hardtop and F70-14, Gran Torino Sport Sportsroof. All tires were belted black sidewall.

Ford: Wheelbase: 121 in. Overall length: 216.2 in. and 219.2 in., station wagons. Tires: F78-15 belted black sidewall, G78-15, Galaxie 500 and LTD and H78-15, station wagons.

Options:

Pinto: 122-cid, 86-hp overhead cam four ($49). Cruise-O-Matic automatic transmission ($170). AM radio ($59). Chrome window moldings, part of Luxury Decor Group ($137). Wheel covers ($23). White sidewall tires ($42). Other Pinto options in 1972 included air conditioning, a consolette with electric clock, a compass, a rear window

1972 Gran Torino fastback

1972 Maverick four-door sedan

1972 Maverick two-door sedan

1972 Maverick "Grabber" two-door sedan

1972 Maverick two-door sedan with Sprint Décor option

1972 Pinto Runabout two-door hatchback

1972 Pinto two-door sedan

1972 Pinto Runabout two-door hatchback

1972 Pinto Squire station wagon

defogger, vinyl or rubber front and rear floor mats, AM push button radio, an AM/FM radio, a two-way citizen's band radio and a rear speaker. A traveling and camping package included a luggage rack, heavy-duty shock absorbers, a trailer hitch, trailer light wiring harness and mirrors. A protective equipment package included air horns, front and rear bumper guards, a locking gas cap, body moldings, a spotlight, a remote trunk release and wheel covers. Available safety equipment included tot guard child safety seats, a fire extinguisher and an emergency flare kit. Other options included a fog lamp, a fold-down rear seats for the base Pinto, pivoting quarter windows and a day-night rear view mirror.

Maverick: 200-cid six-cylinder ($38). 250-cid six-cylinder ($77). 302-cid V-8 engine. Cruise-O-Matic automatic transmission ($177). AM radio ($59). Power steering ($92). White sidewall tires ($34). Other 1972 Maverick options included a floor-mounted three speed manual shifter, Selectaire air conditioning, rear window defogger, tinted glass, power steering, deluxe seat belts, bumper guards, door edge guards, a heavy duty battery, heavy duty suspension, an electric clock, lockable storage consolette, two-tone paint and a vinyl roof. Packages included the Luxury and Décor group which added a vinyl roof, front and rear bumper guards with color-keyed inserts, C78 x 14 whitewall tires, color keyed wheel covers, remote control left-hand exterior mirror, deluxe gas cap and road lamp inserts outside also added a tan interior with cut pile carpeting, padded door trim panels, all-vinyl seats, reclining front bucket seats and a wood grain appliqué on the instrument panel. The convenience group included a color-keyed left side exterior racing mirror and a day-night inside mirror. The protection group offered such items as black vinyl body moldings and front and rear bumper guards.

Torino and Gran Torino: 351-cid, 163-hp "Cleveland" V-8 ($44). 351-cid, 248-hp "Cleveland" V-8, two-door models only ($127). 429-cid, 205-hp V-8 ($99). Cruise-O-Matic automatic transmission, $21 to $211, depending on engine chosen. Four-speed manual transmission ($200). AM radio ($64). AM/FM stereo radio ($208). Power steering ($112). Power tailgate window on station wagons ($34). Luggage rack on station wagons ($77). Vinyl roof ($93). White sidewall tires ($34).

Ford: 400-cid, 172-hp V-8 ($95). 429-cid, 205-hp V-8 ($222). Power front disc brakes, standard on LTDs ($50). Tinted windshield ($53). Air conditioning ($409). Air conditioning with Climate Control ($486). Cruise Control ($99). AM radio ($64). AM/FM stereo radio ($234). Vinyl roof ($110). Vinyl roof on station wagons ($148). White sidewall tires ($34).

History:

The 1972 Ford line was introduced Sept. 24, 1971. New options for 1972 included electric sliding sunroofs, an electric deck lid release, tailgate power lock and body moldings with vinyl inserts. Sun roofs, which Ford referred to consistently as moon roofs, were installed on 0.6 percent of all 1972 Ford Motor Co products, including Lincolns and Mercurys. Engines were no longer rated at brake horsepower. Beginning in 1972, all engines were rated in SAE net horsepower or the theoretical power, deducting for drain caused by the accessories and transmission. Pollution requirements and rising insurance rates, plus the lower compression ratios, meant considerably restricted performance. As a result, 1971 is almost universally considered to be the end of the Ford muscle car era. The Ford model year output peaked at 1,855,201 vehicles this year. The calendar year production total was counted as 1,868,016 units. Henry Ford II was Ford Motor Co. board chairman and Lee Iacocca was the firm's president. Ford Division (also called Ford Marketing Corp.) was headed by J. B. Naughton, who held the title of vice-president and divisional general manager. The model year 1972 was a sales record-breaker and marked the first time in history that Ford dealers sold more than three million cars and trucks.

1973 Ford

Pinto — Four: The Pinto exterior remained basically the same as in the 1972 model year with the exception of front and rear bumpers. Front bumper guards were made standard equipment this year (but deleted in later years). The new bumper treatment lengthened the Pintos by 1.5 inches. Styles included the two-door or three-door, depending on your preference, Runabout. It had a large rear hatch with gas-operated springs. Other body styles continued to be the original two-door Pinto sedan and the station wagon, in its second year. In 1972, Pinto owners could add a larger four-cylinder engine and could add a limited number of options.

Maverick — 6 and V-8: The Maverick series was basically unchanged from the 1972 models. There was, however, a slightly new appearance up front because of the flatter, reinforced bumper. Standard features on the base Maverick again were the 200-cid six, three-speed manual transmission, 14-inch blackwall tires, cowl air induction, curved side glass with rear quarter flip-style windows on two-door models, recessed door handles, a locking glove box, full-width seats with a random striped cloth and vinyl trim, steel guard rails in the side doors, locking steering column with a key reminder buzzer, uni-lock shoulder and lap belts, sound insulation, color-keyed carpeting and a color-keyed steering wheel.

Torino and Gran Torino — 6 and V-8: The 1973 Torino and Gran Torino models were slightly modified from 1972 specifications. A revised grille had a more rectangular opening than the 1972 version and blended well with the large front bumper. Improvements included larger standard rear brakes, an interior hood release and optional spare tire lock. The Torino models were the base trim level and featured chrome-trimmed windshield, rear window and rain gutter moldings, highback bench seats, all-vinyl seat and door trim, floor mats, hubcaps, a 250-cid six-cylinder engine and three-speed manual transmission. The Torino station wagon also included power front disc brakes and Ford's famous three-way tailgate. The Gran Torino was the top trim level for 1973 and included all the Torino trim plus manual front disc brakes, cloth and vinyl trim on seats and interior door panels, carpeting, lower body, wheel well and deck lid moldings, dual note horns, a trunk mat, a deluxe two-spoke steering wheel and chrome trim on the foot pedals. The Gran Torino Squire station wagon also included the 302-cid, 138-hp V-8, deluxe pleated vinyl interior trim, wheel covers and wood grain appliqués on the body, tailgate and instrument panel. The Gran Torino Sport was the daring version of the Gran Torino and included all the Gran Torino features plus the 302-cid, 138-hp V-8, pleated, all-vinyl trim, hood scoops, color-keyed dual racing mirrors and a unique grille

Ford — V-8: Full-size Fords were restyled for the 1973 model year. The emphasis was placed on a more rounded profile, similar to the Torino series. The "Mercedes" grille was the current craze at Ford Motor Co. and big Fords had their own version, complete with a spring-loaded hood ornament on the high trim-level models. At the rear, two rectangular taillights were used on all models and were similar to those used on the lower-priced lines of the 1972 full-size Fords. The Custom 500 was the base trim level Ford in 1973 and included chrome-trimmed windshield and rear window moldings, nylon carpeting, ignition key warning buzzer, the 351-cid V-8, Cruise-O-Matic automatic transmission, power steering and G78-15 belted black sidewall tires. The Galaxie 500 was the intermediate trim level and included all the Custom 500 features plus lower back panel wheel lip moldings, cloth and vinyl seating surfaces, rocker panel moldings and wood grain appliqués on the instrument panel. The LTD was the top trim level and included all the Galaxie 500 features plus deep-cushioned low-back bench seats, an electric clock, a deluxe two-spoke steering wheel, chrome trim on the foot pedals, polished aluminum trim around the rear edge of the hood, body moldings with vinyl inserts and HR78-15 steel-belted radial tires. The LTD Brougham added Flight-Bench seats with center armrests, front door courtesy lights, full wheel covers, cut-pile carpeting, carpeted lower door panels, polished rocker panel moldings and extensions, an automatic seatback release on two-door models, a vinyl roof and color-keyed seat belts. The Ranch Wagon contained all the features of the Galaxie 500 models plus J78-15 tires. The Country Sedan contained Ranch Wagon features plus a dual note horn, wood grain appliqués on the instrument panel and front and rear door panels, a special sound package, body moldings and a chrome-plated grille. The Country Squires contained all the features found in the LTDs plus J78-15 tires and the 400-cid V-8.

VIN:

The 1973 Ford serial number code was broken down as follows: The first symbol indicated the year: 3 = 1973. The second symbol identified the assembly plant: A = Atlanta, Georgia; B = Oakville, Ontario, Canada, E = Mahwah, New Jersey, F = Dearborn, Michigan, G = Chicago, Illinois, H = Lorain, Ohio, J = Los Angeles, California, K = Kansas City, Missouri; N = Norfolk, Virginia, P = Twin Cities (Minneapolis and St. Paul, Minnesota), R = San Jose, California, S = Allen Park Pilot Plant, T = Metuchen, New Jersey, U = Louisville, Kentucky, W = Wayne, Michigan, X = St. Thomas, Ontario, Canada, Y = Wixom, Michigan and Z = St. Louis, Missouri. The third and fourth symbols identified the body series: 63R=Gran Torino Sport fastback. The fifth symbol identified the engine codes: A=460 V-8, F = 302-cid V-8, H = 351-cid V-8, L = 250-cid six-cylinder, N = 429-cid V-8 with four-barrel carb, Q = 351-cid V-8, R = 351-cid Boss V-8, S = 400-cid V-8, T = 200-cid six-cylinder, W=98-cid four-cylinder and X = 122-cid four-cylinder. The last six digits were the unit's production number, beginning at 100001 and up.

1973 LTD four-door hardtop

The Ford Motor Co. body plate changed slightly in 1973. The VIN was on the left side adjacent to the type, Passenger. Along the bottom were six codes from left to right. The first was the body type code, the same as in the VIN. The second was the color code: 6F=Gold Glow. The third code symbol was the trim: BF= Light Ginger with standard cloth and vinyl bench seat. The fourth code was the transmission: W = C4 automatic. The fifth space was the rear axle with 6 = 3.00:1 ratio. Last was the DSO code which listed one of the 33 U. S. Ford districts 74=Seattle or one of the Ford special codes 84 = Home office reserve.

Escort (Four)

Model No.	Body/ Style No.	Body Type & Seating	Factory Price	Shipping Weight	Production Total
20	61D	2-dr. Pony Hatchback-4P	$6,436	2,180 lbs.	Note 1
21	61D	2-dr. GL Hatchback-4P	$6,801	2,187 lbs.	Note 1
25	58D	4-dr. GL Hatchback-4P	$7,022	2,222 lbs.	Note 1
28	74D	4-dr. GL Station Wagon-4P	$7,312	2,274 lbs.	Note 1
23	61D	2-dr. GT Hatchback-4P	$8,724	2,516 lbs.	Note 1

Note 1: For the model year, a total of 206,729 two-door hatchbacks. 102,187 four-door hatchback sedans, and 65,849 station wagons were built.

Pinto (Four)

---	62B	2-dr. Sedan-4P	$1,997	2,124 lbs.	116,146
---	64B	2-dr. Runabout-4P	$2,120	2,162 lbs.	150,603
---	73B	2-dr. Station Wagon-4P	$2,319	2,397 lbs.	217,763

Note: Total Pinto output was 484,512 units.

Maverick (6)

---	54A	4-dr. Sedan-6P	$2,297	2,737 lbs.	Note 1
---	62A	2-dr. Sedan-6P	$2,240	2,642 lbs.	Note 1
---	62D	2-dr. Grabber sedan-6P	$2,419	2,697 lbs.	Note 1

Maverick (V-8)

---	54A	2-dr. Sedan-6P	$2,419	2,900 lbs.	110,382
---	62A	2-dr. Sedan-6P	$2,362	2,800 lbs.	148,943
---	62D	2-dr. Grabber Sedan-6P	$2,541	2,855 lbs.	32,350

Note: Total Maverick output was 291,675 units.

Torino (6)

---	53B	4-dr. Sedan-6P	$2,701	3,597 lbs.	Note 1
---	65B	2-dr. Hardtop-6P	$2,732	3,528 lbs.	Note 1

Torino (V-8)

---	53B	4-dr. Sedan-6P	$2,796	3,683 lbs.	37,524
---	65B	2-dr. Hardtop-6P	$2,826	3,615 lbs.	28,005
---	71B	4-dr. Station Wagon-6P	$3,198	4,073 lbs.	23,982

Gran Torino (6)

---	53D	4-dr. Sedan-6P	$2,890	3,632 lbs.	Note 1
---	65D	2-dr. Hardtop-6P	$2,921	3,570 lbs.	Note 1

1973 Galaxie 500 four-door pillared hardtop

1973 LTD Brougham two-door hardtop

1973 Gran Torino two-door hardtop

1973 LTD Country Squire station wagon

Gran Torino (V-8)

---	53D	4-dr. Sedan-6P	$2,984	3,719 lbs.	98,404
---	65D	2-dr. Hardtop-6P	$3,015	3,656 lbs.	138,962
---	71D	4-dr. Station Wagon-6P	$3,344	4,096 lbs.	60,738
---	71K	4-dr. Squire Station Wagon-6P	$3,559	4,124 lbs.	40,023
---	63R	2-dr. Sport Fastback-6P	$3,154	3,670 lbs.	51,853
---	65R	2-dr. Sport Hardtop-6P	$3,154	3,652 lbs.	17,090

Gran Torino Brougham (6)

---	53K	4-dr. Sedan-6P	$3,051	3,632 lbs.	------
---	65K	2-dr. Hardtop-6P	$3,071	3,590 lbs.	------

Gran Torino Brougham (V-8)

---	53K	4-dr. Sedan-6P	$3,140	3,719 lbs.	------
---	65K	2-dr. Hardtop-6P	$3,160	3,656 lbs.	------

Note: Torino and Gran Torino series output was 496,581 units. Ford Motor Co. didn't break out six or V-8 installations nor did they break out Gran Torino Broughams. Styles 53B, 53D and 53K were called four-door pillared hardtops in 1973.

Custom 500 (V-8)

---	53D	4-dr. Sedan-6P	$3,606	4,078 lbs.	42,549
---	71D	4-dr. Ranch Wagon-6P	$4,050	4,550 lbs.	22,432

Galaxie 500 (V-8)

---	53F	4-dr. Sedan-6P	$3,771	4,110 lbs.	85,654
---	57F	4-dr. Hardtop-6P	$3,833	4,120 lbs.	25,802
---	65F	2-dr. Hardtop-6P	$3,778	4,059 lbs.	70,808
---	71F	4-dr. Country Sedan-6P	$4,164	4,581 lbs.	51,290

LTD (V-8)

---	53H	4-dr. Sedan-6P	$3,958	4,150 lbs.	122,851
---	57H	4-dr. Hardtop-6P	$4,001	4,160 lbs.	28,608
---	65H	2-dr. Hardtop-6P	$3,950	4,100 lbs.	120,864
---	71H	4-dr. Country Squire-6P	$4,401	4,642 lbs.	142,933

LTD Brougham (V-8)

---	53K	4-dr. Sedan-6P	$4,113	4,179 lbs.	49,553
---	57K	4-dr. Hardtop-6P	$4,103	4,189 lbs.	22,268
---	65K	2-dr. Hardtop-6P	$4,107	4,128 lbs.	68,901

Note: Total series output was 941,054 units. The LTD four-door sedan was called a "pillared hardtop."

Engines:

Pinto Base Four: Overhead cam. Cast-iron block. Displacement: 98 cid. B & S: 3.19 x 3.06 in. Compression ratio: 8.0:1. Net hp: 54 at 4800 rpm. Carburetor: Motorcraft one barrel. Five main bearings. Code W.

Pinto Optional Four: Overhead cam. Cast-iron block. Displacement: 122 cid. B & S: 3.58 x 3.03 in. Compression ratio: 8.2:1. Net hp: 86 at 5400 rpm. Carburetor: Ford/Weber two-barrel. Five main bearings. Code X.

Maverick Base Six: Overhead valve. Cast-iron block. Displacement: 200 cid. B & S: 3.68 x 3.13 in. Compression ratio: 8.3:1. Net hp: 84 at 3800 rpm. Carburetor: Motorcraft single-barrel. Seven main bearings. Code T.

Torino Base and Maverick Optional Six: Overhead valve. Cast-iron block. Displacement: 250 cid. B & S: 3.68 x 3.91 in. Compression ratio: 8.0:1. Net hp: 88 at 3200 rpm. Carburetor: Motorcraft single-barrel. Seven main bearings. Code L.

Torino and Gran Torino Base 302 V-8: Overhead valve. Cast-iron block. Displacement: 302 cid. B & S: 4.00 x 3.00 in. Compression ratio: 8.0:1. Net hp: 135 at 4200 rpm. Carburetor: Motorcraft two-barrel. Five main bearings. Code F.

351 "Windsor" V-8: Overhead valve. Cast-iron block. Displacement: 351 cid. B & S: 4.00 x 3.50 in. Compression ratio: 8.0:1. Net hp: 156 at 3800 rpm. Carburetor: Motorcraft two-barrel. Five main bearings.

1973 Gran Torino Squire station wagon

Torino and Gran Torino 351 "Cleveland" V-8: Overhead valve. Cast-iron block. Displacement: 351 cid. B & S: 4.00 x 3.50 in. Compression ratio: 8.0:1. Net hp: 154 at 4000 rpm. Carburetor: Motorcraft two-barrel. Five main bearings. Code H.

351 "Cobra Jet Cleveland" V-8: Overhead valve. Cast-iron block. Displacement: 351 cid. B & S: 4.00 x 3.50 in. Compression ratio: 8.0:1. Net hp: 266 at 5400 rpm. Carburetor: Holley four-barrel. Five main bearings. Code Q.

Ford Optional 400 "Cleveland" V-8: Overhead valve. Cast-iron block. Displacement: 400 cid. B & S: 4.00 x 4.00 in. Compression ratio: 8.0:1. Net hp: 163 at 3800 rpm. Carburetor: Motorcraft two-barrel. Five main bearings. Code S.

Ford Optional Thunderbird 429 V-8: Overhead valve. Cast-iron block. Displacement: 429 cid. B & S: 4.36 x 3.59 in. Compression ratio: 8.0:1. Net hp: 201 at 4400 rpm. Carburetor: Motorcraft four-barrel. Five main bearings. Code N.

Thunderbird 460 V-8: Overhead valve. Cast-iron block. Displacement: 460 cid. B & S: 4.36 x 3.85 in. Compression ratio: 8.0:1. Net hp: 219 at 4400 rpm. Carburetor: Motorcraft four-barrel. Five main bearings. Code A.

Note: Beginning in 1973, Ford rated each engine with two or three different hp ratings, depending on the model each engine was installed in. We show lowest rating for each engine, except the "460's" highest rating. As body size and weight increased, horsepower ratings increased correspondingly. Most engine ratings varied between one and five horsepower. The 460-cid V-8 varied by 17 hp.

Chassis:

Pinto: Wheelbase: 94 in. Overall length: 163 in. Tires: 6.00 x 13 rayon blackwall. A78-13, A70-13 and 175-R13 tires were optional.

Maverick: Wheelbase: 103 in. Overall length: 179.4 in. Tires: 6.45 x 14 tubeless blackwall and C78-14 tubeless blackwall, V-8.

Torino and Gran Torino: Wheelbase: 114 in., two-door sedan and 118 in., four-door sedan. Overall length: 203.7 in., two-door, 207.3 in., four-door and 211.6 in., station wagons. Tires: E78-14, Torino two-door, F78-14, Gran Torino and Torino four-door and H78-14, station wagons. The Gran Torino Sport hardtop used E70-14 tires while the Gran Torino Sport fastback had size F70-14. All tires were belted blackwalls.

Ford: Wheelbase: 121 in. Overall length: 216.2 in. and 219.2 in., station wagons. Tires: F78-15 belted black sidewall and G78-15, Galaxie 500 and LTD as well as H78-15, station wagons.

Options:

Pinto: 122-cid four ($48.53). Cruise-O-Matic automatic transmission ($170). AM radio ($59). Luxury decor group ($137). Wheel covers ($23). White sidewall tires ($42). Sports accent group with radial whitewall tires, a vinyl roof, lower body paint, wheel covers, bright exterior moldings, cut pile carpeting, deluxe seat and door trim and wood tone accents. Four speed transmission. Convenience group ($18). Manual front disc brakes ($31). Electric rear window defroster ($42). AM/FM stereo radio ($190). Color-keyed racing-style mirrors ($12). Tinted glass, all windows ($36). Flip-style quarter windows ($28). Handling suspension ($12).

1973 Gran Torino Brougham four-door sedan

1973 Gran Torino Sport fastback

1973 Maverick Grabber two-door sedan

1973 Maverick two-door sedan

1973 Maverick four-door sedan

1973 Pinto Squire station wagon

1973 Pinto Runabout hatchback

Maverick: 200-cid six-cylinder engine ($77). 302-cid, 135-hp V-8. Cruise-O-Matic automatic transmission ($177). AM radio ($59). Power steering ($92). White sidewall tires ($33). Luxury décor option with grain vinyl roof, body and wheel well moldings, front and rear bumper guards with rubber inserts, bright pillar appliqué, color-keyed wheel covers, deluxe gas cap and DR78 x 14 steel belted whitewall tires. The Luxury décor interior included reclining seats, tan soft vinyl interior, cut pile carpeting, color-keyed instrument panel with wood tone appliqué, deluxe two-spoke steering wheel, sound package and handling package. Other Maverick options included Selectaire air conditioning, high back bucket seats, an AM/FM stereo radio, a vinyl roof, dual racing mirrors, a rear window defogger, a locking jack, tinted glass, heavy-duty suspension, a heavy-duty battery and varied axle ratios. Additional options included an appearance group with door edge guards and floor mats, a deluxe bumper group and forged aluminum wheels. Floor shifts were available with both the three-speed manual and automatic transmission, the latter with bucket seats as well. Wide oval blackwall or raised-white letter tires also were available.

Torino and Gran Torino: 351-cid, 159-hp "Cleveland" V-8 ($44). 400-cid, 168-hp "Cleveland" V-8 ($127). 429-cid, 197-hp V-8 ($99). Cruise-O-Matic automatic transmission ($211). Four-speed manual transmission ($200). AM radio ($64). AM/FM stereo radio ($206). Power steering ($112). Power tailgate window, station wagons ($34). Luggage racks, station wagons ($77). Vinyl roof ($93). White sidewall tires ($34).

Ford: 400-cid, 172-hp V-8 ($95). 429-cid, 205-hp V-8 ($222). 460-cid, 202-hp V-8 ($222). Power front disc brakes, standard on LTDs ($50). Tinted windshield ($53). Air conditioning ($409). Air conditioning with Climate Control ($486). Cruise Control ($99). AM radio ($64). AM/FM stereo radio ($234). Vinyl roof ($110). Vinyl roof on station wagons ($148). White sidewall tires ($34).

History:

The 1973 Ford line was publicly introduced on Sept. 22, 1972. Highlights for 1973 included the new impact-absorbing bumpers and an increased emphasis on making cars theft and vandal-proof. A new fixed-length radio antenna was adopted along with inside hood release mechanisms. A spare tire lock was a new, extra-cost option. The Ford LTD was honored, by *Motor Trend* magazine, as the "Full-size Sedan of the Year" while *Road Test* magazine called it their "Car of the Year." The full-size Fords were the only models to receive significant restyling. The rest of the Ford lines received only minor trim updating. More federally-mandated safety requirements were initiated. They were reflected in massive "park bench" safety bumpers. These were supposed to tolerate a direct impact at five mph without damage. Pollution standards were tightened. The existing engines were further de-tuned or more emissions control equipment was added. Manufacturers began striving for improved mileage at the expense of performance and efficiency in

1973 Pinto Runabout hatchback

the face of further federal regulations. The Arab embargo of oil products imported from the Middle East also brought fuel economy into the spotlight. Ford Motor Co. executives included Board Chairman Henry Ford II, corporate president Lee Iacocca and Ford Marketing Corp. vice-president and Ford Division general manager B. E. Bidwell.

1974 Ford

Pinto — Four: This was the year that energy-absorbing bumpers were added to the Pinto. This brought an obvious change to the front of the car, as the air slot opening in the gravel pan could no longer be seen. Also eliminated was the center-mounted license plate holder. It didn't look right with the massive new bumper, but then, hardly anything else did either. The bumper was plain on the base trim models, but came with rubber-faced vertical guards and a black vinyl impact strip on models with the Deluxe decor package. Pinto station wagons could be outfitted with optional trim packages that included simulated wood grain exterior paneling and roof luggage racks. The Pinto was now in its third full model year and had weathered questions about its gas tank, which in some cases caught fire when punctured in rear impact collisions. While that controversy cast a shadow of doubt over Ford's small car, newer Pintos, especially the station wagon, were popular and versatile cars, especially with growing families.

Maverick — 6 and V-8: The Maverick had a slight frontal restyling for 1974 as energy-absorbing bumpers were adopted this year. A horizontal slot appeared in the center of the face bar, where the license plate indentation had formerly been positioned. Deluxe models featured side moldings with vinyl inserts; wheel cutout trim moldings and, on cars with vinyl roofs, a Maverick nameplate on the rear roof pillar. On all models, a similar nameplate was carried at the left-hand side of the grille. Again in 1974, Maverick was packaged in base trim as an economy model with its 200-cid six-cylinder engine and three-speed manual transmission. Two-door Mavericks came with such no-nonsense features as a cloth and vinyl bench seat, flip-style rear quarter windows, a heater-defroster, locking glove box and a waiting list of options. The four-door Maverick was much the same. The options available were growing as many members of the Baby Boom generation were buying their first cars and wanted a little customization and personalization for the money. It was the fourth full model year for the Maverick, introduced in April 1969.

Torino and Gran Torino — V-8: New grilles, front bumpers and some optional revisions in roof pillar treatments characterized the 1974 Torino editions. The grille used a finer mesh and was now segmented by seven vertical division bars. The bumper had a slightly more prominent center protrusion. Opera window treatments could be ordered, at extra cost, for a fancier looking coupe. Side trim was revised to eliminate the wide, horizontally ribbed decorative panels used on high-trim models the previous season. The Gran Torino Elite arrived at midyear featuring full-length side trim with vinyl inserts; a chrome center molding across the grille; single headlamps in square bezels and parking lamps notched into the corners of the front fenders.. The Torino was the base trim level and featured windshield, rear window and rain gutter moldings, high back bench seats, vinyl upholstery and trim, floor mats, three-speed manual transmission, HR78-14 tires or G78-14 tires on hardtops and a base 302-cid V-8. The Torino station wagon included power front disc brakes, H78-14 tires and a three-way tailgate. The top-level Gran Torino added manual front disc brakes, cloth and vinyl seat trim, carpeting, lower body, wheel well and deck lid moldings, a dual note horn, deluxe two-spoke steering wheel and chrome foot pedal trim. The Gran Torino Squire station wagon added the deluxe pleated vinyl interior trim, wheel covers, wood grain body appliqués and tailgate trim and plus wood grain dashboard inserts. The Gran Torino Sport included all-vinyl trim, hood scoops, color-keyed dual outside racing mirrors and a unique grille.

1974 Gran Torino Brougham two-door hardtop

1974-1/2 Gran Torino Elite two-door hardtop

Ford — V-8: The full-size Fords were slightly re-trimmed versions of the 1973 restyle. The main difference appeared at the front where extension caps were no longer used on the front fender corners, so that the vertical parking lamp lens was taller than the previous type and had a ribbed appearance. The overall shape of the grille was the same but used finer mesh inserts. The central section was surrounded by a rectangular housing that segmented it from the rest of the grille. This hinted at the trendy "Mercedes-Benz" look. Some called it neo-classical styling. To heighten this image, a stand-up hood ornament was added to high-trim Fords. The Custom 500 was the base trim level and included chrome windshield and rear window moldings, nylon carpeting, an ignition key warning buzzer, power steering, automatic transmission, G78-15 belted black sidewall tires and the 351-cid engine. The intermediate Galaxie 500 added wheel lip moldings, cloth and vinyl seats, rocker panel moldings and instrument panel wood grain appliqués. The top-level LTD featured deep cushioned, low-back bench seats, an electric clock, deluxe two-spoke steering wheel, chrome trim on the foot pedals, polished aluminum trim for the rear hood edge; and HR78-15 steel-belted radial tires. The LTD Brougham came with high back Flight-Bench seats with a center armrest, front door courtesy lights, full wheel covers, cut-pile carpeting and carpeted lower door panels, as well as polished rocker panel moldings, an automatic seatback release in two-door styles, a vinyl roof and color-keyed seat belts. The Ranch Wagon rode on J78-15 tires. The Country Sedan added a dual note horn, wood grain instrument panel appliqué, wood grain front and rear door panel trim, special sound insulation, body moldings and a special chrome-plated grille. The Country Squire came with J78-15 tires and the 400-cid V-8.

VIN:

The 1974 Ford serial number code was broken down as follows: The first symbol indicated the year: 4 = 1974. The second symbol identified the assembly plant: A = Atlanta, Georgia; B = Oakville, Ontario, Canada; E = Mahwah, New Jersey, F = Dearborn, Michigan, G = Chicago, Illinois, H = Lorain, Ohio, J = Los Angeles, California, K = Kansas City, Missouri; N = Norfolk, Virginia, P = Twin Cities (Minneapolis and St. Paul, Minnesota), R = San Jose, California, S = Allen Park Pilot Plant, T = Metuchen, New Jersey, U = Louisville, Kentucky, W = Wayne, Michigan, X = St. Thomas, Ontario, Canada, Y = Wixom, Michigan and Z = St. Louis, Missouri. The third and fourth symbols identified the body series: 73B=Pinto station wagon. The fifth symbol identified the engine codes: A=460 V-8, F = 302-cid V-8, H = 351-cid V-8, L = 250-cid six-cylinder, Q = 351-cid Cobra Jet V-8, S = 400-cid V-8, T = 200-cid six-cylinder, X = 122-cid four-cylinder and Y=139-cid four. The last six digits were the unit's production number, beginning at 100001 and up.

Pinto

Model No.	Body/Style No.	Body Type & Seating	Factory Price	Shipping Weight	Production Total
---	62B	2-dr. Sedan-4P	$2,527	2,372 lbs.	132,061
---	64B	2-dr. Hatchback-4P	$2,631	2,402 lbs.	174,754
---	73B	2-dr. Station Wagon-4P	$2,771	2,576 lbs.	237,394

Note: Total Pinto output was 544,209 units. The two-door hatchback coupe was called the Runabout.

Maverick (6)

---	54A	4-dr. Sedan-6P	$2,824	2,851 lbs.	Note 1
---	62A	2-dr. Sedan-6P	$2,742	2,739 lbs.	Note 1
---	62A	2-dr. Grabber sedan-6P	$2,923	2,787 lbs.	Note 1

Maverick (V-8)

---	54A	4-dr. Sedan-6P	$2,982	3,014 lbs.	137,728
---	62A	2-dr. Sedan-6P	$2,949	2,902 lbs.	139,818
---	62A	2-dr. Grabber sedan-6P	$3,081	2,950 lbs.	23,502

Note: Total Maverick output was 301,048 units. Ford Motor Co. did not break out six and V-8 production.

Torino

---	53B	4-dr. Sedan-6P	$3,176	3,793 lbs.	31,161
---	65B	2-dr. Hardtop-6P	$3,310	3,509 lbs.	22,738
---	71B	4-dr. Station Wagon-6P	$3,755	4,175 lbs.	15,393

Gran Torino

---	53D	4-dr. Sedan (Pillared HT)-6P	$3,391	3,847 lbs.	72,728
---	65D	2-dr. Hardtop-6P	$3,485	3,647 lbs.	76,290
---	71D	4-dr. Station Wagon-6P	$3,954	4,209 lbs.	29,866

Gran Torino Sport and Squire

---	71K	4-dr. Squire Station Wagon-6P	$4,237	4,250 lbs.	22,837
---	65R	2-dr. Sport Hardtop-5P	$3,761	3,771 lbs.	23,142

Gran Torino Brougham

---	53K	4-dr. Sedan (Pillared HT)-6P	$3,903	3,887 lbs.	11,464
---	65K	2-dr. Hardtop-5P	$3,912	3,794 lbs.	26,402

Gran Torino Elite

---	65M	2-dr. Hardtop-6P	$4,374	4,092 lbs.	96,604

Note: Total series output was 426,086 units. Styles 53D and 53K were called four-door pillared hardtops.

Custom 500

---	53D	4-dr. Sedan-6P	$3,911	4,180 lbs.	128,941
---	71D	4-dr. Ranch Wagon-6P	$4,417	4,654 lbs.	12,104

Galaxie 500

---	53F	4-dr. Sedan (Pillared HT)-6P	$4,093	4,196 lbs.	49,661
---	57F	4-dr. Hardtop-6P	$4,166	4,212 lbs.	11,526
---	65F	2-dr. Hardtop-6P	$4,140	4,157 lbs.	34,214
---	71F	4-dr. Country Sedan-6P	$4,513	4,690 lbs.	22,400

LTD

---	53H	4-dr. Sedan (Pillared HT)-6P	$4,299	4,262 lbs.	72,251
---	57H	4-dr. Hardtop-6P	$4,367	4,277 lbs.	12,375
---	65H	2-dr. Hardtop-6P	$4,318	4,215 lbs.	73,296
---	71H	4-dr. Country Squire-6P	$4,827	4,742 lbs.	64,047

LTD Brougham

---	53K	4-dr. Sedan (Pillared HT)-6P	$4,576	4,292 lbs.	30,203
---	57K	4-dr. Hardtop-6P	$4,646	4,310 lbs.	11,371
---	65K	2-dr. Hardtop-6P	$4,598	4,247 lbs.	39,084

Note: Total full-size Ford output was 519,916 units. Styles 53F, 53H and 53K were called four-door pillared hardtops. An LTD station wagon was offered but there are production numbers available for it.

Engines:

Pinto Base Four: Overhead cam. Cast-iron block. Displacement: 122 cid. B & S: 3.58 x 3.03 in. Compression ratio: 8.2:1. Net hp: 86 at 5400 rpm. Carburetor: Ford/Weber two-barrel. Five main bearings. Code X.

Pinto Optional Four: Overhead cam. Cast-iron block. Displacement: 139 cid. B & S: 3.78 x 3.13 in. Compression ratio: 8.6:1. Net hp: 80. Carburetor: Motorcraft two-barrel. Five main bearings. Code Y.

Maverick Base Six: Overhead valve. Cast-iron block. Displacement: 200 cid. B & S: 3.68 x 3.13 in. Compression ratio: 8.3:1. Net hp: 84 at 3800 rpm. Carburetor: Motorcraft one-barrel. Seven main bearings. Code T.

Maverick Optional Six: Overhead valve. Cast-iron block. Displacement: 250 cid. B & S: 3.68 x 3.91 in. Compression ratio: 8.0:1. Net hp: 91 at 3200 rpm. Carburetor: Motorcraft one-barrel. Seven main bearings. Code L.

Base Torino and Maverick Optional 302 V-8: Overhead valve. Cast-iron block. Displacement: 302 cid. B & S: 4.00 x 3.00 in. Compression ratio: 8.0:1. Net hp: 140 at 3800 rpm. Carburetor: Motorcraft two-barrel. Five main bearings. Code F.

Torino and Gran Torino Optional 351 "Cleveland" V-8: Overhead valve. Cast-iron block. Displacement: 351 cid. B & S: 4.00 x 3.50

1974 LTD four-door pillared hardtop

1974 Maverick four-door sedan with Luxury package

in. Compression ratio: 8.0:1. Net hp: 162 at 4000 rpm. Carburetor: Motorcraft two-barrel. Five main bearings. Code H.

Torino and Gran Torino Optional 351 "Cobra Jet Cleveland" Four-Barrel V-8: Overhead valve. Cast-iron block. Displacement: 351 cid. B & S: 4.00 x 3.50 in. Compression ratio: 7.9:1. Net hp: 255 at 5600 rpm. Carburetor: Motorcraft four-barrel. Five main bearings. Code Q.

Ford, Torino and Gran Torino Optional 400 V-8: Overhead valve. Cast-iron block. Displacement: 400 cid. B & S: 4.00 x 4.00 in. Compression ratio: 6.0:1. Net hp: 170 at 3400 rpm. Carburetor: Motorcraft two-barrel. Five main bearings. Code S.

Ford, Torino and Gran Torino Optional Thunderbird 460 V-8: Overhead valve. Cast-iron block. Displacement: 460 cid. B & S: 4.36 x 3.85 in. Compression ratio: 8.0:1. Net hp: 220 at 4000 rpm and 215 hp when used in other Ford products. Carburetor: Carter four-barrel. Five main bearings. Code A.

Chassis:

Pinto: Wheelbase: 94.2 inches. Overall length: 169 in and 179 in., station wagon. Tires: 6.00 x 13 and A78-13, station wagon.

Maverick: Wheelbase: 103 in., two-door and 109.9 in., four-door. Overall length: 187 in., two-door and 194 in., four-door. Tires: 6.45 x 14, two-door, C78-14, four door and D70-14, Grabber.

Torino: Wheelbase: 114 in., two-door and 118 in., four-door. Overall length: 212 in., two-door, 216 in., four-door and 222 in., station wagon. Tires: G78-14 belted blackwall on hardtops and H78-14 on other models.

Ford: Wheelbase: 121 in. Overall length: 223 in. and 226 in., station wagons. Tires: G78-15 belted blackwalls, Custom 500, HR78-15 steel-belted radials on LTD and J78-15 belted blackwall tires on station wagons.

Options:

Pinto: 140-cid, 90-hp four ($52). Cruise-O-Matic transmission ($212). AM radio ($61). AM/FM stereo radio ($222). Luxury Decor Group ($137). Full wheel covers ($23). Forged aluminum wheels ($154). White sidewall tires ($44). Vinyl top ($83). Air conditioning ($383). Squire station wagon package ($241).

Maverick: 250-cid six ($42). 302-cid, 140-hp V-8 ($122). Cruise-O-Matic transmission ($212). AM radio ($61). Power steering ($106). White sidewall tires ($33). Vinyl top ($83). Air conditioning ($383). Luxury Decor Group, except Grabber ($332). Leather-wrapped steering wheel. High back bucket seats. Dual color-keyed outside mirrors. Heavy-duty suspension. Heavy-duty battery. Bumper guards with rubber inserts. Metallic glow paints. Manual front disc brakes. Three-speed manual floor shifter with 200-cid six, 302-V-8 and on cars with bucket seats or the Luxury décor option. Option packages included the Protection, Convenience, Deluxe bumper, Exterior décor and Light groups. There also was an all-vinyl seat trim option that was standard on the Grabber and optional on the base two and four-door Mavericks. It was available in Black, Blue Avocado or Tan. Steel-belted radials. Wide-oval tires with raised white letters, standard on Grabber. Steel belted whitewall radial tires. Trim rings and hub caps, standard on Grabber. Forged aluminum wheels.

1974 Pinto Runabout with Luxury package

Torino: 351-cid, 162-hp "Cleveland" V-8 ($46). 400-cid, 170-hp V-8 ($140). 460-cid, 215-hp V-8 ($245). 351 cid, 225-hp "Cleveland" four-barrel V-8 ($132). Cruise-O-Matic transmission; with small V-8 ($219) and with 460 V-8 ($241). AM radio ($67). AM/FM stereo radio ($217). Power steering ($117). Power disc brakes, station wagons and standard on other Torinos ($71). Power tailgate window ($35). Station wagon luggage rack ($80). Vinyl roof ($96). White sidewall tires ($33). Station wagon third passenger seat ($67). Moon roof ($490). AM/FM stereo radio with tape player ($378).

Ford: 400-cid, 170-hp V-8, standard in Country Squire ($94). 460-cid, 215-hp V-8 ($304). Tinted glass ($55). Air conditioning ($426). Climate Control air conditioning ($506). Cruise Control ($103). AM radio ($67). AM/FM radio ($243). Vinyl roof on passenger cars ($115). Vinyl roof on station wagons ($148). Vinyl roof on LTD Brougham, standard. White sidewall tires ($33). AM/FM stereo with tape player ($378). Power seats ($106). Power windows ($134). Moon roof ($516). Country Squire Brougham option ($202). Country Squire Luxury package option ($545). Brougham Luxury Package option ($380).

Note: Cruise-O-Matic automatic transmission and power front disc brakes were standard on Torino station wagons. Automatic transmission, power steering and power front disc brakes were standard on the LTD, Custom 500, Galaxie and Thunderbird. Air conditioning, power windows and an AM radio were also standard in Thunderbirds.

History:

Ford's 1974 model year resulted in 1,843,340 assemblies, including Falcon Club Wagons. Calendar year output was 1,716,975 units again including the Falcon Club Wagon. More federally mandated safety requirements were initiated, primarily in the form of massive rear 'safety' bumpers designed to withstand direct impact, at five mph, without damage. When combined with the front safety bumpers adopted in 1973, the weight of a typical car was up nearly 350 pounds! Pollution standards were also further tightened, which, when combined with the weight increases, made 1974 models generally more sluggish than any available in the recent past. Model year declines of 130,000 units were caused by lagging buyer interest in the larger Fords and Thunderbirds.

1975 Ford

Pinto — 4 and V-6: Changes to the Pinto were minor for 1975. There was little reason to make many changes since the Pinto's good fuel economy was helping to sell the car. The optional 2.8-liter V-6 was available only with Cruise-O-Matic transmission and that combination only in the hatchback and station wagon. Perhaps those limitations made a healthy 84 percent of Pinto buyers avoid it in what would have been a landslide in an election. The unpopular V-6 received only 16 percent of the "vote" of buyers. New accessories for the Pinto included power steering, power front disc brakes and a fuel-economy warning light. The bulwark of the Pinto line was the standard 2.3-liter inline four-cylinder engine, usually equipped with either a four-speed manual or a three-speed automatic transmission.

Maverick — 6 and V-8: Originally scheduled to be replaced by the new Granada, the Maverick's existence was extended after the energy scare of 1973 and 1974. The sedans and the sporty Grabber featured refinements to interior and exterior trim and also had thicker, cut-pile carpeting, a deluxe steering wheel plus the customary 200-cid base six and three-speed manual transmission. Ford block lettering was added along the hood lip and the width of the center slot in the front bumper was slightly decreased. New options included power disc brakes and a deck lid-mounted luggage rack. A catalytic converter was required with the base engine, while the optional 250-cid six or 302-cid V-8 came without the converters. Radial tires were also added to the regular equipment list. Buyers were given a choice of blue, black or tan interior

1975 LTD Landau two-door hardtop coupe with opera windows

1975 Gran Torino Brougham four-door sedan

1975 Elite two-door hardtop

combinations plus a new, light green trim. The base Maverick and more upscale Grabber continued their basic features while more options were available in 1975.

Granada — 6 and V-8: Ford referred to the Granada as a "precision-sized" compact car. Using the four-door platform of the humble Maverick, the Granada emphasized a more upscale look and feel. It came as a two-door coupe and four-door sedan. The luxury inspired styling was heavily influenced by European design themes. Even as a base model, it was quite elegant among cars in its class. The super-rich Ghia-optioned Granada went a step further where luxury was concerned. The 200-cid inline six was the base Granada power plant and was mated with a three-speed manual gearbox. Ghias came standard with a 250-cid inline six, digital clock, deluxe sound package and a wide range of seating surfaces. The base model could be ordered with the bigger six. Two-barrel 302-cid or 351-cid V-8s were offered in both levels. Dealer sales of Granadas in the United States peaked at 241,297 cars, cutting into the popularity of the Mustang II.

Torino, Gran Torino and Elite — V-8: The Torino was the same as the previous year. Torino models were the base trim level and featured chrome-trimmed windshield, rear widow and rain gutter moldings, high back bench seats, all-vinyl seat and door trim, floor mats, hubcaps, a 302-cid V-8 and three-speed manual transmission. The Torino station wagon included power front disc brakes and Ford's three-way tailgate. The 1975 Gran Torino was the intermediate trim level and included manual front disc brakes, cloth and vinyl trim on seats and interior door panels plus carpeting, lower body, wheel well and deck lid moldings, a dual note horn, a trunk mat, deluxe two-spoke steering wheel and chrome trim on the foot pedals. The Gran Torino Squire station wagon used the 351-cid, 148-hp V-8, Cruise-O-Matic automatic transmission, deluxe pleated vinyl interior trim, wheel covers and wood grain appliqués on the body, tailgate and instrument panel. The top level Gran Torino Brougham also had power front disc brakes, power steering; cloth seats, body moldings and a padded vinyl top. The Elite continued to offer its 1974 features for another year.

Ford — V-8: The Custom 500 was the base trim level Ford and it included chrome-trimmed windshield and rear window moldings, nylon carpeting, an ignition key warning buzzer, the 351-cid V-8 engine, Cruise-O-Matic automatic transmission, power steering and G78-15 belted blackwall tires. The LTD included wheel lip moldings, cloth and vinyl seating surfaces, rocker panel moldings and wood grain appliqués on the instrument panel. The top level LTD Brougham had deep-cushioned low back bench seats, an electric clock, deluxe two-spoke steering wheel, chrome trim on the foot pedals, polished aluminum

1975 Maverick two-door sedan

1975 Pinto Runabout two-door hatchback

trim around the rear edge of the hood, body moldings with vinyl inserts and HR78-15 steel-belted radial tires. The LTD Landau added high back Flight Bench seats with center armrests and front door courtesy lights, full wheel covers, cut-pile carpeting, carpeted lower door panels, polished rocker panel moldings, automatic seatback release on two-door models, a vinyl roof and color-keyed seat belts. The Ranch Wagon rode on JR78-15 steel-belted radial tires. The Country Sedan added a dual note horn, wood grain appliqués on the instrument panel and front and rear door panels, a special sound package, body moldings and a chrome-plated grille. The Country Squires added JR78-15 steel-belted radial tires and the 400-cid V-8.

VIN:

The 1975 Ford serial number code was broken down as follows: The first symbol indicated the year: 5 = 1975. The second symbol identified the assembly plant: A = Atlanta, Georgia; B = Oakville, Ontario, Canada, E = Mahwah, New Jersey, F = Dearborn, Michigan, G = Chicago, Illinois, H = Lorain, Ohio, J = Los Angeles, California, K = Kansas City, Missouri; P = Twin Cities (Minneapolis and St. Paul, Minnesota), R = San Jose, California, S = Allen Park Pilot Plant, T = Metuchen, New Jersey, U = Louisville, Kentucky, W = Wayne, Michigan, X = St. Thomas, Ontario, Canada, Y = Wixom, Michigan and Z = St. Louis, Missouri. The third and fourth symbols identified the body series: 66K=Granada Ghia two-door. The fifth symbol identified the engine codes: A=460 V-8, F = 302-cid V-8, H = 351-cid V-8, L = 250-cid six-cylinder, S = 400-cid V-8, T = 200-cid six-cylinder, Y= 139-cid four and Z=169-cid V-6. The last six digits were the unit's production number, beginning at 100001 and up.

Pinto (Four)

Model No.	Body/ Style No.	Body Type & Seating	Factory Price	Shipping Weight	Production Total
---	64B	2-dr. Hatchback-4P	$2,967	2,528 lbs.	Note 1
---	73B	2-dr. Station Wagon-4P	$3,094	2,692 lbs.	Note 1

Pinto (V-6)

---	62B	2-dr. Sedan-4P	$2,769	2,495 lbs.	64,081
---	64B	2-dr. Hatchback-4P	$3,220	2,710 lbs.	68,919
---	73B	2-dr. Station Wagon-4P	$3,347	2,874 lbs.	90,763

Note: Total Pinto output was 223,763 units. Ford Motor Co. did not break out the four and V-6 production for the Pinto.

Maverick (Six)

---	54A	4-dr. Sedan-6P	$3,025	2,820 lbs.	Note 1
---	62A	2-dr. Sedan-6P	$3,061	2,943 lbs.	Note 1
---	62D	2-dr. Grabber-6P	$3,224	2,827 lbs.	Note 1

Maverick (V-8)

---	54A	4-dr. Sedan-6P	$3,147	2,971 lbs.	90,695
---	62A	2-dr. Sedan-6P	$3,183	3,094 lbs.	63,404
---	62D	2-dr. Grabber-6P	$3,346	2,979 lbs.	8,473

Note: Total Maverick output was 162,572 units. Ford Motor Co. did not break out production numbers among six and V-8 editions,

Granada (Six)

---	54H	4-dr. Sedan-6P	$3,756	3,293 lbs.	Note 1
---	66H	2-dr. Sedan-6P	$3,698	3,230 lbs.	Note 1

Granada (V-8)

---	54H	4-dr. Sedan-6P	$3,784	3,355 lbs.	118,168
---	66H	2-dr. Sedan-6P	$3,826	3,306 lbs.	100,810

Granada Ghia (Six)

---	54K	4-dr. Sedan-6P	$4,240	3,361 lbs.	Note 1
---	66K	2-dr. Sedan-6P	$4,182	3,311 lbs.	Note 1

Granada Ghia (V-8)

---	54K	4-dr. Sedan-6P	$4,326	3,423 lbs.	43,652
---	66K	2-dr. Sedan-6P	$4,268	3,373 lbs.	40,028

Note: Total Granada output was 302,649 units. Ford Motor Co. did not break out production numbers among six and V-8 editions,

Torino

---	53B	4-dr. Sedan-6P	$3,957	4,059 lbs.	22,928
---	65B	2-dr. Opera Window Coupe-6P	$3,954	3,987 lbs.	13,394
---	71B	4-dr. Station Wagon-6P	$4,336	4,412 lbs.	13,291

Gran Torino

---	53D	4-dr. Sedan-6P	$4,258	4,090 lbs.	53,161
---	65D	2-dr. Opera Window Coupe-6P	$4,234	3,998 lbs.	35,324
---	71D	4-dr. Station Wagon-6P	$4,593	4,456 lbs.	23,951

Torino Brougham

---	53K	4-dr. Sedan-6P	$4,791	4,163 lbs.	5,929
---	65K	2-dr. Opera Window Coupe-6P	$4,759	4,087 lbs.	4,849

Torino Sport

---	65R	2-dr. Sport Hardtop-5P	$4,744	4,044 lbs.	5,126

Elite

---	65M	2-dr. Hardtop-6P	$4,721	4,160 lbs.	123,372

Note: Total Torino, Gran Torino and Elite production was 318,482 units.

Custom 500

---	53D	4-dr. Sedan-6P	$4,380	4,377 lbs.	31,043
---	71D	4-dr. Ranch Wagon-6P	$4,970	4,787 lbs.	6,930

LTD

---	53H	4-dr. Sedan-6P	$4,615	4,408 lbs.	82,382
---	60H	2-dr. Opera Window Coupe-6P	$4,656	4,359 lbs.	47,432
---	71H	4-dr. Country Sedan-6P	$5,061	4,803 lbs.	22,935

LTD Brougham

---	53K	4-dr. Sedan-6P	$5,016	4,419 lbs.	32,327
---	60K	2-dr. Opera Window Coupe-6P	$5,050	4,391 lbs.	24,005
---	71K	4-dr. Country Squire-6P	$5,340	4,845 lbs.	41,550

LTD Landau

---	53L	4-dr. Sedan-6P	$5,370	4,446 lbs.	32,506
---	60L	2-dr. Opera Window Coupe-6P	$5,401	4,419 lbs.	26,919

Note: Total full-size Ford output was 348,029 units.

Engines:

Pinto Base Four: Overhead cam. Cast-iron block. Displacement: 139 cid. B & S: 3.78 x 3.13 in. Compression ratio: 8.6:1. Net hp: 83. Carburetor: Motorcraft two-barrel. Five main bearings. Code Y.

Pinto Optional V-6: Overhead valve. Cast-iron block. Displacement: 169 cid. B & S: 3.50 x 2.70 in. Compression ratio: 8.0:1. Net hp: 97. Carburetor: Holley two-barrel. Four main bearings. Code Z.

Maverick Base Six: Overhead valve. Cast-iron block. Displacement: 200 cid. B & S: 3.68 x 3.13 in. Compression ratio: 8.3:1. Net hp: 75 at 3200 rpm. Carburetor: Motorcraft one-barrel. Seven main bearings. Code T.

Granada Base and Maverick Optional Six: Overhead valve. Cast-iron block. Displacement: 250 cid. B & S: 3.68 x 3.91 in. Compression ratio: 8.0:1. Net hp: 72 at 2900 rpm. Carburetor: Motorcraft one-barrel. Seven main bearings. Code L.

Torino, Gran Torino and Elite Base 302 V-8: Overhead valve. Cast-iron block. Displacement: 302 cid. Bore and stroke: 4.00 x 3.00 in. Compression ratio: 8.0:1. Net hp: 129 at 3800 rpm. Carburetor: Motorcraft two-barrel. Five main bearings. Code F.

Torino, Gran Torino and Elite Optional 351 "Modified" V-8: Overhead valve. Cast-iron block. Displacement: 351 cid. B & S: 4.00 x

1975 Granada Ghia four-door sedan

1975 Granada four-door sedan

1975 Granada Ghia two-door hardtop

3.50 in. Compression ratio: 8.0:1. Net hp: 148 at 3800 rpm. Carburetor: Motorcraft two-barrel. Five main bearings. Code H.

Ford and Torino, Gran Torino and Elite Optional 400 V-8: Overhead valve. Cast-iron block. Displacement: 400 cid. B & S: 4.00 x 4.00 in. Compression ratio: 8.0:1. Net hp: 158 at 3800 rpm. Carburetor: Motorcraft two-barrel. Five main bearings. Code S.

Ford and Torino, Gran Torino and Elite Optional Thunderbird 460 V-8: Overhead valve. Cast-iron block. Displacement: 460 cid. B & S: 4.36 x 3.65 in. Compression ratio: 8.0:1. Net hp: 218 at 4000 rpm. Carburetor: Motorcraft four-barrel. Five main bearings. Code A.

Chassis:

Pinto: Wheelbase: 94.4 in. and 94.7 in., station wagons. Overall length: 169 in. and 179 in., station wagons. Tires: BR78-13B.

Maverick: Wheelbase: 103 in., two-door and 109.9 in., four-door. Overall length: 187 in., two-door and 194 in., four-door Tires: BR78-14m two-door, CR78-14, four-door and DR70-14, Grabber.

Granada: Wheelbase: 109.9 in. Overall length: 198 in. and 200 in., Ghia. Tires: DR78-14 and ER78-14, Ghia four-door.

Torino, Gran Torino and Elite: Wheelbase: 114.0 in., Torino and Elite and 118.0 in., station wagon. Overall length: 216.0 in., Elite, 217.6 in., Torino and 222.6 in., wagons. Tires: HR78 x 14, Torino and XR78 x 15, Elite.

Ford: Wheelbase: 121 in. Overall length: 224 in. and 226 in., station wagon. Tires: HR78-15.

Options:

Pinto: 169-cid V-6 ($229). Cruise-O-Matic automatic transmission ($212). AM radio ($61). AM/FM stereo radio ($222). Luxury Decor Group ($137). Forged aluminum wheels ($154). White sidewall tires ($33).

Maverick: 302-cid, 129-hp V-8. Cruise-O-Matic automatic transmission ($212). AM radio ($61). Power steering ($106). Luxury decor package ($392). White sidewall tires ($33). Appearance and comfort package. Also packages for the interior, lights, exterior, security and convenience. Selectaire air conditioning. Leather-wrapped steering wheel. AM/FM HiFi stereo. Tinted glass. Metallic glow paint. Power front disc brakes. Space saver spare tire.

Granada: 302-cid, 129-hp V-8 ($85). 351-cid, 143-hp V-8 engine. Cruise-O-Matic automatic transmission ($222). Power steering ($106). Power brakes ($45). AM radio ($61). AM/FM stereo radio ($222). Vinyl roof ($83). Air conditioning ($426). White sidewall tires ($33).

Torino, Gran Torino and Elite: 400-cid, 158-hp V-8 ($54). 460-cid, 218-hp V-8 ($245). AM radio ($67). AM/FM stereo radio ($217). Power steering ($117). Power front disc brakes ($71) and standard on station wagons. Power tailgate window, station wagons ($35). Luggage rack, station wagons ($80). Vinyl top ($96). Air conditioning ($426). White sidewall tires ($33).

Ford: 400-cid, 158-hp V-8 ($94) and standard on Country Squires. 460-cid, 218-hp V-8 ($304). Tinted glass ($55). Air conditioning ($426). Climate Control air conditioning ($506). Cruise control ($103). AM radio ($67). AM/FM stereo radio ($243). Vinyl roof ($115), Vinyl roof on station wagons ($148), Vinyl roof, standard on LTD Landau. White sidewall tires ($33).

History:

The 1975 Ford line was introduced Sept. 27, 1974. Model year sales, by United States dealers, included 282,130 Pintos, 142,964 Mavericks, 241,297 Granadas, 158,798 Torinos, 102,402 Elites, 297,655 LTDs and 37,216 Thunderbirds. The production of 1975 Ford models, in U.S. factories, hit 1,302,205 cars. Calendar year production of Fords, in this country, peaked at 1,302,644 units. The big Fords were attractively face lifted with the addition of a larger Mercedes-style grille and new taillights. The most significant change occurred with the two-door hardtop model. The true pillarless hardtop was replaced by a coupe with fixed quarter windows and large opera windows. The Granada was a new intermediate size car offered in four-door sedan and two-door

sedan versions. As Ford was proud to point out, the four-door had more than a passing resemblance to the Mercedes-Benz. Granadas could be fitted with options that created anything from a taxi to a mini-limousine. They came powered by engines ranging from the sedate 250-cid six-cylinder to the 351-cid V-8, the latter making it one of the fastest Fords. Pollution standards were stiffened once again and, in 1975, all cars were required to burn unleaded gasoline. The majority of the new models came with catalytic converters on the exhaust systems, to help reduce emissions and contaminates. Top executives influencing Ford Division policy were Henry Ford II, Lee Iacocca and B.E. Bidwell. It was the final season for the long-lasting Custom 500 nameplate.

1976 Ford

Pinto — Four and V-6: Ford's subcompact, introduced in 1971, had a new front-end look this year. Appearance changes included a new argent-painted egg-crate grille of one-piece corrosion-resistant plastic, bright bezels for the single round headlamps, bright front lip hood molding, and "Ford" block letters centered above the grille. That new grille was peaked and angled forward slightly, with a tighter crosshatch pattern than before, and held square inset parking lamps. Backup lights were integral with the horizontal tail lamps. Bodies held front and rear side marker lights. For the first time, standard interiors had a choice of all vinyl or sporty cloth-and-vinyl. Four new interior trim fabrics were offered, along with a new bright red interior color. Three four-passenger bodies were offered: two-door sedan, "three-door" Runabout hatchback, and two-door wagon. Wagons had flip-out rear compartment windows and a lift gate-open warning light, as well as tinted glass. Major fuel economy improvements resulted from catalysts, new carburetor calibrations, and a lower (3.18:1) rear axle ratio with the standard 140 cid (2.3-liter) OHC four and fully synchronized four-speed manual gearbox with floor shift lever. Pinto had front disc/rear drum brakes, rack-and-pinion steering, and unibody construction. New this year was a low-budget Pony MPG two-door, wearing minimal chrome trim and plain hubcaps. It had new calibrations for the 2.3-liter engine and a 3.00:1 axle ratio. Pinto standard equipment included a heater/defroster with DirectAire ventilation, bucket seats, mini-console, inside hood release, dome light, glove box, dual padded sun visors, and B78x13 tires. Runabouts and wagons had a fold-down back seat and deluxe seatbelts. Runabouts had a carpeted load area. A new Squire option for Runabouts added simulated wood grain vinyl paneling on body side and the lower back panel, similar to the Squire wagon. Squire also displayed bright surround and B-pillar moldings as well as belt, drip and window frame moldings.

Maverick — Six and V-8: Initially scheduled for disappearance when the new Granada arrived in 1975, Maverick hung on as concern about the fuel crisis continued. This year's grille was a forward-slanting horizontal-bar design, split into two sections by a center vertical divider bar. Rectangular park/signal lamps were mounted in the bright argent plastic grille and backup lights integral with the tail lamps. Single round headlamps continued. The front bumper held twin slots, and the hood showed a sculptured bulge. Front disc brakes were now standard. The base engine was the 200-cid (3.3-liter) inline six with one-barrel carburetor. Options were a 250-cid six or the 302 V-8. All three came with either three-speed manual or automatic transmissions. Maverick's fuel tank had grown from 16 to 19.2 gallons during the 1975 model year.

1976 Pinto Squire hatchback coupe

1976 Pinto Stallion hatchback

Gas mileage was improved with a rear axle ratio at 2.79:1, recalibrating engines and adding back-pressure modulation on the EGR system. Standard equipment included fully-synchronized three-speed column shift, C78 x 14 bias-ply tires, hubcaps, ventless windows with curved glass, front/rear side marker lights. The Maverick had a European-type armrest with door pull assist handle, and lockable glove box. A padded instrument panel held two round cluster pods for gauges. Standard bench seats were trimmed in Random stripe cloth and vinyl. Two-doors had a flipper rear quarter window.

Granada — Six and V-8: For 1976, Granada's fuel economy improved and the "precision-size" compact held a new standard vinyl bench seat and door trim. On each side of the single round headlamps were small, bright vertical sections patterned like the grille. Wide-spaced "Ford" letters stood above the grille. On the fender extensions were wraparound front parking lights and signal/marker lenses. Hoods held a stand-up ornament. Each wraparound tri-color horizontal-style tail lamp was divided into an upper and lower section, with integral side marker lights. Backup lamps sat inboard of the tail lamps. Sporting a tall, squared-off roofline and European-influenced design, the five-passenger Granada strongly resembled a Mercedes up front. Ford bragged: "Its looks and lines remind you of the Mercedes 280 and the Cadillac Seville." Bodies featured bright wraparound bumpers, plus bright moldings on windshield, backlight, drip rail, door belt, doorframe, and wheel lip. Two-door Granadas had distinctive opera windows. Four-doors had a bright center pillar molding with color-keyed insert. Two- and four-door sedans were offered, in base or Ghia trim. Standard equipment included a three-speed manual transmission, front disc/rear drum brakes, heater/defroster, inside hood release. DR78 x 14 black wall steel-belted radials, anti-theft decklid lock, buried walnut wood tone instrument panel appliqués, a locking glove box, two rear seat ashtrays, lighter, and full wheel covers. The base engine was the 200 cid (3.3-liter) inline six.

Granada Ghia — Six and V-8: The Ghia included an ornament on the opera window glass, a color-keyed body side molding with integral wheel lip molding, left-hand remote-control mirror, dual accent paint stripes on the body sides, hood and decklid, trunk carpeting and a lower back panel appliqué, color-keyed to the vinyl roof. Inside Ghia was a "floating pillow" design on independent reclining or flight bench seats, map pockets and an assist handle on back of front seats, a day/night mirror, and a luxury steering wheel with woodnote appliqué on the rim. Under Ghia's hood was the larger 250 cid six-cylinder engine.

Torino — V-8: Nine models made up the mid-size Torino lineup this year; base, Gran Torino and Brougham two- and four-doors, and a trio of wagons. Two-doors rode a 114 in. wheelbase; four-doors measured 118 in. between hubs. Fuel economy was improved by recalibrating engine spark and back-pressure EGR, and lowering the rear axle ratio to 2.75:1. Five body colors were new. Torino got a new saddle interior. Side-by-side quad round headlamps flanked a one-piece plastic grille with tiny crosshatch pattern, divided into six sections by vertical bars. Clear vertical parking/signal lamps hid behind twin matching outer sections,

making eight in all. "Ford" block letters stood above the grille. Two-door Torinos retained the conventional pillarless design, while four-doors were referred to as "pillared hardtops." Bodies held frameless, ventless curved side glass. Standard engine was the 351 cid (5.8-liter) V-8 with two-barrel carburetor and solid-state ignition. SelectShift Cruise-O-Matic, power front disc/rear drum brakes, power steering, and HR78 x 14 steel-belted radial tires were standard. Standard equipment included a cloth/vinyl front bench seat with adjustable head restraints, vinyl door trim panels, recessed door handles, day/night mirror, heater/defroster, and inside hood release. Wagons had a three-way tailgate and locking storage compartment. Squire wagons added a power tailgate window, full wheel covers, and wood grain paneling with side rails.

Gran Torino — V-8: The Gran Torino was the intermediate trim level as the Gran Torino Sport was dropped for 1976. The Gran Torino shared the saddle interior with the Torino. Torino and Gran Torino wore hubcaps.

Torino Brougham — V-8: Broughams had a split bench seat. Broughams added wheel covers, as well as opera windows and a vinyl roof to the Torino and Gran Torino list of standard equipment.

Elite — V-8: The Elite nameplate arrived in 1975 but its body had been called Gran Torino. Appearance changes were slight this year on the pillarless two-door hardtop body, which rode a 114 in. wheelbase. Elite sported a "luxury" sectioned grille with vertical bars and horizontal center bar. A stand-up hood ornament held the Elite crest. Single round headlamps in square housings had bright bezels, while vertical parking/signal lamps sat in front fender tip extensions. Wide vinyl-insert body side moldings were color-keyed to the vinyl roof. Large wraparound tail lamps had bright bezels and integral side marker lights. On the rear roof pillar were two tiny side-by-side opera windows. Bodies also displayed bright tapered wide wheel lip moldings. A standard gold vinyl roof replaced the former brown. Either a full vinyl roof or a new half-vinyl version was available, at no extra charge. The standard axle changed from 3.00:1 to 2.75:1. Standard equipment included the 351 cid (5.8-liter) two-barrel V-8 with SelectShift Cruise-O-Matic, power steering and brakes, four-wheel coil springs, and HR78 x 15 SBR tires. The standard bench seat had Westminster pleated knit cloth and vinyl trim. Woodnote accented the instrument cluster/panel, steering wheel and door panels. Also standard were front bumper guards, heater/defroster, DirectAire ventilation, clock, full wheel covers, and bright window moldings.

LTD/Custom 500 — V-8: LTD was the only full-size Ford available to private buyers this year, as the Custom 500 badge went on fleet models only. The ten-model lineup included two- and four-door base, Brougham and Landau LTD models; Custom 500 four-door and wagon; and base and Country Squire LTD wagons. Four-doors were called "pillared hardtops." Landau and Country squire models had hidden headlamps. Brougham and Landau two-doors carried half-vinyl roofs; four-doors got a "halo" vinyl roof. Front-end appearance changed slightly with a switch to dark argent paint on the secondary surface of the chromed grille. There was a new wheel cover design. LTD's crosshatch grille peaked slightly forward. Headlamp doors held a horizontal emblem. Tri-section wraparound front parking/signal lenses stood at fender tips. On the hood was a stand-up ornament. Two-doors had a six-window design, with narrow vertical windows between the front and rear side windows. Vinyl-insert body side moldings were standard. All models had a reflective rear appliqué. Six body colors were new. At mid-year, Country Squire lost the long horizontal chrome strip along its wood grain side panel. The base engine was the two-barrel 351 cid (5.8-liter) V-8. Wagons carried the 400-cid engine. Standard equipment included power steering and brakes, SelectShift Cruise-O-Matic, steel-belted radials, power ventilation system, and front bumper guards. Brougham, Landau and wagon also had rear guards. Police models with the 460 V-8 and three-speed automatic had first-gear lockout. Rear axle ratios changed to 2.75:1 and engines were recalibrated, in an attempt to boost gas mileage. Wagons had a fuel tank of only 21 gallons, versus 24.3 gallons on hardtops. Wagons now had standard hydro-boost rear brakes. A parking brake warning light became standard on all models. Decklid and ignition switch locks offered improved anti-theft protection.

I.D. Data:

Ford's 1976 11-symbol Vehicle Identification Number (VIN) was stamped on a metal tab on the instrument panel, visible through the windshield. The first digit was a model year code (6=1976). The second letter indicated the assembly plant: A=Atlanta, Georgia, B=Oakville, Ontario, Canada, E=Mahwah, New Jersey, G=Chicago, Illinois, H=Lorain; Ohio, J=Los Angeles, California, K= Kansas City, Missouri, P=Minneapolis-St. Paul, Minnesota, R=San Jose, California, T=Metuchen, New Jersey, U=Louisville, Kentucky, W=Wayne, Michigan and Y=Wixom, Michigan. Digits three and four were the body serial code, which corresponded to the Model Numbers, such as 10=Pinto 2-dr. The fifth symbol was an engine code: Y=140-cid four-cylinder, Z= 170-cid V-6, T=200-cid six-cylinder, L=250-cid six-cylinder, F=302-cid V-8, H=351-cid V-8, S=400-cid V-8, A=460-cid V-8 and C=Police 460-cid V-8. Digits six through 11

1976 Granada Ghia sedan

1976 Gran Torino two-door hardtop

made up the consecutive unit number of cars built at each assembly plant, beginning with 100001. A Vehicle Certification Label on the left front door lock face panel or door pillar showed the manufacturer, month and year of manufacture, GVW, GAWR, certification statement, VIN, body code, color code, trim code, axle code, transmission code, and domestic (or foreign) special order code.

Pinto (Four)

Model No.	Body Style No.	Body Type & Seating	Factory Price	Shipping Weight	Production Total
10	62B	2-dr. Sedan-4P	$3,025	2,452 lbs.	92,264
10	62B	2-dr. Pony Sedan	$2,895	2,450 lbs.	Note 1
11	64B	2-dr. Hatchback- 4P	$3,200	2,482 lbs.	92,540
11	64B	2-dr. Squire Hatch-4P	$3,505	2,518 lbs.	Note 2
12	73B	2-dr. Station Wagon-4P	$3,365	2,635 lbs.	105,328
12	73B	2-dr. Squire Wag-4P	$3,671	2,672 lbs.	Note 2

Pinto V-6

10	62B	2-dr. Sedan-4P	$3,472	2,590 lbs.	92,264
11	64B	2-dr. Hatchback- 4P	$3,647	2,620 lbs.	92,540
11	64B	2-dr. Squire Hatch-4P	$3,592	2,656 lbs.	Note 2
12	73B	2-dr. Station Wagon-4P	$3,865	2,773 lbs.	105,328
12	73B	2-dr. Squire Wag-4P	$4,171	2,810 lbs.	Note 2

Note 1: Pony production included in base sedan figure.
Note 2: Squire Runabout hatchback and Squire Wagon production was included with the standard Runabout and station wagon totals.

Maverick (Six)

91	62A	2-dr. Sedan-4P	$3,117	2,763 lbs.	60,611
92	54A	4-dr. Sedan-5P	$3,189	2,873 lbs.	79,076

Maverick (V-8)

91	62A	2-dr. Sedan-4P	$3,265	2,930 lbs.	60,611
92	54A	4-dr. Sedan-5P	$3,337	3,040 lbs.	79,076

Granada (Six)

82	66H	2-dr. Sedan-5P	$3,707	3,119 lbs.	161,618
81	54H	4-dr. Sedan-5P	$3,798	3,168 lbs.	287,923

Granada (V-8)

82	66H	2-dr. Sedan-5P	$3,861	3,226 lbs.	161,618
81	54H	4-dr. Sedan-5P	$3,952	3,275 lbs.	287,923

Granada Ghia (Six)

84	66K	2-dr. Sedan-5P	$4,265	3,280 lbs.	48,796
83	54K	4-dr. Sedan-5P	$4,355	3,339 lbs.	52,457

Granada Ghia (V-8)

84	66K	2-dr. Sedan-5P	$4,353	3,387 lbs.	48,796
83	54K	4-dr. Sedan-5P	$4,443	3,446 lbs.	52,457

Torino (V-8)

25	65B	2-dr. Hardtop-6P	$4,172	3,976 lbs.	34,518
27	53B	4-dr. Hardtop-6P	$4,206	4,061 lbs.	17,394
40	71B	4-dr. Station Wagon-6P	$4,521	4,409 lbs.	17,281

Gran Torino (V-8)

30	65D	2-dr. Hardtop-6P	$4,461	3,999 lbs.	23,939
31	53D	4-dr. Hardtop-6P	$4,495	4,081 lbs.	40,568
42	71D	4-dr. Station Wagon-6P	$4,769	4,428 lbs.	30,596
43	71K	4-dr. Squire Wagon-6P	$5,083	4,454 lbs.	21,144

Gran Torino Brougham (V-8)

32	65K	2-dr. Hardtop-6P	$4,883	4,063 lbs.	3,183
33	53K	4-dr. Hardtop-6P	$4,915	4,144 lbs.	4,473

Elite (V-8)

21	65H	2-dr. Hardtop-6P	$4,879	4,169 lbs.	146,475

Custom 500 (V-8)

52	60D	2-dr. Pillar Hardtop-6P	----	----	7,037
53	53D	4-dr. Pillar Hardtop-6P	$4,493	4,298 lbs.	23,447
72	71D	4-dr. Ranch Wagon-6P	$4,918	4,737 lbs.	4,633

LTD (V-8)

62	60H	2-dr. Pillar Hardtop-6P	$4,780	4,257 lbs.	62,844
63	53H	4-dr. Pillar Hardtop-6P	$4,752	4,303 lbs.	108,168
74	71H	4-dr. Station Wagon-6P	$5,207	4,752 lbs.	30,237
74	71H	4-dr. DF Rear Seat Wagon-10P	$5,333	4,780 lbs.	Note 3
76	71K	4-dr. Country Squire Wagon-6P	$5,523	4,809 lbs.	47, 329
76	71K	4-dr. DF Seats Squire-10P	$5,649	4,837 lbs.	Note 3

Note 3: Wagons with dual-facing rear seats (a $126 option) are included in standard station wagon and Country Squire wagon totals.

LTD Brougham (V-8)

68	60K	2-dr. Pillar Hardtop-6P	$5,299	4,299 lbs.	20,863
66	53K	4-dr. Pillar Hardtop-6P	$5,245	4,332 lbs.	32,917

LTD Landau (V-8)

65	60L	2-dr. Pillar Hardtop-6P	$5,613	4,346 lbs.	29,673
64	53L	4-dr. Pillar Hardtop-6P	$5,560	4,394 lbs.	35,663

Engines:

Pinto Four: Inline with overhead cam. Cast-iron block and head. Displacement: 140 cid (2.3 liters). B&S: 3.78 x 3.13 in. Compression ratio: 9.0:1 Brake hp: 92 at 5000 rpm. Torque: 121 lbs.-ft. at 3000 rpm. Five main bearings. Hydraulic valve lifters. Carburetor: Holley-Weber 9510 two-barrel. VIN Code: Y.

Pinto Optional V-6: 60-degree, overhead-valve. Cast-iron block and head. Displacement: 170.8 cid (2.8 liters). B&S: 3.66 x 2.70 in. Compression ratio: 8.7:1. Brake hp: 103 at 4400 rpm. Torque: 149 lbs.-ft. at 2800 rpm. Four main bearings. Solid valve lifters. Carburetor: Motorcraft 9510 (D6ZE-BA) two-barrel. VIN Code: Z.

Maverick/Granada Base Six: Inline. Overhead valve. Cast-iron block and head. Displacement: 200 cid (3.3 liters). B & S: 3.68 x 3.13 in. Compression ratio: 8.3:1. Brake hp: 81 at 3400 rpm. Torque: 151 lbs.-ft. at 1700 rpm. Seven main bearings. Hydraulic valve lifters. Carburetor: Carter YFA 9510 one-barrel. VIN Code: T.

Granada Ghia Base Six: (Optional in Maverick and Granada) Inline. Overhead valve. Cast-iron block and head. Displacement: 250 cid (4.1 liters). B & S: 3.68 x 3.91 in. Compression ratio: 8.0:1 Brake hp: 87 at 3600 rpm. (Maverick/Ghia, 90 at 3000). Torque: 190 lbs.-ft. at 2000 rpm. (Ghia, 187 at 1900). Seven main bearings. Hydraulic valve lifters. Carburetor: Carter YFA 9510 one-barrel. VIN Code: L.

Optional V-8 (Maverick, Granada): 90-degree, overhead valve. Cast-iron block and head. Displacement: 302 cid (5.0 liters). B & S: 4.00 x 3.00 in. Compression ratio: 8.0:1. Brake hp: 138 at 3600 rpm. (Granada, 134 at 3600). Torque: 245 lbs.-ft. at 2000 rpm. (Granada, 242 at 2000). Five main bearings. Hydraulic valve lifters. Carburetor: Ford 2150A 9510 two-barrel. VIN Code: F.

Torino, Elite and LTD Base V-8: (Optional Granada) 90-degree, overhead valve. Cast-iron block and head. Displacement: 351 cid (5.8 liters). B & S: 4.00 x 3.50 in. Compression ratio: 8.0:1. (Torino, 8.1:1). Brake hp: 152 at 3800 rpm. (Torino, 154 at 3400). Torque: 274 lbs.-ft. at 1600 rpm. (Torino, 286 at 1800). Five main bearings. Hydraulic valve lifters. Carburetor: Ford 2150A two-barrel. VIN Code: H.

500/LTD wagon Base V-8: (Optional Torino, Elite and LTD) 90-degree, overhead valve. Cast-iron block and head. Displacement: 400 cid (6.6 liters). B & S: 4.00 x 4.00 in. Compression ratio: 8.0:1. Brake hp: 180 at 3800 rpm. Torque: 336 lbs.-ft. at 1800 rpm. Five main bearings. Hydraulic valve lifters. Carburetor: Ford 2150A two-barrel. VIN Code: S.

1976 Ford Elite

1976 Gran Torino Brougham four-door pillared hardtop

1976 Maverick four-door with luxury decor option

Thunderbird Base V-8: (Optional Torino, Elite and LTD) 90-degree, overhead valve. Cast-iron block and head. Displacement: 460 cid (7.5 liters). B & S: 4.36 x 3.85 in. Compression ratio: 8.0:1. Brake hp: 202 at 3800 rpm. Torque: 352 lbs.-ft. at 1600 rpm. Five main bearings. Hydraulic valve lifters. Carburetor: Motorcraft 9510 or Ford 4350A9510, both four-barrel. VIN Code: A.

Note: A Police 460-cid V-8 was also available for the LTD.

Chassis:

Pinto: Wheelbase: 94.5 in. and 94.8 in. on station wagon. Overall length: 169.0 in. and 178.8 in. on station wagon. Tires: A78 x 13 or B78 x 13.

Maverick: Wheelbase: 103.0 in. and 109.9 in. on sedan. Overall length: 187.0 in. and 193.9 in. on sedan. Tires: C78 x 14 and DR78 x 14 with V-8 engine.

Granada: Wheelbase: 109.9 in. Overall length: 197.7 in. Tires: DR78 x 14.

Torino: Wheelbase: 114.0 in. and 118.0 in. on station wagon. Overall length: 213.6 in., 217.6 on the sedan and 222.6 in. on the station wagon. Tires: HR78 x 14.

Elite: Wheelbase: 114.0 in. Overall length: 216.1 in. Tires: HR78 x 15.

LTD/Custom 500: Wheelbase: 121.0 in. Overall length: 223.9 in. and 225.6 in. on the station wagon. HR78 x 15 and JR78 x 15 on station wagon.

Options:

Pinto: A sporty new Stallion option featuring special silver body paint and taping, black window and door moldings, and blacked-out wiper arms, hood, grille and lower back panel. Black tape treatment went on rocker panel and wheel lip areas with Stallion decals on front fenders. Stallion also included dual racing mirrors, styled steel wheels with trim rings, A70 x 13 tires with raised white letters, and a "competition" handling suspension ($283). A Luxury Decor Group included woodnote instrument panel appliqué, custom steering wheel, passenger door courtesy light switch, and rear seat ashtray. ($241). Convenience light group ($70 to $102). Protection group ($73 to $134). Air conditioner ($420). Rear defroster, electric ($70). Tinted glass ($46). Leather-wrapped steering wheel ($33). Dual color-keyed mirrors ($42). Entertainment: AM radio ($71); w/stereo tape player ($192). AM/FM radio ($129). AM/FM stereo radio ($173). Sunroof, manual ($230). Half vinyl roof ($125). Metallic glow paint ($54). Roof luggage rack ($52 to $75). Rocker panel moldings ($19). Wheels: Forged aluminum wheels ($82 to $172). Styled steel wheels ($92 to $119). Wheel covers ($28). Trim rings ($29). SelectShift Cruise-O-Matic: ($186). Power steering: ($117). Power brakes: ($54).

Maverick: A Stallion dress-up package, similar to Pinto's, included black grille and moldings; unique paint/tape treatment on hood, grille, decklid, lower body, and lower back panel; plus large Stallion decal on front quarter panel. The package also included dual outside mirrors, raised white-letter steel-belted radials on styled steel wheels, and "competition" suspension option ($329). Exterior decor group ($99). Interior decor group ($106). Luxury interior decor ($217). Deluxe bumper group ($28 to $61). Convenience group ($34 to $64). Protection group ($24 to $39). Light group ($22 to $34). Security lock group ($16). Air conditioning. ($420). Rear defogger ($40). Tinted glass ($45 to $59). Dual color-keyed mirrors ($13 to $25). AM radio ($71); w/tape player ($192). AM/FM radio ($128). AM/FM stereo radio ($210); w/tape player ($299). Vinyl roof ($94). Metallic glow paint ($54). Decklid luggage rack ($51). Rocker panel moldings ($19). Bumper guards, front or rear ($17). Reclining bucket seats ($147). Cloth bucket seat trim ($24). Vinyl seat trim ($25). Color-keyed deluxe seatbelts ($17). Forged aluminum wheels ($98 to $187). Styled steel wheels ($59 to $89). Hubcap trim rings ($35), no charge with decor group. Space-saver spare ($13) but no charge with radial tires. Automatic transmission ($245). Power brakes: ($53). Sure-Track brakes ($124). Heavy duty suspension: ($16). 250-cid six cylinder engine: ($96).

Granada: Sports sedan option ($482). Exterior decor group ($128). Interior decor group ($181). Luxury decor group ($642). Convenience group ($31 to $75). Deluxe bumper group ($61). Light group ($25 to $37). Protection group ($24 to $39). Visibility group ($30 to $47). Security lock group ($17). Air conditioning ($437). Rear defogger ($43). Rear defroster, electric ($76). Fingertip speed control ($96). Power windows ($95 to $133). Power door locks ($63 to $88). Power four-way seat ($119). Tinted glass ($47). Leather-wrapped steering wheel ($14 to $33). Luxury steering wheel ($18). Tilt steering wheel ($54). Fuel monitor warning light ($18). Digital clock ($40). Dual-note horn ($6). Color-keyed outside mirrors ($29 to $42). Lighted visor vanity mirror ($40). AM radio ($71); w/tape player ($192). AM/FM radio ($142). AM/FM stereo radio ($210); w/tape player ($299). Power moon roof ($786). Power sun roof ($517). Vinyl or half vinyl roof ($102). Metallic glow paint ($54). Rocker panel moldings ($19). Decklid luggage rack ($33). Console ($65). Reclining seats ($60). Leather seat trim ($181). Deluxe cloth seat trim ($88). Trunk carpeting ($20). Trunk dress-up ($33). Color-keyed seatbelts ($17). Styled steel wheels ($41 to $60); w/trim rings ($76 to $95). Lacy spoke aluminum wheels ($112 to $207). 250-cid six ($96). 302-cid V-8 ($154) or ($88), Granada Ghia. 351-cid V-8 ($200) or ($134), Granada Ghia. Automatic transmission ($245). Power brakes ($57). Four-wheel power disc brakes ($210). Sure-Track brakes ($227). Heavy duty suspension ($29). Trailer towing package ($42).

Torino/Elite: Squire Brougham option ($184). Interior decor group: Elite ($384). Accent group: Torino ($45). Deluxe bumper group ($50 to $67). Light group ($41 to $43). Convenience group: Torino ($33 to $84); Elite ($49). Protection group ($26 to $42). Security lock group ($18). Auto-temp control air conditioning ($88). Anti-theft alarm system ($84). Rear defroster, electric ($99). Windshield/rear window defroster, Power windows ($104 to $145). Power tailgate wagon window: ($43). Power door locks ($68 to $109). Electric decklid release ($17). Six-way power seat ($130). Automatic seatback release ($30). Reclining passenger seat ($70). Leather-wrapped steering wheel ($36). Luxury steering wheel ($20). Tilt steering wheel ($59). Fuel sentry vacuum gauge ($13 to $32). Fuel monitor warning light ($20). Electric clock ($18). Dual-note horn ($7). Remote driver's mirror, chrome ($14). Remote-control color-keyed mirrors ($32 to $46). Lighted visor vanity mirror ($43). AM radio ($78). AM/FM stereo radio ($229); w/tape player ($326). AM/FM stereo search radio: Elite ($386). Dual rear speakers ($39). Exterior: Power moon roof: Elite ($859). Power sunroof ($545). Vinyl roof: Torino ($112); Elite. no charge. Opera windows: Torino ($50). Fender skirts: Torino ($41). Rocker panel moldings ($26). Bumper guards, front or rear: Torino ($18). Luggage rack: Torino ($82 to $91). Bucket seats ($146). Rear-facing third seat, station wagon ($104). Vinyl bench seat trim: Torino ($22). Pleated vinyl bench seat trim ($22 to $28). Duraweave vinyl seat trim: Torino ($55). Color-keyed seatbelts ($18). Trunk trim ($36). Deluxe wheel covers: Torino ($37). Luxury wheel covers ($58 to $95). Wire wheel covers: Elite ($99). Magnum 500 wheels w/trim rings: Torino ($141 to $178). Turbine spoke cast aluminum wheels: Elite ($226). 400-cid V-8 ($100). 460-cid V-8 ($292). Heavy duty handling and suspension ($18 to $32), Torino and ($92), Elite. Heavy duty electrical system ($29), Torino and Elite ($80). Medium trailer and towing package ($59). Heavy duty trailer and towing package ($87 to $121), Torino and ($121), Elite.

1976 Maverick Stallion coupe

1976 LTD Landau four-door pillared hardtop

1976 Granada sedan (with Exterior Decor Group option)

LTD: Landau luxury group including concealed headlamps, a convenience group, half vinyl roof (on two-door), front cornering lamps, wide color-keyed body moldings, and unique narrow center pillar windows, padded door panels with woodnote accents, fold-down center armrests, and a digital clock ($472 to $708). Brougham option: wagon ($396); Squire ($266). Harmony color group ($99). Convenience group ($97-$104). Light group ($76 to $79). Deluxe bumper group ($41 to $59). Protection group ($47 to $78). Security lock group ($18). Air conditioning ($353); w/auto-temp control ($486). Anti-theft alarm system ($566). Rear defogger ($43). Rear defroster, electric ($83). Fingertip speed control ($87 to $107). Power windows ($108 to $161). Power mini-vent and side windows ($232). Power door locks ($68-$109). Six-way power driver's seat ($132) or driver and passenger ($259). Automatic seatback release ($30). Tinted glass ($64). Luxury steering wheel ($20). Tilt steering wheel ($59). Fuel monitor warning light ($20). Electric clock ($18). Digital clock ($25 to $43). Cornering lamps ($43). Dual-note horn ($6). Driver's remote mirror ($14). AM radio ($78). AM/FM stereo radio ($229); w/tape player ($326). AM/FM stereo search radio ($386). Dual rear speakers ($39). Sunroof, manual ($632). Full vinyl roof ($126) exc. wagon ($151). Half vinyl roof ($126). Fender skirts ($42). Metallic glow paint ($59). Dual accent paint stripes ($29). Rocker panel moldings ($26). Vinyl-insert body side moldings ($41). Rear bumper guards ($18). Luggage rack ($82 to $96). Dual-facing rear seats, wagon ($126). Split bench seat w/passenger recliner ($141). Leather interior trim ($222). All-vinyl seat ($22). Duraweave vinyl trim ($55). Recreation table ($58). Color-keyed seatbelts ($18). Deluxe cargo area ($83 to $126). Lockable side stowage compartment ($43). Luggage area trim ($36). Full wheel covers ($30). Deluxe wheel covers ($63 to $93). 400-cid V-8 ($100). 460-cid V-8 ($353) and $251 on the LTD station wagon. Four-wheel power disc brakes ($170). Heavy duty suspension ($18). Adjustable air shock absorbers ($43). Extended-range fuel tank ($99). Light duty trailer towing package ($53). Medium duty trailer towing package ($46 to $145). Heavy duty trailer towing package ($132 to $230).

History:

The 1967 Fords were introduced on October 3, 1975. Model year production was 1,861,537, including Mustangs. Calendar year sales by U.S. dealers were 1,682,583, including Mustangs. The total sales gave Ford a 19.9 percent share of the market. Ford sales had declined sharply in the 1975 model year, down over 21 percent. Full-size models had sold best. Even the success of the Granada (new for 1975) wasn't as great as anticipated. Ford had introduced Pinto Pony and Mustang II MPG models late in the 1975 model year. Sales swung upward again for the 1976 model year, even though few major changes were evident in the lineup. Part of the reason was Ford's new "California strategy," that offered special option packages for West Coast buyers to take sales away from the imports. It proved quite successful in 1976. Prices jumped as the model year began, then were cut back in January. Production fell for Pinto, Mustang II and Maverick in 1976, but overall production increased nearly 19 percent, especially due to Granada sales. Model year sales followed a similar pattern, up 18.5 percent. Henry Ford II, Lee Iacocca and B.E. Bidwell were the top Ford executives. Pinto was once described as "a car nobody loved, but everybody bought." This was the last year for the unsafe Pinto gas tank and filler neck. The faulty components had caused a number of highly publicized fires resulting in massive product-liability lawsuits. Granada had proven to be one of the fastest Fords, at least with a "Windsor" 351 cid V-8 under its hood.

1977 Ford

Pinto — Four and V-6: Revised front and rear styling hit Ford's subcompact, offered again in two-door sedan, "three-door" Runabout and station wagon form. A new "soft" nose with sloping hood and flexible fender extension and deflector assembly were up front. At the rear of the two-door sedan and three-door Runabout were new, larger horizontal dual-lens tail lamps. There were new extruded anodized aluminum bumpers front and rear. A new vinyl roof grain was available. Runabouts had a new optional all-glass third door. Inside was new cloth trim, optional on the base high-back bucket seats. A new lower (2.73:1) rear axle ratio went with the standard OHC 140 cid (2.3-liter) four-cylinder engine and a wide-ratio four-speed manual gearbox. The low-budget Pony came with rack-and-pinion steering, front disc brakes, all-vinyl or cloth/vinyl high-back front bucket seats, a mini-console, color-keyed carpeting, and argent hubcaps. The base two-door sedan included a color-keyed instrument panel and steering wheel, bright backlight trim, plus bright drip and belt moldings. Runabouts had a fold-down rear seat, rear lift gate, and rubber load floor mat. All models except the Pony could have a 170.8 cid (2.8-liter) V-6. A new Sports option included a tachometer, ammeter and temperature gauge, new soft-rim spots steering wheel, front stabilizer bar, higher-rate springs, and higher axle ratio. A new Cruising Wagon was aimed at youthful buyers. It included a front spoiler, styled wheels, Sports Rallye equipment, and carpeted rear section.

Maverick — Six and V-8: For its final season, Maverick changed little except for some new body and interior colors, two new vinyl roof colors, and a new vinyl-insert body side molding. New options included wire wheel covers, four-way manual bucket seats, and high-altitude option. The optional 302 V-8 got a variable-Venturi carburetor. All engines gained Dura-Spark ignition. There was also a new wide-ratio three-speed manual shift. Revised speedometers showed miles and kilometers. The Decor Group added a halo vinyl roof. The standard engine was the 200 cid (3.3-liter) six. Standard equipment included front disc brakes (manual), three-speed column-shift manual transmission, a foot parking brake with warning light, and 19.2-gallon gas tank. Also standard were color-keyed carpeting, armrests with a door pull assist handle, flip-open rear quarter windows, bright hubcaps and bright drip rail and wheel lip moldings.

Granada — Six and V-8: Styling of the Mercedes-emulating Granada remained similar to 1976, with nine new body colors available. A new full-synchronized four-speed manual transmission with overdrive fourth gear became standard. That made Granada the first domestic model to offer an overdrive four-speed as standard equipment (except in California, where it was unavailable). The base engine was the 200-cid (3.3-liter) inline six with Dura-Spark ignition. Also standard were front disc brakes, an inside hood release, wiper/washer control on the turn signal lever. The body sported window, drip, belt and wheel lip moldings. Two-doors displayed opera lamps. The Granada Ghia

1977 Pinto three-door Runabout (with optional wire wheels)

added a left-hand remote-control mirror, wide color-keyed vinyl-insert body side moldings (integral with wheel lip moldings), flight bench seats, and unique wire-style wheel covers. A new variable-Venturi carburetor for the 302 V-8 was used only in California. Four models were offered: Granada and Ghia two- and four-door sedans. New Granada options included four-way manual bucket seats, automatic-temperature-control air conditioning, illuminated entry, front cornering lamps, simulated wire wheel covers, white lacy-spoke cast aluminum wheels, wideband whitewall radials, electric trunk lid release, and a high-altitude option.

LTD II — V-8: Serving as a replacement for the abandoned Torino, the new A-bodied LTD II had similar dimensions, and long-hood styling that wasn't radically different. The goal, according to Ford, was to combine "LTD's traditional high level of workmanship with Mustang's sporty spirit." A wide choice of models were offered: S, base and Brougham in the two-door hardtop, a four-door pillared hardtop or a four-door wagon. The wagons were offered only this year, and LTD II would last only into the 1979 model year. Among the more noticeable styling features were vertically-stacked quad rectangular headlamps, and doors with a straight beltline. Sharply-tapered opera windows on the wide roof pillars stood to the rear of the regular quarter windows of two-doors, except the "S" model. Four-doors were also a six-window design. Inside, the LTD II had new seat trim and new-look door trim. The standard engine dropped to a 302 V-8, now with Dura-Spark ignition and a lower axle ratio. Standard equipment on the budget-priced "S" included SelectShift automatic transmission, power steering and brakes and a Kirsten cloth/vinyl bench seat. The basic LTD II had an Ardmore cloth/vinyl flight bench seat, deluxe door trim, rear panel appliqué, hood ornament, and rocker panel and wheel lip moldings. The top-line Brougham added Doral cloth/vinyl split bench seats, dual horns, an electric clock, and wide color-keyed vinyl-insert side moldings. The standard engine was the 302 cid V-8 hooked to SelectShift Cruise-O-Matic.

LTD/Custom 500 — V-8: Rivals may have shrunk their big cars, but the Ford remained full-size once again. According to the factory, that gave LTD a "wider stance, and more road-hugging weight." New colors and fabrics entered LTD interiors this year, but not much else was different. Power train changes included improved 351 and 400 cid V-8s with new Dura-Spark ignition, as well as lower rear axle ratios. New options included illuminated entry, Quadra sonic tape player, simulated wire wheel covers, forged aluminum wheels, and wide whitewall radial tires. The LTD Brougham was dropped, but the top-rung Landau model took its position in the lineup. Six basic models were available: LTD and Landau two- and four-door, LTD wagon, and Country Squire wagon. The Custom 500 was for fleet buyers only. Standard LTD equipment included a 351 cid (5.8-liter) V-8 with Dura-Spark ignition, SelectShift automatic transmission, power brakes and steering, a Redondo cloth/vinyl bench seat, a hood ornament and bright hubcaps. Landau models added concealed headlamps, an Ardmore cloth/vinyl flight bench seat, electric clock, half or full vinyl roof, rear bumper guards, full wheel covers, color-keyed side moldings, and a dual-note horn. A Landau Creme and Blue package was announced for the mid-year, with choice of color combinations. A Creme body color came with a creme or blue vinyl roof. Inside was a Creme super-soft vinyl luxury group, and split bench seats with blue welts.

I.D. Data:

As before, Ford's 11-symbol Vehicle Identification Number (VIN) was stamped on a metal tab fastened to the instrument panel and was visible through the windshield. Coding was similar to 1976. The model year code was 7 = 1977. The Code Y for the Wixom. Michigan, assembly plant was dropped. One engine code was added: Q = the modified 351-cid two-barrel V-8.

Pinto (Four)

Model No.	Body Style No.	Body Type & Seating	Factory Price	Shipping Weight	Production Total
10	62B	2-dr. Sedan-4P	$3,237	2,315 lbs.	48,863
10	62B	2-dr. Pony Sedan-4P	$3,099	2,313 lbs.	Note 1
11	64B	2-dr Hatchback-4P	$3,353	2,351 lbs.	74,237
12	73B	2-dr. Station Wagon-4P	$3,548	2,515 lbs.	79,449
12	73B	2-dr. Squire Wagon-4P	$3,891	2,552 lbs.	Note 2

Pinto (V-6)

10	62B	2-dr. Sedan-4P	$3,519	2,438 lbs.	48,863
11	64B	2-dr. Hatchback- 4P	$3,635	2,414 lbs.	74,237
12	73B	2-dr. Station Wagon-4P	$3,830	2,638 lbs.	79,449
12	73B	2-dr. Squire Wagon-4P	$4,172	2,675 lbs.	Note 2

Note 1: Pony production is included in the base sedan figure.
Note 2: Squire Wagon production is included in the standard station wagon total.
Note: Totals included 22,548 Pintos produced as 1978 models but sold as 1977 models. There were 6,599 two-door sedans, 8,271 hatchback Runabouts and 7,678 station wagons.

Maverick (Six)

91	62A	2-dr. Sedan-4P	$3,322	2,782 lbs.	40,086
92	54A	4-dr. Sedan-5P	$3,395	2,887 lbs.	58,420

Maverick (V-8)

91	62A	2-dr. Sedan-4P	$3,483	2,947 lbs.	40,086
92	54A	4-dr. Sedan-5P	$3,556	3,052 lbs.	58,420

Granada (Six)

82	66H	2-dr. Sedan-5P	$4,022	3,124 lbs.	157,612
81	54H	4-dr. Sedan-5P	$4,118	3,174 lbs.	163,071

Granada (V-8)

82	66H	2-dr. Sedan-5P	$4,209	3,219 lbs.	157,612
81	54H	4-dr. Sedan-5P	$4,305	3,269 lbs.	163,071

Granada Ghia (Six)

84	66K	2-dr. Sedan-5P	$4,452	3,175 lbs.	34,166
83	54K	4-dr. Sedan-5P	$4,548	3,229 lbs.	35,730

Granada Ghia (V-8)

84	66K	2-dr. Sedan-5P	$4,639	3,270 lbs.	34,166
83	54K	4-dr. Sedan-5P	$4,735	3,324 lbs.	35,730

LTD II (V-8)

30	65D	2-dr. Hardtop-6P	$4,785	3,789 lbs.	57,449
31	53D	4-dr. Pillar Hardtop-6P	$4,870	3,904 lbs.	56,704
42	71D	4-dr. Station Wagon-6P	$5,064	4,404 lbs.	23,237
43	71K	4-dr. Squire Wagon-6P	$5,335	4,430 lbs.	17,162

LTD II S (V-8)

25	65B	2-dr. Hardtop-6P	$4,528	3,789 lbs.	9,531
27	53B	4-dr. Pillar Hardtop-6P	$4,579	3,894 lbs.	18,775
40	71B	4-dr. Station Wagon-6P	$4,806	4,393 lbs.	9,636

LTD II Brougham (V-8)

32	65K	2-dr. Hardtop-6P	$5,121	3,898 lbs.	20,979
33	53K	4-dr. Pillar Hardtop-6P	$5,206	3,930 lbs.	18,851

Custom 500 (V-8)

52	60D	2-dr. Pillar Hardtop-6P	----	----	4,139
53	53D	4-dr. Pillar Hardtop-6P	----	----	5,582
72	71D	4-dr. Station Wagon-6P	----	----	1,406

LTD (V-8)

62	60H	2-dr. Pillar Hardtop-6P	$5,128	4,190 lbs.	73,637
63	53H	4-dr. Pillar Hardtop-6P	$5,152	4,240 lbs.	160,255
74	71H	4-dr. Station Wagon-6P	$5,415	4,635 lbs.	90,711
76	71K	4-dr. Country Squire-6P	$5,866	4,674 lbs.	Note 3

Note 3: Country Squire and wagons with dual-facing rear seats are included in basic wagon totals.

LTD Landau (V-8)

65	60L	2-dr. Pillar Hardtop-6P	$5,717	4,270 lbs.	44,396
64	53L	4-dr. Pillar Hardtop-6P	$5,742	4,319 lbs.	65,030

Engines:

Pinto Four: Inline with overhead cam. Cast-iron block and head. Displacement: 140 cid (2.3 liters). B & S: 3.78 x 3.13 in. Compression ratio: 9.0:1. Brake hp: 89 at 4800 rpm. Torque: 120 lbs.-ft. at 3000 rpm. Five main bearings. Hydraulic valve lifters. Carburetor: Motorcraft 5200 two-barrel. VIN Code: Y.

Pinto Optional V-6: 60-degree, overhead-valve. Cast-iron block and head. Displacement: 170.8 cid (2.8 liters). B & S: 3.66 x 2.70 in. Compression ratio: 8.7:1. Brake hp: 93 at 4200 rpm. Torque: 140 lbs.-

1977 Maverick coupe

1977 Maverick sedan

1977 Granada Sports Coupe

1977 Granada sedan

1977-1/2 Granada Sports Coupe (with opera-window louvers)

ft. at 2600 rpm. Four main bearings. Solid valve lifters. Carburetor: Motorcraft 2150 two-barrel. VIN Code: Z.

Maverick, Granada Base Six: Inline and overhead valve. Cast-iron block and head. Displacement: 200 cid (3.3 liters). B & S: 3.68 x 3.13 in. Compression ratio: 8.5:1. Brake hp: 96 at 4400 rpm. Torque: 151 lbs.-ft. at 2000 rpm. Seven main bearings. Hydraulic valve lifters. Carburetor: Carter YFA one-barrel. VIN Code: T.

Granada Ghia Base Six (Optional: Maverick, Granada): Inline. Overhead valve. Cast-iron block and head. Displacement: 250 cid (4.1 liters). B & S: 3.68 x 3.91 in. Compression ratio: 8.1:1. Brake hp: 98 at 3400 rpm. Torque: 182 lbs.-ft. at 1800 rpm. Seven main bearings. Hydraulic valve lifters. Carburetor: Carter YFA one-barrel. VIN Code: L.

LTD II Base V-8 (Optional: Maverick, Granada): 90-degree, overhead valve. Cast-iron block and head. Displacement: 302 cid (5.0 liters). B & S: 4.00 x 3.00 in. Compression ratio: 8.4:1. Brake hp: 130 to 137 at 3400 to 3600 rpm. Torque: 243 to 245 lbs.-ft. at 1600 to 1800 rpm. Five main bearings. Hydraulic valve lifters. Carburetor: Motorcraft 2150 two-barrel. VIN code: F.

Note: Horsepower and torque ratings of the 302 V-8 varied slightly, according to model.

LTD Optional V-8: 90-degree, overhead valve, Cast-iron block and head. Displacement: 351 cid (5.8 liters). B & S: 4.00 x 3.50 in. Compression ratio: 8.3:1. Brake hp: 149 at 3200 rpm. Torque: 291 lbs.-ft. at 1600 rpm. Five main bearings. Hydraulic valve lifters. Carburetor: Motorcraft 2150 two-barrel. Windsor engine. VIN Code: H.

Optional Granada V-8: Same as 351 cid V-8 above, but 135 hp at 3200 rpm. Torque: 275 lbs.-ft. 1600 rpm.

LTD and LTD II wagon V-8 (Optional Granada Ghia and LTD II): Same as 351 cid V-8 above, but the compression ratio is 8.0:1, the brake hp is 161 at 3600 rpm and the torque is 285 lbs.-ft. at 1800 rpm. VIN Code: Q.

LTD wagon Base V-8 (Optional LTD and LTD II): 90-degree, overhead valve. Cast-iron block and head. Displacement: 400 cid (6.6 liters). B & S: 4.00 x 4.00 in. Compression ratio: 8:0.1. Brake hp: 173 at 3800 rpm. Torque: 326 lbs.-ft. at 1600 rpm. Five main bearings. Hydraulic valve lifters. Carburetor: Motorcraft 2150 two-barrel. VIN Code: S.

LTD Optional V-8: 90-degree, overhead valve. Cast-iron block and head. Displacement: 460 cid (7.5 liters). B & S: 4.36 x 3.85 in. Compression ratio: 8.0:1. Brake hp: 197 at 4000 rpm. Torque: 353 lbs.-ft. at 2000 rpm. Five main bearings. Hydraulic valve lifters. Carburetor: Motorcraft 4350 four-barrel. VIN Code: A.

Note: A Police 460-cid V-8 was also available for the LTD.

Chassis:

Pinto: Wheelbase: 94.5 and 94.8, wagon. Overall length: 169.0 in. and 178.8 in., wagon. Tires: A78 x 13.

Maverick: Wheelbase: 103.0 in. and 109.9 in., sedan. Overall length: 187.0 in. and 193.9 in., sedan. Tires: C78 x 14 and DR78 x 14 with V-8.

Granada: Wheelbase: 109.9 in. Overall length: 197.7 in. Tires: DR78 x 14 steel belted radials.

LTD II: Wheelbase: 114.0, two door and 118.0 in, sedan and station wagon. Overall length: 215.5 in., two door, 219.5 in., sedan and 223.1 in. station wagon. Tires: HR78 x 14 steel belted radials.

LTD/Custom 500: Wheelbase: 121.0 in. Overall length: 224.1 in. and 225.6 in., station wagon. Tires: HR78 x 15 and JR78 x 15, station wagon.

Options:

Pinto: Cruising wagon package, including body side tape stripe ($416). Sports Rallye package ($89). Exterior decor group ($122 to $128). Interior decor group ($160). Convenience light group ($73 to $108). Deluxe bumper group ($65). Protection group ($122 to $142). Air conditioner ($446) Rear defroster, electric ($73). Tinted glass ($48). Dual sport mirrors ($45). AM radio ($76), w/stereo tape player ($204). AM/FM radio ($135). AM/FM stereo radio ($184). Sunroof, manual ($243). Flip-up open air roof ($147). Half vinyl roof ($133). Glass third door ($13). Metallic glow paint ($58). Special paint/tape w/luggage rack: cruising wagon ($58). Black narrow vinyl-insert side moldings ($37). Roof luggage rack ($80). Rocker panel moldings ($20). Four-way driver's seat ($33). Load floor carpet ($23). Cargo area cover ($30). Wire wheel covers ($79 to $119). Forged aluminum wheels ($57 to $183). Styled steel wheels ($98 to $127). Wheel covers ($29). 170-cid V-6 ($289). SelectShift Cruise-O-Matic ($196). Optional axle ratio ($14). Power brakes ($58). Power steering ($124). Heavy duty battery ($16). High altitude option ($39).

Maverick: Exterior decor group ($105). Interior decor group ($112). Deluxe bumper group ($65).Convenience group ($49 to $67). Protection group ($34 to $41). Light group ($36). Air conditioning ($446). Rear defogger ($42). Tinted glass ($47 to $63). Dual sport mirrors ($14 to $27). AM radio ($76); w/tape player ($204). AM/FM radio ($135). AM/FM stereo radio ($222); w/tape player ($317). Vinyl roof ($100). Metallic glow paint ($58). Wide vinyl-insert side moldings ($64). Bumper guards, front and rear ($36). Four-way reclining driver's seat ($33). Reclining vinyl bucket seats ($129). Cloth reclining bucket seats ($25). Vinyl seat trim ($27). Wire wheel covers ($86 to $119). Lacy spoke aluminum wheels ($218 to $251). Styled steel wheels ($100 to $131). C78 x 14 white sidewall tires ($33). CR78 x 14 steel belted radial tires ($89). CR78 x 14 white sidewall steel belted tires ($121). DR78 x 14 white sidewall steel belted radial tires ($89 to $112). DR78 x 14 steel-belted white sidewall tires ($121 to $144). Space-saver spare ($14). 250-cid six ($102). 302-cid V-8 ($161). SelectShift Cruise-O-Matic ($259). Power brakes ($57). Power steering ($131). Heavy duty suspension ($17). Heavy duty battery ($16). High altitude option ($39).

LTD II: Squire Brougham option ($203). Sports instrumentation group ($103 to $130). Exterior decor group ($225 to $276). Accent group ($58). Deluxe bumper group ($72). Light group ($46 to $49). Convenience group ($101 to $132). Power lock group ($92 to $125). Air conditioning ($505); w/auto-temp control ($546). Rear defroster, electric ($87). Fingertip speed control ($93 to $114). Illuminated entry system ($51). Tinted glass ($57). Power windows ($114 to $158). Power station wagon tailgate window: ($43). Six-way power seat ($143). Leather-wrapped steering wheel ($39 to $61). Tilt steering wheel ($63). Day/date clock ($20 to $39). Cornering lamps ($43). Remote driver's mirror, chrome ($14). Dual sports mirrors ($51). AM radio ($72). AM/FM radio ($132). AM/FM stereo radio ($192); w/tape player ($266); w/Quadra sonic tape player ($399). AM/FM stereo search radio ($349). Dual rear speakers ($43). Full vinyl roof ($111 to $162). Half vinyl roof ($111). Opera windows ($51). Vinyl-insert side moldings ($39). Rear-facing third seat station wagon ($100). Vinyl seat trim ($22). Color-keyed seatbelts ($18). Deluxe wheel covers ($36). Luxury wheel covers ($59 to $95). Wire wheel covers ($99). Turbine

1977 LTD Landau four-door pillared hardtop

1977 LTD II hardtop coupe

1977 LTD II Brougham pillared hardtop

spoke cast aluminum wheels ($234 to $270). H78 x 14 steel-belted white sidewalls ($45). HR78 x 14 wide-band white sidewall tires ($16 to $61). JR78 x 14 steel-belted white sidewalls ($26 to $71). HR78 x 15 steel-belted white sidewalls ($45). 351-cid V-8 ($66). 400-cid V-8 ($155) and $100, LTD station wagon. Heavy duty handling and suspension ($9 to $33). Heavy duty battery ($17). Heavy duty alternator ($45). Heavy duty trailer towing package ($93 to $111).

LTD: Landau luxury group ($403 to $563). Convenience group ($88 to $136). Light group ($36 to $38). Deluxe bumper group ($43 to $63). Protection group ($50 to $59). Air conditioning ($514), with auto-temp control ($600). Rear defogger ($46). Rear defroster, electric ($88). Fingertip speed control ($92 to $113). Illuminated entry system ($54). Power windows ($114 to $170). Power mini-vent and side windows ($246). Power door locks ($72 to $116) Six-way power driver's seat ($139); driver and passenger seats ($275). Tinted glass ($68). Tilt steering wheel ($63). Electric clock ($20). Digital clock ($26 to $46). Cornering lamps ($46). Driver's remote mirror ($16). AM radio ($83). AM/FM radio ($147). AM/FM stereo radio ($242); with tape player ($346); with Quadra sonic tape player ($450). AM/FM stereo search radio ($409). Dual rear speakers ($42). Full vinyl roof ($134), Landau two-door, no charge. Half vinyl roof ($134). Fender skirts ($45). Rocker panel moldings ($28). Vinyl-insert side moldings ($43). Rear bumper guards ($20). Luggage rack ($101). Dual-facing station wagon rear seats ($134). Split bench seat with passenger recliner ($149). Leather seat trim ($236). All-vinyl seat trim ($23). Duraweave vinyl trim ($59). Color-keyed seatbelts ($20). Lockable side storage compartment ($46). Full wheel covers ($32). Deluxe wheel covers ($67 to $99). Wire wheel covers ($105 to $137). Deep-dish aluminum wheels ($251 to $283). 460-cid V-8 ($297) and ($189) LTD station wagon. Traction-Lok differential ($57). Optional axle ratio ($16). Heavy duty suspension ($20). Heavy duty battery ($18). Heavy duty trailer towing package ($125). High altitude option ($42).

History:

The 1977 Fords were introduced on October 1, 1976. Model year production: 1,840,427, including Mustangs. Calendar year sales by U.S. dealers were 1,824,035, including Mustangs. Both the new LTD II and the shrunken Thunderbird were meant to rival Chevrolet's Monte Carlo and the Pontiac Grand Prix. The LTD cost nearly 7 percent more than in 1976. Since gasoline prices weren't rising, Ford's lineup of relatively small cars wasn't doing as well as hoped. Slight price cuts of smaller models, after their 1977 introduction, didn't help. Plants producing smaller Fords shut down nearly two months earlier for the

1977 LTD Country Squire wagon

'78 changeover than did those turning out full-sized models. During the model year, Maverick production halted and was replaced by the new Fairmont compact. A UAW strike against Ford during the model year didn't affect production. It was nearly identical to the 1976 output. Ford continued the successful California strategy during 1977, offering special models available on the West Coast.

1978 Ford

Pinto — Four and V-6: New body and interior colors made up most of the changes in Ford's rear-drive subcompact Pinto. In 1978, they carried split-cushion bucket rear seats. New options included white-painted forged aluminum wheels and an accent stripe treatment in four color combinations. Seven body colors were available, as well as vinyl roofs in jade or chamois. Pinto's model lineup still included the two-door sedan, three-door hatchback Runabout and station wagon. The base engine remained the 140-cid (2.3-liter) overhead-cam four plus a four-speed manual gearbox. Optional power rack-and-pinion steering added a new variable-ratio system similar to one used on the new Fairmont and Zephyr series. A Sports Rallye Package included a tachometer, sport steering wheel, front stabilizer bar, heavy-duty suspension, and 3.18:1 axle. The Rallye Appearance package contained dual racing mirrors, black front spoiler, gold accent stripes, and blacked-out exterior moldings. The Cruising Wagon option returned, with front spoiler, graphic multi-colored paint striping, cargo area carpeting, styled steel wheels, dual sport mirrors, and steel side panels with round tinted porthole windows. At mid-year a panel delivery Pinto was added. Most regular production options were available on the panel Pinto plus a rear-window security screen.

Fairmont — Four, Six and V-8: A new, more modern compact model, the Fairmont, and its Mercury Zephyr corporate twin, debuted for 1978. They shared the new unitized Fox body/chassis platform that eventually carried a number of other Ford models. Fairmont was designed with an emphasis on efficiency and fuel economy, achieved by means of reduced weight and improved aerodynamics. Ford also made the best use of interior space and offered easy maintenance. The clean styling was influenced by Ford's Ghia design studios in Turin, Italy. Zephyr differed only in grille design and trim details. Under the chassis was a new suspension with MacPherson struts and coil springs up front, and four-link coil spring design at the rear. Front coil springs were mounted on the lower control arms. Rack-and-pinion steering had a power assist available at extra cost. The base engine was the 140 cid (2.3-liter) "Lima" four, also used in Pintos and Mustangs. It was the first four-cylinder in a domestic Ford compact. A four-speed manual gearbox was standard, but V-8 models required automatic. Four-cylinder models had standard low-back bucket seats, while sixes and eights held a bench seat. Standard equipment included B78 x 14 black tires and hubcaps. The Fairmont's wheelbase was 105.5 inches. The opening model lineup included two- and four-door sedans and a station wagon. A Euro styled (ES) option was added later. It included a blacked-out grille, rear quarter window louvers, black window frames and turbine-spoked wheel covers. The Futura Sport Coupe, with roofline reminiscent of Thunderbird, joined the

1978 Pinto station wagon (with Exterior Decor Package)

1978 Pinto three-door hatchback

1978 Pinto three-door Runabout (with Rallye Appearance Package)

original sedans and wagon in December. The coupe borrowed its name from the 1960s Falcon. Inside, the five-passenger Futura were pleated vinyl bucket seats, wood tone appliqué on the dash, and color-keyed seatbelts. William P. Benton, Ford's vice-president (and Ford Division General Manager) said Fairmont Futura "has the best fuel economy in its class, leg, shoulder and hip room of a mid-size car, and responsive handling, plus a rich new look and an array of luxury touches."

Granada Six and V-8: Granada and its twin, the Mercury Monarch, took on a fresh look this year with new bright grilles, rectangular headlamps, parking lamps, a front bumper air spoiler, wide wheel lip moldings, new wraparound tail lamps, and lower back panel appliqués. Also new on two-doors were "window" opera windows split by a bright center bar. This was the first major restyle since 1974 and the first quad rectangular headlamps in the Ford camp. The spoiler and hood-to-grille-opening panel seal, and revised decklid surface, helped reduce aerodynamic drag. A Ford badge went on the lower driver's side of the grille. Rectangular headlamps stood above nearly-as-large rectangular parking lamps, both in a recessed housing. Two-door and four-door sedans were offered again, in base or Ghia trim. Granada Ghia had wide side moldings. A new European Sports Sedan (ESS) option package included a blackout vertical grille texture as well as black rocker panels, door frames and side moldings, black rubber bumper guards and wide rub strips and a unique interior. ESS had color-keyed wheel covers, a heavy-duty suspension, dual sport mirrors, decklid and hood pin striping. It rode on FR78 x 14 steel belted radial tires. The car also had individual reclining bucket seats. Distinctive was the ESS half-covered, louvered quarter windows. Low on the cowl was an ESS badge, above the Granada script. Other options included an AM/FM stereo with cassette tape player, and a 40-channel CB transceiver. Five new Granada colors were offered this year, and a valino vinyl roof came in three new color choices. The base 200 cid six from 1977 was replaced by a 250 cid (4.1-liter) version.

LTD II — V-8: Station wagons left the LTD II lineup this year, since the new Fairmont line included a wagon. Other LTD II models continued with the S base and Brougham series. Broughams had a full-length body trim strip. The standard engine was again the 302 cid (5.0-liter) V-8 with Cruise-O-Matic transmission, power front disc brakes, and power steering. Options included the 351-cid and 400-cid V-8 engines, a heavy-duty trailer towing package (for the 400 V-8), and a Sports Appearance package. Two-doors could either have a solid panel at the rear, or the extra rear coach-style window. A new bumper front spoiler, hood-to-grille-opening panel seal, revised decklid surface, and new fuel tank air deflector were supposed to cut aerodynamic drag and boost economy. Bumper-to-fender shields were new, too. A revised low-restriction fresh-air intake went on V-8 engines. A new mechanical spark control system was limited to the 351M and 400 cid V-8s. Newly optional this year was a 40-channel CB radio. The Mercury Cougar was the corporate twin to the LTD II.

LTD/Custom 500 — V-8: Full-sized Fords were carried over for 1978, with new body colors available but little change beyond a new front bumper spoiler, rear floor pan air deflector, and other aerodynamic additions. The decklid also was new. The LTD still came in two-door or four-door pillared hardtop form, as well as plain-side and Country Squire (simulated wood paneled) station wagons. The Custom 500 was the fleet model and was sold in Canada. Station wagons could now have optional removable auxiliary cushions for the dual facing rear seats. Among the more than 70 options were new two-tone body colors for the LTD Landau. Air conditioners now allowed the driver to control heating and cooling. A downsized LTD arrived for 1979. The 1978 model was the final full-sized version.

I.D. Data:

Just as in 1976 and 1977, Ford's 11-symbol Vehicle Identification Number (VIN) was stamped on a metal tab fastened to the instrument panel and was visible through the windshield. The model year coding changed with the year: 8 = 1978.

Pinto (Four)

Model No.	Body Style No.	Body Type & Seating	Factory Price	Shipping Weight	Production Total
10	62B	2-dr. Sedan-4P	$3,336	2,337 lbs.	62,317
10	62B	2-dr. Pony Sedan-4P	$2,995	2,321 lbs.	Note 1
11	64B	2-dr. Hatchback-4P	$3,451	2,381 lbs.	74,313
12	73B	2-dr. Station Wagon-4P	$3,794	2,521 lbs.	52,269
12	73B	2-dr. Squire Wag-4P	$4,109	2,555 lbs.	Note 2

Pinto (V-6)

10	62B	2-dr. Sedan-4P	$3,609	2,463 lbs.	62,317
11	64B	3-dr. Hatchback-4P	$3,724	2,507 lbs.	74,313
12	73B	2-dr. Station Wagon-4P	$4,067	2,637 lbs.	52,269
12	73B	2-dr. Squire Wag-4P	$4,382	2,672 lbs.	Note 2

Note 1: Pony production was included in the base sedan figure.
Note 2: The Squire Wagon production was included in the standard station wagon total.
Pinto Production Note: Totals do not include 22,548 Pintos produced in 1978 but sold as 1977s.

Fairmont (Four)

93	36R	2-dr. Sport Coupe-5P	$4,044	2,605 lbs.	116,966
91	66B	2-dr. Sedan-5P	$3,589	2,568 lbs.	78,776
92	54B	4-dr. Sedan-5P	$3,663	2,610 lbs.	136,849
94	74B	4-dr. Station Wagon-5P	$4,031	2,718 lbs.	128,390

Fairmont (Six)

93	36R	2-dr. Sport Coupe-5P	$4,164	2,648 lbs.	116,966
91	66B	2-dr. Sedan-5P	$3,709	2,611 lbs.	78,776
92	54B	4-dr. Sedan-5P	$3,783	2,653 lbs.	136,849
94	74B	4-dr. Station Wagon-5P	$4,151	2,770 lbs.	128,390

Note: Prices shown are for four-cylinder and six-cylinder engines. A V-8 cost $199 more than the six.

Granada (Six)

81	66H	2-dr. Sedan-5P	$4,264	3,087 lbs.	110,481
82	54H	4-dr. Sedan-5P	$4,342	3,122 lbs.	139,305

Granada (V-8)

81	66HR	2-dr. Sedan-5P	$4,445	3,177 lbs.	110,481
82	54H	4-dr. Sedan-5P	$4,523	3,212 lbs.	139,305

Granada Ghia (Six)

81	66K	2-dr. Sedan-5P	$4,649	3,147 lbs.	Note 3
82	54K	4-dr. Sedan-5P	$4,728	3,230 lbs.	Note 3

Granada Ghia (V-8)

81	66K	2-dr. Sedan-5P	$4,830	3,237 lbs.	Note 3
82	54K	4-dr. Sedan-5P	$4,909	3,320 lbs.	Note 3

Granada ESS (Six)

81	----	2-dr. Sedan-5P	$4,836	3,145 lbs.	Note 3
82	----	4-dr. Sedan-5P	$4,914	3,180 lbs.	Note 3

Granada ESS (V-8)

81	----	2-dr. Sedan-5P	$5,017	3,235 lbs.	Note 3
82	----	4-dr. Sedan-5P	$5,095	3,270 lbs.	Note 3

Note 3: Granada Ghia and ESS production was included in the base Granada totals.

LTD II (V-8)

30	65D	2-dr. Hardtop-6P	$5,069	3,773 lbs.	76, 285
31	53D	4-dr. Pillared Hardtop-6P	$5,169	3,872 lbs.	64, 133

LTD II S (V-8)

25	65B	2-dr. Hardtop-6P	$4,814	3,746 lbs.	9,004
27	53B	4-dr. Pillared Hardtop-6P	$4,889	3,836 lbs.	21,122

LTD II Brougham (V-8)

30	65K	2-dr. Hardtop-6P	$5,405	3,791 lbs.	Note 4
31	53K	4-dr. Pillared Hardtop-6P	$5,505	3,901 lbs.	Note 4

Note 4: Brougham production was included in the LTD II totals.

LTD Landau (V-8)

| 64 | 60L | 2-dr. Pillared Hardtop-6P | $5,898 | 4,029 lbs. | 27,305 |
| 65 | 53L | 4-dr. Pillared Hardtop-6P | $5,973 | 4,081 lbs. | 39,836 |

Custom 500 (V-8)

52	60D	2-dr. Pillared Hardtop-6P	----	----	1,359
53	53D	4-dr. Pillared Hardtop-6P	----	----	3,044
72	71D	4-dr. Ranch Wagon-6P	----	----	1,196

Note: The Custom 500 was produced for sale in Canada. Totals included an LTD "S" two-door and Ranch wagon for sale in the U.S.

LTD (V-8)

62	60H	2-dr. Pillared Hardtop-6P	$5,335	3,972 lbs.	57,446
63	53H	4-dr. Pillared Hardtop-6P	$5,410	4,032 lbs.	112,392
74	71H	4-dr. Station Wagon-6P	$5,797	4,532 lbs.	71,285
74	71K	4-dr. Country Squire-6P	$6,207	4,576 lbs.	Note 5

Note 5: Country Squire production, and wagons produced with dual-facing rear seats, was included in basic wagon totals.

Engines:

Pinto and Fairmont Base Four: Inline with overhead cam. Cast-iron block and head. Displacement: 140 cid (2.3 liters). B & S: 3.78 x 3.13 in. Compression ratio: 9.0:1. Brake hp: 88 at 4800 rpm. Torque: 118 lbs.-ft. at 2800 rpm. Five main bearings. Hydraulic valve lifters. Carburetor: Motorcraft 5200 two-barrel. VIN Code: Y.

Pinto Optional V-6: 60-degree, overhead-valve. Cast-iron block and head. Displacement: 170.8 cid (2.8 liters). B & S: 3.66 x 2.70 in. Compression ratio: 8.7:1. Brake hp: 90 at 4200 rpm. Torque: 143 lbs.-ft. at 2200 rpm. Four main bearings. Solid valve lifters. Carburetor: Motorcraft 2150 two-barrel. VIN Code: Z.

Fairmont Optional Six: Inline. Overhead valve. Cast-iron block and head. Displacement: 200 cid (3.3 liters). B & S: 3.68 x 3.13 in. Compression ratio: 8.5:1. Brake hp: 85 at 3600 rpm. Torque: 154 lbs.-ft. at 1600 rpm. Seven main bearings. Hydraulic valve lifters. Carburetor: Carter YFA one-barrel. VIN Code: T.

Granada Base Six: Inline. Overhead valve. Cast-iron block and head. Displacement: 250 cid (4.1 liters). B & S: 3.68 x 3.91 in. Compression ratio: 8.5:1. Brake hp: 97 at 3200 rpm. Torque: 210 lbs.-ft. at 1400 rpm. Seven main bearings. Hydraulic valve lifters. Carburetor: Carter YFA one-barrel. VIN Code: L.

LTD and LTD II Base V-8 (Optional in Fairmont and Granada): 90-degree, overhead valve. Cast-iron block and head. Displacement: 302 cid (5.0 liters). B & S: 4.00 x 3.00 in. Compression ratio: 8.4:1. Brake hp: 134 at 3400 rpm. (Fairmont is 139 hp at 3600 rpm.) Torque: 248 lbs.-ft. at 1600 rpm. (Fairmont is 250 lbs.-ft. at 1600 rpm). Five main bearings. Hydraulic valve lifters. Carburetor: Motorcraft 2150 two-barrel. VIN Code: F.

LTD wagon Base V-8 (Optional in LTD and LTD II): 90-degree, overhead valve. Cast-iron block and head. Displacement: 351 cid (5.8 liters). B & S: 4.00 x 3.50 in. Compression ratio: 8.3:1. (LTD compression ratio is 8.0:1). Brake hp: 144 at 3200 rpm. (The LTD was 145 hp at 3400 rpm.) Torque: 277 lbs.-ft. at 1600 rpm. (The LTD was 273 lbs.-ft. at 1800 rpm.) Five main bearings. Hydraulic valve lifters. Carburetor: Motorcraft 2150 two-barrel. Windsor engine. VIN Code: H.

LTD II Optional V-8: Modified version of the 351-cid V-8 with a compression ratio of 8.0:1 and brake hp of 152 at 3600 rpm. Torque: 278 lbs.-ft. at 1800 rpm. VIN Code: Q.

LTD and LTD II Optional V-8: 90-degree, overhead valve. Cast-iron block and head. Displacement: 400 cid (6.6 liters). B & S: 4.00 x 4.00 in. Compression ratio: 8.0:1. Brake hp: 166 at 3800 rpm. (The LTD was 160 hp at 3800 rpm.) Torque: 319 lbs.-ft. at 1800 rpm. (The LTD was 314 lbs.-ft. at 1800 rpm.) Five main bearings. Hydraulic valve lifters. Carburetor: Motorcraft 2150. VIN Code: S.

LTD Optional V-8: 90-degree, overhead valve. Cast-iron block and head. Displacement: 460 cid (7.5 liters). B & S: 4.36 x 3.85 in. Compression ratio: 8.0:1. Brake hp: 202 at 4000 rpm. Torque: 348 lbs.-ft. at 2000 rpm. Five main bearings. Hydraulic valve lifters. Carburetor: Motorcraft 4350 four-barrel. VIN Code: A.

Note: A Police 460-cid V-8 was also available for the LTD series.

Chassis:

Pinto: Wheelbase: 94.5 in. and 94.8 in. on station wagon. Overall length: 169.3 in. and 179.1 in. on station wagon. Tires: A78 x 13.

Fairmont: Wheelbase: 105.5 in. Overall length: 193.8 in. and 195.8 in. on Futura. Tires: B78 x 14 and CR78 x 14 on the station wagon.

Granada: Wheelbase: 109.9 in. Overall length: 197.7 in. Tires: DR78 x 14 steel-belted white sidewall tires and ER78 x 14 on the Granada Ghia.

LTD II: Wheelbase: 114.0 in. and 118.0 in. on the LTD II sedan. Overall length: 215.5 in. and 219.5 in. on the LTD II sedan. Tires: HR78 x 14 steel-belted black wall.

LTD/Custom 500: Wheelbase: 121.0 in. Overall length: 224.1 in., 225.7 in. on the LTD station wagon and 226.8 in. on the LTD Landau. Tires: HR78 x 15, JR78 x 15 on station wagon and GR78 x 15 with the 302-cid V-8.

Options:

Pinto: Cruising wagon option ($365 to $401). Cruising wagon paint/tape treatment ($59). Sports Rallye package ($76 to $96). Rallye appearance package ($176 to $201). Exterior decor group ($30 to $40). Interior decor group ($149 to $181). Interior accent group ($28 to $40). Convenience/light group ($81 to $143). Deluxe bumper group ($70). Protection group ($83 to $135). Air conditioner ($459). Rear defroster, electric ($77). Tinted glass ($53); windshield only ($25). Trunk light ($5). Driver's sport mirror ($16). Dual sport mirrors ($49). Day/night mirror ($7). AM radio ($65); w/digital clock ($47 to $119); with stereo tape player ($119 to $192). AM/FM radio ($48 to $120). AM/FM stereo radio ($89 to $161). Flip-up open air roof ($167). Half vinyl roof ($125). Glass third door ($25). Bumper guards ($37). Roof luggage rack ($69). Rocker panel moldings ($22). Lower body protection ($30). Four-way driver's seat ($33). Load floor carpet ($23). Cargo area cover ($25). Wire wheel covers ($90). Forged aluminum wheels ($173 to $252) and white wheels ($187 to $265). Styled steel wheels ($78). 170-cid V-6 ($273). SelectShift Cruise-O-Matic ($281). Optional axle ratio ($13). Power brakes ($64). Power steering ($131).

Fairmont: ES option: sedan ($300). Squire option ($365). Exterior decor group ($214). Exterior accent group ($96). Interior decor group ($176 to $301). Interior accent group ($89 to $94). Deluxe bumper group ($70). Convenience group ($29 to $60). Appearance protection group ($36 to $47). Light group ($35 to $40). Air conditioning ($465). Floor shift level ($30). Rear defogger ($47). Rear defroster, electric ($84). Tinted glass ($52); windshield only ($25). Sport steering wheel ($36). Electric clock ($18). Interval wipers ($29). Lift gate wiper/washer for station wagon ($78). Trunk light ($4). Left remote mirror ($19). Dual bright mirrors ($13

1978 Fairmont four-door sedan

1978 Fairmont Futura Sport Coupe

1978 Granada Ghia two-door sedan

1978 Granada ESS sedan

to $36). Day/night mirror ($8). AM radio ($72); with an eight-track tape player ($192). AM/FM radio ($120). AM/FM stereo radio ($176); with 8-track or cassette player ($243). Vinyl roof ($89 to $124). Pivoting front vent windows ($37 to $60). Rear quarter vent louvers ($33). Bumper guards, front and rear ($37). Luggage rack ($72). Lower body protection ($30 to $42). Bucket seat, non-reclining ($72). Bench seat ($72 credit). Cloth seat trim ($19-$37). Vinyl seat trim ($22). Lockable side storage box ($19). Hubcaps with trim rings ($34), no charge on Futura. Deluxe wheel covers ($33). Turbine wheel covers ($33 to $66). Wire wheel covers ($48 to $114). Cast aluminum wheels ($210 to $276). 200-cid six ($120). 302-cid V-8 ($319). SelectShift Cruise-O-Matic ($368) and ($281) on the Fairmont station wagon. Power brakes ($63). Power steering ($140). Handling suspension ($30). Heavy duty battery ($17).

Granada: Luxury interior group ($476). Interior decor group ($211). Convenience group ($30 to $89). Deluxe bumper group ($70). Light group ($30 to $43). Cold weather group ($37 to $54). Heavy-duty group ($37 to $54). Protection group ($25 to $43). Visibility group ($4 to $58). Air conditioning ($494); auto-temp ($535). Rear defogger ($47). Rear defroster, electric ($84). Fingertip speed control ($55 to $102). Illuminated entry system ($49). Power windows ($116 to $160). Power door locks ($76 to $104). Power decklid release ($19). Automatic parking brake release ($8). Power four-way seat ($90). Tinted glass ($54); windshield only ($25). Tilt steering wheel ($58). Digital clock ($42). Cornering lamps ($42). Trunk light ($4). Left remote mirror ($14). Dual remote mirrors ($31 to $46). Dual sport mirrors ($42 to $53). Day/night mirror ($8). Lighted right visor vanity mirror ($34). AM radio ($72); w/tape player ($192). AM/FM radio ($135). AM/FM stereo radio ($176); with 8-track or cassette player ($243); w/ Quadrasonic tape ($365). AM/FM stereo search radio ($319). CB radio ($270). Power moon roof ($820). Full or half vinyl roof ($102). Console ($75). Four-way driver's seat ($33). Leather seat trim ($271). Cloth flight bench seat ($54). Deluxe cloth seat/door trim: Ghia/ESS ($99). Color-keyed seatbelts ($19). Deluxe wheel covers ($37) No charge on Ghia and ESS. Wire wheel covers ($59 to $96). Styled steel wheels w/trim rings ($59 to $96). Lacy spoke aluminum wheels ($205 to $242) and white wheels ($218 to $255). 302 V-8 ($181). SelectShift Cruise-O-Matic ($193). Floor shift lever ($30). Power brakes ($63). Four-wheel power disc brakes ($300). Power steering ($148). Heavy duty suspension ($27).

LTD II: Sports appearance package ($216 to $363). Sports instrumentation group ($111 to $138). Sports touring package ($287 to $434). Deluxe bumper group ($76). Light group ($49 to $54). Convenience group ($107 to $139). Power lock group ($100 to $132). Front protection group ($46 to $58). Air conditioning ($543); w/auto-temp control ($588). Rear defroster, electric ($93). Fingertip speed control ($104 to $117). Illuminated entry system ($54). Tinted glass ($62); windshield only ($28). Power windows ($126 to $175). Power door locks ($71 to $101). Six-way power seat ($149). Automatic parking brake release ($9). Leather-wrapped steering wheel ($51 to $64). Tilt steering wheel ($70). Electric clock ($20). Day/date clock ($22 to $42). Cornering lamps ($46). Trunk light ($4). Dual-note horn ($7). Remote driver's mirror ($16). Dual chrome mirrors ($7). Dual sport mirrors ($29 to $58). Lighted visor vanity mirror ($33 to $37). AM radio ($79). AM/FM radio ($132). AM/FM stereo radio ($192); with tape player ($266); with Quadrasonic tape player ($399). AM/FM stereo search radio ($349). CB radio ($295). Dual rear speakers ($46). Full or half vinyl roof ($112). Opera windows ($51). Bucket seats with console ($211), on Brougham ($37). Vinyl seat trim ($24). Cloth/vinyl seat trim ($24). Front floor mats ($20). Heavy-duty floor mats ($9). Color-keyed seatbelts ($21). Deluxe wheel covers ($38). Luxury wheel covers ($62 to $100). Wire wheel covers ($105 to $143), no charge with sports package. Cast aluminum wheels ($196 to $301). HR78 x 14 steel-belted radial white sidewall tires ($46). HR78 x 14 wide-band white sidewalls ($66). HR78 x 14 steel-belted radials ($62). HR78 x 15 steel-belted radials with white sidewalls ($68). Inflatable spare (NC). 351-cid V-8 ($157). 400-cid V-8 ($283). Heavy duty handling suspension ($36). Heavy duty battery ($18). Heavy-duty alternator ($50). Heavy-duty trailer towing package ($184).

LTD: Landau luxury group ($457 to $580). Convenience group ($96 to $146). Light group ($26 to $38). Deluxe bumper group ($50 to $72). Protection group ($45 to $53). Air conditioning ($562), with auto-temp control ($607). Rear defogger ($50). Rear defroster, electric ($93). Fingertip speed control ($104 to $117). Illuminated entry system ($54). Power windows ($129 to $188). Power door locks ($82 to $153). Six-way power driver's seat ($149) or driver and passenger ($297). Tinted glass ($75); windshield only ($28). Tilt steering wheel ($70). Automatic parking brake release ($8). Electric clock ($21). Digital clock ($28 to $49). Cornering lamps ($46). Trunk light ($4). Dual-note horn ($7). Driver's remote mirror ($16). Dual remote mirrors ($32 to $47). Lighted visor vanity mirror ($33 to $37). AM radio ($79). AM/FM radio ($132). AM/FM stereo radio ($192); w/tape player ($266); with Quadrasonic tape player ($399). AM/FM stereo search radio ($349). Dual rear speakers ($46). Power moon roof ($896). Full vinyl roof ($141), no charge on Landau two-door. Half vinyl roof ($141). Rear bumper guards ($22). Luggage rack ($80). Dual-facing rear seats: wagon ($143). Split

bench seat with passenger recliner ($141 to $233). Leather seat trim ($296). All-vinyl seat trim ($24). Duraweave vinyl trim ($50). Color-keyed seatbelts ($21). Lockable side stowage compartment ($33). Full wheel covers ($38). Deluxe or color-keyed wheel covers ($61 to $99). Wire wheel covers ($99 to $137). Deep-dish aluminum wheels ($263 to $301). 351-cid V-8 ($157). 400-cid V-8 ($283). 460-cid V-8 ($428) or ($271) on LTD wagon. Traction-Lok differential ($62). Optional axle ratio ($14). Four-wheel power disc brakes ($187 to $197). Semi-metallic front disc pads ($8). Heavy duty suspension ($65). Adjustable air shock absorbers ($50). Heavy duty battery ($18). Heavy duty alternator ($50). Heavy duty trailer towing package ($139).

History:

The 1978 Fords were introduced on October 7, 1977. The Fairmont Futura premiered December 2, 1977. Model year production was 1,929,254 including Mustangs. Calendar year sales by U.S. dealers were 1,768,753, including Mustangs. The model year sales increased for 1978, though production slipped a bit. Major recalls of more than four million vehicles bruised Ford's reputation. Pintos were recalled for gas tanks that might burst into flame. Many Ford automatic transmissions had a problem with jerking suddenly from park to reverse, a situation that never was resolved. Philip Caldwell replaced Ford president Lee Iacocca. Iacocca emerged within a few months as the new head of Chrysler Corporation. The new compact Fairmont was more popular than the Maverick. There were 417,932 Fairmonts sold versus just 105,156 Mavericks sold in 1977. Fairmont was a better seller than Mustang in its first year. Granada and LTD II sales plummeted for the model year. Fairmont was "the most successful new-car nameplate ever introduced by a domestic manufacturer and Ford's top selling car line in 1978," said Walter S. Walla, Ford Division General Manager. It was also highly rated by the auto magazines. Readers of *Car and Driver* called it "the most significant new American car for 1978." Computer-assisted design techniques were used to develop the Fairmont/Zephyr duo, along with more than 320 hours of wind-tunnel testing. Corporate Average Fuel Economy (CAFE) standards began in 1978. Automakers' fleets were required to meet a specified average miles-per-gallon rating each year for the next decade, with 27.5 mpg the ultimate goal. Fairmont was designed with the CAFE ratings in mind, which required that Fords average 18 mpg. This year's model introduction meetings had been held in the Detroit and Dearborn area for the first time since 1959. More than 15,000 dealers, general managers and spouses attended. The international emphasis was highlighted by a "flags of the world of Ford" display at the world headquarters, in a special ceremony. Ford began to import the front-wheel drive Fiesta from its German plant.

1978 LTD II "S" hardtop coupe

1978 LTD Landau pillared hardtop

1978 Fairmont two-door sedan

1978 Fairmont ES Sport Coupe

1978 Fairmont station wagon

1979 Ford

Pinto — Four and V-6: Restyling brought the subcompact Pinto a new front-end look with single rectangular headlamps in bright housings, as well as a new sloping hood and fenders, and horizontal-style argent grille. New sculptured-look front and rear aluminum bumpers had black rub strips and end sections. Full wheel covers took on a new design. Inside, a new instrument panel and pad held rectangular instrument pods. The redesigned cluster now included a speedometer graduated in miles and kilometers, a fuel gauge and warning lights with symbols. New body and interior colors were available. The two-door sedan, "three-door" hatchback Runabout and station wagon still were offered. A Cruising Package was optional on both Runabouts and wagons, featuring multi-color side paint and tape treatment and black louvers on the wagon's lift gate window. There was also a new ESS option for sedans and Runabouts, with black grille and exterior accents, a black-hinged glass third door, wide black side moldings, and sports-type equipment. Pinto's standard equipment list grew longer this year, adding an AM radio, power brakes, electric rear defroster, and tinted glass. The low-budget Pony lacked some of these extras. The standard engine remained the 140 cid (2.3-liter) overhead-cam four, with a four-speed gearbox. Oil-change intervals were raised to 30,000 miles. The V-6 added a higher-performance camshaft, while the V-6 automatic transmissions offered higher rpm shift points to improve acceleration.

Fairmont — Four, Six and V-8: Appearance of the year-old compact didn't change this year. Model lineup included two-door and four-door sedans, a station wagon, and the Futura coupe. Seven new body colors and four new vinyl roof colors were available. Availability of the distinctive two-tone paint treatment was expanded to sedans, as well as the Futura. A four-speed overdrive manual transmission with new single-rail shifter design replaced the former three-speed, coupled with either the 200 cid (3.3-liter) inline six or 302 cid (5.0-liter) V-8. It was the first time a V-8 was mated with a manual transmission in the Fairmont series. The base engine remained the 140 cid (2.3-liter) four with a non-overdrive

four-speed manual transmission. The six was now offered on wagons sold in California. Ignition and door locks were modified to improve theft-resistance. A lower axle ratio (2.26:1) came with the V-8 and automatic. Inside was a new dark walnut woodtone instrument cluster appliqué. The Fairmont ES package also was offered again. It included a blackout grille, black window frames, dual black sail-mount sport mirrors and turbine wheel covers plus special suspension with rear stabilizer bar.

Granada — Six and V-8: Billed as "An American Classic" and playing on its perceived Mercedes styling origins, Granada changed little for 1979. Few customers had chosen four-wheel disc brakes, so that option was dropped. Both the standard 250 cid (3.3-liter) inline six and 302 cid (5.0-liter) V-8 came with a four-speed overdrive manual gearbox that used a new enclosed single-rail shift mechanism. As before, two- and four-door sedans were produced, in base, Ghia or ESS trim. Base models got all-bright versions of the 1978 Ghia wheel cover. Ghia seats had a new sew style plus all-vinyl door trim with carpeted lower panels. Leather/vinyl trim was now available with bucket seats. New soft Rossano cloth and Wilshire cloth luxury trim also was available. Ignition locks offered improved theft-resistance. New options included tone-on-tone paint in five color combinations. Dropped were white lacy-spoke aluminum wheels, Traction-Lok axle, and the Luxury Interior Group. This year's ESS option was identified by "Granada" script above the "ESS" badge. The Granada ESS had a blacked-out grille, color-keyed wheel covers and dual mirrors, individually reclining bucket seats with Euro headrests and a leather-wrapped steering wheel. Optional speed control for the ESS included a black leather-wrapped steering wheel.

LTD II — V-8: Not enough buyers had found LTD II appealing, so this would be its final season. Not much was new this year, except for a redesigned front bumper spoiler, corrosion-resistant plastic battery tray, and an electronic voltage regulator. Seven body colors were new, as were front and full vinyl roofs. Broughams had new interior fabric selections. All models had standard flight bench seating with a fold-down center armrest. The base engine remained the 302 cid (5.0-liter) V-8, with the 351-cid V-8 optional. The 400-cid V-8 option was discontinued. Automatic transmission was standard. A newly optional 27.5 gallon gas tank suggested LTD II's economy problems hadn't been corrected with either a lighter weight front bumper or by carburetor refinements, Rear bumper guards became standard, and the ignition lock was modified. The Sports Touring Package included two-tone paint, a grille badge and Magnum 500 wheels with HR78 x 14 raised-white-letter tires. A Sports Appearance Group for two-doors had bold tri-color tape stripes. Two-door hardtop and four-door pillared hardtop bodies were offered again. They came in base, Brougham or "S" trim.

LTD — V-8: Substantial downsizing made the 1979 LTD the ninth new full-size model in the company's history. Still built with body-on-frame construction, it was intended to be space-efficient and fuel-efficient. It resulted from more than 270 hours of wind-tunnel testing. Riding a 114.4-inch wheelbase, with seven inches cut, the LTD increased its interior space. A conventional sedan design replaced the pillared hardtop. Door openings were larger and the doors were thinner. Overall, the new design was slightly taller and squarer. Inside, LTD's seating position was higher. A tall, narrow ornament adorned the hood. Two-doors were four-window design with a slim coach-style quarter window. Landaus had new rear-pillar coach lamps. Country Squire wagons showed a new woodtone appliqué treatment. Inside were thin-back seats with foam padding over flex-o-lator cushion support, and a four-spoke soft-rim steering wheel. A steering-column stalk held the dimmer, horn and wiper/washer controls. Door-lock plungers moved to the armrests to improve theft-resistance. Lockable side stowage compartments were standard on wagons. The base engine, except on wagons with California emissions, was the 302 cid (5.0-liter) V-8. That engine had a new single accessory-drive belt operating the fan/water pump, alternator, and power steering pump. A variable-venturi carburetor became standard on both the 302 and the optional 351 V-8 engines. Up front was a new short/long arm coil spring front suspension with link-type stabilizer bar and at the rear was a new four-bar link coil spring setup. Front disc brakes used a new pin-slider design.

1979 Pinto three-door Runabout

1979 Pinto ESS three-door hatchback

Ford's 11-symbol Vehicle Identification Number (VIN) was stamped on a metal tab fastened to the instrument panel and was visible through the windshield. The first digit was the model year code, 9= 1979. The second letter indicated the assembly plant: A=Atlanta, Georgia; B=Oakville, Ontario, Canada; E=Mahwah, New Jersey; G=Chicago, Illinois; H=Lorain, Ohio; J=Los Angeles, California; K=Kansas City, Missouri; S=St. Thomas, Ontario, Canada; T=Metuchen, New Jersey; U=Louisville, Kentucky; W=Wayne, Michigan. Digits three and four corresponded to the Model Numbers: (10=Pinto 2-dr. sedan). The fifth symbol was an engine code: Y=140-cid six, Z=170-cid V-6, T=200-cid six, L=250-cid six, F=302-cid V-8 and H=351 V-8. Digits 6 through 11 made up the unit number of cars built at each assembly plant, beginning with 100001. A Vehicle Certification Label on the left front door lock face panel or door pillar showed the manufacturer, month and year of manufacture, GVW, GAWR, certification statement, VIN, body code, color code, trim code, axle code, transmission code, and special order code.

Pinto (Four)

Model No.	Body Style No.	Body Type & Seating	Factory Price	Shipping Weight	Production Total
10	62B	2-dr. Sedan-4P	$3,629	2,346 lbs.	75,789
10	41E	2-dr. Pony Sedan-4P	$3,199	2,329 lbs.	Note 1
11	64B	3-dr. Hatchback-4P	$3,744	2,392 lbs.	69,383
12	73B	2-dr. Station Wagon-4P	$4,028	2,532 lbs.	53,846
12	41E	2-dr. Pony Wagon-4P	$3,633	----	Note 1
12	73B	2-dr. Squire Wag-4P	$4,343	2,568 lbs.	Note 2

Pinto (V-6)

10	62B	2-dr. Sedan-4P	$3,902	2,446 lbs.	75,789
11	64B	3-dr. Hatchback-4P	$4,017	2,492 lbs.	69,383
12	73B	2-dr. Station Wagon-4P	$4,301	2,610 lbs.	53,846
12	73B	2-dr. Squire Wag-4P	$4,616	2,646 lbs.	Note 2

Note 1: Pony production was included in the base sedan and wagon figures.
Note 2: Squire Wagon production was included in the standard station wagon total.

Fairmont (Four)

93	36R	2-dr. Sport Coupe-5P	$4,071	2,546 lbs.	106,065
91	66B	2-dr. Sedan-5P	$3,710	2,491 lbs.	54,798
92	54B	4-dr. Sedan-5P	$3,810	2,544 lbs.	133,813
94	74B	4-dr. Station Wagon-5P	$4,157	2,674 lbs.	100,691

Pinto (Six)

93	36R	2-dr. Sport Coupe-5P	$4,312	2,613 lbs.	106,065
91	66B	2-dr. Sedan-5P	$3,951	2,558 lbs.	54,798
92	54B	4-dr. Sedan-5P	$4,051	2,611 lbs.	133,813
94	74B	4-dr. Station Wagon-5P	$4,398	2,741 lbs.	100,691

Note: Prices shown are for the four- and six-cylinder engines. A V-8 cost $283 more than the six.

Granada (Six)

81	66H	2-dr. Sedan-5P	$4,342	3,051 lbs.	76,850
82	54H	4-dr. Sedan-5P	$4,445	3,098 lbs.	105,526

Granada (V-8)

81	66H	2-dr. Sedan-5P	$4,625	3,124 lbs.	76,850
82	54H	4-dr. Sedan-5P	$4,728	3,169 lbs.	105,526

Granada Ghia (Six)

81	66K	2-dr. Sedan-5P	$4,728	3,089 lbs.	Note 3
82	54K	4-dr. Sedan-5P	$4,830	3,132 lbs.	Note 3

Granada Ghia (V-8)

602	66K	2-dr. Sedan-5P	$5,011	3,160 lbs.	Note 3
602	54K	4-dr. Sedan-5P	$5,113	3,203 lbs.	Note 3

Granada ESS (Six)

81	----	2-dr. Sedan-5P	$4,888	3,105 lbs.	Note 3
82	----	4-dr. Sedan-5P	$4,990	3,155 lbs.	Note 3

Granada ESS (V-8)

433	----	2-dr. Sedan-5P	$5,161	3,176 lbs.	Note 3
433	----	4-dr. Sedan-5P	$5,273	3,226 lbs.	Note 3

Note 3: Granada Ghia and ESS production totals were included with the base Granada totals.

LTD II (V-8)

30	65D	2-dr. Hardtop-6P	$5,445	3,797 lbs.	18,300
31	53D	4-dr. Pillar Hardtop-6P	$5,569	3,860 lbs.	19,781

LTD II "S" (V-8)

25	65B	2-dr. Hardtop-6P	$5,198	3,781 lbs.	834
27	53B	4-dr. Pillar Hardtop-6P	$5,298	3,844 lbs.	9,649

Note: The LTD "S" was for fleet sales only.

LTD II Brougham (V-8)

30	65K	2-dr. Hardtop-6P	$5,780	3,815 lbs.	Note 4
31	53K	4-dr. Pillar Hardtop-6P	$5,905	3,889 lbs.	Note 4

Note 4: Brougham production was included in the LTD II totals.

LTD (V-8)

62	66H	2-dr. Sedan-6P	$5,813	3,421 lbs.	54,005
63	54H	4-dr. Sedan-6P	$5,913	3,463 lbs.	117,730
74	74H	4-dr. Station Wagon-6P	$6,122	3,678 lbs.	37,955
74	74K	4-dr. Country Squire-6P	$6,615	3,719 lbs.	29,932

Note: Production of wagons with dual-facing rear seats was included in the basic wagon totals. Totals also included Custom 500 production for the Canadian market (2,036 two-doors, 4,567 four-doors and 1,568 wagons).

LTD Landau (V-8)

64	66K	2-dr. Sedan-6P	$6,349	3,472 lbs.	42,314
65	54K	4-dr. Sedan-6P	$6,474	3,527 lbs.	74,599

Engines:

Pinto/Fairmont Four: Inline. Overhead cam. Cast-iron block and head. Displacement: 140 cid (2.3 liters). B & S: 3.78 x 3.13 in. Compression ratio: 9.0:1. Brake hp: 88 at 4800 rpm. Torque: 118 lbs.-ft. at 2800 rpm. Five main bearings. Hydraulic valve lifters. Carburetor: Motorcraft 5200 two-barrel. VIN Code: Y.

Pinto Optional V-6: 60-degree, overhead-valve V-6. Cast-iron block and head. Displacement: 170.8 cid (2.8 liters). B & S: 3.66 x 2.70 in. Compression ratio: 8.7:1. Brake hp: 102 at 4400 rpm. Torque: 138 lbs.-ft. at 3200 rpm. Four main bearings. Solid valve lifters. Carburetor: Motorcraft 2150 or 2700VV two barrel. VIN Code: Z.

1979 Pinto Squire station wagon

1979 Fairmont Squire wagon

1979 Pinto Cruising Wagon

1979 Fairmont Futura sedan

1979 Fairmont two-door sedan

1979 Granada sedan (with optional two-tone paint and cast aluminum wheels)

1979 Granada Ghia coupe

Fairmont Optional Six: Inline. Overhead valve. Cast-iron block and head. Displacement: 200 cid (3.3 liters). B & S: 3.68 x 3.13 in. Compression ratio: 8.5: 1. Brake hp: 85 at 3600 rpm. Torque: 154 lbs.-ft, at 1600 rpm. Seven main bearings. Hydraulic valve lifters. Carburetor: Carter YFA or Holley 1946 single -barrel. VIN Code: T.

Granada Six: Inline. Overhead valve. Cast-iron block and head. Displacement: 250 cid (4.1 liters). B & S: 3.68 x 3.91 in. Compression ratio: 8.6:1. Brake hp: 97 at 3200 rpm. Torque: 210 lbs.-ft. at 1400 rpm. Seven main bearings. Hydraulic valve lifters, Carburetor: Carter YFA single barrel. VIN Code: L.

LTD and LTD II V-8 (Optional Fairmont and Granada): 90-degree, overhead valve. Cast-iron block and head. Displacement: 302 cid (5.0 liters). B & S: 4.00 x 3.00 in. Compression ratio: 8.4:1. Brake hp: 129 at 3600 rpm. in the LTD and 133 at 3400 in the LTD II. It was 140 at 3600 in the Fairmont and 137 at 3600 in the Granada. Torque: 223 lbs.-ft. at 2600 rpm, LTD; 245 at 1600. LTD II; 250 at 1800, Fairmont and 243 at 2000 for the Granada. Five main bearings. Hydraulic valve lifters. Carburetor: Motorcraft 2150 or 2700VV two-barrel. VIN Code: F.

LTD Optional V-8: 90-degree, overhead valve. Cast-iron block and head. Displacement: 351 cid (5.8 liters). B & S: 4.00 x 3.50 in. Compression ratio: 8.3:1. Brake hp: 135 or 142 at 3200 rpm. Torque: 286 lbs.-ft. at 1400 rpm. Five main bearings. Hydraulic valve lifters. Carburetor: Motorcraft 7200VV two-barrel. Windsor engine. VIN Code: H.

LTD and LTD II Optional V-8: The modified version of the 351-cid V-8. Compression: 8.0:1. Brake hp: 151 at 3600 rpm. Torque: 270 lbs.-ft. at 2200 rpm. Carb: Motorcraft 2150 two-barrel. Code: H.

Chassis:

Pinto: Wheelbase: 94.5 in. and 94.8 in. on station wagon. Overall length: 168.8 in. and 178.6 in. on the station wagon. Tires: A78 x 13.

Fairmont: Wheelbase: 105.5 in. Overall length: 193.8 in. and Futura, 195.8 in. Tires: B78 x 14 and CR78 x 14, station wagon.

Granada: Wheelbase: 109.9 in. Overall length: 197.8 in. Tires: DR78 x 14 steel-belted black wall and ER78 x 14 on the Granada Ghia.

LTD II: Wheelbase: 114.0 in., two-door sedan and 118.0 in., four door sedan. Overall length: 217.2 in., two-door sedan and 221.2 in., four-door sedan. Tires: HR78 x 14 steel-belted black wall.

LTD: Wheelbase: 114.4 in. Overall length: 209.0 in. and 212.9 in., LTD station wagon. Tires: FR78 x 14 steel-belted white sidewalls and GR78 x 14 on the LTD station wagon.

Options:

Pinto: ESS package ($236 to $261). Cruising package ($330 to $566); tape delete ($55 credit). Sport package ($96 to $110). Exterior decor group ($20 to $40). Interior decor group ($137 to $207). Interior accent group ($5 to $40). Convenience group ($24 to $61). Deluxe bumper group ($52). Protection group ($33 to $36). Light group ($25 to $37). Air conditioner ($484). Rear defroster ($84). Tinted glass ($59). Trunk light ($5). Driver's sport mirror ($18). Dual sport mirrors ($52). Day/night mirror ($10). AM radio: Pony ($65). AM radio w/digital clock ($47 to $119); w/stereo tape player ($119 to $192). AM/FM radio ($48 to $120). AM/FM stereo radio ($89 to $161); w/cassette player ($157 to $222). Radio flexibility option ($90). Flip-up open air roof ($199). Glass third door ($25). Rear bumper guards ($19). Roof luggage rack ($63). Mud/

stone deflectors ($23). Lower side protection ($30). Interior: Four-way driver's seat ($35). Load floor carpet ($24). Cargo area cover ($28). Wire wheel covers ($99). Forged aluminum wheels ($217 to $289); white wheels ($235 to $307). Lacy spoke aluminum wheels ($217 to $289). Styled steel wheels ($54). A78 x 13 white sidewalls ($43). BR78 x 13 black walls ($148); white sidewalls ($191). BR70 x 13 raised white lettering ($228). 170-cid V-6 ($273). Cruise-O-Matic automatic transmission ($307). Optional axle ratio ($13). Power brakes ($70). Power steering ($141).

Fairmont: Option Packages: ES option, including a blackout grille, black window frames, dual black sail-mount sport mirrors (left remote) and turbine wheel covers ($329). Futura sports group, included unique tape striping, a charcoal argent grille and color-keyed turbine wheel covers ($102). Ghia package ($207 to $498). Squire option ($399). Exterior decor group ($223). Exterior accent group ($82). Interior decor group ($170 to $311). Interior accent group ($80 to $84). Instrumentation group ($77). Deluxe bumper group ($57). Convenience group ($33 to $65). Appearance protection group ($36 to $47). Light group ($27 to $43). Air conditioning ($484). Rear defogger ($51). Rear defroster, electric ($90). Fingertip speed control ($104 to $116). Power windows ($116 to $163). Power door locks ($73 to $101). Power deck lid release ($22). Power seat ($94). Tinted glass ($59); windshield only ($25). Sport steering wheel ($39). Tilt steering ($69 to $81). Electric clock ($20). Interval wipers ($35). Rear wiper/washer ($63). Map light ($7). Trunk light ($7). Left remote mirror ($17). Dual bright mirrors ($37-$43). Day/night mirror ($10). AM radio ($72); with eight-track tape player ($192). AM/FM radio ($120). AM/FM stereo radio ($176); with eight-track or cassette player ($243). Premium sound system ($67). Radio flexibility ($93). Flip-up open air roof ($199). Full vinyl roof ($90). Luggage rack ($76). Lower body protection ($30 to $42). Vinyl bucket seats, non-reclining ($72). Bench seat ($72 credit). Cloth/vinyl seat trim ($20 to $42). Vinyl seat trim ($24). Front floor mats ($18). Lockable side storage box ($20). Hubcaps and trim rings ($37). Deluxe wheel covers ($37). Turbine wheel covers ($39 to $76). Wire wheel covers ($50 to $127). Styled steel wheels ($40 to $116). Cast aluminum wheels ($251 to $327). 200-cid six ($241). 302-cid V-8 ($524). Cruise-O-Matic automatic transmission ($401), Fairmont and ($307) on the Fairmont station wagon. Floor shift lever ($31). Power brakes ($70). Power steering ($149). Heavy duty suspension ($19 to $25). Handling suspension ($41).

Granada: Interior decor group ($211). Convenience group ($35 to $94). Deluxe bumper group ($78). Light group ($41 to $46). Cold weather group ($30 to $60). Heavy-duty group ($18 to $60). Protection group ($24 to $47). Visibility group ($5 to $70). Air conditioning ($514); auto-temp ($555). Rear defogger ($51). Rear defroster, electric ($90). Fingertip speed control ($104 to $116). Illuminated entry system ($52). Power windows ($120 to $171). Power door locks ($78 to $110). Power deck lid release ($22). Automatic parking brake release ($8). Power four-way seat ($94). Tinted glass ($64); windshield only ($25). Tilt steering wheel ($69). Digital clock ($47). Cornering lamps ($43). Trunk light ($5). Left remote mirror ($17). Dual remote mirrors ($37 to $54). Dual sport mirrors ($46 to $63). Day/night mirror ($11). Lighted right visor vanity mirror ($36). AM radio ($72); with tape player ($192). AM/FM radio ($135). AM/FM stereo radio ($176); with eight-track or cassette player ($243); with Quadrasonic tape ($365). AM/FM stereo search radio

1979 Granada ESS sedan

1979 LTD II hardtop coupe (with Sports Appearance Package)

($319). CB radio ($270). Radio flexibility ($93). Power moon roof ($899). Full or half vinyl roof ($106). Lower body protection ($31). Console ($99). Four-way driver's seat ($34). Reclining seats (NC). Leather seat trim ($271). Flight bench seat (NC). Cloth/vinyl flight bench seat ($54). Deluxe cloth/vinyl trim (NC). Front floor mats ($18). Color-keyed seatbelts ($19). Deluxe wheel covers ($41), non charge on the Ghia and ESS. Wire wheel covers ($108), except no charge on the Ghia and ESS ($67). Styled steel wheels with trim rings ($83 to $124). Cast aluminum wheels ($248 to $289). 302-cid V-8 ($283). Cruise-O-Matic automatic transmission ($309). Floor shift lever ($31). Power brakes ($70). Power steering ($155). Heavy duty suspension ($20).

LTD II: Sports appearance package (2-dr.) ($301 to $449). Sports instrumentation group ($121 to $151). Sports touring package (2-dr.) ($379 to $526). Deluxe bumper group ($63). Light group ($51 to $57). Convenience group ($120 to $155). Power lock group ($111 to $143). Protection group ($49 to $61). Air conditioning ($562); with auto-temp control ($607). Rear defroster, electric ($99). Fingertip speed control ($113 to $126). Illuminated entry system ($57). Tinted glass ($70); windshield only ($28). Power windows ($132 to $187). Six-way power seat ($163). Tilt steering wheel ($75). Electric clock ($22). Day/date clock ($22 to $45). Cornering lamps ($49). Dual-note horn ($9). Remote driver's mirror ($18). Dual sport mirrors ($9 to $68). Lighted visor vanity mirror ($34 to $39). AM radio ($79). AM/FM radio ($132). AM/FM stereo radio ($192); with tape player ($266); with Quadrasonic tape player ($399). AM/FM stereo search radio ($349). CB radio ($295). Dual rear speakers ($46). Radio flexibility ($105). Full or half vinyl roof ($116). Opera windows ($54). Front bumper guards ($26). Mud/stone deflectors ($25). Lower body protection ($33 to $46). Bucket seats with console ($211), ($37) for Brougham. Vinyl seat trim ($26). Cloth/vinyl seat trim ($26). Front floor mats ($20). H.D. floor mats ($9). Color-keyed seatbelts ($22). Deluxe wheel covers ($45). Luxury wheel covers ($66 to $111). Wire wheel covers ($116 to $161). no charge with sports package. Cast aluminum wheels ($200 to $361). 351-cid V-8 ($263). Traction-Lok differential ($64). Heavy duty suspension ($41). Heavy duty battery ($18-$21). Heavy duty alternator ($50). Engine block heater ($13 to $14).

LTD: Interior luxury group: Landau ($705); Country Squire ($758). Exterior accent group ($29 to $66). Convenience group ($68 to $99). Light group ($32 to $41). Protection group ($46 to $55). Air conditioning ($597); with auto-temp control ($642). Rear defogger ($57). Rear defroster, electric ($100). Fingertip speed control ($113 to $126). Illuminated entry system ($57). Power windows ($137 to $203). Power door locks ($87 to $161). Power driver's seat ($164); or driver and passenger ($329). Tinted glass ($83); windshield only ($28). Tilt steering wheel ($76). Automatic parking brake release ($8). Electric clock ($24). Digital clock ($32 to $55). Cornering lamps ($49). Trunk light ($4). Dual-note horn ($9). Driver's remote mirror, door or sail mount ($18). Dual remote mirrors ($37 to $55). Lighted visor vanity mirror ($36 to $41). AM radio ($79). AM/FM radio ($132). AM/FM stereo radio ($192); with tape player ($266). AM/FM stereo search radio with Quadrasonic tape player ($432). CB radio ($295). Power antenna ($47). Dual rear speakers ($46). Deluxe sound package ($55); luxury package ($42). Premium sound system ($74 to $158). Radio flexibility ($105). Full or half vinyl roof ($143). Bumper guards, front or rear ($26). Bumper rub strips ($54). Luggage rack ($113).

1979 LTD Landau sedan

1979 LTD Country Squire station wagon

Lower body protection ($33 to $46). Dual-facing rear seats: wagon ($145 to $149). Flight bench seat ($99). Dual flight bench seat recliner ($58). Split bench seat with passenger recliner ($187 to $233). All-vinyl seat trim ($26). Duraweave vinyl trim ($52). Front floor mats ($20). Trunk trim ($41-$46). Color-keyed seatbelts ($24). Full wheel covers ($39). Luxury wheel covers ($64). Wire wheel covers ($145). FR78 x 14 white sidewalls ($47). GR78 x 14 black walls ($30). GR78 x 14 white sidewalls ($47 to $77). HR78 x 14, station wagon, black ($30) or white sidewalls ($77). Conventional spare ($13). 351-cid V-8 ($263). Optional axle ratio ($18). Heavy duty suspension ($22). Handling suspension ($42). Adjustable air shock absorbers ($54). Heavy duty battery ($18 to $21). Heavy duty alternator ($50). Engine block heater ($13 to $14). Heavy duty trailer towing package ($161 to $192).

History:

The 1979 Fords were introduced to the public on Oct. 6, 1978. Model year production was 1,835,937 vehicles including Mustangs. Calendar year sales were 1,499,098. Ford dealers also sold 77,733 German Ford-made Fiestas in 1979. To attempt to meet the CAFE requirement of 19 mpg this year, Ford pushed sales of the new downsized LTD. Buyers seemed to want the big V-8 rather than economical fours and sixes, prompting Ford to increase the price of the V-8 model. LTD sales fell rather sharply, putting the smaller LTD far behind Caprice and Impala. LTD II production ceased in January 1979, amid flagging sales. Sales declined considerably for model year 1979, down 15 percent. A gasoline crisis in mid-year didn't help. Ford had lagged behind other companies in downsizing its big-car lineup. Pinto sales were good, even though the outmoded design rival the new subcompacts. Sales of the new Mustang were impressive — nearly 70 percent above the final figure for its second-generation predecessor. A replacement for the Pinto was scheduled for 1981, dubbed "Erika." That was changed to Escort by the time the new front-drive subcompact was introduced. Ford would have to wait for a true rival to Chevrolet's Chevette. Philip Caldwell was president of Ford Motor Co.

1980 Ford

Pinto — Four: All Pintos had four-cylinder engines for 1980, as the optional V-6 disappeared. The standard 140-cid (2.3-liter) four received improvements to boost its highway gas mileage. Styling was virtually identical to 1979, with seven new body colors and three new interior trim colors available. The low-budget Pony now wore steel-belted radial tires. Batteries were maintenance-free, and the Pintos carried a restyled scissors jack. Radios played a Travelers' Advisory band, and the station wagon's Cruising Package option was revised. This was Pinto's final season, to be replaced by the new front-drive Escort. The Rallye Pack option, introduced late in 1979 on hatchback and wagon, was expanded

1980 Pinto three-door hatchback (with Rallye Pack option)

1980 Fairmont two-door sedan (turbocharged)

this year. The model lineup for the final year included the two-door sedan, three-door hatchback Runabout, two-door station wagon, and Pony sedan or wagon. The Pony lacked the base model's tinted glass, rear window defroster, AM radio, bumper rub strips, and vinyl-insert body moldings, as well as bright window frame, belt and B-pillar moldings.

Fairmont — Four/Six and V-8: The power plants were the major news in the Fairmont line this year. Most notable was the announcement of a turbocharged four. Though it was interesting speculation, it never made production. A new 255-cid (4.2-liter) V-8 did and replaced the former 302 option. It was available only with automatic transmission. Both the 255 and the 200-cid (3.3-liter) inline six had a new lightweight starter. The base engine remained the 140-cid (2.3-liter) four, with a four-speed manual gearbox. Manual-shift transmissions had a new self-adjusting clutch. New high-pressure, P-metric steel-belted radial tires were standard on all models. A mini-spare tire and maintenance-free battery were standard. All radios added a Travelers' Advisory band. Fairmont came in nine new body colors and two new two-tone color schemes (with accent color in the bodyside center). A four-door sedan joined the Futura coupe at mid-year, wearing the unique Futura crosshatch grille. Futuras had standard halogen headlamps (except where prohibited by state laws). Styling was similar to 1978 and 1979. The Futura coupe had a wood grain dash appliqué, quad halogen headlamps, a trunk light, bright window frame moldings, vinyl body moldings, and wheel lip and door belt moldings. The optional sport steering wheel switched from brushed aluminum to black finish.

Granada — Six and V-8: Apart from seven new body colors and three new vinyl roof colors, little changed on the compact Granada sedans. A new lightweight starter went under the hood, a better scissors jack in the trunk, and Ardmore cloth upholstery on the seats. Maintenance-free batteries were standard. Joining the option list were a heavy-duty 54-amp battery, mud/stone guards, and revised electronic search stereo radios and tape players. Ford's "Tu-tone" paint cost $180. The standard engine was the 250-cid (4.1-liter) inline six with a 302-cid (5.0-liter) V-8 optional. California Granadas required the new 255-cid V-8. Granada came in two- or four-door sedan form again with the base, Ghia or ESS trim. Granada Ghia carried dual body/hood/decklid accent stripes, black/argent lower back panel appliqué, a left remote mirror, wide vinyl-insert body moldings, and burled walnut wood tone door trim. The sporty Granada ESS had a blacked-out grille, dual remote mirrors, black rocker panel paint, hood and deck lid paint stripes, bucket seats with chain-mail vinyl inserts, a leather-wrapped steering wheel and louvered opera windows.

LTD — V-8: Reshuffling of the model lineup hit the full-size line for 1980. This year's selections included the budget-priced LTD "S," the base LTD, and the LTD Crown Victoria sedans. An "S" edition also joined the LTD (plain-body) and Country Squire station wagon choices. The Crown Victoria, the same name as the stylish mid-1950s Ford,

1980-1/2 Fairmont Futura sedan

replaced the Landau as the top model. A new four-speed automatic transmission with overdrive top gear became optional on all models. New in 1980 were standard P-metric radial tires with higher pressure, standard maintenance-free battery, and halogen headlamps except the LTD "S." The Crown Victoria and Country Squire carried a new wide hood ornament design, while standard LTDs had no ornament at all. Country Squire wagons had simulated wood panels with planking lines. A new rear half vinyl roof with "frenched" seams and brushed aluminum roof wrap over moldings was on the Crown Victoria. Front bumper guards were standard. The "S" had a different front end and grille, with round headlamps and parking lamps inset into the grille. Other models showed quad headlamps. Two-door opera windows had a more vertical look. The LTD had three police packages available including the 302-cid V-8, the regular 351-cid V-8, and the high-output 351-cid V-8. Police packages included heavy-duty alternators, a 2.26:1 axle for the 5.0 liter or 3.08:1 for the 5.8 liter, a 71 ampere-hour battery, heavy-duty power brakes, 140-mph speedometer, heavy-duty suspension and GR70 x 15 black sidewall police radials. The police automatic transmissions had a first-gear lockout and oil cooler.

I.D. Data:

Ford's 11-symbol Vehicle Identification Number (VIN) was stamped on a metal tab fastened to the instrument panel, visible through the windshield. Coding was the same as 1979, except engine codes (symbol five) changed to: A=140-cid four-cylinder, B=200-cid six-cylinder, C=250-cid six-cylinder, D=255-cid V-8, F=302-cid V-8 and G=351-cid V-8. The model year code was O=1980.

Pinto (Four)

Model No.	Body Style No.	Body Type & Seating	Factory Price	Shipping Weight	Production Total
10	62B	2-dr. Sedan-4P	$4,223	2,385 lbs.	84,053
10	41E	2-dr. Pony Sedan-4P	$3,781	2,377 lbs.	Note 1
11	64B	3-dr. Hatchback-4P	$4,335	2,426 lbs.	61,842
12	73B	2-dr. Station Wagon-4P	$4,622	2,553 lbs.	39,159
12	41E	2-dr. Pony Wagon-4P	$4,284	2,545 lbs.	Note 1
12/604	73B	2-dr. Squire Wagon-4P	$4,937	2,590 lbs.	Note 2

Note 1: Pony production was included in base sedan and wagon figures. Panel delivery Pintos also were produced.
Note 2: Squire Wagon production was included in the standard station wagon total.

Fairmont (Four)

91	66B	2-dr. Sedan-5P	$4,435	2,571 lbs.	45,074
92	54B	4-dr. Sedan-5P	$4,552	2,599 lbs.	143,118
94	74B	4-dr. Station Wagon-5P	$4,721	2,722 lbs.	77,035

Fairmont (Six)

91	66B	2-dr. Sedan-5P	$4,604	-----	45,074
92	54B	4-dr. Sedan-5P	$4,721	-----	143,118
94	74B	4-dr. Station Wagon-5P	$4,890	-----	77,035

Fairmont Futura (Four)

93	36R	2-dr. Sport Coupe-5P	$4,837	2,612 lbs.	51,878
92	----	4-dr. Sedan-5P	$5,070	-----	5,306

Fairmont Futura (Six)

93	36R	2-dr. Sport Coupe-5P	$5,006	-----	51,878
92	----	4-dr. Sedan-5P	$5,239	-----	5,306

Note: Prices shown are for four- and six-cylinder engines. A 255-cid V-8 cost $119 more than the six.

Granada (Six)

81	66H	2-dr. Sedan-5P	$4,987	3,063 lbs.	60,872
82	54H	4-dr. Sedan-5P	$5,108	3,106 lbs.	29,557

Granada (V-8)

81	66H	2-dr. Sedan-5P	$5,025	3,187 lbs.	60,872
82	54H	4-dr. Sedan-5P	$5,146	3,230 lbs.	29,557

Granada Ghia (Six)

81/602	66K	2-dr. Sedan-5P	$5,388	3,106 lbs.	Note 3
82/602	54K	4-dr. Sedan-5P	$5,509	3,147 lbs.	Note 3

Granada Ghia (V-8)

81/602	66K	2-dr. Sedan-5P	$5,426	3,230 lbs.	Note 3
82/602	54K	4-dr. Sedan-5P	$5,547	3,271 lbs.	Note 3

Granada ESS (Six)

81/933	----	2-dr. Sedan-5P	$5,477	3,137 lbs.	Note 3
82/933	----	4-dr. Sedan-5P	$5,598	3,178 lbs.	Note 3

Granada ESS (V-8)

81/933	----	2-dr. Sedan-5P	$5,515	3,261 lbs.	Note 3
82/933	----	4-dr. Sedan-5P	$5,636	3,302 lbs.	Note 3

Note 3: Granada Ghia and ESS production is included in the base Granada totals above.
Note: Prices shown are for the six-cylinder and 255-V-8 engines. A 302-cid V-8 cost $150 more than the 255-cid V-8.

LTD (V-8)

62	66H	2-dr. Sedan-6P	$6,549	3,447 lbs.	15,333
63	54H	4-dr. Sedan-6P	$6,658	3,475 lbs.	51,630
74	74H	4-dr. Station Wagon-6P	$7,007	3,717 lbs.	11,718

LTD "S" (V-8)

----	66D	2-dr. Sedan-6P	-----	-----	553
61	54D	4-dr. Sedan-6P	$6,320	2,464 lbs.	19,283
72	74D	4-dr. Station Wagon-6P	$6,741	3,707 lbs.	3,490

LTD Crown Victoria (V-8)

64	66K	2-dr. Sedan-6P	$7,070	3,482 lbs.	7,725
65	54K	4-dr. Sedan-6P	$7,201	3,524 lbs.	21,962
76	74K	4-dr. Country Squire-6P	$7,426	3,743 lbs.	9,868

Note: Production of wagons with dual-facing rear seats was included in the basic wagon totals.

Engines:

Pinto and Fairmont Base Four: Inline. Overhead cam. Cast-iron block and head. Displacement: 140-cid (2.3 liters). B & S: 3.78 x 3.13 in. Compression ratio: 9.0:1. Brake hp: 88 at 4600 rpm. Torque: 119 lbs.-ft. at 2600 rpm. Five main bearings. Hydraulic valve lifters. Carburetor: Motorcraft 5200 two-barrel. VIN Code: A.

Fairmont Six: Inline. Overhead valve. Cast-iron block and head. Displacement: 200-cid (3.3 liters). B & S: 3.68 x 3.13 in. Compression ratio: 8.6:1. Brake hp: 91 at 3800 rpm. Torque: 160 lbs.-ft. at 1600 rpm. Seven main bearings. Hydraulic valve lifters. Carburetor: Holley 1946 two-barrel. VIN Code: B.

Granada: Inline. Overhead valve. Cast-iron block and head. Displacement: 250 cid (4.1 liters). B & S: 3.68 x 3.91 in. Compression

1980 Fairmont Futura Sport Coupe (turbocharged)

1980 Fairmont Squire station wagon

1980 Granada Ghia sedan

1980 Granada sedan

ratio: 8.6:1. Brake hp: 90 at 3200 rpm. Torque: 194 lbs.-ft. at 1660 rpm. Seven main bearings. Hydraulic valve lifters. Carburetor: Carter YFA one-barrel. VIN Code: C.

Fairmont and Granada Optional V-8: 90-degree, overhead valve. Cast-iron block and head. Displacement: 255 cid (4.2 liters). B & S: 3.68 x 3.00 in. Compression ratio: 8.8:1. Brake hp: 119 at 3800 rpm, Fairmont. Torque: 194 lbs.-ft. at 2200 rpm, Fairmont. Five main bearings. Hydraulic valve lifters. Carburetor: Motorcraft 2150 two-barrel. VIN Code: D.

LTD Base V-8 (Optional Granada): 90-degree, overhead valve. Cast-iron block and head. Displacement: 302 cid (5.0 liters). B & S: 4.00 x 3.00 in. Compression ratio: 8.4:1. Brake hp: 130 at 3600 rpm, LTD and 134 at 3600, Granada. Torque: 230 lbs.-ft. at 1600 rpm, LTD and 232 at 1600, Granada. Five main bearings. Hydraulic valve lifters. Carburetor: Motorcraft 2150 or 2700VV two-barrel. VIN Code: F.

LTD Optional V-8: 90-degree, overhead valve. Cast-iron block and head. Displacement: 351 cid (5.8 liters). B & S: 4.00 x 3.50 in. Compression ratio: 8.3:1. Brake hp: 140 at 3400 rpm. Torque: 265 lbs.-ft. at 2000 rpm. Five main bearings. Hydraulic valve lifters. Carburetor: Motorcraft 7200VV two barrel. Windsor engine. VIN Code: G.
Note: A high-output version of the 351 cid V-8 was available for police use.

Chassis:

Pinto: Wheelbase: 94.5 in. and 94.8 in. on station wagon. Overall length: 170.8 in. and 180.6 in., station wagon. Tires: BR78 x 13 steel-belted radials and A78 x 13, Pony.

Fairmont: Wheelbase: 105.5 in. and 197.4 in. on Futura coupe. Overall length: 195.5 in. and 197.4 in., Futura. Tires: P175/75-R14.

Granada: Wheelbase: 109.9 in. Overall length: 199.7 in. Tires: DR78 x 14 steel-belted radials. ER78 x 14, Ghia and FR78 x 14, ESS.

LTD: Wheelbase: 114.3 in. Overall length: 209.3 in. and 215.0 in., LTD wagon. Tires: P205/75-R14 and P215/75-R14, station wagon.

Options:

Pinto: ESS package, including a charcoal grille and headlamp doors, black windshield and backlight moldings, dual black racing mirrors, glass third door with black hinges, blackout paint treatment, black wheel lip moldings and ESS fender insignia ($281 to $313). Cruising package ($355-$606); tape delete ($70 credit). Rally pack: hatch ($369) or wagon ($625). Sport package ($103 to $118). Exterior decor group ($24 to $44). Interior decor group ($165 to $238). Interior accent group ($5 to $50). Convenience group ($26 to $118). Protection group ($36 to $40). Light group ($41). Air conditioner ($538). Rear defroster, electric ($96). Tinted glass ($65). Trunk light ($5). Driver's remote mirror ($18). Dual sport mirrors ($58). Day/night mirror ($11). AM radio: Pony ($80). AM/FM radio ($65 to $145). AM/FM stereo radio ($103 to $183); with cassette player ($191 to $271). Radio flexibility option ($60). Flip-up open air roof ($206 to $219). Glass third door ($31). Metallic glow paint ($45). Roof luggage rack ($71). Mud/stone deflectors ($25). Lower body protection ($34). Four-way driver's seat ($38). Load floor carpet ($28). Cargo area cover ($30). Front floor mats ($19). Wire wheel covers ($104). Forged aluminum wheels ($225 to $300); white wheels ($256

1980 LTD four-door sedan

1980 LTD Country Squire station wagon

to $331). Lacy spoke aluminum wheels ($225 to $300). Styled steel wheels ($56). BR78 x 13 white sidewall tires ($50). BR70 x 13 raised-white letter tires ($87). Select-Shift automatic transmission ($340). Optional axle ratio ($15). Power brakes ($78). Power steering ($160). Heavy duty battery ($20 to $21). Engine block heater ($15).

Fairmont: ES option, including a blackout grille, dual black remote sport mirrors, turbine wheel covers, black sport steering wheel, rear bumper guards, handling suspension, and black lower back panel ($378). Futura sports group, with color-keyed turbine wheel covers, charcoal/argent grille, and youth-oriented tape stripes ($114). Ghia package: ($193) Futura coupe and standard sedan ($566). Squire option ($458). Exterior decor group ($260). Exterior accent group ($95). Interior decor group ($184 to $346). Interior accent group ($110 to $115). Instrument cluster ($85). Convenience group ($29 to $51). Appearance protection group ($46 to $53). Light group ($30 to $48). Air conditioning ($571). Rear defroster, electric ($101). Fingertip speed control ($116 to $129). Power windows ($135 to $191). Power door locks ($88 to $125). Power deck lid release ($25). Power seat ($111). Tinted glass ($71). Sport steering wheel ($43). Leather-wrapped steering wheel ($44). Tilt steering ($78 to $90). Interval wipers ($39). Rear wiper/washer ($79). Left remote mirror ($19). Dual bright remote mirrors ($54 to $60). AM radio ($93). AM/FM radio ($145). AM/FM stereo radio ($183); with eight-track player ($259); with cassette player ($271). Premium sound system ($94). Radio flexibility ($63). Flip-up open air roof ($219). Full or half vinyl roof ($118). Pivoting front vent windows ($50). Luggage rack ($88). Mud/stone deflectors ($25). Non-reclining bucket seats ($31 to $50). Bench seat ($50 credit). Cloth/vinyl seat trim ($28 to $44). Vinyl seat trim ($25). Front floor mats ($19), Lockable side storage box ($23). Hubcaps with trim rings ($41). Deluxe wheel covers ($41). Turbine wheel covers ($43) and argent color ($43 to $84). Wire wheel covers ($74 to $158). Styled steel wheels ($49 to $133). Cast aluminum wheels ($268 to $351). P175/75-R14 WSW ($50). P185/75-R14 ($31) and white sidewall ($81). Raised white letter tires ($96). Conventional spare ($37). Turbo 140-cid four cylinder ($481). 200-cid six cylinder ($169). 255-cid V-8 ($288). Select-Shift automatic transmission ($340). Floor shift lever ($38). Optional axle ratio ($15). Power brakes ($78). Power steering ($165). Handling suspension ($44). Heavy duty battery ($20 to $21). Engine block heater ($15).

Granada: Interior decor group ($243). Convenience group ($39 to $108). Light group ($46 to $51). Cold weather group ($31 to $65). Heavy-duty group ($20 to $65). Protection group ($29 to $53). Visibility group ($6 to $66). Air conditioning ($571); auto-temp ($634). Rear defroster, electric ($101). Fingertip speed control ($116 to $129). Illuminated entry system ($58). Power windows ($136 to $193). Power door locks ($89 to $125). Power deck lid release ($25). Power four-way seat ($111). Tinted glass ($71). Tilt steering wheel ($78). Digital clock ($54). Cornering lamps ($50). Dual remote mirrors ($41 to $60). Dual sport mirrors ($50 to $69). Lighted right visor vanity mirror ($41). AM radio ($93). AM/FM radio ($145). AM/FM stereo radio ($183); with eight-track player ($259): with cassette ($271). AM/FM stereo search radio ($333); with eight-track ($409); with cassette and Dolby ($421).

Radio flexibility ($63). Power moon roof ($998). Full or half vinyl roof ($118). Mud/stone deflectors ($25). Console ($110). Four-way driver's seat ($38). Reclining bucket seats, no charge. Deluxe cloth/vinyl seat, no charge. Flight bench seat, no charge. Cloth/vinyl flight bench seat ($60). Leather seat trim ($277). Front floor mats ($19). Color-keyed seatbelts ($23). Luxury wheel covers ($46), except Ghia, no charge. Wire wheel covers ($119), except, Ghia and ESS ($73). Styled steel wheels with trim rings ($91 to $138). Cast aluminum wheels ($275 to $321). Inflatable spare ($37). 255-cid V-8 ($38). 302-cid V-8 ($188). Select-Shift automatic transmission ($340). Floor shift lever: ($38). Power brakes ($78). Power steering ($165). Heavy duty suspension ($23). Heavy duty battery ($20 to $21). Engine block heater ($15).

LTD: Interior luxury group ($693 to $741). Convenience group ($68 to $98). Power lock group ($114 to $166). Light group ($33 to $43). Protection group ($48 to $58). Air conditioning ($606); w/auto-temp control ($669). Rear defroster, electric ($103). Fingertip speed control ($116). Illuminated entry system ($58). Power windows ($140 to $208). Power door locks ($89 to $120). Power driver's seat ($168); or driver and passenger ($335). Tinted glass ($85). Autolamp on/off delay ($63). Leather-wrapped steering wheel ($44). Tilt steering wheel ($78). Automatic parking brake release ($10). Electric clock ($24). Digital clock ($38 to $61). Seatbelt chime ($23). Interval wipers ($40). Cornering lamps ($48). Trunk light ($5). Dual-note horn ($10). Driver's remote mirror ($19). Dual remote mirrors ($38 to $56). Lighted right visor vanity mirror ($35 to $41); pair of mirrors ($42 to $83). AM radio ($93). AM/FM radio ($145). AM/FM stereo radio ($183); with eight-track tape player ($259): with cassette ($271). AM/FM stereo search radio ($333); with eight-track ($409); with cassette ($421). CB radio ($316). Power antenna ($49). Dual rear speakers ($40). Premium sound system ($94). Radio flexibility ($66). Full or half vinyl roof ($145). Bumper guards, rear ($26). Bumper rub strips ($56). Luggage rack ($115). Dual-facing rear seats: wagon ($146 to $151). Flight bench seat ($56). Leather split bench seat ($349). Dual flight bench seat recliners ($55). Split bench seat with recliners ($173 to $229). All-vinyl seat trim ($28). Duraweave vinyl trim ($50). Front floor mats ($19); front/rear ($30). Trunk trim ($46 to $51). Trunk mat ($14). Color-keyed seatbelts ($24). Luxury wheel covers ($70). Wire wheel covers ($138). Cast aluminum wheels ($310). P205/75-R14 white sidewall tires ($50). P215/75-R14 blackwall tires ($29); white sidewall tires ($50 to $79). P225/75-R14 white sidewall tires ($79 to $107). P205/75-R15 white sidewalls ($55 to $87). Conventional spare ($37). 351-cid V-8 ($150). Four-speed overdrive automatic transmission ($138). Traction-Lok differential ($69). Optional axle ratio ($19). Handling suspension ($43). Adjustable air shock absorbers ($55). Heavy duty battery ($20 to $21). Engine block heater ($15). Heavy duty trailer towing package ($164 to $169).

History:

The 1980 Fords were introduced on October 12, 1979. Model year production was 1,167,581, including Mustangs. Calendar year sales by U. S. dealers was 1,074,675, including Mustangs. Dealers also sold 68,841 imported Fiestas, made by Ford of Germany. Early in 1980, the "Erika" subcompact was renamed Escort (and Mercury Lynx). Overall Ford sales for the model year fell more than 28 percent, touching every car in the lineup but headed by LTD's 43 percent drop. LTD was advertised during this period as rivaling Rolls-Royce for smooth, quiet ride qualities. The restyled and downsized Thunderbird didn't find many buyers either. Two assembly plants closed during 1980, at Mahwah, New Jersey, and at Los Angeles, California. Ford expected to spend $2 billion for expansion and retooling at other domestic facilities. Foremost hope for the future was the new Escort being readied for 1981 introduction. Philip E. Benton became head of the Ford Division, following the retirement of Walter S. Walla. The 1980 CAFE goal for automakers' fleets was 20 mpg (up from 19 mpg in 1979). Thunderbird was the star of the lineup in its new downsized form. On the power plant front, a turbocharged four was announced as a Fairmont option, but didn't quite materialize, presumably due to mechanical difficulties.

1980 LTD Crown Victoria sedan

1981 Ford

Escort — Four: Ford's international experience influenced the new "world car," the front-wheel-drive Escort. A $3 billion development program had been initiated in the early 1970s to produce Escorts for both the U.S. and Europe. The engine alone cost $1 billion to develop. The U.S. version of the all-new overhead-cam, Compound Valve Hemispherical (CVH) engine had to meet federal emissions standards.. The transverse-mounted engine displaced just 97.6 cid. The cylinder head and intake manifold were aluminum. The CVH design put the spark plug close to the center of the combustion chamber. Escort's maintenance-free features included self-adjusting brakes, lubed-for-life wheel bearings and front suspension, preset carb mixtures, hydraulic valve lifters, fixed caster and camber settings at the front end, and self-adjusting clutches. Three-door hatchback and four-door lift gate bodies were offered. Five trim levels included base, L, GL, GLX and sporty SS. Escort's four-speed manual transaxle was fully synchronized, with wide-ratio gearing. Escort had four-wheel independent suspension, rack-and-pinion steering, standard halogen headlamps and a maintenance-free battery. Front suspension used MacPherson struts with strut-mounted coil springs and a stabilizer bar. At the rear were independent trailing arms with modified MacPherson struts and coil springs, mounted on stamped lower control arms. P-metric (P155/80R) radial tires rode on 13 in. steel wheels. Cast aluminum wheels were optional. Standard equipment included an AM radio, two-speed wipers, three-speed heater/defroster, inside hood release, high-back vinyl front bucket seats, a bench-type folding rear seat, a door-mounted driver's mirror, a day/night mirror, courtesy lights, and semi-styled steel wheels. Options included a console with graphic display module, intermittent wipers, and pivoting front vent windows. Gas mileage estimates reached 30 mpg city and 44 mpg highway. Early criticisms prompted Ford to continually refine the Escort. First-year versions suffered several recalls. Mercury Lynx was Escort's corporate twin.

Fairmont — Four/Six/V-8: In addition to the usual sedans and the Futura coupe, Fairmont delivered a station wagon in 1981 under the Futura badge. The four-door, steel-sided wagon had Futura's bright work and an upgraded interior. Squire (wood grain) trim was available at extra cost. Fairmonts also added new standard equipment, including power front disc brakes, bucket seats, a deluxe sound package, dual-note horn, bright window frames, visor vanity mirror and a glove box lock. The option list expanded to include a console with diagnostic warning lights and digital clock, an illuminated entry system, Traction-Lok rear axle (V-8 only), lighted visor vanity mirror, and Michelin TR type tires. Both the 200-cid (3.3-liter) six and 255-cid (4.2-liter) V-8 now had a viscous-clutch fan drive. The base engine remained the 140-cid (2.3-liter) four, with a four-speed manual gearbox. The four-speed transmission had a self-adjusting clutch. Fairmont's base four-cylinder produced EPA estimates of 34 mpg highway and 23 mpg city. Wide (non-wraparound) tail lamps had vertical ribbing, with backup lenses at inner ends. Four-doors had a six-window design with narrow quarter windows that tapered to a point at the top. Wagons carried vertical wraparound tail lamps.

Granada — Four/Six/V-8: Granada received an aerodynamic restyle that was supposed to deliver a 21 percent improvement in fuel economy. Ford called it "the industry's most changed American-built sedan for 1981." This Granada was three inches shorter than its predecessor, but with more leg, hip and shoulder room inside, and more luggage space. Granada's chassis was based on the familiar "Fox" platform, with coil springs all around. The fully unitized body weighed 400 pounds less than the 1980 version. Drag coefficient rated a low 0.44. Standard was the 140-cid (2.3-liter) OHC four, as in Fairmont and Mustang, with four-speed manual shift. Automatic transmission was standard with the bigger engines. New for 1981 was a MacPherson strut front suspension, a pin-slider front disc brake system, front bucket seats, a revised instrument panel and stalk-mounted controls for turn signals, horn, dimmer, and wiper. P-metric steel-belted radial tires rode on 14 in. stamped steel wheels. Granada also sported halogen headlamps. Three Granada series were offered: L, GL and GLX (replacing base, Ghia and ESS). Body styles included only the two-and four-door sedans. Wide tail lamps had backup lamps toward the center. There was a see-through hood ornament. A square badge was mounted ahead of the front door. Mercury Cougar was Granada's corporate companion.

LTD — V-8: Full-size Fords no longer carried a standard full-size engine. LTD's new standard power train consisted of the 255-cid (4.2-liter) V-8 and automatic overdrive transmission, which had been introduced in 1980 as an option on the LTD and the Thunderbird. That transmission also featured a lockup clutch torque converter. The three-speed automatic was abandoned. A high-output 351-cid V-8, delivering 20 more horsepower, was available only for police cars. LTD's lineup included four-door sedans in base, "S" and Crown Victoria trim. There were two-door sedans in base and Crown Victoria trim and four-door

1981 Escort GLX three-door hatchback

1981 Escort GLX four-door liftgate

wagons in all three series. Switching to a smaller base power plant didn't seem to help mileage that was estimated at just 16 mpg. Standard equipment included halogen headlamps on "S" models, and separate ignition and door keys. Remote mirrors were now door-mounted rather than sail-mounted. Appearance was the same as 1980.

I.D. Data:

Ford had a new 17-symbol Vehicle Identification Number (VIN), again stamped on a metal tab fastened to the instrument panel. It was visible through the windshield. Symbols one to three indicated the manufacturer, make and vehicle type: 1FA=Ford passenger car. The fourth symbol B=the restraint system. The letter P plus two digits that indicated the body type such as 91=Fairmont two-door sedan. Symbol eight indicated the engine type: 2=a 98-cid four cylinder engine, A=the 140-cid four cylinder, B=a 200c-cid six, D= a 255-cid V-8, F=a 302-cid V-8, G=351-cid V-8. The ninth digit was a check digit. Symbol 10 indicated the model year: B=1981. Symbol 11 was the assembly plant: A=Atlanta, Georgia; B=Oakville, Ontario, Canada; G=Chicago, Illinois; H=Lorain, Ohio; K=Kansas City, Missouri; X=St. Thomas, Ontario, Canada; T= Metuchen, New Jersey; U=Louisville, Kentucky and W=Wayne, Michigan. The final six digits made up the sequence number, starting with 100001. A Vehicle Certification Label on the left front door lock face panel or door pillar showed the manufacturer, month and year of manufacture, GVW, GAWR, certification statement, VIN, and codes for such items as body type, color, trim, axle, transmission, and special order information.

Escort (Four)

Model No.	Body Style No.	Body Type & Seating	Factory Price	Shipping Weight	Production Total
05	61D	3-dr. Hatchback-4P	$5,158	1,962 lbs.	Note 1
08	74D	4-dr. Liftgate-4P	$5,731	2,074 lbs.	Note 1
05/60Q	61D	2-dr. L Hatchback-4P	$5,494	1,964 lbs.	Note 1
08/60Q	74D	4-dr. L Liftgate-4P	$5,814	2,075 lbs.	Note 1
05/60Z	61D	2-dr. GL Hatchback-4P	$5,838	1,987 lbs.	Note 1
08/60Z	74D	4-dr. GL Liftgate-4P	$6,178	2,094 lbs.	Note 1
05/602	61D	3-dr. GLX Hatchback-4P	$6,476	2,029 lbs.	Note 1
08/602	74D	4-dr. GLX Liftgate-4P	$6,799	2,137 lbs.	Note 1
05/936	61D	3-dr. SS Hatchback-4P	$6,139	2,004 lbs.	Note 1
08/936	74D	4-dr. SS Liftgate-4P	$6,464	2,114 lbs.	Note 1

Note 1: Escort production totaled 192,554 three-door hatchbacks and 128,173 four-door lift backs. Breakdown by trim levels was not available. Hatchbacks are called two- or three-door and liftgate models also are called station wagons.

Fairmont (Four)

20	66	2-dr. S Sedan-5P	$5,701	-----	-----
20	66B	2-dr. Sedan-5P	$6,032	2,564 lbs.	23,066
21	54B	4-dr. Sedan-5P	$6,151	2,614 lbs.	104,883
23	74B	4-dr. Station Wagon-5P	$6,384	2,721 lbs.	59,154

Fairmont (Six)

20	66	2-dr. S Sedan-5P	$5,914	-----	-----
22	66B	2-dr. Sedan-5P	$6,245	2,617 lbs.	23,066
21	54B	4-dr. Sedan-5P	$6,364	2,667 lbs.	104,883
23	74B	4-dr. Station Wagon-5P	$6,597	2,788 lbs.	59,154

Fairmont Futura (Four)

22	36	2-dr. Coupe-5P	$6,347	2,619 lbs.	24,197
21/605	54B	4-dr. Sedan-5P	$6,361	2,648 lbs.	Note 2
21/605	74B	4-dr. Station Wagon-5P	$6,616	2,755 lbs.	Note 2

Fairmont Futura (Six)

20	36R	2-dr. Coupe-5P	$6,560	2,672 lbs.	24,197
20	54B	4-dr. Sedan-5P	$6,574	2,701 lbs.	Note 2
21	74B	4-dr. Station Wagon-5P	$6,829	2,822 lbs.	Note 2

Note 2: Production totals listed under the base Fairmont sedan and wagon also include Futura models.

Granada (Four)

26	66D	2-dr. L Sedan-5P	$6,474	2,707 lbs.	35,057
27	54D	4-dr. L Sedan-5P	$6,633	2,750 lbs.	86,284
26/602	66D	2-dr. GL Sedan-5P	$6,875	2,728 lbs.	Note 3
27/602	54D	4-dr. GL Sedan-5P	$7,035	2,777 lbs.	Note 3
26/933	66D	2-dr. GLX Sedan-5P	$6,988	2,732 lbs.	Note 3
27/933	54D	4-dr. GLX Sedan-5P	$7,148	2,784 lbs.	Note 3

Granada (Six)

26	66D	2-dr. L Sedan-5P	$6,687	2,797 lbs.	35,057
27	54D	4-dr. L Sedan-5P	$6,848	2,840 lbs.	86,284
26/602	66D	2-dr. GL Sedan-5P	$7,088	2,818 lbs.	Note 3
27/602	54D	4-dr. GL Sedan-5P	$7,248	2,867 lbs.	Note 3
26/933	66D	2-dr. GLX Sedan-5P	$7,201	2,822 lbs.	Note 3
27/933	54D	4-dr. GLX Sedan-5P	$7,361	2,874 lbs.	Note 3

Note 3: Granada GL and GLX production is included in base Granada totals above.
Note: Prices shown are for four-and six-cylinder engines. A 255-cid V-8 cost $50 more than the six.

LTD (V-8)

32	66H	2-dr. Sedan-6P	$7,607	3,496 lbs.	6,279
33	54H	4-dr. Sedan-6P	$7,718	3,538 lbs.	35,932
38	74H	4-dr. Station Wagon-6P	$8,180	3,719 lbs.	10,554
39	74K	4-dr. Country Squire-6P	$8,640	3,737 lbs.	9,443

LTD S (V-8)

31	54D	4-dr. Sedan-6P	$7,522	3,490 lbs.	17,490
37	74D	4-dr. Station Wagon-6P	$7,942	3,717 lbs.	2,465

LTD Crown Victoria (V-8)

34	66K	2-dr. Sedan-6P	$8,251	3,496 lbs.	11,061
35	54K	4-dr. Sedan-6P	$8,384	3,538 lbs.	39,139

Note: Production of wagons with dual-facing rear seats (a $143 option) was included in the basic wagon totals. A prefix P precedes the model number in many reports of 1981 Ford production.

Engines:

Escort Base Four: Inline. Overhead cam. Cast-iron block and aluminum head. Displacement: 97.6 cid (1.6 liters). B & S: 3.15 x 3.13 in. Compression ratio: 8.8:1. Brake hp: 65 at 5200 rpm. Torque: 85 lbs.-ft. at 3000 rpm. Five main bearings. Hydraulic valve lifters. Carburetor: Holley-Weber 5740 two-barrel. VIN Code: 2.

Fairmont and Granada Base Four: Inline. Overhead cam. Cast-iron block and head. Displacement: 140 cid (2.3 liters). B & S: 3.78 x 3.13 in. Compression ratio: 9.0:1. Brake hp: 88 at 4600 rpm. Torque: 118 lbs.-ft. at 2600 rpm. Five main bearings. Hydraulic valve lifters. Carburetor: Holley 6500 two barrel. VIN Code: A.

Fairmont and Granada Optional Engine: Inline. Overhead valve. Cast-iron block and head. Displacement: 200 cid (3.3 liters). B & S: 3.68 x 3.13 in. Compression ratio: 8.6:1. Brake hp: 88 at 3800 rpm. Torque: 154 lbs.-ft. at 1400 rpm. Seven main bearings. Hydraulic valve lifters. Carburetor: Holley 1946 single barrel. VIN Code: B.

LTD Base V-8 (Optional on Fairmont and Granada): 90-degree, overhead valve. Cast-iron block and head. Displacement: 255 cid (4.2 liters). B & S: 3.68 x 3.00 in. Compression ratio: 8.2:1. Brake hp: 115 at 3400 rpm, Fairmont and Granada, and 120 at 3400, LTD. Torque: 195 lbs.-ft. at 2200 rpm, Fairmont and Granada and 205 at 2600, LTD. Five main bearings. Hydraulic valve lifters. Carburetor: Motorcraft 2150 or 7200VV two-barrel. VIN Code: D.

LTD Optional V-8: 90-degree, overhead valve. Cast-iron block and head. Displacement: 302 cid (5.0 liters). B & S:: 4.00 x 3.00 in. Compression ratio: 8.4:1. Brake hp: 130 at 3400 rpm. Torque: 235 lbs.-ft. at 1800 rpm. Five main bearings. Hydraulic valve lifters. Carburetor: Motorcraft 2150 or 7200VV two-barrel. VIN Code: F.

LTD Optional V-8: 90-degree, overhead valve. Cast-iron block and head. Displacement: 351 cid (5.8 liters). B & S: 4.00 x 3.50 in.

1981 Fairmont sedan

1981 Fairmont Futura Squire station wagon

Compression ratio: 8.3:1. Brake hp: 145 at 3200 rpm. Torque: 270 lbs.-ft. at 1800 rpm. Five main bearings. Hydraulic valve lifters. Carburetor: Motorcraft 7200VV two-barrel. Windsor engine. VIN Code: G.

Note: A high-output 351-cid V-8 was available with 165 brake hp at 3600 rpm and 285 lbs.-ft. of torque at 2200 rpm.

Chassis:

Escort: Wheelbase: 94.5 in. Overall length: 163.9 in., hatchback and 165.0 in., lift back. Tires: P155/80-R13 steel-belted radial blackwalls.
Fairmont: Wheelbase: 105.5 in. Overall length: 195.5 in. and Futura coupe, 197.4 in. Tires: P175/75-R14 steel-belted blackwalls.
Granada: Wheelbase: 105.5 in. Overall length: 196.5 in. Tires: P175/75-R14 steel-belted blackwalls.
LTD: Wheelbase: 114.3 in. Overall Length: 209.3 in. and 215.0 in., LTD station wagon. Tires: P205/75-R14 steel-belted white sidewalls and P215/75-R14, LTD station wagon.

Options:

Escort: Squire wagon package ($256). Instrument group ($77). Protection group ($49). Light group ($39). Air conditioner ($530). Rear defroster, electric ($102). Fingertip speed control ($132). Tinted glass ($70); windshield only ($28). Digital clock ($52). Intermittent wipers ($41). Rear wiper/washer ($100). Dual remote sport mirrors ($56). AM/FM radio ($63). AM/FM stereo radio ($100); with cassette player ($187). Dual rear speakers ($37). Premium sound ($91). AM radio delete ($61 credit). Flip-up open air roof ($154 to $228). Front vent windows, pivoting ($55). Remote quarter windows ($95). Vinyl-insert body moldings ($41). Bumper guards, front or rear ($23). Bumper rub strips ($34). Roof luggage rack ($74). Roof air deflector ($26). Lower body protection ($60). Console ($98). Low-back reclining bucket seats ($30). Reclining front seatbacks ($55). Cloth/vinyl seat trim ($28) or vinyl, no charge. Deluxe seatbelts ($23). Wheel trim rings ($44). Aluminum wheels ($193 to $330). P155/80-R13 white sidewall tires ($55). P165/80-R13 blackwalls($19) or white sidewalls ($55 to $74). Optional axle ratio ($15). Power brakes ($79). Power steering ($163). Handling suspension ($37). Extended-range gas tank: Escort ($32). Engine block heater ($16). Automatic transaxle ($344).
Fairmont: Squire option ($200). Interior luxury group ($232 to $256). Instrument cluster ($88). Appearance protection group ($50). Light group ($43). Air conditioning ($585). Rear defroster, electric ($107). Fingertip speed control ($132). Illuminated entry ($60). Power windows ($140 to $195). Power door locks ($93 to $132). Remote deck lid release ($27). Power seat ($122). Tinted glass ($76); windshield only ($29). Leather-wrapped steering wheel ($49). Tilt steering ($80 to $93). Electric clock ($23). Interval wipers ($41). Rear wiper/washer ($85). Map light ($9); dual-beam ($13). Trunk light ($6). Left remote mirror ($15). Dual bright remote mirrors ($55). Lighted visor vanity mirror ($43). AM/FM radio ($51). AM/FM stereo radio ($88); with eight-track player ($162); with cassette player ($174). Twin rear speakers ($37). Premium sound system ($91). Radio flexibility ($61). AM radio delete ($61 credit). Flip-up open air roof ($228). Full or half vinyl roof ($115). Pivoting front vent windows ($55). Lift gate assist handle for station wagon ($16). Rocker panel moldings ($30). Bumper guards, rear ($23). Bumper rub strips ($43). Station wagon luggage rack ($90). Lower body protection ($37 to $49) Interior Console ($168). Bench seat ($24 credit). Cloth seat trim ($28 to $54). Flight bench seat, no charge but

1981 Granada GLX sedan

1981 Escort three-door hatchback

1981 Granada GL coupe

1981 Escort GLX Squire wagon

with vinyl trim ($26). Front floor mats ($18-$20). Locking storage box ($24). Deluxe seatbelts ($23). Wire wheel covers ($76 to $117). Styled steel wheels ($52 to $94). P175/75-R14 whitewall tires($55). P185/75-R14 white sidewalls($86). P190/65-R390 blackwalls on TRX aluminum wheels ($470 to $512). Conventional spare ($39). 200-cid six-cylinder engine ($213). 255-cid V-8 ($263). Floor shift lever ($43). Traction-Lok differential ($67). Select-Shift automatic transmission ($349). Power steering ($168). Heavy-duty suspension ($22). Handling suspension ($45). Heavy-duty battery ($20). Engine block heater ($16).

Granada: Interior sport group ($282 to $295). Light group ($45). Cold weather group ($67). Protection group ($51). Air conditioning ($585). Rear defroster ($107). Fingertip speed control ($89 to $132). Illuminated entry system ($60). Power windows ($140 to $195). Power door locks ($93 to $132). Power deck lid release ($27). Power flight bench seat ($122); split bench ($173). Tinted glass ($76) and windshield only ($29). Sport steering wheel ($26 to $39); leather-wrapped ($49); tilt ($80 to $94). Electric clock ($23). Interval wipers ($41). Cornering lamps ($51). Map light ($13). Trunk light ($6). Remote right mirror ($52). Lighted right visor vanity mirror ($43). AM/FM radio ($51). AM/FM stereo radio ($88); with eight-track player ($162) with cassette ($174). Premium sound ($91). Radio flexibility ($61). AM radio delete ($61 credit). Flip-up open-air roof ($228). Full or half vinyl roof ($115). Pivoting front vent windows ($55). Mud/stone deflectors ($26). Console ($168). Split bench seat: GL/GLX ($178). Cloth seat trim ($45 to $62). Flight bench seat, no charge. Front floor mats ($18 to $20). Color-keyed seatbelts ($23). Luxury wheel covers: L ($43) and GL/GLX, no charge. Wire wheel covers ($124); GL/GLX ($80). Cast aluminum wheels ($308 to $350). P175/75-R14 whitewalls ($55). P185/75-R14 SSW ($32); white sidewalls($86); raised white letters ($102). 190/65-R390 blackwalls on TRX aluminum wheels ($468 to $512). Conventional spare ($39). 200-cid six ($213). 255-cid V-8 ($263). Select-Shift automatic transmission ($349). Floor shift lever ($43). Traction-Lok differential ($67). Optional axle ratio ($16). Power steering ($168). Heavy-duty suspension ($22). Heavy-duty battery ($20). Engine block heater ($16).

LTD: Interior luxury group ($693 to $765). Convenience group ($70 to $101). Power lock group ($93 to $176). Light group ($37). Protection group ($57). Air conditioning ($624); w/auto-temp control ($687). Rear defroster, electric ($107). Fingertip speed control ($135). Illuminated entry system ($59). Power windows ($143 to $211). Power driver's seat ($173) or driver and passenger ($346). Tinted glass ($87); windshield only ($29). Autolamp on/off delay ($65). Leather-wrapped steering wheel ($45). Tilt steering wheel ($80). Automatic parking brake release ($10). Electric clock ($23). Digital clock ($40 to $63). Seatbelt chime ($23). Cornering lamps ($48). Remote right mirror ($39). Lighted right visor vanity mirror ($38) or a pair ($43 to $80). AM/FM radio ($51). AM/FM stereo radio ($88); with eight-track tape player ($162) and Crown Victoria ($74); with cassette ($174) and Crown Victoria ($87). AM/FM stereo search radio ($234) and Crown Victoria ($146); with eight-track ($221 to $309); with cassette ($233 to $321). Power antenna ($48). Dual rear speakers ($39). Premium sound system ($116 to $146).

Radio flexibility ($65). AM radio delete ($61 credit). Full or half vinyl roof ($141). Luggage rack ($84). Dual-facing rear seats on station wagon ($146). Cloth/vinyl flight bench seat ($59). Leather seating ($361). Dual flight bench seat recliners ($56). Cloth/vinyl split bench seating ($178 to $237). All-vinyl seat trim on Crown Victoria and Country Squire ($28) and Duraweave vinyl ($54). Front floor mats ($20). Trunk trim ($45). Luxury wheel covers ($72). Wire wheel covers ($135). Cast aluminum wheels ($338). P215/75-R14 white sidewalls($30). P225/75-14 whitewalls ($30 to $61). P205/75-15 whitewalls ($10 to $40). Puncture-resistant tires ($95 to $125). Conventional spare ($39). 302-cid V-8 ($41). 351-cid V-8 ($83) and ($41) on the LTD wagon. High Output 351-cid V-8 ($139 to $180).). Four-speed overdrive automatic transmission ($162). Traction-Lok differential ($71). Heavy duty suspension ($23). Handling suspension ($45). Adjustable air shock absorbers ($57). Heavy duty battery ($20). Heavy duty alternator ($46). Engine block heater ($16). Heavy duty trailer towing package ($176).

Note: Ford body colors for 1981 were: Black, Bright Bittersweet, Candy Apple Red, Medium or Bright Red, Light Medium Blue, Medium Dark Brown, Bright Yellow, Cream, Chrome Yellow, Tan, Antique Cream, Pastel Chamois, Fawn, and White. Also available was a selection of metallics including: Silver, Medium Gray, Light Pewter, Medium Pewter, Maroon, Dark Blue, Bright Blue, Medium Dark Spruce, Dark Brown, Dark Pine, and Dark Cordovan. Some Ford products were available with nine "Glamour" colors and 16 clear coat paint selections.

History:

The 1981 Fords were introduced on October 3, 1980. The model year production was 1,054,976, including Mustangs. Calendar year sales by U.S. dealers were 977,220, including Mustangs. Dealers also sold 47,707 German-Ford made Fiestas. Escort quickly managed to become the best-selling Ford, selling 284,633 examples. Escort was primed to compete with Chevrolet's five-year-old Chevette. Other Ford sales slumped. The downsized Granada sold better than in 1980, finding 105,743 buyers. Total model year sales were down more than 7 percent. Mustang didn't sell as well as the predictions. It dropped by 29.5 percent for the model year. Calendar year production and sales both fell but not to a shocking level. This was a bad year all around for the industry. Car prices and interest rates rose steadily during this inflationary period, while the country also remained in a recession.

1981 LTD Crown Victoria sedan

Escort evolved from the "Erika" project, first begun in 1972. Both a 1.3-liter and 1.6-liter engine were planned, but only the larger one found its way under North American Escort hoods. Ford spent some $640 million to renovate its Dearborn, Michigan, plant to manufacture Escort's 1.6-liter CVH engine. They were also built at a Ford facility in Wales. Additional future production was planned for Lima, Ohio, and for a Mexican plant.

1982 Ford

Escort — Four: A new four-door hatchback sedan joined Escort's initial "three-door" (actually a two-door) hatchback and four-door liftback wagon. Base and SS wagons were dropped. The L, GL and GLX Escorts now had bright headlamp housings. New stainless steel trim rings (formerly stamped aluminum) arrived on the GL, GLX and GT models. Escort had a new low-restriction exhaust and larger tires (P165/80-R13) in all series. Ford's oval script emblem now appeared on the front and back. An electric hatch release was now standard on GLX hatchbacks. Air-conditioned models included a switch that disconnected the unit for an instant when the gas pedal was floored. Base Escorts included single rectangular halogen headlamps, short black bumper end caps, semi-styled steel wheels with black and argent hub covers, and black wheel nut covers. Inside were vinyl high-back front bucket seats, a black two-spoke steering wheel and color-keyed soft-feel pad. Escort L included bright headlamp doors, an "L" badge on the liftgate, and blackout front end. Escort GL included added deluxe bumper end caps and rub strips and a "GL" badge in back. Inside, the GL had high-back reclining bucket seats and a four-spoke soft-feel color-keyed steering wheel. GLX included dual color-keyed remote sport mirrors, a "GLX" badge and a console with graphic warning display. Escort GT included a front air dam, roof grab handles and a black grille. Escorts had a larger, 11.3-gallon gas tank this year. EPA ratings reached 31 mpg and 47 mpg highway on the base Escort with four-speed.

EXP — Four: First shown at the Chicago Auto Show, then introduced in April as an early 1982 model, EXP was the first two-seater Ford offered in 25 years. Ford Division General Manager Louis E. Latalf said: "We're introducing another two-seater [like the early Thunderbird] but the EXP will be a very affordable, very fuel-efficient car matched to the lifestyles of the '80s." The sporty coupe weighed 1,000 lbs. less than the original Thunderbird. EXP was also two inches lower and five inches shorter. EXP's rakish body rode an Escort/Lynx 94.2-inch wheelbase, with that car's front-drive running gear, four-wheel independent suspension, and dashboard. EXP was longer, lower and narrower than Escort. The EXP weighed about 200 lbs. more than Escort but carried the same small engine. Standard features included steel-belted radial tires, power front disc/rear drum brakes, halogen headlamps, rack-and-pinion steering, reclining high-back bucket seats, four-spoke sport steering wheel, easy-to-read instrument panel and console with full instrumentation. Under the hood was the 97.6 cid (1.6-liter) CVH engine with standard four-speed overdrive manual transaxle. Ford's coupe was a notchback while Mercury's LN7 had a "bubble back" window. The EXP carried an ample list of standard equipment. It included power brakes, tachometer,

1982 Escort GLX five-door hatchback

1982 EXP three-door hatchback

1982 LTD two-door sedan

full carpeting, power hatchback release, digital clock, and cargo area security shade. An optional TR handling package included special wheels and Michelin TRX tires in P165/70R365 size, and a larger-diameter front stabilizer bar. Ford offered an optional (no-extra-cost) 4.05:1 final drive ratio for better performance. In March 1982, an 80-hp edition of the CVH four became available. It included a higher (9.0:1) compression, a bigger air cleaner intake, larger carburetor venturis and a higher-lift camshaft.

Fairmont Futura — Four/Six/V-8: All Fairmont models acquired the Futura name this year as the lineup shrunk to a single series: just a two- and four-door sedan, and sport coupe. The station wagon was dropped, and the 255-cid (4.2-liter) V-8 was available only in police and taxi packages. The base engine was the 140-cid (2.3-liter) four, with the 3.3-liter inline six optional. The optional SelectShift automatic with the six included a new lockup torque converter. Quad rectangular headlamps now stood above quad park/signal lamps, like LTD, but without its wraparound side marker lenses. Fairmont had small marker lenses set low on front fenders. Front fenders held a Futura badge. Interiors held new high-gloss wood tone door trim and instrument panel appliqués. A new deep-well trunk was featured. AM radios added dual front speakers, and a new flash-to-pass feature was added to the headlamp lever. There was also a new gas cap tether. The once optional sweep-hand electric clock was switched to quartz-type, and the available extended-range fuel tank was increased to 20 gallons from 16.

Granada — Four/Six/V-6: Following its major restyle and downsizing for 1981, Granada looked the same this year but added a pair of station wagons (L and GL series). New station wagon options included a luggage rack, two-way liftgate (with flip-up window), rear wiper/washer, and Squire package. Fuel filler caps were now tethered. Flash-to-pass control on the steering column was new this year. Sedans could get an optional extended-range fuel tank. No more V-8s went under Granada hoods. A new optional "Essex" 232-cid (3.8-liter) 112-hp V-6 was said to offer V-8 power. It weighed just four pounds more than the base 140-cid (2.3-liter) four. An inline six also remained available and was standard on wagons. The V-6 got an EPA rating of 19 mpg, city and 26 mpg, highway. A new torque converter clutch that provided a direct connection became standard on the SelectShift automatic for the six and V-6 engines. This would be Granada's final season, but its basic design carried on in the form of a restyled LTD.

LTD — V-8: After a long history, the 351 cid (5.8-liter) V-8 no longer was available for private full-size Fords, but continued as an option for police models. Little changed on this year's LTD lineup, apart from seven new body colors. Ford ovals were added to front grilles and rear deck lids (or tailgates). All monaural radios had dual front speakers and wiring for rear speakers. The sweep-hand clock added quartz operation. A new medium-duty trailer towing option replaced the former heavy-duty one. New optional wire wheel covers incorporated a locking feature. The base engine was a 255-cid (4.2-liter) V-8. Optional was the 302-cid (5.0-liter) V-8. Also optional for 1982 was a Tripminder computer that combined a trip odometer with quartz clock to show vehicle speed, real or elapsed time, and fuel flow. The LTD was the largest Ford with its 114.3-inch wheelbase.

I.D. Data:

Ford's 17-symbol Vehicle Identification Number (VIN) was stamped on a metal tab fastened to the instrument panel, visible through the windshield. The first three symbols: 1FA= manufacturer, make and vehicle type. The fourth symbol: B=the restraint system. The letter "P" plus the model number was the body type, such as P05=Escort two-door hatchback. Symbol eight indicated the engine type: 2=98-cid four-cylinder, A=140-cid four-cylinder, B or T=200-cid six, 3=232-cid V-6, D=255-cid V-8, F=302-cid V-8 and G=351-cid V-8. Next was a check digit. Symbol 10 indicated the model year: C=1982. Symbol 11 was the assembly plant: A=Atlanta, Georgia; B=Oakville, Ontario, Canada; G=Chicago, Illinois; H=Lorain, Ohio; K=Kansas City, Missouri; R=San Jose, California; T=Edison, New

Jersey; W=Wayne, Michigan X=St. Thomas, Ontario, Canada and Z=St. Louis, Missouri. The final six digits made the sequence number, starting with 100001. A Vehicle Certification Label on the left front door lock face panel or door pillar showed the manufacturer, month and year of manufacture as well as the GVW, GAWR, certification statement, VIN, and codes for such items as body type, color, trim, axle, transmission, and special order information.

Escort (Four)

Model No.	Body Style No.	Body Type & Seating	Factory Price	Shipping Weight	Production Total
05	61D	2-dr. Hatchback-4P	$5,462	1,920 lbs.	Note 1
06	58D	4-dr. Hatchback-4P	$5,668	-----	Note 1
05	61D	2-dr. L Hatchback-4P	$6,046	1,926 lbs.	Note 1
06	58D	4-dr. L Hatchback-4P	$6,263	2,003 lbs.	Note 1
08	74D	4-dr. L Station Wagon-4P	$6,461	2,023 lbs.	Note 1
05	61D	2-dr. GL Hatchback-4P	$6,406	1,948 lbs.	Note 1
06	58D	4-dr. GL Hatchback-4P	$6,622	2,025 lbs.	Note 1
08	74D	4-dr. GL Station Wagon-4P	$6,841	2,043 lbs.	Note 1
05	61D	2-dr. GLX Hatchback-4P	$7,086	1,978 lbs.	Note 1
06	58D	4-dr. GLX Hatchback-4P	$7,302	2,064 lbs.	Note 1
08	74D	4-dr. GLX Station Wagon-4P	$7,475	2,079 lbs.	Note 1
05	61D	2-dr. GT Hackback-4P	$6,706	1,963 lbs.	Note 1

Note 1: Total Escort production came to 165,660 two-door hatchbacks, 130,473 four-door hatchbacks, and 88,999 station wagons. Trim level breakdown was not available. Bodies were sometimes called three-door and five-door.

EXP (Four)

01	67D	3-dr. Hackback-2P	$7,387	2,047 lbs.	98,256

Fairmont Futura (Four)

22	36R	2-dr. Sport Coupe-5P	$6,517	2,597 lbs.	17,851
20	66B	2-dr. Sedan-5P	$5,985	2,574 lbs.	8,222
21	54B	4-dr. Sedan-5P	$6,419	2,622 lbs.	101,666

Fairmont Futura (Six)

22	36R	2-dr. Sport Coupe-5P	$7,141	2,682 lbs.	17,851
20	66B	2-dr. Sedan-5P	$6,619	2,659 lbs.	8,222
21	54B	4-dr. Sedan-5P	$7,043	2,707 lbs.	101,666

Granada (Four)

26	66D	2-dr. L Sedan-5P	$7,126	2,673 lbs.	12,802
27	54D	4-dr. L Sedan-5P	$7,301	2,705 lbs.	62,339
28	74D	4-dr. L Station Wagon-5P	-----	-----	45,182
26	66D	2-dr. GL Sedan-5P	$7,543	2,699 lbs.	Note 2
27	54D	4-dr. GL Sedan-5P	$7,718	2,735 lbs.	Note 2
28	74D	4-dr. GL Station Wagon-5P	-----	-----	Note 2
26	66D	2-dr. GLX Sedan-5P	$7,666	2,717 lbs.	Note 2
27	54D	4-dr. GLX Sedan-5P	$7,840	2,753 lbs.	Note 2

Granada (Six and V-6)

26	66D	2-dr. L Sedan-5P	$7,750	2,791 lbs.	12,802
27	54D	4-dr. L Sedan-5P	$7,925	2,823 lbs.	62,339
28	74B	4-dr. L Station Wagon-5P	$7,983	2,965 lbs.	45,182
26	66D	2-dr. GL Sedan-5P	$8,167	2,817 lbs.	Note 2
27	54D	4-dr. GL Sedan-5P	$8,342	2,853 lbs.	Note 2
28	74D	4-dr. GL Station Wagon-5P	$8,399	2,995 lbs.	Note 2
26	66D	2-dr. GLX Sedan-5P	$8,290	2,835 lbs.	Note 2
27	54D	4-dr. GLX Sedan-5P	$8,464	2,871 lbs.	Note 2

Note 2: Granada GL and GLX production is included in basic Granada L totals above.

Prices shown are for four- and six-cylinder engines. The six-cylinder price includes $411 for the required automatic transmission. A 232-cid V-6 cost $70 more than the inline six.

LTD (V-8)

32	66H	2-dr. Sedan-6P	$8,455	3,496 lbs.	3,510
33	54H	4-dr. Sedan-6P	$8,574	3,526 lbs.	29,776
38	74H	4-dr. Station Wagon-6P	$9,073	3,741 lbs.	9,294

LTD S (V-8)

31	54D	4-dr. Sedan-6P	$8,312	3,522 lbs.	22,182
37	74D	4-dr. Station Wagon-6P	$8,783	3,725 lbs.	2,973

LTD Crown Victoria (V-8)

34	66K	2-dr. Sedan-6P	$9,149	3,523 lbs.	9,287
35	54K	4-dr. Sedan-6P	$9,294	3,567 lbs.	41,405
39	74K	4-dr. Country Squire-6P	$9,580	3,741 lbs.	9,626

Engines:

Escort and EXP Base Four: Overhead cam. Cast-iron block and aluminum head. Displacement: 97.6 cid (1.6 liters). B & S: 3.15 x 3.13 in. Compression ratio: 8.8:1. Brake hp: 70 at 4600 rpm. Torque: 89 lbs.-ft. at 3000 rpm. Five main bearings. Hydraulic valve lifters. Carburetor: Motorcraft 740 two-barrel. VIN Code: 2.

Note: An 80-hp high-output version of the 1.6-liter four arrived later in the model year.

Fairmont and Granada Base Four: Inline. Overhead cam. Cast-iron block and head. Displacement: 140-cid (2.3 liters). B & S: 3.78 x 3.13 in. Compression ratio: 9.0:1. Brake hp: 86 at 4600 rpm. Torque: 117 lbs.-ft. at 2600 rpm. Five main bearings. Hydraulic valve lifters. Carburetor: Holley 6500 or Motorcraft 5200 two barrel. VIN Code: A.

Granada Base Six (Optional Fairmont): Inline. Overhead valve. Cast-iron block and head. Displacement: 200 cid (3.3 liters). B & S: 3.68 x 3.13 in. Compression ratio: 8.6:1. Brake hp: 87 at 3800 rpm. Torque: 151 to 154 lbs.-ft. at 1400 rpm. Seven main bearings. Hydraulic valve lifters. Carburetor: Single-barrel Holley 1946. VIN Code: B or T.

Optional Granada V-6: 90-degree, overhead valve. Cast-iron block and aluminum head. Displacement: 232 cid (3.8 liters). B & S: 3.80 x 3.40 in. Compression ratio: 8.65:1. Brake hp: 112 at 4000 rpm. Torque: 175 lbs.-ft. at 2000 rpm. Four main bearings. Hydraulic valve lifters. Carburetor: Motorcraft 2150 two-barrel. VIN Code: 3.

LTD Base V-8: 90-degree, overhead valve. Cast-iron block and head. Displacement: 255 cid (4.2 liters). B & S: 3.68 x 3.00 in. Compression ratio: 8.2:1. Brake horsepower: 122 at 3400 rpm. Torque: 209 lbs.-ft. at 2400 rpm. Five main bearings. Hydraulic valve lifters. Carburetor: Two-barrel Motorcraft 2150 or 7200VV. VIN Code: D.

Note: The 255 cid V-8 was also offered in Fairmont police cars.

LTD Wagon Base V-8 (Optional LTD sedan): 90-degree, overhead valve. Cast-iron block and head. Displacement: 302 cid (5.0 liters). B & S: 4.00 x 3.00 in. Compression ratio: 8.4:1. Brake hp: 132 at 3400 rpm. Torque: 236 lbs.-ft. at 1800 rpm. Five main bearings. Hydraulic valve lifters. Carburetor: Motorcraft 2150A or 7200VV two barrel. VIN Code: F.

LTD High-Output Police V-8: 90-degree, overhead valve. Cast-iron block and head. Displacement: 351 cid (5.8 liters). B & S: 4.00 x 3.50 in. Compression ratio: 8.3:1. Brake hp: 165 at 3600 rpm. Torque: 285 lbs.-ft. at 2200 rpm. Five main bearings. Hydraulic valve lifters. Carburetor: VV two barrel. VIN Code: G.

Chassis:

Escort: Wheelbase: 94.2 in. Overall length: 163.5 in., hatchback and 165.0 in., wagon. Tires: P65/80-R13 steel-belted radial blackwalls.

EXP: Wheelbase: 94.2 in. Overall length: 170.3 in. Tires: P65/80-R13 steel-belted radial blackwalls.

Fairmont: Wheelbase: 105.5 in. Overall length: 195.5 in. and 197.4 in., Futura. Tires: P175/75-R14 steel-belted blackwalls.

Granada: Wheelbase: 105.5 in. Overall length: 196.5 in. Tires: P175/75-R14 steel-belted blackwalls.

LTD: Wheelbase: 114.3 in. Overall Length: 209.3 in., LTD; 215.0 in., LTD wagon and 211.0 in., LTD Crown Victoria. Tires: P205/75-R14 steel-belted white sidewall radials and P215/75-R14, LTD wagon.

Options:

Escort: Squire wagon package ($293). Instrument group ($87). Appearance protection group ($55). Light group ($30). Air conditioner ($611). Rear defroster, electric ($120). Remote liftgate release ($30). Tinted glass ($82); windshield only ($32). Digital clock ($57). Interval wipers ($48). Rear wiper/washer ($117). Dual remote sport mirrors ($66). AM radio ($61). AM/FM radio ($76) and base ($137). AM/FM stereo radio ($106); with cassette or eight-track player ($184) and base ($245). Dual rear speakers ($39). Front vent windows, pivoting ($60). Remote quarter windows ($109). Bumper guards front or rear ($26). Bumper rub strips ($41). Luggage rack ($93). Roof air deflector ($29). Lower body protection ($68). Console ($111). Low-back reclining bucket seats ($33 to $98). High-back reclining bucket seats ($65). Cloth/vinyl seat trim ($29) and vinyl only, no charge. Shearling/leather seat trim ($109 to $138). Deluxe seatbelts ($24). Wheel trim rings ($48). Aluminum wheels ($232 to $377). P165/80R13 WSW ($58). High Output 1.6-liter four ($57). Fuel-saver 1.6-liter four, no charge. Automatic transaxle ($411). Optional axle ratio (no charge). Power brakes ($93). Power steering ($190). Handling suspension ($139 to $187) and ($41), GLX. Heavy-duty battery ($22 to $26). Engine block heater ($17 to $18).

EXP: Appearance protection group ($48). Air conditioner ($611). Fingertip speed control ($151). Tinted glass ($82). Right remote mirror ($41). AM/FM radio ($76). AM/FM stereo radio ($106); with cassette or eight-track player ($184). Premium sound ($105). AM radio delete ($37 credit). Flip-up open air roof ($276). Luggage rack ($93). Lower body protection ($68). Low-back bucket seats ($33). Cloth/vinyl seat trim ($29) and vinyl, no charge.

1982 Fairmont Futura sedan

Leather seat trim ($138). Shearling/leather seat trim ($138). Cast aluminum wheels ($232). P165/80-R13 raised-white letter tires ($72). Automatic transaxle ($411). Optional axle ratio: No charge. Power steering ($190). TR performance suspension package: with TR sport aluminum wheels ($405) or with steel wheels ($204). Heavy-duty battery ($22 to $26). Heavy-duty alternator ($27). Engine block heater ($17 to $18).

Fairmont: Interior luxury group ($282). Instrument cluster ($100). Appearance protection group ($57 to $59). Light group ($49 to $51). Air conditioning ($676). Rear defroster, electric ($124). Fingertip speed control ($155). Illuminated entry ($68). Power windows ($165 to $235). Power door locks ($106 to $184). Remote deck lid release ($32). Power seat ($139). Tinted windshield ($32). Tilt steering ($95). Quartz clock ($32). Interval wipers ($48). Map light ($10). Trunk light ($7). Left remote mirror ($22). Dual bright remote mirrors ($65). AM/FM radio ($39 to $54). AM/FM stereo radio ($85) and with eight-track or cassette player ($172). Twin rear speakers ($39). Premium sound system ($105). AM radio delete ($61 credit). Flip-up open-air roof ($276). Full or half vinyl roof ($137 to $140). Pivoting front vent windows ($63). Rocker panel moldings ($33). Console ($191). Vinyl flight bench seat ($29). Cloth/vinyl seat trim ($29). Flight bench seat, no charge. Front floor mats ($13 to $22). Turbine wheel covers ($54). Styled steel wheels ($54 to $107). P175/75-R14 white sidewall tires ($66). Conventional spare ($51). 200-cd six ($213). Automatic transmission ($411). Floor shift lever ($49). Traction-Lok differential ($76). Power steering ($195). Handling suspension ($52). Heavy-duty battery ($22 to $26). Extended-range gas tank ($46). Engine block heater ($17 to $18).

Granada: Granada Squire option ($282). Cold weather group ($77). Appearance protection group ($57 to $59). Light group ($49 to $51). Air conditioning ($676). Rear defroster, electric ($124). Fingertip speed control ($155). Illuminated entry ($68). Power windows ($165 to $235). Power door locks ($106 to $184). Power split bench seat ($196). Tinted glass ($88). Tinted windshield ($32). Leather-wrapped steering wheel ($55). Tilt steering ($95). Quartz clock ($32). Interval wipers ($48). Liftgate wiper/washer: wagon ($99). Cornering lamps ($59). Map light, dual-beam ($15). Trunk light ($7). Lighted right visor vanity mirror ($46) and pair ($91). AM/FM radio ($39-$54). AM/FM stereo radio ($85); with eight-track or cassette player ($172). Premium sound system ($105). AM radio delete ($61 credit). Flip-up open air roof ($276). Full or half vinyl roof ($137 to $140). Two-way liftgate, wagon ($105). Protective body moldings ($49). Luggage rack ($115). Console ($191). Vinyl seat trim ($29). Flight bench seat (NC). Split bench seat ($230). Front floor mats ($13 to $22). Luxury wheel covers ($49) and GL and GLX, no charge. Wire wheel covers ($80 to $152). Cast-aluminum wheels ($348 to $396). P185/75-R14 blackwalls ($38). P185/75-R14 white walls ($104) and wagon, ($66). P185/75-R14 raised white letter tires ($121) and ($83), wagon. P190/65-R390 blackwalls on TRX aluminum wheels ($529 to $583). Conventional spare ($51). 200-cid six ($213). 232-cid V-6 ($283) exc. wagon ($70). Automatic transmission ($411). Floor shift lever ($49). Traction-Lok differential ($76). Optional axle ratio, no charge. Power steering ($195). Power steering ($195). Heavy-duty suspension ($24). Heavy-duty battery ($22 to $26). Extended-range gas tank ($46). Engine block heater ($17 to $18).

LTD: Interior luxury group ($727 to $807). Convenience group ($90 to $116). Power lock group ($106 to $201). Light group ($43). Protection group ($67). Air conditioning ($695); w/auto-temp control ($761). Rear defroster, electric ($124). Fingertip speed control ($155). Illuminated entry system ($68). Power windows ($165 to $240). Power driver's seat ($198) or driver and passenger ($395). Tinted glass ($102); windshield only ($32). Autolamp on/off delay ($73). Leather-wrapped steering wheel ($51). Tilt steering wheel ($95). Automatic parking brake release ($12). Tripminder computer ($215 to $293). Quartz clock ($32). Digital clock ($46 to $78). Seatbelt chime ($27). Interval wipers ($48). Cornering lamps ($55). Lighted right visor vanity mirrors ($46 to $91). AM/FM radio ($41 to $54). AM/FM stereo radio ($85) and with eight-track or cassette tape player ($172) and Crown Victoria ($87). AM/FM stereo search radio ($232) and Crown Victoria ($146). With eight-track or cassette ($233 to $318). Power antenna ($55). Dual

1982 Granada GL Squire station wagon

rear speakers ($41). Premium sound system ($133 to $167). Full or half vinyl roof ($165). Pivoting front vent windows ($63). Rocker panel moldings ($32). Luggage rack ($104). Dual-facing rear seats, wagon ($167). Leather seating ($412). Dual flight bench seat recliners ($65). Split bench seating ($139 to $204). All-vinyl seat trim ($28); Duraweave vinyl ($62). Front floor mats ($15-$21). Trunk trim ($49). Luxury wheel covers ($82). 15 in. wheel covers ($49). Wire wheel covers ($152). Cast aluminum wheels ($384). P215/75-R14 white sidewalls ($36). P225/75-R14 white sidewalls ($36 to $73). P205/75-15 white sidewalls ($11 to $47). Puncture-resistant tires ($112 to $148). Conventional spare ($51). 302-cid V-8 ($59). Traction-Lok differential ($80). Heavy-duty suspension ($26). Handling suspension ($49). Heavy-duty battery ($22 to $26): Heavy-duty alternator ($52). Engine block heater ($17 to $18). Medium duty trailer towing package ($200 to $251).

History:

The 1982 Fords were introduced on Sept. 24, 1981. The EXP was introduced earlier, on April 9, 1981. Total model year production was 1,035,063, including Mustangs. Calendar year sales by U.S. dealers was 925,490, including Mustangs. The Escort became the best selling domestic car during the model year, finding 321,952 buyers, up more than 13 percent from 1981. Total Ford Division sales for the model year declined by close to 20 percent. The Ford Motor Co. market share held at the 16.5 percent level of the prior year. *Car and Driver* readers had voted Escort "Most Significant New Domestic Car" for 1981, and it beat Chevrolet's Chevette. Granada gained sales but other models did not. Mustang dropped by almost one-third, with Fairmont and Thunderbird dropping by more than 40 percent. EXP did not sell as well as hoped for after its spring 1981 debut. Within a couple of months, incentives were being offered. Sales rose a bit later, partly due to a high-output EXP 1.6-liter engine that debuted in mid-year. Two new plants (San Jose, California, and St. Thomas, Ontario) were assigned to assemble the Escort/EXP subcompacts. Escort was also assembled at Wayne, Michigan, and Edison, New Jersey. As the 1983 model year began, Ford offered low-interest financing (a 10.75 percent rate) to customers who would buy one of the leftover 1982 models. In January 1982, the UAW agreed to an alternating-shift arrangement at certain plants. Workers would work 10 days, then take 10 days off. Ford's advertising theme at this time was: "Have you driven a Ford lately?"

1983 Ford

Escort — Four: America's best selling car in 1982 lost its base model, dropping to four series. That made Escort L the new base model with GL, GLX, and a sporty GT. The new GT was said to be more akin to the high-performance XR3, the image car of the European Escort line. Its 1.6-liter four had multi-port fuel injection. GT also carried five-speed manual shift with 3.73:1 final drive, a TR performance suspension with Michelin TRX tires, functional front and rear spoilers, molded wheel lip

1983 Escort GT three-door hatchback

flares and a tailpipe extension. GT standards also included fog lamps, unique tail lamp treatment, a reclining sport seat, a specially-tuned exhaust, special steering wheel, and console and full instrumentation. The high-output carbureted 97.6-cid (1.6-liter) four was introduced late in the 1982 model year as an option on any Escort except the GT. The 1983 Escort might have any of three suspension levels: base, handling, and TRX performance. All Escorts had all-season steel-belted radial tires and a larger, 13-gallon gas tank. A five-speed gearbox was available with either the high output or EFI engine. Escort's Fuel-Saver package came with economy 3.04:1 final drive and wide-ratio four-speed gearbox. The GLX no longer had front and rear bumper guards. The GL now had standard low-back reclining bucket seats. All except L had a new locking gas filler door with inside release. Optional knit vinyl seat trim replaced regular vinyl on GL and GLX.

EXP — Four: This year's EXP looked the same, but had a wider choice of engines and transaxles. The standard power train was a 97.6-cid (1.6-liter) four with two-barrel carburetor and fast-burn capability. It was hooked to a four-speed manual transaxle with overdrive fourth gear. The high-output 1.6-liter was available with either automatic or a new optional five-speed gearbox. That engine produced 80 hp, versus 70 for the base four. Newly optional this year was a multi-port fuel-injected version of the four. Acceleration to 60 mph was supposed to be cut by three seconds with the new power plant. Five-speed gearboxes came with 3.73:1 final drive ratio. Shift control for the optional automatic transaxle was revised to a straight-line pattern. The EXP had a larger, 13-gallon gas tank. Seats had a new sew style and more porous knit vinyl that would be cooler in summer. A remote-control locking fuel filler door was now standard. New options included a remote fuel door release, sport performance bucket seats, and P175/80-R13 tires. Michelin TRX tires and TR wheels were now available with base suspension.

LTD — Four/Six/V-6: The familiar LTD nameplate took on two forms for 1983: a new, smaller five-passenger model, and the old (larger) LTD Crown Victoria (listed below). This new LTD was built on the "L" body shell. Among its features were gas-pressurized shocks and struts, as introduced in 1982 on the new Continental. LTD came in a single well-equipped series: just a four-door sedan and wagon. Sedans carried the 140 cid (2.3-liter) four with four-speed as base power train; wagons, the 250 cid (3.3-liter) inline six with three-speed automatic. A 3.8-liter "Essex" V-6 became optional, with four-speed overdrive automatic. So was a propane-powered four, intended to attract fleet buyers. The base 2.3-liter engine had a new single-barrel carburetor and fast-burn technology. LTD had rack-and-pinion steering and a wheelbase that was 105.5 inches. It used the Fairmont platform and its aerodynamic design features included a 60-degree rear-window angle and an aero-styled decklid. Its drag coefficient was claimed to be just 0.38. Quad rectangular headlamps were deeply recessed. The sloping rear end held horizontal tri-color wraparound tail lamps with upper and lower segments. The instrument panel evolved from the 1982 Thunderbird. Mercury Marquis was LTD's corporate twin and each was between compact and mid-size.

Fairmont Futura — Four/ Six: For its final season, Fairmont continued with little change. The lineup had been simplified into a single series for the 1982 model year. The 4.2-liter V-8 was dropped completely, leaving only a base four and optional inline-six. The 140-cid (2.3-liter) switched to two-barrel carburetion and added fast-burn technology and a redesigned exhaust manifold. Two- and four-door sedans were offered, along with a two-door coupe. A low-budget "S" series was introduced. The Traction-Lok axle was now available with TR-type tires. One new option was a 100-amp alternator. Flight bench seating and a headlamp-on warning buzzer were added to the interior luxury group. Dual rear speakers were discontinued as an option. Radios got a new look and graphics. In 1984, the rear-drive Fairmont would be replaced by the new front-drive Tempo.

LTD Crown Victoria — V-8: Full-size Fords carried on with little change and a longer name. Initially, the model lineup consisted of two- and four-door sedans and a Country Squire station wagon in just one luxury level. Later came low budget "S" sedans and a plain-bodied wagon. The

base engine was the fuel-injected 302-cid (5.0-liter) V-8 with four-speed overdrive automatic. The Country Squire now had a standard AM/FM radio. All models had a new fuel cap tether. Quad rectangular headlamps stood above rectangular parking lamps, and the assembly continued around the fender tips to enclose signal/marker lenses. Sedans also had a new tail lamp design. The Country Squire had a revised wood tone appearance without the former planking lines. New options included a remote-control locking fuel door, locking wire wheel covers, and new-generation electronic radios. Two trailer-towing packages were offered.

I.D. Data:

Ford's 17-symbol Vehicle Identification Number (VIN) again was stamped on a metal tab fastened to the instrument panel and was visible through the windshield. The first three symbols, 1FA= manufacturer, make and vehicle type. The fourth symbol, B=the restraint system. Next came letter P followed by two digits that indicated the body type. P04=Escort L two-door hatchback. Symbol eight indicated the engine type: 2=98-cid four cylinder; 4=H.O. 98-cid four cylinder; 5=98-cid EFI four cylinder; A=140-cid four cylinder; D=140-cid turbo four cylinder; X=200-cid six; 3=232-cid V-6; F=302-cid V-8 and G=351-cid V-8. Next was a check digit. Symbol 10 indicated the model year: D=1983. Symbol 11 was the assembly plant: A=Atlanta, Georgia; B=Oakville, Ontario, Canada; G=Chicago, Illinois; H=Lorain, Ohio; K=Kansas City, Missouri; R=San Jose, California; T= Edison, New Jersey; W=Wayne, Michigan; X=St. Thomas, Ontario, Canada and Z=St. Louis, Missouri. The final six digits were the sequential number that began with 100001. A Vehicle Certification Label on the left front door lock face panel or door pillar showed the manufacturer, month and year of manufacture, GVW, GAWR, certification statement, VIN, and codes for such items as body type, color, trim, axle, transmission, and special order information.

Escort (Four)

Model No.	Body Style No.	Body Type & Seating	Factory Price	Shipping Weight	Production Total
04	61D	2-dr. L Hatchback-4P	$5,639	1,932 lbs.	Note 1
13	58D	4-dr. L Hatchback-4P	$5,846	1,998 lbs.	Note 1
09	74D	4-dr. L Station Wagon-4P	$6,052	2,026 lbs.	Note 1
05	61D	2-dr. GL Hatchback-4P	$6,384	1,959 lbs.	Note 1
14	58D	4-dr. GL Hatchback-4P	$6,601	2,025 lbs.	Note 1
10	74D	4-dr. GL Station Wagon-4P	$6,779	2,052 lbs.	Note 1
06	61D	2-dr. GLX Hatchback-4P	$6,771	1,993 lbs.	Note 1
15	58D	4-dr. GLX Hatchback-4P	$6,988	2,059 lbs.	Note 1
11	74D	4-dr. GLX Station Wagon-4P	$7,150	2,083 lbs.	Note 1
07	61D	2-dr. GT Hatchback-4P	$7,339	2,020 lbs.	Note 1

Note 1: Total Escort production was 151,386 two-door hatchbacks, 84,649 four-door hatchback sedans, and 79,335 station wagons. Trim level breakdown is not available. Bodies were sometimes called three-door and five-door.

EXP (Four)

01	67D	3-dr. Hatchback-2P	$6,426	2,068 lbs.	19, 697
01/301B	67D	3-dr. HO Coupe-2P	$7,004	------	Note 2
01/302B	67D	3-dr. HO Sport Coupe-2P	$7,794	------	Note 2
01/303B	67D	3-dr. Luxury Coupe-2P	$8,225	------	Note 2
01/304B	67D	3-dr. GT Coupe-2P	$8,739	------	Note 2

Note 2: Production of step-up models is included in basic EXP total above.

Fairmont Futura (Four)

37	36R	2-dr. Coupe-4P	$6,666	2,601 lbs.	7,882
35	66B	2-dr. Sedan-5P	$6,444	2,582 lbs.	3,664
36	54B	4-dr. Sedan-5P	$6,590	2,626 lbs.	69,287

Fairmont Futura (Six)

37	36R	2-dr. Coupe-4P	$7,344	2,720 lbs.	7,882
35	66B	2-dr. Sedan-5P	$7,122	2,701 lbs.	3,664
36	54B	4-dr. Sedan-5P	$7,268	2,745 lbs.	69,287

Fairmont "S" (Four)

35/41K	66B	2-dr. Sedan-5P	$5,985	2,569 lbs.	Note 3
36/41K	54B	4-dr. Sedan-5P	$6,125	2,613 lbs.	Note 3
35/41K	66B	2-dr. Sedan-5P	$6,663	2,688 lbs.	Note 3
36/41K	54B	4-dr. Sedan-5P	$6,803	2,732 lbs.	Note 3

Note 3: Fairmont "S" production is included in Futura sedan totals above.

LTD (Four)

39	54D	4-dr. Sedan-5P	$7,777	2,788 lbs.	111,813
39/60H	54D	4-dr. Brougham-5P	$8,165	2,802 lbs.	Note 4
40	74D	4-dr. Station Wagon-5P	------	------	43,945

1983 EXP HO Sport Coupe

1983 LTD four-door sedan

1983 LTD Country Squire station wagon

LTD (Six)

39	54D	4-dr. Sedan-5P	$8,455	2,874 lbs.	111,813
39/60H	54D	4-dr. Brougham-5P	$8,843	2,888 lbs.	Note 4
40	74D	4-dr. Station Wagon-5P	$8,577	2,975 lbs.	43,945

Note 4: Brougham production is included in basic sedan total.
Note: Prices shown are for four-and six-cylinder engines. The six-cylinder price includes $439 for the automatic transmission. A 232-cid V-6 cost $70 more than the inline-six.

LTD Crown Victoria (V-8)

42	66K	2-dr. Sedan-6P	$10,094	3,590 lbs.	11,414
43	54K	4-dr. Sedan-6P	$10,094	3,620 lbs.	81,859
44	74K	4-dr. Country Squire-6P	$10,253	3,773 lbs.	20,343
43/41K	54K	4-dr. S Sedan-6P	$ 9,130	------	Note 5
44/41K	74K	4-dr. S Station Wagon-6P	$ 9,444	------	Note 5
44/41E	74K	4-dr. Station Wagon-6P	$10,003	------	Note 5

Note 5: Production of S models and the basic station wagon was included in the sedan and Country Squire totals.

Escort and EXP Base Four: Inline and overhead cam. Cast-iron block and aluminum head. Displacement: 98 cid (1.6 liters). B & S: 3.15 x 3.13 in. Compression ratio: 8.8:1. Brake hp: 70 at 4600 rpm. Torque: 88 lbs.-ft. at 2600 rpm. Five main bearings. Hydraulic valve lifters. Carburetor: Motorcraft 740 two-barrel. VIN Code: 2.

Escort and EXP Optional Four: High-output 1.6-liter. Hp: 80 at 5400 rpm. Torque: 88 lbs.-ft. at 3000 rpm. VIN Code: 4.

Escort GT Base Four (Optional in Escort and EXP: Fuel-injected 1.6-liter. Compression ratio: 9.5:1. Hp: 88 at 5400 rpm. Torque: 94 lbs.-ft. at 4200 rpm. VIN Code: 5.

Fairmont and LTD Base Four: Inline. Overhead cam. Cast-iron block and head. Displacement: 140 cid (2.3 liters). B & S: 3.78 x 3.13 in. Compression ratio: 9.0: 1. Brake hp: 90 at 4600 rpm. Torque: 122 lbs.-ft. at 2600 rpm. Five main bearings. Hydraulic valve lifters. Carburetor: Carter YFA single-barrel. VIN Code: A.

Note: A 140-cid (2.3-liter) propane-powered four was also available for LTD.

Fairmont and LTD Optional Six: Inline. Overhead valve. Cast-iron block and head. Displacement: 200 cid (3.3 liters). B & S: 3.68 x 3.13 in. Compression ratio: 8.6:1. Brake hp: 92 at 3800 rpm. Torque: 156 lbs.-ft. at 1400 rpm. Seven main bearings. Hydraulic valve lifters. Carburetor: Holley 1946 single-barrel. VIN Code: X.

LTD Optional V-6: 90-degree, overhead valve. Cast-iron block and aluminum head. Displacement: 232 cid (3.8 liters). B & S: 3.80 x 3.40 in. Compression ratio: 8.65:1. Brake hp: 110 at 3800 rpm. Torque: 175 lbs.-ft. at 2200 rpm. Four main bearings. Hydraulic valve lifters. Carburetor: Motorcraft 2150 or 7200VV two-barrel. VIN Code: 3.

Crown Victoria Base V-8 (Optional LTD): 90-degree, overhead valve. Cast-iron block and head. Displacement: 302 cid (5.0 liters). B & S: 4.00 x 3.00 in. Compression ratio: 8.4:1. Brake hp: 130 at 3200 rpm. Torque: 240 lbs.-ft. at 2000 rpm. Five main bearings. Hydraulic valve lifters. Electronic fuel injection. VIN Code: F.

Note: Crown Victoria also announced a high-output V-8 with 145-hp at 3600 rpm and 245 lbs.-ft. at 2200 rpm.

Crown Victoria High-Output Police V-8: 90-degree, overhead valve. Cast-iron block and head. Displacement: 351 cid (5.8 liters). B & S: 4.00 x 3.50 in. Compression ratio: 8.3:1. Brake hp: 165 at 3600 rpm. Torque: 290 lbs.-ft. at 2200 rpm. Five main bearings. Hydraulic valve lifters. Carburetor: VV two-barrel. VIN Code: G.

Escort: Wheelbase: 94.2 in. Overall length: Escort, 163.9 in. and wagon, 165.0 in. Tires: P165/80-R13 steel-belted blackwalls and P165/70-R365 Michelin TRX on Escort GT.

EXP: Wheelbase: 94.2 in. Overall length: 170.3 in. Tires: P165/80-R13 steel-belted blackwalls and EXP luxury coupe, P165/70-R365 Michelin TRX.

Fairmont: Wheelbase: 105.5 in. Overall length: 195.5 in. and 197.4, Futura coupe. Fairmont: P175/75-R14 steel-belted blackwalls.

LTD: Wheelbase: 105.5 in. Overall length: 196.5. Tires: P185/75-R14 steel-belted blackwalls.

Crown Victoria: Wheelbase: 114.3 in. Overall length: 211.1 in. and 215.0 in., station wagon. Tires: P215/75-R14 steel-belted whitewalls.

Escort: Squire wagon package ($350). Instrument group ($87). Appearance protection group ($39). Light group ($43). Air conditioner ($624). Rear defroster, electric ($124). Fingertip speed control ($170). Tinted glass ($90); windshield only ($40). Digital clock ($57). Interval wipers ($49). Rear wiper/washer ($117). Dual remote sport mirrors ($67). AM radio: L ($61). AM/FM radio ($82) and ($143) on L. AM/FM stereo radio ($109) and ($170) on base. With cassette or eight-track player ($199) and ($260) on L. Premium sound ($117). Flip-up open-air roof ($217 to $310). Pivoting front vent windows ($60). Remote quarter windows ($109). Luggage rack ($93). Lower body protection ($68). Console ($111). Fold-down center armrest ($55). Low-back reclining bucket seats: L ($98). High-back reclining bucket seats: L ($65). Vinyl low-back reclining bucket seats: GL/GLX ($24). Vinyl high-back bucket seats: L ($24). Wheel trim rings ($54). Cast-aluminum wheels ($226 to $383). TR sport aluminum wheels ($568) and ($411) on GLX or ($201), GT. TR styled steel wheels ($210 to $367). H.O. 1.6-liter four ($70 to $73). Close-ratio four-speed trans, no charge. Five-speed manual transmission ($76). Automatic transaxle ($439) and GT ($363). Power brakes ($95). Power steering ($210). Handling suspension ($199) and GLX ($41). Performance suspension: Escort ($41) and with Michelin TRX tires on GT ($41). Heavy duty battery ($26).

EXP: Air conditioner ($624). Rear defroster: base ($124). Tinted glass: H.O. ($90). AM/FM radio ($82). AM/FM stereo radio ($109) and ($199) with cassette or eight-track player or ($90) on luxury coupe. Premium sound ($117). AM radio delete ($37 credit). AM/FM stereo delete: luxury coupe ($145 credit). AM/FM stereo/cassette delete: GT ($235 credit). Flip-up open air roof ($310). Lower body protection ($68). Low-back sport cloth or knit vinyl bucket seats, no charge. Low-back sport performance seats ($173). Leather/vinyl seat trim ($144). Shearling low-back bucket seats ($227). TR sport aluminum wheels on GT, no charge. H.O. 1.6-liter four on GT ($70). Automatic transaxle, base EXP ($439) and ($363), other EXP. Power steering ($210). TR performance suspension with Michelin TRX tires ($41) EXP luxury. Heavy-duty battery ($26). Heavy-duty alternator ($27). Engine block heater ($17 to $18).

Fairmont: Interior luxury group ($294). Instrument cluster ($100). Appearance protection group ($32 to $60). Light group ($55). Air conditioner ($724). Rear defroster, electric ($135). Fingertip speed control ($170). Illuminated entry ($82). Power windows ($180 to $255). Power door locks ($120 to $170). Remote deck lid release ($40). Four-way power seat ($139). Tinted glass ($105). Tinted windshield ($38). Tilt steering ($105). Quartz clock ($35). Interval wipers ($49). Dual bright remote mirrors on S ($68). Lighted visor vanity mirrors, pair ($100). AM radio: S ($61). AM/FM radio ($59 to $120). AM/FM stereo radio ($109 to $170) and ($199 to $260) with eight-track or cassette player. Premium sound system ($117). AM radio delete ($61 credit). Flip-up open air roof ($310). Full or half vinyl roof ($152). Pivoting front vent windows ($63). Console ($191). Cloth/vinyl seat trim ($35). Front floor mats ($15 to $24). Wire wheel covers ($87 to $152). Turbine wheel covers for S ($66). Styled steel wheels ($60 to $126). 200-cid six ($239). Select-Shift automatic transmission ($439). Floor shift lever ($49). Traction-Lok differential ($95). Heavy duty suspension ($24). Heavy-duty battery ($26). Extended-range gas tank ($46).

1984 Ford

1983 LTD Brougham sedan

LTD: Squire option ($282). Brougham decor option: wagon ($363). Power lock group ($170 to $210). Cold weather group ($77). Appearance protection group ($60). Light group ($38). Air conditioner ($724) with auto-temp ($802). Electric rear defroster ($135). Fingertip speed control ($170). Illuminated entry ($76). Autolamp on-off delay ($73). Power windows ($255). Six-way power driver's seat ($207) or dual ($415). Tinted glass ($105). Leather-wrapped steering wheel ($59). Tilt steering ($105). Electronic instrument cluster ($289 to $367). Tripminder computer ($215 to $293). Digital clock ($78). Diagnostic warning lights ($59). Interval wipers ($49). Liftgate wiper/washer, wagon ($99). Cornering lamps ($60). Map light: fleet ($15). AM/FM radio ($59). AM/FM stereo radio ($109) or ($199) with eight-track or cassette player. Electronic-tuning AM/FM stereo radio ($252) and ($396) with cassette. Premium sound system ($117 to $151). AM radio delete ($61 credit). Flip-up open air roof ($310). Full vinyl roof ($152). Two-way liftgate, wagon ($105). Luggage rack, wagon ($126). Console ($100). Individual seats with console ($61). Leather seat trim ($415). Front floor mats ($23). Luxury wheel covers ($55). Wire wheel covers ($159 to $198). Styled wheels ($178). Cast aluminum wheels ($402). Turbo 140-cid four ($896). 200-cid six ($239). 232-cid V-6 ($309) and ($70) on wagon. Select-Shift automatic transmission ($439). Overdrive automatic transmission ($615) and ($176) on wagon. Floor shift lever ($49). Traction-Lok differential ($95). Heavy-duty battery ($26). Extended-range gas tank ($46). Engine block heater ($17 to $18).

Crown Victoria: Interior luxury group ($830 to $911). Convenience group ($95 to $116). Power lock group ($123 to $220). Light group ($48). Protection group ($68). Air conditioning ($724) and ($802) with auto-temp control. Electric rear defroster ($135). Fingertip speed control ($170). Illuminated entry system ($76). Power windows ($180 to $255). Power driver's seat ($210) or driver and passenger ($420). Remote fuel door lock ($24). Tinted glass ($105). Autolamp on/off delay ($73). Leather-wrapped steering wheel ($59). Tilt steering wheel ($105). Tripminder computer ($215 to $261). Quartz clock: S ($35). Digital clock ($61 to $96). Interval wipers ($49). Cornering lamps ($60). Remote right mirror ($43). Lighted visor vanity mirrors ($100). AM/FM stereo radio: S ($106) and ($112 to $218) with eight-track or cassette tape. AM/FM stereo search radio ($166 to $272) or ($310 to $416) with eight-track or cassette. Power antenna ($60). Premium sound system ($145 to $179). AM/FM delete ($152 credit). Luggage rack, Country Squire ($110). Dual-facing rear seats, Country Squire ($167). Leather seat trim ($418). Split bench seating ($139). All-vinyl seat trim ($34); Duraweave vinyl on wagon ($96). Carpeted floor mats ($33). Trunk trim ($49). Luxury wheel covers ($88). Wire wheel covers ($159 to $198). Cast-aluminum wheels ($390). Conventional spare ($63). Traction-Lok differential ($95). Heavy-duty suspension ($26). Handling suspension ($49). Heavy-duty battery ($26). Engine block heater ($17 to $18). Medium-duty trailer towing package ($200 to $251). Heavy-duty trailer towing package ($251 to $302).

History:

The 1983 Fords were introduced on Oct. 14, 1982. The Thunderbird was introduced later, on Feb. 17, 1983. Model year production was 928,146, including Mustangs. Calendar year sales by U.S. dealers was 1,060,314, including Mustangs. Once again, Escort was the best-selling car in the country. That helped Ford's model year sales to rise 12 percent over 1982. Next in line in terms of sales were the new smaller LTD and full-size LTD Crown Victoria. Ford still ranked number two in domestic auto sales with Oldsmobile a potent contender for that spot. Ford was judged second in the industry in quality, behind the Lincoln-Mercury division but ahead of rival GM and Chrysler. Low 10.75 percent financing was extended in December 1982 to include 1983 and leftover 1982 models. Continuing demand kept the big rear-drive Ford alive, as did improved fuel supplies. Tempo was introduced in May 1983 as a new 1984 model.

Escort — Four: Diesel power was news under Ford subcompact hoods, as the company's first passenger-car diesel engine was available on both Escort and Tempo. The Mazda 2.0-liter diesel four came with a five-speed manual (overdrive) transaxle. A little later, a turbocharged, fuel-injected 97.6-cid (1.6-liter) four was ready for the GT model. Turbos hooked up to a five-speed manual gearbox, a package that included firmer suspension and special wheels and tires. Carbureted, high-output and fuel injected versions of the 1.6-liter engines were available. In addition to the carryover L, GL and sporty GT, the LX replaced the GLX. It included the fuel-injected four, TR suspension, an overhead console with digital clock and a five-speed transaxle. Escort GT now sported black polycarbonate bumpers. Inside was a new instrument panel with integral side-window demisters, and a new steering wheel. A new fold-down rear seat was standard on GL, GT and LX. Power ventilation replaced the "ram air" system.

EXP — Four: Turbocharged power brought EXP a strong performance boost for 1984. The new turbo model had a unique front air dam and rear deck lid spoiler. The turbo version included a tighter suspension with Koni shock absorbers, Michelin P185/65-R365 TRX tires on new cast aluminum wheels, and a five-speed manual transaxle. Base power train was upgraded to the high-output 1.6-liter engine, also mated to five-speed manual. EXP had a completely revised exterior. The silhouette was altered dramatically by adding a "bubble back" liftgate. EXP also had new blackout tail lamps, color-keyed bumper rub strips and mirrors, and a revised front air dam. Both the liftgate and tail lamps came from Mercury's former LN7, discontinued for 1984. Inside was a standard overhead console with digital clock and a new instrument panel with performance cluster and tachometer. Styled steel wheels were a new design. New options included a tilt steering wheel, electronic radios with graphic equalizer, clear coat paint, and illuminated visor vanity mirror. Both EXP and Escort had a new clutch/starter interlock system.

Tempo — Four: Ford's replacement for the departed rear-drive Fairmont arrived as an early 1984 model, wearing Ford's "rakish contemporary styling." Aircraft-type door configurations were shared with the 1983 Thunderbird. Door tops extended into the roof to create a wraparound effect. Two- and four-door sedans were offered on a 99.9-inch wheelbase. The four-door sedan had a six-window design and rounded window corners. Tempo came in L, GL and GLX trim. A new 140-cid (2.3-liter) HSC (high swirl combustion) four-cylinder engine was developed specially for Tempo. Displacement was identical to the familiar 2.3-liter four used in the Fairmont and LTD, but the bore and stroke dimensions differed in this OHV design. This was the first production fast-burn engine, controlled by an EEC-IV onboard computer, also used in the Thunderbird Turbo Coupe. Tempo could have either a close-ratio five-speed manual or automatic transaxle. A Fuel Saver four-speed was standard. Tempo had fully independent quadra-link rear suspension using MacPherson struts, a MacPherson strut front suspension and stabilizer bar. Power front disc brakes were standard. Inside, Tempo had low-back bucket seats with cloth trim; color-keyed molded door trim panels with integral storage bins; a storage bin above the radio; color-keyed vinyl sun visors; a carpeted package tray; and a consolette. An optional TR handling package included Michelin

1984 EXP Turbo coupe

1984 Escort GL five-door hatchback

1984 Escort LX station wagon

1984 LTD Brougham sedan

P185/65-R365 TRX tires on new-design cast aluminum wheels, and a special handling suspension. Mercury's Topaz was nearly identical except for trim and the list of options available.

LTD — Four/V-6/V-8: LTD received a few fresh touches that included argent accents on body moldings and optional bumper rub strips plus a revised instrument panel appliqué. A new A-frame steering wheel with center horn button replaced the four-spoke design. Headlamp doors now had dark argent paint, instead of light argent. Parking and turn lamp lenses switched from clear white to amber, and bulbs from amber to clear. The most noteworthy new body feature was the unique formal roof treatment added to the Brougham four-door sedan. It had a distinctive solid rear pillar and "Frenched" back window treatment, and included a full Cambria cloth roof. The inline six-cylinder engine finally disappeared. Manual transmission with the base 140-cid (2.3-liter) four was dropped. A 302-cid (5.0-liter) EFI high-output V-8 was available only on police sedans. That made the fuel-injected 232-cid (3.8-liter) V-6 the only regular option. It was standard on wagons. All engines added EECIV controls. Propane power was available but found few takers. Base and Brougham sedans were offered, along with a station wagon. Power steering and three-speed automatic were standard, with four-speed automatic available in V-6 models. New LTD options included a flight bench seat, the single most requested feature.

LTD Crown Victoria — V-8: The Crown Victoria's new grille featured a light argent second surface, and a new optional Brougham roof for the formal looking, four-door sedan. It included a padded full vinyl top, an upright rear window with "Frenched" treatment, and electro-luminescent coach lamps on the center pillar. Interiors had a new vinyl grain pattern. The full-size Ford was a carryover, available again as a two- or four-door sedan, plus pair of wagons. The Crown Victoria station wagon was just a Country Squire without simulated wood trim. The wide grille had a 12 x 4 hole crosshatch pattern (plus a 2 x 2 pattern within each segment). Amber signal/marker lenses consisted of a large lens above a small one. "LTD Crown Victoria" lettering went ahead of the front door, just above the crease line. The standard engine was the 302-cid (5.0-liter) fuel-injected V-8. The high-performance 351-cid (5.8-liter) V-8 with variable-venturi carburetor was available only with police package.

I.D. Data:

Ford's 17-symbol Vehicle Identification Number (VIN) was stamped on a metal tab fastened on the instrument panel and was visible through the windshield. The first three symbols, 1FA=manufacturer, make and vehicle type. The fourth symbol B=the restraint system. Next came the letter P followed by two digits that indicated the body type. P04=Escort L two-door hatchback. Symbol eight indicated the engine type: 2=98-cid carbureted four cylinder; 4=High Output four; 5=fuel-injected four; 8=98-cid turbo FI four; H=121-cid diesel; A=140-cid four; R or J=HSC four; 6=140-cid propane-fueled four; W=140-cid EFI four; 3=232-cid V-6; F=302-cid V8 and G=351-cid V-8l. Next was a check digit. Symbol 10 indicated the model year: E=1984. Symbol 11 was the assembly plant: A=Atlanta, Georgia; B=Oakville, Ontario, Canada; G=Chicago, Illinois; H=Lorain, Ohio; K=Kansas City, Missouri; T=Edison, New Jersey; W=Wayne, Michigan; X=St. Thomas, Ontario, Canada and Z=St. Louis, Missouri. The final six digits were the sequential number, starting with 100001. A Vehicle Certification Label on the left front door lock face panel or door pillar showed the manufacturer, month and

year of manufacture, GVW, GAWR, certification statement, VIN, and code for body type and color, trim, axle ratio, transmission, and special order data.

Escort (Four)

Model No.	Body Style No.	Body Type & Seating	Factory Price	Shipping Weight	Production Total
04	61D	2-dr. Hatchback-4P	$5,629	1,981 lbs.	Note 1
13	58D	4-dr. Hatchback-4P	$5,835	2,024 lbs.	Note 1
04	61D	2-dr. L Hatchback-4P	$5,885	1,981 lbs.	Note 1
13	58D	4-dr. L Hatchback-4P	$6,099	2,034 lbs.	Note 1
09	74D	4-dr. L Station Wagon-4P	$6,313	2,066 lbs.	Note 1
05	61D	2-dr. GL Hatchback-4P	$6,382	2,033 lbs.	Note 1
14	58D	4-dr. GL Hatchback-4P	$6,596	2,086 lbs.	Note 1
10	74D	4-dr. GL Station Wagon-4P	$6,773	2,115 lbs.	Note 1
15	58D	4-dr. LX Hatchback-4P	$7,848	2,137 lbs.	Note 1
11	74D	4-dr. LX Station Wagon-4P	$7,939	2,037 lbs.	Note 1

Escort GT (Four)

07	61D	2-dr. Hatchback-4P	$7,593	2,103 lbs.	Note 1
07	61D	2-dr. Turbo Hatchback-4P	------	2,239 lbs.	Note 1

Note 1: Total Escort production was 184,323 two-door hatchbacks, 99,444 four-door hatchbacks, and 88,756 station wagons. Trim level breakdown not available. Bodies are referred to as three-door and five-door.

Diesel Note: Diesel-powered Escorts came in L and GL trim, priced $558 higher than gasoline models.

EXP (Four)

01/A80	67D	3-dr. Hatchback-2P	$6,653	2,117 lbs.	23,016
01/A81	67D	3-dr. Luxury Coupe-2P	$7,539	2,117 lbs.	Note 2
01/A82	67D	3-dr. Turbo Coupe-2P	$9,942	2,158 lbs.	Note 2

Note 2: Production of luxury and turbo coupe models is included in basic EXP total above.

Tempo (Four)

18	66D	2-dr. L Sedan-5P	$6,936	2,249 lbs.	Note 3
21	54D	4-dr. L Sedan-5P	$6,936	2,308 lbs.	Note 3
19	66D	2-dr. GL Sedan-5P	$7,159	2,276 lbs.	Note 3
22	54D	4-dr. GL Sedan-5P	$7,159	2,339 lbs.	Note 3
20	66D	2-dr. GLX Sedan-5P	$7,621	2,302 lbs.	Note 3
23	54D	4-dr. GLX Sedan-5P	$7,621	2,362 lbs.	Note 3

Note 3: Total Tempo production came to 107,065 two-doors and 295,149 four-doors.

Diesel note: Diesel-powered Tempos cost $558 more than equivalent gasoline models.

LTD (Four)

39	54D	4-dr. Sedan-5P	$8,605	2,804 lbs.	154,173
39/60H	54D	4-dr. Brougham-5P	$9,980	2,812 lbs.	Note 4
40	74D	4-dr. Station Wagon-5P	------	------	59,569

LTD (V-6)

39	54D	4-dr. Sedan-5P	$9,014	2,881 lbs.	154,173
39/60H	54D	4-dr. Brougham-5P	$10,389	2,889 lbs.	Note 4
40	74D	4-dr. Station Wagon-5P	$9,102	2,990 lbs.	59,569

Note 4: Brougham production is included in basic sedan total.

LTD Crown Victoria (V-8)

42	66K	2-dr. Sedan-6P	$10,954	3,546 lbs.	12,522
43	54K	4-dr. Sedan-6P	$10,954	3,587 lbs.	130,164
44	74K	4-dr. Country Squire-6P	$11,111	3,793 lbs.	30,803
43/41	54K	4-dr. S Sedan-6P	$ 9,826	------	Note 5
44/41K	74K	4-dr. S Station Wagon-6P	$10,136	------	Note 5
44/41E	74K	4-dr. Station Wagon-6P	$10,861	------	Note 5

Note 5: Production of S models and the station wagon was included in the basic sedan and Country Squire totals.

Engines:

Escort Base Four: Inline. Overhead cam. Cast-iron block and aluminum head. Displacement: 97.6 cid (1.6 liters). B & S: 3.15 x 3.13 in. Compression ratio: 9.0:1. Brake hp: 70 at 4600 rpm. Torque: 88 lbs.-ft. at 2600 rpm. Five main bearings. Hydraulic valve lifters. Carburetor: Motorcraft 740 two-barrel. VIN Code: 2.

EXP Base Four (Optional Escort): High-output 1.6-liter. Hp: 80 at 5400 rpm. Torque: 88 lbs.-ft. at 3000 rpm. VIN Code: 4.

Escort LX and GT Base Four (Optional in Escort and EXP): Fuel-injected version of 1.6-liter. Hp: 84 at 5200 rpm. Torque: 90 lbs.-ft. at 2800 rpm. VIN Code: 5.

1984 LTD sedan

1984 LTD Crown Victoria sedan

1984 LTD Country Squire station wagon

1984 Tempo L sedan (with diesel engine)

1984 Tempo GLX coupe

Escort and EXP Turbo Four: 1.6-liter with fuel injection and turbocharger. Compression ratio: 8.0:1. Hp: 120 at 200 rpm. Torque: 120 lbs.-ft. at 3400 rpm. VIN Code: 8.

Escort and Tempo Diesel Four: Inline. Overhead cam. Cast-iron block and aluminum head. Displacement: 121 cid (2.0 liters). B & S: 3.39 x 3.39 in. Compression ratio: 22.5:1. Brake hp: 52 at 4000 rpm. Torque: 82 lbs.-ft. at 2400 rpm. Five main bearings. Solid valve lifters. Fuel injection. VIN Code: H.

Tempo Base Four: Inline. Overhead valve. Cast-iron block and head. Displacement: 140 cid (2.3 liters). B & S: 3.70 x 3.30 in. Compression ratio: 9.0:1. Brake hp: 84 at 4400 rpm. Torque: 118 lbs.-ft. at 2600 rpm. Five main bearings. Hydraulic valve lifters. Carburetor: Holley 6149 single-barrel. High Swirl Combustion (HSC) design. VIN Code: R (U.S.) or J (Mexico).

LTD Base Four: Inline. Overhead cam. Cast-iron block and head. Displacement: 140 cid (2.3 liters). B & S: 3.78 x 3.13 in. Compression ratio: 9.0:1. Brake hp: 88 at 4000 rpm. Torque: 122 lbs.-ft. at 2400 rpm. Five main bearings. Hydraulic valve lifters. Carburetor: Carter YFA single-barrel. VIN Code: A.

LTD Propane Four: 140-cid four for propane fuel. Compression ratio: 10.0:1. Brake hp: 88 at 4000 rpm. Torque: 122 lbs.-ft. at 2400 rpm. VIN Code: 6.

LTD Optional V-6: 90-degree, overhead valve. Cast-iron block and aluminum head. Displacement: 232 cid (3.8 liters). B & S: 3.80 x 3.40 in. Compression ratio: 8.7:1. Brake hp: 120 at 3600 rpm. Torque: 205 lbs.-ft. at 1600 rpm. Four main bearings. Hydraulic valve lifters. Throttle-body fuel injection. VIN Code: 3.

Crown Victoria Base V-8: 90-degree, overhead valve. Cast-iron block and head. Displacement: 302 cid (5.0 liters). B & S: 4.00 x 3.00 in. Compression ratio: 8.4:1. Brake hp: 140 at 3200 rpm. Torque: 250 lbs.-ft. at 1600 rpm. Five main bearings. Hydraulic valve lifters. Electronic fuel injection (TBI). VIN Code: F.

Note: Crown Victoria wagons had a high-output 302-cid, 155-hp V-8 with 265 lbs.-ft. of torque at 2000 rpm.

Crown Victoria High-Output Police V-8: 90-degree, overhead valve. Cast-iron block and head. Displacement: 351 cid (5.8 liters). B & S: 4.00 x 3.50 in. Compression ratio: 8.3:1. Brake hp: 180 at 3600 rpm. Torque: 285 lbs.-ft. at 2400 rpm. Five main bearings. Hydraulic valve lifters. Carburetor: VV two-barrel. VIN Code: G.

Chassis:

Escort Wheelbase: 94.2 in. Overall length: 163.9 in. and 165.0 in., station wagon. Tires: P165/80-R13 steel-belted blackwalls, P165/70-R15 Michelin TRX, Escort GT and P185/65-R15 Michelin TRX, Escort Turbo GT.

EXP Wheelbase: 94.2 in. Overall length: 170.3 in. Tires: P165/80-R13 steel-belted blackwalls.

Tempo Wheelbase: 99.9 in. Overall length: 176.2 in. Tires: P175/80-R13 steel-belted blackwalls.

LTD Wheelbase: 105.9 in. Overall length: 196.5 in. Tires: P185/75-R14 steel-belted blackwalls.

Crown Victoria Wheelbase: 114.3 in. Overall length: 211.1 in. and 215.0 in., station wagon. Tires: P215/75-R14 steel-belted whitewalls.

Options:

Escort: Squire wagon package ($373). Instrument group ($87). Power door lock group ($124 to $176). Light group ($67). Air conditioner ($643). Electric rear defroster ($130). Fingertip speed control ($176). Tinted glass ($95). Tilt steering ($104). Overhead console w/digital clock ($82). Interval wipers ($50). Rear wiper/washer ($120) and LX ($46). Dual remote sport mirrors ($68). AM radio: L ($39). AM/FM radio ($82) and L ($121). AM/FM stereo radio ($109) and L ($148). With cassette player ($204) and L ($243). Electronic-tuning AM/FM stereo ($252 to $291) and w/cassette ($396 to $435). Graphic equalizer ($176). Premium sound ($117). Flip-up open-air roof ($315). Luggage rack ($100). Lower body protection ($68). Console ($111). Vinyl seat trim ($24). Color-keyed front mats ($22). Wheel trim rings ($54). Cast aluminum wheels ($279). TR aluminum wheels ($201). Styled steel wheels ($104 credit). P165/80-R13 steel-belted whitewalls ($59). Fuel-saver 1.6-liter four, no charge. Five-speed manual transmission ($76). Automatic transaxle ($439) and LX and GT ($363). Power brakes ($95). Power steering ($215). Handling suspension: L ($199) and GL ($95). Heavy duty battery ($27).

EXP: Air conditioner ($643). Fingertip speed control ($176). Tinted glass ($95). Tilt steering ($104). Lighted visor vanity mirror ($50). AM/FM stereo radio ($109). With cassette player ($204) and ($95), luxury coupe. Electronic-tuning AM/FM stereo ($252). Luxury coupe ($144) and Turbo ($49). With cassette ($396), luxury coupe ($288) and Turbo ($193). Graphic equalizer ($176). Premium sound ($117). AM radio delete ($39 credit). AM/FM stereo delete: luxury coupe ($148 credit). AM/FM stereo/cassette delete: Turbo ($243 credit). Flip-up open air roof ($315). Lower body protection ($68). Low-back knit vinyl bucket seats, no charge. Sport performance seats ($173). Front floor mats ($22). Wheels: TR aluminum wheels ($369). TR styled steel wheels ($168). Cast aluminum wheels ($238). P165/80-R13 raised white letter tires ($90). P165/70-R365 TRX tires, no charge. Power steering ($215). Heavy duty battery ($27). Heavy duty alternator ($27). Engine block heater ($18).

Tempo: TR performance package with aluminum wheels ($366 to $424). Sport appearance group: GL 2-dr. ($299). Power lock group ($202 to $254). Appearance protection group ($71). Light/convenience group ($50 to $85). Air conditioning ($743). Electric rear defroster, electric ($140). Fingertip speed control ($176). Illuminated entry ($82). Anti-theft system ($159). Power windows ($272). Power deck lid release ($41). Six-way power seat ($224). Tinted glass ($110). Tilt steering ($110). Sport instrument cluster ($71 to $87). Digital clock ($61). Interval wipers ($50). Dual sport remote mirrors ($93). Lighted visor vanity mirrors, pair ($100-$112). AM/FM radio ($59). AM/FM stereo radio ($109) and ($204) with cassette player ($204). Electronic-tuning AM/FM stereo ($252) and with cassette ($396). Premium sound system ($117). AM radio delete ($39 credit). Flip-up open air roof ($315). Console ($111). Fold-down front armrest ($55). Vinyl seat trim ($35). Carpeted front floor mats ($13). Trunk

1984 Tempo GLX sedan

1985 Tempo GL coupe (with Sports option package)

trim ($30). Luxury wheel covers ($59). Styled steel wheels ($59) and no charge, GL and GLX. P175/80-R13 whitewall tires ($72). Five-speed manual transmission ($76). Automatic transaxle ($439). Power steering ($223). Heavy duty suspension, no charge. Soft ride suspension package, no charge. Heavy duty battery ($27). Engine block heater ($18).

LTD: Squire option ($282). Brougham décor, wagon ($363). Interior luxury group ($388). Power lock group ($213 to $254). Cold weather group ($77). Light group ($38). Police package ($859 to $1,387). Taxi pkg. ($860). Fleet package ($210). Air conditioner ($743) and with auto-temp ($809). Electric rear defroster ($140). Fingertip speed control ($176). Illuminated entry ($82). Autolamp on-off delay ($73). Power windows ($272). Six-way power driver's seat ($224) and dual seats ($449). Tinted glass ($110). Leather-wrapped steering wheel ($59). Tilt steering ($110). Electronic instrument cluster ($289 to $367). Tripminder computer ($215 to $293). Interval wipers ($50). Liftgate wiper and washer for wagon ($99). AM/FM stereo radio ($109) and ($204) with cassette player. Electronic-tuning AM/FM stereo radio with cassette ($396). Premium sound system ($151). Full vinyl roof ($152). Luggage rack, wagon ($126). Vinyl seat trim ($35). Split or flight bench seat, no charge. Individual seats with console ($61). Leather seat trim ($415). Luxury wheel covers ($55). Wire wheel covers ($165) and locking ($204). Styled wheels ($178). Styled steel wheels with trim rings ($54). P185/75-R14 whitewalls ($72). P195/75-R14 blackwalls ($38) or whitewalls ($116). Puncture-sealant tires ($240). Conventional spare ($63). Propane 140-cid four ($896). 232-cid V-6 ($409). Overdrive automatic transmission ($237) Heavy-duty battery ($27). Heavy-duty alternator ($52). Extended-range gas tank ($46). Engine block heater ($18). Trailer towing package ($398).

Crown Victoria: Interior luxury group ($954 to $1,034). Convenience group ($109 to $134). Power lock group ($140 to $238). Light group ($48). Protection group ($68). Police package ($279 to $398). Air conditioning ($743) and ($809) with auto-temp control. Electric rear defroster ($140). Fingertip speed control ($176). Illuminated entry system ($82). Power windows ($198 to $272). Power driver's seat ($227) or driver and passenger ($454). Remote fuel door lock ($35). Tinted glass ($110). Autolamp on/off delay ($73). Leather-wrapped steering wheel ($59). Tilt steering wheel ($110). Auto. parking brake release ($12). Tripminder computer ($215 to $261). Digital clock ($61). Interval wipers ($50). AM/FM stereo radio, S ($106) or ($112 to $204) with cassette tape player. Electronic-tuning AM/FM stereo radio with/cassette ($166) and ($416), S. Power antenna ($66). Premium sound system ($151 to $179). Radio delete ($148 credit). Luggage rack ($110). Dual-facing rear seats: Country Squire ($167). Leather seat trim ($418). Split bench seating ($139). All-vinyl seat trim ($34) or Duraweave vinyl ($96). Carpeted front floor mats ($21). Trunk trim ($49). Wire wheel covers ($165) and locking ($204). Cast aluminum wheels ($390). P225/75-R14 whitewalls ($42 to $43). P205/75R15 whitewalls ($17). Puncture-sealant ($178). Conventional spare ($63). Traction-Lok differential ($95). Heavy duty suspension ($26). Heavy duty battery ($27). Engine block heater ($18). Trailer towing package ($200-$251).

History:

The 1984 Fords were introduced on Sept. 22, 1983, except Tempo that debuted in May 1983. Model year production was 1,496,997, including Mustangs. Calendar year sales by U.S. dealers was 1,300,644, including Mustangs. Sales hit their highest mark since 1979 during the 1984 model year, a 27-percent jump over 1983. Escort lost its title as the nation's top-selling car to Chevrolet's Cavalier. EXP sales declined again in 1984. The Escort and Tempo 2.0-liter diesel, from Mazda Motors, showed sluggish sales as well. Edsel B. Ford II was named advertising manager in late 1983. Tempo design had begun in 1979 as the Topaz project. That name ultimately was given to the Mercury version.

1985 Ford

Escort — Four: Reverse gear on the four-and five-speed manual transaxle moved to a new position this year, intended to make shifting easier. Radios had a new flat-face design. Starting in mid-year 1984, clear coat paints were made available on the Escort L and GL. Little was new on Ford's subcompact two- and four-door hatchbacks as the model

year began. Later, a restyled 1985-1/2 Escort appeared, powered by a new 1.9-liter four-cylinder engine. The standard engine for the first series was the CVH 97.6 cid (1.6-liter) carbureted four, with four-speed gearbox. A high-output version was available, as well as one with electronic fuel injection and another with a turbocharger. The 2.0-liter diesel was offered again. Five-speed manual and three-speed automatic transmissions were available. Escort L had a brushed aluminum B-pillar appliqué. Wagons and diesels had standard power brakes. Escort GL added AM radio, low-back seats, and additional bright moldings. Escort LX included power brakes, blackout body treatment, digital clock, fog lamps, TR performance suspension and styled steel wheels. GT models carried wide black body moldings with argent striping, dual black remote racing mirrors, power brakes, TR performance suspension, five-speed transaxle, remote liftgate release, fog lamps, and sport-tuned exhaust. Turbo GT had aluminum TR wheels and standard power steering.

EXP — Four: The two-seater EXP got a revised location for reverse gear (below fifth gear). Radios and cassette players showed a new flat-face design. The base engine was the fuel-injected 97.6-cid (1.6-liter) four. The Turbo Coupe was available again, wearing aluminum wheels with low-profile performance tires and Koni shock absorbers. This was EXP's final season in its original form. Standard equipment included an AM radio, tinted rear-window glass, halogen headlamps, power brakes, tachometer, handling suspension, remote locking fuel door and black moldings. Inside were low-back cloth/vinyl reclining bucket seats. EXP's Luxury Coupe added an AM/FM stereo radio, interval wipers, luxury cloth seats with four-way (manual) driver's side adjuster, dual remote mirrors, rear defroster, and tinted glass. Turbo Coupe included a front air dam, black rocker panel moldings, AM/FM stereo with cassette, power steering, TR suspension and aluminum wheels, wheel spats, and a rear spoiler.

Tempo — Four: Throttle-body fuel injection was added to Tempo's 2300 HSC (High Swirl Combustion) engine after a year of carburetion. A new high-output version had a new cylinder head and intake manifold, and drove a special 3.73:1 final drive ratio. Five-speed manual overdrive transaxles were standard in all Tempo series, with revised reverse gear position (now below fifth gear). GLX Tempos now had a sport instrument cluster, power lock group, light convenience group, tinted glass, AM/FM stereo radio, power steering and tilt steering wheel. There were new see-through reservoirs for brake, power steering and washer fluid levels. The 1985 instrument panel included side window demisters, plus contemporary flat-face radio design and a storage shelf. Tempo again came in three series: L, GL and GLX. Base Tempos came with an AM radio, cloth/vinyl reclining low-back bucket seats, body accent stripes, dual deck lid stripes on two-doors, power brakes, bright bumpers with black end caps, and a black left-hand mirror. GL added a blackout back panel treatment, digital clock, black body moldings, styled wheels, interval wipers, and dual striping on four-door deck lids. A high-performance Sport GL performance option included the high-output (HSO) engine, seven-spoke aluminum wheels with locking lug nuts, improved suspension components, dual remote mirrors and sport performance cloth seats.

LTD — Four/V-6/V-8: Modest restyling gave LTD a new horizontal grille for its third season, plus new sedan tail lamps. Only minor trim changes were evident. Base models wore new deluxe wheel covers. The base 140-cid (2.3-liter) engine added low-friction piston rings, with a boost in compression. Wagons had a standard 232-cid (3.8-liter) V-6.. New options included dual electric remote mirrors and black vinyl rocker panel moldings. Joining the base and Brougham sedan and LTD wagon later in the model year was a new high-performance LX touring sedan. It carried a high-output, fuel-injected 302-cid (5.0-liter) V-8 with a four-speed overdrive automatic transmission. The performance sedan also had a special handling suspension with rear stabilizer bar, 15:1 steering gear, and Goodyear Eagle GT performance tires. LX had a body-colored grille, charcoal and red-orange accents, twin chromed exhaust extensions and styled road wheels. Inside was a center console with floor shifter, tachometer, and unique front bucket seats with inflatable lumbar support. Both base and Brougham sedans had an AM radio, Select Shift automatic transmission, locking glove box, power brakes and steering and a reclining split-bench seating with cloth upholstery,. Brougham added a digital clock, light group, seatback map pockets, lighted visor vanity passenger-side mirror and luxury cloth upholstery.

LTD Crown Victoria — V-8: Except for an aluminum front bumper on station wagons and some new body and vinyl roof colors, full-size Fords showed no significant body change. The Crown Victoria got new gas-filled shock absorbers, pressurized with nitrogen. An ignition diagnostics monitor was added to the EEC-IV electronic engine controls. A single key was now used for door and ignition locks. Lower body panels now had urethane coating for extra corrosion protection. The model lineup for the biggest rear-wheel drives remained: two- and four-door sedan (standard or S, with plain-bodied and Country Squire wagons. The 302-cid (5.0-liter) V-8 engine had fuel injection and came with four-speed automatic overdrive transmission. A new optional automatic load leveling suspension was available later in the model year. With a heavy-duty trailer towing package, Crown Victoria and Country Squire could again tow trailers up to 5,000 lbs. Standard equipment included chrome bumpers, dual-note horn, cloth/vinyl reclining flight bench seating, power steering and brakes, and deluxe wheel covers. The budget-priced S models lacked the padded half (rear) vinyl roof, dual accent tape striping, quartz clock, brushed lower deck lid appliqué and various moldings but had an AM radio. Other models got an AM/FM stereo.

I.D. Data:

Ford's 17-symbol Vehicle Identification Number (VIN) again was stamped on a metal tab that was fastened to the instrument panel and was visible through the windshield. Coding was similar to 1984. The model year code changed to F=1985. The engine code W=HSC 140-cid FI four was added. The 6=propane four was dropped. A Vehicle Certification Label on the left front door lock face panel or door pillar showed the manufacturer, month and year of manufacture, GVW, GAWR, certification statement, VIN, and codes for body type, color, trim, axle, transmission, and special order information.

Escort (Four)

Model No.	Body Style No.	Body Type & Seating	Factory Price	Shipping Weight	Production Total
04/41P	61D	2-dr. Hatchback-4P	$5,620	1,981 lbs.	Note 1
13/41P	58D	4-dr. Hatchback-4P	$5,827	2,034 lbs.	Note 1
04	61D	2-dr. L Hatchback-4P	$5,876	1,981 lbs.	Note 1
13	58D	4-dr. L Hatchback-4P	$6,091	2,034 lbs.	Note 1
09	74D	4-dr. L Station Wagon-4P	$6,305	2,066 lbs.	Note 1
05	61D	2-dr. GL Hatchback-4P	$6,374	2,033 lbs.	Note 1
14	58D	4-dr. GL Hatchback-4P	$6,588	2,086 lbs.	Note 1
10	74D	4-dr. GL Station Wagon-4P	$6,765	2,115 lbs.	Note 1
15	58D	4-dr. LX Hatchback-4P	$7,840	2,137 lbs.	Note 1
11	74D	4-dr. LX Station Wagon-4P	$7,931	2,073 lbs.	Note 1

Escort GT (Four)

07	61D	2-dr. Hatchback-4P	$7,585	2,103 lbs.	Note 1
07/935	61D	2-dr. Turbo Hatchback-4P	$8,680	2,239 lbs.	Note 1

1985-1/2 Escort — Second Series (Four)

31	----	2-dr. Hatchback-4P	$5,856	2,089 lbs.	Note 1
31	----	2-dr. L Hatchback-4P	$6,127	2,096 lbs.	Note 1
36	----	4-dr. L Hatchback-4P	$6,341	2,154 lbs.	Note 1
34	----	4-dr. L Station Wagon-4P	$6,622	2,173 lbs.	Note 1
32	----	2-dr. GL Hatchback-4P	$6,642	2,160 lbs.	Note 1
37	----	4-dr. GL Hatchback-4P	$6,855	2,214 lbs.	Note 1
35	----	4-dr. GL Station Wagon-4P	$7,137	2,228 lbs.	Note 1

Note 1: Ford said the second Escort series production was 100,554 two-door hatchbacks, 48,676 four-door hatchbacks and 36,998 station wagons. Other sources report total Escort production was 112,960 two-doors, 111,385 four-doors, and 82,738 wagons. Trim breakdown was not available. Bodies also called three-door and five-door.

Diesel Note: Diesel-powered Escorts came in L and GL trim and were $558 higher than gasoline models.

1985 EXP Luxury Coupe

EXP (Four)

01/A80	67D	3-dr. Hatchback-2P	$6,697	2,117 lbs.	26,462
01/A81	67D	3-dr. Luxury Coupe-2P	$7,585	2,117 lbs.	Note 2
01/A82	67D	3-dr. Turbo Coupe-2P	$9,997	------	Note 2

Note 2: Production of luxury and turbo coupe models was included in the basic EXP totals.

Tempo (Four)

18	66D	2-dr. L Sedan-5P	$7,052	2,249 lbs.	Note 3
21	54D	4-dr. L Sedan-5P	$7,052	2,308 lbs.	Note 3
19	66D	2-dr. GL Sedan-5P	$7,160	2,276 lbs.	Note 3
22	54D	4-dr. GL Sedan-5P	$7,160	2,339 lbs.	Note 3
20	66D	2-dr. GLX Sedan-5P	$8,253	2,302 lbs.	Note 3
23	54D	4-dr. GLX Sedan-5P	$8,302	2,362 lbs.	Note 3

Note 3: Tempo production was 72,311 two-doors and 266,776 four-doors. A turbocharged Tempo GTX, priced at $9,870, was announced but apparently not produced.

Diesel Note: Diesel-powered Tempos cost $479 more than equivalent gasoline models.

LTD (Four)

39	54D	4-dr. Sedan-5P	$8,874	2,804 lbs.	162,884
39/60H	54D	4-dr. Brougham-5P	$9,262	2,812 lbs.	Note 4
40	74D	4-dr. Station Wagon-5P	------	------	42,642

LTD (V-6)

39	54D	4-dr. Sedan-5P	$9,292	2,881 lbs.	162,884
39/60H	54D	4-dr. Brougham-5P	$9,680	2,889 lbs.	Note 4
40	74D	4-dr. Station Wagon-5P	$9,384	2,990 lbs.	42,642

LTD LX Brougham (V-8)

39/938	54D	4-dr. Sedan-5P	$11,421	------	Note 4

Note 4: Brougham production was included in the basic sedan total.

LTD Crown Victoria (V-8)

42	66K	2-dr. Sedan-6P	$11,627	3,546 lbs.	13,673
43	54K	4-dr. Sedan-6P	$11,627	3,587 lbs.	154,612
44	74K	4-dr. Country Squire-6P	$11,809	3,793 lbs.	30,825
43/41K	54K	4-dr. S Sedan-6P	$10,609	-----	Note 5
44/41K	74K	4-dr. S Station Wagon-6P	$10,956	-----	Note 5
44/41E	74K	4-dr. Station Wagon-6P	$11,559	-----	Note 5

Note 5: Production of S models and basic station wagon was included in sedan and Country Squire totals above.

Police Model: Crown Victoria S police models were $10,929 with the 302-cid V-8 and $11,049 with 351 cid V-8.

Engines:

Escort Base Four: Inline. Overhead cam. Cast-iron block and aluminum head. Displacement: 97.6 cid (1.6 liters). B & S: 3.15 x 3.13 in. Compression ratio: 9.0:1. Brake hp: 70 at 4600 rpm. Torque: 88 lbs.-ft. at 2600 rpm. Five main bearings. Hydraulic valve lifters. Carburetor: Holley 740 two-barrel. VIN Code: 2.

Note: Second Series Escorts carried a 1.9-liter engine. See 1986 listing for specifications.

EXP Base Four (Optional Escort): High-output 1.6-liter. Hp: 80 at 5400 rpm. Torque: 88 lbs.-ft. at 3000 rpm. VIN Code: 4.

Escort LX and GT Base Four (Optional Escort): Fuel-injected 1.6-liter. Hp: 84 at 5200 rpm. Torque: 90 lbs.-ft. at 2800 rpm. VIN Code: 5.

Escort and EXP Turbo Four: Same as 1.6-liter four above, with fuel injection and turbocharger Compression ratio: 8.0:1. Horsepower: 120 at 5200 rpm. Torque: 120 lbs.-ft. at 3400 rpm. VIN Code: B.

Escort and Tempo Diesel Four: Inline. Overhead cam. Cast-iron block and aluminum head. Displacement: 121 cid (2.0 liters). B & S: 3.39 x 3.39 in. Compression ratio: 22.5:1. Brake hp: 52 at 4000 rpm. Torque: 82 lbs.-ft. at 2400 rpm. Five main bearings. Solid valve lifters. Fuel injection. VIN Code: H.

1985 Ford Tempo GLX sedan

1985 Escort (1st series) **GL five-door hatchback** (with diesel engine)

1985 LTD LX Brougham sedan

Tempo Base Four: Inline. Overhead valve. Cast-iron block and head. Displacement: 140 cid (2.3 liters). B & S: 3.70 x 3.30 in. Compression ratio: 9.0:1. Brake hp: 86 at 4000 rpm. Torque: 124 lbs.-ft. at 2800 rpm. Five main bearings. Hydraulic valve lifters. Throttle-body fuel injection. High Swirl Combustion (HSC) design. VIN Code: X.

Tempo Optional Four: High-output version of HSC. Hp: 100 at 4600 rpm. Torque: 125 lbs.-ft. at 3200 rpm. VIN Code: S.

LTD Base Four: Inline. Overhead cam. Cast-iron block and head. Displacement: 140 cid (2.3 liters). B & S: 3.78 x 3.13 in. Compression ratio: 9.5:1. Brake hp: 88 at 4000 rpm. Torque: 122 lbs.-ft. at 2400 rpm. Five main bearings. Hydraulic valve lifters. Carburetor: Carter YFA single-barrel. VIN Code: A.

LTD Propane Four: 140-cid engine with propane fuel. Compression ratio: 10.0:1. Brake hp: 88 at 4000 rpm. Torque: 122 lbs.-ft. at 2400 rpm. VIN Code: 6.

LTD Wagon Base V-6 (Optional LTD): 90-degree: overhead valve. Cast-iron block and aluminum head. Displacement: 232 cid (3.8 liters). B & S: 3.80 x 3.40 in. Compression ratio: 8.7:1. Brake hp: 120 at 3600 rpm. Torque: 205 lbs.-ft. at 1600 rpm. Four main bearings. Hydraulic valve lifters. Throttle-body fuel injection. VIN Code: 3.

Crown Victoria Base V-8: 90-degree, overhead valve. Cast-iron block and head. Displacement: 302 cid (5.0 liters). B & S: 4.00 x 3.00 in. Compression ratio: 8.4:1. Brake hp: 140 at 3200 rpm. Torque: 250 lbs.-ft. at 1600 rpm. Five main bearings. Hydraulic valve lifters. Electronic fuel injection (TBI). VIN Code: F.

LTD LX Base V-8: 302 cid V-8 with compression ratio: 8.3:1. Hp: 165 at 3800 rpm. Torque: 245 lbs.-ft. at 2000 rpm.

Crown Victoria Optional High-Output V-8: 302-cid V-8 with 155 hp at 3600 rpm. Torque: 265 lbs.-ft. at 2000 rpm.

Crown Victoria High-Output Police V-8: 90-degree, overhead valve. Cast-iron block and head. Displacement: 351 cid (5.8 liters). B & S: 4.00 x 3.50 in. Compression ratio: 8.3:1. Brake hp: 180 at 3600 rpm. Torque: 285 lbs.-ft. at 2400 rpm. Five main bearings. Hydraulic valve lifters. Carburetor: 7200VV two-barrel. VIN Code: G.

Escort: Wheelbase: 94.2 in. Overall length: 163.9 in. and 165.0 in., station wagon. Tires: P165/80-R13 steel-belted blackwalls; P175/80-R13, Escort L; P165/70R365 Michelin TRX Escort LX and GT.

EXP: Wheelbase: 94.2 in. Overall length: 170.3 in. EXP P165/80-R13 steel-belted blackwalls and P185/65-R365 Michelin TRX, EXP Turbo.

Tempo: Wheelbase: 99.9 in. Overall length: 176.2 in. Tires: P175/80-R13 steel-belted blackwalls.

LTD: Wheelbase: 105.6 in. Overall length: 196.5 in. Tires: P195/75-R14 SBR BSW and P205/70-HR14 Goodyear Eagle blackwalls for LX and police versions.

Crown Victoria: Wheelbase: 114.3 in. Overall length: 211.0 in. and 215.0 in., station wagon. Tires: P215/75-R14 steel-belted whitewalls.

Escort: Squire wagon package ($373). Instrument group ($87). Convenience group ($206 to $341). Light group ($67). Air conditioner ($643). Electric rear defroster ($139). High-capacity heater ($76). Fingertip speed control ($176). Power door locks ($124 to $176). Tinted glass ($95). Tilt steering ($104). Overhead console w/digital clock ($82). Interval wipers ($50). Rear wiper/washer ($120) and LX ($46). Dual remote sport mirrors ($68). AM radio: base/L ($39). AM/FM radio ($82) and ($121) base/L. AM/FM stereo radio ($109) and ($148) base/L. With cassette player ($148) and ($295), base/L. Electronic-tuning AM/FM stereo with cassette ($409 to $448). Premium sound ($138). Flip-up open-air roof ($315). Luggage rack, wagon ($100). Console ($111). Vinyl seat trim ($24). Cloth/vinyl low-back bucket seats: L ($33). Color-keyed front mats ($22). Wheel trim rings ($54). Cast aluminum wheels ($279). TR aluminum wheels on LX and GT ($201). Styled steel wheels fleet only ($104 credit). P165/80-R13 steel-belted whitewall tires ($59). High-Output 1.6-liter four ($73) Five-speed manual transmission ($76). Automatic transaxle ($439). Power brakes: Escort ($95). Power steering: Escort ($215) Handling suspension, L ($199) and GL ($95). Heavy duty battery ($27). Heavy duty alternator ($27). Engine block heater ($18).

EXP: Air conditioner ($643). Fingertip speed control ($176). Tinted glass ($95). Tilt steering ($104). Lighted visor vanity mirror ($50). AM/FM stereo radio: base ($109) and with cassette player ($256). On luxury coupe ($148). Electronic-tuning AM/FM stereo w/cassette ($409) and ($300) on luxury coupe. On Turbo ($152). Premium sound ($138). AM radio delete ($39 credit). AM/FM stereo delete, luxury coupe ($148 credit). AM/FM stereo/cassette delete, Turbo ($295 credit). Flip-up open-air roof ($315). Four-way driver's seat, base ($55). Low-back vinyl bucket seats, base, no charge. Cloth sport performance seats, luxury coupe ($173). TR aluminum wheels, luxury coupe ($370). TR styled steel wheels, luxury coupe ($168). Cast aluminum wheels, luxury coupe ($238). P165/80-R13 raised white letter tires ($90). P165/70-R365 Michelin TRX, no charge. Automatic transaxle ($363). Power steering ($215). Heavy duty battery ($27). Heavy duty alternator: ($27). Engine block heater ($18).

Tempo: Sport performance package, GL ($900 to $911). Power lock group ($202 to $254). Luxury option group, GL and LX ($755 to $855). Select option group, GL ($401). Air conditioning ($743). Electric rear defroster ($140). Fingertip speed control, GL and GLX ($176). Power windows ($272). Power deck lid release ($40). Remote fuel door release ($26). Six-way power driver's seat ($224). Tinted glass ($110). Tilt steering, GL ($110). Sport instrument cluster ($87). Dual sport remote mirrors ($93). AM/FM stereo radio, L and GL ($109) and $148 to $256 with cassette player. Electronic-tuning AM/FM stereo with cassette ($152 to $409). Graphic equalizer ($107 to $218). AM radio delete ($39 credit). Vinyl seat trim ($35). Leather seat trim, GLX ($300). Styled wheels, L ($73). P175/80-R13 white sidewalls ($72). Power steering ($223). Automatic transaxle ($266 to $363). Engine block heater ($18).

LTD: Squire option ($282). Interior luxury group, wagon ($388). Power lock group ($213 to $254). Light group ($38). Police package ($901 to $1,429). Taxi package ($860). Air conditioning ($743) and auto-temp ($809). Fingertip speed control ($176). Illuminated entry ($82). Autolamp on-off delay ($73). Power windows ($272). Six-way power driver's seat ($224) and dual ($449). Tinted glass ($110). Leather-wrapped steering wheel ($59). Tilt steering ($110). Tripminder computer ($215 to $293). Digital clock ($78). Diagnostic warning lights ($89). Auto. parking brake release LPO ($12). Interval wipers ($50). Liftgate wiper/washer, wagon ($99). Dual electric remote mirrors ($96). Lighted visor vanity mirrors ($57 to $106). AM/FM stereo radio ($109) and with cassette player ($256). Electronic-tuning AM/FM stereo radio with cassette ($409). Premium sound system ($138). Formal roof, cloth or vinyl ($848). Full vinyl roof ($152). Two-way lift gate, wagon ($105). Luggage rack, wagon ($126). Lower body protection ($41). Vinyl seat trim ($35). Flight bench seat, no charge. Luxury wheel covers ($55). Wire wheel covers, locking ($204). Cast aluminum wheels, LX ($224). Styled wheels ($178). Styled steel wheels w/trim rings, fleet ($54). P195/75R14 whitewalls ($72). P205/70-R14 whitewalls ($134). Puncture-sealant P195/75-14 whitewalls ($202). Conventional spare LPO ($63). 232-cid V-6 ($418). First gear lockout delete ($7). Traction-Lok differential ($95). Extended-range gas tank ($46). Engine block heater ($18).

Note: Many LTD options listed above were not available for the LX Brougham.

LTD Crown Victoria: Interior luxury group ($949 to $1,022). Convenience group ($109 to $134). Power lock group ($140 to $238). Light group ($48). Air conditioning ($743) and with auto temp control ($809). Electric rear defroster ($140). Fingertip speed control ($176). Illuminated entry system ($82). Power windows ($198 to $272). Power driver seat ($227) or driver and passenger ($454). Remote fuel door lock ($35). Tinted glass ($110). Autolamp on/off delay ($73). Leather-wrapped steering wheel ($59). Tilt steering wheel ($110). Auto. parking brake release ($12). Tripminder computer ($215 to $261). Quartz clock: S ($35). Digital clock ($61 to $96). Interval wipers ($50). Cornering lamps ($68). Remote right mirror ($46). Lighted visor vanity mirrors ($106). AM/FM stereo radio: S ($109) and with cassette tape Player ($148 to $256). Electronic-

1985 LTD Crown Victoria two-door sedan

tuning AM/FM stereo radio with cassette ($300). Power antenna ($66). Premium sound system ($168). Fully padded Brougham vinyl roof ($793). Luggage rack: wagon ($110). License frames ($9). Dual-facing rear seats: wagon ($167). Leather split bench seat ($418). Cloth/vinyl split bench seating ($139). All-vinyl seat trim ($34) and Duraweave vinyl, wagon ($96). Carpeted front/rear floor mats ($33). Trunk trim ($37). Wire wheel covers, locking ($204). Cast-aluminum wheels ($390). P205/75-R15 whitewalls ($17). Puncture-sealant tires ($178). P215/70-R15 whitewalls ($79). Conventional spare ($63). First gear lockout delete, S ($7). Traction-Lok differential ($95). Heavy-duty suspension ($26). Handling suspension ($49). Automatic load leveling ($200). Engine block heater ($18). Trailer towing package ($251 to $302).

History:

The 1985 Fords were introduced on Oct. 4, 1984. Model year production was 1,265,221, including Mustangs but with incomplete Escort totals from Ford. That total included 24,708 turbo fours, 10,246 diesels, 828,320 four-cylinder engines, 270,461 sixes and 290,322 V-8s. Calendar year sales by U.S. dealers was 1,386,195, including Mustangs. Ford sales rose 14 percent for 1985, partly resulting from incentive programs late in the season. Ford's market share rose to a healthy 17.2 percent, up from 16 percent in the 1984 model year. All seven series showed an increase, led by Escort with a 21 percent rise. Tempo did well, too. Ford raised prices only 1.3 percent on average in 1985, though Crown Victoria had a six percent price increase. Mustangs were actually cheaper.

1986 Ford

Escort — Four: The 1986 Escort actually arrived as a 1985-1/2 model, carrying a bigger (1.9-liter) four-cylinder engine. The model lineup included the LX series replacing the GL, and the temporarily-abandoned GT reintroduced. Pony was the name for the base hatchback. The 2.0-liter diesel engine remained only as an option. Inside was a new black four-spoke steering wheel. Options included tilt steering, speed control, and an instrumentation group. Escort's base engine was carbureted, hooked to a four-speed manual transaxle. Automatic shift was optional. Escort had four-wheel independent suspension. Pony had standard power brakes, day/night mirror, dome light, cloth/vinyl low-back reclining bucket seats, and P175/80-R13 tires. Escort L added an AM radio and load floor carpet. LX included remote fuel door lock, remote lift-gate release, wide vinyl body moldings and styled steel wheels. Escort GT had a high-output 1.9-liter engine with port fuel injection and five-speed manual transaxle plus performance suspension with new front and rear stabilizer bars and eight-spoke aluminum wheels. Also included were fog lamps, a console with graphic display, a leather-wrapped steering wheel, body-color wheel spats with integral rocker panel moldings, a rear spoiler and body-color body moldings. One easy-to-spot styling feature was GT's offset grille. A GT decal sat on the solid passenger side of the grille.

EXP — Four: After a brief absence from the lineup, the two-seater EXP returned in restyled form with a sleek new front-end design, including air dam and aero headlamps. Also new was a bubble-back styled rear hatch with integral spoiler. Large "EXP" recessed lettering was easy to spot on the wide C pillar. Wraparound full-width tail lamps (split by the license plate's recessed housing) were divided into upper/lower segments, and tapered downward to a point on each quarter panel. Luxury Coupe

1986 Escort LX wagon

1986 Tempo LX coupe

1986 Taurus LX sedan

and Sport Coupe versions were offered, with 1.9-liter fast-burn four, five-speed manual transaxle, and four-wheel independent suspension. Luxury Coupe had the carbureted engine, along with a tachometer and trip odometer, reclining low-back bucket seats trimmed in cloth/vinyl (or all vinyl), AM/FM stereo radio, overhead console, and left remote mirror. A fuel-injected high-output version of the four went into the Sport Coupe, which also had special handling components, performance bucket seats, center console with graphic systems monitor, fog lamps and low-profile 15 in. handling tires on cast aluminum wheels.

Tempo — Four: After only two seasons in the lineup, Tempo got new front and rear styling. Tempo also had a color-keyed lower front valence panel. Wide, dark gray body moldings inside bright inserts. Completing the look were aero-style mirrors. Inside was a new-design four-spoke deep-dish steering wheel. A push-pull headlamp switch replaced the toggle unit. New door sill scuff plates were added. A new LX series replaced the GLX. Both GL and LX tires were upgraded to 14-inch size. Sport GL went to 15 inchers, and had red interior accent colors. In addition to the basic GL and LX models, Select GL and Sport GL packages were offered. GL included full cloth reclining front bucket seats, power front disc/rear drum brakes, interval wipers and a digital clock. Tempo LX included styled wheels, tilt steering, power door locks, a full array of courtesy lights, bright argent lower back panel appliqué and AM/FM stereo radio. A Select GL package added power steering, tinted glass, dual sail-mounted remote electric mirrors, and AM/FM stereo radio. Sport GL had a special handling suspension, as well as a high specific output (HSO) version of the standard 2300 HSC (high swirl combustion) four. All had a standard five-speed manual transaxle. Automatic was optional on GL and Select GL. So was the 2.0-liter diesel.

Taurus — Four/V-6: The aerodynamic new mid-size, front-drive Taurus lacked a grille up front. At the rear were wraparound tail lamps. Taurus wagons had narrow vertical tail lamps, and center high-mount stop lamps above the lift gate. Taurus had flush-mounted glass all around. Aero styling gave an impressive drag coefficient, as low as 0.33 for the sedan. Series offered were the L, GL, LX, and, later, a sporty MT5. The base engine was a new 153-cid (2.5-liter) fuel-injected HSC four. Sedans had fully independent MacPherson strut suspension, front and rear. Wagons had independent short and long arm rear suspension. Polycarbonate bumpers were corrosion-proof. The driver-oriented instrument panel featured three analog backlit instrument clusters. Windshield wipers had 20-in. blades and an articulated driver's side arm for a full wipe all the way to the pillar. Standard equipment included power brakes and steering, gas-filled shocks and struts, all-season steel-belted radials, AM radio, and reclining cloth flight bench seats. Wagons had a 60/40 split fold-down rear seat and cargo tie-downs. MT5 came with five-speed manual transaxle and floor shift lever, and included interval wipers, tinted glass, tachometer and bucket seats. The LX included air conditioning, power locks, cloth split bench seats, tilt steering, power windows, and lighted visor vanity mirrors. Taurus looked much like the related Mercury Sable but the sedans shared no sheet metal. They shared drive trains and running gear, plus most equipment.

LTD — Four/V-6: Ford's rear-drive mid-size was scheduled for abandonment at mid-year, now that the front-drive Taurus had arrived.

1986 LTD Crown Victoria Country Squire station wagon

1986 Escort GT hatchback

For its final partial season, the 232-cid (3.8-liter) V-6 became standard (though the four was listed as a credit option). The high-performance LX sedan didn't make the lineup this year, and not much was new apart from the required center high-mount stop lamp. Quite a few low-rate options were dropped. Four-speed automatic overdrive became optional. LTD was virtually identical to Mercury Marquis. Models included base and Brougham sedans, and the base wagon.

LTD Crown Victoria — V-8: Big rear-drives had more than a spark of life remaining in Ford's plans. Crown Victoria added the top-level LX sedan and Country Squire LX wagon. Each incorporated a previously optional interior luxury group. LX had reclining split bench seats upholstered in velour cloth or vinyl. Leather seating was optional. Equipment included power windows and a variety of luxury trim. Sequential multi-port fuel injection was now used on the 302-cid (5.0-liter) V-8 engine coupled with four-speed overdrive automatic. Changes to the 302 engine included fast-burning combustion chambers, higher compression, roller tappets and low-tension piston rings. Wagons now had a mini spare tire rather than the conventional one. Standard equipment included an AM/FM stereo radio with four speakers, quartz clock, front/rear courtesy lights, cloth flight bench seat with dual recliners, and remote driver's mirror. Seven exterior colors were new, along with five vinyl roof colors. Country Squire's simulated wood grain panels switched from cherry to dark cherry. Quad rectangular headlamps stood above amber park/signal lenses. The front end showed a straight, symmetrical design.

I.D. Data:

Ford's 17-symbol Vehicle Identification Number (VIN) was stamped on a metal tab fastened to the instrument panel and was visible through the windshield. The first three symbols 1FA=manufacturer, make and vehicle type. The fourth symbol B=the restraint system. Letter P followed by two digits indicated the body type such as P31=Escort L two-door hatchback. Symbol eight indicated the engine type: 9=113-cid four; J=113-cid H.O four; H=121-cid diesel; X=140-cid HSC four; S=H. O. 140-cid FI four; W=140-cid EFI turbo four; D=153-cid FI four; U=163-cid V-6; 3=232-cid V-6; F=302-cid V-8 and G=351-cid V-8. Next was a check digit. Symbol 10 indicated the model year: G=1986. Symbol 11 was the assembly plant: A=Atlanta, Georgia; B=Oakville, Ontario, Canada; G=Chicago, Illinois; H=Lorain, Ohio; K=Kansas City, Missouri; T=Edison, New Jersey; W=Wayne, Michigan and X=St. Thomas, Ontario, Canada. The final six digits made up the sequential number, starting with 100001. A Vehicle Certification Label on the left front door lock face panel or door pillar showed the manufacturer, month and year of manufacture, GVW, GAWR, certification statement, VIN, and body type, color, trim, axle, transmission, and special order information.

Escort (Four)

Model No.	Body Style No.	Body Type & Seating	Factory Price	Shipping Weight	Production Total
31/41P	------	2-dr. Pony Hatchback-4P	$6,052	2,089 lbs.	Note 1
31	------	2-dr. L Hatchback-4P	$6,327	2,096 lbs.	Note 1
36	------	4-dr. L Hatchback-4P	$6,541	2,154 lbs.	Note 1
34	------	4-dr. L Station Wagon-4P	$6,822	2,173 lbs.	Note 1
32	------	2-dr. LX Hatchback-4P	$7,284	2,160 lbs.	Note 1
37	------	4-dr. LX Hatchback-4P	$7,448	2,214 lbs.	Note 1
35	------	4-dr. LX Station Wagon-4P	$7,729	2,228 lbs.	Note 1
33	------	2-dr. GT Hatchback-4P	$8,112	2,282 lbs.	Note 1

Note 1: A total of 228,013 two-door hatchbacks, 117,300 four-door hatchback sedans, and 84,740 station wagons were produced in 1986. Trim level breakdown is not available. Bodies often called three-door and five-door.

EXP (Four)

01	------	2-dr. Sport Coupe-2P	$7,186	-----	Note 2
01/931	------	2-dr. Luxury Coupe-2P	$8,235	-----	Note 2

Note 2: Total EXP production was 30,978.

Tempo (Four)

19	66D	2-dr. GL Sedan-5P	$7,358	2,363 lbs.	Note 3
22	54D	4-dr. GL Sedan-5P	$7,508	2,422 lbs.	Note 3
20	66D	2-dr. GLX Sedan-5P	$8,578	2,465 lbs.	Note 3
23	54D	4-dr. GLX Sedan-5P	$8,777	2,526 lbs.	Note 3

Note 3: Total Tempo production came to 69,101 two-doors and 208,570 four-doors.

Taurus (Four)

29	54D	4-dr. L Sedan -6P	$9,645	2,749 lbs.	Note 4
30	74D	4-dr. L Station Wagon-6P	-----	-----	Note 4
29/934	54D	4-dr. MT5 Sedan-6P	$10,276	2,154 lbs.	Note 4
30/934	74D	4-dr. MT5 Wagon-6P	$10,741	2,173 lbs.	Note 4
29/60D	54D	4-dr. GL Sedan-6P	------	2,160 lbs.	Note 4
30/60D	74D	4-dr. GL Station Wagon-6P	------	2,214 lbs.	Note 4
29/60H	54D	4-dr. LX Sedan-6P	------	2,228 lbs.	Note 4
30/60H	74D	4-dr. LX Station Wagon-6P	------	2,282 lbs.	Note 4

Taurus (V-6)

29	54D	4-dr. L Sedan -6P	$10,256	2,749 lbs.	Note 4
30	74D	4-dr. L Station Wagon-6P	$10,763	3,097 lbs.	Note 4
29/934	54D	4-dr. MT5 Sedan-6P	-------	-------	Note 4
30/934	74D	4-dr. MT5 Wagon-6P	-------	-------	Note 4
29/60D	54D	4-dr. GL Sedan-6P	$11,322	2,909 lbs.	Note 4
30/60D	74D	4-dr. GL Station Wagon-6P	$11,790	3,108 lbs.	Note 4
29/60H	54D	4-dr. LX Sedan-6P	$13,351	3,001 lbs.	Note 4
30/60H	74D	4-dr. LX Station Wagon-6P	$13,860	3,198 lbs.	Note 4

Note 4: Taurus production came to 178,737 sedans and 57,625 station wagons for 1986.

LTD (Four)

39	54D	4-dr. Sedan-5P	$ 9,538	2,801 lbs.	58,270
39	54D	4-dr. Brougham-5P	$ 9,926	2,806 lbs.	Note 5
40	74D	4-dr. Station Wagon-5P	------	------	14,213

LTD (V-6)

39	54D	4-dr. Sedan-5P	$10,032	2,878 lbs.	58,270
39	54D	4-dr. Brougham-5P	$10,420	2,883 lbs.	Note 5
40	74D	4-dr. Station Wagon-5P	$10,132	2,977 lbs.	14,213

Note 5: Brougham production was included in the basic sedan total.

LTD Crown Victoria (V-8)

42	66K	2-dr. Sedan-6P	$13,022	3,571 lbs.	6,559
43	54K	4-dr. Sedan-6P	$12,562	3,611 lbs.	97,314
44	74K	4-dr. Country Squire-6P	$12,655	3,834 lbs.	20,164
44/41E	74K	4-dr. Station Wagon-6P	$12,405	3,795 lbs.	Note 6
43/41K	54K	4-dr. S Sedan-6P	$12,188	3,591 lbs.	Note 5
44/41K	74K	4-dr. S Station Wagon-6P	$12,468	3,769 lbs.	Note 6

LTD Crown Victoria LX (V-8)

42/60H	66K	2-dr. Sedan-6P	$13,752	3,608 lbs.	Note 6
43/60H	54K	4-dr. Sedan-6P	$13,784	3,660 lbs.	Note 6
44/41E	74K	4-dr. Station Wagon-6P	$13,567	3,834 lbs.	Note 6
44/60H	74K	4-dr. Country Squire-6P	$13,817	3,873 lbs.	Note 6

Note 6: S and LX models and the station wagon are included in the basic sedan and Country Squire totals.

Note: A Police model (P43/41K/55A) S sedan was $11,813 with the 302-cid V-8 or $11,933 with the 351-cid V-8.

Engines:

Escort Base Four: Inline. Overhead cam. Cast-iron block and aluminum head. Displacement: 113 cid (1.9 liters). B & S: 3.23 x 3.46 in. Compression ratio: 9.0:1. Brake hp: 86 at 4800 rpm. Torque: 100 lbs.-ft. at 3000 rpm. Five main bearings. Hydraulic valve lifters. Carburetor: Holley 740 two-barrel. VIN Code: 9.

Escort GT Base Four (Optional Escort): High-output, multi-port fuel-injected 1.9-liter. Hp: 108 at 5200 rpm. Torque: 114 lbs.-ft. at 4000 rpm. VIN Code: J.

Escort and Tempo Diesel Four: Inline. Overhead cam. Cast-iron block and aluminum head. Displacement: 121 cid (2.0 liters). B & S: 3.39 x 3.39 in. Compression ratio: 22.7:1. Brake hp: 52 at 4000 rpm. Torque: 82 lbs.-ft. at 2400 rpm. Five main bearings. Solid valve lifters. Fuel injection. VIN Code: H.

Tempo Base Four: Inline. Overhead valve. Cast-iron block and head. Displacement: 140 cid (2.3 liters). B & S: 3.70 x 3.30 in. Compression ratio: 9.0:1. Brake hp: 86 at 4000 rpm. Torque: 124 lbs.-ft. at 2800 rpm. Five main bearings. Hydraulic valve lifters. Throttle-body fuel injection. High Swirl Combustion (HSC) design. VIN Code: X.

Tempo Optional Four: High-output HSC four. Hp: 100 at 4600 rpm. Torque: 125 lbs.-ft. at 3200 rpm. VIN Code: S.

Taurus (Late) Base Four: Inline. Overhead valve. Cast-iron block and head. Displacement: 153 cid (2.5 liters). B & S: 3.70 x 3.60 in. Compression ratio: 9.0:1. Brake hp: 88 at 4600 rpm. Torque: 130 lbs.-ft. at 2800 rpm. Five main bearings. Hydraulic valve lifters. Electronic fuel injection. VIN Code: D.

Taurus LX and Wagon Base V-6 (Optional Taurus): 60-degree, overhead valve. Cast-iron block and head. Displacement: 183 cid (3.0 liters). B & S: 3.50 x 3.10 in. Compression ratio: 9.25:1. Brake hp: 140 at 4800 rpm. Torque: 160 lbs.-ft. at 3000 rpm. Four main bearings. Hydraulic valve lifters. Multi-port fuel injection. VIN Code: U.

LTD Base V-6: 90-degree, overhead valve. Cast-iron block and aluminum head. Displacement: 232 cid (3.8 liters). B & S: 3.80 x 3.40 in. Compression ratio: 8.7:1. Brake hp: 120 at 3600 rpm. Torque: 205 lbs.-ft. at 1600 rpm. Four main bearings. Hydraulic valve lifters. Throttle-body fuel injection. VIN Code: 3.

Crown Victoria Base V-8: 90-degree, overhead valve. Cast-iron block and head. Displacement: 302 cid (5.0 liters). B & S: 4.00 x 3.00 in. Compression ratio: 8.9:1. Brake hp: 150 at 3200 rpm. Torque: 270 lbs.-ft. at 2000 rpm. Five main bearings. Hydraulic valve lifters. Sequential (port) fuel injection. VIN Code: F.

Crown Victoria High-Output Police V-8: 90-degree, overhead valve. Cast-iron block and head. Displacement: 351 cid (5.8 liters). B & S: 4.00 x 3.50 in. Compression ratio: 8.3:1. Brake hp: 180 at 3600 rpm. Torque: 285 lbs.-ft. at 2400 rpm. Five main bearings. Hydraulic valve lifters. Two-barrel carburetor. VIN Code: G.

Chassis:

Escort: Wheelbase: 94.2 in. Overall length: 166.9 in. and 168.0 in., wagon. Tires: P165/80-R13 steel-belted blackwalls, P175/80-R13, L wagon and LX and P195/60-HR15 blackwalls, Escort GT.

EXP: Wheelbase: 94.2 in. Overall length: 168.4 in. Tires: P185/70-R14 steel-belted blackwalls.

Tempo: Wheelbase: 99.9 in. Overall length: 176.2 in. Tires: P185/80-R14 steel-belted blackwalls.

Taurus: Wheelbase: 106.0 in. Overall length: 188.4 in. and 191.9 in., station wagon. Tires: P195/70-R14 blackwalls and P205/70-R14, GL and LX.

LTD: Wheelbase: 105.6 in. Overall length: 196.5 in. Tires: P195/75-R14 blackwalls.

Crown Victoria: Wheelbase: 114.3 in. Overall length: 211.0 in. and 215.0 in., wagon. Tires: P205/75-R15 steel-belted whitewalls.

Options:

Escort: Instrument group ($87). Climate control/convenience group ($742 to $868). Premium convenience group ($306 to $390). Protection convenience group ($131 to $467). Select L pkg. ($397). Light group ($67). Air conditioner ($657). Electric rear defroster ($135). Fingertip speed control ($176). Tinted glass ($99). Tilt steering ($115). Overhead console with digital clock ($82). Interval wipers ($50). Rear wiper/washer ($126). Dual remote sport mirrors ($68). AM radio ($39). AM/FM stereo radio ($109) and ($148) base. With cassette player ($256) and ($295) base and L. ($148) on the GT ($148). Premium sound ($138). Front vent windows, pivoting ($63). Wide vinyl body moldings ($45). Luggage rack: wagon ($100). Console ($111). Vinyl seat trim ($24). Bright wheel trim rings ($54). Styled wheels ($128 to $195). P165/80-R13 steel-belted whitewalls ($59). Full-size spare ($63). 2.0-liter diesel four ($591). Five-speed manual transmission ($76). Automatic transaxle ($466) and ($390) LX and GT. Power steering ($226). Heavy duty suspension ($26). Heavy duty battery ($27). Heavy duty alternator ($27). Engine block heater ($18).

1986 EXP Sport Coupe

1986 Taurus GL station wagon

EXP: Climate control/convenience group ($841 to $868). Sun/Sound group ($612). Convenience group ($300 to $455). Air conditioner ($657). Rear defroster ($135). Fingertip speed control ($176). Console w/graphic systems monitor ($111). Tinted glass ($99). Tilt steering ($115). Interval wipers ($50). Dual electric remote mirrors ($88). Lighted visor vanity mirror ($50). AM/FM stereo radio with cassette player ($148). Premium sound ($138). Flip-up open-air roof ($315). Cargo area cover ($59). Vinyl seat trim ($24). Automatic transaxle ($390). Power steering ($226). Heavy duty battery ($27). Heavy duty alternator ($27). Engine block heater ($18).

Tempo: Sport GL package ($934). Select GL package ($340 to $423). Power lock group ($207 to $259). Power equipment group ($291 to $575). Convenience group ($224 to $640). Air bag restraint system ($815). Air conditioning ($743). Electric rear defroster ($145). Fingertip speed control ($176). Power windows ($207 to $282). Six-way power driver's seat ($234). Tinted glass ($113). Tilt steering ($115). Sport instrument cluster ($87). Dual electric remote mirrors ($111). AM/FM stereo radio ($109) and with cassette player ($148 to $256). Electronic-tuning AM/FM stereo with cassette ($171 to $279) and ($23) with Sport GL pkg. Premium sound ($138). Deck lid luggage rack ($100). Console ($116). Front center armrest ($55). Vinyl seat trim ($35). Leather seat trim ($300). Styled wheels. P185/70-R14 whitewalls ($72). 2.0-liter diesel four ($509). Automatic transaxle ($448). Power steering ($223). Heavy duty battery ($27). Engine block heater ($18).

Taurus: Exterior accent group ($49 to $99). Power lock group ($180 to $221). Light group ($48 to $51). Air conditioning ($762). Electronic climate control air conditioning: GL ($945) and LX ($183). Rear defroster ($145). Insta-clear windshield ($250). Fingertip speed control ($176). Illuminated entry ($82). Keyless entry ($202). Power windows ($282). Six-way power driver's seat ($237) or dual ($473). Tinted glass: L ($115). Leather-wrapped steering wheel ($59). Tilt steering ($115). Electronic instrument cluster ($305). Autolamp on/off delay ($73). Diagnostic warning lights ($89). Digital clock: L ($78). Interval wipers: L ($50). Rear wiper/washer, wagon ($124). Cornering lamps ($68). Dual electric remote mirrors: L ($59 to $96). Dual lighted visor vanity mirrors ($104-$116). Electronic-tuning AM/FM stereo radio ($157), L and MT5. Electronic-tuning AM/FM stereo with cassette/Dolby ($127 to $284). Power antenna ($71). Premium sound system ($168). Power moon roof ($701). Bucket seats, no charge. Split bench seating: L ($276). Vinyl seat trim ($39). Leather seat trim: LX sedan ($415). Rear-facing third seat: wag ($155). Reclining passenger seat ($45). Luxury wheel covers ($65). Styled wheels, 14 in. ($113 to $178). Cast aluminum wheels, 15 in. ($326 to $390). Conventional spare ($63). 182-cid V-6 ($611). Heavy duty suspension ($26). Heavy duty battery ($27). Extended-range gas tank ($46).

LTD: Squire option ($282). Interior luxury group ($388). Power lock group ($218 to $259). Light group ($38). Air conditioning ($762). Rear defroster ($145). Fingertip speed control ($176). Autolamp on-off delay ($73). Power windows ($282). Six-way power driver's seat ($234). Tinted glass ($115). Leather-wrapped steering wheel ($59). Tilt steering ($115). Overdrive automatic transmission ($245). Digital clock ($78). Auto. parking brake release ($12). Interval wipers ($50). Cornering lamps ($68). Dual electric remote mirrors ($96). Lighted visor vanity mirrors ($57 to $106). AM/FM stereo radio ($109) and ($256) with cassette player. Premium sound system ($138). Pivoting front vent windows ($79). Two-way liftgate, wagon ($105). Luggage rack, wagon ($126). Vinyl seat trim ($35). Flight or split bench seat, no charge. Luxury wheel covers ($55). Wire wheel covers, locking ($212). Styled wheels ($178). Styled steel wheels w/trim rings ($54). Conventional spare ($63). 140-cid four ($494 credit). Heavy duty suspension ($43). Heavy duty battery ($27). Extended-range gas tank ($46). Engine block heater ($18).

LTD Crown Victoria: Convenience group ($109 to $134). Power lock group ($143 to $243). Light group ($48). Police package ($291 to

1986 LTD Crown Victoria sedan

$411). Air conditioning ($762) and ($828) with auto-temp control. Rear defroster, electric ($145). Fingertip speed control ($176). Illuminated entry system ($82). Power windows ($282). Power six-way driver's seat ($237) or driver and passenger ($473). Tinted glass ($115). Autolamp on/off delay ($73). Leather-wrapped steering wheel ($59). Tilt steering wheel ($115). Tripminder computer ($215 to $261). Digital clock ($61 to $96). Interval wipers ($50). Cornering lamps ($68). Remote right convex mirror ($46). Dual electric remote mirrors ($100). AM/FM stereo radio, S ($109) and with cassette tape player ($148-$256). Electronic-tuning AM/FM stereo radio with cassette ($300). Power antenna ($73). Premium sound system ($168). Brougham vinyl roof ($793). Luggage rack, wagon ($110). Dual-facing rear seats, wagon ($167). Leather seat trim ($433). Reclining split bench seats ($144). Duraweave vinyl ($100). Wire wheel covers, locking ($205). Cast aluminum wheels ($390). P205/75-R15 puncture-sealant tires ($161). Conventional spare ($63). Traction-Lok differential ($100). Heavy duty suspension ($26). Handling suspension ($49). Automatic load leveling ($200). Heavy duty battery ($27). Heavy duty alternator ($54). Engine block heater ($18). Trailer towing package ($377-$389).

History:

The 1986 Fords were introduced on Oct. 3, 1985. The Taurus premiered on Dec. 26, 1985. Model year production was 1,559,959, including the Mustangs. Calendar year sales by U.S. dealers was 1,397,141, including Mustangs. The new front-drive, mid-size Taurus was the big news for 1986. Its aerodynamic styling went considerably beyond the Tempo design, taking its cue from European Fords. Taurus hardly resembled the rear-drive LTD that it was meant to replace. Mercury's Sable was similar, but with its own set of body panels and features.

1987 Ford

Escort — Four: Fuel injection replaced the carburetor on Escort's base 1.9-liter four-cylinder engine. As before, Escort GT was powered by a high-output version of the four, with multi-point injection. Some shuffling of model designations and the deletion of the LX series meant this year's offering consisted of Pony, GL and GT models. Automatic motorized front seat belts were introduced during the model year. Joining the option list: a fold-down center armrest and split fold-down rear seat.

EXP — Four: Ford's tiny two-seater came in two forms: Luxury Coupe with the base 1.9-liter four-cylinder engine, or Sport Coupe with the high-output power plant. EXP enjoyed a restyling for reintroduction as

1987 Escort GL four-door hatchback

1987 Taurus LX sedan

a 1986-1/2 model, after a brief departure from the lineup. Rather than a distinct model, EXP was now considered part of the Escort series.

Tempo — Four: Front-drive only through its first three seasons, the compact Tempo added a part-time four-wheel-drive option this year. "Shift-on-the-fly" capability allowed engagement of 4WD while in motion, simply by touching a dashboard switch. Models with that option, which was intended for use only on slippery roads, got an "All Wheel Drive" nameplate. 4WD models also included the high-output version of the 2.3-liter four-cylinder engine. Power steering was now standard on all Tempos, while the driver's airbag became a regular production option (RPO) instead of a limited-production item. A revised three-speed automatic transmission contained a new fluid-linked converter, eliminating the need for a lockup torque converter.

Taurus — Four/V-6: Sales of the aero-styled front-drive Taurus began to take off soon after its mid-1986 debut and little change was needed for the 1987 model year. The basic engine for the L and MT5 series, and the GL sedan, was a 2.5-liter four. A 3.0-liter V-6 was optional in all except the MT5. Other models had the V-6 standard with four-speed overdrive automatic transmission. The MT5 came with a standard five-speed gearbox and the L and GL had a three-speed automatic. Similar Mercury Sables all had V-6 power.

LTD Crown Victoria — V-8: Only a few equipment changes arrived with the 1987 full-size Fords. Air conditioning, tinted glass and a digital clock were now standard equipment. Two- and four-door sedans and a four-door station wagon, in base and LX trim levels, were all powered by a 5.0-liter V-8 with four-speed overdrive automatic transmission.

I.D. Data:

Ford's 17-symbol Vehicle Identification Number (VIN) was stamped on a metal tab fastened to the instrument panel, visible through the windshield. The first three symbols 1FA=manufacturer, make and vehicle type. The fourth symbol B=restraint system. Next came letter P followed by the two-digit model number: P20=Escort Pony two-door hatchback. Symbol eight indicated the engine type. Next was a check digit. Symbol 10 indicated the model year: H=1987. Symbol 11=assembly plant. The final six digits made up the sequence number, starting with 100001.

Escort (Four))

Model No.	Body/Style No.	Body Type & Seating	Factory Price	Shipping Weight	Production Total
20	61D	2-dr. Pony Hatchback-4P	$6,436	2,180 lbs.	Note 1
21	61D	2-dr. GL Hatchback-4P	$6,801	2,187 lbs.	Note 1
25	58D	4-dr. GL Hatchback-4P	$7,022	2,222 lbs.	Note 1
28	74D	4-dr. GL Station Wagon-4P	$7,312	2,274 lbs.	Note 1
23	61D	2-dr. GT Hatchback-4P	$8,724	2,516 lbs.	Note 1

Note 1: For the model year, a total of 206,729 two-door hatchbacks. 102,187 four-door hatchback sedans, and 65,849 station wagons were built.

EXP (Four)

18	----	2-dr. Sport Coupe-2P	$8,831	2,388 lbs.	Note 2
17	----	2-dr. Luxury Coupe-2P	$7,622	2,291 lbs.	Note 2

Note 2: Total EXP production was 25,888.

Tempo (Four)

31	66D	2-dr. GL Sedan-5P	$8,043	2,462 lbs.	Note 3
36	54D	4-dr. GL Sedan-5P	$8,198	2,515 lbs.	Note 3
32	66D	2-dr. LX Sedan-5P	$9,238	2,562 lbs.	Note 3
37	54D	4-dr. LX Sedan-5P	$9,444	2,617 lbs.	Note 3
33	66D	2-dr. Sport GL Sedan-5P	$8,888	2,667 lbs.	Note 3
38	54D	4-dr. Sport GT Sedan-5P	$9,043	2,720 lbs.	Note 3
34	66D	2-dr. AWD Sedan-5P	$9,984	2,667 lbs.	Note 3
39	54D	4-dr. AWD Sedan-5P	$10,138	2,720 lbs.	Note 3

Note 3: Total Tempo production came to 70,164 two-doors and 212,468 four-doors.

Taurus (Four)

50	54D	4-dr. L Sedan-6P	$10,491	-----	Note 4
51	54D	4-dr. MT5 Sedan-6P	$11,966	2,886 lbs.	Note 4
56	74D	4-dr. MT5 Station Wagon-6P	$12,534	3,083 lbs.	Note 4
52	54D	4-dr. GL Sedan-6P	$11,498	-----	Note 4

Taurus (V-6)

50	54D	4-dr. L Sedan-6P	$11,163	2,982 lbs.	Note 4
55	74D	4-dr. L Station Wagon-6P	$11,722	3,186 lbs.	Note 4
52	54D	4-dr. GL Sedan-6P	$12,170	3,045 lbs.	Note 4
57	74D	4-dr. GL Station Wagon-6P	$12,688	3,242 lbs.	Note 4
53	54D	4-dr. LX Sedan-6P	$14,613	3,113 lbs.	Note 4
58	74D	4-dr. LX Station Wagon-6P	$15,213	3,309 lbs.	Note 4

Note 4: Total Taurus production came to 278,562 sedans and 96,201 station wagons.

LTD Crown Victoria (V-8)

70	66K	2-dr. Sedan-6P	$14,727	3,724 lbs.	5,527
73	54K	4-dr. Sedan-6P	$14,355	3,741 lbs.	105,789
78	74K	4-dr. Country Squire-6P	$14,507	3,920 lbs.	17,652
76	74K	4-dr. Station Wagon-6P	$14,235	3,920 lbs.	Note 5
72	54K	4-dr. S Sedan-6P	$13,860	3,708 lbs.	Note 5
75	74K	4-dr. S Station Wagon-6P	$14,228	3,894 lbs.	Note 5

LTD Crown Victoria LX (V-8)

71	66K	2-dr. Sedan-6P	$15,421	3,735 lbs.	Note 5
74	54K	4-dr. Sedan-6P	$15,454	3,788 lbs.	Note 5
77	74K	4-dr. Station Wagon-6P	$15,450	4,000 lbs.	Note 5
79	74K	4-dr. Country Squire-6P	$15,723	4,000 lbs.	Note 5

Note 5: The S, LX and basic station wagons were included in the basic sedan and Country Squire totals.

Engines:

Escort Base Four: Inline. Overhead cam. Cast iron block and aluminum head. Displacement: 113 cid (1.9 liters). B & S: 3.23 x 3.46 in. Compression ratio: 9.0:1. Brake hp: 90 at 4600 rpm. Torque: 106 lbs.-ft. at 3400 rpm. Five main bearings. Hydraulic valve lifters. Throttle-body fuel injection.

Escort GT and EXP Sport Coupe Base Four: High-output, multi-port fuel injection of 1.9-liter. Hp: 115 at 5200 RPM. Torque: 120 lbs.-ft. at 4400 rpm.

Escort Diesel Four: Inline. Overhead cam. Cast iron block and aluminum head. Displacement: 121 cid (2.0 liters). B & S: 3.39 x 3.39 in. Compression ratio: 22.7:1. Brake hp: 58 at 3600 rpm. Torque: 84 lbs.-ft. at 3000 RPM. Five main bearings. Solid valve lifters. Fuel injection.

Tempo Base Four: Inline. Overhead valve. Cast iron block and head. Displacement: 140 cid (2.3 liters). B & S: 3.70 x 3.30 in. Compression ratio: 9.0:1. Brake hp: 86 at 3800 RPM. Torque: 120 lbs.-ft. at 3200 rpm. Five main bearings. Hydraulic valve lifters. Throttle-body fuel injection. High Swirl Combustion (HSC) design.

Tempo AWD or Sport Base Four: High-output version of HSC four. Hp: 94 at 4000 RPM. Torque: 126 lbs.-ft. at 3200 rpm.

Taurus Base Four: Inline. Overhead valve. Cast iron block and head. Displacement: 153 cid (2.5 liters). B & S: 3.70 x 3.60 in. Compression ratio: 9.0:1. Brake hp: 90 at 4400 rpm. Torque: 140 lbs.-ft. at 2800 rpm. Five main bearings. Hydraulic valve lifters. Throttle-body fuel injection.

Taurus LX Base V-6 (Optional Taurus): 60-degree, overhead valve. Cast iron block and head. Displacement: 182 cid (3.0 liters). B & S: 3.50 x 3.10 in. Compression ratio: 9.3:1. Brake hp: 140 at 4800 rpm. Torque: 160 lbs.-ft. at 3000 rpm. Four main bearings. Hydraulic valve lifters. Multi-port fuel injection.

LTD Crown Victoria Base V-8: 90-degree, overhead valve. Cast iron block and head. Displacement: 302 cid (5.0 liters). B & S: 4.00 x 3.00 in. Compression ratio: 8.9:1. Brake hp: 150 at 3200 rpm. Torque: 270 lbs.-ft. at 2000 rpm. Five main bearings. Hydraulic valve lifters. Sequential-port fuel injection.

Chassis:

Escort: Wheelbase: 94.2 in. Overall length: 166.9 in. and 168.0 in., station wagon. Tires: Pony, P165/80-R13; GL 4-dr and station wagon, P165/80-R13 and GT, P195/60-HR15.

EXP: Wheelbase: 94.2 in. Overall length: 168.4 in. Tires: P185/70-R14.

Tempo: Wheelbase: 99.9 in. Overall length: 176.5 in. Tires: P185/70-R14.

Taurus: Wheelbase: 106.0 in. Overall length: 188.4 in. and 191.9 in., station wagon. Tires: P195/70-R14 and P205/70-R14, GLX.

Crown Victoria: Wheelbase: 114.3 in. Overall length: 211.0 in. and 215.0 in, station wagon. Tires: P205/75-R15.

Options:

Escort: Overhead console with digital clock, tachometer, trip odometer and coolant temperature gauge, dual power mirrors, power steering on GL w/gas engine ($496). GL with diesel engine ($409). Overhead console w/clock ($82). Tachometer, trip odometer & coolant temp gauge ($87). Dual power mirrors ($88). Power steering ($235). Air conditioning, heavy-duty battery, rear defogger, tinted glass, intermittent wipers; GL with gas engine ($920). GL with diesel or GT ($893). Air conditioning ($688). Heavy-duty battery ($27). Rear defogger ($145). Tinted glass ($105). Intermittent wipers ($55). Light/Security Group plus front center armrest, cruise control, split folding rear seatback, tilt steering column; GL ($395). Light/Security Group, GL ($91). GT ($67). Front center armrest, Escort ($55). Cruise control ($176). Split folding rear seat ($49). Tilt steering column ($124). Premium Sound System ($138). Luggage rack ($110). AM radio ($39). AM/FM Stereo, Pony ($159). GL ($120). AM/FM Stereo with cassette, AM/FM stereo, Pony ($306). GL ($267). GT ($148). Cast aluminum wheels ($293). Styled road wheels ($195). Rear wiper/washer

1987 LTD Crown Victoria LX sedan

1987 Tempo All-Wheel-Drive sedan

($126). 2.0-liter diesel four, no charge. Five-speed manual transmission ($76). Automatic transaxle, GL ($490). Power steering ($235).

EXP: Overhead console w/clock ($82). Tachometer, trip odometer & coolant temp gauge ($87). Dual power mirrors ($88). Power steering ($235). Air conditioning plus heavy-duty battery, rear defogger, tinted glass, intermittent wipers - Luxury Coupe ($920). Sport Coupe ($893). Air conditioning ($688). Heavy-duty battery ($27). Rear defogger ($145). Tinted glass ($105). Intermittent wipers ($55). Cruise control ($176). Tilt steering column ($124). Cargo area cover, dual power mirrors, dual visor mirrors, (lighted right), cruise control, power steering, tilt steering column, Luxury Coupe ($473). Sport Coupe ($309). Cargo area cover, ($59). Dual power mirrors, ($88). Visor mirrors (lighted right) ($50). Overhead console w/graphic systems monitor, removable sunroof, AM/FM ST w/cassette, premium Sound System, Luxury Coupe ($597). Sport Coupe ($566). Console w/graphic systems monitor ($56). Removable sunroof ($355). AM/FM ST with cassette ($148). Premium Sound System ($138). Luggage rack ($110). Clear coat paint ($91). AM/FM stereo ($148). Cast aluminum wheels ($293). Styled road wheels ($195). Rear wiper/washer ($126). Automatic transaxle ($415). Power steering ($235).

Tempo: Select GL Package with tinted glass, dual power mirrors and AM/FM Stereo ($191). Without radio ($124). Tinted glass ($120). Dual power mirrors ($111). AM/FM Stereo ET radio ($93). Power Lock Group, includes remote fuel filler and trunk releases, power driver's seat, power windows: 2-door GL, Sport or All Wheel Drive ($560). 4-door GL, Sport or All Wheel Drive ($635). LX 2-door ($323). LX 4-door ($347). Power Lock Group, 2-doors ($237). 4-doors ($288). Power driver's seat ($251). Power windows, 2-doors ($222). 4-doors ($296). Front center armrest, Premium Sound System, AM/FM ST ET cassette, speed control, tilt steering column: GL ($643). Select GL ($565). Sport GL ($418). LX ($371). All Wheel Drive ($510). Front center armrest ($55). Premium Sound System ($138). AM/FM Stereo ET cassette, GL ($250). LX or Select GL ($157). Speed control ($176). Tilt steering column ($124). Air conditioning ($773). Console ($116). Rear defogger ($145). Sport instrument cluster ($87). Deck lid luggage rack ($115). AM/FM Stereo ($93). AM/FM Stereo ET cassette, GL ($250). LX, Select GL or All Wheel Drive ($157). Styled road wheels ($178). All vinyl seat trim ($35). Automatic transaxle ($482).

Taurus: Automatic air conditioning, LX ($183). GL ($945). Manual air conditioning ($788). Autolamp system ($73). Heavy-duty battery ($27). Digital clock ($78). Rear defogger ($145). Engine block heater ($18). Remote fuel door and deck lid release ($91) Remote liftgate release, wagons ($41). Extended range fuel tank ($46). Tinted glass ($120). Illuminated entry system ($82). Electronic instrument cluster ($351). Keyless entry system ($202). Power door locks ($195). Dual power mirrors, L sedan ($96). L wagon ($59). Power moon roof ($741). AM/FM Stereo ET radio ($141). AM/FM Stereo w/cassette, L ($268). GL, MT5 & LX ($137). Premium sound system ($168). Power antenna ($76). Rear-facing third seat, wagons ($155). Reclining passenger seat ($45). Power driver's seat ($251). Dual power seats, LX ($502). Others ($251). Speed control ($176). Tilt steering column ($124). Leather-wrapped steering wheel ($59). Rear wiper and washer, wagons ($126). Finned wheel covers, L, GL & MT5 ($65). Locking spoked wheel covers L, GL & MT5 ($205). LX ($140). Aluminum wheels, L, GL & MT5 ($390). LX ($326). Styled road wheels, L, GL & MT5 ($178). LX ($113). Power windows ($296). Intermittent wipers ($55). Split bench seats ($276). Leather seat trim ($415). Vinyl seat trim ($39). 3.0-liter V-6 on L and GL ($672). Heavy duty handling suspension ($26).

1987 LTD Country Squire station wagon

1987 Escort GL station wagon

1987 Taurus LX station wagon

LTD Crown Victoria: Automatic A/C and rear defogger ($211). Autolamp system ($73). Heavy-duty battery ($27). Convenience group with remote deck lid or tailgate release, intermittent wipers, trip odometer, low fuel and oil warning lights (except LX $135) and with Power Lock Group ($85). Cornering lamps ($68). Rear defogger ($145). Engine block heater ($18). Illuminated entry system ($82). Light group ($48). Power lock group: Power door locks, remote fuel door release, two-doors ($207). sedans and wagons ($257). Deluxe luggage rack ($115). AM/FM Stereo w/cassette ($137). Power antenna ($76). Premium Sound System ($168). Power driver's seat ($251). Dual power seats ($502). Dual facing rear seats, wagon ($173). Cruise control ($176). Leather-wrapped steering wheel ($59). Tilt steering column ($124). Tripminder computer ($215). Locking wire wheel covers ($212). Cast aluminum wheels ($390). Power windows & mirrors ($393). Intermittent wipers ($55). Brougham half vinyl roof ($665). Split bench seat ($139). Duraweave vinyl seat trim ($96). Leather seat trim ($418). Traction-Lok differential ($100). Heavy duty handling suspension ($26). Automatic load leveling ($200). Trailer towing package ($387 to $399).

History:

The 1987 Fords were introduced on Oct. 2, 1986. Model year production was 1,474,116, including Mustangs. Calendar year sales by U.S. dealers were 1,389,886 cars, including Mustangs. Once again, Ford's subcompact Escort ranked number one in sales for the model year. Taurus became the second best-selling passenger car in the country. As soon as the mid-size Taurus began its rise to become a hot seller, Ford's LTD left the lineup for good. Sales of the full-size, rear-drive LTD Crown Victoria slid this year, but its place in the lineup was assured.

1988 Ford

Escort — Four: For the first half of the model year, Escort continued with little change except an automatic transmission became optional for the base Pony. The diesel engine option had been dropped. During the model year, motorized automatic front shoulder belts were made standard. A face-lifted Second Series Escort arrived at mid-year. Changes included new fenders, tail lamps, body moldings, quarter panels and plastic bumpers, plus a switch to 14-inch tires. The upgraded GT got a new grille and rear spoiler.

EXP — Four: Only one model remained for the first half of the model year, the Luxury Coupe, as the Sport Coupe was dropped. A Second Series EXP arrived at mid-year, the final season for the subcompact.

Tempo — Four: Restyling of Ford's compact sedans included aero-styled headlamps (integrated with parking lamps and side marker

lenses), wraparound tail lamps, and new bumpers. The four-door also got new body panels and window designs. A new analog instrument panel contained a standard temperature gauge. Under the hood, multi-point fuel injection was used on both the standard and high-output 2.3-liter four-cylinder engines. The standard four got a boost of 12 hp. All Wheel Drive was now available only in the four-door model. The high-output engine was standard in the GLS series and the AWD this year.

Taurus — Four and V-6: Performance fans had a new 3.8-liter V-6 to choose this year. Horsepower was the same as the 3.0-liter V-6, but the engine developed 55 more lbs.-ft. of torque. All models, except the base L and MT5 sedans, could get the 3.8-liter engine. It came only with four-speed overdrive automatic transmission. The MT5 wagon was dropped leaving only the MT5 sedan with the four-cylinder engine and five-speed manual transmission. L and GL sedans also had the four but with three-speed automatic. All station wagons (and the LX sedans) had a standard 3.0-liter V-6 with four-speed automatic.

LTD Crown Victoria — V-8: No two-doors remained in the full-size Ford lineup for 1988. The four-door sedans and wagons got a front and rear restyle (including a new grille and hood, bumpers with rub strips, and trunk lid). Sedans also gained wraparound tail lamps. P215/70-R15 whitewall tires became standard, along with intermittent wipers, a trip odometer, low fuel and oil-level warning lights, an automatic headlamp on/off system, and front-door map pockets. Both base and LX models were powered by a 150-hp, 5.0-liter V-8 engine with four-speed overdrive automatic.

I.D. Data:

Ford's 17-symbol Vehicle Identification Number (VIN) was stamped on a metal tab fastened to the instrument panel and was visible through the windshield. The first three symbols 1FA=manufacturer, make and vehicle type. The fourth symbol=restraint system. Next came letter P followed by two digits that indicated the model number, such as P20=Escort Pony two-door hatchback. Symbol eight indicated the engine type. Next was a check digit. Symbol 10 indicated the model year: J=1988. Symbol 11 was the assembly plant. The final six digits made up the sequence number, starting with 100001.

1988-1/2 Escort GT hatchback coupe

1988 Escort GL three-door hatchback

1988-1/2 Escort LX station wagon

1988 Escort hatchback sedan

Escort (Four))

Model No.	Body/ Style No.	Body Type & Seating	Factory Price	Shipping Weight	Production Total
20	61D	2-dr. Pony Hatchback-4P	$6,632	2,180 lbs.	Note 1
21	61D	2-dr. GL Hatchback-4P	$6,649	2,187 lbs.	Note 1
25	58D	4-dr. GL Hatchback-4P	$7,355	2,222 lbs.	Note 1
28	74D	4-dr. GL Station Wagon-4P	$7,938	2,274 lbs.	Note 1
23	61D	2-dr. GT Hatchback-4P	$9,055	2,516 lbs.	Note 1
90	61D	2-dr. Pony Hatchback-4P	$6,747	------	Note 1
91	61D	2-dr. LX Hatchback-4P	$7,127	2,258 lbs.	Note 1
95	58D	4-dr. LX Hatchback-4P	$7,457	2,295 lbs.	Note 1
98	74D	4-dr. LX Station Wagon-4P	$8,058	2,307 lbs.	Note 1
93	61D	2-dr. GT Hatchback-4P	$9,093	------	Note 1

Note 1: A total of 206,729 two-door hatchbacks. 102,187 four-door hatchback sedans, and 65,849 station wagons were built.

EXP (Four)

17	----	2-dr. Luxury Coupe-2P	$8,073	2,291 lbs.	Note 1

EXP Second Series (Four)

88	----	2-dr. Luxury Coupe-2P	$8,201	2,359 lbs.	Note 1

Tempo (Four)

31	66D	2-dr. GL Sedan-5P	$8,658	2,536 lbs.	Note 2
36	54D	4-dr. GL Sedan-5P	$8,808	2,585 lbs.	Note 2
37	54D	4-dr. LX Sedan-5P	$9,737	2,626 lbs.	Note 2
39	54D	4-dr. AWD Sedan-5P	$10,413	2,799 lbs.	Note 2
33	66D	2-dr. GLS Sedan-5P	$9,249	2,552 lbs.	Note 2
38	54D	4-dr. GLS Sedan-5P	$9,400	2,601 lbs.	Note 2

Note 2: Total Tempo production came to 313,262 or 49,930 two-door and 263,332 four-door sedans.

Taurus (Four)

50	54D	4-dr. L Sedan-6P	$11,699	-----	Note 3
51	54D	4-dr. MT5 Sedan-6P	$12,385	2,882 lbs.	Note 3
52	54D	4-dr. GL Sedan-6P	$12,200	-----	Note 3

Taurus (V-6)

50	54D	2-dr. L Sedan-6P	$12,731	3,005 lbs.	Note 3
55	74D	4-dr. L Station Wagon-6P	$12,884	3,182 lbs.	Note 3
52	54D	4-dr. GL Sedan-6P	$12,872	3,049 lbs.	Note 3
57	74D	4-dr. GL Station Wagon-6P	$13,380	3,215 lbs.	Note 3
53	54D	2-dr. LX Sedan-6P	$15,295	3,119 lbs.	Note 3
58	74D	4-dr. LX Station Wagon-6P	$15,905	3,288 lbs.	Note 3

Note 3: Total Production was 387,577 (294,576 sedans and 93,001 wagons.)

LTD Crown Victoria (V-8)

73	54K	4-dr. Sedan-6P	$15,218	3,779 lbs.	Note 4
72	54K	4-dr. S Sedan-6P	$14,653	3,742 lbs.	Note 4
76	74K	4-dr. Station Wagon-8P	$15,180	3,991 lbs.	Note 4
78	74K	4-dr. Country Squire-8P	$15,613	3,998 lbs.	Note 4

LTD Crown Victoria LX (V-8)

74	54K	4-dr. Sedan-6P	$16,134	3,820 lbs.	Note 4
77	74K	4-dr. Station Wagon-8P	$16,210	3,972 lbs.	Note 4
79	74K	4-dr. Country Squire-8P	$16,643	4,070 lbs.	Note 4

Note 4: Total production came to 110,249 sedans and 14,940 station wagons.

Engines:

Escort Base Four: Inline. Overhead cam. Cast-iron block and aluminum head. Displacement: 113 cid (1.9 liters). B & S: 3.23 x 3.46 in. Compression ratio: 9.0:1. Brake hp: 90 at 4600 rpm. Torque: 106 lbs.-ft. at 3400 rpm. Five main bearings. Hydraulic valve lifters. Throttle-body duel injection.

1988 Tempo sedan with all-wheel-drive

1988 Tempo GLS sedan

Escort GT Base Four: High-output. MFI version of 1.9-liter. Hp: 115 at 5200 rpm. Torque: 120 lbs.-ft. at 4400 rpm.

Tempo Base Four: Inline. Overhead valve. Cast-iron block and head. Displacement: 140 cid (2.3 liter). B & S: 3.70 x 3.30 in. Compression ratio: 9.0:1. Brake hp: 98 at 4400 rpm. Torque: 124 lbs.-ft. at 2200 rpm. Five main bearings. Hydraulic valve lifters. Multi-point fuel injection. High Swirl Combustion (HSC) design.

Tempo AWD and Sport Base Four: High-output version of HSC engine. Hp: 100 at 4400 rpm. Torque: 130 lbs.-ft. at 2600 rpm.

Taurus Base Four: Inline. Overhead valve. Four-cylinder. Cast-iron block and head. Displacement: 153 cid. (2.5 liters). B & S: 3.70 x 3.60 in. Compression ratio: 9.0:1. Brake hp: 90 at 4000 rpm. Torque: 130 lbs.-ft. at 2600 rpm. Five main bearings. Hydraulic valve lifters. Throttle-body fuel injection.

Taurus LX and Wagons V-6 (Optional Taurus L sedan): 60-degree, overhead valve. Cast-iron block and head. Displacement: 182 cid (3.0 liters). B & S: 3.50 x 3.10 in. Compression ratio: 9.3:1. Brake hp: 140 at 4800 rpm. Torque: 160 lbs.-ft. at 3000 rpm. Four main bearings. Hydraulic valve lifters. Multi-port fuel injection.

Taurus Optional V-6: 90-degree, overhead valve. Cast-iron block and aluminum head. Displacement: 232 cid (3.8 liters). B & S: 3.80 x 3.40 in. Compression ratio: 9.0:1. Brake hp: 140 at 3800 rpm. Torque: 215 lbs.-ft. at 2200 rpm. Four main bearings. Hydraulic valve lifters. Multi-point fuel injection.

LTD Crown Victoria Base V-8: 90-degree, overhead valve. Cast-iron block and head. Displacement: 302 cid (5.0 liters). B & S: 4.00 x 3.00 in. Compression ratio: 8.9:1. Brake hp: 150 at 3200 rpm. Torque: 270 lbs.-ft. at 2000 rpm. Five main bearings. Hydraulic valve lifters. Sequential (port) fuel injection.

Chassis:

Escort: Wheelbase: 94.2 in. Overall length: 166.9 in. and 168.0 in, station wagon. Tires: Pony, P175/80-Rl3; GL 4-dr and wagon, P165/80-R13. Second Series Escort: P175/70-Rl4 and GT P195/60-HR15.

EXP: Wheelbase: 94.2 in. Overall length: 168.4 in. Tires: P185/70-R14.

Tempo: Wheelbase: 99.9 in. Overall length: 176.5 in. Tires: P185/70-R14.

Taurus: Wheelbase: 106.0 in. Overall length: 188.4 in. and wagon, 191.9 in. Tires: P195/70-R14 and Taurus LX, P205/70-R14.

Crown Victoria: Wheelbase: 114.3 in. Overall length: 211.0 in. and 216.0 in., station wagon. Tires: P205/70-R15.

Options:

Escort: Escort GT Special Value Pkg. ($815). Four-speed manual Transaxle Package with four-speed manual transaxle, wide vinyl body moldings, electronic AM/FM stereo, electronic digital clock/overhead console, power steering, tinted glass, interval wipers, bumper guards, bumper rub strips and rear window defroster plus instrumentation group, light/security group, dual electric remote control mirrors and trim rings with center hubs ($582). Automatic transaxle package with wide vinyl body moldings, electronic AM/FM stereo radio, digital clock and overhead console, tinted glass, interval wipers, the instrumentation group, the light and security group, dual electric remote-control mirrors

1988 Taurus LX station wagon

1988 Taurus LX sedan

1988 LTD Country Squire station wagon

and trim rings with center hubs ($823). Console with graphic systems monitor ($56). Flip-up open-air roof ($355). Electronic AM/FM stereo radio ($137). Premium sound system ($138). Manual air conditioning ($688). Front center arm rest ($55). Heavy duty battery ($27). Electronic digital clock and overhead console ($82). Rear window defroster ($145). Tinted glass ($105). Instrumentation group ($87). Light and security group, GL ($91) or GT ($67). Deluxe luggage rack ($115). Color-keyed remote-control mirrors ($88). Wide vinyl body moldings ($50). Clear coat paint on GL ($91). AM radio ($39). Electronic AM/FM stereo, Pony ($206) and GL ($167). Electronic AM/FM radio with cassette, Pony ($343); GL ($304) and GT ($137). Premium sound system ($138). Speed control ($182). Split fold down rear seat ($49). Tilt wheel ($124). Styled road wheels ($195). Interval windshield wipers ($55). Rear window wiper and washer ($126). Heavy duty alternator ($27). Engine block heater ($18). Full size spare tire ($73). Five-speed manual transmission ($76). Automatic transaxle, GL ($490). Power steering ($235). Heavy duty handling suspension ($26).

EXP: EXP Special value package ($961). Four-speed manual transaxle package with four-speed manual, vinyl body moldings, AM/FM stereo, digital clock and overhead console, power steering, tinted glass, interval wipers, rear window defroster, instrumentation group, light and security group, dual remote control mirrors and trim rings with center hubs ($582). Automatic transaxle package with vinyl body moldings, AM/FM stereo, digital clock and overhead console, tinted glass, interval wipers, dual remote-control mirrors and trim rings with center hubs ($823). Sun and sound group including console with graphic systems monitor ($56). Flip-up open air roof ($355). AM/FM stereo ($137). Premium sound system, Luxury Coupe ($586). Manual air conditioner ($688). Heavy-duty battery ($27). Rear window defroster ($145). Tinted glass ($105). Instrumentation group ($87).). AM/FM stereo with cassette ($137). Premium sound system ($138). Speed control ($182). Tilt wheel ($124). Trim rings with center hubs ($67). Styled road wheels ($195). Rear window wiper and washer ($126). Heavy-duty alternator ($27). Automatic transaxle ($415). Power steering ($235).

Tempo: Preferred equipment packages: 2-door GL ($245); 4-door GL ($295); 4-door GL ($1,013); 4-door LX ($748) and 4-door LX ($984). Manual air conditioner ($773). Front center armrest ($55). Rear window defroster ($145). Sport instrument cluster ($87). Deck lid luggage rack ($115). Power lock group, 2-door ($237) and 4-door ($287). Dual electric remote control mirrors ($111). AM/FM stereo radio with cassette ($141). Power driver's seat ($251). Premium sound system ($138). Speed control ($182). Tilt steering wheel ($124). Polycast wheels ($176). Power side windows, 4-door ($296). Clear coat metallic paint ($91). All vinyl seat and trim ($37). Heavy duty battery ($27). Engine block heater ($94). Automatic transaxle ($482).

Taurus: Preferred equipment packages: L, 201A=$1,203, 4-door GL sedan, 203A=$1,366, 204A=$1,808, 4-door GL station wagon, 203A=$1,316 and 204A=$1,758. LX, 207A=$559 and 208A=$1,495. MT5 four-door sedan, 212A=$972. Electronic climate control air conditioning, L or GL ($971). LX or Packages 201A, 203A or 204A ($183). Manual air conditioning ($788). Autolamp system ($73). Heavy-duty battery ($27). Cargo area cover ($66). Electronic digital clock ($78). Cornering lamps ($68). Rear window defroster ($145). Engine block heater ($18). Remote fuel door and deck lid release, sedans ($91). Remote fuel door release, station wagons ($41). Extended range fuel tank ($46). Illuminated entry system ($82). Diagnostic ($89). Electronic, LX ($239) and others, except MT5 ($351). Light group ($59).

Load floor ("picnic table") extension ($66). Power door locks ($195). Dual illuminated visor mirrors: L ($116) and GL or MT5 ($104). Power moon roof ($741). Clear coat paint ($183). High level audio system, package 207A ($167) and package 212A ($335). All other Taurus ($472). Electronic AM/FM stereo search radio with cassette ($137). Premium sound system ($168). Power antenna ($76). Rear facing third seat ($155). Six-way power driver's seat ($251). Six-way dual power seats, LX and packages 204A or 212A ($251). All other Taurus ($502). Speed control ($182). Tilt steering column ($124). Leather-wrapped steering wheel ($59). Rear window washer and wiper ($126). Leather seat trim, LX ($415); GL and MT5 ($518). Vinyl seat trim, L ($51) and others ($37). Bolt-on luxury wheel covers with packages 203A or 204A ($21). All other Taurus ($85). Finned wheel covers ($65). Custom 15-inch locking wheel covers, L or GL ($212), LX or packages 203A or 204A ($148) or with packages 207A or 208A ($34) and on the MT5 ($127). Cast aluminum wheels, L or GL ($227), MT5 ($141), LX or packages 203A or 204A ($162) and packages 207A or 208A ($49). Styled road wheels: L or GL ($178), MT5 ($93), LX or packages 203A or 204A ($113). Power side windows ($296). Insta-clear windshield ($250). Interval windshield wipers ($55). 3.0-liter V-6, L ($672). 3.8-liter V-6: LX, L and GL wagons ($396) and other Taurus models ($1,068). Heavy duty handling suspension ($26).

LTD Crown Victoria: Preferred equipment packages: LTD Crown Victoria 4-door, 110A ($472); LTD Crown Victoria LX 4-door, 111A ($699), 112A ($988) and 113A ($1,564); LTD Crown Victoria LTD 4-door and Country Squire station wagon, 130A ($587) and 131A ($1,385); LTD Country Squire 4-door station wagon, 130A ($472) and 131A ($1,270); LTD Country Squire LX 4-door station wagon and LTD Crown Victoria LX 4-door, 132A ($756) and 133A ($1,191) and LTD Crown Victoria S, 120A ($352) and 121A ($1,085). Automatic temperature control air conditioning with packages 110A, 111A, 112A, 130A, 131A or 132A ($66) and all others ($211). High level audio system with package 112A or 132A ($335) and with package 113A or 133A ($167). All other Crown Victorias ($472). Heavy duty battery ($27). Cornering lamps ($68). Rear window defroster ($145). Engine block heater ($18). Illuminated entry system ($82). Light group ($59). Power lock group ($245). Deluxe luggage rack ($115). Vinyl insert body moldings ($66). Electronic AM/FM stereo search radio with cassette and Dolby noise reduction system ($137). Power antenna ($76). Premium sound system ($168). Power six-way driver's seat ($251). Dual control power seats with packages 111A, 112A, 113A, 131A, 132A or 133A ($2,511) and ($502) other models. Dual facing rear seats ($173). Speed control ($182). Leather-wrapped steering wheel ($59). Tilt steering wheel ($124). Tripminder computer ($215). Locking wire wheel covers ($212). Cast aluminum wheels ($390). Power side windows with dual remote mirrors ($379). Insta-clear windshield ($250). Brougham vinyl roof ($665). All vinyl seat trim ($37). Duraweave vinyl seat trim ($96). Leather seat trim ($415). 100 ampere alternator ($52). Remote deck lid release ($50). Deluxe 15-inch wheel covers ($49). Traction-Lok differential ($100). Heavy-duty handling suspension ($26). Auto load leveling ($195). Trailer towing package ($387 to $399).

History:

The 1988 Fords were introduced on Oct. 1, 1987. The Tempo was introduced in November 1987 and the Second Series Escort and EXP debuted on May 12, 1988. Total model year production was 1,606,531, including Mustangs. The calendar year sales by U.S. dealers was 1,527,504, including Mustangs. Escort and EXP started off the year in the same form, but were replaced by a modestly modified Second Series in the spring. For the first time in nearly a decade, the full-size LTD Crown Victoria got a notable restyling. Tempo earned a more

1988 LTD Crown Victoria sedan

modest restyle, while Taurus added some performance with a new engine choice. During 1987, Taurus had become Ford's top seller, displacing the Escort. In addition to the domestic models, Ford now offered a Korean-built Festiva subcompact, designed by Mazda.

1989 Ford

Escort — Four: Following its mild face lift during the 1988 model year, the Escort entered 1989 with little change. With the EXP two-seater gone, the remaining Escort lineup included only the Pony and GT (both in two-door hatchback form only), and the LX (in three body styles). The 1989 models had gas-charged struts. The base 1.9-liter four produced 90 hp, while the GT's high-output version, with its multi-port fuel injection, delivered 115 hp.

Tempo — Four: Little change was evident on this year's compact Tempo sedan. It received a notable aero facelift a year earlier. GL models added nitrogen-pressurized shock absorbers. GLS had a new standard front center armrest. All models got an emissions-system warning light. A stretchable cargo tie-down net went into GLX, LX and All-Wheel-Drive models.

Probe — Four: The new Probe was a separate model with its two-door hatchback body and interior designed by Ford. Its chassis and power train were shared with the Mazda MX-6 coupe, also produced at the Flat Rock, Michigan, plant. The base and GL, powered by a 110-hp Mazda 2.2-liter (12-valve) four and the GT, with a turbocharged/intercooled 145 hp four variant were available. A five-speed manual gearbox was standard while four-speed automatic was optional on the GL/LX. Standard equipment included cloth reclining front bucket seats, power brakes and steering, tachometer, gauges, AM/FM stereo radio and a tinted backlight and quarter windows. The LX added such items as full tinted glass, a tilt steering column, power mirrors and a rear defogger. The sporty GT added front and rear disc brakes, alloy wheels, automatically-adjustable performance suspension and P195/60-VR15 tires on alloy wheels.

Taurus — Four and V-6: Most of the attention this year went to the new Taurus SHO, a high-performance model with special dual-overhead-cam 3.0-liter V-6 (four valves per cylinder) that churned out 220 hp. The engine was built by Yamaha, and the only transmission was a Mazda-built five-speed manual (designed by Ford). SHO also included disc brakes on all four wheels, a special handling suspension, dual exhausts, and P215/65-R15 performance tires on aluminum alloy wheels. The SHO added a set of subtle ground-effects body panels headed by a front air dam with fog lamps. Interior touches included a leather-wrapped steering wheel, analog gauges, power front sport seats with lumbar adjustment, 140-mph speedometer, 8000-rpm tachometer, a rear defogger, console with cup holders and armrest, and power windows. With the demise of the MT5, SHO was the only Taurus with manual shift.

LTD Crown Victoria — V-8: Since it enjoyed a significant facelift a year earlier, the full-size rear-drive Ford returned with few changes for 1989.

1989 Escort GT hatchback coupe

Base and LX trim levels were offered, a four-door sedan and station wagon body styles, all powered by a 150-hp 5.0-liter V-8 with four-speed overdrive automatic. Standard equipment included air conditioning, tinted glass and automatic headlamp on and off. On the dashboard, an engine-systems warning light replaced the former low-oil indicator.

I.D. Data:

Ford's 17-symbol Vehicle Identification Number (VIN) was stamped on a metal tab fastened to the instrument panel and was visible through the windshield. The first three symbols indicated the manufacturer, make and vehicle type. The fourth symbol denoted the restraint system. Next came letter P followed by two digits that indicated the model number, such as P90=Escort Pony two-door hatchback. Symbol eight indicated the engine type. Next was a check digit. Symbol 10 indicated the model year: K=1989. Symbol 11 denoted the assembly plant. The final six digits made up the sequence numbers, starting with 000001 (except Probe, 500001).

Escort (Four))

Model No.	Body/ Style No.	Body Type & Seating	Factory Price	Shipping Weight	Production Total
90	------	2-dr. Pony Hatchback-4P	$6,964	2,235 lbs.	Note 1
91	------	2-dr. LX Hatchback-4P	$7,349	2,242 lbs.	Note 1
95	------	4-dr. LX Hatchback-4P	$7,679	2,313 lbs.	110,631
98	------	4-dr. LX Station Wagon-4P	$8,280	2,312 lbs.	30,888
93	------	2-dr. GT Hatchback-4P	$9,315	2,442 lbs.	Note 1

Note 1: Production of two-door hatchbacks totaled 201,288 with no further breakout available.

Tempo (Four)

Model No.	Body/ Style No.	Body Type & Seating	Factory Price	Shipping Weight	Production Total
31	66D	2-dr. GL Sedan-5P	$9,057	2,529 lbs.	Note 1
36	54D	4-dr. GL Sedan-5P	$9,207	2,587 lbs.	Note 2
37	54D	4-dr. LX Sedan-5P	$10,156	2,628 lbs.	Note 2
39	54D	4-dr. AWD Sedan-5P	$10,860	2,787 lbs.	Note 2
33	66D	2-dr. GLS Sedan-5P	$9,697	2,545 lbs.	Note 1
38	54D	4-dr. GLS Sedan-5P	$9,848	2,603 lbs.	Note 2

Note 1: Production of two-door sedans totaled 23,719 with no further breakout available.
Note 2: Production of four-door sedans totaled 217,185 with no further breakout available.

Probe (Four)

Model No.	Body/ Style No.	Body Type & Seating	Factory Price	Shipping Weight	Production Total
20	------	2-dr. GL Coupe-4P	$10,459	2,715 lbs.	Note 1
21	------	2-dr. LX Coupe-4P	$11,443	2,715 lbs.	Note 1
21	------	2-dr. GT Coupe-4P	$13,593	2,870 lbs.	Note 1

Note 1: Production of two-door coupes totaled 162,889 with no further breakout available.

Taurus (Four)

Model No.	Body/ Style No.	Body Type & Seating	Factory Price	Shipping Weight	Production Total
50	54D	4-dr. L Sedan-6P	$11,778	2,901 lbs.	Note 1
52	54D	2-dr. GL Sedan-6P	$12,202	2,927 lbs.	Note 1

Taurus (V-6)

Model No.	Body/ Style No.	Body Type & Seating	Factory Price	Shipping Weight	Production Total
50	54D	4-dr. L Sedan-6P	$12,450	3,020 lbs.	Note 1
55	74D	4-dr. L Station Wagon-6P	$13,143	3,172 lbs.	Note 2
52	54D	4-dr. GL Sedan-6P	$12,874	3,046 lbs.	Note 1
57	74D	4-dr. GL Station Wagon-6P	$13,544	3,189 lbs.	Note 2
53	54D	2-dr. LX Sedan-6P	$15,282	3,076 lbs.	Note 1
58	74D	4-dr. LX Station Wagon-6P	$16,524	3,220 lbs.	Note 2
54	54D	4-dr. SHO Sedan-6P	$19,739	3,078 lbs.	Note 1

Note 1: Production of four-door sedans totaled 284,175 with no further breakout available.
Note 2: Production of station wagons totaled 87,013 with no further breakout available.

LTD Crown Victoria (V-8)

Model No.	Body/ Style No.	Body Type & Seating	Factory Price	Shipping Weight	Production Total
73	54K	4-dr. Sedan-6P	$15,851	3,730 lbs.	Note 1
72	54K	4-dr. S Sedan-6P	$15,434	3,696 lbs.	Note 1
76	74K	4-dr. Station Wagon-6P	$16,209	3,941 lbs.	Note 2
78	74K	4-dr. Country Squire-6P	$16,527	3,935 lbs.	Note 2

Note 1: Production of four-door sedans totaled 110,437 with no further breakout available.
Note 2: Production of station wagons totaled 12,549 with no further breakout available.

LTD Crown Victoria LX (V-8)

Model No.	Body/ Style No.	Body Type & Seating	Factory Price	Shipping Weight	Production Total
74	54K	4-dr. Sedan-6P	$16,767	3,770 lbs.	Note
77	74K	4-dr. Station Wagon-8P	$17,238	3,915 lbs.	Note
79	74K	4-dr. Country Squire-8P	$17,556	4,013 lbs.	Note

Note: See production figures for Crown Victoria models above.

1989 Taurus SHO sedan

Engines:

Escort Base Four: Inline. Overhead cam. Cast-iron block and aluminum head. Displacement: 113 cid (1.9 liters). B & S: 3.23 x 3.46 in. Compression ratio: 9.0:1. Brake hp: 90 at 4600 rpm. Torque: 106 lbs.-ft. at 3400 rpm. Five main bearings. Hydraulic valve lifters. Throttle-body fuel injection.

Escort GT Base Four: High-output. Multi-port fuel-injected version of 1.9-liter four with 110 hp at 5400 rpm. Torque: 115 lbs.-ft. at 4200 rpm.

Probe Base Four: Inline. Overhead cam. Cast-iron block. Displacement: 133 cid (2.2 liters). B & S: 3.39 x 3.70 in. Compression ratio: 8.6:1. Brake hp: 110 at 4700 rpm. Torque: 130 lbs.-ft. at 3000 rpm. Hydraulic valve lifters. Port fuel injection.

Probe GT Turbocharged Four: Same as 2.2-liter but with turbocharger and intercooler: Compression ratio: 7.8:1. Brake hp: 145 at 4300 rpm. Torque: 190 lbs.-ft. at 3500 rpm.

Tempo Base Four: Inline. Overhead valve. Cast-iron block and head. Displacement: 140 cid (2.3 liters). B & S: 3.70 x 3.30 in. Compression ratio: 9.0:1. Brake hp: 98 at 4400 rpm. Torque: 124 lbs.-ft. at 2200 rpm. Five main bearings. Hydraulic valve lifters. Multi-point fuel injection. High Swirl Combustion (HSC) design.

Tempo AWD and Sport Base Four: High-output version of HSC four with Brake hp: 100 at 4400 rpm. Torque: 130 lbs.-ft. at 2600 rpm.

Taurus Base Four: Inline. Overhead valve. Cast-iron block and head. Displacement: 153 cid (2.5 liters). B & S: 3.70 x 3.60 in. Compression ratio: 9.0:1. Brake hp: 90 at 4400 rpm. Torque: 130 lbs.-ft. at 2600 rpm. Five main bearings. Hydraulic valve lifters. Throttle body fuel injection.

Taurus LX and Taurus wagon Base V-6 (Optional Taurus): 60-degree, overhead valve. Cast-iron block and head. Displacement: 182 cid (3.0 liters). B & S: 3.50 x 3.10 in. Compression ratio: 9.3:1. Brake hp: 140 at 4800 rpm. Torque: 160 lbs.-ft. at 3000 rpm. Four main bearings. Hydraulic valve lifters. Multi-port fuel injection.

Taurus SHO Base V-6: Duel-overhead-cam with 24 valves. Cast-iron block and head. Displacement: 182 cid (3.0 liters). B & S: 3.50 x 3.10 in. Compression ratio: 9.8:1. Brake hp: 220 at 6000 rpm. Torque: 200 lbs.-ft. at 4800 rpm. Four main bearings. Hydraulic valve lifters. Sequential port fuel injection.

Taurus Optional V-6: 90-degree, overhead valve. Cast-iron block and aluminum head. Displacement: 232 cid (3.8 liters). B & S: 3.80 x 3.40 in. Compression ratio: 9.0:1. Brake hp: 140 at 3800 rpm. Torque: 215 lbs.-ft. at 2200 rpm. Four main bearings. Hydraulic valve lifters. Port fuel injection.

1989 LTD Crown Victoria sedan

1989 Taurus LX station wagon

LTD Crown Victoria Base V-8: 90-degree, overhead valve. Cast-iron block and head. Displacement: 302 cid (5.0 liters). B & S: 4.00 x 3.00 in. Compression ratio: 8.9:1. Brake hp: 150 at 3200 rpm. Torque: 270 lbs.-ft. at 2000 rpm. Five main bearings. Hydraulic valve lifters. Sequential port fuel injection.

Chassis:

Escort: Wheelbase: 94.2 in. Overall length: 166.9 in. and 168.0 in., wagon. Tires: Pony, P175/70-R14 and GT P195/60-HR15.

Tempo: Wheelbase: 99.9 in. Overall length: 176.5 in. Tires: P185/70-R14.

Probe: Wheelbase: 99.0 in. Overall length: 177.0 in. Tires: P185/70-SR14 and GT P195/60-VR15.

Taurus: Wheelbase: 106.0 in. Overall length: 188.4 in. and 191.9 in., wagon. Tires: P195/70-R14; LX, P205/70-R14 and SHO, P215/65-R15.

Crown Victoria: Wheelbase: 114.3 in. Overall length: 211.0 in. and 216.0 in., wagon. Tires: P215/70-R15.

Options:

Escort: Escort GT special value package, 330A ($815). Five-speed manual transaxle package with power steering, electronic digital clock, overhead console, rear window defroster, tinted glass plus instrumentation group, light security group, dual electric remote control mirrors, wide vinyl body moldings, electronic AM/FM stereo radio, luxury wheel covers, interval windshield wipers, 2- and 4-door LX hatchback, 320A ($560) and 4-door LX Wagon ($484). Automatic transaxle package includes all of 320A with automatic transaxle replacing five-speed manual, 2- & 4-door LX hatchback, 321A ($938) and 4-door LX wagon ($863). Manual air conditioner ($720). Heavy duty battery ($27). Digital clock and overhead console ($82). Rear window defroster ($150). Tinted glass ($105). Instrumentation group ($87). Light and security group, LX ($91) and GT ($67). Deluxe luggage rack ($115). Color-keyed electronic remote control mirrors ($98). Wide vinyl body moldings ($50). Clear coat paint, LX ($91) and GT, including Tu-Tone ($183). Tu-Tone Paint ($91). AM Radio ($54). Electronic AM/FM stereo, Pony ($206) and LX ($152). Electronic AM/FM with cassette, Pony ($343), LX ($289) and GT ($137). Premium sound system ($138). Speed control ($191). Split fold-down rear seat ($50). Power steering ($235). Tilt steering ($124). Luxury wheel covers ($71). Vinyl trim ($37). Polycast wheels ($193). Interval windshield wipers ($55). Rear window wiper and washer ($126). Heavy duty alternator ($27). Engine block heater ($20). Full size spare tire ($73). P175/70-R14 whitewalls, LX ($73). Five-speed manual transmission, LX sedan ($76). Automatic transaxle ($490) and LX wagon ($415). Power steering ($235).

Tempo: Preferred equip packages: 226A, 2-door GL ($449) and 4-door GL ($499); 227A 4-door GL ($1,250); 229A, 2-door GLS ($1,220); 229A, 4-door GLS ($1,270); 233A 4-door LX ($863); 234A 4-door LX ($1,099) and 232A, 4-door AWD ($352). Manual air conditioner ($807). Rear window defroster ($150). Sport instrument cluster ($87). Deck lid luggage rack ($115). Power lock group, 2-door ($246) and 4-door ($298). Dual electronic remote control mirrors ($121). AM/FM stereo radio with cassette ($137). Power driver's seat ($261). Premium sound system ($138). Speed control ($191). Sports appearance group ($1,178). Tilt steering wheel ($124). Supplemental air bag restraint system, GL ($815) and LX ($751). Polycast wheels ($193). Power side windows, 4-door ($306). Clear coat metallic paint ($91). Lower accent paint treatment ($159). All vinyl Seat and trim ($37). Engine block heater ($20). P185/70-R14 whitewalls ($82). Automatic transaxle ($515).

Probe: Preferred equipment packages: Tinted glass, interval wipers, light group, dual electric remote group, tilt steering column and cluster, rear window defroster, 251A ($334). Electronic instrument cluster, electronic control air conditioner, illuminated entry, leather-wrapped steering wheel and transaxle shift knob, power driver's seat, trip computer, rear washer and wiper, walk-in passenger seat, power windows, speed control, power door locks, AM/FM electronic cassette with premium sound and power antenna, 253A ($2,214). Anti-lock braking system, electronic air conditioning, illuminated entry, leather-wrapped steering wheel and transaxle shift knob, power driver's seat, trip computer, vehicle maintenance monitor with overhead console, rear washer and wiper, walk-in passenger seat, power windows, speed control, power door locks, AM/FM electronic cassette with premium sound system and power antenna, 261A ($2,621). Manual air conditioner with package 250A, including tinted glass ($927). Other Probe models ($807). Rear window defroster ($150). Power door locks ($155). Speed control ($191). Flip-up open-air roof ($355). Aluminum wheels, with GL ($290) and with LX ($237). AM/FM electronic stereo radio w/ premium sound system ($168). AM/FM electronic cassette with premium sound system and power antenna ($344). AM/FM premium electronic cassette with premium sound system, CD player, power antenna, with packages 251A, 252A, or 260A ($1,052); with packages 253A or 261A ($708). Engine block heater ($20). Automatic transaxle ($617).

Taurus: Preferred packages: GL, 204A ($1,749); LX, 207A ($777); 208A, Sedan ($1,913) and wagon ($1,513); SHO, 211A ($533). Electronic

1989 Escort LX station wagon

1989 Tempo AWD sedan

climate control air conditioning package, 202A ($971) and SHO, LX or package 204A ($183). Manual air conditioning ($807). Autolamp system ($73). Heavy duty battery ($27). Cargo area cover ($66). Cornering lamps ($68). Rear window defroster ($150). Engine block heater ($20). Remote fuel door, deck lid or liftgate release ($91). Extended range fuel tank ($46). Illuminated entry system ($82). Diagnostic instrument cluster ($89). Electronic instruments, LX ($239) and GL ($351). Keyless entry system with package 207A or 211A ($137) and on other Taurus models ($218). Light group ($59). Load floor "picnic table" extension ($66). Power door locks ($205). Dual illuminated visor mirrors ($100). Power moon roof ($741). Clear coat paint ($183). Auto parking brake release ($12). High level audio system with package 204A ($335) or package 207A ($167). Other Taurus models ($472). Electronic AM/FM stereo search radio with cassette ($137). Premium sound system ($168). Power radio antenna ($76). JBL audio system ($488). Rear facing third seat ($155). Six-way power driver's seat ($261). Dual six-way power seats, LX or package 204A or 211A ($261). Other Taurus models ($502). Speed control ($191). Tilt steering column ($124). Leather-wrapped steering wheel ($63). Rear window washer and wiper ($126). Finned wheel covers ($65). Custom 15-inch locking wheel covers, with package 202A ($212) or with package 204A ($148). Cast aluminum wheels, L or GL ($279), LX or package 204A ($215) and packages 207A or 208A ($49). Styled road wheels, GL ($193), LX or 204A ($128). Power windows ($306). Insta-clear windshield ($250). Interval windshield wipers ($55). Leather seat trim, LX and SHO ($489) and GL ($593). Vinyl seat trim, L ($51) or GL ($37). Bolt-on luxury wheel covers with package 204A ($21) and other models ($85). P205/70-R14 whitewalls ($82). P205/65-R15 blackwalls ($65). P205/65-R15 whitewalls ($146). Conventional spare tire ($73). Engines: 3.0-liter V-6, L and GL sedan ($672). 3.8-liter V-6: Taurus GL wagon ($400) and other Taurus ($1,072). Heavy duty handling and suspension ($26).

Crown Victoria: Preferred packages: 4-door LTD Crown Victoria LX, 111A ($383); 4-door LTD Crown Victoria LX, 112A ($938); 4-door LTD Crown Victoria LX, 113A ($1,514); 4-door LTD Crown Victoria wagon and Country Squire wagon, 131A ($1,280); 4-door LTD Crown Victoria LX wagon and Country Squire LX wagon, 132A ($688); 4-door LTD Crown Victoria LX Wagon and Country Squire LX wagon, 133A ($1,191); 4-door LTD Crown Victoria S, 120B ($66) and 4-door LTD Crown Victoria S, 121A ($802). Auto temperature control air conditioning with packages 111A, 112A, 131A or 132A ($66). Other Crown Victoria models ($216). High level audio system with packages 112A or 132A ($335) or with packages 113A or 133A ($167). Other Crown Victoria models ($472). Heavy duty battery ($27). Cornering lamps ($68). Rear window defroster ($150). Engine block heater ($20). Illuminated entry system ($82). Light group ($59). Power lock group ($255). Vinyl insert body moldings ($66). Clear coat paint ($226). Electronic AM/FM stereo search radio with cassette tape player and Dolby noise reduction system ($137). Power radio antenna ($76). Premium sound system ($168). Power six-way driver's seat ($261). Dual control power seats with packages 112A, 131A, or 132A ($251) and with other models ($522). Dual facing rear seat, wagons ($173). Speed control ($191). Leather-wrapped steering wheel ($63). Tilt steering wheel ($124). Tripminder computer ($215). Style locking wire wheel covers ($228). Cast aluminum wheels ($40). Power windows and dual electronic remote mirrors ($389). Insta-clear windshield ($250). Brougham half vinyl roof ($665). Duraweave vinyl

1989 Probe GT

seat trim ($96). Leather seat trim ($489). 100 ampere alternator ($52). Electronic digital clock ($96). Remote deck lid release ($50). Deluxe 15-inch wheel covers ($49). Traction-Lok differential ($100). Heavy duty handling and suspension ($26). Auto load leveling ($195). Trailer towing package ($387 to $399).

History:

The 1989 Fords were introduced on Oct. 6, 1988. The Thunderbird premiered on Dec. 26, 1988 and Probe appeared on May 12, 1988. The model year production was 1,505,908, including Mustangs. Calendar year sales by U.S. dealers were 1,433,550, including Mustangs. The sporty new Probe coupe arrived, a product of a joint venture between Ford and Mazda, but built in Michigan. The Thunderbird was restyled, including a Super Coupe with a supercharged V-6 engine. That SC was named *Motor Trend* magazine's "Car Of The Year." Taurus also jumped on the performance bandwagon with the "Super High Output" (SHO) engine in its SHO edition. The car ran the 0-60 mph standard test in the eight-second neighborhood.

1990 Ford

Escort — Four: Not much was new in the Ford subcompact for 1990, since an all-new version was expected for 1991. Rear shoulder belts became standard this year, to complement the motorized front belts. The model lineup was unchanged with a Pony two-door hatchback, the LX in three body styles, and the sporty GT two-door hatchback. The GT version of the 1.9-liter four-cylinder engine produced 110 hp, versus 90 hp for the base power plant.

Tempo — Four: Little was new this year for the popular compact Ford sedans, except the addition of standard floor mats and both foot well and trunk lights. Polycast wheels got a fresh look. Two versions of the 2.3-liter four-cylinder engine were available, and Tempo came in three trim levels plus the All Wheel Drive four-door. A five-speed manual gearbox was standard. The AWD had standard three-speed automatic.

Probe — Four and V-6: The Probe got a new V-6 engine choice. Only the GL came with a standard Mazda-built four-cylinder engine. Probe's GT again carried a turbocharged and intercooled four, and the LX got the 140-hp, 3.8-liter V-6. A GT choice was the four-speed overdrive automatic transmission. Four-wheel disc brakes were standard on the LX and anti-lock brakes were optional. All Probes got new front and rear fascias. New body moldings and cladding adorned the GT. Its alloy wheels were restyled. The GT also got a new soft-feel steering wheel and other models got leather on the wheel and gearshift knob.

1990 Escort GT three-door hatchback

1990 Escort LX station wagon

1990 Probe LX coupe

Taurus — Four and V-6: Anti-lock braking joined the Taurus sedan option list this year, and all models got a standard air bag (with tilt steering) on the driver's side. The instrument panel was revised and now held coin and cup holders. The popular mid-size front-drive sedans and wagons continued in three trim levels plus the performance-oriented SHO. All but the L sedan could have the optional 3.8-liter V-6 engine instead of the 2.5-liter four or 3.0-liter V-6. The V-6 engines came with four-speed overdrive automatic. SHO continued its special double-overhead-cam, 24-valve 3.0-liter V-6, available only with a five-speed manual gearbox.

LTD Crown Victoria — V-8: No major changes were evident in the full-size Ford, but quite a few minor revisions appeared. A driver's side air bag was standard and a coolant temperature gauge went on the revised instrument panel. The glove compartment grew in size. A split bench seat was new and replaced the full bench arrangement. All back seats held shoulder belts. New standard equipment included power windows and mirrors plus tilt steering. Crown Victorias came in a dozen colors this year, including five new ones. The lone power train continued to be the 5.0-liter V-8 with a four-speed overdrive automatic.

I. D. Data:

Ford's 17-symbol Vehicle Identification Number (VIN) was stamped on a metal tab fastened to the instrument panel and was visible through the windshield. The first three symbols indicated the manufacturer, make, and vehicle type. The fourth symbol denoted the restraint system. Next came letter P followed by two digits that indicated the model number, such as P90=Escort Pony two-door hatchback. Symbol eight indicated the engine type. Next was a check digit. Symbol 10 indicated the model year: L=1990. Symbol 11 denoted the assembly plant. The final six digits made up the sequential number, starting with 000001, except the Probe, 500001.

Escort (Four))

Model No.	Body/ Style No.	Body Type & Seating	Factory Price	Shipping Weight	Production Total
90	-----	2-dr. Pony Hatchback-4P	$7,423	2,083 lbs.	-----
91	-----	2-dr. LX Hatchback-4P	$7,827	2,090 lbs.	-----
95	-----	4-dr. LX Hatchback-4P	$8,157	2,144 lbs.	-----
98	-----	4-dr. LX Station Wagon-4P	$8,758	2,177 lbs.	-----
93	-----	2-dr. GT Hatchback-4P	$9,842	2,519 lbs.	-----

Tempo (Four)

31	66D	2-dr. GL Sedan-5P	$9,505	2,418 lbs.	Note 1
36	54D	4-dr. GL Sedan-5P	$9,655	2,467 lbs.	Note 2
37	54D	4-dr. LX Sedan-5P	$10,607	2,508 lbs.	Note 2
39	54D	4-dr. AWD Sedan-5P	$11,330	2,689 lbs.	Note 2
33	66D	2-dr. GLS Sedan-5P	$10,180	2,434 lbs.	Note 1
38	54D	4-dr. GLS Sedan-5P	$10,328	2,483 lbs.	Note 2

Note 1: Production of two-door sedans totaled 8,551. No further breakout was available.

Note 2: Production of four-door sedans totaled 209,875 with no further breakout available.

1990 Ford Taurus SHO sedan

Probe (Four/V-6)

20	-----	2-dr. GL Coupe-4P	$11,574	2,715 lbs.	Note 1
21	-----	2-dr. LX Coupe-4P	$13,113	2,715 lbs.	Note 1
21	-----	2-dr. GT Coupe-4P	$14,838	2,715 lbs.	Note 1

Note: Probe LX had a V-6 engine.

Note 1: Production of two-door coupes totaled 109,898 with no further breakout available.

Taurus (Four)

50	54D	4-dr. L Sedan-6P	$12,594	2,765 lbs.	Note 1
52	54D	4-dr. GL Sedan-6P	$13,067	3,049 lbs.	Note 1

Taurus (V-6)

50	54D	4-dr. L Sedan-6P	$13,290	2,885 lbs.	Note 1
55	74D	4-dr. L Station Wagon-6P	$13,983	3,062 lbs.	Note 2
52	54D	4-dr. GL Sedan-6P	$13,763	3,169 lbs.	Note 1
57	74D	4-dr. GL Station Wagon-6P	$14,433	3,095 lbs.	Note 2
53	54D	4-dr. LX Sedan-6P	$16,095	2,999 lbs.	Note 1
58	74D	4-dr. LX Station Wagon-6P	$17,338	3,233 lbs.	Note 2
54	54D	4-dr. SHO Sedan-6P	$21,505	2,985 lbs.	Note 1

Note 1: Production of four-door sedans totaled 233,153. No further breakout was available.

Note 2: Production of station wagons totaled 75,531 with no further breakout available.

LTD Crown Victoria (V-8)

73	54K	4-dr. Sedan-6P	$17,106	3,611 lbs.	------
72	54K	4-dr. S Sedan-6P	$16,479	3,591 lbs.	------
76	74K	4-dr. Station Wagon-6P	$17,512	3,795 lbs.	------
78	74K	4-dr. Country Squire-6P	$17,830	3,834 lbs.	------

LTD Crown Victory LX (V-8)

74	54K	4-dr. Sedan-6P	$17,743	------	------
77	74K	4-dr. Station Wagon-8P	$18,262	3,834 lbs.	------
79	74K	4-dr. Country Squire-8P	$18,580	3,873 lbs.	------

Engines:

Escort Base Four: Inline. Overhead cam. Cast-iron block and aluminum head. Displacement: 113 cid (1.9 liters). B & S: 3.23 x 3.46 in. Compression ratio: 9.0:1. Brake hp: 90 at 4600 rpm. Torque: 106 lbs.-ft. at 3400 rpm. Five main bearings. Hydraulic valve lifters. Throttle-body fuel injection.

Escort GT Base Four: High-output, multi-port fuel-injected version of 1.9-liter. Brake hp: 110 at 5400 rpm. . Torque: 115 lbs.-ft. at 4200 rpm.

Probe Base Four: Inline. Overhead cam. Cast-iron block. Displacement: 133 cid (2.2 liters). B & S: 3.39 x 3.70 in. Compression ratio: 8.6:1. Brake hp: 110 at 4700 rpm. Torque: 130 lbs.-ft. at 3000 rpm. Hydraulic valve lifters. Port fuel injection.

Probe GT Turbocharged Four: Same as 2.2-liter with turbocharger and intercooler. Compression ratio: 7.8:1. Brake hp: 145 at 4300 rpm. Torque: 190 lbs.-ft. at 3500 rpm.

Tempo Base Four: Inline. Overhead valve. Cast-iron block and head. Displacement: 140 cid (2.3 liters). B & S: 3.70 x 3.30 in. Compression ratio: 9.0:1. Brake hp: 98 at 4400 rpm. Torque: 124 lbs.-ft. at 2200 rpm. Five main bearings. Hydraulic valve lifters. Port fuel injection.

Tempo AWD: High-output HSC engine. Brake hp: 100 at 4400 rpm. Torque: 130 lbs.-ft. at 2600 rpm.

Taurus Base Four: Inline. Overhead valve. Cast-iron block and head. Displacement 153 cid (2.5 liters). B & S: 3.70 x 3.60 in. Compression ratio: 9.0:1. Brake hp: 90 at 4400 rpm. Torque: 130 lbs.-ft. at 2600 rpm. Five main bearings. Hydraulic valve lifters. Throttle-body fuel injection.

Probe LX, Taurus LX and Taurus wagon Base V-6 (Optional Taurus): 60-degree, overhead valve. Cast- iron block and head. Displacement: 182 cid (3.0 liters). B & S: 3.50 x 3.10 in. Compression ratio: 9.3:1. Brake hp: 140 at 4800 rpm. Torque: 160 lbs.-ft. at 3000 rpm. Four main bearings. Hydraulic valve lifters. Multi-port fuel injection.

1990 Tempo sedan

1990 LTD Crown Victoria sedan

Taurus SHO Base V-6: Dual-overhead-cam with 24 valves. Cast-iron block and head. Displacement: 182 cid (3.0 liters). B & S: 3.50 x 3.10 in. Compression ratio: 9.8:1. Brake hp: 220 at 6200 rpm. Torque: 200 lbs.-ft. at 4800 rpm. Four main bearings. Hydraulic valve lifters. Sequential-port fuel injection.

Taurus Optional V-6: 90-degree, overhead valve. Cast-iron block and aluminum head. Displacement: 232 cid (3.8 liters). B & S: 3.80 x 3.40 in. Compression ratio: 9.0:1. Brake hp: 140 at 3800 rpm. Torque: 215 lbs.-ft. at 2200 rpm. Four main bearings. Hydraulic valve lifters. Port fuel injection.

Chassis:

Escort: Wheelbase: 94.2 in. Overall length: 169.4 in. Tires: P175/70-R14 and GT, P195/60-HR15.

Tempo: Wheelbase: 99.9 in. Overall length: 176.7 in., two-door and 177.0 in., four-door Tires: P185/70-R14.

Probe: Wheelbase: 99.0 in. Overall length: 177.0 in. Tires: P185/70-R14, P195/70-R14, LX and P205/60-VR15, GT.

Taurus: Wheelbase: 106.0 in. Overall length: 188.4 in. and 191.9 in., station wagon. Tires: P195/70-14, P205/70-R14, LX and P215/65-R15 SHO.

Crown Victoria: Wheelbase: 114.3 in. Overall length: 211.0 in. and 215.7 in., wagon. Tires: P215/70-R15.

Options:

Escort: LX Series: Five-speed manual transaxle package, electronic digital clock and overhead console, rear window defroster, tinted glass, instrumentation group, including odometer, temp gauge, white graphics, light and security group including illuminated passenger side visor mirror, glove box light, cargo compartment lights, engine compartment light, rear door courtesy light switch (4-door), headlamps-on chimes, remote lift gate release (hatchback), dual electronic remote control mirrors, vinyl body moldings, electronic AM/FM stereo radio, power steering, luxury wheel covers, interval wipers and 2- and 4-door LX hatchback, 302A ($562) and 4-door LX wagon ($486). Automatic transaxle package includes all equipment in 320A with automatic transaxle, 321A, 2- and 4-door LX hatchback ($965) and 4-door LX wagon ($889). Preferred equipment package, GT, includes High-Output four-cylinder engine, five-speed transaxle, air conditioning, rear window defroster, tinted glass, light security group, electronic AM/FM stereo radio with cassette, speed control, tilt steering wheel and interval wipers, 330A ($829). Air conditioner ($720). Heavy duty battery ($27). Electronic digital clock and overhead console ($82). Rear window defroster ($150). Tinted glass ($105). Instrumentation group with tachometer, trip odometer, temp gauge and white graphics ($87). Light and security group with illuminated passenger side visor mirror, glove box light, cargo compartment light, engine compartment light, rear door courtesy light switch (4-door), headlamps-on chimes, remote lift gate release (hatchback), LX ($78); GT ($67). Deluxe luggage rack ($115). Color-keyed electric remote control mirrors ($98). Vinyl body moldings ($50). Clear coat paint, LX ($91) and GT, including two-tone paint ($183). Two-tone paint ($91). AM radio ($54). Electronic AM/FM stereo, Pony ($206) and LX ($152). Electronic AM/FM with cassette tape player, Pony ($343); LX ($289) and GT ($137). Premium sound system ($138). Speed control ($191). Split fold-down rear seat ($50). Tilt steering wheel ($124). Luxury wheel covers ($71). Polycast wheels ($193). Interval windshield wipers ($55). Rear window wiper and washer ($126). Heavy duty alternator ($27). Eng block heater ($20). Full size spare tire ($73). P175/70-R14 whitewall tires, LX ($73). Five-speed manual transmission, LX sedan ($76). Automatic transaxle ($515) and LX wagon ($439). Power steering, Pony and LX ($235).

Probe: Preferred equipment packages including tinted glass, tilt steering column and cluster, rear window defroster, convenience group including interval wipers, light group including glove box light, under-hood lights, fade-to-off dome lamp, headlamps-on warning light, dual electric remote mirrors, 251A ($158). Electronic instrument cluster, electronic air conditioning, illuminated entry, power driver's seat, trip computer, rear washer and wiper, walk-in passenger seat, power windows, speed control, power door locks, AM/FM electronic cassette with premium sound and power antenna plus cargo net, 253A ($2,088). Anti-lock braking system, electronic air conditioning, illuminated entry, power driver's seat, trip computer, vehicle maintenance monitor in overhead console, rear washer and wiper, walk-in passenger seat, power windows, speed control, power door locks, AM/FM electronic cassette player with premium sound and power antenna, dual illuminated visor vanity mirrors and cargo net, 261A ($2,795). Air conditioner with package 250A including tinted glass ($927) and on other Probe models ($807). Rear window defroster ($150). Leather seating surface trim ($489). Power door locks ($155). Speed control ($191). Flip-up open-air roof ($355). Aluminum wheels: with GL, packages 250A or 251A ($313) and with LX, packages 252A or 253A ($252). Power windows ($241). AM/FM electronic stereo radio with premium sound ($168). AM/FM electronic cassette with premium sound and power antenna ($344). AM/FM premium electronic cassette player with premium sound, CD player and power antenna with packages 251A, 252A or 260A ($1,052) and with packages 253A or 261A ($709). Engine block heater ($20). Automatic transaxle ($617). Anti-lock brakes on Probe LX or GT ($924).

Tempo: Preferred equipment packages: 2-door GL including five-speed manual, air conditioning, rear window defroster, light group, power lock group and power deck lid release, remote fuel filler door, dual electric remote control mirrors and tilt wheel, 226A ($486) and ($538), 4-door GL. Special value GLS with five-speed manual, air conditioner, power lock group, power deck lid release, remote fuel filler door, tilt steering wheel, power driver's seat, premium sound system and speed control, 229A 2-door GLS ($1,267) and 4-door GLS ($1,319). Special value LX with automatic transaxle, air conditioner, rear window defroster, and deck lid luggage rack, 4-door LX, 233A ($911). Special value AWD with automatic transaxle, rear window defroster, power lock group, power deck lid release, remote fuel filler door, tilt steering wheel, power windows, 4-door AWD ($378). Air conditioner ($807). Front center armrest ($55). Rear window defroster ($150). Sport instrument cluster ($87). Light group with lights for glove box, engine compartment, dome, door switches & map light ($38). Deck lid luggage rack ($115). Power lock group, power door locks, power deck lid release and remote fuel filler door, 2-door ($246) and 4-door ($298). Dual electric remote control mirrors ($121). Electronic AM/FM stereo radio with cassette ($137). Power driver's seat ($261). Premium sound system with four speakers and amplifier ($138). Speed control ($191). Sports appearance group ($1,178). Tilt steering wheel ($124). Supplemental air bag restraint system, GL ($815) and LX or GL with package 226A ($690). Polycast wheels ($193). Power windows, 4-door ($306). Clear coat metallic paint ($91). All vinyl seat trim ($37). Engine block heater ($20). P185/70-R14 whitewall tires ($82). Automatic transaxle ($539).

Taurus: Preferred equip package, GL, includes 4-cyl. engine, automatic transaxle, air conditioning, speed control, remote deck lid or lift gate and fuel door releases, dual beam map light, engine compartment light, dual courtesy lights, headlamps-on reminder chime, rear window defroster, power door locks, six-way power driver's seat, finned wheel covers and power windows, 202A ($1,688). LX includes 3.0-liter V-6, air conditioning, rear window defroster, power door locks, electronic AM/FM stereo radio with cassette, six-way power driver's seat, power windows, cast aluminum or styled wheels, auto lamp system, illuminated entry system, premium sound system and leather-wrapped steering wheel, 207A ($748). LX sedan includes 3.8-liter V-6, speed control, remote deck lid or lift gate and fuel door releases, dual beam map light, engine compartment light, dual courtesy lights, headlamps-on reminder chime, power door locks, cast aluminum wheels, autolamp system, leather-wrapped steering wheel, electronic climate control air conditioning, anti-lock braking system, high level audio system, electronic instrument cluster, keyless entry system, power antenna and six-way power dual control seats, 208A ($3,099) or ($1,714) LX Wagon. SHO includes DOHC 3.0-liter V-6, five-speed manual, air conditioning, speed control, remote deck lid or lift gate and fuel door releases, dual beam map light, engine compartment light, dual courtesy lights, headlamps-on reminder chime, rear window defroster, power door locks, six-way power driver's seat, power windows, cast aluminum wheels, autolamp system, illuminated entry system, leather-wrapped steering wheel, anti-lock braking system and high level audio system, 211A ($533). DOHC 3.0-liter V-8, five-speed manual transmission, speed control, remote deck lid or lift gate and fuel door releases, light group, rear window defroster,

1990 LTD Country Squire station wagon

power door locks, power windows, cast aluminum wheels, autolamp system, leather-wrapped steering wheel, electronic climate control air conditioning, anti-lock braking system, high level audio system, keyless entry system, power radio antenna, JBL audio system, six-way power dual control seats, leather seat trim and power moon roof, 212A ($2,724). Conventional spare tire ($73). Electronic air conditioning with package 202A ($990) or SHO, LX, or package 204A ($183). Manual air conditioning ($807). Autolamp system ($73). Heavy duty battery ($27). Cornering lamps ($68). Rear window defroster ($150). Engine block heater ($20). Remote deck lid and fuel door, sedans ($91) and wagons ($41). Extended range fuel tank ($46). Illuminated entry system ($82). Diagnostic instrument cluster ($89). Electronic instrument cluster, LX ($239) and GL ($351). Keyless entry system with package 207A or 211A ($137) and other models ($218). Light group ($59). "Picnic table" load floor extension ($66). Power door locks ($205). Dual illuminated visor mirrors ($100). Power moon roof ($741). Clear coat paint ($188). Automatic parking brake release ($12). CD player ($491). High level audio system with package 204A ($335) or with package 207A ($167). Other models ($472). Electronic AM/FM stereo search radio with cassette player ($137). Premium sound system ($168). Power radio antenna ($76). JBL audio system ($488). Rear facing third seat, wagons ($155). Six-way power driver's seat ($261). Dual six-way power seats, LX or packages 204A or 211A ($261) and other models ($522). Speed control ($191). Leather-wrapped steering wheel ($63). Rear window washer and wiper ($126). Finned wheel covers ($65). Cast aluminum wheels, GL ($279), LX or package 204A ($215). Styled Road Wheels, GL ($193) and LX or package 204A ($128). Power windows ($306). Insta-clear windshield ($250). Leather seat trim, LX and SHO ($489) or GL ($593). Vinyl seat trim, L ($51) and GL ($37). P205/70-R14 whitewalls ($82), P205/65-R15 blackwalls ($65) and P205/65-R15 whitewalls ($146). 3.0-liter V-6, L and GL sedan ($696). 3.8-liter V-6, GL wagon and LX sedan ($400) and Taurus GL sedan ($1,096). Variable-assisted power steering ($104). Anti-lock brakes ($985).

LTD Crown Victoria: 4-Dr LTD Crown Victoria LX: Automatic overdrive transmission, rear window defroster, speed control, power lock group, electronic AM/FM stereo radio with cassette and light group, 112A ($420). Equipment in 112A plus six-way power driver's seat, cast aluminum wheels, light group, cornering lamps, illuminated entry system and leather-wrapped steering wheel, 113A ($859).) Automatic overdrive transmission, speed control, power lock group, cast aluminum wheels, light group, cornering lamps, illuminated entry system, leather-wrapped steering wheel, automatic climate control air conditioning, high level audio system, power antenna and dual six-way power Seats, 114A ($1,490). Four-door LTD Crown Victoria and Country Squire wagons: Automatic overdrive transmission, rear window defroster, speed control, power lock group, electronic AM/FM stereo radio with cassette, six-way power driver's seat, dual facing rear seats, 131A ($938). Four-door LTD Crown Victoria LX and Country Squire wagons, package 133A includes all equipment in 131A plus cast aluminum wheels, heavy duty battery, cornering lamps, illuminated entry system and leather-wrapped steering wheel ($779). Package 134A included all equipment in 133A with rear window defroster, electronic AM/FM stereo with cassette, six-way power driver's seat plus auto climate control air conditioning, high level audio, power radio antenna and dual six-way power seats ($1,117). Automatic temperature air conditioner with 112A, 113A, 131A or 133A ($66) and other models ($216). Heavy duty battery ($27). Cornering Lamps ($68). Rear window defroster ($150). Engine block heater ($20). Illuminated entry system ($82). Light group ($59). Power lock group ($255). Vinyl body moldings ($66). Clear coat paint ($230). High level audio system with 112A, 113A, 131A or 133A ($335) and other models ($472). Electronic AM/FM stereo radio with cassette player ($137). Power antenna ($76). Premium sound system ($168). Six-way power driver's seat ($261). Dual six-way power seats with packages 113A, 131A or 133A ($261) and other models ($522). Dual facing rear seats ($173). Speed control ($191). Leather-wrapped steering wheel ($63). Locking wire styled wheel covers ($228). Cast aluminum wheels ($440). Insta-clear windshield ($250). Brougham half vinyl roof ($665). All-Vinyl Seat Trim ($37). Duraweave Vinyl Seat Trim ($96). Leather Seat Trim ($489). Traction-Lok differential ($100). Heavy duty handling and suspension ($26). Auto load leveling ($195). Trailer towing package ($378 to $405).

The 1990 Ford model year production was 1,258,428, including Mustangs. Calendar year sales by U.S. dealers was 1,880,389, including Mustangs. The Fords, Escort and Taurus, were edged out by the popular American-made, Japanese backed Honda Accord as America's best selling car for calendar year 1989. A new Escort was being prepared for 1991. The sporty Probe hatchback coupe, introduced for 1989, gained a V-6 engine in one of its models. Performance continued to play a strong role in the Ford lineup, with the availability of the Taurus SHO, Probe GT and Thunderbird Super Coupe.

1991 Ford

Escort — Four: All new for 1991, the Escort featured a revamped profile with a lower cowl and belt that provided more glass area and improved visibility. The new Escort featured an ergonomically-designed, wraparound instrument panel and a larger interior package with five-passenger seating. The Escort was available in Pony, LX and GT including two- and four-door hatchbacks and station wagons. The Pony and LX versions were powered by the upgraded 1.9-liter four-cylinder engine, rated at 88 hp. The GT used the Mazda-produced 127-hp DOHC 1.8-liter four. The five-speed manual transmission was standard and the four-speed automatic was optional. Four-wheel disc brakes were standard on the GT.

Tempo — Four: Improvements were made to reduce noise and vibration for 1991. Included in these upgrades were front structure enhancements, a new engine mount bracket, new fan and new front spring isolators. The five-passenger Tempo was available in GL (two- and four-door sedans), GLS (two- and four-door sedans), LX (four-door sedan) and the four-door Tempo all-wheel-drive sedan. The 2.3-liter HSC (high swirl combustion) four-cylinder engine was the standard powerplant on GL and LX models. An HSO (higher specific output) version was used with the GLS and four-wheel-drive Tempos. A five-speed manual was the base unit for Tempos except the automatic transaxle-equipped AWD model.

Probe — Four and V-6: The two-door Probe was again offered in GL, LX and GT. Probe GL continued using the 2.2-liter, 12-valve electronically fuel-injected four-cylinder while the Probe LX used the 3.0-liter electronically fuel-injected V-6. The Probe GT was powered by the turbocharged 2.2-liter electronically fuel-injected four. The five-speed manual overdrive transmission was standard and the four-speed automatic with overdrive was optional equipment. Anti-lock brakes were optional on the LX model's four-wheel power disc brakes. The GT model's handling suspension featured sport-tuned performance components and a computerized Automatic Adjusting Suspension.

Taurus — Four and V-6: The Taurus underwent significant improvements. It was available in L, GL, LX and the SHO sedan. The LX sedans and station wagons came with standard anti-lock brakes while the Taurus SHO sedan received new 16-inch cast aluminum wheels with Goodyear GT+4 performance tires. The SHO also got a larger clutch with lower pedal effort and a smoother shifting five-speed transaxle. The new Taurus "L-Plus" was offered and came with air conditioning, rear window defroster, power locks and the automatic transaxle. The

1991 Escort GT three-door hatchback

1991 Escort LX station wagon

1991 Escort GT

Taurus GL's option list included bucket seats, floor-mounted shifter and a console. All Taurus models had standard driver's side air bags. The Taurus L and GL sedans were powered by the 2.5-liter four-cylinder engine. It received sequential electronic multi-port fuel injection and a 15-hp boost to 105 hp. Taurus L and GL station wagons and the LX sedan used the 3.0-liter V-6 engines. They also received sequential electronic multi-port fuel injection. The Taurus SHO sedan came with the 220-hp DOHC 3.0-liter 24-valve V-6. The LX station wagon was powered by the 3.8-liter V-6. All except the aforementioned SHO model used the electronic overdrive four-speed automatic transaxle.

LTD Crown Victoria — V-8: Awaiting the spring 1991 launch of the all-new 1992 Crown Victoria models, the 1991 models were essentially carry-overs. The three series of sedans were again base, S and LX. For the final time, the Crown Victoria and Country Squire station wagons were available. All models were powered by the 5.0-liter V-8 mated to a four-speed automatic overdrive transmission.

I. D. Data:

Ford's 17-symbol Vehicle Identification Number (VIN) was stamped on a metal tab fastened to the instrument panel and was visible through the windshield. The first three symbols indicated the manufacturer, make and vehicle type. The fourth symbol denoted the restraint system. Next came letter P followed by two digits that indicated the model number such as P10=Escort Pony two-door hatchback. Symbol eight indicated the engine type. Next was a check digit. Symbol 10 indicated the model year: M= 1991. Symbol 11 denoted the assembly plant. The final six digits make up the sequential production number, starting with 000001 or 500001, Probe.

Escort (Four)

Model No.	Body/Style No.	Body Type & Seating	Factory Price	Shipping Weight	Production Total
P	10	2-dr. Pony Hatchback-5P	$7,976	2,287 lbs.	Note 1
P	11	2-dr. LX Hatchback-5P	$8,667	2,312 lbs.	Note 1
P	14	4-dr. LX Hatchback-5P	$9,095	2,355 lbs.	114,944
P	15	4-dr. GL Station Wagon-5P	$9,680	2,411 lbs.	57,337
P	12	2-dr. GT Hatchback-5P	$11,484	2,458 lbs.	Note 1

Note 1: Production of two-door hatchback models totaled 182,445 with no further breakout available.

Tempo (Four)

P	30	2-dr. L Sedan-5P	$8,306	------	Note 1
P	35	4-dr. L Sedan-5P	$8,449	------	Note 2
P	31	2-dr. GL Sedan-5P	$9,541	2,529 lbs.	Note 1
P	36	4-dr. GL Sedan-5P	$9,691	2,587 lbs.	Note 2
P	37	4-dr. LX Sedan-5P	$10,663	2,628 lbs.	Note 2
P	39	4-dr. AWD Sedan-5P	$11,390	2,808 lbs.	Note 2
P	33	2-dr. GLS Sedan-5P	$10,358	2,545 lbs.	Note 1
P	38	4-dr. GLS Sedan-5P	$10,506	2,603 lbs.	Note 2

Note 1: Production of two-door sedan models totaled 4,876 and no further breakouts were available.

Note 2: Production of four-door sedan models totaled 180,969 with no further breakouts available.

Probe (Four and V-6 in LX only)

T	20	2-dr. GL Coupe-4P	$11,691	2,730 lbs.	Note 1
T	21	2-dr. LX Coupe-4P	$13,229	2,970 lbs.	Note 1
T	22	2-dr. GT Coupe-4P	$14,964	3,000 lbs.	Note 1

Note 1: Production of two-door coupe models totaled 73,200 with no further breakout available.

Taurus (Four)

P	50	4-dr. L Sedan-6P	$13,352	3,049 lbs.	Note 1
P	55	4-dr. GL Sedan-6P	$13,582	3,062 lbs.	Note 1

Taurus (V-6)

P	50	4-dr. L Sedan-6P	$13,873	3,097 lbs.	Note 1
P	55	2-dr. L Station Wagon-6P	$14,874	3,276 lbs.	Note 2
P	52	4-dr. GL Sedan-6P	$14,103	3,110 lbs.	Note 1
P	57	4-dr. GL Station Wagon-6P	$14,990	3,283 lbs.	Note 2
P	53	4-dr. LX Sedan-6P	$17,373	3,170 lbs.	Note 1
P	58	4-dr. LX Station Wagon-6P	$18,963	3,345 lbs.	Note 2
P	54	4-dr. SHO Sedan-6P	$22,071	3,463 lbs.	Note 1

Note 1: Production of four-door sedans totaled 218,311 and no further breakouts were available.

Note 2: Station wagon production totaled 62,786 with no further breakouts available.

LTD Crown Victoria (V-8)

P	73	4-dr. Sedan-6P	$18,227	3,822 lbs.	Note 1
P	72	4-dr. S Sedan-6P	$17,045	3,822 lbs.	Note 1
P	76	4-dr. Station Wagon-6P	$18,083	4,028 lbs.	Note 2
P	78	4-dr. Country Squire-6P	$18,335	4,027 lbs.	Note 2

LTD Crown Victoria LX (V-8)

P	74	4-dr. Sedan-6P	$18,863	3,841 lbs.	Note 1
P	77	4-dr. Station Wagon-8P	$18,833	4,021 lbs.	Note 2
P	79	4-dr. Country Squire-8P	$19,085	4,082 lbs.	Note 2

Note 1: Production of four-door sedan models totaled 91,315 with no further breakout available.

Note 2: Production of station wagon models totaled 8,000 with no further breakout available.

Engines:

Escort Base Four: Inline. Overhead cam. Cast-iron block and aluminum head. Displacement: 113 cid (1.9 liters). B & S: 3.23 x 3.46 in. Compression ratio: 9.0:1. Brake hp: 90 at 4600 rpm. Torque: 106 lbs.-ft. at 3400 rpm. Five main bearings. Hydraulic valve lifters. Sequential port fuel injection.

Escort GT Base Four: High-output, DOHC multi-port fuel injected version of 1.9-liter. Hp: 127 at 6500 rpm. Torque: 114 lbs.-ft. at 4500 rpm.

Probe Base Four: Inline. Overhead cam. Cast-iron block. Displacement: 133 cid (2.2 liters). B & S: 3.39 x 3.70 in. Compression ratio: 8.6:1. Brake hp: 110 at 4700 rpm. Torque: 130 lbs.-ft. at 3000 rpm. Hydraulic valve lifters. Multi-port fuel injection.

Probe Turbocharged Four: Same as 2.2-liter four but with turbocharger and intercooler. Compression ratio: 7.8:1. Hp: 145 at 4300 rpm. Torque: 190 lbs.-ft. at 3500 rpm.

Tempo Base Four: Inline. Overhead valve. Cast-iron block and head. Displacement: 140 cid (2.3 liters). B & S: 3.70 x 3.30 in. Compression ratio: 9.0:1. Brake hp: 98 at 4400 rpm. Torque: 124 lbs.-ft. at 2200 rpm. Five main bearings. Hydraulic valve lifters. Multi-port fuel injection. High Swirl Combustion (HSC) design.

Tempo AWD Base Four: High-output version of HSC four. Hp: 100 at 4400 rpm. Torque: 130 lbs.-ft. at 2600 rpm.

Taurus Base Four: Inline. Overhead valve. Cast-iron block and head. Displacement: 153 cid (2.5 liters). B & S: 3.70 x 3.60 in. Compression ratio: 9.0:1. Brake hp: 105 at 4400 rpm. Torque: 140 lbs.-ft. at 2400 rpm. Five main bearings. Hydraulic valve lifters. Sequential-port fuel injection.

Probe LX, Taurus L and GL wagons, Taurus LX sedan Base V-6 (Optional Taurus L and GL sedans): 60-degree, overhead. Cast-iron block and head. Displacement: 182 cid (3.0 liters). B & S: 3.50 x 3.10 in. Compression ratio: 9.3:1. Brake hp: Probe LX, 145 at 4800 rpm and 140 at 4800 rpm, all others. Torque: 165 lbs.-ft. at 3400 rpm, Probe LX and 160 lbs.-ft. at 3000 rpm, all others. Four main bearings. Hydraulic valve lifters. Multi-port fuel injection, Probe LX and sequential fuel injection, all others.

Taurus SHO Base V-6: Dual-overhead-cam with 24 valves. Cast-iron block and head. Displacement: 182 cid (3.0 liters). B & S: 3.50 x 3.15 in. Compression ratio: 9.8:1. Brake hp: 220 at 6200 rpm. Torque: 200 lbs.-

1991 Taurus LX sedan

1991 Taurus LX station wagon

1991 Taurus SHO sedan

1991 Tempo GL sedan

ft. at 4800 rpm. Four main bearings. Hydraulic valve lifters. Sequential-port fuel injection.

Optional Taurus GL sedan and wagon and LX sedan V-6: 90-degree, overhead valve. Cast-iron block and aluminum head. Displacement: 232 cid (3.8 liters). B & S: 3.80 x 3.40 in. Compression ratio: 9.0:1. Brake hp: 140 at 3800 rpm. Torque: 215 lbs.-ft. at 2200 rpm. Four main bearings. Hydraulic valve lifters. Sequential-port fuel injection.

LTD Crown Victoria Base V-8: 90-degree, overhead valve. Cast-iron block and head. Displacement: 302 cid (5.0 liters). B & S: 4.00 x 3.00 in. Compression ratio: 8.9:1. Brake hp: 150 at 3200 rpm. Torque: 270 lbs.-ft. at 2000 rpm. Five main bearings. Hydraulic valve lifters. Sequential-port fuel injection.

Chassis:

Escort: Wheelbase: 98.4 in. Overall length: 170.0 in. and 171.3 in., station wagon. Tires: P175/70-R13, Pony and P185/60-HR15, GT.

Tempo: Wheelbase: 99.9 in. Overall length: 176.7 in., two-door and 177.0 in., four-door. Tires: P185/70-R14.

Probe: Wheelbase: 99.0 in. Overall length: 177.0 in. Tires: P185/70-SR14, P195/70-R14, Probe LX and P205/60-VR15, Probe GT.

Taurus: Wheelbase: 106.0 in. Overall length: 188.4 in. and 191.9 in., station wagon. Tires: P205/70R14, P205/70-R14, LX and P215/60-R16, SHO.

LTD Crown Victoria: Wheelbase: 114.3 in. Overall Length: 211.0 in. and 215.7 in. wagon. Tires: P215/70-R15.

Options:

Escort: Preferred equip package, LX: Power steering, light group and electric rear window defroster ($185). Preferred equipment package GT: Electric rear window defroster, manual air conditioning and luxury convenience group ($496). California emission system ($70). Air conditioning, LX and GT ($744). Rear window defroster ($160). Light and convenience group included dual map lights and lighted cargo area, under hood and ignition key plus dual illuminated visor vanity mirrors and dual power mirrors ($290). Luxury convenience group included tilt steering wheel, cruise control, power door locks, tachometer (standard on GT): LX ($251 to $334) and GT ($336). Power moon roof, LX and GT ($549). Clear coat paint ($91). AM/FM stereo radio, Pony ($245). AM/FM radio with cassette player, Pony ($400) and LX ($155). Premium sound system ($138). Power steering, LX and GT ($235). The wagon group package included a deluxe luggage rack and rear window wiper and washer ($241). Four-speed automatic transaxle ($732). Power steering, LX and GT ($235).

Tempo: Preferred equipment package, GL series: Manual air conditioning, light group, dual electric remote control mirrors and tilt steering wheel ($294). Preferred equipment package GL two-door and four-door: All GL items plus rear window defroster, front center armrest, power lock group, electronic AM/FM stereo radio with cassette and clock, automatic FLC transaxle and polycast wheels: two-door ($1,346) and four-door ($1,388). Preferred equip group, SRS GL: Same as GL two-door/four-door equipment minus tilt steering wheel, electronic AM/FM stereo radio with cassette and clock plus polycast wheels ($1,377). Preferred equip package, GLS two-door and four-door: Manual air conditioning, tilt steering wheel and power lock group: two-door ($1,366) and four-door ($1,408). Preferred equip package, LX: Manual air conditioning, rear window defroster, electronic AM/FM stereo radio with cassette and clock plus automatic FLC transaxle ($1,060). Preferred equipment package, AWD: Tilt steering wheel, rear window defroster,

electronic AM/FM stereo radio with cassette and clock plus power lock group ($533). California emissions system ($100). Manual air conditioning ($817). Front center armrest ($55). Rear window defroster ($160). Instrument cluster ($87). Light group ($38). Power lock group, two-door ($276) and four-door ($318). Luggage rack ($115). Dual electric remote control mirrors ($121). Clear coat paint ($91). Electronic AM/FM stereo radio with cassette and clock ($155). Power driver's seat ($290). Premium sound system ($138). Speed control ($210). Tilt steering wheel ($135). Air bag (driver's side only): SRS GL ($815) and LX ($690). Polycast wheels ($193). Power windows, four-door ($315). Engine block heater ($20). P185/70-R14 whitewall tires ($82). Three-speed automatic transaxle, standard in AWD ($563).

Probe: Preferred equipment package, GL: Tinted glass, tilt steering column and cluster, rear window defroster, convenience group including interval wipers, light group, dual electric remote control mirrors ($179). Preferred equipment package, LX: Manual air conditioning, illuminated entry system, rear washer and wiper, walk-in passenger seat, power windows, speed control, power door locks, electronic AM/FM radio with cassette and premium sound system plus power antenna and cargo net ($1,545). Preferred equipment package, GT: Same as LX ($1,645). Manual air conditioning and tinted glass ($937). Electronics group: LX ($82) and GT ($182). Rear window defroster ($160). Leather bucket seats, LX and GT ($489). Power driver's seat, LX and GT ($290). Power door locks ($195). Speed control ($210). Anti-lock brakes, LX and GT ($924). Flip-up open-air roof, LX and GT ($355). Aluminum wheels, GL ($313) and LX ($376). Power windows, LX and GT ($260). Tinted glass ($120) and standard on LX and GT. Electronic AM/FM stereo radio with cassette player and premium sound system ($368). AM/FM electronic stereo with CD player, premium sound system and power antenna ($709). California emissions system ($100). Engine block heater ($20). Four-speed automatic transaxle ($732). Anti-lock brakes, LX and GT ($924).

Taurus: Preferred equipment package L Plus: Power door locks, manual air conditioning, rear window defroster and paint stripe ($964). Preferred equipment package GL sedan and wagon: Power door locks, manual air conditioning, rear window defroster, paint stripe, power windows and power six-way driver's seat, GL sedan ($1,804) and GL wagon ($1,754). Preferred equip package LX: Rear window defroster, paint stripe, electronic AM/FM stereo radio with cassette, speed control, cast aluminum wheels and P205 15-in. tires, autolamp system, leather-wrapped steering wheel, illuminated entry system and premium sound system ($795). Preferred equipment package LX sedan and wagon: Rear window defroster, paint stripe, speed control, cast aluminum wheels and P205 15-in. tires, autolamp system, leather-wrapped steering wheel, anti-lock brakes, electronic climate control air conditioning, high-level audio system, keyless entry, power antenna, dual control six-way power seats, electronic instrument cluster, variable speed sensitive power steering and 3.8-liter V-6 with automatic overdrive transmission: sedan ($3,336) and LX Wagon ($2,781). Preferred equipment package, SHO sedan: Electronic climate control air conditioning, dual control six-way power seats, autolamp system, keyless entry system, high level audio system and power radio antenna ($724). Conventional spare tire ($73). Electronic air conditioning: GL ($1,000) or SHO and LX ($183). Manual air conditioning ($817). Autolamp system ($73). Heavy duty battery ($27). Cornering lamps ($68). Rear window defroster ($160). Engine block heater ($20). Remote deck lid and fuel door, sedans ($91) and wagons (fuel door) ($41). Extended range fuel tank ($46). Illuminated entry system ($82). Electronic instrument cluster, LX ($239) and GL ($351). Keyless entry system, GL or LX ($218). Light group for L or GL ($59). "Picnic table" wagon load floor extension ($66). Power door locks, L Plus ($226). Dual illuminated visor mirrors ($100). Power moon roof ($776). Clear coat paint ($188). Automatic parking brake release ($12). Electronic AM/FM stereo radio with cassette player ($155). Power antenna ($82). Rear facing third seat, wagons ($155). Dual control six-way power seats ($290). Speed control ($210). Leather-wrapped steering wheel ($63). Rear window washer and wiper, wagons ($126). Heavy duty suspension ($26). Variable speed sensitive power steering ($104). Finned wheel covers ($65). Cast aluminum wheels, LX ($279) and GL or L Plus ($344). Styled road wheels: LX ($128) and GL or L Plus ($193). Insta-clear windshield ($305). California emissions system ($100). Leather bucket seats with console, LX or SHO ($489) and

1991 LTD Country Squire station wagon

($593). Vinyl split bench seat, L or GL ($37). P205/70-R14 whitewalls ($82). 3.0-liter V-6, L and GL sedan ($521). 3.8-liter V-6, GL ($1,276). Anti-lock brakes ($985).

LTD Crown Victoria: The options were the same as those listed in the 1990 section. The new, 1992 LTD Crown Victoria was launched in spring 1991. That car's equipment is listed in the 1992 Ford section. Some selected 1991 options included: Traction-Lok differential ($100). Heavy duty handling and suspension ($26). Automatic load leveling suspension ($250). Trailer towing package ($405).

History:

U.S. model year production in 1991 totaled 1,162,256, including Mustangs. Ford's market share was 14.2 percent of the industry. The Taurus, Escort and Tempo all ranked in the Top 10-second, fifth and tenth, respectively-in U.S. car sales for calendar year 1991. Coming off a year where Ford's U.S. automotive operations lost a reported $17 million, and predictions for an even tougher year for sales in 1991, Ford maintained a high level of product development. The new 1992 Crown Victoria was introduced in early 1991. It followed the 1991 Escort, launched in the spring of 1990. The Escort's new design was primarily contributed by Mazda Motor Corp. The car was built in both Mexico and domestically in Wayne, Michigan.

1992 Ford

Escort — Four: The Escort was basically unchanged for 1992, the second year for its redesign look. The lineup was revamped with the Escort Pony dropped and the LX sedan and performance-minded LX-E sedan added. The lineup now consisted of the base three-door hatchback, the LX three and five-door hatchbacks, four-door sedan and station wagon, the LX-E four-door sedan and the GT three-door hatchback. The new LX and LX-E sedans came standard with split fold-down rear seats. The LX model also came standard with 14-inch wheels, two-speed interval wipers, four-wheel independent suspension, rack-and-pinion steering, color-keyed bumpers and an AM/FM stereo radio. The LX-E sedan shared the 16-valve DOHC 1.8-liter four-cylinder engine found in the GT. Standard LX-E equipment included 14-inch styled aluminum wheels, modified GT front seats and door trim, four-wheel disc brakes and sport suspension. A five-speed manual transaxle was standard on Escorts, with the electronic four-speed automatic overdrive transaxle optional.

1992 Tempo GLS sedan

1992 Tempo GLS coupe

1992 Probe GT coupe

Tempo — Four: The big news for 1992 Tempo buyers was the 140-hp 3.0-liter V-6, standard on the GLS and optional on the GL and LX series. All V-6-equipped Tempos offered a touring suspension with performance tires, tuned gas shock absorbers and a rear stabilizer bar. The Tempo GLS had sport suspension. The four-wheel-drive Tempo offered previously was discontinued. Tempo was available as a two- or four-door sedan in the GL series, a two- or four-door sedan in the GLS series, and a four-door sedan in the LX series. The base engine was the 2.3-liter four-cylinder and it added sequential electronic fuel injection as an upgrade. Both the GL and LX series received minor exterior refinements plus a single-belt accessory drive system to reduce noise and vibration. The GLS was restyled with new bumper and body cladding, fog lamps, bright exhaust tips, 15-inch aluminum wheels and performance tires. A rear deck spoiler was used on the two-door GLS. Other 1992 Tempo refinements included a color-keyed grille and color-keyed body moldings that gave Tempo a monochromatic look. Standard equipment included the five-speed manual transaxle.

Probe — Four and V-6: Probe returned with its three series lineup in 1992, GL, LX and GT, but added an LX Sport option model that featured a rear deck spoiler, 15-inch aluminum wheels and performance tires. Two new "tropical" colors were offered to Probe buyers, Calypso green and Bimini blue. Probe GL continued using the 2.2-liter, 12-valve electronically fuel-injected four-cylinder engine. The LX and LX Sport were powered by a 3.0-liter electronically fuel-injected V-6 engine. The Probe GT used the turbocharged 2.2-liter electronically fuel-injected four. The five-speed manual overdrive transaxle was standard and the four-speed automatic with overdrive was optional equipment. Anti-lock brakes were optional on the LX, LX Sport and GT, all equipped with four-wheel power disc brakes as standard equipment. The same trio of coupes also came equipped with tilt steering column/instrument panel, while the LX driver's seat offered manual adjustments for tilt, lumbar support and side bolsters.

Taurus — V-6: The 1992 Taurus had a virtually all-new body as well as receiving improvements in interior appointments. The Taurus SHO sedan was also restyled to emphasize its performance character. The 1992 Taurus consisted of four-door sedans and station wagons in the L, GL and LX series as well as the SHO sedan. The Taurus exterior trim included ornamentation, bumpers and rocker panel moldings. The Taurus' overall length was increased 3.8 inches for 1992. Nine new exterior colors were offered and other additions included tinted outside rearview mirrors, new wheel covers and new aluminum wheels. Inside the Taurus, additions included an optional passenger side air bag, a "flow-through" dashboard, more legible gauges and larger, illuminated power window switches. A four-cylinder engine was no longer available in a Taurus. The standard power train for the L, GL and LX sedans and L and GL wagons was the 140-hp 3.0-liter V-6 with sequential electronic fuel injection and the electronically controlled four-speed automatic overdrive transaxle. The LX wagon was powered by the 3.8-liter V-6, optional on other Taurus models. It also used the four-speed automatic. The SHO sedan used a DOHC 220-hp 24-valve 3.0-liter V-6 and a five-speed manual transaxle. The redesign of the SHO sedan included a more aggressive look with color-keyed body and rocker panel moldings, integrated fog lamps, a special rear bumper and 16-inch aluminum wheels.

Crown Victoria — V-8: The new, 1992 Crown Victoria was introduced in the spring of 1991. A Touring Sedan was added to the lineup in 1992, but the station wagon models were discontinued. A revision of the name was in order as the Crown Vic line no longer used the LTD prefix. The three-model line consisted of four-door sedans in base, LX

1992 Crown Victoria Touring Sedan

and Touring Sedan trim levels. The Crown Victoria models all featured speed-sensitive steering, four-wheel disc brakes, a rear stabilizer bar and standard driver's side air bag. Anti-lock brakes and traction control were standard equipment on the Touring Sedan and optional on the base and LX sedans. Options included a rear air-suspension and passenger side air bag. Performance and efficiency were improved due to a new 4.6-liter modular V-8, rated at 190 hp. The Touring Sedan was powered by a 210-hp 4.6-liter V-8. The four-speed automatic overdrive transmission was used in all Crown Vics.

I. D. Data:

Ford's 17-symbol Vehicle Identification Number (VIN) was stamped on a metal tab fastened to the instrument panel and was visible through the windshield. The first three symbols indicated the manufacturer, make and vehicle type. The fourth symbol denoted the restraint system. Next came letter P followed by two digits that indicated the model number, such as P10=Escort two-door hatchback. Symbol eight indicated the engine type. Next was a check digit. Symbol 10 indicated the model year: N=1992. Symbol 11 denoted the assembly plant. The final six digits make up the sequence number, starting with 000001.

Escort (Four)

Model No.	Body/ Style No.	Body Type & Seating	Factory Price	Shipping Weight	Production Total
P	10	2-dr. Hatchback-5P	$8,355	2,287 lbs.	Note 1
P	11	2-dr. LX Hatchback-5P	$9,055	2,312 lbs.	Note 1
P	14	4-dr. LX Hatchback-5P	$9,483	2,355 lbs.	57,651*
P	13	4-dr. LX Sedan-5P	$9,795	2,364 lbs.	Note 2
P	15	4-dr. LX Station Wagon-5P	$10,067	2,411 lbs.	58,950*
P	16	4-dr. LX-E Sedan-5P	$11,933	2,464 lbs.	Note 2
P	12	2-dr. GT Hatchback-5P	$11,871	2,458 lbs.	Note 1

Note 1: Production of two-door hatchback models totaled 81,023* and no further breakout was available.
Note 2: Production of four-door sedan models totaled 62,066* with no further breakout available.
* All Escort total production figures included 1993 models that were introduced early in 1992.

Tempo (Four)

P	31	2-dr. GL Sedan-5P	$9,987	2,532 lbs.	Note 1
P	36	4-dr. GL Sedan-5P	$10,137	2,600 lbs.	Note 2
P	37	4-dr. LX Sedan-5P	$11,115	2,626 lbs.	Note 2

Tempo (V-6 in GLS only)

P	33	2-dr. GLS Sedan-5P	$12,652	2,601 lbs.	Note 1
P	38	4-dr. GLS Sedan-5P	$12,800	2,659 lbs.	Note 2

Note 1: Production of two-door sedan models totaled 35,149 with no further breakout available.
Note 2: Production of four-door sedan models totaled 172,191 with no further breakout available.

Probe (Four)

T	20	2-dr. GL Coupe-4P	$12,257	2,730 lbs.	Note 1
T	22	2-dr. GT Coupe-4P	$14,857	3,000 lbs.	Note 1

Probe LX (V-6)

T	21	2-dr. LX Coupe-4P	$13,257	2,970 lbs.	Note 1

Note 1: Production of two-door coupe models totaled 41,035* with no further breakout available.
* **Note:** Probe total production figure included 1993 models that were introduced early in 1992.

Taurus (V-6)

P	50	4-dr. L Sedan-6P	$14,980	3,111 lbs.	Note 1
P	55	2-dr. L Station Wagon-6P	$16,013	3,262 lbs.	Note 2
P	52	4-dr. GL Sedan-6P	$15,280	3,117 lbs.	Note 1
P	57	4-dr. GL Station Wagon-6P	$16,290	3,264 lbs.	Note 2
P	53	4-dr. LX Sedan-6P	$17,775	3,193 lbs.	Note 1
P	58	4-dr. LX Station Wagon-6P	$19,464	3,388 lbs.	Note 2
P	54	4-dr. SHO Sedan-6P	$23,839	3,309 lbs.	Note 1

Note 1: Production of four-door sedan models totaled 274,289 and no further breakout was available.
Note 2: Production of station wagon models totaled 67,828 with no further breakout available.

Crown Victoria (V-8)

P	73	4-dr. Sedan-6P	$19,563	3,748 lbs.	Note 1
P	74	4-dr. LX Sedan-6P	$20,887	3,769 lbs.	Note 1
P	75	4-dr. Touring Sedan-6P	$23,832	3,850 lbs.	Note 1

Note 1: Production of four-door sedan models totaled 136,949 with no further breakout available.

1992 Taurus SHO sedan

Engines:

Escort Base Four: Inline. Overhead cam. Cast-iron block and aluminum head. Displacement: 113 cid (1.9 liters). B & S: 3.23 x 3.46 in. Compression ratio: 9.0:1. Brake hp: 88 at 4400 rpm. Torque: 108 lbs.-ft. at 3800 rpm. Five main bearings. Hydraulic valve lifters. Sequential electronic fuel injection.

Escort GT Base Four: High-output, DOHC multi-port fuel injection version of 1.9-liter four. Hp: 127 at 6500 rpm. Torque: 114 lbs.-ft. at 4500 rpm.

Probe Base Four: Inline. Overhead cam. Cast-iron block. Displacement: 133 cid (2.2 liters). B & S: 3.39 x 3.70 in. Compression ratio: 8.6:1. Brake hp: 110 at 4700 rpm. Torque: 130 lbs.-ft. at 3000 rpm. Hydraulic valve lifters. Multi-port fuel injection.

Probe GT Turbocharged Four: Same as 2.2-liter four with added turbocharger and intercooler. Compression ratio: 7.8:1. Hp: 145 at 4300 rpm. Torque: 190 lbs.-ft. at 3500 rpm.

Tempo Base Four: Inline. Overhead valve. Cast-iron block and head. Displacement: 140 cid (2.3 liters). B & S: 3.70 x 3.30 in. Compression ratio: 9.0:1. Brake hp: 96 at 4400 rpm. Torque: 128 lbs.-ft. at 2600 rpm. Five main bearings. Hydraulic valve lifters. Sequential electronic fuel injection.

Probe LX, Tempo GLS, Taurus L, GL and LX sedan - Base V-6 (Optional on Tempo GL and LX): 60-degree, overhead valve. Cast-iron block and head. Displacement: 182 cid (3.0 liters). B & S: 3.50 x 3.10 in. Compression ratio: 9.3:1. Brake hp: 145 at 4800 rpm, Probe LX and 140 at 4800 rpm, all others. Torque: 165 lbs.-ft. at 3400 RPM, Probe LX and 165 lbs.-ft. at 3000 rpm, all others. Four main bearings. Hydraulic valve lifters. Multi-port fuel injection, Probe LX and sequential electronic fuel injection, all others.

Taurus SHO Base V-6: Dual-overhead-cam with 24 valves. Cast-iron block and head. Displacement: 182 cid (3.0 liters). B & S: 3.50 x 3.15 in. Compression ratio: 9.8:1. Brake hp: 220 at 6200 rpm. Torque: 200 lbs.-ft. at 4800 rpm. Four main bearings. Hydraulic valve lifters. Sequential electronic fuel injection.

Taurus GL and LX sedan Optional V-6: 90-degree, overhead valve. Cast-iron block and aluminum head. Displacement: 232 cid (3.8 liters). B & S: 3.80 x 3.40 in. Compression ratio: 9.0:1. Brake hp: 140 at 3800 rpm. Torque: 215 lbs.-ft. at 2200 rpm. Four main bearings. Hydraulic valve lifters. Sequential electronic fuel injection.

Crown Victoria Base V-8: Modular, overhead valve. Displacement: 281 cid (4.6 liters). B & S: 3.60 x 3.60. Compression ratio: 9.0:1. Brake hp: 190 at 4200 rpm. Torque: 260 lbs.-ft. at 3200 rpm.

Chassis:

Escort: Wheelbase: 98.4 in. Overall length: 170.0 in. and 171.3 in., station wagon. Tires: P175/70-R13 or P175/65-R14, LX; P185/65R14 LX-E and P185/60R15, GT.

Tempo: Wheelbase: 99.9 in. Overall length: 176.7 in., two-door and 177.0 in., four-door. Tires: P185/70-R14.

Probe: Wheelbase: 99.0 in. Overall length: 177.0 in. Tires: P195/70-R14 and P205/60-VR15, GT.

Taurus: Wheelbase: 106.0 in. Overall length: 192.0 in. and 193.1 in., station wagon. Tires: P205/70-R14 and P215/60-R16, SHO.

Crown Victoria: Wheelbase: 114.4 in. Overall length: 212.4 in. Tires: P215/70-R15.

Options:

Escort: Preferred equipment package for LX included: Power steering, light group with dual electric remote control mirrors and rear window defroster ($248). Preferred equip package for LX-E included: Manual air conditioning, rear window defroster and the luxury convenience group

1992 Probe LX coupe

($554). GT preferred equipment package GT ($759). Rear window defroster ($170). Light and convenience group with dual electric remote control mirrors and remote fuel door and deck lid releases ($317). Luxury convenience group included a tilt steering wheel, cruise control, power door locks, and tach, standard on GT and LX, LX-E sedan and GT ($369) and for LX, LX-E hatchback and wagon ($428). Power moon roof for LX, LX-E and GT ($549). Clear coat paint ($91). Dual electric remote control mirrors ($98). Remote fuel door and deck lid release ($101). Comfort group with air conditioning and power steering for base Escort ($841). AM/FM stereo radio, base Escort ($312). AM/FM cassette radio, base Escort ($467) or ($155), LX. Premium sound system ($138). Power steering, LX ($261). Wagon group included deluxe luggage rack, the light and convenience group and the rear window wiper and washer, LX wagon ($250). Four-speed automatic transaxle: Escort ($732).

Tempo: Preferred equipment package, GL two-door and four-door included rear window defroster, front center armrest, power lock group, electronic AM/FM stereo radio with cassette and clock, automatic transaxle and polycast wheels ($1,305), GL two-door and GL four-door ($1,345). Preferred equip package GLS two-door and four-door included tilt steering wheel, rear window defroster, dual electric remote control mirrors, premium sound system and the power lock group ($642), GLS two-door and ($682), GLS four-door. Preferred equipment package, LX included manual air conditioning, rear window defroster, electronic AM/FM stereo radio with cassette and clock and automatic transaxle ($1,755). California emissions system ($100). Manual air conditioner ($817). Front center armrest ($59). Rear window defroster ($170). Floor mats front and rear ($33). Instrument cluster ($87). Light group ($38). Power lock group, two-door ($311) and four-door ($351). Luggage rack ($115). Dual electric remote control mirrors ($115). Clear coat paint ($91). Electronic AM/FM stereo radio with cassette and clock ($155). Power driver's seat ($305). Premium sound system ($138). Speed control ($224). Tilt steering wheel ($145). Air bag, driver's side, GL ($369) and LX ($224). Polycast wheels ($193). Power windows, four-door ($330). Engine block heater ($20). P185/70-R14 whitewalls ($82).

Probe: Preferred equipment, GL: Tinted glass, tilt steering column and cluster, rear window defroster, dual illuminated visor vanity mirrors, convenience group with interval wipers, light group and dual electric remote mirrors ($308). Preferred equip package, LX and GT: Same as GL equipment plus air conditioning and electronic AM/FM radio with cassette and premium sound plus power antenna ($1,842), LX and GT ($1,397). Manual air conditioning with tinted glass ($937). Rear window defroster ($170). Leather bucket seats, LX and GT ($523). Power driver's seat, LX and GT ($305). Power door locks, GL ($210). Speed control ($224). Anti-lock brakes, LX and GT ($595). Flip-up open-air roof, LX and GT ($355). Aluminum wheels, GL only ($313). Power windows, LX and GT ($485). Vehicle maintenance monitor ($146). Trip computer ($215). Tilt steering column with gauge cluster ($205). Sport option, LX ($445). Illuminated entry system, LX and GT ($82). Convenience group I ($213). Convenience group II, GL ($188) and LX or GT ($323). Instrument cluster ($463). Tinted glass, GL ($120). Electronic AM/FM stereo radio with cassette and premium sound ($372). AM/FM electronic radio with CD player, premium sound and power antenna ($1,080). California emissions system ($72). Engine block heater ($20). Four-speed automatic transaxle ($732). Anti-lock brakes, LX and GT ($595). 3.0-liter V-6, GL and LX sedans ($685).

Taurus: Preferred equipment package, L: Manual air conditioning and rear window defroster ($686). Preferred equipment package, GL: Power door locks, manual air conditioner, rear window defroster, electronic AM/FM stereo radio with cassette, speed control, deluxe wheel covers, cargo net, front and rear floor mats, light group, power windows and six-way power driver's seat ($2,023). Preferred equipment package, LX sedan: rear window defroster, speed control, front and rear floor mats, leather-wrapped steering wheel, electronic AM/FM stereo radio with cassette, keyless entry system and power antenna ($454). Preferred equipment

package, LX wagon: same as LX Sedan plus cargo area cover, "picnic table" load floor extension and rear window washer and wiper ($655). Preferred equipment package, SHO sedan: Electronic climate control air conditioning and keyless entry system ($219). Conventional spare tire ($73). Electronic air conditioning, LX and SHO ($183). Manual air conditioning, L and GL ($841). Passenger side air bag ($488). Anti-lock brakes ($595). CD player ($491). High level audio system ($502). Cargo area cover, wagons ($66). Cargo Net, GL ($44). Rear window defroster ($170). Engine block heater ($20). Floor mats front and rear ($45). Remote deck lid and fuel door release, GL ($101). Remote keyless entry system, LX and SHO ($146). Light group, GL ($59). "Picnic Table" load floor extension, wagons ($90). Power door locks, L and GL ($257). Power moon roof, LX and SHO ($776). Electronic AM/FM stereo radio with cassette ($171). Power antenna, LX ($102). Rear facing third seat, wagons ($155). Dual control six-way power seats, LX and SHO ($305). Six-way power driver's seat, GL ($305). Speed control ($224). Leather-wrapped steering wheel ($96). Rear window washer and wiper, wagons ($135). Cast aluminum wheels, GL ($239). Heavy duty battery ($27). California emissions system ($100). Leather bucket seats with console, LX ($515) or GL ($618). Leather split bench seat, LX ($515). Leather bucket seats, SHO sedan ($515). Front floor mats ($26). P205/65-R15 blackwall tires, GL ($150). 3.8-liter V-6, GL and LX sedans ($555). Anti-lock brakes, Taurus ($595).

Crown Victoria: Preferred equip package, base: Rear window defroster, color-keyed front and rear floor mats, illuminated entry system, light and decor group, power lock group, electronic AM/FM stereo radio with cassette, remote fuel door release, six-way power driver's seat, leather-wrapped steering wheel, speed control, spare tire cover, trunk cargo net and locking spoked wheel covers ($943). Preferred equipment package, LX: Rear window defroster, color-keyed front and rear floor mats, illuminated entry system, power lock group, electronic AM/FM stereo radio with cassette, power antenna, six-way power driver's seat, leather-wrapped steering wheel, speed control, cornering lamps and cast aluminum wheels ($827). Preferred equipment package, Touring Sedan: Rear window defroster, power lock group, cornering lamps, power antenna, high level audio system and illuminated keyless entry system ($961). California emissions system ($100). Leather split-bench seat, LX ($555) and Touring Sedan ($339). Conventional spare tire ($85). Passenger air bag ($488). Anti-lock brakes, standard on Touring Sedan ($695). Heavy duty battery ($27). Cornering lights ($68). Electric rear window defroster ($170). Electronic group ($516). Color-keyed front and rear floor mats ($46). Handling and performance package including electronic traction control, cast aluminum wheels, aluminum driveshaft and dual exhausts, 41G ($1,172). Engine block heater ($25). Illuminated entry system ($82). Illuminated keyless entry system ($146). Light and decor group, base Crown Victoria only ($222). Power lock group ($310). Electronic AM/FM stereo radio with cassette ($155). High level audio system, LX ($335) or Touring Sedan ($490). Ford JBL audio system ($526). Power antenna ($85). Rear air suspension ($285). Remote fuel door release, base Crown Victoria ($41). Six-way power driver's seat ($305). Dual six-way power seat ($779). Cruise control with leather-wrapped steering wheel ($321). Trailer towing package, base Crown Victoria ($490) or LX ($205). Trunk cargo net ($44). Cast aluminum wheels: LX ($440) and Touring Sedan, no charge. Locking spoked wheel covers, base Crown Victoria ($311). Insta-clear windshield ($305), not available on base Crown Victoria. Trailer towing package ($205).

History:

The 1992 U. S. model year production totaled 758,865, including Mustangs. Ford Motor Co. held 16.3 percent of the industry's market share. The Taurus was the best selling car in the United States in 1992, with 409,751, compared to 329,751 for the second place Honda Accord. In addition to the all-new, 1992 Crown Victoria introduced in the spring of 1991, Ford's 1992 lineup included a redesigned Taurus series, two new four-door Escort sedans as well as a Crown Victoria Touring Sedan.

1992 Escort GT three-door hatchback

1992 Escort LX-E sedan

1993 Ford

1993 Escort LX five-door hatchback

1993 Tempo GL sedan

Escort — Four: For the 1993 model year, Escort's lineup consisted of base (three-door hatchback), LX (three- and five-door hatchbacks, four-door sedan and station wagon), LX-E (four-door sedan) and GT (three-door hatchback). Key design refinements included six new exterior colors, new grilles, tail lamp treatment, wheel covers and color-keyed bumpers and body moldings on many models. The LX three-door hatchback was offered with a Sport Appearance group option that included a rear spoiler, 14-inch aluminum wheels, full cloth seats, tachometer and sport steering wheel. The Escort GT featured both a new rear spoiler and new aluminum wheels and a sport steering wheel. Standard equipment on all 1993 Escorts included side-window demisters, electronic engine controls and ignition, an engine-malfunction indicator light, tinted glass, inside hood release and front and rear stabilizer bars. The standard engine for the base and LX Escorts was the 1.9-liter four with sequential fuel injection. A five-speed manual transaxle was standard on Escorts, with the electronic four-speed automatic overdrive transaxle optional. The LX-E sedan shared the 16-valve DOHC 1.8-liter four-cylinder engine found in the GT model.

Tempo — Four: Tempo's ranks were thinned a bit in 1993 with the previous GLS series being discontinued. The lineup now consisted of two- and four-door GL sedans and a four-door LX sedan. Tempo's base power plant was the 2.3-liter four-cylinder with sequential electronic fuel injection. The five-speed manual transaxle was standard with the three-speed automatic transaxle optional. Also optional was a 3.0-liter V-6. Standard equipment included an AM/FM stereo radio with digital electronic clock. Models with the five-speed manual transaxle received a new leather-wrapped shift knob. The Tempo LX featured dual electric remote control mirrors, polycast 14-inch wheels, performance tires, an illuminated entry system, the power lock group, a trip odometer and tachometer plus upgraded cloth seat trim with seatback pockets.

Probe — Four and V-6: Originally introduced in 1988, by 1993 the Probe was all-new with an increase in length, width, wheelbase and tread. The Probe now used a cab forward design, which moved the passenger compartment closer to the front of the car and resulted in a shorter front overhang plus increased windshield slope and greater interior space. The sporty coupe was available in base or GT series. The base coupe was powered by a new DOHC 2.0-liter four-cylinder engine with four valves per cylinder and an aluminum cylinder head. It was rated at 115 hp. The GT coupe used a DOHC 2.5-liter V-6 with four valves per cylinder and a cast-aluminum engine block and cylinder head. It was rated at 164 hp. A five-speed manual transaxle was standard on both coupes and an electronically controlled four-speed automatic transaxle was optional. A driver's side air bag was standard equipment on the Probe. The GT version's standard equipment included a leather-wrapped steering wheel, adjustable power lumbar and seat-back side bolster front seats, fog lamps, a cargo net and four-wheel disc brakes. Anti-lock brakes were optional on both coupes. A new center console with armrest and storage area was standard on the GT and optional on the base Probe.

Taurus — V-6: Taurus for 1993 underwent several refinements after undergoing a major redesign the year previous. For the first time, an optional automatic transaxle was offered on the SHO sedan. This automatic unit was coupled to a DOHC 3.2-liter V-6 with four valves per cylinder. The DOHC 3.0-liter V-6 mated to a five-speed manual transaxle remained as the base powertrain for the SHO model. Among other changes for the SHO model was the addition of a decklid spoiler with an integrated light-emitting diode (LED) stop lamp. In addition to the SHO sedan, Taurus was offered in both sedan and station wagon versions in the GL and LX series. The L series offered the year previous was discontinued. The GL sedan and wagon and LX sedan were again powered by the 3.0-liter V-6 with sequential electronic fuel injection. The LX wagon was again powered by the 3.8-liter V-6, which was optional on other Taurus models (except the SHO sedan). The four-speed automatic overdrive transaxle was the standard unit on Taurus with the five-speed manual unit optional, just the opposite of the SHO sedan. Body-color bumpers and bodyside moldings as well as new seat trim were added to the GL series. On the LX, exterior color choices expanded from six to ten monochromatic colors, and a new floor-mounted console was added. A driver's side air bag was standard equipment on all Taurus models with the passenger-side air bag and anti-lock brakes (standard on SHO sedan) both optional.

Crown Victoria — V-8: With the Touring Sedan discontinued for 1993, the 1993 Crown Victoria lineup was now two series: the base and the LX, with each offering a four-door sedan. The modular 4.6-liter V-8 again was the standard engine, now coupled to an electronically controlled four-speed automatic overdrive transmission. The unit featured an overdrive lockout function for improved acceleration. The Crown Victoria again offered such standard equipment as speed-sensitive steering, four-wheel disc brakes and a driver's side air bag. A passenger-side air bag, anti-lock brakes and traction control were optional. The Crown Victoria's trunk provided 20 cubic feet of space - the largest in its class. The optional trailer-towing package included a dual exhaust system that boosted horsepower to 210 and allowed a Class III towing capacity up to 5,000 lbs. The LX sedan featured new cloth seats and optional cast aluminum wheels in both 15- or 16-inch sizes. An important safety feature was the brake shift interlock, which required the brake to be depressed before the car could be put into gear.

1993 Escort LX three-door hatchback

1993 Probe GT coupe

Ford's 17-symbol Vehicle Identification Number (VIN) was stamped on a metal tab fastened to the instrument panel and visible through the windshield. The first three symbols indicated the manufacturer, make and vehicle type. The fourth symbol denoted the restraint system. Next came letter P followed by two digits that indicated the model number, such as P10= Escort two-door hatchback. Symbol eight indicated the engine type. Next was a check digit. Symbol 10 indicated the model year: P=1993. Symbol 11 denoted the assembly plant. The final six digits make up the sequential number, starting with 100001.

Escort (Four))

Model No.	Body/Style No.	Body Type & Seating	Factory Price	Shipping Weight	Production Total
P	10	2-dr. Hatchback-5P	$8,355	2,285 lbs.	Note 1
P	11	2-dr. LX Hatchback-5P	$9,364	2,306 lbs.	Note 1
P	14	4-dr. LX Hatchback-5P	$9,797	2,354 lbs.	58,909
P	13	4-dr. LX Sedan-5P	$10,041	2,359 lbs.	Note 2
P	15	4-dr. LX Station Wagon-5P	$10,367	2,403 lbs.	157,239
P	16	4-dr. LX-E Sedan-5P	$11,933	2,440 lbs.	Note 2
P	12	2-dr. GT Hatchback-5P	$11,871	2,440 lbs.	Note 1

Note 1: Production of two-door hatchback models totaled 89,761 with no model breakouts available.
Note 2: Production of four-door sedan models totaled 69,796 with no further breakout available.

Tempo (Four)

P	31	2-dr. GL Sedan-5P	$10,267	2,511 lbs.	52,129
P	36	4-dr. GL Sedan-5P	$10,267	2,569 lbs.	Note 1
P	37	2-dr. LX Sedan-5P	$12,135	2,613 lbs.	Note 1

Note 1: Production of four-door sedan models totaled 154,762 and no further breakout was available.

Probe (Four)

T	20	2-dr. Coupe-4P	$12,845	2,619 lbs.	Note 1

Probe (V-6)

T	22	2-dr. GT Coupe-4P	$15,174	2,815 lbs.	Note 1

Note 1: Production of two-door coupe models totaled 119,769 with no breakout available.

Taurus (V-6)

P	52	4-dr. GL Sedan-6P	$15,491	3,083 lbs.	Note 1
P	57	4-dr. GL Station Wagon-6P	$16,656	3,255 lbs.	Note 2
P	53	2-dr. LX Sedan-6P	$18,300	3,201 lbs.	Note 1
P	58	4-dr. LX Station Wagon-6P	$19,989	3,368 lbs.	Note 2
P	54	4-dr. SHO Sedan-6P	$24,829	3,354 lbs.	Note 1

Note 1: Production of four-door sedan models totaled 350,802 with no further breakout available.
Note 2: Production of station wagon models totaled 76,502 with no further breakout available.

Crown Victoria (V-8)

P	73	4-dr. Sedan-6P	$19,972	3,793 lbs.	Note 1
P	74	4-dr. LX Sedan-6P	$21,559	3,799 lbs.	Note 1

Note 1: Production of four-door sedan models totaled 100,179 with no further breakout available.

Escort Base Four: Inline. Overhead cam. Cast-iron block and aluminum head. Displacement: 113 cid (1.9 liters). B & S: 3.23 x 3.46 in. Compression ratio: 9.0:1. Brake hp: 88 at 4400 rpm. Torque: 108 lbs.-ft. at 3800 rpm. Five main bearings. Hydraulic valve lifters. Sequential electronic fuel injection.

Escort LX-E and GT Base Four: High-output. Inline. Dual overhead cam. Cast-iron block and aluminum head. Displacement: 109 cid (1.8 liters). B & S: 3.27 x 3.35 in. Compression ratio: 9.0:1. Brake hp: 127 at 6500 rpm. Torque: 114 lbs.-ft. at 4500 rpm. Five main bearings. Hydraulic valve lifters. Multi-port fuel injection.

Probe Base Four: Inline. Dual overhead cam. Cast-iron block and aluminum head. Displacement: 122 cid (2.0 liters). B & S: 3.27 x 3.62 in. Compression ratio: 9.0:1. Brake hp: 115 at 5500 rpm. Torque: 124 lbs.-ft. at 3500 rpm. Hydraulic valve lifters. Sequential electronic fuel injection.

Tempo Base Four: Inline. Overhead valve. Cast-iron block and head. Displacement: 140 cid (2.3 liters). B & S: 3.70 x 3.30 in. Compression ratio: 9.0:1. Brake hp: 96 at 4200 rpm. Torque: 126 lbs.-ft. at 2600 rpm. Five main bearings. Hydraulic valve lifters. Sequential electronic fuel injection.

Probe GT Base V-6: Dual overhead cam with 24 valves. Aluminum block and head. Displacement: 153 cid (2.5 liters). B & S: 3.33 x 2.92 in.

1993 Taurus SHO sedan

1993 Taurus LX station wagon

Compression ratio: 9.2:1. Brake hp: 164 at 6000 rpm. Torque: 156 lbs.-ft. at 4000 rpm. Four main bearings. Hydraulic valve lifters. Sequential electronic fuel injection.

Taurus GL and LX sedan Base V-6 (Optional Tempo GL and LX): 60-degree, overhead valve. Cast-iron block and head. Displacement: 182 cid (3.0 liters). B & S: 3.50 x 3.10 in. Compression ratio: 9.3:1. Brake hp: 135 at 4800 rpm. Torque: 165 lbs.-ft. at 3250 rpm. Four main bearings. Hydraulic valve lifters. Sequential electronic fuel injection.

Taurus SHO Base V-6: Dual-overhead-cam with 24 valves. Cast-iron block and head. Displacement: 182 cid (3.0 liters). B & S: 3.50 x 3.15 in. Compression ratio: 9.8:1. Brake hp: 220 at 6200 rpm. Torque: 200 lbs.-ft. at 4800 rpm. Four main bearings. Hydraulic valve lifters. Sequential electronic fuel injection.

Taurus LX wagon Base V-6 (Optional: Taurus GL and LX sedan): 90-degree, overhead valve. Cast-iron block and aluminum head. Displacement: 232 cid (3.8 liters). B & S: 3.80 x 3.40 in. Compression ratio: 9.0:1. Brake hp: 140 at 3800 rpm. Torque: 215 lbs.-ft. at 2200 rpm. Four main bearings. Hydraulic valve lifters. Sequential electronic fuel injection.

Crown Victoria Optional V-8: Same as 281 cid (4.6-liter) V-8 but with brake hp: 210 at 4600 rpm and torque at 270 lbs.-ft. at 3400 rpm.

Escort: Wheelbase: 98.4 in. Overall length: 170.0 in. and 171.3 in., station wagon. Tires: P175/70-R13; P175/65-R14, LX; P185/60-R14, LX-E and P185/60-R15, GT.

Tempo: Wheelbase: 99.9 in. Overall length: 176.7 in., two-door and 177.0 in., four-door. Tires: P185/70-R14.

Probe: Wheelbase: 102.9 in. Overall length: 178.9 in. Tires: P195/65-14 and P225/50-VR16, GT.

Taurus: Wheelbase: 106.0 in. Overall length: 192.0 in. and 193.1 in., wagon. Tires: P205/70-R14; P205/65-R15, LX and P215/60-R16, SHO.

Crown Victoria: Wheelbase: 114.4 in. Overall length: 212.4 in. Tires: P215/70-R15.

Escort: Preferred equipment package, LX: Power steering, light group including dual electric remote control mirrors and a rear window defroster ($248). Preferred equipment package, LX-E: Manual air conditioning, rear window defroster, speed control, tilt steering and tach ($554). Preferred equipment package, GT: Manual air conditioning, rear window defroster, speed control, tilt steering and tach ($554). California emissions system ($72). Air conditioning, LX, LX-E and GT ($759). Rear window defroster ($170). Light and convenience group including dual electric remote control mirrors, remote fuel door release and remote deck lid release ($317). Luxury convenience group includes tilt steering wheel, cruise control, power door locks, and tach (standard on GT), LX-E and GT ($369) and LX ($428). Power moon roof ($549). Clear coat paint ($91). Dual electric remote control mirrors, LX ($98). Remote fuel door and deck lid release ($101). Comfort group including air conditioning and power steering, base Escort ($841). AM/FM stereo radio, base Escort ($312). AM/FM cassette radio, base Escort ($467) and LX ($155). Premium sound system ($138). Power steering, LX ($261). Wagon group including deluxe luggage

1993 Crown Victoria sedan

1993 Escort LX station wagon

1993 Taurus LX sedan

rack, light and convenience group and rear window wiper and washer, LX wagon ($250). Sport appearance group including 14-inch aluminum wheels, GT steering wheel and tach, full cloth seats, lift gate spoiler and appliqués ($757). Iris decor group, GT, included clear coat Iris exterior color, color-keyed wheels, leather-wrapped steering wheel plus seat, door and front floor mats with embroidered GT trim ($365). Four-speed automatic transaxle ($732).

Tempo: Preferred equipment package I, GL Manual air conditioning, light group, dual electric remote control mirrors and tilt steering wheel ($304). Preferred equipment package II, GL two-door and four-door included: All GL items plus rear window defroster, front center armrest, front and rear floor mats, power lock group, electronic AM/FM stereo with cassette and clock, automatic transaxle and polycast wheels ($1,305), two-door and four-door, ($1,345). Preferred equipment group SRS GL: Same as GL plus driver's side air bag and without tilt steering wheel, electronic AM/FM stereo radio with cassette and clock or polycast wheels: two-door ($1,081) and four-door ($1,121). Preferred equipment package, LX: Manual air conditioning, rear window defroster, electronic AM/FM stereo radio with cassette and clock and automatic transaxle ($1,005). California emissions system ($100). Manual air conditioning ($817). Front center armrest ($59). Rear window defroster ($170). Front and rear floor mats ($33). Instrument cluster ($87). Light group ($38). Lock group: two-door ($311) and four-door ($351). Luggage rack ($115). Dual electric remote mirrors ($121). Clear coat Paint ($91). Electronic AM/FM stereo radio with cassette and clock ($155). Power driver's seat ($305). Premium sound system ($138). Speed control ($224). Tilt steering wheel ($145). Driver's side air bag: GL ($369) and LX ($224). Polycast wheels ($193). Power windows, four-door ($330). Engine block heater ($20). P185/70-R14 whitewall tires ($82). 3.0-liter V-6 ($685). Three-speed automatic transaxle ($563).

Probe: Preferred equipment base, 251A: Tilt steering column, rear window defroster, convenience group including interval wipers, light group and dual electric remote mirrors ($395). Preferred equipment package base, 253A: Same as 251A plus manual air conditioning, electronic AM/FM radio with cassette and premium sound, color-keyed body moldings, remote keyless entry, speed control and power group ($2,421). Preferred equipment package, GT, 261A: Same as 251A plus manual air conditioning and electronic AM/FM radio with cassette and premium sound system ($1,451). Preferred equipment package, GT, 263A: Same as 253A plus anti-lock brakes, rear wiper and washer plus heated dual electric remote control mirrors ($2,898). Manual air conditioner ($817). Rear window defroster ($170). Leather bucket seats: base ($712) and GT ($523). Cloth bucket seats, standard on GT ($189). Power driver's seat ($305). Speed control ($224). Anti-lock brakes, base ($774) and GT ($595). Power sliding roof ($648). Keyless entry system ($137). Anti-theft system ($200). Convenience group including tinted glass, interval wipers, courtesy lights and headlamp warning chime ($374). Power group including power door locks and power windows with dual express down ($510). Light group including dual illuminated visor vanity mirrors, fade-to-off dome lamp and illuminated entry ($249). Front color-keyed floor mats ($33). Dual electric remote control mirrors ($106). Color-keyed body moldings ($50). Rear wiper and washer system ($182). Manual driver's seat adjustment ($37). Power antenna ($85). Electronic AM/FM stereo radio with cassette and premium sound system ($339). AM/FM electronic stereo with CD player and premium sound ($840). California emissions system ($100). Engine block heater ($20). P205/55-R15 blackwall tires, base ($450). Four-speed automatic transaxle ($732). Anti-lock brakes, GT ($595).

Taurus: Preferred equipment package, GL, 203A: Manual air conditioning and rear window defroster ($686). Preferred equipment package, GL, 204A: Same as 203A plus power door locks, electronic AM/FM stereo radio with cassette, speed control, deluxe wheel covers, cargo net, front and rear floor mats, light group, power windows and six-way power driver's seat ($2,412). Preferred equipment package, LX: Rear window defroster, speed control, front and rear floor mats, leather-wrapped steering wheel, electronic AM/FM stereo radio with cassette, cargo area cover and "picnic table" load floor extension in wagons, keyless entry system and power antenna ($501). Conventional spare tire ($73). Electronic air conditioning, LX ($183). Manual air conditioning, GL ($841). Passenger side air bag ($488). Anti-lock brakes, standard on

SHO sedan ($595). Cargo area cover, wagons ($66). Cargo net, GL ($44). Rear window defroster ($170). Engine block heater ($20). Front and rear floor mats ($45). Remote deck lid and fuel door release, GL ($101). Remote keyless entry system, LX and SHO ($193). Light group, GL ($59). "Picnic table" load floor extension, wagons ($90). Power door locks, GL ($257). Power moon roof, LX and SHO ($776). Electronic AM/FM stereo radio with cassette ($171). Audio digital CD player ($491). JBL audio system ($526). Power antenna, LX ($102). Rear facing third seat, wagons ($155). Dual control six-way power seats ($305). Six-way power driver's seat, GL ($305). Speed control ($224). Leather-wrapped steering wheel ($96). Rear window washer and wiper, wagons ($135). Cellular phone ($779). Luxury convenience group with JBL audio system, power moon roof and dual power seats ($1,407). GL decor equipment group including upgraded cloth trim, speed sensitive power steering, paint stripe and dual visor mirrors ($389). Cast aluminum wheels ($239). Heavy duty battery ($27). California emissions system ($100). Leather bucket seats with console: LX ($515) and GL ($618). Leather split bench seat, LX ($515). Leather bucket seats, SHO sedan ($515). Heavy duty suspension, not available on SHO ($26). Front floor mats ($45). P205/65R-15 blackwall tires ($150). 3.8-liter V-6, GL and LX sedans ($555). Anti-lock brakes, standard on SHO ($595).

Crown Victoria: Preferred equipment package, base, 111A: Color-keyed front and rear floor mats, illuminated entry and convenience group ($559). Preferred equipment package, LX, 113A: Same as 111A plus audio group, exterior decor group, leather-wrapped steering wheel and light/décor group ($1,082). Preferred equip package, LX, 114A: Same as 113A plus LX luxury group ($3,581). California emissions system ($100). Leather split-bench seat ($555). Conventional spare tire ($85). Passenger side air bag ($488). Anti-lock brakes with electronic traction assistance ($695). 41G handling and performance package, LX including electronic traction control, revised springs, shocks and stabilizer bar, power steering cooler, P225/60-R16 blackwall touring tires, 16-inch cast aluminum wheels and dual exhausts ($1,905). Engine block heater ($25). Illuminated entry system ($82). Keyless illuminated entry system ($196). Light and decor group, base ($240). Cellular phone ($779). Exterior decor group, LX ($508). Convenience group including rear window defroster, power lock group, speed control and trunk cargo net: base ($807) and LX ($704). Exterior decor group, LX, including cast aluminum wheels and cornering lamps ($508). Electronic AM/FM stereo radio with cassette ($171). High level audio system, LX ($335). Ford JBL audio system ($526). LX luxury group including anti-lock brakes with electronic traction assist, high level audio system, electronic group, rear air suspension, remote keyless entry and dual power seats ($2,820). Rear air suspension ($285). Leather-wrapped steering wheel, LX ($96). Trailer towing package: base ($490) and LX ($205). Six-way power driver's seat, base ($305). Dual power seats, LX ($504). Trailer towing package ($205).

History:

U.S. model year production of Fords totaled 1,118,265, including Mustang. For the second consecutive year, Taurus was the best selling car in the United States in 1993, with 360,448 units sold compared to 330,030 for the second place Honda Accord. Leading the "what's new" parade at Ford in 1993 was the total redesign of the Probe. It now featured a cab forward design and was available in base and GT versions. The Probe series used two new power plants, a 2.0-liter 16-valve DOHC four-cylinder engine or a 2.5-liter 24-valve DOHC V-6. Alex J. Trotman was named chairman and CEO of Ford Motor Co. on Nov. 1, 1993. He succeeded Harold A. "Red" Poling who retired.

1994 Ford

Escort — Four: Escort's 1994 lineup was the same as the year previous except for the discontinuance of the LX-E four-door sedan. Returning were the base (three-door hatchback), LX (three- and five-door hatchbacks, four-door sedan and station wagon) and GT (three-door hatchback). A driver's side air bag became standard equipment. A compact disc player was optional on the GT model. The standard engine for base and LX model Escorts was the 1.9-liter four-cylinder version with sequential electronic fuel injection. A five-speed manual transaxle was standard on Escorts, with the electronic four-speed automatic overdrive transaxle optional. The GT model used the 16-valve DOHC 1.8-liter four-cylinder engine with multi-port fuel injection.

Tempo — Four: In its final half year, before production halted in spring 1994, Tempo returned unchanged from 1993. The lineup again consisted of two- and four-door sedans in the GL series and a four-door sedan in LX trim. Tempo's base engine was the 2.3-liter four-cylinder with sequential electronic fuel injection. The five-speed manual transaxle was standard equipment with the three-speed automatic transaxle optional, except on the GL two-door sedan. Again optional across-the-board was a 3.0-liter V-6. A driver's side air bag was optional on all Tempos equipped with the 2.3-liter four.

Probe — Four and V-6: After its redesign in 1993, Probe returned in 1994 with its lineup unchanged. Probe was again available in base or GT. The base coupe was powered by the DOHC 2.0-liter four-cylinder engine. The GT coupe used the all-aluminum DOHC 2.5-liter V-6. A five-speed manual transaxle was standard on both coupes and an electronically controlled four-speed automatic transaxle was optional. Along with a driver's side air bag, a passenger side supplemental restraint system (SRS) was now standard equipment on Probe.

Taurus — V-6: The lineup for Taurus in 1994 remained unchanged from 1993. Taurus was again offered in both sedan and station wagon versions in the GL and LX series as well as the SHO sedan. The GL sedan and wagon and LX sedan were powered by the 3.0-liter V-6 with sequential electronic fuel injection. The LX wagon was powered by the 3.8-liter V-6, again the option engine for many Taurus models except the SHO sedan. The four-speed automatic overdrive transaxle was standard on GL and LX models. The SHO sedan used the DOHC 3.0-liter V-6 coupled to a five-speed manual transaxle. The DOHC 3.2-liter V-6 was the optional engine on SHO models and was mated to a four-speed automatic overdrive transaxle. The passenger side supplemental restraint system (SRS) was standard equipment on all 1994 Taurus models.

Crown Victoria — V-8: The Crown Vic returned in 1994 with the base and LX, each offering a four-door sedan. The modular 4.6-liter V-8 again was the standard engine, coupled to an electronically controlled four-speed automatic overdrive transmission. A passenger's side air bag was standard on 1994 Crown Victorias.

I. D. Data:

Ford's 17-symbol Vehicle Identification Number (VIN) was stamped on a metal tab fastened to the instrument panel and was visible through the windshield. The first three symbols indicated the manufacturer, make and vehicle type. The fourth symbol indicated the restraint system. Next came letter P followed by two digits that indicated the model number such as P10=Escort two-door hatchback. Symbol eight indicated the engine type. Next was a check digit. Symbol 10 indicated model year R=1994. Symbol 11 revealed the assembly plant. The final six digits made up the sequence number, starting with 100001.

Escort (Four)

Model No.	Body/Style No.	Body Type & Seating	Factory Price	Shipping Weight	Production Total
P	10	2-dr. Hatchback-5P	$9,035	2,304 lbs.	Note 1
P	11	2-dr. LX Hatchback-5P	$9,890	2,325 lbs.	Note 1
P	14	4-dr. LX Hatchback-5P	$10,325	2,419 lbs.	39,837
P	13	4-dr. LX Sedan-5P	$10,550	2,371 lbs.	49,052
P	15	4-dr. LX Station Wagon-5P	$10,880	2,419 lbs.	108,372
P	12	2-dr. GT Hatchback-5P	$12,300	2,447 lbs.	Note 1

Note 1: Production of two-door hatchback models totaled 87,888 with no further breakout available.

Tempo (Four)

P	31	2-dr. GL Sedan-5P	$10,735	2,511 lbs.	32,050
P	36	4-dr. GL Sedan-5P	$10,735	2,569 lbs.	Note 1
P	37	4-dr. LX Sedan-5P	$12,560	2,569 lbs.	Note 1

Note 1: Production of four-door sedan models totaled 110,399 with no further breakout available.

Probe (Four)

T	20	2-dr. Coupe-4P	$13,685	2,690 lbs.	Note 1

Probe (V-6, GT only)

T	22	2-dr. GT Coupe-4P	$16,015	2,921 lbs.	Note 1

Note 1: Production of two-door coupe models totaled 85,505 with no further breakout available.

Taurus (V-6)

P	52	4-dr. GL Sedan-6P	$16,140	3,104 lbs.	Note 1
P	57	4-dr. GL Station Wagon-6P	$17,220	3,253 lbs.	Note 2
P	53	4-dr. LX Sedan-6P	$18,785	3,147 lbs.	Note 1
P	58	4-dr. LX Station Wagon-6P	$20,400	3,296 lbs.	Note 2
P	54	4-dr. SHO Sedan-6P	$24,715	3,395 lbs.	Note 1

Note 1: Production of four-door sedan models totaled 288,737 and there were no other breakouts available.
Note 2: Production of station wagon models totaled 55,135 with no further breakout available.

Crown Victoria (V-8)

P	73	4-dr. Sedan-6P	$19,300	3,786 lbs.	Note 1
P	74	4-dr. LX Sedan-6P	$20,715	3,794 lbs.	Note 1

Note 1: Production of four-door sedan models totaled 100,983 with no further breakout available.

Engines:

Escort Base Four: Inline. Overhead cam. Cast-iron block and aluminum head. Displacement: 113 cid (1.9 liters). B & S: 3.23 x 3.46 in. Compression ratio: 9.0:1. Brake hp: 88 at 4400 rpm. Torque: 108 lbs.-ft. at 3800 rpm. Five main bearings. Hydraulic valve lifters. Sequential electronic fuel injection.

Escort GT Base Four: High-output. Inline. Dual overhead cam. Cast-iron block and aluminum head. Displacement: 109 cid (1.8 liters). B & S: 3.27 x 3.35 in. Compression ratio: 9.0:1. Brake hp: 127 at 6500 rpm. Torque: 114 lbs.-ft. at 4500 rpm. Five main bearings. Hydraulic valve lifters. Multi-port fuel injection.

Probe Base Four: Inline. Dual overhead cam. Cast-iron block and aluminum head. Displacement: 122 cid (2.0 liters). B & S: 3.27 x 3.62 in. Compression ratio: 9.0:1. Brake hp: 118 at 5500 rpm. Torque: 127 lbs.-ft. at 4500 rpm. Hydraulic valve lifters. Multi-port fuel injection.

1994 Escort LX sedan

1994 Tempo LX sedan

1994 Taurus SHO sedan

1994 Taurus GL sedan

1994 Probe GT coupe

1994 Taurus GL station wagon

1994 Crown Victoria sedan

Tempo Base Four: Inline. Overhead valve. Cast-iron block and head. Displacement: 140 cid (2.3 liters). B & S: 3.70 x 3.30 in. Compression ratio: 9.0:1. Brake hp: 96 at 4200 rpm. Torque: 126 lbs.-ft. at 2600 rpm. Five main bearings. Hydraulic valve lifters. Sequential electronic fuel injection.

Probe GT Base V-6: Dual overhead cam with 24 valves. Aluminum block and head. Displacement: 153 cid (2.5 liters). B & S: 3.33 x 2.92 in. Compression ratio: 9.2:1. Brake hp: 164 at 5600 rpm. Torque: 160 lbs.-ft. at 4000 rpm. Four main bearings. Hydraulic valve lifters. Multiport fuel injection.

Taurus GL and LX sedan Base V-6 (Optional Tempo GL and LX): 60-degree, overhead valve. Cast-iron block and head. Displacement: 182 cid (3.0 liters). B & S: 3.50 x 3.15 in. Compression ratio: 9.3:1. Brake hp: 140 at 4800 rpm. Torque: 165 lbs.-ft. at 3250 rpm. Four main bearings. Hydraulic valve lifters. Sequential electronic fuel injection.

Taurus SHO Base V-6: Dual-overhead-cam V-6 (24-valve). Cast-iron block and head. Displacement: 182 cu. in. (3.0 liters). Bore & stroke: 3.50 x 3.15 in. Compression ratio: 9.8:1. Brake horsepower: 220 at 6200 rpm. Torque: 200 lbs.-ft. at 4800 rpm. Four main bearings. Hydraulic valve lifters. Sequential electronic fuel injection.

Taurus LX wagon Base V-6 (Optional: Taurus GL and LX sedans): 90-degree, overhead valve. Cast-iron block and aluminum head. Displacement: 232 cid (3.8 liters). B & S: 3.80 x 3.40 in. Compression ratio: 9.0:1. Brake hp: 140 at 3800 rpm. Torque: 215 lbs.-ft. at 2200 rpm. Four main bearings. Hydraulic valve lifters. Sequential electronic fuel injection.

Crown Victoria Base V-8: Modular, overhead valve. Displacement: 281 cid (4.6 liters). B & S: 3.60 x 3.60. Compression ratio: 9.0:1. Brake hp: 190 at 4600 rpm. Torque: 260 lbs.-ft. at 3200 rpm. Sequential electronic fuel injection.

Chassis:

Escort: Wheelbase: 98.4 in. Overall length: 170.0 in. and 171.3 in., wagon. Tires: P175/70-R13; P175/65-R14, LX and P185/60-R15, GT.

Tempo: Wheelbase: 99.9 in. Overall length: 176.7 in., two-door and 177.0 in., four-door. Tires: P185/70-R14.

Probe: Wheelbase: 102.8 in. Overall length: 178.7 in. Tires: P195/65-R14 and P225/50-VR16, GT.

Taurus: Wheelbase: 106.0 in. Overall length: 192.0 in. and 193.1 in., wagon. Tires: P205/65-R15 and P215/60-ZR16, Taurus SHO.

Crown Victoria: Wheelbase: 114.4 in. Overall length: 212.4 in. Tires: P215/70-R15.

Options:

Escort: Preferred equipment package, LX, 320A: Power steering, light and convenience group plus rear window defroster ($235). Preferred equipment package, LX, 321A: Manual air conditioning, rear window defroster, light and convenience group, power steering, electronic AM/FM stereo radio with cassette and clock, clear coat paint and wagon additions of luggage rack and rear window wiper and washer ($1,850). Preferred equip package, GT: Manual air conditioning, rear window defroster plus luxury and convenience group ($530). California emissions system ($70). Air conditioning, LX and GT only ($725). Rear window defroster ($160). Light and convenience group including dual electric remote control mirrors, remote fuel door and deck lid releases ($205). Luxury convenience group including tilt steering wheel, speed control and tach, standard on GT ($410). Power moon roof ($525). Clear coat paint ($85).

Comfort group with air conditioning and power steering, base Escort ($800). AM/FM stereo radio, base ($300). AM/FM cassette radio, base ($465) and LX ($165). Electronic AM/FM stereo radio with CD player: base ($740); LX ($445) and GT ($280). Premium sound system ($138). Power steering, LX ($250). Wagon group with deluxe luggage rack, light and convenience group and rear window wiper and washer, LX wagon ($240). Sport appearance group including 14-inch aluminum wheels, tach, full cloth seats, lift gate spoiler and appliqués ($720). Sunrise Red decor group, GT including clear coat Sunrise Red exterior color, color-keyed wheels, cloth bucket seats and front floor mats with embroidered GT trim ($350). Anti-lock Brakes ($565). Power equipment group including power door locks, power windows and tach ($520). Four-speed automatic transaxle ($790). Anti-lock brakes ($565).

Tempo: Preferred equipment package, GL, 225A: Manual air conditioning, light group, dual electric remote control mirrors and rear window defroster ($310). Preferred equipment package, GL, 226A: Same as 225A plus electronic AM/FM stereo radio with cassette and clock, auto transaxle, front center armrest, front and rear floor mats, power lock group, polycast wheels and tilt steering wheel ($1,255). Preferred equipment package, GL, 227A: Same as 226A plus driver's side air bag ($1,190). Preferred equipment package, LX: Manual air conditioning, rear window defroster, 3.0-liter V-6 and automatic transaxle, electronic AM/FM stereo radio with cassette and clock plus deck lid luggage rack ($960). California emissions system ($95). Manual air conditioner ($780). Front center armrest ($55). Rear window defroster ($160). Front and rear floor mats ($45). Instrument cluster ($85). Light group ($35). Power lock group: two-door ($295) and four-door ($335). Luggage rack ($110). Dual electric remote mirrors ($115). Clear coat paint ($85). Electronic AM/FM stereo radio with cassette and clock ($150). Power driver's seat ($290). Premium sound system ($135). Speed control ($215). Tilt steering wheel ($140). Driver's side air bag: GL ($465) and LX ($325). Polycast wheels ($185). Power windows, four-door ($315). Engine block heater ($20). P185/70-R14 whitewall tires, GL and LX ($80). 3.0-liter V-6 ($655). Three-speed automatic transaxle ($535).

Probe: Preferred equipment package, base, 251A: Tilt steering column, rear window defroster, convenience group including interval wipers, light group, dual electric remote mirrors and tinted glass ($370). Preferred equipment package, base, 253A: Same as 251A plus manual air conditioning, electronic AM/FM radio with cassette and premium sound, color-keyed body moldings, illuminated entry system, speed control, power group and fade-to-off dome lamp ($2,340). Preferred equip package, GT, 261A: Manual air conditioning, electronic AM/FM stereo radio with cassette and premium sound, tilt steering column, rear window defroster, convenience group including interval wipers, light group, dual electric remote mirrors and tinted glass ($1,385). Preferred equipment package, GT, 263A: Same as 261A plus color-keyed body moldings, illuminated entry system, speed control, power group and fade-to-off dome lamp ($2,790). Manual air conditioning ($780). Leather bucket seats, GT ($500). Power driver's seat ($290). Anti-lock brakes, base ($735) and GT ($565). Power sliding roof ($615). Feature car package, GT including Wild Orchid exterior finish and unique floor mats and bucket seat trim ($215). Sport edition option, base, includes GT fascia, with fog lamps, 15-inch aluminum wheels and P205/55-R15 tires ($760). Anti-theft system ($190). Power group including power door locks and power windows with dual express down ($700). Light group including dual illuminated visor vanity mirrors, fade-to-off dome lamp and illuminated entry ($395). Color-keyed front floor mats ($30). Dual electric remote control mirrors ($175). Color-keyed body moldings ($50). Rear wiper and washer system ($175). Manual driver's seat height

1994 Taurus LX sedan

1994 Taurus LX station wagon

adjustment ($35). Power antenna ($80). Electronic AM/FM stereo radio with cassette and premium sound ($325). Electronic AM/FM stereo radio with CD player and premium sound ($800). California emissions system ($95). Engine block heater ($20). P205/55-R15 blackwall tires, base ($430). Four-speed automatic transaxle ($790).

Taurus: Preferred equipment package, GL, 203A: Manual air conditioning and rear window defroster ($650). Preferred equip package, GL, 204A: Same as 203A plus power door locks, electronic AM/FM stereo radio with cassette, speed control, deluxe wheel covers, front and rear floor mats, power windows and power six-way driver's seat ($2,070). Electronic air conditioning, LX ($175). Anti-lock brakes, standard on SHO sedan, ($565). Engine block heater ($20). Front and rear floor mats ($45). Keyless remote entry system: GL ($390) and LX ($215). "Picnic table" load floor extension, wagons ($85). Power door locks, GL ($245). Electronic AM/FM stereo radio with cassette ($165). High level audio system, LX and SHO ($315). CD player, LX and SHO ($470). JBL audio system, LX and SHO ($500). Rear-facing third seat, wagons ($150). Dual control power seats, LX ($290). Six-way power driver's seat ($290). Speed control ($215). Cellular phone ($500). Luxury convenience group including JBL audio system, power moon roof, keyless entry system and dual power seats ($1,555). LX convenience group including power moon roof and dual power seats ($1,030). Cast aluminum wheels, GL ($230). California emissions system ($95). Leather bucket seats with console: LX ($495) and GL ($595). Leather split-bench seat, LX ($495). Leather bucket seats, SHO sedan ($495). Heavy duty suspension, not available on SHO ($26). Heavy-duty battery, not available on SHO ($30). Conventional Spare Tire, LX ($70). Power windows ($340). 3.8-liter V-6: GL and LX sedans ($630). Anti-lock brakes: Taurus, standard on SHO ($565).

Crown Victoria: Preferred equipment package, base: Color-keyed front and rear floor mats, rear window defroster, power lock group, trunk cargo net, speed control, illuminated entry system and spare tire cover ($695). Preferred equipment package, LX, 113A: Color-keyed front and rear floor mats, rear window defroster, power lock group, cornering lamps, speed control, illuminated entry system, leather-wrapped steering wheel, electronic AM/FM stereo radio with cassette player, power antenna, cast aluminum wheels, and light and décor group ($295). Preferred equipment package, LX, 114A: Same as 113A plus dual control power seats, high level audio system, anti-lock brakes with electronic traction assist, rear air suspension, automatic temperature control air conditioning, trip minder computer, electronic digital instrumentation, heavy duty battery, keyless remote entry and electric automatic dim mirror ($2,295). California emissions system ($95). Leather split-bench seat, LX ($625). Conventional spare tire ($80). Anti-lock brakes with electronic traction assist ($665). 41G handling and performance package, LX including electronic traction control, revised springs, shocks and stabilizer bar, power steering cooler, P225/60-R16 blackwall touring tires, 16-inch cast aluminum wheels and dual exhausts ($1,765). Engine block heater ($25). Illuminated entry system ($80). Keyless remote entry system, LX ($215). Light and décor group, LX ($225). Cellular phone, LX ($745). Exterior decor group, LX ($485). Convenience group including rear window defroster, power lock group, speed control and trunk cargo net: base ($770) and LX ($670). Exterior decor group, LX, including cast aluminum wheels and cornering lamps ($485). Electronic AM/FM stereo radio with cassette player ($165). High level audio system, LX ($315). Ford JBL audio system ($500). LX luxury group with anti-lock brakes and electronic traction assist, high

level audio system, rear air suspension, keyless remote entry and dual power seats ($2,720). Rear air suspension, LX ($270). Leather-wrapped steering wheel, LX ($90). Trailer towing package, LX ($395). Six-way power driver's seat ($290). Dual power seats, LX ($480). Deluxe wheel covers ($45). Rear window defroster ($160). Color-keyed front and rear floor mats ($45). Rear air suspension, LX ($270). Trailer towing package ($690). Anti-lock brakes with electronic traction assist ($665).

History:

The U.S. model year production totaled 1,307,534, including Mustang. Ford Motor Co. held 18.5 percent of the industry market share. That was the third consecutive year with that percentage. Taurus was the best selling car in the United States in 1994, with 397,037 units sold compared to 367,615 for the second place Honda Accord. Ford Motor Co. recorded an auto industry-record net income of $5.308 billion for 1994, more than double its 1993 net of $2.5 billion. Production geared up for the all-new Contour when the Tempo was discontinued in spring of 1994. The Contour debuted as a 1995 model along with the South Korean-produced Aspire, which replaced the Ford Festiva. The Escort LX-E model offered previously was discontinued. Dual air bags became standard equipment on the Probe, Taurus, Crown Victoria and Thunderbird. A driver's side air bag was standard on the Escort and Tempo.

1995 Ford

Escort — Four: The six Escort models offered the previous year returned in 1995. The lineup was the base three-door hatchback, the LX three- and five-door hatchback, four-door sedan and station wagon and the GT three-door hatchback. The passenger-side air bag was standard equipment. All models featured a new instrument panel. The LX sedan's tachometer was discontinued. The standard engine for the base and LX Escorts was the 1.9-liter four-cylinder with sequential electronic fuel injection. A five-speed manual transaxle was standard and the electronic four-speed automatic overdrive transaxle was optional. The GT model continued to use the 16-valve DOHC 1.8-liter four-cylinder engine with multi-port fuel injection.

Contour — Four and V-6: The Contour was Ford's replacement for the discontinued Tempo. It was the company's initial "global car" using the expertise of Ford's worldwide operations to produce vehicles for multiple markets. The front-wheel-drive Contour was offered in GL, LX and SE series, each a four-door sedan with five-passenger capacity. The Contour featured "safety cell" body construction, with high-tensile boron steel door beams, a cross-car beam running between the windshield pillars and a reinforced subframe. The Contour's cab-forward design offered a low 0.31 drag coefficient (Cd). The GL and LX sedans used the Zetec DOHC, 16-valve 2.0-liter, 125 hp four-cylinder engine. The SE sedan was powered by the all-aluminum, modular Duratec 2.5-liter V-6. Both used Ford's engine controller EEC-IV, and featured an ignition without a distributor plus mass-air flow and knock sensors. The base transaxle on all Contours was the MTX75 five-speed manual while the CD4E electronically-controlled four-speed automatic was optional. Dual

1995 Escort LX station wagon

1995 Escort GT three-door hatchback

1995 Contour GL sedan

airbags were standard along with solar reflective glass that reduced interior heat build-up.

Probe — Four and V-6: Probe's lineup again consisted of a coupe in base or GT series. Changes for 1995 included a minor interior redesign, modified tail lamps and rear bumper. The T sported new aluminum wheels. The base coupe was again powered by the DOHC 2.0-liter four-cylinder engine. The GT coupe used the all-aluminum DOHC 2.5-liter V-6. A five-speed manual transaxle was again standard equipment on both coupes and an electronically controlled four-speed automatic transaxle was optional.

Taurus — V-6: The addition of an SE series sedan meant six models in four series for the 1995 Taurus. They were the GL, SE, LX and SHO. The SE and SHO each offered a four-door sedan while the GL and LX series offered a sedan and station wagon. The base 3.0-liter V-6 offered in the GL and SE series and LX sedan received an upgrade. New standard equipment included a rear window defroster, manual air conditioning, tinted glass and a low fuel light. The LX wagon was powered by the 3.8-liter V-6, the optional engine on all other Taurus models except the SHO sedan. The four-speed automatic overdrive transaxle was the standard on the GL, SE and LX models. The SHO sedan used the DOHC 3.0-liter V-6 as its base unit and was coupled to a five-speed manual transaxle. The SHO sedan was also available with the DOHC 3.2-liter V-6 with the four-speed automatic overdrive transaxle. A re-designed Taurus was launched in June 1995.

Crown Victoria — V-8: The Crown Victoria four-door sedan was available in base or LX series for the second consecutive model year. The Crown Victoria was revised inside and out as it received a new instrument panel, door panels and seats as well as modified tail lamps, grille, bumpers and body moldings. New standard features included a battery saver and heated rearview mirror. The modular 4.6-liter V-8 and electronically controlled four-speed automatic overdrive transmission were again the standard power train offered with the 1995 Crown Victorias.

I. D. Data:

Ford's 17-symbol Vehicle Identification Number (VIN) was stamped on a metal tab fastened to the instrument panel and was visible through the windshield. The first three symbols indicated the manufacturer, make and vehicle type. The fourth symbol denoted the restraint system. Next came letter P followed by two digits that indicated the model number, such as P10=Escort two-door hatchback. Symbol eight indicated the engine type. Next was a check digit. Symbol 10 indicated the model year S=1995. Symbol 11 denoted the assembly plant. The final six digits made up the sequential number, starting with 100001 or 000001 on the Contour.

Escort (Four)

Model No.	Body/ Style No.	Body Type & Seating	Factory Price	Shipping Weight	Production Total
P	10	2-dr. Hatchback-5P	$9,560	2,316 lbs.	Note 1
P	11	2-dr. LX Hatchback-5P	$10,415	2,355 lbs.	Note 1
P	14	4-dr. LX Hatchback-5P	$11,020	2,385 lbs.	50,233
P	13	4-dr. LX Sedan-5P	$10,850	2,404 lbs.	62,713
P	15	4-dr. LX Station Wagon-5P	$11,405	2,451 lbs.	115,960
P	12	2-dr. GT Hatchback-5P	$12,700	2,459 lbs.	Note 1

Note 1: Production of two-door hatchback models totaled 91,875 with no further breakout available.

Contour (Four)

P	65	4-dr. GL Sedan-5P	$13,310	2,769 lbs.	Note 1
P	66	4-dr. LX Sedan-5P	$13,995	2,808 lbs.	Note 1

Contour (V-6)

P	65	4-dr. GL Sedan-5P	$14,390	2,769 lbs.	Note 1
P	66	4-dr. LX Sedan-5P	$15,040	2,808 lbs.	Note 1
P	67	4-dr. SE Sedan-5P	$15,695	2,994 lbs.	Note 1

Note 1: Production of four-door sedan models totaled 178,832 with no further breakout available.

1995 Probe GT coupe

Probe (Four)

T	20	2-dr. Coupe-4P	$14,180	2,690 lbs.	Note 1

Probe GT (V-6)

T	22	2-dr. GT Coupe-4P	$16,545	2,921 lbs.	Note 1

Note 1: Production of two-door coupe models totaled 58,226 with no further breakout available.

Taurus (V-6)

P	52	4-dr. GL Sedan-6P	$17,585	3,118 lbs.	Note 1
P	57	4-dr. GL Station Wagon-6P	$18,680	3,285 lbs.	Note 2
P	52	4-dr. SE Sedan-6P	$17,955	3,118 lbs.	Note 1
P	53	4-dr. LX Sedan-6P	$19,400	3,186 lbs.	Note 1
P	58	4-dr. LX Station Wagon-6P	$21,010	3,363 lbs.	Note 2
P	54	4-dr. SHO Sedan-6P	$25,140	3,377 lbs.	Note 1

Note 1: Production of four-door sedan models totaled 345,244 and no further breakouts were available.

Note 2: Production of station wagon models totaled 50,494 with no further breakout available.

Crown Victoria (V-8)

P	73	4-dr. Sedan-6P	$20,160	3,762 lbs.	Note 1
P	74	4-dr. LX Sedan-6P	$21,970	3,779 lbs.	Note 1

Note 1: Production of four-door sedan models totaled 98,309 with no further breakout available.

Engines:

Escort Base Four: Inline. Overhead cam. Cast-iron block and aluminum head. Displacement: 113 cid (1.9 liters). B & S: 3.23 x 3.46 in. Compression ratio: 9.0:1. Brake hp: 88 at 4400 rpm Torque: 108 lbs.-ft. at 3800 rpm. Five main bearings. Hydraulic valve lifters. Sequential electronic fuel injection.

Escort GT Base Four: High-output. Inline. Dual overhead cam. Cast-iron block and aluminum head. Displacement: 109 cid (1.8 liters). B & S: 3.27 x 3.35 in. Compression ratio: 9.0:1. Brake hp: 127 at 6500 rpm. Torque: 114 lbs.-ft. at 4500 rpm. Five main bearings. Hydraulic valve lifters. Multi-port fuel injection.

Probe Base Four: Inline. Dual overhead cam. Cast-iron block and aluminum head. Displacement: 122 cid (2.0 liters). B & S: 3.27 x 3.62 in. Compression ratio: 9.0:1. Brake hp: 118 at 5500 rpm. Torque: 127 lbs.-ft. at 4500 rpm. Hydraulic valve lifters. Multi-port fuel injection.

Contour Base Four: Inline. Dual overhead cam with 16 valves. Cast-iron block and aluminum head. Displacement: 121 cid (2.0 liters). B & S: 3.34 x 3.46 in. Compression ratio: 9.6:1. Brake hp: 125 at 5500 rpm. Torque: 125 lbs.-ft. at 4500 rpm. Sequential electronic fuel injection.

Probe GT Base V-6: Dual overhead cam V-6 (24-valve). Aluminum block and head. Displacement: 153 cu. in. (2.5 liters). B & S: 3.33 x 2.92 in. Compression ratio: 9.2:1. Brake horsepower: 164 at 5600 RPM. Torque: 160 lbs.-ft. at 4000 rpm. Four main bearings. Hydraulic valve lifters. Multi-port fuel injection.

Contour SE Base V-6 (Optional Contour GL and LX): Modular, dual overhead cam with 24 valves. Aluminum block and head. Displacement: 155 cid (2.5 liters). B & S: 3.24 x 3.13 in. Compression ratio: 9.7:1. Brake hp: 170 at 6200 rpm. Torque: 165 lbs.-ft. at 5000 rpm. Sequential electronic fuel injection.

Taurus GL, SE and LX Base V-6: Overhead valve. Cast-iron block and head. Displacement: 182 cid (3.0 liters). B & S: 3.50 x 3.15 in. Compression ratio: 9.3:1. Brake hp: 140 at 4800 rpm. Torque: 165 lbs.-ft. at 3250 rpm. Four main bearings. Hydraulic valve lifters. Sequential electronic fuel injection.

Taurus SHO Base V-6: Dual-overhead-cam with 24 valves. Cast-iron block and head. Displacement: 182 cid (3.0 liters). B & S: 3.50 x 3.15 in. Compression ratio: 9.8:1. Brake hp: 220 at 6200 rpm. Torque: 200 lbs.-ft. at 4800 rpm. Four main bearings. Hydraulic valve lifters. Sequential electronic fuel injection.

Taurus LX wagon Base V-6 (Optional Taurus GL, SE and LX sedan): 90-degree, overhead valve. Cast-iron block and aluminum head. Displacement: 232 cid (3.8 liters). B & S: 3.80 x 3.40 in. Compression

1995 Taurus SE sedan

1995 Crown Victoria LX sedan

1995 Contour LX sedan

ratio: 9.0:1. Brake hp: 140 at 4800 rpm. Torque: 215 lbs.-ft. at 2200 rpm. Four main bearings. Hydraulic valve lifters. Sequential fuel injection.

Crown Victoria Base V-8: Modular, overhead valve. Displacement: 281 cid (4.6 liters). B & S: 3.60 x 3.60. Compression ratio: 9.0:1. Brake hp: 190 at 4250 rpm. Torque: 260 lbs.-ft. at 3200 rpm. Sequential electronic fuel injection.

Chassis:

Escort: Wheelbase: 98.4 in. Overall length: 170.0 in. and 171.3 in., station wagon. Tires: P175/70-R13; P175/65-R14, LX and P185/60-R15. GT.

Contour: Wheelbase: 106.5 in. Overall length: 183.9 in. Tires: P185/70-R14S and P205/60-R15T, SE.

Probe: Wheelbase: 102.8 in. Overall length: 178.7 in. Tires: P195/65-R14 and P225/50-VR16, GT.

Taurus: Wheelbase: 106.0 in. Overall length: 192.0 in. Tires: P205/65-R15 and P215/60-ZR16, SHO.

Crown Victoria: Wheelbase: 114.4 in. Overall length: 212.4 in. Tires: P215/70-R15.

Options:

Escort: Preferred equipment package, LX, 320M: Power steering, light and convenience group, sport appearance group and rear window defroster ($190). Preferred equipment package, LX, 321M: Manual air conditioning, rear window defroster, light and convenience group, sport appearance group, power steering, electronic AM/FM stereo radio with cassette and clock plus, in wagons, luggage rack and rear window wiper and washer ($1,185). Preferred equipment package, LX, 322M: Automatic transmission, manual air conditioner, rear window defroster, light and convenience group, sport appearance group, power steering, electronic AM/FM stereo radio with cassette and clock plus, in wagons, luggage rack and rear window wiper and washer ($2,000). Preferred equipment package, GT: Manual air conditioner and rear window defroster ($435). California emissions system ($95). Integrated child seat, LX, ($135). Air conditioning, LX and GT ($785). Rear window defroster ($160). Light and convenience group with dual electric remote control mirrors, LX ($160). Luxury convenience group including tilt steering wheel, speed control and tach, LX ($410) and GT ($460). Power moon roof ($525). Clear coat paint ($85). Comfort group with air conditioning and power steering, base ($860). Electronic AM/FM stereo radio, base ($300). Electronic AM/FM stereo radio with cassette, base ($465) and LX ($165). Electronic AM/FM stereo radio with CD player, base ($625), LX ($325) and GT ($160). Premium sound system ($60). Power steering, LX ($250). Deluxe luggage rack, light and convenience group and rear window wiper and washer, LX wagon ($240). Sport appearance group with 14-inch aluminum wheels, tach, full cloth seats, lift gate spoiler and appliqués ($720). Ultra Violet decor group, GT with clear coat metallic Ultra Violet, color-keyed wheels, cloth bucket seats and front floor mats with embroidered GT trim ($400). Anti-lock brakes, GT ($565). Electric dual remote control mirrors ($95). Power equipment group with power door locks, power windows and tach ($520). Four-speed automatic transaxle ($815). Power steering, LX ($250). Anti-lock brakes ($565).

Contour: Preferred equipment package, GL, 235A: Manual air conditioner, rear window defroster, heated exterior mirrors, AM/FM stereo radio with cassette and full-length console ($850). Preferred

equipment package, GL, 236A: Same as 235A plus power door locks, light group including dual illuminated visor mirrors and illuminated entry system ($1,310). Preferred equip package, GL, 240A: Same as 236A plus power windows and 2.5-liter V-6 engine ($2,530). Preferred equip package, LX, 237A: Manual air conditioner, rear window defroster, power locks, power windows, light group with dual illuminated visor mirrors and illuminated entry system ($1,350). Preferred equipment package, LX, 238A: Same as 237A plus 2.5-liter V-6 Engine ($2,245). Preferred equip package, SE 239A: Air conditioning, rear window defroster, power windows, power door locks, light group with dual illuminated visor mirrors and illuminated entry system ($1,350). California emissions system ($95). Door lock and light group including power door locks, dual illuminated visor mirrors and illuminated entry system ($345). Lock system with keyless remote ($160). Power moon roof ($595). Power driver's seat, LX ($330) and SE ($290). Power windows ($340). Electronic AM/FM stereo radio with cassette player ($130). Electronic AM/FM stereo radio with CD player ($270). All- speed traction control with anti-lock Brakes ($800). Anti-lock brakes ($565). Manual air conditioner ($780). Rear window defroster ($160). Front and rear carpeted floor mats ($45). Leather bucket seats, LX ($645) or SE ($595). Speed control ($215). 14-inch aluminum wheels, GL and LX ($265). 2.5-liter DOHC V-6: GL ($1,080) and LX ($1,045). Four-speed automatic transaxle ($815). Anti-lock brakes ($565).

Probe: Preferred equipment base series, 251A: Manual air conditioner, AM/FM stereo radio with cassette and tinted glass ($560). Preferred equipment package, base, 253A: Same as 251A plus tilt steering, interval wipers, dual remote power mirrors, rear window defroster and console ($2,545). Preferred equipment package, GT, 261A: Manual air conditioner, electronic AM/FM stereo radio with cassette and premium sound, tilt steering, rear window defroster, interval wipers, speed control, color-keyed body moldings, tinted glass, front and rear color-keyed floor mats and dual electric remote mirrors ($1,790). Preferred equipment package, GT, 263A: Same as 261A plus anti-lock brakes, keyless remote entry system, dual illuminated visor mirrors, power windows, power driver's seat and fade-to-off dome lamp ($3,495). Manual air conditioner ($895). Leather bucket seats, GT ($500). Power driver's seat, GT ($290). Anti-lock brakes, base ($735) or GT ($565). Anti-theft system, GT ($190). Electronic AM/FM stereo radio with cassette and clock, base ($165). Electronic AM/FM stereo radio with cassette player and premium sound ($405). Electronic AM/FM stereo radio with CD player and premium sound, base ($430) and GT ($270). Color-keyed body moldings ($50). Color-keyed front and rear floor mats ($30). Power sliding roof ($615). Rear deck lid spoiler ($235). Rear window wiper and washer system, GT ($130). SE appearance package with GT front fascia, 15-inch aluminum wheels, P205/55-R15 blackwall tires and SE Graphics ($530). California emissions system ($95). Engine block heater ($20). 15-inch aluminum wheels, base ($450). 16-inch chrome wheels, GT ($390).

Taurus: Preferred equipment package, GL, 204A: Power door locks, electronic AM/FM stereo radio with cassette, speed control, deluxe wheel covers, front and rear floor mats, power windows and six-way driver's seat ($775) and with 3.8-liter V-6 ($1,275). Preferred equipment package, SE, 205A including power door locks, power windows, Electronic AM/FM stereo radio with cassette, power driver's seat, sport bucket seats, cast aluminum wheels, front and rear floor mats and console ($1,045) or with 3.8-liter engine ($1,545). Preferred equipment package, LX, 208A including speed control, keyless remote entry, electronic AM/FM stereo radio with cassette player and power antenna, leather-wrapped steering wheel, front and rear floor mats and for wagon, rear window washer and wiper, load floor extension and cargo area cover ($545). Electronic air conditioner, LX ($175). Anti-lock brakes, standard on SHO sedan ($565). Engine block heater ($20). Front and rear floor mats ($45). Keyless remote entry system, GL ($295); SE ($390) and LX or SHO ($215). "Picnic table" load floor extension, wagons ($85). Power door locks, GL and SE ($245). Electronic AM/FM stereo radio with cassette ($165). High level audio system, LX and SHO ($315). Audio digital CD player, LX and SHO ($375). JBL audio system, LX and SHO ($500). Rear facing third seat, wagons ($150). Dual control power seats, LX and SHO ($290). Six-way power driver's seat, LX ($290). Speed control ($215). Cellular phone ($500). Luxury convenience group with JBL audio system, power moon roof, keyless entry system and dual power seats ($1,555). LX convenience group including power moon roof and dual power seats

1995 Contour SE sedan

1996 Escort LX three-door hatchback (with Sport Appearance package)

($1,030). GL equipment group with speed sensitive power steering, paint stripe, dual visor mirrors and secondary visor ($245). Deck lid spoiler, SE ($270). Power side windows, GL and SE ($340). Cast aluminum wheels, GL ($230). California emissions system ($95). Leather bucket seats with console, LX ($495) or GL ($595). Leather split bench seat, LX ($495). Leather bucket seats, SE and SHO sedan only ($495). Heavy duty suspension, not available on SHO ($26). Heavy duty battery, not available on SHO ($30). Deluxe wheel covers, GL ($80). Conventional spare tire, GL and LX ($70). 3.8-liter V-6: GL, SE and LX sedan ($630).

Crown Victoria: Preferred equipment package, base, 111A: Color-keyed front and rear floor mats, power lock spoked wheel covers, speed control and illuminated entry system ($745). Preferred equipment package, LX, 113A including color-keyed front and rear floor mats, power lock group, cornering lamps, speed control, illuminated entry system, leather-wrapped steering wheel, electronic AM/FM stereo radio with cassette, cast aluminum 12-spoke wheels and light and decor group ($320). Preferred equipment package, LX, 114A: Same as 113A plus dual control power seats, high level audio system, anti-lock brakes with electronic traction assist, rear air suspension, automatic temperature control air conditioning, trip minder computer, digital electronic instrumentation, heavy duty battery, keyless remote entry and electric auto-dimming mirror ($2,300). Electronic automatic temperature control air conditioning ($175). California emissions system ($95). Leather split-bench seat, LX ($645). Conventional spare tire ($80). Anti-lock brakes with electronic traction assist ($665). 41G handling and performance package, LX, with revised springs, shocks and stabilizer bar, power steering cooler, P225/60-R16 blackwall touring tires, 16-inch cast aluminum wheels and dual exhausts ($1,100). Engine block heater ($25). Keyless remote entry system, LX ($215). Light and decor group, LX ($225). Electronic AM/FM stereo radio with cassette ($185). High level audio system, LX ($360). Ford JBL audio system ($500). Rear air suspension, base ($270). Trailer towing package, base ($500) and LX ($795). Six-way power driver's seat, base ($360). Dual power seats ($360). Color-keyed front and rear floor mats ($45). P215/70-R15 whitewall tires ($80). Trailer towing package ($795).

History:

U.S. model year production totaled 1,179,436, including Mustang but excluding Crown Victoria. U. S. calendar year production totaled 1,010,997, including Mustang, for 15.9 percent of the automotive industry market share. In 1995, for the fourth consecutive year, the Taurus was the best selling car in the United States with 366,266 units sold compared to 341,384 for the second place Honda Accord. With the Tempo discontinued, its 1995 replacement debuted early in 1994, the Contour. The Contour was an example of Ford's new wave of "World Cars" with the Mercury Mystique and European Ford Mondeo all based on the same platform. The cars also had similar styling. The Contour used either the Zetec 2.0-liter four-cylinder engine in the GL or LX sedans or the Duratec 2.5-liter V-6, the engine used in the SE sedan. The Taurus SE sedan was another new model in the Ford lineup. The Crown Victoria received several revisions including a modified grille and tail outside and a new instrument panel inside.

1996 Ford

Escort — Four: With an all-new design, the 1997 Escort was to be launched in spring 1996. That meant that the 1995 Escort lineup was carried over early in the 1996 model year. That lineup was again the base three-door hatchback, the LX three- and five-door hatchbacks, the LX four-door sedan and station wagon and the GT three-door hatchback. Escort's drive ratio was increased from 3.55:1 to 4.06:1 for improved acceleration in 1996. Integrated child seats were an option on

all Escort models. The sport appearance package was now available on LX series models. The standard engine for base and LX Escorts was the 1.9-liter four-cylinder with sequential electronic fuel injection. A five-speed manual transaxle was again standard with the electronic four-speed automatic overdrive transaxle an option. The GT model continued to use the 16-valve DOHC 1.8-liter four-cylinder engine, equipped in 1996 with electronic fuel injection.

Contour — Four and V-6: The Contour was basically unchanged from its debut the year previous. It was again offered as a four-door sedan in GL, LX and SE series. The Contour's seats were revised to increase rear passenger legroom. The GL and LX sedans repeated their use of the Zetec DOHC, 16-valve 2.0-liter four-cylinder engine. The SE sedan was powered by the modular, DOHC Duratec 2.5-liter V-6, the optional engine for the GL and LX models. Contours again used the five-speed manual transaxle as a base unit and the electronically controlled four-speed automatic transaxle as the option unit.

Probe — Four and V-6: Half of the option packages offered previously on Probe's base or GT coupes were discontinued, leaving only two packages, one for each series, in 1996. The base coupe was again powered by the DOHC 2.0-liter four-cylinder engine. The GT coupe again used the DOHC 2.5-liter V-6. A five-speed manual transaxle was again standard equipment on both coupes and an electronically controlled four-speed automatic transaxle was optional.

Taurus — V-6: The all-new 1996 Taurus was launched in September 1995 and was available in three series: GL, LX and SHO. The GL and LX series each included a sedan and station wagon while the SHO model was a four-door sedan. This new Taurus was longer, wider and more rounded than the previous year's version. Standard features included an integrated control panel that governed audio and climate systems, electronic four-speed automatic transaxle and dual air bags. Anti-theft and air filtration systems were standard on both the LX and SHO models. GL models were capable of seating six due to a front flip-fold central console seat. Anti-lock brakes were optional for the GL and LX. The GL series used the revised Vulcan 3.0-liter 145 hp V-6. LX models were powered by the 200 hp Duratec DOHC 3.0-liter V-6. The SHO sedan used the 240-hp DOHC 3.4-liter V-8. The optional engine for the GL sedan was a flex-fuel 3.0-liter V-6. The electronically-controlled four-speed automatic transaxle was standard on all Taurus models except the SHO sedan which used the five-speed manual transaxle.

Crown Victoria — V-8: Base or LX four-door sedans comprised the Crown Victoria lineup, returning for 1996 basically unchanged after undergoing refinement for the 1995 model year. Changes included the Crown Victoria's upgraded variable assist power steering receiving and an additional engine option, the 178-hp 4.6-liter natural gas-fueled V-8. The base power train was again the modular 4.6-liter V-8 with an electronically controlled four-speed automatic overdrive transmission.

I. D. Data:

Ford's 17-symbol Vehicle Identification Number (VIN) was stamped on a metal tab fastened to the instrument panel and was visible through the windshield. The first three symbols indicated the manufacturer, make and vehicle type. The fourth symbol denoted the restraint system. Next came letter P followed by two digits that indicated the model number, such as P10=Escort two-door hatchback. Symbol eight indicated the engine type. Next was a check digit. Symbol 10 indicated the model year: T=1996. Symbol 11 noted the assembly plant. The final six digits made up the sequential production number, starting with 100001.

Escort (Four)

Model No.	Body/Style No.	Body Type & Seating	Factory Price	Shipping Weight	Production Total
P	10	2-dr. Hatchback	$10,065	2,323 lbs.	Note 1
P	11	2-dr. LX Hatchback-5P	$10,910	2,356 lbs.	Note 1
P	14	4-dr. LX Hatchback-5P	$11,345	2,398 lbs.	11,807
P	13	4-dr. LX Sedan-5P	$11,515	2,378 lbs.	13,439
P	15	4-dr. LX Station Wagon-5P	$11,900	2,444 lbs.	35,199
P	12	2-dr. GT Hatchback-5P	$13,205	2,455 lbs.	Note 1

Note 1: Production of two-door hatchback models totaled 64,964 with no further breakout available.

1996 Taurus GL sedan

Contour (Four)

| P | 65 | 4-dr. GL Sedan-5P | $13,785 | 2,773 lbs. | Note 1 |
| P | 66 | 4-dr. GL Sedan-5P | $14,470 | 2,815 lbs. | Note 1 |

Contour (V-6)

P	65	4-dr. GL Sedan-5P	$14,865	2,875 lbs.	Note 1
P	66	4-dr. GL Sedan-5P	$15,515	2,939 lbs.	Note 1
P	67	4-dr. SE Sedan-5P	$16,170	2,934 lbs.	Note 1

Note 1: Production of four-door sedan models totaled 167,555 with no further breakout available.

Probe (Four)

| T | 20 | 2-dr. Coupe-4P | $13,930 | 2,690 lbs. | Note 1 |

Probe GT (V-6)

| T | 22 | 2-dr. GT Coupe-4P | $16,450 | 2,921 lbs. | Note 1 |

Note 1: Production of two-door coupe models totaled 30,125 with no further breakout available.

Taurus (V-6)

P	52	4-dr. GL Sedan-6P	$18,600	3,347 lbs.	Note 1
P	57	4-dr. GL Station Wagon-6P	$19,680	3,511 lbs.	Note 2
P	53	4-dr. LX Sedan-6P	$20,980	3,355 lbs.	Note 1
P	58	4-dr. LX Station Wagon-6P	$22,000	3,531 lbs.	Note 2

Taurus SHO (V-8)

| P | 54 | 4-dr. SHO Sedan-6P | $25,930 | 3,544 lbs. | Note 1 |

Note 1: Production of four-door sedan models totaled 348,671 and no further breakout was available.
Note 2: Production of station wagon models totaled 45,439 with no further breakout available.

Crown Victoria (V-8)

| P | 73 | 4-dr. Sedan-6P | $20,955 | 3,780 lbs. | Note 1 |
| P | 74 | 4-dr. LX Sedan-6P | $22,675 | 3,791 lbs. | Note 1 |

Note 1: Production of four-door sedan models totaled 108,252 with no further breakout available.

Engines:

Escort Base Four: Inline. Overhead cam. Cast-iron block and aluminum head. Displacement: 113 cid (1.9 liters). B & S: 3.23 x 3.46 in. Compression ratio: 9.0:1. Brake hp: 88 at 4400 rpm. Torque: 108 lbs.-ft. at 3800 rpm. Five main bearings. Hydraulic valve lifters. Sequential electronic fuel injection.

Escort GT Base Four: High-output. Inline. Dual overhead cam. Cast-iron block and aluminum head. Displacement: 109 cid (1.8 liters). B & S: 3.27 x 3.35 in. Compression ratio: 9.0:1. Brake hp: 127 at 6500 rpm. Torque: 114 lbs.-ft. at 4500 rpm. Five main bearings. Hydraulic valve lifters. Electronic fuel injection.

Probe Base Four: Inline. Dual overhead cam. Cast-iron block and aluminum head. Displacement: 122 cid (2.0 liters). B & S: 3.27 x 3.62 in. Compression ratio: 9.0:1. Brake hp: 118 at 5500 rpm. Torque: 127 lbs.-ft. at 4500 rpm. Hydraulic valve lifters. Sequential electronic fuel injection.

Contour Base Four: Inline. Dual overhead cam with 16 valves. Cast-iron block and aluminum head. Displacement: 121 cid (2.0 liters). B & S: 3.34 x 3.46 in. Compression ratio: 9.6:1. Brake hp: 125 at 5500 rpm. Torque: 125 lbs.-ft. at 4500 rpm. Sequential electronic fuel injection.

Probe GT Base V-6: Dual overhead cam with 24 valves. Aluminum block and head. Displacement: 153 cid (2.5 liters). B & S: 3.33 x 2.92 in. Compression ratio: 9.2:1. Brake hp: 164 at 5600 rpm. Torque: 160 lbs.-ft. at 4000 rpm. Four main bearings. Hydraulic valve lifters. Sequential electronic fuel injection.

Contour SE Base V-6 (Optional on Contour GL and LX): Modular, dual overhead cam with 24 valves. Aluminum block and head. Displacement: 155 cid (2.5 liters). B & S: 3.24 x 3.13 in. Compression ratio: 9.7:1. Brake hp: 170 at 6200 rpm. Torque: 165 lbs.-ft. at 5000 rpm. Sequential electronic fuel injection.

1996 Taurus GL station wagon

Taurus GL Base V-6: Overhead valve. Cast-iron block and head. Displacement: 182 cid (3.0 liters). B & S: 3.50 x 3.15 in. Compression ratio: 9.3:1. Brake hp: 140 at 4800 rpm. Torque: 165 lbs.-ft. at 3250 rpm. Four main bearings. Hydraulic valve lifters. Sequential electronic fuel injection.

Taurus LX Base V-6: Dual-overhead-cam with 24 valves. Aluminum block and head. Displacement: 182 cid (3.0 liters). B & S: 3.50 x 3.15 in. Compression ratio: 9.3:1. Brake hp: 200 at 5750 rpm. Torque: N/A. Four main bearings. Hydraulic valve lifters. Sequential electronic fuel injection.

Taurus SHO Base V-8: Dual overhead cam with 32 valves. Aluminum block and head. Displacement: 207 cid (3.4 liters). B & S: 3.50 x 3.15 in. Compression ratio: 9.8:1. Brake hp: 224 at 6500 rpm. Torque: N/A. Sequential electronic fuel injection.

Crown Victoria Base V-8: Modular, overhead valve V-8. Displacement: 281 cid (4.6 liters). B & S: 3.60 x 3.60. Compression ratio: 9.0:1. Brake hp: 190 at 4250 rpm. Torque: 260 lbs.-ft. at 3200 rpm. Sequential electronic fuel injection.

Chassis:

Escort: Wheelbase: 98.4 in. Overall length: 170.0 in. and 171.3 in., wagon. Tires: P175/70-R13; P175/65-R14, LX and P185/60-R15, GT.

Contour: Wheelbase: 106.5 in. Overall length: 183.9 in. Tires: P185/70-R14S and P205/60-R15T SE.

Probe: Wheelbase: 102.8 in. Overall length: 178.7 in. Tires: P195/65-R14 and P225/50-VR16, GT.

Taurus: Wheelbase: 108.5 in. Overall length: 197.5 in. Tires: P205/65-R15 and P225/55-VR16, SHO.

Crown Victoria: Wheelbase: 114.4 in. Overall length: 212.0 in. Tires: P215/70-R15.

Options:

Escort: Preferred equipment package, LX, 320M: Power steering, light and convenience group, sport appearance group and rear window defroster: two-door ($250) and four-door ($200). Preferred equipment package, LX, 321M: Manual air conditioner, electronic AM/FM stereo radio with cassette and clock and in wagons: luggage rack and rear window wiper and washer, two-door ($1,195); four-door sedan ($590); four-door hatchback ($760) and wagon ($205). Preferred equipment package, LX, 322M: Automatic transmission, manual air conditioner, electronic AM/FM stereo radio with cassette and clock plus, in the wagons, luggage rack and rear window wiper and washer, two-door ($2,010); four-door sedan ($1,405); four-door hatchback ($1,575) and wagon ($1,020). Preferred equipment package, GT: Manual air conditioner and rear window defroster ($445). California emissions system ($100). Integrated child seat, LX ($135). Air conditioner ($785). Rear window defroster ($170). Light and convenience group including dual electric remote control mirrors ($160). Luxury convenience group with tilt steering wheel, leather-wrapped steering wheel, speed control and tach: LX ($465) or GT ($460). Power moon roof ($525). Clear coat paint ($85). Comfort group with air conditioning and power steering, base ($860). Electronic AM/FM stereo radio, base ($300). Electronic AM/FM stereo radio with cassette, base ($465) and LX ($165). Electronic AM/FM stereo radio with CD player: base ($625); LX ($325) and GT ($160). Premium sound system ($60). Power steering ($250). Luggage rack, light and convenience group and rear window wiper and washer, LX wagon ($240). Sport appearance group with 14-inch aluminum wheels, tach, lift gate spoiler and appliqués ($720). Anti-lock brakes, GT ($570). Electric dual remote control mirrors ($95). Power equipment group with power door locks, power windows and tach: LX ($520) and GT ($460). Integrated child's seat, LX ($135). Four-speed automatic transaxle ($815). Power steering ($250).

Contour: Preferred equipment package, GL, 235A: Manual air conditioner, rear window defroster, heated exterior mirrors, AM/FM stereo radio with cassette and full-length console ($870). Preferred equipment package, GL, 236A: Same as 235A with power door locks,

1996 Taurus SHO sedan

1996 Crown Victoria LX sedan

1996 Probe SE coupe

light group with dual illuminated visor mirrors and illuminated entry system plus speed control ($1,330). Preferred equipment package, GL, 240A: Same as 236A plus power windows and 2.5-liter V-6 ($3,365). Preferred equipment package, LX, 238A: 2.5-liter V-6, air conditioner, rear window defroster, speed control, power locks, power windows, light group, dual illuminated visor mirrors and illuminated entry system ($3,060). Preferred equipment package, SE, 239A: Air conditioner, rear window defroster, speed control, power windows, power door locks, light group with dual illuminated visor mirrors and illuminated entry system ($1,370). California emissions system ($100). Door lock and light group including power door locks, dual illuminated visor mirrors and illuminated entry system ($345). Keyless remote lock system ($190). Power moon roof ($595). Power windows ($340). Electronic AM/FM stereo radio with cassette player ($130). Electronic AM/FM stereo radio with CD player ($270). All-speed traction control with anti-lock brakes ($805). Anti-lock brakes ($570). Manual air conditioner ($780). Rear window defroster ($170). Carpeted front and rear floor mats ($45). Power driver's seat, LX and SE ($330). Leather bucket seats: LX ($645) and SE ($595). Split fold-down rear seat, GL ($205). Sport package, GL ($495) or LX ($420). Speed control ($215). 15-inch aluminum wheels, GL and LX ($425). 2.5-liter DOHC V-6, GL ($1,080) and LX ($1,045). Four-speed automatic transaxle ($815). Anti-lock brakes ($570).

Probe: Preferred equipment package, base: SE appearance package, manual air conditioner, AM/FM stereo radio with cassette player, interval wipers, rear window defroster and tinted Glass ($1,120). Preferred equipment package, GT: Manual air conditioner, rear window defroster, interval wipers, tinted glass, anti-lock brakes, power windows, power door locks, deck lid spoiler and dual electric remote mirrors ($1,905). Manual air conditioner ($895). Leather bucket seats, GT ($500). Power driver's seat, GT ($290). Convenience group with dual power mirrors, base ($740) and GT ($570). Power convenience group with power door locks and power windows ($485). Driver comfort group including tilt steering and speed control ($355). Anti-lock brakes: base ($740) and GT ($570). Electronic AM/FM stereo radio with cassette and clock, base ($165). Electronic AM/FM stereo radio with CD player and premium sound ($430). Color-keyed body moldings ($50). Color-keyed front and rear floor mats ($30). Power sliding roof, GT ($615). Keyless remote entry ($270). Rear deck lid spoiler ($235). Interval wipers ($60). SE appearance package with GT front fascia, 15-inch aluminum wheels, P205/55-R15 blackwall tires and SE graphics ($530). California emissions system ($100). Engine block heater ($20). 16-inch chrome wheels, GT ($390). Four-speed automatic transaxle ($815). Anti-lock brakes: ($740) and GT ($570).

Taurus: Preferred equipment package, GL, 204A: Power door locks, AM/FM stereo radio with cassette, speed control, air filtration system plus front and rear floor mats ($240). Preferred equipment package, GL, 205A: Same as 204A plus power driver's seat, light group, cargo net and aluminum wheels: sedan ($840) and wagon ($880). Preferred equipment package, LX, 208A: Speed control and front and rear floor mats ($150). Preferred equipment package, LX, 209A: Same as 208A plus four-wheel disc brakes with anti-lock and keyless remote entry system and perimeter anti-theft system ($860). Preferred equip package, LX, 210A: Same as 209A plus electronic temperature control air conditioning, aluminum wheels and sound system upgrade: sedan ($1,915) and wagon ($1,730). Preferred equipment package, SHO: Power moon roof, electronic temperature control air conditioning, keyless remote entry with perimeter anti-theft system and JBL audio system ($1,325). Electronic temperature control air conditioning, LX and SHO ($175). Anti-lock brakes, ($570). Power moon roof, LX and SHO ($740). Air filtration system, GL ($30). Daytime running lights ($40). Keyless remote entry system ($190). Electronic AM/FM stereo radio with cassette, GL ($175). Electronic AM/FM stereo radio with cassette and premium sound, LX wagon ($315). Trunk-mounted

CD changer, LX and SHO ($595). JBL audio system, LX and SHO sedans ($500). Rear-facing third seat, wagons ($200). Power driver's seats, GL ($340). Cellular phone ($650). Light group, GL ($45). Rear window washer and wiper plus and cargo cover ($255). Chrome wheels, LX and SHO ($580). Cast aluminum wheels, GT ($315). California emissions system ($100). Leather seats with console, LX ($990). Leather sport bucket seats, SHO sedan ($1,190). Heavy duty suspension, GL wagon ($25). Conventional spare tire, GL and LX ($125). Flex-fuel (methanol or ethanol) 3.0-liter V-6 ($1,165). Heavy duty suspension, GL wagon ($25).

Crown Victoria: Preferred equipment package, base, 111A: Color-keyed front and rear floor mats, power lock group, spoked wheel covers, speed control and illuminated entry system ($60). Preferred equipment package, LX, 113A: Color-keyed front and rear floor mats power lock group, cornering lamps, speed control, illuminated entry system, leather-wrapped steering wheel, electronic AM/FM stereo radio with cassette, cast aluminum 12-spoke wheels and light and decor group ($640). Preferred equip package, LX, 114A: Same as 113A plus dual control power seats, high level audio system, anti-lock brakes with electronic traction assist, air suspension, automatic temperature controlled air conditioning, trip minder computer, digital electronic instrumentation, heavy duty battery, keyless remote entry and electric auto dimming mirror ($3,385). Natural gas-fueled 4.6-liter V-8, base ($6,165). Electronic automatic temperature- controlled air conditioning ($175). California emissions system ($100). Leather split-bench seat, LX ($645). Conventional spare tire ($80). Anti-lock brakes with electronic traction assist ($670). 41G handling and performance package, LX, including revised springs, shocks and stabilizer bar plus power steering cooler, P225/60-R16 blackwall touring tires, 16-inch cast aluminum wheels and dual exhausts ($1,100). Engine block heater ($25). Keyless remote entry system, LX ($240). Light and decor group, LX ($225). Electronic AM/FM stereo radio with cassette player ($185). High level audio system, LX ($360). Rear air suspension, LX ($270). Speed control with natural gas-fueled 4.6-liter V-8 ($215). Power lock group with natural gas-fueled 4.6-liter V-8 ($305). Six-way power driver's seat, base ($360). Dual power seats ($360). Color-keyed front and rear floor mats ($45). P215/70-R15 whitewall tires ($80). Natural gas-powered 4.6-liter V-8, base ($6,165). Trailer towing package ($795). Anti-lock brakes with electronic traction assist ($670).

History:

U.S. model year production totaled 829,427, including Mustang but excluding Crown Victoria. U.S. calendar year production totaled 1,069,764, including Mustang and gave the Ford Motor Co. 17.6 percent of the industry market share. For the fifth consecutive year, Taurus was the best selling car in the United States in 1996, with 401,049 units sold compared to 382,298 for the Honda Accord, once again finishing in second place. The Escort was ranked as the best-selling small car with 284,644 units sold compared to 278,574 for the second place Saturn. Crown Victoria buyers could order a 4.6-liter V-8 fueled by natural gas. The Escort had several refinements even though an all-new 1997 model would debut in May 1996.

1997 Ford

Escort — Ford: The all-new Escort featured one-piece body construction, which allowed 25 percent more torsional rigidity and better road "feel" over the previous version. Available in four-door sedan (base and LX versions as well as an LX sedan with optional Sport Package) and station wagon (LX only) models, the 1997 Escort featured side impact protection and dual air bags as standard equipment. Four inches longer than before, the Escort sedan provided 100 cubic feet of interior space while the Escort station wagon offered 120 cubic feet. The Escort featured an Integrated Control Panel that put audio and climate controls in easy-to-use locations as well as solar-tinted glass to reduce glare. Ford's new small car offered 100,000-mile tune-up intervals on its new 2.0-liter four-cylinder engine with Split Port Induction, rated at 110 hp and 125 lbs.-ft. of torque. The standard five-speed manual transaxle and the optional four-speed automatic transaxle were both improved for better shift quality and improved performance. Optional equipment included four-wheel anti-lock brakes, a trunk-mounted CD player and remote keyless entry.

Contour — Four and V-6: The addition of a base four-door sedan and an optional Sport model in GL or LX trim topped the list of changes for the 1997 Contour. Offered in base, GL, LX and SE series, all four-door sedans, the new features for Contour included an interior trunk light, a tilt-column steering wheel, power antenna, illuminated visor mirrors (LX and SE sedans only) and optional 15-inch alloy wheels (GL and LX sedans only). The Contour Sport featured an exclusive Alpine green clear coat body color (as well as standard Contour colors), leather-wrapped steering wheel and shift knob, 15-inch alloy wheels, fog lamps, Sport badging and Sport graphics on front floor mats. The base, GL and LX sedans were powered by the DOHC 2.0-liter four-cylinder engine. The SE sedan was powered by the modular, DOHC 2.5-liter V-6, the optional engine for the GL and LX models. Contours used the five-speed manual transaxle as standard equipment while the electronically-controlled four-speed automatic transaxle was optional.

Probe — Four and V-6: In its final year of production, the nine-year-old Probe was again offered in base and GT coupe versions. An optional GTS sport appearance package was added to the GT coupe for 1997, and consisted of dual racing stripes running the length of the car, GTS decals, a rear spoiler and 16-inch chrome wheels. The base coupe was powered by the DOHC 2.0-liter four-cylinder engine. The GT coupe used the DOHC 2.5-liter V-6. A five-speed manual transaxle was standard equipment on all Probes and an electronically-controlled four-speed automatic transaxle was optional.

Taurus — V-6 and V-8: The introduction of a base G four-door sedan at midyear in 1996 expanded the 1997 Taurus lineup, that now was comprised of the G, GL, LX and SHO four-door sedans as well as GL and LX station wagons. In its second year of a re-design, the 1997 Taurus was only slightly revised. The GL series Vulcan 3.0-liter V-6

received an upgraded catalytic configuration, engine recalibrations and a secondary air-injection system that enabled it to qualify as a low-emission vehicle (LEV) in California. This 3.0-liter V-6 also offered two flexible fuel packages (introduced midyear in 1996). One permitted use of up to 85 percent methanol and the other permitted use of up to 85 percent ethanol. Taurus offered 101.5 cubic feet of interior room. The G and GL series used the Vulcan 3.0-liter V-6. The LX series was powered by the Duratec DOHC 3.0-liter V-6. The SHO sedan used the DOHC 3.4-liter V-8. The AX4N electronically-controlled four-speed automatic transaxle was standard unit on all Taurus models. Features of the SHO sedan included a color-keyed rear spoiler, flared rocker panel design, 16-inch/five-spoke cast aluminum wheels and dual exhaust.

Crown Victoria — V-8: Four-door sedan models in base or LX trim were the Crown Victoria offerings for 1997. New features included an improved steering gear to enhance on-center road "feel" and stability as well as several new color selections. The Crown Victoria natural gas vehicle (NGV) returned after being introduced in 1996. Using a modified version of the Crown Victoria's standard 4.6-liter V-8, the NGV model produced 175 hp at 4500 rpm and 235 lbs.-ft. of torque at 3500 rpm. The electronically-controlled four-speed automatic overdrive transmission was used in all Crown Victorias once again during the 1997 model year.

I.D. Data:

Ford's 17-symbol Vehicle Identification Number (VIN) was stamped on a metal tab fastened to the instrument panel and was visible through the windshield. The first three symbols indicated the manufacturer, make and vehicle type. The fourth symbol denoted the restraint system. Next came letter P followed by two digits that indicated the model number such as P10=Escort four-door sedan. Symbol eight indicated the engine type. Next was a check digit. Symbol 10 indicated the model year: V=1997. Symbol 11 showed the assembly plant. The final six digits made up the sequential production number, starting with 000001.

Escort (Four)

Model No.	Body/ Style No.	Body Type & Seating	Factory Price	Shipping Weight	Production Total
P	10	4-dr. Sedan-5P	$11,015	2,457 lbs.	Note 1
P	13	4-dr. LX Sedan-5P	$11,515	2,503 lbs.	Note 1
P	15	4-dr. LX Station Wagon-5P	$12,065	2,571 lbs.	71,610

Note 1: Production of four-door sedan models totaled 251,894 with no further breakout available.

Contour (Four)

P	65	4-dr. Sedan-5P	$13,460	2,769 lbs.	Note 1
P	65	4-dr. GL Sedan-5P	$14,285	2,769 lbs.	Note 1
P	66	4-dr. LX Sedan-5P	$14,915	2,769 lbs.	Note 1

Contour (V-6)

P	65	4-dr. GL Sedan-5P	$15,520	------	Note 1
P	66	4-dr. LX Sedan-5P	$16,115	2,908 lbs.	Note 1
P	67	4-dr. SE Sedan-5P	$16,115	2,994 lbs.	Note 1

Note 1: Production of four-door sedan models totaled 79,951 with no further breakout available.

Probe (Four)

T	20	2-dr. Coupe-4P	$14,280	2,690 lbs.	Note 1

Probe GT (V-6)

T	22	2-dr. GT Coupe-4P	$16,780	2,921 lbs.	Note 1

Note 1: Production of two-door coupe models totaled 16,821 with no further breakout available.

Taurus (V-6)

P	51	4-dr. G Sedan-6P	$17,995	3,329 lbs.	Note 1
P	52	4-dr. GL Sedan-6P	$18,985	3,329 lbs.	Note 1
P	57	4-dr. GL Station Wagon-6P	$20,195	3,480 lbs.	Note 2
P	53	4-dr. LX Sedan-6P	$21,610	3,326 lbs.	Note 1
P	58	4-dr. LX Station Wagon-6P	$22,715	3,480 lbs.	Note 2

Taurus SHO (V-8)

P	54	4-dr. SHO Sedan-6P	$26,460	3,440 lbs.	Note 1

Note 1: Production of four-door sedan models totaled 384,844 and no further breakouts were available.
Note 2: Production of station wagon models totaled 13,958 with no further breakout available.

Crown Victoria (V-8)

P	73	4-dr. Sedan-6P	$21,475	3,776 lbs.	Note 1
P	74	4-dr. LX Sedan-6P	$23,195	3,780 lbs.	Note 1

Note 1: Production of four-door sedan models totaled 123,833 with no further breakout available.

1997 Escort LX sedan

1997 Escort LX station wagon

Escort Base Four: Inline. Overhead cam. Cast-iron block and aluminum head. Displacement: 122 cid (2.0 liters). B & S: 3.33 x 3.46 in. Compression ratio: 9.2:1. Brake hp: 110 at 5000 rpm. Torque: 125 lbs.-ft. at 3750 rpm. Sequential electronic fuel injection.

Probe Base Four: Inline. Dual overhead cam. Cast-iron block and aluminum head. Displacement: 122 cid (2.0 liters). B & S: 3.27 x 3.62 in. Compression ratio: 9.0:1. Brake hp: 118 at 5500 rpm. Torque: 127 lbs.-ft. at 4500 rpm. Sequential electronic fuel injection.

Contour Base Four: Inline. Dual overhead cam. Cast-iron block and aluminum head. Displacement: 121 cid (2.0 liters). B & S: 3.34 x 3.46 in. Compression ratio: 9.6:1. Brake hp: 125 at 5500 rpm. Torque: 130 lbs.-ft. at 4000 rpm. Sequential electronic fuel injection.

Probe GT Base V-6: Dual overhead cam with 24 valves. Aluminum block and head. Displacement: 153 cid (2.5 liters). B & S: 3.33 x 2.92 in. Compression ratio: 9.2:1. Brake hp: 164 at 5600 rpm. Torque: 160 lbs.-ft. at 4000 rpm. Sequential electronic fuel injection.

Contour Base V-6 (Optional Contour GL and LX): Modular, dual overhead cam with 24 valves. Aluminum block and head. Displacement: 155 cid (2.5 liters). B & S: 3.24 x 3.13 in. Compression ratio: 9.7:1. Brake hp: 170 at 6250 rpm. Torque: 165 lbs.-ft. at 4250 rpm. Sequential electronic fuel injection.

Taurus G and GL Base V-6: Overhead valve. Cast-iron block and head. Displacement: 182 cid (3.0 liters). B & S: 3.50 x 3.15 in. Compression ratio: 9.3:1. Brake hp: 145 at 5250 rpm. Torque: 170 lbs.-ft. at 3250 rpm. Sequential electronic fuel injection.

Taurus LX Base V-6: Dual-overhead-cam with 24 valves. Aluminum block and head. Displacement: 182 cid (3.0 liters). B & S: 3.50 x 3.15 in. Compression ratio: 9.3:1. Brake hp: 200 at 5750 rpm. Torque: 200 lbs.-ft. at 4500 rpm. Sequential electronic fuel injection.

Taurus SHO Base V-8: 60-degree, dual overhead cam with 32 valves. Aluminum block and head. Displacement: 207 cid (3.4 liters). B & S: 3.50 x 3.15 in. Compression ratio: 9.8:1. Brake hp: 235 at 6100 rpm. Torque: 230 lbs.-ft. at 4800 rpm. Sequential electronic fuel injection.

Crown Victoria Base V-8: Modular, overhead valve. Displacement: 281 cid (4.6 liters). B & S: 3.60 x 3.60. Compression ratio: 9.0:1. Brake hp: 190 at 4250 rpm. Torque: 265 lbs.-ft. at 3200 rpm. Sequential electronic fuel injection.

Escort: Wheelbase: 98.4 in. Overall length: 174.7 in. and 172.7 in., station wagon. Tires: P185/65-R14.

Contour: Wheelbase: 106.5 in. Overall length: 183.9 in. Tires: P185/70-R14 and P205/60-R15, SE.

Probe: Wheelbase: 102.8 in. Overall length: 183.9 in. Tires: P195/65-R14 and P225/50-R16, GT.

Taurus: Wheelbase: 108.5 in. Overall length: 197.5 in. and 199.6 in., station wagon. Tires: P205/65-R15 and P225/55-VR16, SHO.

Crown Victoria: Wheelbase: 114.4 in. Overall length: 212.0 in. Tires: P215/70-R15.

Escort: Preferred equipment package, LX, 317A: Air conditioning, driver's door remote entry and rear window defroster ($765). Preferred equipment package, LX, 318A: Air conditioning, driver's door remote entry, dual power mirrors, power locks with anti-theft feature, power windows and rear window defroster ($1,390). California emissions system ($170). Integrated child seat, LX ($135). Air conditioner ($795). Rear window defroster ($190). Electronic AM/FM stereo radio with cassette ($165). Electronic AM/FM stereo radio with CD player, LX ($515). Luggage rack and rear window wiper and washer, LX wagon ($240). Sport package including 14-inch aluminum wheels, oval-tipped exhausts, unique sport seats with rear integrated headrests, tach, lift gate spoiler and appliqués ($495). Anti-lock brakes ($570). Dual power mirrors, LX ($95). Front and rear floor mats ($45). Four-speed automatic transaxle ($815). Anti-lock brakes ($570).

Contour: Preferred equipment package, base, 230A: Rear window defroster, full-length console and electronic AM/FM stereo radio with cassette ($410). Preferred equipment package, GL, 236A: Rear window defroster, full-length console, speed control, light group, power door locks and electronic AM/FM stereo radio with cassette ($1,310). Preferred equipment package, GL, 240A: Same as 236A plus power windows and 2.5-liter V-6 ($2,685). Preferred equipment package, LX, 238A: Power windows, 2.5-liter V-6, rear window defroster, full-length console, speed control, light group, power door locks and electronic AM/FM stereo radio with cassette ($2,415). Preferred equipment package, SE, 239A: Power windows, rear window defroster, full-length console, speed control, light group, power door locks and electronic AM/FM stereo radio with cassette ($1,385). California emissions system ($100). Keyless remote entry system ($190). Power moon roof ($595). Power windows, LX and SE ($340). Electronic AM/FM stereo radio with cassette and premium

1997 Probe GT coupe

1997 Crown Victoria LX sedan

sound: GL ($315) or LX and SE ($130). Electronic AM/FM stereo radio with CD player and premium sound: GL ($455) or LX and SE ($270). Anti-lock brakes ($570). Air conditioning ($795). Rear window defroster ($190). Carpeted front and rear floor mats ($45). Power driver's seat, LX and SE ($330). Leather bucket seats: LX ($645) and SE ($595). Rear split fold-down seat, GL ($205). Sport package with 15-inch, six-spoke aluminum wheels, leather-wrapped steering wheel and shift knob, plus fog lamps and tach: GL ($495) or LX ($420). Speed control ($215). 15-inch aluminum wheels, GL and LX ($425). 2.0-liter four-cylinder gaseous fuel prep ($260). 2.5-liter DOHC V-6: GL ($1,235) or LX ($1,200). Four-speed automatic transaxle ($815). Anti-lock brakes ($570).

Probe: Preferred equipment package, base: Air conditioning and AM/FM stereo radio with cassette and clock ($740). Preferred equipment package, GT: Air conditioning and AM/FM stereo radio with cassette and clock ($740). California emissions system ($170). Manual air conditioner with tinted glass ($895). Leather bucket seats ($500). Power driver's seat ($290). Convenience group with interval wipers, speed control, tilt steering and console, base ($430) or GT ($375). Luxury group including power windows, power door locks, electric dual remote mirrors and keyless remote and illuminated entry ($615). Anti-lock brakes, base ($820) or GT ($650). Electronic AM/FM stereo radio with cassette and clock ($165). Electronic AM/FM stereo radio with cassette and premium sound system ($170). Electronic AM/FM stereo radio with CD player and premium sound system ($620). Color-keyed body moldings ($60). Color-keyed front floor mats ($30). Power sliding roof ($615). Rear deck lid spoiler ($235). GTS sport appearance group with rear deck lid spoiler, tape stripes, 16-inch chrome wheels and P225/50-VR15 blackwall tires ($745). 15-inch aluminum wheels with P205/55-HRX15 blackwall tires, base, ($470). 16-inch chrome wheels with P225/50-VRX16 blackwall tires ($390). Four-speed automatic transaxle ($895). Anti-lock brakes ($820) or Probe GT ($650).

Taurus: Preferred equipment package, GL, 204A: Power door locks, AM/FM stereo radio with cassette, speed control, air filtration system and front and rear floor mats ($250). Preferred equipment package, GL, 205A: Same as 204A plus power driver's seat, light group and aluminum wheels ($850). Preferred equipment package, LX, 209A: Four-wheel anti-lock disc brakes, speed control, front and rear floor mats, air filtration system and keyless remote entry system perimeter anti-theft features ($720). Preferred equipment package, LX, 210A: Same as 209A plus electronic temperature controlled air conditioning, aluminum wheels and sound system upgrade: sedan ($1,710) and wagon ($1,630). Preferred equipment package, SHO: Power moon roof, electronic temperature-controlled air conditioning, power heated mirrors, keyless remote entry with perimeter anti-theft system and MACH audio system ($1,210). California emissions system ($170). Electronic temperature-controlled air conditioner ($210). Anti-lock brakes, standard on SHO ($600). Power moon roof, LX and SHO ($740). Air filtration system ($30). Daytime running lights ($40). Remote entry system, GL ($190). Remote entry system with perimeter anti-theft system, LX and SHO ($440). Electronic AM/FM stereo radio with cassette, G and GL ($185). Trunk-mounted CD changer, LX and SHO ($595). MACH audio system, LX sedan ($400) and LX wag and SHO ($320). Rear facing third seat, wagons ($200). Power driver's seat, GL ($340). Cellular phone ($650). Light group, GL ($45). Wagon group including rear window washer and wiper plus cargo cover ($295). Chrome wheels, LX and SHO ($580). Cast-aluminum

1997 Taurus LX sedan

1997 Taurus GL station wagon

wheels, GL ($315). Leather seats with console, LX ($990). Leather sport bucket seats with console, SHO sedan ($1,190). Heavy duty suspension, GL wagon ($25). Flex-fuel (methanol or ethanol) 3.0-liter V-6: Taurus GL sedan only ($1,165). Heavy duty suspension, GL wagon ($25). Anti-lock brakes ($600).

Crown Victoria: Preferred equipment package, base, 111A: Color-keyed front and rear floor mats, power lock group, spoked wheel covers, speed control and illuminated entry system ($60). Preferred equipment package, LX, 113A: Color-keyed front and rear floor mats, power lock group, cornering lamps, speed control, illuminated entry system, leather-wrapped steering wheel, electronic AM/FM stereo radio with cassette, cast aluminum 12-spoke wheels and light and decor group ($640). Preferred equipment package, LX, 114A: Same as 113A plus electronic automatic temperature controlled air conditioning, anti-lock brakes with electronic traction assist, power passenger seat, high level audio system, digital electronic instrumentation, keyless remote entry and electric auto dim mirror ($2,965). California emissions system ($170). Natural gas-fueled 4.6-liter V-8 ($6,165). Electronic automatic temperature controlled air conditioning ($175). Leather split bench seat, LX ($735). Anti-lock brakes with electronic traction assist ($695). 41G handling and performance package, LX, including revised springs, shocks and stabilizer bar power steering cooler, P225/60-RX16 blackwall touring tires, 16-inch cast aluminum wheels and dual exhausts ($1,100). Engine block heater ($25). Keyless remote entry system, LX ($240). Light and decor group ($225). Electronic AM/FM stereo radio with cassette player ($185). High level audio system, base ($545) or LX ($360). Six-way power driver's seat ($360). Power passenger seat, LX ($360). Color-keyed front and rear floor mats ($45). Conventional spare tire ($80). P215/70-RX15 whitewall tires ($80). Natural gas-powered 4.6-liter V-8 ($6,165). Anti-lock brakes with electronic traction assist ($695).

History:

U.S. model year production totaled 1,116,975 cars, including Mustang. The newly-designed 1997 Escort sedan and station wagon models made their debut in the spring of 1996. The lineup was trimmed considerably and offered a base four-door sedan or LX four-door sedan or station wagon. Contour's changes were minimal for 1997. A Sport Package was optional on the Contour GL or LX models, which included aluminum wheels, fog lamps and Sport badging. The Probe GT also received a GTS sport appearance group that included dual racing stripes, a rear deck spoiler and 16-inch chrome wheels. This was the final year for Probe production. Taurus added a base G sedan in 1996. The Ford Aspire, not covered in this catalog due to its import status, was also in its last year of sale in the United States.

1997 Contour SE sedan

1998 Ford

Escort — Four: The Escort lineup was revised for 1998. The base Escort and LX station wagon were discontinued and a new SE series was introduced. Escort was now available as an LX four-door sedan or SE four-door sedan or station wagon. Ford also introduced an all-new two-door coupe named the ZX2, affiliated with the Escort because the two cars shared key components. This performance coupe was aimed at younger buyers and was available in "Cool" or "Hot" versions. The ZX2 used the Zetec 2.0-liter four-cylinder engine, rated at 130 hp, mated to a five-speed manual transaxle. Optional equipment included anti-lock brakes, premium sound system, power windows, power moon roof, remote entry system and automatic transaxle. A sport package was also offered with the ZX2 and it featured 15-inch aluminum wheels, a rear spoiler, fog lamps, upgraded bucket seats and special badging. The Escort, after being totally redesigned in 1997, received several improvements. The upgrades included a new electronically-controlled four-speed automatic transaxle that provided for more throttle response. The car also had chrome-plated wheel covers, a sensor added to the power plant to reduce noise and emissions controls added to contain the non-tailpipe hydrocarbons. The SE's list of standard equipment included air conditioning, rear window defroster, driver's door remote entry system and dual power mirrors. The Escort used the 2.0-liter four-cylinder engine with Split Port Induction. The standard transaxle was the five-speed manual with the option unit including the electronically controlled four-speed automatic with overdrive.

Contour — Four and V-6: Ford touted the 1998 Contour's more than 100 customer-driven refinements. The biggest change was the base and GL sedans were dropped. Contour's lineup now was an LX or SE four-door sedan. Buyers could opt for the limited edition Contour SVT four-door sports sedan. Ford's Special Vehicle Team (SVT) announced it would build 5,000 Contour SVT sports sedans per year, each fitted with a 195-hp version of the Duratec DOHC 2.5-liter V-6 with 10.0:1 compression ratio and 2.25-inch stainless steel dual exhausts and coupled to a MTX-75 five-speed manual transaxle. Top speed of the SVT sports sedan was 143 mph. Standard SVT features included four-wheel disc brakes with a four-channel and four-sensor antilock system, five-spoke cast aluminum wheels and various leather interior surfaces. Standard LX and SE sedan equipment included air conditioning, dual power mirrors and full wheel covers. The SE added color-keyed mirrors, a rear window defroster, power locks and windows and speed control. The LX and SE sedans were again powered by the Zetec DOHC 2.0-liter four-cylinder engine. The modular, DOHC 2.5-liter V-6 was the optional engine for both. The five-speed manual transaxle was standard while the electronically controlled four-speed automatic transaxle was optional.

Taurus — V-6 and V-8: The Taurus lineup was overhauled in 1998 with the G and GL models discontinued and the SE series introduced. Taurus was now available as an LX four-door sedan, SE four-door sedan or station wagon or the high-performance SHO sedan. The LX and SE models received a more assertive fascia and a more consistent monochrome treatment for tail lamps and rear appliqué. A new sport group was available on the SE sedan and it included the Duratec V-6, SecuriLock anti-theft system, rear deck lid spoiler and chrome bolt-on wheel covers. The LX and SE used the Vulcan 3.0-liter V-6, rated at 145 hp, and four-speed automatic overdrive transaxle. Optional for both was the 200-hp Duratec 3.0-liter V-6 coupled to the electronically controlled AX4N non-synchronous four-speed automatic overdrive transaxle. The SHO sedan again used the DOHC 3.4-liter V-8 mated to the AX4N four-speed automatic. The two flex fuel (methanol or ethanol) 3.0-liter V-6 engines that debuted in 1997 were offered in LX or SE sedans. Taurus models also received the second generation driver and passenger air bags as standard equipment.

Crown Victoria — V-8: The Crown Victoria offered the lone unchanged Ford car in 1998. Available as a four-door sedan in base or LX trim, several new features were added to the Crown Victoria including all-new Watt's linkage rear and revised front suspensions, larger front

1998 Escort SE sedan (with Sport Package)

brakes and new 16-inch tires, the SecuriLock anti-theft system and an optional all-speed traction control. The Crown Victoria's exterior was redesigned with a new front fascia and larger headlamps as well as new wraparound taillamps. The 4.6-liter V-8, rated at 200 hp, and the electronically controlled four-speed automatic overdrive transmission were the standard power train. Buyers opting for the Handling & Performance Package (41G) received 215 hp (15 extra) and 10 additional lbs.-ft. of torque. The Crown Victoria NGV (powered by a 4.6-liter natural gas V-8) was also offered again in 1998.

I. D. Data:

Ford's 17-symbol Vehicle Identification Number (VIN) was stamped on a metal tab fastened to the instrument panel and was visible through the windshield. The first three symbols indicated the manufacturer, make and vehicle type. The fourth symbol showed the restraint system. Next came letter P followed by two digits that indicated the model number such as P10=Escort LX four-door sedan. Symbol eight indicated the engine type. Next was a check digit. Symbol 10 revealed the model year: W=1998. Symbol 11 indicated the assembly plant. The final six digits made up the sequential production number, starting with 000001.

Escort (Four))

Model No.	Body/ Style No.	Body Type & Seating	Factory Price	Shipping Weight	Production Total
P	10	4-dr. LX Sedan-5P	$11,280	2,468 lbs.	-----
P	13	4-dr. SE Sedan-5P	$12,580	------	-----
P	15	4-dr. SE Station Wagon-5P	$13,780	2,531 lbs.	-----

Escort ZX2 (Four)

| P | 11/41V | 2-dr. Cool Coupe-5P | $11,580 | 2,478 lbs. | ----- |
| P | 11 | 2-dr. Hot Coupe-5P | $13,080 | ------ | ----- |

Contour (Four)

| P | 66 | 4-dr. LX Sedan-5P | $14,460 | 2,811 lbs. | ----- |
| P | 67 | 4-dr. SE Sedan-5P | $15,785 | 3,030 lbs. | ----- |

Contour (V-6)

| P | 68 | 4-dr. SVT Sport Sedan-5P | $22,405 | 3,068 lbs. | 5,000 |

Note: No actual production figure for SVT sport sedan was available.

Taurus (V-6)

P	52	4-dr. LX Sedan-6P	$18,245	3,353 lbs.	-----
P	52/60E	4-dr. SE Sedan-6P	$19,445	3,294 lbs.	-----
P	57	4-dr. SE Station Wagon-6P	$21,105	3,497 lbs.	-----

Taurus SHO (V-8)

| P | 54 | 4-dr. SHO Sedan-6P | $28,920 | ------ | ----- |

Crown Victoria (V-8)

| P | 73 | 4-dr. Sedan-6P | $20,935 | ------ | ------ |
| P | 74 | 4-dr. LX Sedan-6P | $23,135 | ------ | ------ |

1998 Escort ZX2 coupe

1998 Taurus LX sedan

Engines:

Escort Base Four: Inline. Overhead cam. Cast-iron block and aluminum head. Displacement: 122 cid (2.0 liters). B & S: 3.33 x 3.46 in. Compression ratio: 9.2:1. Brake hp: 110 at 5000 rpm. Torque: 125 lbs.-ft. at 3750 rpm. Split port induction.

Escort ZX2 Base Four: Inline. Dual overhead cam. Cast-iron block and aluminum head. Displacement: (2.0 liters). B & S: N/A. Compression ratio: 9.6:1. Brake hp: 130 at 5750 rpm. Torque: 127 lbs.-ft. at 4250 rpm. Sequential electronic fuel injection.

Contour Base Four: Inline. Dual overhead cam. Cast-iron block and aluminum head. Displacement: 121 cid (2.0 liters). B & S: 3.34 x 3.46 in. Compression ratio: 9.6:1. Brake hp: 125 at 5500 rpm. Torque: 130 lbs.-ft. at 4000 rpm. Sequential electronic fuel injection.

Contour SVT Base V-6: 60-degree dual overhead cam. Aluminum block and head. Displacement: 155 cid (2.5 liters). B & S: 3.21 x 3.08 in. Compression ratio: 10.0:1. Brake hp: 195 at 6625 rpm. Torque: 165 lbs.-ft. at 5625 rpm. Sequential electronic fuel injection.

Contour LX and SE Optional V-6: Modular, dual overhead cam. Aluminum block and head. Displacement: 155 cid (2.5 liters). B & S: 3.24 x 3.13 in. Compression ratio: 9.7:1. Brake hp: 170 at 6250 rpm. Torque: 165 lbs.-ft. at 4250 rpm. Sequential electronic fuel injection.

Taurus Base V-6: Overhead valve. Cast-iron block and head. Displacement: 182 cid (3.0 liters). B & S: 3.50 x 3.15 in. Compression ratio: 9.3:1. Brake hp: 145 at 5250 rpm. Torque: 170 lbs.-ft. at 3250 rpm. Sequential electronic fuel injection.

Taurus Optional V-6: Dual-overhead-cam. Aluminum block and head. Displacement: 182 cid (3.0 liters). B & S: 3.50 x 3.15 in. Compression ratio: 9.3:1. Brake hp: 200 at 5750 rpm. Torque: 200 lbs.-ft. at 4500 rpm. Sequential electronic fuel injection.

Taurus SHO Base V-8: 60-degree, dual overhead cam. Aluminum block and head. Displacement: 207 cid (3.4 liters). B & S: 3.50 x 3.15 in. Compression ratio: 9.8:1. Brake hp: 235 at 6100 rpm. Torque: 230 lbs.-ft. at 4800 rpm. Sequential electronic fuel injection.

Crown Victoria Base V-8: Modular, overhead valve. Displacement: 281 cid (4.6 liters). B & S: 3.60 x 3.60. Compression ratio: 9.0:1. Brake hp: 190 at 4250 rpm. Torque: 265 lbs.-ft. at 3200 rpm. Sequential electronic fuel injection.

Chassis:

Escort and ZX2: Wheelbase: 98.4 in. Overall length: 174.7 in. and 172.7 in., station wagon or 175.2 in., ZX2. Tires: P185/65-R14.

Contour: Wheelbase: 106.5 in. Overall length: 184.6 in. Tires: P185/70-R14 and P205/55-ZR16, SVT.

Taurus: Wheelbase: 108.5 in. Overall length: 197.5 in. and 199.6 in., station wagon. Tires: P205/65-R15 and P225/55-ZR16, SHO.

Crown Victoria: Wheelbase: 114.4 in. Overall length: 212.0 in. Tires: P225/60-SR16.

Options:

Escort: Appearance group including leather-wrapped steering wheel, 14-inch chrome bolt-on wheel covers and bright tip exhaust, 51S: SE sedan ($155) or SE wagon ($120). Comfort group including speed control, tilt steering column, dual map lights and dual visor mirrors, 50A, SE ($345). Power group including power locks, power windows and all-door remote entry with anti-theft system, 60A, SE ($395). SE wagon group including deluxe luggage rack, rear window wiper and washer plus cargo area cover, 51W ($295). Sport group including 14-inch aluminum wheels, rear spoiler, tach, bright tip exhausts and rear seats with integrated headrest, 434, SE sedan ($495). California emissions system ($170). Manual air conditioner ($795). Integrated child's seat, SE wagon ($135). Rear window defroster ($190). Electronic AM/FM stereo radio with cassette ($185). Electronic AM/FM stereo radio with cassette player and premium sound ($255). Electronic AM/FM stereo radio with cassette player, premium sound and CD changer, SE sedan ($515). Driver's door remote entry with panic alarm ($135). Anti-lock Brakes ($400). Front and rear floor mats ($55). 14-inch aluminum wheels, SE ($265). Four-speed automatic transaxle ($815).

Escort ZX2: Manual air conditioner ($795). Comfort group with speed control, tilt steering column, dual map lights and dual visor mirrors, 50A, Hot Coupe ($345). Appearance group including leather-wrapped steering wheel, 14-inch chrome bolt-on wheel covers and bright tipped exhausts, 51S, Hot Coupe ($155).) Sport package including 15-inch aluminum wheels, fog lamps, spoiler, bright tipped exhausts and upgraded seats, 41G, Hot Coupe, ($595). Driver's door remote entry with panic alarm, Cool Coupe ($135). Power group with power locks, power windows and all-door remote entry with anti-theft system, 60A, Hot Coupe ($395). Power sliding moon roof, Hot Coupe ($595). Rear window defroster ($190). California emissions system ($170). Front and rear floor mats, Hot Coupe ($55). Electronic AM/FM stereo radio with

1998 Taurus SE station wagon

1998 Contour SVT sedan

cassette player ($185). Electronic AM/FM stereo radio with cassette player and premium sound ($255). Electronic AM/FM stereo radio with cassette player, premium sound and CD changer, Hot Coupe ($515). 14-inch, five-spoke aluminum wheels ($265). Four-speed automatic transaxle ($815). Anti-lock brakes ($400).

Contour: SE comfort group with 10-way power driver's seat, eight-spoke aluminum wheels, leather-wrapped steering wheel, fog lights, intermittent wipers, dual illuminated vanity mirrors and power antenna, 53C, SE ($795). SE sport group with Duratec 2.5-liter V-6, P205/60-TGR15 blackwall tires, 12-spoke aluminum wheels, tach, leather-wrapped steering wheel, sport floor mats, rear spoiler, intermittent wipers, fog lights, dual illuminated vanity mirrors and sport cloth bucket seats, 53S, SE ($1,000). California emissions system ($170). Rear window defroster ($190). Anti-lock brakes ($500). 2.0-liter four-cylinder gaseous fuel prep, LX and SE ($260). Keyless remote entry system, SE ($190). Front and rear carpeted floor mats ($55). Power moon roof, SE and SVT ($595). Leather seats with split-fold rear seat, SE ($895). 60/40 split-fold rear seat, SE ($205). 10-way power driver's seat ($350). Electronic AM/FM stereo radio with cassette player and premium sound, SE ($135). Electronic AM/FM stereo radio with premium sound system and CD player, SE ($275) or SVT ($140). Power antenna, SE ($95). Integrated child's seat ($135). 15-inch, eight-spoke aluminum wheels, SE ($425). 15-inch wheels with simulated bolt-on covers, SE ($135). 2.5-liter DOHC V-6: Contour LX and SE ($495). Four-speed automatic transaxle: LX and SE ($815). Anti-lock brakes: LX and SE ($500).

Taurus: SE sport group with Duratec 3.0-liter V-6, rear spoiler and chrome wheel covers, 60S, SE sedan ($695). SE comfort group with Duratec 3.0-liter V-6, power driver's seat, electronic temperature controlled air conditioning, 12-spoke aluminum wheels, leather-wrapped steering wheel, power antenna, remote entry keypad with perimeter anti-theft and illuminated passenger side visor mirror, P53, SE sedan ($1,450) and SE wagon ($1,285). SE comfort and sport group including the P53 and 60S packages plus 12-spoke chrome wheels, P53/60S, SE sedan ($2,000). California emissions system ($170). Anti-lock brakes, standard on SHO ($600). Power moon roof, standard on SHO ($740). Daytime running lights ($40). Front and rear floor mats, standard on SHO ($55). Light group including dual courtesy lights, standard on SHO ($45). Power dual heated mirrors, SE ($35). Power door locks, LX ($275). Keyless remote entry system with key fobs, LX ($190). Electronic AM/FM stereo radio with cassette player, LX ($185). CD changer, SE ($350). MACH audio system, SE sedan ($400) or SE wagon ($320). Cloth bucket seats, SE ($105). Leather bucket seats, SE ($895). Power driver's seat, SE ($350). Dual power seats, SE ($350). Integrated child's seat, SE wagon ($135). Cargo area cover and cargo net, SE wagon ($140). Rear facing third seat, SE wagon ($200). Heavy duty suspension, SE wagon ($25). Conventional spare tire ($105). Five-spoke aluminum wheels, LX and SE ($315). Flex-fuel (methanol or ethanol) 3.0-liter V-6: Taurus LX/Taurus SE sedan ($1,165). Duratec 3.0-liter V-6: Taurus LX/Taurus SE ($495). Anti-lock brakes, standard on SHO ($600).

1998 Crown Victoria LX sedan

Crown Victoria: Comfort group including electronic automatic temperature controlled air conditioning, 12-spoke aluminum wheels, power passenger seat and leather-wrapped steering wheel, 65C, LX ($900). Comfort group plus including 65C options plus electronic instrumentation, anti-lock brakes with traction control and premium audio system, 65E, LX ($2,200). California emissions system ($170). Anti-lock brakes with traction control ($775). Handling and performance package, 41G, LX, with revised springs, shocks and stabilizer bar plus P225/60-TR16 blackwall touring tires and 16-inch cast aluminum wheels, rear air suspension and dual exhausts, LX ($935). Keyless remote entry system, base ($240). Electronic AM/FM stereo radio with cassette player, base ($185). Electronic AM/FM stereo radio with CD player, LX ($140). Premium audio system ($360). Six-way power driver's seat, base ($360). Leather split-bench seat, LX ($735). Color-keyed front and rear floor mats ($55). Conventional spare tire ($120). P225/60-SR16 whitewall tires ($80). P225/60-VR16 whitewall tires, natural gas-powered vehicles ($170). Universal garage door opener, LX ($115). Natural gas-powered 4.6-liter V-8 ($6,165). Anti-lock brakes with electronic traction control ($775).

History:

The four-door Taurus was selected as the model to replace the discontinued Thunderbird on the NASCAR circuit. This was the first time in NASCAR's history a production four-door automobile was allowed as an accepted body style. It reflected the fact that after 42 years of production, Ford's venerable Thunderbird was not continued for the 1998 model year. Ford Motor Co. juggled its lineups from 1997. Also discontinued after nine years of production was the Probe. New models from the blue oval were the Escort ZX2 two-door coupe, available in either the base "Cool" or the upscale "Hot" versions. The high-performance Contour SVT four-door sedan was a limited edition product of Ford's Special Vehicle Team. The second-generation driver and passenger air bags became standard equipment on all models. The SecuriLock anti-theft immobilizer also became standard equipment on most Ford automobiles.

1999 Ford

Escort — Four: The 1999 Escort combined style and fun in its small-size. With the optional ZX2 Sport Group the Escort buyer received special wheels, special seats and a spoiler. For those who considered performance a priority, the ZX2 featured a 130-hp, 16-valve, dual overhead cam Zetec engine and a sporty suspension. The wagon model increased the Escort's rear cargo area to 63.4 cu. ft. Standard equipment for the Escort LX included power-assisted front disc/rear drum brakes, the 2.0-liter split port induction (SPI 2000) four-cylinder engine, flush tinted windshield and tinted windows and backlight, a

1999 Escort SE four-door sedan

1999 Escort ZX2 Hot Series coupe

1999 Contour SE Sport four-door sedan

1999 Taurus SE Sport four-door sedan

flow-through ventilation system with a four-speed blower, a soft "vinyl feel" dashboard with knee bolsters, an integrated climate control and audio control panel, a clock, a storage bin, child safety rear door locks, an AM/FM stereo with premium speakers, low-back cloth front seats, split-folding 60/40 rear seat with dual release pull tabs, a four-spoke steering wheel, power rack-and-pinion steering, a temperature gauge, P185/65-R14 black sidewall tires, a five-speed manual transmission, a trip odometer, two-speed windshield wipers with intermittent feature and 14 x 5.5-in. semi styled steel wheels. The Escort SE included CFC-free manual temperature control air conditioning, a rear window defroster, an AM/FM cassette stereo with premium speakers and keyless remote entry with perimeter anti-theft. The Cool series coupe also included the 2.0-liter DOHC 16-valve Zetec four-cylinder engine, low-back cloth front bucket seats with driver side memory recline, a tachometer, a temperature gauge, and a trip odometer. The Hot series coupe added CFC-free manual temperature control air conditioning, a rear window defroster, a stereo cassette system with premium speakers and a remote keyless entry system with panic alarm.

Contour — Four and Contour SVT-V-6: In its 1999 sales catalog, Ford Motor Co. noted the Contour had been named an "All Star" by *Automobile Magazine* for four years in a row. Contour offerings now consisted only of the LX or SE four-door sedans. A European front suspension design was adopted for improved ride and handling in the SVT Sport Sedan. The front seats were redesigned to give more rear seat foot and leg room. Second generation air bags, redesigned front brakes and a larger fuel tank, which were made standard late in 1998, continued in use on the 1999 models. Standard equipment on the Contour LX included dual second generation air bags, air conditioning, power front disc and rear drum brakes, an electric digital clock, the 2.0-liter DOHC Zetec 16-valve I-4, a heater and defroster with a four-speed blower control, a soft touch dashboard with knee bolsters and four positive shutoff registers, analog gauges (including a trip odometer, a fuel gauge, a high-beam warning light, a coolant temperature gauge and a low-oil-pressure light, turn signal indicator lights, a handbrake-on warning light, a catalyst malfunction light and a seat belt reminder light), a day/night rearview mirror, an AM/FM stereo, individual manual two-way adjustable front bucket seats with reclining seat backs, tilt steering column, power rack-and-pinion steering, P185/70-R14S blackwall tires, a five-speed manual transmission with overdrive, single-speed windshield wipers with intermittent feature and fluidic washers and 14-in. wheel covers. The Contour SE featured a rear window defroster, power door locks, an AM/FM stereo radio with cassette player, speed control, power windows, rear window lockout, illuminated switches on all doors and a tachometer. The Contour SVT featured power four-wheel disc brakes with Dacromat finished rotors and unique front calipers, an antilock braking system, the 2.5-liter DOHC high-output Duratec 24-valve V-6 with passive anti-theft system (PATS), a unique Quasi-Dual exhaust system with low back pressure mufflers, a white-faced 160-mph speedometer, an electronic AM/FM stereo radio with cassette player and premium sound system, a 10-way power driver's seat, a split-folding 60/40 rear seat, a leather-wrapped

steering wheel, P215/50-R16Z directional-rated tires and five-spoke 16-in. cast-aluminum wheels.

Taurus — V-6 and V-8: For 1999, five-passenger seating became standard in the Taurus, but six-passenger seating was a no-charge option. The suspension was revised for a smoother ride and the 16-in. wheels used on the SHO model were available at extra cost on the LX and SE. Standard LX equipment included dual second generation air bags, CFC-free manual temperature control air conditioning, power front disc/rear drum brakes, a rear window defroster and defogger, the 3.0-liter two-valve six-cylinder engine, Solar-Tinted glass, a full-width windshield defroster and side window demisters, a dual grain instrument panel finish for reduced glare, a temperature gauge, a fuel gauge, a 110-mph speedometer, a warning light for low brake, a "fluids-low" alert light, a tachometer, an interior day/night mirror, an electronic AM/FM stereo radio, five-passenger seating with dual recliners, two-way headrests, a mini console, a tilt steering column, power rack-and-pinion steering with variable assist, P205/65-R15 all-season tires, an electronic four-speed automatic transmission with overdrive, two-speed intermittent windshield wipers and full wheel covers. The SE featured remote keyless entry, illuminated door controls for power accessories, an electronic AM/FM stereo with full logic stereo cassette player and four speakers and a 60/40 split-folding rear seat. The SE wagon featured a power antenna, four-wheel disc brakes, a unique lift gate latch and a rear washer/wiper. The Taurus SHO Sport Sedan included electronic temperature control air conditioning, four-wheel disc brakes, the 3.4-liter four-valve V-8, a MACH audio system with six speakers, a six-way power leather driver's sport bucket seat with adjustable lumbar support, the SecuriLock™ passive anti-theft system with coded key, a leather-wrapped four-spoke steering wheel, precision power rack-and-pinion steering with ZF variable assist, P225/55-ZR16 all-season, low-profile sport tires, an automatic transmission with overdrive lockout switch and aerodynamic Autobahn windshield wipers.

Crown Victoria — V-8: The 1999 Crown Victorias got antilock brakes as standard equipment and traction control became a free-standing option. The Crown Victoria could be ordered as a dedicated natural gas-fueled vehicle. Standard equipment on the base Crown Victoria included manual air conditioning with positive shut-off registers, a radio antenna hidden in the rear window defroster, the SecuriLock™ passive anti-theft system, power four-wheel disc antilock brakes, an electric digital clock with dimming feature, the 4.6-liter OHC sequential fuel-injected V-8, a stainless steel exhaust system, a gauge cluster with analog gauges (voltmeter, oil pressure, water temperature and fuel), full Solar-Tinted glass, wood grain instrument panel appliqués, power door locks, a day/night inside rearview mirror, an electronic AM/FM stereo with cassette and door-mounted speakers, a sound insulation package, speed control, speed sensitive variable-assist power steering, a tilt steering column with stalk-mounted controls, P225/60-SR16 all-season blackwall tires, an ECT automatic transmission with overdrive lockout, dual-jet interval windshield wipers, deluxe wheel covers and HSLA 16 x 7-in. wheel rims. The LX featured remote keyless entry, a split bench seat with fold-down center armrest and chrome-plated, locking cross-spoke wheel covers.

I.D. Data:

Ford's 17-symbol Vehicle Identification Number (VIN) was stamped on a metal tab fastened to the instrument panel and was visible through the windshield. The first symbol indicates the nation of origin: 1=United States; 2=Canada; 3=Mexico. The second symbol indicated the manufacturer: F=Ford Motor Co. The third symbol indicated the vehicle type: A=passenger car. The fourth symbol indicated the restraint system. The fifth symbol indicated the designation: P=Ford or T=Imported from outside North America or non-Ford car marketed by Ford. The sixth and seventh symbols indicated the body type such as : 10=Escort LX four-door sedan; 13=Escort SE four-door sedan;

15=Escort SE four-door station wagon; 52=Taurus LX four-door sedan; 53=Taurus SE two-valve four-door sedan; 54=Taurus SE four-valve four-door sedan; 58=Taurus SE four-door station wagon; 65=Contour LX four-door sedan; 67=Contour SE four-door sedan; 68=Contour SVT four-door sedan; 71=Crown Victoria Police Interceptor four-door sedan; 72=Crown Victoria "S" (Fleet) four-door sedan; 73=Crown Victoria four-door sedan; 74=Crown Victoria LX four-door sedan.) The eighth symbol indicated the engine: Escort, P=2.0-liter I-4 with EFI; Taurus, S=3.0-liter DOHC V-6 with EFI; U=3.0-liter V-6 with EFI; 2=Flexible fuel 3.0-liter V-6 with EFI. Contour, G=2.5-liter DOHC V-6 with EFI; L=2.5-liter DOHC V-6 with EFI; Z=2.0-liter DOHC I-4 with EFI and 3=2.0-liter DOHC I-4 with EFI. Crown Victoria, W=4.6-liter SOHC V-8 with EFI (Romeo engine plant). The ninth symbol was a check digit. The 10th symbol indicated the model year: Y=2000. The 11th symbol indicated the assembly plant: A=Hapeville (Atlanta), Georgia; F=Dearborn, Michigan; G=Chicago, Illinois.; K=Claycomo (Kansas City), Missouri.; M=Cuautitlan, Mexico; R=Hermosillo, Mexico; W=Wayne, Michigan and X=Talbotville (St. Thomas), Ontario, Canada. The last six symbols were the sequential production numbers starting at 100001 at each factory.

Escort LX (Four)

Model No.	Body/ Style No.	Body Type & Seating	Factory Price	Shipping Weight	Production Total
P	10	4-dr. Sedan-5P	$11,870	2,468 lbs.	Note 1

Escort SE (Four)

P	13	4-dr. Sedan-5P	$13,350	2,468 lbs.	Note 1
P	15	4-dr. Station Wagon-5P	$14,550	2,531 lbs.	Note 2

Escort ZX2 Cool Series (Four)

P	11/41V	2-dr. Coupe-5P	$12,075	2,478 lbs.	Note 3

Escort ZX2 Hot Series (Four)

P	11	2-dr. Coupe-5P	$13,755	2,478 lbs.	Note 3

Note 1: Model year production in the U.S., Canada and Mexico of four-door sedans was 170,715.
Note 2: Model year production in the U.S., Canada and Mexico of four-door wagons was 22,621.
Note 3: Model year production in the U.S., Canada and Mexico of two-door coupes was 94,175.
Total Escort model year production in the U.S., Canada and Mexico was 287,511—all were sold in the U.S.

Contour LX (Four)

P	65	4-dr. Sedan-5P	$14,995	2,744 lbs.	Note 4

Contour LX (V-6)

P	65	4-dr. Sedan-5P	$15,590	------	Note 4

Contour SE (Four)

P	66	4-dr. Sedan-5P	$16,490	2,744 lbs.	Note 4

Contour SE (V-6)

P	66	4-dr. Sedan-5P	$16,890	------	Note 4

Contour SVT (V-6)

P	68	4-dr. Sports Sedan-5P	$22,940	3,068 lbs.	Note 5

Note 4: Model year production in the U.S., Canada and Mexico for the U.S. market of four-door sedans was 139,380.
Note 5: Approximately 5,000 Contour SVT Sports Sedans were assembled.

Taurus LX (V-6)

P	52	4-dr. Sedan-6P	$17,995	3,329 lbs.	Note 6

Taurus SE (V-6)

P	53	4-dr. Sedan-6P	$18,995	3,329 lbs.	Note 6
P	58	4-dr. Station Wagon-6P	$18,995	3,480 lbs.	Note 7

Taurus SE Comfort (V-6)

P	53	4-dr. Sedan-6P	$20,495	3,353 lbs.	Note 6
P	58	4-dr. Station Wagon-6P	$21,495	3,480 lbs.	Note 7

Taurus SHO (V-8)

P	54	4-dr. Sedan-6P	$29,550	3,326 lbs.	Note 6

Note 6: Model year production in the U.S., Canada and Mexico for the U.S. market of four-door sedans was 385,227.
Note 7: Model year production in the U.S., Canada and Mexico for the U.S. market of four-door wagons was 38,129.
Total Taurus model year production in the U.S., Canada and Mexico for the U.S. market was 423,356.

Crown Victoria (V-8)

P	73	4-dr. Sedan-6P	$22,510	3,917 lbs.	Note 8

Crown Victoria LX (V-8)

P	74	4-dr. Sedan-6P	$24,530	3,917 lbs.	Note 8

Crown Victoria (Natural Gas V-8)

P	73	4-dr. Sedan-6P	$28,675	------	Note 8

Crown Victoria LX (Natural Gas V-8)

P	74	4-dr. Sedan-6P	$30,695	------	Note 8

Note 8: Model year production in the U.S., Canada and Mexico for the U.S. market of four-door sedans was 118,882.

Engines:

Escort LX and SE Base Four: Inline. Overhead cam. Cast-iron block and aluminum head. Displacement: 122 cid. (2.0 liters). B & S: 3.33 x 3.46 in. Compression ratio: 9.2:1. Brake hp: 110 at 5000 rpm. Torque: 125 lbs.-ft. at 3750 rpm. Split port induction.

ZX2 Base Four: Inline. Double overhead cam. Cast-iron block and aluminum head. Displacement: 121 cid (2.0 liters). B & S: 3.34 x 3.46 in. Compression ratio: 9.6:1. Brake hp: 130 at 5750 rpm. Torque: 127 lbs.-ft. at 4250 rpm. Sequential electronic fuel injection.

Contour LX and SE Base Four: Inline. Dual overhead cam. Cast-iron block and aluminum head. Displacement: 121 cid (2.0 liters). B & S: 3.34 x 3.46 in. Compression ratio: 9.6:1. Brake hp: 125 at 5500 rpm. Torque: 130 lbs.-ft. at 4000 rpm. Sequential electronic fuel injection.

Contour SVT Base V-6: Dual overhead cam. Aluminum block and head. Displacement: 155 cid (2.5 liters). B & S: 3.24 x 3.13 in. Compression ratio: 10.0:1. Brake hp: 200 at 6625 rpm. Torque: 165 lbs.-ft. at 5625 rpm. Sequential electronic fuel injection.

Contour LX and SE Optional V-6: Modular, dual overhead cam. Aluminum block and head. Displacement: 155 cid (2.5 liters). B & S: 3.24 x 3.13 in. Compression ratio: 9.7:1. Brake hp: 170 at 6250 rpm. Torque: 165 lbs.-ft. at 4250 rpm. Sequential electronic fuel injection.

Taurus LX and SE Base V-6: Overhead valve. Cast-iron block and head. Displacement: 182 cid. (3.0 liters). B & S: 3.50 x 3.15 in. Compression ratio: 9.3:1. Brake hp: 145 at 5250 rpm. Torque: 170 lbs.-ft. at 3250 rpm. Sequential electronic fuel injection.

Taurus LX and SE Optional V-6: Dual overhead cam. Aluminum block and head. Displacement: 182 cid (3.0 liters). B & S: 3.50 x 3.15 in. Compression ratio: 10.0:1. Brake hp: 200 at 5750 rpm. Torque: 200 lbs.-ft. at 4500 rpm. Sequential electronic fuel injection.

Taurus LX and SE Optional Ethanol V-6: Dual overhead cam, flexible-fuel engine. Aluminum block and head. Displacement: 182 cid (3.0 liters). B & S: 3.50 x 3.15 in. Compression ratio: 10.0:1. Brake hp: 200 at 5750 rpm. Torque: 200 lbs.-ft. at 4500 rpm. Ethanol fuel.

Taurus SHO Base V-8: 60-degree, dual overhead cam. Aluminum block and head. Displacement: 207 cid (3.4 liters). B & S: 3.2 x 3.1 in. Compression ratio: 9.8:1. Brake hp: 235 at 6100 rpm. Torque: 230 lbs.-ft. at 4800 rpm. Sequential electronic fuel injection.

1999 Contour SE four-door sedan

1999 Taurus SE station wagon

1999 Escort SE station wagon

Crown Victoria Base V-8: Modular, overhead valve. Displacement: 281 cid. (4.6 liters). B & S: 3.60 x 3.60. Compression ratio: 9.0:1. Brake hp: 190 at 4250 rpm. Torque: 265 lbs.-ft. at 3200 rpm. Sequential electronic fuel injection.

Chassis:

Escort: Wheelbase: 98.4 in. Overall length: (LX and SE sedan) 174.7 in. and (SE wagon) 172.7 in. (ZX2 coupe) 175.2 in. Tires: P185/65-R14.

Contour: Wheelbase: 106.5 in. Overall length: 184.6 in. Tires: P185/70-R14S and P185/50-R16Z.

Taurus: Wheelbase: 108.5 in. Overall length: (sedan) 197.5 in. and (wagon) 199.6 in. Tires: P205/65-R15 and P225/55-ZR16, SHO sedan.

Crown Victoria: Wheelbase: 114.7 in. Overall length: 212 in. Tires: P225/60-SR16.

Options:

Escort: Air conditioning, standard in SE ($795). Antilock braking system ($400). Rear window defroster, standard in SE ($190). California emissions system, no cost. Front and rear floor mats ($55). Engine block heater ($20). AM/FM stereo with cassette player ($185). ETR AM/FM stereo with cassette player and premium sound system, ZX2 Hot coupe ($95). AM/FM stereo cassette with premium sound system and six-disc CD changer ($295). Remote keyless entry ($165). SE comfort group, includes speed control, tilt steering and dual map lights, SE ($345). SE power group, includes power locks and power windows ($345). Unique sport bucket seats. Sport package including 14-in. aluminum wheels, rear deck lid spoiler, bright exhaust pipe tips, unique seats with rear integrated headrests, leather-wrapped steering wheel and sport badging, SE sedan ($495). Four-speed overdrive automatic transmission ($815). 14-in. aluminum wheels ($265). ZX2 Hot Coupe series power group, with power windows and power door locks ($345). ZX2 Hot Coupe sport group including rear deck lid spoiler, bright exhaust tips, unique seats with rear headrests with ZX2 script, 15-in. aluminum wheels, sport badging and leather-wrapped steering wheel ($595). Power sliding moon roof for Hot Coupe ($595). Rear deck lid spoiler for coupes ($195). Four-speed automatic transmission with 16-valve Zetec 2.0-liter DOHC engine, ZX2 ($815). Aluminum wheels for Hot Coupe ($265). Wheels and tunes package, includes 14-in. aluminum wheels, radio, floor mats and spoiler for ZX2, not available on Hot coupe ($450).

Contour: Antilock braking system, standard on SVT ($500). Rear window defroster ($190). California emissions system (no cost). High-altitude emissions system (no cost). 2.0-liter four-cylinder gaseous fuel preparation package, includes four-wheel disc brakes and P195/65-R14 tires and requires automatic transmission ($260). 2.5-liter Duratec V-6, includes tachometer, P195/65-R15 blackwall performance tires, four-wheel anti-lock brakes and SecuriLock anti-theft system ($70 credit). Engine block heater ($20). Front and rear floor mats ($55). Moon roof, SE ($595). Premium sound system with ETR AM/FM stereo, cassette player and amplifier ($135). ETR AM/FM stereo with CD player and premium sound, SE ($275) and no charge, SVT. AM/FM stereo cassette player, LX ($185). Power antenna ($95). Remote keyless entry, includes illuminated entry system ($190). SE comfort group, includes power driver's seat, 15-in. 12-spoke aluminum wheels, leather-wrapped steering wheel, fog lamps, variable interval windshield wipers, illuminated visor mirror and power antenna ($795). Sport group, included with 2.5-liter V-6, five-speed manual transmission, 15-in. eight-spoke aluminum wheels, a tachometer, a leather-wrapped steering wheel, rear deck lid spoiler, variable fixed interval windshield wipers, an illuminated vanity mirror, fog lamps, sport cloth bucket seats and sport badging ($1,000). Leather seating surfaces ($895). 60/40 split folding rear seat, SE ($205). Six-way power driver's seat, SE ($350). Speed control, LX ($215). Traction control, requires 2.5-liter engine and antilock brakes ($175). ECT automatic transmission, LX and SE ($815). 15-in. eight-spoke cast-aluminum wheels, includes P205/60-R15 black sidewall tires, SE ($425).

1999 Crown Victoria LX four-door sedan

1999 Crown Victoria four-door sedan

Taurus: Antilock braking system, standard on SHO ($600). Power door locks, LX ($275). California emissions system (no cost). High-altitude emissions system, no charge. 3.0-liter flexible fuel (ethanol) V-6 on LX/SE, with column shift only ($1,165). Engine block heater ($35). Light group ($45). Front and rear floor mats ($55). Heated exterior mirrors, standard on SHO ($35). Power moon roof, with map lamps in overhead console ($740). ETR AM/FM stereo and cassette player with four speakers ($185). Ford Mach audio system with six speakers, SE ($320 and no charge, SHO). Trunk-mounted six-disc CD changer ($350). Keyless remote entry ($190). SE comfort group, includes 3.0-liter four, overdrive automatic transmission, power driver's seat with adjustable lumbar support, electronic temperature control air conditioning, 12-spoke bright cast aluminum wheels, leather-wrapped steering wheel, remote entry with keypad and perimeter anti-theft, illuminated visor mirrors, five-passenger seating, floor console and floor shift ($1,000 with sport group; $1,500 without sport group). SE sport group with 3.0-liter four-valve V-6, automatic overdrive transmission, rear deck lid spoiler, five-spoke aluminum wheels, five-passenger seating, floor console and floor shift ($750). Five-passenger seating with center seating console, column shift and secondary power point ($105). Six-passenger seating with center seating console, column shift and secondary power point, no cost. Leather bucket seats, requires power seat ($895). Power driver's seat with power lumbar adjustment, SE ($395). Dual power seats in SE, requires SE comfort package ($350). Rear facing vinyl third seat, wagon ($200). Integrated rear child seat, SE wagon ($135). Speed control ($215). Conventional spare tire ($125). Cargo net and cargo area cover, SE wagon ($140). Five-spoke aluminum wheels, includes locking lug nut package, LX and SE ($395). Chrome 12-spoke wheels, includes locking lug nut kit, no cost. 16-in. bright cast-aluminum five-spoke wheels, with P225/55-ZR16 all-season low-profile tires ($580).

Crown Victoria: LX comfort group with electronic automatic temperature control air conditioning, 12-spoke aluminum wheels, power passenger seat with power lumbar and recliners, auto dim mirror with compass and leather-wrapped steering wheel ($900). LX comfort plus group, comfort group plus electronic instrumentation, leather trim seats and premium sound system ($2,150). California emissions, no cost. 4.6-liter natural gas engine with engine compression light and P225/60-VR16 tires, ($6,165). Handling and performance package with revised springs, shocks and stabilizer bar, P225/60-TR16 black sidewall touring tires, 16-in. cast-aluminum wheels, rear air suspension, dual exhausts and 3.27:1 axle ($615 to $935 depending upon other options ordered). Front color-keyed carpeting ($30). Rear color-keyed carpeting ($25). Single CD player replacing cassette ($140). Trunk-mounted six-disc CD changer ($350). Premium sound system ($360). Remote keyless entry ($240). Leather seating surfaces on split bench seat ($735). Six-way power driver's seat, including power lumbar and recliner ($360). Conventional spare tire ($120). P225/60-R16 white sidewall tires ($80 above regular tires). T23 P225/60-VR15 white sidewall tires with requires natural gas engine, no cost. Traction control ($175). Universal garage door opener ($115).

Jack Nasser, a 30-year Ford Motor Co. veteran and former president of Ford Automotive Operations took over as corporate president and chief executive officer on Jan. 1, 1999. At the time it was announced he would work with 41-year-old William Clay Ford, Jr., who was named non-executive chairman. It was predicted Nasser would run day-to-day operations of the company for the next 14 years, although things turned out differently. Nasser was eventually fired by Ford Jr. Ford Motor Company's outlook was rosy in 1999, with $14.9 billion of cash in the bank and plans to acquire a number of automakers to expand the company's line of vehicles. Ford purchased Sweden's Volvo car operations in March of 1999 at a cost of $6.45 billion. Nasser envisioned Volvo and other brands as part of a new Premier Automotive Group within the Ford family. He also hooked up with Microsoft's MSN CarPoint service, teamed with Priceline.com to test market a name-your-price car-buying plan in Florida and opened a plant in Norway to build a two-passenger thermoplastic vehicle named the "Th!nk."

2000 Ford

Focus — Four: The Focus was introduced during 2000 as an all-new small car intended to replace the Escort and, eventually, the Contour. It was available in three body styles: a three-door hatchback coupe, a four-door sedan and a four-door wagon. Standard equipment on the ZX3 hatchback included a 2.0-liter DOHC inline four-cylinder engine, a five-speed manual transmission, P195/60-R15 tires, a space saver spare tire, a steel spare wheel, four-wheel disc brakes, front and rear stabilizer bars, front seat belt pre-tensioners, child seat anchors, an emergency release in the trunk, two front headrests, a remote vehicle anti-theft system, front fog lights, intermittent windshield wipers, a rear window wiper and defogger, front bucket seats, premium cloth upholstery, a height-adjustable driver's seat, a split bench rear seat with split-folding back, rear seat heat ducts, an AM/FM CD stereo and four speakers, power steering, remote control dual outside mirrors, front and rear cup holders, front door pockets, a 12-volt power outlet, a front storage console, a leather-wrapped steering wheel, front and rear floor mats, a tachometer, a clock and a low-fuel indicator. The LX sedan also included a four-cylinder SOHC engine, P185/65-R14 tires, full wheel covers, a front stabilizer bar only, rear door child safety locks and an AM/FM cassette stereo. The SE sedan featured P195/60-R15 tires, variable intermittent wipers, remote power door locks, power windows, power outside rearview mirrors and an AM/FM stereo radio and a multi-CD player. The SE wagon featured a four-speed automatic transmission, rear door child safety locks, variable intermittent wipers, a roof rack, remote power door locks, one-touch power windows, power mirrors and air conditioning. The Focus ZTS four-door sedan featured P205/50-R16 tires, antilock brakes, rear door child safety locks, variable intermittent wipers, a driver's seat with adjustable lumbar support, remote power door locks, one-touch power windows, power mirrors, cruise control, a tilt/telescope steering column, air conditioning, front reading lights, simulated wood dash trim and simulated wood door trim.

Escort — Four: The 2000 Escort had no major design changes but the station wagon was dropped. Standard equipment for the Escort SE included dual second-generation air bags, power-assisted front disc/rear drum brakes, side window demisters, a rear window defroster, the 2.0-liter split port induction (SPI 2000) four-cylinder engine, single exhaust with tip, flush Solar-Tinted windshield and tinted windows, a heater and defroster, CFC-free manual temperature control air conditioning, a soft "vinyl feel" dashboard, an integrated climate control and audio control panel, a clock, a storage bin, child safety rear door locks, an AM/FM cassette stereo radio with premium speakers, keyless remote entry with perimeter anti-theft, low-back cloth front seats, split-folding 60/40 rear seat, a four-spoke steering wheel, power rack-and-pinion steering, P185/65-R14 blackwall tires, a five-speed manual transmission, a trip

2000 Focus four-door sedan

odometer, two-speed windshield wipers with intermittent feature and 14 x 5.5 in. semi-styled steel wheels. The ZX2 coupe included the 2.0-liter DOHC 16-valve Zetec four-cylinder engine, frameless door glass, low-back cloth front bucket seats with driver side memory recline, a tachometer, a temperature gauge, an AM/FM stereo cassette, power mirrors, a rear window defroster, a rear spoiler and a trip odometer. A performance-oriented S/R package was optional on the Escort ZX2 and the Sport-optioned version now featured a 60/40 split-folding seatback, a passive anti-theft system and remote keyless entry. Leather seats were no longer available.

Contour — Four and SVT — V-6: The Contour LX was dropped from the 2000 series lineup. The only four-cylinder model available was the SE four-door sedan. This model was also available in a three-car V-6 series, along with the Contour Sport four-door sedan and the Contour SVT four-door sedan. Standard equipment on the Contour SE included dual second generation air bags, air conditioning, rear window defroster, power door locks, power front disc and rear drum brakes, an electric digital clock, childproof rear door locks, the 2.0-liter DOHC Zetec 16-valve I-4, semi flush exterior glass with Solar-Tint, a heater and defroster with a four-speed blower control, a soft touch dashboard, a backlit cluster with 130-mph speedometer, analog gauges (including a trip odometer, a fuel gauge, a high-beam warning light, a coolant temperature gauge and a low oil pressure light, turn signal indicator lights, a handbrake-on warning light, a catalyst malfunction light and a seat belt reminder light), left- and right-hand power body-color exterior mirrors, a day/night rearview mirror, an AM/FM stereo with cassette player, speed control, one-touch power windows, illuminated door switches, manual two-way adjustable front bucket seats with reclining seat backs and a driver's side armrest attached to the seat, a tilt steering column, a tachometer, a soft touch steering wheel with center horn control, power rack-and-pinion steering, P185/70-R14S blackwall tires, a five-speed manual transmission with overdrive, single-speed windshield wipers with intermittent feature and fluidic washers and 14-in. wheel covers. The Contour SVT featured power four-wheel disc brakes with Dacromat finished rotors and unique front calipers, an antilock braking system, the 2.5-liter DOHC high-output Duratec 24-valve V-6, a passive anti-theft system (PATS), a unique quasi-dual exhaust system with low back pressure mufflers, a white-faced 160-mph speedometer, an electronic AM/FM stereo radio with cassette player and premium sound system, unique sport front seats with a 10-way power driver's seat, a split-folding 60/40 rear seat with integral headrests, carpeted rear seat backs, a leather-wrapped steering wheel, P215/50-R16Z directional rated tires, variable intermittent windshield wipers with fluidic washers and five-spoke 16-in. cast-aluminum wheels.

Taurus — V-6 and V-8: The big news for 2000 was the high-performing SHO model was dropped. The remaining cars were redesigned and offered in two trim levels: LX and SE. Both engines used in these cars — the 3.0-liter Vulcan V-6 and the 3.8-liter Duratec V-6 — had higher horsepower and torque ratings. Trunk space in the Taurus sedan was significantly increased thanks to a new rear deck design. A restyled roofline increased interior headroom in the front and rear. Sedans had new front and rear fascias, while wagons had a new front fascia. Ford introduced a new "Personal Safety System" that included dual-stage air bags, a crash severity sensor, a belt-use sensor and a driver seat position sensor. Child seat tether anchors and the SecuriLock™ passive anti-theft system were made standard on all Taurus models. New options included front side-impact air bags and all-speed traction control combined with antilock braking. A new power adjustable pedal system was available. Standard LX equipment included a V-6 engine, a four-speed automatic transmission, P215/60-R16 all-season tires, a space saver spare, full wheel covers, four-wheel independent suspension and a front stabilizer bar, front and rear solid disc brakes, front seat belt pre-tensioners, rear door child safety locks, child seat anchors, an emergency trunk release, two front headrests, variable intermittent windshield wipers, a rear defogger, five-passenger seating with cloth upholstered bucket front seats and rear bench seat, rear seat heating ducts, power door locks, one-touch power windows, power mirrors, an AM/FM stereo system with four speakers, speed-proportional power steering, a tilt-adjustable steering wheel, a remote trunk lid release, front seatback storage, a front 12-volt power outlet, air conditioning, front reading lights, dual visor-vanity mirrors, a trunk light, a tachometer, a clock and a low-fuel warning indicator. The SE sedan included alloy rims, remote power door locks, an AM/FM cassette stereo system and cruise control. The SES sedan also added ABS brakes, six-passenger seating with a split front bench seat, a six-way power driver's seat with adjustable lumbar support, an AM/FM stereo radio with CD and cassette players and dual illuminating vanity mirrors. The SEL sedan added the Duratec V-6, a remote vehicle anti-theft system, dusk-sensing headlights, digital keypad power door locks, heated mirrors, an AM/FM stereo with cassette player and a six CD system, a climate control system and a leather-wrapped steering wheel. The SE station wagon featured alloy rims, front and rear stabilizer bars, front disc/rear drum brakes, a front center lap belt,

2000 Escort ZX2 coupe

a roof rack, rear window wipers, six-passenger seating with a split front bench seat and a split-folding rear seat, remote power door locks, an AM/FM stereo with cassette system, a power radio antenna, cargo area lighting and cargo tie downs.

Crown Victoria — V-8: The 2000 Crown Victoria got a new emergency interior trunk release and rear child seat anchors. Standard equipment on the base Crown Victoria included dual air bags, manual air conditioning, a radio antenna hidden in the rear window defroster, the SecuriLock™ passive anti-theft system, a brake/shift interlock, power four-wheel disc antilock brakes, rear seat child safety latches, an electric digital clock with dimming feature, a rear window defroster, the 4.6-liter OHC sequential fuel-injected V-8, a stainless steel exhaust system, a gauge cluster with analog gauges (voltmeter, oil pressure, water temperature and fuel), full Solar Tinted glass, instrument panel appliqués, side window demisters, power door locks, dual remote-control fold-away power exterior mirrors, a day/night inside rearview mirror, an electronic AM/FM stereo with cassette player and door-mounted speakers, a cloth-trimmed split bench front seat with center fold-down armrest and reclining seatbacks, a sound insulation package, speed control, a color-keyed steering wheel, speed-sensitive variable-assist power steering (not available in cars with the natural gas engine), cloth-covered sun visors, a tilt steering column with stalk-mounted controls, P225/60-SR16 all-season blackwall tires, an ECT automatic transmission with overdrive, a trip odometer, dual-jet interval windshield wipers, deluxe wheel covers, HSLA 16 x 7-in, wheel rims and power windows with driver side express down. The LX featured remote keyless entry (except with natural gas engine), a split bench seat with fold-down center armrest trimmed in luxury cloth (with power lumbar adjustment and six-way power adjustment on the driver's side, plus a power back recliner) and chrome-plated, locking cross-spoke wheel covers.

I. D. Data:

Ford's 17-symbol Vehicle Identification Number (VIN) was stamped on a metal tab fastened to the instrument panel, visible through the windshield. The first symbol indicated the nation of origin: 1=United States; 2=Canada; 3=Mexico. The second symbol indicated the manufacturer: F=Ford Motor Co. The third symbol indicated the vehicle type: A=passenger car. The fourth symbol indicated the type of restraint system: B=driver and passenger air bags and active belts (except Escort ZX2 coupe); F=driver and passenger air bags and active belts; K= driver and passenger air bags and active belts in all outboard positions. The fifth symbol indicated the designation: P=Ford; T=Imported from outside North America or non-Ford car marketed by Ford in North America. The sixth and seventh symbols indicated the body type: 13=Escort LX four-door sedan; 30=Focus ECO three-door coupe; 31=Focus ZX3 three-door coupe; 33=Focus LX four-door sedan; 34=Focus SE four-door sedan; 36=Focus SE four-door station wagon; 38=Focus ZTS four-door sedan; 52=Taurus LX four-door sedan; 53=Taurus SE two-valve four-door sedan; 54=Taurus SE four-valve four-door sedan; 55=Taurus SE SVG four-door sedan; 56=Taurus SE four-door Comfort sedan; 58=Taurus SE four-door station wagon; 59=Taurus SE four-door Comfort station wagon; 66=Contour SE four-door sedan; 68=Contour SVT four-door sedan; 71=Crown Victoria Police Interceptor four-door sedan; 72=Crown Victoria "S" (Fleet) four-door sedan; 73=Crown Victoria four-door sedan; 74=Crown Victoria LX four-door sedan. The eighth symbol indicated the engine: Escort, P=2.0-liter I-4 with EF/SPI; Taurus, S=3.0-liter DOHC V-6 with EFI; U=3.0-liter V-6 with EFI; 2=flexible fuel 3.0-liter V-6 with EFI. Contour, G=2.5-liter DOHC V-6 with EFI; L=2.5-liter DOHC V-6 with EFI; Z=2.0-liter DOHC I-4 with EFI; 3=2.0-liter DOHC I-4 with EFI. Crown Victoria, W=4.6-liter SOHC V-8 with EFI (Romeo engine plant). The ninth symbol was a check digit. The 10th symbol indicated the model year: Y=2000. The 11th symbol indicated the assembly plant: A=Hapeville (Atlanta), Georgia; F=Dearborn, Michigan; G=Chicago, Illinois; K=Claycomo (Kansas City), Missouri; M=Cuautitlan, Mexico; R=Hermosillo, Mexico; W=Wayne, Michigan; X=Talbotville (St. Thomas), Ontario, Canada. The last six symbols were the sequential production numbers starting at 100001 at each factory.

Focus ZX3 (Four)

Model No.	Body/ Style No.	Body Type & Seating	Factory Price	Shipping Weight	Production Total
P	31	3-dr. Hatchback-5P	$12,280	2,551 lbs.	------

Focus LX (Four)

P	33	4-dr. Sedan-5P	$12,540	2,564 lbs.	------

Focus SE (Four)

P	34	4-dr. Sedan-5P	$13,980	2,564 lbs.	------
P	36	4-dr. Station Wagon-5P	$15,795	2,717 lbs.	------

Focus ZTS (Four)

P	38	4-dr. Sedan-5P	$15,580	2,564 lbs.	------

Escort SE (Four)

P	13	4-dr. Sedan-5P	$12,440	2,468 lbs.	------

Escort ZX2 (Four)

P	11	2-dr. Coupe-5P	$12,200	2,478 lbs.	------

Contour SE (Four)

P	66	4-dr. Sedan-5P	$17,290	2,769 lbs.	------

Contour SE (Four)

P	66	4-dr. Sedan-5P	$22,365	2,850 lbs.	------

Contour SE (V-6)

P	66	4-dr. Sedan-5P	$17,785	2,774 lbs.	------

Contour SE Sport option (V-6)

P	66	4-dr. Sedan-5P	$17,405	2,774 lbs.	------

Contour SVT (V-6)

P	68	4-dr. Sedan-5P	$23,275	3,068 lbs.	------

Taurus LX (V-6)

P	52	4-dr. Sedan-6P	$18,245	3,329 lbs.	------

Taurus SE (V-6)

P	53	4-dr. Sedan-6P	$19,295	3,329 lbs.	------
P	58	4-dr. Station Wagon-6P	$20,450	3,480 lbs.	------

Taurus SE (Flexible Fuel V-6)

P	---	4-dr. Sedan-6P	$19,295	------	------
P	---	4-dr. Station Wagon-6P	$20,450	------	------

Taurus SES (V-6)

P	55	4-dr. Sedan-6P	$20,170	3,353 lbs.	------

Taurus SEL (V-8)

P	56	4-dr. Sedan-6P	$21,445	3,340 lbs.	------

Crown Victoria Police Interceptor (V-8)

P	71	4-dr. Sedan-6P	-----	-----	------

Crown Victoria S-Fleet option (V-8)

P	72	4-dr. Sedan-6P	-----	-----	------

Crown Victoria (V-8)

P	73	4-dr. Sedan-6P	$22,635	3,908 lbs.	------

Crown Victoria (Natural Gas V-8)

P	73	4-dr. Sedan-6P	$28,800	3,990 lbs.	------

Crown Victoria LX (V-8)

P	74	4-dr. Sedan-6P	$24,750	3,908 lbs.	------

Crown Victoria LX (Natural Gas V-8)

P	74	4-dr. Sedan-6P	$30,915	3,990 lbs.	------

Engines:

Focus LX, SE and ZX3 Base Four: Inline. Overhead cam. Cast-iron block and aluminum head. Displacement: 121 cid (2.0 liters). B & S: 3.39 x 3.52 in. Compression ratio: 9.4:1. Brake hp: 110 at 5000 rpm. Torque: 125 lbs.-ft. at 3750 rpm. Split port induction.

Focus ZTS Base Four: Inline. Dual overhead cam. Cast-iron block and aluminum head. Displacement: 121 cid (2.0 liters). B & S: 3.39 x 3.52 in. Compression ratio: 9.6:1. Brake hp: 130 at 5750 rpm. Torque: 135 lbs.-ft. at 4500 rpm. Sequential electronic fuel injection.

Escort SE Base Four: Inline. Overhead cam. Cast-iron block and aluminum head. Displacement: 121 cid (2.0 liters). B & S: 3.39 x 3.52 in. Compression ratio: 9.4:1. Brake hp: 110 at 5000 rpm. Torque: 125 lbs.-ft. at 3750 rpm. Split port induction.

Escort ZX2 Base Four: Inline. Dual overhead cam. Cast-iron block and aluminum head. Displacement: 121 cid (2.0 liters). B & S: 3.39 x 3.52 in. Compression ratio: 9.6:1. Brake hp: 130 at 5750 rpm. Torque: 135 lbs.-ft. at 4500 rpm. Sequential electronic fuel injection.

Contour SE Base Four: Inline. Dual overhead cam. Cast-iron block and aluminum head. Displacement: 121 cid (2.0 liters). B & S: 3.39 x 3.52 in. Compression ratio: 9.6:1. Brake hp: 125 at 5500 rpm. Torque: 130 lbs.-ft. at 4000 rpm. Sequential electronic fuel injection.

Contour SVT Base Four: 60-degree dual overhead cam. Aluminum block and head. Displacement: 155 cid (2.5 liters). B & S: 3.24 x 3.13 in. Compression ratio: 10.0:1. Brake hp: 200 at 6625 rpm. Torque: 167 lbs.-ft. at 5625 rpm. Sequential electronic fuel injection.

Contour SE Optional V-6: Modular. Dual overhead cam. Aluminum block and head. Displacement: 155 cid (2.5 liters). B & S: 3.24 x 3.13 in. Compression ratio: 9.7:1. Brake hp: 170 at 6250 rpm. Torque: 165 lbs.-ft. at 4250 rpm. Sequential electronic fuel injection.

Taurus LX and SE Base V-6: Overhead valve. Cast-iron block and head. Displacement: 182 cid (3.0 liters). B & S: 3.50 x 3.15 in. Compression ratio: 9.3:1. Brake hp: 155 at 4900 rpm. Torque: 185 lbs.-ft. at 3950 rpm. Sequential electronic fuel injection.

Taurus SE and Comfort Wagon Optional V-6: Dual overhead cam. Aluminum block and head. Displacement: 182 cid (3.0 liters). B & S: 3.50 x 3.15 in. Compression ratio: 10.0:1. Brake hp: 200 at 5750 rpm. Torque: 200 lbs.-ft. at 4500 rpm. Sequential electronic fuel injection. VIN code: S.

Taurus SE SVG Optional V-6: Dual overhead cam, flexible-fuel engine. Aluminum block and head. Displacement: 182 cid (3.0 liters). B & S: 3.50 x 3.15 in. Compression ratio: 10.0:1. Brake hp: 200 at 5750 rpm. Torque: 200 lbs.-ft. at 4500 rpm.

Crown Victoria Base V-8: Modular, overhead valve. Displacement: 281 cid (4.6 liters). B & S: 3.60 x 3.60. Compression ratio: 9.0:1. Brake hp: 200 at 4250 rpm. Torque: 275 lbs.-ft. at 3000 rpm. Sequential electronic fuel injection.

Crown Victoria Natural Gas V-8: Modular, overhead valve. Displacement: 281 cid (4.6 liters). B & S: 3.60 x 3.60. Compression ratio: 9.0:1. Brake hp: 175 at 4250 rpm. Torque: 235 lbs.-ft. at 3000 rpm. Natural gas engine.

Chassis:

Focus: Wheelbase: 103 in. Overall length: 168.1 in., hatchback; 174.9 in., sedan and 174.9 in., station wagon. Tires: P185/65-R14, LX sedan; P195/60-R15, SE sedan and wagon and ZX3 and P205/50-R16, ZTS sedan.

Escort: Wheelbase: 98.4 in. Overall length: 174.7 in., SE sedan and 175.2 in., ZX2 coupe. Tires: P185/65-R14.

Contour: Wheelbase: 106.5 in. Overall length: 184.6 in. Tires: P185/70-R14S, SE and P15/50-R16Z, SVT.

Taurus: Wheelbase: 108.5 in. Overall length: 197.5 in, sedan and 199.6 in., station wagon. Tires: P215/60-R16.

Crown Victoria: Wheelbase: 114.7 in. Overall length: 212 in. Tires: P225/60-SR16.

Options:

Focus: ZX3 hatchback: Four-speed overdrive automatic transmission ($815). AdvanceTrac ($1,225). Air conditioning ($795). Antilock braking system ($400). California emissions requirements, no cost. Manual moon roof ($446). Non-California emissions, no cost. Power group ($740). Premium group ($1,095). Side air bags ($350). **LX sedan:** Four-speed overdrive automatic transmission ($815). Air conditioning ($795). Antilock braking system ($400). California emissions requirements , no cost. Non-California emissions, no cost. Side air bags ($350). **SE sedan:** Four-speed overdrive automatic transmission ($815). Antilock braking system ($400). California emissions requirements, no cost. Non-California emissions, no cost. SE Comfort group ($345). SE sports group ($470). Side air bags ($350). **ZTS sedan:** Four-speed overdrive automatic transmission ($815). AdvanceTrac ($1,225). California emissions requirements, no cost. Non-California emissions, no cost. Side air bags ($350). Low-back bucket seats with leather trim and map pockets ($695). **SE wagon:** Five-speed manual transmission, no cost. Antilock braking system ($400). California emissions requirements, no cost. Non-California emissions, no cost. SE Comfort group ($345). Side air bags ($350).

Escort: Air conditioning, standard in SE ($795). Antilock braking system ($400). Rear window defroster, standard in SE ($190). California emissions, no cost. Front and rear floor mats ($55). Engine block heater ($20). AM/FM stereo with cassette player ($185). ETR AM/FM stereo and cassette player with premium sound, ZX2 Hot Coupe ($95). AM/FM stereo and cassette player with premium sound and six disc CD changer ($295). Keyless remote entry ($165). SE comfort group, includes speed control, tilt steering and dual map lights, SE ($345). SE power group with power locks and power windows ($345). Sport bucket seats, no cost. Sport package includes 14-in. aluminum

2000 Escort four-door sedan

2000 Crown Victoria four-door sedan

wheels, rear deck lid spoiler, bright exhaust pipe tips, unique seats with rear integrated headrests, leather-wrapped steering wheel and sport badging, SE sedan ($495). Four-speed overdrive automatic transmission ($815). 14-in. aluminum wheels ($265). ZX2 Hot Coupe power group with power windows and power door locks ($345). ZX2 Hot Coupe sport group with rear deck lid spoiler, bright exhaust tips, unique seats and rear headrests with ZX2 script, 15-in. aluminum wheels, sport badging and leather-wrapped steering wheel ($595). Power sliding moon roof for Hot Coupe ($595). Rear deck lid spoiler, coupes, requires 41G if ordered for Hot coupe ($195). Four-speed automatic overdrive transmission with 16-valve Zetec 2.0-liter DOHC engine, ZX2 ($815). Aluminum wheels for Hot Coupe ($265). Wheels and tunes package with 14-in. aluminum wheels, radio, floor mats and spoiler, ZX2 but not available on Hot coupe ($450).

Contour: Antilock braking system, standard on SVT ($500). Rear window defroster ($190). California emissions system, no cost. High-altitude emissions system, no cost. 2.0-liter four-cylinder gaseous fuel preparation package, included four-wheel disc brakes and P195/65-R14 tires and required automatic transmission ($260). 2.5-liter Duratec V-6, included tachometer, P195/65-R15 blackwall performance tires, four-wheel antilock brakes and SecuriLock™ anti-theft system, SE only ($70 credit). Engine block heater ($20). Front and rear floor mats ($55). Moon roof, SE ($595) and no charge, SVT. Premium sound system with ETR AM/FM stereo, cassette player and amplifier ($135). ETR AM/FM stereo with CD player and premium sound, SE ($275) and no charge, SVT. AM/FM stereo cassette, LX, standard in SE ($185). Power antenna ($95). Keyless remote entry with illuminated entry system ($190). SE Comfort group with power driver's seat, 15-in. 12-spoke aluminum wheels, leather-wrapped steering wheel, leather shift knob, fog lamps, variable interval windshield wipers, illuminated visor mirror and power antenna ($795). Sport group included the 2.5-liter V-6, five-speed manual transmission, 15-in. eight-spoke aluminum wheels, tachometer, leather-wrapped steering wheel, sport floor mats, a rear deck lid spoiler, variable fixed interval windshield wipers, fog lamps, sport cloth bucket seats and sport badging ($1,000). Leather seating ($895). 60/40 split-folding rear seat, SE ($205). Six-way power driver's seat, SE ($350). Speed control, LX ($215). Traction control with 2.5-liter engine and antilock brakes ($175). ECT automatic transmission, LX and SE ($815). 15-in. eight-spoke cast-aluminum wheels and P205/60-R15 black sidewall tires, SE ($425).

Taurus: Antilock braking system, standard on SHO ($600). Power door locks, LX ($275). California emissions system, no cost. High-altitude emissions system, no cost. 3.0-liter flexible fuel (ethanol) V-6, LX and SE with column shift ($1,165). Engine block heater ($35). Light group ($45). Front and rear floor mats ($55). Heated exterior mirrors, standard on SHO ($35). Power moon roof with map lamps in overhead console ($740). ETR AM/FM stereo with cassette player and four speakers ($185). Ford Mach audio system with six speakers, SE ($320) and no charge, SHO. Trunk-mounted six-disc CD changer ($350). Keyless remote entry ($190). SE comfort group, included 3.0-liter four, overdrive automatic transmission, power driver's seat with adjustable lumbar support, electronic temperature control air conditioning, 12-spoke bright cast aluminum wheels, leather-

2000 Taurus SE Sport four-door sedan

2000 Contour SVT four-door sedan

wrapped steering wheel, automatic headlamps, remote entry with keypad and perimeter anti-theft, light group, illuminated visor mirrors, five-passenger seating, floor console and floor shift ($1,000 with sport group and $1,500 without sport group). SE sport group with 3.0-liter four-valve V-6, automatic overdrive transmission, rear deck lid spoiler, five-spoke aluminum wheels, five-passenger seating, floor console and floor shift ($750). Five-passenger seating with center seating console, column shift and secondary power point ($105). Six-passenger seating with center seating console, column shift and secondary power point, no cost. Leather bucket seats with required power seat ($895). Power driver's seat with power lumbar adjustment in SE ($395). Dual power seats, SE with required SE comfort package ($350). Rear facing vinyl third seat, wagon ($200). Integrated rear child seat, SE wagon ($135). Speed control ($215). Conventional spare tire ($125). Cargo net and cargo area cover, SE wagon ($140). Five-spoke aluminum wheels with locking lug nut package, LX and SE ($395). Chrome 12-spoke wheels, with locking lug nut kit, no cost. 16-in. bright cast-aluminum five-spoke wheels with P225/55-ZR16 all-season tires ($580).

Crown Victoria: LX comfort group, included electronic automatic temperature control air conditioning, 12-spoke aluminum wheels, power passenger seat with power lumbar and recliners, auto dim mirror with compass and leather-wrapped steering wheel ($900). LX comfort plus group, included comfort group plus electronic instrumentation, leather trim seats and premium sound system ($2,150). California emissions, no cost. 4.6-liter natural gas engine, included engine compression light and P225/60-VR16 tires, but deleted standard auto headlamp system and SecuriLock™ anti-theft system, plus remote keyless entry on LX ($6,165). The handling and performance package included revised springs, shocks and stabilizer bar, P225/60-TR16 blackwall touring tires, 16-in. cast-aluminum wheels, rear air suspension, dual exhausts and 3.27:1 axle ($615 to $935 depending upon other options ordered). Color-keyed front carpeting ($30). Color-keyed rear carpeting ($25). Single CD player replacing cassette ($140). Trunk-mounted six-disc CD changer ($350). Premium sound system ($360). Keyless remote entry ($240). Leather seating surfaces on split bench seat ($735). Six-way power driver's seat, included power lumbar and recliner ($360). Conventional spare tire ($120). P225/60-R16 white sidewall tires ($80 above regular tires). P225/60-VR15 white sidewall tires, required natural gas engine, no cost. Traction control ($175). Universal garage door opener ($115).

History:

In 2000, Ford Motor Co. had substantial accomplishments, but also faced unprecedented challenges. The automaker achieved record volume, revenue and operating earnings per share and generated strong operating profits. Individual product successes included the Ford Focus, the world's best-selling car. During 2000, Ford acquired the strong global brand Land Rover and successfully integrated it into the company's overall business. The Automotive Consumer Services Group — Ford's principal source of vehicle service and customer support worldwide — had record revenues and was a strong contributor to customer satisfaction. Ford Financial — which included Ford Credit and Primus Financial Services — achieved earnings of $1.54 billion, up 22 percent. Ford's Hertz rental car unit posted a record income for the ninth year in a row. A major challenge for Ford in 2000 was the headline-making Firestone tire recall. Ford dealers, suppliers and union partners were called upon to identify bad tires and find replacements months ahead of the original Firestone schedule. Ford Motor Company's official statement was "Customer safety guided all of our actions," but the recall severed Ford's longstanding relationship with Firestone that dated back to the Model T and Henry Ford's personal friendship with the Firestone family. Ford changed to covering tires under its vehicle warranty program, not a common industry practice before the Firestone recall. The company planned to introduce a tire pressure monitoring system in the 2002 Ford Explorer and eventually in all of its light trucks and sport utility vehicles. Ford also worked with the U.S. government and the auto industry to create an "early warning system" with a linked computer database of tire information. During 2000, Ford Motor Co. continued to be overly dependent on its North American earnings. With business conditions softening and U. S. competition getting more intense, correcting this imbalance became a critical goal for the automaker, which implemented a long-term European Turnaround Strategy. It included the introduction of at least 45 new products in the next five years and the taking of action to improve its performance in South America.

2001 Ford

Focus — Four: The 2001 Ford Focus featured "smart design and spirited driving" according to Ford. It was a sophisticated compact aimed at the worldwide market and available in three-door hatchback, four-door sedan and four-door wagon styles. The sedan was merchandised in LX, SE and ZTS trim lines. Standard equipment for the ZX3 hatchback included a 2.0-liter DOHC 16-valve 130-hp four-cylinder engine, a five-speed manual transmission, front-wheel drive, four-wheel independent suspension with front and rear stabilizer bars, a tachometer, a low-fuel indicator, a clock, 15-in. alloy wheel rims, P195/60-R15 tires, a space saver spare on a steel spare wheel, intermittent windshield wipers, a rear window wiper, a rear defogger, ventilated front disc/rear drum brakes, child seat anchors, a center rear three-point safety belt, front seat belt pre-tensioners, an emergency interior trunk release, two front seat headrests, power steering, front and rear cup holders, a front 12-volt power outlet, remote driver and passenger mirrors, a front console with storage space, five-passenger seating with premium cloth-trimmed front bucket seats, height adjustable driver and passenger seats, a split rear bench seat with split-folding seatbacks, rear seat heating ducts, dual visor-vanity mirrors, alloy trim on the gearshift knob, a leather-wrapped steering wheel, front and rear floor mats, an AM/FM CD stereo and a four-speaker sound system. The Focus LX sedan included most of the same standard features plus a 2.0-liter SOHC eight-valve 110-hp four-cylinder engine, 14-in. wheel rims, P185/65-R14 tires, front door pockets, a front console with storage space, five-passenger seating with cloth-trimmed front bucket seats, height-adjustable driver and passenger seats, a split rear bench seat with split-folding seatbacks, rear seat heating ducts, dual visor-vanity mirrors, front and rear floor mats, an AM/FM cassette stereo and a four-speaker sound system. Along with the standard equipment, the Focus SE sedan added 15-in. alloy wheel rims, P195/60-R15 tires, remote power door locks, one touch power windows, power mirrors, power steering, air conditioning, an AM/FM CD stereo and a four-speaker sound system. The Focus Street sedan carried the standard features listed above with 16-in. wheel rims and P205/65-R16 tires an AM/FM six CD stereo with multi-CD located in dash and a four-speaker sound system. Along with the Focus standard equipment, the ZTS sedan included a 2.0-liter DOHC 16-valve 130-hp four-cylinder engine, air conditioning, front reading lights, a leather-wrapped steering wheel, simulated wood dash trim, simulated wood door trim and an AM/FM CD stereo and a four-speaker sound system. Standard equipment for the Focus SE station wagon included a 2.0-liter DOHC 16-valve 130-hp four-cylinder engine, a four-speed automatic

2001 Taurus station wagon

transmission, 15-in. wheel rims and P195/60-R15 tires, a roof rack, a rear window wiper and ventilated front disc/rear drum brakes. Standard equipment for the Focus Street wagon included a 2.0-liter DOHC 16-valve 130-hp four-cylinder engine, a four-speed automatic transmission, 16-in. wheel rims, P205/50-R16 tires, a roof rack, remote power door locks, one touch power windows, power steering, air conditioning, dual visor-vanity mirrors, an AM/FM six CD stereo with in-dash multi-CD and a four-speaker sound system.

Escort — Four: The only Escort model remaining in 2001 was the ZX2 two-door coupe. It came in a few new colors, the extent of any changes. The S/R high-performance option was no longer available. Standard equipment included a 2.0-liter DOHC 16-valve 130-hp four-cylinder engine, a five-speed manual transmission, front-wheel drive, four-wheel independent suspension with front and rear stabilizer bars, a tachometer, a low-fuel indicator, a clock, an external temperature indicator, 15-in. wheel rims, P185/60-TR15 tires, a space saver spare on a steel spare wheel, variable intermittent windshield wipers, a rear defogger, a rear spoiler, front disc/rear drum brakes, child seat anchors, an emergency interior trunk release, daytime running lights, power door locks, power mirrors, power steering, front cup holders, a front 12-volt power outlet, front door pockets, a front console with storage space, four-passenger seating with cloth-trimmed front bucket seats, a split-folding rear seat, rear seat heating ducts, dual visor-vanity mirrors and an AM/FM cassette stereo.

Taurus — V-6 and V-8: After being restyled in 2000, the Taurus had minor changes for 2001. A LATCH (lower anchor and tether for children) arrangement for child safety belts was standard on all models. A new Spruce Green Metallic color was offered and fuel tank capacity was increased to 18 gallons. Standard equipment in the Taurus LX sedan included a 3.0-liter 12-valve 155-hp V-6 engine, a four-speed automatic transmission, front-wheel drive, four-wheel independent suspension, a front stabilizer bar, a tachometer, a low-fuel indicator, a clock, P215/60-R16 all-season tires on 16-in. steel rims, a space saver spare on a spare steel wheel, full wheel covers, variable intermittent wipers, a rear defogger, ventilated front disc/rear drum brakes, front seat belt pre-tensioners, rear door child safety locks, child seat anchors, an emergency inside trunk release, a center rear lap belt, two front headrests, an engine immobilizer, power door locks, one-touch power windows, power mirrors, speed-proportional power steering, a tilt-adjustable steering wheel, front cup holders, a remote trunk lid release, front seatback storage, a front 12-volt power outlet, a front console with storage space, retained accessory power, five-passenger seating with cloth-trimmed front bucket seats, a rear bench seat, rear seat heating ducts, air conditioning, front reading lights, dual visor-vanity mirrors, a trunk light, an AM/FM stereo, a mast antenna and a four-speaker sound system. The Taurus SE sedan added air conditioning, front reading lights, dual visor-vanity mirrors, a trunk light, an AM/FM cassette stereo, a mast antenna and a four-speaker sound system. In addition to Taurus standard equipment listed above, the Taurus SEL sedan included a 3.0-liter 24-valve 200-hp V-6 engine, ventilated front disc/rear drum ABS brakes, dusk-sensing headlights, digital keypad power door locks, one-touch power windows, heated power mirrors, cruise control, speed-proportional power steering, an AM/FM cassette six-CD stereo with multi-CD located in dash, a mast antenna and a four-speaker sound system. The Taurus SES sedan added a 3.0-liter 12-valve 155-hp V-6 engine, six-passenger seating with cloth-trimmed front split bench seat with six-way power and adjustable lumbar support on driver's side, a trunk light, an AM/FM cassette CD stereo, a mast antenna and a four-speaker sound system. Standard equipment in the Taurus SE wagon included a 3.0-liter 12-valve 155-hp V-6 engine, a roof rack, a rear window wiper, one-touch power windows, power mirrors, cruise control, speed-proportional power steering, a tilt-adjustable steering wheel, air conditioning, front reading lights, dual illuminated visor-vanity mirrors, a cargo area light, an AM/FM cassette CD stereo, a power antenna and a four-speaker sound system.

Crown Victoria — V-8: The 2001 Crown Victoria offered a more powerful V-8 engine. There were also minor interior improvements and an optional adjustable pedal assembly. A crash sensor, safety belt

2001 Escort ZX2 coupe

2001 Taurus LX Sport sedan

2001 Crown Victoria four-sedan

pre-tensioners, dual-stage air bags and seat-position sensor enhanced the safety of the driver and passengers. Standard equipment for the base Crown Victoria included a 4.6-liter SOHC 16-valve 220-hp V-8, a four-speed automatic transmission, rear-wheel drive, front independent suspension, front and rear stabilizer bars, a clock, a low-fuel indicator, P225/60-SR16 all-season tires on 16 x 7-in. steel rims, a space saver spare tire on a steel spare wheel, variable intermittent windshield wipers, a rear window defogger, front disc/rear drum brakes, front seat belt pre-tensioners, rear door child safety locks, an emergency interior trunk release, front and rear center lap belts, two front headrests, an engine immobilizer, one-touch power windows, power door locks, power mirrors, cruise control, speed-proportional power steering, a tilt-adjustable steering wheel, steering wheel mounted cruise controls, a remote trunk release, front door map pockets, six-passenger seating with a cloth-trimmed split front bench seat, a rear bench seat, air conditioning, a trunk light, a wood-trimmed dash, an AM/FM cassette stereo with four speakers and an element radio antenna. Standard equipment for the base Crown Victoria LX included a 4.6-liter SOHC 16-valve 220-hp V-8, a four-speed automatic transmission, rear-wheel drive, a front independent suspension, front and rear stabilizer bars, a clock, a low-fuel indicator, P225/60-SR16 all-season tires on 16 x 7-in. steel rims, a space saver spare tire on a steel spare wheel, variable intermittent windshield wipers, a rear window defogger, front disc/rear drum brakes, front seat belt pre-tensioners, rear door child safety locks, an emergency interior trunk release, front and rear center lap belts, two front headrests, an engine immobilizer, one-touch power windows, remote power door locks, power mirrors, cruise control, speed-proportional power steering, a tilt-adjustable steering wheel, steering wheel mounted cruise controls, a remote trunk release, front door map pockets and seatback storage, six-passenger seating, a cloth-trimmed split front bench seat with six-way power and adjustable lumbar support on driver's side, a rear folding center armrest, air conditioning, front reading lights, dual illuminated visor-vanity mirrors, a trunk light, a wood-trimmed dash, an AM/FM cassette stereo with four speakers and an element radio antenna.

I.D. Data:

Ford's 17-symbol Vehicle Identification Number (VIN) was stamped on a metal tab fastened to the instrument panel and was visible through the windshield. The first symbol indicated the nation of origin: 1=United States; 2=Canada; 3=Mexico. The second symbol indicated the manufacturer: F=Ford Motor Co. The third symbol indicated the vehicle type: A=passenger car. The fourth symbol indicated the type of restraint system: B=driver and passenger air bags and active belts (except Escort ZX2 coupe); F=driver and passenger air bags and active belts; K= driver and passenger air bags and active belts in all outboard positions. The fifth symbol indicated the designation: P=Ford and T=Imported from outside North America or non-Ford car marketed by Ford in North America. The sixth and seventh symbols indicated the body type: 11=Escort ZX2 two-door coupe; 31=Focus ZX3 three-door coupe; 33=Focus LX four-door sedan; 34=Focus SE/Focus Street four-door sedan; 36=Focus SE/Focus Street four-door station wagon; 38=Focus ZTS four-door sedan; 52=Taurus LX four-door sedan; 53=Taurus SE two-valve four-door sedan; 55=Taurus SE SVG four-door sedan; 56=Taurus SEL four-door sedan; 58=Taurus SE four-door station wagon; 73=Crown Victoria four-door sedan and 74=Crown Victoria LX four-door sedan. The eighth symbol indicated the engine: Escort, P=2.0-liter I-4 with EF/SPI; Taurus, S=3.0-liter DOHC V-6 with EFI; U=3.0-liter V-6 with EFI; 2=flexible fuel 3.0-liter V-6 with EFI; Contour G=2.5-liter DOHC V-6 with EFI; L=2.5-liter DOHC V-6 with EFI; Z=2.0-liter DOHC I-4 with EFI; 3=2.0-liter DOHC I-4 with EFI; Crown Victoria W=4.6-liter SOHC V-8 with EFI (Romeo engine plant). The ninth symbol was a check digit. The 10th symbol indicated the model year: Z=2001. The 11th symbol revealed the assembly plant: A=Hapeville (Atlanta), Georgia; F=Dearborn, Michigan; G=Chicago, Illinois; K=Claycomo (Kansas City), Missouri; M=Cuautitlan Mexico; R=Hermosillo, Mexico; W=Wayne, Michigan and X=Talbotville (St. Thomas), Ontario, Canada. The last six symbols were the sequential production numbers starting at 100001 at each factory.

Focus ZX3 (Four)

Model No.	Body/ Style No.	Body Type & Seating	Factory Price	Shipping Weight	Production Total
P	31	3-dr. Hatchback-5P	$12,905	2,551 lbs.	------

Focus LX (Four)

P	33	4-dr. Sedan-5P	$13,220	2,564 lbs.	------

Focus SE (Four)

P	34	4-dr. Sedan-5P	$14,320	2,564 lbs.	------
P	36	4-dr. Station Wagon-5P	$17,015	2,717 lbs.	------

Focus Street (Four)

P	34	4-dr. Sedan-5P	$14,810	2,564 lbs.	------
P	36	4-dr. Station Wagon-5P	$17,015	2,717 lbs.	------

Focus ZTS (Four)

P	38	4-dr. Sedan-5P	$16,030	2,564 lbs.	------

Escort ZX2 (Four)

P	11	2-dr. Coupe-5P	$12,830	2,478 lbs.	------

Taurus LX (V-6)

P	52	4-dr. Sedan-6P	$19,275	3,354 lbs.	------

Taurus SE (V-6)

P	53	4-dr. Sedan-6P	$19,325	3,354 lbs.	------
P	58	4-dr. Station Wagon-6P	$21,105	3,516 lbs.	------

Taurus SES (V-6)

P	55	4-dr. Sedan-6P	$20,965	3,354 lbs.	------

Taurus SEL (V-8)

P	56	4-dr. Sedan-6P	$22,450	3,354 lbs.	------

Crown Victoria (V-8)

P	73	4-dr. Sedan-6P	$22,935	3,946 lbs.	------

Crown Victoria LX (V-8)

P	74	4-dr. Sedan-6P	$25,050	3,946 lbs.	------

Engines:

Focus LX, SE and Street Sedan Base Four: Inline. Overhead cam. Cast-iron block and aluminum head. Displacement: 121 cid (2.0 liters). B & S: 3.39 x 3.52 in. Compression ratio: 9.4:1. Brake hp: 110 at 5000 rpm. Torque: 125 lbs.-ft. at 3750 rpm. Split port induction.

Focus ZX3 Hatchback, ZTS sedan and SE wagon Base Four: Inline. Dual overhead cam. Four-cylinder. Cast-iron block and aluminum head. Displacement: 121 cid (2.0 liters). B & S: 3.39 x 3.52 in. Compression ratio: 9.6:1. Brake hp: 130 at 5750 rpm. Torque: 135 lbs.-ft. at 4500 rpm. Sequential electronic fuel injection.

Escort ZX2 Base Four: Inline. Dual overhead cam. Four-cylinder. Cast-iron block and aluminum head. Displacement: 121 cid (2.0 liters). B & S: 3.39 x 3.52 in. Compression ratio: 9.6:1. Brake hp: 130 at 5750 rpm. Torque: 135 lbs.-ft. at 4500 rpm. Sequential electronic fuel injection.

2001 Focus ZX3 three-door hatchback

2001 Taurus SEL four-door sedan

2001 Taurus SES Sport sedan

Taurus LX and SE Base V-6: Overhead valve. Cast-iron block and head. Displacement: 182 cid (3.0 liters). B & S: 3.50 x 3.15 in. Compression ratio: 9.3:1. Brake hp: 155 at 4900 rpm. Torque: 185 lbs.-ft. at 3950 rpm. Sequential electronic fuel injection.

Taurus SEL Base V-6: Dual overhead cam, flexible-fuel. Aluminum block and head. Displacement: 182 cid (3.0 liters). B & S: 3.50 x 3.15 in. Compression ratio: 10.0:1. Brake hp: 200 at 5750 rpm. Torque: 200 lbs.-ft. at 4500 rpm.

Crown Victoria Base V-8: Modular, overhead valve. Displacement: 281 cid (4.6 liters). B & S: 3.60 x 3.60. Compression ratio: 9.0:1. Brake hp: 220 at 4750 rpm. Torque: 265 lbs.-ft. at 4000 rpm. Sequential electronic fuel injection.

Chassis:

Focus: Wheelbase: 103 in. Overall length: 168.1 in., hatchback; 174.9 in., sedan and 174.9 in., station wagon. Overall width: 66.9 in. Overall height: 56.3 in. and 53.9 in., station wagon. Tires: P185/65-R14, LX sedan; P195/60-R15, ZX3, SE sedan and station wagon; P205/65-R16, Street and ZTS sedans; P205/50-R16, Street station wagon.

Escort: Wheelbase: 98.4 in. Overall length: 175.2 in. Overall width: 67.4 in. Overall height: 52.3 in. Front tread: 56.5 in. Rear tread: 56.5 in. Tires: P185/60-TR15.

Taurus: Wheelbase: 108.5 in. Overall length: 197.5 in. sedan and 199.6 in., station wagon Overall width: 73 in. Overall height: 56.1 in., sedan and 58 in., station wagon. Front tread: 61.6 in. Rear tread: 61.4 in. Tires: P215/60-R16.

Crown Victoria: Wheelbase: 114.7 in. Overall length: 212 in. Overall width: 78.2 in. Overall height: 56.8 in. Front tread: 62.8 in. Rear tread: 63.3 in. Tires: 225/60-SR16.

Options:

Focus: Four-speed overdrive automatic transmission, ($815). AdvanceTrac ($1,225). Air conditioning ($795). Antilock braking system ($400). California emissions requirements, no cost. Non-California emissions requirements, no cost. Power group ($740). Premium group ($1,095). Side air bags ($350). Manual moon roof, ZX3 hatchback ($446). SE sports group ($470). SE comfort group ($345). Street Edition Feature Car package, Street sedan, 67A ($775). Low-back bucket seats with unique leather trim and map pockets, ZTS sedan ($695).

Escort: 14-in. five-spoke chrome wheels ($595). Four-speed overdrive automatic transmission ($815). AM/FM stereo cassette with six-disc compact CD changer ($295). Antilock braking system ($400). California emissions requirements, no cost. Non-California emissions requirements, no cost. Comfort group ($395). Front and rear floor mats ($55). Manual air conditioning ($795). Power group ($395). Power moon roof ($595). Unique leather sport bucket seats ($395).

Taurus: 3.0-liter flexible fuel ethanol V-6, 992/44L, no cost. Six-passenger seating, no cost. Antilock braking system ($600). California emissions requirements, no cost. Non-California emissions requirements, no cost. Front floor mats ($30). Rear floor mats ($25). Side impact air bags ($390). AM/FM stereo single CD player ($140). Adjustable pedals ($120). All-Speed traction control ($175). Antilock braking system

2001 Focus SE station wagon

($600). Power driver's seat with manual lumbar adjustment ($395). 60/40 split-folding rear seat ($140). Five-passenger seating, SEL and SES sedans ($105). Leather seating surfaces, SEL sedan ($895). MACH premium sound system, SEL sedan ($320). Power passenger's seat, SEL sedan ($350). Rear spoiler, SEL and SES sedans ($230). 3.0-liter four-valve V-6 99S/44L ($695). All-Speed traction control ($175). Heated mirrors, SES sedan ($35). Power moon roof, SES sedan ($890). Premium audio group, SES sedan ($530). AM/FM stereo single CD player ($140). Antilock braking system ($600). Premium audio group ($530). SES group ($1,040). Wagon group, 96W ($300).

Crown Victoria: 4.6-liter natural gas V-8 with automatic overdrive transmission ($6,165). Six-way power driver's seat ($360). Antilock braking system ($600). Antilock braking system with traction control ($775). California emissions requirements, no cost. Non-California emissions requirements, no cost. Conventional spare tire ($120). Electronic AM/FM stereo with single CD player ($140). Front and rear floor mats ($55). Handling and performance package ($935). P225/60-SR15 white sidewall tires ($80). Keyless remote entry system ($240). Five-passenger sport appearance package ($995). Comfort group, 65C ($900). Comfort Plus group, 65E ($1,900). Electronic AM/FM stereo with single CD player ($140). Front and rear floor mats ($55). Handling and performance package, 41G ($615 to $740). Split bench seat with leather seating surfaces ($795). Power adjustable pedals, 59C ($120). Premium electronic AM/FM stereo with cassette, 586 ($360). Trunk-mounted six-disc CD changer ($350). Universal garage door opener ($115).

History:

On Tuesday Oct. 30, 2001, Ford Motor Co. Chairman William Clay Ford, Jr., forced the resignation of Jacques Nasser, the company's president and chief executive officer. Ford Jr. hinted the company had lost its focus in several areas. Nasser's resignation ended a stormy three-year relationship between the earthy and outspoken native of the Middle East, who grew up in Australia, and the 44-year-old Ford family member. It also highlighted a stressful season for Ford, which lost more than $1 billion between April and November and had no clear sign that things would improve during 2002. Ford Jr. said the company needed to focus on its core business of making cars and trucks. The troubles started with the massive Firestone tire recall during 2000. With millions of dollars of lost sales for one of its most profitable vehicles, the Explorer SUV, Nasser went on the offensive against Firestone leading to a split between the two companies. It ended one of the oldest business and personal relationships in U.S. corporate history. Henry Ford and Harvey Firestone were Bill Ford's great-grandfathers. The quality of Ford's cars and trucks also deteriorated and productivity at its manufacturing facilities slipped. The introductions of the new Ford Escape mini-SUV and the redesigned 2002 Ford Explorer were delayed. With Nasser's resignation, Ford, Jr., became chairman and CEO. Nick Scheele, a group vice president at the company's North American operations, was named chief operating officer and began work immediately on a recovery plan. Carl Reichardt, a retired chairman and CEO of Wells Fargo & Co., was named vice chairman of the board and chairman of the finance committee. Reichardt, an old friend of the Ford family, took charge of Ford's financial operations. Ford Motor Co. did have something to celebrate, the centennial of Ford motor sports during 2001. It was a big celebration that took place at the Henry Ford Museum and Greenfield Village during September.

2001 Crown Victoria LX sedan

2002 Ford

Focus — Four: Since its introduction in Europe in 1999 and in the U.S. in the 2000 model, the Focus won praise for its performance, handling and package ingenuity. The 2002 Focus came in four distinct body styles: a ZX3 two-door hatchback, a four-door sedan, a four-door wagon and a new ZX5 five-door hatchback. New features for the 2002 Focus included a Personal Safety System. The all-new ZX5 five-door hatchback had the European styling of the ZX3 with the versatility of four doors. The new ZTW wagon included a sporty package that added more style to the versatile wagon. Available for the first time on all body styles was a power moon roof and a six-disc in-dash CD changer. Inside, Focus buyers found improved cup holders designed to accept larger cups, an added rear-seat map pocket on LX, SE and ZX3 models and "kangaroo" seat pouches on the ZTS. Colors added for 2002 included Grabber Green Clear coat Metallic, French Blue Clear coat Metallic and Liquid Grey Clear coat Metallic. The high roofline increased front and rear headroom, while the long wheelbase offered greater interior volume and contributed to a smoother ride. A 2.0L SOHC in-line four-cylinder was standard on Focus LX and SE. It produced 110 hp and 125 lb.-ft. of torque. This engine was matched with an IB5 five-speed manual transaxle that used synthetic lubricant to help ensure durability and smooth shifting in cold weather. The 2.0-liter DOHC Zetec inline four-cylinder engine was standard on Focus ZX3, ZTS and wagon models and optional on the Focus SE sedan. It delivered 130 hp and 135 lb.-ft. of torque. This engine was matched with a MTX75 five-speed manual transaxle designed with low-friction needle-roller bearings and using low-viscosity mineral oil to help improve fuel economy and performance. A four-speed electronic automatic overdrive transaxle was optional for all models. Common to 2002 Focus models were a bumper-color 5-mph front bumper, a black deck lid handle, black door handles with integral front key locks, fog lamps, a flush windshield and backlight with Solar-Tint glass, semi-flush side glass, fixed rear quarter glass, aerodynamic halogen headlamps, front side markers in bumper and front turn indicators in grille, color-keyed door frame moldings, a PVC coating on the lower body sides, a PVC underbody coating, clear coat paint, 15-in. five-spoke aluminum wheels, dual front second-generation air bags, LATCH system, a full-length center console with two front cup holders, pen storage, a storage area with cup holder, an alloy shift knob (manual transmission only), courtesy lights with theater dimming feature, soft feel vinyl door trim, vinyl covered door trim insert panels, a non-locking glove box, front and rear grab handles, a soft feel instrument panel with climate and radio controls in center stack position, a storage tray, a coin holder and trinket tray, alloy appearance on center stack bezel, a carpeted and removable package tray cover, an AM/FM stereo single disc CD player with digital clock and four speakers, sport bucket seats with tip/slide feature and driver-side height adjustment, a four-spoke leather-wrapped sport steering wheel, a tachometer, driver and passenger visor-vanity mirrors with flap closings, a 110-amp. alternator, a maintenance-free battery, a battery saver, a power-assisted front disc/rear drum brake system, a self-energizing rear linkage clutch, a rear window defroster, side window demisters, electronic engine controls, an electronic ignition system, the 2.0-liter Zetec four-cylinder engine, front-wheel drive, a 13.2-gallon fuel tank, a headlamps-on warning chime, an inside hood release, a single-note horn, an interior trunk or lift gate release, a low-fuel warning light, a 12V-power point, rear seat heat ducts, the SecuriLock™ passive anti-theft system, front and rear stabilizer bars, power rack-and-pinion steering, a MacPherson strut independent front suspension, a control blade short/long arm independent rear suspension, P195/60-R15 tires, a mini spare tire, a five-speed transaxle, two-speed windshield wipers with fixed intermittent feature and a rear window wiper and washer. The Focus LX sedan was similarly equipped to the ZX but included the 2.0-liter SPI four cylinder engine with a five-speed manual transaxle and P185/65-R14 tires. The Focus SE sedan offered such features as one-touch power windows and air conditioning as well as P195/60-R15 tires. The ZTS sedan included power door locks, an AM/FM stereo single disc CD player with digital clock and four speakers, low-back cloth bucket seats with driver's seat height adjustment and lumbar support, dual map pockets and "kangaroo" pouch, a 60/40 split-folding rear seat with flip-up rear cushion, the 2.0-liter Zetec four-cylinder engine and P2-5/50-R16 tires. The Focus ZX5 hatchback included Focus standard features plus power door locks, an AM/FM stereo with six disc in-dash CD player with digital clock and four speakers, sport bucket seats with driver's seat height adjustment, dual map pockets and "kangaroo" pouch, a tachometer, and P205/50R16 tires. The SE and ZTW station wagons offered the host of standard Focus features plus such features as power rack and pinion steering, four-speed automatic transmission and a rear window wiper and washer on both station wagon models.

Escort — Four: The Escort didn't make it into Ford Motor Co.'s 2002 electronic press kits, but you could still get one in 2002. It was essentially a carryover model with few, if any, changes from 2001. It

2002 Focus ZX5 five-door hatchback

2002 Focus ZX3 three-door hatchback

2002 Focus ZTW station wagon

was offered in ZX2 coupe, Deluxe ZX2 coupe and Premium ZX2 coupe trim levels. All used the same regular-grade-fuel 2.0-liter 16-valve inline four-cylinder gasoline engine that produced 130 hp at 5300 rpm and 135 ft.-lbs. of torque at 4500 rpm. Standard equipment common to all Escort models included a 2.0-liter DOHC 16-valve 130-hp four-cylinder engine, a five-speed manual transmission, front-wheel drive, four-wheel independent suspension, front and rear stabilizer bars, a tachometer, a low-fuel indicator, a clock, 15-in. alloy wheel rims, P185/60R15 all-season tires, a space saver spare on a steel spare wheel, variable intermittent windshield wipers, a rear defogger, a rear spoiler, front disc/rear drum brakes, power mirrors, power steering, front and rear cupholders, a remote trunk release, front door pockets, a front 12-volt power outlet, a front console with storage space, four-passenger seating with cloth trimmed sport bucket seats, a split-folding rear seat, dual visor-vanity mirrors and an AM/FM cassette stereo with four speakers. The ZX2 Deluxe added cruise control, front reading lights and a leather-wrapped tilt-adjustable steering wheel. The ZX2 premium added everything the others carried plus one-touch power windows and remote power door locks.

Taurus — V-6 and V-8: The 2002 Taurus remained an outstanding family vehicle with a focus on safety, quality, convenience and comfort. It was available in two body styles, a four-door sedan and a four-door wagon. The 3.0-liter OHV Vulcan V-6 produced 155 hp and 185 lbs.-ft. of torque, while the 3.0-liter DOHC 24-valve Duratec V-6 produced 200 hp and 200 lbs.-ft. of torque. A flexible fuel version of the Vulcan engine that ran on E-85 ethanol, regular unleaded gasoline or any combination of the two in the same tank was optional. The sedan came with a choice of five- or six-passenger seating and offered available 60/40 split fold-down rear seatbacks for flexibility in carrying passengers and cargo. A rear-facing third seat was available on the wagon. Taurus' Personal Safety System was able to adjust the deployment of the dual-stage front air bags to help protect the front occupants. The system used an electronic crash severity sensor, a PSS restraint control module, a driver's seat position sensor, safety belt pre-tensioners, energy management retractors and front outboard safety belt usage sensors to help it protect the driver and right front passenger in certain frontal collisions. The Taurus also offered an optional side airbag supplemental restraint system for enhanced protection. The new LATCH child-safety seat system (Lower Anchors and Tethers for Children) helped to improve the connection of a LATCH-compatible child safety seat. The SecuriLock™ passive anti-theft system used an electronically coded ignition key to start the vehicle. The vehicle would not start if the key did not have the code. An available perimeter anti-theft system monitored the doors, hood and deck lid against unauthorized entry. An auto-dimming rearview mirror with a compass was available on SES and SEL models. Security approach lamps were standard on SE, SES and SEL models. An AM/FM stereo single CD player was a new no-cost option on SE sedans and wagons. Floor mats became standard in all series. SE, SES and SEL models got a new cargo net.

Added colors for 2002 included Matador Red Clear coat Metallic, True Blue Clear coat Metallic, Arizona Beige Clear coat Metallic and Dark Shadow Grey Clear coat Metallic. All Taurus models had an 18-gallon fuel tank. Standard equipment included 5-mph front and rear bumpers, body-color flush mounted door handles, a body-color front fascia, black-finished electric control mirrors, clear coat paint, locking wheel covers, color-keyed 13.5-oz. Carpeting with a built-in foot rest and an electronic digital clock with a dimmer feature, a color-keyed integral center console with cup holders and cassette storage, two-tone instrument panel with backlit cluster, positive shut-off climate control registers, side window demisters, a windshield defroster, a rear defroster, a light group with dual-beam map and dome lamps, day/night rearview mirrors, dual second-generation air bags, an electronic AM/FM full-logic stereo with four speakers, six-passenger seating with dual recliners, a center seat console, seat belts, a tilt steering column, a color-keyed four-spoke steering wheel, cloth covered sun visors, dual visor-vanity mirrors, air conditioning, quarter panel air extractors, a 130-amp/ alternator, a 58-amp. low-maintenance battery, a battery saver, power assisted front disc/rear drum brakes, a crash-severity sensor, the 3.0-liter two-valve Vulcan V-6, front-wheel drive, an 18-gallon fuel tank, Solar-Tinted glass, rear seat heat ducts, a hood with gas-assist struts and a remote release, a dual-note horn, instrumentation (including temperature and fuel gauges, a 110-mph speedometer, a low brake fluid warning, a trip odometer, an odometer and a tachometer), rear door child safety locks, illuminated power door lock controls, a foot-operated parking brake, two 12-volt power points (outlets), the SecuriLock™ passive anti-theft system, a column-mounted gearshift with soft feel handle, power rack-and-pinion steering, MacPherson strut independent front suspension with nitrogen gas pressurized struts and a front stabilizer bar, an independent rear quadra-link suspension with nitrogen gas pressurized struts, P215/60-R16 all-season tires, a mini spare tire, an electronic four-speed automatic overdrive transaxle, a transaxle oil cooler, two-speed variable intermittent windshield wipers and one-touch power windows with lock-out switch and illuminated controls.

Crown Victoria — V-8: Standard equipment on the base Crown Victoria included a 4.6-liter SOHC 16-valve 220-hp V-8, a four-speed automatic transmission, rear-wheel drive, a front independent suspension, front and rear stabilizer bars, a clock, a low-fuel indicator, P225/60-SR16 all-season tires on 16 x 7-in. steel rims, a space saver spare tire on a steel spare wheel, variable intermittent windshield wipers, a rear window defogger, front disc/rear drum brakes, front seat belt pre-tensioners, rear door child safety locks, an emergency interior trunk release, front and rear center lap belts, two front headrests, an engine immobilizer, one-touch power windows, power door locks, power mirrors, cruise control, speed-proportional power steering, a tilt-adjustable steering wheel, steering wheel mounted cruise controls, a remote trunk release, front door map pockets, six-passenger seating with a cloth-trimmed split front bench seat, a rear bench seat, air conditioning, a trunk light, a wood-trimmed dash, an AM/FM cassette stereo with four speakers and an element radio antenna. The base Crown Victoria LX carried a 4.6-liter SOHC 16-valve 220-hp V-8, a four-speed automatic transmission, rear-wheel drive, a front independent suspension, front and rear stabilizer bars, a clock, a low-fuel indicator, P225/60-SR16 all-season tires on 16 x 7-in. steel rims, a space saver spare tire on a steel spare wheel, variable intermittent windshield wipers, a rear window defogger, front disc/rear drum brakes, front seat belt pre-tensioners, rear door child safety locks, an emergency interior trunk release, front and rear center lap belts, two front headrests, an engine immobilizer, one touch power windows, remote power door locks, power mirrors, cruise control, speed-proportional power steering, a tilt-adjustable steering wheel, steering wheel mounted cruise controls, a remote trunk release, front door map pockets, front seatback storage, six-passenger seating with a cloth-trimmed split front bench seat with six-way power and adjustable lumbar support on driver's side, a rear bench seat with folding center armrest, air conditioning, front reading lights, dual illuminated visor-vanity mirrors, a trunk light, a wood-trimmed dash, an AM/FM cassette stereo with four speakers and an element radio antenna.

2002 Focus ZX3 Premium hatchback

I. D. Data:

Ford's 17-symbol Vehicle Identification Number (VIN) was stamped on a metal tab fastened to the instrument panel and was visible through the windshield. The first symbol indicated the nation of origin: 1=United States; 2=Canada; 3=Mexico. The second symbol indicated the manufacturer: F=Ford Motor Co.; The third symbol indicated the vehicle type: A=passenger car. The fourth symbol indicated the type of restraint system: B=driver and passenger air bags and active belts (except Escort ZX2 coupe); F=driver and passenger air bags and active belts; K=driver and passenger air bags and active belts in all outboard positions. The fifth symbol indicated the: P=Ford and T=Imported from outside North America or non-Ford car marketed by Ford in North America. The sixth and seventh symbols indicated the body type: 11=Escort ZX2 two-door coupe; 31=Focus ZX3 three-door coupe; 33=Focus LX four-door sedan; 34=Focus SE/Focus Street four-door sedan; 36=Focus SE/Focus Street four-door station wagon; 38=Focus ZTS four-door sedan; 52=Taurus LX four-door sedan; 53=Taurus SE four-door sedan; 55=Taurus SE SVG four-door sedan; 56=Taurus SEL four-door sedan; 58=Taurus SE four-door station wagon; 73=Crown Victoria four-door sedan; 74=Crown Victoria LX four-door sedan. The eighth symbol indicated the engine: Escort, P=2.0-liter I-4 with EF/SPI; Taurus, S=3.0-liter DOHC V-6 with EFI; U=3.0-liter V-6 with EFI and 2=flexible fuel 3.0-liter V-6 with EFI. Contour, G=2.5-liter DOHC V-6 with EFI; L=2.5-liter DOHC V-6 with EFI; Z=2.0-liter DOHC I-4 with EFI and 3=2.0-liter DOHC I-4 with EFI. Crown Victoria, W=4.6-liter SOHC V-8 with EFI (Romeo engine plant). The ninth symbol was a check digit. The 10th symbol indicated the model year: Z=2001. The 11th symbol indicated the assembly plant: A=Hapeville (Atlanta), Georgia; F=Dearborn, Michigan; G=Chicago, Illinois; K=Claycomo (Kansas City), Missouri; M=Cuautitlan, Mexico; R=Hermosillo, Mexico; W=Wayne, Michigan and X=Talbotville (St. Thomas), Ontario, Canada. The last six symbols were the sequential production numbers starting at 100001 at each factory.

Focus ZX3 (Four)

Model No.	Body/Style No.	Body Type & Seating	Factory Price	Shipping Weight	Production Total
P	31	3-dr. Hatchback-5P	$12,935	2,551 lbs.	------

Focus ZX3 Power Premium (Four)

P	31	3-dr. Hatchback-5P	$14,970	2,551 lbs.	------

Focus ZX3 Premium (Four)

P	31	3-dr. Hatchback-5P	$14,030	2,551 lbs.	------

Focus LX (Four)

P	33	4-dr. Sedan-5P	$13,250	2,551 lbs.	------

Focus LX Premium (Four)

P	33	4-dr. Sedan-5P	$14,095	2,551 lbs.	------

Focus SE (Four)

P	34	4-dr. Sedan-5P	$14,840	2,551 lbs.	------
P	36	4-dr. Station Wagon-5P	$17,045	2,551 lbs.	------

Focus SE Comfort (Four)

P	34	4-dr. Sedan-5P	$15,185	2,551 lbs.	------
P	36	4-dr. Station Wagon-5P	$17,390	2,551 lbs.	------

Focus SE Comfort (Zetec Four)

P	34	4-dr. Sedan-5P	$15,435	2,551 lbs.	------

Focus ZTS (Four)

P	38	4-dr. Sedan-5P	$15,760	2,551 lbs.	------

Focus ZK5 (Four)

P	---	5-dr. Hatchback-5P	$16,135	2,600 lbs.	------

Focus ZTW (Four)

P	38	4-dr. Station Wagon-5P	$18,225	2,551 lbs.	------

2002 Taurus SEL sedan

Escort ZX2 (Four)

P	11	2-dr. Coupe-5P	$12,990	2,478 lbs.	------

Escort ZX2 Deluxe (Four)

P	11	2-dr. Coupe-5P	$14,035	2,478 lbs.	------

Escort ZX2 Premium (Four)

P	11	2-dr. Coupe-5P	$14,490	2,478 lbs.	------

Taurus LX (V-6)

P	52	4-dr. Sedan-6P	$19,375	3,336 lbs.	------

Taurus SE (V-6)

P	53	4-dr. Sedan-6P	$20,185	3,336 lbs.	------
P	58	4-dr. Station Wagon-6P	$22,120	3,502 lbs.	------

Taurus SE Deluxe (V-6)

P	58	4-dr. Station Wagon-6P	$22,745	3,502 lbs.	------

Taurus SE Premium (V-6)

P	58	4-dr. Station Wagon-6P	$23,435	3,502 lbs.	------

Taurus SES (V-6)

P	55	4-dr. Sedan-6P	$21,200	3,336 lbs.	------

Taurus SES Deluxe (V-6)

P	55	4-dr. Sedan-6P	$22,300	3,336 lbs.	------

Taurus SEL Deluxe (V-8)

P	55	4-dr. Sedan-6P	$23,070	3,336 lbs.	------
P	58	4-dr. Station Wagon-6P	$23,320	3,502 lbs.	------

Taurus SEL Premium (V-8)

P	56	4-dr. Sedan-6P	$23,640	3,336 lbs.	------

Crown Victoria (V-8)

P	73	4-dr. Sedan-6P	$22,935	3,946 lbs.	------

Crown Victoria LX (V-8)

P	74	4-dr. Sedan-6P	$25,050	3,946 lbs.	------

In 2002, Ford produced 49,371 Crown Victorias, 81,659 Escorts, 252,249 Focuses, 136,303 Mustangs, 321,020 Taurus' and 25,143 Tunderbirds.

Engines:

Focus LX and SE Sedan Base Four: Inline. Overhead cam. Cast-iron block and aluminum head. Displacement: 121 cid (2.0 liters). B & S: 3.39 x 3.52 in. Compression ratio: 9.4:1. Brake hp: 110 at 5000 rpm. Torque: 125 lbs.-ft. at 3750 rpm. Split port induction.

Focus Hatchback, ZTS sedan and station wagon Four: Inline. Dual overhead cam. Cast-iron block and aluminum head. Displacement: 121 cid (2.0 liters). B & S: 3.39 x 3.52 in. Compression ratio: 9.6:1. Brake hp: 130 at 5300 rpm. Torque: 135 lbs.-ft. at 4500 rpm. Sequential fuel injection.

Escort ZX2 Four: Inline. Dual overhead cam. Cast-iron block and aluminum head. Displacement: 121 cid (2.0 liters). B & S: 3.39 x 3.52 in. Compression ratio: 9.6:1. Brake hp: 130 at 5750 rpm. Torque: 135 lbs.-ft. at 4500 rpm. Sequential fuel injection.

Taurus LX and SE Base V-6: Overhead valve. Cast-iron block and head. Displacement: 182 cid (3.0 liters). B & S: 3.50 x 3.15 in. Compression ratio: 9.3:1. Brake hp: 155 at 4900 rpm. Torque: 185 lbs.-ft. at 3950 rpm. Sequential electronic fuel injection.

Taurus SEL Base V-6: Dual overhead cam flexible-fuel engine. Aluminum block and head. Displacement: 182 cid (3.0 liters). B & S: 3.50 x 3.15 in. Compression ratio: 10.0:1. Brake hp 200 at 5750 rpm. Torque: 200 lbs.-ft. at 4500 rpm.

Crown Victoria Base V-8: Modular, overhead valve. Displacement: 281 cid (4.6 liters). B & S: 3.60 x 3.60. Compression ratio: 9.0:1. Brake hp: 220 at 4750 rpm. Torque: 265 lbs.-ft. at 4000 rpm. Sequential electronic fuel injection.

2002 ZX2 Premium coupe

2002 Taurus SEL Premium sedan

2002 Taurus SEL station wagon

Chassis:

Focus: Wheelbase: 103 in. Overall length: 168.1 in. Tires: P195/60-R15.

Escort: Wheelbase: 98.4 in. Overall length: 175.2 in. Tires: P 185/60-R15.

Taurus: Wheelbase: 108.5 in. Overall length: 197.6 in., sedan and 197.7 in., wagon. Tires: P215/60-R16.

Crown Victoria: Wheelbase: 114.7 in. Overall Length: 212 in. Tires: P225/60-SR16.

Options:

Focus: Air conditioning, 572 ($795). Anti-lock braking system, 522 ($400). California emissions requirements, 422, no cost. Side air bags, 59M ($350). Four-speed overdrive automatic transmission, 44A ($815). ABS brakes with AdvanceTrac, 47D ($1,625). Power moon roof, 13B ($595). AM/FM stereo with six-disc in-dash CD player, 581 ($280). In-dash CD changer regional discount, B3W ($280 credit). Five-speed manual transmission, 445 ($815). Leather seating ($695).

Escort: Four-speed overdrive automatic transmission, 44T ($815). Anti-lock braking system, 552 ($400). California emissions requirements, 422, no cost. Front and rear floor mats, 12Y ($55). Manual air conditioning, 572 ($795). Power moon roof, 13B, ZX2 Deluxe and Premium, ($595). 14-in. five-spoke chrome wheels, 64A, ZX2 Premium ($595). AM/FM cassette with six-disc CD changer, 919, ZX2 Premium ($295). Unique leather sport bucket seats, ZX2 Premium ($367).

Taurus: AM/FM stereo with cassette player, 58H ($185). Anti-lock braking system, 552 ($600). California emissions, 422, no cost. Non-California emissions, 93N, no cost. Adjustable pedals, 59C ($120). No charge SE Value package discount, 53S ($535 credit). Safety package, 85R ($565). 60/40 split-folding rear seat 46S ($140). Adjustable pedals, 59C ($120). Leather seating surfaces, J ($895). Luxury and Convenience package, 96L ($185). No-cost power moon roof discount, 13B ($895 credit). No-cost power moon roof and leather seating surfaces discount, J ($895 credit). Premium audio group, 53A ($530). SES sport package, 90T ($290). Six-passenger seating with flip-fold center console, 184, ($105 credit). MACH premium sound system, 916 ($320). Rear deck lid spoiler, 13K ($230). Duratec engine package, 53D ($1,120). MACH premium sound system, SEL Premium sedan ($320 credit). Power moon roof discount, SEL Premium ($895 credit). Power passenger seat, 21J ($350).

Crown Victoria: 4.6-liter natural gas V-8 with automatic overdrive transmission, 999 ($6,165). Six-way power driver's seat, 21A ($360). Anti-lock braking system, 552 ($600). Anti-lock braking system with traction control, 553 ($775). California emissions, 422, no cost. Conventional spare tire, 508 ($120). Electronic AM/FM stereo with single CD player, 585 ($140). Front and rear floor mats, 12Y ($55). Handling and Performance package, 41G ($935). Non-California emissions, 93N, no cost. P225/60-SR15 white sidewall tires, T2A ($80). Keyless remote entry system, 144 ($240). Five-passenger sport appearance package, LX sedan, 60R ($995). Anti-lock braking system with traction control, LX sedan, 553 ($775). Comfort group, 65C ($900). Comfort Plus group, 65E ($1,900). Handling and Performance package, LX sedan ($615 to $740). Split bench seat with leather seating surfaces, L ($795). Power adjustable pedals, 59C ($120). Premium electronic AM/FM stereo with cassette player, 586 ($360). Trunk-mounted six-disc CD changer, 919, LX sedan ($350). Universal garage door opener, 175, LX sedan ($115).

History:

Ford Motor Co. entered 2002 with William Clay Ford Jr. at its helm. The Thunderbird Custom — a one-of-a-kind project car that brought a new look to the roadster through subtle design changes — was introduced at the 2001 Pebble Beach Concours d'Elegance in Monterey, Calif. The Custom was designed to be a contemporary interpretation of the customizing and hot-rod movement of the 1950s. Ford designers were asked to develop design renderings of new possibilities for the future. One sketch featured a blacked-out grille, more pronounced belt line and big chrome wheels with knock-off hubs. The sketch looked so good, Ford

decided to build it. Changes included doubling the size of the recesses for the characteristic chevrons on the Thunderbird's front fender and adding a black mesh insert behind them to accentuate their presence. The car was painted with several coats of Dark Shadow Gray Metallic lacquer for a deep glossy finish. The iconic egg-crate grille was recessed slightly — an old customizer's trick — and painted in the same color as the body. To achieve a longer, more relaxed exterior appearance, the design team lowered the coil-spring suspension by one inch front and rear making it appear higher in front and lower in the rear. The retuned exhaust system gave the car a low "burble" at idle and a performance tone during acceleration. Chrome tailpipe extensions — two and one-half inches in diameter at the tip — were prominent from the side or rear view. Halibrand created a unique interpretation of its classic "Kidney Bean 5" polished chrome wheel featuring five spokes with kidney bean-shaped "windows" that created a strobing effect through the wheel when the car was in motion. Aggressively treaded Michelin Pilot Sport Z-rated 18-in. tires finished the look, virtually filling the wheel wells. The Thunderbird Custom had a black convertible top that stored below a removable two-piece, ebony leather-wrapped tonneau cover. The interior featured a two-tone theme with sienna and ebony leather, set off by engine-turned aluminum accent panels. The door panels featured sienna leather armrests and upper sills with engine-turned aluminum accents. The bucket seats were covered in sienna leather and featured plush side bolsters and adjustable head restraints. The steering wheel and shift knob were tightly wrapped and stitched in sienna leather. The center stack was finished in Dark Shadow Gray matching the exterior. It flowed into a one-of-a-kind white-on-black Thunderbird instrument cluster. On November 12, in Las Vegas, Nevada, the 2002 Ford Thunderbird captured *Motor Trend* magazine's "Car of the Year" award. The award was announced during the *Motor Trend* International Auto Show. In the 50-year lifespan of *Motor Trend,* no other model won more "Car of the Year" honors than the Thunderbird, with twice as many wins as its closest competitor. "We're especially honored that Ford Thunderbird was chosen with the *Motor Trend* "Car of the Year" for the fourth time," said Jim O'Connor, Ford Div. president. "The all-new Thunderbird celebrates Ford's heritage of innovation and reaffirms our goal to build the best cars on the planet — cars that invoke passion and touch people's hearts and souls."

2002 Crown Victoria LX Sport sedan

1955 Thunderbird

Thunderbird — Series H — (V-8): The original Ford Thunderbird had many outstanding selling features. Its styling was less radical than that of the other American sports cars. L.D. Crusoe, Ford Motor Company vice president and general manager of Ford Division insisted that the new car be based on a full-sized Ford for "family" identity and to ensure that major parts would be interchangeable with other 1955 Fords. Parts sharing cut development time, too. Designers were able to skip the time-consuming job of making mock-ups or models, going straight to the creation of full-sized drawings of the T-Bird's profile instead. The car's dimensions were based on those of the Corvette and the Jaguar XK-120. To save even more time, a used Ford sedan was obtained to serve as a designers' "mule." It was cut down with a torch and re-welded to fashion a small Ford with a 102-inch wheelbase. Ford's chief engineer William Burnett decided to go at the project this way. Those involved with it called the car the "Burnetti" after him. They thought this name had an Italian sports car ring to it. The first plan was to call the production version the Fairlane (after Henry Ford's estate in Michigan). Crusoe was said to prefer "Savile," but he proposed a contest in which FoMoCo employees could suggest names. The winner was offered a prize of $250, but actually won a suit worth $75-$100. Designer Alden "Gib" Giberson, a native of the Southwest, suggested the name "Thunderbird." In Indian mythology, the Thunderbird helped humans by flapping its wings, bringing thunder, lightning and rain to alleviate a drought. On February 15, 1954, the name was made official. The T-Bird nickname may well have stemmed from Ford ads referring to the car's introductory date as "T-day." Although the car-buying public got a few peeks at the T-Bird early in 1954, it wasn't until October 22 that the production version was officially unveiled. Its introductory retail price was $2,695, less federal taxes and delivery and handling charges. This compared to $2,700 for a 1955 Corvette. Later, the price was increased when a fiberglass hardtop became standard equipment. Looking very much like a scaled-down Ford, the Thunderbird was trim, though not sub-compact. The standard telescoping steering wheel allowed large T-Bird drivers to get comfortable inside the car. The styling of the car was quite pleasing. Its "frenched" headlamps gave it a forward-thrusting look at the front, while the crisp tail fins seemed to "flip-off" a little message to every slower car passed on the highway. They seemed to be saying, "I'm the latest and the greatest thing for the young and the young at heart." In its September 1955 issue, *Motor Trend* selected the Thunderbird as one of the six best-looking cars of 1955. "Overall consistency of design. Width, height, length ratios show excellent proportion," noted *Motor Trend*. "It's small Hardtop version has a very classic look." The low, square Ford-look emphasized the car's width and the production version featured only minimal use of chrome. "Pretty well de-chromed and clean-looking," *Motor Trend* said. "First and foremost a car for comfort and looks." For a 1955 American car, the Thunderbird offered excellent driving characteristics. Vision over the hood was exceptionally good, as the cowl stood just 37.2 inches above the surface of the road. The wraparound windshield created some distortion at the corners. Inside, the operator was greeted with a modern-looking dashboard featuring a tachometer, "idiot lights" (to monitor oil pressure and electrical output) and a clock with a sweep second hand that was great for rallying. A firm ride made the first Thunderbird feel like a sports car. Still, it was somewhat prone to under steering and would break loose in a tight turn, before drifting around it like a competition racer. However, it hung in the corners well enough to take them at 10 to 15 mph faster than most contemporary, full-size American cars. Standard equipment on the Thunderbird included: 292-cid Y-block V-8 engine, four-barrel carburetor, dual exhausts, 6-volt electrical system, 40-amp generator, 90 amp-hr 6-volt battery, three-speed manual transmission with all-helical gears and floor-mounted shift lever Hotchkiss drive, ball-joint front suspension, 5-leaf spring rear suspension, five 6.70 x 15 tubeless tires, vinyl upholstery, Astra-Dial control panel with illuminated control knobs, 150-mph Astra-Dial speedometer, parcel compartment with locking-type push-button latch, inside hood release, tachometer, Telechron (GE) electric clock with sweep second hand, power seat, left-hand outside rear view mirror, full-width seat with foam rubber padding, adjustable steering wheel, built-in arm rests, floor carpet, ash tray, 4-way illuminated starter-ignition switch, cigar lighter, panel courtesy light with integral switch and automatic door switches, rear view mirror on windshield upper molding, dual horns, half-circle steering wheel horn ring, and (as a running addition) glass-fibre hardtop. Some Thunderbirds shipped to Europe had metric speedometers that read from 0-240 km/hr, which was basically the same as 0-150 mph.

VIN:

The VIN plate was located on the left door pillar. The first symbol denoted the engine: P=292 cid/193 hp four-barrel Thunderbird Special V-8 (manual transmission). P=292 cid/193 hp four-barrel Thunderbird Special V-8 (overdrive transmission). P=292 cid/198 hp four-barrel Thunderbird

1955 Ford Thunderbird Convertible (OCW)

Special V-8. (automatic transmission). The second symbol indicated the model-year: 5=1955. The third symbol denoted the assembly plant: F=Dearborn, Michigan. The fourth symbol revealed the body type: H=Thunderbird convertible. The fifth though 10th symbols denoted the sequential production numbers of the specific vehicle starting at 100001. The body number plate was located on the firewall. The serial number was the same as the number on the left door pillar tag. Symbols below "BODY" were the body symbol code: 40A=Thunderbird. The symbols below "COLOR" were the paint color code. Symbols below "TRIM" were the trim combination code. Symbols below "PRODUCTION DATE" were the production date code. The numerical prefix indicated the date of the month the car was made. The letters indicated the month of manufacture: A=January, B=February, C=March, D=April, E=May, F=June, G=July, H=August, J=September, K=October, L=November, M=December. The numerical suffix indicated the production sequence.

Thunderbird (V-8)

Model No.	Body/Style No.	Body Type and Seating	Factory Price	Shipping Weight	Production Total
H	40A	2-dr. Convertible-2P	$2,944	2,980 lbs.	16,155

Engines:

Thunderbird Base V-8 (with synchromesh or overdrive): 90-degree. Overhead valves. Cast-iron block. B & S: 3.75 x 3.30 in. Displacement: 292 cid. Compression ratio: 8.1:1. Brake hp: 193 at 4400 rpm. Taxable hp: 45. Torque: 280 lbs.-ft. at 2600 rpm. Five main bearings. Solid valve lifters. Crankcase capacity: 5 qt. (add 1 qt. with new oil filter). Cooling system capacity: 19 qt. Carburetor: Holley four-barrel. Code P.

(Early reports gave the horsepower rating of this engine as 190 hp).

Thunderbird Base V-8 (with Ford-O-Matic): Overhead valve. Cast-iron block. Bore and stroke: 3.75 x 3.30 inches. Displacement: 292 cid. Compression ratio: 8.50:1. Brake hp: 198 at 4400 rpm. Taxable hp: 45. Torque: 286 at 2500 rpm. Five main bearings. Solid valve lifters. Crankcase capacity: 5 qt. (add 1 qt. with new oil filter). Cooling system capacity: 19 qt. Carburetor: Holley four-barrel. Code P.

Chassis:

Wheelbase: 102 in. Overall length: 175.3 in. Overall width: 70.3 in. Overall height: 50.2 in. Ground clearance: 5.5 in. Front and rear tread: 56 in. Front headroom: (with hardtop) 32.2 in. Front hip room: 58.8 in. Front shoulder room: 53.3 in. Front leg room: 45.4 in. Top of door height: 34.2 in. Tires: 6.70 x 15 4-ply.

Technical:

Brake swept area: 175 sq. in. Turning diameter: 36 ft. Turns lock-to-lock: 3.5. Steering ratio: 20.0:1. Steering wheel: 17 in. diameter. Weight distribution: 50/50. Chassis type: X-frame. Front suspension: Ball-joints, coil springs, tube shocks and stabilizer. Rear suspension: Composite axle, five-leaf springs, double-acting shock absorbers. Steering: Symmetrical linkage type. Steering wheel: Three-inch in-and-out adjustable. Front brakes: 11-in. diameter double-sealed. Rear brakes: 11-in. diameter double-sealed. Standard transmission: Three-speed synchromesh with helical gears, ratios: (First) 2.32, (Second) 1.48, (Third) 1:1 and (Reverse) 2.82. Optional transmission: Planetary overdrive with planetary gears, 27-mph cut-in speed and 0.70 ratio. Optional transmission: Ford-O-Matic torque converter transmission with planetary gears, ratios: (Drive) 1.48 and 1.00 x torque converter with a 2.1 maximum ratio at stall, (Low) 2.44 x torque converter, (Reverse) 2.0 x torque converter. Standard rear axle with synchromesh transmission: 3.73, optional 4.10 axle was optional. Standard rear axle with overdrive: 3.92. Standard rear axle with Ford-O-Matic transmission: 3.31.

Options:

Full-flow oil filter. Oil bath air cleaner. 4-way power seat. Swift-Sure power brakes ($40). Master-Guide power steering.($92). Power-Lift windows ($70). I-Rest tinted safety glass ($25). Ford-O-Matic Drive ($215). Overdrive ($110). White sidewall tires ($30). Tachometer. Electric clock. Cigarette lighter. Convertible fabric top in lieu of hardtop

1955 Ford Thunderbird Convertible with hardtop (OCW)

($75). Convertible fabric top in addition to hardtop was originally $290 until glass-fibre hardtop became standard equipment. Special fuel and vacuum pump unit. MagicAire Heater ($85). Radio ($100). Rear fender shields. Full wheel covers. Simulated wire wheels. Engine dress-up kit ($25) Windshield washers ($10).

History:

At the beginning of the 1955 model-year, Ford Motor Company projected that it would sell 10,000 Thunderbirds, a conservative estimate. Dealers reportedly took 4,000 orders on October 22, 1954, the first day it was available. The *1956 Ward's Automotive Yearbook* listed September 7, 1954 as the day that Thunderbird production began, but the Classic Thunderbird Club International reports that the earliest production unit had serial number P5FH100005 and was made on September 9, 1954. This car was referred to in the October 4, 1954, issue of *Sports Illustrated*, which carried three pages of Thunderbird coverage entitled "America's newest Sports Car." The writer documented that the car was "not a pilot model Thunderbird, but the Number 1 production model." In the summer of 1965, a Thunderbird owner named George Watts found the remains of serial number P5FH100005 sitting outside a small, Southern California body shop. It had only 78,000 miles on its odometer, but had deteriorated from obvious neglect and improper storage. The car's upholstery was bad, both tops were missing and it had been repainted several times. Originally black, the car showed evidence of being refinished twice, once in white and a second time in blue. The man who owned the car had an unsatisfied loan with a finance company. He also owed the body shop owner for some work he had commissioned. The bills on the car totaled $500. This situation helped Watts purchase the remains for a price he considered fair. After towing the T-Bird home, Watts checked the serial number. He found it was very low. He thought it was the fifth 1955 T-Bird made. A restoration was carried out while his research into the car's background continued. In February 1966, a letter from Ford Motor Company's General Counsel arrived at Watts' home. It revealed that he had the first production Thunderbird. Watts put 10,000 additional miles on the car, driving it until 1973. He then did a restoration and repainted P5FH100005 in its original Raven Black color. Automotive historian James F. Petrik researched Thunderbird factory records and reported that a Thunderbird with serial number P5FH100004 had been discovered, but the Classic Thunderbird Club International agrees that P5FH100005 is considered the first *production* vehicle. According to *Ward's*, Thunderbird production ended August 26, 1955. However, James F. Petrik discovered that a Thunderbird with serial number P5FH260557 was the last 1955 Ford product built. He found that the invoice for this car was typed on September 14, 1955 and that it was constructed on September 16, 1955. The first Thunderbird received good press reviews. "Perhaps the outstanding feature of the new Ford Thunderbird is the clever wedding of sports car functionalism with American standards of comfort," wrote *Motor Trend's* Detroit editor Don MacDonald. "Rather than being the first in the field, much was gained by a period of watchful waiting, typical of shrewd L.D. Crusoe, Ford Motor Company Vice President and General Manager of Ford Division." In a variety of contemporary magazine road tests, the Thunderbird with the 198-hp version of the 292-cid V-8 did 0 to 60 mph in 8.8 seconds, 9.5 seconds, 10.75 seconds and 11 seconds. Typical quarter-mile times were given as 16.9 seconds, 17.1 seconds and 17.75 seconds (at 83 mph). Top speed was recorded as 120 mph. Thunderbirds were being raced before the year ended. They became fairly popular in the "A" Sports Cars class at drag races across the country. At the NHRA Regional Drags in Sioux City, Iowa, in the summer of 1955, Charlie Ward took Class A honors with a T-Bird that hit 81.32 mph in the quarter mile. That was the fifth fastest run of the event out of 15 winners in a wide assortment of classes. That summer, during a 100-degree heat wave, John Hale topped the same class, in a T-Bird, during Columbus, Ohio's first organized drag event. His speed in the quarter was an even 80 mph. Other T-Birds drag raced at Lake City, Florida (Calvin Partin/80.86 mph), Memphis, Tennessee (Marshall Robillio/82.34 mph) and San Antonio, Texas (E.L. Kendrick/87.37

mph). The T-Birds got noticeably faster after firms such as Edelbrock Equipment Company began offering dual four-barrel and triple two-barrel carburetor intake manifolds and high-speed distributors designed specifically for Thunderbirds.

1956 Thunderbird

Thunderbird — Series H — (V-8): Most exterior alterations to the 1956 Thunderbird were not very obvious ones. The emblem on the front of the car, above the grille, was changed from crossed checkered racing flags to a stylized rendition of the American Indian thunderbird symbol. The headlight doors now had a rib under the hooded area. The badges behind the simulated louver trim on the front fenders were revised from V-8 insignias to Ford crests. Door-like air vents were added to the sides of the Thunderbird's cowl to improve interior cooling. Also added for the same reason were wind-wings on the car's chrome windshield frame. The standard continental tire kit on the rear of the car was the most obvious update. "The Thunderbird's brand-new, rear spare-tire mounting folds back handily, as quick as a wink," advertisements boasted. "It adds greatly to your luggage space as it does to the overall beauty of the car." Cars built before November 14, 1955 had their continental spare tires raised for added ground clearance. Later, Ford dealers had to recall these cars to change the height of the continental kits by 1-3/8 inches. The 1956 frame had to be modified for this feature, since the original 1955 frame couldn't tolerate the "cantilever" effect of the heavy continental kit at the extreme rear of the vehicle. A new, vented gas cap was used on the center-fill gas tank's neck. The door that the gas filler hid behind was devoid of the checkered flag emblem used to dress it up in 1955. Slight modifications were made to the Thunderbird's taillights. Though still large and circular, the rear red lenses had a wider center protrusion with more elaborate chrome trim. The arch-shaped area above the round red lens was also restyled. A small circular reflector was added to the chrome molding right at the top of the arch. Back-up lamps could again be ordered in place of the metal filler plate. Offered again was the same glass-fibre hardtop used in 1955. A new version, with "port" windows in its side panels, was also available for 1956. The hardtop in matching body color (with or without port windows) was optional at no extra cost. Having the top finished in a contrasting color did cost extra, though. Some Ford dealers added the porthole windows to the standard-style hardtop when buyers found their Thunderbirds claustrophobic or complained about blind spots. The 1956 Thunderbird's interior door panels had new "stitching" embossments molded into the seams in the vinyl. The patterning on the seats, supplied by McInerney Spring & Wire Company, was also changed. In 1955, the vertically ribbed insert sections of the seats were separate from each other. The 1956 design brought the ribs across the center of the backrest. They ran nearly the full width of the seat back and gave the visual impression that the seat had been widened. A three-spoke Lifeguard deep-dish steering wheel was standard equipment in the Thunderbird. It replaced the flat, two-spoke steering wheel used the previous year. This steering wheel required alterations to the signal lamp stalk and the steering column adjusting collar. Also standard were Lifeguard door latches that were not supposed to open in a serious accident. Other Ford Lifeguard features, such as seat belts, a ribbed padded dash and padded sun visors were optional. Ford's Lifeguard safety program was a reaction to Cornell University Medical College's assertion that 1955 automobiles were no safer than those built between 1940-1949. Ford spent months researching auto safety. Auto accident statistics and data were gathered from safety research centers including the Cornell Medical College. As a result, Ford isolated injury-causing components of cars and set up a test lab to redesign such components. As an extra-cost item, the safety features were a flop, but *Motor Trend* magazine presented Ford with its "1st annual *Motor Trend* Award," for making the most significant advancement on a United States production car. "Rising high in stature, above all other (advances), however, is the progress toward automotive safety made by the Ford Motor Co.," wrote Walt Woron and engineering editor John Booth. "This company, and each of its divisions, is not alone in its pursuit of those elusive qualities we'd like to see built into all cars. What

1956 Ford Thunderbird Convertible (PH)

this company has initiated is without a doubt the biggest step forward in 1956." There were a few additional "running" production changes in 1956 Thunderbirds. With the spare tire out of the trunk, changes were made in the way that the luggage compartment was trimmed. A curtain made of material similar to the ribbed rubber trunk mat was added at first. Later, the rubber trim was replaced with trim made of a composition material called Burtex and the curtain was no longer used. At mid model year, a dual four-barrel carburetor "competition kit" was released for Thunderbirds with manual transmission. Engines fitted with the kit, which was intended for serious racing, were rated at 260 hp. Standard features included: a 292-cid Y-block V-8 engine, automatic choke, 12-volt electrical system, dual exhausts, three-speed manual transmission, Hotchkiss drive, ball-joint front suspension, 5-leaf spring rear suspension, five 6.70 x 15 tubeless tires, all-vinyl interiors with harmonizing looped-rayon carpeting, 17-in. diameter deep-center Lifeguard steering wheel with 2-in. adjustment, Lifeguard double-grip door latches, Lifeguard rear view mirror, Astra-Dial control panel with illuminated control knobs, parcel compartment with locking-type push-button latch, 4-way illuminated starter-ignition switch, panel courtesy light with integral switch and automatic door switches, dual horns, half-circle steering wheel horn ring, and glass-fibre hardtop.

VIN:

The VIN was located on a plate on the left door pillar. The first symbol denoted the engine: M=292-cid/202-hp four-barrel Thunderbird V-8 (manual transmission), P=312-cid/215-hp four-barrel Thunderbird Special V-8 (overdrive transmission), P=312-cid/225-hp four-barrel Thunderbird Special V-8 (automatic transmission), P=312-cid/260-hp dual four-barrel Thunderbird Special V-8 (overdrive transmission). The second symbol indicated the model-year: 6=1956. The third symbol was the assembly plant: F=Dearborn, Michigan. The fourth symbol denoted the body type: H=Thunderbird convertible. The fifth through 10th symbols denoted the sequential production numbers of the specific vehicle starting at 100001. The body number plate was located on the firewall. The serial number was the same as the number on the left door pillar tag. Symbols below "BODY" were the body symbol code: 40A=Thunderbird. Symbols below "COLOR" were the paint color code. Symbols below "TRIM" were the trim combination code. Symbols below "PRODUCTION CODE" were the production date code. The numerical prefix indicated the date of the month the car was made. The letters indicated the month of manufacture: A=January, B=February, C=March, D=April, E=May, F=June, G=July, H=August, J=September, K=October, L=November, M=December. The numerical suffix was the sequence the car was built in.

Thunderbird (V-8)

Model No.	Body/ Style No.	Body Type and Seating	Factory Price	Shipping Weight	Production Total
H	40B	2-dr. Hardtop-2P	$3,158	3,297 lbs.	Note 1
H	40A	2-dr. Convertible-2P	$3,233	3,159 lbs.	Note 1

Note 1: Combined production of both models was 15,631.

Ward's 1956 Automotive Yearbook showed an introductory price of $2,842 for the Thunderbird, but most 1956 models were sold for about $300 more than that. The base price in June 1956 was $3,147.60. That included the suggested retail price at the main factory, federal tax and delivery and handling (but not freight).

Engines:

Thunderbird Base V-8 (with manual transmission): Overhead valve. Cast-iron block. B & S: 3.75 x 3.30 in. Displacement: 292 cid. Compression ratio: 8.40:1. Brake hp: 202 at 4600 rpm. Taxable hp: 45. Torque: 289 lbs.-ft. at 2600 rpm. Five main bearings. Solid valve lifters. Crankcase capacity: 5 qt. (add 1 qt. with new oil filter). Cooling system capacity: 19 qt. Carburetor: Holley 4000 four-barrel. Code M.

Thunderbird Special V-8 (with overdrive): Overhead valve. Cast-iron block. B & S: 3.80 x 3.44 in. Displacement: 312 cid. Compression ratio: 8.4:1. Brake hp: 215 at 4600 rpm. Taxable hp: 45. Torque: 317 lbs.-ft. at 2600 rpm. Five main bearings. Crankcase capacity: 5 qt. (add 1 qt. with new oil filter). Cooling system capacity: 19 qt. Carburetor: Holley 4000 four-barrel. Code P.

Thunderbird Special V-8 (with Ford-O-Matic or overdrive): Overhead valve. Cast-iron block. B & S: 3.80 x 3.44 in. Displacement: 312 cid. Compression ratio: 9.0:1. Brake hp: 225 at 4600 rpm. Taxable hp: 45. Torque: 324 at 2600 rpm. Five main bearings. Crankcase capacity: 5 qt. (add 1 qt. with new oil filter). Cooling system capacity: 19 qt. Carburetor: Holley 4000 four-barrel. Code L.

Thunderbird Special Dual Four-Barrel V-8 (with manual transmission): Overhead valve. Cast-iron block. B & S : 3.80 x 3.44 in. Displacement: 312 cid. Compression ratio: 9.5:1. Brake hp: 260 at unknown rpm. Taxable hp: 45. Torque: unknown. Five main bearings. Crankcase capacity: 5 qt. (add 1 qt. with new oil filter). Cooling system capacity: 19 qt. Carburetor: Two Holley four-barrel. Code P.

Chassis:

Wheelbase: 102 in. Overall length: 185.1 in. Overall width: 70.3 in. Overall height (top of glass-fibre hardtop to ground): 50.2 in. Road clearance: 5.9

in. Front tread: 56 in. Rear tread: 56 in. Front headroom: (with hardtop) 33.1 or 33.6 in. Hip room: 58.8 in. Front shoulder room: 53.3 in. Front legroom: 45.1 in. Top of door height: 34.2 in. Tires: 6.70 x 15 4-ply.

Technical:

Standard hypoid axle: (Manual transmission) 3.73:1, (Overdrive transmission) 3.92:1, (Ford-O-Matic) 3.31:1. Wheel studs: 5.5 in. Wheel stud circle: 4.5 in. diameter. Brake swept area: 175.5 sq. in. Turning diameter: 36 ft. Steering ratio: 23.0:1. Weight distribution: 49.4/50.6. Chassis type: X-frame. Front suspension: Ball-joints, coil springs, tube shocks and stabilizer. Rear suspension: Composite axle, four-leaf springs, double-acting shock absorbers. Steering: Parallel linkage type. Steering wheel: Three-inch in-and-out adjustable. Front brakes: 11-in. diameter double-sealed. Rear brakes: 11-in. diameter double-sealed. Standard transmission: Three-speed synchromesh with helical gears. Optional transmission: Planetary overdrive with planetary gears. Optional transmission: Ford-O-Matic torque converter transmission with planetary gears. Standard rear axle ratio with manual transmission: 3.73. Standard rear axle with overdrive: 3.92. Standard rear axle with Ford-O-Matic transmission: 3.31.

Options:

Full-flow oil filter. Four -way power seat ($65). Swift Sure power brakes ($34). Master-Guide power steering ($64). Power-Lift windows ($70). I-Rest tinted safety glass. Ford-O-Matic Drive ($215). Overdrive ($146). White sidewall tires. Fuel and vacuum pump unit. MagicAire Heater ($84). Radio ($107). Rear fender shields (the type of fender skirts with an edge molding and gravel shield, as used mostly from April 1955 on). Full wheel covers. Simulated wire wheel covers. Engine dress-up kit. Auto-Wipe windshield washers. Turn signals. Lifeguard seat belts (Match 1956). Lifeguard padded sun visors and Lifeguard instrument panel padding starting in March 1956 ($22-$32). Thunderbird 312-cid four-barrel V-8. Thunderbird 312-cid dual four-barrel V-8. Convertible fabric top alone ($75). Convertible top and hardtop ($290). Tonneau cover.

History:

Henry Ford II was President of Ford Motor Company in 1956. Earnest R. Breech was Chairman of the Board. Robert S. McNamara, who later went on to become United States Secretary of Defense, was a FoMoCo Vice President and General Manager of Ford Division. A man who would later become an automotive industry legend, Lee Iacocca, was Ford Division's Truck Marketing Manager this year. The 1956 Thunderbird bowed on September 23, 1955. Ford announced that its target was to built 20,000 of the cars in 1956. They were often used to attract attention to other Fords. Thunderbirds appeared in many FoMoCo ads featuring Mainline, Customline and Fairlane models. The 202-hp "Thunderbird Y-8" was mentioned in many advertisements. Ford ultimately produced 15,631 T-Birds, which was below its target, but only 524 less than in 1955, which was a record year for the auto industry. *Motor Trend* did its second annual Thunderbird versus Corvette comparison road test in June 1956. The magazine noted that GM had added "more fuel to an old duel" by adding a hardtop, roll-up windows and more power to the Corvette's equipment. "But don't get the idea that Ford has been lulled into a no-progress policy by their sales leadership with the Thunderbird," advised editor Walt Woron. "The No. 1 sales position is hard to come by and is jealously guarded." *Hot Rod* magazine did a "Rod Test" of the 1956 Thunderbird in July and expanded it to discuss Thunderbird modifications. According to editor Racer Brown, the car's popularity "was soon resolved into a matter of appearance." He believed that horsepower, performance, fuel economy, economics and utilitarian value had little to do with the appeal of Ford's two-seater. "It was the bold American lines that captivated the majority (of buyers)," he opined. "Yet, these lines have been restrained by good taste." Under the test car's hood was the 312.7-cid V-8 in its 225-hp "power pack" format. It went from 0-to-60 mph in an average 9.1 seconds and hit zero to 80 mph in an average 15.5 seconds with Brown "shifting" the automatic transmission. Keeping the gear-shifter in drive range only, the comparable times were 9.8 seconds and 16.6 seconds. The car averaged 77 mph for the standing-start quarter-mile. Despite Ford's early attempts to discourage people from racing its products, some of the hottest U.S. production sports cars at the Daytona International Speed Trials/NASCAR Speedweek in February 1956 were Thunderbirds. Chuck Daigh's streamlined Thunderbird with bullet-shaped headlight covers, no bumpers or windshield, smooth Moon Disc hubcaps and a tonneau cover over its cockpit hit an average top speed of 85.308 mph for the standing-start mile early in the trials, then averaged 92.142 mph three days later. It beat out a Corvette driven by Zora Arkus-Duntov. However, both vehicles were disqualified. The two car builders had misunderstood the rules and over-bored their engines. Since the misunderstanding was not intentional, Daigh was permitted to replace his Thunderbird's over-size engine with a stock one. He worked for almost 48 hours straight making his power plant change. The result was a factory-spec 312-cid block fitted with the racing kit that Ford offered stock car racers. It consisted of a dual four-barrel

1956 Ford Thunderbird Convertible (OCW)

intake manifold and a pair of special Holley four-barrel carburetors, plus 10.0:1 high-compression heads with larger intake and exhaust ports, a limited advance distributor, a special cam and lifters and tubular push rods, rocker arms and valve springs. Daigh wound up with an average of 88.779 mph performance for the standing mile. Another Thunderbird, driven by William Norkert, was second with an 87.869 mph two-way run. A Thunderbird built by Andy Hotten, of Dearborn Steel Tubing Company, had a faster official time. Both Hotten and Suzanne La Fountain drove the car. It ran 134 mph, for a third-place in the flying mile with Hotten behind the wheel. Bill Borkett's 1955 Thunderbird was fourth with 133.087 mph and Merritt Brown took his 1956 Thunderbird to fifth place with a 122.491 mph performance. Other Thunderbirds were entered at Daytona by Bob Wallis and Jack Horsley. The latter, with its weird two-stage McCulloch blower, was also seen in the July issue of *Hot Rod*. Later, Chuck Daigh equipped his car with a 4.56 rear end gear, Hi-Tork differential, eight shock absorbers and a synchromesh gearbox. It ran the quarter-mile at just over 100 mph. Another drag racer, Bill Williams, turned 105 mph in a supercharged "312" Thunderbird with Ford-O-Matic. The Thunderbird's racetrack potential was beginning to evolve more fully, at least in drag racing. "A well-modified 'Bird out there holds all the local drag strip records in the modified sports car class," noted Racer Brown. "Top time: 108 mph and there's more where that came from." Despite its stance against racing, FoMoCo produced a film entitled "Thunder Beach" that told the tale of the Daytona stock car races. Ford also wrote the results from Speedweek into a mid-1956 advertisement that promoted the Thunderbird as a "Mink coat for Father." The ad boasted "Talking of speed, have you heard how a Thunderbird dusted off all U.S. and foreign production sports cars in the acceleration tests at the Daytona Speed Trials? From a standing start it covered a mile in 40.5 seconds . . . was pushing 150 mph when it took the flag. If you'd like to sample some of this sizzle, take a whirl in a Thunderbird with an over-square 225-hp Thunderbird Special V-8, floor-mounted three-speed transmission and 3.73:1 final drive." At the Rocky Mountain Regional drag races in Pueblo, Colorado, a 1955 Thunderbird piloted by William Burkhart of Phoenix, Arizona took "A" Sports Car honors with a quarter-mile run of 15.15 seconds at 96.35 mph. There was also a Thunderbird at the Bonneville (Utah) Speed Trials in August 1956. Another dragging Thunderbird was the 1955 hardtop campaigned in "A" Sports class by Kirk White, of Glenside, Pennsylvania. With a McCulloch supercharged 292-cid V-8 blowing through triple two-barrel carburetors, it turned 98.74 mph in the National Hot Rod Association's "1956 National Championship Drags" in Kansas City. In December 1956, *Hot Rod* magazine printed an article called "300 Honest HP." It detailed a series of different steps taken to up the power output of a 312-cid Mercury V-8 (identical to the Thunderbird power plant). After 17 separate modifications and dynamometer tests, the engine was churning out 303 hp at 5,350 rpm and maximum torque of 360 ft.-lbs. at 3500 rpm. *Motor Trend* honored the international appeal of Thunderbird styling by selecting it as the year's "most beautiful sports-type car." The magazine stated, "A neo-classic, blending a modern feeling with the crisp, sharp-edged look reminiscent of the '30s, the Thunderbird has a huge number of admirers both here and in other countries. Though it could do with less chrome and applied trim, these are more nearly a part of the overall design than in almost any other car. Here's another trend-setter, heralding smaller cars."

1957 Thunderbird

Thunderbird — Series H — (V-8): There were big styling changes to the 1957 Thunderbird, but only minor mechanical alterations. New appearance features included a larger, stronger front bumper incorporating rectangular parking lamps. A larger front grille was said to improve engine cooling. The shape of the front wheel cut outs was modified. Chrome "Thunderbird" name scripts were added to the front fenders, ahead of the louver decorations. Tail fins were added to the T-Bird. A body side feature line curved up and over the door handles, then swept to the rear atop the outward-canted fins. A higher deck lid

had a reverse-angle shape at its rear. The longer 1957 body provided more luggage space. After being externally mounted in 1956, the spare tire was moved back inside the six-inch longer trunk. This made getting into the trunk a lot easier. Ford said that it also helped enhance handling, due to improvements in weight distribution caused by the extra poundage at the rear. The spare tire sat at an upright angle in the trunk's tire well. The Thunderbird's longer, larger, finned rear fenders ended with large round taillights. The rear bumper was also enlarged and had more curves than in the past. Built-in exhaust outlets were featured at either side. The license plate was mounted in the center of the rear bumper. A badge on the center of the rear deck lid, shaped like a stylized Thunderbird, identified the model. The new Thunderbird had a firmer ride than big sedans of its era due mainly to its shorter wheelbase. However, it was plush, comfortable and soft riding in comparison to European sports cars. For 1957, the ride was improved through a lowered center of gravity and the use of recalibrated shock absorbers. Five-leaf rear springs were reintroduced, after being dropped in favor of four-leaf springs in 1956. Despite the fact that smaller wheels were employed in 1957, the front brakes were enlarged. The smaller new 14-in. diameter safety rim wheels with 7.50 x 14 tires mounted brought the car closer to the ground. They were dressed up with handsome new louvered full-wheel disks. The 1957 frame was virtually the same as before. However, the number four cross-member was changed to box section (instead of channel section) design. This provided added strength to support the extra bulk of the bigger body. The Hardtop model was again really a convertible with a detachable fiberglass top. Ford literature still described it as a "glass-fibre standard hardtop." The standard top had port windows in 1957. Optional at no extra cost was the hardtop without port windows. Both were available in contrasting or matching colors. Some 75 percent of all 1957s had the porthole tops, which had no trim badges. The non-porthole tops featured round emblems with V-shaped Thunderbird insignias. Both hardtops used a revised clamping mechanism. The Convertible came with a folding fabric top. Modifications were made to the top mechanism to make it easier to operate. Two types of fabric tops were offered. The canvas convertible top was available in three colors, while an optional vinyl top came only in one color. Many owners preferred both hard and soft tops. In this case, the Convertible model was purchased with the hardtop as a separate option. In October 1956, the Thunderbird was offered in 10 single colors. All 10 colors were also offered on the fiberglass hardtops with specific body and interior color combinations. Inside, the 1957 T-Bird had modest interior alterations. The dashboard was based on the one used in full-size 1957 Fords with a simulated engine-turned face panel added. The visor above the instrument panel no longer had a transparent "window." A tachometer was mounted low at the driver's left and a bit hard to see. "Idiot" lights monitored oil pressure and the battery's state of charge. The seats were redesigned. They had separate sections for the driver and passenger. New springs that gave better spine support and much improved lateral support were employed. The seats were the same basic size and shape as in 1956, but the new springs were said to reduce driver fatigue. The door panels were also changed. A "Dial-O-Matic" seat was optional. Dash-mounted buttons permitted adjusting the seat to the driver's favorite position. When the ignition was turned off, it automatically moved to its rearmost position. When the ignition was turned on, the seat moved automatically to the pre-selected driving position. A new idea in radios was a speed-sensitive receiver. There was an electronic device built into the circuit between the radio volume control and the distributor. It automatically increased volume as the car speed got higher. As the engine speed increased, a capacitor wired in series with the distributor lead raised the volume. This maintained the listening level at a constant level at all times and kept the radio from blasting loudly when the car was idling at a traffic light. A safety feature added to the 1957 Thunderbird was a reflecting strip along the rear edge of the left door. When the door was opened at night, headlights from oncoming cars were reflected from the strip, warning drivers of another car's presence. The doors also had heavier hinges than those used

1957 Ford Thunderbird Convertible (PH)

1957 Ford Thunderbird Convertible (OCW)

in previous years. Standard equipment included: 292-cid Y-block V-8 engine, automatic choke, Super-Filter air cleaner with reusable paper element (effective Feb. 1957), 12-volt electrical system, dual exhausts, three-speed manual transmission, Hotchkiss drive, ball-joint front suspension, 5-leaf spring rear suspension, five 7.50 x 14 tubeless tires, Safety-Contoured 14-in. wheel rims, pleated all-vinyl Tu-Tone interiors or all-vinyl monochromatic interiors with harmonizing looped-rayon carpeting, standard glass-fibre hardtop with port windows or optional glass-fibre hardtop without port windows (in contrasting or matching colors), Lifeguard cushioned sun visors and Lifeguard instrument panel padding, deep-center Lifeguard steering wheel, Lifeguard double-grip door latches, Lifeguard rear view mirror, parcel compartment with locking-type push-button latch, 4-way illuminated starter-ignition switch, panel courtesy light with integral switch and automatic door switches, dual horns, and half-circle steering wheel horn ring.

VIN:

Located on plate on left door pillar. First symbol denotes engine: C=292-cid/206-hp V-8 (manual transmission) or 212-hp V-8 (Ford-O-Matic transmission) four-barrel Thunderbird V-8, D=312-cid/245-hp four-barrel Thunderbird Special V-8, E=312-cid/270-hp dual four-barrel Thunderbird Special V-8, F=312-cid/300-hp supercharged Thunderbird Special V-8. Second symbol denotes model-year: 7=1957 Third symbol denotes the assembly plant: F=Dearborn, Michigan. Fourth symbol denotes body type: H=Thunderbird convertible. Fifth thru tenth symbols denote sequential production number of specific vehicle starting at 100001. Body number plate located on firewall. Serial number: Same as number on left door pillar tag. Symbols below "BODY" are body symbol code: 40=Thunderbird. Symbols below "COLOR" are paint color code. See the table below. Symbols below "TRIM" are trim combination code. See the table below. Symbols below "PRODUCTION CODE" are the production date code. The numerical prefix indicates the date of the month the car was made. The letters indicate month of manufacture: A=January, B=February, C=March, D=April, E=May, F=June, G=July, H=August, J=September, K=October, L=November, M=December. The numerical suffix indicates production sequence.

Thunderbird (V-8)

Model No.	Body/Style No.	Body Type and Seating	Factory Price	Shipping Weight	Production Total
H	40A	2-dr. Convertible-2P	$3,548	3,134 lbs.	Note 1
H	40B	2-dr. Hardtop-2P	$3,383	3,299 lbs.	Note 1

Note 1: Combined production of both models was 16,155.

Engines:

Thunderbird Base V-8 (Manual transmission): Overhead valve. Cast-iron block. B & S: 3.75 x 3.30 in. Displacement: 292 cid. Compression ratio: 9.10:1. Brake hp: 212 at 4500 rpm. Torque: 297 lbs.-ft. at 2700 rpm. Taxable hp: 45.0. Five main bearings. Solid valve lifters. Crankcase capacity: 5 qt. (add 1 qt. with new oil filter). Cooling system capacity: 19 qt. Carburetor: Holley two-barrel. Code C.

Thunderbird Special V-8 (Overdrive or Ford-O-Matic transmission): Overhead valve. Cast-iron block. B & S: 3.80 x 3.44 in. Displacement: 312 cid. Compression ratio: 9.70:1. Brake hp: 245 at 4500 rpm. Taxable hp: 45.0. Torque: 332 lbs.-ft. at 3200 rpm. Five main bearings. Crankcase capacity: 5 qt. (add 1 qt. with new oil filter). Cooling system capacity: 19 qt. Carburetor: Single Holley four-barrel. Code D.

Thunderbird Super V-8 (with dual four-barrel carburetors, all transmissions): Overhead valve. Cast-iron block. B & S: 3.80 x 3.44 in. Displacement: 312 cid. Compression ratio: 9.70:1 (10.0:1 with racing kit installed). Brake hp: 270 at 4800 rpm. Taxable hp: 45.0. Torque: 336 lbs.-ft. at 3400 rpm. Five main bearings. Solid valve lifters. Crankcase capacity: 5 qt. (add 1 qt. with new oil filter). Cooling system capacity: 19 qt. Carburetor: Two Holley four-barrel. Code E.

Thunderbird Super V-8 (Racing kit version, all transmissions): Overhead valve. Cast-iron block. B & S: 3.80 x 3.44 in. Displacement:

312 cid. Compression ratio: 9.70:1 (10.0:1 with racing kit installed). Brake hp: 285 at 5200 rpm. Taxable hp: 45.0. Torque: 343 lbs.-ft. at 3500 rpm. Five main bearings. Solid valve lifters. Crankcase capacity: 5 qt. (add 1 qt. with new oil filter). Cooling system capacity: 19 qt. Carburetor: Two Holley four-barrel. Code E.

Thunderbird Special Supercharged V-8 (All transmissions): Overhead valve. Cast-iron block. B & S: 3.80 x 3.44 in. Displacement: 312 cid. Compression ratio: 8.5:1. Brake hp: 300 at 4800 rpm. Taxable hp: 45.0. Torque: 340 at 5300 rpm. Five main bearings. Solid valve lifters. Crankcase capacity: 5 qt. (add 1 qt. with new oil filter). Cooling system capacity: 19 qt. Carburetor: Holley four-barrel with McCulloch/Paxton centrifugal supercharger. Code F.

Chassis:

Wheelbase: 102 in. Overall length: 181.4 in. Overall width: 72.8 in. Overall height: 49.6 in. Front and rear tread: 56 in. Front headroom: (with hardtop) 33.1 in., (with convertible top) 33.6 in. Front hip room: 58.8 in. Front shoulder room: 53.3 in. Front legroom: 44.9 in. Top of door height: 34.2 in. Top of soft top height: 51.8 in. Tires: 7.50 x 14 4-ply.

Technical:

Standard hypoid axle: (Manual transmission) 3.56:1, (Overdrive transmission) 3.70:1, (Ford-O-Matic) 3.10:1. Wheels: 14-in. Safety Contour. Wheel studs: 5.5 in. Wheel stud circle: 4.5 in. diameter. Brake swept area: 175.5 sq. in. Turning diameter: 36 ft. Steering wheel: 17-in. Lifeguard type. Steering wheel adjustment: 2 in. Turns lock-to-lock: 4.5. Steering ratio: 23.0:1. Weight distribution: 50/50. Chassis type: X-frame. Front suspension: Ball-joints, coil springs, tube shocks and stabilizer. Rear suspension: Composite axle, five-leaf springs, double-acting shock absorbers. Steering: Parallel linkage type. Steering wheel: Three-inch in-and-out adjustable. Front brakes: 11-in. diameter double-sealed. Brake swept area: 176 sq. in. Rear brakes: 11-in. diameter double-sealed. Standard transmission: Three-speed synchromesh with helical gears. Optional transmission: Planetary overdrive with planetary gears. Optional transmission: Ford-O-Matic torque converter transmission with planetary gears. Axle ratios: (manual transmission) 3.56:1, (overdrive transmission) 3.70:1 and (automatic transmission) 3.10:1. Gas tank: 20 gallons.

Options:

Dial-O-Matic four-way power seat. Swift Sure power brakes ($38). Master-Guide power steering ($68). Power-Lift windows ($70). I-Rest tinted safety glass. Ford-O-Matic Drive ($215). Overdrive ($108). White sidewall tires. Special fuel and vacuum pump unit for positive-action windshield wipers. MagicAire Heater. Volumatic radio. Deluxe antenna. Rear fender shields. Back-up lights. Locking gas cap. Hooded mirror. Auto-Home electric shaver. Turbine wheel covers. Simulated wire wheel covers. Engine dress-up kit ($25). Aquamatic windshield wipers/washers. Thunderbird 312-cid four-barrel V-8. Thunderbird 312-cid Super V-8. Convertible fabric top. Tonneau cover. Seat belts. Full-flow oil filter (left off some early literature). Super Filter air cleaner (changed to standard equipment effective Feb. 1957).

History:

Henry Ford II was President of Ford Motor Company in 1957. Earnest R. Breech was Chairman of the Board. J. O. Wright was a FoMoCo Vice President and General Manager of Ford Division. A man who would later become an automotive industry legend, Lee Iacocca, was promoted to Car Marketing Manager this year. Production of 1957 Thunderbirds began on September 14, 1956 with car number D7FH100010. Model introductions took place on October 3, 1956. Ford continued building these cars after full-size Fords underwent the normal model changeover late in the summer of 1957. The company had set a production target of 20,000 units, but the '57s were popular and orders ran higher than expected. Model-year production eventually hit 21,380. The extended model run allowed Ford to "build out" the two-seat T-Bird and use up parts in inventory before switching to four-seat model production for the 1958 model year. The last 1957 model, reportedly owned by David Koto of Michigan, had serial number E7FH395813. Ford Motor Company boasted that the T-Bird had outsold all other sports-type personal cars combined. According to *Popular Mechanic's 1957 Car Facts Book*, during 1956 it outsold its principal domestic competitor, the Chevrolet Corvette, by more than 10 to 1. Even though the Corvette had whipped the T-Bird in sports car racing, the T-Bird was the big winner on the boulevards of America. By the time the extended 1957 season came to a close, the three-year total of T-Bird production stood at 53,166 units. That compared to just 14,446 Corvettes built in five years. Most car magazines test drove early versions of the 1957 Thunderbird. The cars Ford loaned them for the tests seemed to have many convenience options like Ford-O-Matic transmission, an adjustable steering wheel, a four-way power seat and power windows. Usually the 245-hp Thunderbird Special engine was under the hood. *Motor Life's* Ken Fermoyle found this T-Bird's performance, "Frankly disappointing." He said he had trouble believing that the car needed 11.5 seconds to go from 0-to-60 mph. In

May 1957, *Speed Age* did an "Expert Test" comparing the Corvette, T-Bird, and Studebaker Golden Hawk. Of the three, the T-Bird was slowest. However, it registered an 8.49-second 0-to-60 time and a top speed of 119.3 mph. "Any car that will accelerate from 0-60 in under nine seconds these days is fairly quick," said writer Bob Veith. "The take-off response up to 70 mph was neck-snapping all right and the engine continued to deliver a good punch even on the high end." As you can guess, the existence of a factory racing kit and a NASCAR version of the "F" engine encouraged some people to race 1957 Thunderbirds. For the 1957 Daytona Speed Weeks, Danny Eames took his modified T-Bird to an acceleration mark of 97.933 mph. He did the Flying Mile at 160.356 mph. There was also a factory-sponsored racing effort featuring 1957 models known as the "Battlebirds." One of these cars has been restored. Numerous aftermarket continental kits were offered for the few buyers who felt they needed a continental spare tire. Eastern Auto Company, of Los Angeles, advertised one of these for $119.50. A chrome tire ring was $10 extra. Many other non-factory accessories were also available. The manufacturer of the Traction-Masters suspension levelers used a cartoon T-Bird in its advertising. Camshaft wizard Ed Iskenderian showed a photo of a 1957 T-Bird at the top of one ad, with testimonials from drivers who raced them. De Ville Sports Car Accessories offered tonneau covers for T-Birds. The tan and black versions sold for $39.95, while the white cover was $5 extra. These had a zipper down the center, so the cockpit could be left uncovered. A press release in the September 1957 issue of *Motor Trend* introduced two new "Thunderbird conversions." One was the Town Car kit that allowed owners to carry their detachable hardtop on the rear deck and move it over the driver's head in less than 15 seconds if it rained. Tie-down straps and standard toggle bolts were used to attach the top. In profile, this made the Thunderbird look like an old-fashioned town car. This kit was sold by Sanco, Inc. of Atlanta, Ga., as well as by Ford dealers, which made it "semi-factory" equipment. It originally cost $89.50. Also featured in the same release was the better known Thunderbird "rumble seat" marketed by Birdnest of Burbank, California. Made of pressed body steel, this accessory replaced the original trunk deck with a swiveling lid that had a naugahyde-upholstered seat and side panels on its inner surface. When swiveled to the "seat-up" position, it could accommodate two adults or several kids on its in-the-trunk seat. The original price of the Birdnest was $239. Performance results recorded in car magazines varied. A test of the 312-cid 225-hp T-Bird registered a 0-to-60 mph time of 11.5 seconds. In two different tests of cars with the 312-cid 245-hp V-8, the 0-to-60 mph times were 8.49 seconds and 12.7 seconds, respectively. A fourth test of a T-Bird with the 312-cid 270-hp engine recorded a 9.5-second 0-to-60 mph time. Top speed of the 245-hp version was estimated at 116 mph.

1958 Thunderbird

Thunderbird — Series H/J — (V-8): The 1958 four-seat Thunderbird was one of the most totally changed cars in history. Much larger than the two-seat T-Bird, it also featured unit-body construction. A two-door hardtop was the only model offered at first. This was a true pillarless coupe, rather than a convertible with an add-on fiberglass top like the 1955-1957 "Hardtop" model. A convertible was introduced in mid 1958. It had the first power-operated cloth top on a T-Bird, but the ragtop was not fully automatic in its operation. The new car had a square "Ford" look that led to the nickname "Squarebird." Angular, sculptured feature lines characterized the hood scoop, the front fenders, the body side "projectiles" and the twin "jet-pod" rear end. There were two headlights on each side up front. Chrome decorations included Thunderbird scripts on the front fender sides with bombsight ornaments atop both fenders. The integral bumper-grille had twin guards mounted on the lower part of the grille frame. The insert was a piece of stamped sheet metal with round holes punched into it in diagonal rows. Five cast-metal ornaments with groups of chrome hash marks decorated the projectiles on the lower body sides. Each rear jet-pod held two large, round taillights set into small painted grilles with inserts matching the front grille. Back-up lights were optional. The rear license plate was in the center. Small tail fins graced the top of the rear fenders. They ran from ahead of the door handles, canting slightly outwards at the rear. The center area of the deck lid had a wide depression with a chrome Thunderbird emblem in

its center. The formal-roof hardtop had a long and low appearance. The roof sail panels carried small round Thunderbird medallions. Bright metal strips with horizontal ribbing decorated the bottom of the roof pillars. The standard full wheel disks had turbine-fins with large flat centers. Vent windows were a new feature. Approval to make the 1958 Thunderbird Convertible was delayed until May 1957 and it bowed in June 1958. Its top disappeared completely into the trunk leaving no fabric exposed and a smooth, unbroken trunk line. Top operation was by two hydraulic cylinders that derived pressure from an electrically-operated rotor pump. To stack the top, the operator had to release the header clamps, unsnap eight fasteners in the quarter window area (above the side rails) and unlatch the luggage compartment door. When the latches were released by forward pressure on the cylinder of the luggage compartment door latch lock, the operator had to release the door safety catch and raise the door by hand. After the door had been raised upright, the upper back finish panel had to be raised in position to avoid damage when the lid was lowered with the top stacked. The panel had to be raised and locked. A release-knob plunger was provided. The top could then be lowered by means of a safety switch located in the luggage compartment. After the top was stacked, the luggage compartment door had to be lowered by hand and latched by putting pressure on the door, near the latches. This procedure was reversed to raise the top. Inside, the T-Bird was also totally redesigned. It was the first American car to come standard with bucket seats and a center console. To keep overall height as low as possible, the passenger compartment had a deeper-than-usual well described as a "sunken living room." The transmission/drive shaft tunnel was high and the full-length console was used to make it functional. The console housed controls for a heater (and optional air conditioner), the power window switches, the radio speaker and front and rear ashtrays. Each of the four seats was virtually a separate "cubicle." The dashboard had "twin pods" for driver and passenger. There was a deep-dish steering wheel, safety-padded instrument panel, padded sun visors and a service-tray glove box door. Molded door and side panels were also new. Overall, the interior design was very attractive. Powering 1958 T-Birds was a new 352-cid "Interceptor" V-8. A 430-cid 375-hp engine mentioned in some literature and ads did not materialize. Also new was an angle-poised ball-joint front suspension. The 1958 model was also the only Thunderbird to have a coil spring rear suspension prior to 1967. Standard equipment included [December 1957 for Hardtop only] 300-hp 352-cid Thunderbird Special V-8, four-barrel carburetor, dual exhausts, full-flow oil filtration, automatic choke, three-speed manual transmission, Lifeguard padded instrument panel, cushioned sun visors, cigarette lighter, horn ring, dual horns, automatic dome light, turn signals. [Jan. 1958 for Hardtop only] 300-hp 352-cid Thunderbird Special V-8, four-barrel carburetor, dual exhausts, full-flow oil filtration, automatic choke, three-speed manual transmission, Lifeguard padded instrument panel, cushioned sun visors, double-grip door locks, safety-swivel inside rear view mirror, deep-center steering wheel with horn ring, manually-adjustable driver's seat, automatic dome light, cigarette lighter, coat hooks in rear compartment, dual horns, turn signals. [May 1958 for Hardtop and Convertible] 300-hp 352-cid Thunderbird Special V-8, four-barrel carburetor, dual exhausts, full-flow oil filtration, automatic choke, Cruise-O-Matic drive, Lifeguard padded instrument panel, cushioned sun visors, double-grip door locks, safety-swivel rear view mirror, deep-center steering wheel, manually-adjustable front seats, electric clock, automatic dome light in Hardtop and courtesy light in Convertible, cigarette lighter, gun sight front fender ornaments, dual horns and turn signals.

VIN:

The VIN plate was located on the left door pillar. The first symbol denoted the engine: H=352-cid/300-hp Thunderbird Special V-8. The second symbol indicated the model-year: 8=1958. The third symbol denoted the assembly plant: Y=Wixom (Novi), Michigan. The fourth symbol indicated the body type: H=Thunderbird Tudor Hardtop, J=Thunderbird two-door convertible. The fifth thru 10th symbols denoted sequential production number of the specific vehicle starting at 100001. The body number plate was located on the left front door hinge post. The serial number was the same as number on the VIN tag. Symbols below "BODY" were the body symbol code: 63A=Thunderbird Hardtop, 76A=Thunderbird Convertible. Symbols below "COLOR" were the paint color code. The first symbol indicated the lower body color. The second symbol, if used, indicated the upper body color on cars with two-tone paint. Symbols below "TRIM" were the trim combination code. Symbols below the "DATE" were the production date code. The number indicated the date of the month the car was made. The letters indicated the month of manufacture: A=January, B=February, C=March, D=April, E=May, F=June, G=July, H=August, J=September, K=October, L=November, M=December. Symbols below "TRANS" were the transmission code: 1-conventional three-speed manual transmission, 2=three-speed manual transmission with overdrive, 4=Cruise-O-Matic transmission. Symbols below "AXLE" were the axle code: 1=3.10, 3=3.70.

1958 Ford Thudebird two-door Sport Coupe (FMC)

1958 Ford Thunderbird two-door Convertible (PH)

Thunderbird (V-8)

Model No.	Body/ Style No.	Body Type and Seating	Factory Price	Shipping Weight	Production Total
H	63A	Tudor-4P	$3,631	3,708 lbs.	35,758
J	76A	2-dr. Convertible-4P	$3,914	3,733 lbs.	2,134

Engines:

Thunderbird Base V-8 (All transmissions): Overhead valve. Cast-iron block. B & S: 4.00 x 3.50 in. Displacement: 352 cid. Compression ratio: 10.2:1. Brake hp: 300 at 4600 rpm. Taxable hp: 51.2. Torque: 395 lbs.-ft. at 2800 rpm. Five main bearings. Valve lifters: solid (early) and hydraulic (late). Crankcase capacity: 5 qt. (add 1 qt. with new oil filter). Cooling system capacity: 19.5 qt. Dual exhausts. Carburetor: Ford-Holley Model B8A-9510-E four-barrel or Carter numbers 2640S-SA-SC four-barrel. Code H.

Chassis:

Wheelbase: 113.2 in. Overall length: 205.4 in. Overall width: 77.0 in. Overall height: (Hardtop) 54.5 in., (Convertible) 53.1 in. Front headroom (Hardtop): 34.5 in. Rear headroom (Hardtop): 33.3 in. Front seat cushion to floor height (Hardtop): 11 in. Rear seat cushion to floor height (Hardtop): 13.1 in. Front shoulder room (Hardtop): 56.2 in. Rear shoulder room (Hardtop): 54.1 in. Front hip room (Hardtop): 59.6 in. Rear hip room (Hardtop): 48.7 in. Front leg room (Hardtop): 43.4 in. Rear leg room (Hardtop): 38.1 in. Road clearance: 5.8 in. Front tread: 60 in. Rear tread: 57 in. Tires: 8.00 x 14 4-ply. Turning diameter: 39 ft.

Technical:

Steering ratio: 25.0:1. Chassis type: Welded, integral body and frame. Front suspension: Ball-joints, coil springs and tube shocks. Rear suspension: Trailing arm type with coil springs, rubber-mounted pivots and double-acting shock absorbers. Steering: Re-circulating ball type. Turning circle, curb-to-curb: 40.32 ft. Front brakes: 11-in. diameter double-sealed, ceramic linings. Rear brakes: 11-in. diameter double-sealed, ceramic linings. Brake swept area: (standard) 168.98 sq. in., (optional) 193.5 sq. in. sq. in. Standard transmission: Three-speed synchromesh with helical gears. Optional transmission: Planetary overdrive with planetary gears. Optional transmission: Cruise-O-Matic torque converter transmission with planetary gears. Standard rear axle ratio: (manual and overdrive) 3.70, (Cruise-O-Matic): 3.10. Gas tank: 20 gallons (premium fuel required).

Options:

Manually adjustable front passenger seat (Manually-adjustable front seats became standard in May 1958). Power brakes ($37). Overdrive transmission ($108). Power windows ($101). Four-way power driver's seat ($64). Tube-type radio ($77). Signal-seeking radio ($99). Five 8.00 x 14 whitewall tires in place of black sidewall ($36). I-Rest Tinted glass ($20). Windshield washers-wipers ($12). Back-up lights ($10). Power steering ($69). MagicAire heater ($95). SelectAire conditioner (N/A). Leather interior ($106). Radio antennas. Seat belts. Positive windshield wipers. Electric clock (became standard after May 1958). Outside mirrors. Rear fender shields. Fashion-Ray wheel covers. Locking gas cap (first offered in January 1958). Gun sight front fender ornaments (became standard in May 1958). Cruise-O-Matic transmission (Sale literature said "optional, it was installed in production" after May 1958).

History:

Henry Ford II remained President of Ford Motor Company in 1958 and Earnest R. Breech remained Chairman of the Board. Robert S. McNamara was a Ford Motor Company Group Vice President and President of the Car and Truck Division. J. O. Wright was a FoMoCo Vice President and General Manager of Ford Division. The new four-passenger Thunderbird entered production on Jan. 13, 1958. It was built in the brand new Wixom factory near Novi, Michigan. alongside the 1958 Lincoln and Continental Mark III. Since it was all-new, it arrived in showrooms later than other 1958 Ford products. Dealer introductions took place on Feb. 13, 1958. The convertible was added to the line on May 1, 1958. T-Bird product planner Tom Case had wanted to continue the two-passenger model (with a new power top) and add a four-passenger model. This was guaranteed to bring a sales increase, but there was no guarantee profits would go up. Robert S. McNamara, the new general manager of Ford Division told Case to drop the two-car idea. McNamara fought with the board of directors to get the four-passenger car he knew would bring higher profits. The T-Bird became one of only two U.S. cars to increase sales in 1958. "Despite a late introduction and the fact that 1958 was a miserable flop as a year for selling cars, the '58 T-Bird sold 37,000 units and dealers ended up at changeover time with orders backlogged for 800 cars," is how *Hot Rod* magazine put it in July 1959. *Ward's Automotive Yearbook* reported that Thunderbird sales climbed from 1.3 percent to 3.8 percent of Ford's sales total. Optional power plants had been considered for the 1958 Thunderbird, since the long list of engines offered in 1957 had helped to sell cars. One plan was to use the 361-cid Edsel V-8 with a choice of four horsepower ratings. However, the total budget for styling, engineering and tooling work was only $50 million. After tooling costs absorbed 90 percent of the money, the plan was changed to one offering only one engine. A 430-cid V-8 was mentioned in some T-Bird literature and advertisements. It is believed that this engine was not used in production cars. It was a Lincoln V-8 suitable only for use with Cruise-O-Matic (Lincoln called it Turbo-Drive) transmission. *Motor Trend* tested a prototype Thunderbird with this engine and shaved about two seconds off normal 0-60 times. The 352-cid-powered 1958 T-Bird hardtop was tested at 12.9 seconds for 0-to-60 mph and 17.6 seconds for the quarter mile. The 1958 Thunderbird was only 511 lb. heavier than a Ford Custom Tudor V-8, but lacked the Ford's ladder frame and had a shorter wheelbase. Gutted of its console and other goodies, the T-Bird held promise as a stock car racer. This wasn't lost on NASCAR fans. Some car builders wanted to start constructing competition versions of the four-seat T-Bird right away. As things turned out, the "Square-Bird" would go stock car racing, but not in 1958. A one-year-only coil spring rear suspension was introduced in anticipation of using the "Ford Aire" system — an early type of air suspension — in the T-Bird. When Ford Aire proved unreliable, the idea of using it on the T-Bird was dropped, but Ford was stuck with the coil springs for 1958. T-Birds went back to leaf springs in 1959. *Motor Trend* magazine picked the 1958 Thunderbird to win its "Car of the Year" award. Ford Motor Company produced its 50 millionth vehicle of all time on March 17, 1958 (hopefully it was green).

1959 Thunderbird

Thunderbird — Series H/J — (V-8): The 1959 T-Bird was changed very little from 1958. A new horizontal louver pattern filled the "air scoop" grille and was repeated in the recessed taillight panels. Instead of hash marks, the body-side projectiles had a chrome arrowhead at the front of the bulge. Thunderbird nameplates were moved from the front fenders to the doors and decorated the projectiles. The round medallion seen on the rear window pillar of the 1958 hardtop was replaced by a sculptured Thunderbird medallion. The convertible's top was power operated and folded completely into the trunk. The base 352-cid V-8 had ignition improvements and a new Holley model 9510 four-barrel carburetor. A 430-cid Thunderbird Special V-8 was optional, but only with SelectShift Cruise-O-Matic transmission. This V-8 did not have a conventional combustion chamber in the cylinder head. The valves seated on a flat head surface and the combustion chamber was formed between the tops of the pistons and the top of the block, which was milled 10 degrees from perpendicular to the cylinder bore.

1959 Ford Thunderbird two-door Sport Coupe (OCW)

Dual exhausts were standard with both V-8s. Other technical revisions in T-Birds included a new radiator fan, a new auxiliary coolant tank, a relocated windshield washer system, an "Angle-Poised" ball-joint front suspension, four-foot wide doors, 20 cu. ft. of trunk space and individually adjustable front seats. The T-Bird bucket seats had a kind of rounded and overstuffed look. The front passenger seat folded to permit entry into the rear from the curb side of the car. The 1959 instruments and gauges had white faces, instead of the previous black ones. The T-Bird's unit-constructed body had the floor pan, frame, body side panels, front and rear fenders, roof panel and cross braces all welded together into one durable unit of double-walled sculptured steel. There was a new leaf-spring rear suspension with longitudinal springs on either side that gave a more evenly balanced ride with slightly less lean in the corners. Standard equipment included: Built-in armrests, floor carpets, individually-adjusted seats with deep-foam rubber seat cushions and backs, full folding front passenger seat, optional choice of deep-pleated all-vinyl interior or linen seat inserts with vinyl bolsters, padded dash and sun visors, front and rear ashtrays, cigarette lighter, electric clock, courtesy lights, dual exhausts, fuel filter, a deep-center "Lifeguard" steering wheel with a horn ring, turn signals, dual horns with horn ring, spare tire and bumper jack.

VIN:

The VIN plate was located on the left door pillar. The first symbol denoted the engine: H=352-cid/300-hp Thunderbird Special V-8, J=430-cid/350-hp Thunderbird Special V-8. The second symbol indicated the model-year: 9=1959. The third symbol denoted the assembly plant: Y=Wixom (Novi), Michigan. The fourth symbol was the body type: H=Thunderbird Tudor Hardtop, J=Thunderbird two-door convertible. The fifth thru 10th symbols denoted the sequential production number of the specific vehicle starting at 100001. The body number plate was located on the left front door hinge post. The serial number was the same as the number on the VIN tag. Symbols below "BODY" were the body symbol code: 63A=Thunderbird Hardtop, 76A=Thunderbird Convertible. Symbols below "COLOR" were the paint color code. The first symbol indicated the lower body color. The second symbol, if used, indicated the upper body color on cars with two-tone paint. Symbols below "TRIM" were the trim combination code. Symbols below "DATE" were the production date code. The number indicated the date of the month the car was made: A=January, B=February, C=March, D=April, E=May, F=June, G=July, H=August, J=September, K=October, L=November, M=December. Symbols below "TRANS" were the transmission code: 1=conventional three-speed manual transmission, 2=three-speed manual transmission with overdrive, 4=Cruise-O-Matic transmission. Symbols below "AXLE" were the axle code: 1=3.10, 3=3.70 and 0=2.91:1.

Thunderbird (V-8)

Model No.	Body/Style No.	Body Type and Seating	Factory Price	Shipping Weight	Production Total
H	63A	Tudor-4P	$3,368	3,813 lbs.	57,195
J	76A	2-dr. Convertible-4P	$3,631	3,903 lbs.	10,261

Engine:

Thunderbird 352 Special V-8 (All transmissions): Overhead valve. Cast-iron block. B & S: 4.00 x 3.50 in. Displacement: 352 cid. Compression ratio: 9.6:1. Brake hp: 300 at 4600 rpm. Taxable hp: 51.2. Torque: 395 lbs.-ft. at 2800 rpm. Five main bearings. Hydraulic valve lifters. Crankcase capacity: 5 qt. (add 1 qt. with new oil filter). Cooling system capacity: 19.5 qt. Dual exhausts. Carburetor: Ford four-barrel Model 5752304 and 5752305 or Holley four-barrel. Code H.

Thunderbird 352 Special V-8 (Cruise-O-Matic only): Overhead valve. Cast-iron block. B & S: 4.30 x 3.70 in. Displacement: 430 cid. Compression ratio: 10.0:1. Brake hp: 350 at 4600 rpm. Taxable hp: 51.2. Torque: 490 lbs.-ft. at 2800 rpm. Five main bearings. Hydraulic valve lifters. Crankcase capacity: 5 qt. (add 1 qt. with new oil filter). Cooling system capacity: 19.5 qt. Dual exhausts. Carburetor: Holley four-barrel Model 4160-C. Code J.

Chassis:

Wheelbase: 113 in. Overall length: 205.3 in. Overall width: 77.0 in. Overall height: (Hardtop) 54.2 in., (Convertible) 53.1 in. Front headroom (Hardtop): 34.5 in. Rear headroom (Hardtop): 33.3 in. Front seat cushion to floor height (Hardtop): 11 in. Rear seat cushion to floor height (Hardtop): 13.1 in. Front shoulder room (Hardtop): 56.2 in. Rear shoulder room (Hardtop): 54.1 in. Front hip room (Hardtop): 59.6 in. Rear hip room (Hardtop): 48.7 in. Front leg room (Hardtop): 43.4 in. Rear leg room (Hardtop): 38.1 in. Road clearance: 5.80 in. Front tread: 60 in. Rear tread: 57 in. Tires: 8.00 x 14 4-ply.

Technical:

Steering ratio: 25.0:1. Chassis type: Welded, integral body and frame. Front suspension: Ball-joints, coil springs and tube shocks. Rear suspension: Outboard-mounted rear leaf springs, shackles and wind-up control rubber bumpers over springs with double-acting shock

1959 Ford Thunderbird two-door Convertible (OCW)

absorbers. Steering: Re-circulating ball type. Turning circle, curb-to-curb: 40.32 ft. Front brakes: 11-in. diameter double-sealed, ceramic linings. Rear brakes: 11-in. diameter double-sealed, ceramic linings. Brake swept area: 194.0 sq. in. sq. in. Standard transmission: Three-speed synchromesh with helical gears. Optional transmission: Planetary overdrive with planetary gears. Optional transmission: Cruise-O-Matic torque converter transmission with planetary gears. Standard rear axle ratio with manual transmission: 3.70. Standard rear axle with overdrive: 3.70. Standard rear axle ratio with 352-cid V-8 and Cruise-O-Matic: 3.10. Standard rear axle ratio with 430-cid V-8 and Cruise-O-Matic: 2.91. Gas tank: 20 gallons (premium fuel required).

Options:

Cruise-O-Matic ($242). Overdrive ($145). Radio ($105). Signal seeker radio ($92.60*). Rear seat speaker ($13.50*). Power brakes ($43). Fresh air heater and defroster ($83). Driver's side power seat ($86). Select Air Conditioner ($446). 350-hp engine ($177). Genuine leather interior ($106). Rear fender shields ($27). Two seat belts ($26). White sidewall tires ($36). Full wheel disks ($17). Back up lights ($10). Tinted glass ($38). Power windows ($102). Windshield washers ($14). Left-hand OSRV mirror ($5) Tu-Tone paint ($26). Two-speed electric wipers ($7.10*). Pair of regular floor mats ($3.50*). Pair of contoured floor mats ($7.95*). Equa-Lock differential ($32.15*). Heavy-duty 70-amp battery ($8). Door-mounted side view mirror ($5.95*). Fender-mounted side view mirror ($8.95*). Visor-vanity mirror ($1.95*). Factory undercoating ($15*). Tu-Tone paint ($22*). Clear plastic seat covers ($29.95*). Antifreeze ($6.95*). Tissue dispenser ($6.75 *)

*Note: This indicates a dealer wholesale price since retail prices for these items are unknown.

History:

Henry Ford II was President of Ford Motor Company again in 1959. Earnest R. Breech remained Chairman of the Board. Robert S. McNamara was a Ford Motor Company Group Vice President and President of the Car and Truck Division. J. O. Wright was a FoMoCo Vice President and General Manager of Ford Division. The 1959 T-Bird was introduced on October 17, 1958, ten days later than other Fords. Despite a 116-day steel workers strike, Ford continued operating the Thunderbird assembly lines with minimum downtime. Thunderbird production for the calendar year improved by 42 percent. *Hot Rod* magazine did a test of the 430-cid Thunderbird in its July 1959 issue. With the 430-cid 350-hp V-8 the T-Bird hardtop did 0-to-60 mph in 9.0 seconds and covered the quarter mile in 17.0 seconds at 86.57 mph. The offering of a larger V-8 had a big influence on the Thunderbird's role in professional motor sports. The unit-bodied T-Bird was shorter in wheelbase and lighter in weight than standard Fords with ladder-type frames, which enhanced its racing potential. Ford formed an association with Holman & Moody, of Charlotte, N.C., for the construction of several very hot 1959 T-Bird stock cars that made their racing debut at the new 2.5-mile International Daytona International Speedway in February. After completion by Holman & Moody, these cars were sold to the public. In race-ready form, the cars went for $5,500. T-Bird driver Johnny Beauchamp, of Harlan, Iowa was named the unofficial winner of the Daytona 500. Beauchamp's T-Bird, Lee Petty's Oldsmobile and Joe Weatherly's Chevrolet crossed the finish line neck-and-neck. Weatherly was one lap down, so Beauchamp and Petty were the leaders. When photos of the finish were reviewed by NASCAR officials, the camera showed that Petty had crossed the line first. Beauchamp was credited with second. T-Birds also held positions eight, nine and 13. The AMT model company offered a choice of 10 special AMT 3 in 1 Daytona Beach Race Car Kits for only $1.39 or $1.49 each. The 1960 Thunderbird model was one of the three higher-priced kits, along with the Buick and Corvette of the same year. Like the full-size racers, the models carried decals on their body for the hot 350-hp Thunderbird V-8. At least two of the Holman & Moody Thunderbird race cars survive. In 1989, Billy Cooper & Associates of Barnwell, S.C. obtained one of the cars in exchange for a complete restoration. This car was restored to like-new condition and displayed at the Klassics Auto Museum in Daytona Beach, Florida. A few years ago, a second car with the special racing equipment, but non-racing trim, showed up at the Barrett-Jackson Classic Car Auction in Scottsdale, Arizona.

1960 Thunderbird

Thunderbird — Series 7 — (V-8): The four-passenger "Squarebird" styling of 1958 and 1959 was carried forward for one more year in 1960. There was a new grille. It had a large, horizontal main bar that was intersected by three vertical bars. Behind the bars was a grid-pattern insert. There was a trio of chrome hash marks, each consisting of three vertical bars, decorating the rear fenders. They were positioned towards the rear, just ahead of new taillight clusters that had three round lenses on each side. The hardtop model's rear roof pillars had elongated Thunderbird emblems. There was also a winged badge on the trunk, just above the license plate. The lower body side projectiles now carried chrome Thunderbird scripts. A manually-operated sliding sunroof was a new option for hardtops. Cars with sun roofs were known as Golde Top models. Golde was the name of the German company that licensed the sun roof design to Ford. A large, circular chrome fixture inside the car locked the sliding panel in place. It was the first sunroof offered on a postwar domestic production cars. Only 2,536 buyers ordered it. Inside the 1960 Thunderbird had the same kind of dual-pod dash, front bucket seats and a panel console. There were several new upholstery options. One two-tone design had large squares stitched into the seat inserts and upper door panels. Another choice had lengthwise pleating on the seats, vertical pleats on the upper door panels and monochromatic color schemes. The rear seats had built-in armrests. Also new was a polarized day/night inside rearview mirror. There were two 1960 T-Bird engines, the 352-cid Thunderbird Special V-8 and the 350-hp Thunderbird 430 Special V-8 that won so many 1959 stock car races. A chrome dress-up kit was available to make the engine compartments shine. Ford cleverly advertised "Precision Fuel Induction" for the larger engine, which actually used a conventional Holley four-barrel carburetor with "precision fuel metering." Ford promoted that Cruise-O-Matic Drive was optional with either engine, although it was actually *mandatory* with the 430-cid Lincoln motor. The 352-cid V-8 also came with a three-speed manual gearbox or three-speed manual with overdrive. Standard equipment included: Built-in dual exhausts, fuel filter, oil filter, 352-cid four-barrel V-8 engine, padded instrument panel and sun visors, electric clock with sweep second hand, courtesy lights, turn signals, deep-center steering wheel, dual horns and horn rings, individually-adjustable front seats, day-night tilt type rearview mirror, double-grip door locks, wheel covers, built-in arm rests, floor carpets, full-width foam rubber seat, all-vinyl upholstery, ash tray, cigar lighter, air cleaner and five black 8.00 x 14 tubeless tires.

VIN:

The die was stamped on top of the front fender crossbar to right of hood lock striker plate. The first symbol denoted the model-year: 0=1960. The second symbol denoted the assembly plant: Y=Wixom (Novi), Michigan. The third symbol denoted the car-line: 7=Thunderbird. The fourth symbol revealed the body type: 1=Thunderbird Tudor Hardtop, 3=Thunderbird two-door convertible. The fifth symbol indicated the engine: Y=352-cid/300-hp Interceptor V-8, J=430-cid/350-hp Thunderbird Special V-8. The sixth through 11th symbols were the sequential production numbers of the specific vehicle starting at 100001. The body number plate was located on the left front body pillar. The serial number was the same as the number on the VIN tag. Symbols above "BDY" were the body symbol code: 63A=Thunderbird Hardtop, 76A=Thunderbird Convertible. Symbols above "CLR" were the paint color code. The first symbol indicated the lower body color. The second symbol, if used, indicated the upper body color on cars with two-tone paint. Symbols above "TRM" were the trim combination code. Symbols below "DT" were the production date code. The number indicated the date of the month the car was made. The letters indicated the month of manufacture: A=January, B=February, C=March, D=April, E=May, F=June, G=July, H=August, J=September, K=October, L=November, M=December, N=January and P=February, etc. (Ford listed two-year codes in case the 1960 model run was extended). Symbols above DSO indicated information including the Ford Motor Co. Sales District Code. Symbols above AX indicated the rear axle. Axles used on 1960 Thunderbirds were: 3=3.10:1, 9=3.70:1. Symbols above TR indicate type of transmission: 1=Three-

speed manual, 2=Three-speed manual with overdrive and 4=SelectShift Cruise-O-Matic. Vinyl convertible tops came in Black (except with trims 52 and 72), White (with all trims), and Blue (with trims 52 and 72 only). All convertible tops included a black headlining.

Thunderbird (V-8)

Model No.	Body/ Style No.	Body Type and Seating	Factory Price	Shipping Weight	Production Total
73	63A	Tudor-4P	$3,426	3,799 lbs.	78,447
71	76A	2-dr. Convertible-4P	$3,860	3,897 lbs.	11,860
73	63B	2-dr. Golde Top-4P	$3,638	3,805 lbs.	2,536

Engines:

Interceptor Special V-8 (Base Thunderbird V-8): Overhead valve. Cast-iron block. B & S: 4.00 x 3.50 in. Displacement: 352 cid. Compression ratio: 9.6:1. Brake hp: 300 at 4600 rpm. Taxable hp: 51.2. Torque: 381 lbs.-ft. at 2800 rpm. Five main bearings. Hydraulic valve lifters. Crankcase capacity: 5 qt. (add 1 qt. with new oil filter). Cooling system capacity: 19.5 qt. Dual exhausts. Carburetor: Carburetor: Ford-Holley four-barrel Model COAE-9510-J with standard transmission or COAE-9510-K with automatic transmission. Code Y.

Note: Not mentioned in early 1960 Ford literature were the aluminum intake and Holley carburetor. These were not available in cars with power steering or power brakes.

Thunderbird Special V-8 (Optional Thunderbird V-8): Overhead valve. Cast-iron block. B & S: 4.30 x 3.70 in. Displacement: 430 cid. Compression ratio: 10.0:1. Brake hp: 350 at 4600 rpm. Taxable hp: 59.15. Torque: 490 at 2800 rpm. Five main bearings. Hydraulic valve lifters. Crankcase capacity: 5 qt. (add 1 qt. with new oil filter). Cooling system capacity: 20 qt. with heater (16.5 qt. without heater). Dual exhausts. Carburetor: Carter AFB No. 2992S. Cruise-O-Matic mandatory. Code J.

Chassis:

Wheelbase: 113 in. Overall length: 205.32 in. Overall width: 77.0 in. Overall height: (Hardtop) 54.5 in., (Convertible) 53.1 in. Front headroom (Hardtop): 34.5 in. Rear headroom (Hardtop): 33.3 in. Front shoulder room: 56.2 in. Rear shoulder room: 54.1 in. Front hip room: 59.6 in. Rear hip room: 48.7 in. Front legroom: 43.4 in. Rear legroom: 38.1 in. Road clearance: 5.80 in. Front tread: 60 in. Rear tread: 57 in. Tires: 8.00 x 14 4-ply.

Technical:

Steering ratio: 25.0:1. Chassis type: Welded, integral body and frame. Front suspension: Ball-joints, coil springs and tube shocks. Rear suspension: Outboard-mounted rear leaf springs, shackles and wind-up control rubber bumpers over springs with double-acting shock absorbers. Steering: Re-circulating ball type. Turning circle, curb-to-curb: 40.32 ft. Front brakes: 11-in. diameter double-sealed, ceramic linings. Rear brakes: 11-in. diameter double-sealed, ceramic linings. Brake swept area: 194.0 sq. in. sq. in. Standard transmission: Three-speed synchromesh with helical gears. Optional transmission: Planetary overdrive with planetary gears. Optional transmission: Cruise-O-Matic torque converter transmission with planetary gears. Standard rear axle ratio with manual transmission: 3.70. Standard rear axle with overdrive: 3.70. Standard rear axle ratio with 352-cid V-8 and Cruise-O-Matic: 3.10. Standard rear axle ratio with 430-cid V-8 and Cruise-O-Matic: 2.91. Gas tank: 20 gallons (premium fuel required).

Options:

Cruise-O-Matic drive ($242). Overdrive ($144.50). Central console radio and antenna ($112.80). MagicAire heater and defroster ($82.90). Air conditioner ($465.80). Tinted glass ($37.90). 8.00 x 14 rayon whitewall tires ($35.70). 8.00 x 14 nylon white sidewall tires ($63.50). 8.50 x 14 white sidewall tires (Price not available). 350-hp V-8 engine ($177). Master Guide power steering ($75.30). Power windows ($102.10). Swift Sure power brakes ($43.20). Four-way power driver's seat ($92.10). Left- or right-hand OSRV mirror ($5.10). Back-up lights ($9.50). Windshield washers ($13.70). Rear fender shields — skirts ($26.60). Front seat belts ($22.80). Leather interior ($106.20). Heavy-duty 70-amp battery in Hardtop ($7.60). Tu-Tone paint ($25.80). Underseal ($14.10). Sliding sun roof ($212.40). Two seat belts ($22.80). Two-speed electric windshield wipers (Price not available). Pair of regular floor mats (Price not available). Pair of contoured floor mats (Price not available). Equa-Lock differential (Price not available). Fender-mounted side view mirror (Price not available). Visor-vanity mirror (Price not available). Clear plastic seat covers (Price not available). Antifreeze (Price not available). Tissue dispenser (Price not available). Full wheel covers (Price not available). Note: Based on model-year production.

History:

Henry Ford II was President of Ford Motor Company again in 1959. Earnest R. Breech remained Chairman of the Board. Robert S. McNamara was a Ford Motor Company Group Vice President and President of the Car and Truck Division. J. O. Wright was a FoMoCo Vice President and General Manager of Ford Division. A total of 92,843

1960 Ford Thunderbird two-door Convertible (PH)

T-Birds, representing 1.5 percent of total industry, were produced for the model year. Calendar year output of 87,218 T-Birds was up 15.2 percent over 75,723 in 1959 and represented an all-time high for the nameplate. Calendar year dealer sales were 81,555 T-Birds, which was 5.8 percent of total Ford sales. Research shows that the sun roof model and the Golde Top model were the same car. Production of 1960 T-Birds ended earlier than usual, in July 1960. The model changeover was pushed up because a total redesign was coming in 1961. Almost as soon as production ended, two special Thunderbirds were built. They had stainless steel bodies. Allegheny-Ludlum Steel Co. and Budd Body Co. teamed up to make the two cars as a showcase for their product lines. The "Stainless Steel T-Birds" had to be built as the last 1959 production units, since fabricating the stainless steel bodies wrecked the dies. As in 1959, the 430-powered T-Bird was capable of a nine second 0-60 runs, but *Motor Trend* said of the T-Bird, "What it does have is originality, freshness and newness of concept. This is its secret. It has, more than any other current domestic car, the spirit and quality that made the classic roadsters and tourers of the 1930s such memorable favorites." "Uncle" Tom McCahill, the famous automotive writer, said the Thunderbird made him picture a well-off "club woman" arriving at a fancy piano concert in a Duesenberg. "For many people, owning a new T-Bird is a last backwards look at their fleeting youth," he said. "And if they get a bounce out of it, I'm all for it." After the 1957 Automobile Manufacturer's Association ban on factory participation in auto racing, President Robert S. McNamara was happy to eliminate Ford's racing budget. Over half of the Thunderbird stock cars that raced in 1960 were 1959 models. At least some of these were cars built and prepped by racers John Holman and Ralph Moody. Ford sold its racing parts to Holman & Moody, who continued building Ford race cars. The six 1959 Thunderbirds with 430-cid/350-hp V-8s built by Holman & Moody passed into different hands in 1960. A few 1960 T-Birds were also campaigned by private teams. Fords wound up with 15 national wins, but none were earned by Thunderbirds. Pontiacs had become dominant in stock car racing, with Chevrolets and Plymouths running close behind them. Two new super-speedways, Charlotte and Atlanta, opened in 1960. Together with Daytona and Darlington, that brought the number of major races to four. It was the first year that stock car races were televised nationally. Ford's advertising and public relations people were aware of the opportunity for product exposure. When newly elected U.S. President John F. Kennedy picked McNamara to serve as his Secretary of Defense, the door was opened for Ford's "Total Performance" program. This was launched, under Lee A. Iacocca — a real automotive enthusiast — in 1961.

1960 Ford Thunderbird two-door Sport Coupe (FMC)

1961 Thunderbird

Thunderbird — Series 7 — (V-8): The 1961 T-Bird was all new. Instead of corners and angles, it had smooth, curving lines. Ford's personal-luxury car had a new chassis and a larger, more powerful engine. "To many Thunderbird owners, the greatly restyled 1961 model will look like a bird from another nest," said *Science and Mechanics* magazine in December 1960. "Because this is an age of aerodynamics, high speeds and rockets, we must keep in tune with the times," said George Walker, Ford's vice president of styling. The downward-curved hood seemed to be moving forward while the car was standing still. Two headlights appeared on either side and were nicely integrated into the upper edge of the grille. Gone were the "eyebrows" that shielded the 1958 to 1960 headlights. A swept-under grille blended in smoothly with the rest of the torpedo-shaped car. Walker said that sculpturing was dropped from

1961 Ford Thunderbird two-door Sport Coupe (OCW)

the T-Bird because it added nothing to aerodynamic design. Despite its departure from earlier T-Birds, the new model did have some traditional design elements like a sloped nose and a hood scoop. The roof was fairly flat. The rear roof pillars had a "formal" T-Bird-like appearance. Although updated inside, it remained a four-place automobile with bucket seats and a center console. Short, outward-canted rear fins and round taillights were continued. Unit construction remained a T-Bird benefit. The frame and body components were welded into an integral unit, rather than bolted together. Ford actually made the car of two unitized sections with a rigid, box-sectioned joint at the cowl area. For the first time, the T-Bird hood was hinged at the rear. It was wider than the 1960 hood, while the fenders were narrower and were bolted on to make body repairs simpler. A new, thin-pillared "straight line" windshield was seen. Ford offered 19 different "Diamond Lustre" exterior colors and 30 two-tones (including seven reversible combinations). The "Luxury Lounge" interior came in 16 different upholstery combinations and six colors. The 25-percent-smaller center console added legroom. One new idea was gluing the rearview mirror to the windshield. The convertible featured a fully-automatic top-retracting mechanism operated by the turn of a switch on the inside of the left-hand door. The lifting mechanism and pump assembly were relocated to the quarter panels, instead of behind the seat. To raise the top, the trunk lid opened to the rear and powerful motors lifted the top, extending it nearly straight up until it lowered over the passenger compartment. This isolated the top-riser mechanism from the passengers and made top operation quieter. A drawback was a noticeable lack of storage space in the trunk when the top was folded and stored there. Standard equipment included: Built-in dual exhausts, fuel filter, oil filter, 390-cid four-barrel V-8 engine, Lifeguard padded instrument panel and cushioned sun visors, electric clock with sweep second hand, automatic courtesy lights, turn signals, deep-center steering wheel, dual horn and horn rings, individually-adjustable front seats, Safety-Swivel day-night tilt type mirror, double-grip door locks, full wheel covers, built-in armrests, floor carpets, full-width foam rubber seat, all-vinyl upholstery, ash tray, cigar lighter, air cleaner, and five black 8.00 x 14 tubeless tires, Cruise-O-Matic transmission, power brakes, power steering, two-speed electric windshield wipers, undercoating, safety belt anchors, coat hooks, parking brake light, glove box light, ash tray light, back-up lights, fully-lined luggage compartment with light and positive crankcase ventilation system on California cars only.

VIN:

The VIN was die-stamped on top of front fender cross-bar to right of hood lock striker plate. The first symbol denoted the model-year: 1=1961. The second symbol indicated the assembly plant: Y=Wixom (Novi), Michigan. Pilot models possibly were built at the Pilot Plant, Dearborn, Mich. (Plant code S). The third symbol denoted the car-line: 7=Thunderbird. The fourth symbol indicated the body type: 1=Thunderbird Tudor Hardtop, 3=Thunderbird two-door convertible. The fifth symbol indicated the engine: R=390-cid/275-hp low-compression export-only V-8, Z=390-cid/300-hp Thunderbird V-8, Z 0r Q=390-cid/375-hp Thunderbird Special V-8, Z=390-cid/401-hp Thunderbird Special 6V V-8. Sixth thru 11th symbols denote sequential production number of specific vehicle starting at 100001. The body number plate was located on the left front body pillar. The serial number was the same as the number on the VIN tag. Symbols above "BDY" were the body symbol code: 63A=Thunderbird Hardtop, 76A=Thunderbird Convertible. Symbols above "CLR" were the paint color code. The first symbol indicated the lower body color. The second symbol, if used, indicated the upper body color on cars with two-tone paint. Symbols above "TRM" were the trim combination code. Symbols above "DT" were the production date code. The number indicated the date of the month the car was made. The letters indicated the month of manufacture: A=January, B=February, C=March, D=April, E=May, F=June, G=July, H=August, J=September, K=October, L=November, M=December, N=January and P=February, etc. (Ford listed two-year codes in case the model run was extended). Symbols above DSO indicated information including the Ford Motor Co. Sales District Code. Symbols above AX indicate rear axle. Axles used on 1961 Thunderbirds were: 1=2.91:1 (also noted as 3.00:1 and 3.56:1), 3=3.10:1, 6=3.00:1, A=3.56:1 Equa-Lock, F=3.56:1 Equa-Lock and H=2.91:1 Equa-Lock. Symbols above TR indicated the type of transmission: All Thunderbirds from 1961 until the 1980s came only with SelectShift Cruise-O-Matic Drive.

1961 Ford Thunderbird two-door Convertible (OCW)

Thunderbird (V-8)

Model No.	Body/ Style No.	Body Type and Seating	Factory Price	Shipping Weight	Production Total
7	63A	2-dr. Hardtop-4P	$4,170	3,958 lbs.	62,535
7	76A	2-dr. Convertible-4P	$4,637	4,130 lbs.	10,516

Engines:

Thunderbird 390 Special Base V-8: Overhead valve. Cast-iron block. B & S: 4.05 x 3.78 in. Displacement: 390 cid. Brake hp: 275. Taxable hp: 52.49. Five main bearings. Hydraulic valve lifters. Crankcase capacity: 5 qt. (add 1 qt. with new oil filter). Cooling system capacity: 19 qt. Carburetor: Ford four-barrel Model CIAE-9510-AG with standard transmission or CIAE-9510-AH with automatic transmission. Code Z.

Thunderbird 390 Special Base V-8: Overhead valve. Cast-iron block. B & S: 4.05 x 3.78 in. Displacement: 390 cid. Compression ratio: 9.60:1. Brake hp: 300 at 4600 rpm. Taxable hp: 52.49. Torque: 427 lbs.-ft. at 3200 rpm. Five main bearings. Hydraulic valve lifters. Crankcase capacity: 5 qt. (add 1 qt. with new oil filter). Cooling system capacity: 19 qt. Carburetor: Ford four-barrel Model CIAE-9510-AG with standard transmission or CIAE-9510-AH with automatic transmission. Code Z.

Thunderbird 390 Special Optional V-8: Overhead valve. Cast-iron block. B & S: 4.05 x 3.78 in. Displacement: 390 cid. Compression ratio: 10.60:1. Brake hp: 375 at 6000 rpm. Taxable hp: 52.49. Torque: 427 lbs.-ft. at 3400 rpm. Five main bearings. Solid valve lifters. Crankcase capacity: 5 qt. (add 1 qt. with new oil filter). Cooling system capacity: 19 qt. Carburetor: Ford four-barrel Model CIAE-9510-AG with standard transmission or CIAE-9510-AH with automatic transmission. Code Q.

Note: Some cars were delivered with the intake manifold and carburetors in the trunk.

Thunderbird 390 Special 6-V Optional V-8: Overhead valve. Cast-iron block. B & S: 4.05 x 3.78 in. Displacement: 390 cid. Compression ratio: 10.60:1. Brake hp: 401 at 6000 rpm. Taxable hp: 52.49. Torque: 430 lbs.-ft. at 3500 rpm. Five main bearings. Solid valve lifters. Crankcase capacity: 5 qt. (add 1 qt. with new oil filter). Cooling system capacity: 19 qt. Carburetor: Three two-barrel carburetors. Code Q (Early versions may use code Z).

Chassis:

Wheelbase: 113 in. Overall length: 205 in. Overall width: 75.9 in. Overall height (hardtop): 53.9 in. Front headroom (hardtop): 34.2 in. Rear headroom (hardtop): 33.1 in. Front shoulder room (hardtop): 58 in. Rear shoulder room (hardtop): 55.6 in. Front hip room (hardtop): 59 in. Rear hip room (hardtop): 52.3 in. Front leg room (hardtop): 44.4 in. Rear leg room (hardtop): 57.7 in. Front tread: 61 in. Rear tread: 60 in. Tires: 8.00 x 14 4-ply.

Technical:

Steering ratio: 20.31:1. Turns lock-to-lock: 4.5. Turning circle, curb-to-curb: 40.2 ft. Chassis type: Welded, integral body and frame. Front suspension: Independent SLA (short-and-long-arm) with ball joints and coil springs. Rear suspension: Hotchkiss. Front brakes: 11.03 x 3.00-in. drums. Rear brakes: 11.03 x 2.50-in. drums. Brake swept area: 233.75 sq. in. Standard transmission: SelectShift Cruise-O-Matic Drive. Gas tank: 20 gallons (premium fuel required). Weight distribution: 66 percent front/44 percent rear. Fuel economy: 13-21 mpg. Driving Range: 260 to 420 miles.

Options:

Push-button radio and antenna ($112.80). MagicAire fresh air heater ($82.90). SelectAire conditioner ($462.80). I-Rest tinted glass ($43). 8.00 x 14 rayon whitewall tires ($42.10). 8.00 x 14 nylon white sidewall tires ($70.40). Power windows ($106.20). Four-way power driver's seat ($92.10). Four-way power passenger's seat ($92.10). Left- or right-hand OSRV mirror ($5.10). Electric windshield washers ($13.70). Rear fender shields — skirts ($26.60). Lifeguard front seat safety belts ($22.80). Leather interior ($106.20). Heavy-duty 70-amp battery ($7.60). Tu-Tone paint ($25.80). Equa-Lock differential axle ($38.60). Movable Swing-Away steering column ($25.10).

History:

Henry Ford II was Board Chairman of Ford Motor Company. John Dykstra was President of FoMoCo. Lee Iacocca was a FoMoCo Vice President and General Manager of Ford Division. M.S. McLaughlin was general sales manager of Ford Division. A total of 73,051 T-Birds, representing 1.4 percent of total industry, was produced for the model year in the Wixom plant. Calendar year output of 88,207 T-Birds represented another all-time high for the nameplate. Calendar year dealer sales were 85,142 T-Birds, which was 6.2 percent of total Ford sales. *Motor Trend* made a "Special Report" on the all-new 1961 T-Bird in its December 1960 issue, picturing the car with a 1957 two-seat model. Associate editor John Lawlor had praise for everything from the Swing-Away steering wheel to the new springs and wider tread width. He found that riders were well-insulated from road shocks and vibrations. The car cornered with less lean than previous T-Birds and had improved brakes. Lawlor was unable to get any hard performance figures, as he was driving a pre-production car at Ford's Dearborn test track. "On the basis of the prototype, though, I believe the '61 model shows a new level of sophistication in its engineering," he wrote. "Without diminishing the particular appeal of the old two-seater nor the trailblazing of the previous four-seater, the latest Thunderbird looks to me like the best one yet." In February 1961, *Motor Trend* followed up its initial review with a road test article entitled "Thunderbird: A Real Change ... For the Better." The title said it all, as the report praised just about everything except luggage accommodations in the convertible. *Cars* magazine tested a pre-production convertible. A full-bore test of the '61 T-Bird's performance wasn't possible with the prototype. "Those figures registered indicated to our satisfaction that this 300-bhp T-Bird will hold its own with the hottest Detroit machinery, excepting the Corvette," said the editors. "We were assured by Ingram Taylor, quality analysis technician and former Ford test driver, that a '61 'Bird in good tune should attain a maximum speed in excess of 130 mph." Other tests recorded a 0-to-60 mph time of 8.5 seconds for a convertible with the 390-cid 300-hp V-8. Despite its performance numbers, the '61 T-Bird was not competitive in stock car racing. However, some 1959-1960 models continued to race. Many of the cars were battle-worn and fell into the hands of lesser known drivers with smaller budgets. Lenny Page did a good job racking up his number 3 Thunderbird in the 1961 Charlotte 400 race. The car spun out and slammed head-first into the guard rail. It then did a "180" and tail-boned into the guard rail again. Page's T-Bird was then hit by car number 35, a 1960 Pontiac Ventura, which inflicted more damage than the guard rail. The driver was injured in the accident, which was captured in a film sequence seen in the Feb. 1961 edition of *Motor Life*. The magazine advised that Page did recover from head injuries and neck lacerations that he endured during his wild ride.

1962 Thunderbird

Thunderbird — Series 8 — (V-8): Both T-Bird body styles carried over from 1961 had the same "projectile" front end and twin-jet-tube rear design. A reworked radiator grille featured four rows of shiny metal "drawer pulls" between thin horizontal bars. Replacing the four moldings stacked on the rear fender of the '61 model were horizontal "dashes" of ribbed chrome. Late in the spring, some cars were built with a horizontal chrome accessory strip on their body sides. The trademark large round taillights changed from 1961 and also had more chrome to dress them up. The hardtop model's roof was again slightly on the formal side. The convertible had a flip-up deck and "accordion" top mechanism that Tom McCahill joked about in *Mechanix Illustrated*. "The first time I lowered the top, I thought the car was about to eat itself," he said. "Deck flips open, panels unfold, the top shoots up, all to the accompaniment of a whining noise similar to launching a guided missile. The sight of this operation is enough to cause a coronary in a slightly inebriated 3rd Avenue playboy. The total operation makes Buck Rogers look like a rail-splitting partner of Abe Lincoln's and the end result, though successful in concealing the top, leaves less trunk room than you'll find in a Volkswagen." A new Landau or Landau Hardtop model featured a black or white vinyl top that looked

1962 Ford Thunderbird two-door Sport Coupe (OCW)

1962 Ford Thunderbird two-door Landau Hardtop (OCW)

like a leather-padded carriage top. To further this impression, it had landau irons on the sides of its rear roof panels. An English magazine, *The Motor Sport,* reported, "It's a very pleasing combination, with genuine leather upholstery optional on order." The number of Landaus built was not recorded separately, but the model pushed overall sales of the Thunderbird hardtop up by 7,000 units. Another new model called the Sports Roadster had a tonneau cover over the rear seats and Kelsey-Hayes wire wheels. Tom McCahill said, "Ford has fielded a convertible T-Bird, called a Sports Roadster, with some real wild innovations that are bound to have eyes popping in Peoria." The tonneau cover could be added or removed in less than three minutes. The headrest section was horseshoe-shaped and fit over the Thunderbird's bucket seats. A quick-release catch secured it to the transmission tunnel between the front seats. Sliding it under the deck lid secured it at the rear. It was possible to raise or lower the convertible top with the tonneau in place. The seat back recessed into the headrest for a smooth, aerodynamic fit. A gap between the bottom edge of the tonneau and the rear seat was provided. You could slide small items under the cover and onto the rear seat cushion for storage after folding the front seat forward. *Car Life* magazine compared the Sport Roadster's long rear end to the deck of the aircraft carrier *USS Enterprise.* "As a prestige car in the true Midwest culture school, this little item should be hard to beat," chimed McCahill. "It won't get a second glance from the Ferrari and E-Jag buffs, but it will singe a lot of wheat in Nebraska." Fender skirts were not used on Sports Roadsters due to clearance problems with the knock-off hub hubs — although restorers have found ways to get around this. The open fenders also looked more sports car-like and facilitated brake cooling. The wire wheels did not work well with tubeless tires and required the use of inner tubes. T-Birds had about 45 lbs. of sound-deadening materials, including aluminum insulation, fiber or mastic felt, undercoating and fiberglass applied to the hood, wheel well housings, dashboard, passenger and trunk floors, roof panels, package tray and quarter panels. On the underbody, the zinc-coated metal had better rust-proofing including a zinc-rich coating, three coats of primer and two finish coats of "never wax" enamel. The aluminized muffler was improved and stainless steel parts were used in some critical places in the exhaust system, such as the resonators. T-Bird engines featured revised manifolding. There were 15 improvements to carburetors alone, plus a disposable fuel filter designed to function for 30,000 miles. Oil filter life was also extended to 4,000-6,000 mile intervals by eliminating a crossover valve. T-Birds came with permanent antifreeze that gave protection to minus 35-degrees and had to be changed only every two years or 30,000 miles. A larger master cylinder was said to increase braking efficiency, while reducing pedal pressure. For better durability and fade resistance, new brake lining materials were used. T-Bird seats were low and soft. As in 1961, heater controls and a glove compartment were incorporated into the center console between the seats. A Swing-Away steering wheel moved 10 inches to make getting in and out of the car easier. It functioned only when the gear selector was in Park. In addition to the 390-cid 300-hp base V-8, a limited-edition option was available in 1962. "I am told that under the pressure of thumb-screw and with the possible aid of your congressman, you might be able to order a 'Bird with a hotter engine," joked Tom McCahill. It was a version of the 390 with three progressively linked Holley two-barrel carburetors known as the M-code power plant. Although the T-Bird was sports-car fast, it came nowhere near handling or braking like a sports car according to *Car and Driver. Motor Trend* rated the car higher, but criticized under steer and body roll. The brakes functioned fine under all conditions, but the linings heated up quickly and caused severe fade if the car was driven hard. Standard equipment included: Built-in dual exhausts, fuel filter, oil filter, 390-cid four-barrel V-8, Lifeguard padded instrument panel, cushioned sun visors, safety belt anchors, electric clock with sweep second hand, automatic courtesy lights, turn signals, a deep-center steering wheel, dual horns and horn ring, individually adjustable individual front bucket seats, Safety-Swivel day-night tilt type inside rearview mirror, double-grip door locks, coat hooks, full wheel covers, built-in arm rests, floor carpet, full-width foam rubber seats, all-vinyl upholstery, fully-lined

luggage compartment, ashtray, cigar lighter, air cleaner, Cruise-O-Matic automatic transmission, power brakes, power steering, two-speed electric windshield wipers, undercoating, parking brake, glove box, ash tray, back-up and luggage compartment lights, heater and defroster, movable steering column, console between the front seats, and five black 8.00 x 14 tires. The Convertible Sports Roadster also included the molded tonneau cover with padded headrests, real Kelsey-Hayes chrome wire wheels with knock-off hub caps, a front passenger grab handle with color-keyed vinyl insert, a special insignia under the Thunderbird front fender script and no fender skirts. A Swing-Away steering wheel was standard, except on very early 1961 models.

VIN:

The VIN was die-stamped on top of the front fender cross-bar to right of hood lock striker plate. The first symbol denoted the model-year: 2=1962. The second symbol revealed the assembly plant: Y=Wixom (Novi), Michigan. The third symbol indicated the car-line: 8=Thunderbird. The fourth symbol denoted the body type: 3=Thunderbird Tudor Hardtop, 5=Thunderbird two-door convertible. The fifth symbol indicated the engine: Z=390 cid/300-hp Thunderbird V-8, M=390 cid/340-hp Thunderbird Special Six-Barrel V-8. (The M code engine was introduced in January 1962.) The sixth thru 11th symbols denoted the sequential production numbers of the specific vehicle starting at 100001. The body number plate was located on the left front body pillar. The serial number was the same as the number on the VIN tag. The symbols above "BDY" were the body symbol code: 63A=Hardtop, 63B=Landau Hardtop, 76A=Convertible, 76B=Sport Roadster. Symbols above CLR were the paint color code. The first symbol indicated the lower body color. The second symbol indicated the upper body color. Symbols above TRM were the trim combination code. Symbols above "DT" were the production date code. The number indicated the date of the month the car was made. The letters indicated the month of manufacture: A=January, B=February, C=March, D=April, E=May, F=June, G=July, H=August, J=September, K=October, L=November, M=December, N=January and P=February. Symbols above DSO indicate information including the Ford Motor Co. Sales District Code. Symbols above AX indicated the rear axle. 1=3.00:1. Symbols above TR indicated the type of transmission: All 1962 Thunderbirds came only with Code 4 SelectShift Cruise-O-Matic Drive.

Thunderbird (V-8)

Model No.	Body/ Style No.	Body Type and Seating	Factory Price	Shipping Weight	Production Total
83	63A	2-dr. Hardtop-4P	$4,321	4,132 lbs.	57,845
87	63B	2-dr. Landau-4P	$4,398	4,144 lbs.	10,282
85	76A	2-dr. Convertible-4P	$4,788	4,370 lbs.	8,457
89	76B	2-dr. Sport Roadster-4P	$5,439	4,471 lbs.	1,427

Engines:

Thunderbird 390 Special V-8: Overhead valve. Cast-iron block. B & S: 4.05 x 3.78 in. Displacement: 390 cid. Compression ratio: 9.60:1. Brake hp: 300 at 4600 rpm. Taxable hp: 52.49. Torque: 427 lbs.-ft. at 2800 rpm. Five main bearings. Hydraulic valve lifters. Crankcase capacity: 5 qt. (add 1 qt. with new oil filter). Cooling system capacity: 19 qt. Carburetor: Ford four-barrel Model CIAE-9510-AG with standard transmission or CIAE-9510-AH with automatic transmission. Code Z.

Thunderbird 390 Special 6-V V-8: Overhead valve. Cast-iron block. Displacement: 390 cid. B & S: 4.05 x 3.78 in. Compression ratio: 10.50:1. Brake hp: 340 at 5000 rpm. Torque: 430 lbs-ft. at 3200 rpm. Five main bearings. Hydraulic valve lifters. Carburetor: Holley three two-barrels. Cooling system capacity: 20.5 qt. with heater. Crankcase capacity: 5 qt. (add 1 qt. with new oil filter). Dual exhausts. Code M.

Chassis:

Wheelbase: 113 in. Overall length: 205 in. Overall width: 76 in. Overall height (hardtop): 54.2 in. Front seat headroom (hardtop): 34.3 in. Rear seat headroom (hardtop): 33.1 in. Front seat legroom (hardtop): 44.9 in. Rear seat legroom (hardtop): 37.3 in. Front seat shoulder room (hardtop): 58.1 in. Rear seat shoulder room (hardtop): 55.6 in. Front seat hip room (hardtop): 58.8 in. Rear seat hip room (hardtop): 52.3 in. Front tread: 61 in. Rear tread: 60 in. Road axle road clearance: 5.3 in. Body road clearance: 7.2 in. Tires: 8.00 x 14 4-ply.

Technical:

Steering ratio: 20.7:1. Turning diameter: 40.2 ft. Chassis type: Welded, integral body and frame. Front suspension: Independent wishbone type with ball joints and coil springs. Rear suspension: Live rear axle attached to semi-elliptic rear springs. Standard rear axle: 3.00:1. Optional rear axle: 3.00:1 Equal-Lock. Front brakes: 11.0-in. drums. Rear brakes: 11.0-in. drums. Brake swept area: 234 sq. in. Standard transmission: SelectShift Cruise-O-Matic Drive. Gas tank: 20 gallons (premium fuel required). Weight distribution: 66 percent front/44 percent rear. Fuel economy: 11-20 mpg. Driving range: 230 to 420 miles

1962 Ford Thunderbird two-door Convertible (OCW)

1962 Ford Thunderbird two-door Sport Roadster (AA)

Options:

Push-button radio and antenna ($112.80). Rear seat radio speaker with reverb ($15.50). MagicAire heater ($82.90). Thunderbird 390-cid V-8 with triple two-barrel carburetors ($242.10). SelectAire conditioner ($415.10). I-Rest tinted glass ($43). 8.00 x 14 rayon whitewalls ($42.10). 8.00 x 14 nylon whitewalls ($70.40). Power windows ($106.20). One 4-way power front seat ($92.10). Outside rear view mirror ($5.10). Electric windshield washers ($13.70). Rear fender shields ($26.60). Lifeguard front seat belts ($22.80). Leather seat ($106.20). Heavy-duty 70-amp battery ($.7.60) Tu-Tone paint ($25.80). Chrome wire wheels ($372.30). Automatic speed control ($80.50). Deluxe wheel covers with simulated knock-off hubs ($15.60). Automatic vacuum door locks ($34.10). Sports side trim ($34.80). Equa-Lock differential ($38.60). Note: Leather seats included leather seat inserts and bolsters.

History:

Henry Ford II was Board Chairman of Ford Motor Company. John Dykstra was President of FoMoCo. Lee Iacocca was a FoMoCo Vice President and General Manager of Ford Division. M.S. McLaughlin was general sales manager of Ford Division. A total of 78,011 T-Birds, representing 1.4 percent of total industry, were produced for the model year in the Wixom plant. Calendar year output of 75,536 T-Birds represented the first decline in several seasons. Calendar year dealer sales were 74,306 T-Birds, which was 4.8 percent of total Ford sales. The rare "M" code V-8 had a $171 dealer cost and added $242.10 to retail price. It was truly hard to get, with a reported total of just 120 M-code Sports Roadsters being put together. An "M" Roadster could move from 0-60 in approximately 8.5 seconds and hit a top speed of 125 mph. Most contemporary car magazines dwelled on T-Bird brake fade and the fact that once the brakes faded, they took a long time to cool off and come back. If T-Birds had trouble stopping, it must have spilled over to the sales department, since there was no stopping the steady increase in demand for '62s. From their introduction on October 12, 1961, the cars sold well. The combination of good looks, advanced styling, many creature comforts, luxury appointments, and reliable performance was a winner in the early 1960s. "Ford's plush style setter has its share of faults and shortcomings," said *Motor Trend*'s technical editor Jim Wright. "But, it's still the classic example of a prestige car." In addition, other than the limited-production Chrysler 300 letter car, the Thunderbird had the personal-luxury niche to itself. There was no Buick Riviera to contend with in 1962, and the new Pontiac Grand Prix had not yet developed the distinctive styling that would make it a big hit in 1963. On the other hand, Thunderbird's two added models helped fill out the niche and boosted production by 5,000 units.

1963 Thunderbird

Thunderbird — Series — (V-8): The 1963 model retained the previous styling with a new sculptured body side feature line, a modestly revised "electric shaver" grille, new taillights, new side trim and new wheel covers. Inside, buyers found medal-clad brake and accelerator pedals. New options included an AM/FM radio and a tachometer. This was the first T-Bird to use hydraulic windshield wipers powered by the power steering pump. The brakes were more fade-resistant and nearly 100 pounds of sound-deadening materials were added. Suspension and exhaust

improvements, lifetime chassis lubrication and an alternator in place of a generator were other updates. The grille incorporated a concealed hood latch, eliminating the old cable-operated release. The front fenders had a horizontal crease line that started just behind the grille, passed over the front wheel opening and continued past the middle of the door where it slanted downwards for a few inches and faded into the door. Just below the crease line, near the center of the door, were three groupings of forward-slanting chrome hash marks with five strips in each group. *Motor Trend* (October 1962) said these were supposed to remind one of turbine waste gates. Chrome Thunderbird scripts were moved to the rear fenders. New deep-dish wheel covers followed the turbine motif. There weren't any big changes to the inside of the basic models, although the inner door panels had new white and red courtesy lights for added safety when passengers were entering or exiting the car. Models were the same as in 1962 until February 7, 1963, when a special Limited-Edition Landau made its debut A single exhaust system was now used with the base 390-cid V-8. It was supposedly a quieter and longer lasting system featuring 2.0-in. diameter laminated tubing (double pipes, one inside the other) and an asbestos-wrapped, aluminized steel muffler. A 1.78-in. diameter tailpipe was employed. The 1963 T-Bird front suspension was lubricated for the "life of the car," which Ford estimated as 100,000 miles or seven years. Road noise and vibrations were reduced through use of a newly-developed rubber compression-type shock mount for the steering box, plus a flexible coupling between the gear assembly and the steering shaft. Standard features included: Built-in dual exhausts, fuel filter, oil filter, 390-cid four-barrel V-8, padded instrument panel, padded sun visors, electric clock with sweep second hand, courtesy lights, turn signals, deep-center steering wheel, dual horns and horn rings, individually adjustable front seats, day-night tilt type mirror, double-grip door locks, full wheel covers, built-in arm rests, floor carpet, full-width foam rubber seats, all-vinyl upholstery, ash tray, cigar lighter, air cleaner, automatic transmission, power brakes, power steering, electric windshield wipers, undercoating, parking brake, glove box, ash tray, luggage, back-up, and compartment lights, heater and defroster, movable steering column, console between front seats, AM radio and antenna, remote-control left-hand outside rear view mirror, and five black 8.00 x 14 tubeless tires. The Convertible Sports Roadster, which came only in eight colors, also included special front fender insignias, a molded tonneau cover with padded headrests, bolt-on chrome wire wheels with simulated knock-off hubs, a Swing-Away steering wheel, a passenger-assist handle and no fender skirts. The 1963 Landau offered Black, White, Brown and Blue vinyl tops, simulated walnut interior trim and a simulated walnut steering wheel. The Limited-Edition Landau featured White leather upholstery, a white steering wheel, simulated rosewood interior trim, a Rose Beige (maroon) vinyl top and special wheel covers with simulated knock-off hubcaps.

VIN:

The VIN was die-stamped on top of the front fender cross-bar to right of hood lock striker plate. First symbol denoted the model-year: 3=1963. The second symbol indicated the assembly plant: Y=Wixom (Novi), Michigan. The third symbol revealed the car-line: 8=Thunderbird. The fourth symbol denoted the body type: 3=Thunderbird Tudor Hardtop, 5=Thunderbird two-door convertible, 7=Two-door Landau Hardtop, 9=Sports Roadster. The fifth symbol indicated the engine: 9=390-cid low-compression Thunderbird V-8 (for export), Z=390 cid/300-hp Thunderbird V-8, M=390 cid/340-hp Thunderbird Special Six-Barrel V-8. Sixth thru 11th symbols denote sequential production number of specific vehicle starting at 100001. The body number plate was located on the left front body pillar. The serial number was the same as the VIN tag. Symbols

1963 Ford Thunderbird two-door Sport Coupe (OCW)

1963 Ford Thunderbird two-door Landau Hardtop (OCW)

1963 Ford Thunderbird two-door Sport Roadster (AA)

1963 Ford Thunderbird two-door Convertible (OCW)

above "BDY" were body symbol codes: 63A=Hardtop, 63B=Landau Hardtop, 76A=Convertible, 76B=Sport Roadster. Symbols above CLR were the paint color code. The first symbol indicated the lower body color. The second symbol indicated the upper body color. Symbols above TRM were the trim combination code. Symbols above "DT" were the production date code. The number indicated the date of the month the car was made. The letters indicated the month of manufacture: A=January, B=February, C=March, D=April, E=May, F=June, G=July, H=August, J=September, K=October, L=November, M=December. Symbols above DSO indicated information including the Ford Motor Co. Sales District Code. Symbols above AX indicated the rear axle. 1=3.00:1. Symbols above TR indicated the type of transmission: All 1963 Thunderbirds came only with SelectShift Cruise-O-Matic Drive Code 4.

Thunderbird (V-8)

Model No.	Body/Style No.	Body Type and Seating	Factory Price	Shipping Weight	Production Total
83	63A	2-dr. Hardtop-4P	$4,445	4,195 lbs.	42,806
87	63B	2-dr. Landau-4P	$4,548	4,320 lbs.	14,139
85	76A	2-dr. Convertible-4P	$4,912	4,205 lbs.	5,913
89	76B	2-dr. Sports Roadster-4P	$5,463	4,395 lbs.	455

Note 1: A total of 2,000 Limited-Edition "Princess Grace" Landau Hardtops are included above.

Engines:

Interceptor 390 Base V-8: Overhead valve. Cast-iron block. Displacement: 390 cid. B & S: 4.05 x 3.78 in. Compression ratio: 9.60:1. Brake hp: 300 at 4600 rpm. Torque: 427 lbs.-ft. at 2800 rpm. Five main bearings. Hydraulic valve lifters. Carburetor: Ford four-barrel C2AF-9510. Cooling system capacity: 20.5 qt. with heater. Crankcase capacity: 5 qt. (add 1 qt. with new oil filter). Dual exhaust. Code Z.

Thunderbird Special 390 6-V Optional V-8: Overhead valve. Cast-iron block. Displacement: 390 cid. B & S: 4.05 x 3.78 in. Compression ratio: 10.50:1. Brake hp: 340 at 5000 rpm. Torque: 430 lbs.-ft. at 3200 rpm. Five main bearings. Hydraulic valve lifters. Carburetor: Holley three Model 2300 two-barrel. Cooling system capacity: 20.5 qt. with heater. Crankcase capacity: 5 qt. (add 1 qt. with new oil filter). Dual exhaust. Code M.

Chassis:

Wheelbase (all): 113.2 in. Overall length (all): 205 in. Overall width (all): 76.5 in. Overall height (hardtop): 52.5 in. Front tread: 61 in. Rear tread: 60 in. Front seat headroom (hardtop): 34.3 in. Rear seat headroom (hardtop): 33.1 in. Front seat legroom (hardtop): 44.9 in. Rear seat legroom (hardtop): 37.3 in. Front Hip Room: 2 x 21.5 in. Rear Hip Room: 52.3 in. Front Overhang: 38.3 in. Box Volume: 476 cu. ft. Front Overhang: 38.3 in. Front Approach Angle: 20.6 degrees. Rear Overhang: 53.6 in. Rear Departure Angle: 12.7 degrees. Road axle road clearance: 5.6 in. Body road clearance: 7.2 in. Tires: 8.00 x 14 4-ply.

Technical:

Steering: Power-assisted link type 3.6 turns lock-to-lock. Steering ratio: 20.3:1. Turning diameter: 40.2 ft. Chassis type: Welded, integral body and frame. Front suspension: Independent wishbone type with ball joints and coil springs (with a ride rate of 105 lb.-in.) and 0.660-in. anti-roll bar. Rear suspension: Live rear axle attached to 2.5 x 60-in. semi-elliptic rear springs with ride rate of 105 lb.-in. Telescoping 1/19-in. piston diameter shocks were mounted on the T-Bird suspension front and rear. Standard rear axle: 3.00:1. Front brakes: 11 x 3-in. drums. Rear brakes: 11 x 2.5-in. drums. Brake swept area: 234 sq. in. Weight Distribution: 56

percent front/44 percent rear. Electrical: Autolite alternator with 2.25:1 drive ratio and maximum 40-amp. charge rate. Standard transmission: SelectShift three-element Cruise-O-Matic automatic transmission with Park/Reverse/Neutral/Drive-1/Drive-2/Low quadrant layout, 2.10:1 stall ratio and 5.04:1 ratio at breakaway. Transmission gears: (first) 2.40:1 (second) 1.47:1, (third) 1.0:1 and (reverse) 2.00:1. The transmission had a maximum up shift speed of 70 mph and a maximum kick-down speed of 65 mph. Gas tank: 20 gallons (premium fuel required). Fuel economy: 11 to 20 mpg. Driving Range: 230 to 420 miles.

Options:

Rear speakers in Hardtop and Landau ($15.60). AM/FM push-button radio and antenna ($83.70). Rear radio speaker, hardtop only ($15.50). Reverb-type rear radio speaker, hardtops only ($54.10). Thunderbird 390-cid 340-hp 6V V-8, includes dual exhaust ($242.10). Dual exhaust system with standard V-8 ($31.90). SelectAire Air Conditioner, except with 6V engine ($415.10). Banded tinted glass ($43). Concentric whitewall tires ($51.90). Five 8.00 x 14 rayon whitewalls ($42.10). Five 8.00 x 14 nylon whitewalls ($70.40). Power windows ($106.20). One 4-way power front seat ($92.10). Power door locks ($34.10). Windshield washers ($13.70). Rear fender shields, except with wire wheels ($26.60). Front seat belts ($16.80). Leather seat ($106.20). Heavy-duty 70-amp battery ($7.60). Tu-Tone paint ($25.80). Chrome wire wheels ($372.30). Automatic speed control system ($80.50). Sports tachometer ($56.80). Deluxe wheel covers with simulated knock-off hubs ($15.60). Note: Leather seats included leather seat inserts and bolsters. Heavy-duty alternator.

History:

Henry Ford II was Board Chairman of Ford Motor Company. Arjay R. Miller was President of FoMoCo. Lee Iacocca was a FoMoCo Vice President and General Manager of Ford Division. O.F. Yand was general sales manager of Ford Division. A total of 63,313 T-Birds, representing .09 percent of total industry, were produced for the model year in the Wixom plant. Calendar year output of 66,681 T-Birds represented .09 percent of industry. Calendar year dealer sales were 66,681 T-Birds, which was 4.1 percent of total Ford sales. The four carryover T-Bird models were introduced to the public on September 28, 2002. On February 7, 1963, the special 1963-1/2 Limited-Edition Thunderbird Landau made its debut in the Principality of Monaco. Princess Grace of Monaco was given car number one. This model was then dubbed the "Princess Grace" model by Ford salesmen. Only 2,000 were built and all were painted white. One Thunderbird factory "dream car" was built this year for display at auto shows. It was called the Italien and had to be one of the sleekest T-Bird styling exercises ever built. When viewed from the side it looked like a fastback, but it actually had a notchback roofline like the original 1965 Mustang 2+2. This car had wire wheels, unique taillight trim and special trim on the front fenders and doors. The 1963 Thunderbird is considered by many to be the best-looking of the three-year group, primarily because of its new grille. Unfortunately, the party was over. With new competitors in the marketplace, the '63s sold the worst of the bunch. Hardtop deliveries tumbled to just 42,806 units. The total output of regular Landaus was recorded separately this year and came to 12,139. That did not include the 2,000 "Princess Grace" Limited-Edition Landaus. The regular Convertible saw production of 5,913 units. Only 455 Sports Roadsters were built, including a mere 37 with the optional M-code engine. Overall, nearly 15,000 fewer Thunderbirds were built.

1964 Thunderbird

Thunderbird — Series 8 — (V-8): The 1964 T-Bird had new styling with a longer hood and shorter roofline. The hood was raised and blended in with the front fenders. There were "mirror-image" upper and lower feature lines at the belt line and lower body sides. *Car Life* (October 1963) noted "While the basic under-structure — unit-body inner and floor pan sections — probably do remain much the same as the '63s (and the '61s-62s, too), virtually all of the outer sheet metal stampings are new and different." The convertible had an all-vinyl, wrinkle-resistant top that retracted under the power-operated deck lid. It was automatically stacked in the trunk, eliminating the need for an outside top boot. Options could be purchased to turn the convertible into a Sports Roadster type car. Ford dealers sold wire wheels for $415 and a new headrest Sports Tonneau cover was $269. The factory produced a few dozen cars with both options. A "Chinese pagoda" shape characterized the Thunderbird's grille and textured horizontal bars made up the grille insert. "Thunderbird" was spelled out along the lip of the hood in widely-spaced chrome letters. Amber-colored rectangular parking lamps were recessed into the bumper directly under the headlamps. The dual headlamps sat side by side under the sculptured eyebrows. A dual directional light indicator system was standard. There were little indicator lamps on the front fenders for the driver to visualize when turning. Side sculpturing created a kind of flat "Parker pen" shaped indentation on the upper body sides. Thunderbird styling trademarks included a scooped hood (with a larger scoop) chrome Thunderbird script nameplates behind the front wheel openings and a formal-style roof. The hardtop's wide sail panels were decorated with T-Bird emblems. Full wheel covers of a new design were standard. The rear of the car was shaped like an electric razor without blades. The large, rectangular taillights sported bright frames and a T-Bird symbol in the middle. Some said they were the industry's largest taillights because Ford planned to make them flash sequentially. The company had this technology ready to go, but some state laws prohibited sequential lamps in 1964. Between the taillights was a white center piece bearing the Thunderbird name. An optional Safety-Convenience panel had toggle switches for safety flashers and automatic door locks, plus lights to indicate low fuel, door ajar and safety flasher operation. A restyled "Flight-Deck" instrument panel was one of the 1964 T-Bird's big selling features. The complete interior sported an aircraft look. The instruments were mounted in separate pods and illuminated by soft green lighting. New thin-shell front bucket seats with headrests were featured. A front passenger seat with a fully-reclining back rest was optional. The bucket seats were mounted on pedestals, which increased rear passenger legroom. Wider doors and a difference in the roofline made getting in and out of the T-Bird noticeably easier. New crank-type vent windows aided ventilation. The "Silent-Flo" fresh air circulation system let air into the car through vents at the base of the windshield. It exited through a grille vent just below the rear window. A new asymmetric full-length console was offset to the driver's side, where it blended into the instrument panel. Between the front seats, the console rose up to double as a center foam-padded armrest. It also separated the all-new wraparound Lounge style rear seats, which had a fold-down center armrest. Safety and convenience were stressed in the new interior. A two-spoke steering wheel made the controls and gauges easier to see. It incorporated a padded hub. The dashboard and sun visors were also padded. The speedometer was of drum design with progressive illumination. A red indicator light grew in size as speed increased. All control levers, buttons and wheels for operating the heater, air conditioner, cruise control, radio, air vents and power windows were clustered around the console. The gearshift lever was on the steering column for greater safety. There were stronger new "bear hug" door latches to hold the larger doors shut. Flood-type reading lamps, mounted in the rear roof pillars behind the seats, enhanced both safety and convenience. New inertia reels were provided to retract the outboard front seat belts and make them easier to store and use. The Landau model's vinyl top now had corner creases that gave it a crisper appearance. The only engine changes included microscopically smaller intake and exhaust valve diameters, a reduction in exhaust pipe diameter from 2.5 in. to 2.0 in., a corresponding reduction in tailpipe diameter from 2.0 in. to 1.75 in. and some ignition timing revisions. Another improvement was that the main bearing thrust surface was increased 1/4 in. in diameter for increased durability and ruggedness. A transistorized ignition system was a new option. Ford said it could increase ignition points and spark plug life to 48,000 miles. Part of the fuel system was a new 22-gallon gas tank. One of its biggest advantages was that its new location provided a deep, wide well and more space in the luggage compartment. Continuing its quest of the "lifetime" car, Ford promoted 24,000-mile wheel bearing lubrication intervals, 100,000-mile chassis lubes and 6,000-mile oil changes for T-Birds this year. The smooth-shifting Cruise-O-Matic transmission had no specifications changes. There was a new integral power steering system. T-Birds switched to 15-in. wheels and 8.15 x 15 low-profile tires. These had a special tread and composition developed specifically for T-Birds. Convertibles with optional wire wheels used 8.00 x 14 tires. Another change in 1964 was the availability of a long list of rear axle options. Standard equipment included: A 300-hp 390-cid four-barrel V-8, Cruise-O-Matic transmission, power steering, power brakes, movable steering column, padded instrument panel, padded sun visors, hydraulic windshield wipers, electric clock, push-button radio and antenna, heater, automatic parking brake release, turn signals, seat belts with retractors, wheel covers, undercoating, back-up lights, glove box light, ash tray light, courtesy light, map light, luggage compartment light, remote-control mirror, windshield wipers-washers, alternator, full instrumentation, automatic parking brake release and Silent-Flow fresh-air circulation system. The Landau model had a padded vinyl top and had landau bars attached to its roof sail panels. Although they had the traditional S-shape with chrome finish, the landau irons carried a new horizontal oval badge at their center. The Landau Hardtop's vinyl top came in Black, White, Brown, and Blue. Simulated walnut graining on the

1964 Ford Thunderbird two-door Sport Coupe (OCW)

1964 Ford Thunderbird two-door Landau Hardtop (OCW)

instrument panel and interior doorsills returned, but Rosewood trim was no longer offered.

VIN:

The VIN was die-stamped on the top of front fender cross-bar to right of hood lock striker plate. The first symbol denoted the model-year: 4=1964. The second symbol indicated the assembly plant: Y=Wixom (Novi), Michigan. The third symbol revealed the car-line: 8=Thunderbird. The fourth symbol denoted the body type: 3=Thunderbird Tudor Hardtop, 5=Thunderbird two-door convertible, 7=Two-door Landau Hardtop. The fifth symbol indicated the engine: 9=390-cid low-compression Thunderbird V-8 (for export), Z=390 cid/300-hp Thunderbird V-8. The sixth thru 11th symbols denoted the sequential production numbers of the specific vehicle starting at 100001. The body number plate was located on the left front body pillar. The serial number was the same as the number on the VIN tag. Symbols above "BDY" were the body symbol code: 63A=Hardtop, 63B=Landau Hardtop, 76A=Convertible. Symbols above CLR were the paint color code. The first symbol indicated the lower body color. The second symbol indicated the upper body color. Symbols above TRM were the trim combination code. Symbols above "DT" were the production date code. The number indicated the date of the month the car was made. The letters indicated the month of manufacture: A=January, B=February, C=March, D=April, E=May, F=June, G=July, H=August, J=September, K=October, L=November, M=December. Symbols above DSO indicate information including the Ford Motor Co. Sales District Code. Symbols above AX indicated the rear axle. 1=3.00:1, 4=3.25:1, A=3.00:1 Equa-Lock and D=3.25:1 Equa-Lock. Symbols above TR indicates the type of transmission: All 1964 Thunderbirds came only with SelectShift Cruise-O-Matic Drive code 4.

Thunderbird (V-8)

Model No.	Body/ Style No.	Body Style and Seating	Factory Price	Shipping Weight	Production Total
83	63A	2-dr. Hardtop-4P	$4,486	4,452 lbs.	60,552
87	63B	2-dr. Landau-4P	$4,589	4,460 lbs.	22,715
85	76A	2-dr. Convertible-4P	$4,953	4,547 lbs.	9,198

Note 1: A total of 45 convertibles left the factory with wire wheels and a sports tonneau

Engines:

Thunderbird 390 V-8 (Low-compression, for export only): Overhead valve. Cast-iron block. Displacement: 390 cid. B & S: 4.05 x 3.78 in. Compression ratio: 9.6:1. Brake hp: 275. Five main bearings. Hydraulic valve lifters. Carburetor: Four-barrel. Cooling system capacity: 20 qt. with heater. Crankcase capacity: 5 qt. (add 1 qt. with new oil filter). Dual exhausts. Code Z.

Thunderbird 390 Base V-8: Overhead valve. Cast-iron block. Displacement: 390 cid. B & S: 4.05 x 3.78 in. Compression ratio: 10.8:1. Brake hp: 300 at 4600 rpm. Torque: 427 lbs-ft. at 2800 rpm. Five main bearings. Hydraulic valve lifters. Carburetor: Four-barrel. Cooling system capacity: 20 qt. with heater. Crankcase capacity: 5 qt. (add 1 qt. with new oil filter). Dual exhausts. Code Z.

Chassis:

Wheelbase (all): 113.2 in. Overall length (all): 205.4 in. Overall width (all): 77.1 in. Overall height (hardtop and Landau Hardtop): 52.5 in., (convertible) 53.3 in. Front tread: 61 in. Rear tread: 60 in. Front Hip Room: 2 x 21.5 in. Rear Hip Room: 49.9 in. Box volume: 482 cu. ft. Front area: 22.4 sq. ft. Front Overhang: 37.7 in. Front Approach Angle: 19.5 degrees. Rear Overhang: 54.5 in. Rear Departure Angle: 12.9 degrees. Road axle road clearance: 5.56 in. Body road clearance: 9.0 in. Tires: 8.15 x 15 4-ply (8.00 x 14 with wire wheels).

Technical:

Steering: Power-assisted link type 3.6 turns lock-to-lock. Steering ratio: 20.3:1. Turning diameter: 40.2 ft. Chassis type: Welded, integral body and

1964 Ford Thunderbird two-door Convertible (OCW)

1965 Thunderbird

Thunderbird — Series 8 — (V-8): The 1965 T-Bird had no drastic appearance changes. Thunderbird lettering on the edge of the hood was replaced with a stylized T-Bird emblem. Wide-spaced vertical moldings were added to the former horizontal-bars grille. The script plate with the model name moved from the front fender to the rear fender. There were dummy air vents (Ford called them "simulated waste gates") on both sides of the body, just behind the front wheel openings. New emblems with a stylized Thunderbird partly encircled by a chrome ring adorned the roof sail panels. The center section of the rear bumper had a Thunderbird crest replacing the name spelled out across it. The broad taillights were divided into six square segments by short vertical chrome moldings. The doors could now be locked without using a key and the keys went into the door locks with either edge up. A "fasten seat belt" light now went off when the driver's belt was pulled out and latched. (In 1964, the light had stayed lit.) The engine was virtually the same as 1964 and earlier 390s, but the oil filler tube in front of the manifold was replaced with a breather cap and filler tube on the driver's side valve cover. Two engine mount bosses were added on each side of the block casting, due to the use of a new engine-mounting system. A vacuum-operated trunk release was a new accessory. The headrest-style Sports Tonneau cover was dropped. However, the '64 Sports Tonneau fit the '65 Convertible and, for buyers who demanded one, a cover could often be obtained from some Ford dealer's parts inventory. Red band tires, another new option, were $44 extra. Only 15-in. tires were offered in 1965. New disc brakes did not work with wire wheels, so that option was dropped. The hardtop, Landau hardtop and convertible models returned. A limited-edition Special Landau was released in March 1965. Inside the T-Bird was an instrument panel inspired by aircraft design motifs. *Car Life* quipped that driving a T-Bird for the first time at night could "remind its driver of the main drag of Las Vegas, if all the lights are blinking in front of him." At the rear, new sequential taillights were a real attention getter. They operated through an arrangement of multiple taillight bulbs that flashed, in order, from the inner side of the broad red lens to its outer edge. The T-Bird's 390-cid 300-hp V-8 had a new carburetor. Standard equipment included: Built-in dual exhausts and aluminized stainless steel muffler, fuel filter, oil filter, 390-cid 300-hp four-barrel V-8, Cruise-O-Matic Drive, double-sided keys, keyless door locking, variable-speed hydraulic windshield wipers, electric windshield washers, crank-type vent windows, front seat belts, padded instrument panel, padded sun visors, electric clock with sweep second hand, courtesy lights, safety-courtesy door lights, sequential turn signals, Swing-Away deep-center steering wheel, dual horns and horn rings, individually adjustable shell-contour front bucket seats, front armrest on top of center console, rear center folding armrest, floating day-night tilt type mirror, double-grip door locks, full wheel covers, power front disc brakes, built-in armrests, floor carpet, full-width foam rubber seats, MagicAire heater and defroster, Silent-Flo ventilation system (except convertible), all-vinyl upholstery, ashtray, cigar lighter, air cleaner, automatic transmission, power brakes, integral power steering, undercoating, automatic parking brake release, map light, glove box light, ignition light, ashtray light, fully-lined luggage compartment, luggage compartment light, back-up lights, compartment lights, convertible roof bow light, transistor-type AM radio and antenna, remote-control left-hand outside rearview mirror, five black 8.15 x 15 tubeless tires, full wheel covers, rear fender shields (fender skirts) and shielded alternator. The limited-edition Thunderbird Special Landau also featured Ember-Glo exterior finish, Ember-Glo dashboard trim, Ember-Glo carpeting, special

frame. Front suspension: Independent wishbone type with ball joints and coil springs. Rear suspension: Live rear axle attached to semi-elliptic rear springs. Telescoping shocks were mounted on the T-Bird suspension front and rear. Standard rear axle: 3.00:1. Front brakes: 11.09 x 3-in. drums. Rear brakes: 11 x 2.5-in. drums. Brake swept area: 381 sq. in. Weight Distribution: 56 percent front/44 percent rear. Standard transmission: SelectShift three-element Cruise-O-Matic automatic transmission. Gas tank: 22 gallons (premium fuel required). Fuel economy: 11.1 (averaged 8.3 mpg to 14.5 mpg. Driving Range: 242 to 308 miles.

Options:

Four-way power driver's seat ($92.10). 4-way power driver and passenger seats ($184.10) Power windows ($106.20). SelectAire air conditioner ($415.10). AM/FM push-button radio with antenna ($83.70). Rear seat speaker ($15.50). StudioSonic reverb sound system ($54.10). 8.15 x 15 white sidewall tires ($42.10). Tu-Tone paint ($25.80). Sports side trim ($34.80). Tonneau cover, for convertible only ($269). Contoured vinyl floor mats ($15.25). Sports tachometer ($43.10). Kelsey-Hayes sports-style chrome wire wheels and 8.00 x 14 white sidewall tires ($415.20). Deluxe wheel covers ($15.60). Leather seat trim ($106.20). Reclining passenger seat with adjustable headrest ($38.60). Heavy-duty battery ($7.60). Rear fender shields ($26.60). Tinted with banded windshield glass ($43). Transistorized ignition system ($51.50). Safety Convenience Control Panel, includes vacuum door locks, door ajar warning light, low fuel warning light, simultaneous flashing parking and taillights ($45.10). Speed control system ($63.40). Equa-Lock limited-slip rear axle. Optional rear axle ratios: 3.00:1, 3.25:1, 3.00:1 Equa-Lock and 3.25:1 Equa-Lock. Right-hand outside rearview mirror ($6.95). Door edge guards ($4.40). License plate frame ($6.10). Accent striping ($13.90).

History:

Henry Ford II was Board Chairman of Ford Motor Company. Arjay R. Miller was President of FoMoCo. Lee Iacocca was a FoMoCo Vice President and General Manager of Ford Division. M.S. McLaughlin was back as general sales manager of Ford Division. The Thunderbird posted a 26 percent retail sales increase and celebrated its 10th anniversary on October 21, 1964. Calendar-year output leaped 35 percent. A total of 92,465 T-Birds, representing 1.2 percent of total industry output, were produced for the model year in the Wixom factory. That just missed the all-time record, set in 1960, of 92,843. Calendar year output of 90,239 T-Birds represented 1.1 percent of industry. Calendar year dealer sales were 90,239 T-Birds, which was a huge two percent gain. "What it is is a heavy, luxurious, prestige four-seater that gives its owner a soft, smooth ride and every imaginable creature comfort," *Motor Trend* said in February 1964. "Granted, it's not everyone's cup of tea, but for 'Bird lovers, it's the 'only way to fly.'" Magazines aimed at 1960s sports car buffs always seemed to be a bit more critical of the T-Bird. *Car and Driver* (August 1964), complained, "The Thunderbird is 205.5 in. of steel and chrome with one purpose: gratification of the ego." Along with the rest of Ford Motor Company's Total Performance Products, the Thunderbird shared *Motor Trend* magazine's "Car of the Year" award for "the best possible use of high-performance testing in bringing to the motoring public a product that lives up to the claims of the maker: Total Performance." A Thunderbird show car called the "Golden Palomino" made its way around the circuit this year. It was a Landau with roof sections that flipped-up. The car had both genuine wire wheels and fender skirts. While touring the country it was put on display at many Ford dealerships nationwide.

1965 Ford Thunderbird two-door Sport Coupe (OCW)

1965 Ford Thunderbird two-door Landau Hardtop (OCW)

1965 Ford Thunderbird two-door Special Landau Hardtop (OCW)

1965 Ford Thunderbird two-door Convertible (OCW)

wheel discs with Ember-Glo trim, a Parchment vinyl roof, a Parchment steering wheel, Parchment dashboard and console trim, a Parchment headliner, Parchment vinyl upholstery, burled walnut vinyl accents on the doors and instrument panel and a plate affixed to the console with the owner's name and "Limited Edition" engraved on it. (Note: At least one Thunderbird Special Landau had White finish.)

VIN:

The VIN was die-stamped on top of the front fender cross-bar to right of the hood lock striker plate. The first symbol denoted the model-year: 5=1965. The second symbol indicated the assembly plant: Y=Wixom (Novi), Michigan. The third symbol revealed the car-line: 8=Thunderbird. The fourth symbol was the body type: 1=Two-door Landau Special Hardtop, 3=Thunderbird Tudor Hardtop, 5=Thunderbird two-door convertible, 7=Two-door Landau Hardtop. The fifth symbol denoted the engine: 9=390-cid low-compression Thunderbird V-8 (for export), Z=390 cid/300-hp Thunderbird V-8. The sixth through 11th symbols denoted the sequential production numbers of the specific vehicle starting at 100001. The body number plate was located on the left front body pillar. The serial number was the same as the number on the VIN tag. Symbols above "BDY" were the body symbol code: 63A=Hardtop, 63B=Landau Hardtop, 63D=Landau Special Hardtop and 76A=Convertible. Symbols above "CLR" were the paint color code. The first symbol indicated the lower body color. The second symbol indicated the upper body color. Symbols above TRM were the trim combination code. Symbols above "DT" were the production date code. The number indicated the date of the month the car was made. The letters indicated the month of manufacture: A=January, B=February, C=March, D=April, E=May, F=June, G=July, H=August, J=September, K=October, L=November, M=December. Symbols above DSO indicated the information including the Ford Motor Co. Sales District Code. Symbols above AX indicated the rear axle. 1=3.00:1, 4=3.25:1, 5=3.50:1, 6=2.80:1, A=3.00:1 Equa-Lock, D=3.25:1 Equa-Lock, E=3.50:1 and F=2.80:1. Symbols above TR indicated the type of transmission. All 1965 Thunderbirds came only with SelectShift Cruise-O-Matic Drive, code 4 or code 6.

Thunderbird (V-8)

Model No.	Body/ Style No.	Body Type and Seating	Factory Price	Shipping Weight	Production Total
8	63A	2-dr. Hardtop-4P	$4,396	4,470 lbs.	42,652
8	63B	2-dr. Landau-4P	$4,495	4,478 lbs.	20,974
8	63D	2-dr. Special Landau-4P	$4,639	4,460 lbs.	4,500
8	76A	2-dr. Convertible-4P	$4,851	4,588 lbs.	6,846

Engines:

Thunderbird Special Base V-8: Overhead valve. Cast-iron block. Displacement: 390 cid. B & S: 4.05 x 3.78 in. Compression ratio: 10.0:1. Brake hp: 300 at 4600 rpm. Torque: 427 lbs.-ft. at 2800 rpm. Five main bearings. Hydraulic valve lifters. Carburetor: Four-barrel. Cooling system capacity: 20 qt. with heater. Crankcase capacity: 5 qt. (add 1 qt. with new oil filter). Engine weight: 660 lbs. Dual exhausts. Code Z. (Code 9 low-compression engine used in export units).

Chassis:

Wheelbase: 113.2 in. Overall length: 205.4 in. Overall width: 77.1 in. Overall height (hardtop): 52.5 in., (Landau) 52.7 in., (convertible) 53.3 in. Front tread: 61 in. Rear tread: 60 in. Front Hip Room: 2 x 21.5 in. Rear Hip Room: 49.9 in. Box volume: 482 cu. ft. Front area: 22.5 sq. ft. Front Overhang: 37.7 in. Front Approach Angle: 19.5 degrees. Rear overhang: 54.5 in. Rear departure angle: 12.9 degrees. Road axle road clearance: 5.5 in. Body road clearance: 9.0 in. Tires: 8.15 x 15 4-ply.

Technical:

Steering: Power-assisted link type 3.6 turns lock-to-lock. Steering ratio: 20.4:1. Turning diameter: 40.2 ft. Chassis type: Welded, integral body and frame. Front suspension: Independent wishbone type with coil springs. Rear suspension: Live rear axle attached to semi-elliptic rear springs. Telescoping shocks were mounted on the T-Bird suspension front and rear. Standard rear axle: 3.00:1. Front brakes: 11.87-in.Kelsey-Hayes ventilated 4-piston caliper discs. Rear brakes: 11 x 2.5-in. drums with 412 sq. in. of swept area. Brake lining gross area: 133 sq. in. Weight Distribution: 56 percent front/44 percent rear. Standard transmission:

SelectShift three-element Cruise-O-Matic automatic transmission. Gas tank: 22 gallons (premium fuel required). Average fuel economy: 11.1 mpg (averaged 8.3 mpg to 14.5 mpg.) Driving range: 242 to 308 miles.

Options:

SelectAire air conditioner ($424.90). Heavy-duty 70-amp battery ($7.60). California type closed emission system ($5.30). Automatic deck lid release, except Convertible ($12.90). Limited-slip differential ($47.70). Extra-cooling package ($7.90). Rear fender shields — skirts ($32.70). Tinted glass with banded windshield ($43). Leather seat bolsters and inserts ($106.20). Tu-tone paint ($25.80). Sports side trim ($34.80). Retracting power antenna ($29.60). 4-way power driver's seat ($92.10). Four-way power driver and passenger seats ($184.10). Power windows and power vent windows ($159.40). Power windows ($106.20). AM/FM push-button radio and antenna ($83.70). Safety Convenience Control Panel includes vacuum door locks, door ajar light, low fuel light, and safety flashers ($58). Reclining passenger seat with headrest ($45.10). Rear seat speaker ($16.90). Studiosonic rear seat speaker ($54.10). Speed control system ($63.40). Heavy-duty suspension with front and rear heavy-duty springs and shock absorbers ($28.60). Five rayon 8.15 x 15 whitewall tires ($43.90). Five rayon 8.15 x 15 Red Band tires ($51.98 l). Transistorized ignition system ($76). Deluxe wheel covers with simulated knock-off hubs ($15.60). Automatic headlamp dimmer ($45.60). Extra-cooling package ($7.90). Color-keyed floor mats ($15.25). Door edge guards ($4.40). Right-hand outside rearview mirror ($6.95). License plate frame ($6.10). Fuel filler door edge guard ($3.35).

History:

Henry Ford II was Board Chairman of Ford Motor Company. Arjay R. Miller was President of FoMoCo. Donald N. Frey was a FoMoCo Vice President and the new General Manager of Ford Division. Lee A. Iacocca became moved to the Ford Truck Group. M.S. McLaughlin was now Assistant General Manager of Ford Division Sales and Marketing. Calendar-year output fell to 75,710 units representing 0.81 percent of industry. A total of 74,972 T-Birds, representing 0.9 percent of total industry output, were produced for the model year in the Wixom factory. Calendar year dealer sales were 72,132 T-Birds, representing 0.8 percent of industry sales. Despite the calendar year sales and production declines, Ford built more Thunderbirds in October 1965 than in any other single month in T-Bird history. The 10,339 cars sold that month (mostly 1966 models) beat the previous monthly sales record of 9,753 units set in October 1962. *Car Life* found the 1965 T-Bird's optional thin-shell bucket seats "an aid to the continual ease of riding" and strongly recommended the optional reclining passenger seat with pull-up headrest. "The seats provide a fine compromise between wrap-around support and lounge chair squirm room," reported *Car Life*. "Once tried, the 'Bird's accommodations actually invite long (and normally dreary) drives, rather than discouraging them." The new Kelsey-Hayes vented disc brakes featured 4-piston calipers and brought a vast improvement in T-Bird braking performance. "Deceleration rates and stopping distances are nothing short of phenomenal for a 5,000-lb. car," said *Car Life*. The disc brake system was the same one used in the Lincoln Continental, except that the T-Bird did not have a front wheel pressure-limiting valve. A proportioning valve was used in the system to balance pressure to the lightly loaded rear wheels. The disc brake pads were advertised to last 30,000 miles. With countless gadgets and accessories running, *Car Life* reported, "So quiet and effortless was the running that the red ribbon type speedometer all too often crept past the 80 mph mark." As usual, the T-Bird was assessed as being "hard-pressed to exhibit much control with less than ideal road surfaces." But the magazine said that the car had to be admired for inspiring "dozens of lesser imitations which, by their very imitation, prove the 'Bird a better beast."

1966 Thunderbird

Thunderbird — Series 8 — (V-8): The headlights on the 1966 T-Bird had a bright metal faceplate around them and the rest of the front end had a more aggressive wedge shape. The hood grew longer and the hood scoop was flatter and more sharply pointed. The front lip of the hood had no decorative trim and the heavy chrome grille surround was eliminated.

1966 Ford Thunderbird two-door Hardtop (OCW)

1966 Ford Thunderbird two-door Landau Hardtop (OCW)

1966 Ford Thunderbird two-door Town Landau Hardtop (OCW)

An "ice cube tray" grille carried a big stylized T-Bird ornament right in its center. There was a much slimmer bumper with the splash pan showing below it and parking lamps in the splash pan. Ford removed the fake "waste gates" from the front fenders, but the "Thunderbird" name stayed on the rear body sides. Thin chrome moldings highlighted the front and rear wheel openings. Fender skirts were optional. When skirts were ordered, the rear wheel arch moldings were eliminated and the skirts had chrome bottom moldings. A full-width rear end treatment had the back-up lights in the middle of the sequential taillight lenses. The taillights had a series of side-by-side square segments, but the individual squares no longer had chrome moldings. New pentastar wheel covers with a "mag" wheel look and color-coordinated sections that matched the body color were used on some new models. The Town Hardtop and Town Landau were new models with a roof featuring wider sail panels and no rear quarter windows. Both carried Thunderbird insignias on the roof sail panels, while the Town Landau carried S-shaped landau irons in the same location. The Landau Hardtop was dropped. The 390-cid engine was tuned to give 315 hp and a new 428-cid 345-hp V-8 was optional. Another new option was a stereo tape player that was built into the AM radio. It provided up to 80 minutes of music per cartridge. Four speakers were included with this sound system. A Safety-Convenience control panel was standard in "Town" models and optional in hardtops and convertibles. In the Town Hardtop and Town Landau it was incorporated into an overhead roof console. Standard equipment included: Built-in dual exhausts with aluminized stainless steel mufflers, fuel filter, oil filter, 390-cid 315-hp four-barrel V-8, Cruise-O-Matic Drive, double-sided keys, keyless door locks, retractable front seat belts with reminder light, color-keyed rear seat belts, front and rear folding center armrests, padded instrument panel, padded sun visors, crank-type vent windows, automatic parking brake release, electric clock with sweep second hand, courtesy lights, sequential turn signals, shielded alternator, Safety-Courtesy door lights, deep-center steering wheel, dual horns and horn rings, individually adjustable shell-contour front bucket seats, floating type day-night tilt type mirror, double-grip door locks, full wheel covers, built-in arm rests, floor carpet, full-width foam rubber seats, all-vinyl upholstery, ash tray, cigar lighter, air cleaner, automatic transmission, power front disc brakes, integral power steering, variable-speed hydraulic windshield wipers, electric windshield washers, undercoating, parking brake light, map light, glove box light, ashtray light, fully-lined luggage compartment with light, roof bow light (convertible only), back-up lights, compartment lights, MagicAire heater and defroster, Swing-Away movable steering column, transistorized AM push-button radio with antenna, remote-control left-hand outside rearview mirror, five black 8.15 x 15 tubeless tires, Silent Flo ventilation system (except convertible), complete underbody sound coating and full wheel covers. [Town Models] Overhead Safety Panel.

VIN:

The VIN was die-stamped on the top of front fender cross-brace to right of hood lock striker plate. First symbol denotes model-year: 6=1966. The second symbol denoted the assembly plant: Y=Wixom (Novi), Michigan. The third symbol indicated the car-line: 8=Thunderbird. The fourth revealed the body type: 1=Two-door Town Hardtop (blind rear roof quarters with painted top), 3=Two-door Hardtop, 5=Thunderbird two-door convertible, 7=Two-door Town Landau (blind rear roof quarters with vinyl top). The fifth symbol denotes engine: Z=390 cid/300-hp Thunderbird V-8, 8=428-cid/265-hp V-8 for export only, Q=428-cid/345-hp Thunderbird Special V-8. The sixth through 11th symbols indicated the sequential production number of specific vehicle starting at 100001.

The body number plate was located on the left front body pillar. The serial number was the same as the number on the VIN tag. Symbols above "BDY" were the body symbol code: 63A=Hardtop, 63C=Town Hardtop, 63D=Town Landau Hardtop and 76A=Convertible. Symbols above CLR were the paint color code. The first symbol indicated the lower body color. The second symbol indicated the upper body color. Symbols above TRM were trim combination code. Symbols above "DT" were the production date code. The number indicated the date of the month the car was made. The letters indicated the month of manufacture: A=January, B=February, C=March, D=April, E=May, F=June, G=July, H=August, J=September, K=October, L=November, M=December. Symbols above DSO indicated information including the Ford Motor Co. Sales District Code. Symbols above AX indicated the rear axle. The rear axles used were: 1=3.00:1, 3=3.20:1, 6=2.80:1, 01=3.00:1, 11=3.00:1, A=3.00:1 Equa-Lock, F=2.80:1 Equa Lock, 0A=3.00:1 Equa-Lock, 1A=3.00:1 Equa Lock and 6A=2.80:1 Equa Lock. Symbols above TR indicated the type of transmission: All 1966 Thunderbirds came only with SelectShift Cruise-O-Matic Drive code 4 or code 8.

Thunderbird (V-8)

Model No.	Body/Style No.	Body Type and Seating	Factory Price	Shipping Weight	Production Total
Z/Q	63A	2-dr. Hardtop Coupe-4P	$4,395	4,386 lbs.	13,389
Z/Q	63B	2-dr. Hardtop Town Sedan-4P	$4,451	4,359 lbs.	15,633
Z/Q	63D	2-dr. Landau-4P	$4,552	4,367 lbs.	35,105
Z/Q	76A	2-dr. Convertible-4P	$4,895	4,496 lbs.	5,049

Engines:

Thunderbird Special 390 Base V-8: Overhead valve. Cast-iron block. Displacement: 390 cid. B & S: 4.05 x 3.78 in. Compression ratio: 10.5:1. Brake hp: 315 at 4600 rpm. Torque: 427 lbs.-ft. at 2800 rpm. Five main bearings. Hydraulic valve lifters. Carburetor: Four-barrel. Cooling system capacity: 20.5 qt. with heater. Crankcase capacity: 4 qt. (add 1 qt. with new oil filter). Dual exhausts. Code Z.

Thunderbird Special 428 Export V-8: Overhead valve. Cast-iron block. Displacement: 428 cid. B & S: 4.13 x 3.98 in. Compression ratio: 8.9:1. Brake hp: 265 at 4400 rpm. Torque: 462 lbs.-ft. at 2800 rpm. Five main bearings. Hydraulic valve lifters. Carburetor: Four-barrel. Cooling system capacity: 20.5 qt. with heater. Crankcase capacity: 4 qt. (add 1 qt. with new oil filter). Dual exhausts. Engine weight: 680 lbs. Code 8.

Thunderbird Special 428 Base V-8: Overhead valve. Cast-iron block. Displacement: 428 cid. Bore and stroke: 4.13 x 3.98 in. Compression ratio: 10.50:1. Brake hp: 345 at 4600 rpm. Torque: 462 lbs.-ft. at 2800 rpm. Five main bearings. Hydraulic valve lifters. Carburetor: Four-barrel. Cooling system capacity: 20.5 qt. with heater. Crankcase capacity: 4 qt. (add 1 qt. with new oil filter). Dual exhausts. Engine weight: 680 lbs. Code Q.

Chassis:

Wheelbase (all): 113.0 in. Overall length (all): 205.4 in. Overall width (all): 77.3 in. Overall height: (hardtop) 52.5 in., (Town Hardtop) 52.6 in., (Town Landau) 52.7 in., (convertible) 52.5 in. Front tread: 61 in. Rear tread: 60 in. Front Hip Room: 2 x 21.5 in. Front Shoulder Room: 57 in. Front headroom: 37.4 in. Rear hip room: 49.9 in. Rear shoulder Room: 54 in. Rear Leg Room: 33.2 in. Rear headroom: 37.6 in. Road axle road clearance: 6.4 in. Body Road Clearance: 9.0 in. Box volume: 482 cu. ft. Front area: 22.5 sq. ft. Front overhang: 37.7 in. Front approach angle: 19.5 degrees. Rear Overhang: 54.5 in. Rear Departure Angle: 12.9 degrees. Tires: 8.15 x 15 4-ply.

Technical:

Steering: Power-assisted link type 3.6 turns lock-to-lock. Turning diameter: 42.6 ft. Steering ratio: 20.4:1. Front suspension: Independent wishbone type with coil springs and ball joints. Rear suspension: Live rear axle attached to semi-elliptic rear springs. Telescoping shocks were mounted on the T-Bird suspension front and rear. Front brakes: 11.87-in.Kelsey-Hayes ventilated 4-piston caliper discs. Rear brakes: 11.09 x 2.50 -in. drums with 412 sq. in. of swept area. Weight Distribution: (with 390-cid V-8) 56 percent front/44 percent rear. Weight Distribution: (with 428-cid V-8) 53.9 percent front/56.1 percent rear. Standard transmission: SelectShift three-element Cruise-O-Matic automatic transmission. Gas tank: 22 gallons (premium fuel required). Average fuel economy: 11.1 mpg (averaged 8.3 mpg to 14.5

1966 Ford Thunderbird two-door Convertible (OCW)

1967 Thunderbird

mpg.) Driving Range: 242-308 miles. Axle (390 V-8): 3.00 (standard), 3.25 (optional), Axle (428 V-8): 2.80 (standard), 3.00/3.50 (optional). Average Fuel Economy: (390 V-8) 13 to 16 mpg, (428 V-8) 12 to 14 mpg. Driving Range: (390 V-8) 286 to 352 miles, (428 V-8) 264 to 308 miles.

Options:

428-cid 345-hp V-8 ($64.77). 6-way power driver's seat ($96.62). 6-way power driver and passenger seats ($193.73). Power windows ($103.95). Power windows including vent windows ($156.40). Retracting power antenna ($29.60). Heavy-duty 80-amp battery, standard with 428-cid V-8 ($7.44). Limited-slip differential ($46.35). Transistorized ignition system with 428-cid V-8 only ($75.50). Highway-Pilot speed control ($128.72). Safety Convenience Control includes vacuum door locks, door ajar light, low fuel light, and safety flashers, standard in Town Hardtop and Town Landau ($56.36). Tinted glass ($42.09). SelectAire conditioner ($412.90). AM/FM radio with antenna ($81.55). Remote deck lid release, except convertible ($12.90). AM radio and Stereosonic 8-track tape player ($127.54). Rear fender shields — skirts ($32.70). License plate frames ($6.10). Leather seat trim, includes reclining seat ($147.03). Tu-Tone paint ($25.07). White sidewall tires ($42.93). White sidewall tires with red band ($51.98). Deluxe wheel covers with simulated knock-off hubs ($15.60). Reclining passenger seat with headrest ($43.83). Rear seat speaker ($16.90). StudioSonic rear seat speaker ($53.50). California closed crankcase emissions control system ($5.30). Exhaust emissions control system ($49.45). Extra-cooling package ($7.90). Heavy-duty suspension ($28.60). Right-hand outside rearview mirror ($6.95). Chrome deck lid luggage rack ($32.44). Retractable rear seat belts ($7.10). Door edge guards ($4.40). Fuel filler door edge guard ($3.35). Contour floor mats ($15.25). Body side moldings ($34.80). Special order paint ($34.70).

History:

Henry Ford II was Board Chairman of Ford Motor Company. Arjay R. Miller was President of FoMoCo. Donald N. Frey was a FoMoCo Vice President and the new General Manager of Ford Division. Lee A. Iacocca became moved to the Ford Truck Group. M.S. McLaughlin was now Assistant General Manager of Ford Division Sales and Marketing. Calendar-year output was 72,734 units representing 0.8 percent of industry. A total of 69,176 T-Birds, representing 0.8 percent of total industry output, were produced for the model year in the Wixom factory. Calendar year dealer sales were 68,816 T-Birds, representing 0.8 percent of industry sales. The flying-carpet-on-autopilot" is how *Car Life* (June 1966) referred to the Thunderbird that it tested. "Aladdin himself would be astounded at the things this Ford-built 'jinni' can do — and without all that tiresome rubbing of lamps." The writers, of course, were referring to the car's "bells and whistles," which they had the opportunity to try out during a cruise from Los Angeles to Las Vegas. Their "magic carpet" was described as a Town Landau carrying "Aquamarine Blue lower body paint, a pebbled White vinyl-covered top with aluminized plastic landau bars at the windowless rear quarter panel, special tires with both red and white striping, Beige leather-like vinyl upholstery, interior trim of chromium and walnut, loop pile nylon carpeting in a matching blue-green shade and a Beige molded fiberglass headliner." It was loaded with the 428-cid V-8, air conditioning, California emission controls, vacuum door locks, a door warning light, a low-fuel warning lamp, emergency flashers, power seats, speed control, and a special steering wheel for the speed control. Naturally, this was all in addition to such standard features as Cruise-O-Matic transmission, power steering, power front disc brakes, AM radio, bonded mirror, heater, hydraulic wipers, and Swing-Away steering wheel. *Car Life*, in its test, had nothing but praise for the Thunderbird. This included advice that the car with power front discs drew quickly to a halt, in a straight line, hardly screeching the tires. The steering was assessed as "a definite surprise when compared to mushy, imprecise, and slow-turning assisted systems." The magazine liked the car's "steering only" (with speed control on) operation, plus its Swing-Away steering wheel, electric seat, power windows and air conditioning system. It did, however, note the shortage of rear seat legroom and some wind rumble at speeds above 60 mph). With the big engine the car could do 0 to 30 mph in 3.1 seconds, 0 to 50 in 6.8 seconds, and 0 to 100 in 29 seconds. Moving from 30-70 mph in passing gear took 9.3 seconds.

Thunderbird — Series 8 — V-8: The 1967 T-Bird was completely redesigned with a perimeter frame, a semi-unit body and an all-coil-spring suspension. The convertible was replaced by a four-door Landau. The sporty four-door, with center-opening doors, was viewed as competitor for sales with the Jaguar Mark II and the Maserati Quattroporte. Also available was a two-door hardtop and two-door Landau. The new T-birds had long-hood/short-deck styling with a long front overhang. Full-radius wheel openings and the lack of fender skirts gave an "open-wheel" look. A full-width oval bumper housed a lattice-work grille, "Hide-Away" headlights and a T-Bird-shaped center trim piece. One-piece curved door glass eliminated vent windows. Two-door hardtops had rear quarter windows that retracted by sliding horizontally. Both Landau models had roofs with wide "C" pillars that gave them a close-coupled appearance. All models had a "Coke bottle" profile and wall-to-wall sequential taillights at the rear. Landaus had vinyl tops and S-shaped landau irons with center medallions. The T-Bird interior had a smoother and cleaner dashboard with four dials across the dash. A new Tilt-Away steering wheel swung aside or tilted to make it easy for the driver to enter or leave the car. The 1967 T-Bird took driver and passenger safety to new levels. In addition to a padded, shock-absorbing steering wheel, padded dashboard and back-up braking system, Ford provided front seat shoulder harnesses that stowed above the doors with Velcro fasteners, plus recessed sun visors, pliable rubber door grab handles and front fender trim pieces. Underneath, the '67s were the first T-Birds in 10 years not to have unit-body construction. Computer-tuned mounting pads carried the T-Bird's semi-unit body on the frame, allowing it to "float" on the mountings. The '67 T-Bird had a steering column gear selector with a shift pattern similar to the Fairlane GTA's, which was arranged like a manual gearshift. The '67s were described as "quiet-riding cars on the highway." The new bodies were extremely rigid, due to their stamped-in floor pan stiffeners, heavy sheet metal cross members and full-length drive shaft tunnel. A 14-point body mounting system reduced noise and vibration. All mounts were of bridge-type design and all were located ahead of or behind the passenger compartment. The T-Bird's disc brakes continued to get high marks. The new four-door Landau was initially a big success, with production higher than the combined total of 1964-1966 T-Bird convertibles. Standard equipment includes: Comfort Stream ventilation system, MagicAire heater and defroster, Unipane side glass, sliding quarter windows in coupes, reversible keys, keyless door locking, ignition lock light, suspended accelerator pedal, retractable headlamp doors, built-in dual exhausts, windshield washers, front and rear seat belts with front retractors and warning light, 4-way emergency flashers, signal lights with lane-change feature, automatic brake release, impact-absorbing steering wheel, padded instrument panel, padded sun visors, padded windshield pillars, electric clock, instrument panel courtesy light, sequential turn signals, adjustable front bucket seats, front seat center console with lighted ashtray and stowage compartment, rear seat folding center armrest, door courtesy lights, non-glare day-night tilt-type mirror, full wheel covers, SelectShift Cruise-O-Matic drive, dual hydraulic brake system, self-adjusting power front disc/rear drum brakes, power steering, variable-speed hydraulic windshield wipers, undercoating, parking brake light, map light, glove box light, ashtray light, luggage compartment light, back-up lights, heater and defroster, Tilt-Away movable steering column, AM push-button radio and antenna, fully-trimmed luggage compartment, remote-control left-hand OSRV mirror, Safety-Yoke door latches, positive locking door buttons, five 8.15 x 15 tubeless tires, 390-cid 315-hp V-8 engine, alternator, and all standard FoMoCo safety features. Landau models came with a vinyl top as standard equipment.

The VIN was die-stamped on the right-hand side of cowl top panel tab. The first symbol denoted the model-year: 7=1967. The second symbol indicated the assembly plant: Y=Wixom (Novi), Michigan. The third symbol noted the car-line: 8=Thunderbird. The fourth symbol was

1967 Ford Thunderbird two-door Landau Hardtop (OCW)

1967 Ford Thunderbird two-door Hardtop (OCW)

1967 Ford Thunderbird four-door Landau Sedan (OCW)

the body type: 1=Two-door hardtop painted roof, 2=Two-door Landau, 4=four-door Landau. The fifth symbol denoted the engine: Z=390 cid/315-hp Thunderbird V-8, Q=428-cid/345-hp Thunderbird Special V-8, 8=428-cid Thunderbird Special low-compression V-8 for export. The sixth through 11th symbols were the sequential production numbers of the specific vehicle starting at 100001. The body number plate was located on the front body pillar. The serial number was the same as the VIN tag. Symbols above "BODY" were the body symbol code: 65A=Hardtop, 65B=Landau Hardtop and 57B=Landau Sedan. Symbols above CLR were the paint color code. The first symbol indicated the lower body color. The second symbol indicated the upper body color. Symbols above TRM were the trim combination code. Symbols above "DT" were the production date code. The number indicated the date of the month the car was made. The letter indicated the month of manufacture: A=January, B=February, C=March, D=April, E=May, F=June, G=July, H=August, J=September, K=October, L=November, M=December. Symbols above DSO indicated information including the Ford Motor Co. Sales District Code. Symbols above AX indicated the rear axle: 1=3.00:1 conventional, 6=2.80:1 conventional and A=3.00:1 limited-slip. Symbols above TR indicated the type of transmission: All 1967 Thunderbirds came only with C6 SelectShift Cruise-O-Matic Drive, code U.

Thunderbird (V-8)

Model No.	Body/ Style No.	Body Type and Seating	Factory Price	Shipping Weight	Production Total
1	65A	2-dr. Hardtop-4P	$4,603	4,348 lbs.	15,567
2	65C	2-dr. Landau-4P	$4,704	4,526 lbs.	37,422
4	57D	4-dr. Landau-4P	$4,552	4,348 lbs.	24,967

Note: Hardtop production included five "Apollos" built for Abercrombie & Fitch. See History section.

Engines:

Thunderbird Special 390 Base V-8: Overhead valve. Cast-iron block. Displacement: 390 cid. B & S: 4.05 x 3.78 in. Compression ratio: 10.5:1. Brake hp: 315 at 4600 rpm. Torque: 427 lbs.-ft. at 2800 rpm. Five main bearings. Hydraulic valve lifters. Carburetor: Single four-barrel C7AF-AD. Cooling system capacity: 20.5 qt. with heater. Crankcase capacity: 4 qt. (add 1 qt. with new oil filter). Dual exhausts. Code Z.

Thunderbird Special 428 Base V-8: Overhead valve. Cast-iron block. Displacement: 428 cid. B & S: 4.13 x 3.98 in. Compression ratio: 10.50:1. Brake hp: 345 at 4600 rpm. Torque: 462 lbs.-ft. at 2800 rpm. Five main bearings. Hydraulic valve lifters. Carburetor: Single four-barrel C7AF-AD. Cooling system capacity: 20.5 qt. with heater. Crankcase capacity: 4 qt. (add 1 qt. with new oil filter). Dual exhausts. Code Q. (The 428-cid export V-8 was also available in export units.)

Chassis:

Wheelbase (two-door): 114.7 in., (four-door) 117.2 in. Overall length (two-door): 206.9 in., (four-door) 209.4. Overall width (all): 77.2 in. Overall height (two-door): 52.8 in., (four-door) 53.7 in. Front tread: 62 in. Rear tread: 62 in. Front Hip Room: 2 x 22.5 in. Effective headroom: 38.4 in. Rear Hip Room: 54.3 in. Box volume: 505.1 cu. ft. Front area: 22.8 sq. ft. Tires: 8.15 x 15 4-ply.

Technical:

Wheelbase (two-door): 114.7 in., (four-door) 117.2 in. Overall length (two-door): 206.9 in., (four-door) 209.4. Overall width (all): 77.2 in. Overall height (two-door): 52.8 in., (four-door) 53.7 in. Front tread: 62 in. Rear tread: 62 in. Front hip room: 2 x 22.5 in. Effective headroom: 38.4 in. Rear hip room: 54.3 in. Box volume: 505.1 cu. ft. Front area: 22.8 sq. ft. Tires: 8.15 x 15 4-ply. Steering: Power-assisted link type. Steering ratio: 20.4:1. Turn diameter: 40.2 ft. Front suspension: Independent SLA type with drag strut, ball joints and rubber-bushed stabilizer. Rear suspension: Three-link type with coil springs and rubber-bushed lateral track bar. Telescoping shocks were mounted on the T-Bird suspension front and rear. Standard rear axle: 3.00:1. Front brakes: 11.87 x 1.125 in. power front disc. Rear brakes: 11.03-in. X 2.25 in. drums. Effective area 398 sq. in. Standard transmission: SelectShift three-element Cruise-O-Matic automatic transmission. Gas tank: 24.1 gallons (premium fuel required).

Options:

Body side accent stripe ($13.90). SelectAire air conditioner ($421.49). Tinted glass ($47.49). 80-amp heavy-duty battery ($7.44). Limited-slip differential ($46.69). California type emissions control system with EECS only ($5.19). Exhaust emission control system, California type ($49.45). 428-cid 345-hp V-8 with Cruise-O-Matic transmission, extra charge over base V-8 ($90.68). Extra heavy-duty cooling package, standard with air conditioning ($7.73). Tinted glass with banded windshield ($47.49). Tu-Tone paint, on Tudor Hardtop only ($25.25). Retracting power antenna ($28.97). Power deck lid release ($12.63). 6-way power driver's seat ($97.32). Power windows ($103.95). Two-door Protection group ($25.28). Four-door Protection group ($29.17). Note: Protection Groups include front and rear color-keyed floor mats, license plate frames, and door edge guards. AM/FM Multiplex stereo radio with speakers ($163.17). AM manual Stereosonic tape system ($128.49). AM/FM radio with dual rear speakers ($89.94). Overhead Convenience Control Panel, includes speed-actuated power door locks, door ajar light, low-fuel light, and emergency flashers ($77.73 for two-door models, $101.10 for four-door models). Reclining passenger seat with headrest ($57.08). Shoulder harness ($27.27). Dual rear speaker for AM radio only ($33.07). Highway Pilot fingertip speed control, including specific steering wheel ($129.55). Heavy-duty suspension includes front and rear heavy springs and shocks ($27.99). 8.15 x 15 four-ply tires, whitewall with red band ($51.98). 8.15 x 15 four-ply tires, whitewall ($43.12). Split leather trim interior with unique seat trim style and wood-grain accents ($201.06). Deluxe wheel covers with spinners ($19.48). Styled steel wheel covers with chrome lug nuts ($35.70).

History:

The 1967 Thunderbird was introduced on September 22, 1966. Henry Ford II was Board Chairman of Ford Motor Company. Arjay R. Miller was President of FoMoCo. Donald N. Frey was a FoMoCo Vice President and the new General Manager of Ford Division. M.S. McLaughlin was now Vice President and General Manager of Ford Division. J.B. Naughton was assistant general sales manager. Calendar-year output was 59,640 units or 0.8 percent of industry. This was a 16.7 percent drop from the previous year, although much of this was due to a 61-day strike against Ford. A total of 77,956 T-Birds, representing 1 percent of industry output, were produced for the model year in the Wixom factory. Model-year output was up 12.7 percent from 1966. Calendar year dealer sales amounted to 57,913 T-Birds, representing 0.7 percent of industry sales. The 1967 Thunderbird was a fairly good performer. With the optional 428-cid engine, it was even more fun to drive. "While no dragster, the (428) test car's accelerative ability was at least adequate for all present-day driving needs," noted *Car Life*. "Zero to 60 mph acceleration in 10 seconds will take care of the exigencies of on-ramp maneuvering, while sprinting to 82 mph within a quarter-mile's space certainly implies more briskness than most drivers will ever require or employ." Five Thunderbird two-door hardtops were specially-ordered by Abercrombie & Fitch for display in the company's department stores in New York, San Francisco, Chicago, Miami and Palm Beach. These cars were converted into two-door Landau models with sliding sunroofs, with the work being done by Andy Hotten's Detroit Steel Tubing Company at a cost of approximately $15,000 per car. They were loaded up with options and painted Apollo Blue. The cars had serial numbers 7Y81Q122570-7Y81Q122574. At least three of them survive.

1968 Thunderbird

Thunderbird — Series 8 — V-8: The 1968 was mildly revised. The full-width grille had more-widely-spaced openings. Instead of a large T-Bird emblem in the center, there were smaller ones on the grille sides of the rotating headlight doors. The lower part of the narrower new two-piece bumper was painted body color and had large slots below it, one on each side, that provided increased air flow. The parking lamps were set into these slots. A two-door hardtop and two- and four-door Landaus returned along with a new four-door Town Sedan. The Town Sedan's roof was painted, instead of vinyl, and wider S-shaped Landau bars decorated its sail panels. Federally-mandated front fender side marker lamps were seen. The rear fenders had red reflectors that served a similar purpose. Much thinner rocker panel moldings were used. Other new government-required safety features included a non-tilting energy-absorbing steering column (the Tilt-Away wheel became optional equipment), hazard flasher lights, recessed instruments and windshield washers. Shoulder belts, which were previously a $23.38 option, were added to the standard equipment list effective January 1, 1968. A three-passenger Flight Bench front seat was now standard. Bucket seats, a center console and a console-mounted gear selector lever were optional. The T-Bird also featured new squeeze-type inside door handles. Rear seat legroom was increased due to a lower floor tunnel, which was made possible by a new type of universal joint. At the start of the model-year the 390-cid V-8 was base engine. A new IMCO exhaust emission control system was used. It incorporated a different carburetor with a preheated air feature and ignition modifications designed to provide more complete fuel combustion. A new option was a 429-cid "Thunderjet" thin-wall V-8 rated at 360 hp. Based on Ford's lightweight 289-cid V-8, this "big-block" version provided more horsepower with lower emissions. Effective January 1, 1968, the 429 became standard equipment in T-Birds and the 390 was discontinued. Other technical changes for 1968 included new "floating" caliper front disc/rear drum brakes. There were no major changes in the 1968 T-Bird chassis. *Motor Trend* (November 1967) described it as "the ideal car for pleasant journeying." Standard features included: Comfort Stream ventilation system, MagicAire heater and defroster, Unipane side glass, sliding quarter windows in coupes, reversible keys, keyless door locking, ignition switch light, suspended accelerator pedal, retractable headlight doors, built-in dual exhausts, dual-stream windshield wipers, front and rear seat belts with front retractors and warning light, shoulder belts for front outboard passengers (effective January 1, 1968), 4-way emergency flashers, front side marker lights and rear side reflectors, sequential turn signal instrument panel indicator (early production only), signal lights with lane-change feature, automatic brake release, impact-absorbing steering wheel, energy-absorbing instrument panel, padded safety sun visors, padded windshield pillars, electric clock, instrument panel courtesy light, interior rear courtesy light, sequential turn signals, full-width three-passenger front seat, self-locking folding seats, front seat center console with lighted ashtray and stowage compartment, rear seat folding center armrest, door courtesy lights, non-glare day-night tilt-type mirror, full wheel covers, SelectShift Cruise-O-Matic drive, dual hydraulic brake system, self-adjusting power front disc/rear drum brakes, power steering, variable-speed hydraulic windshield wipers, underbody sound coating, parking brake light, map light, glove box light, ashtray light, luggage compartment light, back-up lights, heater and defroster, AM push-button radio and antenna, fully-trimmed luggage compartment, remote-control left-hand OSRV mirror, corrosion-resistant brake lines, Safety-Yoke door latches, positive locking door buttons, five 8.15 x 15 tubeless tires on two-door models or five 8.45 x 15 four-ply-rated black sidewall tires on four-door models, (early) Thunderbird 390 Special 315-hp V-8 engine, (after January 1) Thunderjet 429 360-hp V-8, alternator, and all standard FoMoCo safety features. Landau models came with a vinyl top as standard equipment.

VIN:

The VIN was stamped on an aluminum tab riveted to the dashboard on passenger side and was observable through the windshield from outside the car. The first symbol denoted the model-year: 8=1968. Second symbol indicated the assembly plants: Y=Wixom (Novi), Michigan and J=Los Angeles, California. Third symbol was the car-line: 8=Thunderbird. The fourth symbol denoted the body type: 3=Two-door hardtop, 4=Two-door Landau, 7=four-door Landau. The fifth symbol indicated the engine: Z=390 cid/315-hp Thunderbird V-8, N=429-cid/360-hp Thunder-Jet V-8. The sixth through 11th symbols were the sequential production numbers of the specific vehicle starting at 100001. The body number plate was located on the front door hinge pillar. The serial number was the same as the number on the VIN tag. The symbols above "BODY" were the body symbol code: 65C=Hardtop, 65D=Landau Hardtop and 57C=Landau

Sedan. Symbols above CLR were the paint color code. The first symbol indicated the lower body color. The second symbol indicated the upper body color. Symbols above TRM were the trim combination code. Symbols above "DT" were the production date code. The number indicated the date of the month the car was made. The letters indicated the month of manufacture: A=January, B=February, C=March, D=April, E=May, F=June, G=July, H=August, J=September, K=October, L=November, M=December. Symbols above DSO indicated information including the Ford Motor Co. Sales District Code. Symbols above AX indicated the rear axle: 0=standard 2.50:1, 3=optional 2.80:1, 5=optional 3.0:1, C=optional 2.80:1 limited-slip and E=optional 3.00:1 limited-slip. The TR code indicated the type of transmission: All 1968 T-Birds came only with SelectShift Cruise-O-Matic Drive code U.

Thunderbird (V-8)

Model No.	Body/ Style No.	Body Type and Seating	Factory Price	Shipping Weight	Production Total
8	65A	2-dr. Hardtop-4P	$4,716	4,327 lbs.	9,977
8	65B	2-dr. Landau-4P	$4,845	4,337 lbs.	33,029
8	57B	4-dr. Landau-4P	$4,924	4,427 lbs.	21,925

Note: The production total included 5,420 Model 65A with bucket seats, 19,105 Model 65B with bucket seats and 4,674 Model 57B with bucket seats.

Engines:

Thunderbird 390 Four-Barrel Base V-8: Overhead valve. Cast-iron block. Displacement: 390 cid. B & S: 4.05 x 3.78 in. Compression ratio: 10.5:1. Brake hp: 315 at 4600 rpm. Torque: 427 lbs.-ft. at 2800 rpm. Five main bearings. Hydraulic valve lifters. Carburetor: Four-barrel. Cooling system capacity: 20.5 qt. with heater. Crankcase capacity: Mid-size and Mustang 4 qt. and full-size and T-Bird 5 qt. (add 1 qt. with new oil filter). Dual exhausts. Code Z.

Thunder Jet 429 V-8: Overhead valve. Cast-iron block. Displacement: 429 cid. B & S: 4.36 x 3.59 in. Compression ratio: 10.50:1. Brake hp: 360 at 4600 rpm. Torque: 480 lbs.-ft. at 2800 rpm. Five main bearings. Hydraulic valve lifters. Carburetor: Motorcraft four-barrel. Cooling system capacity: 18.6 qt. with heater (T-bird 19.4 qt.). Crankcase capacity: 5 qt. (add 1 qt. with new oil filter). Dual exhausts. Code N.

Chassis:

Wheelbase (two-door): 114.7 in., (four-door) 117.2 in. Overall length (two-door): 206.9 in., (four-door) 209.4. Overall width (all): 77.3 in. Overall height: (two-door) 52.6 in., (four-door) 53.4 in. Front tread: 62 in. Rear tread: 62 in. Front Hip Room: 2 x 22.5 in. Effective headroom: 38.1 in. Rear hip room: 54.3 in. Box volume: 505.1 cu. ft. Front area: 22.8 sq. ft. Tires: 8.15 x 15 4-ply.

Technical:

Steering: Power-assisted link type. Ratio: 21.9:1. Turning diameter: 42.0 ft. Front suspension: Independent SLA type with coil springs and ball joints. Rear suspension: Four-link type with coil springs. Telescoping shocks were mounted on the T-Bird suspension front and rear. Standard rear axle: 3.00:1. Front brakes: 11.80 x 1.125 in. power front disc. Rear brakes: 11.03-in. X 2.25 in. drums. Effective area 373 sq. in. Standard transmission: SelectShift three-element Cruise-O-Matic automatic transmission. Gas tank: 24.0 gallons (premium fuel required).

Options:

429-cid ThunderJet V-8 engine, prior to January 1, 1968 ($53.18). Limited-slip rear axle ($46.69). High-ratio axle, standard with 429-cid engine ($46.69). Heavy-duty battery, standard with 429-cid engine ($7.44). Two-door Brougham interior trim with bucket seats ($129.54). Four-door Brougham interior trim with bench seats ($161.98). Brougham leather interior for models with Black or Saddle colored bucket seats ($194.31). Note: Brougham interior trim includes unique seat trim style, wood-grain appointments, door courtesy lights, cut-pile carpets, unique door trim panels, door pull handles, and rear seat center arm rest. Deluxe front or rear shoulder belts ($15.59). Deluxe front shoulder belts ($18.22). Deluxe rear shoulder belts ($18.22). Passenger side reclining seat ($41.49). Adjustable front headrests ($42.75). Tilt-Away

1968 Ford Thunderbird two-door Hardtop (OCW)

1968 Ford Thunderbird two-door Landau Hardtop (OCW)

1968 Ford Thunderbird four-door Landau Sedan (OCW)

1969 Thunderbird

steering wheel ($66.14). Heavy-duty suspension with front and rear heavy springs and shocks ($27.99). Deluxe wheel covers ($57.08). Extra charge for non-standard tires on two-door models without air conditioning: 8.15 x 15 4-ply whitewalls ($43.12). 8.15 x 15 4-ply red band whitewalls ($51.98). 8.45 x 15 4-ply black sidewalls ($18.07). 8.45 x 15 4-ply whitewalls ($61.26). 8.45 x 15 4-ply red band whitewalls ($70). 8.45 x 15 (215 R15) radial-ply whitewalls ($117.64). Extra charge for non-standard tires on two-door models with air conditioning and all four-door models: 8.45 x 15 4-ply whitewalls ($43.19). 8.45 x 15 4-ply red band whitewalls ($52.04). 8.45 x 15 (215 R15) radial-ply whitewalls ($101.30). Appearance Protection Group, including door edge guards, license plate frame and vinyl floor mats front and rear, on tow-door ($25.28), on four-door ($29.17). Body side protection molding ($45.40). Spare Tire Cover ($5.25). Styled steel wheel covers with chrome lug nuts ($35.70). Body accent stripe in Red, White or Black ($13.90). Supplemental brake lamp ($33.70) Front Cornering Lamps ($33.70). Convenience Check Group 2 Door ($77.73), 4 Door ($101.10). Rear Lamp Monitor ($25.91). Four-note horn ($15.59). Rear window defogger ($22.33). Complete tinted glass ($47.49). SelectAire Conditioner ($427.07). SelectAire Conditioner with Automatic Climate Control ($499.22). Dual rear seat speakers with AM radio only ($33.07). AM-FM push-button stereo radio ($150.29). AM push-button radio/StereoSonic tape system ($128.49). Power radio antenna ($28.97). Highway Pilot speed control, *requires* Tilt-Away steering wheel ($97.21). Power deck lid release ($14.85). 6-Way power seat, bench or driver's side bucket ($97.32). Power windows ($103.95). Visor-vanity mirror ($3.79). Automatic headlight dimmer ($51.20 special order). Automatic ride control ($89.94).

History:

The 1968 T-Bird was introduced on September 22, 1967. Henry Ford II was Board Chairman of Ford Motor Company. Arjay R. Miller was Vice Chairman. J.B. Naughton was a FoMoCo Vice President and the new General Manager of Ford Division. G.B. MacKenzie was assistant general sales manager. Lee A Iacocca was named Executive Vice President in charge of North American Operations for Ford Motor Company. Calendar-year output was 76,789 units or 0.9 percent of industry. This was a 28.8 percent rise from the previous year. A total of 64,391 T-Birds, representing 0.8 percent of industry output, were produced. Only 51,429 of these cars were made in the Wixom assembly plant. The additional 13,502 cars were made in Ford's Los Angeles, California factory. Model-year output was down 16.7 percent from 1967. Calendar year dealer sales amounted to 67,373 T-Birds, representing 0.8 percent of industry sales and a 17.6 percent gain over '67. In December 1967, *Motor Trend* magazine published an article titled "How the 429 really performs." In it, editor Steve Kelly drove a 429-powered 1968 T-Bird two-door Landau at the Ford test track in Dearborn, Michigan. The car had only 500 miles on its odometer. A 2.80:1 final drive ratio allowed it to cruise at 27.6 mph per 1000 rpm, keeping engine speed down and gas mileage up. With two people on board, 150 lb. of test equipment, and a full tank of gas, the car moved from 0-60 mph in 9.5 seconds and covered the quarter-mile in 17.4 seconds at 84 mph. "The times were very good, but below those of a 428-cid V-8-powered 'Bird tested in the August '67 *MT*," said Kelly. "The 428 car, though, had nearly 5,000 miles of careful break-in, and from what we learned of the new engine from behind the wheel and from the engineering department, we can safely predict that the 429 will reveal itself a better performer than the earlier 428. In our judgment, not only is the 429 V-8 a breakthrough in low emission design power plants, it is an amazingly good performer with reserve power and reliability." A historical milestone was marked this year when T-Birds were produced in two different factories. Another significant event in the history of Ford Motor Co. occurred this year in the hiring of "Bunkie" Knudsen, a veteran General Motors executive, as FoMoCo's new president. He came to Dearborn on February 6, 1968. This was too late to influence product changes scheduled for 1969, but — even though his tenure at Ford turned out to be very brief — Knudsen would have a role in planning the fifth-generation T-Birds that bowed in 1970.

Thunderbird — Series 8 — (V-8): Ford's new boss, "Bunkie" Knudsen, arrived too late to change the 1969 T-Bird in any significant way. The front and rear were modestly updated for the new model year. A new formal roof treatment with wider "C" pillars graced the Landau coupe, giving it a more stately look. A new die-cast radiator grille featured a full-width horizontal center bar and three widely-spaced vertical bars that crossed it to form eight slim rectangular segments. Each segment had a horizontally textured background and the outer grille segments (actually the headlamp doors) had additional segmentation. There was a large Thunderbird emblem in the center of the grille. The front bumper had indentations cut into the air slots for housing the rectangular parking lamps. At the rear of the car, full-width taillights were gone. Instead a single, large, red rectangular lens on each side carried the T-Bird emblem in its center. Sequential taillight bulbs were used, but the center rear panel section that had the Thunderbird name lettered across it was no longer illuminated. New front side marker lamps had a simpler design and the red reflectors on the rear fenders were smaller. Three body styles were offered again. Like all 1969 Ford products, T-Birds came with FoMoCo's package of "Lifeguard Design Safety Features." This was the name for some two dozen safety items, some required by federal law. They ranged from outside rearview mirrors to "safety" coat hooks. Another new safety feature found on all Ford front seats were headrests. There were standard vinyl bench and bucket seat options, Brougham bucket and bench options and a Brougham leather option for bucket seat interiors only. A center console was included when bucket seats were ordered. The consoles swept upwards, in front, to integrate with the dashboard and included two extra storage boxes to supplement the glove compartment in the dash. Bucket seats with standard vinyl trim were not provided in four-door Landaus, but you could get bucket seats with fancier trims in that model. Reclining seat mechanisms were optional and available on all seats at extra cost. Specific seat trims were available in up to six color choices and vinyl tops came in Black, White, Dark Blue and Ivy Gold. Interiors included a recessed, five-pod gauge cluster with full instrumentation as standard equipment. Also standard in Thunderbirds was a 429-cid 360-hp V-8 and SelectShift Cruise-O-Matic automatic transmission. The big engine featured dual exhausts as regular equipment. Ford's biggest automatic transmission had a P-R-N-D-2-1 shift pattern that provided a choice of manual-style or fully-automatic gear selection. Several new options were introduced this year. One was a wire-in-glass type rear window defroster and the other was a push-button sliding electric sunroof. Constructed entirely of metal, the sunroof (last offered in 1960) was power-operated. A small button on the bottom portion of the dash activated it. *Motor Trend* (February 1969) said, "The roof itself is a solid, well-built unit that seals tightly into place when closed." Also noted was a lack of turbulence with the roof open and the fact that the car stayed warm when the roof was rolled back on chilly, but sunny days. A crank was provided to operate the roof in case of electrical failure. Technical improvements for 1969 were mainly refinements. All T-Birds came equipped with an Autolite "Sta-Ful" battery, Autolite "Power-Tip" spark plugs, Autolite shock absorbers and an Autolite 6,000-mile oil filter. Ford promoted "Twice-A-Year Maintenance" based on the fact that recommended oil change intervals were 6,000 miles or six months. Coolant replacement was called for at 24 months and major chassis lubrication was supposed to be good for 36,000 miles. "The '69 Thunderbird needs so little service it's just good sense to see that it gets the best — at your Ford dealer's," said the sales catalog. There were some important suspension modifications on 1969 two-door models and all T-Birds were lowered one-half inch. Coupes got what amounted to a heavy-duty suspension package. It included stiffer springs with a ride rate of 135 lb.-in. up front and 123 lb.-in. in the rear, larger shock absorbers and a fatter 0.812-in. diameter anti-roll bar. While this gave a ride that was still on the traditional "T-Bird-soft" side, it was firmer than in the past. "Ride and handling characteristics are vastly improved in the two-door models due to suspension modifications," *Motor Trend* reported. "The change in suspension has reduced roll and gives a flatter, smoother ride when cornering." Standard equipment included: ThunderJet 429-cid 360-hp V-8, SelectShift Cruise-O-Matic drive, Unipane side glass, reversible keys, keyless locking, lighted ignition switch, full-width three-passenger front seat, power steering, AM radio, electric clock, MagicAire heater and defroster, suspended accelerator pedal, lockable lighted glove box, map light, instrument panel courtesy light, rear interior courtesy lights, power front disc/rear drum brakes, sequential turn signals, lined and lighted luggage compartment, underbody sound coating, full wheel covers, dual hydraulic brake system with warning light, front and rear seat belts with front outboard retractors, floating day/night breakaway inside rearview mirror, energy-absorbing instrument panel, padded safety sun visors, variable-speed hydraulic windshield wipers, windshield washers, 4-way emergency flasher, back-up lights, side marker lights, self-locking folding front seat backs, shoulder belts

1969 Ford Thunderbird two-door Hardtop (OCW)

for outboard front seat passengers, remote-control left-hand outside rearview mirror, retractable headlight doors that open automatically if vacuum system fails, power ventilation, directional signals with lane-change feature, adjustable headrests (after January 1, 1969) and cornering side lights (optional on very early-production cars).

VIN:

The VIN was stamped on an aluminum tab riveted to the dashboard on the passenger side and observable through the windshield from outside the car. The first symbol denoted the model-year: 9=1969. The second symbol indicate the assembly plants: Y=Wixom (Novi), Michigan and J=Los Angeles, California. The third symbol was the car-line: 8=Thunderbird. The fourth symbol denoted the body type: 3=Two-door hardtop, 4=Two-door Landau, 7=four-door Landau. The fifth symbol indicated the engine: N=429-cid/360-hp Thunder-Jet V-8. The sixth through 11th symbols were the sequential production numbers of the specific vehicle starting at 100001. The body number plate was located on the front body pillar. The serial number was the same as the number on the VIN tag. Symbols above "BODY" were body symbol codes: 65A=two-door hardtop with bucket front seat, 65C=two-door Hardtop with front bench seat; 65B=two-door Landau with blind quarter roof and front bucket seats; 65D=two-door Landau with blind rear quarter roof and front bench seat; 57B=four-door Landau with front bucket seats; 57C=four-door Landau with front bench seat. Symbols above CLR are paint color code. The first symbol indicated the lower body color. The second symbol indicated the upper body color. Symbols above TRM were trim combination codes. Symbols above "DT" were the production date codes. The number indicates the date of the month the car was made. The letters indicate month of manufacture: A=January, B=February, C=March, D=April, E=May, F=June, G=July, H=August, J=September, K=October, L=November, M=December. Symbols above DSO indicated information including the Ford Motor Co. Sales District Code. Symbols above AX indicated the rear axle: 4=2.80:1, 6=3.00:1, M=2.80:1 limited-slip and O=3.00:1 limited-slip. Symbols above TR indicated the type of transmission: All 1968 T-Birds came only with SelectShift Cruise-O-Matic Drive C6 (Code U) or SelectShift a Automatic C6 Special (Code Z).

Thunderbird (V-8)

Model No.	Body/ Style No.	Body Type and Seating	Factory Price	Shipping Weight	Production Total
8	65A/65C	2-dr. Hardtop-4P	$4,807	4,348 lbs.	5,913
8	65B/65D	2-dr. Landau-4P	$4,947	4,360 lbs.	27,664
8	57B/57C	4-dr. Landau-4P	$5,026	4,460 lbs.	15,650

Note: 65A=two-door hardtop with bucket front seat, 65C=two-door Hardtop with front bench seat; 65B=two-door Landau with blind quarter roof and front bucket seats; 65D=two-door Landau with blind rear quarter roof and front bench seat; 57B=four-door Landau with front bucket seats; 57C=four-door Landau with front bench seat.

Prices increased by $17 on February 1, 1969 after front headrests became standard federally-mandated equipment.

Production totals above include 2,361 Model 65A with bucket seats, 12,125 Model 65B with bucket seats and 1,983 Model 57B with bucket seats.

Engines:

Thunder Jet 429 Four-Barrel V-8: Overhead valve. Cast-iron block. Displacement: 429 cid. B & S: 4.36 x 3.59 in. Compression ratio: 10.50:1. Brake hp: 360 at 4600 rpm. Torque: 480 lbs.-ft. at 2800 rpm. Five main bearings. Hydraulic valve lifters. Carburetor: Motorcraft four-barrel. Cooling system capacity: 18.6 qt. with heater (T-bird 19.4 qt.). Crankcase capacity: 5 qt. (add 1 qt. with new oil filter). Dual exhausts. Code N.

Chassis:

Wheelbase (two-door): 114.7 in., (four-door) 117.2 in. Overall length (two-door): 206.9 in., (four-door) 209.4. Overall width (all): 77.3 in. Overall height (two-door) 52.3 in., (four-door) 53.4 in. Front tread: 62 in. Rear tread: 62 in. Front hip room: 2 x 23 in. Front headroom: 37.1 in. Rear hip room: 53.5 in. Rear headroom: 36.7 in. Door opening width: 40.5 in. Tires: 8.45 x 15 4-ply.

Technical:

Steering: Integral with power-assist, 4.0 turns lock-to-lock. Steering ratio: 21.8 to 1. Turning diameter: 42 ft. Front suspension: Independent wishbone type with coil springs and ball joints. Rear suspension: Four-link type with coil springs. Telescoping shocks were mounted on the T-Bird suspension front and rear. Standard rear axle: 3.00:1. Front brakes: 11.72 x 1.77 in. power front disc. Rear brakes: 11.03-in. X 2.25 in. drums. Rear brake swept area 373.2 sq. in. Standard transmission: SelectShift three-element Cruise-O-Matic automatic transmission. Gas tank: 24.1 gallons (premium fuel required).

Options:

SelectAire air conditioner ($427.07). SelectAire conditioner with automatic climate control ($499.22). Electric sun roof in Landau model ($453.30). Sure Track anti-lock braking system ($194.31). Flight Bucket seats and console ($64.77). Reclining front passenger seat ($41.49). 6-Way power seat ($98.89). Power window lifts ($109.22). Power trunk lid release ($14.85). Power retracting antenna ($28.97). Rear window defogger ($22.23). Electric defroster and tinted rear window ($84.25). Tinted glass ($47.49). Highway-Pilot speed control, requires Tilt-Away steering wheel ($97.21). Tilt-Away steering wheel ($66.14). Four-door convenience group ($101.10). Two-door convenience group ($77.73). AM/FM stereo with speakers ($150.29). Stereo sonic AM radio with tape player ($128.49). Dual rear speakers, standard with stereo sonic or stereo ($33.07). Limited-slip differential axle ($46.69) Four-note horn ($15.59). Brougham cloth and vinyl interior trim with bucket seats ($129.54). Brougham cloth and vinyl interior trim with bench seats ($161.98). Brougham vinyl and leather interior for models with Black or Saddle colored bucket seats ($194.31). Note: Brougham interior trim includes unique seat trim style, wood-grain appointments, door courtesy lights, cut-pile carpets, unique door trim panels, door pull handles, and rear seat center arm rest. Deluxe seat belts with warning light ($15.59). Deluxe front and rear shoulder belts ($15.60). Rear lamp monitor ($25.91). High-level rear window brake lamp, supplemental, four-door Landaus only ($33.70). Two-door Protection group ($25.28). Four-door protection group ($29.17). Heavy-duty suspension ($27.99). Deluxe wheel covers ($57.08). Simulated styled wheel covers with chrome lug nuts, finished in Argent Silver, Brittany Blue, Candy apple Red, Champagne Gold, Midnight Aqua or Oxford Gray ($35.70). Extra charge for non-standard tires: 8.55 x 15 whitewalls ($42.88). 8.55 x 15 red band whitewalls ($52.04). Size 215-B15 A (6.55 x 15) steel-belted radial whitewall tires ($101.30). Fiberglass-belted white sidewall tires ($75.43). 215R15 Michelin radial-ply white sidewall tires ($101.30). Goodyear Power-Cushion Life Guard dual-chamber tires with unique whitewall design ($196.80). Adjustable head restraints prior to January 1, 1969 ($17). Cornering sidelights ($33.70, but became standard early in the production run). Rear lamp monitor ($25.91). Rear shoulder belts ($27.06). Body side protection moldings ($45.40). Spare tire cover ($5.25). Body accent stripe in Red, White or Black ($13.90). Right-hand outside rearview mirror ($6.95). Visor-vanity mirror ($3.79). Deck lid luggage rack ($32.45). Automatic headlight dimmer, special order ($51.20) and Automatic Red Control ($89.94).

History:

The 1968 T-Bird was introduced on September 27, 1968. Henry Ford II was Board Chairman of Ford Motor Company. Arjay R. Miller was Vice Chairman. Lee A Iacocca was Executive Vice President of Ford Motor Company. J.B. Naughton was a FoMoCo Vice President and the new General Manager of Ford Division. G.B. MacKenzie was assistant general sales manager. Calendar-year output was 50,143 units. This was a 34.7 percent drop from the previous year. A total of 49,272 T-Birds, representing 0.6 percent of industry output, were produced in the model year. This was a decline of 24.1 percent. Of these units, 40,571 were made in the Wixom assembly plant and 8,701 were made in Ford's Los Angeles, California factory. Calendar year dealer sales amounted to 49,381 T-Birds, representing 0.58 percent of industry sales and a 26.7 percent drop from 1968. The 1969 T-Bird was designed to do battle with personal-luxury cars like the Buick Riviera, Cadillac Eldorado, Oldsmobile Toronado, Dodge Charger and Pontiac Grand Prix, all of which had arrived in the market since 1962. Considering that the T-Bird was the "old buzzard" of the bunch, the competition actually strengthened its image. "Ford hasn't just 'added on' the '69 'Bird, but has made definite and worthwhile improvements right down the line — in ride, handling, comfort and convenience," *Motor Trend* reported. "It has that elusive, diffident air known as class." While the 1969 T-Bird was the "class of its class," it was still basically a 1967 model and its aging did have a negative effect on sales in a new-product-driven marketplace. In fact, Thunderbird model-year production dropped to its lowest point since 1958. It included 1,983 four-door Landaus with bucket seats, 13,712 four-door Landaus with bench seats, 2,361 two-door Hardtops with bucket seats, 3,552 two-door Hardtops with bench seats, 12,425 two-door Landaus with bucket seats and 15,239 two-door Landaus with bench seats. Even this low production total — 49,272 units — outpaced the production of front-wheel-drive Eldorados (27,100) and Toronados (28,500) and came within striking distance of the 52,700 Rivieras built. However, the less expensive Charger (69,000) and the all-new Pontiac Grand Prix

1969 Ford Thunderbird two-door Landau Hardtop (OCW)

(112,500) found many more buyers. Change was needed and was on its way. Unfortunately, coming T-Bird revisions did not last very long for two reasons. First, they had virtually no effect on the car's popularity. Sales climbed microscopically in 1970, then plummeted again in 1971. Second, they were changes that Ford's new general manager "Bunkie" Knudsen brought in with his GM thinking and Knudsen was fired even before they hit the market. In August 1969, the former GM executive was let go after a personality conflict with FoMoCo Chairman Henry Ford II erupted in Dearborn. Some observers blamed his firing on the fact that Knudsen wanted to involve Ford in motor sports and HFII did not want to go that route. Others said that Knudsen's management concepts went against the Ford family's concept of centralized control of the company. Whatever the reason, Knudsen's departure was probably good for the Thunderbird, since he seemed incapable of understanding what made the car sell.

1970 Thunderbird

Thunderbird — Series 8 — (V-8): The 1970 T-Birds are often called "Bunkie" Birds because their bold, dramatically-different formal appearance reflected the influence of Semon E. "Bunkie" Knudsen. Knudsen had left General Motors to take over the reins at Ford, but he clashed with Henry Ford II and his tenure at the firm bearing HFII's name was very short. He did, however, stick around long enough to help develop the 1970 T-Bird. With all-new front end sheet metal, the T-Bird was six inches longer and one inch lower to the ground. Its new radiator grille stuck way out and came to a point. Some said it had a Pontiac-like look. Unfortunately, its protruding center section proved prone to damage, inspiring insurance companies to charge T-Bird owners' higher premiums. Hide-Away headlights were discontinued, but the radio antenna and windshield wipers were now tucked out of sight. Full-width taillights returned. They had a new inverted-U appearance and sequential turn signals. The length and lowness of the T-Bird was accented by a single horizontal feature line along the mid body sides. A full-width vinyl "Flight Bench" front seat was standard. A Special Brougham option featured hopsack-and-vinyl upholstery. Ford's "better idea" Swing-Away steering wheel was gone. A Tilt-Away type was optional. Color-keyed wheel covers added to the rich look of T-Birds with the Brougham package. The T-Bird engine was again the 429-cid 360-hp V-8. Dual exhausts and SelectShift Cruise-O-Matic transmission were standard. The T-Bird's strong body-on-frame design consisted of a front end assembly, a rear end assembly and four torque box assemblies connected by formed center rails (which were longer on the four-door model). The frame featured rugged ladder-type construction with five reinforced cross members. Node-point body mounting at 14 computer-designed positions resulted in superior noise and vibration suppression characteristics. Up front, the suspension used drag-struts and ball joints, plus a rubber-bushed stabilizer bar. The rear suspension was by a three-link coil spring system with a long-and short mounting link arrangement. A lateral track bar centered the axle. All of the links, as well as the track bar, had rubber bushings. Integral-design power steering was featured. The self-adjusting brakes used floating caliper discs in front and drum-shoe brakes at the rear. The drums were cross-ribbed and flared. True-Center wheels on precision-machined hubs carried the radial-ply tires. Standard equipment included: ThunderJet 429-cid 360-hp V-8, SelectShift Cruise-O-Matic transmission, integral Fluidic-Control power steering, self adjusting front disc/rear drum brakes, dual exhausts, full instrumentation, remote-control left hand outside rearview mirror, radial tires, Flight Bench seats with fold-down center armrest, power ventilation system, concealed electric windshield wipers, Uni-Lock safety harness, sequential turn signals, cornering lights, ventless side glass, reversible keys, keyless door locking, electric clock, MagicAire heater and defroster, lockable lighted glove box, map light with automatic time delay (early production units), lined and lighted luggage compartment, full wheel covers, articulated accelerator pedal, front and rear ashtrays, back-up lights, cigarette lighter, coat hooks, courtesy lights, floor carpeting, all-vinyl color-keyed headlining, day/night rearview mirror, teak-toned appliqué on instrument panel and all Ford Motor Company Lifeguard Design safety features.

VIN:

The VIN was stamped on an aluminum tab riveted to the dashboard on the passenger side and was observable through the windshield from outside the car. The prefix indicated the manufacturer: F=Ford. The first symbol denoted the model-year: 0=1970. The second symbol indicated the assembly plant: Y=Wixom (Novi), Michigan and J=Los Angeles, California. The third symbol was the car-line: 8=Thunderbird. The fourth symbol indicated the body type: 3=Two-door hardtop, 4=Two-door Landau, 7=Four-door Landau. The fifth symbol was the engine: N=429-cid/360-hp Thunder-Jet V-8. The sixth through 11th symbols were the sequential production numbers of the specific vehicle starting at 100001. Body certification label located on rear face of driver's door. The top part of the label indicated the Thunderbird was manufactured by the Ford Motor Company. Directly below this was the month and year of manufacture, plus a statement that the car conformed to the federal motor vehicle safety standard in effect on the indicated date of manufacture. The VIN appears first on the first line of encoded information. It matches the 1st to 11th symbols on VIN tag. The body style code appeared to the right of the VIN on the same line. The Thunderbird codes for this model-year were: 57B=four-door Landau with front split-bench seat; 57C=four-door Landau with front bench seat; 65A=two-door Hardtop with front bucket seats; 65B=two-door Landau with front bucket seats; 65C=two-door Hardtop with front bench seat; 65D=two-door Landau with front bench seat. The color code(s) appeared to the right of the body style code. Conventional colors were identified by a single letter or number. Optional Glamour Paints are identified by two numbers. The trim code appeared on the far left-hand side of the second line of encoded information. The axle code appeared to the right of the trim code in the second position on the second line of encoded information. Axle codes were: 2=2.75:1, 4=2.80:1, 6=3.00:1, K=2.75:1 limited-slip, M=2.80:1 limited-slip and O=3.00:1 limited-slip. Transmission codes were: U=SelectShift Cruise-O-Matic C6 three-speed automatic, Z= SelectShift Cruise-O-Matic C6 special three-speed automatic. The transmission code appeared to the right of the axle code in the third position on the second line of encoded information. The District Special Equipment (DSO) code appeared to the right of the transmission code in the far right-hand position on the second line of encoded information. The abbreviations VIN/BDY/CLR/TRM/AX/TR/DSO did not appear on the certification label itself. The specific application of the codes was determined by where they are located on the vehicle certification label.

Thunderbird (V-8)

Model No.	Body/ Style No.	Body Type and Seating	Factory Price	Shipping Weight	Production Total
8	65A/65C	2-dr. Hardtop-4P	$4,916	4,354 lbs.	5,116
8	65B/65D	2-dr. Landau-4P	$5,104	4,630 lbs.	36,847
8	57B/57C	4-dr. Landau-4P	$5,182	4,464 lbs.	8,401

Note: 65A=two-door hardtop with bucket front seat, 65C=two-door Hardtop with front bench seat; 65B=two-door Landau with blind quarter roof and front bucket seats; 65D=two-door Landau with blind rear quarter roof and front bench seat; 57B=four-door Landau with front split-bench seats; 57C=four-door Landau with front bench seat. Production totals above include 1,925 Model 65A with bucket seats, 16,953 Model 65B with bucket seats and 5,005 Model 57B with bucket seats.

Engines:

Thunder Jet 429 Four-Barrel V-8: Overhead valve. Cast-iron block. Displacement: 429 cid. B & S: 4.36 x 3.59 in. Compression ratio: 10.50:1. Brake hp: 360 at 4600 rpm. Torque: 480 lbs.-ft. at 2800 rpm. Five main bearings. Hydraulic valve lifters. Carburetor: Motorcraft four-barrel. Cooling system capacity: 18.6 qt. with heater (T-bird 19.4 qt.). Crankcase capacity: 5 qt. (add 1 qt. with new oil filter). Dual exhausts. Code N.

Chassis:

Wheelbase (two-door): 114.7 in., (four-door) 117.2 in. Overall length (two-door): 212.5 in., (four-door) 215 in. Overall width: (two-door) 78 in. and (four-door) 77.4 in. Overall height (two-door): 51.4 in., (four-door) 53.6 in. Front tread: 62 in. Rear tread: 62 in. Tires: 215R15 radial.

Technical:

Steering: Integral with power-assist, 3.6 turns lock-to-lock. Overall steering ratio: 21.9 to 1. Turning diameter: (two-door) 42.7 ft., (four-door) 43.4 ft. Front suspension: Coil spring and drag-strut ball-joint type with rubber-bushed stabilizer. Rear suspension: Three-link coil-spring with

1970 Ford Thunderbird two-door Hardtop (OCW)

1970 Ford Thunderbird two-door Hardtop (OCW)

long-and-short mounting link and lateral track bar (all rubber-bushed). Telescopic shock absorbers front and rear. Standard rear axle: 2.8:1. Front brakes: Power front disc. Rear brakes: Power drums.

Options:

SelectAire air conditioner ($427.07). SelectAire conditioner with automatic climate control ($499.22). Electric sun roof in Landau model ($453.30). Sure Track anti-lock braking system ($194.31). Flight Bucket seats and console ($64.77). Reclining front passenger seat ($41.49). 6-Way power seat ($98.89) Power window lifts ($109.22). Power trunk lid release ($14.85). Power retracting antenna ($28.97). Rear window defogger ($22.23). Electric defroster ($84.25). Tinted windows ($47.49). Highway-Pilot speed control, requires Tilt-Away steering wheel ($97.21). Tilt-Away steering wheel ($66.14). Four-door convenience group ($101.10). Two-door convenience group ($77.73). AM/FM stereo with speakers ($150.29). Stereo sonic AM radio with tape player ($128.49). Dual rear speakers, standard with stereo sonic or stereo ($33.07). Limited-slip differential axle ($46.69) Four-note horn ($15.59). Brougham cloth and vinyl interior trim with bucket seats ($129.54). Brougham cloth and vinyl interior trim with bench seats ($161.98). Brougham vinyl and leather interior for models with Black or Saddle colored bucket seats ($194.31). Note: Brougham interior trim includes unique seat trim style, wood-grain appointments, door courtesy lights, cut-pile carpets, unique door trim panels, door pull handles, and rear seat center arm rest. Deluxe seat belts with warning light ($15.59). Rear lamp monitor ($25.91). High-level rear window brake lamp, supplemental, four-door Landaus only ($33.70). Two-door Protection group ($25.28). Four-door protection group ($29.17). Heavy-duty suspension ($27.99). Simulated styled steel wheel covers ($57.08). Extra charge for non-standard tires: 8.55 x 15 whitewalls ($42.88). 8.55 x 15 red band whitewalls ($52.04). Size 215-B15 A (6.55 x 15) steel-belted radial whitewall tires ($101.30).

History:

The 1970 T-Bird was introduced on September 19, 1969. Henry Ford II was Board Chairman of Ford Motor Company. Lee A Iacocca was the new Executive Vice president and President of North American Auto Operations. J.B. Naughton was a Vice President and General Manager of Ford Division. G.B. MacKenzie was General Marketing manager for Ford Division. Calendar-year output was 40,512 units. This was a 23.8 percent drop from the previous year. A total of 50,364 T-Birds were produced in the model year. Of these units, 30,830 were made in the Wixom assembly plant and 19,534 were made in Ford's Los Angeles, California factory. Calendar year dealer sales amounted to 40,868 T-Birds, representing 0.6 percent of industry sales. In November 1969, *Motor Trend* did a comparison road test pitting the T-Bird against the Chevrolet Monte Carlo and Pontiac Grand Prix. "The '70 'Bird is practically an entirely new car, even without what should be called a major change" suggested writer Bill Sanders with a bit of wordsmithing. He was talking about its lower height and new body-hugging roofline. "The first thing that comes to mind when looking at the two-door in profile is the beautiful custom work of the late '40s and early '50s," chimed Sanders. "The '70 'Bird is reminiscent of some of those early creations and looks like it has been chopped and channeled." Mentioned in the article was the T-Bird's adoption of the Lincoln Mark III's sound insulation package to reduce noise inside the car, the fact that the seats had additional comfort padding, and the use of an in-the-windshield wire-type radio antenna. Despite its larger size and heavier weight, the 1970 model performed almost exactly the same as the 1969 edition. "Unlike the Monte Carlo or Grand Prix, the 'Bird is not specifically a performance-oriented car, but is more at home with the luxury aspects," said Sanders. "For instance, acceleration may not be as rapid, but it is fluid smooth with no quick shifting movements." With its new suspension and radial tires, the car was a better handler than previous Thunderbirds. It had very little under

1970 Ford Thunderbird four-door Landau Sedan (OCW)

steer and driver control was described as "uncanny." All in all, the car was summarized as combining a custom luxury feeling with outstanding ride and handling abilities.

1971 Thunderbird

Thunderbird — Series 8 — (V-8): The 1971 Thunderbird was the 1970 model with minor trim revisions. The grille had slightly wider bright metal blades at every third rung, which gave it a horizontally-segmented look. There were nine vertical bars in the new grille. Front side marker lamps with a one-piece lens were introduced. In addition, the front bumper had more massive wraparound edges. A few bits of chrome were revised. Some new exterior appearance options were color-keyed wheel covers, body side moldings with color-keyed protective vinyl inserts and wheel opening moldings. These all came as part of the Brougham interior option. The same three Thunderbird body styles were offered. H78 x 15 belted bias-ply tires were standard. Michelin 215R15 steel-belted radials were standard with the Special Brougham option. In 1971, the T-Bird was the only U.S. car offered with radial tires as an option. This was the only year that the four-door Landau model was not available with optional front bucket seats. A front bench seat was also standard in two-door models, but bucket seats were optional. Front seating options included standard vinyl bench seats (all models), vinyl bucket seats (optional in two-door models), Brougham bench seat (optional in two-door models), Brougham split bench seat (optional in four-door models), Brougham leather bucket seats (optional in two-door models), Brougham leather bench seat (optional in four-door models) and Special Brougham bucket seats (optional in two-doors models). All standard FoMoCo safety, anti-theft, convenience items and emissions control equipment, sequential rear turn signals, Uni-Lock harness, remote-control left-hand OSRV mirror, locking steering column with ignition key reminder buzzer, electric clock, front cornering lights, AM radio, power ventilation, 100 percent Nylon carpeting, automatic parking brake release, carpeting, padded five-pod instrument panel cluster with full gauges, non-reversing odometer, Safety Design front end, head rests or high-back seats and shoulder belts for front outboard passengers, padded sun visors, energy-absorbing steering column, yield-away day/night inside rearview mirror, fuel evaporative emission control system, hydraulic wipers with electric washers, courtesy lights, energy-absorbing steering column, 4-way emergency flasher, back-up lights, flashing side marker lights, safety coat hooks. MagicAire heater and defroster, glove box light, map light, luggage compartment light, Flight Bench seats with bright seat shields, front seat center arm rest, pleated all-vinyl interior fabric, SelectShift Cruise-O-Matic transmission, power steering, power front disc brakes, dual hydraulic master cylinder, brake warning light, 429-cid 360-hp four-barrel V-8 engine and H78-15 black sidewall bias-ply tires. Landau models included a Cayman Grain vinyl roof.

VIN:

The VIN was stamped on an aluminum tab riveted to the dashboard on the passenger side and was observable through the windshield. The prefix indicated the manufacturer: F=Ford. The first symbol denoted the model-year: 1=1971. The second symbol indicated the assembly plants: Y=Wixom (Novi), Michigan and J=Los Angeles, California. The third symbol denoted the car-line: 8=Thunderbird. The fourth symbol was the body type: 3=Two-door hardtop, 4=Two-door Landau, 7=Four-door Landau. The fifth symbol indicated the engine: N=429-cid/360-hp Thunder-Jet V-8. The sixth through 11th symbols were the sequential production numbers of the specific vehicle starting at 100001. The body certification label was located on the rear face of the driver's door. The top part of the label indicated the Thunderbird was manufactured by Ford Motor Company. Directly below this was the month and year of manufacture, plus a statement that the car conformed to federal motor vehicle safety standards in effect on the indicated date of manufacture. The VIN appeared on the first line of encoded information. It matched the first through 11th symbols on the VIN tag. The body style code appeared to the right of the VIN on the same line. The Thunderbird codes for this model-year were: 57B=four-door Landau with front split-bench seat; 57C=four-door Landau with front bench seat; 65A=two-

1971 Ford Thunderbird two-door Landau Hardtop (OCW)

door Hardtop with front bucket seats; 65B=two-door Landau with front bucket seats; 65C=two-door Hardtop with front bench seat; 65D=two-door Landau with front bench seat. The color code(s) appeared to the right of the body style code. Conventional colors were identified by a single letter or number. Optional glamour paints were identified by two numbers. The trim code appeared on the far left-hand side of the second line of encoded information. The axle code appeared to the right of the trim code in the second position on the second line of encoded information: 2=2.75:1, 4=2.80:1, 6=3.00:1, K=2.75:1 limited-slip, M=2.80:1 limited-slip and O=3.00:1 limited-slip. The transmission code appeared to the right of the axle code in the third position on the second line of encoded information: U=SelectShift Cruise-O-Matic C6 three-speed automatic, Z=SelectShift Cruise-O-Matic C6 special three-speed automatic. The District Special Equipment (DSO) code appeared to the right of the transmission code in the far right-hand position on the second line of encoded information. The abbreviations VIN/BDY/CLR/TRM/AX/TR/DSO were not appear on the certification label itself. The specific application of the codes was determined by where they are located on the vehicle certification label.

Thunderbird (V-8)

Model No.	Body/ Style No.	Body Type and Seating	Factory Price	Shipping Weight	Production Total
8	65A/65C	2-dr. Hardtop-4P	$5,295	4,399 lbs.	9,146
8	65B/65D	2-dr. Landau-4P	$5,438	4,370 lbs.	20,356
8	57B/57C	4-dr. Landau-4P	$5,516	4,509 lbs.	6,553

Note: 65A=two-door hardtop with bucket front seat, 65C=two-door Hardtop with front bench seat; 65B=two-door Landau with blind quarter roof and front bucket seats; 65D=two-door Landau with blind rear quarter roof and front bench seat; 57B=four-door Landau with front bucket seats; 57C=four-door Landau with front bench seat. Production totals above include 2,992 Model 65A with bucket seats, 8,133 Model 65B with bucket seats and 4,238 Model 57B with split bench seats.

Engine:

Thunder Jet 429 Four-Barrel V-8: Overhead valve. Cast-iron block. Displacement: 429 cid. B & S: 4.36 x 3.59 in. Compression ratio: 10.50:1. Brake hp: 360 at 4600 rpm. Torque: 480 lbs.-ft. at 2800 rpm. Five main bearings. Hydraulic valve lifters. Carburetor: Motorcraft four-barrel. Cooling system capacity: 18.6 qt. with heater (T-bird 19.4 qt.). Crankcase capacity: 5 qt. (add 1 qt. with new oil filter). Dual exhausts. Code N.

Chassis:

Wheelbase (two-door): 114.7 in., (four-door) 117.2 in. Overall length (two-door): 212.5 in., (four-door) 215 in. Overall width; (two-door) 78 in., (four-door) 77.4 in. Overall height (two-door): 51.9 in., (four-door) 53.7 in. Front tread: 62 in. Rear tread: 62 in. Tires: H78 x 15.

Technical:

Steering: Integral with power-assist, 3.6 turns lock-to-lock. Overall ratio: 21.9:1. Turning diameter: (two-door) 42.7 ft., (four-door) 43.4 ft. Front suspension: Coil spring and drag-strut ball-joint type with rubber-bushed stabilizer. Rear suspension: Three-link coil-spring with long-and-short mounting link and lateral track bar (all rubber-bushed). Telescopic shock absorbers front and rear. Standard rear axle: 3.0:1. Front brakes: Power front disc. Rear brakes: Power drums.

Options:

SelectAire conditioner ($448). Automatic temperature control with 55-amp alternator and electric rear window defroster ($519). Traction-Lok differential ($49). Sure Track brake control system ($194). Rear window defogger ($26). Electric rear window defroster, includes interior light located in the heater control ($84). Complete tinted glass ($52). Glamour paint ($130). Front and rear bumper guards with rubber inserts ($20). Vinyl-insert body side protection moldings, includes wheel lip moldings, but standard with Brougham package and exterior appearance group ($34). Power antenna ($31). 6-way power full-width seat or 6-way power driver's high-back bucket seat ($104). 6-way power driver and passenger high-back bucket seats ($207). Power side windows ($133). AM/FM stereo radio including dual front and rear seat speakers ($150). Vinyl roof, except standard on Landau models ($141). High-back bucket seats and center console for two-door Thunderbirds, except standard with Brougham option ($78). Manual reclining passenger seat, except standard with Turnpike group ($41). Dual rear seat speakers, standard with AM/FM stereo radio or tape system ($33). Fingertip speed control

including rim-blow deluxe three-spoke steering wheel (standard with Turnpike group, otherwise ($97). Tilt steering wheel ($52). Trailer towing package ($50). Stereophonic tape system with AM radio only ($150). Power-operated sun roof, requires vinyl roof on Hardtop ($518). Heavy-duty suspension with heavy front and rear springs and shocks, front stabilizer bar ($28). Deluxe wheel covers, not available with Special Brougham package or Exterior Appearance group ($52). Power trunk lid release ($14). Exterior appearance group, included with Special Brougham option ($78). Deluxe color-keyed seat belts ($16). Convenience check group including seat belt light, low fuel flasher and door ajar light, vacuum power door locks, front lights-on warning light and buzzer, and automatic seat back release, for two-doors only ($101). Michelin single-band white sidewall steel-belted radial tires, standard with Turnpike Convenience group ($101). Dual-band white sidewall bias-belted tires, standard with Special Brougham option ($30). Turnpike convenience group includes fingertip speed control, manual reclining passenger seat, and Michelin steel-belted radial-ply whitewall tires with 40,000-mile tread life guarantee on Thunderbirds with Brougham option ($196). Turnpike convenience group includes fingertip speed control, manual reclining passenger seat, and Michelin steel-belted radial-ply whitewall tires with 40,000-mile tread life guarantee on Thunderbirds without Brougham option ($227). Exterior appearance group includes color-keyed stone shields and grille finish panels, body side moldings with color-keyed vinyl inserts, color-keyed wheel covers, and wheel lip moldings ($61 only with specific selected exterior colors and not available teamed with special wheel covers, Brougham option, or special paint colors). Protection group includes color-keyed floor mats, license plate frames, and door edge guards for two-doors ($26), for four-doors ($30). Special Brougham option for two-door, includes Hopsack-and-Vinyl high-back bucket seats, matching door panels, center rear armrest, 3-spoke Rim-Blow deluxe steering wheel, plush cut-pile carpeting, door-pull handles, courtesy lights, color-keyed stone shield and grille finish panels, full-length color-keyed body side moldings, wheel-lip moldings, bias-belted double-band white sidewall tires and color-coordinated wheel covers. Brougham low-back bench seat cloth-and-vinyl interior for two-door models ($162). Brougham high-back split-bench seat cloth-and-vinyl interior for four-door models ($162). Brougham bucket seat leather-and-vinyl interior for two-door models ($227). Brougham split-bench seat leather-and-vinyl interior for two-door models ($227).

History:

The 1971 T-Bird was introduced on September 18, 1970. Henry Ford II was Ford's Chairman of the Board. Lee A Iacocca was promoted to President of Ford Motor Company. J.B. Naughton was a Vice President and General Manager of Ford Division. G.B. MacKenzie was General Marketing manager for Ford Division. Calendar-year output was 46,277 units. A total of 36,055 T-Birds were produced in the model year. Of these units, 29,733 were made in Michigan and 6,322 were made in California. Calendar year dealer sales amounted to 41,801 T-Birds, representing 0.5 percent of industry sales. The T-Bird was the only 1971 Ford to increase calendar-year dealer sales over 1970. In December 1970, *Motor Trend* published an article by Jim Brokaw entitled "Almost a Limousine." It was a comparison road test featuring 1971 versions of the "boattail" Riviera, the front-drive Oldsmobile Toronado and the Brougham-optioned Thunderbird two-door Landau. It was the first of a series of annual articles that compared various cars, but almost always included the T-Bird. The 1971 model tested had a list price of $6,649.71, which compared to $6,667.72 for the Buick and $6,457.15 for the Oldsmobile. "These cars are expensive," said the writer. "If you have to check your budget to see whether you can handle the payments, you can't afford one." The five-page story pointed out that the Thunderbird's four-coil suspension differed from that of the other two cars in how the lateral and longitudinal restraints were handled with drag-strut bars up front and three control arms and one track bar at the rear. The T-Bird's system was rated the firmest, but it also exhibited much less roll control than the "Riv" and the "Toro." Brokaw concluded, "The 'Bird requires a bit of attention going into a corner at high speed, but produces no surprises after the initial turn is passed." Of the three cars, the T-Bird was fastest in the quarter-mile acceleration test and the quickest to stop from 30 mph (27 ft.) and 60 mph (129 ft.). Part of the reason for the model year's poor showing may have been that sales of the "Bunkie" Knudsen-designed 1971 models were the responsibility of Lee A. Iacocca, who had a totally different concept of what a Thunderbird should be. Iacocca would soon give the car a new personality and turn the sales trend around.

1971 Ford Thunderbird two-door Hardtop (OCW)

1972 Thunderbird

Thunderbird — Series 8 — (V-8): The 1972 T-Birds were restyled. They were the biggest T-Birds ever. Lee Iacocca created these cars on the "the bigger-is-better" principal. He based them on a new Lincoln Continental Mark IV. The two cars shared chassis and sheet metal. Only a two-door hardtop with a long hood and short rear deck was offered. The grille had a neo-classic look with horizontal bars above and below a massive bumper. The horizontal-bars texture was also used in the headlamp housings. There was a Thunderbird emblem on the car's nose. Notches in the leading edges of the front fenders held the parking lamps, which doubled as side marker lamps. Separate side marker lights and signal lights for the front fender sides were optional. The T-Bird's large, thick doors had guard beams built into them to protect occupants during side-impact collisions. A low semi-fastback roof bridged the extremely wide "C" pillars. A single wall-to-wall taillight lens contributed to a very massive rear end appearance. There were 10 taillight bulbs that lit up the car like a light bar. T-Birds came in 24 colors and the optional Glamour colors — Burgundy Fire, Blue Fire, Green Fire, Lime Fire, Walnut Fire, Cinnamon Fire, Copper Fire and Gold Fire — were particularly brilliant. They came in packages that included color-coordinated wheel covers and moldings, hood and body side pin striping and tooled-silver S-shaped landau bars on cars with vinyl tops. There was a new dashboard and full instrumentation was abandoned in favor of warning lights. The T-Bird's 429-cid four-barrel V-8 was de-tuned to operate on unleaded gas and rated at 212 net horsepower. The T-Bird body was mounted at computer-designated points for noise and vibration suppression characteristics. A new rear stabilizer bar improved roll stiffness. T-Bird brakes had now been accepted as perhaps the best system in the sports-personal car market segment. ABS brakes were optional. A heavier-duty 9.38-in. rear axle ring gear was used with this system, as ABS tended to create some rear axle chattering that could wreck the standard 9-in. ring gear. Standard equipment included: 429-cid V-8, SelecShift Cruise-O-Matic transmission, power steering, power front disc brakes, automatic parking brake release, Michelin 40,000-mile black sidewall steel-belted radial tires, electric clock, split bench front seat, front seat center armrest, seat belt reminder buzzer, cut-pile floor carpeting, power ventilation system, MagicAire heater and defroster, remote-control left-hand outside rearview mirror, vinyl-insert body side moldings, dome light, door courtesy lights, under dash light, glove compartment light, front ash tray light, fully insulated body, fully-trimmed trunk, luggage compartment light, full wheel covers, side-guard door rails, energy-absorbing steering column, energy-absorbing steering wheel, energy-absorbing instrument panel, padded sun visors, two-speed electric windshield wipers, windshield washers, 4-way hazard flasher, back-up lights, self-locking front seat backs, non-reversing odometer, locking steering column and ignition key buzzer.

VIN:

The VIN was stamped on an aluminum tab riveted to the dashboard on the passenger side and was observable through the windshield from outside the car. The prefix indicated the manufacturer: F=Ford. The first symbol denoted the model-year: 2=1972. The second symbol indicated the assembly plant: Y=Wixom (Novi), Michigan and J=Los Angeles, California. Third symbol was the car-line: 8=T-Bird. The fourth symbol denoted the body type: 7=Two-door hardtop. The fifth symbol was the engine: N=429-cid/212-hp Thunderbird V-8, A=460-cid/224 hp Thunderbird V-8. The sixth through 11th symbols were the sequential production numbers of the specific vehicle starting at 100001. The body certification label was located on the rear face of the driver's door. The top part of the label indicated the T-Bird was manufactured by Ford Motor Company. Directly below this was the month and year of manufacture, plus a statement that the car conformed to federal motor vehicle safety standards in effect on the indicated date of manufacture. The VIN appeared on the first line of the encoded information. It matched the first through 11th symbols on the VIN tag. The body style code appeared to the right of the VIN on the same line. The T-Bird code for this model-year was: 65K=two-door Hardtop. The color code(s) appeared to the right of the body style code. Conventional colors were identified by a single letter or number. Optional glamour paints were identified by two numbers. The trim code appeared on the far left-hand side of the second line of encoded information. The axle code appeared to the right of the trim code in the second position on the second line of encoded information: K=2.75:1 Traction-Lok, M=2.80:1 Traction-Lock, O=3.00:1 Traction-Lok, R=3.25:1 Traction-Lok, 2=2.75:1, 4=2.80:1, 6=3.00:1 and 9=3.25:1. The transmission code appeared to the right of the axle code in the third position on the second line of encoded information: U=C-6 three-speed automatic, Z=C-6 special three-speed automatic. The District Special Equipment (DSO) code appeared to the right of the transmission code in the far right-hand position on the second line of encoded information.

1972 Ford Thunderbird two-door Hardtop (OCW)

The abbreviations VIN/BDY/CLR/TRM/AX/TR/DSO did not appear on the certification label itself. The specific application of the codes was determined by the location on the vehicle certification label.

Thunderbird (V-8)

Model No.	Body/ Style No.	Body Type and Seating	Factory Price	Shipping Weight	Production Total
8	65K	2-dr. Hardtop-4P	$5,293	4,420 lbs.	57,814

Engines:

Thunderbird 429 Four-Barrel V-8: Overhead valve. Cast-iron block. Displacement: 429 cid. B & S: 4.36 x 3.59 in. Compression ratio: 8.50:1. Brake hp: 212 at 4400 rpm. Torque: 327 lbs.-ft. at 2600 rpm. Five main bearings. Hydraulic valve lifters. Carburetor: Four-barrel. Cooling system capacity: 18.8 qt. with heater. Crankcase capacity: 5 qt. (add 1 qt. with new oil filter). Dual exhausts. Code N.

Thunderbird 460 Four-Barrel V-8: Overhead valve. Cast-iron block. Displacement: 429 cid. B & S: 4.36 x 3.85 in. Compression ratio: 8.50:1. Brake hp: 224 at 4400 rpm. Torque: 342 lbs.-ft. at 2600 rpm. Five main bearings. Hydraulic valve lifters. Carburetor: Four-barrel. Cooling system capacity: 18.8 qt. with heater. Crankcase capacity: 5 qt. (add 1 qt. with new oil filter). Dual exhausts. Code A.

Chassis:

Wheelbase: 120.4 in. Overall length: 216. Overall width: 79.3. Overall height: 51.3 in. Trunk volume: 13.9 cu. ft. Front tread: 63 in. Rear tread: 62.8 in. Tires: 215R-15 steel-belted radial.

Technical:

Steering: Integral with power-assist. Turning diameter: 43 ft. Front suspension: Independent drag-strut, ball-joint type with coil springs. Rear suspension: Four-link rubber-cushioned with integral stabilizer bar. Standard rear axle: 2.75:1. Front brakes: Power front disc brakes, swept area 232 sq. in. Rear brakes: Power drums, swept area: 155.9 sq. in. Total swept area: 387.9 sq. in. Fuel tank capacity: 22.5 gal.

Options:

SelectAire conditioner ($436.52). Automatic temperature control with 61-amp alternator and electric rear window defroster ($505.68). Traction-Lok differential ($47.71 without optional axle ratio, $60.33 with optional axle ratio). Deluxe seat belts with warning light ($35.94). Bumper guards front and rear, except standard with protection group ($36.97). Electric rear window defroster, includes 65-amp alternator and panel light ($81.91). 460-cid four-barrel V-8, air conditioning required ($75.97). California emissions system ($15.14). Complete tinted glass ($50.74). Rocker panel moldings ($25.37). Color Glow paint ($37.99). Dual accent body side stripes ($12.62). Power antenna ($30.17). Door lock group, includes remote deck lid release ($59.45). 6-way power driver's seat ($101.34). 6-way power driver and passenger seats ($201.67). Power side windows ($129.60). Power trunk lid release ($13.63). AM/FM stereo radio including dual front and rear seat speakers ($146.14). Vinyl roof ($137.43). Note: Vinyl roof includes "S" landau bars with wood-grain inserts (or tooled silver landau bar inserts when Glamour paint is ordered) on T-Birds. Manual reclining passenger seat, except standard with Turnpike group ($40). High-back bucket seats and console ($75.97). Spare tire cover ($86.32). Dual rear seat speakers, standard with AM/FM stereo radio or tape system ($32.18). Fingertip speed control including rim-blow deluxe three-spoke steering wheel (standard with Turnpike group, otherwise $103.14). Deluxe three-spoke rim-blow steering wheel ($37.99). Tilt steering wheel ($50.74). Stereosonic tape system with AM radio only ($146.14). Power-operated sun roof, requires vinyl roof on Hardtop ($504.80). Heavy-duty suspension with heavy front and rear springs and shocks, front stabilizer bar ($27.26). Leather trim for split-bench seats ($63.65). Deluxe wheel covers, except not available with Glamour Paint option ($87.07). Intermittent windshield wipers, requires

1972 Ford Thunderbird two-door Hardtop (OCW)

recessed windshield wipers ($25.37). Convenience group includes low fuel and door ajar light and buzzer, dual overhead map lights, engine compartment light ($43.79). Glamour Paint option, includes color-keyed wheel covers, dual body side and hood paint stripes, tooled silver landau bar inserts without vinyl roof ($161.79). Protection group includes color-keyed floor mats, license plate frames, and door edge guards ($25.37). Heavy-duty trailer towing package, includes heavy-duty suspension, extra-cooling package, wiring harness, high-ratio axle, and trailer towing decal ($45.82). Turnpike convenience group includes fingertip speed control, manual reclining passenger seat, and trip odometer ($132.51). Michelin 215 15R steel-belted radial-ply single band whitewall tires with 40,000-mile tread life guarantee (Michelin black sidewalls were standard and the whitewalls were $31.17 extra).

History:

The 1972 T-Bird was introduced on September 24, 1971. Henry Ford II was Ford's Chairman of the Board. Lee A Iacocca was promoted to President of Ford Motor Company. J.B. Naughton was a Vice President and General Manager of Ford Division. G.B. MacKenzie became General Sales manager for Ford Division. Calendar-year output was 58,582 units. A total of 57,814 T-Birds were produced in the model year. This represented 0.7 percent of the industry total. Of these units, 35,585 were made in Michigan and 22,229 were made in California. Calendar year dealer sales amounted to 58,731 T-Birds, representing 0.6 percent of industry sales. Ford had originally planned to use a 400-cid two-barrel V-8 as the standard 1972 T-Bird power plant. Sales catalog no. 5303 dated 8/71 lists this smaller engine as standard equipment and the 429-cid four-barrel V-8 as an option. However, a new version of the 429-4V was used and Lincoln's big 460-cid four-barrel V-8 was optional. "Evidently, the 400-2V engine's performance was not what they hoped it would be," said *Road Test* magazine. "The 460-4V can be expected to give slightly better acceleration, but decreased gas mileage." Body and frame construction was reintroduced in the new model. The 429-4V normally averaged about 9.0 to 9.1 mpg. *Road Test* magazine averaged 10.6 mpg for its entire trial, but had a low figure of 8.2 mpg during acceleration testing. *Motor Trend* (December 1971) averaged 11.67 mpg, also with the 429-4V. The 460-4V engine was good for 10-10.6 mpg on average. When the '72 models were about 10 years old, the editors of *Consumer Guide* said that the T-Bird was "A possible collector's item one day, but awful mileage means you'll spend more time looking at it than driving it." *Motor Trend's* December article was an unusual three-way comparison between the Buick Riviera, the T-Bird, and the Jaguar XJ6. The buff book made the point that America's personal luxury cars had grown as large as its four-door sedans, thereby justifying — in its "editorial mind" at least — stacking the pair of destroyer-sized domestics against one of Britain's hottest "sports saloon" models (saloon meaning four-door sedan in the King's English.). The conclusion arrived at through this methodology was nearly as unique as the underlying concept. "You can bet your bottom dollar that the next generation of both Thunderbird and Riviera will be smaller and will handle better," predicted writer Jim Brokaw. "...take a peek at tomorrow and promote a ride in an XJ6." A significant historical milestone was marked during the year when the one millionth T-Bird ever built was assembled. It was specially finished with Anniversary Gold paint and wore a White vinyl-clad landau roof. The wheel covers had color-coordinated gold accents. Up front was a gold-finished radiator grille. Commemorative "Millionth Thunderbird" emblems were found on the right-hand side of the instrument panel, and in the center of the S-shaped landau bars on either side of the roof. The car was presented to a member of the Classic Thunderbird Club International to use for one year. The following year it was purchased by George Watts, the collector who owns the earliest production T-Bird known to have been built.

1973 Thunderbird

Thunderbird — Series 8 — (V-8): The 1973 T-Bird continued sharing the Lincoln Mark IV body. There was a new eggcrate grille, plus a stand-up hood ornament. The grille no longer showed through below a new energy-absorbing bumper that was designed to withstand 5-

1973 Ford Thunderbird two-door Hardtop (OCW)

mph impacts. This massive "Twin I-Beam" bumper had a shelf-like appearance and added nearly three inches of length. Vertical guards near the center of the bumper were standard. The Thunderbird name was spelled out on the car's nose. The dual headlamps were mounted in separate square bezels on each side of the grille. New three-deck parking lights were notched into the front fenders and viewable from the side. Wider body side moldings with color-keyed protective vinyl inserts were seen. Initially, opera windows were optional and they eliminated a blind spot caused by massive "C" pillars. The opera windows were basically of a low, rectangular shape, but the trailing edge was slanted to match the rear roofline. A midyear sales catalog (5402 Rev. 6/73) added opera windows as standard equipment, along with SelectAire air conditioning, tinted glass, power side windows, an automatic seatback release (that unlatched the seat when you opened the door to simplify entering the car with bulky packages), power steering and a vinyl roof. Landau bars were no longer offered. The 1973 wheel covers had some detail changes. Wall-to-wall taillights again graced the T-Bird's rear end, with a winged Thunderbird emblem in the center of each lens. The huge lens had more of a wedge shape than an inverted U-shape. The "vacation-size" trunk offered 13.9 cu. ft. of luggage capacity. The rear bumper was massive and wrapped around the body corners. Two large vertical guards flanked a huge license plate "frame" in the center. The energy-absorbing rear bumper system met new Federal safety standards. Exteriors could be finished in any of 15 standard colors or eight optional Glamour paints. The Glamour paints contained a higher amount of metallic particles for greater reflectivity and iridescence. Odense Grain vinyl tops (available on cars having the Exterior Decor Group option) came in Copper, White, Blue, Green and Brown. Individually adjustable, deep-cushioned split bench front seats with fold-down armrests were standard in all T-Birds. Also featured was cut-pile carpeting on the floor, lower seatbacks and lower door panels. Cloth-and-vinyl interior trims were standard for the split bench seat. Optional all-vinyl trim was available in all seven colors. Leather-and-vinyl trim was available for the split bench seat. Optional bucket seats came only in cloth-and-vinyl. The 1973 T-Birds had an improved impact-absorbing laminated safety glass windshield. Other product improvements included suspension system refinements, increased front and rear headroom and whitewall steel-belted radial tires as standard equipment. An inside hood release and spare tire lock were also new. The standard 429-cid four-barrel V-8 was designed to operate on regular gasoline with an octane rating of at least 91 (Research Method) with the engine adjusted to factory specifications. The 460-cid four-barrel V-8 was optional. Standard equipment included: All regulation safety, anti-theft, convenience items and emissions control equipment, dual hydraulic brake system with warning light, Uni-Lock shoulder and lap belts with reminder, side-door steel guard rails, energy-absorbing front and rear bumpers, 429-cid four-barrel regular fuel V-8, SelectShift Cruise-O-Matic transmission with uniform transmission shift quadrant, power front disc/rear drum brakes, rubber-insert-type front bumper guards, body side moldings with protective vinyl inserts, bright window reveal moldings, remote-control left-hand OSRV mirror, full wheel covers, individually adjustable split-bench front seat with two folding armrests, self-locking front seat backs with padding, non-reversing odometer, Aurora cloth seat trim with vinyl facings, headrests or high-back seats for front outboard passengers, cut-pile carpeting, energy-absorbing steering column and wheel, locking steering column with warning buzzer, two-speed windshield wipers, windshield washers, 4-way hazard warning flashers, turn signals with lane-change feature, fully-lined and lighted luggage compartment, wood-tone interior dress up accents, deluxe arm rests, interior courtesy lights (dome, door, under-panel, glove box and front ashtray), steel-belted radial white sidewall tires, power front disc/rear drum brakes, power ventilation system, 80-amp battery, inside the car hood release, constant-ratio power steering, AM radio, MagicAire heater and defroster, electric clock, spare tire lock, back-up lights, side marker lights, unique T-Bird identification and ornamentation, hood ornament, bright moldings at rear of hood, door belts, drip rails and wheel lips, 61-amp alternator maintains battery charge even at low engine speeds, automatic parking brake release, aluminized muffler with stainless steel components and

1973 Ford Thunderbird two-door Hardtop (OCW)

choice of 23 exterior colors. Added to standard equipment list on June 11, 1973 were SelectAire conditioner, opera windows, power windows, tinted glass, vinyl roof and automatic seat back release.

VIN:

The VIN was stamped on an aluminum tab riveted to the dashboard on the passenger side and was visible through the windshield from outside the car. The prefix indicated the manufacturer: F=Ford. The first symbol denoted the model-year: 3=1973. The second symbol indicated the assembly plants: Y=Wixom (Novi), Michigan and J=Los Angeles, California. The third symbol was the car-line: 8=T-Bird. The fourth symbol denoted the body type: 7=Two-door hardtop. The fifth symbol indicated the engine: N=429-cid/208-hp Thunderbird V-8 and A=460-cid/219 hp Thunderbird V-8. The sixth through 11th symbols were the sequential production numbers of the specific vehicle starting at 100001. The suffix denoted the manufacturer, F=Ford. The body certification label was located on the rear face of driver's door. The top part of the label indicated the T-Bird was manufactured by Ford Motor Company. Directly below this was the month and year of manufacture, plus a statement that the car conformed to federal motor vehicle safety standards in effect on the date of manufacture. The VIN appeared on the first line of the encoded information. It matched the first to 11th symbols on the VIN tag. The body style code appeared to the right of the VIN on the same line. The T-Bird code for this model-year was: 65K=two-door Hardtop. The color code(s) appeared to the right of the body style code. Conventional colors were identified by a single letter or number. Optional glamour paints were identified by two numbers. The trim code appeared on the far left-hand side of the second line of encoded information. The axle code appeared to the right of the trim code in the second position on the second line of encoded information: 2=2.75:1, 6=3.00:1, 9=3.25:1, K=2.75:1 Traction Lok, O=3.00:1 Traction Lock and R=3.25:1 Traction Lok. The transmission code appeared to the right of the axle code in the third position on the second line of encoded information: U=SelectShift Cruise-O-Matic three-speed automatic and Z=SelectShift Cruise-O-Matic Special three-speed automatic. The District Special Equipment (DSO) code appeared to the right of the transmission code in the far right-hand position on the second line of encoded information. The abbreviations VIN/BDY/CLR/TRM/AX/TR/DSO did not appear on the certification label itself. The specific application of the codes was determined by where they are located on the vehicle certification label.

Thunderbird (V-8)

Model No.	Body/ Style No.	Body Type and Seating	Factory Price	Shipping Weight	Production Total
7	65K	2-dr. Hardtop-4P	$5,577	4,572 lbs.	87,269

Note: The price increased to $6,414 when six additional items listed above became standard equipment on June 11, 1973.

Engines:

Thunderbird 429 Four-Barrel V-8: Overhead valve. Cast iron block. Displacement: 429 cid. B & S: 4.36 x 3.59 in. Compression ratio: 8.50:1. Brake hp: 201 at 4400 rpm. Torque: 327 lbs.-ft. at 2800 rpm. Five main bearings. Hydraulic valve lifters. Carburetor: Four-barrel. Cooling system capacity: 18.8 qt. with heater. Crankcase capacity: 5 qt. (add 1 qt. with new oil filter). Dual exhausts. Code N.

Thunderbird 460 Four-Barrel V-8: Overhead valve. Cast-iron block. Displacement: 429 cid. B & S: 4.36 x 3.85 in. Compression ratio: 8.50:1. Brake hp: 219 at 4400 rpm. Torque: 338 lbs.-ft. at 2600 rpm. Five main bearings. Hydraulic valve lifters. Carburetor: Four-barrel. Cooling system capacity: 18.8 qt. with heater. Crankcase capacity: 5 qt. (add 1 qt. with new oil filter). Dual exhausts. Code A.

Chassis:

Wheelbase: 120.4 in. Overall length: 218.9. Overall width: 79.7. Overall height: 53.1 in. Trunk volume: 13.9 cu. ft. Front tread: 63 in. Rear tread: 63.1 in. Tires: 230R-15 steel-belted radial.

Technical:

Steering: Integral with power-assist, 21.73:1 overall ratio. Turning diameter: 43 ft. Ground clearance: 5.4 in. Front suspension: Coil springs, stabilizer, shocks, axial strut. Rear suspension: Coil spring, shocks and stabilizer. Standard rear axle: 2.75:1. Front brakes: Power front disc brakes, swept area 232 sq. in. Rear brakes: Power drums, swept area: 155.9 sq. in. Total swept area: 387.9 sq. in. Fuel tank capacity: 22.5 gal.

Options:

Power side windows, prior to June 11, 1973 ($129.60). 460-cid 219-hp V-8 engine ($75.79). Vinyl roof, prior to June 11, 1973 ($137). SelectAire Conditioner, prior to June 11, 1973 ($436.52). SelectAire Conditioner with automatic temperature control ($505.68). Traction-Lok differential with standard axle ratio ($47.71). Traction-Lok differential with high-ratio axle ($60.33). Sure-Track brake control system ($197). Deluxe bumper group including front and rear bumper guards with rubber inserts and full-width rub strips ($51). Opera windows, prior to June 11, 1973 ($81.84). Glamour Paint Group, includes higher amount of metallic particles in paint, dual body side stripes, twin hood stripes and color-keyed wheel covers ($161.79). Electric rear window defroster, including panel indicator light and 70-amp alternator ($81.91). California emissions testing ($21). Dual exhaust system, including sound package ($53). Dual body side and hood stripes ($18). Fire Metallic paint ($131). Starfire Metallic paint ($172). Dual body side accent stripes ($18). Power antenna ($30.17). Power door locks group including remote trunk release ($59.45). 6-way power full-width driver and passenger seats ($201.67). 6-way power driver seat ($1,201.34). Power sunroof, vinyl top required ($504.80). AM/FM stereo radio ($146). AM/FM stereo radio with tape player ($311). Dual rear seat speakers (standard with stereo radio or tape system, otherwise $32.18). Manual reclining passenger seat, standard with Turnpike convenience group ($40). High-back bucket seats with central console ($75.97). Fingertip speed control, including rim-blow steering wheel and standard with Turnpike convenience group ($103.14). Rim-blow steering wheel alone ($37.99). Tilt steering wheel ($51). Heavy-duty suspension includes heavy front and rear springs and shocks ($27.26). Heavy-duty trailer-towing package, includes heavy-duty suspension ($45.82). Front cornering lamps ($43). Deluxe bumper group ($51). Super-soft vinyl seat trim ($35). Luggage compartment trim ($57). Leather and vinyl trim ($35). Deluxe wheel covers ($64). Convenience Light Group including high-intensity map lights, warning lights for headlamps on, low fuel warning light, door ajar light, headlamps on buzzer and engine compartment light ($43.79). Tinted glass ($50.74). Turnpike convenience group, including visor-vanity mirror, interval windshield wipers, right- and left-hand remote-control mirrors, speed control, manual reclining passenger seat, and trip odometer ($132.51). Theft-Foil alarm system with alarm and decals ($79). Interval windshield wipers ($25.37). Deluxe color-keyed seat belts ($50.49). Remote-control right-hand rearview mirror ($26.67). Vinyl seat trim ($35). Rim-blow steering wheel ($37.99). Appearance Protection group with door edge guards, license plate frames, spare tire lock and cover, and front and rear floor mats with carpet inserts (with exterior decor group $68, without exterior decor group $75). Class III trailer towing package with heavy-duty handling suspension, heavy-duty alternator, wiring harness, extra-cooling package, coolant recovery system, heavy-duty frame, and trailer towing decal ($48, but not offered for cars registered in California). LR78 steel-belted radial-ply whitewall tires ($33 extra). Burgundy luxury group, including Burgundy Victorian velour or Red leather seats and door trim, deluxe luggage compartment trim, gold insert Thunderbird opera window ornaments, Burgundy Fire Metallic paint, simulated wire wheel covers, gold paint stripes, and Dark Red Odense grain vinyl roof ($411).

History:

The 1973 T-Bird was introduced on September 22, 1972. Henry Ford II (Chairman) and. Lee A Iacocca (President) again held the top two corporate positions at Ford Motor Company. B.E. Bidwell was Ford Division's new Vice President and General Manager W.J. Oben became General Sales manager for the division. Calendar-year output was 90,404 units. A total of 87,269 T-Birds were produced in the model year. This represented 0.9 percent of the industry total. Of these units, 46,676 were made in Michigan and 40,593 were made in California. Calendar year dealer sales amounted to 74,759 T-Birds, representing 0.8 percent of industry sales. With the government and insurance companies cracking down on automotive performance, 1973 Ford sales catalogs said nothing about horsepower or torque ratings. *Motor Trend* did a four-car comparison (June 1973) of a T-Bird, Pontiac Grand Prix, Buick Riviera and Oldsmobile Toronado. The T-Bird was the most expensive of the quartet. Although it used the optional 460-4V engine, it had the lowest horsepower rating. Nevertheless, it was second fastest from 0-60 mph. It also had the second fastest terminal speed in the quarter-mile, but the third lowest elapsed time. Writer Jim Brokaw found the T-Bird's handling good, but sensitive to tire inflation. He joked about its cigarette lighter having more stages than a Saturn V rocket and said, "If you threw it out the window in Belfast, you'd clear the streets in three seconds." Brokaw especially noted the 460-cid V-8 was a good low-end torquer that could easily burn rubber. He actually rated it second highest in performance, next to the 455-cid 250 hp Grand Prix. Criticisms were directed at a too small ashtray and glove box and excessive wind noise for a Ford product. He also gave the T-Bird his top rating in the "prestige" department. Model-year production was nearly 30,000 units higher than the previous year, an impressive endorsement of the Lincoln-like "T-Bird." Ford published separate T-Bird literature for dealers in Canada, although all of the 1973 models were built in the United States. Under a free trade agreement that went into effect around 1970, cars could be shipped across the border, in either direction, duty-free. This allowed automakers to avoid sourcing cars from both countries to avoid tariffs and helped them make more efficient use of their production facilities. There are no dramatic differences in the wording of the U.S. and Canadian sales catalogs, although at least three small differences appear in Canadian literature. First, the phrase "1973 Federal Motor Vehicle Standards" is changed to "1973 Canadian Motor Vehicle Standards." Second, instead of mentioning specific mileage intervals for service operations Canadian catalogs say "details are contained in the Owner's Manual." Third, instead of listing a "22.5-gallon" fuel tank, the Canadian literature says "18.7 gallons."

1974 Thunderbird

Thunderbird — Series 8 — (V-8): In most details, the 1974 T-Bird was changed very little from 1973, but there were a number of refinements. The bumpers and bumper guards were slightly altered and there was a new rear appearance with the addition of an impact-absorbing bumper and redesigned full-width taillights. The 460-cid four-barrel V-8 became standard equipment. It had a new solid-state ignition system and a 220-hp rating. The solid-state ignition replaced ignition parts like the points, cam and condenser with highly reliable, low-maintenance electronic components. The results were a stronger spark, reduced maintenance, more dependable cold weather starting, lower emissions and the virtual elimination of misfiring. New luxury options included an electrically-heated quick-defrost windshield and rear window, plus a transparent moon roof. T-Bird interiors featured simulated woodtone accents and deluxe seat belts. On the outside all T-Birds had full wheel covers, a unique T-Bird hood ornament, moldings on the hood edge, doors, belt line, drip rails and wheel openings and vinyl-insert body side moldings. Initially, 21 exterior colors were offered on '74 T-Birds and eight were optional Glamour Colors. In January 1974, the Autumn Fire Glamour Paint color was deleted. Also in January, a pair of Special Edition T-Birds was added. The Burgundy Luxury Group model included all basic T-Bird equipment, plus dual body side and hood stripes, special body side moldings and simulated wire wheel covers. An exclusive Dark Red Odense grain vinyl top was also featured. The White and Gold Special Edition Thunderbird came with color-coordinated wide body side moldings, color-keyed wheel covers, body side accent stripes, hood and deck lid accent stripes and an exclusive Gold Levant grain vinyl top. Both special T-Birds also offered Glamour colors and luggage compartment trim as standard equipment. All Comfort and Convenience features found on mid-1973 T-Birds were standard including the adjustable split-bench front seat with fold-down center armrest. Front outboard retractable lap/shoulder belts with the infamous starter interlock system, as required by the National Highway Traffic Safety Administration (NHTSA) were so unpopular that the new safety rule was canceled by the U.S. Congress at the end of the year. The ignition interlock system prevented an engine from starting if belts for occupied front seats were not buckled in the proper sequence. A warning buzzer (after January a warning light and buzzer) reminded outboard passengers to buckle up. Additionally, a logic circuit prevented the engine from starting if passengers attempted to beat the system by extending the harness before sitting or by buckling the belts together. Standard features included: All regulation safety, anti-theft, convenience items and emissions control equipment, Thunderbird hood ornament, power steering, solid-state ignition, power windows, power ventilation system, automatic seatback release, inside hood release, dome light,

door courtesy light, underpanel light, glove box light, front ashtray light, ignition light, map lights, SelectShift transmission, 460-cid V-8 engine, power front disc/rear drum brakes, AM radio, electric clock, cut-pile carpeting, Odense vinyl roof, opera windows, individually-adjustable split bench front seat with fold-down center armrests, Aurora cloth and vinyl interior trim, woodtone accents, extensive soundproofing, seat belt-ignition interlock system, remote-control left-hand OSRV mirror, deluxe seat belts, protective body side moldings with vinyl inserts, lined and lighted trunk, LR78/15 steel-belted radial white sidewall tires, spare tire lock, full wheel covers, manual SelectAire conditioner, tinted glass, rear hood edge molding, door belt moldings, drip rail moldings, wheel lip moldings, 61-amp. alternator, automatic parking brake release, front bumper guards and full coil spring suspension.

VIN:

The VIN was stamped on an aluminum tab riveted to the dashboard on the passenger side and was observable through the windshield. The prefix indicated the manufacturer: F=Ford. The first symbol denoted the model-year: 4=1974. The second symbol indicated the assembly plants: Y=Wixom (Novi), Michigan and J=Los Angeles, California. The third symbol was the car-line: 8=T-Bird. The fourth symbol indicated the body type: 7=Two-door hardtop. The fifth indicated the engine: A=460-cid/220 hp Thunderbird V-8. The sixth through 11th symbols denoted the sequential production numbers of specific vehicles starting at 100001. The suffix denoted the manufacturer, F=Ford. The body certification label was located on the rear face of the driver's door. The top part of the label indicated the T-Bird was manufactured by Ford Motor Company. Directly below this was the month and year of manufacture, plus a statement that the car conformed to federal motor vehicle safety standards in effect on the indicated date of manufacture. The VIN appeared on the first line of encoded information. It matched the first to 11th symbols on VIN tag. The body style code appeared to the right of the VIN. The T-Bird code for this model-year was 65K=two-door Hardtop. The color code(s) appeared to the right of the body style code. Conventional colors were identified by a single letter or number. Optional glamour paints were identified by two numbers. The trim code appeared on the far left-hand side of the second line of encoded information. The axle code appeared to the right of the trim code in the second position on the second line of encoded information: K=2.75:1 limited-slip, O=3.00:1 limited-slip, R=3.25:1 limited-slip, 2=2.75:1, 6=3.00:1 and 9=3.25:1. The transmission code appeared to the right of the axle code in the third position on the second line of encoded information: U=C6 SelectShift three-speed automatic, Z=C6 special SelectShift three-speed automatic. The District Special Equipment (DSO) code appeared to the right of the transmission code in the far right-hand position on the second line of encoded information. The abbreviations VIN/BDY/CLR/TRM/AX/TR/DSO did not appear on the certification label itself. The specific application of the codes was determined by where they are located on the vehicle certification label.

Thunderbird (V-8)

Model No.	Body/ Style No.	Body Type and Seating	Factory Price	Shipping Weight	Production Total
7	65K	2-dr. Hardtop-4P	$7,221	5,033 lbs.	58,443

Engine:

Thunderbird 460 Four-Barrel V-8: Overhead valve. Cast-iron block. Displacement: 429 cid. B & S: 4.36 x 3.85 in. Compression ratio: 8.00:1. Brake hp: 220 at 4000 rpm. Torque: 355 lbs.-ft. at 2600 rpm. Five main bearings. Hydraulic valve lifters. Carburetor: Four-barrel. Cooling system capacity: 18.8 qt. with heater. Crankcase capacity: 5 qt. (add 1 qt. with new oil filter). Dual exhausts. Code A.

Chassis:

Wheelbase: 120.4 in. Overall length: 224.8. Overall width: 79.7. Overall height: 53.in. Trunk volume: 13.4 cu. ft. Front tread: 63 in. Rear tread: 63.1 in. Tires: 230R-15 steel-belted radial.

Technical:

Steering: Integral with power-assist. Turning diameter: 43 ft. Front suspension: Coil springs, stabilizer, shocks and axial strut. Rear suspension: Coil spring, shocks and stabilizer. Standard rear axle: 3.00:1. Front brakes: Power disc. Rear brakes: Power drum. Fuel tank capacity: 26 gallons.

Options:

Automatic temperature control air conditioner ($74). Traction-Lok differential ($50). Deluxe bumper group including front and rear bumper guards with rubber inserts and full-width rub strips ($51). Quick-defrost windshield and rear window ($315). Electric rear window de-icer including panel indicator light and 70-amp alternator ($85). California emissions testing ($21). Dual exhaust system, including sound package ($53). Dual body side and hood stripes ($18). Fire Metallic paint ($131). Starfire Metallic paint ($172). Power antenna ($31). Power door locks group

1974 Ford Thunderbird two-door Hardtop (PH)

including remote trunk release ($62). 6-way power full-width seat ($210). 6-way power split-bench seat, driver's side only ($105). Front cornering lamps, included in Exterior Décor Group ($43). Power Moon roof ($798). Power mini -vent windows ($70). AM/FM stereo radio ($152). AM/FM stereo radio with tape player ($311). Dual rear seat speakers (standard with stereo radio or tape system, otherwise $33). Manual reclining passenger seat, standard with Turnpike convenience group ($42). High-back bucket seats with central console ($120). Fingertip speed control, including rim-blow steering wheel and standard with Turnpike convenience group ($103). Rim-blow steering wheel alone ($40). Tilt steering wheel ($53). Power-operated sun roof ($525). Sure-Track brake control system ($197). Heavy-duty suspension includes heavy front and rear springs and shocks ($28). Trailer equalizing hitch, requires trailer towing package ($90). Super-soft vinyl seat trim ($35). Deluxe luggage compartment trim ($57). Picardy velour cloth trim ($64). Leather seat trim ($105). Deluxe wheel covers ($64). Color-keyed standard wheel covers ($20). Simulated wire wheel covers ($85). Rear window quick defrost ($315). Anti-Theft Group, includes lockable hood latch ($79). Auto Lamp on/off delay system, included in Light Group ($34). Convenience group, including interval windshield wipers and right-hand remote-control OSRV mirror ($53). Turnpike convenience group, including visor-vanity mirror, interval windshield wipers, right- and left-hand remote-control mirrors, speed control, manual reclining passenger seat, and trip odometer ($138). Convenience light group, including illuminated visor mirror, headlights-on light and buzzer, low fuel warning light, door opening warning light, overhead map light, and engine compartment light ($138). Light Group includes dual overhead map lights, illuminated visor vanity mirror, warning lights for headlamps on, buzzer for headlamps on, low-fuel light, door ajar light, engine compartment light and Autolamp system ($160). Exterior decor group, including partial wheel lip moldings, front cornering lights, and wide lower body side moldings with padded grain-tone vinyl inserts ($141). Protection group with door edge guards, license plate frames, spare tire lock and cover, and front and rear floor mats with carpet inserts (with exterior decor group $68, without exterior decor group $75). Class III trailer towing package with heavy-duty handling suspension, heavy-duty alternator, wiring harness, extra-cooling package, coolant recovery system, heavy-duty frame, and trailer towing decal ($48, but not offered for cars registered in California). Theft-Foil alarm system with alarm and decals ($79). LR78 steel-belted radial-ply whitewall tires ($33 extra). Burgundy luxury group, including Burgundy Victorian velour or Red leather seats and door trim, deluxe luggage compartment trim, gold insert Thunderbird opera window ornaments, Burgundy Fire Metallic paint, simulated wire wheel covers, gold paint stripes, and Dark Red Odense grain vinyl roof ($411). White and Gold Luxury Group ($546). Space Saver spare tire ($86).

The 1974 T-Bird was introduced on September 20, 1973. Henry Ford II (Chairman) and. Lee A Iacocca (President) again held the top two corporate positions at Ford Motor Company. B.E. Bidwell was Ford Division's new Vice President and General Manager. W.J Oben was General Sales manager for the division. Calendar-year output was 49,074 units. A total of 58,443 T-Birds were produced in the model year. This represented 0.72 percent of the industry total. Of these units, 37,943 were made in Michigan and 20,500 were made in California. Calendar year dealer sales amounted to 54,112 T-Birds, representing 0.6 percent of industry sales. The 460-4V engine retained its 8.0:1 compression ratio to permit operation on 91 octane gas. Although the 1974 T-Bird averaged just 11.6 mpg on a 73-mile loop of city, suburban, freeway and hilly roads driving conducted by *Motor Trend* magazine (March 1974), Ford sales literature included a list of "Economy and Durability" features. Self-adjusting brakes, two-year coolant, a long-life Motorcraft Sta-Ful battery, a corrosion-resistant aluminized muffler, zinc-coatings on underbody parts and the fact that the 460 operated on regular fuel were highlighted as "economy" features. In the durability department, Ford promoted its 36,000-mile major chassis lubrication, 6,000-mile oil changes and 12,000-mile (after the first time) oil filter changes. This year's Jim Brokaw road test in *Motor Trend* continued the practice of comparing the T-Bird to other American personal-luxury cars. It featured eight vehicles — the most ever — of which three were new models. The T-Bird had faced off against the Riviera, Toronado, Grand Prix and Monte Carlo in previous competitions. Now it was also being stacked up against the AMC Matador "Oleg Cassini" model, the Mercury Cougar and the Ford Torino Elite. The T-Bird was the most expensive and heaviest car in the group. It had the most cubic inches, but only the sixth highest net horsepower rating. Though tied for second in torque, the T-Bird's fuel economy was on the very bottom. Brokaw concluded that all eight models shared the same basic features and a high level of execution. "It's really a matter of product loyalty and styling tastes," he felt about picking one over the other. After the Arab oil embargo caused a severe energy shortage in the U.S. from January-March 1974, the big T-Bird's long-term popularity dropped. The 1974 T-Bird lost about 30,000 customers and two-tenths of a point of market share. No T-Birds were built in Canada, although a separate Canadian sales catalog was issued in August 1973. It was

the same as the July 1973 U.S. catalog, except for one difference that some collectors might be interested in ... cars sold in Canada (although made in the U.S.) were *not* required to have the seat belt/starter interlock system. Ford described the '74 T-Bird as "A magnificent expression of personal car luxury, which has long been a hallmark of Thunderbird." An informative piece of factory literature entitled *Thunderbird: An engineering achievement*, talked about the engineers, designers and assembly line workers who built the car and their desire to achieve a higher standard of quality. It suggested that this was reflected in the fit of T-Bird parts, the look of the paint, an exceptionally smooth and quiet ride and painstaking attention to detail.

1975 Thunderbird

Thunderbird — Series 7 — (V-8): The physical appearance of the 1975 T-Bird was virtually unchanged from 1974, except that the front bumper guards were spaced further apart to improve the car's crash worthiness. There was also a new steering wheel with a center hub with outer ends that angled downward. Separate body and frame construction was featured. The T-Bird's strong, durable frame featured closed box-section members and five cross-members. Self-adjusting rear brakes, a long-life battery, an aluminized muffler and zinc-coated chassis parts were standard equipment. All 1975 T-Birds were considered "20th Anniversary" models. Twenty exterior colors were originally offered, but others were added during the year. The standard interior featured Aurora cloth-and-vinyl trim in four colors. Picton velour cloth-and-vinyl, Super Soft vinyl and leather seats with vinyl trim were available. The standard Odense grain vinyl roof came in 11 colors: Black, White, Blue, Silver Blue, Green, Brown, Tan, Gold, Red, Copper and Silver. Silver and Copper Luxury trim options joined last year's Gold and White Luxury options. To make the 20th Anniversary T-Bird more distinctive, Ford added a Jade Luxury Group option at midyear. This package featured new colors, new textures and new fabrics in three exterior and two interior decor combinations. The All-Jade version had a Normande grain padded vinyl half-top, color-keyed vinyl-clad rear window moldings, color-keyed roof moldings, a silver Thunderbird opera window insignia, color-keyed wide body side moldings, Jade Starfire glamour finish, dual hood and body side stripes and wire wheel covers. In addition to the all-green version, the Jade Thunderbird came in two alternate combinations. One featured Polar White exterior finish smartly topped with a Jade half-vinyl roof. Another offered Jade Starfire glamour finish with a white half-vinyl top. Jade Thunderbirds also featured a choice of White leather seating surfaces or Jade Media Velour upholstery, both with Jade vinyl trim and color-keyed components. A half-vinyl roof was standard with Copper, Silver and Jade Luxury groups. The T-Bird engine was again the 460-cid four-barrel V-8. Horsepower wasn't given in sales catalogs and various sources show different ratings. Standard features included: All regulation safety, anti-theft, convenience items, and emissions control equipment, body and frame construction with closed box-section members and five cross-members, power steering, ignition and map lights, Cruise-O-Matic transmission, 460-cid V-8 engine, self-adjusting power front disc/rear drum brakes, three-year coolant and antifreeze, long-life Motorcraft Sta-Ful battery, corrosion-resistant aluminized muffler, zinc-coated underbody parts, AM radio, electric clock, split-bench front seat, vinyl roof, opera windows, full front seat with arm rests, standard cloth and vinyl seat trim, cut-pile carpeting, remote-control left-hand OSRV mirror, protective body side moldings with vinyl inserts, all courtesy lights, all door light switches, ash tray and trunk lights, LR78/15 steel-belted radial white sidewall tires, full wheel covers, SelectAire conditioner, tinted glass, front bumper guards and full coil spring suspension. Copper Starfire or White exterior, Copper padded vinyl half roof with color-coordinated wrap-over moldings, color-keyed vinyl insert body side moldings, Gold-toned T-Bird insignia. The Copper Luxury Group substituted or added: Copper Starfire or Polar White exterior finish, Copper Odense grain padded vinyl half roof with

1975 Ford Thunderbird two-door Copper Luxury Hardtop (OCW)

color-coordinated wrap-over moldings, color-keyed vinyl insert body side moldings, Gold-toned T-Bird insignia on opera windows, color-accented cast-aluminum wheels, color-keyed pin stripes on hood and body belt, Copper velour cloth or Copper leather interior trim, Copper dash, door panel and headliner accents, Copper floor carpeting, Copper colored trunk compartment trim. The Silver Luxury Group substituted or added: Silver Starfire exterior finish, Silver Odense grain padded vinyl half roof with color-coordinated wrap-over moldings, color-keyed vinyl insert body side moldings, silver silk-screened T-Bird insignia on opera windows, choice of Red velour, Red leather or Silver leather deluxe interior trim and color-coordinated trunk compartment trim. The Jade Luxury Group substituted or added: Choice of Polar White exterior body finish with Jade Green half vinyl roof, or Jade Starfire Glamour paint exterior body finish with Jade Green half vinyl roof, or Jade Starfire Glamour paint exterior body finish with White half vinyl roof, plus wide body side molding color-keyed to roof, opera window Thunderbird insignia, rear window and roof moldings also color-keyed, dual hood and body side paint stripes, wire wheel covers and rich White leather seating (code P5) with Jade vinyl trim and components or deep-cushioned seats tailored in plush Jade Green Media velour cloth trim (Code NR) with Jade vinyl trim and color-keyed components.

VIN:

The VIN was stamped on an aluminum tab riveted to the dashboard on the passenger side and was visible through the windshield. The prefix indicated the manufacturer: F=Ford. The first symbol denoted the model-year: 5=1975. The second symbol indicated the assembly plants: Y=Wixom (Novi), Michigan and J=Los Angeles, California. The third symbol was the car-line: 8=T-Bird. The fourth symbol denoted the body type: 7=Two-door hardtop. The fifth symbol indicate the engine: A=460-cid/220-hp Thunderbird V-8. The sixth through 11th symbols denoted the sequential production numbers of specific vehicles starting at 100001. The suffix showed the manufacturer: F=Ford. The body certification label was located on the rear face of the driver's door. The top part of the label indicated the T-Bird was manufactured by Ford Motor Company. Directly below this was the month and year of the manufacture, plus a statement that the car conformed to federal motor vehicle safety standards in effect on the indicated date of manufacture. The VIN appeared on the first line of encoded information. It matched the first to 11th symbols on the VIN tag. The body style code appeared to the right of the VIN on the same line. The T-Bird code for this model-year was 65K=two-door Hardtop. The color code(s) appeared to the right of the body style code. Conventional colors were identified by a single letter or number. Optional glamour paints were identified by two numbers. The trim code appeared to the right of the color and vinyl roof codes in the third position on the second line of encoded information. The transmission code appeared to the right of the trim code in the fourth position on the second line of encoded information: U=C6 XPL automatic transmission, Z=C6 Special XPL automatic transmission. The axle code appeared to the right of the transmission code in the fifth position on the second line of encoded information: K=2.75:1 limited-slip, 2=2.75:1 and 6=3.00:1. The District Special Equipment (DSO) code appeared to the right of the transmission code in the far right-hand position on the second line of encoded information. The abbreviations VIN/BDY/CLR/TRM/AX/TR/DSO did not appear on the certification label itself. The specific application of the codes was determined by where they were located on the vehicle certification label.

Thunderbird (V-8)

Model No.	Body/ Style No.	Body Type and Seating	Factory Price	Shipping Weight	Production Total
7	65K	2-dr. Hardtop-4P	$7,701	5,101 lbs.	42,685

Engine:

Thunderbird 460 Four-Barrel V-8: Overhead valve. Cast-iron block. Displacement: 460 cid. B & S: 4.36 x 3.85 in. Compression ratio: 8.50:1. Brake hp: 194 at 3800 rpm. Torque: 355 lbs.-ft. at 2600 rpm. Five main bearings. Hydraulic valve lifters. Carburetor: Four-barrel. Cooling system capacity: 18.8 qt. with heater. Crankcase capacity: 5 qt. (add 1 qt. with new oil filter). Dual exhausts. Code A.

Chassis:

Wheelbase: 120.4 in. Overall length: 225.8. Overall width: 79.7. Overall height: 53 in. Trunk volume: 13.4 cu. ft. Front tread: 62.9 in. Rear tread: 62.8 in. Tires: 230R-15 steel-belted radial.

Technical:

Steering: Integral with power-assist. Turning diameter: 43 ft. Front suspension: Coil springs, stabilizer, shocks and axial strut. Rear suspension: Coil spring, shocks and stabilizer. Standard rear axle: 3.00:1. Front brakes: Power disc. Rear brakes: Power drum. Fuel tank capacity: 26.5 gallons.

Options:

Copper Luxury Group ($624). Silver Luxury Group ($337). Power-operated glass moon roof ($798). Power-operated sunroof ($617). AM/FM stereo radio with tape player ($249). Power antenna ($32). Dual body side and hood paint stripes ($33). Trunk dress-up kit ($59). Protection Group with color-coordinated carpet-insert floor mats front and rear, license plate frames, door edge guards, rocker panel moldings and spare tire cover ($79 on cars with trunk dress-up kit; on other cars includes parts of the trunk dress-up kit and costs $87). Wide vinyl-insert body side moldings ($121). Deluxe wheel covers ($67, but included with Silver Luxury Group). Simulated wire wheel covers ($88). Deep-dish aluminum wheels ($251, but standard with Copper Luxury Group). Wide-band white sidewall tires ($59). Leather seating with vinyl trim ($239, but available at no extra cost for cars with Silver Luxury Group or Copper Luxury Group). Picton velour cloth trim ($96, but standard with Silver Luxury Group). Super-Soft vinyl trim ($55). Anti-theft alarm system, includes inside locking hood release ($84). Security lock group, includes inside locking hood release and locking gas cap ($18). Manual reclining passenger seat ($70). Tilt steering wheel ($68). Convenience Group, includes remote-control right-hand outside rearview mirror and interval windshield wipers ($84). Fingertip speed control ($120). Light Group, includes Autolamp on/off delay system, lighted visor-vanity mirror, twin overhead map lights, low fuel reminder, door-ajar warning light, headlights-on warning light and buzzer and underhood light ($164). Power lock group, includes electric door locks and electric trunk lid release ($86). 6-Way power driver's seat ($132). Six-Way power front seats for driver and passenger ($250). Power mini-vent windows ($79). Space-Saver spare tire ($86). Optional ratio axles ($14). Traction-Lok differential ($54). Four-wheel disc brakes ($184). Sure-Track brake control system, includes four-wheel disc brakes ($378). Dual exhausts ($53). Heavy-duty suspension ($28). Fuel monitor warning light ($20). Class II trailer tow package ($48). Automatic Temperature Control system ($74). Quick-Defrost windshield and rear window ($355). Electric rear window defroster ($99). Starfire glamour paint ($204). Turnpike Group, including manually-reclining passenger seat, Fingertip speed control and trip odometer ($180).

History:

The 1974 T-Bird was introduced on September 27, 1974. Henry Ford II (Chairman) and. Lee A Iacocca (President) again held the top two corporate positions at Ford Motor Company. W.P. Benton was Ford Division's new Vice President and General Manager. W.J. Oben was General Sales manager for the division. Calendar-year output was 37,557 units. A total of 42,685 T-Birds were produced in the model year. This represented 0.65 percent of the industry total. Of these units, 24,455 were made in Michigan and 18,230 were made in California. Calendar year dealer sales amounted to 36,803 T-Birds, representing 0.5 percent of industry sales. According to *Ward's Automotive Yearbook 1975* the specification was 194 nhp at 3800 rpm. Other sources say 216 hp, 218 hp and 220 hp. In reality, the early net horsepower ratings used in the industry were relative to vehicle weight, so the fully-loaded T-Bird could, theoretically, have less horsepower than the base model. Therefore, all of these ratings could be "correct." The biggest technical innovation of 1975 was an optional four-wheel disc brake system powered by Ford's new Hydro-Boost hydraulic brake booster. It included the Sure Trac rear brake anti-skid package. In addition, the anti-freeze was now advertised to last three years, instead of two. All 1975 T-Birds were manufactured in U.S. plants, but not all were produced for the U.S. market. Export units may have had minor differences. For instance, the sales literature issued by Ford of Canada did not include a paragraph that appeared in U.S. catalogs saying that T-Birds were designed to operate on unleaded gas. Also, the American literature specified mileage intervals for oil changes and major chassis lubrication, while Canadian catalogs eliminated such references. Sales and production saw another decline and the Thunderbird's share of market dropped, too. Model-year production was about 15,800 less than the previous year.

1976 Thunderbird

Thunderbird — Series 7 — (V-8): Ford described the 1976 T-Bird as "Possibly the best luxury car buy in the world today." No drastic product changes were made. The T-Bird came only as a roomy two-door hardtop on the same chassis as before. It had a cavernous trunk. Seventeen exterior colors were offered and seven were optional Starfire finishes. Odense grain or Creme Normande grain vinyl roofs were standard. Four styles of wheel covers were available: Base, Deluxe (not available with Luxury groups), simulated wire (included with Bordeaux and Lipstick Red Luxury groups) and deep-dish aluminum wheels (included with the Crème and Gold Luxury package). Buyers of the latter could swap the aluminum wheels for the simulated wire wheels and receive a credit. Silky Aurora nylon cloth-and-vinyl trim was standard on the deep-cushioned split-bench seats. The interior included assist straps, burled walnut wood-tone appliqués and plush cut-pile carpeting. Kasman cloth trim, which had the look and feel of cashmere, was optional in four colors. T-Bird buyers could also pick from super-soft vinyl trims in 11 single and two-tone combinations or over a dozen optional trims featuring genuine leather seating surfaces. A new Lipstick Red and White Luxury group, as listed in the 1976 Color & Trim book, had a Lipstick Red Normande grain half-vinyl roof with Lipstick Red exterior finish. Also featured in this package were color-keyed body side, border and back window moldings and color-keyed paint and tape stripes. White with Lipstick Red accents were available in both vinyl or vinyl-and-leather interiors. If the buyer wanted the optional Silver moon roof, a color-keyed full vinyl roof was required. A "feature car" for 1976 was the T-Bird with a Lipstick Red Luxury group that included the same Lipstick Red exterior color, but came with a Bright Red Odense grain vinyl half-top, color-keyed border and wide body moldings, dual body and hood paint stripes, wire wheel covers, White leather seating surfaces or White super-soft vinyl upholstery, Red and White door trim panels, color-keyed interior components, 24-oz. cut-pile carpeting, and color-keyed luggage compartment trim. The Bordeaux luxury package included Bordeaux Starfire exterior finish, a Dark Red or Silver Odense grain vinyl half-top, color-keyed border and wide body side moldings, dual body and hood paint stripes, wire wheel covers, rich Red leather or plush Red velour Media cloth seats, color-keyed interior components, 24-oz. cut-pile carpeting and a color-keyed luggage compartment. The Creme and Gold luxury group was an ultra-luxurious option. It included Gold Starfire glamour paint on the body sides, Creme paint on the hood, deck and front half of the roof, unique double tape stripes along the upper fender edges, a fully-padded Gold Odense grain half-vinyl roof, color-keyed border moldings, wide Creme body side moldings, Gold Thunderbird emblems in the opera windows and deep-dish aluminum wheels. Interior touches included Creme and Gold leather seating or plush Gold velour Media cloth trim, a gold instrument panel appliqué, color-keyed 24-oz. cut-pile carpeting and a luggage compartment dress-up package. Under the T-Bird's hood was a huge 7.5-liter V-8 with a four-barrel carburetor. Road testers were able to chirp the tires with this engine and Cruise-O-Matic transmission. Standard features included: 460-cid V-8, solid-state ignition, SelectShift Cruise-O-Matic transmission, power steering, power front disc brakes, manual SelectAire Conditioning, automatic parking brake release, AM radio with driver and front passenger door speakers, power window lifts, heavy-duty 61-amp alternator, burled walnut woodtone interior appliqués, inside hood release, power ventilation system, door courtesy lights, under panel light, glove box light, front ashtray light, individually-adjustable split-bench seat with dual folding center armrest, Aurora cloth-and-vinyl upholstery, electric clock, 24-oz. cut-pile carpeting, color-keyed deluxe safety belts, sound insulation, Odense Grain full vinyl roof, opera windows with T-Bird emblems, remote-control left-hand outside rearview mirror, stand-up hood ornament, hood rear edge molding, door belt molding, bright drip rail moldings, bright body side moldings with color-keyed vinyl inserts, partial wheel opening moldings, Deluxe bumper group (including front and rear bumper guards with white insert strips), steel-belted radial white sidewall tires and full wheel covers.

VIN:

The VIN was stamped on an aluminum tab riveted to the dashboard on the passenger side and was visible through the windshield. The prefix indicated the manufacturer: F=Ford. The first symbol denoted the model-year: 6=1976. The second symbol indicated the assembly plants: Y=Wixom (Novi), Michigan and J=Los Angeles, California. The third symbol was the car-line: 8=T-Bird. The fourth symbol indicated the body type: 7=Two-door hardtop. The fifth symbol was the engine: A=460-cid/202-hp Thunderbird V-8. The sixth through 11th symbols denoted the sequential production numbers of specific vehicles starting at 100001. The suffix showed the manufacturer: F=Ford. The body certification label was located on the rear face of the driver's door. The top part of the label indicated the T-Bird was manufactured by Ford Motor Company. Directly below this was the month and year of manufacture, plus a statement that the car conformed to federal motor vehicle safety standards in effect on the indicated dates of manufacture. The VIN appeared on the first line of encoded information. It matched the first to 11th symbols on the VIN tag. "PASSENGER" now appeared to the right of the VIN to and indicated a passenger vehicle. The body style code appeared on the far left-hand side of the second line of encoded information. The only Thunderbird code for this model-year was: 65K = 2-door Hardtop. The color and vinyl roof type/color code appeared to the right of the body style code in the second position on the second line of encoded information. The trim code appears to the right of the color and vinyl roof codes in the third position on the second line of encoded information. The transmission code appeared to the right of the trim code in the fourth position on the second line of encoded information:

1976 Ford Thunderbird two-door Hardtop (F)

U=XPL C6 three-speed automatic, Z=XPL C6 Special three-speed automatic. The axle code appeared to the right of the transmission code in the fifth position on the second line of encoded information: K=2.75:1 limited-slip, L=2.79:1 limited-slip, M=3.18:1 limited-slip, N=3.07:1 limited-slip, O=3.00:1 limited-slip, P=3.40:1 limited-slip, R=3.25:1 limited slip. The District Special Equipment code appeared to the right of the transmission code in the far right-hand position on the second line of encoded information. The abbreviations VIN/BDY/CLR/TRM/TR/AX/DSO did not appear on the certification label itself. The specific application of the codes was determined by where they are located on the vehicle certification label.

Thunderbird (V-8)

Series No.	Body/Style No.	Body Type and Seating	Factory Price	Shipping Weight	Production Total
7	65K	2-dr. Convertible-4P	$7,790	4,808 lbs.	52,935

Engine:

Thunderbird 460 Four-Barrel V-8: Overhead valve. Cast-iron block. Displacement: 429 cid. B & S: 4.36 x 3.85 in. Compression ratio: 8.50:1. Brake hp: 202 at 3800 rpm. Torque: 352 lbs.-ft. at 1600 rpm. Five main bearings. Hydraulic valve lifters. Carburetor: Four-barrel Motorcraft 9510 or Ford 4350A 9510. Cooling system capacity: 18.8 qt. with heater. Crankcase capacity: 5 qt. (add 1 qt. with new oil filter). Dual exhausts. Code A.

Chassis:

Wheelbase: 120.4 in. Overall length: 225.7. Overall width: 79.7. Overall height: 52.8 in. Trunk volume: 13.9 cu. ft. Front tread: 63 in. Rear tread: 63.1 in. Tires: JR78-15 steel-belted radial.

Technical:

Steering: Integral with power-assist. Turning diameter: 43 ft. Front suspension: Coil springs, stabilizer, shocks and axial strut. Rear suspension: Coil spring, shocks and stabilizer. Steering: Integral power-assist. Standard rear axle: 3.00:1. Front brakes: Power disc. Rear brakes: Power drum. Fuel tank capacity: 26.5 gallons.

Options:

Bordeaux luxury group ($624-$700). Creme and Gold luxury group ($717 to $793). Lipstick luxury group ($337-$546). Turnpike group ($180). Convenience group including remote-control right-hand outside rearview mirror, interval windshield wipers and automatic seatback release ($84). Protection group including front and rear color-keyed floor mats with carpet inserts, license plate frames, door edge guards, spare tire cover and rocker panel moldings ($79 without rocker panel molding or $87 with). Light group including Autolamp On/Off delay system, passenger lighted visor-vanity mirror, dual overhead map/dome lights, engine compartment light, low fuel and door ajar warning lights, headlamps-on alert buzzer and automatic headlamp dimmer ($164). Power lock group including electric door locks and trunk opener ($86). Security lock group including locking gas cap, spare tire lock and lockable inside hood release ($18). Automatic temperature control air conditioning ($488). Anti-theft alarm system ($84). Electric rear defroster ($99). Electric windshield/rear window defroster ($355). Fingertip speed control ($120). Tinted glass ($29-$66). Power mini-vent windows ($79). Power six-way power driver's seat ($132). Power six-way driver and passenger seat ($250). Power lumbar support seats ($86). Manual reclining passenger seat ($70). Automatic seat back release ($30). Tilt steering wheel ($68). Fuel monitor warning light ($20). Front cornering lamps ($43). Lighted driver's visor vanity mirror ($43). AM/FM stereo radio ($145). AM/FM stereo radio with tape player ($249). AM/FM stereo radio with search function ($298). AM/FM quadrosonic radio with tape player ($382). Power antenna ($32). Power-operated glass moon roof in Gold, Silver, Brown or Rose ($879). Power-operated sunroof ($716). Starfire Glamour paint ($204). Wide color-keyed vinyl insert body side moldings ($121). Dual body side and hood paint stripes ($33). Leather seat trim ($239). Kasman cloth seat trim ($96). Super-soft vinyl seat trim ($55). Trunk dress-up package

($59). Deluxe wheel covers ($67). Simulated wire wheel covers, except with Gold and Creme package ($88). Simulated wire wheel covers (with Gold and Creme package $163 credit). Deep-dish aluminum wheels, except with Bordeaux/Lipstick groups ($251). Deep-dish aluminum wheels with Bordeaux/Lipstick groups ($163). JR78 x 15 steel-belted radial whitewall tires ($41). LR78 x 15 steel-belted radial wide white sidewall tires ($59). Space-Saver spare tires ($ 86). Optional axle ratio ($14). Traction-Lok axle ($55). Four-wheel disc brakes ($184). Sure-Track brake control system, includes four-wheel disc brakes ($378). Dual exhaust system ($72). Engine block heater ($18). Heavy-duty suspension ($29).

History:

The 1976 T-Bird was introduced on October 3, 1975. Henry Ford II (Chairman) and. Lee A Iacocca (President) again held the top two corporate positions at Ford Motor Company. W.P. Benton was Ford Division's Vice President and General Manager. W.J. Oben was General Sales manager for the division. Calendar-year output was 106,962 units and included production of the all-new, down-sized 1977 T-Bird. A total of 52,935 T-Birds were produced in the model year. This represented 0.65 percent of the industry total. Of these units, 37,777 were made in Michigan and 15,158 were made in California. Calendar year dealer sales amounted to 100,658 T-Birds, representing 1.2 percent of industry sales. During late June and early July of 1976, the country was in a fever pitch with the Bicentennial Celebration theme. It was from this celebration that a "Commemorative" model T-Bird evolved. Only 32 of these cars were made. These cars had many special features and a sticker price of nearly $10,000. *Motor Trend's* Tony Swan said that his deepest affection for the T-Bird surfaced while stuck in rush hour traffic jams or dashing across Interstate highways through Nebraska. He described the T-Bird as "a car for people who like to ride, not drive." It was the best-insulated and quietest car built by Ford at the time. The silence experienced in the interior helped to isolate the driver from his or her surroundings. The conclusion reached in *Motor Trend* was "Big Birds rank high in the lists of all-time opulent glamour boats and they're habit-forming in the extreme. They'll be missed." Other experts found the car's performance "pretty good." Its recall history and repair record were also not all that bad. Overall reliability of the 1976 model was rated "better than average" by *Consumer Guide*. In his *Illustrated Thunderbird Buyer's Guide*, Ford expert Paul G. McLaughlin writes, "The 1976 T-Birds were fine cars in their own right, but the time had come for them to take on a new image, an image more in tune with the needs of late-1970s society. The T-Birds that would follow were smaller, more agile, lighter and more performance-oriented. They'll never be more luxurious, though, because as far as luxury goes in a T-Bird package, the epitome was reached in 1976."

1977 Thunderbird

Thunderbird — Series 7 — (V-8): The all-new 1977 T-Bird was a mid-size — rather than full-size — luxury car with the same six-passenger accommodations as before. All new sheet metal and sharp styling hid the fact that the shrunken T-Bird was based on the Ford LTD II. The car's profile was pleasantly different. A chrome wrap-over roof molding and small opera windows with beveled-glass decorated the "B" pillars, which separated the front door windows from large coach windows at the far rear end of the "greenhouse." Distinctive T-Bird features included concealed headlights (hidden behind large flip-up doors) and functional front fender louvers. The chrome crosshatch grille had the same design theme, but horizontal bars were more dominant. It had a bright surround and a lower edge designed to swing back, under impact, to avoid slow-speed collision damage. The parking and signal light lenses were notched into the front fender tips. At the rear of the car were tall, full-width taillights and a sculptured deck lid. A Thunderbird nameplate dressed up the deck section that extended down between the taillights. A 302-cid (5.0-liter) V-8 with DuraSpark ignition was standard. California cars came with a cleaner-burning 351-cid V-8. Both 351- and 400-cid V-8s were optional in federal (non-California) cars. To improve handling, the 1977 T-Bird had higher-rate springs, a larger front stabilizer bar and a standard rear stabilizer bar. There was less standard equipment overall, but a coolant recovery system was added. The T-Bird interior featured bench seats with Wilshire cloth and vinyl upholstery. There was a new five-pod instrument cluster with European-type graphics. Instruments included an 85-mph speedometer, a trip odometer, a 0-6000-rpms tachometer, an amp gauge, a fuel gauge, a temperature gauge, an oil pressure gauge and a clock. Warning lights were provided as directional signal and high-beam indicators. Other lights indicated when the hand-brake was on, if the door was ajar, when the seat belts were in use and whether the rear defogger was being used. Simulated engine-turned trim or simulated burled wood-grain accents were used on the dashboard. The stitching pattern on the standard bench seat was brand new. A split-bench seat or bucket seats were optional. Also available was a front center console with twin storage bins. An optional exterior decor package could be ordered to accent the T-Bird's roof. Also optional was an interior decor group option. It contained Ardmore and Kasman knit cloth upholstery choices, fold-down center arm rests, a reclining passenger seat, a visor vanity mirror and color-keyed seat belts. Two personalized versions of the T-Bird arrived in the spring. One was the Silver/Lipstick Feature Package and the other was an all-new T-Bird Town Landau. The Silver/Lipstick feature package was basically a paint and vinyl trim option. A flyer showed the base vehicle price of $5,063, and prices for three separate options (vinyl roof at $132, interior decor group at $299, and all-vinyl trim at $22). They added up to $5,516. However, the same flyer also noted that a vinyl roof was not required, so you could get a Silver or Lipstick decor car with an all-steel roof for as little as $5,384. It's doubtful that many (if any) were ordered without a vinyl roof, which was a popular feature. The decor package's actual content included a Silver Metallic exterior color or Lipstick Red exterior color. Both were usually combined with a vinyl roof in a choice of the matching or contrasting color. This added up to six combinations, since buyers could get either color of paint without a vinyl top or with a choice of a Silver or Lipstick Red vinyl top. You also got a Dove Grey all-vinyl interior with a choice of a split bench seat or bucket seats up front. This interior featured Lipstick Red accent straps and welts, Dove Grey door and quarter trim with Lipstick Red carpets, moldings, and components, plus Dove Grey trim above the belt line. This package could be teamed with all other T-Bird regular production options except leather seat trims and Tu-tone paint treatments. The Town Landau was a separate model. Standard features included: All standard FoMoCo safety, anti-theft, convenience items, and emissions control equipment, 302-cid two-barrel V-8 (or 352-cid 149-hp V-8 in California), DuraSpark ignition system, SelectShift automatic transmission, power steering, power front disc/rear drum brakes, HR78 x 15 black sidewall belted radial tires, chrome-plated swing-away grille, fender louvers, concealed two-speed windshield wipers, wiper-mounted washer jets, coolant recovery system, inside hood release, concealed headlights, full-width taillights, opera windows, dual note horn, bright rocker panel moldings, bright wheel lip moldings, full wheel covers, bright window, door belt, and roof drip moldings, heater and defroster, full-flow ventilation, deluxe steering wheel, day/night mirror, bench seats, carpeting, instrument panel with wood-grain appliqués, inside hood release, and cigar lighter.

1977-1/2 Thunderbird Town Landau: The Town Landau had most of the features above, with these differences or additions: A brushed aluminum roof wrap-over appliqué, color-keyed roof cross-over moldings (when optional vinyl top is ordered), color-coordinated translucent hood ornament insert, four cast aluminum wheels with accent paint, opera windows with a Town Landau insignia, accent stripes on body sides, hood, and grille opening panel, deck lid, headlight doors, and fender louvers, whitewall steel-belted radial tires, wide color-keyed vinyl insert body side moldings with partial wheel lip moldings, front cornering lamps, deluxe bumper group (including front and rear bumper guards and horizontal rub strips), a luxury sound insulation package, Town Landau insignia on instrument panel appliqué, 22-karat gold finish plaque engraved with owner's name, 6-way power driver's seat, power side windows, power lock group (including door locks and remote trunk release), manual-control SelectAire Conditioner, Interior luxury group including convenience group (with left- and right-hand remote control mirrors, interval windshield wipers, automatic parking brake release, and trip odometer) and light group (with dual-beam map lights, under-dash lights, glove box light, ash tray light, trunk light, engine compartment light, door ajar light, and headlights on light), tinted glass, AM/FM stereo search radio (with twin front door mounted speakers and dual rear speakers) and a tilt steering wheel.

VIN:

The VIN was stamped on an aluminum tab riveted to the dashboard on the passenger side and was visible through the windshield. The prefix indicated the manufacturer: F=Ford. The first symbol denoted the model-year: 7=1977. The second symbol indicated the assembly plants: G=Chicago, Illinois and J=Los Angeles, California. The third symbol was the car-line: 8=T-Bird. The fourth symbol denoted the body type: 7=Two-door hardtop. The fifth symbol indicated the engine: F = 302 cid (5.0L)/130- to 137-hp V-8, H = 351 cid (5.8L)/149-hp V-8, Q = Modified 351 cid (5.8L)/152-hp V-8, S = 400 cid (6.6L)/173-hp V-8. The sixth through 11th symbols were the sequential production numbers of the specific vehicle starting at 100001. The suffix denoted the manufacturer: F=Ford. The body certification label was located on the rear face of the driver's door. The top part of the label indicated the T-Bird was manufactured by Ford Motor Company. Directly below this was the month and year of manufacture, plus a statement that the car conformed to federal motor vehicle safety standard in effect on the indicated date of manufacture. The vehicle certification label was located on the rear face of driver's door. The top part of the label indicated the Thunderbird was manufactured by Ford Motor Company. Directly below this was the month and year of manufacture, plus a statement that the car conformed to federal motor vehicle safety standards in effect on the indicated date of manufacture.

1977 Ford Thunderbird two-door Town Landau Coupe (F)

The VIN appeared on the first line of encoded information. It matched the first to 11th symbols on the VIN tag. PASSENGER appeared to the right of the VIN to denote passenger vehicle. The body style code appeared on the far left-hand side of the second line of encoded information. The only Thunderbird code for this model-year was: 60H=2-door Pillared Hardtop. The color and vinyl roof type/color code appeared to the right of the body style code in the second position on the second line of encoded information. The trim code appeared to the right of the color and vinyl roof codes in the third position on the second line of encoded information. The transmission code appeared to the right of the trim code in the fourth position on the second line of encoded information. The axle code appeared to the right of the transmission code in the fifth position on the second line of encoded information. The District Special Equipment code appeared to the right of the transmission code in the far right-hand position on the second line of encoded information. The abbreviations VIN/BDY/CLR/TRM/TR/AX/DSO did not appear on the certification label itself. The specific application of the codes was determined by where they are located on the vehicle certification label.

Thunderbird (V-8)

Series No.	Body/Style No.	Body Type and Seating	Factory Price	Shipping Weight	Production Total
87	60H	2-dr. Hardtop-4P	$5,063	3,907 lbs.	Note 1
87	60H	2-dr. Town Hardtop-4P	$7,990	4,104 lbs.	Note 1

Note 1: Production of both models combined was 318,140.

Engines:

Thunderbird Base V-8 (Federal): 90-degree, overhead valve V-8. Cast-iron block and head. Displacement: 302 cid (5.0 liters). B & S: 4.00 x 3.00 in. Compression ratio: 8.4:1. Brake hp: 130-137 at 3400-3600 rpm. Torque: 243-245 lbs.-ft. at 1600-1800 rpm. Five main bearings. Hydraulic valve lifters. Carburetor: Motorcraft 2150 two-barrel. Serial number code: F.

Thunderbird Base V-8 (California): 90-degree, overhead valve V-8, Cast-iron block and head. Displacement: 351 cid (5.8 liters). B & S: 4.00 x 3.50 in. Compression ratio: 8.3:1. Brake hp: 149 at 3200 rpm. Torque: 291 lbs.-ft. at 1600 rpm. Five main bearings. Hydraulic valve lifters. Carburetor: Motorcraft 2150 two-barrel. Windsor engine. Serial number code: H.

Thunderbird Optional V-8 (Federal): 90-degree, overhead valve V-8, Cast-iron block and head. Displacement: 351 cid (5.8 liters). B & S: 4.00 x 3.50 in. Compression ratio: 8.0:1. Brake hp: 161 at 3600 rpm. Torque: 285 lbs.-ft. at 1800 rpm. Five main bearings. Hydraulic valve lifters. Carburetor: Motorcraft 2150 two-barrel. Windsor engine. Serial number code: Q.

Thunderbird Optional V-8 (Federal): 90-dgree, overhead valve V-8. Cast-iron block and head. Displacement: 400 cu. in (6.6 liters). B & S: 4.00 x 4.00 in. Compression ratio: 8:0.1. Brake hp: 173 at 3800 rpm. Torque: 326 lbs.-ft. at 1600 rpm. Five main bearings. Hydraulic valve lifters. Carburetor: Motorcraft 2150 two-barrel. Serial number code: S.

Technical:

Wheelbase: 114 in. Overall length: 215.5. Overall width: 78.5. Overall height: 53 in. Front headroom: 37.3 in. Front legroom: 42.1 in. Rear headroom: 36.2 in. Rear legroom: 32.6 in. Trunk capacity: 15.6 cu. ft. Front tread: 63.2 in. Rear tread: 63.1 in. Wheels: 15 x 6.5 in. Tires: H78-15 steel-belted radial.

Chassis:

Steering: Integral with power-assist. Steering ratio: 21.9:1. Turning diameter: 43.1 ft. Front suspension: Independent, upper and lower control arms, coil springs, tubular shocks and anti-roll bar. Rear suspension: Live axle, four-link control arms, coil springs, tubular shocks, anti-roll bar. Steering: Recirculating ball, power-assist. Standard rear axle: 2.50:1. Weight distribution: 57/43. Front brakes: Power vented disc. Rear brakes: Power drum. Brakes swept area: 372.3 sq. in. Fuel tank capacity: 21 gallons.

Options:

351-cid 161-hp V-8 engine ($66). 400-cid V-8 engine ($155). Manual air conditioner ($505). Automatic air conditioner in base Hardtop ($546). Automatic air conditioner in Town Landau or Diamond Jubilee (N/A) Heavy-duty 90-amp alternator ($45). Optional ratio axle ($14). Traction-Lok differential axle ($54). Heavy-duty 77-amp. battery ($17). Color-keyed deluxe seat belts ($18). Front license plate bracket (no charge). Deluxe bumper group ($72). Day and date clock ($20). Convenience group for models with bucket seat and floor shift ($88), for other models ($96). Front cornering lights ($43). Exterior decor group for models with convenience group or interior luxury group ($317), for other models ($368). Interior decor group ($299). Electric rear window defroster ($87). California emissions equipment ($70). Illuminated entry system ($51). Complete tinted glass ($61). High-altitude equipment ($22). Instrumentation group for Sports models with convenience group ($103), for other models ($111). Light group ($46). Power lock group ($92). Interior luxury group ($724). Dual sport mirrors from models with convenience or interior luxury groups (no charge), for other models ($51). Remote-control left OSRV chrome mirror ($14). Illuminated right-hand visor-vanity mirror for models with interior decor group ($42), for other models ($46). Black vinyl insert body side moldings ($39). Bright wide body side moldings ($39). Color-keyed wide body side moldings ($51). Power moon roof ($888). Metallic glow paint ($62). Protection group for models with front license plate bracket ($47), for other models ($43). AM/FM manual radio ($59). AM/FM stereo radio ($120). AM/FM stereo search radio ($276). AM/FM radio with quadrosonic tape player in base Hardtop ($326), in Town Landau ($50). AM/FM stereo with tape player ($193). Two-piece vinyl roof ($132). Six-way power full-width front seat ($143). Six-way power driver's seat only ($143). Bucket seats and console with interior decor group (no charge), all others ($158). Automatic seat back release ($52). Space Saver spare tire (no charge to $13 credit, depending on type of tires). Dual rear seat speakers ($43). Fingertip speed control in models with sports instrumentation group or interior luxury group ($93), all other models ($114). Leather steering wheel in models with sports instrumentation group ($39), all other models ($61). Tilt steering wheel ($63). Handling suspension ($79). Dual accent paint stripes ($39). Heavy-duty trailer towing package ($138). Leather seat trim ($241). Vinyl seat trim ($22). Tu-Tone paint treatment ($49). Wire wheel covers with exterior decor group ($47 credit), other models ($99). Four turbine-spoke cast aluminum wheels, with exterior decor group ($88), all other models ($234). Power side windows ($114). AM radio delete ($72 credit). Tire options (followed by extra charge for models having five HR78 x 15 steel-belted black sidewall tires as standard equipment): HR78 x 15 radial whitewalls ($45 extra), HR78 x 15 radial white band whitewalls ($61 extra), and HR70 x 17 white oval whitewalls ($67 extra).

History:

The 1977 T-Bird was introduced on September 30, 1976. Henry Ford II (Chairman) and. Lee A Iaccoca (President) again held the top two corporate positions at Ford Motor Company. W.P. Benton was Ford Division's Vice President and General Manager. W.J. Oben was General Sales manager for the division. Demand for T-Birds soared and Ford scrambled to keep up with a six-fold increase in production. Calendar-year output was 365,986 units. A total of 318,144 T-Birds were produced in the model year. This represented 3.49 percent of the industry total. Of these units, 235,884 were made in Chicago and 82,256 were made in Los Angeles. Calendar year dealer sales amounted to 325,153 T-Birds, representing 3.6 percent of industry sales. "New Ford Thunderbird: The Best in 15 Years," announced the cover of the April 1977 issue of *Road Test* magazine. The magazine explained that Ford had made the right decision by taking the T-Bird "off the hill of the custom built homes" and rolling it down the road "where it can punch it out with all the Monte Carlos, Grand Prixs, Cordobas and Cougars." The magazine was loaned a Sport version of the T-Bird with a 400-cid V-8 that averaged 17 mpg. While summing up the T-Bird's appearance as "practically every styling cliché known to civilized Western man," the magazine stressed how much T-Bird buyers were getting for the car's now-more-affordable price tag. It said that the car was "qualitatively no different" than a Ford or a Mercury Cougar. "But in a market where you sell quantity, this new T-Bird is a lot of car," the testers concluded. "You can roll that thing into your driveway and the whole neighborhood can tell it says Thunderbird." On a scale of 0-100, *Road Test* rated acceleration at 79 points. The brakes were scored 89 points. Handling warranted 73 points. Interior noise levels (92 points) and tire reserve (100 points) where the highest-rated categories. Fuel economy got 30 points. Overall, the 1977 T-Bird earned 76 points. This was only two to three points under the three best cars that had been tested , which were the VW Super Scirocco, the Saab EMS and the Porsche Turbo Carrera. From a contemporary buyer's standpoint, these cars were a vast improvement over the "Big 'Birds" of the past few years in terms of maneuverability and economy. The cars had no major mechanical problems, but the bodies of the 1977 models proved very prone to rust.

The 1978 and 1979 editions had improved rust protection. Cars of 1977 vintage with tilt steering were also the subject of a recall, since some had been built with Ford truck tilt steering parts. This caused some of the cars to start with the gear selector in neutral. While these T-Birds lack the degree of distinction from other Ford products that earlier T-Birds reflected, they were tremendously well received by the car-buying public and T-Bird production saw a huge increase. The Los Angeles assembly plant put together more 'Birds than it had in the last three years combined. This was over twice as many T-Birds as had ever been made there in a single year. The grand total of 318,144 T-Birds in the model year over 60,000 higher than Ford had built in the first six years of the T-Bird's history. Of these, 295,779 were made for the U.S. market and the rest were shipped to Canada and other countries.

1978 Thunderbird

Thunderbird Series 7 — (V-8): Ford added T-Bird emblems to the headlight doors in 1978. Six new body colors, four added vinyl roof colors, bold striped cloth bucket seat trim and a new Russet interior option were promoted. Technical improvements included a more efficient torque converter, a new lighter weight battery, revisions to the engine air induction system and a new lighter weight power steering pump with quick-disconnect hydraulic fittings. A T-roof convertible option was a midyear innovation. However, the biggest news of the year was the limited-availability Diamond Jubilee Edition commemorating Ford's 75th year of making cars. New options included a power radio antenna and a 40-channel CB radio. The 302-cid V-8 was again base engine. A slightly hotter "modified" version of the 351-cid V-8 with a four-barrel carburetor, plus the 400-cid (actually 402 cid) two-barrel V-8 remained optional. The base engine provided about 15.1 mpg on average. The 351 used as standard equipment in California cars averaged around 14.1 mpg. The more powerful version of the 351-cid V-8 was good for about 13.6 mpg overall. The larger 400-cid engine averaged around 12.8 mpg. T-Birds came with deep-cushioned bench seats wearing knit-cloth-and-vinyl trim. Heavy carpeting, full-length door armrests and burled walnut wood tone accents gave even the base model a rich look inside. Optional bucket seats came in all-vinyl or cloth and vinyl. An interior decor package with special door panels was a separate option. A front split-bench seat was included with the Town Landau model and the interior luxury group option. It came with either standard velour cloth trim or optional Ultra-Soft leather-and-vinyl trim and both included interior decor type door trim panels. The Diamond Jubilee Edition T-Bird featured an interior done in one of two exclusive colors of luxury cloth with a split bench style front seat. New this year was a sports decor option that added a bold grille with blacked-out vertical bars, unique imitation deck lid straps, paint stripes, twin remote sport mirrors, spoke-style road wheels, HR70 x 15 raised white letter tires, polycoated Chamois color paint and a tan vinyl roof with color-keyed rear window moldings. The Thunderbird Town Landau returned in 1978 and came in 14 body colors. Crushed velour upholstery and a split-bench seat with fold-down center armrest were part of the Town Landau interior package. Billed as "the most exclusive Thunderbird you can buy," the $10,106 Diamond Jubilee anniversary model included several items never before offered on a Thunderbird. It had an exclusive monochromatic exterior done in Diamond Blue Metallic or Ember Metallic paint. Diamond Blue models had blue luxury cloth upholstery. Diamond Ember models had chamois-colored cloth seats. Some collectors say the production totals included just under 19,000 Diamond Jubilee Editions. Standard equipment included: All standard FoMoCo safety, anti-theft, convenience items, and emissions control equipment, 302-cid two-barrel V-8 (or 352-cid 149-hp V-8 in California), DuraSpark ignition system, SelectShift automatic transmission, power steering, power front disc/rear drum brakes, front and rear stabilizer bars, H78 x 15 black sidewall belted radial tires, chrome-plated swing-away grille, fender louvers, concealed two-speed windshield wipers, wiper-mounted washer jets, coolant recovery system, inside hood release, concealed headlights, full-width taillights, opera windows, dual note horn, bright rocker panel moldings,

bright wheel lip moldings, full wheel covers, bright window, door belt, and roof drip moldings, heater and defroster, full-flow ventilation, deluxe steering wheel, day/night mirror, deep-cushioned bench seats with knit cloth/vinyl trim, color-keyed 10-oz. cut-pile carpeting, full-length door arm rests, all-vinyl door trim with burled walnut wood-tone appliqués, instrument panel with burled walnut wood-tone appliqués, inside hood release, cigar lighter, AM radio, and electric clock.

Thunderbird Town Landau: Standard equipment for the Town Landau included most of the features above, with these differences or additions: Brushed aluminum roof wrap-over appliqué, color-keyed roof cross-over moldings (when optional vinyl top is ordered), color-coordinated translucent hood ornament insert, four cast aluminum wheels with accent paint, opera windows with a Town Landau insignia, accent stripes on body sides, hood, and grille opening panel, deck lid, headlight doors, and fender louvers, whitewall steel-belted radial tires, wide color-keyed vinyl insert body side moldings with partial wheel lip moldings, front cornering lamps, deluxe bumper group (including front and rear bumper guards and horizontal rub strips), a luxury sound insulation package, Town Landau insignia on instrument panel appliqué, 22-karat gold finish plaque engraved with owner's name, 6-way power driver's seat, power side windows, power lock group (including door locks and remote trunk release), manual-control SelectAire Conditioner, Interior luxury group including convenience group (with left- and right-hand remote control mirrors, interval windshield wipers, automatic parking brake release, and trip odometer) and light group (with dual-beam map lights, under-dash lights, glove box light, ash tray light, trunk light, engine compartment light, door ajar light, and headlights on light), tinted glass, AM/FM stereo search radio (with twin front door mounted speakers and dual rear speakers), and a tilt steering wheel.

Thunderbird Diamond Jubilee Edition: Standard equipment on the Diamond Jubilee Edition included most of the Thunderbird features above except/or in addition: An exclusive monochromatic exterior done in Diamond Blue Metallic or Ember Metallic paint, a matching thickly padded vinyl roof, a color-keyed grille texture, a Diamond Jubilee opera window insignia, the owner's initials on the door, color-keyed cast aluminum wheels, color-keyed bumper rub strips, a power radio antenna, an illuminated left-hand visor-vanity mirror, an instrumentation cluster with Ebony wood-tone appliqué, unique front split-bench seat with biscuit design all cloth trim and Thunderbird ornamentation on the upper seat bolsters, door and front seat-back assist straps, hand-stitched leather-covered pad on instrument panel, ebony wood-tone appliqués on instrument panel, knobs, door and quarter trim panels, and steering wheel, molded door and quarter trim arm rests with extra padding, 36-oz. cut-pile floor carpeting, bright metal pedal trim accents, unique car keys with wood-tone inserts, color-keyed 18-oz. trunk carpets, molded rear deck liner, and seat belt warning chime.

VIN:

The VIN was stamped on an aluminum tab riveted to the dashboard on passenger side and was visible through the windshield. The prefix indicated the manufacturer: F=Ford. The first symbol denoted the model-year: 8=1978. The second symbol indicated the assembly plants: G=Chicago, Illinois and J=Los Angeles, California. The third symbol was the car-line: 8=T-Bird. The fourth symbol denoted the body type: 7=Two-door hardtop. The fifth symbol indicated the engine: F=302 cid (5.0L)/134-hp V-8, H=351 cid (5.8L)/144-hp V-8, Q = Modified 351 cid (5.8L)/152-hp V-8, and S = 400 cid (6.6L)/173-hp V-8. The sixth through the 11th symbols were the sequential production numbers of specific vehicles starting at 100001. The suffix denoted the manufacturer: F=Ford. The body certification label was located on the rear face of the driver's door. The top part of the label indicated the T-Bird was manufactured by Ford Motor Company. Directly below this was the month and year of manufacture, plus a statement the car conformed to federal motor vehicle safety standards in effect on the indicated date of manufacture. The vehicle certification label was located on the rear face of the driver's door. The top part of the label indicated the Thunderbird was manufactured by Ford Motor Company. Directly below this was the month and year of manufacture, plus a statement that the car conforms to federal motor vehicle safety standard in effect on the indicated date of manufacture. The VIN appeared on the first line of encoded information. It matched the first to 11th symbols on the VIN tag. PASSENGER appeared to the right of the VIN to denote passenger vehicle. The body style code appeared on the far left-hand side of the second line of encoded information. The only Thunderbird code for this model-year was: 60H=2-door Pillared Hardtop. The color and vinyl roof type/color code appeared to the right of the body style code in the second position on the second line of encoded information. The trim code appeared to the right of the color and vinyl roof codes in the third position on the second line of encoded information. The transmission code appeared to the right of the trim code in the fourth position on the second line of encoded information. The axle code appeared to the right of the transmission code in the fifth position on the second line of encoded information. The District Special

1978 Ford Thunderbird two-door T-roof Convertible (OCW)

1978 Ford Thunderbird two-door Diamond Jubilee Edition (OCW)

Equipment code appeared to the right of the transmission code in the far right-hand position on the second line of encoded information. The abbreviations VIN/BDY/CLR/T RM/TR/AX/DSO did not appear on the certification label. The specific application of the codes was determined by their location on the vehicle certification label.

Thunderbird

Series No.	Body/Style No.	Body Type and Seating	Factory Price	Shipping Weight	Production Total
87	60H	2-dr. Hardtop-4P	$5,411	3,907 lbs.	Note 1

Town Landau

87	60H	2-dr. Hardtop-4P	$8,420	4,104 lbs.	Note 1

Diamond Jubilee Edition

87	60H	2-dr. Hardtop-4P	$10,106	4,200 lbs.	18,994

Note 1: Production of both the Thunderbird and Thunderbird Town Landau combined was 333,757.

Engines:

Thunderbird Base V-8 (Federal): 90-degree, overhead valve V-8. Cast-iron block and head. Displacement: 302 cid (5.0 liters). B & S: 4.00 x 3.00 in. Compression ratio: 8.4:1. Brake hp: 134 at 3400 rpm. Torque: 248 lbs.-ft. at 1600 rpm. Five main bearings. Hydraulic valve lifters. Carburetor: Motorcraft 2150 two-barrel. Serial number code: F.

Thunderbird Base V-8 (California): 90-degree, overhead valve. Cast-iron block and head. Displacement: 351 cid (5.8 liters). B & S: 4.00 x 3.50 in. Compression ratio: 8.3:1. Brake hp: 145 at 3400 rpm. Torque: 277 lbs.-ft. at 1600 rpm. Five main bearings. Hydraulic valve lifters. Carburetor: Motorcraft 2150 two-barrel. Windsor engine. Serial number code: H.

Thunderbird Optional V-8 (Federal): 90-degree, overhead valve. Cast-iron block and head. Displacement: 351 cid (5.8 liters). Bore and stroke: 4.00 x 3.50 in. Compression ratio: 8.0:1. Brake horsepower: 152 at 3600 rpm. Torque: 278 at 1800 rpm. Five main bearings. Hydraulic valve lifters. Carburetor: Motorcraft 2150 two-barrel. Windsor engine. Serial number code: Q.

Thunderbird Optional V-8 (Federal): 90-dgree, overhead valve. Cast-iron block and head. Displacement: 400 cu. in (6.6 liters). B & S: 4.00 x 4.00 in. Compression ratio: 8:0.1. Brake hp: 166 at 3800 rpm. Torque: 319 lbs.-ft. at 1800 rpm. Five main bearings. Hydraulic valve lifters. Carburetor: Motorcraft 2150 two-barrel. Serial number code: S.

Chassis:

Wheelbase: 114 in. Overall length: 215.5. Overall width: 78.5. Overall height: 53 in. Front headroom: 37.3 in. Front legroom: 42.1 in. Rear headroom: 36.2 in. Rear legroom: 32.6 in. Trunk capacity: 15.6 cu. ft. Front tread: 63.2 in. Rear tread: 63.1 in. Wheels: 15 x 6.5 in. Tires: HR78-15 steel-belted radial.

Technical:

Steering: Integral with power-assist. Steering ratio: 21.9:1. Turning diameter: 43.1 ft. Front suspension: Independent, upper and lower control arms, coil springs, tubular shocks and anti-roll bar. Rear suspension: Live axle, four-link control arms, coil springs, tubular shocks, anti-roll bar. Steering: Recirculating ball, power-assist. Standard rear axle: 2.50:1. Weight distribution: 57/43. Front brakes: Power vented disc. Rear brakes: Power drum. Brakes swept area: 372.3 sq. in. Fuel tank capacity: 21 gallons.

Options:

351-cid 161-hp V-8 engine ($157). 400-cid V-8 engine ($283). Traction-Lok differential axle ($50). Manual air conditioner ($543). Automatic air conditioner in base Hardtop ($588). Automatic air conditioner in Town Landau or Diamond Jubilee ($45) Power antenna ($45). Heavy-duty battery ($18). Color-keyed deluxe seat belts ($21). Front license plate bracket (no charge). Deluxe bumper group ($78). Day and date clock ($22). Convenience group for models with bucket seat and floor shift ($93), for other models ($103). Front cornering lights ($46). Exterior

decor group for models with convenience group or interior luxury group ($332), for other models ($382). Interior decor group ($316). Sports decor group for models with convenience group ($396), for other models ($446). Electric rear window defroster ($93). California emissions equipment ($75). T-roof convertible option ($699). Illuminated entry system $54). Complete tinted glass ($66). Sports instrumentation group for models with convenience group ($111), for other models ($118). Luxury sound insulation package ($29). Light group ($49). Power lock group ($100). Interior luxury group ($783). Dual sport mirrors for models with convenience or interior luxury groups ($8), for other models ($58). Remote-control left OSRV mirror ($16). Illuminated visor-vanity mirror for models with interior decor group ($33), for other models ($37). Rocker panel moldings ($29). Bright wide body side moldings ($42). Color-keyed wide body side moldings ($54). Power moon roof ($691). Metallic glow paint ($62). Protection group for models with front license plate bracket ($50), for other models ($46). AM/FM monaural radio ($53). AM/FM stereo radio ($113). AM/FM stereo search radio ($270). 40-channel Citizens Band radio ($295). AM/FM radio with quadrasonic tape player in base Hardtop ($320), in Town Landau and Diamond Jubilee models ($50). AM/FM stereo with tape player ($187). Radio flexibility group ($105). Two place vinyl roof ($138). Bucket seats and console with interior decor group ($37), all others ($211). Automatic seat back release ($33). Dual rear seat speakers ($46). Fingertip speed control, Town Landau or Diamond Jubilee with sports instrumentation group or interior luxury group ($104), all other models ($117). Leather steering wheel in models with sports instrumentation group ($51), all other models ($64). Tilt steering wheel ($70). Heavy-duty suspension ($20) Dual accent paint stripes ($46). Inflatable spare tire with HR78 black sidewall tires (no charge). Heavy-duty trailer towing package ($184). Leather and vinyl seat trim ($296). Luggage compartment trim ($39). Vinyl seat trim ($24). Tu-Tone paint treatment ($79). Wire wheel covers ($112). Four styled road wheels ($159). Four cast aluminum wheels on models with exterior decor group ($132), all other models ($291). Power side windows ($126). Heavy-duty alternator ($50). Front and rear bumper guards ($42). Sports instrumentation group on Town Landau or models with interior luxury group ($75), models with convenience group ($111), all other models ($118). Vinyl body side moldings ($42). Tinted windshield glass ($28) Front floor mats ($20). Tire options for base Hardtop with five GR78 x 15 tires as standard equipment included GR78 x 15 radial whitewalls ($46), HR78 x 15 black sidewalls ($22), HR78 x 15 radial whitewalls ($68), HR78 x 15 radial white-band whitewalls ($88), and HR70 x 17 white oval whitewalls ($90). Tire options for the Diamond Jubilee with five standard HR78 x 15 steel-belted whitewall radials as standard equipment included HR78 x 15 radial wide band whitewalls ($20), and HR70 x 15 whitewall wide oval radials ($22).

History:

The 1978 T-Bird was introduced on October 6, 1977. Henry Ford II (Chairman), Phillip Caldwell (Vice Chairman) and. Lee A Iacocca (President) held the top three corporate positions at Ford Motor Company. W.S. Walla was Ford Division's Vice President and General Manager. B.L. Crumpton was General Sales manager for the division. Demand for T-Birds was the highest ever and set a new all-time production record for an annual model. Calendar-year output was 326,873 units. A total of 352,751 T-Birds were produced in the model year. This represented 3.94 percent of the industry total. Of these units, 260,792 were made in Chicago and 91,959 were made in Los Angeles. Calendar year dealer sales amounted to 304,430 T-Birds, representing 3.3 percent of industry sales. An estimated 20,000 of the T-Birds made in the U.S. were destined for the export market and were shipped to Canada and other countries. These offered almost the same equipment, color schemes, and trim as the cars made for the U.S. market. However, they were not necessarily 100 percent identical. For example the "California" version of the 351-cid two-barrel V-8 was not offered in cars marketed in Canada. Also the Canadian version of the Diamond Jubilee Edition did not include a power antenna. In Canadian literature the gas tank capacity was expressed in Imperial gallons (17.3), the trunk space was expressed in liters (402), and other measurements were given in millimeters. Interestingly, service mileage intervals used in the U.S. did not apply to Canadian cars, but the cars sold in Canada were backed by a no-extra-charge Duraguard system that offered 36-month protection against sheet metal rust-through. There was no such program offered in the U.S. During calendar-year 1978, a total of 144 additional Thunderbirds were actually put together in a factory in Canada. As far as we can tell, these were the first cars bearing the Thunderbird name to be manufactured in Canada. They were early 1979 Models, however, and not 1978 models. It was, however, the 1977 Thunderbird that brought the marque back into NASCAR racing. Drivers Bobby Allison, Dick Brooks, and Jody Ridley found the new down-sized T-Bird well-suited to Grand National competition with the proper modifications. It had been 18 years — since 1960 — since the T-Bird's last appearance in a stock car race. 1978 would be only the beginning of the T-Bird's latter-day motorsports history. Allison's number 15 T-Bird, built by Bud Moore, took the checkered flag in events like the NAPA 400 at Riverside, California. That

1978 Ford Thunderbird two-door Diamond Jubilee Edition (OCW)

particular event was conducted in 103-degree weather, and Allison's car held up until his clutch linkage broke. However, he managed to keep the T-Bird going and came home 32.9 seconds in front of Darrell Waltrip.

1979 Thunderbird

Thunderbird — Series 7 — (V-8): A bolder, heavier-looking grille greeted T-Bird customers in 1979. It had a neo-classic look with a heavy chrome shell around it. Three thin horizontal moldings crossed three vertical bars to form large rectangular openings arranged in a four across by four high pattern. The hidden headlight doors were double-framed with chrome moldings and had large chrome Thunderbird insignias at their centers. There was a script nameplate on the left one. A massive, angular front bumper carried heavy, low bumper guards. A new spoiler went below the front bumper. Clear fender-notched parking lamp lenses with adjoining amber-colored marker lenses each held three horizontal divider strips. Each front fender sported a set of six simulated vertical louvers just behind the front wheel opening. Horizontal cornering lamps that mounted low on the fenders, just ahead of the wheel opening, were optional or included as part of decor packages. A forward-slanting wrap-over roof was becoming a T-Bird trademark. The wrap-over section showed narrow, slanting opera windows. Standard inside the base T-Bird was a comfort-contoured Flight Bench front seat with Rossano cloth seating surfaces and vinyl trim. A large, fold-down armrest hid in the center of the seat back. There were six solid interior colors and five Tu-Tone combinations with White as the base color. Specific color choices were offered in various materials: Vinyl, vinyl and cloth, standard cloth, luxury cloth or ultra-soft leather. Eight body colors, five vinyl roof colors, and four interior colors were all-new for 1979. Bucket seats in vinyl or cloth and vinyl were an extra-cost item. Optional split-bench seats came with these same materials, plus regular cloth, luxury cloth or ultra-soft leather. On the floor was 10-oz. cut-pile carpeting color-keyed to match the upholstery. The door panels had full-length armrests. At the rear of most models were large, swept-back side windows. Separate large, rectangular-shaped two-piece taillights characterized the rear of 1979 T-Birds. These replaced the former full-width units and looked like rectangles within rectangles. A winged T-Bird emblem was in the center. A single back-up light stood between the taillights. It was centered over the new rear bumper guards, which were standard equipment. Ford's 75th anniversary year had ended and the Diamond Jubilee model disappeared. A new Heritage Edition T-Bird was designed to take its place. Two monochromatic color schemes were available for this luxury car. One was Maroon and the other Light Medium Blue. A matching Lugano grain formal-style padded vinyl roof was featured. The split-bench seats had unique biscuit design all-cloth upholstery and a T-Bird insignia on the upper seat back bolsters. The Heritage Edition's roof had a unique solid quarter panel appearance instead of rear quarter windows. Chrome Heritage scripts decorated the solid panels. Returning as a Thunderbird option package was the Sports decor group. It included a Chamois vinyl roof with color-keyed backlight moldings; Chamois dual accent paint stripes; Chamois hood/GOP and fender louver paint stripes, Chamois deck lid straps, styled road wheels with Chamois paint accents, dual sport mirrors, and blacked-out vertical grille bars. It was available on cars with Black, Polar White, Midnight Blue Metallic, Dark Cordovan Metallic, Burnt Orange Glow, Dark Jade Metallic, or Pastel Chamois exterior finish. Chamois-colored interior trims were available with all exterior body colors. Chamois and White trims were offered with Polar White or Dark Cordovan Metallic exteriors. Chamois or Cordovan trims came in cars with Dark Cordovan Metallic exteriors. Also available were Chamois or Jade upholstery trims in cars with Dark Jade Metallic bodies. The deck lid straps gave these cars a hint of the classic image embodied in the sporty Stutz and Bentley touring coupes of the 1930s. On the technical front, T-Birds had a new electronic voltage regulator. The carburetor on the base 302-cid V-8 was also a refined two-barrel design. Door and ignition locks were modified for better theft protection. Corrosion protection was also becoming a factor in the U.S. market. Ford used pre-coated steels — such as galvanized steel and chromium/zinc-rich primer coated steel — vinyl sealers, aluminized wax and enamel top coats to combat rust. Standard features included: All standard FoMoCo safety, anti-theft, convenience items, and emissions control equipment,

302-cid two-barrel V-8 (or 352-cid 149-hp V-8 in California), DuraSpark ignition system, SelectShift automatic transmission, power steering power front disc/rear drum brakes, front and rear stabilizer bars, GR78 x 15 black sidewall belted radial tires, chrome-plated swing-away grille chrome plated front and rear bumpers, chrome plated rear bumper guards, fender louvers, concealed two-speed windshield wipers, wiper-mounted washer jets, coolant recovery system, inside hood release concealed headlights, full-width taillights, opera windows, dual note horn, bright rocker panel moldings, bright wheel lip moldings, full wheel covers, bright window, door belt, and roof drip moldings, heater and defroster, full-flow ventilation, deluxe steering wheel, day/night mirror Flight Bench seat, three-point seat and shoulder belts with retractors color-keyed 10-oz. cut-pile carpeting, full-length door arm rests, all-vinyl door trim with burled walnut wood-tone appliqués, instrument panel with burled walnut wood-tone appliqués, inside hood release, cigar lighter AM radio, and electric clock.

Town Landau: Standard Town Landau equipment included most of the features above, with these differences or additions: HR78 x 15 steel-belted radial whitewall tires, air conditioning, luxury sound insulation package, power lock group, 6-way driver's power seat, power side windows, tilt steering wheel, tinted glass, trip odometer, windshield wipers with interval control, deluxe bumper group, dual sport remote-control mirrors, wide color-keyed vinyl insert body side moldings integral partial wheel lip moldings, brushed aluminum roof wrap-over appliqué, cast aluminum wheels, upgraded carpeting, quartz crystal day and date clock, illuminated visor-vanity mirror on passenger side, AM/FM stereo radio, split bench seat with manual recliner, and automatic seat back releases.

Heritage Edition: Standard Heritage Edition equipment included most of the features above with these differences or additions to base equipment: HR78 x 15 whitewall steel-belted radial tires, air conditioning, illuminated entry system, luxury sound insulation package, power antenna, power lock group, 6-way power driver's seat, power side windows, speed control, tilt steering wheel, tinted glass, trip odometer, interval windshield wipers, deluxe bumper group, dual remote-control mirrors, wide color-keyed vinyl body side moldings, integral wheel lip moldings, vinyl roof, cast aluminum wheels, upgraded carpeting, illuminated visor-vanity mirrors on both sides, AM/FM stereo search radio, split bench seat with manual recliner, automatic seat back release, and sport instrumentation.

VIN:

The VIN was stamped on an aluminum tab riveted to the dashboard on the passenger side and was visible through the windshield. The prefix indicated the manufacturer: F=Ford. The first symbol denoted the model-year: 9=1979. The second symbol indicated the assembly plants G=Chicago, Illinois and J=Los Angeles, California. The third symbol was the car-line: 8=T-Bird. The fourth symbol denoted the body type: 7=Two-door pillared hardtop. The fifth symbol denoted the engine: F=302 cid (5.0L)/133-hp V-8, H=351 cid (5.8L)/135-142-hp V-8 and Q = Modified 351 cid (5.8L)/151-hp V-8. The sixth through 11th symbols denoted the sequential production numbers of the specific vehicle starting at 100001. The body certification label was located on the rear face of driver's door. The top part of the label indicated the T-Bird was manufactured by Ford Motor Company. Directly below this was the month and year of manufacture, plus a statement that the car conformed to federal motor vehicle safety standards in effect on the indicated date of manufacture. The VIN appeared on the first line of encoded information. It matched the first to 11th symbols on the VIN tag. PASSENGER appeared to the right of the VIN to denote a passenger vehicle. The color and vinyl roof type/color code appeared in the far left-hand position on the second line of encoded information. The District Special Order code appeared to the right of the body style code in the second position on the second line of encoded information. The body style code appeared on the far left-hand side of the second line of encoded information. The only Thunderbird code for this model-year was: 60H=2-door Pillared Hardtop. The trim code appeared to the right of the body style code in the fourth position on the second line of encoded information. The Scheduled Build Date was a new code. It appeared to the right of the trim code in the fifth position on the second line of encoded information. The axle code appeared to the right of the

1979 Ford Thunderbird two-door Heritage Edition (F)

1979 Ford Thunderbird two-door Hardtop Coupe (OCW)

Scheduled Build Date in the sixth position on the second line of encoded information. The transmission code appeared to the right of the axle code in the seventh position on the second line of encoded information. The air conditioning code appeared to the right of the transmission code in the eighth position on the second line of encoded information. The abbreviations VIN/BDY/CLR/TRM/TR/AX/DSO did not appear on the certification label. The specific application of the codes was determined by where they are located on the vehicle certification label.

Thunderbird (V-8)

Series No.	Body/ Style No.	Body Type and Seating	Factory Price	Shipping Weight	Production Total
87	60H	2-dr. Hardtop-4P	$5,877	3,893 lbs.	Note 1

Town Landau (V-8)

87	60H	2-dr. Hardtop-4P	$8,866	4,284 lbs.	Note 1

Heritage Edition (V-8)

87	60H	2-dr. Hardtop-4P	$10,687	4,178 lbs.	Note 1

Note 1: Production of the three models combined was 284,141.

Engines:

Thunderbird Base V-8 (Federal): 90-degree, overhead valve. Cast-iron block and head. Displacement: 302 cid (5.0 liters). B & S: 4.00 x 3.00 in. Compression ratio: 8.4:1. Brake hp: 133 at 3400 rpm. Torque: 245 lbs.-ft. at 1600 rpm. Five main bearings. Hydraulic valve lifters. Carburetor: Motorcraft 2150 two-barrel. Serial number code: F.

Thunderbird Base V-8 (California): 90-degree, overhead valve. Cast-iron block and head. Displacement: 351 cid (5.8 liters). B & S: 4.00 x 3.50 in. Compression ratio: 8.3:1. Brake hp: 135-142 at 3200 rpm. Torque: 286 lbs.-ft. at 1400 rpm. Five main bearings. Hydraulic valve lifters. Carburetor: Motorcraft 2150 two-barrel. Windsor engine. Serial number code: H.

Thunderbird Optional V-8 (Federal): 90-degree, overhead valve. Cast-iron block and head. Displacement: 351 cid (5.8 liters). B & S: 4.00 x 3.50 in. Compression ratio: 8.0:1. Brake hp: 151 at 3600 rpm. Torque: 270 lbs.-ft. at 2200 rpm. Five main bearings. Hydraulic valve lifters. Carburetor: Motorcraft 2150 two-barrel. Windsor engine. Serial number code: Q.

Chassis:

Wheelbase: 114 in. Overall length: 217.2. Overall width: 78.5. Overall height: 52.8 in. Front headroom: 37.3 in. Front legroom: 42.1 in. Rear headroom: 36.2 in. Rear legroom: 32.6 in. Trunk capacity: 15.6 cu. ft. Front tread: 63.2 in. Rear tread: 63.1 in. Wheels: 15 x 6.5 in. Tires: 215-R15 steel-belted radial.

Technical:

Steering: Integral with power-assist. Steering ratio: 21.9:1. Turning diameter: 43.1 ft. Front suspension: Independent, upper and lower control arms, coil springs, tubular shocks and anti-roll bar. Rear suspension: Live axle, four-link control arms, coil springs, tubular shocks, anti-roll bar. Steering: Recirculating ball, power-assist. Standard rear axle: 2.50:1. Weight distribution: 57/43. Front brakes: Power vented disc. Rear brakes: Power drum. Brakes swept area: 372.3 sq. in. Fuel tank capacity: 21 gallons.

Options:

351-cid 161-hp V-8 engine ($263). Traction-Lok differential axle ($64). Auto Temperature Control air conditioner, in base Hardtop ($607); in Town Landau or Heritage Edition ($45) Manual air conditioner ($562). Heavy-duty battery ($20). Color-keyed deluxe seat belts ($22). Lower body side protection, models with rocker panel moldings ($33); other models ($46). Front license plate bracket (no charge). Bumper rub strips ($37). Day and date clock ($24). Convenience group for models with bucket seat and floor shift ($108); for other models ($117). Front cornering lights ($49). Exterior decor group with convenience group or interior luxury group ($346); for other models ($406). Interior decor group ($322). Sports decor group for models with convenience group ($459); for other models($518). Mud and stone deflectors ($25). Electric rear window defroster ($99). California emissions equipment ($83). High-altitude emissions system ($83). Extended range fuel tank ($36). Illuminated entry system ($57). Complete tinted glass ($70). Sports instrumentation group for Town Landau or cars with interior luxury group ($88), for models with convenience group ($121); for other models ($129). Light group ($51). Power lock group ($111). Luggage compartment trim ($43). Luxury sound insulation package ($30). Interior luxury group ($816). Illuminated passenger side visor-vanity mirror for cars with interior decor group ($34), for other cars ($39). Left-hand remote-control OSRV mirror ($18). Color-keyed wide body side moldings ($54). Dual sport mirrors, on models with convenience group or interior luxury group ($9), on other models ($68). Rocker panel moldings ($29). Wide bright body side moldings ($42). Power moon roof ($691). Metallic glow paint ($64). Protection group for models with front license plate bracket ($53); for other models ($49). Power radio antenna ($47). AM radio delete ($79 credit). AM/FM monaural radio ($59). AM/FM stereo radio ($120). AM/FM stereo search radio ($276). AM/FM radio with 8-track tape player ($193). 40-channel Citizens Band radio ($329). AM/FM radio with quadrosonic tape player in base Hardtop ($326); in Town Landau and Heritage Edition models ($50). AM/FM stereo with cassette tape player, in two-door Hardtop ($187), in Town Landau or Heritage Edition ($83 credit). Radio flexibility group ($105). Two-piece vinyl roof ($132). Seat belt warning chime ($22). Bucket seats and console with interior decor group ($37); all others ($211). Automatic seat back release ($37). Dual rear seat speakers ($46). Fingertip speed control, Town Landau or Heritage Edition with sports instrumentation group or interior luxury group ($1134); all other models ($126). Tilt steering wheel ($75). Heavy-duty suspension ($22) Dual accent paint stripes ($46). Inflatable spare tire with HR78 black sidewall tires (no charge). All-vinyl seat trim ($26). Ultra-soft leather seat trim, in Heritage Edition ($243), in other models ($309). T-roof convertible option ($747). Tu-Tone paint treatment ($62). Wire wheel covers ($118). Four styled road wheels ($132). Four cast aluminum wheels on models with exterior decor group ($150); all other models ($316). Power side windows ($132). Tire options for base Hardtop with five GR78 x 15 steel-belted radial black sidewall tires as standard equipment included GR78 x 15 radial whitewalls ($47 extra); HR78 x 15 black sidewalls ($25 extra); HR78 x 15 radial whitewalls ($72 extra); and HR70 x 17 white oval whitewalls ($100 extra). Tire options cards with five standard HR78 x 15 steel-belted whitewall radials as standard equipment included HR70 x 15 whitewall wide oval radials ($29 extra);. Color-keyed front floor mats ($20). Tinted windshield only ($28). Engine block heater ($14). Vinyl body side moldings ($42).

History:

The 1979 T-Bird was introduced on October 6, 1978. Henry Ford II (Chairman), Phillip Caldwell (Vice Chairman) and William O'Borke (Executive VP of North American Automotive Operations) were the top three executives at Ford Motor Company after Lee Iacocca was fired from the presidency by HFII. William Clay Ford was named Chairman of the Executive Committee and Vice President of Product Design. Walter S. Walla was Ford Division's Vice President and General Manager and Bernard L. Crumpton was General Sales manager for the division. Demand for T-Birds dropped off a bit. Calendar-year output was 264,451 units. A total of 284,141 T-Birds were produced in the model year. This represented 3.09 percent of the industry total. Of these units, 208,248 were made in Chicago and 75,893 were made in Los Angeles. Calendar year dealer sales amounted to 215,698 T-Birds, representing 2.6 percent of industry sales. As might be expected after three years, the down-sized Thunderbird was no longer the newest thing to hit the market and did not benefit from a sales campaign, such as the Diamond Jubilee promotion, to help bring extra buyers into Ford showrooms. As a result, sales declined. In addition, the second Arab oil embargo occurred this year, chasing American car buyers' away from V-8-powered cars. Bobby Allison continued to race a T-Bird for the Bud Moore NASCAR team. He encountered his share of disappointments such as finishing 16th in the Busch Nashville 420, after starting in second place. In the World 600, at Charlotte Motor Speedway, he crossed the line in 22nd position, after spending 38 minutes doing an engine change. Allison did manage to claim second spot at the Southern 500 in Bristol, Tenn., coming in between the Monte Carlos of Dale Earnhardt and Darrell Waltrip. A historical milestone of sorts was marked in 1979 with the firing of Lee Iacocca by Henry Ford II. Iacocca in October 1978. A month later, he was working for Chrysler Corp. in nearby Highland Park. As things turned out, the "father" of the Ford Mustang would go on to save the No. 3 automaker from doom. Both the creation of the Mustang and the salvation of Chrysler are accomplishments that Iacocca deserves tremendous credit for, but don't overlook the fact that nearly a million of his 1977-1979 T-Birds were sold. Taking a nameplate that was selling 60,000 copies a year up to 300,000 copies a year represented another great automotive marketing achievement.

1980 Thunderbird

Thunderbird — Series 7 — (V-8): To celebrate its 25th year the T-Bird had a new size and a new standard engine. It was 17 in. shorter and 700 lb. lighter than its immediate predecessor. This 'Bird was created by stretching the Ford Fairmont/Mercury Zephyr platform and was identical to the 1980 Mercury Cougar XR-7. For the first time in 15 years, the T-Bird featured unitized body construction. Jack Telnack, who later gained fame for his Taurus, was the head designer of the new T-Bird. William P. Boyer, who had helped create the original two-seat T-Birds, was also assigned to the project. Arthur I. Querfield, another member of the original T-Bird design team, was also involved. They were considered four-passenger models. The base Hardtop and Town Landau returned along with a midyear Silver Anniversary model. The latter featured a Silver Glow exterior highlighted by black accents, a special padded rear-half vinyl roof, a high-gloss roof wrap-over molding and distinctive horizontal coach lamps with Silver Anniversary scripts. In addition to the featured Anniversary Silver paint color, Black, Light Gray, Red Glow and Midnight Blue Metallic solid exterior finishes could be substituted. There was also a special two-tone combination mating Black with Anniversary Silver. In each case, the color of the roof wrap-over bands, vinyl tops, body side accent stripes, body side moldings and bumper rub strips were coordinated with the exterior color selected. Inside the Silver Anniversary model was a thickly cushioned split-bench front seat upholstered in velvet-like knit-velour and color-keyed 36-oz. carpets. There were burled rosewood wood-tone instrument panel appliqués, a special leather-wrapped steering wheel, and dual illuminated visor-vanity mirrors. The car owner was also sent a bright rhodium nameplate with his or her name engraved on it. Traditional T-Bird styling trademarks such as hidden headlights and wrap-over roof styling were blended into the T-Bird's new appearance. The body also featured strong sculpturing along the main body side feature lines, single opera windows to the rear of the wrap-over roof band and solid-panel roof pillars like the previous Heritage Edition. The grille was again neo-classic in shape, but had a new eggcrate pattern insert. Some of the grille texture showed below the bumper. Soft, color-keyed urethane-clad bumpers were used up front and in the rear. Bumper guards were optional. The large rectangular headlight covers were integral with the huge signal/parking lights that wrapped around the body corners to double as side marker lights. Ford very wisely used many T-Bird hallmarks to give this new model a strong identity that loyal buyers would recognize. At the rear of the body, wraparound wall-to-wall taillights returned. The general shape was like an upside-down telephone receiver. At each end, the red lens had a white back-up light lens in its center and these carried a stylized winged T-Bird logo. The entire unit followed the forward slant of the rear deck lid and the lenses wrapped around the rear body corners to function as side markers. Above the right-hand lens was T-Bird lettering. A modified McPherson strut front suspension was used, with four-bar-link coil springs at the rear. Along with the 700-lb. weight loss came higher axle ratios for better fuel economy. Power-assisted, variable-ratio rack-and-pinion steering was another technological advance. A new 255-cid V-8 was known as the 4.2-liter and was considered standard equipment. It carried the same stroke as the 302-cid (5.0-liter) V-8, but had a smaller bore. The 5.0-liter V-8 was optional. The 4.2-liter V-8 typically delivered 17-20 mpg and the 5.0-liter V-8 was good for 16-19 mpg. Late in the year, a new in-line six-cylinder was made available as a delete option. It was the first time a six-cylinder engine was ever offered in a T-Bird. A new four-speed overdrive automatic transmission was available with the 5.0-liter V-8. Standard features include: All standard FoMoCo safety, anti-theft, convenience items, and emissions control equipment, 4.2-liter (255-cid) two-barrel V-8, automatic transmission, variable-ratio power rack and pinion steering, power front disc/rear drum brakes, DuraSpark ignition system, maintenance-free battery, coolant recovery system, modified McPherson strut front suspension, four-bar link-type rear suspension, front and rear stabilizer bars, three-speed heater and defroster, concealed rectangular headlights, wraparound parking lamps, soft urethane covered bumpers, chrome-plated egg-crate grille, quarter windows, moldings on wheel lips, hood, rocker panels, windshield, drip rail, and door belt, full wheel covers, Flight Bench seating with cloth and vinyl trim, 10-oz. color-keyed cut-pile carpeting, and vinyl door trim with wood-tone accents, push-button AM radio, 4-spoke deluxe steering wheel, trip odometer, self-regulating illuminated electric clock, cigar lighter, day-night rear view mirror, glove box and ash tray lights, inertia seat back releases, continuous loop belts, luggage compartment map, mini spare tire, and P185/75R14 black sidewall tires.

Town Landau: Standard Equipment adds or substitutes air conditioning, tinted glass, power side windows, 6-way power driver's seat, power lock group, tilt steering wheel, interval windshield wipers, TR type white

1980 Ford Thunderbird two-door Town Landau (PH)

sidewall radial tires, auto lamp on and off delay system, electronic instrument cluster, front cornering lamps, padded rear half-vinyl roof with wrap-over band and coach lamps, wide door belt moldings, color-keyed rear window moldings, striping on hood, body sides and rear deck lid, dual remote-control mirrors, color-keyed vinyl insert body side moldings with partial wheel lip moldings, cast-aluminum wheels, split-bench seats with dual recliners, velour seat trim, luxury door panel trim with cloth or vinyl inserts, courtesy lamps in quarter trim panels, and front door arm rests, electronic AM/FM search stereo radio, illuminated visor-vanity mirror (passenger side), 18-oz. cut-pile luxury carpeting, wood-tone instrument panel appliqués, luxury steering wheel, color-keyed deluxe seat belts, luxury luggage compartment trim, light group with dual-beam lights, map light, instrument panel courtesy lights, engine compartment light, and luggage compartment light.

VIN:

The VIN was stamped on an aluminum tab riveted to the dashboard on the passenger side and was visible through the windshield. The first symbol denoted the model-year: 0=1980. The second symbol indicated the assembly plants: G=Chicago, Illinois and H=Lorain, Ohio. The third symbol was the car-line: 8=T-Bird. The fourth symbol denoted the body type: 7=Two-door pillared hardtop. The fifth symbol was the engine: B=200 cid (3.3L) 6-cyl, D=255 cid (4.2L)/115-hp V-8, F = 302 cid (5.0L)/131-hp V-8 and G=351 cid. The sixth through 11th symbols denoted the sequential production numbers of the specific vehicle starting at 100001. The vehicle certification label was located on the rear face of the driver's door. The top part of the label indicated the Thunderbird was manufactured by Ford Motor Company. Directly below this was the month and year of manufacture, plus a statement that the car conformed to the federal motor vehicle safety standards in effect on the indicated date of manufacture. The VIN appeared on the first line of encoded information. It matched the first to 11th symbols on the VIN tag. Some other codes also appeared. TYPE: On left side of label, indicated the body type. PASSENGER. EXT. COLOR: This line carried the exterior paint color(s) code. DSO: The District Special Order code appeared above "DSO" to the right of the exterior paint color code. BODY: The body style code appeared to the extreme left of the bottom line. The only Thunderbird code for this model-year was: 66D=2-door Pillared Hardtop. VR: The vinyl roof type/color code was to the right of the body code. MLDG: The molding code was to the right of the vinyl roof code. INT. TRIM: The interior trim code was to the right of the molding code. A/C: The air conditioning code was to the right of the interior trim code. Cars with air conditioning had "A" stamped here. R: The radio code was to the right of the A/C code. S: The sun roof code appeared to the right of the radio code. AX: The axle code appeared to the right of the sun roof code. TR: The transmission code appeared to the right of the axle code. The terms and abbreviations shown in capitals appeared on the line above the actual codes.

Thunderbird (V-8)

Series No.	Body/ Style No.	Body Type and Seating	Factory Price	Shipping Weight	Production Total
87	60D	2-dr. Hardtop-4P	$6,432	3,118 lbs.	Note 1

Town Landau (V-8)

87/607	60D	2-dr. Hardtop-4P	$10,036	3,357 lbs.	Note 1

Thunderbird Silver Anniversary (Six and V-8)

87/603	66D	2-dr. Hardtop-4P	$11,679	3,225 lbs.	Note 1

Note 1: Production of the three models combined was 156,803.

Engines:

Thunderbird Base V-8: 90-degree, overhead valve. Cast-iron block and head. Displacement: 255 cid (4.2 liters). B & S: 3.68 x 3.00 in. Compression ratio: 8.8:1. Brake hp: 115 at 3800. Torque: 194 lbs.-ft. at 2200. Five main bearings. Hydraulic valve lifters. Carburetor: Motorcraft 2150 two-barrel. Serial number code: D.

1980 Ford Thunderbird two-door Silver Anniversary Coupe (PH)

Thunderbird Delete Option Inline Six: Overhead valve inline. Cast-iron block and head. Displacement: 200 cid (3.3 liters). B & S: 3.68 x 3.13 in. Compression ratio: 8.6:1. Brake hp: 88 at 3800. Torque: 154 lbs.-ft. at 1400. Seven main bearings. Hydraulic valve lifters. Carburetor: Holley one-barrel. Serial number code: B.
Note: Used in a limited number of late 1980 model year Thunderbirds.

Thunderbird Optional V-8: 90-degree, overhead valve. Cast-iron block and head. Displacement: 302 cid (5.0 liters). B & S: 4.00 x 3.00 in. Compression ratio: 8.4:1. Brake hp: 131 at 3600 rpm. Torque: 231 lbs.-ft. at 1600 rpm. Five main bearings. Hydraulic valve lifters. Carburetor: Motorcraft 2150 or 2700VV two-barrel. Serial number code: F.

Thunderbird Optional V-8: 90-degree, overhead valve. Cast-iron block and head. Displacement: 351 cid (5.8 liters). B & S: 4.00 x 3.50 in. Compression ratio: 8.3:1. Brake hp: 140 at 3400 rpm. Torque: 265 lbs.-ft. at 2000 rpm. Five main bearings. Hydraulic valve lifters. Carburetor: Motorcraft 7200VV two-barrel. Windsor engine. Serial number code: G.

Chassis:

Wheelbase: 108.4 in. Overall length: 200.4. Overall width: 74.1. Overall height: 53 in. Front headroom: 37.1 in. Front legroom: 41.6 in. Rear headroom: 36.3 in. Rear legroom: 36.5 in. Trunk capacity: 17.7 cu. ft. Front tread: 58.1 in. Rear tread: 57.2 in. Ground clearance: 6 in. Tires: P185/75R14 steel-belted radial.

Technical:

Steering: Integral with power-assist. Turning diameter: 40.1 ft. Turns lock-to-lock: 3.4. Front suspension: Modified McPherson strut. Rear suspension: Four-link-bar with coil springs. Steering: Variable-ratio power rack and pinion. Standard rear axle: 2.79:1. Front brakes: 10-inch power vented disc. Rear brakes: 9-inch power assisted drums. Fuel tank capacity: 21 gallons.

Options:

5.0-liter (302-cid) two-barrel V-8 ($150). 351-cid V-8 engine. In-line six-cylinder engine. Automatic overdrive transmission ($138). Automatic temperature control air conditioner in Hardtop ($634). Automatic temperature control air conditioner in Town Landau or Silver Anniversary models ($63). Manual temperature control air conditioner ($571). Auto lamp on and off delay system ($63). Heavy-duty battery ($20). Color-keyed deluxe seat belts ($23). Lower body side protection with rocker panel moldings ($34). Lower body side protection on models without rocker panel moldings ($46). Front license plate bracket (no charge). Electronic digital clock ($38). Front cornering lamps ($50). Exterior decor group ($359). Interior decor group ($348). Mud and stone deflectors ($25). Electric rear window defroster ($101). Diagnostic warning lights ($50). California emissions system ($238). High-altitude emissions system ($36). Garage door opener with illuminated visor and vanity mirror in Town Landau or models with interior luxury group ($130). Garage door opener with illuminated visor and vanity mirror in models with interior decor group ($165). Garage door opener with illuminated visor and vanity mirror in all other models ($171). Tinted glass ($71). Engine block immersion heater ($15). Dual note horn ($9). Illuminated entry system ($58). Electronic instrument cluster in Hardtop with interior luxury group ($275). Electronic instrument cluster in all other models ($313). Keyless entry system with Recaro bucket seats ($106). Keyless entry system without Recaro bucket seats ($119). Light group ($35). Power lock group ($113). Luggage compartment trim ($44). Exterior luxury group ($489). Interior luxury group ($975) Passenger side illuminated visor and vanity mirror with interior decor group ($35). Passenger side illuminated visor and vanity mirror without interior decor group ($41). Left-hand remote-control OSRV mirror ($18). Dual remote-control mirrors ($69). Rocker panel moldings ($30). Wide door belt moldings with interior luxury group ($31). Wide door belt moldings without interior luxury group ($44). Wide vinyl insert body side moldings ($54). Metallic Glow paint ($60). Tu-Tone paint and striping treatment on Town Landau ($106). Tu-Tone paint and striping

treatment on Hardtop with exterior luxury or exterior luxury groups ($123). Tu-Tone paint and striping treatment on base Hardtop ($163). Automatic parking brake release ($10). Protection group on models with front license plate bracket ($43). Protection group on models without front license plate bracket ($39). Power radio antenna ($49). AM radio delete ($81 credit). AM/FM monaural radio ($53). AM/FM stereo radio ($90). AM/FM stereo radio with 8-track tape player ($166). AM/FM stereo radio with cassette tape player ($179). Electronic AM/FM stereo search radio ($240). Electronic AM/FM stereo search radio with 8-track tape player in Hardtop ($316). Electronic AM/FM stereo search radio with 8-track tape player in Town Landau or Silver Anniversary Hardtops ($76). 40-channel CB radio ($316) Electronic AM/FM stereo search radio with cassette tape player and Dolby noise reduction system in Hardtop ($329). Electronic AM/FM stereo search radio with cassette tape player and Dolby noise reduction system in Town Landau or Silver Anniversary Hardtops ($89). Radio flexibility package ($66). Flip-up open air roof ($219). Vinyl rear half roof ($133). 6-way power driver's seat ($166). 4-way full-width power seat ($111). Bucket seats and console with interior luxury group (no charge). Bucket seats and console without interior luxury group ($176).Recaro bucket seats and console in Town Landau (no charge). Recaro bucket seats and console in Hardtop with interior luxury group ($166). Recaro bucket seats and console in Hardtop without interior luxury group ($254). Premium sound system, with conventional radio ($119). Premium sound system with electronic radio ($150). Conventional spare tire ($37). Dual rear seat speakers ($38). Fingertip speed control in Town Landau or Hardtop with interior luxury group ($116). Fingertip speed control in base Hardtop ($129). Leather-wrapped steering wheel ($44). Tilt steering wheel ($78). Dual accent body side stripes ($40). Hood and body side accent stripes with exterior decor or exterior luxury groups ($16). . Hood and body side accent stripes without exterior decor or exterior luxury groups ($56). Heavy-duty handling suspension ($23). All-vinyl seat trim ($26). Ultra-soft leather seat trim in Silver Anniversary model ($318). Ultra-soft leather seat trim in all models except Silver Anniversary ($349). Luxury wheel covers ($88). Simulated wire wheel covers with exterior luxury group ($50). Simulated wire wheel covers without exterior luxury group ($138). Power side windows ($136). Interval windshield wipers ($39). P195/75R x 14 steel-belted radial-ply black sidewall tires on base Hardtop ($26). P195/75R x 14 steel-belted radial-ply white sidewall tires on base Hardtop ($59). TR type radial whitewall tires with exterior decor and including aluminum wheels on Town Landau and Silver Anniversary models ($441). TR type radial whitewall tires without exterior decor ($528). Front floor mats ($19) Luggage compartment light ($29). Electronic instrument cluster delete on Town Landau or Silver Anniversary only ($275 credit).

History:

The 1980 T-Bird was introduced on October 12, 1979. Phillip Caldwell became Chairman of the Board of Ford Motor Co. in 1980. Donald E. Petersen was President. Harold A. Poling was Executive Vice President of North American Automotive Operations. Philip E. Benton Jr. was Ford Division's Vice President and General Manager. Bernard L. Crumpton remained General Sales manager for the division. Demand for T-Birds continued to drop. Calendar-year output was 117,856 units. A total of 156,803 T-Birds were produced in the model year. This represented 2.31 percent of the industry total. Of these units, 93,634 were made in Chicago and 63,169 were made in Lorain, Ohio. Calendar year dealer sales amounted to 127,248 T-Birds, representing 1.9 percent of industry sales. The new T-Bird had some teething problems. It guzzled more gas than some other cars in its class and was not as agile as some of its competitors. The new unit body made the car slightly noisier. Ford also wrestled with claims that the T-Bird's automatic transmission slipped gears. The company made an out of court settlement of those claims. It also recalled some 1980 T-Birds that were built with Mustang brakes, which were too small. In addition to the brakes, electrical and body integrity problems were other shortcomings of the new car. Cars with the 5.0-liter V-8 using a variable-venturi carburetor were also trouble-prone. *Motor Trend* put two 1980 T-Birds on the cover of its September 1979 issue. One was a monotone Red Glow car with no vinyl roof, white stripe tires and spoke-style wheel covers. The second was a Chamois and Bittersweet Glow two-toned version with a luxury half-vinyl roof and simulated wire wheel covers. "All-New ... Split Personality: Performance, Luxury," read the cover blurb. Peter Frey's article about the new car was a positive review sub-titled, "A living legend rises from the ashes of obesity to reclaim its heritage." The article gave specifications for the 1980 model, but no performance numbers. In its third "Country Wide Test" in June 1980, *Motor Trend* tried out a T-Bird with the 5.0-liter V-8, four-speed overdrive transmission, luxury exterior group, Recaro bucket seats, electronic instrumentation and Bittersweet Glow Metallic finish. This car was driven on both coasts and made two cross-country trips in the course of four months. Nearly 15,000 miles were driven during the evaluation. Various editors took stints behind the wheel. "Down-sizing has unquestionably improved the breed," said associate editor Bob Nagy. "The fact that, in not many more years, no one will produce a car like this makes me sad," Washington editor Ted Orme noted. However, executive editor Jim McGraw felt differently. "We'd rather spend $11,000 buying an original Thunderbird restoration," he headlined his report that criticized the car's exterior and interior designs. (Unfortunately, two seat T-Birds were selling for $15,000-$18,000 at the time, so McGraw would have had a hard time getting one on his budget.) Associate editor Peter Frey said the T-Bird made him smile and engineering editor Chuck Nerpel — who had road tested a '55 model for *Motor Trend* — said, "It has better handling than any T-Bird of the past." Though popular with most magazine editors, the 1980 T-Bird had the misfortune of bowing at a time when Americans were rethinking what they needed and wanted in automobiles. It's true that the automobile industry, as well as the national economy, was in a slump at this time. However, even in a weakened market, the T-Bird's slice of the smaller pie was shrinking. The nameplate owned 3.09 percent of the total market in 1979, but only 2.31 percent in 1980. Records show that 18,702 U.S.-built T-Birds were made for the export market and many of these were shipped to Canada. By looking at optional equipment installations, it was easy to tell the type of transition the T-Bird had gone through in its 25 years. What had started out as a fancy two-seat sporty car had become an ostentatious luxury coupe. In racing, there were big questions about the future of Grand National stock car racing at this time. The new down-sized cars coming out of Detroit were too small for the Grand National wheelbase and size specifications. Nevertheless, the October 1979 issue of *Motor Trend* featured a sketch of Bobby Allison's proposed 1980 T-Bird stock car, saying in the caption that it was unclear if the new model would be approved by NASCAR. A few of these cars did eventually race, but without the much-needed factory backing.

1981 Thunderbird

Thunderbird — Series 7 — (V-8): The 1981 T-Bird looked like the 1980, except the grille texture no longer showed below the bumper. The license plate sat in a recessed opening low on the bumper. Huge full-width taillights again had T-Bird emblems on each side. The deck lid protruded halfway between each taillight half. New options included a Carriage Roof that made a car look like a convertible, a Traction-Lok axle, pivoting front vent windows, a convex remote-control left-hand rearview mirror and self-sealing puncture-resistant tires. The in-line six-cylinder engine that was a delete-option in a small number of late-1980 T-Birds became the base engine for the 1981 series. It was attached to the conventional SelectShift automatic transmission. The 4.2-liter and 5.0-liter V-8s were both extra-cost items. The base hardtop had more standard equipment and upgraded trimmings. Some of the ingredients had formerly been part of the exterior luxury group package. A Flight Bench front seat was standard with a choice of all-vinyl or cloth and vinyl upholstery. The Town Landau had "Town Landau" fender scripts. Its Valino grain vinyl roof came in half and luxury half styles with a choice of seven colors. The Town Landau interior offered standard split-bench seat with dual recliners and knit-cloth fabric upholstery. Town Landaus came in seven colors: Black, White, Midnight Blue, Fawn, Medium Red, Bittersweet and Silver with color-coordinated roof wrap-over moldings and specific color (Black or Silver) accent tape on the opera windows. The top T-Bird was the Heritage Edition hardtop with its padded rear half vinyl roof with brushed aluminum wrap-over band, coach lamps, a "Frenched" backlight, distinctive "arrowheads" at the forward end of the body stripes, a unique hood ornament with a "cut-glass" look and a split-bench seat with velour cloth trim. Standard equipment included: All standard FoMoCo safety, anti-theft, convenience items, and emissions control equipment, 3.3-liter (200-cid) one-barrel six-cylinder engine, three-speed automatic transmission, variable-ratio power rack and pinion steering, power front disc/rear drum brakes, DuraSpark ignition system, halogen headlights, maintenance-free 36AH battery, coolant recovery system, modified McPherson strut front suspension with stabilizer bar, four-bar link-type rear suspension with stabilizer bar, three-speed heater and defroster, concealed rectangular headlights, inside hood release, power ventilation system, dual-note horn, chrome-plated egg-crate grille, hood ornament, soft color-keyed urethane covered bumpers with bright bumper rub strips, bright moldings on rear of hood, windshield, drip rail, door belt, and rear window, wide vinyl insert body side moldings with integral partial wheel lip moldings, quarter windows, full wheel covers, electric clock, cigar lighter, locking glove box, push-button AM radio, 4-spoke deluxe steering wheel, inside day-night rear view mirror, Flight Bench seat with adjustable head restraints, color-keyed seat belts with reminder chime, anti-theft door locks, 10-oz. color-keyed cut-pile carpeting, luggage compartment light, mini spare, and P195/75R14 white sidewall steel-belted radial tires.

Town Landau: Standard Equipment additions or substitutes for the Town Landau included a padded half-vinyl roof with color-coordinated

wrap-over band and coach lamps, hood and body side accent stripes, right-hand remote-control OSRV mirror, luxury wheel covers, wide door belt moldings, split-bench seats with dual fold-down arm rests,, 18-oz. luxury color-keyed cut-pile carpets, Coco Bola wood-tone appliqué around instrument panel, light group, tilt steering wheel, interval wipers, and diagnostic warning light system.

Heritage Edition: Standard Equipment additions or substitutes for the Heritage Edition included a padded rear half-vinyl roof with brushed aluminum wrap-over band and coach lamps, "Frenched" vinyl roof treatment around rear window, dual body side stripes, deck lid accent stripes, bright rocker panel moldings, wire wheel covers, electronic AM/FM stereo search radio, bright rhodium engraved owner's nameplate, luxury steering wheel with wood-tone insert, illuminated passenger side visor and vanity mirror, velour cloth seat trim in luxury sew style, luxury door trim panels with cloth inserts, burled rosewood wood-tone instrument panel appliqués, luxury luggage compartment trim, 4.2-liter (255-cid) V-8 engine, air conditioning with manual temperature control, tinted glass, power side windows, 6-way power driver's seat, power door locks, remote control deck lid release, auto lamp on and off delay system, electronic instrument cluster, and front cornering lamps.

VIN:

The VIN was stamped on an aluminum tab riveted to the dashboard on the passenger side and was visible through the windshield. The first symbol, 1, denoted U. S. built. The second symbol, F, indicated Ford. The third symbol, A, meant a Ford passenger vehicle. The fourth symbol was the type of restraint system. The fifth symbol, P = passenger-type vehicle. The sixth symbol 4 = Thunderbird. The seventh symbol 2 = 2-door coupe. The eighth symbol denoted the engine: B=200-cid (3.3L) 115-hp six-cylinder, D=255-cid (4.2L)/115-hp V-8 and F=302-cid (5.0L)/131-hp V-8. The ninth symbol was the check digit. The 10th symbol B=1981 model year. The 11th symbol was the assembly plant. All T-Birds were made at plant H in Lorain, Ohio. The 12th through 17th symbols were the sequential production numbers of specific vehicles starting at 100001. The vehicle certification label was located on the rear face of the driver's door. The top part of the label indicated the Thunderbird was manufactured by Ford Motor Company. Directly below this was the month and year of manufacture, plus a statement that the car conformed to federal motor vehicle safety standards in effect on the indicated date of manufacture. VIN: The VIN appeared on the first line of encoded information. It matched the first to 11th symbols on the VIN tag. Some other codes also appeared. TYPE: On left side of label, indicates PASSENGER. EXT. COLOR: This line carried the exterior paint color(s) code. DSO: The District Special Order code now appeared above "DSO" to the right of the exterior paint color code. BODY: The body style code appeared to the extreme left of the bottom line. The only Thunderbird code for this model-year was: 66D=2-door Pillared Hardtop. VR: The vinyl roof type/color code was to the right of the body code. MLDG: The molding code was to the right of the vinyl roof code. INT. TRIM: The interior trim code was to the right of the molding code. A/C: The air conditioning code was to the right of the interior trim code. Cars with air conditioning had an "A" stamped here. R: The radio code was to the right of the A/C code. S: The sun roof code appears to the right of the radio code. AX: The axle code appears to the right of the sun roof code. TR: The transmission code appeared to the right of the axle code. The terms and abbreviations shown in capitals appeared on the line above the actual codes. The terms and abbreviations shown in capitals appeared on the line above the actual codes.

Thunderbird (Six)

Series No.	Body/Style No.	Body Type and Seating	Factory Price	Shipping Weight	Production Total
42	66D	2-dr. Hardtop-4P	$7,551	3,004 lbs.	Note 1

Thunderbird (V-8)

Series No.	Body/Style No.	Body Type and Seating	Factory Price	Shipping Weight	Production Total
42	66D	2-dr. Hardtop-4P	$7,601	3,124 lbs.	Note 1

Town Landau (Six)

Series No.	Body/Style No.	Body Type and Seating	Factory Price	Shipping Weight	Production Total
42/60T	66D	2-dr. Hardtop-4P	$8,869	3,067 lbs.	Note 1

Town Landau (V-8)

Series No.	Body/Style No.	Body Type and Seating	Factory Price	Shipping Weight	Production Total
42/60T	66D	2-dr. Hardtop-4P	$8,739	3,187 lbs.	Note 1

Heritage Edition (V-8)

Series No.	Body/Style No.	Body Type and Seating	Factory Price	Shipping Weight	Production Total
42/607	66D	2-dr. Hardtop-4P	$11,355	3,303 lbs.	Note 1

Note 1: Production of the three models combined was 86,693.

Engines:

Thunderbird Base Six: In-line. Cast-iron block and head. Displacement: 200 cid (3.3 liters). B & S: 3.68 x 3.13 in. Compression ratio: 8.6:1. Brake hp: 88 at 3800. Torque: 154 lbs-ft. at 1400. Seven main bearings. Hydraulic valve lifters. Carburetor: Holley 1946 one-barrel. Serial number code: B.

Thunderbird Base V-8: 90-degree, overhead valve. Cast-iron block and head. Displacement: 255 cid (4.2 liters). B & S: 3.68 x 3.00 in. Compression ratio: 8.2:1. Brake hp: 115 at 3400. Torque: 195 lbs.-ft. at 2200. Five main bearings. Hydraulic valve lifters. Carburetor: Motorcraft 2150 or 7200VV two-barrel. Serial number code: D.

Thunderbird Optional V-8: 90-degree, overhead valve. Cast-iron block and head. Displacement: 302 cid (5.0 liters). B & S: 4.00 x 3.00 in. Compression ratio: 8.4:1. Brake hp: 130 at 3400 rpm. Torque: 235 lbs.-ft. at 1600 rpm. Five main bearings. Hydraulic valve lifters. Carburetor: Motorcraft 2150 or 7200VV two-barrel. Serial number code: F.

Chassis:

Wheelbase: 108.4 in. Overall length: 200.4. Overall width: 74.1. Overall height: 53 in. Front headroom: 37.1 in. Front legroom: 41.6 in. Rear headroom: 36.3 in. Rear legroom: 36.5 in. Trunk capacity: 17.7 cu. ft. Front tread: 58.2 in. Rear tread: 57.0 in. Ground clearance: 6 in. Tires: P185/75R14 steel-belted radial.

Technical:

Steering: Integral with power-assist. Turning diameter: 40.1 ft. Turns lock-to-lock: 3.4. Front suspension: Modified McPherson strut. Rear suspension: Four-link-bar with coil springs. Steering: Variable-ratio power rack and pinion. Standard rear axle: 2.79:1. Front brakes: 10-inch power vented disc. Rear brakes: 9-inch power assisted drums. Fuel tank capacity: 18 gallons.

Options:

4.2-liter (255-cid) two-barrel V-8, but standard in Heritage Edition ($50). 5.0-liter (302-cid) two-barrel V-8 in Heritage Edition ($41). 5.0-liter (302-cid) two-barrel V-8 in all except Heritage Edition ($91). Four-speed automatic overdrive transmission ($162). Traction-Lok rear axle ($67). Automatic temperature control air conditioner in Hardtop and Town Landau ($652). Automatic temperature control air conditioner in Heritage Edition ($67). Manual temperature control air conditioner ($585). Auto lamp on and off delay system ($65). Heavy-duty battery ($20). Lower body side protection on Heritage Edition ($34). Lower body side protection on other models ($48). Front license plate bracket (no charge). Electronic digital clock ($40). Front cornering lamps ($51). Mud and stone deflectors ($26). Electric rear window defroster ($107). Diagnostic warning lights ($51). California emissions system ($46). High-altitude emissions system ($38). Exterior decor group ($341). Garage door opener with illuminated visor and vanity mirror in Heritage Edition or models with interior luxury group ($134). Garage door opener with illuminated visor and vanity mirror in all other models ($177). Tinted glass ($76). Engine block immersion heater ($16). Illuminated entry system ($60). Electronic instrument cluster in Hardtop with interior luxury group ($282). Electronic instrument cluster in all other models ($322). Electronic instrument cluster delete ($282 credit). Interior decor group ($349). Interior luxury group in Town Landau ($584). Interior Luxury group in other models ($1,039). Keyless entry system ($122). Light group ($30). Power lock group ($120). Luggage compartment trim ($44). Passenger side illuminated visor and vanity mirror ($41). Right-hand remote-control OSRV mirror ($52). Rocker panel moldings ($30). Wide door belt moldings ($45). Tu-Tone paint and striping treatment on Heritage Edition ($111). Tu-Tone paint and striping treatment on Hardtop with exterior decor group ($139). Tu-Tone paint and striping treatment on base Hardtop ($180). Automatic parking brake release ($10). Protection group ($45). Power radio antenna ($48). AM radio delete ($61 credit). Dual rear speakers with AM radio ($37). AM/FM monaural radio ($51). Dual rear speakers with AM/FM monaural radio ($37). AM/FM stereo radio ($88). AM/FM stereo radio with 8-track tape player in Town Landau ($74). AM/FM stereo radio with 8-track tape player in base Hardtop ($162) AM/FM stereo radio with cassette tape player in Town Landau ($87). AM/FM stereo radio with cassette tape player in other models ($174). Electronic AM/FM stereo search radio in Town Landau ($146). Electronic AM/FM stereo search radio in other models ($234). Electronic AM/FM stereo search radio with 8-track tape player in Heritage Edition ($74). Electronic AM/FM stereo search radio with 8-track tape player in Town Landau ($221). Electronic AM/FM stereo search radio with 8-track tape player in other models than Town

1981 Ford Thunderbird two-door Town Landau Coupe (F)

1981 Ford Thunderbird Heritage Edition two-door Hardtop(F)

Landau ($309). Electronic AM/FM stereo search radio with cassette tape player and Dolby noise reduction system in Heritage Edition ($87). Electronic AM/FM stereo search radio with cassette tape player and Dolby noise reduction system in Town Landau ($233). Electronic AM/FM stereo search radio with cassette tape player and Dolby noise reduction system in models other than Town Landau or Heritage Edition ($321). Radio flexibility package ($65). Flip-up open air roof ($228). 6-way power driver's seat ($173). 4-way full-width power seat ($122). Premium sound system, with conventional radio ($116). Premium sound system with electronic radio ($146). Fingertip speed control ($132). Leather-wrapped luxury steering wheel ($45). Tilt steering wheel ($80). Dual accent body side stripes ($41). Hood and body side accent stripes with exterior decor group ($16). Hood and body side accent stripes without exterior decor groups ($57). Heavy-duty handling suspension ($23). Pivoting front vent windows ($55). Luxury wheel covers ($98). Simulated wire wheel covers with Town Landau or exterior decor group ($38). Simulated wire wheel covers without exterior decor group ($135). Power side windows ($140). Interval windshield wipers ($41). P195/75R x 14 puncture-resistant self-sealing steel-belted radial-ply black sidewall tires ($85). TR type radial whitewall tires with exterior decor and including aluminum wheels on Heritage Edition model ($428). TR type radial whitewall tires with exterior decor and including aluminum wheels on Town Landau model ($466). TR type radial whitewall tires without exterior decor ($563). Metallic Glow paint ($70). Color-keyed and carpeted front floor mats ($20). Vinyl front floor mats ($13). Bucket seats and console with Town Landau and interior decor group (no charge). Bucket seats and console without Town Landau or interior decor group ($182). Recaro bucket seats and console in Heritage Edition ($213). Recaro bucket seats and console in Hardtop with interior luxury group ($376). Recaro bucket seats and console in Town Landau and Hardtop with interior decor group ($461). All-vinyl seat trim ($28). Ultra-soft leather seat trim ($309). Carriage roof ($902). Rear half-vinyl roof ($130). Tinted windshield ($29).

History:

The 1981 T-Bird was introduced on October 3, 1980. Phillip Caldwell was Chairman of the Board of Ford Motor Co. William Clay Ford was Vice Chairman and Donald E. Petersen was President. Louis E. Lataif was Ford Division's General Manager. Bernard L. Crumpton remained General Sales manager for the division. Calendar-year output was 64,328 units. A total of 86,693 T-Birds were produced in the model year. This represented 1.30 percent of the industry total. Of these units, all were made in Lorain, Ohio. Calendar year dealer sales amounted to 69,775 T-Birds, representing 1.1 percent of industry sales. The T-Bird's share of market continued to decline in 1981. This year the number of cars with luxury features went up across the board, while sporty options like bucket seats and sun roofs continued to lose favor with those who were still purchasing T-Birds. A larger 16.4 percent of those purchasing 1981 models opted for the in-line six. Neil Bonnett drove the Wood Brother's 1981 T-Bird during the year's NASCAR Winston Cup stock car racing series. Without factory help, there were very few 'Birds of this vintage on the circuit.

1982 Thunderbird

Thunderbird — Series 7 — (V-8): The 1982 T-Bird had carryover front and rear end styling. The cross-hatched grille had an 8 x 6 pattern of wide holes. Lettered into the grille header was the T-Bird name. A wide see-through hood ornament held a T-Bird insignia. That insignia also highlighted the roof sail panels and the taillight lenses. The same models were offered: Base T-Bird, Town Landau and Heritage. Technical changes in 1982 models started with engines. The 3.3-liter in-line six was the base power plant in the base 'Bird and Town Landau. A 3.8-liter V-6 was now standard equipment in the Heritage. In fact, it was the only engine offered for that upscale model. Buyers could get the V-6 as an option in the base 'Bird and Town Landau. These two cars, but not the Heritage Hardtop, could also have the 4.2-liter V-8 installed under the hood at extra cost. SelectShift automatic was standard in the base T-Bird and Town Landau, while automatic overdrive transmission was standard in the Heritage edition. The three-speed SelectShift transmission used this year had noticeable improvements for smoother, more efficient operation, but the four-speed automatic overdrive gave much better fuel economy. It was optional in the base 'Bird and the Town Landau. The gas tank was also enlarged to 21-gal. A new optional was a Tripminder computer that showed time and speed and calculated elapsed time, distance traveled, fuel used, average speed and current or average mpg. Also, a new luxury vinyl roof treatment was standard on the Town Landau. The Carriage Roof was not available on the Town Landau teamed with the flip-up sunroof, keyless entry system, or wide door belt molding packages. The base type rear half-vinyl roof was standard with the exterior decor group, but not available on Town Landau or Heritage models. When used on the base 'Bird, wide door belt moldings were required, too. Standard equipment included: All standard FoMoCo safety, anti-theft, convenience items, and emissions control equipment, 3.3-liter (200-cid) one-barrel six-cylinder engine, electronic ignition, maintenance-free battery, coolant recovery system, automatic transmission, variable-ratio power rack and pinion steering, power front disc/rear drum brakes, P195/75R14 white sidewall steel-belted radial tires, three-speed heater and defroster, modified McPherson strut front suspension with stabilizer bar, four-bar link-type rear suspension with stabilizer bar, left-hand remote-control OSRV mirror, chrome-plated egg-crate grille, concealed rectangular halogen headlights, soft color-keyed urethane covered bumpers with black bumper rub strips with white accent stripes, black door window frames, bright moldings on windshield, drip rail, door belt, and rear window, black vinyl insert body moldings with partial wheel lip moldings, full wheel covers, illuminated quartz electric sweep hand clock, cigarette lighter, locking glove box, AM radio with dual front speakers, deluxe 4-spoke deluxe steering wheel, inside day-night rear view mirror, Flight Bench seat, 10-oz. color-keyed cut-pile carpeting, luggage compartment light, and mini spare tire.

Town Landau: Thunderbird Town Landau standard equipment added or substituted a tilt steering wheel, interval windshield wipers, diagnostic warning light system, luxury padded vinyl roof with color-keyed wrap-over molding and coach lights, hood and body side accent stripes, right-hand remote-control OSRV mirror, luxury wheel covers, wide door belt moldings, split-bench seats with fold-down arm rests, adjustable head restraints, and dual recliners, decor door trim panels, AM/FM stereo radio, 18-oz. luxury color-keyed cut-pile carpets, and light group.

Heritage Edition: Thunderbird Heritage Edition standard equipment added or substituted a 3.8-liter (232-cid) two-barrel V-6 engine, automatic overdrive transmission, air conditioning with manual temperature control, tinted glass, power side windows, 6-way power driver's seat, power door locks, remote-control deck lid, auto lamp on and off delay system, electronic instrument cluster with digital read-out, front cornering lamps, automatic parking brake release, padded rear half-vinyl top with brushed aluminum wrap-over appliqué and coach lamps, deck lid accent stripes, bright rocker panel moldings, wire wheel covers, special "cut-glass" look hood ornament, electronic AM/FM stereo search radio,, bright rhodium engraved owner's nameplate, luxury level steering wheel with wood-tone insert, dual illuminated visor and vanity mirrors, velour cloth seat trim in luxury sew style, luxury door trim panels with cloth and burled rosewood wood-tone inserts, burled rosewood wood-tone instrument panel appliqués, and luxury luggage compartment trim.

VIN:

The VIN was stamped on an aluminum tab riveted to the dashboard on the passenger side and was visible through the windshield. The first symbol, 1, denoted built in the United States. The second symbol, F, meant Ford. The third symbol A = a Ford passenger vehicle. The fourth symbol was the type of restraint system. The fifth symbol, P, indicated a passenger-type vehicle. The sixth symbol 4 = Thunderbird. The seventh symbol, 2 = 2-door coupe. The eighth symbol denoted the engine: B=200-cid (3.3L) 115-hp six-cylinder, 3=232-cid (3.8L)/115-hp V-6 and D=255-cid (4.2L)/131-hp V-8. The ninth symbol was the check digit. The 10th symbol C=1982 model year. The 11th symbol was the assembly plant. All T-Birds were made at plant H in Lorain, Ohio. The 12th through 17th symbols were the sequential production numbers of the specific vehicle starting at 100001. The vehicle certification label was located on the rear face of the driver's door. The top part of the label indicated the Thunderbird was manufactured by Ford Motor Company. Directly below this was the month and year of manufacture, plus a statement that the car conformed to federal motor vehicle safety standards in effect on the indicated date of manufacture. VIN: The VIN appeared on the first line of encoded information. It matched the first to 11th symbols on the VIN tag. Some other codes also appeared. PASSENGER. EXT. COLOR: This line carried the exterior paint color(s) code. DSO: The District Special Order code appeared above "DSO" to the right of the exterior paint color code. BODY: The body style code appeared to the extreme left of the bottom line. The only Thunderbird code for this model-year was: 66D=2-door Pillared Hardtop. VR: The vinyl roof type/color code

was to the right of the body code. MLDG: The molding code was to the right of the vinyl roof code. INT. TRIM: The interior trim code was to the right of the molding code. A/C: The air conditioning code was to the right of the interior trim code. Cars with air conditioning had "A" stamped here. R: The radio code was to the right of the A/C code. S: The sun roof code appeared to the right of the radio code. AX: The axle code appeared to the right of the sun roof code. TR: The transmission code appeared to the right of the axle code. The terms and abbreviations shown in capitals appeared on the line above the actual codes.

Thunderbird (Six)

Series No.	Body/ Style No.	Body Type and Seating	Factory Price	Shipping Weight	Production Total
42	66D	2-dr. Hardtop-4P	$8,492	3,000 lbs.	Note 1

Thunderbird (V-8)

42	66D	2-dr. Hardtop-4P	$8,733	3,137 lbs.	Note 1

Town Landau (Six)

42/60T	66D	2-dr. Hardtop-4P	$9,703	3,063 lbs.	Note 1

Town Landau (V-8)

42/60T	66D	2-dr. Hardtop-4P	$9,944	3,200 lbs.	Note 1

Heritage Edition (Six)

42/607	66D	2-dr. Hardtop-4P	$12,742	3,235 lbs.	Note 1

Heritage Edition (V-8)

42/607	66D	2-dr. Hardtop-4P	$12,742	3,361 lbs.	Note 1

Note 1: Production of the three models combined was 45,142.

Engines:

Thunderbird Base Six (Not available in Heritage Edition): In-line. Cast-iron block and head. Displacement: 200 cid (3.3 liters). B & S: 3.68 x 3.13 in. Compression ratio: 8.6:1. Brake hp: 88 at 3800. Torque: 154 lbs.-ft. at 1400. Seven main bearings. Hydraulic valve lifters. Carburetor: Holley 1946 one-barrel. Serial number code: B.

Thunderbird Base V-6 (Heritage Edition): 90-degree, overhead valve. Cast-iron block and aluminum head. Displacement: 232 cid (3.8 liters). B & S: 3.80 x 3.40 in. Compression ratio: 8.65:1. Brake horsepower: 112 at 4000. Torque: 175 at 2000. Four main bearings. Hydraulic valve lifters. Carburetor: Motorcraft 2150 two-barrel. Serial number code: 3.

Thunderbird Base V-8: 90-degree, overhead valve. Cast-iron block and head. Displacement: 255 cid (4.2 liters). B & S: 3.68 x 3.00 in. Compression ratio: 8.2:1. Brake hp: 120 at 3400. Torque: 205 lbs.-ft. at 1600. Five main bearings. Hydraulic valve lifters. Carburetor: Motorcraft 2150 or 7200VV two-barrel. Serial number code: D.

Chassis:

Wheelbase: 108.4 in. Overall length: 200.4. Overall width: 74.1. Overall height: 53.3 in. Front headroom: 37.1 in. Front legroom: 41.6 in. Rear headroom: 36.3 in. Rear legroom: 36.5 in. Trunk capacity: 17.7 cu. ft. Front tread: 58.1 in. Rear tread: 57.0 in. Ground clearance: 6 in. Tires: P195/75R14 steel-belted radial.

Technical:

Steering: Integral with power-assist. Turning diameter: 40.1 ft. Turns lock-to-lock: 3.4. Front suspension: Modified McPherson strut. Rear suspension: Four-link-bar with coil springs. Steering: Variable-ratio power rack and pinion. Standard rear axle: 2.73:1. Front brakes: 10-inch power vented disc. Rear brakes: 9-inch power assisted drums. Fuel tank capacity: 21 gallons.

Options:

3.8-liter (232-cid) two-barrel V-6 engine, except standard on Heritage Edition ($241). 4.2-liter (255-cid) two-barrel V-8, no charge in Heritage Edition, in other models ($241). Traction-Lok rear axle ($76). Automatic temperature control air conditioner in Hardtop and Town Landau ($754).

1982 Ford Thunderbird two-door Town Landau Coupe (F)

Automatic temperature control air conditioner in Heritage Edition ($78). Manual temperature control air conditioner ($676). Auto lamp on and off delay system ($73). Heavy-duty battery ($24). Lower body side protection on Heritage Edition ($39). Lower body side protection on other models ($54). Front license plate bracket (no charge). Electronic digital clock ($46). Front cornering lamps ($59). Electric rear window defroster ($126). Diagnostic warning lights ($59). California emissions system ($46). High-altitude emissions system (no charge). Exterior decor group ($385). Tinted glass ($88). Engine block immersion heater ($17). Illuminated entry system ($68). Electronic instrument cluster with interior luxury group ($321). Electronic instrument cluster without interior luxury group ($367). Electronic instrument cluster delete ($321 credit). Interior decor group ($372). Interior luxury group in Town Landau ($683). Interior Luxury group in other models ($1,204). Keyless entry system ($139). Light group ($35). Power lock group ($138). Luxury luggage compartment trim ($48). Dual illuminated visor and vanity mirrors in Heritage or with interior luxury group ($46). Dual illuminated visor and vanity mirrors without interior luxury group ($91). Right-hand remote-control OSRV mirror ($60). Rocker panel moldings ($33). Wide door belt moldings ($51). Tu-Tone paint and striping treatment on Heritage Edition ($128). Tu-Tone paint and striping treatment on Hardtop with exterior decor group ($157). Tu-Tone paint and striping treatment on base Hardtop ($206). Automatic parking brake release ($12). Appearance protection group ($51). Power radio antenna ($55). AM radio delete ($61 credit). AM radio with rear speakers ($39). AM/FM monaural radio ($54). Dual rear speakers with AM/FM monaural radio ($39). AM/FM stereo radio ($85). AM/FM stereo radio with 8-track tape player in Town Landau ($87). AM/FM stereo radio with 8-track tape player in base Hardtop ($172) AM/FM stereo radio with cassette tape player in Town Landau ($87). AM/FM stereo radio with cassette tape player in other models ($172). Electronic AM/FM stereo search radio in Town Landau ($146). Electronic AM/FM stereo search radio in other models ($232). Electronic AM/FM stereo search radio with 8-track tape player in Heritage Edition ($87). Electronic AM/FM stereo search radio with 8-track tape player in Town Landau ($233). Electronic AM/FM stereo search radio with 8-track tape player in other models than Town Landau ($318). Electronic AM/FM stereo search radio with cassette tape player and Dolby noise reduction system in Heritage Edition ($87). Electronic AM/FM stereo search radio with cassette tape player and Dolby noise reduction system in Town Landau ($233). Electronic AM/FM stereo search radio with cassette tape player and Dolby noise reduction system in models other than Town Landau or Heritage Edition ($318). Premium sound system, with conventional radio ($133). Premium sound system with electronic radio ($167). Flip-up open air roof ($276). 6-way power driver's seat ($198). Fingertip speed control ($155). Leather-wrapped luxury steering wheel ($51). Tilt steering wheel ($95). Dual accent body side stripes ($49). Hood and body side accent stripes with exterior decor group ($16). Hood and body side accent stripes without exterior decor groups ($65). Heavy-duty handling suspension ($26). TripMinder computer with Heritage, interior luxury group or electronic instrument cluster ($215).TripMinder computer without Heritage, interior luxury group or electronic instrument cluster ($261). Pivoting front vent windows ($63). Luxury wheel covers ($107). Simulated wire wheel covers with Town Landau or exterior decor group ($45). Simulated wire wheel covers without exterior decor group ($152). Power side windows ($165). Interval windshield wipers ($48). P195/75R x 14 puncture-resistant self-sealing steel-belted radial-ply black sidewall tires ($106). TR type radial whitewall tires including aluminum wheels on Heritage Edition model ($490). TR type radial whitewall tires with exterior decor and Town Landau model ($535).TR type radial whitewall tires without exterior decor ($643). Metallic Glow paint ($80). Color-keyed and carpeted front floor mats ($22). Bucket seats and console with Town Landau and interior decor group (no charge). Bucket seats and console without Town Landau or interior decor group ($211). Recaro bucket seats and console in Heritage Edition ($222). Recaro bucket seats and console in Hardtop with interior luxury group ($405). Recaro bucket seats and console in Town Landau and Hardtop with interior decor group ($523). Split-bench seat ($216). Luxury split-bench seat ($124). All-vinyl seat trim ($28). Super-soft vinyl split-bench seat trim ($30). Ultra-soft leather seat trim ($409). Carriage roof with exterior decor group ($766). Carriage roof without exterior decor group ($973). Rear half-vinyl roof with exterior decor group ($163). Rear half-vinyl roof without exterior decor group ($320). Tinted windshield ($32). Electronic digital clock ($38). Front cornering lamps.

History:

The 1982 T-Bird was introduced on September 24, 1981. Phillip Caldwell remained as Chairman of the Board of Ford Motor Co.. Once again, William Clay Ford was Vice Chairman and Donald E. Petersen was President. Louis E. Lataif continued as Ford Division's General Manager. Bernard L. Crumpton remained General Sales manager for the division. Calendar-year output was 29,336 units. A total of 45,142 T-Birds were produced in the model year. This represented 0.88 percent of the industry total. Of these units, all were made in Lorain, Ohio. Calendar year dealer sales amounted to 47,903 T-Birds, representing 0.9 percent of industry sales. For 1982 T-Birds, Ford recommended an engine oil change every

7,500 miles, a spark plug change every 30,000 miles, air filter replacement every 30,000 miles and engine coolant replacement at 52,500 miles or every three years. *Consumer Report's* overall trouble index rated the T-Bird a "good" car, although it was slightly costlier than average to fix when repairs were required. *Consumer Reports* also found the seats extremely comfortable, the car quiet and smooth riding, the comfort control system excellent, the power adequate and the brakes impressive. With the 3.8-liter V-6, the car used 675 gallons of fuel in 15,000 miles. It averaged 16 mpg in the city and 29 mpg on the highway. "These rear-wheel-drive Ford products are our models of choice in the domestic specialty coupe field," said the magazine. "Primarily because of their relatively good overall repair records." Dale Earnhardt — the NASCAR driver better known as "Mr. Chevrolet" — piloted a 1982 T-Bird this year. He drove the Bud Moore car to victory in events like the Rebel 500 at Darlington, which was his first checkered flag since winning the 1980 Winston Cup Championship. Bill Elliott, who would play a bigger role in racing the next generation of 'Birds against Earnhardt's Monte Carlo, also raced a 1982 T-Bird. He spent most of his time, this year, chasing other cars across the finish line, such as in the Winston 500 at Talladega, where he placed 26th in his Melling Tool Co. sponsored car.

1983 Thunderbird

Thunderbird — Series 46 — (V-8): The all-new 10th-generation Thunderbird had a slick aero look. Although down-sized again, the T-Bird was only three inches shorter and narrower than the 1982 model, with a 2.8 in. shorter wheelbase. The front compartment was larger, the rear compartment was tighter-fitting and cargo volume dropped from 17.7 cu. ft. to 14.6 cu. ft. At first, some traditional T-Bird buyers had a negative reaction to the new "Dearborn jelly bean" and preferred the 1982 model, but the new "Aero 'Bird" ultimately tripled the popularity of T-Birds. Much curvier than before, the new T-Birds looked very radical. Exposed quad rectangular halogen headlamps flanked a small, bright, neo-classic egg-crate grille with an 8 x 6 pattern. A T-Bird insignia was stamped on the header bar. The grille and headlight surrounds sloped backwards, as did the cornering lamps (which doubled as side markers). The center of the hood had a tapered bulge. A curved, urethane-clad front bumper held slit-like rectangular parking lights. The windshield slanted back at a rakish angle. It was a very slippery-looking car with a low 0.35 coefficient of drag. Decorative trim was minimal. Wide, color-keyed moldings were optional on the base model and standard on others. They continued the bumper line around the smooth, curving body sides. Full-width wraparound taillights met the recessed rear license plate housing in a sloping back panel. T-Bird insignias and back-up lights were in the center of each taillight lens. Three distinct models were merchandised, The base Thunderbird coupe, the old Heritage coupe and a midyear Turbo Coupe with a high-tech 2.3-liter (140-cid) turbocharged four-cylinder MPEFI engine. A Garrett AlResearch T-03 turbocharger helped it produce 145-hp at 5000 rpm. A unique front fascia with an air dam and Marchal fog lamps gave the Turbo Coupe instant recognition. It wore unique 14-in. aluminum wheels and P205/70HR14 performance tires. Bumper rub strip extensions, wide body side moldings, and striping on the body side and deck lid were also included. Turbo Coupes were offered in Black, Pastel Charcoal, Bright Red, Desert Tan, Silver Metallic Clearcoat, Dark Charcoal Metallic Clearcoat, and Medium Red Metallic Clearcoat. The clear coat paint colors were optional. A special Turbo Coupe paint scheme featured Dark Charcoal accents around the entire lower body perimeter. It was available with all Turbo Coupe colors except Black, Light Desert Tan, and Dark Charcoal Clearcoat Metallic. A five-speed manual transmission, special handling suspension and Traction-Lok axle were included. Inside were special Lear-Siegler articulated bucket seats with back rest and bolster adjustments, a leather-clad floor shifter, fishnet map pockets on the door panels, a few other goodies and some exclusive options. The T-Bird Turbo Coupe was the darling of the automotive press at the time. Other 1983 Thunderbirds came in a choice of 13 exterior finishes. Five were extra-cost Metallic Clearcoat colors. Base interiors featured individually reclining bucket seats with knit cloth-and-vinyl trim, plus a padded console with a flocked and illuminated interior and a removable trash bin. The standard all-vinyl door trim panels had assist straps and storage bins. The fancier Heritage model had the interior luxury group, a wood-grained steering wheel and clock and sound system upgrades. The basic 1983 T-Bird had a modified McPherson strut front suspension with gas-filled struts. At the rear was a four-bar-link suspension with gas-filled shock absorbers. Steering was again rack-and-pinion type with power-assist. The base and Heritage models used a variable-ratio system, while the Turbo Coupe featured increased power steering effort and a 15.1:1 non-variable ratio. Standard equipment included a 3.8-liter (232-cid) V-6 engine, three-speed automatic transmission, power brakes, power steering, electronic ignition and voltage regulator, dual-note horn, halogen headlamps, left-hand remote-control OSRV mirror, vinyl insert body side moldings, deluxe wheel covers, seat belt reminder chimes, analog quartz clock, center console, vinyl door panels, full carpeting including trunk, AM radio with dual front speakers, individual reclining front seats, four-spoke luxury steering wheel, cloth and vinyl upholstery, trip odometer.

Heritage Edition: Thunderbird Heritage Edition standard equipment added or substituted an Auto lamp on and off delay system, tinted glass, illuminated entry system, power lock group, automatic parking brake release, diagnostic warning light display, power door windows, interval wipers, electroluminescent coach lamps, front cornering lamps, dual electric remote-control door mirrors, wide body side moldings, accent tape stripes, wire wheel covers, luxury floor carpeting, carpeted seat cushion side facings, cloth insert door panel trim, wood-tone instrument cluster appliqués, electronic instrument cluster, quarter panel courtesy lights, light group, seat back map pockets, dual illuminated visor-vanity mirrors, premium sound system with AM/FM electronic stereo search radio, and velour cloth upholstery.

Thunderbird Turbo Coupe: Thunderbird Town Landau standard equipment added or substituted a 2.3-liter (140-cid) turbocharged four-cylinder engine with fuel-injection, five-speed overdrive manual transmission, and special handling suspension.

VIN:

The VIN was stamped on an aluminum tab riveted to the dashboard on the passenger side and was visible through the windshield. The first symbol 1 = built in the United States. The second symbol, F = Ford. symbol three, A = a Ford passenger vehicle. The fourth symbol was the type of restraint system. The fifth symbol P = a passenger-type vehicle. The sixth symbol 4 = Thunderbird. The seventh symbol, 6 = 2-door coupe. The eighth symbol was the engine: D=140 cid (2.3L) 142 hp turbocharged four-cylinder, 3=232 cid (3.8L)/110-hp V-6 and F=302 cid (5.0L)/130-hp V-8. The ninth symbol was the check digit. The 10th symbol D=1983 model year. The 11th symbol denoted the assembly plants: A=Atlanta, Georgia or H=Lorain, Ohio. The 12th through 17th symbols were the sequential production numbers of specific vehicles starting at 100001. The vehicle certification label was located on the rear face of the driver's door. The top part of the label indicated that the Thunderbird was manufactured by Ford Motor Company. Directly below this was the month and year of manufacture, plus a statement that the car conformed to federal motor vehicle safety standards in effect on the indicated date of manufacture. VIN: The VIN appeared on the first line of the encoded information. It matched the first to 11th symbols on the VIN tag. Some other codes also appeared. PASSENGER. EXT. COLOR: This line carried the exterior paint color(s) code. DSO: The District Special Order code now appeared above "DSO" to the right of the exterior paint color code. BODY: The body style code appeared to the extreme left of the bottom line. The only Thunderbird code for this model-year was: 66D=2-door Pillared Hardtop. VR: The vinyl roof type/color code was to the right of the body code. MLDG: The molding code was to the right of the vinyl roof code. INT. TRIM: The interior trim code was to the right of the molding code. A/C: The air conditioning code was to the right of the interior trim code. Cars with air conditioning had "A" stamped here. R: The radio code was to the right of the A/C code. S: The sun roof code appeared to the right of the radio code. AX: The axle

code appeared to the right of the sun roof code. TR: The transmission code appeared to the right of the axle code. The terms and abbreviations shown in capitals appear on the line above the actual codes.

Thunderbird (V-6)

Series No.	Body/ Style No.	Body Type and Seating	Factory Price	Shipping Weight	Production Total
46	66D	2-dr. Hardtop-4P	$9,197	2,905 lbs.	Note 1

Thunderbird (V-8)

46	66D	2-dr. Hardtop-4P	$9,485	2,936 lbs.	Note 1

Heritage Edition (V-6)

46/607	66D	2-dr. Hardtop-4P	$12,228	3,027 lbs.	Note 1

Heritage Edition (V-8)

46/607	66D	2-dr. Hardtop-4P	$12,516	------	Note 1

Turbo Coupe (Four)

46/934	66D	2-dr. Hardtop-4P	$11,790	------	Note 1

Note 1: Production of all models combined was 121,999.

Engines:

Thunderbird Base V-6: 90-degree, overhead valve. Cast-iron block and aluminum head. Displacement: 232 cid (3.8 liters). B & S: 3.80 x 3.40 in. Compression ratio: 8.65:1. Brake hp: 114 at 4000. Torque: 175 lbs.-ft. at 2200. Four main bearings. Hydraulic valve lifters. Carburetor: Motorcraft 2150 or 7200VV two-barrel. Code: 3.

Thunderbird Turbo Coupe Base Turbo Four: In-line. Overhead valve. Cast-iron block and head. Displacement: 140 cid (2.3 liters). B & S: 3.78 x 3.13 in. Compression ratio: 8.0:1. Brake hp: 142 at 5000. Torque: 172 lbs.-ft. at 3800. Five main bearings. Hydraulic valve lifters. Induction: Multi-Port Electronic Fuel injection. Garrett AIResearch T-03 turbocharger. Code: D.

Thunderbird Optional V-8: 90-degree, overhead valve. Cast-iron block and head. Displacement: 302 cid (5.0 liters). B & S: 4.00 x 3.00 in. Compression ratio: 8.4:1. Brake hp: 130 at 3200 rpm. Torque: 240 lbs.-ft. at 2000 rpm. Five main bearings. Hydraulic valve lifters. Induction: Electronic Fuel injection. Code: F.

Chassis:

Wheelbase: 104 in. Overall length: 197.6. Overall width: 71.1. Overall height: 53.2 in. Front headroom: 37.7 in. Front legroom: 42 in. Front shoulder room: 55.2 in. Rear headroom: 36.7 in. Rear legroom: 34.3 in. Trunk capacity: 14.6 cu. ft. Front tread: 58.1 in. Rear tread: 58.5 in. Tires: P195/75R14 steel-belted radial.

Technical:

Steering: Variable-ratio, power, rack and pinion. Steering ratio: 15.0-13.0:1. Turning diameter: 38.6 ft. Turns lock-to-lock: 2.5. Front suspension: Modified McPherson strut. Rear suspension: Four-link-bar. Weight distribution: 56/44 percent front/rear. Power to Weight ratio: 20.56 lb./hp. Steering: Variable-ratio power rack and pinion. Standard rear axle: 2.73:1. Front brakes: Power vented disc. Rear brakes: Power-assisted drums. Brakes Swept/1000 lb.275.6 sq. in. Rear axle (with five-speed manual transmission): 3.45:1. Rear Axle (with three-speed automatic transmission): 2.47:1. Rear axle (four-speed automatic transmission): 3.08:1. Fuel tank capacity: 18 gallons.

Options:

5.0-liter EFI V-8 engine, except in Turbo Coupe ($288). Four-speed overdrive automatic transmission, except in Turbo Coupe ($176). Traction-Lok axle ($95). Exterior accent group ($343). Automatic temperature control air conditioning ($802). Manual control air conditioning ($724). Anti-theft system ($159). Auto lamp on and off delay system, standard in Heritage ($73). Heavy-duty battery ($26). Lower body side protection on Turbo Coupe ($39). Lower body side protection, except Turbo Coupe ($54). Bumper rub strip extensions ($52). Electronic digital clock ($61). Front cornering lamps ($60). Electric rear window defroster ($135). Diagnostic warning lights, standard in Heritage ($59). Carpeted front floor mats ($22). Remote locking fuel filler door ($26). Full tinted glass ($105). Engine block immersion heater ($17). Illuminated entry system, standard in Heritage ($76). Electronic instrument cluster with interior luxury group ($321). Electronic instrument cluster without interior luxury group ($3820). Electronic instrument cluster standard in Heritage, delete option ($321 credit). Keyless entry system in Heritage ($88). Keyless entry system, except in Heritage ($163). Light group, standard in Heritage ($35). Power lock group, standard on Heritage ($160). Luxury carpet group in Turbo Coupe ($48). Luxury carpet group except in Turbo Coupe ($72). Interior luxury group ($1,170). Electronic dimming rear view mirror ($77). Dual illuminated visor-vanity mirrors, standard in Heritage ($100). Dual electric remote-control door mirrors, standard on Heritage ($94). Bright rocker panel moldings ($33). Wide body side moldings, standard on Heritage

1983 Ford Thunderbird two-door Coupe (F)

1983 Ford Thunderbird two-door Turbo Coupe (JG)

($51). Two-tone paint and tape treatment on Heritage ($148). Two-tone paint and tape treatment with exterior accent group ($163). Two-tone paint and tape treatment without exterior accent group ($218). Automatic parking brake release, standard in Heritage ($12). Power antenna ($60). AM radio delete ($61 credit). AM/FM stereo radio ($109). AM/FM stereo with 8-track or cassette tape in Turbo Coupe ($90). AM/FM stereo with 8-track or cassette tape except in Turbo Coupe and Heritage ($199). AM/FM stereo electronic search radio, in base Coupe ($252. AM/FM stereo electronic search radio, in Turbo Coupe ($144). Note: Previous radio standard in Heritage Edition. AM/FM stereo electronic search radio and cassette, in base Coupe ($396). AM/FM stereo electronic search radio and cassette, in Turbo Coupe ($288). AM/FM stereo electronic search radio and cassette, in Heritage Coupe ($144). Premium sound system ($179). Flip-up open air roof ($310). 6-way power driver's seat ($210). Dual-control power seat ($420). Fingertip speed control ($170). Leather-wrapped luxury steering wheel ($59). Tilt steering wheel ($105). Dual accent body side striping an d deck lid stripes ($55). Hood, body side and deck lid stripes ($71). Hood stripe ($16). Heavy-duty suspension, except not available in Turbo Coupe ($26). Medium-duty trailer tow package ($251). Traveler's assistance kit ($65). TripMinder computer with Heritage, luxury interior group, or electronic instrument cluster ($215). TripMinder computer except with Heritage, luxury interior group, or electronic instrument cluster ($276). Pivoting front vent windows ($76). Electronic voice alert ($67). Luxury wheel covers ($113). Locking wire wheel covers with Heritage ($20). Locking wire wheel covers with exterior accent group ($84). Locking wire wheel covers with all others ($198). Wire wheel covers with exterior accent group ($45). Wire wheel covers without exterior accent group ($159). Styled road wheels with exterior accent group ($65). Styled road wheels without exterior accent group ($178). Power side windows, standard in Heritage ($180). Interval wipers ($49). Articulated seats with interior luxury group ($183). Articulated seats without interior luxury group ($427). Vinyl seat trim ($37). Ultra-soft leather trim with Turbo Coupe or with articulated seats ($659). Ultra-soft leather trim without articulated seats or Turbo Coupe ($415).

History:

The 1983 T-Bird was introduced on February 17, 1983 and the Thunderbird Turbo was introduced on April 1, 1983. Phillip Caldwell remained as Chairman of the Board of Ford Motor Co. Once again, William Clay Ford was Vice Chairman and Donald E. Petersen was President. Louis E. Lataif continued as Ford Division's General Manager. Bernard L. Crumpton remained General Sales manager for the division. The new aerodynamically-styled T-Bird rose 107 percent in sales to a respectable 99,176 units, up from 47,903 in 1982. A Ford official said "Thunderbird did all we could have expected of it." He pointed out that T-Bird sales were even strong in the traditionally import-intensive coastal regions. Calendar-year output was 186,566 units. A total of 121,999 T-Birds were produced in the model year. This represented 2.14 percent of the industry total. Of these units, 45,994 were made in Atlanta, Georgia, and 76,005 were made in Lorain, Ohio. Calendar year dealer sales amounted to 134,710 T-Birds, representing 6 percent of industry sales. Seven cars competed for *Motor Trend* magazine's "Car of the Year Award" in 1983 and the new T-Bird was among them. Each of the cars was rated in eight categories, including styling and design, comfort and convenience, ride and drive, quality control, instrumented performance, fuel economy, handling and value. The Thunderbird V-6 placed third overall, but came in first in handling and second in the appearance, quality and value categories. The car did 0-60 in 13.07 seconds and the quarter-mile in 19.04 seconds at 72.90 mph. *Motor Trend* featured the T-Bird Turbo Coupe in its June 1983 issue. "Three decades later, the T-Bird finally becomes what it started out to be," crowed writer Ron Grable, who loved both the form and functioning of the Turbo Coupe. His test car had the five-speed manual gear box (the sole Turbo option) and a 3.45:1 rear axle. With a curb weight of 2,982 lb. it did 0-60 in 8.56 seconds. The standing quarter-mile took 16.45 seconds at 81 mph. Top speed was 142 mph. It didn't take long for race car builders to realize the competition potential of the powerful, great-handling, wind-cheating Aero 'Birds. In stock car racing, Dale Earnhardt, Buddy Baker and Bill Elliott were among the drivers who got new T-Birds to campaign during the 1983 season. The cars did handle well and got plenty of factory support, but some developmental problems and bad racing luck worked against them. By summer, *Motor Trend* was referring to the cars as "a group of promising but still teething T-Birds." At midyear, NASCAR made some rules changes, outlawing certain valve train modifications that worked to the advantage of cars with Chevrolet V-8s. Then the tides started to turn. Driving the Wood Brother's T-Bird, Buddy Baker took first place in Daytona's Firecracker 400. A week later, Dale Earnhardt was victorious at Nashville in the 'Bird that Bud Moore built for him. Earnhardt also took his T-Bird to a checkered flag at Talladega two races later. The final race of the season was the Winston Western 500 (km) at Riverside, Calif. It was in this event that driver Bill Elliott collected his first Winston Cup win with the Melling Ford T-Bird.

1984 Thunderbird

Thunderbird — Series 46 — (V-8): New T-Bird features for 1984 included electronic controls and fuel-injection on all engines, an automatic transmission for Turbo Coupes and new Elan and FILA models. All models now had bumper rub strip extensions as standard equipment. A slightly curved 8 x 6-hole cross-hatched grille with a T-Bird insignia on the header characterized the front end. Staggered, exposed and recessed dual headlights flanked side of the grille. Set into the bumper were new, clear plastic parking lights. Small amber wraparound marker light lenses were used at each front body corner. T-Bird insignias dressed up the roof sail panels. Wraparound wall-to-wall taillights again lit the rear of the T-Bird. The T-Bird insignias on the taillight lenses had a new molded appearance. The model line up was revised. The Heritage became the Elan name. It had the same 3.8-liter EFI V-6 as the base 'Bird. The 5.0-liter V-8 was optional. A new FILA model was developed in conjunction with FILA Sports, Inc., an Italian manufacturer of apparel for active leisure sports such as skiing and tennis. The FILA model had exclusive Pastel Charcoal paint with Dark Charcoal Metallic lower accents and unique red and blue tape stripes like the company logo. Bright trim was minimal. Instead of chrome, the grille and wheels had distinctive body-color finish. Charcoal windshield and backlight moldings were also featured. Inside, the FILA edition had Charcoal trim components. Its articulated bucket seats were done in Oxford White leather with perforated leather inserts or in Oxford Gray luxury cloth with perforated cloth inserts. Turbo Coupes added Charcoal greenhouse moldings and a new viscous clutch fan, as well as a starter/clutch interlock system and oil temperature warning switch. The Turbo Coupe now came with automatic transmission, as well as the five-speed manual gear box. The Turbo Coupe used a non-variable ratio to increase power steering effort for better high-speed control. Standard equipment included a 3.8-liter two-barrel EFI V-6 engine, SelectShift automatic transmission with locking torque converter, variable-ratio rack and pinion steering, power front disc/rear drum brakes, DuraSpark electronic ignition, electronic voltage regulator, maintenance-free battery, McPherson strut front suspension with gas-filled struts, four-bar-link rear suspension with gas-filled shocks, dual fluidic windshield washer system, P195/75R15 all-season white sidewall tires, concealed drip moldings, quad rectangular halogen headlamps, left-hand remote-control OSRV mirror, soft urethane-covered front and rear bumpers, charcoal bumper rub strips with extensions, deluxe wheel covers, individually reclining seats, padded console with illuminated interior and removable litter bin, 10-oz. color-keyed cut-pile carpeting, all-vinyl door trim panels with assist straps and storage bins, luxury steering wheel with center horn blow, trip odometer, quartz electric (sweep-hand) clock, glove box and ash tray lights, color-keyed cloth headlining and sun visors, utility strap on driver's visor, visor-vanity mirror on passenger visor, inertia seat back releases, color-keyed deluxe seat belts with comfort regulator feature and reminder chime, and AM radio (may be deleted for credit).

Thunderbird Elan: The Elan model adds or substitutes the following features over base Thunderbird equipment: an automatic parking brake release, dual electric remote-control OSRV mirrors, wide body side moldings, front cornering lamps, hood stripes, body side and deck lid accent stripes, styled road wheels, luxury carpet group, quarter panel courtesy lights, electronic digital clock, electronic AM/FM stereo search radio, premium sound system, power lock group, interval windshield wipers, power windows, complete tinted glass, tilt steering wheel, Autolamp on and off delay system, illuminated entry system, electronic instrument cluster, diagnostic warning lights, and light group.

Thunderbird FILA: The FILA model adds or substitutes the following features over base Thunderbird equipment: an automatic overdrive transmission, special handling package, P205/70HR14 black sidewall performance tires, automatic parking brake release, dual electric remote-control mirrors, wide body side moldings, front cornering lamps, 14-in. aluminum wheels, articulated seats, luxury carpet group, quarter panel courtesy lights, leather-wrapped steering wheel, electronic digital

1984 Ford Thunderbird FILA two-door Coupe (JG)

1984 Ford Thunderbird two-door Turbo Coupe (PH)

clock, electronic AM/FM stereo search radio with cassette player and Dolby noise reduction system, premium sound system, power lock group, 6-way power driver's seat, complete tinted glass, tilt steering wheel, fingertip speed control, Autolamp on and off delay system, illuminated entry system, diagnostic warning lights, and light group.

Turbo Coupe: The Turbo Coupe adds or substitutes the following features over base Thunderbird equipment: 2.3-liter overhead cam EFI turbocharged four-cylinder engine, five-speed manual overdrive transmission, special handling package, tachometer with boost and over-boost lights, Traction-Lok rear axle, P205/70HR14 black sidewall performance tires, dual electric remote-control mirrors, wide body side moldings, body side and deck lid accent stripes, unique front fascia with air dam and fog lights, 14-in. aluminum wheels, articulated seats, luxury carpet group, leather-wrapped sports steering wheel, electronic digital clock, AM/FM stereo radio, diagnostic warning lights, and light group.

VIN:

The VIN was stamped on an aluminum tab riveted to the dashboard on the passenger side and was visible through the windshield. First symbol 1 = built in the United States. The second symbol F = Ford. The third symbol A = Ford passenger vehicle. The fourth symbol was the type of restraint system. The fifth symbol P = passenger-type vehicle. The sixth symbol 4 = Thunderbird. The seventh symbol 6 = 2-door coupe. The eighth symbol was the engine: W=140 cid (2.3L) 145 hp turbocharged four-cylinder, 3=232 cid (3.8L)/120-hp V-6 and F=302 cid (5.0L)/140-hp V-8. The ninth symbol was the check digit. The 10th symbol E=1984 model year. The 11th symbol indicated the assembly plant: A=Atlanta, Georgia or H=Lorain, Ohio. The 12th through 17th symbols were sequential production numbers of the specific vehicle starting at 100001. The vehicle certification label was located on the rear face of the driver's door. The top part of the label indicated the Thunderbird was manufactured by Ford Motor Company. Directly below this was the month and year of manufacture, plus a statement that the car conformed to federal motor vehicle safety standards in effect on the indicated date of manufacture. VIN: The VIN appeared on the first line of encoded information. It matched the first to 11th symbols on the VIN tag. Some other codes also appeared. PASSENGER. EXT. COLOR: This line carried the exterior paint color(s) code. DSO: The District Special Order code now appeared above "DSO" to the right of the exterior paint color code. BODY: The body style code appeared to the extreme left of the bottom line. The only Thunderbird code for this model-year was: 66D=2-door Pillared Hardtop. VR: The vinyl roof type/color code was to the right of the body code. MLDG: The molding code was to the right of the vinyl roof code. INT. TRIM: The interior trim code was to the right of the molding code. See table below. A/C: The air conditioning code was to the right of the interior trim code. Cars with air conditioning had "A" stamped here. R: The radio code was to the right of the A/C code. S: The sun roof code appeared to the right of the radio code. AX: The axle code appeared to the right of the sun roof code. TR: The transmission code appeared to the right of the axle code. Note: The terms and abbreviations shown in capitals appear on the line above the actual codes.

Thunderbird (V-6)

Series No.	Body/Style No.	Body Type and Seating	Factory Price	Shipping Weight	Production Total
46	66D	2-dr. Hardtop-4P	$9,633	2,890 lbs.	Note 1

Thunderbird (V-8)

46	66D	2-dr. Hardtop-4P	$9,633	2,890 lbs.	Note 1

Thunderbird (V-6)

46/607	66D	2-dr. Hardtop-4P	$12,661	2,956 lbs.	Note 1

1984 Ford Thunderbird Elan two-door Coupe (JG)

Thunderbird (V-8)

46/607	66D	2-dr. Hardtop-4P	$13,281	3,163 lbs.	Note 1

Thunderbird FILA (V-6)

46/606	66D	2-dr. Hardtop-4P	$14,471	3,061 lbs.	Note 1

Thunderbird FILA (V-8)

46/606	66D	2-dr. Hardtop-4P	$14,854	3,268 lbs.	Note 1

Turbo Coupe (Four)

46/934	66D	2-dr. Hardtop-4P	$12,330	2,938 lbs.	Note 1

Note 1: Production of the all models combined was 170,533.

Engine:

Thunderbird Base V-6: 90-degree, overhead valve. Cast-iron block and aluminum head. Displacement: 232 cid (3.8 liters). B & S: 3.80 x 3.40 in. Compression ratio: 8.7:1. Brake hp: 120 at 3600. Torque: 205 lbs.-ft. at 1600. Four main bearings. Hydraulic valve lifters. Induction: Throttle Body Injection. Code: 3.

Thunderbird Turbo Coupe Base Turbo Four: In-line. Overhead valve. Cast-iron block and head. Displacement: 140 cid (2.3 liters). B & S: 3.78 x 3.13 in. Compression ratio: 8.0:1. Brake hp: 145 at 4600. Torque: 180 lbs.-ft. at 3600. Five main bearings. Hydraulic valve lifters. Induction: Multi-Point Electronic Fuel injection. Garrett AIResearch T-03 turbocharger. Code: W.

Thunderbird Optional V-8: 90-degree, overhead valve. Cast-iron block and head. Displacement: 302 cid (5.0 liters). B & S: 4.00 x 3.00 in. Compression ratio: 8.4:1. Brake hp: 140 at 3200 rpm. Torque: 250 lbs.-ft. at 1600 rpm. Five main bearings. Hydraulic valve lifters. Induction: Throttle Body Injection. Code: F.

Chassis:

Wheelbase: 104 in. Overall length: 197.6. Overall width: 71.1. Overall height: 53.2 in. Front headroom: 37.7 in. Front legroom: 42 in. Front shoulder room: 55.2 in. Rear headroom: 36.7 in. Rear legroom: 34.3 in. Trunk capacity: 14.6 cu. ft. Front tread: 58.1 in. Rear tread: 58.5 in. Tires: P195/75R14 white sidewall steel-belted radial.

Technical:

Steering: Variable-ratio, power, rack-and-pinion. Steering ratio: 15.0-13.0:1. Turning diameter: 38.6 ft. Turns lock-to-lock: 2.5. Front suspension: Modified McPherson strut. Rear suspension: Four-link-bar. Weight distribution: 56/44 percent front/rear. Power to Weight ratio: 20.56 lb./hp. Steering: Variable-ratio power rack and pinion. Standard rear axle: 2.73:1. Front brakes: Power disc. Rear brakes: Power drum. Brakes Swept/1000 lb.275.1 sq. in. Rear axle (with five-speed manual transmission): 3.45:1. Rear Axle (with three-speed automatic transmission): 2.47:1. Rear axle (four-speed automatic transmission): 3.08:1. Fuel tank capacity: 21 gallons.

Options:

AM/FM stereo radio ($98). AM/FM stereo radio with cassette tape player. Electronic AM/FM stereo search radio, Electronic AM/FM stereo search radio with cassette tape player and Dolby noise reduction system, Premium sound system (stereo radios only). Wide body side moldings. Exterior accent group. Luxury carpet group. Dual body side and deck lid tape stripes. Tu-Tone paint/tape treatments. Charcoal lower accent treatment. Charcoal Metallic paint. Electroluminescent coach lamps. Autolamp on and off delay system. Diagnostic warning lights. Electronic instrument cluster. TripMinder computer. Electronic voice alert. Traveler's assistance kit. Front cornering lamps. Electric rear window defroster ($126). Remote-control locking fuel door. Dual electric remote-control mirrors ($86). Pivoting front vent windows. Keyless entry system including illuminated entry system. Illuminated entry system. Interval windshield wipers ($45). Flip-up Open-Air roof ($284). SelectAire conditioner with automatic control ($669). SelectAire conditioner with manual control. Automatic parking brake release. Electronic digital clock. Complete tinted glass ($99). Light group. Fingertip speed control ($158). Electronic dimming day/night rear view mirror. Leather-wrapped luxury steering wheel. Tilt steering wheel ($99). Interior luxury group. Articulated seats. Ultrasoft leather trim. Anti-theft system. Lower body sides protection. Bright rocker panel moldings. Front floor mats. Front license plate bracket. License plate frames. Power lock group ($159). Power radio antenna. 6-way power driver's seat. Dual 6-way power seats. Power side windows ($178). Luxury wheel covers. Locking wire wheel style wheel covers. Styled road wheel covers. TRX aluminum wheels including Michelin TRX tires. 5.0-liter V-8 with EFI optional in all models, except Super Coupe. SelectShift automatic transmission with locking torque converter, standard in T-Bird and Elan, optional in Super Coupe ($284). Automatic overdrive transmission, optional in T-Bird and Elan, standard in FILA, not available in Super coupe. Traction-Lok differential, standard in Super Coupe. Medium-duty trailer towing package. Heavy-duty battery. Heavy-duty suspension. Special handling package (standard in FILA and Super Coupe). Engine block immersion heater. California emissions system.

History:

The 1984 T-Bird was introduced on September 22, 1983. Phillip Caldwell remained as Chairman of the Board of Ford Motor Co. Once again, William Clay Ford was Vice Chairman and Donald E. Petersen was President. Louis E. Lataif continued as Ford Division's General Manager. Bernard L. Crumpton remained General Sales manager for the division. Some reshuffling of the executive staff would occur by the start of 1985. Calendar-year output was 146,186 units. A total of 170,551 T-Birds were produced in the model year. This represented 2.10 percent of the industry total. Of these units, 34,250 were made in Atlanta, Georgia, and 136,301 were made in Lorain, Ohio. Calendar year dealer sales amounted to 156,583 T-Birds, representing 2 percent of industry sales. This year the Turbo Coupe was merchandised heavily in both the U.S. and Canada. Starting on March 16, 1984 three Special Value Packages with a discount were available. Each package included the same 11 basic extras. Collectors are likely to find many well-loaded 1984 Turbo Coupes today because of this promotion. *Motor Trend* (April 1984) tested the Turbo Coupe, describing it as a "show and go that you can afford to keep on the road." The car traveled from 0-60 mph in 8.98 seconds and ran the quarter-mile in 16.73 seconds at 80.9 mph. Writer Jim Hall focused on its economy of operation. In 13,257.3 miles of long-term use, the Silver T-Bird cost $987.65 (7.4 cents per mile) to operate. The total included $55.45 in maintenance costs and $932.20 worth of gas. Surging upon acceleration and pinging on climbing steep hills were two problems. After 1,000 miles of use, the surging went away. The pinging was minimized by use of unleaded premium fuel. An air conditioning compressor was also replaced under the factory warranty. The T-Bird was summarized as a "good looking performance car that won't cost the driver an arm and a leg during the first year of ownership." In an interesting comparison report, *Motor Trend's* long-term Turbo test car was later (July 1984 issue) compared to a Turbo-Bird modified by Creative Car Products (CCP) of Hawthorne, Calif. The CCP Thunderbird featured a front air dam, side skirts, rear valance panel, rear spoiler, and a Turbo Auto intercooler atop its engine. Additional upgrades included chrome-silicon coil springs front and rear, larger anti-roll bars, and Koni adjustable shocks, plus special Hayashi wheels and Goodyear tires. The magazine described the car's overall look as "reminiscent of the NASCAR Grand National cars." At Sears Point Raceway, the CCP Thunderbird took 9.11 seconds to do 0-60, and covered the quarter-mile in 16.86 seconds at 80.4 mph. Although it was slower-accelerating than the stock Turbo because of its "stickier" tires, the sleek CCP 'Bird performed better in braking and handling tests. In addition to street-performance modifications, the new-generation Aero 'Birds were also gaining the attention of the race car set. In stock car racing, Ford's Special Vehicle Operations (SVO) parts pipeline was funneling hardware to race car builders that made the T-Birds even more competitive in 1984. Bill Elliott took his Coors Melling T-Bird to the first back-to-back victories in the 1984 NASCAR Winston Cup Series in October, putting him third in the overall point standings with two races to go. Other stock car drivers racing T-Birds this year included Benny Parsons in the number 55 Copenhagen car, Ricky Rudd in the Wrangler T-Bird, Dick Brooks in the Chameleon Sunglasses T-Bird, Kyle Petty's 7-Eleven car, Kenny Schrader in the Sunny King/Honda Bird, and Buddy Baker in the Valvoline T-Bird. In sports car racing, John Bauer campaigned his number 77 T-Bird. The blue and white car, with Ford/Motorcraft sponsorship, dominated GTO competition. At Pikes Peak, Leonard Vahsholtz and Larry Overholser raced T-Birds up the mountain with mixed success. They were competitive in the event, but wound up in second and fourth place, respectively. Finally, in drag racing, Chief Auto Parts announced its principal sponsorship of Bob Glidden's Pro Stock T-Bird. The 30th anniversary of the T-Bird's introduction was celebrated in the fall of 1984, and by the end of the year, there would be more to celebrate as model-year production in the U.S. leaped to 170,551, a gain of nearly 50,000 over 1983.

1985 Thunderbird

Thunderbird — Series 46 — (V-8): Ford celebrated the 30th Anniversary of the T-Bird with a special limited-edition commemorative model with unique exterior and interior trim. Regular T-Birds got a new color-keyed grille and full-width taillights with inboard back-up lights. There was also a new T-Bird emblem on the taillight lenses, the "C" pillars and the grille header bar. The base Coupe, the Elan Coupe and the FILA Coupe returned. The 1985 Turbo Coupe was "dechromed" to give it a more purposeful look. It also got larger tires on aluminum wheels. Ford offered 14 colors for the exterior of T-Birds. Seven were standard colors and seven were Clearcoat Metallics. Seven color-coordinated paint stripe colors were used. The Turbo Coupe first came in three standard colors and five clear coats, all with a Dark Charcoal lower accent treatment. However a 1985-1/2 running change offered three of the same exterior colors (Bright Canyon Red, Oxford White, or Medium Regatta Blue Clearcoat Metallic) in a Monotone treatment without Dark Charcoal lower accenting. The FILA model again offered a Pastel Charcoal exterior with Dark Charcoal lower accent treatment. However, the Red and Blue tape stripes of 1984 were changed to Red Orange and Dark Blue. Three other Monotone color options were added: Black, Bright Canyon Red, and Medium Charcoal Metallic Clearcoat. All three also came with the same FILA tape stripes. The most collectible car of the year was the 30th Anniversary Limited-Edition T-Bird. It came exclusively with Medium Regatta Blue Metallic exterior finish highlighted with Silver Metallic graduated paint stripes. Interior changes included a new instrument panel with a digital speedometer and analog gauges. Also revised were the door trim panels. The front center console was shortened and a third seat belt was added in the rear for five-passenger seating. A total of 33 interior trim options were listed in 1985. They included a special Regatta Blue luxury cloth split-bench seat interior for the 30th Anniversary T-Bird. The Turbo Coupe received a modified 2.3-liter four-cylinder engine with electronic boost control and higher flow-rate fuel injectors to increase power. The improvements were the result of research and development done for the Merkur XR4Ti, built by Ford of Germany, which used the same engine. There was also a new five-speed manual transmission with new gear ratios, plus an automatic transmission designed to handle the Turbo Coupe's high-revving capabilities. When the driver accelerated quickly, it stayed in low gear right through the power curve, not shifting until higher performance could be gained by going to a higher gear. Standard equipment included: a 3.8-liter two-barrel EFI V-6 engine, SelectShift automatic transmission with locking torque converter, variable-ratio rack and pinion steering, power front disc/rear drum brakes, electronic voltage regulator, McPherson strut front suspension with gas-filled struts, four-bar-link rear suspension with gas-filled shocks, P205/70R14 all-season black sidewall tires, concealed drip moldings, halogen headlamps, luxury wheel covers, individually reclining split-bench seats with cloth seating surfaces and consolette, 16-oz. color-keyed cut-pile carpeting, luxury steering wheel with center horn blow, quartz electric (sweep-hand) clock, AM radio (may be deleted for credit).

Thunderbird Elan: The Elan model adds or substitutes the following features over base Thunderbird equipment: an automatic parking brake release, dual electric remote-control OSRV mirrors, wide body side moldings, body side and deck lid accent stripes, rear seat center folding arm rest, luxury door and quarter panel trim, quarter panel courtesy lights, electronic digital clock, AM/FM stereo cassette tape player, interval windshield wipers, power windows, complete tinted glass, diagnostic warning lights, light group, and remote-locking fuel door.

Thunderbird FILA: The FILA model adds or substitutes the following features over base Thunderbird equipment: an automatic overdrive transmission, automatic parking brake release, dual electric remote-control mirrors, wide body side moldings, body side and deck lid striping, cornering lamps, 14-in. aluminum wheels, articulated seats, rear seat center folding arm rest, luxury door and quarter trim panels, quarter panel courtesy lights, leather-wrapped steering wheel, electronic digital clock, electronic AM/FM stereo search radio with cassette player and Dolby noise reduction system, premium sound system, power lock group, interval wipers, 6-way power driver's seat, complete tinted glass, tilt steering wheel, speed control, Autolamp on and off delay system, illuminated entry system, diagnostic warning lights, light group, and remote locking fuel door.

Super Coupe: The Super Coupe adds or substitutes the following features over base Thunderbird equipment: 2.3-liter overhead cam EFI turbocharged four-cylinder engine, five-speed manual overdrive transmission, full analog instrumentation with tachometer and boost and over-boost lights, Traction-Lok rear axle, P225/60VR15 black sidewall performance tires, dual electric remote-control mirrors, wide body side moldings, cornering lamps, unique front fascia with air dam and Marchal fog lights, 15-in. aluminum wheels, articulated seats, rear seat center folding arm rest, performance instrumentation, luxury door

1985 Ford Thunderbird Elan two-door Coupe (JG)

and quarter trim panels, quarter panel courtesy lights, leather-wrapped steering wheel, electronic digital clock, AM/FM stereo radio, interval wipers, tinted glass complete, diagnostic warning lights, light group, and remote locking fuel door.

The VIN was stamped on an aluminum tab riveted to dashboard on the passenger side and was visible through the windshield. The first symbol 1 = built in the United States. The second symbol F = Ford. Symbol three A = a Ford passenger vehicle. The fourth symbol was the type of restraint system. The fifth symbol P= a passenger-type vehicle. The sixth symbol 4 = Thunderbird. The seventh symbol 6 = 2-door coupe. The eighth symbol was the engine: W=140 cid (2.3L) 155 hp turbocharged four-cylinder, 3=232 cid (3.8L)/120-hp V-6 and F=302 cid (5.0L)/140-hp V-8. The ninth symbol was the check digit. The 10th symbol F=1985 model year. The 11th symbol was the assembly plant: A=Atlanta, Georgia or H=Lorain, Ohio. The 12th through 17th symbols were the sequential production numbers of the specific vehicles starting at 100001. The vehicle certification label was located on the rear face of the driver's door. The top part of the label indicated the Thunderbird was manufactured by Ford Motor Company. Directly below this was the month and year of manufacture, plus a statement that the car conformed to federal motor vehicle safety standards in effect on the indicated date of manufacture. VIN: The VIN appeared on the first line of encoded information. It matched the first to 11th symbols on the VIN tag. Some other codes also appeared. PASSENGER. EXT. COLOR: This line carried the exterior paint color(s) code. DSO: The District Special Order code appeared above "DSO" to the right of the exterior paint color code. BODY: The body style code appeared to the extreme left of the bottom line. The only Thunderbird code for this model-year was: 66D=2-door Pillared Hardtop. VR: The vinyl roof type/color code was to the right of the body code. MLDG: The molding code was to the right of the vinyl roof code. INT. TRIM: The interior trim code was to the right of the molding code. A/C: The air conditioning code was to the right of the interior trim code. Cars with air conditioning had "A" stamped here. R: The radio code was to the right of the A/C code. S: The sunroof code appeared to the right of the radio code. AX: The axle code appeared to the right of the sun roof code. TR:The transmission code appeared to the right of the axle code. Note: The terms and abbreviations shown in capitals appeared on the line above the actual codes.

Thunderbird (V-6)

Series No.	Body/ Style No.	Body Type and Seating	Factory Price	Shipping Weight	Production Total
46	66D	2-dr. Hardtop-4P	$10,249	2,890 lbs.	Note 1

Thunderbird (V-8)

46	66D	2-dr. Hardtop-4P	$10,884	3,097 lbs.	Note 1

Thunderbird Elan (V-6)

46/607	66D	2-dr. Hardtop-4P	$11,916	2,956 lbs.	Note 1

Thunderbird Elan (V-8)

46/607	66D	2-dr. Hardtop-4P	$12,551	3,163 lbs.	Note 1

Thunderbird FILA (V-6)

46/606	66D	2-dr. Hardtop-4P	$14,974	3,061 lbs.	Note 1

Thunderbird FILA (V-8)

46/606	66D	2-dr. Hardtop-4P	$15,609	3,268 lbs.	Note 1

Turbo COUPE (Four)

46/934	66D	2-dr. Hardtop-4P	$13,365	2,938 lbs.	Note 1

Note 1: Production of the all models combined was 151,852.

Engine:

Thunderbird Base V-6: 90-degree, overhead valve. Cast-iron block and aluminum head. Displacement: 232 cid (3.8 liters). B & S: 3.80 x 3.40 in. Compression ratio: 8.7:1. Brake hp: 120 at 3600. Torque: 205 lbs.-ft. at 1600. Four main bearings. Hydraulic valve lifters. Induction: Throttle Body Injection. Code: 3.

1985 Ford Thunderbird Turbo two-door Coupe (PH)

Thunderbird Turbo Coupe Base Turbo Four: In-line. Overhead valve. Cast-iron block and head. Displacement: 140 cid (2.3 liters). B & S: 3.78 x 3.13 in. Compression ratio: 8.0:1. Brake hp: 155 at 4600. Torque: 190 lbs.-ft. at 2800. Five main bearings. Hydraulic valve lifters. Induction: Multi-Point Electronic Fuel injection. Garrett AIResearch T-03 turbocharger. Code: W.

Thunderbird Optional V-8: 90-degree, overhead valve. Cast-iron block and head. Displacement: 302 cid (5.0 liters). B & S: 4.00 x 3.00 in. Compression ratio: 8.4:1. Brake hp: 140 at 3200 rpm. Torque: 250 lbs.-ft. at 1600 rpm. Five main bearings. Hydraulic valve lifters. Induction: Throttle Body Injection. Code: F.

Chassis:

Wheelbase: 104 in. Overall length: 197.6. Overall width: 71.1. Overall height: 53.2 in. Front headroom: 37.7 in. Front legroom: 42 in. Front shoulder room: 55.2 in. Rear headroom: 36.7 in. Rear legroom: 34.3 in. Trunk capacity: 14.6 cu. ft. Front tread: 58.1 in. Rear tread: 58.5 in. Tires: P195/75R14 white sidewall steel-belted radial.

Technical:

Steering: Variable-ratio, power, rack-and-pinion. Steering ratio: 15.0-13.0:1 (15.1:1 on Turbo Coupe). Turning diameter: 38.6 ft. Turns lock-to-lock: 2.5. Front suspension: Modified McPherson strut. Rear suspension: Four-link-bar (quad shocks on Turbo Coupe). Weight distribution: 56/44 percent front/rear. Power to Weight ratio: 20.56 lb./hp. Steering: Variable-ratio power rack and pinion. Standard rear axle: 2.73:1. Front brakes: Power disc. Rear brakes: Power drum. Brakes swept area: 275.6 sq. in. Rear axle (with five-speed manual transmission): 3.45:1. Rear Axle (with three-speed automatic transmission): 2.47:1. Rear axle (four-speed automatic transmission): 3.08:1. Fuel tank capacity: 21 gallons.

Options:

AM/FM stereo radio with cassette tape player ($133). Electronic AM/FM stereo search radio with cassette tape player and Dolby noise reduction system. Premium sound system (stereo radios only). Graphic equalizer. Wide body side moldings. Dual body side and deck lid tape stripes. Hood stripes. Tu-Tone paint/tape treatments. Clearcoat Metallic paint. Front cornering lamps. Rear window defroster. Dual electric remote-control mirrors ($86). Pivoting front vent windows. Keyless entry system including illuminated entry system ($105). Illuminated entry system. Interval windshield wipers. Flip-up Open-Air roof ($284). SelectAire conditioner with electronic control ($686). SelectAire conditioner with manual control. Automatic parking brake release. Electronic digital clock. Complete tinted glass ($104). Light group. Speed control ($158). Electronic dimming day/night rear view mirror. Dual illuminated visor mirrors. Leather-wrapped luxury steering wheel. Tilt steering wheel ($104). Heated driver and passenger seat. Articulated seats. Ultrasoft leather seat trim. Anti-theft system. Bright rocker panel moldings. Front floor mats. Front license plate bracket. License plate frames. Power lock group ($198). Power radio antenna. 6-way power driver's seat ($214). Dual 6-way power seats. Power seat recliners. Power side windows ($186). Locking wire wheel style wheel covers. Styled road wheel covers. Alloy wheels. 5.0-liter V-8 with EFI and automatic overdrive transmission optional in all models, except Super Coupe ($448 engine/$213 transmission). SelectShift automatic transmission with locking torque converter, standard in T-Bird and Elan, optional in Super Coupe ($284). Traction-Lok differential, standard in Super Coupe. Medium-duty trailer towing package. Heavy-duty battery. Heavy-duty suspension. Engine block immersion heater. California emissions system. Note: Incomplete options pricing date at time of publication.

History:

The 1985 T-Bird was introduced on October 4, 1984. Donald E. Petersen became Chairman of the Board and CEO of Ford Motor Co. William Clay Ford remained Vice Chairman and Harold A. Poling was President and Chief Operating Officer. Ford Vice President Robert L. Rewey took over as Ford Division's General Manager. Phillip M. Novell was General Sales manager for the division. Calendar-year output was 170,541 units. A total of 151,852 T-Birds were produced in the model year. This represented 1.94 percent of the industry total. Of these units, 20,637 were made in Atlanta, Georgia, and 131,215 were made in Lorain, Ohio. Calendar year dealer sales amounted to 169,770 T-Birds, representing 2.1 percent of industry sales. In racing, the T-Birds were flying high this season, with Ricky Rudd's Bud Moore-built Motorcraft T-Bird making him one of the most promising newcomers in NASCAR events. The T-Birds were so dominant that Chevy buff Junior Johnson convinced Winston Cup officials that he would be able to lower here his Monte Carlos to the same roof height specs applied to T-Birds (50 in. instead of 51 in.). At midyear, NASCAR established a new uniform minimum roof height dimension of 50 in. It didn't matter. Bill Elliott's Coors-sponsored T-Bird continued to "rule" NASCAR and set a record qualifying speed in its next outing. That was the Winston 500 at Talladega Superspeedway, a race in which T-Birds finished 1-2-3. Elliott took the checkered flag with a mind-blowing average speed of 186.288 mph. He also won the Daytona 500, the Transouth 500 at Darlington, the Budweiser 500 at Dover, Del., the Pocono Summer 500, the Champion Spark Plug 500 at Michigan International, and the Southern 500 at Darlington. His victory in the latter event made Elliott the winner of the new Winston Million series, which earned him a check for $1 million from R.J. Reynolds. Ultimately, Darrell Waltrip would come from behind to take the 1985 points championship, which created a bit of controversy over the way the scoring was handled. Elliott, though, had become the first driver to ever win 11 Winston Cup super speedway races in a single season. It was still a great year for Bill's pocketbook and the T-Bird's long performance history. Cale Yarborough (Hardees Ranier T-Bird), Kyle Petty (Woods Brothers T-Bird), and Bobby Allison were other T-Bird pilots in NASCAR. In drag racing, Rickie Smith's Motorcraft T-Bird broke the 180 mph and eight second barriers in Pro Stock competition. This car was a star on both the NHRA and IHRA circuits in 1985. In a third venue, Darin Brassfield had success with his Brooks Racing T-Bird in the IMSA Camel GT Series.

1986 Thunderbird

Thunderbird — Series 46 — (V-8): T-Bird styling was similar to 1985, except for a new high-mounted stop lamp. A new electronic climate control system was announced and an electronically-tuned AM/FM stereo became standard equipment in the base model. The T-bird hood had counter-balanced springs to hold it open instead of inconvenient prop rods. Larger 215/70R14 tires and a collapsible spare with an on-board compressor to inflate it were other changes. Added to the options list were a power-operated moon roof and a specially-designed Tot-Guard child seat. Ford switched to a three-year unlimited mileage warranty on major power train components. The base and Elan models returned. Five conventional finishes and eight extra-cost Clearcoat paints were offered for base and Elan models. Five colors were available in two-tone combinations. There were nine color-keyed striping colors. The Turbo Coupe came in three regular colors and five Clearcoat Metallics. Four (including Black) were available in combination with Dark Charcoal lower body accents. Five interior colors were listed for base and Elan models. A sixth color, called Raven, was only for Elans with articulated seats. Articulated sports seats were available in the Elan and Turbo Coupe. Turbos came with only three interior colors. A wood-tone instrument panel appliqué was added to the interior. The 3.8-liter fuel-injected V-6 hooked to a three-speed SelectShift automatic transmission was standard. New hydraulic engine mounts made the car smoother running. The 5.0-liter V-8 now featured sequential fuel-injection, roller tappets, low-tension piston rings, fast-burn combustion chambers and hydraulic engine mounts. A four-speed automatic overdrive transmission and upgraded rear axle were standard with the V-8. The Turbo Coupe featured a standard 2.3-liter turbocharged engine and five-speed manual transmission. Standard features included: a 3.8-liter (232-cid) TBI V-6 engine, three-speed automatic transmission, power brakes, power steering, dual note horn, halogen headlamps, left-hand remote-control door mirror, vinyl insert body side moldings, deluxe wheel covers, seat belt reminder chimes, analog quartz clock, center console, vinyl door panels, full carpeting including trunk, AM/FM stereo radio, individual reclining front seats, luxury steering wheel, cloth upholstery, trip odometer, P215/70R14 tires.

1986 Ford Thunderbird two-door Turbo Coupe (PH)

Thunderbird Elan: The Elan model adds or substitutes the following features over base Thunderbird equipment: Power windows, folding rear seat arm rest, tinted glass, light group, dual electric remote-control OSRV mirrors, wide body side moldings, AM/FM cassette stereo, intermittent windshield wipers.

Thunderbird Turbo Coupe: The Turbo Coupe model adds or substitutes the following features over base Thunderbird equipment: an 2.3-liter (140-cid) turbocharged four-cylinder PFI engine, 5-speed manual overdrive transmission, and special handling suspension.

VIN:

The VIN was stamped on an aluminum tab riveted to the dashboard on the passenger side and was visible through the windshield. The first symbol 1 = built in the United States. The second symbol F = Ford. The third symbol A = a Ford passenger vehicle. The fourth symbol denoted the type of restraint system. The fifth symbol P = a passenger-type vehicle. The sixth symbol 4 = Thunderbird. The seventh symbol 6 = 2-door coupe. The eighth symbol was the engine: W=140 cid (2.3L) 145 hp turbocharged four-cylinder/automatic, W=140 cid (2.3L) 155 hp turbocharged four-cylinder/manual, 3=232 cid (3.8L)/120-hp V-6 and F=302 cid (5.0L)/150-hp V-8. The ninth symbol was the check digit. The 10th symbol G=the 1986 model year. The 11th symbol denoted the assembly plant: H=Lorain, Ohio. The 12th through 17th symbols were the sequential production numbers of the specific vehicle starting at 100001. The vehicle certification label was located on the rear face of the driver's door. The top part of the label indicated the Thunderbird was manufactured by Ford Motor Company. Directly below this was the month and year of manufacture, plus a statement that the car conformed to federal motor vehicle safety standards in effect on the indicated date of manufacture. VIN: The VIN appeared on the first line of encoded information. It matches the first to 11th symbols on VIN tag. Some other codes also appeared. PASSENGER. EXT. COLOR: This line carried the exterior paint color(s) code. DSO: The District Special Order code now appeared above "DSO" to the right of the exterior paint color code. BODY: The body style code appeared to the extreme left of the bottom line. The only Thunderbird code for this model-year was: 66D=2-door Pillared Hardtop. VR: The vinyl roof type/color code was to the right of the body code. No T-Birds had vinyl tops. MLDG: The molding code was to the right of the vinyl roof code. INT. TRIM: The interior trim code was to the right of the molding code. A/C: The air conditioning code was to the right of the interior trim code. Cars with air conditioning had "A" stamped here. R: The radio code was to the right of the A/C code. S: The sunroof code appeared to the right of the radio code. AX: The axle code appeared to the right of the sun roof code. TR: The transmission code appeared to the right of the axle code. Note: The terms and abbreviations shown in capitals appeared on the line above the actual codes.

Thunderbird (V-6)

Series No.	Body/Style No.	Body Style and Seating	Factory Price	Shipping Weight	Production Total
46	66D	2-dr. Hardtop-4P	$11,020	2,923 lbs.	Note 1

Thunderbird (V-8)

Series No.	Body/Style No.	Body Style and Seating	Factory Price	Shipping Weight	Production Total
46	66D	2-dr. Hardtop-4P	$11,805	3,101 lbs.	Note 1

Thunderbird Elan (V-6)

Series No.	Body/Style No.	Body Style and Seating	Factory Price	Shipping Weight	Production Total
46/607	66D	2-dr. Hardtop-4P	$12,554	2,977 lbs.	Note 1

Thunderbird Elan (V-8)

Series No.	Body/Style No.	Body Style and Seating	Factory Price	Shipping Weight	Production Total
46/607	66D	2-dr. Hardtop-4P	$13,339	3,155 lbs.	Note 1

Turbo Coupe (Four)

Series No.	Body/Style No.	Body Style and Seating	Factory Price	Shipping Weight	Production Total
46/934	66D	2-dr. Hardtop-4P	$14,143	3,016 lbs.	Note 1

Note 1: Production of the all models combined was 163,965.

Engines:

Thunderbird Base V-6: 90-degree, overhead valve. Cast-iron block and aluminum head. Displacement: 232 cid (3.8 liters). B & S: 3.80 x 3.40 in. Compression ratio: 8.7:1. Brake hp: 120 at 3600. Torque: 205 lbs.-ft. at 1600. Four main bearings. Hydraulic valve lifters. Induction: Throttle Body Injection. Code: 3.

Thunderbird Turbo Coupe Base Turbo Four (Automatic): In-line. Overhead valve. Cast-iron block and head. Displacement: 140 cid (2.3 liters). B & S: 3.78 x 3.13 in. Compression ratio: 8.0:1. Brake hp: 145 at 4400. Torque: 180 lbs.-ft. at 3000. Five main bearings. Hydraulic valve lifters. Induction: Multi-Point Electronic Fuel injection. Garrett AIResearch T-03 turbocharger. Code: W.

Thunderbird Turbo Coupe BASE Turbo Four: In-line. Overhead valve. Cast-iron block and head. Displacement: 140 cid (2.3 liters). B & S: 3.78 x 3.13 in. Compression ratio: 8.0:1. Brake hp: 155 at 4600. Torque: 190 at 2800. Five main bearings. Hydraulic valve lifters.

Induction: Multi-Point Electronic Fuel injection. Garrett AIResearch T-03 turbocharger. Code: W.

Thunderbird Optional V-8: 90-degree, overhead valve. Cast-iron block and head. Displacement: 302 cid (5.0 liters). B & S: 4.00 x 3.00 in. Compression ratio: 8.9:1. Brake hp: 150 at 3200 rpm. Torque: 270 lbs.-ft. at 2000 rpm. Five main bearings. Hydraulic valve lifters. Induction: Sequential (port) fuel injection. Code: F.

Chassis:

Wheelbase: 104 in. Overall length: 197.6. Overall width: 71.1. Overall height: 53.2 in. Front headroom: 37.7 in. Front legroom: 42 in. Front shoulder room: 55.2 in. Rear headroom: 36.7 in. Rear legroom: 34.3 in. Trunk capacity: 14.6 cu. ft. Front tread: 58.1 in. Rear tread: 58.5 in. Tires: P195/70-R14 white sidewall steel-belted radial.

Technical:

Steering: Variable-ratio, power, rack-and-pinion. Steering ratio: 15.0-13.0:1 (15.1:1 on Turbo Coupe). Turning diameter: 38.6 ft. Turns lock-to-lock: 2.5. Front suspension: Modified McPherson strut. Rear suspension: Four-link-bar (quad shocks on Turbo Coupe). Weight distribution: 56/44 percent front/rear. Power to Weight ratio: 20.56 lb./hp. Steering: Variable-ratio power rack and pinion. Standard rear axle: 2.73:1. Front brakes: Power disc. Rear brakes: Power drum. Brakes swept area: 275.6 sq. in. Rear axle (with five-speed manual transmission): 3.45:1. Rear Axle (with three-speed automatic transmission): 2.47:1. Rear axle (four-speed automatic transmission): 3.08:1. Fuel tank capacity: 21 gallons.

Options:

5.0-liter PFI V-8 ($505). Three-speed automatic transmission in Turbo Coupe ($290). Four-speed automatic transmission in T-Bird and Elan ($220). Traction-Lok axle ($920). Inflatable spare tire ($112). Conventional spare tire ($58). Automatic air conditioning ($850). Air conditioning ($700). Anti-theft system ($145). Autolamp system ($67). Heavy-duty battery ($25). Digital clock ($56). Cornering lamps ($63). Rear defogger ($133). Diagnostic alert lights ($82). Tinted glass ($106). Engine block immersion heater ($17). Illuminated entry system ($75). Electronic instrument cluster in T-Bird ($305). Electronic instrument cluster in T-Bird Elan coupe ($250). Remote keyless entry system ($182). Light group ($32). Power lock group ($200). Front floor mats ($20). Dual illuminated sun visor mirrors ($98). Dual remote-control OSRV mirrors ($88). Wide body side moldings ($52). Power-operated moon roof ($645). Two-tone exterior paint on T-Bird ($200). Two-tone exterior paint on T-Bird Elan Coupe ($150). Metallic clear coat paint ($168). Power antenna ($65). AM/FM stereo delete option ($167 credit). AM/FM electronically-tuned stereo with cassette tape player ($117). Graphic equalizer ($200). Premium sound system ($155). Articulated sport seats ($168). 6-way power driver's seat ($220). Dual 6-way power seats ($440). Dual power recliners ($174). Speed control ($162). Leather steering wheel ($54). Tilt steering column ($106). Vinyl seat trim ($34). Leather seat trim ($380). TripMinder computer in T-Bird ($255). TripMinder computer in Elan Coupe and Turbo Coupe ($198). Front vent windows ($73). Locking wire wheel covers ($195). Cast-aluminum wheels ($315). Styled road wheels ($164). Power windows ($190). Intermittent windshield wipers ($46). California emissions system ($81), and tinted windshield ($44).

History:

The 1986 T-Bird was introduced on October 3, 1985. Donald E. Peterseen was again Chairman of the Board and CEO of Ford Motor Co. William Clay Ford remained Vice Chairman and Harold A. Poling stayed on as President and Chief Operating Officer of the corporation. Ford Vice President Robert L. Rewey was again the Ford Division's General Manager and Phillip M. Novell continued as divisional General Sales manager. Calendar-year output was 131,383 units. A total of 163,965 T-Birds were produced in the model year. This represented 2.07 percent of the industry total. Of these units, all were made in Lorain, Ohio. Calendar year dealer sales amounted to 144,577 T-Birds, representing 1.8 percent of industry sales. *Motor Trend* tested a Turbo and announced, "There is almost nothing to dislike about the Ford Thunderbird Turbo Coupe." Writer Daniel Charles Ross averaged 18.23 mpg with the car during the 2,493 miles he drove it. His test T-Bird had the three-speed automatic transmission, which came with a slightly less powerful engine. It developed 145 hp at 4400 rpm and 180 lb.-ft. of torque at 3000 rpm. "The car looks like it was designed by someone with an engineering degree from MIT and an art degree from the Sorbonne," Ross wrote. He managed 0-60 mph in 9.29 seconds and estimated that times in the eight second range would be possible with 91 octane gas or premium unleaded fuel. Turbo lag, usually in stop-and-go traffic, was the only problem experienced with the car. NASCAR enacted a number of rules changes affecting the racing T-Birds in 1986. One changed the allowable dimensions for rear spoilers to increase down force. This helped the narrow T-Bird stick better in the corners. Front air dams and larger carburetors were also allowed. Bill Elliott had his frustrations this season, but he managed to take the checkered flag (and $240,000 in prize money) in the Winston 500 at Atlanta International Raceway. T-Birds continued to win stock car races,

1986 Ford Thunderbird two-door Coupe (FMC)

as well as other events, but the Thunderbird dominance of 1985 was not apparent this season. Nevertheless, Ford did a great job promoting its 1985 wins and managed to translate those victories into new-car sales. Thunderbird output for model-year 1986 increased. Ford even exported 2,002 T-Birds to Mexico during calendar 1986.

1987 Thunderbird

Thunderbird — Series 46 — (V-8): Evolutionary styling changes were very apparent on the 1987 T-Bird. The front and rear ends were totally new, along with the hood, roof, rear deck lid, doors and quarter panels. Flush aero-style headlights, notched-in full-width taillights that wrapped around the body corners (to function as side markers) and aerodynamic flush side glass were all new. Antilock brakes and automatic ride control were standard. Standard in the base coupe and LX were a 3.8-liter fuel-injected V-6 and four-speed automatic overdrive transmission. The fancier LX also featured the V-6. A sequentially-injected 5.0-liter V-8 with a four-speed overdrive automatic transmission was optional in these models and standard in a new Sport model. The Turbo Coupe got an air-to-air intercooler. Four standard exterior colors and a record nine Clearcoat Metallic colors were offered for non-Turbo models. Specific stripes were used with specific exterior/interior color combinations. Four interior colors were offered in Turbos, six for other models. Two-tone paint treatments were not available for Turbos. The Turbo Coupe featured a grille less front end and functional hood scoops. There was a large T-Bird emblem on the car's nose. Its engine upgrades reflected research and development done by Ford's SVO (Special Vehicle Operations) branch. It had a new IHI turbocharger designed to optimize low-end and mid-range response and to minimize turbo lag. Also featured were new higher-flow manifolds and a dual exhaust system. The improvements boosted engine output to 190 hp. Standard features included: Air conditioning, diagnostic alert lights (LX, Turbo). Traction-Lok axle (Turbo), maintenance free battery, power front disc/rear drum brakes (except Turbo), four-wheel disc brakes with ABS (Turbo), electronic ignition, 3.8-liter V-6 (except Sport and Turbo), 5.0-liter V-8 (Sport), 2.3-liter EFI turbocharged four-cylinder engine (Turbo), hydraulic engine mounts, remote-control fuel door (Turbo), tinted glass, three-speed heater and defroster, illuminated entry system (LX), high-mount rear brake light, power lock group (LX), automatic ride control (Turbo), gas pressurized shock absorbers, speed control (LX), power steering, tilt steering wheel (LX), special handling package (Sport and Turbo), P215/70R14 black sidewall tires (Base T-Bird and LX), P215/70HR14 black sidewall tires (Sport), P225/60VR16 black sidewall Goodyear Gatorback tires (Turbo). SelectShift automatic transmission (Base T-Bird and LX), automatic overdrive transmission (Sport), 5-speed manual overdrive transmission (Turbo), windshield washer, two-speed electric windshield wipers, halogen headlights, hood scoops (Turbo), fog lamps (Turbo), left-hand remote-control OSRV mirror (Base T-Bird), dual electric remote-control mirrors (Sport, LX and Turbo), luxury wheel covers (Base T-Bird), cast-aluminum wheels (Turbo), styled road wheels (Sport and LX).

VIN:

The VIN was stamped on an aluminum tab riveted to the dashboard on the passenger side and was visible through the windshield. The first symbol 1 = built in the United States. The second symbol F = Ford. The third symbol A = Ford passenger vehicle. The fourth symbol was the type of restraint system. The fifth symbol P = a passenger-type vehicle. The sixth symbol 6 = Thunderbird. The seventh symbol indicated the body type: 0=Standard Coupe, 1=Sport Coupe, 2=LX Coupe and 4=Turbo Coupe. The eighth symbol was the engine: W=140 cid (2.3L) 190 hp turbocharged four-cylinder/manual, W=140 cid (2.3L) 150 hp turbocharged four-cylinder/automatic, 3=232 cid (3.8L)/120-hp V-6 and F=302 cid (5.0L)/150-hp V-8. The ninth symbol was the check digit. The 10th symbol H=the 1987 model year. The 11th symbol denoted the assembly plant: H=Lorain, Ohio. The 12th through 17th symbols were the sequential production numbers of the specific vehicle starting at 100001. The vehicle certification label was located on the rear face of the driver's door. The top part of the label indicates the Thunderbird was manufactured by Ford Motor Company. Directly below this was the month and year of manufacture, plus a statement that the car conformed to federal motor vehicle safety standards in effect on the indicated date of manufacture. VIN: The VIN appeared on the first line of the encoded information. It matched the first to 11th symbols on the VIN tag. Some other codes also appeared. PASSENGER. EXT. COLOR: This line carried the exterior paint color(s) code. DSO: The District Special Order code appeared above "DSO" to the right of the exterior paint color code. BODY: The body style code appeared to the extreme left of the bottom line. The only Thunderbird code for this model-year was: 66D=2-door Pillared Hardtop. VR: The vinyl roof type/color code was to the right of the body code. No T-Birds had vinyl tops. MLDG: The molding code was to the right of the vinyl roof code. INT. TRIM: The interior trim code was to the right of the molding code. A/C: The air conditioning code was to the right of the interior trim code. Cars with air conditioning had "A" stamped here. R: The radio code was to the right of the A/C code. S: The sunroof code appeared to the right of the radio code. AX: The axle code appeared to the right of the sun roof code. TR:The transmission code appeared to the right of the axle code. **Note:** The terms and abbreviations shown in capitals appeared on the lline above the actual codes.

Thunderbird (V-6)

Series No.	Body/ Style No.	Body Type and Seating	Factory Price	Shipping Weight	Production Total
60	66D	2-dr. Coupe-4P	$12,972	3,133 lbs.	Note 1

Thunderbird (V-8)

60	66D	2-dr. Coupe-4P	$13,611	3,272 lbs.	Note 1

Thunderbird Sport (V-8)

61	66D	2-dr. Coupe-4P	$15,079	3,346 lbs.	Note 1

Thunderbird LX (V-6)

62	66D	2-dr. Coupe-4P	$15,383	3,176 lbs.	Note 1

Thunderbird LX (V-8)

62	66D	2-dr. Coupe-4P	$16,022	3,315 lbs.	Note 1

Turbo Coupe (Four)

64	66D	2-dr. Coupe-4P	$16,805	3,380 lbs.	Note 1

Note 1: Production of the all models combined was 128,135.

Engines:

Thunderbird Base V-6: 90-degree, overhead valve. Cast-iron block and aluminum head. Displacement: 232 cid (3.8 liters). B & S: 3.80 x 3.40 in. Compression ratio: 8.7:1. Brake hp: 120 at 3600. Torque: 205 lbs.-ft. at 1600. Four main bearings. Hydraulic valve lifters. Induction: Throttle Body Injection. Code: 3.

Thunderbird Turbo Coupe Base Turbo Four (Automatic): In-line. Overhead valve. Cast-iron block and head. Displacement: 140 cid (2.3 liters). B & S: 3.78 x 3.13 in. Compression ratio: 8.0:1. Brake hp: 150 at 4400. Five main bearings. Hydraulic valve lifters. Induction: Multi-Point Electronic Fuel injection. Garrett AIResearch T-03 turbocharger. Code: W.

Thunderbird Turbo Coupe Base Turbo Four: In-line. Overhead valve. Cast-iron block and head. Displacement: 140 cid (2.3 liters). B & S: 3.78 x 3.13 in. Compression ratio: 8.0:1. Brake hp: 190 at 4600. Torque: 240 lbs.-ft. at 3400. Five main bearings. Hydraulic valve lifters. Induction: Multi-Point Electronic Fuel injection. Garrett AIResearch T-03 turbocharger. Code: W.

Thunderbird Optional V-8: 90-degree, overhead valve. Cast-iron block and head. Displacement: 302 cid (5.0 liters). B & S: 4.00 x 3.00 in. Compression ratio: 8.9:1. Brake hp: 150 at 3200 rpm. Torque: 270 lbs.-ft. at 2000 rpm. Five main bearings. Hydraulic valve lifters. Induction: Sequential (port) fuel injection. Code: F.

1987 Ford Thunderbird two-door Coupe (FMC)

Chassis:

Wheelbase: 104.2 in. Overall length: 202.1. Overall width: 71.1. Overall height: 53.4 in. Front headroom: 37.7 in. Front legroom: 42 in. Front shoulder room: 55.2 in. Rear headroom: 36.7 in. Rear legroom: 34.3 in. Trunk capacity: 14.6 cu. ft. Front tread: 58.1 in. Rear tread: 58.5 in. Tires: P195/75R14 white sidewall steel-belted radial.

Technical:

Steering: Variable-ratio, power, rack-and-pinion. Steering ratio: 15.0-13.0:1 (15.1:1 on Turbo Coupe). Turning diameter: 38.6 ft. Turns lock-to-lock: 2.5. Front suspension: Modified McPherson strut. Rear suspension: Four-link-bar (quad shocks on Turbo Coupe). Weight distribution: 53/47 percent front/rear. Power to Weight ratio: 20.56 lb./hp. Steering: Variable-ratio power rack and pinion. Standard rear axle: 2.73:1. Front brakes: Power disc. Rear brakes: Power drum. Brakes swept area: 275.6 sq. in. Rear axle (with five-speed manual transmission): 3.45:1. Rear Axle (with three-speed automatic transmission): 2.47:1. Rear axle (four-speed automatic transmission): 3.08:1. Fuel tank capacity: 18.2 gallons.

Options:

5.0-liter V-8, except standard on Sport ($639). 4-speed automatic overdrive transmission, optional on Turbo ($515). P215/70R14 tires on standard Base T-Bird and LX ($72 extra). Conventional spare tire ($73). Heavy-duty 54-amp. battery ($27). Electronic equipment group, on Base T-Bird ($634), on Sport and Turbo ($365), on LX ($577). Front floor mats ($30). Luxury light and convenience group, on Base T-Bird ($461), on Base T-Bird with electronic equipment group ($379), on Sport and Turbo ($426), on Sport and Turbo with electronic equipment group ($344), on LX ($244). Dual power seat, on Base T-Bird and LX and Sport ($302), on Turbo or LX with articulated seats ($251). Power antenna ($76). Front license plate bracket (no charge). Electronic digital clock ($61). Rear window defroster ($145). Engine block immersion heater ($18). Power lock group ($249). Dual electric remote-control mirrors ($96). Moon roof, on Base T-Bird, Turbo or Sport ($801), on LX or with luxury and lights package ($741). Premium luxury package, standard on models with value option package 151A, on Sport model with 154A ($829), on Turbo with 157A ($717), AM/FM stereo credit ($206). Electronic AM/FM stereo with cassette tape player ($137). Graphic equalizer ($218). Premium sound system ($168). 6-way power driver's seat ($251). Speed control ($176). Leather-wrapped luxury steering wheel ($59). Tilt steering wheel ($124). Body side and deck lid stripes ($55). Locking wire style wheel covers, on LX or with 151A package, above price of road wheels ($90), with standard Base T-Bird over price of luxury wheel covers ($212). Cast aluminum wheels, on LX or Sport with 151A package ($89), on Base T-Bird ($211). Styled road wheels ($122). Power side windows ($222). California emissions system ($55). High-altitude emissions system ($99). Two-tone paint treatment Base T-Bird, cost over body side and deck lid striping or LX ($218), on LX with 151A package ($163). Clearcoat paint ($183). Articulated Sport seats ($183). Vinyl trim ($37). Leather trim ($415). Base T-Bird Value Option Package151A (($1,329-$1,402). Sport Value Option Package 154A (#$986-$1,009). LX Value Option Package 161A (no charge to $73). Select LX Value Option Package 162A (($807-$830). Turbo Value Option Package 157A (no charge to $72).

History:

The 1987 T-Bird was introduced on October 2, 1986. Donald E. Peterseen was Chairman of the Board and CEO of Ford Motor Co. William Clay Ford was Vice Chairman. Harold A. Poling was President and Chief Operating Officer of the corporation. Ford Vice President Robert L. Rewey was the Ford Division's General Manager and Phillip M. Novell was divisional General Sales manager. Calendar-year output was 157,507 units. A total of 128,135 T-Birds were produced in the model year. This represented 1.74 percent of the industry total. Of these units, all were made in Lorain, Ohio. Calendar year dealer sales amounted to 126,767 T-Birds, representing 1.7 percent of industry sales. A "Preview Test" by Gary Witzenberg in the October 1986 issue of *Motor Trend* put the 1987 T-Bird Turbo Coupe through its paces. Witzenberg did some brief measured tests at Ford's proving grounds in Romeo, Michigan and recorded 0-to-60-mph performance at 8.4 seconds. The car did the standing quarter-mile in 16.13 seconds and 81.8 mph. It also exhibited improved handling and braking, as well as an outstanding "high-performance" premium sound system. "We've liked Ford's T-Bird — especially the sleek-looking, smart-handling Turbo Coupe — since its '83 reincarnation," said Witzenberg in his summary. "We like it even better for 1987, and we'll likely go on liking it for some time to come. Think of it as the average man's 635csi and you won't be far wrong." *Motor Trend* gave the 1987 T-Bird Turbo Coupe its "Car of the Year" award. *Road & Track* (August 1987) also wrung out the Turbo. The handling and braking abilities of the T-Bird were highly praised and the writer said it had an "attractive shape." The magazine liked the handsome body design, the ABS brakes and the advantage

1987 Ford Thunderbird Turbo two-door Coupe (FMC)

of a large dealer network. In racing, Bill Elliott and Kyle Petty were two of the leading drivers of T-Bird stock cars. In fact, Ford's ads were still making hay over the records Elliott established during 1985. Davey Allison, driver of the number 28 Havoline T-Bird, was 1987 "Rookie of the Year" and the first driver to ever win more than one Winston Cup event in his first season on the circuit. In drag racing, Ford had the winningest driver in the history of NHRA competition. Bob Glidden's bright red 1987 Pro Stock T-Bird helped him become the only seven-time NHRA World Champion. Unfortunately, not everyone liked the '87 T-Birds as much as *Motor Trend*, although production totals clearly suggest that the "Car of the Year" honors helped Ford sell more Turbo models that year. Overall output dropped to 128,135 T-Birds and a 1.74 percent share of industry in model-year 1987. The Lorain, Ohio factory accounted for all 128,135 units. Of these, 122,059 were made for sale in the U.S. This total included 59.2 percent with a V-6 and 22.2 percent with a V-8. However, Turbo Coupe output climbed to an all-time high of 23,833 cars or 18.6 percent of all domestic-market T-Birds. Accordingly, a record high 12 percent had five-speed transmissions this season.

1988 Thunderbird

Thunderbird — Series 46 — (V-8): Minor changes, many hidden, separated 1987 and 1988 T-Birds. The 1988 model was available in base Coupe and LX (V-6 or V-8), Sport (V-8 only) and Turbo Coupe (four-cylinder turbocharged) models. Sport models now had analog gauges and came with articulated sport seats. Five regular and nine Clearcoat Metallic colors were offered for base and LX models and five could be had in two-tone combinations. Eight different color-coordinated stripes were used, but only in specific combinations. There were five monotone interiors. Sport models could only be had in two of the 14 exterior hues and with four interior shades only. Turbo Coupes came in just two conventional colors and five Clearcoat Metallics. A Raven-colored interior was exclusive to this model, but the Medium Gray and Cinnabar interiors could not be ordered for the Turbo. Multi-point fuel injection replaced the former single-point system in the T-Bird's base V-6 engine this year. This boosted horsepower by 20. Inside the engine was a new balance shaft that produced smoother-running operation. Dual exhausts were now standard with the 5.0-liter V-8, which was standard in the Sport model and optional in the base and LX models. Standard features included: All standard FoMoCo safety, anti-theft, convenience items, and emissions control equipment, 3.8-liter MPEFI V-6, automatic overdrive transmission, power rack and pinion steering, front disc/rear drum brakes, modified McPherson strut front suspension with variable rate springs and gas-pressurized struts, four-bar-link rear suspension with variable-rate springs and gas-pressurized shock absorbers, P215/70Rx14 black sidewall all-season tires, dual aerodynamic halogen headlamps, wide body side moldings, luxury wheel covers, bright windshield moldings, bright side window moldings, bright back window moldings, black bumper rub strips and extensions with bright insert, left-hand remote-control mirror, air conditioning, tinted glass, safety belt reminder chimes, deep-well trunk with mini spare tire, luggage compartment light, 16-oz. color-keyed cut-pile carpeting, electronic digital clock, ash tray lights, continuous color-keyed safety belts with comfort regulator feature, LCD speedometer with trip odometer, and electronic AM/FM stereo radio with four speakers (may be deleted for credit.

Thunderbird Sport: The Thunderbird Sport model adds or substitutes the following features over base Thunderbird equipment: an 5.0-liter EFI V-8 engine, handling suspension including quadra-shock rear suspension, heavy-duty battery, Traction-Lok axle, dual-note Sport-tuned horn, P215/70HRx14 speed-rated handling tires, styled road wheels, black windshield moldings, black side window moldings, black rear window moldings, adjustable articulated sport seats, 24-oz. luxury carpeting, light group with dual beam map light, instrument panel courtesy lights, and

1988 Ford Thunderbird two-door Coupe (FMC)

engine compartment light, full analog instrumentation, Systems Sentry diagnostic alert lights, leather-wrapped steering wheel, tunnel-mounted shift with leather-wrapped handle, full console with covered storage compartment lid/arm rest, and speed control.

Thunderbird LX: The Thunderbird LX model adds or substitutes the following features over base Thunderbird equipment: an automatic parking brake release, body side and deck lid accent stripes, dual remote-control electric mirrors, luxury cloth split-bench seats in special sew style with 4-way headrests, 24-oz, luxury carpet, light group with dual beam map light, instrument panel courtesy lights, and engine compartment light, luxury door and quarter trim panels, Systems Sentry diagnostic alert lights, leather-wrapped steering wheel, electronic AM/FM stereo radio with four speakers and cassette tape player, illuminated entry system, power side windows, interval windshield wipers, speed control, tilt steering, power lock group with power door locks, remote deck lid release in glove box, and remote fuel filler door release in glove box, and power driver's seat.

Thunderbird Turbo Coupe: The Thunderbird Turbo Coupe model adds or substitutes the following features over base Thunderbird equipment: an 2.3-liter overhead cam turbocharged engine with EFI, air-to-air intercooler, and regular/premium fuel selection, 5-speed manual overdrive transmission, power 4-wheel disc brakes with electronic antilock system (ABS), special handling package including automatic ride control and quadra-shock rear suspension, heavy-duty battery, Traction-Lok rear axle, remote-control fuel filler door release, dual-note Sport-tuned horn, automatic parking brake release, P225/60VRx16 black sidewall performance tires and unique 16 x 7-in. diameter aluminum wheels, unique front fascia with Hella fog lights, black windshield, side window and rear window moldings, red insert replacing bright metal insert on black bumper rub strips, dual intercooler hood scoops, dual remote-control electric mirrors, adjustable articulated sport seats, 24-oz. luxury carpet, light group with dual beam map light, instrument panel courtesy lights, and engine compartment light, luxury door and quarter trim panels, full analog instrumentation, Systems Sentry diagnostic alert lights, Soft Feel steering wheel, tunnel-mounted shift with leather-wrapped handle, full Console with covered storage compartment lid/arm rest, power side windows, and interval windshield wipers.

VIN:

The VIN was stamped on an aluminum tab riveted to the dashboard on the passenger side and was visible through the windshield. The first symbol 1 = built in the United States. The second symbol F = Ford. The third symbol A meant a Ford passenger vehicle. The fourth symbol was the type of restraint system. The fifth symbol P = a passenger-type vehicle. The sixth symbol 6 = Thunderbird. The seventh symbol denoted the body type: 0=Standard Coupe, 1=Sport Coupe, 2=LX Coupe and 4=Turbo Coupe. The eighth symbol indicated the engine: W=140 cid (2.3L) 190 hp turbocharged four-cylinder/manual, W=140 cid (2.3L) 150 hp turbocharged four-cylinder/automatic, 3=232 cid (3.8L)/140-hp V-6 and F=302 cid (5.0L)/155-hp V-8. The ninth symbol was the check digit. The 10th symbol J = the1988 model year. The 11th symbol denoted the assembly plant: H=Lorain, Ohio. The 12th through 17th symbols were the sequential production numbers of the specific vehicle starting

1988 Ford Thunderbird LX two-door Coupe

at 100001. The vehicle certification label was located on the rear face of the driver's door. The top part of the label indicated the Thunderbird was manufactured by Ford Motor Company. Directly below this was the month and year of manufacture, plus a statement that the car conformed to the federal motor vehicle safety standards in effect on the indicated date of manufacture. VIN: The VIN appeared on the first line of encoded information. It matched the first to 11th symbols on the VIN tag. Some other codes also appeared. PASSENGER. EXT. COLOR: This line carried the exterior paint color(s) code. DSO: The District Special Order code appeared above "DSO" to the right of the exterior paint color code. BODY: The body style code appeared to the extreme left of the bottom line. The only Thunderbird code for this model-year was: 66D=2-door Pillared Hardtop. VR: The vinyl roof type/color code was to the right of the body code. No T-Birds had vinyl tops. MLDG: The molding code was to the right of the vinyl roof code. INT. TRIM: The interior trim code was to the right of the molding code. A/C: The air conditioning code was to the right of the interior trim code. Cars with air conditioning had "A" stamped here. R: The radio code was to the right of the A/C code. S: The sunroof code appeared to the right of the radio code. AX: The axle code appeared to the right of the sun roof code. TR: The transmission code appeared to the right of the axle code. Note: The terms and abbreviations shown in capitals appeared on the line above the actual codes.

Thunderbird (V-6)

Series No.	Body/Style No.	Body Type and Seating	Factory Price	Shipping Weight	Production Total
60	66D	2-dr. Coupe-4P	$13,599	3,215 lbs.	Note 1

Thunderbird (V-8)

Series No.	Body/Style No.	Body Type and Seating	Factory Price	Shipping Weight	Production Total
60	66D	2-dr. Coupe-4P	$14,320	3,345 lbs.	Note 1

Thunderbird Sport (V-8)

Series No.	Body/Style No.	Body Type and Seating	Factory Price	Shipping Weight	Production Total
61	66D	2-dr. Coupe-4P	$16,030	3,450 lbs.	Note 1

Thunderbird LX (V-6)

Series No.	Body/Style No.	Body Type and Seating	Factory Price	Shipping Weight	Production Total
62	66D	2-dr. Coupe-4P	$15,885	3,529 lbs.	Note 1

Thunderbird LX (V-8)

Series No.	Body/Style No.	Body Type and Seating	Factory Price	Shipping Weight	Production Total
62	66D	2-dr. Coupe-4P	$16,606	3,389 lbs.	Note 1

Turbo Coupe (Four)

Series No.	Body/Style No.	Body Type and Seating	Factory Price	Shipping Weight	Production Total
64	66D	2-dr. Coupe-4P	$17,250	3,415 lbs.	Note 1

Note 1: Production of the all models combined was 147,243.

Engines:

Thunderbird Base V-6: 90-degree, overhead valve. Cast-iron block and aluminum head. Displacement: 232 cid (3.8 liters). B & S: 3.80 x 3.40 in. Compression ratio: 9.0:1. Brake hp: 140 at 3800. Torque: 215 lbs.-ft. at 2400. Four main bearings. Hydraulic valve lifters. Induction: Throttle Body Injection. Code: 3.

Thunderbird Turbo Coupe Base Turbo Four (Automatic): In-line. Overhead valve. Cast-iron block and head. Displacement: 140 cid (2.3 liters). B & S: 3.78 x 3.13 in. Compression ratio: 8.0:1. Brake hp: 150 at 4400. Five main bearings. Hydraulic valve lifters. Induction: Multi-Point Electronic Fuel injection. Garrett AIResearch T-03 turbocharger. Code: W.

Thunderbird Turbo Coupe Base Turbo Four: In-line. Overhead valve. Cast-iron block and head. Displacement: 140 cid (2.3 liters). B & S: 3.78 x 3.13 in. Compression ratio: 8.0:1. Brake hp: 190 at 4600. Torque: 240 lbs.-ft. at 3400. Five main bearings. Hydraulic valve lifters. Induction: Multi-Point Electronic Fuel injection. Garrett AIResearch T-03 turbocharger. Code: W.

Thunderbird Optional V-8: 90-degree, overhead valve. Cast-iron block and head. Displacement: 302 cid (5.0 liters). B & S: 4.00 x 3.00 in. Compression ratio: 8.9:1. Brake hp: 155 at 3400 rpm. Torque: 265 lbs.-ft. at 2200 rpm. Five main bearings. Roller cam. Induction: Sequential (port) fuel injection. Code F.

Chassis:

Wheelbase: 104.2 in. Overall length: 202.1. Overall width: 71.1. Overall height: 53.4 in. Front headroom: 37.7 in. Front legroom: 42 in. Front shoulder room: 55.2 in. Rear headroom: 36.7 in. Rear legroom: 34.3 in. Trunk capacity: 14.6 cu. ft. Front tread: 58.1 in. Rear tread: 58.5 in. Tires: P195/75R14 white sidewall steel-belted radial.

Technical:

Steering: Variable-ratio, power, rack-and-pinion. Steering ratio: 15.0-13.0:1 (15.1:1 on Turbo Coupe). Turning diameter: 38.6 ft. Turns lock-to-lock: 2.5. Front suspension: Modified McPherson strut. Rear suspension: Four-link-bar (quad shocks on Turbo Coupe). Weight distribution: 53/47 percent front/rear. Power to Weight ratio: 20.56 lb./hp. Steering: Variable-ratio power rack and pinion. Standard rear axle: 2.73:1. Front brakes: Power disc. Rear brakes: Power

1988 Ford Thunderbird Turbo two-door Coupe (PH)

drum. Brakes swept area: 275.6 sq. in. Rear axle (with five-speed manual transmission): 3.45:1. Rear Axle (with three-speed automatic transmission): 2.47:1. Rear axle (four-speed automatic transmission): 3.08:1. Fuel tank capacity: 21 gallons.

Options:

5.0-liter V-8, except standard in Sport and Turbo Coupe ($639). 4-speed automatic overdrive transmission, optional on Turbo ($515). Heavy-duty battery in base T-Bird and LX ($27). Styled road wheels on base T-Bird ($122). Cast aluminum wheels, on LX or Sport with 151A package ($89), on Base T-Bird ($211). Locking wire style wheel covers, on LX or base T-Bird with 151A package, above price of road wheels ($90), with standard Base T-Bird over price of luxury wheel covers ($212). Body side and deck lid stripes on base T-Bird or Sport models ($55). Two-tone paint treatment on base T-Bird, cost over body side and deck lid striping or LX ($218), on LX with 151A package ($163). Dual electric remote-control mirrors on base T-Bird or Sport ($96). Moon roof, on Base T-Bird, Turbo or Sport ($801), on LX or with luxury and lights package ($741). Leather trim, except base T-Bird ($415). Light group, on Base T-Bird (N/A). Systems Sentry diagnostic alert lights, on base T-Bird (N/A). Electronic AM/FM stereo with cassette tape player, on all except LX ($137). Premium sound system, optional all models ($168). Graphic equalizer , optional all models ($218). Illuminated entry system, except LX (N/A). Power side windows in base T-Bird and Sport ($222). Interval windshield wipers, in base T-Bird or Sport (N/A). Speed control on base T-Bird or Turbo Coupe ($176). Tilt steering wheel, except LX ($124). Power lock group, except LX ($249). 6-way power driver's seat, except LX ($251). Power antenna, all ($76). Luxury light and convenience group, on Base T-Bird ($461), on Base T-Bird with electronic equipment group ($379), on Sport and Turbo ($426), on Sport and Turbo with electronic equipment group ($344), on LX ($244). Electronic equipment group, on Base T-Bird ($634), on Sport and Turbo ($365), on LX ($577). Dual power seat, on Base T-Bird and LX and Sport ($302), on Turbo or LX with articulated seats ($251). Front floor mats ($30).PEP 140A includes P215/70R14 tires, automatic overdrive transmission, and dual electric mirrors for base T-Bird (N/A). PEP 141A includes P215/70R14 tires, automatic overdrive transmission, dual electric mirrors, light group, electronic AM/FM stereo with cassette, interval wipers, premium sound system, front floor mats, and styled road wheels for base T-Bird (N/A). PEP 142A includes P215/70R14 tires, automatic overdrive transmission, dual electric mirrors, light group, electronic AM/FM stereo with cassette, interval wipers, premium sound system, front floor mats, styled road wheels, and manual temperature control air conditioning for base T-Bird (N/A). PEP 145A includes P215/70HRx14 handling tires, automatic overdrive transmission, dual electric mirrors, light group, electronic AM/FM stereo with cassette, interval windshield wipers, styled road wheels, manual air conditioning, power lock group, power side windows, tilt steering, speed control, and 6-way power driver's seat for Sport T-bird (N/A). PEP 150A includes P215/70Rx14 all-season tires, automatic overdrive transmission, dual electric mirrors, light group, electronic AM/FM stereo with cassette, interval windshield wipers, styled road wheels, power lock group, power side windows, tilt steering, speed control, and 6-way power driver's seat for LX T-bird (N/A). Extra Value Package 151A includes P215/70Rx14 all-season tires, automatic overdrive transmission, dual electric mirrors, light group, electronic AM/FM stereo with cassette, interval windshield wipers, front floor mats, manual air conditioning, power lock group, power side windows, tilt steering, speed control, dual power seats with recliners, power radio antenna, keyless entry system, luxury light and convenience group, graphic equalizer, and wire wheel covers for LX T-bird (N/A).

Extra Value Package 155A includes 5-speed manual overdrive transmission, P225/60VRx16 black sidewall tires, power side windows, dual electric mirrors, interval wipers, manual air conditioning, light group, power lock group, electronic AM/FM stereo with cassette, speed control, tilt steering, and power driver's seat for T-Bird Turbo Coupe (N/A). Extra Value Package 156A includes 5-speed manual overdrive transmission, P225/60VRx16 black sidewall tires, power side windows, dual electric mirrors, interval wipers, manual air conditioning, light group, front floor mats, luxury light and convenience group, premium sound system, power radio antenna, power lock group, electronic AM/FM stereo with cassette, speed control, tilt steering, and power driver's seat for T-Bird Turbo Coupe (N/A).

History:

The 1987 T-Bird was introduced on October 1, 1987. Donald E. Peterseen was Chairman of the Board and CEO of Ford Motor Co. William Clay Ford was Vice Chairman. Harold A. Poling was President and Chief Operating Officer of the corporation. Ford Vice Thomas J. Wagner was the Ford Division's new General Manager and Richard L. Fenstermacher was divisional General Sales manager. Calendar-year output was 111,760 units. A total of 147,243 T-Birds were produced in the model year. This represented 2.11 percent of the industry total. Of these units, all were made in Lorain, Ohio. Calendar year dealer sales amounted to 117,866 T-Birds, representing 5.8 percent of industry sales. *Motor Trend's* December 1987 issue was a special issue devoted to Ford and included a "Retrospect" on the 1955 T-Bird. Included in the issue was a road test of the T-Bird Turbo Coupe. The article written by Don Fuller carried a Ford-friendly title, "Thunderbird Turbo Coupe: Redefining the American high-tech performance car." Fuller described the Turbo as "the dream of every enthusiast who has waited for all the positive elements of the modern age to be wrapped up in one American roadburner." One of the highlights of the article was a fabulous, two-page 3/4-front view phantom illustration of the 1988 Turbo Coupe drawn by David Kimble. Ford's factory racing efforts were also covered. In NASCAR racing Bill Elliott won the 1988 Winston Cup with his Coors/Melling T-Bird. However, his most exciting experience of the year probably came two days after he took the checkered flag at the 1988 *Atlanta Journal* 500 race. That's when he went to Dobbin Air Force Base, in Marietta, Ga., to film a recruiting commercial for the U.S. Air Force. Like many race car drivers, Elliott is a pilot and has an interest in flying. He was offered the opportunity to take an "orientation" flight in an F-16 fighter aircraft. During this flight, the F-16 was attempting a maneuver and struck a Georgia National Guard F-15 Eagle. The pilot bailed out of the damaged Eagle, while USAF Major Wayne F. Conroy was able to get the F-16, with Elliott aboard, back safely. "I think I'll go home and have a nervous breakdown," Elliott cracked, after being asked to compare the crash to driving a race car. Although Elliott took the cup, Chevrolet was able to walk off with the Manufacturer's Championship again in 1988. However, the margin of winning was a slim two (2) points. Other 1988 Ford drivers included Davey Allison of Hueytown, Ala., Kyle Petty of High Point, N.C., Ralph Jones of Upton, Ken., Derrike Cope of Charlotte, N.C., Benny Parsons of Ellerbe, N.C., Brett Bodine of Chemung, N.Y., Phil Barkdoll of Phoenix, Ariz., Mark Martin of Batesville, Ar., and Alan Kulwicki of Concord, N.C. Kulwicki won his first Winston Cup race during 1988. Another name associated with Ford was that of IHRA driver Floyd Cheek. His dragracing T-'Bird was champion in the 8.90-second class.

1989 Thunderbird

Thunderbird — Series 46 — (V-8): The 1989 T-Bird was a completely redesigned rear-drive model with a longer wheelbase and lower profile. A "grille-less" front end emphasized lowness and width. New flush-fitting headlights were of low-profile, composite design. The parking lamps swept around the body corners to function as side marker lights. The hood dipped between the headlights and carried a T-Bird emblem on its center. A unique trapezoid-shaped greenhouse featured increased glass area. Thin rear roof pillars minimized blind spots. The full-width taillights had a T-Bird insignia on each side. A new Super Coupe (replacing the Turbo Coupe) featured a different frontal treatment with a large horizontal air intake below each headlight and "SC" embossed in the bumper. It also had a front spoiler, narrow body side skirting, a lower rear valance incorporating an air extractor and a supercharged 3.8-liter V-6 coupled to a five-speed manual gear box. A four-speed automatic transmission was extra. The base Coupe came loaded and the LX added fancier trim, electronic instrumentation, power locks, a cassette player and styled road wheel covers. The Super Coupe had 16-in. cast aluminum wheels, fat performance tires and front fog lights. A new T-Bird interior featured reclining bucket seats, a floor-length console, a floor shift and new motorized front seat belts Cloth seating surfaces and vinyl trim was standard. The LX included luxury cloth seat trim, a leather-wrapped steering wheel and a six-way power driver's seat. The articulated seats used in the Super Coupe had power lumbar and seat back bolster adjustments. A total of 11 exterior finishes (seven Metallic Clearcoats) and four different color-keyed interiors were offered on base and LX

models. Three regular and two Metallic Clearcoat colors were available for the Super Coupe, which also had three interior color options. The 3.8-liter V-6 received friction-reducing roller tappets, light-weight magnesium rocker covers and an aluminum-hub crankshaft damper. Sequential operation of the multi-port EFI system enhanced the precision of fuel delivery system. A new "distributorless" ignition system used electronic engine controls. For exceptionally smooth operation, Ford used hydraulic engine mounts and isolation in the third cross member. The Super Coupe engine used a custom-made Roots-type positive displacement supercharger for its power boost. The engine crankshaft drove the 90-cid supercharger via a poly v-belt running at 2.6 times crankshaft speed. This produced a maximum boost of 12 psi at 4000 rpm. Twin three-lobe helical rotors helped the blower do its work more smoothly and quietly. It also had an engine oil cooler and an intercooler to lower intake air temperature. T-Birds had a new four-wheel independent suspension. On standard and LX models, a long-spindle short and long arm (SLA) setup was used in front, along with variable-rate coil springs, double-acting gas-pressurized shocks, and a .27-mm stabilizer bar. At the rear there was also an SLA setup with toe control link, plus variable-rate springs, gas shocks and a .25-mm diameter stabilizer. The Super Coupe added Automatic Ride Control to the front and rear suspensions, plus beefier stabilizer bars at both ends. Power rack-and-pinion steering with a 14.1:1 ratio on center was standard. It was speed-sensitive on the LX and Super Coupe. Standard features include: all standard FoMoCo safety, anti-theft, convenience items and emissions control equipment, 3.8-liter V-6, automatic overdrive transmission, power-assisted antilock braking system, four-wheel disc brakes, 15 x 6-in. stamped steel wheels, P205/70R15 black sidewall tires, air conditioning, tinted glass, power steering, power brakes, power windows, side window defoggers, interval windshield wipers, front automatic seat belt restraint system, full-length console with floor-mounted shifter, vinyl door trim with storage bins, cloth bucket seats with recliners, analog instrumentation, electronic AM/FM stereo search radio with digital clock (may be deleted for credit), left-hand remote-control OSRV mirror, wide body side protection moldings, deluxe wheel covers, all-season radial tires and 5-mph color-keyed bumpers.

Thunderbird LX: The Thunderbird LX model adds or substitutes the following features over base Thunderbird equipment: Luxury cloth seats with recliners, six-way power driver's seat, luxury door trim and carpeting, electronic instrument cluster, instrument panel upper storage compartment, illuminated entry system and convenience lights, speed control and tilt steering wheel, speed-sensitive power steering, leather-wrapped luxury steering wheel, illuminated visor mirrors, power lock group, electronic AM/FM stereo search radio with cassette and digital clock, rear seat center arm rest, vehicle maintenance monitor, remote release fuel door, dual electric remote-control mirrors, bright window moldings and styled road wheel covers.

Thunderbird Super Coupe: The Thunderbird Super Coupe model adds or substitutes the following features over base Thunderbird equipment: 3.8-liter supercharged and inter-cooled V-6 with dual exhausts, five-speed manual transmission, automatic ride control system, heavier front and rear stabilizer bars, Traction-Lok differential, 16 x 7-in. cast-aluminum wheels, Goodyear Eagle P225/60VR16 performance tires, articulated sports seats with power lumbar and power seat back bolster adjustments, sport soft-feel steering wheel, luxury door trim and carpeting, instrument panel upper storage compartment, performance instrumentation, vehicle maintenance monitor, fog lamps, narrow body side moldings and lower body side cladding, anti-lock braking system with 4-wheel disc brakes, Traction-Lok differential, speed-sensitive power steering, dual electric remote-control mirrors, heavy-duty battery and heavy-duty alternator.

VIN:

The VIN was stamped on an aluminum tab riveted to the dashboard on the passenger side and was visible through the windshield. The first symbol 1 = built in the United States. The second symbol F = Ford. The third symbol A = Ford passenger vehicle. The fourth was the type of restraint system. The fifth symbol P meant a passenger-type vehicle.

1989 Ford Thunderbird two-door Super Coupe

The Sixth symbol (6) denoted Thunderbird. The seventh symbol was the body type: 0=Standard Coupe, 2=LX Coupe and 4=Super Coupe. The eighth symbol indicated the engine: 4=232 cid (3.8L) 140 hp V-6 and R=232 cid (3.6L) 210 hp supercharged V-6. The ninth symbol was the check digit. The 10th symbol K=1989 model year. The 11th symbol revealed the assembly plant: H=Lorain, Ohio. The 12th through 17th symbols were the sequential production numbers of the specific vehicles starting at 100001. The vehicle certification label was located on the rear face of the driver's door. The top part of the label indicated the Thunderbird was manufactured by Ford Motor Company. Directly below this was the month and year of manufacture, plus a statement that the car conformed to the federal motor vehicle safety standards in effect on the indicated date of manufacture. VIN: The VIN appeared on the first line of encoded information. It matched the first to 11th symbols on the VIN tag. Some other codes also appeared. PASSENGER. EXT. COLOR: This line carried the exterior paint color(s) code. DSO: The District Special Order code now appeared above "DSO" to the right of the exterior paint color codes. BODY: The body style code appeared to the extreme left of the bottom line. The only Thunderbird code for this model-year was: BS2=2-door Pillared Hardtop. VR: The vinyl roof type/color code was to the right of the body code. No T-Birds had vinyl tops. MLDG: The molding code was to the right of the vinyl roof code. INT. TRIM: The interior trim code was to the right of the molding code. A/C: The air conditioning code was to the right of the interior trim code. Cars with air conditioning had "A" stamped here. R: The radio code was to the right of the A/C code. S: The sunroof code appeared to the right of the radio code. AX: The axle code appeared to the right of the sun roof code. TR: The transmission code appeared to the right of the axle code. Note: The terms and abbreviations shown in capitals appeared on the line above the actual codes.

Thunderbird (V-6)

Series No.	Body/ Style No.	Body Type and Seating	Factory Price	Shipping Weight	Production Total
60	66D	2-dr. Convertible-2P	$14,612	3,542 lbs.	Note 1

Thunderbird LX (V-6)

Series No.	Body/ Style No.	Body Type and Seating	Factory Price	Shipping Weight	Production Total
62	66D	2-dr. Coupe-4P	$16,817	3,554 lbs.	Note 1

Thunderbird LX (V-6)

Series No.	Body/ Style No.	Body Type and Seating	Factory Price	Shipping Weight	Production Total
64	66D	2-dr. Coupe-4P	$19,823	3,701 lbs.	Note 1

Note 1: The production total was not available.

Engines:

Thunderbird Base V-6: 90-degree, overhead valve. Cast-iron block and aluminum head. Displacement: 232 cid (3.8 liters). B & S: 3.80 x 3.40 in. Compression ratio: 9.0:1. Brake hp: 140 at 3800. Torque: 215 lbs.-ft. at 2400. Four main bearings. Hydraulic valve lifters. Induction: Throttle Body Injection. Code: 4.

Thunderbird Super Coupe Supercharged V-6: 90-degree, overhead valve V-6. Cast-iron block and aluminum head. Displacement: 232 cid (3.8 liters). B & S: 3.80 x 3.40 in. Compression ratio: 8.3:1. Brake hp: 210 at 4000. Torque: 315 lbs.-ft. at 2600. Four main bearings. Hydraulic valve lifters. Induction: Sequential Electronic Fuel Injection (Supercharged). Code: R.

Chassis:

Wheelbase: 113 in. Overall length: 198.7. Overall width: 72.7. Overall height: 52.7 in. Front tread: 61.6 in. Rear tread: 60.2 in. Tires: P205/70R14 white sidewall steel-belted radial.

Technical:

Steering ratio: 14.1:1. Turning diameter: 38.6 ft. Turns lock-to-lock: 2.5. Front suspension: Independent, upper and lower control arms, coil springs, tubular shocks and anti-roll bar. Rear suspension Live axle, four-link control arms, coil springs, adjustable tubular shocks and anti-roll bar. Weight distribution: 53/47 percent front/rear. Power to Weight ratio: 20.56 lb./hp. Front brakes: Power vented disc. Rear brakes: Power drum. Fuel tank capacity: 19 gallons.

Options:

Four-speed overdrive transmission on Super Coupe ($539). P205/75R15 white sidewall tires ($73). Eagle GT + 4 P225/60VR16 black sidewall all-season performance tires, Super Coupe only ($73). Conventional spare tire in base T-Bird and LX ($73). Traction-Lok axle for base T-Bird and LX ($100). Optional 3.27:1 axle ratio for Super Coupe ($21). Premium luxury group for base T-Bird ($420), for Super Coupe with 157A ($761). Antilock braking system, except standard on Super Coupe ($1,085). Anti-theft system ($183). Moon roof ($741-$841 depending on options teamed with). Clearcoat paint system ($183). Ford JBL audio system ($488). Compact disc player ($491). Radio-delete credits ($245-$382). Locking wire wheel covers, on base T-Bird ($212), as option on others ($127). Cast aluminum wheels on base T-Bird ($299), as option on

1989 Ford Thunderbird two-door Super Coupe (FMC)

others ($213). California emissions ($100). High-altitude emissions (no charge). LX leather trim ($489). Super Coupe leather trim ($622). Front license plate bracket (no charge). Cold weather group on Super Coupe ($18), on others ($45). Preferred equipment package 151B ($1,235). Preferred equipment package 162A ($735). Luxury group ($735). Preferred equipment group 157B for Super Coupe (no charge).

History:

The 1989 Fords were introduced on October 6, 1987, but the all-new 1988 Thunderbird did not bow until the day after Christmas. Donald E. Petersen was Chairman of the Board and CEO of Ford Motor Co. William Clay Ford was Vice Chairman. Harold A. Poling was President and Chief Operating Officer of the corporation. Ford Vice Thomas J. Wagner was the Ford Division's new General Manager and Richard L. Fenstermacher was divisional General Sales manager. Calendar-year output was 137,326 units. A total of 114,868 T-Birds were produced in the model year. This represented 1.61 percent of the industry total. Of these units, all were made in Lorain, Ohio. Calendar year dealer sales amounted to 120,645 T-Birds. The T-Bird was one of the year's most outstanding new vehicles and took "Car of the Year" honors from *Motor Trend* magazine. Ford Chairman Donald Petersen received lots of credit for turning the T-Bird into a world-class "image" car for his company and was promoted by year's end. Over $1 billion was spent to develop the new body, chassis, suspension, engine and interior package. By January 1989, Ford had 20,000 orders for the new Super Coupe, which had been appearing on the cover of (and inside) enthusiasts magazines since the middle of the previous summer. The Super Coupe's introduction was delayed due to durability problems with production versions of the original Duracast crankshaft. Duracast metal — actually a kind of cast iron — had tested fine in pre-production prototype engines. However, Ford found out later that the manufacturer had custom-selected the cranks used in the prototypes. The metal in production versions, which were manufactured for an engine that had been considerably upgraded, did turn out to be too porous to stand up in severe use and decided to use a forged crankshaft. This change in plan was accomplished in near-record time and the supercharged V-6 entered production on January 30, 1989 at a FoMoCo plant in Essex, Ontario, Canada. Ford then announced that it would build 300 engines daily (up from a planned 200-per-day schedule) and ship 600 by the end of February. Ford actually tested some of the earliest production supercharged engines by installing 15 of them in fleet vehicles and police cars. The cop cars were 1988 Thunderbird LXs. Three belonged to the police department in Dearborn, Michigan, where Ford has its headquarters. This allowed the automaker to monitor the engine's performance in a cold environment. Seven more were installed in Arizona Highway Patrol cars for the opposite reason. A Dallas, Texas courier service also got five engines. *AutoWeek* magazine got to try out two of the Dearborn Police Department cars and did a report in its February 20, 1989 issue. Myron Stokes' side bar story revealed that two cars had also been given to a testing service in Flint, Michigan and three were assigned to Ford's Arizona Proving Grounds. *Motor Trend* gave the Super Coupe preliminary coverage in its October 1988 issue. The report, by Daniel Charles Ross, called it "a remarkable step forward for a car that was already impressively potent." A spy report, by *Car and Driver's* Rich Ceppos (July 1988), hinted that the Super Coupe would do 0-60 mph in the low-seven-second bracket and hit 145 mph at top end. New T-Bird race cars came out of the gate running strong, though not ahead of the entire pack. Davey Allison put his Robert Yates/Havoline T-Bird across the finish line second at Daytona. Ford stock cars had their longest winning streak in 20 years and Ford driver Mark Martin ultimately took third in the standings, with two other Fords in the top 10. In NHRA Funny Car competition Tom Heney's T-Bird racked up 7,774 points to earn him an eighth place national ranking. At Pike's Peak, Leonard Vasholtz pushed his T-Bird up the 12.42-mile, 156-turn course in 12:23:31 to win the Stock Cars class. Also, in October 1988, a specially-prepared 1989 T-Bird circled Alabama International Motor Speedway with Lyn St. James at the wheel and set 21 new records.

1990 Thunderbird

Thunderbird — Series 46 — (V-8): After its dramatic restyling, *Motor Trend's* 1989 "Car of the Year" changed very little. Two new option groups were offered in 1990, the Power Equipment Group and the Luxury Group. To celebrate the Thunderbird's 35th birthday, a limited-edition 35th Anniversary commemorative package was made available in January for the Super Coupe and 5,000 copies were planned. Anniversary models used the same supercharged 3.8-liter V-6 as the standard Super Coupe. They featured unique Black and Titanium two-tone paint, blue accent stripes, black road wheels and commemorative fender badges. A special interior trim featured suede-and-leather bucket seats, a split fold-down rear seat and commemorative badges on the interior door panels. Also standard was an anti-lock brake system, a handling package with automatic ride control and a Traction-Lok axle. The 35th Anniversary package (option no. 563) carried a dealer cost of $1,584. Its factory-suggested retail price added $1,863 to the regular cost of a Super Coupe. Two new exterior colors were offered for 1990 T-Birds, Alabaster and Sandalwood Frost Clearcoat Metallic. The regular Super Coupe came in the same five colors as last season, three of which were extra-cost Clearcoat Metallic finishes. Interiors were color-coordinated with the exterior finishes. On base Coupes and LXs, as total of four colors was offered: Crystal Blue, Currant Red, Black and Light Sandalwood. There were 18 different interior trims. Standard features include: All standard FoMoCo safety, anti-theft, convenience items, and emissions control equipment, 3.8-liter V-6, 4-speed automatic overdrive transmission, daytime running lights, rear window defroster, 72-amp battery, 65-amp alternator, wide body side protection moldings, deluxe wheel covers, full-length console with floor-mounted shift, vinyl door trim with storage bins, cloth bucket seats with recliners, air conditioning, tinted glass, analog instrumentation, electronic AM/FM search radio with digital clock (may be deleted for credit), power steering, all-season radial tires, power windows and interval windshield wipers.

Thunderbird LX: The Thunderbird LX model adds or substitutes the following features over base Thunderbird equipment: power lock group, dual electric remote-control mirrors, bright window moldings, electronic AM/FM stereo radio with cassette and clock, speed control system, tilt steering wheel, styled road wheel covers, illuminated entry system, fog lamps, luxury-level door trim and carpeting, convenience lights, instrument panel upper storage compartment, illuminated visor mirrors, luxury cloth bucket seats with recliners, rear seat center arm rest, leather-wrapped luxury steering wheel, vehicle maintenance monitor, remote-release fuel door, electronic instrument cluster and speed-sensitive power steering.

Thunderbird Super Coupe: The Thunderbird Super Coupe model adds or substitutes the following features over base Thunderbird equipment: 3.8-liter EFI supercharged V-6 engine, five-speed manual overdrive transmission, power lock group, dual electric remote-control mirrors, electronic AM/FM stereo radio with cassette and clock, speed control system, tilt steering wheel, fog lamps, narrow body side moldings, lower body side cladding, 16-in. cast aluminum wheels, P255/60R16 black sidewall performance tires, luxury door trim and carpeting, articulated sports seat with power lumbar and power seat back bolster adjustments, Sport soft-feel steering wheel, heavy-duty alternator, automatic ride control adjustable suspension and performance instrumentation.

The VIN was stamped on an aluminum tab riveted to the dashboard on the passenger side and was visible through the windshield. The first symbol 1 = built in the United States. The second symbol F = Ford. The third symbol A = Ford passenger vehicle. The fourth was the type of restraint system. The fifth symbol P meant a passenger-type vehicle. The Sixth symbol 6 denoted Thunderbird. The seventh symbol was the body type: 0=Standard Coupe, 2=LX Coupe and 4=Super Coupe. The eighth symbol indicated the engine: 4=232 cid (3.8L) 140 hp V-6 and R=232 cid (3.6L) 210 hp supercharged V-6. The ninth symbol was the check digit. The 10th symbol K=1990 model year. The 11th symbol revealed the assembly plant: H=Lorain, Ohio. The 12th through 17th symbols were the sequential production numbers of the specific vehicles starting at 100001. The vehicle certification label was located on the rear face of the driver's door. The top part of the label indicated the Thunderbird was manufactured by Ford Motor Company. Directly below this was the month and year of manufacture, plus a statement that the car conformed to the federal motor vehicle safety standards in effect on the indicated date of manufacture. VIN: The VIN appeared on the first line of encoded information. It matched the first to 11th symbols on the VIN tag. Some other codes also appeared. PASSENGER. EXT. COLOR: This line carried the exterior paint color(s) code. DSO: The District Special Order code now appeared above "DSO" to the right of the exterior paint color codes. BODY: The body style code appeared to the extreme left of the bottom line. The only Thunderbird code for this model-year was: BS2=2-door Pillared Hardtop. VR: The vinyl roof type/color code was to the right

1990 Ford Thunderbird two-door Super Coupe (OCW)

of the body code. No T-Birds had vinyl tops. MLDG: The molding code was to the right of the vinyl roof code. INT. TRIM: The interior trim code was to the right of the molding code. A/C: The air conditioning code was to the right of the interior trim code. Cars with air conditioning had "A" stamped here. R: The radio code was to the right of the A/C code. S: The sunroof code appeared to the right of the radio code. AX: The axle code appeared to the right of the sun roof code. TR: The transmission code appeared to the right of the axle code. Note: The terms and abbreviations shown in capitals appeared on the line above the actual codes.

Thunderbird (V-6)

Series No.	Body/ Style No.	Body Type and Seating	Factory Price	Shipping Weight	Production Total
60	66D	2-dr. Coupe-4P	$14,980	3,581 lbs.	Note 1

Thunderbird (V-6)

62	66D	2-dr. Coupe-4P	$17,263	3,618 lbs.	Note 1

Super Coupe (Four)

64	66D	2-dr. Coupe-4P	$20,390	3,809 lbs.	Note 1

Note 1: Production of the all models combined was 113,957.

Thunderbird Base V-6: 90-degree, overhead valve. Cast-iron block and aluminum head. Displacement: 232 cid (3.8 liters). B & S: 3.80 x 3.40 in. Compression ratio: 9.0:1. Brake hp: 140 at 3800. Torque: 215 lbs.-ft. at 2400. Four main bearings. Hydraulic valve lifters. Induction: Throttle Body Injection. Code: 4.

Thunderbird Super Coupe Supercharged V-6: 90-degree, overhead valve. Cast-iron block and aluminum head. Displacement: 232 cid (3.8 liters). B & S: 3.80 x 3.40 in. Compression ratio: 8.3:1. Brake hp: 210 at 4000. Torque: 315 lbs.-ft. at 2600. Four main bearings. Hydraulic valve lifters. Induction: Sequential Electronic Fuel Injection (Supercharged). Code: R.

Wheelbase: 113 in. Overall length: 198.7. Overall width: 72.7. Overall height: 52.7 in. Front tread: 61.6 in. Rear tread: 60.2 in. Tires: P225/60VR16

Front suspension: Independent, upper and lower control arms, coil springs, tubular shocks and anti-roll bar. Rear suspension Live axle, four-link control arms, coil springs, adjustable tubular shocks and anti-roll bar. Steering: Power rack-and-pinion, speed-sensitive on LX. Front Brakes: Power vented disc. Rear Brakes: Power drum. Fuel tank capacity: 19 gal. Seating capacity: Five (5). Fuel Economy: 17-24 mpg. Transmission: 4-speed automatic. Wheels: 16 in.

Four-speed overdrive transmission on Super Coupe ($539). P205/75R15 white sidewall tires ($73). Eagle GT + 4 P225/60VR16 black sidewall all-season performance tires, Super Coupe only ($73). Conventional spare tire in base T-Bird and LX ($73). Traction-Lok axle for base T-Bird and LX ($100). Optional 3.27:1 axle ratio for Super Coupe ($21). Premium luxury group for base T-Bird ($420), for Super Coupe with 157A ($761). Antilock braking system, except standard on Super Coupe ($1,085). Anti-theft system ($183).Keyless entry system for base T-Bird ($219), for others ($137). Front carpeted floor mats ($33) Luxury and lights convenience group ($26). Moon roof (($741-$841 depending on options teamed with). Clearcoat paint system ($188). Electronic premium cassette radio ($305-$442). Ford JBL audio system ($488). Compact disc player ($491). Radio-delete credits ($245). Power antenna ($76). Locking wire wheel covers, on base T-Bird ($228), as option on others ($143). Cast aluminum wheels on base T-Bird ($298), as option on others ($213). California emissions ($100). High-altitude emissions (no charge). LX leather trim ($489). Super Coupe leather trim ($622). Front license plate bracket (no charge). Cold weather group on most ($168-$195), on others ($18-$45). Preferred equipment package 151A ($1,288). Preferred equipment package 155A ($819). Preferred equipment group 157B for Super Coupe (no charge).

1990 Ford Thunderbird 35th Anniversary Edition Super Coupe (OCW)

Harold A. Poling was Chairman of the Board and CEO of Ford Motor Co. Phillip E. Benton, Jr. was President and Chief Operating Officer of the corporation. Allan D. Gilmour was Executive Vice President and President of the Ford Automotive Group. Ford Vice Thomas J. Wagner continued as the Ford Division's General Manager and Phillip M. Novell was divisional General Sales manager. Calendar-year output was 107,430 units. A total of 113,957 T-Birds was produced in the model year. This represented 1.82 percent of the industry total. Of these units, all were made in Lorain, Ohio. Calendar year dealer sales amounted to 106,124 for a 12.1 percent share of the domestic Large Specialty class. *Motor Trend* magazine road tested the 1990 T-Bird Super Coupe in its September 1990 issue. The car moved from 0-60 mph in 7.4 seconds and covered the quarter-mile in 15.8 seconds at 90.8 mph. During lateral acceleration the car pulled .82g. It took 136 ft. to come to a complete halt from 60 mph. Its average EPA city mileage rating was 17 mpg. In racing, it was a good year for Thunderbirds, with five Fords in NASCAR's top 10 Winston Cup standings. Dale Earnhardt's nine victories gave Chevrolet its eighth manufacturer's title in a row. However, the T-Birds were really nipping at the heels of his number 3 Lumina. Earnhardt had only a 26-point margin over Mark Martin's Folgers Coffee Ford. Martin took checkered flags at Richmond. Michigan and North Wilkesboro. Bill Elliott's Coor's Ford was third, although his only win was at Dover. Geoff Bodine's Budweiser 'Bird was fourth. It had two victories at Martinsville and one at Pocono. Morgan Shepard's Motorcraft Ford was sixth, although he came in first only at Atlanta in the fall. The other Ford was Alan Kulwicki's Zerex Ford in eighth place, including a win at Rockingham.

1991 Thunderbird

Thunderbird — Series 46 — (V-8): Very few revisions were made to 1991 T-Birds. The biggest change was the reinstatement of a V-8 engine. A new 200-hp version of the 5.0-liter Mustang V-8 was made optional in standard and LX models. The standard T-Bird also received some interior upgrades. Leather seat facings and cloth-and-vinyl door panel inserts were added on the LX model. The LX also had bright window moldings, dual electric remote control mirrors, styled road wheel covers, luxury level door trim and carpeting, an illuminated entry system with convenience lights, an upper storage compartment for the instrument panel, illuminated visor mirrors, luxury cloth bucket seats with recliners, a front seat center armrest, a leather-wrapped luxury steering wheel, a power lock group, speed control, tilt steering and speed-sensitive power steering. The top-of-the-line Super Coupe had seats with a T-Bird insignia embroidered into them and under its hood was the 210-hp supercharged V-6. Standard features included: all standard FoMoCo safety, anti-theft, convenience items and emissions control equipment, 3.8-liter V-6, 4-speed automatic overdrive transmission, daytime running lights, rear window defroster, 72-amp battery, 65-amp alternator, wide body side protection moldings, deluxe wheel covers, full-length console with floor-mounted shift, vinyl door trim with storage bins, cloth bucket seats with recliners, air conditioning, tinted glass, analog instrumentation, electronic AM/FM search radio with digital clock (may be deleted for credit), power steering, all-season radial tires, power windows and interval windshield wipers.

Thunderbird LX: The Thunderbird LX model adds or substitutes the following features over base Thunderbird equipment: power lock group, dual electric remote-control mirrors, bright window moldings, electronic AM/FM stereo radio with cassette and clock, speed control system, tilt steering wheel, styled road wheel covers, illuminated entry system, fog lamps, luxury-level door trim and carpeting, convenience lights, instrument panel upper storage compartment, illuminated visor mirrors, luxury cloth bucket seats with recliners, rear seat center arm rest, leather-wrapped luxury steering wheel, vehicle maintenance monitor, remote-release fuel door, electronic instrument cluster and speed-sensitive power steering.

Super Coupe: The Thunderbird Super Coupe model adds or substitutes the following features over base Thunderbird equipment: 3.8-liter EFI supercharged V-6 engine, five-speed manual overdrive transmission, power lock group, dual electric remote-control mirrors, electronic AM/FM stereo radio with cassette and clock, speed control system, tilt steering wheel, fog lamps, narrow body side moldings, lower body side cladding, 16-in. cast aluminum wheels, P255/60R16 black sidewall performance tires, luxury door trim and carpeting, articulated sports seat with power lumbar and power seat back bolster adjustments, Sport soft-feel steering wheel, heavy-duty alternator, automatic ride control adjustable suspension and performance instrumentation.

The VIN was stamped on an aluminum tab riveted to the dashboard on the passenger side and was visible through the windshield. The first symbol 1 = built in the United States. The second symbol F = Ford. The third symbol A = Ford passenger vehicle. The fourth was the type of restraint system. The fifth symbol P meant a passenger-type vehicle. The Sixth symbol 6 denoted Thunderbird. The seventh symbol was the body type: 0=Standard Coupe, 2=LX Coupe and 4=Super Coupe. The eighth symbol indicated the engine: 4=232 cid (3.8L) 140 hp V-6 and R=232 cid (3.6L) 210 hp supercharged V-6. The ninth symbol was the check digit. The 10th symbol M= the 1991 model year. The 11th symbol revealed the assembly plant: H=Lorain, Ohio. The 12th through 17th symbols were the sequential production numbers of the specific vehicles starting at 100001. The vehicle certification label was located on the rear face of the driver's door. The top part of the label indicated the Thunderbird was manufactured by Ford Motor Company. Directly below this was the month and year of manufacture, plus a statement that the car conformed to the federal motor vehicle safety standards in effect on the indicated date of manufacture. VIN: The VIN appeared two lines above the UPC. It matched the first to 11th symbols on the VIN tag. Some other codes also appeared. TYPE: The type appeared on the left side of the label on a line above the UPC. It indicated PASSENGER. UPC: The scannable bar code carried the UPC information. EXT. COLOR: This line carried the exterior paint color(s) code. DSO: The District Special Order code appeared above "DSO" to the right of the exterior paint color codes. BODY: The body style code appeared to the extreme left of the bottom line. The only Thunderbird code for this model-year was: BS2=2-door Pillared Hardtop. VR: The vinyl roof type/color code was to the right of the body code. No T-Birds had vinyl tops. MLDG: The molding code was to the right of the vinyl roof code. INT. TRIM: The interior trim code was to the right of the molding code. A/C: The air conditioning code was to the right of the interior trim code. TAPE: The tape treatment code appeared to the right of the interior trim code. R: The radio code was to the right of the A/C code. S: The sunroof code appeared to the right of the radio code. AX: The axle code appeared to the right of the sun roof code. TR: The transmission code appeared to the right of the axle code.

Thunderbird (V-6)

Series No.	Body/ Style No.	Body Type and Seating	Factory Price	Shipping Weight	Production Total
60	66D	2-dr. Coupe-4P	$15,318	3,550 lbs.	Note 1

Thunderbird (V-8)

Series No.	Body/ Style No.	Body Type and Seating	Factory Price	Shipping Weight	Production Total
60	66D	2-dr. Coupe-4P	$16,398	3,732 lbs.	Note 1

Thunderbird LX (V-6)

Series No.	Body/ Style No.	Body Type and Seating	Factory Price	Shipping Weight	Production Total
62	66D	2-dr. Coupe-4P	$17,734	3,572 lbs.	Note 1

Thunderbird LX (V-8)

Series No.	Body/ Style No.	Body Type and Seating	Factory Price	Shipping Weight	Production Total
62	66D	2-dr. Coupe-4P	$18,814	3,742 lbs.	Note 1

Super Coupe (V-8)

Series No.	Body/ Style No.	Body Type and Seating	Factory Price	Shipping Weight	Production Total
64	66D	2-dr. Coupe-4P	$20,999	3,767 lbs.	Note 1

Note 1: Production of the all models combined was 82,973.

Thunderbird Base V-6: 90-degree, overhead valve. Cast-iron block and aluminum head. Displacement: 232 cid (3.8 liters). B & S: 3.80 x

1991 Ford Thunderbird two-door Coupe (FMC)

3.40 in. Compression ratio: 9.0:1. Brake hp: 140 at 3800. Torque: 215 lbs.-ft. at 2400. Four main bearings. Hydraulic valve lifters. Induction: Throttle Body Injection. Code: 4.

Thunderbird Super Coupe Supercharged V-6: 90-degree, overhead valve. Cast-iron block and aluminum head. Displacement: 232 cid (3.8 liters). B & S: 3.80 x 3.40 in. Compression ratio: 8.3:1. Brake hp: 210 at 4000. Torque: 315 lbs.-ft. at 2600. Four main bearings. Hydraulic valve lifters. Induction: Sequential Electronic Fuel Injection (Supercharged). Code R.

Thunderbird LX Optional V-8: 90-degree, overhead valve V-8. Cast-iron block and head. Displacement: 302 cid (5.0 liters). B & S: 4.00 x 3.00 in. Compression ratio: 8.9:1. Brake hp: 200 at 4000 rpm. Torque: 275 lbs.-ft. at 3000 rpm. Five main bearings. Roller cam. Induction: Sequential fuel injection.

Chassis:

Wheelbase: 113 in. Overall length: 198.7. Overall width: 72.7. Overall height: 52.7 in. Tires: P215/70R15. Trunk capacity: 14.7 cu. ft. Front tread: 61.6 in. Rear tread: 60.2 in.

Technical:

Front suspension: Independent, upper and lower control arms, coil springs, tubular shocks and anti-roll bar. Rear suspension Live axle, four-link control arms, coil springs, adjustable tubular shocks and anti-roll bar. Steering: Power rack-and-pinion, speed-sensitive on LX. Front Brakes: Power vented disc. Rear Brakes: Power drum. Fuel tank capacity: 18 gal. Seating capacity: Five (5). Fuel Economy: 17-24 mpg. Transmission: 4-speed automatic. Wheels: 15 in. Fuel Economy: [Base V-6] 19 mpg city/27 mpg highway, [Supercharged V-6] 17 mpg city/24 mpg highway and [V-8] 15 mpg city/23 mpg highway.

Options:

5.0-liter V-8 in base T-Bird and LX ($1,080). Four-speed overdrive transmission on Super Coupe ($595). P205/75R15 white sidewall tires ($73). Eagle GT + 4 P225/60VR16 black sidewall all-season performance tires, Super Coupe only ($73). Conventional spare tire in base T-Bird and LX ($73). Traction-Lok axle for base T-Bird and LX ($100). Premium luxury group for base T-Bird ($420), for Super Coupe with 157A ($761). Antilock braking system including Traction-Lok axle, except standard on Super Coupe ($1,085). Anti-theft system ($245). Auto lamp group ($176). Keyless entry system for base T-Bird ($219), for others ($137). Front carpeted floor mats ($33) Luxury group ($$345-$627)). Moon roof (($776-$876 depending on options teamed with). Cornering lamps ($68). Rear window defroster ($160). Electronic auto temperature control ($162). Electronic premium cassette radio ($305-$460). Ford JBL audio system ($488). Illuminated entry system ($82). Compact disc player ($491). Radio-delete credits ($245). Power lock group ($245). Light convenience group ($100-$146). Luxury group ($345-$627). Power antenna ($82). 6-way power driver's seat ($290). 6-way power passenger seat ($290). Speed control and tilt steering ($345). Vehicle maintenance monitor ($89). Locking wire wheel covers, on base T-Bird ($228), as option on others ($143). Cast aluminum wheels on base T-Bird ($299), as option on others ($214). LX leather trim ($489). Super Coupe leather trim ($622). Front license plate bracket (no charge). Cold weather group on most ($178-$205), on others ($18-$45). Preferred equipment package 151A ($796). Preferred equipment package 155A ($977). Preferred equipment group 157A for Super Coupe ($739).

History:

The new T-Birds were released on September 17, 1990. Harold A. Poling was Chairman of the Board and CEO of Ford Motor Co. Phillip E. Benton, Jr. was President and Chief Operating Officer of the corporation. Allan D. Gilmour was Executive Vice President and President of the Ford Automotive Group. Ford Vice Thomas J. Wagner continued as the Ford Division's General Manager and Phillip M. Novell was divisional General Sales manager. Calendar-year output was 71,395 units. A total of 82,973 T-Birds was produced in the model year. This represented

1991 Ford Thunderbird LX two-door Coupe (OCW)

1991 Ford Thunderbird two-door Super Coupe (OCW)

1.43 percent of the industry total. Of these units, all were made in Lorain, Ohio. Calendar year dealer sales amounted to 74,189 for a 11.0 percent share of the domestic Large Specialty class. T-Bird enthusiasts helped bring the V-8 engine back in 1991 by asking Ford dealers for the type of engine that was traditional in their favorite car. The company stuffed the 5.0-liter Mustang engine into the T-Bird's smaller engine bay and created an optional hood with a "power bulge." This appeared in an *Autoweek* spy photo as early as May 1, 1989 and didn't look bad, but designer Jack Telnack didn't like it. He killed the idea of putting a bulge on the hood, so Ford redesigned the 5.0-liter V-8. Its length was shortened by 2-1/2 in. and its height was lowered by redesigning the intake manifold. *Road & Track* road tested the 1991 T-Bird LX Coupe and published the results in its April 1991 issue. The car, as tested, priced out at $23,181. It was equipped with the four-speed automatic transmission. In the acceleration category, the car did 0-60 mph in 9.0 seconds. The quarter-mile took 16.7 seconds. The car's top speed was 140 mph. Braking performance was also good, with 255 ft. required to stop the car from 80 mph. It averaged 60.3 mph through the slalom. T-Birds also turned in impressive performances in various types of racing events during 1991. Hot-driving NASCAR competitors running Fords included Davey Allison, Mark Martin and Sterling Marlin. Ford was a close second to Chevrolet in the battle for the Manufacturer's Cup. Also, for the first time since 1988, Ford managed a super speedway triumph in ARCA stock car racing when Greg Trammell put his Melling-Elliott T-Bird across the finish line first in the March 16 race at Atlanta Motor Speedway. He averaged a blistering 131.532 mph to set an event record. Bobby Bowsher placed third in his Don Thompson Excavating T-Bird. In NHRA drag racing, Bob Glidden's Pro Stock T-Bird struggled to a fifth place finish.

1992 Thunderbird

Thunderbird — Series 46 — (V-8) Minor changes were seen on 1992 T-Birds. The LX and Sport models now had the same aggressive front fascia used on the Super Coupe, but without the "SC" initials embossed in the bumper. Four colors — Cayman Green Clearcoat Metallic, Dark Plum Clearcoat Metallic, Opal Grey and Silver — were new for 1992. Standard features included: all standard FoMoCo safety, anti-theft, convenience items, and emissions control equipment, 3.8-liter 140-hp MPEFI V-6, automatic overdrive transmission, long-spindle SLA front suspension with variable-rate coil springs, double-acting gas-pressurized shock absorbers and 1.1-in. diameter stabilizer bar, independent H-arm rear suspension with toe control link, variable-rate springs, double-acting gas-pressurized shocks, and 1.04-in. diameter stabilizer bar, power rack and pinion steering with 14.1:1 ratio on center, power front disc/rear drum brakes, 15 x 6-in. stamped steel wheels, deluxe wheel covers, P205/70R15 steel-belted black sidewall all-season radial tires, new long-lasting LED taillights, body side protection moldings with bright insert, (U.S.) fully-automatic shoulder belt restraint system with manual lap belt, full-length console with floor-mounted shifter, vinyl door trim with storage bins, cloth bucket seats with recliners, map and dome lights, luggage compartment light, ash tray light, driver's foot well light, air conditioning, tinted glass, analog instruments, electronic AM/FM stereo search radio with digital clock (may be deleted for credit), power windows, interval windshield wipers, (Canada) heavy-duty battery and (Canada) electric rear window defroster.

LX: The Thunderbird LX model adds or substitutes the following features over base Thunderbird equipment: Speed-sensitive variable-assist power steering with 14.1:1 ratio on center, styled road wheel covers, dual electric remote-control OSRV mirrors, luxury level door trim and carpeting, power lock group with power door locks, remote deck lid release, and remote-control for fuel filler door in glove box, analog performance instrumentation with tachometer, fog lamps, illuminated entry system and convenience lights, illuminated visor mirrors, luxury cloth/leather/vinyl bucket seats with recliners and 6-way power driver's

1992 Ford Thunderbird LX two-door Coupe (FMC)

1992 Ford Thunderbird Sport two-door Coupe (FMC)

seat, rear seat center arm rest, leather-wrapped luxury steering wheel, electronic AM/FM stereo search radio with cassette and digital clock and speed control with tilt steering wheel.

Sport: The Thunderbird Sport model adds or substitutes the following features over base Thunderbird equipment: 5.0-liter EFI V-8, automatic overdrive transmission, cast aluminum wheels, P215/70R15 black sidewall tires, speed-sensitive variable-assisted power steering with 14.1:1 ratio on center, handling suspension, performance analog instrument cluster and leather-wrapped steering wheel.

Super Coupe: The Thunderbird Super Coupe model adds or substitutes the following features over base Thunderbird equipment: 3.8-liter 210-hp supercharged and intercooled SMPEFI, 5-speed manual overdrive transmission, automatic ride control suspension in addition to standard suspension (includes 1.12-in. diameter front stabilizer bar and .9-in. diameter solid rear stabilizer bar, Traction-Lok rear axle, speed-sensitive variable-assist power steering with 14.1:1 ratio on center, four-wheel power disc brakes with anti-lock braking system, cast-aluminum 16 x 7.0-in. wheels and P225/60 performance tires, fog lamps, narrow body side moldings and lower body side cladding, dual electric remote-control mirrors, luxury door trim and carpeting, articulated sport seats with power lumbar and seat back bolster adjustments, sport soft-feel steering wheel, heavy-duty battery and alternator and analog performance instrumentation with tachometer.

VIN:

The VIN was stamped on an aluminum tab riveted to the dashboard on the passenger side and was visible through the windshield. The first symbol 1 = built in the United States. The second symbol F = Ford. The third symbol A = Ford passenger vehicle. The fourth was the type of restraint system. The fifth symbol P meant a passenger-type vehicle. The Sixth symbol 6 denoted Thunderbird. The seventh symbol was the body type: 0=Standard Coupe, 2=LX Coupe and 4=Super Coupe. The eighth symbol indicated the engine: 4=232 cid (3.8L) 140 hp V-6, R=232 cid (3.6L) 210 hp supercharged V-6 and T = 302-cid (5.0 L) 200-hp V-8. The ninth symbol was the check digit. The 10th symbol N= the 1992 model year. The 11th symbol revealed the assembly plant: H=Lorain, Ohio. The 12th through 17th symbols were the sequential production numbers of the specific vehicles starting at 100001. The vehicle certification label was located on the rear face of the driver's door. The top part of the label indicated the Thunderbird was manufactured by Ford Motor Company. Directly below this was the month and year of manufacture, plus a statement that the car conformed to the federal motor vehicle safety standards in effect on the indicated date of manufacture. VIN: The VIN appeared two lines above the UPC. It matched the first to 11th symbols on the VIN tag. Some other codes also appeared. TYPE: This appeared on the left side of the label on the line above the UPC and indicated PASSENGER. UPC: A scannable bar code carried the UPC. EXT. COLOR: This line carried the exterior paint color(s) code. DSO: The District Special Order code now appeared above "DSO" to the right of the exterior paint color codes. BODY: The body style code appeared to the extreme left of the bottom line. The Thunderbird codes for this model-year were: BS2=2-door Base Coupe, LX2=2-door LX coupe and SC2=2-door Super Coupe. VR: The vinyl roof type/color code was to the right of the body code. No T-Birds had vinyl tops. MLDG: The molding code was to the right of the vinyl roof code. INT. TRIM: The interior trim

code was to the right of the molding code. A/C: The air conditioning code was to the right of the interior trim code. TAPE: The tape treatment code appeared to the right of the interior trim code. R: The radio code was to the right of the A/C code. S: The sunroof code appeared to the right of the radio code. AX: The axle code appeared to the right of the sun roof code. TR: The transmission code appeared to the right of the axle code. Note: The terms and abbreviations shown in capitals appeared on the line above the actual codes.

Thunderbird (V-6)

Series No.	Body/Style No.	Body Type and Seating	Factory Price	Shipping Weight	Production Total
60	66D	2-dr. Coupe-4P	$16,345	3,514 lbs.	Note 1

Thunderbird (V-8)

60	66D	2-dr. Coupe-4P	$17,425	3,772 lbs.	Note 1

Thunderbird Sport Coupe (V-8)

60	66D	2-dr. Coupe-4P	$18,611	3,686 lbs.	Note 1

Thunderbird LX (V-6)

62	66D	2-dr. Coupe-4P	$18,783	3,566 lbs.	Note 1

Thunderbird LX (V-8)

62	66D	2-dr. Coupe-4P	$19,863	3,719 lbs.	Note 1

Super Coupe (Four)

64	66D	2-dr. Coupe-4P	$22,046	3,768 lbs.	Note 1

Note 1: Production of the all models combined was 77,789.

Engines:

Thunderbird Base V-6: 90-degree, overhead valve. Cast-iron block and aluminum head. Displacement: 232 cid (3.8 liters). B & S: 3.80 x 3.40 in. Compression ratio: 9.0:1. Brake hp: 140 at 3800. Torque: 215 lbs.-ft. at 2400. Four main bearings. Hydraulic valve lifters. Induction: Throttle Body Injection. Code: 4.

Thunderbird Super Coupe Supercharged V-6: 90-degree, overhead valve. Cast-iron block and aluminum head. Displacement: 232 cid (3.8 liters). B & S: 3.80 x 3.40 in. Compression ratio: 8.3:1. Brake hp: 210 at 4000. Torque: 315 lbs.-ft. at 2600. Four main bearings. Hydraulic valve lifters. Induction: Sequential Electronic Fuel Injection (Supercharged). Code: R.

Thunderbird LX Optional V-8: 90-degree, overhead valve V-8. Cast-iron block and head. Displacement: 302 cid (5.0 liters). B & S: 4.00 x 3.00 in. Compression ratio: 8.9:1. Brake hp: 200 at 4000 rpm. Torque: 275 lbs.-ft. at 3000 rpm. Five main bearings. Roller cam. Induction: Sequential fuel injection.

Chassis:

Wheelbase: 113 in. Overall length: 198.7. Overall width: 72.7. Overall height: 52.7 in. Front legroom: 41.5 in. Trunk capacity: 14.7 cu. ft. Front tread: 61.6 in. Rear tread: 60.2 in. Tires: P215/70R15.

Technical:

Front suspension: Independent, upper and lower control arms, coil springs, tubular shocks and anti-roll bar. Rear suspension Live axle, four-link control arms, coil springs, adjustable tubular shocks and anti-roll bar. Steering: Power rack-and-pinion, speed-sensitive on LX. Turning circle: 37.5 ft. Front Brakes: Power vented disc. Rear Brakes: Power drum. Fuel tank capacity: 18 gal. Seating capacity: Five (5). Fuel Economy: 17-24 mpg. Transmission: 4-speed automatic. Wheels: 15 in. Fuel Economy: [Base V-6] 19 mpg city/27 mpg highway, [Supercharged V-6] 20 mpg city/27 mpg highway and [V-8] 15 mpg city/23 mpg highway. Weight distribution: 57/43 percent.

Options:

5.0-liter HO V-8 in base T-Bird and Sport ($1,080). Four-speed overdrive transmission on in T-Bird and Sport ($595). California emissions ($100). P225/60ZR16 black sidewall all-season performance tires, Super Coupe only ($73). Conventional spare tire in base T-Bird and LX ($73). Leather bucket seating surfaces in LX ($515). Leather bucket seating surfaces in Super Coupe ($648). Anti-lock braking system, includes Traction-Lok axle ($695). Anti-theft system ($245). Autolamp group ($193). Traction-Lok axle for base T-Bird, Sport and LX ($100). CD player, requires premium cassette radio ($491). Cornering lights ($68). Rear window defroster ($170). Automatic air conditioning for LX and Super Coupe ($162). Electronic instrument cluster for LX ($270). Electronic premium cassette radio ($305-$460). AM/FM ETR (stereo) with cassette in base T-Bird and LX ($155). Ford JBL audio system ($526). Radio-delete credits ($245). Keyless entry, including illuminated entry system and power lock group ($146-$228). Light convenience group ($100-$146). Power lock group ($311). Luxury group ($$311-$561). Moon roof (($776-$876 depending on options teamed with). Power antenna ($85). 6-way power driver's seat ($305). 6-way power passenger seat ($305). Vehicle maintenance

1992 Ford Thunderbird two-door Super Coupe (FMC)

monitor ($89). Cast aluminum wheels on base T-Bird ($306), as option on others ($221). Front license plate bracket (no charge). Cold weather group on most ($178-$205), on others ($18-$45). Preferred equipment package 151A ($762). Preferred equipment package 155A ($1,038). Preferred equipment group 157A for Super Coupe ($858).

History:

Harold A. Poling was Chairman of the Board and CEO of Ford Motor Co. Phillip E. Benton, Jr. was President and Chief Operating Officer of the corporation. Allan D. Gilmour was Executive Vice President and President of the Ford Automotive Group. Ross Roberts became the Ford Division's General Manager and Phillip M. Novell remained divisional General Sales manager. Calendar-year output was 97,822 units. A total of 77,789 T-Birds was produced in the model year. This represented 1.38 percent of the industry total. Of these units, all were made in Lorain, Ohio. Calendar year dealer sales amounted to 84,186 for a 11.2 percent share of the domestic Large Specialty class. "For some of us who love cars, the most intriguing models are not racing cars or sports cars, but big coupes. Grand Touring Cars. Cars with powerful engines, good road manners, style, and grace," said *Road & Track's Complete '92 Car Buying Guide*. "A gentleman's car like the Jensen Interceptor III, Facel-Vega HK 500, Aston Martin DB4. If there is a modern successor to these machines, it is the Ford T-Bird." In racing, the 1992 T-Birds proved more reliable. They came out of the gate strong in 1992 NASCAR Winston Cup racing, earning consecutive wins in the first nine races. Between the Charlotte race in the fall of 1991, and the spring 1992 Winston Cup event at the same track, Ford drivers netted 14 checkered flags. Still, the season wound up being another cliff-hanger. Back-to-back Geoff Bodine victories finally clinched the Winston Cup Manufacturer's Championship for Ford. Bodine's number 15 Bud Moore/Motorcraft T-Bird race car crossed the line first at Martinsville and North Wilkesboro, taking both events on Mondays after Sunday rain-outs. It was the first time in nine years that the blue oval cars wrestled the Manufacturer's Cup away from Chevrolet. The coup de grace came at season's end, when Bill Elliott put his T-Bird across the line first in the Hooters 500 at Atlanta Motor Speedway in Ford's 400th NASCAR victory, and Ford pilot Alan Kulwicki captured the Winston Cup Championship with his Hooters T-Bird. That gave Kulwicki, Elliott and Davey Allison the top three places in the point standings. In all, the Fords had 16 wins on the season, led the most laps, took a dominating 57 top-five finishes, and ran in the top 10 places 142 times! Another flock of 'Bird jockeys — led by title-winner Bobby Bowsher — performed nearly as well in 1992 ARCA competition. A win by another Ford in the last race of the season settled the title bout between Bowsher, and Chrysler LeBaron driver Bob Keselowski. This came in the Motorcraft 500K race at Atlanta, which Loy Allen, Jr. won with his Robert Yates-built number 2 Hooters T-Bird. Ford drivers struggled in NHRA drag racing, with Bob Glidden's Pro Stock T-Bird placing only third at the Keystone Nationals and second at Topeka. Glidden managed to pull out a late-season win at Dallas and finished fifth in the point standings again. In IHRA competition, Glen May's "Cranberry Connection" T-Bird did become the first "door-slammer" car to break the 220-mph barrier.

1993 Thunderbird

Thunderbird — Series 46 — (V-8): The standard T-Bird Coupe and the Sport Coupe disappeared from the T-Bird model lineup. Prices on some of the remaining models were slightly lowered. The 1993 retail prices ranged from $16,292 to $22,525 and compared to the 1992 price range of $16,763 to $22,457. Standard features included: all standard FoMoCo safety, anti-theft, convenience items and emissions control equipment, 3.8-liter 140-hp SMPEFI V-6, automatic overdrive transmission, long-spindle SLA front suspension with variable-rate coil springs, double-acting gas-pressurized shock absorbers and 1.1-in. diameter stabilizer bar, independent H-arm rear suspension with toe control link, variable-rate springs, double-acting gas-pressurized shocks and 1.04-in. diameter stabilizer bar, speed-sensitive variable-assist power steering, power front disc/rear drum brakes, 15 x 6-in. stamped steel wheels, styled road wheel covers, P205/70R15 steel-belted black sidewall radial tires, long-lasting LED taillights, body color body side

protection moldings, full-length console with floor-mounted leather-wrapped shifter, map/dome, luggage compartment, ash tray and driver's foot well lights, air conditioning and tinted glass, power windows, power door locks, remote deck lid, remote fuel filler door release, interval windshield wipers, dual electric remote-control mirrors, luxury level door trim and carpeting, analog performance instrumentation with tachometer, integral fog lamps in front fascia, illuminated entry system, rear seat courtesy lights, luxury cloth/leather/vinyl bucket seats with recliners and 6-way power for driver, rear seat center arm rest, leather-wrapped luxury steering wheel, electronic AM/FM stereo search radio with cassette tape player and digital clock and speed control with tilt steering wheel.

Super Coupe: The Thunderbird Super Coupe model adds or substitutes the following features over base Thunderbird equipment: 3.8-liter 210-hp supercharged and intercooled SMPEFI V-6 with dual exhausts, 5-speed manual overdrive transmission, supercharger boost gauge in instrument cluster, automatic ride control suspension in addition to standard suspension, Handling components including 1.10-in. (28 mm) diameter solid front stabilizer bar and 0.90-in. (23 mm) diameter solid rear stabilizer bar, Traction-Lok rear axle, four-wheel power disc brakes with anti-lock system, directional cast-aluminum 16 x 7.0-in. wheels and P225/60ZR black sidewall performance tires, narrow black body side moldings, lower body side cladding, unique rear fascia, sport soft-feel steering wheel, light convenience group with instrument panel courtesy light and engine compartment light, all-cloth articulated sport seats with power lumbar and seat back bolster adjustments, plus 4-way adjustable head restraints (up/down/forward/back).

VIN:

The VIN was stamped on an aluminum tab riveted to the dashboard on the passenger side and was visible through the windshield. The first symbol 1 = built in the United States. The second symbol F = Ford. The third symbol A = Ford passenger vehicle. The fourth symbol was the type of restraint system. The fifth symbol P = passenger-type vehicle. The sixth symbol 6 = Thunderbird. The seventh symbol = the body type: 2=LX Coupe and 4=Super Coupe. The eighth symbol was the engine: 4=232 cid (3.8L) 140 hp V-6, R=232 cid (3.6L) 210 hp supercharged V-6 and T=302 cid (5.0L) 200 hp V-8. The ninth symbol was the check digit. The 10th symbol P= the 1993 model year. The 11th symbol indicated the assembly plant: H=Lorain, Ohio. The 12th through 17th symbols were the sequential production numbers of the specific vehicle starting at 100001. The vehicle certification label was located on the rear face of the driver's door. The top part of the label indicated the Thunderbird was manufactured by Ford Motor Company. Directly below this was the month and year of manufacture, plus a statement that the car conformed to federal motor vehicle safety standards in effect on the indicated date of manufacture. VIN: The VIN appeared two lines above the UPC. It matched the first through 11th symbols on the VIN tag. Some other codes also appeared. TYPE: Appeared on the left side of label on a line above the UPC, and indicated PASSENGER. UPC: A scannable bar code carried the UPC. EXT. COLOR: This line carried the exterior paint color(s) code. DSO: The District Special Order code appeared above "DSO" to the right of the exterior paint color code. BODY: The body style code appeared to the extreme left of the bottom line. The Thunderbird codes for this model-year were: LX2 = 2-door LX Coupe and SC2 = 2-door Super Coupe. VR: The vinyl roof type/color code was to the right of the body code. No T-Birds had vinyl tops. MLDG: The molding code was to the right of the vinyl roof code. INT. TRIM: The interior trim code was to the right of the molding code. TAPE: The tape treatment code appeared to right of the interior trim code. R: The radio code was to the right of the A/C code, A. S: The sun roof code was to the right of the radio code. AX: The axle code appeared to the right of the sun roof code. TR: The transmission code appeared to the right of the axle code. The terms and abbreviations shown in the left-hand column appeared on the line above the actual codes.

Thunderbird LX (V-6)

Series No.	Body/ Style No.	Body Type and Seating	Factory Price	Shipping Weight	Production Total
62	66D	2-dr. Coupe-4P	$15,797	3,536 lbs.	Note 1

Thunderbird LX (V-8)

Series No.	Body/ Style No.	Body Type and Seating	Factory Price	Shipping Weight	Production Total
62	66D	2-dr. Coupe-4P	$16,883	3,673 lbs.	Note 1

Super Coupe (Four)

Series No.	Body/ Style No.	Body Type and Seating	Factory Price	Shipping Weight	Production Total
64	66D	2-dr. Coupe-4P	$22,030	3,760 lbs.	Note 1

Note 1: Production of the all models combined was 134,111.

Engines:

Thunderbird Base V-6: 90-degree, overhead valve. Cast-iron block and aluminum head. Displacement: 232 cid (3.8 liters). B & S: 3.80 x 3.40 in. Compression ratio: 9.0:1. Brake hp: 140 at 3800. Torque: 215 lbs.-ft. at 2400. Four main bearings. Hydraulic valve lifters. Induction: Throttle Body Injection. Code: 4.

1993 Ford Thunderbird LX two-door Coupe (OCW)

Thunderbird Super Coupe Supercharged V-6: 90-degree, overhead valve. Cast-iron block and aluminum head. Displacement: 232 cid (3.8 liters). B & S: 3.80 x 3.40 in. Compression ratio: 8.3:1. Brake hp: 210 at 4400. Torque: 315 lbs.-ft. at 2500. Four main bearings. Hydraulic valve lifters. Induction: Sequential Electronic Fuel Injection (Supercharged). Code: R.

Thunderbird LX Optional V-8: 90-degree, overhead valve. Cast-iron block and head. Displacement: 302 cid (5.0 liters). B & S: 4.00 x 3.00 in. Compression ratio: 8.9:1. Brake hp: 200 at 4000 rpm. Torque: 275 at 3000 rpm. Five main bearings. Roller cam. Induction: Sequential fuel injection.

Chassis:

Wheelbase: 113 in. Overall length: 198.7. Overall width: 72.7. Overall height: 52.5 in. Front headroom: 38.1 in. Rear headroom: 37.5 in. Front legroom: 42.5 in. Rear legroom: 35.8 in. Front shoulder room: 59 in. Rear shoulder room: 58.9 in. Trunk capacity: 15.1 cu. ft. Front tread: 61.6 in. Rear tread: 60.2 in. Wheels: 15 in. Tires: (LX) P205/70R15 black sidewall, (Super Coupe) P225/60ZR16 black sidewall.

Technical:

Front suspension: Long spindle SLA type, variable-rate coil springs, tubular gas shocks and stabilizer bar. Rear Suspension Independent, H-arm design with toe control link, variable-rate coil springs, gas shocks and stabilizer bar. Steering: Power rack-and-pinion. Turning circle: 39 ft. Brakes: Power front disc/rear drum on LX, Power four-wheel disc with ABS on Super Coupe. Fuel tank capacity: 18 gal. Seating capacity: Five (5). Fuel Economy: 17-24 mpg. Transmission: 4-speed automatic. Fuel Economy: [Base V-6] 19 mpg city/27 mpg highway, [Supercharged V-6] 20 mpg city/27 mpg highway and [V-8] 15 mpg city/23 mpg highway. Weight distribution: 57/43 percent.

Options:

5.0-liter HO V-8 in T-Bird LX only ($1,086). Four-speed overdrive transmission in T-Bird Super Coupe ($595). Power lock group ($311). Moon roof (($776-$876 depending on options teamed with). 6-way power driver's seat ($305). 6-way power passenger seat ($305). CD player, requires premium cassette radio ($491). Electronic premium cassette radio with premium sound system ($305). Ford JBL audio system ($526). Power antenna ($85). Radio-delete credits ($400). Automatic air conditioning for LX and Super Coupe ($162). Anti-lock braking system, includes Traction-Lok axle ($695). Anti-theft system ($245). Autolamp group ($193). Traction-Lok axle for base T-Bird LX ($100). Front license plate bracket (no charge). Cold weather group on LX and Super Coupe ($178-$205 depending on transmission and if car has PEP 157A). Rear window defroster included in PEPs and Cold Weather Group and required in New York state ($170). California emissions ($100). High-altitude emissions (no charge). Front carpeted floor mats ($33). Illuminated entry system in Super Coupe ($82). Electronic instrument cluster in LX ($270). Keyless entry, including illuminated entry system and power lock group in LX ($196), in Super Coupe ($278). Light convenience group with instrument panel courtesy light and engine compartment light, standard in Super Coupe ($46). Dual illuminated visor-vanity mirrors ($100). Speed control and tilt steering ($369). Leather seating surfaces in LX ($515). Leather seating surfaces in Super Coupe, includes fold-down rear seat and requires power seats and locks ($648). Vehicle maintenance monitor ($89). Directional cast aluminum wheels with up-size P215/70R15 black sidewall tires on T-Bird LX ($221). P225/60ZR16 black sidewall all-season performance tires on Super Coupe ($73 extra). Preferred equipment package 155A ($1,086).

History:

Harold A. Poling was Chairman of the Board and CEO of Ford Motor Co. Allan D. Gilmour was Vice Chairman of the corporation. Alexander J. Trotman was President and Chief Operating Officer of the corporation. Louis R. Ross was Vice Chairman and Chief Technical Officer of the Ford Automotive Group. Ross Roberts was again Ford Division's General Manager and Phillip M. Novell remained divisional General

Sales manager. Calendar-year output was 125,659 units. A total of 134,111 T-Birds was produced in the model year. This represented 2.24 percent of the industry total. Of these units, all were made in Lorain, Ohio. Calendar year dealer sales amounted to 122,415. The 1993 stock car racing season caused frustration for T-Bird fans, as Ford lost the battle for the Manufacturer's Cup by one point after winning seven of the final 12 Winston Cup events. Drivers piloting T-Birds this season included Bill Elliott, Mark Martin and Ernie Irvan. Driving the Texaco/Robert Yates car, Irvan won his fourth race as a Ford driver when he took the checkered flag at Martinsville on September 26. A sad note for Ford motorsports was the death of Ford driver Alan Kulwicki in an April 1 small-plane crash near Bristol Speedway. Geoff Bodine later purchased Kulwicki's T-Bird to drive for the Bud Moore/Motorcraft team in 1994. Towards the end of 1993, Bill Stroppe — the builder of many Ford and Lincoln race cars from the early 1950s on — launched a new Winston Cup effort with three T-Birds and Parnelli Jones' son as one driver. Venable Racing also entered NASCAR Winston West competition with a pair of T-Birds. Bob Glidden continued campaigning a 429-powered T-Bird Pro Stocker in NHRA drag racing, while finishing work on a new Pro Stock Mustang. In addition, "Animal" Jim Feuer, made news with a new Pro Mod car called the "Wunderbird," which didn't last long. Late in the 1993 season, the Wunderbird disintegrated after smashing into a guardrail at Maryland International Raceway. As usual, efforts like the Ford motorsports program kept interest in the new T-Birds at a peak.

1994 Thunderbird

Thunderbird — Series 46 — (V-8): The first major T-Bird styling changes in five years were seen in 1994. The LX and Super Coupe both had more rounded front and rear ends. More pronounced air intake slots characterized the frontal appearance. A T-Bird badge "floated" in the slot between the new Aero-design halogen headlights. Engine cooling air was now taken from under the bumper, rather than through a grille. Integrated flush bumpers enhanced the streamlined appearance. An all-new hood was shorter and the front fenders curved into the hood line to enhance aerodynamics. The doors merged into the roofline and the drip rails were fully concealed. New aero-designed rearview mirrors completed the sleek-looking body package. Fine-tuning the body surface directed airflow to create more down-force to improve handling. The totally restyled "organic" interior featured an aircraft-inspired look with twin "pods" for driver and front passenger. Analog gauges were standard. The console swept up into the instrument panel and its curved feature line continued smoothly through to the door panel. A large glove box and dual cup holders in the console were new. Easy-twist round knobs controlled many driving functions. Back-lit instrument panel switches, dual air bags and a CPC-free manual air conditioner were standard. A new Electronic Traction Assist system that linked to the 4-wheel anti-lock brakes was optional. Minor electronic improvements were made to the base V-6 engine in LXs, but the big news was Ford's new 4.6-liter Modular V-8 becoming an option. This single overhead cam engine developed 205 hp. It came attached to an electronically-controlled four-speed automatic transmission that provided "seamless" part-throttle shifts and positive full-throttle gear-shifting. In addition to being more refined than the previous 5.0-liter push rod engine, the new V-8 was also cleaner-burning and more fuel efficient. It increased gas mileage by one to two miles per gallon. The 1994 Super Coupe also had a couple of engine refinements. A new Eaton supercharger with low-drag Teflon-coated rotors was used. In addition to being quieter, it upped output by 10 percent to 230 hp. Torque also increased by five percent. Also new were an improved camshaft, a cam-over-cable throttle linkage and heftier pistons, rods and cylinder heads to complement the harder-working motor. A five-speed manual gearbox remained standard fare, but the electronic four-speed automatic overdrive transmission was optional. Standard features included: all standard FoMoCo safety, anti-theft, convenience items and emissions control equipment, 3.8-liter 140-hp SMPEFI V-6, EEC IV electronic engine controls, automatic overdrive transmission, long-spindle SLA front suspension with variable-rate coil springs, double-acting gas-pressurized shock absorbers and 1.1-in. diameter stabilizer bar, independent H-arm rear suspension with toe control link, variable-rate coil springs, double-acting gas-pressurized shocks and 1.04-in. diameter stabilizer bar, speed-sensitive variable-assist power steering, power front disc/rear drum brakes, 15 x 6-in. stamped steel wheels, styled road wheel covers, P205/70R15 steel-belted black sidewall all-season radial tires, mini spare tire, long-lasting LED taillights, full-length console with floor-mounted leather-wrapped shifter, dual cup holders, manual air conditioning and tinted glass, power windows, power door lock group (LX only), 130-amp. alternator, remote deck lid, remote fuel filler door release, interval windshield wipers, dual electric remote-control mirrors, luxury level door trim with courtesy lights and door bins, 24-oz. cut-pile luxury carpeting, analog performance instrumentation with trip odometer, oil pressure gauge, fuel gauge, temperature gauge and voltmeter, integral fog lamps in front fascia, illuminated entry system,

1994 Ford Thunderbird LX two-door Coupe (OCW)

Thunderbird LX (V-6)

Series No.	Body/ Style No.	Body Type and Seating	Factory Price	Shipping Weight	Production Total
62	66D	2-dr. Coupe-4P	$16,830	3,570 lbs.	Note 1

Thunderbird LX (V-8)

62	66D	2-dr. Coupe-4P	$17,860	3,711 lbs.	Note 1

Super Coupe (4-CYL)

64	66D	2-dr. Coupe-4P	$22,240	3,758 lbs.	Note 1

Note 1: Production of the all models combined was 123,757.

rear seat courtesy lights, luxury cloth bucket seats with 6-way power for driver, rear seat center arm rest, leather-wrapped luxury steering wheel, electronic AM/FM ETR stereo search radio with cassette tape player and digital clock, tilt steering wheel, speed control (LX only), dual-note horn, illuminated entry system (LX only), dome, map, luggage compartment, ash tray, driver's side foot well and glove box lights, rear seat courtesy lights, carpeted low lift over luggage compartment, dual supplemental airbags restraint system, 3-point passive restraint system with active front lap belt and 3-point active restraints in rear outboard position and center rear lap belt, seat belt reminder chime, black moldings on windshield, side windows and rear window, side window defoggers, soft color-keyed front and rear bumpers, integral fog lamps in front fascia, double-spear-shaped body color body side protection moldings, aerodynamic halogen headlights and parking lights, dual covered visor mirrors with headliner pocket and styled road wheel covers.

Super Coupe: The Thunderbird Super Coupe model adds or substitutes the following features over base Thunderbird equipment: 3.8-liter 210-hp supercharged and intercooled SMPEFI V-6 engine with dual exhaust, 5-speed manual overdrive transmission, 4-wheel disc brakes with ABS, hand-operated console-mounted parking brake, indicator light and supercharger boost gauge in instrument cluster, automatic ride control suspension in addition to standard suspension, Handling components including 1.10-in. (28 mm) diameter solid front stabilizer bar and 0.90-in. (23 mm) diameter solid rear stabilizer bar, Traction-Lok rear axle, 110-amp heavy-duty alternator, 58-amp maintenance-free battery (72-amp with automatic overdrive), directional cast-aluminum 16 x 7.0-in. wheels with locking lug nuts and P225/60ZR16 black sidewall performance tires, lower body side cladding, unique rear fascia, sport soft-feel steering wheel, light convenience group with instrument panel courtesy light and engine compartment light, all-cloth articulated sport seats with seat back pockets and power lumbar and seat back bolster adjustments, plus 4-way adjustable head restraints (up/down/forward/back), electronic semi-automatic temperature control, driver's foot rest and adjustable suspension with "firm ride" indicator light.

VIN:

The VIN was stamped on an aluminum tab riveted to the dashboard on the passenger side and was visible through the windshield. The first symbol, 1 = built in the United States. The second symbol, F = Ford. The third symbol, A = a Ford passenger vehicle. The fourth symbol indicated the type of restraint system. The fifth symbol, P = passenger-type vehicle. Symbol six was 6 = Thunderbird. The seventh symbol was the body type: 2=LX Coupe and 4=Super Coupe. The eighth symbol was the engine: 4=232 cid (3.8L) 140 hp V-6, R = 232 cid (3.6L) 230 hp supercharged V-6 and W = 281 cid (4.6L) 205 hp V-8. The ninth symbol was the check digit. The 10th symbol Q= the 1994 model year. The 11th symbol was the assembly plant: H=Lorain, Ohio. The 12th through 17th symbols were the sequential production numbers of the specific vehicle starting at 100001. The vehicle certification label was located on the rear face of the driver's door. The top part of the label indicated the Thunderbird was manufactured by Ford Motor Company. Directly below this was the month and year of manufacture, plus a statement that the car conformed to federal motor vehicle safety standards in effect on the indicated date of manufacture. VIN: The VIN appeared two lines above the UPC. It matched the first through 11th symbols on the VIN tag. Some other codes also appeared. TYPE: Appeared on the left side of the label on the line above the UPC, and indicated PASSENGER. UPC: A scannable bar code carried the UPC. EXT. COLOR: This line carried the exterior paint color(s) code. DSO: The District Special Order code appeared above "DSO" to the right of the exterior paint color code. BODY: The body style code appeared to the extreme left of the bottom line. The Thunderbird codes for this model-year were: LX2 = 2-door LX Coupe and SC2 = 2-door Super Coupe. VR: The vinyl roof type/color code was to the right of the body code. No T-Birds had vinyl tops. MLDG: The molding code was to the right of the vinyl roof code. INT. TRIM: The interior trim code was to the right of the molding code. TAPE: The tape treatment code appeared to right of the interior trim code. R: The radio code was to the right of the A/C code, A. S: The sun roof code was to the right of the radio code. AX: The axle code appeared to the right of the sun roof code. TR: The transmission code appeared to the right of the axle code. The terms and abbreviations shown in left-hand column appeared on the line above the actual codes.

Engines:

Thunderbird Base V-6: 90-degree, overhead valve. Cast-ron block and aluminum head. Displacement: 232 cid (3.8 liters). B & S: 3.80 x 3.40 in. Compression ratio: 9.0:1. Brake hp: 140 at 3800. Torque: 215 lbs.-ft. at 2400. Four main bearings. Hydraulic valve lifters. Induction: Throttle Body Injection. Code: 4.

Thunderbird Super Coupe Supercharged V-6: 90-degree, overhead valve. Cast-iron block and aluminum head. Displacement: 232 cid (3.8 liters). B & S: 3.80 x 3.40 in. Compression ratio: 8.3:1. Brake hp: 210 at 4400. Torque: 315 lbs.-ft. at 2500. Four main bearings. Hydraulic valve lifters. Induction: Sequential Electronic Fuel Injection (Supercharged). Code: R.

Thunderbird LX Optional V-8: Modular, overhead cam V-8. Single overhead cam. Displacement: 281 cid (4.6 liters). B & S: 3.60 x 3.60. Compression ratio: 9.0:1. Brake hp: 205 at 4500 rpm. Torque: 265 lbs.-ft. at 3200 rpm. Hydraulic valve lifters. Induction: Sequential fuel injection.

Chassis:

Wheelbase: 113 in. Overall length: 200.3. Overall width: 72.7. Overall height: 52.5 in. Front headroom: 38.1 in. Rear headroom: 37.5 in. Front legroom: 42.5 in. Rear legroom: 35.8 in. Front shoulder room: 59 in. Rear shoulder room: 58.9 in. Trunk capacity: 15.1 cu. ft. Front tread: 61.6 in. Rear tread: 60.2 in. Wheels: 15 in. Tires: (LX) P205/70R15 black sidewall, (Super Coupe) P225/60ZR16 black sidewall.

Technical:

Front suspension: Long spindle SLA type, variable-rate coil springs, tubular gas shocks and stabilizer bar. Rear Suspension Independent, H-arm design with toe control link, variable-rate coil springs, gas shocks and stabilizer bar. Steering: Power rack-and-pinion. Turning circle: 39 ft. Brakes: Power front disc/rear drum on LX, Power four-wheel disc with ABS on Super Coupe. Fuel tank capacity: 18 gallons. Seating capacity: Five (5). Fuel Economy: 17-24 mpg. Transmission: 4-speed automatic. Fuel Economy: [Base V-6] 19 mpg city/27 mpg highway, [Supercharged V-6] 20 mpg city/27 mpg highway and [V-8] 15 mpg city/23 mpg highway. Weight distribution: 57/43 percent.

Options:

4.6-liter V-8 ($515 net). Four-speed overdrive transmission in T-Bird Super Coupe ($790). California emissions ($85). High-altitude emissions (no charge). P225/60ZR16 black sidewall all-season performance tires on Super Coupe ($70 extra). Leather seating surfaces in LX ($490). Leather seating surfaces in Super Coupe, includes fold-down rear seat and requires power seats and locks ($615). Anti-lock braking system, includes Traction-Lok axle ($565). Anti-theft system ($245). Cold weather group on LX and Super Coupe, including engine block heater, 72-amp battery, rear window defroster and 3.27:1 Traction-Lok rear axle ($18-$20-$300 depending on transmission and if car has PEPs 155A or 157A). Front floor mats ($30). Keyless entry, including illuminated entry system and power lock group in LX or Super Coupe with luxury group ($215), in Super Coupe ($295). Power moon roof ($740). Hands Free cellular telephone ($530). Traction assist in LX only ($210). Tri-coat paint ($225). Electronic premium cassette radio with premium sound system and power antenna ($370). Ford JBL audio system ($500). Trunk mounted compact disc changer ($785). Group 2 (RPO 411) includes lock group, power group, speed control and 6-way power driver's seat for Super Coupe only ($800). Group 2 (RPO 432) includes semi-automatic temperature control and rear window defroster ($160 for Super Coupe and $315 for

1994 Ford Thunderbird two-door Super Coupe (FMC)

LX). Group 3 includes cast-aluminum wheels, P215/70RX15 tires for LX only, plus dual illuminated vanity mirrors ($95 for Super Coupe or $305 for LX). Luxury group includes Autolamp on and off delay, illuminated entry system for Super Coupe only, light group for LX only, 6-way power passenger seat and Integrated warning lamp module for LX only ($580 for LX and $555 for Super Coupe). Preferred equipment package 155A for LX ($620, but no charge with applicable Group 2 discounts). Preferred equipment package 157A for Super Coupe ($1,055, but no charge with applicable Group 2 discounts).

History:

Alexander J. Trotman was Chairman of the Board and CEO of Ford Motor Co. Allan D. Gilmour was Vice Chairman of the corporation. Louis R. Ross was Vice Chairman and Chief Technical Officer of the Ford Automotive Group. Ross Roberts was again Ford Division's General Manager and Phillip M. Novell remained divisional General Sales manager. Calendar-year output was 146,846 units. A total of 123,757 T-Birds was produced in the model year. This represented 2.05 percent of the industry total. Of these units, all were made in Lorain, Ohio. Calendar year dealer sales amounted to 130,713. *Motor Trend* road tested the V-8-optioned LX. It moved from 0-60 mph in 8.5 seconds and did the quarter-mile in 16.4 seconds at 87.6 mph. It braked from 60-0 mph in 139 feet. In stock car racing, T-Birds had a super year in 1993, led by Rusty Wallace in his number 2 Miller Genuine Draft Ford. Wallace took 10 first place finishes. Geoff Bodine (three wins) and Mark Martin and Jimmy Spencer (two wins each) also put in strong performances all year long. Bill Elliott and Ricky Rudd both had a win apiece, while Brett Bodine, Morgan Shepard, Rick Mast and Lake Speed contributed valuable Winston Cup points. In 31 contests, Fords sat on the pole 25 times and won 20 checkered flags. They also established 17 new track records. However, it became a clear case of winning the battles and losing the war, as Chevy pilot Dale Earnhardt nailed his seventh Winston Cup points championship with his consistent high-place finishes. One thing that hurt the blue oval effort was Ernie Irvan's wreck of his Texaco T-Bird. The car was a hot contender, with three victories during the first half of '94, but the wreck put Irvan out for the season and longer. Ford did capture NASCAR's Manufacturer's Cup.

1995 Thunderbird

Thunderbird — Series 46 — (V-8): The 1995 T-Birds had few changes from the 1994 models. The LX and the Super Coupe returned. Both models had modest weight changes. The LX continued to utilize the 3.8-liter 140-hp V-6 as its standard power plant, with the Modular V-8 as an option. The Super Coupe included a 230-hp supercharged version of the V-6, plus a standard five-speed manual transmission and anti-lock brakes. Dual air bags are standard in both models and a Traction Control system was optional with both. Conventional power steering was standard in the LX. Variable-assist steering was standard in LXs with the optional V-8 and in Super Coupes. An anti-theft alarm, an engine block heater, a Traction-Lok axle and a heavy-duty battery were no longer offered. Standard features included: Front and rear soft color-keyed 5-mph bumpers, flush windshield, door quarter window and backlight glass, aerodynamic halogen headlights and parking lamps, dual color-keyed remote-control electric mirrors, black windshield, window, door quarter window and backlight moldings, body-color double-spear-shaped body side protection moldings, Bolfon design road wheel styled wheel covers, air bag supplemental restraint system, 3-point safety belts with active-restraints in all outboard positions and center rear belt and reminder chime, foot-operated parking brake, 24-oz. cut-pile carpeting, full-length console with floor-mounted leather-wrapped gear shift handle and storage compartment, dual console-mounted cup holders, luxury level door trim with courtesy lights and illuminated switches, front floor mats, driver's side foot well lights, illuminated entry system, map/dome, luggage compartment, front ash tray, glove box and rear seat courtesy lights, low liftover design carpeted luggage compartment, dual visor mirrors, luxury cloth bucket seats with 6-way power driver's seat, luxury leather-wrapped tilt steering wheel, manual air conditioner with rotary controls, 130-amp alternator, 58-amp maintenance-free battery, power front disc/rear drum brakes, digital clock, EEC-IV electronic engine controls system, 3.8-liter SMPEFI V-6 engine, 18-gallon fuel tank, tethered gas filler cap, complete tinted glass and dual note horn.

Super Coupe: The Thunderbird Super Coupe model adds or substitutes the following features over base Thunderbird equipment: Unique rear bumper treatment, lower body side cladding, integral fog lamps in front fascia, 16 x 7-in. directional cast-aluminum wheels with locking lug nuts, console-mounted hand-operated parking brake with leather-wrapped handle, driver's foot rest, integrated warning lamp module, light group

1995 Ford Thunderbird LX two-door Coupe (OCW)

including right-hand panel courtesy light and engine compartment light, articulated bucket seats in cloth/leather/vinyl trim with power adjustable lumbar support and seat back bolsters, rear seat head rests, electronic air conditioner with semi-automatic temperature control, 110-amp alternator, Traction-Lok rear axle, 58-amp (72-amp with automatic overdrive) Maintenance-Free battery, antilock braking system with 4-wheel disc brakes, 3.8-liter SMPEFI supercharged and intercooled V-6 with dual exhausts and speed control deletion.

VIN:

The VIN was stamped on an aluminum tab riveted to the dashboard on the passenger side and was visible through the windshield. The first symbol, 1= built in the United States. The second symbol, F = Ford. The third symbol, A = Ford passenger vehicle. The fourth symbol indicated the type of restraint system. The fifth symbol P denoted a passenger-type vehicle. The sixth symbol, 6 = Thunderbird. The seventh symbol was the body type. 2=LX Coupe and 4=Super Coupe. The eighth symbol indicated the engine: 4=232 cid (3.8L) 140 hp V-6, R = 232 cid (3.6L) 230 hp supercharged V-6 and W = 281 cid (4..6L) 205 hp V-8. The ninth symbol was the check digit. The 10th symbol R= the 1995 model year. The 11th symbol was the assembly plant: H=Lorain, Ohio. The 12th through 17th symbols were the sequential production numbers of the specific vehicle starting at 100001. The vehicle certification label was located on the rear face of the driver's door. The top part of the label indicated the Thunderbird was manufactured by Ford Motor Company. Directly below this was the month and year of manufacture, plus a statement that the car conformed to federal motor vehicle safety standards in effect on the indicated date of manufacture. VIN: The VIN appeared two lines above the UPC. It matched the first to 11th symbols on the VIN tag. Some other codes also appeared. TYPE: Appeared on the left side of the label on the line above the UPC and indicated PASSENGER. UPC: A scannable bar code carried the UPC. EXT. COLOR: This line carried the exterior paint color(s) code. DSO: The District Special Order code appeared above "DSO" to the right of the exterior paint color code. BODY: The body style code appeared to the extreme left of the bottom line. The Thunderbird codes for this model-year were: LX2 = 2-door LX Coupe, SC2 = 2-door Super Coupe. VR: The vinyl roof type/color code was to the right of the body code. No T-Birds had vinyl tops. MLDG: The molding code was to the right of the vinyl roof code. INT. TRIM: The interior trim code was to the right of the molding code. TAPE: The tape treatment code appeared to right of the interior trim code. R: The radio code was to the right of the A/C, code A. S: The sun roof code was to the right of the radio code. AX: The axle code appeared to the right of the sun roof code. TR: The transmission code was to the right of the axle code. The terms and abbreviations shown in the left-hand column appeared on the line above the actual codes.

Thunderbird LX (V-6)

Series No.	Body/Style No.	Body Type and Seating	Factory Price	Shipping Weight	Production Total
62	66D	2-dr. Coupe-4P	$17,225	3,536 lbs.	Note 1

Thunderbird LX (V-8)

| 62 | 66D | 2-dr. Coupe-4P | $18,355 | 3,673 lbs. | Note 1 |

Super Coupe (V-8)

| 64 | 66D | 2-dr. Coupe-4P | $22,735 | 3,758 lbs. | Note 1 |

Note 1: Production of the all models combined was 116,069.

Engines:

Thunderbird Base V-6: 90-degree, overhead valve. Cast-iron block and aluminum head. Displacement: 232 cid (3.8 liters). B & S: 3.80 x 3.40 in. Compression ratio: 9.0:1. Brake hp: 140 at 3800. Torque: 215 lbs.-ft. at 2400. Four main bearings. Hydraulic valve lifters. Induction: Throttle Body Injection. Code: 4.

Thunderbird Super Coupe Supercharged V-6: 90-degree, overhead valve. Cast-iron block and aluminum head. Displacement: 232 cid (3.8 liters). B & S: 3.80 x 3.40 in. Compression ratio: 8.3:1. Brake hp: 230 at 4400. Torque: 330 lbs.-ft. at 2500. Four main bearings. Hydraulic valve lifters. Induction: Sequential Electronic Fuel Injection (Supercharged). Code: R.

Thunderbird LX Optional V-8: Modular, overhead cam. Single overhead cam. Displacement: 281 cid (4.6 liters). B & S: 3.60 x 3.60. Compression ratio: 9.0:1. Brake hp: 205 at 4500 rpm. Torque: 265 lbs.-ft. at 3200 rpm. Hydraulic valve lifters. Induction: Sequential fuel injection.

Chassis:

Wheelbase: 113 in. Overall length: 200.3. Overall width: 72.7. Overall height: 52.5 in. Front headroom: 38.1 in. Rear headroom: 37.5 in. Front legroom: 42.5 in. Rear legroom: 35.8 in. Front shoulder room: 59.1 in. Rear shoulder room: 58.9 in. Trunk capacity: 15.1 cu. ft. Front tread: 61.6 in. Rear tread: 60.2 in. Wheels: 15 in. Tires: (LX) P205/70R15 black sidewall, (Super Coupe) P225/60ZR16 black sidewall.

Technical:

Front suspension: Long spindle SLA type, variable-rate coil springs, tubular gas shocks and stabilizer bar. Rear Suspension Independent, H-arm design with toe control link, variable-rate coil springs, gas shocks and stabilizer bar. Steering: Power rack-and-pinion. Turning circle: 39 ft. Brakes: Power front disc/rear drum on LX, Power four-wheel disc with ABS on Super Coupe. Fuel tank capacity: 18 gallons. Seating capacity: Five (5). Fuel Economy: 17-24 mpg. Transmission: 4-speed automatic. Fuel Economy: [Base V-6] 19 mpg city/27 mpg highway, [Supercharged V-6] 20 mpg city/27 mpg highway and [V-8] 15 mpg city/23 mpg highway. Weight distribution: 57/43 percent.

Options:

4.6-liter V-8, including heavy-duty battery and speed-sensitive power steering for LX only ($615 net). Four-speed overdrive transmission in T-Bird Super Coupe ($790). California emissions ($95). High-altitude emissions (no charge). P225/60ZR16 black sidewall all-season performance tires on Super Coupe ($70 extra). Leather seating surfaces in LX ($490). Leather seating surfaces in Super Coupe, includes fold-down rear seat and requires power seats and locks ($615). Option Group 1 includes power lock group, speed control and 6-way power driver's seat for Super Coupe ($800). Option Group 2 includes rear window defroster for both models and semi-automatic temperature control for LX ($160 for Super Coupe and $315 for LX). Option Group 3 includes cast-aluminum wheels and P21570R15 black sidewall tires ($210). Anti-lock braking system, includes Traction-Lok axle ($565). Traction-Lok rear axle (standard on Super Coupe with 5-speed, otherwise $95). Front license plate bracket (no charge). Front floor mats ($30). Remote keyless entry, including illuminated entry system two remotes LX or Super Coupe with luxury group ($215), in Super Coupe ($295). Luxury group includes Autolamp on and off delay, power antenna, illuminated entry system for Super Coupe only, light group for LX only and dual illuminated visor mirrors and integrated warning lamp module for LX only ($350 for LX and $325 for Super Coupe). Power-operated moon roof, requires luxury group and PEP 155A or PEP 157A ($740). 6-way power passenger seat, requires Option Group 1 ($290). Hands Free cellular telephone ($530). Traction-Assist, requires ABS and luxury group and not available for Super Coupe with 5-speed (standard for Super Coupe with automatic transmission, otherwise $210). Tri-Coat paint ($225). AM/FM stereo ETR with cassette and premium sound system ($290). AM/FM stereo ETR with compact disc player and premium sound system ($430). Heavy-duty 72-amp battery ($25). Engine block heater ($20). 155A for LX ($620, but no charge with applicable Group 2 discounts). Preferred equipment package 157A for Super Coupe ($1,055, but no charge with applicable Group 2 discounts).

History:

Alexander J. Trotman was Chairman of the Board and CEO of Ford Motor Co. Louis R. Ross was Vice Chairman and Chief Technical Officer. Ross Roberts was again Ford Division's General Manager and Phillip M. Novell remained divisional General Sales manager. Calendar-year output was 94,027 units. A total of 116,069 T-Birds was produced in the model year. This represented 1.72 percent of the industry total. Of these units, all were made in Lorain, Ohio. Calendar year dealer sales amounted to 104,254. After capturing its second NASCAR Manufacturer's Cup in a row, Ford entered 1995 with a dramatic television ad promoting its latest stock cars as the most ominous thing to come from "bird-dom" since Alfred Hitchcock's classic thriller film "The Birds." It was a fitting throwback to the era in which the first T-Birds was created and a reminder to many of the marque's continuing vitality on its 40th birthday. As the '95 Ford sales catalog asked, "How many cars on the road today can you identify at a glance, whose badges elicit instant recognition and admiration? There certainly aren't many, but one should readily come to mind. It's the familiar Thunderbird wide wingspan."

1996 Thunderbird

Thunderbird — Series 46 — (V-8): With the discontinuation of the Super Coupe for 1996, T-Bird was reduced to a one-model series. Remaining was the LX Coupe. It didn't take a genius to read the writing on the wall. Ford was taking at hard look at the future of the T-Bird in a changing marketplace. The T-Bird received a mild face-lift for the 1996 model year, but remained one of Ford's best chassis. The T-Bird handled well when leaned on for a big (16.7 ft.-long) car. It was larger than the Contour four-door sedan. The 1996 LX received a mild restyling in the hood, grille, headlight and bumper cover areas. Wide body cladding and now door handles were color-keyed to match the exterior paint for what Ford called "a sporty, monochromatic look." The standard 3.8-liter V-6 was upgraded and was now rated at 145 hp. Optional at no cost was a package consisting of rear window defroster, P215/70R15 tires and cast aluminum wheels. An antitheft system and traction control system returned to the optional equipment list after not being offered the year previous. A four-speed automatic overdrive transmission was standard. Standard features included: Dual front air bags, manual air conditioning, 130-amp alternator, rear seat center armrest, 58-amp maintenance-free battery, power front disc/rear drum brakes, soft, color-keyed front and rear bumpers, 18-oz. cut-pile carpeting, lower body side cladding with integral body-color body side molding, digital clock, full-length console with floor-mounted shift, storage and dual cupholders, power remote deck lid release, power door locks with illuminated switches, luxury level door trim with courtesy lights, stowage bins and illuminated door switches, 145-hp, 3.8-liter SMPEFI V-6 engine, EEC-IV electronic engine control system, 18-gallon fuel tank with tethered cap, solar-tinted glass, aerodynamic halogen complex-reflector head- and parking lamps, rear seat heating ducts, analog instrument cluster with speedometer, trip odometer, voltmeter, oil pressure gauge, fuel gauge and temperature gauge, Interior lights - dome/map, luggage compartment, ashtray, driver's side foot well, glove box and engine compartment, low liftover carpeted luggage compartment, dual electric remote-controlled color-keyed mirrors, black moldings on windshield, backlight, door and quarter windows, foot-operated parking brake, 3-point seat belts with front and rear outboard positions, center lap belt and reminder chime, rear-wheel drive, luxury cloth bucket seats, leather shift knob, mini spare tire, speed control, AM/FM/stereo/cassette ETR sound system with four speakers, power steering, tilt steering wheel, long-spindle SLA front suspension with stabilizer bar, variable rate springs, lower control arm and tension strut, independent H-arm rear suspension with variable rate springs and stabilizer bar, full-width taillights, P205/70R15 black sidewall all-season radial tires, four-speed ECT automatic transmission with overdrive and overdrive lockout, styled road wheel covers, power windows with illuminated switches and variable interval windshield wipers.

VIN:

The VIN was stamped on an aluminum tab riveted to the dashboard on the passenger side and was visible through the windshield. The first symbol, 1: = built in the United States. The second symbol, F = Ford. The third symbol, A = Ford passenger vehicle. The fourth symbol was the type of restraint system. The fifth symbol, P = passenger-type vehicle. The sixth symbol, 6 = Thunderbird. The seventh symbol was the body type: 2=LX Coupe. The eighth symbol was the engine: 4=232 cid (3.8L) 145 hp V-6 and W = 281 cid (4.6L) 205 hp V-8. The ninth symbol was the check digit. The 10th symbol T= the 1996 model year. The 11th symbol was the assembly plant: H=Lorain, Ohio. Symbols 12 through 17 were the sequential production numbers of the specific vehicle starting at 100001. The vehicle certification label was located on the rear face of the driver's door. The top part of the label indicated the Thunderbird was manufactured by Ford Motor Company. Directly below this was the month and year of manufacture, plus a statement that the car conformed to federal motor vehicle safety standards in effect on the indicated date of manufacture. VIN: The VIN appeared two lines above the UPC. It matched the first to 11th symbols on the VIN tag. Some other codes also appeared. TYPE: Appeared on the left side of label on line above the UPC and indicated PASSENGER. UPC: A scannable bar code carried the UPC. EXT. COLOR: This line carried the exterior paint color(s) code. DSO: The District Special Order code appeared above "DSO" to the right of the exterior paint color code. BODY: The body style code appeared to the extreme left of the bottom line. The only Thunderbird code for this model-year was LX2 = 2-door LX Coupe. VR: The vinyl roof type/color code was to the right of the body code. No T-Birds had vinyl tops. MLDG: The molding code was to the right of the vinyl roof color code. INT. TRIM: The interior trim code was to the right of the molding code. TAPE: The tape treatment code appeared to right of the interior trim code. R: The radio code was to the right of the A/C code, A. S: The sun roof code was to the right of the radio code. AX: The axle code appeared to the right of the sun roof code. TR: The transmission code appeared to the right of the axle code. The terms and abbreviations shown in the left-hand column appeared on the line above the actual codes.

1996 Ford Thunderbird LX two-door Coupe (OCW)

Thunderbird LX (V-6)

Series No.	Body/ Style No.	Body Type and Seating	Factory Price	Shipping Weight	Production Total
62	66D	2-dr. Coupe-4P	$17,485	3,561 lbs.	Note 1

Thunderbird LX (V-8)

62	66D	2-dr. Coupe-4P	$18,615	3,689 lbs.	Note 1

Note 1: Production of the all models combined was 82,010.

Engines:

Thunderbird Base V-6: 90-degree, overhead valve. Cast-iron block and aluminum head. Displacement: 232 cid (3.8 liters). B & S: 3.80 x 3.40 in. Compression ratio: 9.0:1. Brake hp: 140 at 3800. Torque: 215 lbs.-ft. at 2400. Four main bearings. Hydraulic valve lifters. Induction: Throttle Body Injection. Code: 4.

Thunderbird LX Optional V-8: Modular, overhead cam. Single overhead cam. Displacement: 281 cid (4.6 liters). B & S: 3.60 x 3.60. Compression ratio: 9.0:1. Brake hp: 205 at 4500 rpm. Torque: 265 lbs.-ft. at 3200 rpm. Hydraulic valve lifters. Induction: Sequential fuel injection.

Chassis:

Wheelbase: 113 in. Overall length: 200.3. Overall width: 72.7. Overall height: 52.5 in. Front headroom: 38.1 in. Rear headroom: 37.5 in. Front legroom: 42.5 in. Rear legroom: 35.8 in. Front shoulder room: 59.1 in. Rear shoulder room: 58.9 in. Trunk capacity: 15.1 cu. ft. Front tread: 61.6 in. Rear tread: 60.2 in. Wheels: 15 in. Tires: (LX) P205/70R15 black sidewall.

Technical:

Front suspension: Long spindle SLA type, variable-rate coil springs, tubular gas shocks and stabilizer bar. Rear Suspension Independent, H-arm design with toe control link, variable-rate coil springs, gas shocks and stabilizer bar. Steering: Power rack-and-pinion. Turning circle: 39 ft. Brakes: Power front disc/rear drum on LX, Power four-wheel disc with ABS on Super Coupe. Fuel tank capacity: 18 gallons. Seating capacity: Five (5). Transmission: 4-speed automatic. Fuel tank: 18 gallons. Fuel Economy: [Base V-6] 19 mpg city/27 mpg highway, [V-8] 15 mpg city/23 mpg highway. Weight distribution: 57/43 percent.

Options:

Preferred Equipment Packages: (155A) rear window defroster, P215/70R15 tires and cast aluminum wheels (NC). (157A) 4.6-liter SOHC V-8 including speed-sensitive power steering, heavy-duty battery, 6-way power driver's seat, illuminated entry system and leather-wrapped steering wheel ($835 net). California emissions system ($100). Leather-faced bucket seats ($490). Remote keyless entry ($270). Front floor mats ($30). Electronic AM/FM stereo radio with cassette and premium sound ($290). Electronic AM/FM stereo radio with CD player and premium sound ($430). Anti-lock brakes ($570). Anti-theft system ($145). Power moon roof ($740). Sport Option: includes 16-inch aluminum wheels, P225/65R16 BSW tires, modified stabilizer bars and revised spring rates ($210). Tri-coat paint ($225). Traction assist ($210). Traction-Lok axle ($95). Power driver's seat ($290). Luxury Group: includes electronic semi-automatic temperature control air conditioning, dual illuminated visor mirrors, light group, integrated warning lamp module and power antenna ($495). 15-inch chrome wheels ($580).

History:

Alexander J. Trotman was Chairman of the Board and CEO of Ford Motor Co. Ross Roberts was again Ford Division's General Manager and Phillip M. Novell remained divisional General Sales manager. Calendar-year output was 77,094 units. A total of 82,010 T-Birds was produced in the model year. This represented 1.60 percent of the industry total. Of these units, all were made in Lorain, Ohio. Calendar year dealer sales amounted to 79,721. Ford Motor Company's board of directors asked Alex Trotman to stay on as Chairman of the Board for a year and a half past his 60th birthday, but Jacques A. Nasser, a native of Lebanon raised in Australia, emerged in 1995 as Trotman's successor.

Nasser was promoted to the position of President of Ford Automotive Operations in October 1996. Nasser immediately initiated a product review that concluded that the Thunderbird should be dropped from the model lineup. This was done following the 1997 model year.

2001 Thunderbird Concept

Thunderbird Series — (V-8): An automotive legend was re-born when the T-Bird made its return as an all-new concept car at the North American International Auto Show on January 3, 1999. The all-new Thunderbird concept drew on the T-Bird's rich heritage in introducing a modern interpretation of an automotive legend. It incorporated the trademark design cues that set the original T-Bird apart from a crowd of 1955 sports cars and made it an American cultural. "The Ford Thunderbird has an emotional hold on the American public that spans decades and generations," said Jac Nasser, Ford's president and chief executive officer at the time. "This timeless classic is an important part of Ford Motor Company's heritage and, indeed, this country's automotive history. The new concept car is an indication of where we're headed with the Thunderbird when it goes back into production for the new millennium." The new concept car featured design elements from T-Birds of 1955-1957 and 1961-1962 simplified into contemporary forms. Its design cues included port-hole windows, aluminum-finished chevrons, a hood scoop and a trademark Thunderbird badge. "The design of the Thunderbird concept reflects the attitude of a simpler time," J Mays - Ford's vice president of Design — stated at the show in Detroit, Michigan. "The unbridled optimism and the confident attitude of the 1950's comes through in an absolutely modern design." The Thunderbird concept's stance was designed to be relaxed and confident. Mays achieved this attitude via a negative-wedge design in which the front of the vehicle appears to be set slightly higher than the rear. The 18-inch, eight-spoke aluminum wheels and P245R50-18 tires gave the Sunmist Yellow show car a sporty stance. A circular design theme ran throughout the vehicle, starting with the round headlamps and fog lamps and back to the round taillights. The removable hard-top, with its porthole windows, was the signature cue from the original Thunderbird. "This is an aspirational design," Mays told the press. "Simple shapes combined with timeless materials and textures conveys a relaxed, confident look and a feel that is the true essence of the original Thunderbird." The oval grille opening remained true to the original with an aluminum finished egg-crate design. Two large fog lamps were set into the front bumper, with a secondary grille opening below them. The scoop was integrated into the hood design — rather than serving merely as a prominent addition. The porthole windows were functional, allowing additional light to enter the vehicle and providing better rearward visibility when the top is on. The chrome slash marks decorating the show car's front quarter panels were cut into the sheet metal and represented a modern interpretation of the chrome chevrons on the original car. The concept car also featured cues from 1961-1962 Thunderbirds, which were more equally proportioned than their predecessors. The show car's interior continued the design theme by combining modern materials and a two-tone color combination. Two, black leather-wrapped bucket seats were specially stitched with a washboard-like pattern. The interior door panels were covered in black leather with yellow leather inserts and brushed aluminum accents. The instrument panel sported white gauges with turquoise pointers. The upper instrument panel, steering wheel and floor-mounted shifter were covered in black leather. The lower instrument panel and glove box were accented in yellow leather, matching the car's Sunmist Yellow exterior. A black leather wrapped tonneau cover was visible when the show car's hardtop was removed. Aluminum-finished Thunderbird body badges featured a turquoise insert across the wings. They appeared prominently on the vehicle's nose, rear and across the front seatbacks. An aluminum finished Thunderbird script stretched across both rear quarter panels. Standard equipment was very similar to 2002 Premium production version.

VIN:

It was undetermined for this concept car, but probably was around 1FAHP60A11Y100001.

2001 Thunderbird Concept

Series No.	Body/ Style No.	Body Type & Seating	Factory Price	Shipping Weight	Production Total
6	0	2-dr. Roadster-4P	—	—	Note 1

Note 1: Calendar 2001 production of 5,177 T-Birds did not include this concept car. Those cars were early 2002 production models.

Engine:

Thunderbird V-8: Double overhead cam. 32 valve. Aluminum block and heads. Displacement: 240 cid (3.9 liters). B & S: 3.39 x 3.35 in. Compression ratio: 10.55:1. Brake hp: 252 at 6100 rpm. Torque: 261 at 4300 rpm. Sequential multiport electronic fuel injection.

2001 Ford Thunderbird two-door Roadster (FMC)

Wheelbase: 107.2-in. Overall length: 186.3. Overall width: 72. Overall height: 52.1 in. Front headroom: 37.2 in. Front legroom: 43.7 in. Front hip room: 53.7. Front shoulder room: 57.3 in. Luggage capacity: 8.5 cu. ft. Front tread: 61.6 in. Rear tread: 60.2 in. Front suspension: short and long arm type with aircraft-grade forged or cast aluminum control arms and stabilizer bar. Rear suspension: short and long arm type with stabilizer bar. Steering: Power rack-and-pinion. Brakes: Power four-wheel disc with ABS. Fuel tank capacity: 18 gallons. Transmission: Five-speed automatic. Wheels: 17 x 7.5-in. alloy rims. Tires: P235/50-VR17. Fuel tank: 18 gallons.

Options:

Not applicable to this concept car.

History:

The new Ford Thunderbird concept vehicle was a modern interpretation of a classic American icon – a phenomenon that Ford labeled "modern-heritage" in its first press kit for the all-new T-Bird. "Styling heritage comes from the soul of a great automotive nameplate," stated J Mays, Ford's Vice President of Design. "There are only a select few nameplates that have earned their way into the hearts of the motoring public by establishing a true heritage. Thunderbird is certainly one of them." Styling elements of the Thunderbird concept car had meaning beyond mere sheet metal. With the Thunderbird concept, Ford designers had a wealth of styling cues to call upon. The project direction was to recreate the enthusiasm of the original car by building a two-seat roadster with Thunderbird elements in a distinctly modern interpretation. The modern Thunderbird concept saluted the original, but also symbolized turn-of-the-millennium automotive styling. Mays insisted, "It's not retro, while the Thunderbird concept is loaded with heritage cues, it is a decidedly modern machine. This hint's at the direction we plan to take when we bring back the production car early in the next century."

2002 Thunderbird

Thunderbird Series — (V-8): After a four-year absence, the T-Bird returned in 2001 as an all-new 2002 "retro" model. It was a throwback to the original roadster-convertible that wore the T-Bird name. The new car came only as a two-seat roadster with a modern interpretation of the styling themes of the original 1955 Thunderbird. The car was built on the Lincoln LS platform and powered by Lincoln's 3.9-liter double overhead camshaft V-8. It had a fully-independent suspension, four-wheel disc brakes and an antilock braking system. The styling was characterized by a machined egg-crate grille, aluminum finished decorative chevrons, a scooped hood, rounded headlights, large round taillights, fog lamps and port hole windows in the optional removable hardtop. Traditional-looking turquoise blue Thunderbird emblems identified the car. The wraparound windshield was set at a rakish 64-degree angle and surrounded by a wide band of chrome. The doors were set to the center, rather than to the rear, and a crisp feature line runs from the headlights straight back to the taillights creating the hint of a '50s-style tail fin. The T-Bird interior continued the back-to-the-'50s design theme

by combining modern materials and finishes with the flair of the past and two-tone upholstery options. The standard black leather-wrapped bucket seats had a "Thunderbird tuck-and-roll" look. With the two-tone interior the door panels were covered in black leather with colored leather inserts and brushed aluminum accents. The upper instrument panel, steering wheel and floor-mounted shifter were black leather. The lower instrument panel and glove box carried color accents. When the package was ordered for Yellow, Red or Blue cars, the color accents matched. In Black or White cars, the color accents were red. A black leather tonneau cover was visible when the hardtop was removed. Standard equipment varied according to level of trim as follows:

Deluxe: 3.9-liter DOHC V-8, a new-generation power train electronic controller (PTEC), a specially-engineered close-ratio five-speed automatic transmission, 17 x 7.5 cast-aluminum rims, P235/50VR17 all-season tires, a space saver spare tire, four-wheel independent suspension, front and rear stabilizer bars, front and rear ventilated disc brakes, antilock braking system with electronic brake force distribution, vented rotors and dual-piston calipers, an airbag deactivation switch, child seat anchors, emergency release in trunk, leather upholstery, front bucket seats with headrests, 6-way power driver's seat with adjustable lumbar support, 2-way power passenger seat, remote vehicle antitheft system, auto-delay-off headlights, variable intermittent windshield wipers, power-operated convertible top, glass rear window, rear window defogger, remote power door locks, one-touch power windows, dual power outside rearview mirrors, AM/FM cassette 6-CD stereo, multi-CD changer located in dash, 180-watts stereo output, eight speakers, element antenna, cruise control, power steering, tilt-and-telescopic steering wheel with built-in cruise and audio controls, front cupholders, front door pockets, front seat console with storage provisions, retained accessory power, dual-zone climate control system, front reading lights, dual visor-vanity mirrors, leather-wrapped steering wheel, front floor mats, trunk light, tachometer, trip computer, clock and low-fuel warning.

Premium: In addition to or instead of deluxe equipment, the Premium model includes chrome alloy wheel rims and traction control.

Nieman Marcus: In addition to or instead of premium equipment, this model included a special Black-and-Silver paint scheme, a removable hardtop, an element antenna, Neiman Marcus emblems on the instrument panel, front floor mats with Neiman Marcus emblems and a special vehicle identification number as a guarantee of authenticity.

VIN:

The VIN was stamped on an aluminum tab riveted to the dashboard on the passenger side and was visible through the windshield. The first symbol, 1 = built in the United States. The second symbol, F = Ford. The third symbol A = Ford passenger vehicle. The fourth symbol indicated a type of restraint system: B=Active belts, F=Driver and passenger airbags and side airbags and active belts and H=Driver and passenger airbags and side airbags, curtains or canopies and active belts. The fifth symbol, P = passenger-type vehicle. The sixth and seventh symbols were the body style: 60=Thunderbird base convertible and 64=Neiman Marcus Thunderbird convertible. The eighth symbol denoted the engine: A=3.9-liter EFI double overhead cam V-8. The ninth symbol was the check digit. The 10th symbol was 2=2002 model year. The 11th symbol was the assembly plant: Y=Wixom, Michigan. Symbols 12 through 17 were the sequential production numbers of specific vehicles starting at 100001.

Deluxe Thunderbird (V-8)

Series No.	Body/ Style No.	Body Type and Seating	Factory Price	Shipping Weight	Production Total
6	0	2-dr. Roadster-4P	$34,965	3,775 lbs.	Note 1

Deluxe Thunderbird (V-8)

6	0	2-dr. with Hardtop-4P	$35,965	3,863 lbs.	Note 1

Nieman Marcus Edition Thunderbird (V-8)

6	0	2-dr. with Hardtop-4P	$41,995	3,863 lbs.	Note 1

Premium Thunderbird (V-8)

6	0	2-dr. Roadster-4P	$38,465	3,775 lbs.	Note 1

Premium Thunderbird (V-8)

6	0	2-dr. with Hardtop-4P	$41,465	3,863 lbs.	Note 1

Note 1: Calendar 2001 production of the all models combined was 5,177. Model-year production for 2002 models was 31,121 units. This included 8,686 cars in Evening Black (including Neiman Marcus editions), 7,353 in Thunderbird Blue, 7,184 in Torch Red, 4,149 in Whisper White and 3,749 in Inspiration Yellow.

Engine:

Thunderbird V-8: Double overhead cam V-8. 32 valve. Aluminum block and heads. Displacement: 240 cid (3.9 liters). B & S: 3.39 x 3.35 in. Compression ratio: 10.55:1. Brake hp: 252 at 6100 rpm. Torque: 261 lbs.-ft. at 4300 rpm. Sequential multiport electronic fuel injection. VIN code A.

Chassis:

Wheelbase: 107.2-in. Overall length: 186.3. Overall width: 72. Overall height: 52.1 in. Front headroom: 37.2 in. Front legroom: 43.7 in. Front hip room: 53.7. Front shoulder room: 57.3 in. Luggage capacity: 8.5 cu. ft. Front tread: 60.5 in. Rear tread: 60.2 in. Wheels: 17 x 7.5-in. alloy rims. Tires: P235/50-VR17.

Technical:

Front suspension: Independent, unequal-length control arms made of aircraft-grade forged or cast aluminum, coil springs, shock absorbers and stabilizer bar. Rear Suspension Independent, unequal-length control arms with anti-lift design, coil springs, shock absorbers and stabilizer bar. Steering: Power, speed-sensitive, variable-assist rack-and-pinion with 18.0:1 overall ratio and 35.2-ft. curb-to-curb turn circle. Turns lock-to-lock: 3. Frame: Cross-car beam and three bolted-on X-braces. Front brakes: Power disc with ABS, outside rotor diameter 11.8 in., inside rotor diameter 7.17 in., total swept area 277 sq. in. Rear brakes: Power disc with ABS, outside rotor diameter 11.3 in., inside rotor diameter 7.83 in., total swept area 211.1 sq. in. Fuel tank capacity: 18 gal. Transmission: Special close-ratio 5-speed automatic with overdrive. Fuel tank: 18 gallons.

Options:

153 front license plate bracket (no cost). 422 California emissions requirements (no cost). 428 high-altitude principal use (no cost). 51P supplemental parking lamps (no cost). 553 traction control ($230). 68B black accent package, includes black accent on steering wheel and shift handle, not available with 68C or 68D ($295). 68C full-color interior package, not available with 68A or 68D ($800). 68D partial interior color accent package, not available with 68A or 68C ($595).

History:

Dressed in a formal design for a very special occasion, The Thunderbird Custom made its official debut at the 50th Annual Concours d'Elegance in Pebble Beach in August 2000. This one-of-a-kind project car brought a new look to the roadster through subtle design changes. The Custom was designed to be a contemporary interpretation of the customizing and hot rod movement of the 1950s. It started as a 2002 Ford Thunderbird. Ford designers were asked to develop design renderings of new styling possibilities for future years. One sketch featured several unique elements including a blacked-out grille, a more pronounced belt line and big chrome wheels with knock-off hubs. The sketch looked so good, Ford decided to build it. Changes included doubling the size of the recesses for the characteristic chevrons on the T-Bird's front fenders and adding a black mesh insert behind them to accentuate their presence. The Custom was painted with several coats of Dark Shadow Gray Metallic lacquer for a deep, glossy finish. The iconic egg-crate grille was recessed slightly and painted the same color as the body. It was further accentuated with a chrome bezel surrounding the grille. To achieve a longer, more relaxed exterior appearance for the project car, the design team lowered the coil-spring suspension one-inch front and rear, making it look higher in front and lower in the rear. The exhaust system was re-tuned to give it a low "baritone burble" at idle and a more aggressive performance tone during acceleration. Chrome tailpipe extensions — t2-1/2 in. in diameter at the tip — were prominent in the side view. Halibrand created a unique interpretation of its classic "Kidney Bean 5" polished chrome wheel featuring five spokes with kidney-bean-shaped "windows" that created a strobing effect when the car was in motion. The wheel hubs were set off with three-arm knock-offs, a classic customizing touch. Aggressively treaded Michelin Pilot Sport Z-rated 18-in. tires finished the look, virtually filling the project car's wheel wells. The Thunderbird Custom had a black convertible top that stored below a removable two-piece, Ebony-leather-wrapped tonneau cover. The interior featured a two-tone theme with Sienna and Ebony leather set off by engine-turned aluminum accent

2002 Ford Thunderbird two-door Roadster (FMC)

2002 Ford Thunderbird two-door Roadster (FMC)

panels. The door sill plate was wrapped in a thin layer of Sienna leather with an opening in the middle displaying the Thunderbird logo etched in aluminum. The door panels featured Sienna leather armrests and upper sills with engine-turned aluminum accents. The bucket seats were covered in Sienna leather and featured plush side bolsters and adjustable head restraints. The seating surfaces were covered with perforated Sienna leather in the familiar Thunderbird tuck-and-roll style. The steering wheel and shift knob were tightly wrapped and stitched in Sienna leather. The shifter bezel featured an engine-turned aluminum background. The center stack was finished in Dark Shadow Gray matching the exterior. It flowed into a one-of-a-kind White-on-Black Thunderbird instrument cluster that was precision stitched in Ebony leather. At Pebble Beach, Ford announced that it would offer 200 uniquely-designed Neiman Marcus Edition Thunderbirds exclusively through the specialty retailer's "Christmas Book" which came out in September 2000. The Neiman Marcus Edition Thunderbird featured Black–and-Silver finish with a removable Silver top. The removable top was highlighted with the Thunderbird insignia etched into the porthole glass. Chrome 17-inch wheels matched the A-pillars. The hood scoop was adorned with trim accents and a chrome bezel. The Black-and-Silver theme was carried through to the interior. The steering wheel and shift knob were painted silver to match the exterior roof and accent colors. The lower door panel was silver to match the aluminum molding and inserts on the padded instrument panel. The seats contained a perforated, silver leather insert surrounded by black leather. The Neiman Marcus Thunderbird was made available exclusively through the Neiman Marcus Christmas Book beginning on September 25th at a price of $41,995. All 200 copies sold in two hours and 15 minutes. The cars were not delivered until production actually started in the summer of 2001. Ford officially opened the order banks for the 2002 Thunderbird on Monday, January 8, 2001, the day that the car made its regular-production debut at the North American International Auto Show in Detroit, Michigan. The regular-production "new" T-Bird was originally slated to go on sale in June of 2001 as a 2002 model, but the first real sales were not concluded and counted until August of the year 2001. Sales for calendar-year 2001 still amounted to 5,177 units. This included 243 cars sold in August 2001, 340 cars sold in September, 1,315 cars sold in October, 1,421 cars sold in November and 1,858 cars sold in December 2001. Calendar-year 2001 output of 2002 T-Birds was 7,955 units. Of these units, all were made in Wixom, Michigan. By the end of 2002, Jacques Nasser's rein at Ford ended abruptly with his dismissal for failure to control financial losses. William Clay Ford, Jr., took over as Chief Executive Officer and Nick Scheele assumed the role of President and Chief Operating Officer. Alan Gilmour was Chief Financial Officer. The January 1, 2001 issue of *Automotive News* had a picture of a Red Thunderbird with a White interior to promote the Detroit Auto Show. This show car had a matching Torch Red tonneau cover. It was themed after the '60s T-Bird Sport Roadster and used the same name. A Nieman Marcus Thunderbird was shown at the 2001 Los Angeles Auto Show. On November 12, 2001, at the SEMA Show in Las Vegas, *Motor Trend* announced that it had picked the 2002 Thunderbird as "Car of the Year." It was the fourth time that *Motor Trend* had bestowed this honor on the T-Bird. "We're especially honored that the Ford Thunderbird was chosen *Motor Trend's* 'Car of the Year' for the fourth time," said Ford Division President Jim O'Connor. "The all-new Thunderbird celebrates Ford's heritage of innovation and reaffirms our goal to build the best cars on the planet — cars that evoke passion and touch people's hearts and souls." Motor Week later selected the Thunderbird as "Best Convertible for 2002," Women Journalists picked it as their "Favorite Car of the Year" and *Auto Interiors* selected it for "Best Interior" honors.

1964-1/2 Mustang

Mustang — Six and V-8: The biggest news for 1964 was not the restyled Galaxie, Fairlane, Falcon or Thunderbird, but, rather, the later introduction of a small, sporty Ford Mustang, which caught the rest of the automotive industry totally off guard as well as catching the hearts of the American car buying public. The Mustang was the midyear model that set records, which have yet to be broken. It combined sporty looks, economy and brisk performance in a package that had a base price of $2,345. Mustangs could be equipped to be anything from absolute economy cars to luxury sports cars. The Mustang, with its extended hood, shortened rear deck, sculptured body panels and sporty bucket seats provided a family-size sedan for grocery-getting mothers, an appearance for those people who yearned for another two-seat Thunderbird and plenty of power and handling options for the performance Ford enthusiast. So successful was the Mustang that a whole assortment of similar cars, by competing manufacturers, came to be known as 'pony cars' or, in other words, cars in the original Mustang image. Mustangs came powered by everything from the tame 170-cid 101-hp six-cylinder engine to a wild, solid-lifter high-performance 289-cid/271-hp V-8 available only with a four-speed manual transmission. The basic standard equipment package found on all 1964-1/2 Mustangs included a three-speed manual transmission with floor lever controls, front bucket seats, a padded instrument panel, full wheel covers, cloth-and-vinyl (hardtop) or all-vinyl (convertible) upholstery, color-keyed carpeting, a Sports steering wheel, a cigarette lighter, door courtesy lights, a glove box light and a heater and defroster.

1964-1/2 Ford Mustang two-door Convertible GT (OCW)

1964-1/2 Ford Mustang two-door Convertible (IMS)

VIN:

The vehicle identification number was die-stamped on the top of the front inner fender apron. The first symbol indicated the model year: 5=1965 (all 1964-1/2 Mustangs were considered 1965 models). The second symbol was a letter designating the assembly point: F = Dearborn, Michigan, R = San Jose, California or T = Metuchen, New Jersey. The next two symbols were the body code: 65A=two-door hardtop coupe, 65B=two-door luxury hardtop coupe, 65C=two-door hardtop coupe with bench seats, 76A=two-door convertible, 76B=two-door luxury convertible and 76C=two-door convertible with bench seat. The fifth symbol was an engine code, listed with the engine breakouts below. The next group of symbols were the consecutive unit numbers, beginning with 100001 and up at each factory.

Mustang (Six)

Model No.	Body/ Style No.	Body Type and Seating	Factory Price	Shipping Weight	Production Total
07	65A	2-dr. Hardtop -4P	$2,345	2,449 lbs.	27,430
08	76A	2-dr. Convertible-4P	$2,587	2,625 lbs.	5,255

Mustang (V-8)

| 07 | 65A | 2-dr. Hardtop -4P | $2,461 | 2,718 lbs. | 62,275 |
| 08 | 76A | 2-dr. Convertible-4P | $2,703 | 2,894 lbs. | 23,578 |

Engines:

Six: Overhead valve. Cast-iron block. Displacement: 170 cid. B & S: 3.50 x 2.94 in. Compression ratio: 8.7:1. Brake hp: 101 at 4400 rpm. Seven main bearings. Hydraulic valve lifters. Carburetor: Ford (Autolite) one-barrel Model C30F-9510-G. Code U.

Challenger 260 V-8: Overhead valve. Cast-iron block. Displacement: 260 cid. B & S: 3.80 x 2.87 in. Compression ratio: 8.8:1. Brake hp: 164 at 4400 rpm. Torque: 258 lbs.-ft. at 2200 rpm. Five main bearings. Hydraulic valve lifters. Carburetor: Two-barrel. Cooling system capacity: 15.5 qt. with heater. Crankcase capacity: 4 qt. (add 1 qt. with new oil filter). Code F.

Challenger 289 V-8: Overhead valve. Cast-iron block. Displacement: 289 cid. B & S: 4.00 x 2.87 in. Compression ratio: 9.30:1. Brake hp: 200 at 4400 rpm. Torque: 282 lbs.-ft. at 2400 rpm. Five main bearings. Hydraulic valve lifters. Carburetor: Two-barrel. Cooling system capacity: 16 qt. with heater. Crankcase capacity: 4 qt. (add 1 qt. with new oil filter). Code C.

Challenger 289 V-8: Overhead valve. Cast-iron block. Displacement: 289 cid. B & S: 4.00 x 2.87 in. Compression ratio: 10.0:1. Brake hp: 225 at 4800 rpm. Torque: 305 lbs.-ft. at 3200 rpm. Five main bearings. Hydraulic valve lifters. Carburetor: Four-barrel. Cooling system capacity: 16 qt. with heater. Crankcase capacity: 4 qt. (add 1 qt. with new oil filter). Code A.

High-Performance Challenger 289 V-8: Overhead valve. Cast-iron block. Displacement: 289 cid. B & S: 4.00 x 2.87 in. Compression ratio: 10.50:1. Brake hp: 271 at 6000 rpm. Torque: 312 lbs.-ft. at 3400 rpm. Five main bearings. Solid valve lifters. Carburetor: Four-barrel. Cooling system capacity: 16 qt. with heater. Crankcase capacity: 4 qt. (add 1 qt. with new oil filter). Code K.

Chassis:

Wheelbase: 108 in. Overall length: 181.6 in. Tires: (with V-8) 7.00 x 13 four-ply tubeless, (with high-performance 289-cid V-8) 7.00 x 14 four-ply tubeless black sidewall, (other models) 6.50 x 13 four-ply tubeless blackwall.

Options:

Accent Group ($27.70). Ford air conditioner ($283.20). Heavy-duty battery ($7.60). Front disc brakes ($58). Full-length center console ($51.50). Console with air conditioning ($32.20). Equa-Lock limited slip differential ($42.50). California-type closed emissions system ($5.30). Challenger V-8 ($108). Challenger four-barrel V-8 engine ($162). Challenger high-performance four-barrel V-8 ($442.60). Early year only, 260-cid V-8 ($75). Emergency flashers ($19.60). Tinted glass with banded windshield ($30.90). Banded, tinted windshield only ($21.55). Back-up lights ($10.70). Rocker panel moldings ($16.10). Power brakes ($43.20). Power steering ($86.30). Power convertible top ($54.10). Push-button radio with antenna ($58.50). Rally-Pac instrumentation with clock and tachometer ($70.80). Deluxe retractable front seat safety belts ($7.55). Special Handling Package ($31.30). Padded sun visors ($5.70). Cruise-O-Matic transmission, with six ($179.80), with 200-hp and 225-hp V-8s ($189.60). Four-speed manual transmission with six ($115.90), with V-8 ($75.80). Hardtop vinyl roof ($75.80). Visibility Group including remote-control mirror, day/nite mirror, two-speed electric wipers and windshield washers ($36). Wheel covers with simulated knock-off hubs ($18.20). Wire wheel covers, 14 inch ($45.80). Styled steel wheels, 14 inch ($122.30). NOTE: The MagicAire heater ($32.20 credit) and front seat belts ($11 credit) were 'delete options.' Size 6.50 x 13 whitewalls with six ($33.90). Size 6.95 x 14 tires, black sidewall with six ($7.40), whitewall with six ($41.30), whitewall with V-8s, except high-performance type ($33.90), black nylon, except with high-performance V-8 ($15.80), Red Band nylon with V-8s except high-performance V-8 ($49.60), Black nylon or white sidewall nylon with high-performance V-8 (no charge).

History:

Mustang was introduced April 17, 1964. Model year production peaked at 121,538 units. Lee Iacocca headed an eight-man committee that conceived the idea for the new car. Stylists Joe Oros, Gail Halderman and David Ash designed the car. So cleanly styled was the new Mustang that it was awarded the Tiffany Award for Excellence in American Design, the first and only automobile ever to be so honored by Tiffany & Co. Not only did the design purists like the new Mustang, so did the public. More than 100,000 were sold in the first four months of production, followed by 500,000 more in the next 12 months. More than 1,000,000 found buyers in less than 24 months. This set an automotive industry sales record that has yet to be equaled or eclipsed. A 1964-1/2 Mustang convertible was also selected as the Indianapolis 500 pace car. Out of all the Mustangs built in the 1964 model run, some 49.2 percent featured an automatic transmission, 19.3 percent four-speed manual transmission, 73.1 percent V-8 engines, 26.9 percent six-cylinder engines, 77.8 percent radio, 99:1 percent heater, 30.9 percent power steering, 7.7 percent power brakes, 88.2 percent whitewalls, 48.3 percent windshield washers, 22.4 percent tinted windshields only and 8.0 percent all tinted glass, 44.6 percent back-up lights and 6.4 percent air conditioning.

1964-1/2 Ford Mustang two-door Hardtop (OCW)

1965 Mustang

1965 Ford Mustang GT two-door Convertible (OCW)

Mustang — Six and V-8: One brand-new model and a number of minor revisions were seen in the 1965 Mustang lineup. A 2+2 fastback body joined the hardtop and convertible, creating an expanded stable of three pony cars. Perhaps the most significant change for 1965 was the use of an alternator in the place of the previously used generator. Engine choices remained the same as in late 1964, with one exception. The old workhorse I-block, 170-cid engine was replaced by the 200-cid version as base six-cylinder power plant. A number of small changes and some new options were seen on the 1965 models. While interior door handles on the earliest Mustangs were secured by 'C' type clips, Allen screw attachments were a running production change adopted for later cars. Also, the spacing between the letters in the lower body side nameplates was modified, giving them a five-inch measurement or about one-quarter-inch longer than before. The push-down door lock buttons were chrome plated, in contrast to the 1964-1/2 type, which were colored to match the interior. Front disc brakes were one new option. So was the GT Package that included racing stripes as a standard feature that could be deleted. The standard equipment list for 1965 was much the same as before, including a heater and defroster, dual sun visors, Sports-type front bumpers, full wheel covers, vinyl upholstery, seat belts, a padded instrument panel, automatic courtesy lights, a cigarette lighter, front and rear carpets, foam-padded front bucket seats, self-adjusting brakes, a Sports steering wheel, five 6.50 x 13 four-ply tubeless black sidewall tires, and the 200-cid 120-hp six. The 289-cid V-8 and 6.95 x 14 size tires were standard in the Mustang V-8 series.

VIN:

The vehicle identification number was die-stamped on the top of the front inner fender apron. The first symbol indicated the model year: 5=1965. The second symbol was a letter designating the assembly point: F = Dearborn, Michigan, R = San Jose, California and T = Metuchen, New Jersey. The next two symbols were the body code: 63A=two-door 2+2 fastback, 63B=two-door luxury 2+2 fastback, 65A=two-door hardtop coupe, 65B=two-door luxury hardtop coupe, 65C=two-door hardtop coupe with bench seats, 76A=two-door convertible, 76B=two-door luxury convertible and 76C=two-door convertible with bench seat. The fifth symbol was an engine code, listed with the engine specifications below. The next group of symbols were the consecutive unit numbers, beginning with 100001 and up at each factory.

Mustang (Six)

Model No.	Body/ Style No.	Body Type and Seating	Factory Price	Shipping Weight	Production Total
07	65A	2-dr. Hardtop-4P	$2,321	2,465 lbs.	167,025
08	63A	2-dr. 2 + 2 Hardtop-4P	$2,533	2,515 lbs.	12,271
08	76A	2-dr. Convertible-4P	$2,558	2,650 lbs.	19,595

Mustang (V-8)

Model No.	Body/ Style No.	Body Type and Seating	Factory Price	Shipping Weight	Production Total
07	65A	2-dr. Hardtop-4P	$2,427	2,735 lbs.	242,235
08	63A	2-dr. 2 + 2 Hardtop-4P	$2,639	2,785 lbs.	64,808
08	76A	2-dr. Convertible-4P	$2,663	2,920 lbs.	53,517

Note 1: Total model year output was 559,451 units. This figure includes 5,776 Luxury fastbacks, 22,232 Luxury hardtops, 14,905 bench seat-equipped hardtops, 5,338 Luxury convertibles and 2,111 convertibles equipped with bench seats.

1965 Ford Mustang two-door Hardtop (OCW)

Engines:

Six: Overhead valve. Cast iron block. Displacement: 200 cid. Bore and stroke: 3.68 x 3.13 inches. Compression ratio: 9.2:1. Brake hp: 120 at 4400 rpm. Seven main bearings. Hydraulic valve lifters. Carburetor: Ford (Autolite) two-barrel Model C5OF-9510-E. Serial number code T.

Challenger 289 V-8: Overhead valve. Cast-iron block. Displacement: 289 cid. B & S: 4.00 x 2.87 in. Compression ratio: 9.30:1. Brake hp: 200 at 4400 rpm. Torque: 282 lbs.-ft. at 2400 rpm. Five main bearings. Hydraulic valve lifters. Carburetor: Two-barrel. Cooling system capacity: 16 qt. with heater. Crankcase capacity: 4 qt. (add 1 qt. with new oil filter). Code C.

Challenger 289 Four-Barrel V-8: Overhead valve. Cast-iron block. Displacement: 289 cid. B & S: 4.00 x 2.87 in. Compression ratio: 10.0:1. Brake hp: 225 at 4800 rpm. Torque: 305 lbs.-ft. at 3200 rpm. Five main bearings. Hydraulic valve lifters. Carburetor: Four-barrel. Cooling system capacity: 16 qt. with heater. Crankcase capacity: 4 qt. (add 1 qt. with new oil filter). Code A.

Challenger 289 High-Performance Four-Barrel V-8: Overhead valve. Cast-iron block. Displacement: 289 cid. B & S: 4.00 x 2.87 in. Compression ratio: 10.5:1. Brake hp: 271 at 6000 rpm. Torque: 312 lbs.-ft. at 3400 rpm. Five main bearings. Solid valve lifters. Carburetor: Four-barrel. Cooling system capacity: 16 qt. with heater. Crankcase capacity: 4 qt. (add 1 qt. with new oil filter). Code K.

Chassis:

Wheelbase: 108 in. Overall length: 181.6 in. Tires: (V-8) 7.00 x 13 four-ply tubeless black sidewall, (high-performance 289 V-8) 7.00 x 14 four-ply tubeless black sidewall, (other models) 6.50 x 13 four-ply tubeless black sidewall.

Options:

Accent Group, on hardtop and convertible ($27.70), on fastback coupe ($14.20). Ford air conditioner ($283.20). Heavy-duty battery ($7.60). Front disc brakes with V-8 and manual brakes only ($58). Full-length center console ($51.50). Console for use with air conditioner ($32.20). Equa-Lock limited-slip differential ($42.50). California-type closed emissions system ($5.30). Challenger 200-hp V-8 ($108). Challenger four-barrel 225-hp V-8 ($162). Challenger 271-hp high-performance V-8 including Special Handling Package and 6.95 x 14 nylon tires ($442.60). Emergency flashers ($19.60). Tinted glass with banded windshield ($30.90). Tinted-banded windshield glass ($21.55). Back-up lights ($10.70). Rocker panel moldings, except fastback coupe ($16.10). Power brakes ($43.20). Power steering ($86.30). Power convertible top ($54.10). Push-button radio with antenna ($58.50). Rally-Pac instrumentation with clock and tachometer ($70.80). Deluxe retractable front seat safety belts ($7.55). Special Handling package, with 200-hp or 225-hp V-8s ($31.30). Padded sun visors ($5.70). Cruise-O-Matic transmission, with six ($179.80), with 200-hp and 225-hp V-8s ($189.60). Four-speed manual transmission, with six ($115.90), with V-8 ($188). Vinyl roof, on two-door hardtop only ($75.80). Visibility Group, includes remote-control outside rearview mirror, day/nite inside rearview mirror, two-speed electric wipers and windshield washers ($36). Wheel covers with knock-off hubs ($18.20). Fourteen-inch wire wheel covers ($45.80). Fourteen-inch styled steel wheels ($122.30).

History:

The 1965 Mustang was officially introduced on October 1, 1964. Model year production peaked at 559,451 cars. An interesting historical point is that Mustangs made in Germany were called Ford T-5 models, since the right to the Mustang name in that country belonged to another manufacturer.

1965 Ford Mustang two-door Convertible (OCW)

1965 Ford Mustang two-door 2+2 Hardtop (PH)

1966 Mustang

1966 Mustang — (Six and V-8): The 1966 Mustang continued to sell like 'hot cakes,' in spite of only minor restyling in the trim department. The grille featured a floating Mustang emblem in the center, with no horizontal or vertical dividing bars. Brand new trim, on the rear fender, featured three chrome steps leading into the simulated scoop. This was the first year of federally mandated safety standards and all 1966 Fords included front and rear seat belts, padded instrument panel, emergency flashers, electric wipers, and windshield washers as standard equipment. In addition, the list of regular Mustang features was comprised of the following: front bucket seats, pleated vinyl upholstery and interior trim, Sports-type steering wheel, five dial instrument cluster, full carpeting, heater and defroster, left-hand door outside rearview mirror, back-up lamps, door courtesy lights, rocker panel moldings, full wheel covers, three-speed manual transmission with floor lever control, and 200-cid 120-hp six-cylinder engine. The fastback coupe also came with special Silent-Flo ventilation and the base V-8 engine was the 200-hp version of the 289.

VIN:

The vehicle identification number was die-stamped on the top of the front inner fender apron. The first symbol indicated the model year: 6=1966. The second symbol was a letter designating the assembly point: F = Dearborn, Michigan, R = San Jose, California and T = Metuchen, New Jersey. The next two symbols were the body code: 63A=two-door 2+2 fastback, 63B=two-door luxury 2+2 fastback, 65A=two-door hardtop coupe, 65B=two-door luxury hardtop coupe, 65C=two-door hardtop coupe with bench seats, 76A=two-door convertible, 76B=two-door luxury convertible and 76C=two-door convertible with bench seat. The fifth symbol was an engine code, listed with the engine specifications below. The next group of symbols was the consecutive unit number, beginning with 100001 and up at each factory.

Mustang (Six)

Model No.	Body/Style No.	Body Type and Seating	Factory Price	Shipping Weight	Production Total
07	65A	2-dr. Hardtop-4P	$2,416	2,488 lbs.	224,942
09	63A	2-dr. 2 + 2 Hardtop-4P	$2,607	2,519 lbs.	4,403
08	76A	2-dr. Convertible-4P	$2,653	2,650 lbs.	23,867

1966 Ford Mustang two-door Convertible (OCW)

Mustang (V-8)

07	65A	2-dr. Hardtop-4P	$2,522	2,733 lbs.	274,809
09	63A	2-dr. 2 + 2 Hardtop-4P	$2,713	2,764 lbs.	31,295
08	76A	2-dr. Convertible-4P	$2,758	2,895 lbs.	48,252

Note 1: Total series output was 607,568 units. This figure included 7,889 Luxury fastbacks, 55,938 Luxury hardtops, 21,397 hardtops equipped with bench seats, 12,520 Luxury convertibles and 3,190 convertibles equipped with bench seats.

Engines:

Six: Overhead valve. Cast-iron block. Displacement: 200 cid. B & S: 3.68 x 3.12 in. Compression ratio: 9.2:1. Brake hp: 120 at 4400 rpm. Seven main bearings. Hydraulic valve lifters. Carburetor: Ford (Autolite) one-barrel Model C6OF-9510-AD. Code T.

Challenger 289 V-8: Overhead valve. Cast-iron block. Displacement: 289 cid. B & S: 4.00 x 2.87 in. Compression ratio: 9.30:1. Brake hp: 200 at 4400 rpm. Torque: 282 lbs.-ft. at 2400 rpm. Five main bearings. Hydraulic valve lifters. Carburetor: Two-barrel. Cooling system capacity: 15 qt. with heater. Crankcase capacity: 4 qt. (add 1 qt. with new oil filter). Code C.

Challenger 289 Four-Barrel V-8: Overhead valve. Cast-iron block. Displacement: 289 cid. B & S: 4.00 x 2.87 in. Compression ratio: 10.0:1. Brake hp: 225 at 4800 rpm. Torque: 305 lbs.-ft. at 3200 rpm. Five main bearings. Hydraulic valve lifters. Carburetor: Four-barrel. Cooling system capacity: 15 qt. with heater. Crankcase capacity: 4 qt. (add 1 qt. with new oil filter). Code A.

Challenger 289 High-Performance Four-Barrel V-8: Overhead valve. Cast-iron block. Displacement: 289 cid. B & S: 4.00 x 2.87 in. Compression ratio: 10.5:1. Brake hp: 271 at 6000 rpm. Torque: 312 lbs.-ft. at 3400 rpm. Five main bearings. Hydraulic valve lifters. Carburetor: Four-barrel. Cooling system capacity: 15 qt. with heater. Crankcase capacity: 4 qt. (add 1 qt. with new oil filter). Code K.

Chassis:

Wheelbase: 108 in. Overall length: 181.6 in. Tires: 6.95 x 14 four-ply tubeless black sidewall, (high-performance V-8) 7.00 x 14 four-ply tubeless black sidewall.

Options:

Challenger 289-cid V-8 ($105.63). Challenger four-barrel 289 cid/225 hp V-8 ($158.48). High-performance 289 cid/271 hp V-8, in standard Mustang ($433.55), in Mustang GT ($381.97). Note: The total cost of the high-performance engine was $327.92 on regular Mustangs and $276.34 on Mustang GTs, plus the cost of the base V-8 attachment over the six (which was $105.63). Cruise-O-Matic automatic transmission with six ($175.80), with standard V-8s ($185.39), with high-performance V-8 ($216.27). Four-speed manual floor shift transmission, with six ($113.45), with all V-8s ($184.02). Power brakes ($42.29). Power steering ($84.47). Power convertible top ($52.95). Heavy-duty 55-amp battery ($7.44). Manual disc brakes, with V-8 only ($56.77). GT Equipment group, with high-performance V-8 only, includes: dual exhaust, fog lamps, special ornamentation, disc brakes, GT racing stripes (rocker panel moldings deleted), and Handling Package components ($152.20). Limited-slip differential ($41.60). Rally-Pack instrumentation, includes clock and tachometer ($69.30). Special Handling Package, with 200-hp and 225-hp V-8 engines, includes increased rate front and rear springs, larger front and rear shocks, 22:1 overall steering ratio and large diameter stabilizer bar ($30.84). Fourteen-inch styled steel wheels, on V-8 models only ($93.84). Two-speed electric windshield wipers ($12.95). Tinted-banded windshield only ($21.09). All glass tinted with banded windshield ($30.25). Deluxe, retractable front seat safety belts and warning lamp ($14.53). Visibility Group, includes remote-control outside rearview mirror, day/nite inside mirror and two-speed electric wipers ($29.81). Ford air conditioner ($310.90). Stereo tape player, AM radio mandatory ($128.49). Full-width front seat with armrest for Styles 65A and 76A only ($24.42). Rear deck luggage rack, except fastback ($32.44). Radio and antenna ($57.51). Accent striping, less rear quarter ornamentation ($13.90). Full-length center console ($50.41). Console for use with air conditioning ($31.52). Deluxe steering wheel with simulated wood-grain rim ($31.52). Interior Decor Group, includes special interior trim, Deluxe wood-grain steering wheel, rear window door courtesy lights and pistol grip door handles

1966 Ford Mustang two-door Hardtop (PH)

1966 Ford Mustang GT two-door 2+2 Hardtop (OCW)

1966 Ford Mustang Shelby GT 350 2+2 (OCW)

Mustang (Six)

Model No.	Body/Style No.	Body Type and Seating	Factory Price	Shipping Weight	Production Total
01	65A/B/C	2-dr. Hardtop-4P	$2,461	2,578 lbs.	126,583
03	63A/B	2-dr. 2 + 2 Hardtop-4P	$2,592	2,605 lbs.	4,192
02	76A/C	2-dr. Convertible-4P	$2,698	2,738 lbs.	10,782

Mustang (V-8)

01	65A/B/C	2-dr. Hardtop-4P	$2,567	2,766 lbs.	229,688
03	63A/B	2-dr. 2 + 2 Hardtop-4P	$2,698	2,793 lbs.	66,850
02	76A/C	2-dr. Convertible-4P	$2,804	2,926 lbs.	34,026

Note 1: Total series output was 472,121 units. This figure included 17,391 Luxury fastbacks body style 63B, 22,228 Luxury hardtops body style 65B, 8,190 hardtops equipped with bench seats body style 65C, 4,848 Luxury convertibles body style 76B and 3,190 convertibles equipped with bench seats body style 76C.

Engines:

Six: Overhead valve. Cast-iron block. Displacement: 200 cid. B & S: 3.68 x 3.12 in. Compression ratio: 9.2:1. Brake hp: 120 at 4400 rpm. Seven main bearings. Hydraulic valve lifters. Carburetor: Ford (Autolite) one-barrel Model C6OF-9510-AD. Serial number code T.

Challenger 289 V-8: Overhead valve. Cast-iron block. Displacement: 289 cid. B & S: 4.00 x 2.87 in. Compression ratio: 9.30:1. Brake hp: 200 at 4400 rpm. Torque: 282 lbs.-ft. at 2400 rpm. Five main bearings. Hydraulic valve lifters. Carburetor: Two-barrel. Cooling system capacity: 15 qt. with heater. Crankcase capacity: 4 qt. (add 1 qt. with new oil filter). Code C.

Challenger 289 Four-Barrel V-8: Overhead valve. Cast-iron block. Displacement: 289 cid. B & S: 4.00 x 2.87 in. Compression ratio: 10.0:1. Brake hp: 225 at 4800 rpm. Torque: 305 lbs.-ft. at 3200 rpm. Five main bearings. Hydraulic valve lifters. Carburetor: Four-barrel. Cooling system capacity: 15 qt. with heater. Crankcase capacity: 4 qt. (add 1 qt. with new oil filter). Code A.

Challenger 289 High-Performance Four-Barrel V-8: Overhead valve. Cast-iron block. Displacement: 289 cid. B & S: 4.00 x 2.87 in. Compression ratio: 10.5:1. Brake hp: 271 at 6000 rpm. Torque: 312 lbs.-ft. at 3400 rpm. Five main bearings. Solid valve lifters. Carburetor: Four-barrel. Cooling system capacity: 15 qt. with heater. Crankcase capacity: 4 qt. (add 1 qt. with new oil filter). Code K.

Mustang GT/GTS V-8: Overhead valve. Cast-iron block. Displacement: 390 cid. B & S: 4.05 x 3.78 in. Compression ratio: 10.5:1. Brake hp: 320 at 4600 rpm. Torque: 427 lbs.-ft. at 3200 rpm. Five main bearings. Hydraulic valve lifters. Carburetor: Holley four-barrel. Cooling system capacity: 20.5 qt. with heater. Crankcase capacity: 4 qt. (add 1 qt. with new oil filter). Dual exhausts. Code S.

Chassis:

Wheelbase: 108 inches. Overall length: 183.6 inches. Tires: 6.95 x 14 four-ply tubeless black sidewall.

Options:

200-hp V-8 ($106). 225-hp V-8 ($158). 271-hp V-8, included with GT Equipment Group ($434). 320-hp V-8 ($264). Cruise-O-Matic three-speed automatic transmission with six-cylinder ($188), with 200-hp and 225-hp V-8s ($198), with 271-hp and 320-hp V-8s ($232). Four-speed manual transmission, with six-cylinder or 225-hp V-8 ($184), with other V-8s ($233). Heavy-duty three-speed manual, required with 390-cid V-8 ($79). Power front disc brakes ($65). Power steering ($84).

1967 Ford Mustang two-door Convertible (OCW)

($94.13). Vinyl top, on hardtop ($74.36). Simulated wire wheel covers ($58.24). Wheel covers with simulated knock-off hubs ($19.48). Closed crankcase emissions system, except with high-performance V-8 ($519). Exhaust emissions control system, except with high-performance V-8 ($45.45). Tire options, exchange prices listed indicate cost above base equipment: 6.95 x 14 four-ply rated whitewall ($33.31), nylon black sidewall ($15.67), nylon whitewall ($48.89), nylon with dual red band design, on cars with high-performance V-8 (no charge), all other ($48.97). No charge for substitution of nylon black sidewalls or whitewalls on cars with high-perfomance V-8. MagicAire heater could be deleted for $45.45 credit. Air conditioning, three-speed manual transmission, power steering and U.S. Royal tires not available in combination with high-performance V-8. Power brakes and accent striping not available with GT Equipment Group. Full-width front seat not available in cars with Interior Decor Group, or Model 63A or cars with console options.

History:

The 1966 Mustangs were introduced October 1, 1965, the same day as all other Fords. Model-year production hit 607,568 Mustangs with the little "pony" pulling down a significant 7.1 percent share of all American car sales. Henny Ford II was Ford Motor Co. board chairman and Arjay Miller was the president. The Ford Division, which was actually responsible for Mustang sales, was headed by M.S. McLaughlin who had the titles of vice-president and general manager. For 1966, Mustang was the third best-selling individual nameplate in the American industry, an outstanding achievement for a car only three model years old.

1967 Mustang

Mustang — (Six and V-8): For the first time since its mid-1964 introduction the Mustang was significantly changed. The styling was similar to the original in its theme, but everything was larger. The grille featured a larger opening. The feature lines on the side led to a larger simulated scoop. The taillights took the form of three vertical lenses on each side of a concave indentation panel, with a centrally located gas cap. Standard equipment included all Ford Motor Co. safety features plus front bucket seats, full carpeting, floor-mounted shift, vinyl interior trim, heater, wheel covers and cigarette lighter. The fastback came with wheel covers, special emblems, and rocker panel moldings. There were five engine choices ranging from a 200-cid/120-hp six to a 390-cid/320-hp V-8. New options available included SelectShift Cruise-O-Matic.

VIN:

The VIN for Mustangs was die-stamped on the top upper flange of the left-hand front fender apron. The first symbol indicates year: 7=1967. The second symbol identifies assembly plant, as follows: F=Dearborn, Michigan, R=San Jose, California, T=Metuchen, New Jersey. The third and fourth symbols identify body series code: 01=two-door hardtop, 02=two-door convertible, 03=two-door fastback. The fifth symbol identifies engine code, as follows: T=200-cid six-cylinder, C=289-cid two-barrel V-8, A=289-cid four-barrel V8, K=289-cid four-barrel high-performance V-8 and S=390-cid four-barrel V-8. The last six digits are the unit's production number, beginning at 100001 and going up, at each of the assembly plants.

1967 Ford Mustang two-door 2+2 Fastback (OCW)

1967 Ford Mustang two-door Hardtop (OCW)

Power top, convertible ($53). GT Equipment Group, V-8s only ($205). Limited-slip differential ($42). Competition Handling Package, with GT Group only ($62). Styled steel wheels, 2+2 ($94), other models ($115). Tinted windows and windshield ($30). Convenience control panel ($40). Fingertip speed control, V-8 and Cruise-O-Matic required ($71). Remote-control left door mirror, standard 2+2 ($10). Safety-glass rear window, convertible ($32). Select-Aire conditioning ($356). Push-button AM radio ($58). Push-button AM/FM radio ($134). Stereo-Sonic tape system, AM radio required ($128). "Sport Deck" option with folding rear seat and access door for 2+2 ($65). Full-width front seat, not available with 2+2 ($24). Tilt-Away steering wheel ($60). Deck lid luggage rack not available on 2+2 ($32). Comfort-weave vinyl trim, not available on convertible ($25). Center console, radio required ($50). Deluxe steering wheel ($32). Exterior Decor Group ($39). Lower back panel grille ($19). Interior Decor Group for convertible ($95), for other models ($108). Two-tone paint, lower back grille ($13). Accent stripe ($14). Vinyl roof, hardtop ($74). Wheel covers, standard on 2+2 ($21). Wire wheel covers, 2+2 ($58), other models ($80). Typical whitewall tire option ($33). Rocker panel moldings, standard on 2+2 ($16). Magic-Aire heater delete option ($32 credit).

History:

The 1967 Mustang was introduced September 30, 1966. Model-year output peaked at 472,121 units. Dealer sales totaled 377,827 units, a 31.2 percent decline due to increased competition in the sports/personal car market, plus a strike in the final business quarter. Henry Ford II was chairman of Ford Motor Co. Mustang's creator, Lee Iacocca, was an executive vice-president in charge of North American Operations and was definitely on his way up the corporate ladder, thanks to the success his "pony car" had seen.

1968 Mustang

Mustang — (Six and V-8): The 1968 Mustang continued to use the same body shell introduced the previous year, with minor trim changes. The Mustang emblem appeared to float in the center of the grille, with no horizontal or vertical bars attached to the emblem. Also, the side scoop had much cleaner chrome trim than the previous year, with no horizontal stripes connected to it. Standard equipment included all Ford safety features, front bucket seats, full carpeting, a floor-mounted gear shifter, vinyl interior trim, a heater, full wheel covers and a cigarette lighter, The 2+2 Fastback model also included full wheel covers and rocker panel moldings.

Mustang GT — (V-8): Cars with a 302-cid four-barrel V-8 or 390-cid V-8 could get the GT equipment package, which added a dual exhaust system with bright extensions, fog lamps, a special grille bar and GT ornamentation, power disc brakes, special handling components, a GT stripe, a heavy-duty suspension and six-inch wide wheel rims with Wide-Oval white sidewall tires.

Competition Handing — (V-8): Also available on a limited production was the Competition Handling package which included more rigid front and rear springs, 1-3/16-inch adjustable shock absorbers, an extra-heavy stabilizer bar, 16:1 ratio manual steering, a high-ratio rear axle, unique wheel covers, six-inch wide wheel rims, 6.50 x 15 or 6.70 x 15 Sports 200 nylon tires and the 320-hp (or higher) V-8.

VIN:

The VIN was stamped on an aluminum tab riveted to the instrument panel close to the windshield on the passenger side of the car and was viewable from the outside of the car. The first symbol indicated the year: 8=1968. The second symbol identified the assembly plant: F=Dearborn, Michigan, R=San Jose, California, and T=Metuchen, New Jersey. The third and fourth symbols identified the body series code: 01=two-door hardtop, 02=two-door convertible and 03=two-door fastback. The fifth symbol identified the engine code: T=200-cid six-cylinder, C=289-cid two-barrel V-8, F=302-cid two-barrel V-8, J=302-cid four-barrel V-8, X=390-cid two-barrel V-8, S=390-cid four-barrel V-8 and R=428-cid four-barrel V-8. The last six digits were the unit's production numbers, beginning at 100001 and going up, at each of the assembly plants.

Mustang (Six)

Model No.	Body/Style No.	Body Type and Seating	Factory Price	Shipping Weight	Production Total
01	65A/B/C	2-dr. Hardtop-4P	$2,602	2,635 lbs.	84,175
03	63A/B	2-dr. 2 + 2 Hardtop-4P	$2,712	2,659 lbs.	2,360
02	76A/C	2-dr. Convertible-4P	$2,814	2,745 lbs.	5,241

Mustang (V-8)

01	65A	2-dr. Hardtop-4P	$2,707	2,843 lbs.	155,410
03	63A	2-dr. 2 + 2 Hardtop-4P	$2,818	2,867 lbs.	32,304
02	76A	2-dr. Convertible-4P	$2,920	2,953 lbs.	16,796

Mustang Deluxe (Six)

01	65A/B/C	2-dr. Hardtop-4P	$2,726	2,635 lbs.	870
03	63A/B	2-dr. 2 + 2 Hardtop-4P	$2,836	2,659 lbs.	98
02	76A/C	2-dr. Convertible-4P	$2,924	2,745 lbs.	145

Mustang Deluxe (V-8)

01	65A	2-dr. Hardtop-4P	$2,831	2,843 lbs.	8,992
03	63A	2-dr. 2 + 2 Hardtop-4P	$2,942	2,867 lbs.	7,819
02	76A	2-dr. Convertible-4P	$3,030	2,953 lbs.	3,194

Engines:

Six: Overhead valve. Cast-iron block. Displacement: 200 cid. B & S: 3.68 x 3.12 in. Compression ratio: 9.2:1. Brake hp: 120 at 4400 rpm. Seven main bearings. Hydraulic valve lifters. Carburetor: Ford (Autolite) one-barrel Model C6OF-9510-AD. Code T.

Challenger 289 V-8: Overhead valve. Cast-iron block. Displacement: 289 cid. B & S: 4.00 x 2.87 in. Compression ratio: 8.70:1. Brake hp: 195 at 4400 rpm. Torque: 282 lbs.-ft. at 2400 rpm. Five main bearings. Hydraulic valve lifters. Carburetor: Two-barrel. Cooling system capacity: 15 qt. with heater. Crankcase capacity: 4 qt. (add 1 qt. with new oil filter). Code C.

302 Two-Barrel V-8: Overhead valve. Cast-iron block. Displacement: 302 cid. B & S: 4.00 x 3.00 in. Compression ratio: 9.50:1. Brake hp: 220 at 4600 rpm. Torque: 300 lbs.-ft. at 2600 rpm. Five main bearings. Hydraulic valve lifters. Carburetor: Two-barrel. Cooling system capacity: (Mid-size/Mustang)15 qt. with heater, (Full-size) 15.4 qt. with heater. Crankcase capacity: 4 qt. (add 1 qt. with new oil filter). Code F.

302 Two-Barrel V-8: Overhead valve. Cast-iron block. Displacement: 302 cid. B & S: 4.00 x 3.00 in. Compression ratio: 10.0:1. Brake hp: 230 at 4800 rpm. Five main bearings. Hydraulic valve lifters. Carburetor: Two-barrel. Cooling system capacity: 15 qt. with heater. Crankcase capacity: 4 qt. (add 1 qt. with new oil filter). Code J.

Thunderbird 390 Two-Barrel V-8: Overhead valve. Cast-iron block. Displacement: 390 cid. B & S: 4.05 x 3.78 in. Compression ratio: 10.5:1. Brake hp: 280 at 4400 rpm. Torque: 403 lbs.-ft. at 2600 rpm. Five main bearings. Hydraulic valve lifters. Carburetor: Holley two-barrel. Cooling system capacity: 20.5 qt. Crankcase capacity: 4 qt. (add 1 qt. with new oil filter). Dual exhausts. Code X.

Thunderbird 390 Four-Barrel V-8: Overhead valve. Cast-iron block. Displacement: 390 cid. B & S: 4.05 x 3.78 in. Compression ratio: 10.5:1. Brake hp: 320 at 4600 rpm. Torque: 427 lbs.-ft. at 3200 rpm. Five main bearings. Hydraulic valve lifters. Carburetor: Four-barrel. Cooling system capacity: 20.5 qt. with heater. Crankcase capacity: 4 qt. (add 1 qt. with new oil filter). Dual exhausts. Code S.

Cobra-Jet 428 V-8: Overhead valve. Cast-iron block. Displacement: 428 cid. B & S: 4.13 x 3.98 in. Compression ratio: 10.70:1. Brake hp: 335 at 5600 rpm. Torque: 440 lbs.-ft. at 3400 rpm. Hydraulic valve lifters. Carburetor: Holley four-barrel. Cooling system capacity: 20.5 qt. Crankcase capacity: 4 qt. Dual exhausts. Code R.

Chassis:

Wheelbase: 108 in. Overall length: 183.6 in. Tires: 6.95 x 14 four-ply tubeless black sidewall (E70-14 four-ply tubeless black sidewall, with

1968 Ford Mustang two-door Convertible (OCW)

1968 Ford Mustang two-door 2+2 Fastback (OCW)

1968 Ford Mustang two-door Hardtop (OCW)

Wide-Oval Sport tire option).

Options:

289 cid/195 hp two-barrel V-8 ($106). 302 cid/230 hp four-barrel ($172). 390 cid/325 hp four-barrel V-8 ($158). 427 cid/390 hp four-barrel V-8 ($775). 428 cid/335 hp four-barrel Cobra-Jet V-8 ($245). SelectShift Cruise-O-Matic three-speed automatic with six-cylinder ($19), with 289 V-8 ($201), with '390' V-8 ($233). Four-speed manual, not available with six-cylinder, with 289 V-8 ($184), with '390' V-8 ($233). Power front disc brakes, V-8s only, required with '390' V-8 or GT Equipment Group ($54). Power steering ($84). Power top, convertible ($53). GT Equipment Group, 230-hp or 325-hp V-8s with power brakes not available with Sports Trim Group of optional wheel covers ($147). Tachometer, V-8s only ($54). Limited-slip differential, V-8s only ($79). Glass backlight, convertible ($39). Tinted glass ($30). Convenience Group, console required with Select-Aire ($32). Fingertip speed control, V-8 and SelectShift required ($74). Remote-control left door mirror ($10). Select-Aire conditioner ($360). Push-button AM radio ($360). AM/FM stereo radio ($61). Stereo-Sonic Tape System, AM radio required ($181). Sport deck rear seat, 2+2 only ($65). Full-width front seat, hardtop and 2+2 only, not available with console ($32). Tilt-Away steering wheel ($66). Center console, radio required ($54). Interior Decor Group in convertibles and models with full-width front seat ($110), in others without full-width front seat ($124). Two-tone hood paint ($19). Accent paint stripe ($14). Vinyl roof, hardtop ($74). Wheel covers, not available with GT or V-8 Sports Trim Group ($34). Whitewall tires ($33).

History:

The 1968 Mustangs were introduced in September 1967. Model year production peaked at 317,148 units. The 427-powered Mustang was capable of moving from 0-to-60 mph in around six seconds. The price for this engine was $775 above that of the base Mustang V-8. The 427 was rare, but 428 V-8s were installed in 2,854 Mustangs built this model year. Side marker lights and other new federally mandated safety features were required on all Mustangs built this year. Ford went through a 60-day strike from late September to late November 1967. This had a negative effect on sales and production. A collectible model-option produced this year was the highly sought after "California Special," a variant of the coupe with special features such as Shelby-type taillights. There was also the "High-Country Special," a similar regional edition

1969 Mustang

Mustang — (Six and V-8): The Mustang was different for 1969. It was considerably enlarged and significantly restyled for the new year. For the first time, Mustangs had quad headlights, the outboard units being mounted in deeply recessed openings at the outer edges of the fenders. The inboard units were mounted inside the grille opening. The side scoop was now located high on the rear fenders of fastback models. It was in the same location as before on the hardtops and convertibles but now faced rearward. High-performance was the theme for Ford in 1969 and the hot new Mustangs were in the spotlight. The sizzling Mach 1 came with a 351-cid V-8 as standard equipment. The 390-cid V-8 and 428 Cobra Jet V-8 engines were optional. Trans-Am road racing was popular at this time. To compete with the Chevrolet Camaro race cars Ford introduced the famous and powerful Boss 302 Mustang. The top engine option for 1969 Mustangs became the huge

Boss 429. Even though these monsters came with a factory horsepower rating of 375, actual output was much higher. They were definitely not machines for the weak-spirited individual. Standard equipment included all Ford safety features, front bucket seats, a sports steering wheel, ornamentation, a louvered hood with integral turn signals, full carpeting, a floor-mounted gear shifter, a heater, a cigarette lighter and a 115-hp six-cylinder engine or 195-hp V-8.

Mustang —(V-8): The Mustang GT included a dual exhaust system with bright extensions, fog lamps, GT ornamentation, special handling components, a C stripe or triple GT stripe, a heavy-duty suspension, Argent styled wheels with chrome rings, F70 x 14 Wide-Oval white sidewall tires, a pop-open gas cap and chrome engine trim on 390- or 427-cid V-8s. Power discs brakes were a required option, at extra cost, if the 390- or 427-cid V-8s were ordered.

VIN:

The VIN was stamped on an aluminum tab riveted to the instrument panel close to the windshield on the passenger side of the car and was viewable from the outside of the car. The first symbol indicated the year: 9=1969. The second symbol identified the assembly plant: F=Dearborn, Michigan, R=San Jose, California and T=Metuchen, New Jersey. The third and fourth symbols identified the body series code: 01=two-door hardtop, 02=two-door convertible, 03=two-door fastback, 04=Grandé hardtop and 05=Mach 1 Sportsroof. The fifth symbol identified the engine code: T=200-cid six-cylinder, L=250-cid six-cylinder, F=302-cid two-barrel V-8, G=302-cid four-barrel Boss V-8, H=351-cid two-barrel V-8, M=351-cid four-barrel V-8, S=390-cid four-barrel V-8, Q=428-cid four-barrel Cobra-Jet V-8, R=428-cid four-barrel Super-Cobra-Jet V-8 and Z=429-cid four-barrel Boss V-8. The last six digits were the unit's production number, beginning at 100001 and going up, at each of the assembly plants. Mustangs were not built at all Ford plants.

Mustang (Six)

Model No.	Body/Style No.	Body Type and Seating	Factory Price	Shipping Weight	Production Total
01	65A	2-dr. Hardtop-4P	$2,618	2,690 lbs.	-----
03	63A	2-dr. 2 + 2 Hardtop-4P	$2,618	2,713 lbs.	-----
02	76A	2-dr. Convertible-4P	$2,832	2,800 lbs.	-----
04	65E	2-dr. Grandé Hardtop-4P	$2,849	2,981 lbs.	-----

Mustang (V-8)

Model No.	Body/Style No.	Body Type and Seating	Factory Price	Shipping Weight	Production Total
01	65A	2-dr. Hardtop-4P	$2,723	2,690 lbs.	127,954
03	63A	2-dr. 2 + 2 Hardtop-4P	$2,723	2,713 lbs.	61,980
02	76A	2-dr. Convertible-4P	$2,937	2,800 lbs.	14,746
04	65E	2-dr. Grandé Hardtop-4P	$2,954	2,981 lbs.	22,182
05	63C	2-dr. Mach 1-4P	$3,122	3,122 lbs.	72,458

Note 1: Production column shows combined six-cylinder and V-8 totals.

Engines:

Six: Overhead valve. Cast-iron block. Displacement: 200 cid. B & S: 3.68 x 3.12 in. Compression ratio: 9.2:1. Brake hp: 120 at 4400 rpm. Seven main bearings. Hydraulic valve lifters. Carburetor: Ford (Autolite) one-barrel Model C6OF-9510-AD. Code T.

1969 Ford Mustang two-door Sportsroof Fastback (OCW)

1969 Ford Mustang two-door Hardtop (OCW)

1969 Ford Mustang two-door **Convertible** (OCW)

1969 Ford Mustang two-door **Mach 1 Sportsroof Fastback** (OCW)

1969 Ford Mustang two-door **Boss 302 Sportsroof Fastback** (PH)

Six: Overhead valve. Cast-iron block. Displacement: 250 cid. B & S: 3.68 x 3.91 in. Compression ratio: 9.0:1. Brake hp: 155 at 4400 rpm. Seven main bearings. Hydraulic valve lifters. Carburetor: Ford Motorcraft one-barrel. Code L.

302 Two-Barrel V-8: Overhead valve. Cast-iron block. Displacement: 302 cid. B & S: 4.00 x 3.00 in. Compression ratio: 9.50:1. Brake hp: 220 at 4600 rpm. Torque: 300 lbs.-ft. at 2600 rpm. Five main bearings. Hydraulic valve lifters. Carburetor: Two-barrel. Cooling system capacity: (Mid-size/Mustang)15 qt. with heater, (Full-size) 15.4 qt. with heater. Crankcase capacity: 4 qt. (add 1 qt. with new oil filter). Code F.

351 Two-Barrel V-8: Overhead valve. Cast-iron block. Displacement: 351 cid. B & S: 4.00 x 3.50 in. Compression ratio: 9.50:1. Brake hp: 250 at 4600 rpm. Torque: 355 lbs.-ft. at 2600 rpm. Five main bearings. Hydraulic valve lifters. Carburetor: Motorcraft two-barrel. Cooling system capacity: (Mid-size/Mustang) 15 qt., (Full-size) 16.5 qt. with heater. Crankcase capacity: (Mid-size/Mustang) 4 qt., (Full-Size/T-Bird) 5 qt. (add 1 qt. with new oil filter). Code H.

Boss 302 V-8: Overhead valve. Cast-iron block. Displacement: 302 cid. B & S: 4.00 x 3.00 in. Compression ratio: 10.50:1. Brake hp: 290 at 5800 rpm. Torque: 290 lbs.-ft. at 4300 rpm. Five main bearings. Solid valve lifters. Carburetor: Holley four-barrel. Cooling system capacity: (Mid-size/Mustang)15 qt. with heater, (Full-size) 15.4 qt. with heater. Crankcase capacity: (Mid-size/Mustang) 4 qt., (Full-Size/T-Bird) 5 qt. (add 1 qt. with new oil filter). Code G.

351 Four-Barrel V-8: Overhead valve. Cast-iron block. Displacement: 351 cid. B & S: 4.00 x 3.50 in. Compression ratio: 10.70:1. Brake hp: 290 at 4800 rpm. Torque: 385 lbs.-ft. at 3200 rpm. Five main bearings. Hydraulic valve lifters. Carburetor: Motorcraft four-barrel. Cooling system capacity: (Mid-size/Mustang) 20.5 qt., (Full-size) 20.1 qt. with heater. Crankcase capacity: (Mid-size/Mustang) 4 qt., (Full-Size/T-Bird) 5 qt. (add 1 qt. with new oil filter). Code M.

Thunderbird 390 Four-Barrel V-8: Overhead valve. Cast-iron block. Displacement: 390 cid. B & S: 4.05 x 3.78 in. Compression ratio: 10.5:1. Brake hp: 320 at 4600 rpm. Torque: 427 lbs.-ft. at 3200 rpm. Five main bearings. Hydraulic valve lifters. Carburetor: Four-barrel. Cooling system capacity: (Mid-size/Mustang) 20.5 qt., (Full-size) 20.1 qt. with heater. Crankcase capacity: (Mid-size/Mustang) 4 qt., (Full-Size/T-Bird) 5 qt. (add 1 qt. with new oil filter). Dual exhausts. Code S.

Cobra-Jet 428 V-8: Overhead valve. Cast-iron block. Displacement: 428 cid. B & S: 4.13 x 3.98 in. Compression ratio: 10.60:1. Brake hp: 335 at 5200 rpm. Torque: 440 lbs.-ft. at 3400 rpm. Five main bearings. Hydraulic valve lifters. Carburetor: Holley four-barrel. Cooling system capacity: (Mid-size/Mustang) 20.5 qt., (Full-size) 20.1 qt. with heater. Crankcase capacity: (Mid-size/Mustang) 4 qt., (Full-Size/T-Bird) 5 qt. (add 1 qt. with new oil filter). Dual exhausts. Code Q.

Super-Cobra-Jet 428 V-8: Overhead valve. Cast-iron block. Displacement: 428 cid. B & S: 4.13 x 3.98 in. Compression ratio: 10.50:1. Brake hp: 360 at 5400 rpm. Torque: 460 lbs.-ft. at 3200 rpm. Five main bearings. Solid valve lifters. Carburetor: Holley four-barrel. Cooling system capacity: (Mid-size/Mustang) 20.5 qt., (Full-size) 20.1 qt. with heater. Crankcase capacity: (Mid-size/Mustang) 4 qt., (Full-Size/T-Bird) 5 qt. (add 1 qt. with new oil filter). Dual exhausts. Code R.

Boss 429 V-8: Overhead valve. Cast-iron block. Displacement: 429 cid. B & S: 4.36 x 3.59 in. Compression ratio: 11.30:1. Brake hp: 375 at 5600 rpm. Torque: 450 lbs.-ft. at 3400 rpm. Five main bearings. Solid or hydraulic valve lifters. Carburetor: Holley four-barrel. Cooling system capacity: 18.6 qt. with heater (T-bird 19.4 qt.). Crankcase capacity: 5 qt. (add 1 qt. with new oil filter). Dual exhausts. Code Z.

Chassis:

Wheelbase: 108 in. Overall length: 187.4 in. Tires: C78-14 four-ply tubeless black sidewall (E78-14 four-ply on small V-8-equipped models and F70-14 four-ply on large V-8-equipped models).

Options:

302-cid/220-hp two-barrel V-8, not available in Mach 1 ($105). 351-cid/250-hp two-barrel V-8, standard in Mach 1 ($163 in other models). 351-cid/290-hp four-barrel V-8, in Mach 1 ($26), in other models ($189). 390-cid/320-hp four-barrel V-8, in Mach 1 ($100), in other models ($158). 428-cid/335-hp four-barrel V-8, in Mach 1 ($224), in other models ($288). 428-cid four-barrel Cobra Jet V-8 including Ram Air, in Mach 1 ($357), in other models ($421). SelectShift Cruise-O-Matic transmission, six-cylinder engines ($191), 302 and 351 V-8s ($201), 390 and 428 V-8s ($222). Four-speed manual, 302 and 351 V-8s ($205), 390 and 428 V-8s ($254). Power disc brakes, not available with 200-cid inline six ($65). Power steering ($95). Power top convertible ($53). GT Equipment Group, not available on Grandé or with six-cylinder or 302-cid V-8, ($147). Tachometer, V-8s only ($54). Handling suspension, not available on Grandé or with six-cylinder and 428 V-8 engines ($31). Competition suspension, standard on Mach 1 and GT, 428 V-8 required ($31). Glass backlight, convertible ($39). Limited slip differential, 250 inline six and 302 V-8 ($42). Traction-Lok differential, not available on sixes and 302 V-8s ($64). Intermittent windshield wipers ($17). High-back front bucket seats, not available in Grandé ($85). Color-keyed dual racing mirrors, standard in Mach 1 and Grandé, ($19). Power ventilation, not available with Select-Aire ($40). Electric clock, standard in Mach 1 and Grandé ($16). Tinted windows and windshield ($32). Speed control, V-8 and automatic transmission required ($74). Remote-control left door mirror ($13). Select-Aire conditioner, not available with 200 inline six or 428 V-8 with four-speed ($380). Push-button AM radio ($61). AM/FM stereo radio ($181). Stereo-Sonic tape system, AM radio required ($134). Rear seat speaker, hardtop and Grandé ($13). Rear seat deck, Sportsroof and Mach 1 ($97). Full-width front seat, hardtop, not available with console ($32). Tilt-Away steering wheel ($66). Rim Blow Deluxe steering wheel ($36). Console ($54). Interior Decor Group, not available on Mach 1 and Grandé ($101), with dual racing mirrors ($88). Deluxe Interior Decor Group, Sportsroof and convertible ($133), with dual racing mirrors ($120). Deluxe seat belts with reminder light ($16). Vinyl roof, hardtop ($84). Wheel covers, not available on Mach 1, Mustang GT or Grandé, but included with exterior Decor Group ($21). Wire wheel covers, not available with Mach 1 and Mustang GT, standard on Grandé, with Exterior Decor Group ($58), without Exterior Decor Group ($80). Exterior Decor Group, not available on Mach 1 and Grandé, ($32). Chrome styled steel wheels, standard on Mach 1, not available on Grandé or with 200 inline six ($117), with GT Equipment Group ($78), with Exterior Decor Group ($95). Adjustable head restraints, not available on Mach 1 ($17).

History:

The 1969 Mustangs were introduced in September 1968. Model year production peaked at 299,824 units. The new fastback styling was called the "Sportsroof" treatment. The fantastic Boss 302 Mustang was styled and detailed by Larry Shinoda. Its standard equipment included the special competition engine, staggered shock absorbers, heavy-duty springs, CJ four-speed gearbox, power front disc brakes, heavy-duty rear drums, special ignition system (with high rpm cut-out feature), and F60-15 Goodyear Polyglas tires. A total of 1,934 Boss 302 Mustangs were built, almost twice as many as needed to qualify the model for Trans-Am racing. Bunkie Knudsen was the chief executive officer of the company this year, but was in his last year at the helm. Ford Motor Co. chairman Henry Ford II fired Knudsen in August. Knudsen, of course, was famous for creating Pontiac's performance image in the early 1960s. Part of his problem at FoMoCo was that auto sales were becoming less relative

1969 Ford Mustang two-door Grandé Hardtop (OCW)

1969 Ford Mustang two-door Boss 429 Sportsroof Fastback (PH)

1970 Ford Mustang two-door Hardtop

1970 Ford Mustang two-door Sportsroof Fastback (OCW)

to high-performance marketing techniques in the early 1970s. Others, however, suggested that Knudsen was the victim of Ford's traditional family controlled management system. He had tried to overstep the limits of his power and, for doing this, was dismissed on short notice.

1970 Mustang

Mustang — (Six and V-8): For 1970, Mustangs were slightly revised versions of the 1969 models. The biggest change was the return to single headlights. They were located inside the new, larger grille opening. Simulated air intakes were seen where the outboard lights were on the 1969 models. The rear was also slightly restyled. There were flat taillight moldings and a flat escutcheon panel, taking the place of the concave panel and lights used in 1969. The year 1970 saw the introduction of the famous 351-cid "Cleveland" V-8 in two-barrel and four-barrel configurations. Standard equipment in Mustangs included vinyl high-back bucket seats, carpeting, a floor-mounted shift lever, instrument gauges, E78-15 tires and either the 200-cid six-cylinder engine or the 302-cid V-8.

Mustang Grandé — (Six and V-8): The Grandé came with all the above plus Deluxe two-spoke steering wheel, color-keyed racing mirrors, wheel covers, electric clock, bright exterior moldings, dual outside paint stripes, and luxury trim bucket seats. Convertibles had power-operated tops.

Mustang MACH 1 —(V-8): The Mach 1 featured vinyl bucket seats, a hood scoop, a competition suspension, color-keyed racing mirrors, console-mounted gearshift controls, a deluxe steering wheel with rim-blow feature, rocker panel moldings, a rear deck lid tape stripe, deep-dish sport wheel covers, carpeting, E70-15 fiberglass-belted whitewall tires and the 351-cid 250-hp two-barrel V-8.

Mustang Boss 302 — (V-8): The Mustang Boss 302 had, in addition to the above, quick-ratio steering, a functional front spoiler, a Space Saver spare tire and the 302-cid Boss V-8 engine.

1970 Ford Mustang two-door Convertible (OCW)

VIN:

The VIN was stamped on an aluminum tab riveted to the instrument panel and was viewable through the windshield. The first symbol indicated the year: 0=1970. The second symbol identified the assembly plant: F=Dearborn, Michigan, R=San Jose, California and T=Metuchen, New Jersey. The third and fourth symbols identified the body series code: 01=two-door hardtop, 02=two-door convertible, 03=two-door Sportsroof, 04=Grandé hardtop and 05=Mach 1 Sportsroof. The fifth symbol identified the engine code: T=200-cid six-cylinder, L=250-cid six-cylinder, F=302-cid two-barrel V-8, G=302-cid four-barrel Boss V-8, H=351-cid two-barrel V-8, M=351-cid four-barrel V-8, Q=428-cid four-barrel Cobra-Jet V-8, R=428-cid four-barrel Super-Cobra-Jet V-8 and Z=429-cid four-barrel Boss V-8. The last six digits were the unit's production number, beginning at 100001 and going up, at each of the assembly plants.

Mustang (Six)

Model No.	Body/ Style No.	Body Type and Seating	Factory Price	Shipping Weight	Production Total
01	65A/B/C	2-dr. Hardtop-4P	$2,712	2,721 lbs.	-------
03	63A/B	2-dr. 2 + 2 Hardtop-4P	$2,771	2,745 lbs.	-------
02	76A/C	2-dr. Convertible-4P	$3,025	2,830 lbs.	-------
04	65E	2-dr. Grandé Hardtop-4P	$2,926	3,008 lbs.	-------

Mustang (V-8)

Model No.	Body/ Style No.	Body Type and Seating	Factory Price	Shipping Weight	Production Total
01	65A	2-dr. Hardtop-4P	$2,822	2,923 lbs.	82,569
03	63A	2-dr. Sportsroof-4P	$2,872	2,947 lbs.	45,934
02	76A	2-dr. Convertible-4P	$3,126	3,033 lbs.	7,673
04	65E	2-dr. Grandé Hardtop-4P	$3,028	3,008 lbs.	13,581
05	63C	2-dr. Mach 1-4P	$3,271	3,240 lbs.	40,970

Note 1: Production column shows combined six-cylinder and V-8 totals.

Engines:

Six: Overhead valve. Cast-iron block. Displacement: 200 cid. B & S: 3.68 x 3.12 in. Compression ratio: 9.2:1. Brake hp: 115 at 3800 rpm. Seven main bearings. Hydraulic valve lifters. Carburetor: Ford Motorcraft one-barrel. Code T.

Six: Overhead valve. Cast-iron block. Displacement: 250 cid. B & S: 3.68 x 3.91 in. Compression ratio: 9.0:1. Brake hp: 155 at 4400 rpm. Seven main bearings. Hydraulic valve lifters. Carburetor: Ford Motorcraft one-barrel. Code L.

302 Two-Barrel V-8: Overhead valve. Cast-iron block. Displacement: 302 cid. B & S: 4.00 x 3.00 in. Compression ratio: 9.50:1. Brake hp: 220 at 4600 rpm. Torque: 300 lbs.-ft. at 2600 rpm. Five main bearings. Hydraulic

1970 Ford Mustang two-door Grandé Hardtop (PH)

1970 Ford Mustang Grandé two-door Hardtop

valve lifters. Carburetor: Two-barrel. Cooling system capacity: 15 qt. with heater. Crankcase capacity: 4 qt. (add 1 qt. with new oil filter). Code F.

351 Two-Barrel V-8: Overhead valve. Cast-iron block. Displacement: 351 cid. B & S: 4.00 x 3.50 in. Compression ratio: 9.50:1. Brake hp: 250 at 4600 rpm. Torque: 355 lbs.-ft. at 2600 rpm. Five main bearings. Hydraulic valve lifters. Carburetor: Motorcraft two-barrel. Cooling system capacity: 15 qt. with heater. Crankcase capacity: 4 qt. (add 1 qt. with new oil filter). Code H.

Boss 302 V-8: Overhead valve. Cast-iron block. Displacement: 302 cid. B & S: 4.00 x 3.00 in. Compression ratio: 10.50:1. Brake hp: 290 at 5800 rpm. Torque: 290 lbs.-ft. at 4300 rpm. Five main bearings. Solid valve lifters. Carburetor: Holley four-barrel. Cooling system capacity: 15 qt. with heater. Crankcase capacity: 4 qt.,(add 1 qt. with new oil filter). Code G.

351 Four-Barrel V-8: Overhead valve. Cast-iron block. Displacement: 351 cid. B & S: 4.00 x 3.50 in. Compression ratio: 10.70:1. Brake hp: 290 at 4800 rpm. Torque: 385 lbs.-ft. at 3200 rpm. Five main bearings. Hydraulic valve lifters. Carburetor: Motorcraft four-barrel. Cooling system capacity: 20.5 qt. with heater. Crankcase capacity: 4 qt. (add 1 qt. with new oil filter). Code M.

Cobra-Jet 428 V-8: Overhead valve. Cast-iron block. Displacement: 428 cid. B & S: 4.13 x 3.98 in. Compression ratio: 10.60:1. Brake hp: 335 at 5200 rpm. Torque: 440 lbs.-ft. at 3400 rpm. Five main bearings. Hydraulic valve lifters. Carburetor: Holley four-barrel. Cooling system capacity: 20.5 qt. with heater. Crankcase capacity: 4 qt., 5 qt. (add 1 qt. with new oil filter). Dual exhausts. Code Q.

Super-Cobra-Jet 428 V-8: Overhead valve. Cast-iron block. Displacement: 428 cid. B & S: 4.13 x 3.98 in. Compression ratio: 10.50:1. Brake hp: 360 at 5400 rpm. Torque: 460 lbs.-ft. at 3200 rpm. Five main bearings. Solid valve lifters. Carburetor: Holley four-barrel. Cooling system capacity: 20.5 qt. Crankcase capacity: 4 qt. (add 1 qt. with new oil filter). Dual exhausts. Code R.

Boss 429 V-8: Overhead valve. Cast-iron block. Displacement: 429 cid. B & S: 4.36 x 3.59 in. Compression ratio: 11.30:1. Brake hp: 375 at 5600 rpm. Torque: 450 lbs.-ft. at 3400 rpm. Five main bearings. Solid or hydraulic valve lifters. Carburetor: Holley four-barrel. Cooling system capacity: 18.6 qt. with heater. Crankcase capacity: 5 qt. (add 1 qt. with new oil filter). Dual exhausts. Code Z.

Chassis:

Wheelbase: 108 in. Overall length: 187.4 in. Tires: C78-14 four-ply tubeless black sidewall (E78-14 four-ply on cars equipped with small V-8s and F70-14 four-ply on those with large V-8s). Boss 302s and Boss 429s used F70-15 tires.

Options:

351-cid/250-hp V-8, in Mach 1 (standard), in other Mustangs ($45). 351-cid/300-hp V-8 in Mach 1 ($48), in other Mustangs ($93). 428-cid/335-hp Cobra Jet V-8 engine with Ram Air induction, in Mach 1 ($376), in other Mustangs ($421). Cruise-O-Matic automatic transmission ($222). Four-speed manual transmission ($205). Power steering ($95). Power front disc brakes ($65). Limited slip differential ($43). Styled steel wheels ($58). Magnum 500 chrome wheels ($129). AM radio ($61). AM/FM stereo radio ($214). AM/8-track stereo ($134). Center console ($54). Tilt steering wheel ($45). Exterior Decor Group ($78). Vinyl roof ($84), on

1970 Ford Mustang two-door Boss 302 Sportsroof Fastback (PH)

1970 Ford Mustang two-door Mach 1 Sportsroof Fastback (PH)

Grandé ($26). Wheel covers ($26). Rocker panel moldings ($16).

History:

The 1970 Mustangs were introduced in September 1969. Model-year production peaked at 190,727 units. Ford ceased its official racing activities late in the 1970 calendar year. Before getting out of racing,

1971 Mustang

Mustang — (Six and V-8): The 1971 Mustangs were completely restyled. They were over two inches longer and had a new hood and concealed windshield wipers. The styling left little doubt that the cars were Mustangs, but they were lower, wider and heavier than any previous models. A full-width grille, incorporating the headlights within its opening, was used. The Mustang corral was again seen in the center. The roof had a thinner appearance. New door handles fit flush to the body. New on the options list were the Special Instrumentation Group package, electric rear window defogger, and a Body Protection Group package that included side moldings and front bumper guards. The fastback-styled "Sportsroof" was now available dressed in a vinyl top. Sadly, two of the most exotic engines were gone. The Boss 302 and Boss 429 power plants bit the dust. Although rumors persist that five cars were assembled with the 'Boss 429,' they are unconfirmed. There was a new Boss 351 Mustang that provided a more refined package, with a better weight distribution layout than the front-heavy Boss 429. Standard equipment on base Mustangs included color-keyed nylon carpeting, floor-shift, high-back bucket seats, steel guardrail door construction, DirectAire ventilation system, concealed windshield wipers with cowl air inlets, mini console with ashtray, armrests, courtesy lights, cigar lighter, heater and defroster, all-vinyl interior, glove box, E78-14 belted black sidewall tires, power convertible top and either the 250-cid six or 302-cid V-8.

Mustang Grandé — (Six and V-8): The Mustang Grandé coupe had the same basic features plus bright pedal pads, Deluxe high-back bucket seats in cloth trim, Deluxe instrument panel, Deluxe two-spoke steering wheel, electric clock, molded trim panels with integral pull handles and armrests, right rear quarter panel trim with ashtray, dual paint accent stripes, dual color-keyed racing mirrors (left remote-control), rocker panel moldings, vinyl roof, wheel covers, and wheel lip moldings.

Mustang MACH 1 — (V-8): The Mustang Mach 1 had all of the basic equipment plus color-keyed spoiler, hood moldings, fender moldings, and racing mirrors, a unique grille with Sportlamps, competition suspension,

1971 Ford Mustang two-door Sportsroof Fastback (PH)

1971 Ford Mustang two-door Mach 1 Sportsroof Fastback (OCW)

1971 Ford Mustang two-door Hardtop (OCW)

trim rings and hubcaps, high-back bucket seats, honeycomb texture back panel appliqué, pop open gas cap, deck lid paint stripe, black or Argent Silver finish on lower bodysides (with bright molding at upper edge), E70-14 whitewalls, and the two-barrel 302-cid V-8. A NASA-styled hood scoop treatment was a no-cost option.

Mustang Boss 351 — (V-8): The Mustang Boss 351 had even more extras. In addition to the basic equipment, this model featured a functional NASA hood scoop, black or Argent Silver painted hood, hood lock pins, Ram-Air engine call-outs, color-keyed racing mirrors (left remote-controlled), unique grille with Sportslamps, hubcaps with trim rings, body side tape stripes in black or Argent Silver, color-keyed hood and front fender moldings, Boss 351 call-out nomenclature, dual exhaust, power disc brakes, Space Saver spare tire, competition suspension with staggered rear shocks, 3.91:1 rear axle gear ratio with Traction Lok differential, electronic rpm limiter, functional front spoiler (finished in black and shipped 'knocked-down'), 80-ampere battery, Instrumentation Group, F60-15 raised white letter tires, High-Output 351 cid/330 hp V-8 with four-barrel carburetion, special cooling package, and wide ratio four-speed manual gearbox with Hurst shifter.

VIN:

The VIN was stamped on an aluminum tab riveted to the instrument panel and was viewable through the windshield. The first symbol indicated the year: 1=1971. The second symbol identified the assembly plant: F=Dearborn, Michigan and T=Metuchen, New Jersey. The third and fourth symbols identified the body series code: 01=two-door hardtop, 02=two-door convertible, 03=two-door Sportsroof, 04=Grandé hardtop and 05=Mach 1 Sportsroof. The fifth symbol identified the engine code: L=250-cid six-cylinder, F=302-cid two-barrel V-8, H=351-cid two-barrel V-8, M=351-cid four-barrel V-8, R=351-cid four-barrel Boss V-8, C=429-cid four-barrel Cobra-Jet V-8 and J=429-cid four-barrel Super-Cobra-Jet V-8. The last six digits were the unit's production number, beginning at 100001 and going up, at each of the assembly plants.

Mustang (Six)

Model No.	Body/Style No.	Body Type and Seating	Factory Price	Shipping Weight	Production Total
01	65D	2-dr. Hardtop-4P	$2,911	2,937 lbs.	------
03	63D	2-dr. 2 + 2 Hardtop-4P	$2,973	2,907 lbs.	------
02	76D	2-dr. Convertible-4P	$3,227	3,059 lbs.	------
04	65F	2-dr. Grandé Hardtop-4P	$3,117	2,963 lbs.	------

Mustang (V-8)

01	65D	2-dr. Hardtop-4P	$3,006	3,026 lbs.	65,696
03	63D	2-dr. Sportsroof-4P	$3,068	2,993 lbs.	23,956
02	76D	2-dr. Convertible-4P	$3,322	3,145 lbs.	6,121
04	65F	2-dr. Grandé Hardtop-4P	$3,212	3,049 lbs.	17,406
05	63R	2-dr. Mach 1-4P	$3,268	3,220 lbs.	36,449

Note 1: Production column shows combined six-cylinder and V-8 totals.

Engines:

Six: Overhead valve. Cast-iron block. Displacement: 250 cid. B & S: 3.68 x 3.91 in. Compression ratio: 9.0:1. Brake hp: 145 at 4000 rpm. Seven main bearings. Hydraulic valve lifters. Carburetor: Ford

1971-1/2 Ford Mustang two-door Hardtop With Sport Appearance (OCW)

1971 Ford Mustang two-door Grandé Hardtop (PH)

1971 Ford Mustang two-door Boss 351 Sportsroof Fastback (OCW)

Motorcraft one-barrel. Code L.

Base Mustang V-8: Overhead valve. Cast-iron block. Displacement: 302 cid. B & S: 4.00 x 3.00 in. Compression ratio: 9.00:1. Brake hp: 210 at 4600 rpm. Torque: 296 lbs.-ft. at 2600 rpm. Five main bearings. Hydraulic valve lifters. Carburetor: Motorcraft two-barrel. Cooling system capacity: 13.5 qt. with heater. Crankcase capacity: 4 qt. (add 1 qt. with new oil filter). Code F.

351 "Windsor" V-8: Overhead valve. Cast-iron block. Displacement: 351 cid. B & S: 4.00 x 3.50 in. Compression ratio: 9.00:1. Brake hp: 240 at 4600 rpm. Torque: 350 lbs.-ft. at 2600 rpm. Hydraulic valve lifters. Carburetor: Motorcraft two-barrel. Cooling system capacity: 14.6 with heater. Crankcase capacity: 4 qt. (add 1 qt. with new oil filter). Code H.

351 "Cleveland" Four-Barrel V-8 (Cobra-Jet after May 1971): Overhead valve. Cast-iron block. Displacement: 351 cid. B & S: 4.00 x 3.50 in. Compression ratio: 10.7:1. Brake hp: 285 at 5400 rpm. (280 hp after May 1971) Torque: 370 lbs.-ft. at 3400 rpm. Five main bearings. Hydraulic valve lifters. Carburetor: Four-barrel. Cooling system capacity: 14.6 with heater. Crankcase capacity: 4 qt. (add 1 qt. with new oil filter). Code M.

Boss 351 H.O. Four-Barrel V-8: Overhead valve. Cast-iron block. Displacement: 351 cid. B & S: 4.00 x 3.50 in. Compression ratio: 11.7:1. Brake hp: 330 at 5400 rpm. Torque: 370 lbs.-ft. at 4000 rpm. Five main bearings. Hydraulic valve lifters. Carburetor: Holley four-barrel. Cooling system capacity: 14.6 with heater. Crankcase capacity: 4 qt. Code R.

429 Cobra-Jet V-8: Overhead valve. Cast-iron block. Displacement: 429 cid. B & S: 4.36 x 3.59 in. Compression ratio: 11.30:1. Brake hp: 370 at 5400 rpm. Torque: 450 lbs.-ft. at 3400 rpm. Five main bearings. Hydraulic valve lifters. Carburetor: Four-barrel. Cooling system capacity: 19 with heater. Crankcase capacity: 4 qt. (add 1 qt. with new oil filter). Dual exhausts. Code C.

429 Super-Cobra-Jet V-8: Overhead valve. Cast-iron block. Displacement: 429 cid. B & S: 4.36 x 3.59 in. Compression ratio: 11.50:1. Brake hp: 375 at 5600 rpm. Torque: 450 lbs.-ft. at 3400 rpm. Five main bearings. Solid valve lifters. Carburetor: Holley four-barrel. Cooling system capacity: 19 with heater. Crankcase capacity: 4 qt. (add 1 qt. with new oil filter). Dual exhausts. Code J.

Chassis:

Wheelbase: 109 in. Overall length: 189.5 in. Width: 75 in. Tires: E78-14

1971 Ford Mustang two-door Convertible (OCW)

belted black sidewall.

History:

The 1971 Mustangs were introduced September 19, 1970. Model-year production peaked at 149,678 units. Calendar-year sales of 127,062 cars were recorded. J.B. Naughton was the chief executive officer of the Ford Division this year. This branch of the corporation was also known as Ford Marketing Corp. Of all Mustangs built in the model year 1971, some 5.3 percent had four-speed manual transmissions, 5.6 percent had stereo eight-track tape players, 1.9 percent had power windows

1972 Mustang

Mustang — (Six and V-8): The Mustang was a versatile package. The original 1964-1/2 Mustang was promoted as a sports/personal car. Later, the Mustang became a luxury automobile. Still later, it became a high-performance machine. Actually, the basic car itself changed very little in overall concept. Yet, for 1972, it was suddenly being called Ford's "Sports Compact." It came in five two-door styles, two hardtops, two Sportsroofs (fastbacks) and a convertible. Styling was generally unaltered, the only appearance refinements were a color-keyed front bumper and a redesigned deck latch panel nameplate. The color-keyed bumper was standard on Mach 1s, while other models continued to use chrome front bumpers as standard equipment. A lot of customers ordered the monochromatic bumpers at slight extra-cost. Instead of spelling Mustang in block letters on the rear, a chrome signature script was used. The powerful 429-cid V-8 was no longer offered. The Cleveland 351-cid four-barrel carbureted V-8 was the hairiest power plant around. Standard equipment in all body styles included concealed windshield wipers, rocker panel moldings, wheel lip moldings, a lower back panel appliqué with bright moldings, color-keyed dual racing mirrors, recessed exterior door handles, wheel covers, DirectAire ventilation, a heater and defroster, high-back bucket seats and bonded door trim panels with pull-type handles and armrests. At this point, the specific equipment in different styles varied.

Hardtop/Sportsroof — (Six and V-8): The hardtop and Sportsroof featured carpeting, mini-consoles, courtesy lights, a deluxe two-spoke steering wheel with wood-toned inserts, a three-speed floor shift, E78-14 black belted tires and a base 250-cid six-cylinder engine. In addition to all of this, the Sportsroof also featured fixed rear quarter windows (except with power lifts) and a tinted backlight.

1972 Ford Mustang two-door Hardtop (OCW)

Convertible — (Six and V-8): The Mustang convertible also had a five-ply power-operated top, a color-keyed top boot, a tinted windshield, a tinted-glass backlight, bright, upper back panel moldings, knitted vinyl seat trim, molded door handles, and black instrument panel appliqués.

Grandé — (Six and V-8) The Mustang Grandé featured — in addition to the above — a vinyl top with Grandé script nameplates, unique body side tape stripes, unique wheel covers, a floor mat in the trunk, Lambeth cloth-and-vinyl interior trim, bright pedal moldings, a deluxe camera-grain instrument panel with wood-toned appliques, a panel-mounted electric clock and rear ashtrays.

Mach 1 — (V-8): The Mach 1 Sportsroof featured the following standard extras: a competition suspension, NASA-type hood scoops (listed as a no-cost option on all Mach 1s, but essentially standard for the model), a front spoiler-type bumper, color-keyed hood and rear fender moldings, a black-finished grille with integral Sportslamps, a back panel appliqué, black or Argent Silver painted lower body, front and rear valance panels, rear tape stripes with Mach 1 decals, wheel trim rings and hubcaps, E70-14 bias-belted whitewall tires and a base 302-cid two-barrel carbureted V-8.

VIN:

The VIN was stamped on an aluminum tab riveted to the instrument panel and was viewable through the windshield. The first symbol indicated the year: 2=1972. The second symbol identified the assembly plant: F=Dearborn, Michigan. The third and fourth symbols identified the body series code: 01=two-door hardtop, 02=two-door convertible, 03=two-door Sportsroof, 04=Grandé hardtop and 05=Mach 1 Sportsroof. The fifth symbol identified the engine code: L=250-cid six-cylinder, F=302-cid two-barrel V-8, H=351-cid two-barrel V-8, Q=351-cid four-barrel V-8 and R=351-cid four-barrel V-8. The last six digits were the unit's production number, beginning at 100001 and going up.

Mustang (Six)

Model No.	Body/ Style No.	Body Type & Seating	Factory Price	Shipping Weight	Production Total
01	65D	2-dr. Hardtop-4P	$2,729	2,941 lbs.	—
03	63D	2-dr. Sportsroof-4P	$2,786	2,909 lbs.	—
02	76D	2-dr. Convertible-4P	$3,015	2,965 lbs.	—
04	65F	2-dr. Grandé Hardtop-4P	$2,915	2,965 lbs.	—

Mustang (V-8)

01	65D	2-dr. Hardtop-4P	$2,816	3,025 lbs.	57,350
03	63D	2-dr. Sportsroof-4P	$2,873	3,025 lbs.	15,622
02	76D	2-dr. Convertible-4P	$3,101	3,147 lbs.	6,401
04	65F	2-dr. Grandé Hardtop-4P	$3,002	3,051 lbs.	18,045
05	63R	2-dr. Mach 1-4P	$3,053	3,046 lbs.	27,675

Note 1: Production column shows combined six-cylinder and V-8 totals.

Engines:

Note: Starting in 1972 horsepower and torque ratings are net, as installed in the vehicle.

Six: Overhead valve. Cast-iron block. Displacement: 250 cid. B & S: 3.68 x 3.91 in. Compression ratio: 8.0:1. Brake hp: 98 at 3400 rpm. Seven main bearings. Hydraulic valve lifters. Carburetor: Ford Motorcraft one-barrel. Code L.

302 Two-Barrel V-8: Overhead valve. Cast-iron block. Displacement: 302 cid. B & S: 4.00 x 3.00 in. Compression ratio: 8.50:1. Brake hp: 140 at 4000 rpm. Torque: 239 at 2000 rpm. Five main bearings. Hydraulic valve lifters. Carburetor: Motorcraft two-barrel. Cooling system capacity with air conditioning: 15.5 qt. Crankcase capacity: 4 qt (add 1 qt. with new oil filter. Code F.

351 Two-Barrel V-8: Overhead valve. Cast-iron block. Displacement: 351 cid. B & S: 4.00 x 3.50 in. Compression ratio: 8.60:1. Brake hp: 168. Five main bearings. Hydraulic valve lifters. Carburetor: Motorcraft two-barrel. Cooling system capacity with air conditioning: 15.75 qt. Crankcase capacity: 4 qt (add 1 qt. with new oil filter). Code H.

351 "Cleveland " Four –Barrel H.O. V-8: (Optional Compact, Intermediate Ford and Mustang): Overhead valve. Cast-iron block. Displacement: 351 cid. B & S: 4.00 x 3.50 in. Compression ratio:

1972 Ford Mustang two-door Grandé Hardtop (OCW)

1972 Ford Mustang two-door Convertible (OCW)

1972 Ford Mustang two-door Sprint Hardtop (OCW)

8.60:1. Brake hp: 266 at 5400 rpm. Torque: 301 at 3600 rpm. Five main bearings. Solid valve lifters. Carburetor: Motorcraft four-barrel. Cooling system capacity with air conditioning: 15.75 qt. Crankcase capacity: 5 qt. (add 1 qt. with new oil filter). Code R.

351 Cobra-Jet Four-Barrel V-8: Overhead valve. Cast-iron block. Displacement: 351 cid. B & S: 4.00 x 3.50 in. Compression ratio: 8.60:1. Brake hp: 275 at 6000 rpm. Torque: 286 at 3800 rpm. Five main bearings. Hydraulic valve lifters. Carburetor: Motorcraft four-barrel. Cooling system capacity with air conditioning: 15.75 qt. Crankcase capacity: 5 qt. (add 1 qt. with new oil filter). Code Q.

Chassis:

Wheelbase: 109 in. Overall length: 189.5 in. Width: 75 in. Tires: E78-14. (Note: Additional tire sizes are noted in text when used as standard equipment on specific models.)

Options:

351-cid/177-hp Cleveland V-8 ($41). 351-cid/266-hp Cleveland V-8 engine ($115). 351-cid/275-hp High-Output V-8 with four-barrel carburetion ($841-$870). Cruise-O-Matic transmission ($204). Four-speed manual transmission ($193). Power steering ($103). Power front disc brakes ($62). Limited-slip differential ($43). Magnum 500 chrome wheels ($108-$139). Center console ($53-$97). Vinyl roof ($79). White sidewall tires ($34).

History:

The 1972 Mustangs were introduced September 24, 1971. Calendar-year sales by United States dealers stopped at 120,589 units, a decline from the previous season. Ford had already stopped building Mustangs in San Jose, Calif., in 1971. Now, the Metuchen, New Jersey, factory was converted to Pinto production, leaving the sole Mustang assembly line in Dearborn, Michigan. This would not last long, though. Sales took a sudden leap from 127,062 to 238,077 units and Mustang II production was soon resumed at San Jose, California. Model-year production stopped at 111,015 cars. There were no changes in top Ford management, although B.E. Bidwell would soon be named vice president and general manager of Ford Marketing Corporation.

1972 Ford Mustang two-door Mach 1 Sportsroof Fastback (PH)

1972 Ford Mustang two-door Sprint Convertible (BB)

1973 Mustang

Mustang — (Six and V-8): The 1973 Mustangs were virtually the same as the 1972 models. The Mustang convertible was the only car of that body style still offered by Ford. It was also one few remaining ragtops in the entire industry. All Mustangs featured a high-impact molded urethane front bumper that was color-keyed to the body. One design change for the new season was a revised cross-hatch texture for the grille insert. New Mustang exterior colors and interior trims were provided. New options included forged aluminum wheels and steel-belted radial-ply tires. Headlights, still of single-unit design, were housed inside square panels that flanked the grille on each side. New features of the grille itself included a "floating" pony badge at the center and an eggcrate-style insert with vertical parking lights in the outboard segments. A new front valance panel was of an un-slotted design.

Hardtop — (Six and V-8): Standard equipment included the 250-cid six-cylinder engine or 302-cid V-8, a three-speed manual transmission, a floor-mounted gearshift, E78-14 black sidewall tires, rocker panel moldings, wheel lip moldings, a lower back panel appliqué with a bright molding, a chrome-plated rectangular left-hand door mirror, all-vinyl upholstery and door trim, a mini front console, color-keyed loop-pile carpeting, a deluxe two-spoke steering wheel with a wood-tone insert, a cigarette lighter, a seat belt reminder system and door courtesy lamps.

Sportsroof — (Six and V-8): The Sportsroof style also included a tinted back window and fixed rear quarter windows.

Convertible — (Six and V-8): The convertible added under-dash courtesy lights, power-operated vinyl top, glass backlight, knit-vinyl seat trim and power front disc brakes.

Grandé — (Six and V-8): Standard extras on the Mustang Grandé, in addition to base equipment, was comprised of dual, color-keyed racing mirrors, a vinyl roof, body side tape striping, special wheel covers, a trunk mat, Lambeth cloth-and-vinyl seat trim, molded door panels with integral armrests, bright pedal pads, a deluxe instrument panel and an electric clock.

Mach 1 — (V-8): Also available was the Mustang Mach 1, which came with all of the following: a competition suspension package, the choice of two hood designs (one with NASA-type hood scoops), size E70-14 whitewall tires of bias-belted Wide-Oval construction, color-keyed dual racing mirrors, a black-finished grille, a black back panel appliqué, a back panel tape stripe, wheel trim rings and hubcaps, a tinted back window, all-vinyl upholstery and trim (with high-back bucket seats) and the 136-hp version of the two-barrel carbureted 302-cid V-8.

VIN:

The VIN was stamped on an aluminum tab riveted to the instrument panel and was viewable through the windshield. The first symbol indicated the year: 3=1973. The second symbol identified the assembly plant:

1973 Ford Mustang two-door Convertible (OCW)

F=Dearborn, Michigan. The third and fourth symbols identified the body series code: 01=two-door hardtop, 02=two-door convertible, 03=two-door Sportsroof, 04=Grandé hardtop and 05=Mach 1 Sportsroof. The fifth symbol identified the engine code: L=250-cid six-cylinder, F=302-cid two-barrel V-8, H=351-cid two-barrel V-8 and Q=351-cid four-barrel V-8. The last six digits were the unit's production number, beginning at 100001 and going up, at each of the assembly plants.

Mustang (Six)

Model No.	Body/ Style No.	Body Type & Seating	Factory Price	Shipping Weight	Production Total
01	65D	2-dr. Hardtop-4P	$2,760	2,984 lbs.	—
03	63D	2-dr. Sportsroof-4P	$2,820	2,991 lbs.	—
02	76D	2-dr. Convertible-4P	$2,946	3,106 lbs.	—
04	65F	2-dr. Grandé Hardtop-4P	$2,915	2,982 lbs.	—

Mustang (V-8)

01	65D	2-dr. Hardtop-4P	$2,847	3,076 lbs.	51,430
03	63D	2-dr. Sportsroof-4P	$2,907	3,083 lbs.	10,820
02	76D	2-dr. Convertible-4P	$3,189	3,198 lbs.	11,853
04	65F	2-dr. Grandé Hardtop-4P	$3,033	3,074 lbs.	25,274
05	63R	2-dr. Mach 1-4P	$3,088	3,090 lbs.	35,440

Note 1: Production column shows combined six-cylinder and V-8 totals.

Engines:

Six: Overhead valve. Cast-iron block. Displacement: 250 cid. B & S: 3.68 x 3.91 in. Compression ratio: 8.0:1. Brake hp: 98 at 3400 rpm. Seven main bearings. Hydraulic valve lifters. Carburetor: Ford Motorcraft one-barrel. Code L.

302 Two-Barrel V-8: Overhead valve. Cast-iron block. Displacement: 302 cid. B & S: 4.00 x 3.00 in. Compression ratio: 8.0:1. Net hp: 140 at 4000 rpm. Net torque: 232 at 2200. Carburetor: Motorcraft two-barrel. Five main bearings. Cooling system capacity with air conditioning: 15.25 qt. Crankcase capacity: 4 qt (add 1 qt. with new oil filter). Code F.

351 "Cleveland" Two-Barrel V-8: Overhead valve. Cast-iron block. Displacement: 351 cid. B & S: 4.00 x 3.50 in. Compression ratio: 8.6:1. Net hp: 177 at 3800 rpm. Net torque: 256 at 2400. Carburetor: Motorcraft two-barrel. Five main bearings. Cooling system capacity with air conditioning: 15.75 qt. Crankcase capacity: 4 qt (add 1 qt. with new oil filter). Code H.

351 Cobra-Jet Four-Barrel V-8: Overhead valve. Cast-iron block. Displacement: 351 cid. B & S: 4.00 x 3.50 in. Compression ratio: 8.0:1. Net hp: 246 at 5400 rpm (248 at 5400 rpm in Mustang). Net torque, 312 lbs.-ft. at 3600. Carburetor: Holley four-barrel. Five main bearings. Cooling system capacity with air conditioning: (Mustang) 15.75 qt., (Torino) 16.75 qt., (Full-size) 16.25 qt. Crankcase capacity: 4 qt (add 1 qt. with new oil filter). Code Q.

Chassis:

Wheelbase: 109 in. Overall length: 189.5 in. Width: 75 in. Tires: E78-14. (Note: Additional tire sizes are noted in text when used as standard equipment on specific models.)

Options:

302-cid two-barrel V-8 standard in Mach 1, in other models ($87). 351-cid two-barrel V-8 ($128). 351-cid four-barrel V-8, including 55-amp alternator, heavy-duty 55-amp battery, special intake manifold, special valve springs and dampers, large-capacity 4300-D carburetor, 25-inch diameter dual exhaust outlets, modified camshaft and four-bolt main bearing caps. Requires Cruise-O-Matic 3.25:1 axle ratio or four-speed manual transmission, 3.50:1 axle combination, power front disc brakes

1973 Ford Mustang two-door Grandé Hardtop (OCW)

and competition suspension ($194). California emission testing ($14). SelectShift Cruise-O-Matic transmission ($204). Four-speed manual transmission with Hurst shifter, not available with six-cylinder ($193). Power front disc brakes, standard on convertible, required with 351-cid V-8 ($62). Power windows ($113). Power steering, required with Tilt-Away steering wheel ($103). SelectAire conditioning, including extra cooling package, not available on six-cylinder with three-speed manual transmission ($368). Console, in Grandé ($53), in other models ($68). Convenience Group, including trunk light, glove compartment light, map light, under hood light, lights-on warning buzzer, automatic seatback releases, under-dash courtesy lights (standard on convertible), parking brake warning light, and glove compartment lock ($46). Electric rear window defroster, not available with convertible or six-cylinder ($57). Tinted glass, convertible ($14), others ($36). Instrumentation Group, including tachometer, trip odometer and oil pressure, ammeter and temperature gauges, included with Mach 1 Sports Interior, not available on six-cylinders, in Grandé without console ($55), in other models ($71). Color-keyed dual racing mirrors, standard on Grandé, Mach 1 ($23). AM radio ($59). AM/FM stereo radio ($191). Sport deck rear seat Sportsroof, Mach 1 only ($86). Deluxe three-spoke Rim-Blow steering wheel ($35). Tilt-Away steering wheel, power steering required ($41). Deluxe leather-wrapped two-spoke steering wheel ($23). Stereo-Sonic Tape System, AM radio required ($120). Intermittent windshield wipers ($23). Optional axle ratios ($12). Traction-Lok differential ($43). Heavy-duty 70-amp-hour battery, standard hardtop and convertible with 351-cid two-barrel V-8 in combination with Instrument Group or SelectAire ($14). Extra cooling package, standard with SelectAire, not available on six-cylinder ($13). Dual Ram Induction, '351' two-barrel V-8, including functional NASA-type hood with black or argent two-tone paint, hood lock pins, "Ram-Air" engine decals ($58). Rear deck spoiler, with Sportsroof or Mach 1 only ($29). Competition suspension, including extra heavy-duty front and rear springs, extra heavy-duty front and rear shock absorbers, standard with Mach 1 and not available with six-cylinder engine ($28). Deluxe seat and shoulder belts package, standard without shoulder belts in convertible ($15). Deluxe Bumper Group including rear rubber bumper inserts and full-width horizontal strip ($25). Rear bumper guards ($14). Decor Group, including black or argent lower body side paint with bright upper edge moldings, unique grille with Sportslamps, trim rings with hubcaps [deletes rocker panel and wheel lip moldings with Decor Group] ($51). Door edge guards, included with Protection Group ($6). Color-keyed front floor mats ($13). Metallic Glow paint ($35). Two-tone hood paint, for Mach 1 ($18), for other models ($34). Protection Group including vinyl-insert bodyside moldings, spare tire lock, door edge guards [deletes bodyside tape stripe] on Grandé ($23), on other models ($36), but not available on Mach 1 or Mustangs with Decor Group. Vinyl roof on hardtops, including C-pillar tri-color ornament [standard on Grandé] ($80). Three-quarter vinyl roof for Sportsroofs only ($52). Mach 1 Sports Interior, for Mach 1 and V-8 Sportsroof only, including knitted vinyl trim, high-back bucket seats with accent stripes, Instrumentation Group, door trim panels with integral pull handles and armrests, color-accented, deep-embossed carpet runners, Deluxe black instrument panel appliqué with wood-tone center section, bright pedal pads and rear seat ashtray ($115). Black or argent bodyside stripes, with Decor Group only ($23). Trim rings with hubcaps [standard on Mach 1 and Mustangs with Decor Group], for Grandé ($8), for other models ($31). Sports wheel covers on Grandé ($56), on Mach 1 or Mustangs with Decor Group ($48), on other models ($79). Forged aluminum wheels on Grandé ($119), on Mach 1 or Mustangs with Decor Group ($111), on other models ($142).

History:

Most 1973 Mustangs, 90.4 percent were equipped with the automatic, 6.7 percent had the three-speed manual, 2.9 percent had the four-speed manual, 92.9 percent had power steering, 77.9 percent had power brakes, 5.6 percent had a tilting steering wheel, 62.8 percent had tinted glass, 3.2 percent had power windows and 56.2 percent were sold with an air conditioner.

1974 Mustang

Mustang II — (Four and V-6): Ford Motor Co. introduced its all-new Mustang II in 1974. It was billed as the "right car at the right time." The new "pony car" measured seven inches shorter than the original 1964-1/2 Mustang and was a full 13 inches shorter than the 1973 model. Sales of the new entry were sluggish at first, since the company loaded most cars in the early mix with a lot of optional equipment. It didn't take long, however, for the marketing men to see that the car had its greatest appeal as an economy model. The Mustang II was a combination of design motifs derived from both sides of the Atlantic. The Italian coach building firm of Ghia, recently acquired by Ford Motor Co., did some of the primary design work. Other ingredients came straight from the Ford/Mercury/Lincoln styling studios. Four models were available: the notch

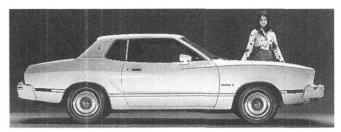

1974 Ford Mustang II two-door coupe

1974 Ford Mustang II two-door 2+2 hatchback (PH)

1974 Ford Mustang II Mach 1 two-door 2+2 hatchback

back coupe, three-door fastback, Ghia notch back coupe and fastback Mach 1. Standard equipment included a 2.3-liter four-cylinder engine, a four-speed manual transmission with floor-mounted gear shifter, a solid-state ignition system, front disc brakes, a tachometer, steel-belted white sidewall tires, low-back front bucket seats, vinyl upholstery and door trim, color-keyed carpeting, a wood-tone instrument panel appliqué, European-type armrests and full wheel covers.

Mustang II 2+2— (Four and V-6): The 2+2 model added a fold-down rear seat and styled steel wheels.

Mustang II Ghia – (Four and V-6): The Ghia notch back coupe also had, in addition to the base equipment, color-keyed Deluxe seat belts, dual color-keyed remote-control door mirrors, Super Sound Package, shag carpeting, wood-tone door panel accents, digital clock, super soft vinyl or Westminster cloth interior trim, color-keyed vinyl roof, and spoke-style wheel covers.

Mustang II Mach 1— (V-6): The Mach 1 had all 2+2 equipment plus a 2.8-liter V-6 engine, dual color-keyed remote-control door mirrors, Wide-Oval steel-belted black sidewall radial tires, black lower body side paint, deck lid striping and styled steel wheels with trim rings.

VIN:

The VIN was stamped on an aluminum tab riveted to the instrument panel and was viewable through the windshield. The first symbol indicated the year: 4=1974. The second symbol identified the assembly plant: F=Dearborn, Michigan and R=San Jose, California. The third and fourth symbols identified the body series code: 02=two-door coupe, 03=two-door hatchback, 04=two-door Ghia Coupe and 05=Mach 1 hatchback. The fifth symbol identified the engine code: Y=140-cid two-barrel four-cylinder and Z=171-cid two-barrel V-6. The last six digits were the unit's production number, beginning at 100001 and going up, at each of the assembly plants.

Mustang (Four)

Model No.	Body/ Style No.	Body Type & Seating	Factory Price	Shipping Weight	Production Total
02	60F	2-dr. Coupe-4P	$3,081	2,620 lbs.	177,671
03	69F	2-dr. 2 + 2 -4P	$3,275	2,699 lbs.	74,799
04	60H	2-dr. Ghia Coupe-4P	$3,427	2,866 lbs.	89,477

Mustang (V-6)

Model No.	Body/ Style No.	Body Type & Seating	Factory Price	Shipping Weight	Production Total
05	69R	2-dr. Mach 1 2 + 2-4P	$3,621	2,787 lbs.	44,046

Engines:

Mustang Four: Overhead cam. Cast-iron block. Displacement: 140 cid. B & S: 3.78 x 3.13 in. Compression ratio: 8.4:1. SAE Net hp: 85. Carburetor: Motorcraft two-barrel. Five main bearings. Code Y.

Mustang V-6: Overhead valve. Cast-iron block. Displacement: 169 cid. B & S: 3.66 x 2.70 in. Compression ratio: 8.0:1. SAE Net hp: 105.

Carburetor: two-barrel. Code Z.

Mustang Mach 1 V-6: Overhead valve. Cast-iron block. Displacement: 171 cid. B & S: 3.66 x 2.70 in. Compression ratio: 8.7:1. SAE Net hp: 109. Carburetor: two-barrel.

Chassis:

Wheelbase: 96.2 in. Overall length: 175 in. Width: 70.2 in. Tires: B78-13 belted black sidewall (BR78-13 on Ghia model).

Options:

2.8-liter (171 cid/109 hp) V-6, standard in Mach I, in other Mustang IIs ($299). SelectShift Cruise-O-Matic ($212). Convenience Group includes: dual color-keyed remote control door mirrors, right visor vanity mirror, inside day/night mirror, parking brake boot and rear ashtray, on Mustangs with Luxury Interior Group ($41), on Mach 1 or Mustangs with Rallye Package ($21), on other Mustangs ($57). Light Group includes: under hood, glove box, map, ashtray and instrument panel courtesy lights, plus trunk or cargo area courtesy light and warning lamps for parking brake, 'door ajar' and 'headlamps-on' ($44). Luxury Interior Group includes: super-soft vinyl upholstery, Deluxe door panels with large armrests and wood-tone accents, Deluxe rear quarter trim, 25-ounce cut-pile carpeting, sound package, parking brake boot, door courtesy lamps, rear ashtray, standard in Ghia, in other Mustangs ($100). Maintenance Group includes: shop manual, spare bulbs, fire extinguisher, flares, warning flag, fuses, tire gauge, bungee cord, lube kit, trouble light, pliers, screwdriver and crescent wrench ($44). Rallye Package, 2.8-liter V-8 required [not available on Ghia], includes Traction-Lok differential, steel-belted raised white letter tires, extra-cooling package, competition suspension, dual color-keyed remote-control door mirrors, styled steel wheels, Sport exhaust system, digital clock and leather-wrapped steering wheel, on Mach 1 ($150), on 2+2 ($284), on others ($328). SelectAire conditioning ($383). Anti-theft alarm system ($75). Traction-Lok differential ($45). Heavy-duty battery ($14). Color-keyed Deluxe seat belts, standard in Ghia, in others ($17). Front and rear bumper guards ($37). Digital clock, standard in Ghia, in others ($36). Console ($43). Electric rear window defroster ($59). California emission equipment ($19). Full tinted glass ($37). Dual color-keyed door mirrors, standard in Ghia and Mach 1, in others ($36). Rocker panel moldings ($14). Vinyl-insert body side moldings ($50). Glamour paint ($36). Pin stripes ($14). Power brakes ($45). Power steering ($106). Radios, AM ($61), AM/FM monaural ($124), AM/FM stereo ($222), AM/FM stereo with tape player ($346). Competition suspension, including heavy-duty springs, adjustable shocks, rear anti-roll bar and 195/70 BWL tires ($37). Flip-out quarter windows, for 2+2 and Mach 1 fastbacks only ($29). Vinyl roof, hardtop only, standard on Ghia, on other models ($83). Fold-down rear seat ($61). Super Sound Package, standard in Ghia, in others ($22). Leather-wrapped steering wheel ($30). Sun roof ($149). Luggage compartment trim ($28). Picardy velour cloth trim, Ghia ($62). Wheel trim rings, standard on Ghia, on others ($32).

History:

The new Mustang II was initially released as a luxury subcompact in mid-1973 and by the end of model year 1974 had recorded an impressive record of 338,136 assemblies, which compared to only

1975 Mustang

Mustang II — (Four and V-6): Throughout its five years of availability, the Mustang II would see little change. A 'moon roof' option and extra-cost V-8 engine were the major revisions for 1975. The design of the steering wheel was modified. A two-spoke-type was used again, but the spokes bent downward at each end instead of running nearly straight across as in the 1974 models. Ghia models had a new roofline with thicker, 'blind' rear quarters. This made the opera windows somewhat smaller. Another Ghia addition was a stand-up hood ornament. New hubcaps were featured with most decor-levels and, on cars with catalytic converters, unleaded fuel decals were affixed to the gas filler cap. In midyear, several changes took effect. The first was a slightly plainer Ghia coupe with restyled hubcaps and no hood ornament. The second was the Mustang II MPG, an economy leader that gave 26-28 highway miles per gallon. Standard equipment on the basic notch back hardtop included a solid-state ignition system, front disc brakes, a tachometer, steel-belted BR78-13 black sidewall tires, low-back front bucket seats, vinyl upholstery and trim, woodgrained dash appliqués, armrests, full wheel covers, a four-speed manual transmission with floor shift and the 2.3-liter four-cylinder engine.

Mustang II 2+2— (Four and V-6): The 2+2 model added a fold-down rear seat and styled steel wheels.

Mustang II Ghia — (Four and V-6): The Ghia notchback coupe also had, in addition to the base equipment, color-keyed Deluxe seat belts, dual color-keyed remote-control door mirrors, Super Sound Package, shag carpeting, wood-tone door panel accents, digital clock, super soft vinyl or Westminster cloth interior trim, color-keyed vinyl roof, and spoke-style wheel covers.

Mustang II Mach 1— (V-6): The Mach 1 had all 2+2 equipment plus a 2.8-liter V-6 engine, dual color-keyed remote-control door mirrors, Wide-Oval steel-belted black sidewall radial tires, black lower body side paint, deck lid striping and styled steel wheels with trim rings.

VIN:

The VIN was stamped on an aluminum tab riveted to the instrument panel and was viewable through the windshield. The first symbol indicated the year: 5=1975. The second symbol identified the assembly plant: F=Dearborn, Michigan and R=San Jose, California. The third and fourth symbols identified the body series code: 02=two-door coupe, 03=two-door hatchback, 04=two-door Ghia Coupe and 05=Mach 1 hatchback. The fifth symbol identified the engine code: Y=140-cid (2.3-liter) two-barrel four-cylinder, Z=171-cid (2.8-liter) two-barrel V-6 and F=302-cid (5.0-liter) two-barrel V-8. The last six digits were the unit's production numbers, beginning at 100001 and going up, at each of the assembly plants.

Mustang (Four)

Model No.	Body/ Style No.	Body Type & Seating	Factory Price	Shipping Weight	Production Total
02	60F	2-dr. Coupe-4P	$3,529	2,660 lbs.	—
03	69F	2-dr. 2 + 2-4P	$3,818	2,697 lbs.	—
04	60H	2-dr. Ghia Coupe-4P	$3,938	2,745 lbs.	—

Mustang (V-6)

02	60F	2-dr. Coupe-4P	$3,801	2,775 lbs.	85,155
03	69F	2-dr. 2 + 2-4P	$4,090	2,812 lbs.	30,038
04	60H	2-dr. Ghia Coupe-4P	$4,210	2,947 lbs.	52,320
05	69R	2-dr. Mach 1 2 + 2-4P	$4,188	2,879 lbs.	21,062

Note 1: Production column shows combined four-cylinder, V-6 and optional V-8 totals.

Engines:

2.3-Liter Four: Inline. Overhead valve and camshaft. Cast-iron block. Displacement: 140 cid. B & S: 3.78 x 3.13 in. Compression ratio: 8.4:1. SAE Net hp: 83. Hydraulic valve lifters. Carburetor: Motorcraft two-barrel Model 5200. Code Y.

2.8-Liter V-6: Overhead valve and camshaft. Cast-iron block. Displacement: 171 in. B & S: 3.66 x 2.70 in. Compression ratio: 8.7:1. SAE Net hp: 97. Carburetor: Motorcraft two-barrel Model 5200. Code Z.

1975 Ford Mustang II two-door coupe

1975 Ford Mustang two-door Ghia Coupe (OCW)

1975 Ford Mustang II two-door 2+2 hatchback

Optional 5.0-Liter V-8: Overhead valve. Cast-iron block. Displacement: 302 cid. B & S: 4.00 x 3.00 in. Compression ratio: 8.0:1. SAE Net hp: 122. Carburetor: Motorcraft two-barrel Model 2150. Code F.

Chassis:

Wheelbase: 96.2 in. Overall length: 175 in. Front tread: 55.6 in. Rear tread: 55.8 in. Tires: Various.

Options:

Exterior Accent Group ($151). Select-Aire conditioning ($401). Anti-Theft alarm system ($71). Deluxe color-keyed seat belts in Ghia (standard), in other models ($51). Front and rear bumper guards ($31). Digital quartz electric clock ($37). Console ($63). Electric rear window defroster ($59). California emissions equipment ($41). Fuel monitor warning light ($14). Deck lid luggage rack ($43). Dual color-keyed outside rearview door mirrors, standard Ghia/Mach 1, on others ($36). Rocker panel moldings ($14). Color-keyed vinyl insert type bodyside moldings ($51). Power steering ($111). Glass moon roof ($422). Radio, AM ($63), AM/FM ($124), AM/FM stereo ($213), same with 8-track ($333). Glamour paint ($43). Vinyl roof for hardtop coupe, standard with Ghia, on others ($83). Fold-down rear seat, standard in fastbacks, on others ($61). Leather-wrapped steering wheel ($30). Pin striping ($18). Sun roof ($195). Competition suspension, includes heavy-duty springs, adjustable shock absorbers, rear anti-roll bar, and 195/70 blackwall or White Line tires on Ghia or others with Exterior Accent Group ($43), on Mach 1 ($25), on others ($55). Velour cloth interior trim ($63). Flip-out rear quarter windows on fastbacks ($31). Four-speed manual transmission with floor shift (standard), Select-Shift Cruise-O-Matic ($227). Mach 1 2.8-liter/171 cid V-6 engine, in Mach 1 (no charge), in other models ($253). 5.0-liter/302 cid V-8 engine, in Mach 1 ($172), in other models ($199). Traction-Lok differential ($46). Heavy-duty battery ($14). Extended range fuel tank ($18).

Option Packages: Convenience-Group, included dual, color-keyed, remote-controlled outside rearview door mirrors, right-hand visor/vanity mirror, inside day/night mirror, parking brake boot, and rear ashtray, with Luxury Interior Group ($48), on Mach 1 or models with Rallye Package or Exterior Accent Group ($29), on other models ($65). Light Group, includes under hood glove box, ashtray, dashboard courtesy lights, plus map, "door ajar" and "headlamps-on" warning lights ($33). Security Lock Group, included locking gas cap, inside hood release lock and spare tire lock ($14). Luxury Interior Group, includes Super-Soft vinyl seats, door trim with large armrests, Deluxe rear quarter trim, door courtesy lights, color-keyed seat belts, shag carpets, parking brake boot, rear ashtray and Super-Sound package ($100). Ghia Silver Luxury Group (for Ghia coupe only), included Silver metallic paint, silver Nommande-grain half vinyl roof, stand-up hood ornament, Cranberry striping, Silver bodyside moldings, all-Cranberry interior in Media velour cloth, color-keyed sun visors and headliner, plus center console ($151). Maintenance Group, included shop manual, bulbs, fire extinguisher, flares, warning flag, fuses, tire gauge, bungee cord, lube kit, trouble light, pliers, screwdriver, and crescent wrench ($45). Rallye Package, included Traction-Lok differential, 195/70 raised white letter tires, extra-cooling package, bright exhaust tips, competition suspension package, dual color-keyed, remote-control outside rearview door mirrors, leather-

1975 Ford Mustang II Mach 1 two-door 2+2 hatchback (PH)

wrapped steering wheel, and styled steel wheels with trim rings, on Mach 1 ($168), on 2+2 ($218), on other models ($262). Protection Group, included door edge guards, front floor mats, and license plate frames, on Mach 1 ($19), on others ($27).

History:

The 1975 Mustang II lineup was introduced in September 1974, with the plainer Ghia coupe and Mustang II MPG bowing at midyear. Model year production of 188,575 cars was recorded. Lee Iacocca was chief executive officer of the company this year. The new Mustang II V-8 was capable of a top speed above 105 mph and could cover the standing-start quarter-mile in 17.9 seconds with a terminal speed of 77 mph.

1976 Mustang

Mustang II — (Four and V-6): The 1976 Mustang II again came in two basic body styles, a two-door hardtop and three-door 2+2 hatchback. The two-door was commonly referred to by Ford as a sedan, but was really a coupe. Ford simply used the term "sedan" to distinguish it from the old (larger) coupe design. The "three-door" model had only two doors for people. It was designated either a hatchback or fastback, both terms accurately describing the sloping lift-up rear end design. Coupes came in base or Ghia trim and fastbacks came in base or Mach 1 form. The Fastback had fold-down rear seats, while the hardtop displayed a formal-looking roof line. The MPG series, carrying fewer standard items and a smaller price tag, was continued in 1976. This year's highlights include significant fuel economy gains, some new options and a new sport exterior dress-up package for the 2+2 and Mach 1. The former horizontal stainless steel bumper inserts were replaced by black bumper rub strips with white stripes. The wiper/washer control had moved to the turn signal lever in mid-year 1975, and continued there this year. To improve economy, Mustang II got a lower optional 2.79:1 axle ratio. An optional wide-ratio transmission was available with that rear-end ratio. New options included sporty plaid trim on seating surfaces, expanded availability of Ghia luxury coupe colors, whitewall tires, and an AM radio with stereo tape player. Styling was similar to 1975, except for a new air scoop below the front bumper. Rectangular parking/signal lamps were inset right into the forward-slanting grille, which had a 14 x 6-holes crosshatch pattern. The grille was narrower at the top than at the base, with a traditional Mustang (horse) emblem in its center. Separate "Ford" block letters stood above the grille, facing upward. Single round headlamps were recessed into squarish housings. The front bumper protruded forward in the center, matching the width of the grille. Rub strips wrapped only slightly onto the bumper sides. The door sheet metal had a sculptured, depressed area that began near the back and extended for a short distance on the quarter panel, following the contour of the wheel opening. The curvaceous body side crease ran below the door handle. Coupes had a "B" pillar and conventional quarter window. Fastbacks had sharply-tapered quarter windows that came to a point at the rear. Each European-style taillight consisted of three side-by-side sections, with a small back-up lens at the bottom of each center section and larger amber turn signal lenses. Large "F-O-R-D" block letters stood on the panel between the taillights, above the license plate housing. The bodies had a one-piece fiberglass-reinforced front end and color-keyed urethane-coated bumpers. Standard features included wheel lip moldings, side marker lights with die-cast bezels, recessed door handles and slim high-luster exterior trim moldings. Inside were low-back all-vinyl front bucket seats with full-width head restraints, a tachometer, a speedometer, an ammeter, fuel and temperature gauges, European-type armrests with integral pull handles, a two-spoke steering wheel and a lockable glove box. Simulated burled walnut wood tone

1976 Ford Mustang II two-door Ghia Coupe (FMC)

accents went on the instrument panel and shift knob. The Mustang had a unitized body and chassis with a front isolated mini-frame, Hotchkiss-type rear suspension and rack-and-pinion steering. The rear suspension consisted of longitudinal semi-elliptic leaf springs (four leaves), while the independent front suspension used ball joints, a stabilizer bar, and compression-type struts. The standard engine was a 140-cid (2.3-liter) four with four-speed floor shift. A 302-cid (5.0-liter) V-8 with Cruise-O-Matic transmission or 171-cid (2.8-liter) V-6 with four-speed manual were options. Three Luxury Groups were available: Silver, Tan Glow, and Silver Blue Glow (the latter two colors new this year). Two special option packages were offered: a new Stallion group intended to appeal to youthful buyers, and the more notorious Cobra II.

Mustang II Ghia — (Four and V-6): Ghias included a quartz design clock, body side molding. BR78 x 13 steel-belted radial whitewalls, padded half or full vinyl roof, hood ornament, dual remote mirrors, crushed velour seats surfaces, full console, and body side paint stripes. Ghias had wire-type wheel covers, Mach 1 included wheel trim rings.

Mustang II Silver Stallion — (Four and V-6): The sporty silver Stallion package featured a two-tone paint and tape treatment (on fastback models), a large Stallion decal on front fenders (at the cowl), dual racing mirrors, styled steel wheels with raised-white-letter tires and a competition suspension. Black paint highlighted the greenhouse, lower body, hood, grille, deck lid and lower back panel.

Mustang II Mach 1— (V-6): Mach 1 had the V-6 as standard. A four-speed manual gearbox became available with the V-8 later in the season. Front disc brakes were standard, power brakes (and steering) optional. Mach 1 added the 2.8-liter V-6, dual remote racing mirrors, BR70 x 13 raised-white-letter tires on styled steel wheels and rear tape and fender decals. Black paint went on the lower bumpers, lower body side and between rear taillights.

Mustang II Cobra II —(V-6): On the ultimate option, large 'Cobra II' decal lettering at the door bottoms was easy to spot from a distance. Cobra II sported a black grille with cobra emblem, front air dam, simulated hood scoop, rear spoiler, and rocker-panel racing stripes. Dual wide stripes ran from the grille, over the hood and roof, onto the deck area. Front fenders displayed large cobra (snake) decals. Louvers covered the triangular flip-out quarter windows. Inside was a sport steering wheel and brushed-aluminum trim on dash and door panels, plus dual remote-control mirrors. Cobra II carried a standard V-6 engine and four-speed, with raised-white-letter tires on styled steel wheels. Only one body color scheme was offered at first, white with blue striping.

VIN:

The VIN was stamped on an aluminum tab riveted to the instrument panel and was viewable through the windshield. The first symbol indicated the year: 6=1976. The second symbol identified the assembly plant: F=Dearborn, Michigan and R=San Jose, California. The third and fourth symbols identified the body series code: 02=two-door coupe, 03=two-door hatchback, 04=two-door Ghia Coupe and 05=Mach 1 hatchback. The fifth symbol identified the engine code: Y=140-cid (2.3-liter) two-barrel four-cylinder, Z=171-cid (2.8-liter) two-barrel V-6 and F=302-cid (5.0-liter) two-barrel V-8. The last six digits were the unit's production numbers, beginning at 100001 and going up, at each of the assembly plants.

Mustang (Four)

Model No.	Body/ Style No.	Body Type & Seating	Factory Price	Shipping Weight	Production Total
02	60F	2-dr. Coupe-4P	$3,525	2,678 lbs.	—
03	69F	2-dr. 2 + 2-4P	$3,781	2,706 lbs.	—
04	60H	2-dr. Ghia Coupe-4P	$3,859	2,729 lbs.	—

Mustang (V-6)

Model No.	Body/ Style No.	Body Type & Seating	Factory Price	Shipping Weight	Production Total
02	60F	2-dr. Coupe-4P	$3,791	2,756 lbs.	78,508
03	69F	2-dr. 2 + 2-4P	$4,047	2,784 lbs.	62,312
04	60H	2-dr. Ghia Coupe-4P	$4,125	2,807 lbs.	37,515

1976 Ford Mustang two-door Cobra II 2+2 (OCW)

| 05 | 69R | 2-dr. Mach 1 2 + 2-4P | $4,209 | 2,822 lbs. | ------ |

Mustang (V-8)

| 05 | 69R | 2-dr. Mach 1 2 + 2-4P | $4,154 | 2,879 lbs. | 9,232 |

Note 1: The production column shows combined V-6 and V-8 totals for Cobra II and combined four-cylinder and V-6 totals for other models.

Engines:

2.3-Liter Four: Inline. Overhead valve and camshaft. Cast-iron block. Displacement: 140 cid (2.3 liters). B & S: 3.78 x 3.13 in. Compression ratio: 9.0:1. Brake hp: 92 at 5000 rpm. Torque: 121 lbs.-ft. at 3000 rpm. Five main bearings. Hydraulic valve lifters. Carburetor: Holley-Weber 9510. Code Y.

2.8-Liter V-6: 60-degree, overhead valve. Cast-iron block and head. Displacement: 170.8 cid (2.8 liters). B & S: 3.66 x 2.70 in. Compression ratio: 8.7:1. Brake hp: 103 at 4400 rpm. Torque: 149 lbs.-ft. at 2800 rpm. Four main bearings. Solid valve lifters. Carburetor: Holley-Weber 9510 two-barrel. German Ford-built. Code Z.

Optional 5.0-Liter V-8: 90-degree, overhead valve. Cast-iron block and head. Displacement: 302 cid (5.0 liters). B & S: 4.00 x 3.00 in. Compression ratio: 8.0:1. Brake hp: 134 at 3600 rpm. Torque: 247 lbs.-ft. at 1800 rpm. Five main bearings. Hydraulic valve lifters. Carburetor: Motorcraft 9510 two-barrel. Code F.

Chassis:

Wheelbase: 96.2 in. Overall length: 175.0 in. Height: (Coupe) 50.0 in., (2+2) 49.7 in. Width: 70.2 in. Front Tread: 55.6 in. Rear Tread: 55.8 in. Wheel Size: 13 x 5 in. Tires: B78 x 13, base, BR78 x 13, Ghia and BR70 x 13 steel-belted radial with raised white letters, Mach 1. Sizes CR70 x 13 and 195/70R13 were also available.

Technical:

Transmissions: Four-speed manual transmission (floor shift) standard. Gear ratios: (1st) 4.07:1, (2nd) 2.57:1, (3rd) 1.66:1, (4th) 1.00:1, (Rev) 3.95:1. Four-cylinder four-speed, (1st) 3.50:1, (2nd) 2.21:3, (3rd) 1.43:1, (4th) 1.00:1, (Reverse) 3.38:1. Select-Shift three-speed automatic optional (initially were standard with the V-8). Four-cylinder: (1st) 2.47:1, (2nd) 1.47:1, (3rd) 1.00:1, (Reverse) 2.11:1. V-6/V-8 automatic: (1st) 2.46:1, (2nd) 1.46:1, (3rd) 1.00:1, (Reverse) 2.20:1. Standard final drive ratio: 2.79:1 with four-speed manual, 3.18:1 with automatic transmission, (V-6) 3.00:1, (V-8) 2.79:1. Steering: Rack and pinion. Front suspension: Compression strut with lower trailing links, stabilizer bar and coil springs. Rear suspension: Hotchkiss rigid axle with semi-elliptic leaf springs (four leaves) and anti-sway bar. Brakes: Front disc, rear drum. Disc diameter: 9.3 in. outer, 6.2 in. inner. Drum diameter: 9.0 in. Ignition: Electronic. Body construction: Unibody with front isolated mini-frame. Fuel tank: 13 gallons.

Options:

140-cid four-cylinder engine ($272 credit from base V-6 price). Cruise-O-Matic transmission ($239). Optional axle ratio ($13). Traction-Lok differential ($48). Power brakes ($54). Power steering ($117). Competition suspension ($29-$191). Heavy-duty 53-amp battery ($14). Extended-range fuel tank ($24). Engine block heater ($17). California emission system ($49). Cobra II package ($325). Cobra II modification package ($287). Rallye package for Mach 1 ($163). Rally package for Coupe ($267-$399). Ghia luxury group ($177). Stallion option ($72). Exterior accent group ($169). Luxury interior group ($117). Convenience group ($35). Light group ($28-$41). Protection group ($36-$43). Air conditioning ($420). Electric rear defroster ($70). Tinted glass ($46). Leather-wrapped steering wheel ($33). Electric clock ($17). Digital clock ($40). Fuel monitor warning light ($18). Anti-theft alarm ($83). Security lock group ($16). Dual-note horn ($6). Color-keyed mirrors ($42). AM radio ($71). AM radio with tape player ($192). AM/FM radio ($128). AM/FM stereo radio ($173). AM/FM stereo radio with tape player ($299). Glass moon roof ($470). Manual sunroof ($230). Vinyl roof ($86). Half-vinyl roof on Ghia (NC). Glamour paint ($54). Two-tone paint and tape ($84). Pinstriping ($27). Front and rear bumper guards ($34). Color-keyed vinyl-insert body

side molding ($60). Rocker panel moldings ($19). Pivoting rear quarter windows ($33). Deck lid luggage rack ($51). Console ($71). Fold-down rear seat ($72). Velour cloth trim ($99). Color-keyed deluxe seat belt ($17). Cast-aluminum spoke wheels ($96-$182). Forged aluminum wheels ($96-$182). Styled steel wheels for 2+2 and HT ($51). Styled wheels for Ghia (no cost). Trim rings ($35). B78 x 13 black sidewall ($84). B78 x 13 white sidewall ($33-$52). BR78 x 13 black sidewall ($97). BR78 x 13 white sidewall ($33 to $130). BR70 x 13 raised white letter ($30 to $160). CR70 x 13 white sidewall ($10 to $169). 195/70R13 white sidewall ($22 to $191). 195/70R13 raised white letter ($12 to $203). 195/70R13 wide white sidewall ($5 to $208).

History:

Introduced October 3, 1975. Model-year production (U.S.): 187,567. Total production for the U.S. market of 172,365 included 91,886 four-cylinder, 50,124 V-6, and 30,361 V-8 Mustangs. Calendar-year production (U.S.): 183,369. Calendar-year sales: 167,201. Mustang, America's best selling small specialty car, had been outselling Monza, Starfire and Skyhawk combined. The optional V-6, also used on the

1977 Mustang

Mustang II — (Four and V-6): No significant styling changes were evident on the Mustang for 1977, although new colors were offered and both the four-cylinder and V-6 engines lost power. As before, hardtop (notchback) and three-door fastback models were available. Simulated pecan replaced the burled walnut woodgrain interior appliqués. California models used a variable-venturi carburetor. Joining the option list were simulated wire wheel covers, painted cast aluminum spoke wheels, a flip-up removable sunroof, four-way manual bucket seats, and high-altitude option. The bronze-tinted glass sunroof panels could either be propped partly open or removed completely for storage in the trunk. That T-Bar roof package included a wide black band across the top (except with the Cobra II). Mustang's engine/transmission selection continued as before. Neither a V-6, nor a V-8 with four-speed manual gearbox was offered in California. The basic two-door hardtop carried a standard 140 cid (2.3-liter) four-cylinder engine with Dura-Spark ignition, four-speed manual gearbox, front disc brakes. color-keyed urethane bumpers, low-back bucket seats with vinyl trim, B78 x 13 tires, and full wheel covers. Bright moldings highlighted the windshield, drip rail, belt, back window and center pillar. Mustang 2+2 hatchbacks included a front spoiler at no extra cost (which could be deleted), along with a sport steering wheel, styled steel wheels, B78 x 13 bias-belted raised-white-letter or 195R/70 whitewall tires, black-out grille, and brushed aluminum instrument panel appliqués.

Mustang II Rally 2+2 — (Four and V-6): The later-arriving 2+2 Rally Appearance Package replaced the Stallion option. It included dual gold accent stripes on hood and bodysides, flat black wiper arms, door handles, lock cylinders, and antenna, dual black sport mirrors, and argent styled steel wheels with trim rings. A gold-color surround molding highlighted the black grille (which lost its horse emblem). Also included gold taillamp accent moldings and dual gold accent stripes in bumper rub strips. A black front spoiler was a no-cost option. Black and Polar White body colors were offered with the package. Inside were black or

1977 Ford Mustang II two-door coupe

1977 Ford Mustang II two-door 2+2 hatchback

white vinyl seats with gold ribbed velour Touraine cloth inserts and gold welting, and gold accent moldings on door panels.

Mustang II Ghia — (Four and V-6): Ghia added a half-vinyl roof, pinstripes, unique wheel covers, and body side moldings with color-keyed vinyl inserts. Ghia interiors could have Media Velour cloth with large armrests. Ghia's Sports Group was available with black or tan body, including a vinyl roof and many color-coordinated components in black or chamois color. Also included was a three-spoke sports steering wheel, cast aluminum wheels with chamois-color spokes, and trunk luggage rack with straps and buckles.

Mustang II Mach 1—(V-6): Stepping up another notch, Mach 1 carried a standard 2.8-liter V-6 and sported a black paint treatment on lower body side and back panel. Also included: dual sport mirrors, Mach I emblem, and raised-white-letter BR70 x 13 (or 195R/70) steel-belted radial tires on styled steel wheels with trim rings.

Mustang II Cobra II —(V-6): Cobra II changed its look after the model year began. Big new tri-color tape stripes went on the full bodyside and front spoiler, front bumper, hood, hood scoop, roof, deck lid and rear spoiler. "Cobra II" block lettering was low on the doors at first, later halfway up as part of the huge center bodyside tape stripe. The deck lid spoiler displayed a Cobra snake decal, and another snake highlighted the black grille. Early Cobras also had snake cowl decals. Flat black greenhouse moldings, vertical-style quarter-window louvers (without the snake) and rear-window louvers also became standard. So was a narrow band of flat black along the upper doors. Cobra II equipment also included dual black sport mirrors, rear-opening hood scoop, BR70 or 195/R70 x 13 raised white letter tires, and brushed aluminum door trim inserts. The required power brakes cost extra. Cobra II was now offered in four color choices, not just the original white with blue striping. Selections were white body with red, blue or green stripes, or black with gold stripes. A new Rallye package included dual racing mirrors, heavy-duty springs and cooling, adjustable shocks, and rear stabilizer bar. Mustang's Sports Performance package included a 302 cu. in. V-8 with two-barrel carb, heavy-duty four-speed manual gearbox, power steering and brakes, and P195R/70 radial tires.

VIN:

The VIN was stamped on an aluminum tab riveted to the instrument panel and was viewable through the windshield. The first symbol indicated the year: 7=1977. The second symbol identified the assembly plant: F=Dearborn, Michigan and R=San Jose, California. The third and fourth symbols identified the body series code: 02=two-door coupe, 03=two-door hatchback, 04=two-door Ghia Coupe and 05=Mach 1 hatchback. The fifth symbol identified the engine code: Y=140-cid (2.3-liter) two-barrel four-cylinder, Z=171-cid (2.8-liter) two-barrel V-6 and F=302-cid (5.0-liter) two-barrel V-8. The last six digits were the unit's production numbers, beginning at 100001 and going up, at each of the assembly plants.

Mustang (Four)

Model No.	Body/Style No.	Body Type & Seating	Factory Price	Shipping Weight	Production Total
02	60F	2-dr. Coupe-4P	$3,702	2,627 lbs.	—
03	69F	2-dr. 2 + 2 -4P	$3,901	2,672 lbs.	—
04	60H	2-dr. Ghia Coupe-4P	$4,119	2,667 lbs.	—

Mustang (V-6)

02	60F	2-dr. Coupe-4P	$3,984	2,750 lbs.	67,793
03	69F	2-dr. 2 + 2-4P	$4,183	2,795 lbs.	49,161
04	60H	2-dr. Ghia Coupe-4P	$4,401	2,709 lbs.	29,510
05	69R	2-dr. Mach 1 2 + 2-4P	$4,332	2,785 lbs.	-----

Mustang (V-8)

05	69R	2-dr. Mach 1 2 + 2-4P	$4,284	2,879 lbs.	6,719

Notes: The production column shows combined V-6 and V-8 totals for Cobra II and combined four-cylinder and V-6 totals for other models. The totals shown include 20,937 Mustangs produced as 1978 models. but sold as 1977 models: 9,826 model 02 coupes, 7,019 model 03 2 + 2, 3,209 Ghia coupes and 883 Mach 1 models.

Engines:

2.3-Liter Four: Inline. Overhead valve and camshaft. Cast-iron block. Displacement: 140 cid (2.3 liters). B & S: 3.78 x 3.13 in. Compression ratio: 9.0:1. Brake hp: 89 at 4800 rpm. Torque: 120 lbs.-ft. at 3000 rpm. Five main bearings. Hydraulic valve lifters. Carburetor: Motorcraft 5200. Code Y.

2.8-Liter V-6: 60-degree, overhead valve. Cast-iron block and head. Displacement: 170.8 cid (2.8 liters). B & S: 3.66 x 2.70 in. Compression ratio: 8.7:1. Brake hp: 93 at 4200 rpm. Torque: 140 lbs.-ft. at 2600 rpm. Four main bearings. Solid valve lifters. Carburetor: Motorcraft 2150 two-barrel. German Ford-built. Code Z.

Optional 5.0-Liter V-8: 90-degree, overhead valve. Cast-iron block and head. Displacement: 302 cid (5.0 liters). B & S: 4.00 x 3.00 in.

1977 Ford Mustang II two-door Ghia Coupe (FMC)

1977 Ford Mustang two-door Cobra II 2+2 (FMC)

Compression ratio: 8.0:1. Brake hp: 139 at 3600 rpm. Torque: 247 lbs.-ft. at 1800 rpm. Five main bearings. Hydraulic valve lifters. Carburetor: Motorcraft 2150 two-barrel. Code F.

Chassis:

Wheelbase: 96.2 in. Overall length: 175.0 in. Height: (Coupe) 50.3 in., (2+2) 50.0 in. Width: 70.2 in. Front Tread: 55.6 in. Rear Tread: 55.8 in. Tires: BR78 x 13, Ghia, BR70 x 13, Mach I and B78 x 13, other Mustangs.

Technical:

Transmission: Four-speed manual transmission (floor shift) standard. V-8 gear ratios: (1st) 2.64:1, (2nd) 1.89:1, (3rd) 1.34:1, (4th) 1.00:1, (Reverse) 2.56:1. Four and V-6 four-speed: (1st) 3.50:1, (2nd) 2.21:1, (3rd) 1.43:1, (4th) 1.00:1, (Reverse) 3.38:1. Select-Shift three-speed automatic optional. Four-cylinder: (1st) 2.47:1, (2nd) 1.47:1, (3rd) 1.00:1: (Reverse) 2.11:1. V-8 automatic: (1st) 2.46:1, (2nd) 1.46:1, (3rd) 1.00:1, (Reverse) 2.19:1. Standard final drive ratio: (four) 3.18:1, (V-6/V-8) 3.00:1. Fuel tank: 13 gallons and V-8, 16.5 gallons.

Options:

140-cid four-cylinder ($289 credit from base V-6 price). 170-cid V-6 ($289). 302-cid V-8 ($230). Cruise-O-Matic trans. ($253). Power brakes ($58). Power steering ($124). Heavy-duty battery ($16). California emission system ($52). High-altitude emissions ($39). Cobra II package. ($535). Sports performance package ($451 to $607). Sports performance package for Mach 1 ($163). Rallye package ($43-$88). Ghia sports group ($422). Exterior accent group ($216). Appearance decor group ($96 to $152). Luxury interior group ($124). Convenience group ($37 to $71). Light group ($29 to $43). Protection group ($39 to $46). Air conditioning ($446). Electric rear window defroster ($73). Tinted glass ($48). Leather-wrapped steering wheel ($35 to $49). Digital clock ($42). Dual sport mirrors ($45). Entertainment: AM radio ($76). AM radio with tape player ($204). AM/FM radio ($135). AM/FM stereo radio ($184). AM/FM stereo radio with tape player ($317). Exterior: Flip-up open air roof ($147). Manual sunroof ($243). Full vinyl roof ($90). Front spoiler (no charge). Metallic glow paint ($58). Pinstriping ($28). Color-keyed vinyl-insert body side moldings ($64). Rocker panel moldings ($20). Deck lid luggage rack ($54). Console ($76). Four-way driver's seat ($33). Fold down rear seat ($77). Media velour cloth trim ($105). Color-keyed deluxe seat belts ($18). Wire wheel covers ($33 to $86). Forged aluminum wheels ($102 to $193). Lacy spoke aluminum wheels ($102 to $193). Lacy spoke white wheels ($153 to $243). Styled steel wheels ($37 to $90). Trim rings ($37). B78 x 13 black sidewall/white sidewall. BR78 x 13 black sidewall/white sidewall. BR70 x 13 raised white letter. 195/70R13 white sidewall/wide white sidewall/raised white letter.

History:

Introduced October 1, 1976. Model-year production (U.S.): 153,173. Total production for the U.S. market of 141,212 included 71,736 four-cylinder Mustangs, 33,326 Mustang V-6s and 36,150 Mustang V-8s. Calendar-year production (U.S.): 170,315. Calendar-year sales: 170,659. Model-year sales by U.S. dealers: 161,513. After a strong showing following the 1974 restyle, Mustang sales began to sag in 1975 and 1976. The Cobra packages looked dramatic, and performed well enough with a V-8, but Mustang couldn't find enough customers in this form. Production declined significantly this year. A four-cylinder Mustang with manual four-

1978 Mustang

Mustang II — (Four and V-6): New colors and interior trims made up most of the changes for 1978. The 2.8-liter V-6 got a plastic cooling fan. A new electronic voltage regulator gave longer-life reliability than the old electromechanical version. New this year was optional variable-ratio power steering, first introduced on the Fairmont. New inside touches included separate back-seat cushions, revised door and seat trim, new carpeting, and new tangerine color. Six new body colors added late in the 1977 model year were carried over this time. As before, clear rectangular horizontal parking lamps were set into the crosshatch black grille. Angled outward at its base, that grille had a 14 x 6 hole pattern, with Mustang (horse) badge in the center. Separate "Ford" letters stood above the grille. Single round headlights continued this year. Engine choices were the same as in 1977. So were the two body styles: two-door hardtop (coupe) or "three-door" 2+2 fastback. Base and Ghia coupes were offered as were base and Mach 1 hatchbacks. Standard equipment included the 140-cid (2.3-liter) four-cylinder engine with electronic ignition, a four-speed manual transmission, front disc brakes, rack-and-pinion steering, a tachometer and an ammeter. A Fashion Accessory Group, aimed at women, consisted of a four-way adjustable driver's seat, striped cloth seat inserts, illuminated entry, lighted driver's vanity visor mirror, coin tray, and door pockets. It came in nine body colors. The simulated convertible T-Roof, with dual removable tinted glass panels, was now entering its first full model year as an option on the 2+2 and Mach 1 hatchbacks.

Mustang II Ghia — (Four and V-6): Ghia added a half-vinyl roof, pinstripes, unique wheel covers, and body side moldings with color-keyed vinyl inserts. Ghia interiors could have Media Velour cloth with large armrests. Mustang's Ghia sports group came with black, blue or chamois body paint and a chamois or black vinyl half-roof, along with vinyl-insert body side moldings and pinstripes. Aluminum wheels had chamois-color lacy spokes. Inside was all-vinyl chamois or black seat trim, black "engine-turned" dash appliqués, and a leather-wrapped steering wheel.

Mustang II Mach 1—(V-6): Stepping up another notch, Mach 1 carried a standard 2.8-liter V-6 and sported a black paint treatment on lower body side and back panel. Also included were dual sport mirrors, Mach I emblems and raised-white-letter BR70 x 13 (or 195R/70) steel-belted radial tires on styled steel wheels with trim rings.

Mustang II Cobra II —(V-6 and V-8): Mustang's Cobra II package (for the 2+2 only) continued in the form introduced at mid-year in 1977. Tri-color tape stripes decorated the body sides, front spoiler, front bumper, hood, hood scoop, roof, deck lid and rear spoiler. Huge "Cobra" block letters went on the center body side tape stripe and deck lid spoiler. There was a Cobra decal on the back spoiler and a Cobra II snake emblem on the black grille. The package also included flat black greenhouse moldings, black quarter-window, black backlight louvers, black rocker panels, dual racing mirrors, a narrow black band along upper doors, a rear-opening hood scoop, a Rallye package and flip-open quarter windows (except with T-Roof option). Styled steel wheels with trim rings held BR70 raised white letter tires (195/70R with a V-8 or with the V-6 engine and air conditioning).

Mustang II King Cobra II — (V-8): King Cobra, new this year, might be viewed as a regular Cobra and more of the same and plenty of striping and lettering. The King did without the customary body side striping, but sported a unique tape treatment, including a giant snake decal on the hood and pinstriping on the greenhouse, deck lid, wheel lips, rocker panels, belt, over-the-roof area, and around the side windows. Up front

was a tough-looking spoiler. The 302-cid (5.0-liter) V-8 was standard in the King Cobra. It also had a four-speed transmission, power brakes and power steering. A "King Cobra" nameplate went on each door and the back spoiler. There was also a 5.0L badge on the front hood scoop. The King Cobra also had rear quarter flares, a black grille, black moldings and color-keyed dual sport mirrors. Raised-white-letter tires rode lacy spoke aluminum wheels with twin rings and Cobra symbol on the hubs.

VIN:

The VIN was stamped on an aluminum tab riveted to the instrument panel and was viewable through the windshield. The first symbol indicated the year: 8=1978. The second symbol identified the assembly plant: F=Dearborn, Michigan and R=San Jose, California. The third and fourth symbols identified the body series code: 02=two-door coupe, 03=two-door hatchback, 04=two-door Ghia Coupe and 05=Mach 1 hatchback. The fifth symbol identified the engine code: Y=140-cid (2.3-liter) two-barrel four-cylinder, Z=171-cid (2.8-liter) two-barrel V-6 and F=302-cid (5.0-liter) two-barrel V-8. The last six digits were the unit's production numbers, beginning at 100001 and going up, at each of the assembly plants.

Mustang (Four)

Model No.	Body/ Style No.	Body Type & Seating	Factory Price	Shipping Weight	Production Total
02	60F	2-dr. Coupe-4P	$3,555	2,608 lbs.	—
03	69F	2-dr. 2 + 2-4P	$3,798	2,654 lbs.	—
04	60H	2-dr. Ghia Coupe-4P	$3,972	2,646 lbs.	—

Mustang (V-6)

Model No.	Body/ Style No.	Body Type & Seating	Factory Price	Shipping Weight	Production Total
02	60F	2-dr. Coupe-4P	$3,768	2,705 lbs.	81,304
03	69F	2-dr. 2 + 2-4P	$4,011	2,751 lbs.	68,408
04	60H	2-dr. Ghia coupe-4P	$4,185	2,743 lbs.	34,730
05	69R	2-dr. Mach 1 2 + 2-4P	$4,253	2,733 lbs.	------

Mustang (V-8)

Model No.	Body/ Style No.	Body Type & Seating	Factory Price	Shipping Weight	Production Total
05	69R	2-dr. Mach 1 2 + 2-4P	$4,401	2,879 lbs.	7,968

Notes: The production column shows combined V-6 and V-8 totals for Cobra II and the combined four-cylinder and V-6 totals for other models. The totals shown do not include 20,937 Mustangs produced as 1978 models, but sold as 1977 models.

Engines:

2.3-Liter Four: Inline. Overhead valve and camshaft. Cast-iron block. Displacement: 140 cid (2.3 liters). B & S: 3.78 x 3.13 in. Compression ratio: 9.0:1. Brake hp: 89 at 4800 rpm. Torque: 120 lbs.-ft. at 3000 rpm. Five main bearings. Hydraulic valve lifters. Carburetor: Motorcraft 5200. Code Y.

2.8-Liter V-6: 60-degree, overhead valve. Cast-iron block and head. Displacement: 170.8 cid (2.8 liters). B & S: 3.66 x 2.70 in. Compression ratio: 8.7:1. Brake hp: 93 at 4200 rpm. Torque: 140 lbs.-ft. at 2600 rpm. Four main bearings. Solid valve lifters. Carburetor: Motorcraft 2150 two-barrel. German Ford-built. Code Z.

Optional 5.0-Liter V-8: 90-degree, overhead valve. Cast-iron block and head. Displacement: 302 cid (5.0 liters). B & S: 4.00 x 3.00 in. Compression ratio: 8.0:1. Brake hp: 139 at 3600 rpm. Torque: 247 lbs.-ft. at 1800 rpm. Five main bearings. Hydraulic valve lifters. Carburetor: Motorcraft 2150 two-barrel. Code F.

Chassis:

Wheelbase: 96.2 in. Overall length: 175.0 in. Height: (Coupe) 50.3 in., (2+2) 50.0 in. Width: 70.2 in. Front Tread: 55.6 in. Rear Tread: 55.8 in. Tires: BR78 x 13 steel belted radial, Ghia, BR70 x 13 steel belted radial raised white letter, Mach 1 and B78 x 13, other Mustangs.

Technical:

Transmission: Four-speed manual transmission (floor shift) standard. V-8 gear ratios: (1st) 2.64:1, (2nd) 1.89:1, (3rd) 1.34:1, (4th) 1.00:1, (Reverse) 2.56:1. Four-cylinder four-speed: (1st) 3.50:1, (2nd) 2.21:1, (3rd) 1.43:1, (4th) 1.00:1, (Reverse) 3.38:1. V-6 four-speed: (1st)

1978 Mustang II 2 + 2 hatchback

1978 Mustang II Ghia coupe

1978 Ford Mustang II two-door coupe

1978 Ford Mustang II two-door Cobra 2+2 (PH)

4.07:1, (2nd) 2.57:1, (3rd) 1.66:1, (4th) 1.00:1, (Reverse) 3.95:1. Select-Shift three-speed automatic, optional. Four-cylinder: (1st) 2.47:1, (2nd) 1.47:1, (3rd) 1.00:1, (Reverse) 2.11:1. V-6/V-8 automatic: (1st) 2.46:1, (2nd) 1.46:1, (3rd) 1.00:1, (Reverse) 2.19:1. Standard final drive ratio: (four) 3.18:1, (V-6) 3.00:1 with four-speed, 3.40:1 with automatic, (V-8) 2.79:1. Steering/suspension/brakes/body: same as 1976-77. Fuel tank: 13 gallon with V-8 engine, 16.5 gallons.

Engine/Transmission: 140-cid four-cylinder ($213 credit from base V-6 price). 170-cid V-6 ($213). 302--cid V-8 ($361 except Mach 1), 302-cid Mach 1 ($148). Cruise-O-Matic transmission ($281). Power brakes ($64). Power steering ($131). Engine block heater ($12). California emission system ($69). High-altitude emissions (no charge). Option Packages: Cobra II package for 2+2 ($677 to $700). King Cobra package for 2+2 ($1,253). Fashion accessory package for two-door ($207). Rally package ($43 to $93). Rally appearance package ($163). Ghia sports group ($361). Exterior accent group: pinstripes, wide body side moldings, dual remote sport mirrors, and whitewalls on styled wheels ($163-$245). Appearance decor group: lower body two-tone, pinstripes, styled wheels, brushed aluminum dash appliqué ($128-$167). Luxury interior group ($149 to $155). Convenience group including interval wipers, vanity and day/night mirrors and pivoting rear quarter windows on hatchback ($34 to $81). Light group ($40 to $52). Appearance protection group ($24 to $36). Air conditioning ($459). Electric rear defroster ($77). Tinted glass ($53). Leather-wrapped steering wheel ($34 to $49). Digital clock ($43). Trunk light ($4). Color-keyed driver's sport mirror ($16). Dual sport mirrors ($49). Day/night mirror ($7) AM radio ($72). AM radio tape player ($192). AM/FM radio ($120). AM/FM stereo radio ($161). AM/FM stereo radio with 8-track or cassette tape player ($229. T-Roof "convertible" option ($587 to $629). Flip-up open air roof ($167). Full vinyl roof ($99). Front spoiler ($8). Metallic glow paint ($40). Pinstriping ($30). Color-keyed body side moldings ($66). Rocker panel moldings ($22). Bumper guards, front and rear ($37). Lower body side protection ($30). Console ($75). Four-way driver's seat ($33). Fold-down rear seat ($90). Wilshire cloth trim ($100). Ashton cloth-and-vinyl trim ($12). Color-keyed deluxe seat belts ($18). Wire wheel covers ($12 to $90). Forged aluminum wheels ($173 to $252). White wheels ($187 to $265). Lacy spoke aluminum wheels ($173 to $252). Lacey spoke white wheels ($187 to $265). Styled steel wheels ($59 to $78). Trim rings ($39). B78 x 13 white sidewall. BR78 x 13 black sidewall/white sidewall. BR70 x 13 raised white letter. 195/70R13 white sidewall/wide white sidewall/raised white letter.

Introduced October 7, 1977. Model-year production: 192,410. Total production for the U.S. market of 173,423 units included 85,312 four-cylinder, 57,060 V-6, and 31,051 V-8 Mustangs. Calendar-year production: 240,162. Calendar-year sales by U.S. dealers: 199,760. Model-year sales by U.S. dealers: 179,039. This would be the final year for Mustang II, as an all-new Mustang was planned for 1979. Although plenty of Mustangs were built during the 1974 through 1978 period, Cobra II production was modest. The King Cobra, offered only for 1978,

1978 Ford Mustang II two-door King Cobra 2+2 (OCW)

1979 Mustang

Mustang— (Four and V-6): All-new sheet metal created what appeared to be an all-new Mustang for 1979. Its chassis came from the Fairmont, although it was shortened and modified to hold the new body metal. The familiar curved crease in the body side was gone. At a time when most cars were shrinking, the new Mustang managed to gain four inches in length and 20 percent more passenger space. Soft urethane bumpers added to the illusion of length. The weight of the Mustang dropped by some 200 pounds, however. The aerodynamic wedge design featured a sloping front and hood and a sculptured roofline. A lowered window line gave Mustang large glass area for improved visibility. As in the prior version, two-door notchback and three door hatchback bodies were offered in base and Ghia levels. There was also a Sport package and a high-performance TRX package. As before, Ford generally referred to the two-door model as a sedan, while the third door of the "three-door" car was a hatchback, rather than an entryway for people. The new hatchback did not have the sharply-angled fastback shape of the former Mustang. The conventional or notchback two-door did look more like a sedan than its predecessor, though enthusiasts still tended to view it as a coupe (especially since a convertible would appear a few years later). A similar Mercury Capri was offered only in hatchback form. Both bodies had sail-shaped quarter windows that were wider at the base, but the hatchback's were much narrower at the top and almost triangle shaped. Both models had a set of tall, louver-like ribs formed in a tapered panel on the "C" pillar. They were angled to match the quarter window's rear edge, but the hatchback had one more of them. Staggered, recessed quad rectangular headlights replaced the former single round units. The outer units sat a little farther back than the inner pair. The new black crosshatch grille (with a 10 x 5 pattern of openings) angled forward at the base and no longer held a Mustang badge. It did have "Ford" lettering at the driver's side. Rectangular amber parking/signal lamps were mounted in the bumper, just below the outboard headlights. Narrow, amber-colored front side marker lenses followed the angle of front fender tips. Well below the front bumper was an air scoop with five holes. On the hood, above the grille, was a round tri-color Mustang emblem. A badge on front fenders, at the cowl ahead of the door, denoted the type of engine under the hood. The taillights were wider than before and now wrapped around each quarter panel. In addition to the German-built 170-cid (2.8-liter) V-6 and the 302-cid (5.0-liter) V-8 carried over from 1978, there was a new engine option: a 140-cid (2.3 liter) turbocharged four. The base engine remained a non-turbo four-cylinder four. Later in the year, Ford's inline six replaced the V-6 as first option above the base model. The turbo was also optional in other Mustangs. V-8 powered Mustangs could have a new four-speed manual overdrive transmission with a peppy 3.07:1 first gear and 0.70:1 overdrive. A single (serpentine) belt now drove engine accessories. A new front suspension used a hydraulic shock strut to replace the conventional upper arm. The rear suspension was a new four-bar link-and-coil system that replaced the old leaf-spring Hotchkiss design. Two handling/suspension options were offered. The basic handling suspension with 14-inch radial tires included different

1979 Mustang two-door hatchback

1979 Ford Mustang two-door coupe (OCW)

spring rates and shock valving, stiffer bushings in front suspension and upper arm in the rear and a special rear stabilizer bar. The second level package came with a Michelin TRX tire option. The TRX was an ultra-low aspect ratio tire (390 MM) introduced on the European Granada. Its 15.35-inch size demanded special metric wheels. The package also included unique shock valving, increased spring rates and wider front and rear stabilizer bars. All Mustangs had full instrumentation including a tachometer, a trip odometer and gauges for fuel, oil pressure, alternator and temperature. Mustangs also had front bucket seats, a simulated wood grain instrument panel appliqué and stalk-mounted controls for the horn, headlight dimmer switch and windshield wiper/washer. Standard chassis equipment included rack-and-pinion steering, manual front disc brakes and a front stabilizer bar. Also standard were vinyl door trim with carpeted lower panels, a squeeze-open lockable glove box, a day/night inside rearview mirror, a cigarette lighter, a black remote-control driver's mirror and full wheel covers. Fastbacks had black rocker panel moldings, full wraparound body side moldings with dual accent stripe inserts and semi-styled wheels with black sport hub covers and trim rings. Quite a few options joined the list, including a sport-tuned exhaust, cruise control, tilt steering, leather seat trim and interval windshield wipers.

Ghia — (Four and V-6): Ghia models featured many color-keyed components including dual remote-control mirrors, quarter louvers and body side molding inserts. Ghias also had turbine-style wheel covers, BR78 x 14 radial tires, pin stripes, body-color window frames, a Ghia badge on the deck lid or hatch, low-back bucket seats with European-type headrests and convenience pockets in color-keyed door panels. Interiors came in six leather colors and five soft cloth colors.

Cobra — (Turbo Four and V-8): The costly ($1,173) Cobra package included a 2.3-liter turbocharged four, turbo hood scoop with "Turbo" nameplate, 190/65R x 390 TRX tires on metric forged aluminum wheels, and special suspension. A 302-cid V-8 was available instead of the turbo. Cobras had blacked-out greenhouse trim, black lower body side tape treatment and wraparound body side moldings with dual color-keyed inserts. Also included were a color-keyed grille and quarter louvers, dual sport mirrors, black bumper rub strips with dual color-keyed inserts, an 8,000-rpm tachometer, an engine-turned instrument cluster panel, a sport-tuned exhaust system and a bright tailpipe extension. Rocker panel moldings were deleted. Optional hood graphics cost $78 extra.

VIN:

The VIN was stamped on an aluminum tab riveted to the instrument panel and was viewable through the windshield. The first symbol indicated the year: 9=1979. The second symbol identified the assembly plant: F=Dearborn, Michigan and R=San Jose, California. The third and fourth symbols identified the body series code: 02=two-door coupe, 03=two-door hatchback, 04=two-door Ghia Coupe and 05= Ghia hatchback. The fifth symbol identified the engine code: Y=140-cid (2.3-liter) two-barrel SOHC four-cylinder, W=140-cid (2.3-liter) two-barrel SOHC turbocharged four-cylinder, Z=171-cid (2.8-liter) two-barrel V-6, T=200-cid (3.3-liter) one-barrel inline six-cylinder and F=302-cid (5.0-liter) two-barrel V-8. The last six digits were the unit's production numbers, beginning at 100001 and going up, at each of the assembly plants.

Mustang (Four)

Model No.	Body/Style No.	Body Type & Seating	Factory Price	Shipping Weight	Production Total
02	66B	2-dr. Coupe-4P	$4,071	2,431 lbs.	—
03	61R	2-dr. 2 + 2 -4P	$4,436	2,451 lbs.	—
04	66H	2-dr. Ghia coupe-4P	$4,642	2,539 lbs.	—

Mustang (V-6)

02	66B	2-dr. Coupe-4P	$4,344	2,511 lbs.	156,666
03	61R	2-dr. 2 + 2-4P	$4,709	2,531 lbs.	120,535
04	66H	2-dr. Ghia coupe-4P	$4,915	2,619 lbs.	56,351

Mustang (Turbo Four)

05	61H	2-dr. Mach 1 2 + 2-4P	$4,824	2,628 lbs.	36,384

Mustang (V-8)

05	61H	2-dr. Mach 1 2 + 2-4P	$5,097	2,628 lbs.	36,384

Note 1: The production column shows body style production totals for (all engines).

Engines:

Four: Inline, overhead cam. Cast-iron block and head. Displacement: 140-cid (2.3 liters). B & S: 3.78 x 3.13 in. Compression ratio: 9.0:1 Brake hp: 88 at 4800 rpm Torque: 118 lbs.-ft. at 2800 rpm. Five main bearings. Hydraulic valve lifters. Carburetor: two-barrel Motorcraft 5200. Code Y.

Turbo Four: Same as 140-cid four above, but with turbocharger. Brake hp: 140 at 4800 rpm. Torque: N/A. Carburetor: two-barrel Holley 6500. Code W.

V-6: 60-degree, overhead valve. Cast-iron block and head. Displacement: 170.8-cid (2.8 liters). B & S: 3.66 x 2.70 in. Compression ratio: 8.7:1. Brake hp: 109 at 4800 rpm. Torque: 142 lbs.-ft. at 2800 rpm. Four main bearings. Solid valve lifters. Carburetor: two-barrel Ford 2150 or Motorcraft 2700VV. German Ford-built. Code Z.

Six: Inline, overhead valve. Cast-iron block and head. Displacement: 200-cid (3.3 liters). B & S: 3.68 x 3.13 in. Compression ratio: 8.6:1. Brake hp: N/A. Torque: N/A. Seven main bearings. Hydraulic valve lifters. Carburetor: two-barrel Holley 1946. Code T.

V 8: 90-degree, overhead valve. Cast-iron block and head. Displacement: 302-cid (5.0 liters). B & S: 4.00 x 3.00 in. Compression ratio: 8.4:1. Brake hp: 140 at 3600 rpm. Torque: 250 lbs.-ft. at 1800 rpm. Five main bearings. Hydraulic valve lifters. Carburetor: two-barrel Motorcraft 2150. Code F.

Chassis:

Wheelbase: 100.4 in. Overall length: 179.1 in. Height: 51.8 in. Width 69.1 in. Front tread: 56.6 in. Rear tread: 57.0 in. Tires: B78 x 13 black sidewall and BR78 x 14 steel belted radial black sidewall, Ghia.

Technical:

Four-speed manual (floor shift) standard on four-cylinder. Gear ratios: (1st) 3.98:1, (2nd) 2.14:1, (3rd) 1.42:1, (4th) 1.00:1, (reverse) 3.99:1. Turbo four-speed: (1st) 4.07:1, (2nd) 2.57:1, (3rd) 1.66:1, (4th) 1.00:1, (reverse) 3.95:1. Four-speed overdrive manual transmission standard on V-8. Gear ratios: (1st) 3.07:1, (2nd) 1.72:1, (3rd) 1.00:1, (4th) 0.70:1, (reverse) 3.07:1. Select Shift three-speed automatic, optional. Four cylinder: (1st) 2.47:1, (2nd) 1.47:1, (3rd) 1.00:1, (reverse) 2.11:1. V-6/V-8 automatic: (1st) 2.46:1, (2nd) 1.46:1, (3rd) 1.00:1, (reverse) 2.18:1 or 2.19:1. Standard final drive ratio: 308:1 except 3.45:1 with turbo, 2.47:1 w/V-8 and auto. (early models differed). Steering: Rack and pinion. Front suspension: Modified MacPherson hydraulic shock struts with coil springs and stabilizer bar. Rear suspension: Four-bar link and coil spring system: anti-sway bar with V-8. Brakes: Front disc, rear drum. Disc diameter: 9.3 in. (10.4 in. with V-8). Rear drum diameter: 9 in. Ignition: Electronic. Body construction: unibody with front isolated mini-frame. Fuel tank 11.5 gallons and 12.5 gallons with V-6/V-8.

Options:

Engine/Transmission Turbo 140-cid four ($542). 170-cid V-6 ($273). 302-cid V-8 ($514). Sport-tuned exhaust ($34). Automatic transmission ($307). Power brakes ($70). Variable-ratio power steering ($141) Handling suspension ($33). Engine block heater ($13). Heavy-duty battery ($18). California emission system ($76). High-altitude emissions ($33). Cobra package ($1,173). Cobra hood graphics ($78). Sport option ($175). Exterior accent group ($72). Interior accent group ($108 to $120). Light group ($25 to $37). Protection group ($33 to $36). Power lock group ($99). Air conditioning ($484). Electric rear window defroster ($84) Fingertip speed control ($104 to $116). Tinted glass ($59). Tinted windshield only ($25). Leather-wrapped steering wheel ($41 to $53). Tilt steering wheel ($69-$81). Interval windshield wipers ($35). Rear windshield wiper and washer ($63). Trunk light ($5). Driver's remote-control inside rearview mirror ($18). Dual remote mirrors ($52). AM radio ($72). AM radio with digital clock ($119). AM radio with tape player

1979 Ford Mustang two-door Sport Option hatchback (FMC)

1979 Ford Mustang two-door Cobra hatchback (OCW)

1979 Ford Mustang two-door Cobra Turbo hatchback (OCW)

($192). AM/FM radio ($120). AM/FM stereo radio ($176). AM/FM stereo radio with eight-track or cassette tape player ($243). Premium sound system ($67). Dual rear speakers ($42) Radio flexibility option ($90). Flip-up open air roof ($199). Full vinyl roof ($102). Metallic glow paint ($41). Lower two-tone paint ($78). Body side/deck lid pinstripes ($30). Wide body side moldings ($66). Narrow vinyl-insert body side moldings ($39). Rocker panel moldings ($24). Mud and stone deflectors ($23). Lower body side protection ($30). Console ($140). Four-way driver's seat ($35). Cloth seat trim ($20). Ghia cloth seat trim ($42). Accent cloth seat trim ($29). Leather seat trim ($282). Front floor mats ($18). Color-keyed deluxe seat belts ($20). Wire wheel covers ($60 to $99). Turbine wheel covers ($10 to $39). Forged metric aluminum wheels ($259 to $298). Cast-aluminum wheels ($251 to $289). Styled steel wheels with trim rings ($55 to $94). B78 x 13 white sidewall tires ($43). C78 x 13 black sidewall tires ($25). C78 x 13 white sidewall tires ($69). B78 x 14 white sidewall tires ($66). C78 x 14 black sidewall tires ($48). BR78 x 14 black sidewall tires ($124). BR78-14 white sidewall tires ($43 to $167). CR78 x 14 white sidewall tires ($69 to $192). CR78 x 14 raised white letter tires ($86 to $209). TRX 190/65R 390 Michelin black sidewall tires ($117 to $241). The lower tire prices are for the Mustang Ghia.

History:

Introduced, October 6, 1978. Model-year production: 369,936 Total production for the U.S. market of 332,024 units included 181,066 four-cylinder (29,242 with turbocharger), 103,390 sixes, and 47,568 V-8 Mustangs. Calendar-year production, 365,357. Calendar-year sales by U.S. dealers: 304,053. Model-year sales by U.S. dealers: 302,309. If the second-generation Mustang had lacked some of the pizzazz of the original pony car, the "new breed" third-generation edition offered a chance to boost the car's image. The optional turbocharged 2.3-liter four was said to offer "V-8 performance without sacrificing fuel economy." In Ford tests, the Mustang turbo went 0-55 mph in just over 8 seconds (a little quicker than a V-8). Gas mileage reached well into the 20s. A V-8 version was named pace car for the Indy 500, prompting the production of a Pace Car Replica later in the year. Ready for the 1980s, Mustang now offered a pleasing blend of American and European design. Of many styling proposals, the final one came from a team led by Jack Telnack of the Light Truck and Car Design Group. Plastic and aluminum components helped cut down the car's weight and it was considerably roomier inside than the former Mustang II. Drag coefficient of 0.44 (for the fastback) was the best Ford had ever achieved. Customers must

1979 Ford Mustang two-door Indy Pace Car hatchback (PH)

1980 Mustang

Mustang — (Four and Six): The appearance of the modern, re-sized Mustang changed little in its second season, except for a new front and rear end appearance on the sporty Cobra model. Two-door notchback coupes also had an aerodynamic revision to their deck lids. The Mustang taillights consisted of five sections on each side, plus an inboard back-up lens section (positioned toward the license plate). A larger section at the outside wrapped around onto each quarter panel. The deck lid held "Ford" and "Mustang" lettering. The body side moldings stretched all the way around the car, meeting bumper strips. Body striping came down ahead of the front marker lenses. Four-cylinder models had no fender identifier, others were marked with an engine displacement call-out in liters. Base and Ghia models were again offered in notchback or hatchback form. Base notchbacks had black bumper rub strips, while hatchback bumpers had dual argent silver stripe inserts. Hatchbacks also had full wraparound-style wide black body side moldings with dual argent silver inserts. Both models carried high-back vinyl bucket seats. On the notchback coupe the rear pillar louvers were color-keyed, while on the hatchback they were black. A 255-cid (4.2-liter) V-8 replaced the former 302-cid (5.0-liter) V-8. The 200-cid (3.3-liter) inline six introduced for 1979 was the only six-cylinder engine used in 1980. Both the non-turbocharged 2.3-liter four and inline six could have a four-speed manual gearbox (overdrive fourth with the six), while all engines could have an automatic. All models now had high-pressure P-metric radial tires and halogen headlights. Maintenance-free batteries were standard equipment and Mustang radios added a Travelers' Advisory Band. Semi-metallic front disc brake pads were used on Mustangs with optional engines. Two suspension options were available, a standard package and a modified "Special Suspension System" that included Michelin TRX tires on special forged aluminum wheels. A new Carriage Roof option for the notchback model was supposed to resemble a convertible, even though the car had a solid "B" pillar. It used diamond-grain vinyl. Other new options included a roof luggage rack, a cargo area cover (for the hatchback), lift back window louvers and Recaro adjustable seat back bucket seats with improved thigh support. The Mustang's inside door handles were relocated to the upper door.

Ghia — (Four and Six): The Mustang Ghia model added low-back bucket seats with Euro-style headrests, a roof assist handle, color-keyed window frames, dual remote mirrors, pin striping, 14-inch tires, turbine wheel covers and a Ghia insignia on the rear deck lid or hatch back opening.

Cobra — (Turbo Four and V-8): Available again was the Cobra option. It was raised in price. The Cobra's slat-style three-holes grille, its hood scoop (with simulated rear opening), its front air dam (with built-in fog lamps) and its rear spoiler were all restyled. The new appearance was patterned after the 1979 Indy Pace Car replica. The Cobra's tape treatment was also revised and it carried the TRX suspension. Standard Cobra features included a black lower Tu-Tone treatment, special body side and quarter window taping, dual black sport mirrors, a sport-tuned exhaust system with a bright tailpipe extension, black bumper rub strips. 190/65R x 390 TRX tires on forged metric aluminum wheels, an engine-turned instrument cluster panel with a Cobra medallion, a body side molding with dual color-keyed accent stripes, an 8,000-rpm tachometer and the turbo engine. "Cobra" lettering decorated the quarter windows.

VIN:

The VIN was stamped on an aluminum tab riveted to the instrument panel and was viewable through the windshield. The first symbol indicated the year: 0=1980. The second symbol identified the assembly plant: F=Dearborn, Michigan and R=San Jose, California. The third and fourth symbols identified the body series code: 02=two-door coupe, 03=two-door hatchback, 04=two-door Ghia Coupe and 05= Ghia hatchback. The fifth symbol identified the engine code: A=140-cid (2.3-liter) two-barrel SOHC four-cylinder, W=140-cid (2.3-liter) two-barrel turbocharged SOHC four-cylinder, T=200-cid (3.3-liter) one-barrel inline six-cylinder and D=255-cid (4.2-liter) two-barrel V-8. The last six digits were the unit's production numbers, beginning at 100001 and going up, at each of the assembly plants.

1980 Ford Mustang two-door coupe (JG)

Mustang (Four)

Model No.	Body/Style No.	Body Type & Seating	Factory Price	Shipping Weight	Production Total
02	66B	2-dr. Coupe-4P	$4,884	2,497 lbs.	—
03	61R	2-dr. 2 + 2-4P	$5,194	2,531 lbs.	—
04	66H	2-dr. Ghia coupe-4P	$5,369	2,565 lbs.	—

Mustang (Six)

Model No.	Body/Style No.	Body Type & Seating	Factory Price	Shipping Weight	Production Total
02	66B	2-dr. Coupe-4P	$5,103	2,532 lbs.	128,893
03	61R	2-dr. 2 + 2-4P	$5,413	2,566 lbs.	98,497
04	66H	2-dr. Ghia coupe-4P	$5,588	2,600 lbs.	23,647

Mustang (Turbo Four)

Model No.	Body/Style No.	Body Type & Seating	Factory Price	Shipping Weight	Production Total
05	61H	2-dr. Mach 1 2 + 2-4P	$5,512	2,588 lbs.	------

Mustang (V-8)

Model No.	Body/Style No.	Body Type & Seating	Factory Price	Shipping Weight	Production Total
05	61H	2-dr. Mach 1 2 + 2-4P	$5,731	2,623 lbs.	20,285

Note 1: The production column shows body style totals for all engines.

Engines:

Four: Inline, overhead cam. Cast-iron block and head. Displacement: 140-cid (2.3 liters). B & S: 3.78 x 3.13 in. Compression ratio: 9.0:1 Brake hp: 88 at 4600 rpm Torque: 119 lbs.-ft. at 2600 rpm. Five main bearings. Hydraulic valve lifters. Carburetor: two-barrel Motorcraft 5200. Code A.

Turbo Four: Same as 140-cid four above, but with turbocharger. Brake hp: 150 at 4800 rpm. Torque: N/A. Carburetor: two-barrel Holley 6500. Code W.

Six: Inline, overhead valve. Cast-iron block and head. Displacement: 200-cid (3.3 liters). B & S: 3.68 x 3.13 in. Compression ratio: 8.6:1. Brake hp: 91 at 4000 rpm. Torque: N/A. Seven main bearings. Hydraulic valve lifters. Carburetor: two-barrel Holley 1946. Code T.

V-8: 90-degree. overhead valve. Cast-iron block and head. Displacement: 255-cid (4.2 liters). B & S: 3.68 x 3.00 in. Compression ratio: 8.8:1. Brake hp: 119 at 3800 rpm. Torque: 194 lbs.-ft. at 2200 rpm. Five main bearings. Hydraulic valve lifters. Carburetor: two-barrel Motorcraft 2150. Code D.

Chassis:

Wheelbase: 100.4 in. Overall length: 179.1 in. Height: 51.4 in. Width: 69.1 in. Front tread: 56.6 in. Rear tread: 57.0 in. Tires: P185/80R13 black sidewall and P175/75R14 black sidewall, Ghia.

Technical:

Four-speed manual (floor shift) standard on four-cylinder. Gear ratios: (1st) 3.98:1; (2nd) 2.14:1, (3rd) 1.42:1, (4th) 1.00:1, (Reverse) 3.99:1. Turbo four-speed: (1st) 4.07:1, (2nd) 2.57:1, (3rd) 1.66:1, (4th) 1.00:1, (Reverse) 3.95:1. Four-speed overdrive manual transmission standard on six. Gear ratios: (1st) 3.29:1, (2nd) 1.84:1, (3rd) 1.00:1, (4th) 0.81:1, (Reverse) 3.29:1. Select Shift three-speed automatic, optional. Four-cylinder: (1st) 2.47:1, (2nd) 1.47:1, (3rd) 1.00:1, (Reverse) 2.11:1. Turbo/six/V-8 automatic: (1st) 2.46:1, (2nd) 1.46:1, (3rd) 1.00:1, (Reverse) 2.19:1. Standard final drive ratio: 3.08:1 with four, 2.26:1 with V-8 and automatic transmission, 3.45:1 with turbo, Steering: Rack and pinion. Front suspension: Modified MacPherson hydraulic shock struts with coil springs and stabilizer bar. Rear suspension: Four-bar link and coil spring system. Brakes: Front disc, rear drum. Ignition: Electronic. Body construction: Unibody with front isolated mini-frame. Fuel tank: 11.5 gallons and 12.5 gallons with V-8.

Options:

Turbo 140-cid four-cylinder ($481). 200-cid six-cylinder ($219). 255-cid V-8 ($338), except with Cobra package ($144 credit). Sport-tuned exhaust: V-8 ($38). Select-shift automatic transmission ($340). Optional axle ratio ($18). Power brakes ($78). Power steering ($160). Handling suspension ($35). Engine block heater ($15). Heavy-duty battery ($20). California emission system ($253). High-altitude emissions ($36). Cobra package ($1,482). Cobra hood graphics ($88). Sport option includes black rocker panel moldings, black belt moldings, black door frames, black window frames, full wraparound body side molding with dual argent stripe insert, sport wheel trim rings and steering wheel ($168-$186). Exterior accent group ($63). Interior accent group ($120 to $134). Light group ($41). Appearance protection group ($38 to $41). Power lock group ($113). Air conditioning ($583). Electric rear defroster ($96). Fingertip speed control ($116 to $129). Tinted glass ($65). Tinted windshield only ($29). Leather-wrapped steering wheel ($44 to $56). Tilt steering wheel ($78 to $90). Interval wipers ($39). Rear wiper/washer ($79). Lighting and Mirrors: Trunk light ($5). Driver's remote mirror ($19). Dual remote mirrors ($58). AM radio ($93). AM/FM radio ($145). AM/FM stereo radio ($183). AM/FM stereo radio with eight-track tape player ($259). AM/FM stereo radio with cassette player

1980 Ford Mustang two-door Cobra Turbo hatchback (PH)

1980 Ford Mustang two-door "carriage top" coupe (FMC)

($271). Premium sound system ($94). Dual rear speakers ($38). Radio flexibility option ($63). Flip-up open air roof ($204 to $219). Carriage roof ($625). Full vinyl roof ($118). Metallic glow paint ($46). Lower two-tone paint ($88). Body side and deck lid pinstripes ($34). Accent tape stripes ($19-$53). Hood scoop ($31). Lift gate louvers ($141). Narrow vinyl-insert body side moldings ($43). Wide vinyl-insert body side moldings ($74). Rocker panel moldings ($30). Roof luggage rack ($86). Mud and stone deflectors ($25). Lower body side protection ($34). Console ($166). Four-way driver's seat ($38). Recaro high-back bucket seats ($531). Cloth-and-vinyl bucket seats ($21 to $46). Vinyl low-back bucket seats (NC). Accent cloth/vinyl seat trim ($30). Leather low-back bucket seats ($345). Cargo area cover ($44). Front floor mats ($19). Color-keyed seat belts ($23). Wire wheel covers ($79 to $121). Turbine wheel covers ($10 to $43). Forged metric aluminum wheels ($313 to $355). Cast aluminum wheels ($279 to $321). Styled steel wheels with trim rings ($61 to $104). P185/80R13 white sidewall tires ($50). P175/75R14 black sidewall tires ($25). P175/75R14 white sidewall tires ($50 to $75). P185/75R14 black sidewall tires ($25 to $49). P185/75R14 white sidewall tires ($75 to $100). P185/75R14 raised white letter ($92 to $117). TRX 190/65 x 390 black sidewall ($125 to $250).

History:

Introduced October 12, 1979. Model-year production: 271,322. Total production for the U.S. market of 241,064 units included 162,959 four-cylinder (12,052 with turbocharger), 71,597 sixes, and 6,508 V-8 Mustangs. Calendar-year production: 232,517. Calendar-year sales by U.S. dealers: 225,290. Model-year sales by U.S. dealers: 246,008. Mustang's base 2.3-liter four-cylinder engine was said to deliver an ample boost in gas mileage this year. Short supplies of the German-made V-6 had prompted Ford to switch to the familiar inline six during the 1979 model year. After a whopping sales increase for 1979, Mustang slackened this year. Still, most observers felt the new model showed a vast improvement over the Mustang II and would give Ford

1981 Mustang

Mustang — (Four and Six): Ford made very few modifications to the Fox-bodied Mustang in its sophomore year. The base four-cylinder engine enjoyed a 23 percent fuel economy improvement and there minor changes to the turbocharged version. As might be expected, the appearance of the modernized and re-sized Mustang changed little. The sporty Cobra model received a specific front/rear aerodynamic treatment to further distinguish it from cheaper models. Base Mustang notchbacks had black bumper rub strips. The hatchback model's bumpers wore dual Argent Silver stripe inserts. Hatchbacks also had full wraparound, wide

1981 Ford Mustang two-door T-top coupe (FMC)

1981 Ford Mustang two-door coupe (PH)

1981 Ford Mustang two-door "Air Roof" coupe (PH)

black body side moldings with dual Argent Silver inserts. Both models carried high-back vinyl bucket seats. On the notchback Coupe, the rear pillar louvers were color-keyed, while the hatchbacks were black. All models now rode on high-pressure P-metric radial tires and benefited from halogen headlights. Maintenance-free batteries were standard and Mustang radios gained a Travelers' Advisory Band. Semi-metallic front disc brake pads were included with optional engines. A new Carriage Roof option for the Coupe was supposed to make it resemble a convertible, even though the car had a solid "B" pillar. It used diamond-grain vinyl. Other new options included a roof luggage rack, cargo area cover (hatchback), lift back window louvers and Recaro adjustable seatback bucket seats with improved thigh support. The inside door handles were relocated to the upper door.

Mustang Ghia — (Four and Six): Ghia added low-back bucket seats with Euro-style headrests, a roof assist handle, color-keyed window frames, dual remote mirrors, pin striping, 14-inch tires, turbine wheel covers and a "Ghia" insignia on the rear deck lid or hatch back door.

Mustang Cobra — (Turbo four and V-8): The Cobra's slat-style three-hole grille, hood scoop (with simulated rear opening), front air dam (with built-in fog lamps) and rear spoiler were restyled with the 1979 Indy Pace Car replica in mind. The tape treatment was also revised and all Cobras came standard with TRX suspension. Features included black lower Tu-Tone treatment, special body side and quarter window taping, dual black sport outside rearview mirrors, a sport-tuned exhaust system with a bright tailpipe extension, black bumper rub strips, 190/65R-390 TRX tires on forged metric aluminum wheels, an engine-turned instrument cluster panel with a Cobra medallion, a body side molding with dual color-keyed accent stripes, an 8000-rpm tachometer and the turbocharged engine. "Cobra" lettering appeared on quarter windows.

VIN:

The VIN was stamped on an aluminum tab riveted to the instrument panel and was viewable through the windshield. The first symbol indicated the country of origin: 1=U.S.A. The second symbol identified the manufacturer: F=Ford. The third symbol indicated the vehicle type: A=passenger car. The fourth symbol indicated the restraint system: B=active belts. The fifth symbol indicated the division: P=Ford. The sixth symbol indicated the series: 1-Mustang. The seventh symbol indicated the body style: 0 or 4=Coupe, 5=Hatchback, 2=Ghia Coupe and 3=Ghia Hatchback. The eighth symbol indicated the engine: A=140-cid (2.3-liter) SOHC four-cylinder two-barrel, B=200-cid (3.3-liter) in-line six-cylinder one-barrel and D=255-cid (4.2-liter) V-8 two-barrel. The ninth symbol was a check digit. The 10th symbol indicated the model year: B=1981. The 11th symbol indicated the assembly plant: F=Dearborn, Michigan. The last six digits were the unit's production numbers, beginning at 100001 and going up, at each of the assembly plants.

Mustang (Four)

Model No.	Body/ Style No.	Body Type & Seating	Factory Price	Shipping Weight	Production Total
10	66B	2-dr. Coupe-4P	$6,171	2,524 lbs.	—
15	61R	2-dr. Hatchback-4P	$6,408	2,544 lbs.	—

Mustang Ghia (Four)

12	66H	2-dr. Coupe-4P	$6,645	2,558 lbs.	—
15	61H	2-dr. Hatchback-4P	$6,729	2,593 lbs.	—

Mustang (Six)

10	66B	2-dr. Coupe-4P	$6,384	2,551 lbs.	77,458
15	61R	2-dr. Hatchback-4P	$6,621	2,571 lbs.	77,399

Mustang Ghia (Six)

12	66H	2-dr. Coupe-4P	$6,858	2,585 lbs.	13,422
15	61H	2-dr. Hatchback-4P	$6,729	2,593 lbs.	14,273

Notes: The production column shows body style totals for all engines. A V-8 and

a Cobra package were options.

Engines:

Four: Inline, overhead cam. Cast-iron block and head. Displacement: 140-cid (2.3 liters). B & S: 3.78 x 3.13 in. Compression ratio: 9.0:1 Brake hp: 88 at 4600 rpm Torque: 118 lbs.-ft. at 2600 rpm. Five main bearings. Hydraulic valve lifters. Carburetor: two-barrel Motorcraft 5200 or Holley 6500. Code A.

Turbo Four: Same as 140-cid four above, but with turbocharger. Brake hp: 150 at 4800 rpm. Torque: N/A. Carburetor: two-barrel Holley 6500. Code W.

Six: Inline, overhead valve. Cast-iron block and head. Displacement: 200-cid (3.3 liters). B & S: 3.68 x 3.13 in. Compression ratio: 8.6:1. Brake hp: 94 at 4000 rpm. Torque: 158 lbs.-ft. at 1400 rpm. Seven main bearings. Hydraulic valve lifters. Carburetor: two-barrel Holley 1946. Code T.

V-8: 90-degree, overhead valve. Cast-iron block and head. Displacement: 255-cid (4.2 liters). B & S: 3.68 x 3.00 in. Compression ratio: 8.8:1. Brake hp: 115 at 3400 rpm Torque: 195 lbs.-ft. at 2200 rpm. Five main bearings. Hydraulic valve lifters. Carburetor: two-barrel Motorcraft 2150 or 7200VV. Code D.

Chassis:

Wheelbase: 100.4 in. Overall length: 179.1 in. Height: 51.4 in. Width 69.1 in. Front tread: 56.6 in. Rear tread: 57.0 in. Standard tires: P185/80R13 black sidewall and P175/75R14 black sidewall, Ghia.

Technical:

Transmission: Four-speed manual (floor shift) standard on four-cylinder. Gear ratios: (1st) 3.98:1, (2nd) 2.14:1, (3rd) 1.42:1, (4th) 1.00:1, (Reverse) 3.99:1. Turbo four-speed: (1st) 4.07:1, (2nd) 2.57:1, (3rd) 1.66:1, (4th) 1.00:1, (Reverse) 3.95:1. Four-speed overdrive manual transmission standard on six. Gear ratios: (1st) 3.29:1, (2nd) 1.84:1, (3rd) 1.00:1, (4th) 0.81:1, (Reverse) 3.29:1. Other models: (1st) 3.98:1, (2nd) 2.14:1, (3rd) 1.42:1, (4th) 1.00:1, (Reverse) 3.99:1. Five-speed manual overdrive optional: (1st) 4.05:1, (2nd) 2.43:1, (3rd) 1.48:1, (4th) 1.00:1, (5th) 0.82:1, (Reverse) 3.90:1. Turbo five-speed: (1st) 3.72:1, (2nd) 2.23:1, (3rd) 1.48:1, (4th) 1.00:1, (5th) 0.76:1, (Reverse) 3.59:1. Select-Shift three-speed automatic optional: (1st) 2.46:1 or 2.47:1, (2nd) 1.46:1 or 1.47:1, (3rd) 1.00:1, (Reverse) 2.11:1 or 2.19:1. Standard final drive ratio: (four) 3.08:1 and 3.45:1 with five-speed, (six) 3.45:1 with four-speed, 2.73:1 w/auto., (V-8) 2.26:1. Steering: Rack and pinion. Front suspension: Modified MacPherson struts with lower control arms, coil springs and stabilizer bar. Rear suspension: Four-bar link and coil spring system with lower trailing arms and transverse linkage bar. Brakes: Front disc, rear drum. Ignition: Electronic. Body construction: Unibody. Fuel tank: 12.5 gallons.

Options:

Turbo 140-cid four-cylinder engine ($610). 200-cid six-cylinder engine ($213). 255-cid V-8 ($263) except with Cobra package ($346 credit). Sport-tuned exhaust: V-8 ($39 with Turbo and automatic). (NC). Five-

1981 Ford Mustang two-door Cobra Turbo hatchback

speed manual transmission ($152). Select-shift automatic transmission ($349). Traction-Lok differential ($63). Optional axle ratio ($20). Power brakes ($76). Power steering ($163). Handling suspension ($43). Engine block heater ($16). Heavy-duty battery ($20). California emission system ($46). High-altitude emissions ($38). Cobra package ($1,588). Cobra package with tape delete ($65 credit). Cobra hood graphics ($90). Sport option ($52 to $72). Interior accent group ($126 to $139). Light group ($43). Appearance protection group ($41). Power lock group ($93 to $120). Air conditioning ($560). Electric rear defroster ($107). Fingertip speed control ($132). Power windows ($140). Tinted glass ($76). Tinted windshield only ($29). Leather-wrapped steering wheel ($49 to $61). Tilt steering wheel ($80 to $93). Interval wipers ($41). Rear wiper/washer ($85). Trunk light ($6). Driver's remote mirror ($20). Dual remote mirrors ($56) AM/FM radio ($51). AM/FM stereo radio ($88). AM/FM stereo radio with 8-track tape player ($162). AM/FM stereo radio with cassette player ($174). Premium sound system ($91). Dual rear speakers ($37). Radio flexibility option ($61). AM radio delete ($61 credit). T-Roof ($874). Flip-up open air roof ($213 to $228). Carriage roof ($644). Full vinyl roof ($115). Metallic glow paint ($48). Two-tone paint ($121 to $155). Lower two-tone paint ($90). Pin striping ($34). Accent tape stripes ($54). Hood scoop ($32). Lift gate louvers ($145). Rocker panel moldings ($30). Roof luggage rack ($90). Mud and stone deflectors ($26). Lower body side protection ($37). Console ($168). Recaro high-back bucket seats ($732). Cloth and vinyl bucket seats ($22 to $48). Accent cloth-and-vinyl seat trim ($30). Leather low-back bucket seats ($359). Cargo area cover for hatchback ($45). Front floor mats ($18 to $20). Color-keyed seat belts ($23). Wire wheel covers ($77 to $118). Turbine wheel covers ($10 to $41). Forged metric aluminum wheels ($340). Cast aluminum wheels ($305). Styled steel wheels w/trim rings ($60 to $101). P185/80R13 white sidewall tires ($49). P175/75R14 black sidewall tires ($24). P175/75R14 white sidewall tires ($49 to $73). P185/75R14 black sidewall tires ($24 to $49). P185/75R14 black sidewall tires ($73 to $97). P185/75R14 raised white letter tires ($90 to $114). TRX 190/65R x 390 black sidewall tires ($122 to $146).

History:

Introduced: October 3, 1980. Model-year production: 182,552. Total production for the U.S. market of 162,593 Mustangs included 101,860 four-cylinder, 55,406 sixes and only 5,327 V-8 engines. Calendar-year production: 153,719. Calendar-year sales by U.S. dealers: 154,985. Model-year sales by U.S. dealers: 173,329. Mustang prices rose sharply this year, as did those of other Ford products. The new T-Roof met all federal body structure regulations as a result of body modifications that included the use of H-shaped reinforcements. Both production and sales slipped considerably, but this was a weak period for the industry as a whole. After more than a decade spent avoiding factory involvement in motorsports, Ford renewed its interest in 1980. The initials of the International Motor Sports Association were used on a concept car called the Mustang IMSA. Powered by a hopped-up version of the turbo four, the IMSA wore fat Pirelli tires and a lot of competition-like flares, spoilers and air dams. Ford envisioned a return to the glory days of the 1960s, when its parts branch created a tidy profit center merchandising bolt-on performance hardware to enthusiasts. Englishman Michael Kranefuss, Ford's European competition director, was brought to Dearborn to organize a Special Vehicle Operations (SVO) group. The purpose of the SVO team was threefold. First, it would help interested race drivers build up competition versions of the new Mustang. Second was the creation of a series of specialty "image" cars to generate interest in GT sports car racing. Third on the list was to help conceive/create kits of bolt-on parts that could be purchased by average Mustang owners to modify their street cars for road-and-track use in IMSA or SCCA events. The McLaren Mustang was introduced with lots of fanfare later in the year, including a cover on *Motor Trend* and articles in many buff books. The $25,000 car looked like the IMSA Mustang concept vehicle, with many extensive body modifications and many special accessories like Euro-style BBS alloy wheels. The power

1982 Mustang

Mustang — (Four, Six and V-8): "The Boss is Back!" declared Ford ads for the 1982 Mustang. The biggest news of the year was indeed the return of the 302-cid V-8, which soon became better known as the "5.0" (5,0-liter) engine. The Turbo Four temporarily disappeared. Appearance changed little for 1982, but the Mustang model designations were revised. The new lineup included an L, a GL and a GLX, as well as a GT that replaced the former Cobra option.

Mustang L — (Four, Six and V-8): Mustang L was the new base model, with full wheel covers, full wraparound body side moldings and an AM radio. New standard equipment included seat belts with tension relievers, a remote-control left-hand mirror, a new flash-to-pass headlight feature and a new screw-on gas cap tethered to the gas filler neck. Ford switched to 14-inch wheels with P175/75R14 P-Metric steel-belted radial tires. Four-cylinder Mustangs with air conditioning had an electro-drive cooling fan. Mustang radios had dual front speakers, plus wiring for two more.

Mustang GL — (Four, Six and V-8): The GL was slightly above the L model in terms of standard equipment and exterior trim. It also had more options available.

Mustang GLX – (Four, Six and V-8): The GLX replaced the former Ghia and had about the same distinctions the Ghia had.

Mustang GT — (Four, V-6 and V-8): The GT — which was first called the SS — added P185/75R14 black sidewall steel-belted radial tires on cast-aluminum wheels, a handling suspension, dual black-finished remote-control outside rearview mirrors and built-in fog lamps. Styling features included a body-colored front fascia with an integral spoiler and air dam, a three-slot grille, a color-keyed rear spoiler and a body-color cowl grille. GT identification was seen on the lift gate. Body-color headlight frames replaced the black doors on other models. The black body side moldings had a black plastic insert and aluminum end caps. Standard equipment included a Traction-Lok differential, power brakes, power steering, a console with a digital clock and a diagnostic warning module. The Mustang continued to use a black-out treatment on interior components. An optional TR performance package could enhance the handling qualities of all Mustang models. It included Michelin TRX tires on forged metric aluminum wheels and a handling suspension with a rear stabilizer bar.

VIN:

The VIN was stamped on an aluminum tab riveted to the instrument panel and was viewable through the windshield. The first symbol indicated the country of origin: 1=U.S.A. The second symbol identified the manufacturer: F=Ford. The third symbol indicated the vehicle type: A=passenger car. The fourth symbol indicated the restraint system: B=active belts. The fifth symbol indicated the division: P=Ford passenger car. The sixth symbol indicated the series: 1-Mustang. The seventh symbol indicated the body style: 0=L or GL Coupe, 6=GL or GT Hatchback, 2=GLX Coupe and 3=GLX Hatchback. The eighth symbol indicated the engine: A=140-cid (2.3-liter) SOHC four-cylinder two-barrel, B=200-cid (3.3-liter) in-line six-cylinder one-barrel, D=255-cid (4.2-liter) V-8 two-barrel and F=302-cid (4.0-liter) V-8 two-barrel. The ninth symbol was a check digit. The 10th symbol indicated the model year: C=1982. The 11th symbol indicated the assembly plant: F=Dearborn, Michigan. The last six digits were the unit's production numbers, beginning at 100001 and going up, at each of the assembly plants.

Mustang L (Four)

Model No.	Body/Style No.	Body Type & Seating	Factory Price	Shipping Weight	Production Total
10	66B	2-dr. Coupe-4P	$6,345	2,511 lbs.	—

Mustang GL (Four)

Model No.	Body/Style No.	Body Type & Seating	Factory Price	Shipping Weight	Production Total
10	66B	2-dr. Coupe-4P	$6,844	2,528 lbs.	—
16	61B	2-dr. Hatchback-4P	$6,979	2,565 lbs.	-----

1982 Ford Mustang two-door Sport Option coupe (JG)

Mustang GLX (Four)

12	66H	2-dr. Coupe-4P	$6,980	2,543 lbs.	—
16	61H	2-dr. Hatchback-4P	$7,101	2,579 lbs.	-----

Mustang L (Six)

10	66B	2-dr. Coupe-4P	$7,062	2,524 lbs.	Note

Mustang GL (Six)

10	66B	2-dr. Coupe-4P	$7,468	2,652 lbs.	45,316
16	61B	2-dr. Hatchback-4P	$7,390	2,689 lbs.	69,348

Mustang GLX (Six)

12	66H	2-dr. Coupe-4P	$7,604	2,667 lbs.	5,828
15	61H	2-dr. Hatchback-4P	$7,725	2,703 lbs.	9,926

Notes: The production column showed total body styles figures for all engines. Two V-8s were optional.

Production of the L Coupe was included in the GL Coupe totals.

Production of the GT option (23,447) was included with the GL Hatchback total.

Engines:

Four: Inline, overhead cam. Cast-iron block and head. Displacement: 140-cid (2.3 liters). B & S: 3.78 x 3.13 in. Compression ratio: 9.0:1 Brake hp: 86 at 4600 rpm. Torque: 117 lbs.-ft. at 2600 rpm. Five main bearings. Hydraulic valve lifters. Carburetor: two-barrel Motorcraft 5200 or Holley 6500. Code A.

Six: Inline, overhead valve. Cast-iron block and head. Displacement: 200-cid (3.3 liters). B & S: 3.68 x 3.13 in. Compression ratio: 8.6:1. Brake hp: 87 at 3800 rpm. Torque: 154 lbs.-ft. at 1400 rpm. Seven main bearings. Hydraulic valve lifters. Carburetor: two-barrel Holley 1946. Code T.

V-8: 90-degree, overhead valve. Cast-iron block and head. Displacement: 255-cid (4.2 liters). B & S: 3.68 x 3.00 in. Compression ratio: 8.2:1. Brake hp: 120 at 3400 rpm. Torque: 205 lbs.-ft. at 1600 rpm. Five main bearings. Hydraulic valve lifters. Carburetor: two-barrel Motorcraft 2150 or 7200VV. Code D.

V-8: 90-degree, overhead valve. Cast-iron block and head. Displacement: 302-cid (5.0 liters). B & S: 4.00 x 3.00 in. Compression ratio: 8.3:1. Brake hp: 157 at 4200 rpm. Torque: 240 lbs.-ft. at 2400 rpm. Five main bearings. Hydraulic valve lifters. Carburetor: two-barrel Motorcraft 2150 or 7200VV. Code F.

Chassis:

Wheelbase: 100.4 in. Overall length: 179.1 in. Height: 51.4 in. Width 69.1 in. Front tread: 56.6 in. Rear tread: 57.0 in. Tires: P175/75R14 BSW and P185/75R14, GT.

Technical:

Four-speed manual (floor shift) standard with four-cylinder. Gear ratios: (1st) 3.98:1, (2nd) 2.14:1, (3rd) 1.49:1, (4th) 1.00:1, (Reverse) 3.99:1. Four-speed overdrive manual transmission standard with V-8. Gear ratios: (1st) 3.07:1, (2nd) 1.72:1, (3rd) 1.00:1, (4th) 0.70:1, (Reverse) 3.07:1. Five-speed manual overdrive optional: (1st) 3.72:1, (2nd) 2.23:1, (3rd) 1.48:1, (4th) 1.00:1, (5th) 0.76:1, (Reverse) 3.59:1. Select Shift three-speed automatic optional with four-cylinder, standard with six, (1st) 2.47:1, (2nd) 1.47:1, (3rd) 1.00:1, (Reverse) 2.11:1. Converter clutch automatic available with six or V-8: (1st) 2.46:1, (2nd) 1.46:1, (3rd) 1.00:1, (Reverse) 2.19:1. Standard final drive ratio: 2.73:1 and four with five-speed, 3.45:1, four with automatic transmission, 302 V-8 with four-speed 3.08:1. Body construction: unibody. Fuel tank: 15.4 gallons.

Options:

200-cid six-cylinder ($213). 255-cid V-8 ($263, except $57 credit with GT). 302-cid V-8 ($452, except $402 with TR performance package). Five-speed manual transmission ($196). Select Shift automatic transmission ($411). Traction-Lok differential ($76). Optional axle ratio (NC). Power brakes ($93). Power steering ($190). TR performance suspension package ($533 to $583, except $105 with GT). Handling suspension ($50). Engine block heater ($17). Heavy-duty battery ($24). California emission system ($46). High-altitude emissions system (NC). Light group ($49). Appearance protection group ($48). Power lock group ($139). Air conditioning ($676). Electric rear window defroster ($124). Fingertip speed control ($155). Power windows ($165). Tinted glass ($88). Tinted windshield only ($32). Leather-wrapped steering wheel ($55). Tilt steering wheel ($95). Interval wipers ($48). Rear wiper/washer ($101). Trunk light ($7). Remote right mirror ($41). AM/FM radio ($76). AM/FM stereo radio ($106). AM/FM stereo radio 8-track or cassette player ($184). Premium sound system ($105). Dual rear speakers ($39). AM radio delete ($61 credit). T-Roof ($1,021). Flip-up open air roof ($276). Carriage roof ($734). Full vinyl roof ($137). Metallic glow paint ($54). Two-tone paint ($138 to $177). Lower two-tone paint ($104). Accent tape stripes ($62). Hood scoop ($38). Lift gate louvers ($165).

1982 Ford Mustang two-door GT Hatchback (BB)

Black rocker panel moldings ($33). Lower body side protection ($41). Console ($191). Recaro high-back bucket seats ($834). Cloth and vinyl seats ($23 to $51). Leather low-back bucket seats ($409). Cargo area cover ($51). Carpeted front floor mats ($22). Wire wheel covers ($91 to $141). Cast-aluminum wheels ($348 to $398). Styled steel wheels with trim rings ($72 to $122). P175/75R14 white sidewall tires ($66). P185/75R14 black sidewall tires ($30). P185/75R14 white sidewall tires ($66 to $96). P185/75R14 raised white letter tires ($85 to $116).

History:

Introduced September 24, 1981. Model-year production: 130,418. Total production for the U.S. market of 119,314 Mustangs included 54,444 four-cylinder, 37,734 six-cylinder and 27,136 V-8 engines. Calendar-year production: 127,370. Calendar-year sales by U.S. dealers: 119,526. Model-year sales by U.S. dealers: 116,804. Option prices rose sharply this year, by around 20 percent on the average. Production of V-8 engines also rose sharply, with five times as many coming off the line as in 1981. Mustang sales declined by almost one-third in the 1982 model year. A convertible model was announced, but it didn't appear

1983 Mustang

Mustang L — (Four, Six and V-8): A restyled nose and rear end improved the Mustang's aerodynamics, but otherwise the "pony car" was essentially a carryover model in 1983. All Mustangs had a new angled-forward front end and new front fascia with deeply-recessed headlight housings. A narrower grille design tapered inward slightly at the base, with a Ford oval in its center. The Mustang's rectangular parking lights stood at bumper level, as before. They were positioned below the outboard headlamps. The taillights were restyled, but again had a wraparound design. The use of galvanized and zincro-metal coatings was expanded. A 232-cid "Essex" V-6 was offered in the Mustang for the first time and delivered a two-second improvement in 0-60 mph time over the previous 3.3-liter inline six-cylinder engine. The high-output 302-cid V-8 with a four-speed manual gearbox returned, but now used a four-barrel carburetor and had more horsepower. The V-8 also got an aluminum intake manifold and freer-flowing exhaust system. The base 140-cid four-cylinder engine switched from two-barrel to single-barrel carburetion. Later in the season, a new 140-cid overhead cam turbocharged four-cylinder engine arrived. It had multi-port fuel injection. Turbo models could not have air conditioning. Both the inline six-cylinder engine and the 255-cid V-8 were dropped. A new manual five-speed gearbox, optional with the four-cylinder engine, had Ford's U-shaped shift motion between fourth and fifth gear. An up-shift indicator light option was available in cars with manual transmission. It indicated the most fuel-efficient shift points. All Mustang tires increased by at least one size, while the optional handling suspension got tougher anti-sway bars and re-tuned springs and shock absorbers. Mustangs were now available without the formerly-required Michelin TRX tires. Joining the option list were: cloth sport performance low-back bucket seats, turbine wheel covers, restyled wire wheel covers, a convex right-hand outside rearview mirror, a new special two-tone paint and tape treatment and TRX tires and wheels without the TR performance suspension. Several options were deleted, including the rear windshield wiper and washer, dual rear seat radio speakers, the carriage roof, lift gate louvers, accent tape stripes and Recaro seats. Standard equipment on the base Mustang L included black bumper rub strips, halogen headlights, a three-speed heater and defroster, a wood tone instrument panel appliqué, quarter-window louvers, a black-finished remote-control left-hand outside rearview mirror, an AM radio, a four-spoke steering wheel with a wood grain insert and a four-speed manual gearbox, full wheel covers, Argent Silver accent striping, a cigarette lighter and high-back reclining bucket seats with vinyl upholstery. Cars optioned with the high-output 302-cid V-8 featured a new hood scoop design.

Mustang GL — (Four, Six and V-8): The Mustang GL added black rocker panel finish, black door frame moldings, black window frame moldings, dual accent body side pinstripes, a black-finished sport steering wheel, carpeted lower door trim panels, a right-hand visor vanity mirror and low-back bucket seats.

Mustang GLX – (Four, Six and V-8): The Mustang GLX came with dual bright remote-control outside rearview mirrors, a four-spoke steering wheel with wood grain insert, bright rocker panel moldings, map pockets in the driver's door trim panel and a light group. A new convertible was part of the GLX series and was available with any power train except the 2.3-liter four with automatic transmission. The Mustang convertible included a glass backlight, roll-down quarter windows, a power top, power brakes, tinted glass, dual black remote-control outside rearview mirrors, black rocker panel moldings and automatic transmission.

Mustang GT —V-8: The Mustang GT carried a standard Traction-Lok rear axle, power brakes and steering, black grille, rear spoiler, black hood scoop, handling suspension, and five-speed manual gearbox, GT models could have Michelin TRX tires on cast aluminum wheels and a console with digital clock and diagnostic module, but no dual accent body side pin striping. Black windshield, window and door frames completed the GT's appearance. The V-8 engine was standard in the GT. Later, a Borg-Warner T5 close-ratio five-speed became available for GTs, which had a 3.27:1 final drive ratio.

VIN:

The VIN was stamped on an aluminum tab riveted to the instrument panel and was viewable through the windshield. The first symbol indicated the country of origin: 1=U.S.A. The second symbol identified the manufacturer: F=Ford. The third symbol indicated the vehicle type: A=passenger car. The fourth symbol indicated the restraint system: B=active belts. The fifth symbol indicated the division: P=Ford passenger car. The sixth and seventh symbols indicated the body style: 26=Coupe, 27=Convertible and 28=Hatchback. The eighth symbol indicated the engine: A=140-cid (2.3-liter) SOHC four-cylinder one-barrel, T=140-cid (2.3-liter) SOHC four-cylinder two-barrel with electronic fuel injection and turbocharger, 3=232-cid (3.8-liter) V-6 two-barrel and F=302-cid (5.0-liter H.O.) V-8 four-barrel. The ninth symbol was a check digit. The 10th symbol indicated the model year: D=1983. The 11th symbol indicated the assembly plant: F=Dearborn, Michigan. The last six digits were the unit's production numbers, beginning at 100001 and going up, at each of the assembly plants.

Mustang L (Four)

Model No.	Body/ Style No.	Body Type & Seating	Factory Price	Shipping Weight	Production Total
26	66B	2-dr. Coupe-4P	$6,727	2,532 lbs.	—

Mustang GL (Four)

26	66B	2-dr. Coupe-4P	$7,264	2,549 lbs.	—
28	61B	2-dr. Hatchback-4P	$7,439	2,584 lbs.	-----

Mustang GLX (Four)

26	66H	2-dr. Coupe-4P	$7,398	2,552 lbs.	—
28	61H	2-dr. Hatchback-4P	$7,557	2,587 lbs.	-----
27	---	2-dr. Cnnvertible-4P	-----	-----	-----

Mustang L (Six)

26	66B	2-dr. Coupe-4P	$7,036	2,621 lbs.	—

Mustang GL (Six)

26	66B	2-dr. Coupe-4P	$7,573	2,638 lbs.	Note 1
28	61B	2-dr. Hatchback-4P	$7,748	2,673 lbs.	Note 1

Mustang GLX (Six)

26	66B	2-dr. Coupe-4P	$7,707	2,641 lbs.	Note 1
28	61B	2-dr. Hatchback-4P	$7,866	2,676 lbs.	Note 1
27	----	2-dr. Convertible-4P	$9,449	2,759 lbs.	Note 1

Mustang GT (V-8)

28/932	61B	2-dr. Hatchback-4P	$ 9,328	2,891 lbs.	Note 1
26/932	66B	2-dr. Convertible-4P	$13,479	-----	Note 1

Mustang Turbo GT (Four)

28/932	61B	2-dr. Hatchback-4P	$ 9,714	------	Note 1

Note 1: The production column shows the body style totals for all engines. Ford reported total production of 33,201 coupes, 64,234 hatchbacks and 23,438 convertibles.

Engines:

Four: Inline, overhead cam. Cast-iron block and head. Displacement: 140-cid (2.3 liters). B & S: 3.78 x 3.13 in. Compression ratio: 9.0:1. Brake hp: 90 at 4600 rpm. Torque: 122 lbs.-ft. at 2600 rpm. Five main bearings.

1983 Ford Mustang GT two-door Convertible (OCW)

Hydraulic valve lifters. Carburetor: Carter YFA one-barrel. Code A.

Turbo Four: Inline, overhead cam, turbocharged, EFI. Cast-iron block and head. Displacement: 140-cid (2.3 liters). B & S: 3.78 x 3.13 in. Compression ratio: 8.0:1 Brake hp: 142 at 5000 rpm. Torque: 172 lbs.-ft. at 3800 rpm. Five main bearings. Hydraulic valve lifters. Induction: Electronic fuel injection. Code D.

V-6: 90-degree, overhead valve. Cast-iron block and aluminum head. Displacement: 232-cid (3.8 liters). B & S: 3. 80 x 3.40 in. Compression ratio: 8.7:1. Brake hp: 112 at 4000 rpm. Torque: 175 lbs.-ft. at 2600 rpm. Four main bearings. Hydraulic valve lifters. Carburetor: two-barrel Motorcraft 2150. Code 3.

V-8: 90-degree, overhead valve. Cast-iron block and head. Displacement: 302-cid (5.0 liters). B & S: 4.00 x 3.00 in. Compression ratio: 8.3:1. Brake hp: 175 at 4000 rpm. Torque: 245 lbs.-ft. at 2400 rpm. Five main bearings. Hydraulic valve lifters. Carburetor: Holley 4180 four-barrel. Code F.

Chassis:

Wheelbase: 100.4 in. Overall length: 179.1 in. Height: 51.9 in. Width 69.1 in. Front tread: 56.6 in. Rear tread: 57.0 in. Tires: P185/75R14 steel-belted radial black sidewall and P205/70HR14 or Michelin P220/55R390 TRX, GT.

Technical:

Transmission: Four-speed manual (floor shift) standard with four-cylinder. Gear ratios: (1st) 3.98:1, (2nd) 2.14:1, (3rd) 1.49:1, (4th) 1.00:1, (Reverse) 3.99:1. Four-speed overdrive manual transmission standard with V-8. Gear ratios: (1st) 3.07:1, (2nd) 1.72:1, (3rd) 1.00:1, (4th) 0.70:1 (Reverse) 3.07:1. Five-speed manual overdrive optional: (1st) 3.72:1, (2nd) 2.23:1, (3rd) 1.48:1, (4th) 1.00:1, (5th) 0.76:1 (Reverse) 3.59:1. Turbo five-speed: (1st) 4.03:1, (2nd) 2.37:1, (3rd) 1.50:1, (4th) 1.00:1, (5th) 0.86:1, (Reverse) 3.76:1. Alternate turbo five-speed: (1st) 3.76:1, (2nd) 2.18:1, (3rd) 1.36:1, (4th) 1.00:1, (5th) 0.86:1, (Reverse) 3.76:1. V-8 five-speed: (1st) 2.95:1 (2nd) 1.94:1, (3rd) 1.34:1, (4th) 1.00:1, (5th) 0.73:1, (Reverse) 2.76:1. Select Shift three-speed automatic transmission optional with four-cylinder, standard with six-cylinder: (1st) 2.47:1, (2nd) 1.47:1, (3rd) 1.00:1 , (Reverse) 2.11:1 V-6 ratios: (1st) 2.46:1, (2nd) 1.46:1, (3rd) 1.00:1, (Reverse) 2.19:1. Standard final drive ratio: 3.08:1 with four-speed, 3.45:1 with five-speed, 3.08:1 or 2.73:1 with automatic. Steering: Rack and pinion. Front suspension: Modified MacPherson struts with lower control arms and stabilizer bar. Rear suspension: Rigid axle w/four-bar link and coil springs. Brakes: Front disc, rear drum. Ignition: Electronic. Body construction: Unibody. Fuel tank: 15.4 gallons.

Options:

232-cid V-6 ($309). 302-cid V-8 ($1,343, except in convertibles ($595). Five-speed manual transmission ($124). Select-shift automatic transmission. ($439). Traction-Lok differential ($95). Optional axle ratio (NC). Power brakes ($93). Power steering ($202). Handling suspension ($252). Engine block heater ($17). Heavy-duty battery ($26). California emission system ($76). High-altitude emissions (NC). Sport performance package ($196). Light group ($55). Appearance protection group ($60). Power lock group ($160). Air conditioning ($724). Electric rear defroster ($135). Fingertip speed control ($170). Power windows ($180). Tinted glass ($105). Tinted windshield only ($38). Leather-wrapped steering wheel ($59). Tilt steering wheel ($105). Interval windshield wipers ($49). Remote right-hand outside rearview mirror ($44). AM/FM radio ($82) AM/FM stereo radio ($109). AM/FM stereo radio with 8-track or cassette player ($199). Premium sound system ($117). AM radio delete ($61 credit). T-Roof ($1,055). Flip-up open air roof ($310). Metallic glow paint ($54). Two-tone paint ($150 to $189). Lift gate louvers for hatchback ($171). Rocker panel moldings ($33). Lower body side protection ($41). Console ($191). Cloth-and-vinyl seats ($29 to $57). Leather low-back bucket seats ($415). Carpeted front floor mats ($22). Wire wheel covers ($98 to $148). Turbine wheel covers (NC). Cast-aluminum wheels ($354 to $404). Styled steel wheels with trim rings ($78 to $128). P185/75R14 white sidewall tires ($72). P195/75R14 white sidewall tires

1983 Ford Mustang GLX two-door Hatchback (OCW)

1983 Ford Mustang GLX two-door Convertible (OCW)

($108). P205/75R14 black sidewall tires ($224). TRX P220/55R390 black sidewall tires ($327 to $551).

History:

Most models were introduced Oct. 14, 1982. The convertible was introduced on Nov. 5, 1982. Model-year production: 108,438 Total production for the U.S. market of 108,438 Mustangs included 27,825 four-cylinder, 47,766 sixes, and 32,847 V-8 engines. Calendar-year production: 124,225. Calendar-year sales by U.S. dealers: 116,976. Model-year sales by U.S. dealers: 116,120. The Mustang convertible actually began life as a steel-topped notchback and was modified by an outside contractor. The car itself was assembled at Dearborn, then sent to Cars & Concepts, in Brighton, Michigan, for installation of the top and interior trim. The Mustang GT was said to deliver a seven-second 0-60 mph time (quickest of any standard domestic model), as well as

1984 Mustang

Mustang L — (Four, Six and V-8): Standard models looked the same as in 1983. Throughout the line were new steering wheels with a center horn, new instrument panel appliqués and split folding rear seats. All manual transmissions now had a clutch/starter interlock so the engine couldn't start unless the clutch was depressed. Mustang instrument panels had red lighting this year. Buyers could also select a more modest turbo model, without the intercooler. The L series previously offered only the two-door notchback, but now included a three-door hatchback. On the power plant front, the optional 3.8-liter V-6 switched to throttle-body fuel injection and gained some horsepower. A fuel-injected high-output 5.0-liter V-8 came with an automatic overdrive transmission. A higher-output version of the four-barrel V-8, producing 205 hp, was announced for December arrival but then got delayed.

Mustang GLX — (Four, Six and V-8): The GL and GLX models of 1983 were gone and replaced by a single LX series. A convertible was offered again this year in the LX series.

Mustang GT — (V-8 and Turbo Four): GT customers had a choice of V-8 engines and an available overdrive automatic transmission. GTs displayed a new front air dam and road lamps were available. The GT also added gas-filled shock absorbers and a handling suspension. A GT Turbo had been introduced in spring 1983 and was continued for 1984.

Mustang SVO — (Turbo Four) Performance-minded "Mustangers" enjoyed fresh temptation this year in the new SVO. Developed by Ford's Special Vehicle Operations department, the hot-performing SVO model carried an air-to-air intercooler on its turbocharged four-cylinder engine. Standard SVO equipment included an 8,000-rpm tachometer, quick-ratio power steering, a Traction-Lok rear axle, a leather-wrapped steering wheel, a shift knob and brake handle, unique instrument panel appliqués, narrow body side moldings and unique C-pillar and taillight treatments. A premium/regular fuel switch recalibrated the ignition instantly. Revised pedal positioning allowed heel-and-toe downshifting and had a footrest for the left foot during hard cornering. The SVO package included a Borg-Warner T5 five-speed manual gearbox with Hurst linkage, four-wheel disc brakes, a performance suspension with adjustable Koni gas-filled shocks, P225/50VR16 Goodyear NCT tires on 16 x 7-in. cast-aluminum

wheels and a functional hood scoop. Ford claimed the SVO could do 134 mph and get to 60 mph in just 7.5 seconds. Inside were multi-adjustable articulated leather bucket seats. The SVO shock absorbers and struts had three settings: cross-country (for front and rear), GT (front only) and competition (front and rear). Four-wheel disc brakes were standard. The SVO had a much different front-end look than the standard Mustang with a grille-less front fascia and integrated fog lamps. Just a single slot stood below the hood panel, which contained a Ford oval. Large, deeply-recessed single rectangular headlights were flanked by large wraparound lenses. A polycarbonate dual-wing rear spoiler was meant to increase rear-wheel traction, while rear-wheel "spats" directed airflow around the wheel wells. The SVO was offered only in three-door hatchback form and only in Black, Silver Metallic, Dark Charcoal Metallic or Red Metallic. The interiors were charcoal. Only six major options were available for SVO, because it had so much standard equipment. The available extras were: air conditioning, power windows, power door locks, a cassette player, a flip-up sun roof and leather seat trim.

VIN:

The VIN was stamped on an aluminum tab riveted to the instrument panel and was viewable through the windshield. The first symbol indicated the country of origin: 1=U.S.A. The second symbol identified the manufacturer: F=Ford. The third symbol indicated the vehicle type: A=passenger car. The fourth symbol revealed the restraint system: B=active belts. The fifth symbol indicated the division: P=Ford passenger car. The sixth and seventh symbols were the body style: 26=Coupe, 27=Convertible and 28=Hatchback. The eighth symbol indicated the engine: A=140-cid (2.3-liter) SOHC four-cylinder two-barrel, T= Turbo GT 140-cid (2.3-liter) SOHC four-cylinder with electronic fuel injection and turbocharger, W=SVO Turbo 140-cid (2.3-liter) SOHC four-cylinder with electronic fuel injection and turbocharger, 3=232-cid (3.8-liter) V-6 with electronic fuel injection, F=302-cid (5.0-liter) V-8 with electronic fuel injection and M=302-cid (5.0-liter H.O.) V-8 with four-barrel. The ninth symbol was a check digit. The 10th symbol indicated the model year: E=1984. The 11th symbol showed the assembly plant: F=Dearborn, Michigan. The last six digits were the unit's production numbers, beginning at 100001 and going up, at each of the assembly plants.

Mustang L (Four)

Model No.	Body/Style No.	Body Type & Seating	Factory Price	Shipping Weight	Production Total
26	66B	2-dr. Coupe-4P	$7,098	2,538 lbs.	—
28	61B	2-dr. Hatchback-4P	$7,269	2,584 lbs.	—

Mustang LX (Four)

Model No.	Body/Style No.	Body Type & Seating	Factory Price	Shipping Weight	Production Total
26/602	66H	2-dr. Coupe-4P	$7,290	2,559 lbs.	—
28/602	61B	2-dr. Hatchback-4P	$7,496	2,605 lbs.	—

Mustang L (Six)

Model No.	Body/Style No.	Body Type & Seating	Factory Price	Shipping Weight	Production Total
26	66B	2-dr. Coupe-4P	$7,507	2,646 lbs.	Note 1
28	61B	2-dr. Hatchback-4P	$7,678	2,692 lbs.	Note 1

Mustang LX (Six)

Model No.	Body/Style No.	Body Type & Seating	Factory Price	Shipping Weight	Production Total
26/602	66H	2-dr. Coupe-4P	$7,699	2,667 lbs.	Note 1
28/602	61B	2-dr. Hatchback-4P	$7,905	2,713 lbs.	Note 1
27/602	66B	2-dr. Convertible-4P	$11,849	2,873 lbs.	Note 1

Note 1 : The 302-cid four-barrel V-8 engine cost $1,165 more than the V-6 and it was $318 more on the LX convertible.

Mustang GT (Turbo Four)

Model No.	Body/Style No.	Body Type & Seating	Factory Price	Shipping Weight	Production Total
28/932	61B	2-dr. Hatchback-4P	$ 9,762	2,753 lbs.	Note 2
27/932	66B	2-dr. Convertible-4P	$13,245	2,921 lbs.	Note 2

Mustang GT (V-8)

Model No.	Body/Style No.	Body Type & Seating	Factory Price	Shipping Weight	Production Total
28/932	61B	2-dr. Hatchback-4P	$ 9,578	2,899 lbs.	Note 2
27/932	66B	2-dr. Convertible-4P	$13,051	3,043 lbs.	Note 2

Mustang SVO (Turbo Four)

Model No.	Body/Style No.	Body Type & Seating	Factory Price	Shipping Weight	Production Total
28/939	61B	2-dr. Hatchback-4P	$15,596	2,881 lbs.	Note 2

Note 2: Ford reported production of 37,680 Coupes, 86,200 Hatchbacks and 17,600 Convertibles.

Engines:

Four: Inline, overhead cam. Cast-iron block and head. Displacement: 140-cid (2.3 liters). B & S: 3.78 x 3.13 in. Compression ratio: 9.0:1 Brake hp: 88 at 4400 rpm Torque: 122 lbs.-ft. at 2400 rpm. Five main bearings. Hydraulic valve lifters. Carburetor: Carter YFA one-barrel. Code A.

Turbo Four: Inline, overhead cam, turbocharged, EFI. Cast-iron block and head. Displacement: 140-cid (2.3 liters). B & S: 3.78 x 3.13 in. Compression ratio: 8.0:1 Brake hp: 145 at 4600 rpm. Torque: 180 lbs.-

1984 Ford Mustang GT 5.0-Liter Sport Coupe (JG)

1984 Ford Mustang GT-350 20th Anniversary Convertible (FMC)

1984 Ford Mustang SVO two-door Coupe (OCW)

ft. at 3600 rpm. Five main bearings. Hydraulic valve lifters. Induction: Electronic fuel injection. Code T.

SVO (Turbo Four): Inline, overhead cam, turbocharged, EFI. Cast-iron block and head. Displacement: 140-cid (2.3 liters). B & S: 3.78 x 3.13 in. Compression ratio: 8.0:1 Brake hp: 175 at 4400 rpm. Torque: 210 lbs.-ft. at 3000 rpm Five main bearings. Hydraulic valve lifters. Induction: Electronic fuel injection (TBI). Code W.

V-6: 90-degree, overhead valve. Cast-iron block and aluminum head. Displacement: 232-cid (3.8 liters). B & S: 3. 80 x 3.40 in. Compression ratio: 8.7:1. Brake hp: 120 at 3600 rpm. Torque: 205 lbs.-ft. at 1600 rpm. Four main bearings. Hydraulic valve lifters. Induction: Electronic fuel injection (TBI). Code 3.

5.0-Liter V-8: 90-degree, overhead valve. Cast-iron block and head. Displacement: 302-cid (5.0 liters). B & S: 4.00 x 3.00 in. Compression ratio: 8.3:1. Brake hp: 165 at 3800 rpm. Torque: 245 lbs.-ft. at 2000 rpm. Five main bearings. Hydraulic valve lifters. Induction: Electronic fuel injection (TBI). Code F.

5.0-Liter HO V-8: 90-degree, overhead valve. Cast-iron block and head. Displacement: 302-cid (5.0 liters). B & S: 4.00 x 3.00 in. Compression ratio: 8.3:1. Brake hp: 175 at 4000 rpm. Torque: 245 lbs.-ft. at 2400 rpm. Five main bearings. Hydraulic valve lifters. Carburetor: Holley 4180C four-barrel. Code M.

Chassis:

Wheelbase: 100.5 in. Overall length: 179.1 in. except SVO, 181.0 in. Height: 51.9 in. Width: 69.1 in. Front tread: 56.6 in. except SVO, 57.8 in. Rear tread: 57.0 in. except SVO, 58.3 in. Tires: P185/75R14 steel-belted radial with black sidewall. Tires—GT: P205/70HR14.

Technical:

Transmission: Four-speed manual (floor shift) standard on four-cylinder. Gear ratios: (1st) 3.98:1, (2nd) 2.14:1, (3rd) 1.49:1, (4th) 1.00:1, (Reverse) 3.99:1. Standard turbo five-speed: (1st) 4.03:1, (2nd) 2.37:1, (3rd) 1.50:1, (4th) 1.00:1, (5th) 0.86:1, (Reverse) 3.76:1. Standard V-8 five-speed: (1st) 2.95:1, (2nd) 1.94:1, (3rd) 1.34:1, (4th) 1.00:1, (5th) 0.63:1, (Reverse) 2.76:1. Select Shift three-speed automatic optional on four-cylinder: (1st) 2.47:1, (2nd) 1.47:1, (3rd) 1.00:1, (Reverse) 2.11:1. Four-speed overdrive automatic standard on V-6: (1st) 2.40:1, (2nd) 1.47:1, (3rd) 1.00:1, (4th) 0.67:1, (Reverse) 2.00:1. Standard final drive ratio: (four) 3.08:1 with 4-speed transmission, 3.27:1 with automatic transmission, (V-6) 3.08:1 (V-8) 3.08:1 with 5-speed transmission, 2.73:1 with 3-speed transmission, 3.27:1 with 4-speed automatic transmission., (turbo) 3.45:1. Steering: Rack-and-pinion. Front Suspension: Modified MacPherson struts with lower control arms and stabilizer bar, SVO added adjustable gas-pressurized shocks. Rear Suspension: Rigid axle with 4-bar link and coil springs, SVO and GT Turbo added an anti-sway bar. Brakes: Front disc, rear drum except SVO, four-wheel disc brakes. Ignition: Electronic. Body construction: Unibody. Fuel tank: 15.4 gallons.

Options:

232 cid V-6 ($409). 302 cid V-8 package ($1574) except LX convertible ($727). Five-speed manual transmission (NC). Three-speed automatic transmission ($439). Four-speed overdrive automatic transmission ($551). Traction-Lok differential ($95). Optional axle ratio (no cost). Power brakes ($93). Power steering ($202). Handling suspension ($252) except with VIP package ($50). Engine block heater ($18). Heavy-duty battery ($27). California emission system ($99). High-altitude option (no cost). SVO competition preparation package: delete air conditioning, power locks, AM/FM/cassette and power windows ($1,253 credit). VIP package for L/LX with AM/FM stereo or tilt wheel ($93), both ($196). VIP package for GT ($110). 20th anniversary VIP package: GT ($25-$144). Light/convenience group ($55-$88). Power lock group ($177). Air conditioning ($743). Rear defroster, electric ($140). Fingertip speed control ($176). Power windows ($198). Tinted glass ($110).

Tilt steering wheel ($110). Interval wipers ($50). Remote right mirror ($46). Entertainment: AM/FM stereo radio ($109), with cassette player ($222) except SVO or with VIP package ($113). Premium sound system ($151). AM radio delete ($39 credit). T-Roof ($1,074) except with VIP package ($760). Flip-up open air roof ($315). Metallic glow paint ($54). Two-tone paint: L/LX ($150 to $189). Lower two-tone paint ($116). Lift gate louvers: hatch ($171). Rocker panel moldings ($39). Lower body side protection ($41). Console ($191). Articulated sport seats ($196). High-back vinyl bucket seats: L ($29), low-back, LX/GT ($29). Leather bucket seats ($189). Front floor mats, carpeted ($22). Wire wheel covers ($98). Cast aluminum wheels ($354). Styled steel wheels with trim rings ($78). P185/75R14 white sidewall ($72). P195/75R14 white sidewall ($108). P205/75R14 black sidewall ($224). TRX P220/55R390 black sidewall ($327-$551) except GT ($27 credit).

History:

Introduced September 22, 1983. Model-year production was 141,480 cars. Total production for the U.S. market of 129,621 Mustangs included 46,414 four-cylinder, 47,169 sixes and 36,038 V-8 engines. Calendar-year production: 140,338. Calendar-year sales by U.S. dealers: 138,296. Model-year sales by U.S. dealers: 131,762. Ford's Special Vehicle Operations Department was formed in 1981 to supervise the company's renewed involvement in motorsports (among other duties), and to develop special limited-edition high-performance vehicles. SVO was the first of those offered as a production model. *Motor Trend* called SVO "the best driving street Mustang the factory has ever produced." *Road & Track* claimed that SVO "outruns the Datsun 280ZX, outhandles the Ferrari 308

1985 Mustang

Mustang LX — (Four, V-6 and V-8): Changes for 1985 focused mainly on Mustang's front end and mechanical matters. All models wore a new front-end look with a four-hole integral air dam below the bumper. It was flanked by low, rectangular parking lamps. A "grille" similar to the SVO type — essentially one wide slot with angled sides in a sloping front panel — appeared on all Mustangs. The panel displayed a Ford oval. The taillight were of a full-width design (except for the license plate opening) and had back-up lenses at the upper portion of each inner section. A Ford script oval stood above the right taillight. Most Mustang exterior trim and accents switched from black to a softer charcoal shade. All models had new charcoal front and rear bumper rub strips and body side moldings. Also new was a charcoal hood paint/tape treatment and a revised rear deck lid decal, The base L series was dropped, making the LX the bottom-level Mustang. Standard LX equipment now included power brakes, power steering, a remote-control right-side mirror, a dual-note horn, interval windshield wipers and an AM/FM stereo radio. New standard interior features included a console, and low-back bucket seats, The convertible's quarter trim panels were revised to accommodate a refined seat belt system. Mechanical radio faces switched to a contemporary flat design. All Mustangs had larger tires this year and they added urethane lower body side protection. Added to the options list was a new electronic AM/FM stereo radio with cassette player. The 140-cid (2.3-liter) four remained standard, but buyers had quite a choice of other power plants, as usual. Both the 3.8-liter V-6 and 5.0-liter V-8 had new oil warning lights. The high-output, fuel-injected V-8 also reached 180 hp.

Mustang GT —(V-8): The Mustang GT had integral fog lamps and GT nomenclature (where applicable) molded into the body side moldings. The GT line offered hatchback and convertible models. New standard interior features included a console, articulated sport seats, luxury door trim panels and covered visor mirrors. The GT now had Goodyear Eagle unidirectional Gatorback tires on 15 x 7-in. cast-aluminum wheels. The Mustang GT's high-output carbureted 302-cid (5.0-liter) V-8 gained a high-performance camshaft, plus roller tappets and a two-speed accessory drive system. That engine now produced 210 hp, while its mating five-speed manual gearbox had a tighter shift pattern and new gear ratios.

Mustang SVO — (Turbo Four): The turbocharged SVO returned a little late and now wearing Eagle 50-series tires on 16-inch wheels.

VIN:

The VIN was stamped on an aluminum tab riveted to the instrument panel and was viewable through the windshield. The first symbol indicated the country of origin: 1=U.S.A. The second symbol identified the manufacturer: F=Ford. The third symbol revealed the vehicle type: A=passenger car. The fourth symbol indicated the restraint system: B=active belts. The fifth symbol indicated the division: P=Ford passenger car. The sixth and seventh symbols indicated the body style: 26=Coupe, 27=Convertible and 28=Hatchback. The eighth symbol was the engine: A=140-cid (2.3-liter) SOHC four-cylinder one-barrel, W=Turbo 140-cid (2.3-liter) SOHC turbocharged four-cylinder SVO with electronic fuel injection, 3=232-cid (3.8-liter) V-6 with electronic fuel injection, F=302-cid (5.0-liter) V-8 with electronic fuel injection and M=302-cid (5.0-liter H.O.) V-8 with four-barrel. The ninth symbol was a check digit. The 10th symbol indicated the model year: F=1985. The 11th symbol indicated the assembly plant: F=Dearborn, Michigan. The last six digits were the unit's production numbers, beginning at 100001 and going up, at each of the assembly plants.

Mustang LX (Four)

Model No.	Body/Style No.	Body Type & Seating	Factory Price	Shipping Weight	Production Total
26/602	66B	2-dr. Coupe-4P	$6,885	2,559 lbs.	Note 1
28/602	61B	3-dr. Hatchback-4P	$7,345	2,605 lbs.	Note 1

Mustang LX (V-6)

Model No.	Body/Style No.	Body Type & Seating	Factory Price	Shipping Weight	Production Total
26/602	66H	2-dr. Coupe-4P	$8,017	2,667 lbs.	Note 1
28/602	61B	3-dr. Hatchback-4P	$8,477	2,713 lbs.	Note 1
27/602	66B	2-dr. Convertible-4P	$11,985	2,873 lbs.	Note 1

Note: The 302-cid four-barrel V-8 engine cost $561 more than the V-6. It was $152 more on the LX convertible.

Mustang GT (V-8)

Model No.	Body/Style No.	Body Type & Seating	Factory Price	Shipping Weight	Production Total
28/932	61B	3-dr. Hatchback-4P	$ 9,885	2,899 lbs.	Note 2
27/932	66B	2-dr. Convertible-4P	$13,585	3,042 lbs.	Note 2

Mustang SVO (Turbo Four)

Model No.	Body/Style No.	Body Type & Seating	Factory Price	Shipping Weight	Production Total
28/939	61B	3-dr. Hatchback-4P	$ 14,521	2,881 lbs.	Note 2

Note 1: Ford reported production of 56,781 Coupes, 84,623 Hatchbacks and 15,110 Convertibles.

Engines:

Four: Inline, overhead cam. Cast-iron block and head. Displacement: 140-cid (2.3 liters). B & S: 3.78 x 3.13 in. Compression ratio: 9.0:1 Brake hp: 88 at 4400 rpm Torque: 122 lbs.-ft. at 2400 rpm. Five main bearings.

1985 Ford Mustang GT 5.0-Liter Hatchback (PH

1985 Ford Mustang SVO Coupe (JG)

Hydraulic valve lifters. Carburetor: Carter YFA one-barrel. Code A.

SVO Turbo Four: Inline, overhead cam, turbocharged, EFI. Cast-iron block and head. Displacement: 140-cid (2.3 liters). B & S: 3.78 x 3.13 in. Compression ratio: 8.0:1 Brake hp: 205 at 5000 rpm. Torque: Torque: 210 lbs.-ft. at 3000 rpm. Five main bearings. Hydraulic valve lifters. Induction: Electronic fuel injection (TBI). Code W.

V-6: 90-degree, overhead valve. Cast-iron block and aluminum head. Displacement: 232-cid (3.8 liters). B & S: 3. 80 x 3.40 in. Compression ratio: 8.7:1. Brake hp: 120 at 3600 rpm Torque: 205 lbs.-ft. at 1600 rpm. Four main bearings. Hydraulic valve lifters. Induction: Electronic fuel injection (TBI). Code 3.

5.0-Liter V-8: 90-degree, overhead valve. Cast-iron block and head. Displacement: 302-cid (5.0 liters). B &S: 4.00 x 3.00 in. Compression ratio: 8.3:1. Brake hp: 165 at 4200 rpm Torque: 245 lbs.-ft. at 2000 rpm. Five main bearings. Hydraulic valve lifters. Induction: Electronic fuel injection (TBI). Code F.

5.0-Liter HO V-8: 90-degree, overhead valve. Cast-iron block and head. Displacement: 302-cid (5.0 liters). B & S: 4.00 x 3.00 in. Compression ratio: 8.3:1. Brake hp: 210 at 4400 rpm Torque: 270 lbs.-ft. at 3200 rpm. Five main bearings. Hydraulic valve lifters. Carburetor: Holley 4180C four-barrel. Code M.

Chassis:

Wheelbase: 100.5 in. Overall length: 179.3 in. and SVO, 180.8 in. Height: 52.1 in. Width: 69.1 in. Front tread: 56.6 in. and SVO, 57.8 in. Rear tread: 57.0 in. and SVO, 58.3 in. Tires: P195/75R14 steel-belted radial with black sidewall, P225/60VR15, GT and P225/50VR16 Eagle, SVO.

Options:

232 cid V-6 in LX ($439). 302-cid V-8 package ($552). 302-cid V-8 package in LX convertible ($152). Five-speed manual transmission in LX ($124). Three-speed automatic transmission in LX ($439). Four-speed overdrive automatic transmission in LX ($676). Four-speed overdrive automatic transmission in GT ($551). Traction-Lok differential ($95). Optional axle ratio (NC). Handling suspension in LX ($258). Engine block heater ($18). Heavy-duty battery ($27). California emission system ($99). High-altitude option (NC). SVO competition preparation package with air conditioner delete, power locks, AM/FM stereo/cassette and power windows ($1,417 credit). Light and convenience group ($55). Power lock group ($177 to $210). Air conditioning ($743). Electric rear defroster ($140). Fingertip speed control ($176). Power windows, except convertible ($198). Power windows, convertible ($272). Tinted glass ($110). Tilt steering wheel in LX ($110). AM/FM stereo radio with cassette player in LX and GT ($148). Electronic AM/FM stereo with cassette in LX and GT ($300). Premium sound system in LX and GT ($138). Radio delete ($148 credit). T-Roof for hatchback ($1,074). Flip-up open air roof for hatchback ($315). Lower two-tone paint ($116). Single wing spoiler on SVO (NC). Console ($191). Low-back vinyl bucket seats in LX ($29). Leather sport performance bucket seats in LX convertible ($780). Leather sport performance bucket seats in GT convertible ($415). Leather sport performance bucket seats in SVO ($189). LX wire wheel covers ($98). Styled steel wheels ($178). P205/75R14 white sidewall tires ($109). P205/70VR14 black sidewall tires ($238). P225/60VR15 steel-belted radial black-sidewall tires ($665).

History:

Introduced: October 4, 1984. Model-year production: 156,514. Total production for the U.S. market of 143,682 Mustangs included 79,885 four-cylinder, 18,334 sixes and 45,463 V-8 engines. Calendar-year production: 187,773. Calendar-year sales by U.S. dealers: 157,821. Model-year sales by U.S. dealers: 159,741. This year's GT proved that the V-8 had a future under Mustang hoods, even with the turbocharged SVO available. For one thing, the GT was a lot cheaper. It also performed more sedately than a turbo under ordinary conditions, yet was able to deliver impressive performance whenever needed. *Motor Trend* applauded the arrival of the potent 210-hp V-8 for delivering

1986 Mustang

Mustang LX — (Four, V-6 and V-8): The Mustang LX had full body side striping, power brakes and steering and such extras as interval wipers, a luxury sound package and an AM/FM stereo radio (which could be deleted for credit). The base engine remained the 2.3-liter overhead cam four with a four-speed manual gearbox. V-8 engines now had sequential port fuel injection. The 3.8-liter V-6 with throttle-body injection was optional again, but standard on the LX convertible. The appearance of the Mustang LX was essentially the same as in 1985. The sloping center front-end panel held a Ford oval at the top and a single wide opening below. The quad rectangular headlights were deeply recessed. The parking lights stood far down on the front end. The side marker lenses were angled to match the front fender tips. The taillights were distinctly divided into upper and lower sections by a full-width divider bar. "Mustang" lettering stood above the left taillight lens with a Ford oval above the right. Three new body colors were offered. Turbine wheel covers switched from bright-and-Argent Silver finish to bright-and-Black. The Mustang's rear axle was upgraded to 8.7 inches with the standard 2.73:1 axle ratio (8.8 inch with others) for use with the 5.0-liter V-8. Viscous engine mounts were added on the 3.8-liter V-6 and the V-8, as used on the turbo four starting in midyear 1985. One key now operated the door locks and the ignition. The two-door LX notchback had a high-mounted stop light added to the rear package tray. Hatchback LX models added a spoiler to house the stop light, while LX and GT convertibles installed a luggage rack with an integral stop light. Preferred Equipment Packages included such items as air conditioning, styled wheels and a Premium Sound System.

Mustang GT —(V-8): The Mustang GT had integral fog lamps and GT nomenclature (where applicable) molded into the body side moldings. The high-mounted stop light was in the spoiler. GT convertibles also installed a luggage rack with integral brake light. The Mustang GT carried a new high-output 5.0-liter V-8 with multi-port fuel injection. Rated at 200 hp with EECIV electronic engine controls, it was hooked to a five-speed manual (overdrive) transmission or an automatic overdrive. The GT included a special suspension, Goodyear Eagle VR performance tires, quick-ratio power steering and articulated front sport seats. The four-barrel V-8 was abandoned. All Mustang V-8s with a five-speed manual transmission also added an up-shift indicator light.

Mustang SVO — (Turbo Four): SVO, the "Ultimate Mustang," carried a computer-controlled 200-hp 2.3-liter four with an intercooled turbocharger and multi-port fuel injection. A five-speed transmission with a Hurst shifter that offered short, quick throws was standard. Disc brakes were employed all around.

The VIN was stamped on an aluminum tab riveted to the instrument panel and was viewable through the windshield. The first symbol indicated the country of origin: 1=U.S.A. The second symbol identified the manufacturer: F=Ford. The third symbol indicated the vehicle type: A=passenger car. The fourth symbol revealed the restraint system: B=active belts. The fifth symbol indicated the division: P=Ford passenger car. The sixth and seventh symbols indicated the body style: 26=Coupe, 27=Convertible and 28=Hatchback. The eighth symbol was the engine: A=140-cid (2.3-liter) SOHC four-cylinder one-barrel, W=Turbo 140-cid (2.3-liter) SOHC turbocharged four-cylinder SVO with electronic fuel injection, 3=232-cid (3.8-liter) V-6 with electronic fuel injection and M=302-cid (5.0-liter) H.O. V-8 with electronic fuel injection. The ninth symbol was a check digit. The 10th symbol indicated the model year: G=1986. The 11th symbol indicated the assembly plant:

1986 Ford Mustang GT 5.0-Liter Convertible (JG)

F=Dearborn, Michigan. The last six digits were the unit's production numbers, beginning at 100001 and going up.

Mustang LX (Four)

Model No.	Body/ Style No.	Body Type & Seating	Factory Price	Shipping Weight	Production Total
26	66B	2-dr. Coupe-4P	$7,189	2,601 lbs.	Note 1
28	61B	3-dr. Hatchback-4P	$7,744	2,661 lbs.	Note 1

Mustang LX (V-6)

26	66B	2-dr. Coupe-4P	$8,153	2,722 lbs.	Note 1
28	61B	3-dr. Hatchback-4P	$8,708	2,782 lbs.	Note 1
27	66B	2-dr. Convertible-4P	$12,821	2,908 lbs.	Note 1

Note 1: The 302-cid four-barrel V-8 engine cost $1,120 more than the V-6 and was $106 more on the LX convertible.

Mustang GT (V-8)

| 28 | 61B | 3-dr. Hatchback-4P | $10,691 | 2,976 lbs. | Note 2 |
| 27 | 66B | 2-dr. Convertible-4P | $14,523 | 3,103 lbs. | Note 2 |

Mustang GT (V-8)

| 28/939 | 61B | 3-dr. Hatchback-4P | $15,272 | 3,028 lbs. | Note 2 |

Note 2: Ford reported production of 84,774 coupes, 22,946 convertibles and 117,690 hatchbacks.

Engines:

Four: Inline, overhead cam. Cast-iron block and head. Displacement: 140-cid (2.3 liters). B & S: 3.78 x 3.13 in. Compression ratio: 9.0:1 Brake hp: 88 at 4400 rpm Torque: 122 lbs.-ft. at 2400 rpm. Five main bearings. Hydraulic valve lifters. Carburetor: Carter YFA one-barrel. Code A.

SVO Turbo Four: Inline, overhead cam, turbocharged, EFI. Cast-iron block and head. Displacement: 140-cid (2.3 liters). B & S: 3.78 x 3.13 in. Compression ratio: 8.0:1. Brake hp: 205 at 5000 rpm. Torque: 210 lbs.-ft. at 3000 rpm. Five main bearings. Hydraulic valve lifters. Induction: Electronic fuel injection (TBI). Code W.

V-6: 90-degree, overhead valve. Cast-iron block and aluminum head. Displacement: 232-cid (3.8 liters). B & S: 3. 80 x 3.40 in. Compression ratio: 8.7:1. Brake hp: 120 at 3600 rpm. Torque: 205 lbs.-ft. at 1600 rpm. Four main bearings. Hydraulic valve lifters. Induction: Electronic fuel injection (TBI). Code 3.

5.0-Liter HO V-8: 90-degree, overhead valve. Cast-iron block and head. Displacement: 302-cid (5.0 liters). B & S: 4.00 x 3.00 in. Compression ratio: 8.3:1. Brake hp: 200 at 4000 rpm Torque: 285 lbs.-ft. at 3000 rpm. Five main bearings. Hydraulic valve lifters. Induction: Electronic fuel injection. Code M.

Chassis:

Wheelbase: 100.5 in. Overall length: 179.3 in. and 180.8 in., SVO. Height: 52.1 in. (convertible 51.9 in). Width: 69.1 in. Front tread: 56.6 in. and 57.8 in., SVO. Rear tread: 57.0 in. and 58.3 in., SVO. Tires: P195/75R14 steel-belted radial with black sidewall, GT and P225/60VR15, GT and P225/50VR16 "Gatorback," SVO.

Technical:

Four-speed manual (floor shift) standard on four-cylinder. Five-speed manual standard on turbo and V-8. Select Shift three-speed automatic optional on four-cylinder, standard on V-6. Gear ratios (not available). Gear ratios: (1st) 2.47:1, (2nd) 1.47:1, (3rd) 1.00:1, (Reverse) 2.11:1. V-6 three-speed automatic: (1st) 2.46:1, (2nd) 1.46:1, (3rd) 1.00:1, (Reverse) 2.19:1. Four-speed overdrive automatic available with V-8: (1st) 2.40:1, (2nd) 1.47:1, (3rd) 1.00:1, (4th) 0.67:1, (Reverse) 2.00:1. Standard final drive ratio: (four) 3.08:1 with four-speed manual, 3.27:1 with automatic, (V-6) 2.73:1, (V 8) 2.73:1 with five-speed manual, 3.27:1 with four-speed automatic, (turbo) 3.73:1. Steering: Rack and pinion, power-assisted. Front Suspension: Modified MacPherson struts with lower control arms and stabilizer bar, SVO added adjustable gas-pressurized shocks. Rear Suspension: Rigid axle w/four-bar link and coil springs, GT/SVO added an anti-sway bar and dual shocks on each side. Brakes: Front disc, rear drum (power-assisted) except SVO, four-wheel disc brakes. Ignition: Electronic. Body construction: Unibody. Fuel tank: 15.4 gallons.

Options:

232-cid V-6 in LX ($454). 302-cid V-8 package ($1,120). 302-cid V-8 in LX convertible ($106). Five-speed manual transmission in LX ($124). Three-speed automatic transmission in LX ($510), but standard in convertible). Four-speed overdrive automatic transmission in LX ($746). Four-speed overdrive automatic transmission in GT ($622). Engine block heater ($18). Heavy-duty battery ($27). California emission system ($102). High-altitude option (NC). SVO competition preparation package with equipment deleted ($1,451 credit). Light and convenience group ($55). Power lock group ($182 to $215). Air conditioning ($762). Electric

1986 Ford Mustang GT 5.0-Liter Coupe (PH)

1986 Ford Mustang LX 5.0-Liter California Highway Patrol car (BB)

rear defroster ($145). Fingertip speed control ($176). Power windows ($207). Power windows in convertible ($282). Tinted glass ($115). Tilt steering wheel in LX ($115). AM/FM stereo radio with cassette player in LX or GT ($148). Electronic seek/scan AM/FM stereo with cassette in LX or GT ($300). Premium sound system ($138), Radio delete ($148 credit). T-Roof for hatchback ($1,100). Flip-up open air roof for hatchback ($315). Lower charcoal accent paint ($116). Single wing spoiler for SVO (NC). Console with clock and systems monitor ($191). Vinyl bucket seats in LX ($29). Articulated leather sport bucket seats in LX convertible ($807). Articulated leather sport bucket seats in GT convertible ($429). Leather seat upholstery in SVO ($189). Wire wheel covers for LX ($98). Styled steel wheels ($178). P205/75R14 white sidewall tires ($109) P225/60VR15 tires on cast-aluminum wheels ($665).

History:

Introduced: October 3, 1985. Model-year production: 224,410. Total production for the U.S. market of 198,358 Mustangs included 107,340 four-cylinder, 38.422 sixes and 52,596 V-8 engines. Calendar-year production: 177,737. Calendar-year sales by U.S. dealers: 167,699. Model-year sales by U.S. dealers: 175,598. Mustang was the only Ford model to show a sales increase for 1986. Mercury's similar Capri would not return for another year, but Mustang was prepared to carry on in ordinary and high-performance trim. Turbocharging forced a hefty amount of horsepower out of SVO's small four-cylinder engine,

1987 Mustang

Mustang LX — (Four and V-8) Mercury's Capri was out of the lineup after 1986, leaving Mustang as Ford's sole pony car. The turbocharged SVO Mustang also departed, leaving only the LX and GT models. The V-6 engine was also gone. Ford's pony car got a fresh look for 1987 with a significant restyling — the first one since its debut in 1979. Changes included new front and rear fascias, a switch to aero headlights and the addition of substantial lower body side moldings. The GT had a lower air dam with integrated fog lamps and air scoops, as well as Mustang GT lettering formed into its flared rocker panel moldings and rear fascia. On the inside, all Mustangs had a new instrument panel with a more European took and a new two-spoke steering wheel. Multi-point fuel injection replaced a carburetor on the base four-cylinder engine. A five-speed manual gearbox was now standard, with four-speed overdrive automatic optional.

1987 Ford Mustang LX 5.0-Liter Coupe (PH)

1987 Ford Mustang GT 5.0-Liter Convertible (PH)

Mustang GT — (V-8) The GT hatchback also had a large spoiler that held the required high-mounted stop lamp. Wide taillights on the GT were covered by a louver-like slotted appliqué. The V-8 got a boost from 200 to 225 hp.

VIN:

The VIN was stamped on an aluminum tab riveted to the instrument panel and was viewable through the windshield. The first symbol indicated the country of origin: 1=U.S.A. The second symbol identified the manufacturer: F=Ford. The third symbol indicated the vehicle type: A=passenger car. The fourth symbol was the restraint system: B=active belts. The fifth symbol indicated the division: P=Ford passenger car. The sixth and seventh symbols indicated the body style: 40=LX Coupe, 41=LX Hatchback, 42=GT Hatchback, 44=LX Convertible and 45=GT Convertible. The eighth symbol indicated the engine: A=140-cid (2.3-liter) SOHC four-cylinder with electronic fuel injection and M=302-cid (5.0-liter) V-8 with electronic fuel injection. The ninth symbol was a check digit. The 10th symbol indicated the model year: H=1987. The 11th symbol indicated the assembly plant: F=Dearborn, Michigan. The last six digits were the unit's production number, beginning at 100001 and going up, at each of the assembly plants.

Mustang LX (Four)

Model No.	Body/ Style No.	Body Type and Seating	Factory Price	Shipping Weight	Production Total
40	66B	2-dr. Coupe-4P	$ 8,043	2,724 lbs.	Note 1
41	61B	3-dr. Hatchback-4P	$ 8,474	2,782 lbs.	Note 1
44	66B	2-dr. Convertible-4P	$12,840	2,921 lbs.	Note 1

Mustang LX (V-8)

40	66B	2-dr. Coupe-4P	$ 9,928	3,000 lbs.	Note 1
41	61B	3-dr. Hatchback-4P	$10,359	3,058 lbs.	Note 1
44	66B	2-dr. Convertible-4P	$14,725	3,197 lbs.	Note 1

Note: The 302-cid four-barrel V-8 engine cost $1,120 more than the V-6 and $106 more on the LX convertible.

Mustang GT (V-8)

42	61B	3-dr. Hatchback-4P	$11,836	3,080 lbs.	Note 1
45	66B	2-dr. Convertible-4P	$15,724	3,214 lbs.	Note 1

Note 1: Ford reported total production 43,257 coupes, 94,441 hatchbacks and 32,074 convertibles.

Engines:

Four: Inline, overhead cam. Cast-iron block and head. Displacement: 140-cid (2.3 liters). B & S: 3.78 x 3.13 in. Compression ratio: 9.5:1 Brake hp: 90 at 3800 rpm. Torque: 130 lbs.-ft. at 2800 rpm. Five main bearings. Hydraulic valve lifters. Induction: Port fuel injection. Code: A.

5.0-Liter HO V-8: 90-degree, overhead valve. Cast-iron block and head. Displacement: 302-cid (5.0 liters). B & S: 4.00 x 3.00 in. Compression ratio: 9.2:1. Brake hp: 225 at 4000 rpm. Torque: 300 lbs.-ft. at 3200 rpm. Five main bearings. Hydraulic valve lifters. Induction: Sequential fuel injection. Code: M.

Chassis:

Wheelbase: 100.5 in. Overall length: 179.6 in. Height: 52.1 in. (convertible 51.9 in. Width: 69.1 in. Front tread: 56.6 in. Rear tread: 57.0 in. Standard tires: P195/75-R14 steel-belted radial with black sidewall. Tires, GT: P225/50VR16 "Gatorback."

Technical:

Five-speed manual (floor shift) standard. Four-speed overdrive automatic available. Rack and pinion steering, power-assisted. Modified MacPherson strut front suspension with lower control arms and stabilizer bar (gas shocks on GT). Rigid rear axle with four links and coil springs (stabilizer bar on GT). Brakes: Front disc, rear drum (power-assisted). Body construction: Unibody. Fuel tank: 15.4 gallons.

Options:

5.0-liter V-8 package for LX ($1,885). Four-speed overdrive automatic

1987 Ford Mustang GT 5.0-Liter Hatchback (OCW)

transmission ($515). Climate Control Group including air conditioning, heavy-duty battery, rear defogger and tinted glass for LX coupe with four-speed manual transmission ($1,005). Climate Control Group including air conditioning, heavy-duty battery, rear defogger and tinted glass for LX coupe with V-8 ($978). Climate Control Group including air conditioning, heavy-duty battery, rear defogger and tinted glass for LX convertible with four-sped manual transmission ($740). Climate Control Group including air conditioning, heavy-duty battery, rear defogger and tinted glass for LX coupe with V-8 ($713). Climate Control Group including air conditioning, heavy-duty battery, rear defogger and tinted glass for GT coupe ($858). Climate Control Group including air conditioning, heavy-duty battery, rear defogger and tinted glass for GT convertible ($713). Air conditioning ($788). Heavy-duty battery ($27). Rear defogger ($145). Tinted glass ($120). Climate Control Group with Premium Sound instead of rear defogger in LX coupes with four-speed manual transmission ($1,028). Climate Control Group including air conditioning, heavy-duty battery, rear defogger and tinted glass for LX coupes with V-8 ($1,001). Climate Control Group including air conditioning, heavy-duty battery, rear defogger and tinted glass for LX convertible with four-speed manual transmission ($908). Climate Control Group including air conditioning, heavy-duty battery, rear defogger and tinted glass for LX convertible with GT V-8 ($881). Climate Control Group with Custom Equipment Group and Premium Sound instead of rear defogger for LX coupes with four-speed manual transmission ($860). Climate Control Group with Custom Equipment Group and Premium Sound instead of rear defogger for LX coupes with V-8 ($833). Climate Control Group with Custom Equipment Group and Premium Sound instead of rear defogger for LX convertible with four-speed manual transmission ($740). Climate Control Group with Custom Equipment Group and Premium Sound instead of rear defogger for LX convertible with GT V-8 ($713). Custom Equipment Group including Graphic Equalizer, dual power mirrors, lighted visor mirrors, tilt steering column and power windows for LX coupe ($624). Custom Equipment Group including Graphic Equalizer, dual power mirrors, lighted visor mirrors, tilt steering column and power windows for LX convertible ($538). Custom Equipment Group including Graphic Equalizer, dual power mirrors, lighted visor mirrors, tilt steering column and power windows for GT coupe ($500). Custom Equipment Group including Graphic Equalizer, dual power mirrors, lighted visor mirrors, tilt steering column and power windows for GT convertible ($414). Graphic equalizer ($218). Dual power mirrors ($60). Lighted visor mirrors ($100). Tilt steering column for LX ($124). Power windows in coupe ($222). Power windows in convertible ($296). Power Lock Group includes remote fuel filler and deck lid/hatch releases, AM/FM radio with cassette, speed control and styled road wheels for LX with V-8 ($735). Power Lock Group includes remote fuel filler and deck lid/hatch releases, AM/FM radio with cassette, speed control and styled road wheels for GT ($519). Power Lock Group for LX ($244). Power Lock Group for GT ($206). AM/FM Stereo Radio with cassette ($137). Speed control ($176). Styled road wheels on LX ($178). Body side molding insert stripe ($49). AM/FM Stereo delete ($206 credit). Flip-up/open-air sun roof ($355). T-Roof for LX ($1737). T-roof for LX with Climate Control Group ($1,667). T-roof

for LX with Special Value Group ($1,543). T-roof for LX with Custom Equipment Group ($1,505). T-roof for GT ($1,608). T-roof for GT with Special Value Group ($1,401). T-roof for GT with Custom Equipment Group ($1,341). Premium Sound System ($168). Wire wheel covers on LX ($98). Leather articulated sport seats for LX convertible ($780). Leather articulated sport seats for GT convertible ($415).

History:

Introduced: October 2, 1986. Model-year production: 159,145. Calendar-year production: 214,153. Calendar -ear sales by U.S. dealers: 172,602.

1988 Mustang

Mustang LX — (Four and V-8) In the wake of the 1987 restyling, Mustang entered this model year with minimal change. As in 1987, two power plants were available for the Ford pony car: a 2.3-liter four-cylinder engine rated 90 hp. A five-speed manual floor shift was standard, with four-speed overdrive automatic optional.

Mustang GT — (V-8) The GT hatchback also had a large spoiler that held the required high-mounted stop lamp. Wide taillights on the GT were covered by a louver-like slotted appliqué. The V-8 was standard.

VIN:

The VIN was stamped on an aluminum tab riveted to the instrument panel and was viewable through the windshield. The first symbol indicated the country of origin: 1=U.S.A. The second symbol was the manufacturer: F=Ford. The third symbol indicated the vehicle type: A=passenger car. The fourth symbol revealed the restraint system: B=active belts. The fifth symbol was the division: P=Ford passenger car. The sixth and seventh symbols indicated the body style: 40=LX Coupe, 41=LX Hatchback, 42=GT Hatchback, 44=LX Convertible and 45=GT Convertible. The eighth symbol indicated the engine: A=140-cid (2.3-liter) SOHC four-cylinder with electronic fuel injection and M=302-cid (5.0-liter) V-8 with electronic fuel injection. The ninth symbol was a check digit. The 10th symbol indicated the model year: J=1988. The 11th symbol indicated the assembly plant: F=Dearborn, Michigan. The last six digits were the unit's production number, beginning at 100001 and going up, at each of the assembly plants.

Mustang LX (Four)

Model No.	Body/ Style No.	Body Type and Seating	Factory Price	Shipping Weight	Production Total
40	66B	2-dr. Coupe-4P	$8,726	2,751 lbs.	Note 1
41	61B	3-dr. Hatchback-4P	$9,221	2,818 lbs.	Note 1
44	66B	2-dr. Convertible-4P	$13,702	2,953 lbs.	Note 1

Mustang LX (V-8)

40	66B	2-dr. Coupe-4P	$10,611	3,037 lbs.	Note 1
41	61B	3-dr. Hatchback-4P	$11,106	3,105 lbs.	Note 1
44	66B	2-dr. Convertible-4P	$15,587	3,209 lbs.	Note 1

Mustang GT (V-8)

42	61B	3-dr. Hatchback-4P	$12,745	3,193 lbs.	Note 1
45	66B	2-dr. Convertible-4P	$16,610	3,341 lbs.	Note 1

Note 1: Ford reported total production 53,221 coupes, 125,930 hatchbacks, and 32,074 convertibles.

Engines:

Four: Inline, overhead cam. Cast-iron block and head. Displacement: 140-cid (2.3 liters). B & S: 3.78 x 3.13 in. Compression ratio: 9.5:1 Brake hp: 90 at 3800 rpm Torque: 130 lbs.-ft. at 2800 rpm Five main bearings. Hydraulic valve lifters. Induction: Port fuel injection. Code: A.

5.0-Liter HO V-8: 90-degree, overhead valve. Cast-iron block and head. Displacement: 302-cid (5.0 liters). B & S: 4.00 x 3.00 in. Compression ratio: 9.5:1. Brake hp: 225 at 4200 rpm Torque: 300 lbs.-ft. at 3200 rpm. Five main bearings. Hydraulic valve lifters. Induction: Sequential fuel injection. Code: M.

Chassis:

Wheelbase: 100.5 in. Overall length: 179.6 in. Height: 52.1 in. (convertible 51.9 inches). Width: 69.1 in. Front tread: 56.6 in. Rear tread: 57.0 in. Tires: P195/75R14 steel-belted radial with black sidewall and P225/60VR16 Goodyear Eagle GT "Gatorback," GT.

Technical:

Five-speed manual (floor shift) standard. Four-speed overdrive automatic available. Rack and pinion, power-assisted steering. Modified MacPherson struts front suspension with lower control arms and stabilizer bar (gas shocks on GT). Rigid rear axle with four links and coil springs (stabilizer bar on GT). Front disc, rear drum (power-assisted)

1988 Ford Mustang LX Convertible (PH)

1988 Ford Mustang GT 5.0-Liter Convertible (OCW)

1988 Ford Mustang GT Hatchback (OCW)

brakes. Unibody. 15.4 gallon fuel tank.

1989 Ford Mustang LX 5.0-Liter Coupe (OCW)

1989 Ford Mustang LX 5.0-Liter Hatchback (OCW)

Options:

5.0-liter V-8 package for LX ($1885). Four-speed overdrive automatic transmission ($515). Preferred equipment packages for LX coupe or hatchback with four-speed manual transmission (NC). Preferred equipment packages for LX coupe or hatchback with V-8 ($615). Preferred equipment packages for LX convertible with four-speed manual transmission (NC). Preferred equipment packages for LX convertible with V-8 ($555). Preferred equipment packages for GT Hatchback ($615). Preferred equipment packages for GT Convertible ($555). Manual control air conditioning ($788). Power side Windows ($222). Tilt steering wheel ($124). Dual illuminated visor-vanity mirror ($100). Custom Equipment Group for LX ($1,034). Custom Equipment Group for LX Convertible ($934). Custom Equipment Group for GT ($910). Custom Equipment Group for GT convertible ($810). Body side molding insert stripe ($49). Rear window defroster ($145). Graphic equalizer ($218). Power lock group ($237). Dual electric remote-control mirrors ($60). Electronically-tuned AM/FM radio with cassette ($137). Flip-up open air roof ($355). T-roof for LX ($1,800). T-roof for LX with Preferred Equipment package. ($1,505. T-roof for LX with Custom equipment group ($1,459). T-roof for LX with Custom Equipment group and Preferred Equipment package ($1,163). T-roof for GT ($1,659). T-roof for LX with Preferred Equipment package ($1,363). T-roof for LX with Custom Equipment group ($1,437). T-roof for LX with Custom Equipment group and Preferred Equipment package ($1,141). Premium sound system ($168). Speed control ($182). Wire style wheel covers ($178). Styled road wheels ($178). Front license plate bracket (NC). Engine block heater ($18). California emission system ($99). High-altitude emissions system (NC). Lower titanium accent treatment exterior paint for GT (NC). Leather articulated Sport seats for LX convertible ($780). Leather articulated Sport seats for GT convertible ($415). Vinyl seat trim ($37). P195/75R14 white sidewall tires ($82).

History:

Introduced: October 1, 1987. Model-year production: 211,225 (total). Calendar-year production: 200,089. Calendar-year sales by U.S.

1989 Mustang

Mustang LX — (Four and V-8): Ford's pony car entered the 1989 marketplace with little change, except that the LX, when equipped with the available V-8 engine, was now called "LX 5.0L Sport." Once again, two power plants were available for Ford's pony car. When installed in the LX, the V-8 package included articulated sport seats. The convertible model now had standard power windows and door locks.

Mustang GT — (V-8): The GT had the V-8, aero body components and articulated sport seats among its standard equipment features. The convertible had standard power windows and door locks.

VIN:

The VIN was stamped on an aluminum tab riveted to the instrument panel and viewable through the windshield. The first symbol indicated the country of origin: 1=U.S.A. The second symbol identified the manufacturer: F=Ford. The third symbol indicated the vehicle type: A=passenger car. The fourth symbol revealed the restraint system: B=active belts. The fifth symbol indicated the division: P=Ford passenger car. The sixth and seventh symbols indicated the body style: 40=LX Coupe, 41=LX Hatchback, 42=GT Hatchback, 44=LX Convertible and 45=GT Convertible. The eighth symbol indicated the engine: A=140-cid (2.3-liter) SOHC four-cylinder with electronic fuel injection and M=302-cid (5.0-liter) V-8 with electronic fuel injection. The ninth symbol was a check digit. The 10th symbol indicated the model year: K=1989. The 11th symbol revealed the assembly plant: F=Dearborn, Michigan. The last six digits were the unit's production number, beginning at 100001 and going up.

Mustang LX (Four)

Model No.	Body/ Style No.	Body Type and Seating	Factory Price	Shipping Weight	Production Total
40	66B	2-dr. Coupe-4P	$9,050	2,754 lbs.	Note 1
41	61B	3-dr. Hatchback-4P	$9,556	2,819 lbs.	Note 1
44	66B	2-dr. Convertible-4P	$14,140	2,966 lbs.	Note 1

Mustang LX (V-8)

40	66B	2-dr. Coupe-4P	$11,410	3,045 lbs.	Note 1
41	61B	3-dr. Hatchback-4P	$12,265	3,110 lbs.	Note 1
44	66B	2-dr. Convertible-4P	$17,001	3,257 lbs.	Note 1

Mustang GT (V-8)

42	61B	3-dr. Hatchback-4P	$13,272	3,194 lbs.	Note 1
45	66B	2-dr. Convertible-4P	$17,512	3,333 lbs.	Note 1

Note 1: Ford reported total production 50,560 coupes, 116,965 hatchbacks, and 42,244 convertibles.

Engines:

Four: Inline, overhead cam. Cast-iron block and head. Displacement: 140-cid (2.3 liters). B & S: 3.78 x 3.13 in. Compression ratio: 9.5:1 Brake hp: 90 at 3800 rpm Torque: 130 lbs.-ft. at 2800 rpm Five main bearings. Hydraulic valve lifters. Induction: Port fuel injection. Code: A.

5.0-Liter HO V-8: 90-degree, overhead valve. Cast-iron block and head. Displacement: 302-cid (5.0 liters). B & S: 4.00 x 3.00 in. Compression ratio: 9.5:1. Brake hp: 225 at 4200 rpm Torque: 300 lbs.-ft. at 3200 rpm. Five main bearings. Hydraulic valve lifters. Induction: Sequential fuel injection. Code: M.

Chassis:

Wheelbase: 100.5 in. Overall length: 179.6 in. Height: 52.1 in. (convertible 51.9 inches). Width: 69.1 in. Front tread: 56.6 in. Rear tread: 57.0 in. Tires: P195/70R14 steel-belted radial with black sidewall and 225/60VR15, GT and LX with V-8.

Technical:

Five-speed manual (floor shift) standard. Four-speed overdrive automatic available. Rack and pinion, power-assisted steering. Modified MacPherson struts front suspension with lower control arms and stabilizer bar (gas shocks on GT). Rigid rear axle with four links and coil springs (stabilizer bar on GT). Front disc, rear drum (power-assisted)

1989 Ford Mustang GT 5.0-Liter Hatchback (OCW)

brakes. Unibody. 15.4 gallon fuel tank.

Options:

Four-speed overdrive auto trans. ($515). Preferred equipment package for LX with four-cylinder engine. Special value group. Power door locks group. Dual electric remote-control mirrors. AM/FM radio with cassette player and clock. Speed control. Styled road wheels. Power side windows for LX coupe or hatchback. Power side windows for LX convertible. Manual control air conditioning. Dual illuminated visor mirrors. Tilt steering wheel. Premium sound system for coupe or hatchback ($1,006). Premium sound system for convertible ($487). Body side molding insert stripe ($61). Rear window defroster ($150). Flip-up open air roof ($355). Wire style wheel covers ($193). California emission system ($100). High-altitude emissions system (NC). Lower titanium accent treatment for exterior paint on GT (NC). Leather articulated sport seats in LX convertible ($855). Leather articulated sport seats in LX V-8 sport convertible or GT convertible ($489). Vinyl seat trim ($37). Front license plate bracket (NC). P195/75R14 white sidewall Tires ($82).

History:

Introduced: October 6, 1988. Model-year production: 209,769. Calendar-

1990 Mustang

Mustang LX — (Four and V-8): Safety led Mustang into 1990, as a driver's airbag and rear shoulder belts became standard on all models. Otherwise, the familiar rear-drive pony car continued as before, for its 12th season in this form. Body styles and power trains were the same as prior years: coupe, hatchback and convertible with 2.3-liter four or 5.0-liter V-8. No longer did the Mustang interior include a tilt steering column or console armrest, but the door panels now had map pockets. The LX 5.0L, with V-8 engine, came with the heftier suspension and bigger tires from the GT, but lacked the GT's spoilers and air dams. Clear coat paint was now optional, as was leather interior trim for the hatchback with the V-8. The convertible included standard power windows and door locks.

Mustang GT — (V-8): The GT had the V-8, aero body components like spoilers and air dams and articulated sport seats among its standard equipment features. It also had a heftier suspension.

VIN:

The VIN was stamped on an aluminum tab riveted to the instrument panel and was viewable through the windshield. The first symbol indicated the country of origin: 1=U.S.A. The second symbol identified the manufacturer: F=Ford. The third symbol indicated the vehicle type: A=passenger car. The fourth symbol indicated the restraint system: C=air bags with active belts. The fifth symbol indicates the division: P=Ford passenger car. The sixth and seventh symbols were the body style: 40=LX Coupe, 41=LX Hatchback, 42=GT Hatchback, 44=LX Convertible and 45=GT Convertible. The eighth symbol indicated the engine: A=140-cid (2.3-liter) SOHC four-cylinder with electronic fuel injection and M=302-cid (5.0-liter) V-8 with electronic fuel injection. The ninth symbol was a check digit. The 10th symbol indicated the model year: L=1990. The 11th symbol showed the assembly plant: F=Dearborn, Michigan. The last six digits were the unit production numbers beginning at 100001 and going up.

1990 Ford Mustang LX 5.0-Liter Hatchback (OCW)

Mustang LX (Four)

Model No.	Body/Style No.	Body Type and Seating	Factory Price	Shipping Weight	Production Total
40	66B	2-dr. Coupe-4P	$ 9,638	2,634 lbs.	Note 1
41	61B	3-dr. Hatchback-4P	$10,144	2,634 lbs.	Note 1
44	66B	2-dr. Convertible-4P	$14,495	2,871 lbs.	Note 1

Mustang LX (V-8)

40	66B	2-dr. Coupe-4P	$12,107	2,715 lbs.	Note 1
41	61B	3-dr. Hatchback-4P	$12,950	2,715 lbs.	Note 1
44	66B	2-dr. Convertible-4P	$17,681	2,952 lbs.	Note 1

Mustang GT (V-8)

42	61B	3-dr. Hatchback-4P	$13,929	3,065 lbs.	Note 1
45	66B	2-dr. Convertible-4P	$18,303	3,213 lbs.	Note 1

Note 1: Ford reported total production 22,503 coupes, 78,728 hatchbacks, and 26,958 convertibles.

Engines:

Four: Inline, overhead cam. Cast-iron block and head. Displacement: 140-cid (2.3 liters). B & S: 3.78 x 3.13 in. Compression ratio: 9.5:1 Brake hp: 88 at 4000 rpm Torque: 132 lbs.-ft. at 2600 rpm Five main bearings. Hydraulic valve lifters. Induction: Port fuel injection. Code A.

5.0-Liter HO V-8: 90-degree, overhead valve. Cast-iron block and head. Displacement: 302-cid (5.0 liters). B & S: 4.00 x 3.00 in. Compression ratio: 9.5:1. Brake hp: 225 at 4200 rpm Torque: 300 lbs.-ft. at 3200 rpm. Five main bearings. Hydraulic valve lifters. Induction: Sequential fuel injection. Code M.

Chassis:

Wheelbase: 100.5 in. Overall length: 179.6 in. Height: 52.1 in. Width: 68.3 in. Front tread: 56.6 in. Rear tread: 57.0 in. Tires: P195/75R14 steel-belted radial with black sidewall and P225/60VR15, GT and LX with V-8.

Technical:

Five-speed manual (floor shift) standard. Four-speed overdrive automatic available. Rack and pinion, power-assisted steering. Modified MacPherson struts front suspension with lower control arms and stabilizer bar (gas shocks on GT). Rigid rear axle with four links and coil springs (stabilizer bar on GT). Front disc, rear drum (power-assisted) brakes. Unibody. 15.4 gallon fuel tank.

Options:

Four-speed overdrive automatic transmission ($539). Preferred equipment package for LX four-cylinder includes special value group, power lock group, dual electric remote mirrors, AM/FM radio with cassette player and clock, speed control, styled road wheels and power side windows (no charge). Preferred equipment package for LX V-8 Sport GT includes special value group, power lock group, dual electric remote mirrors, AM/FM radio with cassette player and clock, speed control, styled road wheels, power side windows, custom equipment group, air conditioning, dual illuminated visor mirrors, tilt wheel, premium sound system for the coupe or hatchback ($1,003). Preferred equipment package for LX V-8 Sport GT includes special value group, power lock group, dual electric remote mirrors, AM/FM radio with cassette player and clock, speed control, styled road wheels, power side windows, custom equipment group, air conditioning, dual illuminated visor mirrors, tilt wheel, premium sound system for the convertible ($496). Group options including custom equipment group, dual illuminated visor mirrors, tilt wheel and premium sound system for four-cylinder LX coupe or hatchback ($907). Group

1990 Ford Mustang LX 5.0-Liter Convertible (OCW)

1990 Ford Mustang GT 5.0-Liter Hatchback (OCW)

1990 Ford Mustang GT 5.0-Liter Convertible (OCW)

1991 Ford Mustang LX 5.0-Liter Convertible (PH)

options including custom equipment group, dual illuminated visor mirrors, tilt wheel and premium sound system for four-cylinder LX convertible ($807). Rear window defroster ($150). Flip-up open-air roof ($355). Wire style wheel covers ($193). Premium sound system with six premium speakers, 4-channel amplifier and 80 watts ($168). California emission system ($100). High-altitude emissions (no charge). Clear coat exterior paint ($91). Lower titanium accent treatment for GT ($159). Leather seating surfaces on articulated sport seats ($489). Vinyl seat trim ($37). Front license plate bracket (no charge). Engine block heater ($20). P195/75R-14 white sidewall tires ($82).

History:

Model-year production: 128,189. Calendar-year sales by U.S. dealers: 124,135. Model-year sales by U.S. dealers: 120,486.

1991 Mustang

Mustang LX — (Four and V-8): The 1991 Mustang was available in two series: Mustang LX and GT. A new twin-plug version of the 2.3-liter engine improved base Mustang horsepower from 86 to 105 for heightened performance. Power train availability in LX models included this 2.3-liter electronically fuel-injected engine and the 5.0-liter HO (High Output) engine. Both were available with either five-speed manual (standard) or four-speed automatic (optional) transmissions. The LX 5.0-liter models got new, upsized 16-inch five-spoke aluminum wheels. New P225/55ZR16 all-season performance tires were made standard on the LX 5.0-liter. The convertible received a lowered top-down stack height for a cleaner, more attractive appearance. For interior changes, new cloth seat materials on the 2.3-liter LX models were added. Other improvements included vinyl door trim panel inserts added to power window-equipped units. An articulated sport seat was made standard on the LX 5.0-liter sedan. Options added for 1991 included a cargo tie down net, front floor mats, a graphic equalizer, 15-inch cast-aluminum wheels with P205/65R15 black sidewall tires on the 2.3-liter LX and 14-inch styled road wheels. A driver's-side airbag supplemental restraint system and rear-passenger manual lap/shoulder belts were now included as standard equipment.

Mustang GT — (V-8): The GT came standard with the V-8 engine, aero body components, spoilers, air dams and articulated sport seats. It also had a heavier-duty suspension. GT models also got the new upsized 16-inch five-spoke aluminum wheels. The new P225/55ZR16 all-season performance tires were optional on the GT.

VIN:

The VIN was stamped on an aluminum tab riveted to the instrument panel and was viewable through the windshield. The first symbol indicated the country of origin: 1=U.S.A. The second symbol identified the manufacturer: F=Ford. The third symbol showed the vehicle type: A=passenger car. The fourth symbol revealed the restraint system: C=air bags with active belts. The fifth symbol indicates the division: P=Ford passenger car. The sixth and seventh symbols indicated the body style: 40=LX Coupe, 41=LX Hatchback, 42=GT Hatchback, 44=LX Convertible and 45=GT Convertible. The eighth symbol revealed the engine: S=140-cid (2.3-liter) SOHC four-cylinder with electronic fuel injection and E=302-cid (5.0-liter)

V-8 with electronic fuel injection. The ninth symbol was a check digit. The 10th symbol indicated the model year: M=1991. The 11th symbol indicated the assembly plant: F=Dearborn, Michigan. The last six digits were the unit production numbers beginning at 100001 and going up.

Mustang LX (Four)

Model No.	Body/ Style No.	Body Type and Seating	Factory Price	Shipping Weight	Production Total
40	66B	2-dr. Coupe-4P	$10,157	2,759 lbs.	Note 1
41	61B	3-dr. Hatchback-4P	$10,663	2,824 lbs.	Note 1
44	66B	2-dr. Convertible-4P	$16,222	2,960 lbs.	Note 1

Mustang LX (V-8)

40	66B	2-dr. Coupe-4P	$13,270	3,037 lbs.	Note 1
41	61B	3-dr. Hatchback-4P	$14,055	3,102 lbs.	Note 1
44	66B	2-dr. Convertible-4P	$19,242	3,238 lbs.	Note 1

Mustang GT (V-8)

42	61B	3-dr. Hatchback-4P	$15,034	3,191 lbs.	Note 1
45	66B	2-dr. Convertible-4P	$19,864	3,327 lbs.	Note 1

Note 1: Ford reported total production 19,447 coupes, 57,777 hatchbacks, and 21,513 convertibles.

Engines:

Four: Inline, overhead cam. Cast-iron block and head. Displacement: 140-cid (2.3 liters). B & S: 3.78 x 3.12 in. Compression ratio: 9.5:1 Brake hp: 105 at 4600 rpm Torque: 135 lbs.-ft. at 2600 rpm Five main bearings. Hydraulic valve lifters. Induction: Port fuel injection. Code: S.

5.0-Liter HO V-8: 90-degree, overhead valve. Cast-iron block and head. Displacement: 302-cid (5.0 liters). B & S: 4.00 x 3.00 in. Compression ratio: 9.0:1. Brake horsepower 225 at 4200 rpm Torque: 300 lbs.-ft. at 3200 rpm. Five main bearings. Hydraulic valve lifters. Induction: Sequential fuel injection. Code: E.

Chassis:

Wheelbase: 100.5 in. Overall length: 179.6 in. Height: 52.1 in. Width: 68.3 in. Front tread: 56.6 in. Rear tread: 57.0 in. Tires: P195/75R14 steel-belted radial with black sidewall and P225/55ZR16, GT and LX with V-8.

Technical:

Five-speed manual (floor shift) standard. Four-speed overdrive automatic available. Rack and pinion, power-assisted steering. Modified MacPherson struts front suspension with lower control arms and stabilizer bar (gas shocks on GT). Rigid rear axle with four links and coil springs (stabilizer bar on GT). Front disc, rear drum (power-assisted) brakes. Unibody. 15.4 gallon fuel tank.

Options:

Four-speed automatic overdrive transmission ($595). Preferred equipment package for LX sedan and hatchback including power-operated dual remote-control electric mirrors, power side windows, power lock group, cargo tie-down net, front floor mats, speed control, electronically-controlled AM/FM radio with cassette player and clock and styled road wheels ($222). Preferred equipment package for LX convertible, including power-operated dual remote-control electric mirrors, power side windows, power lock group, cargo tie-down net, front floor mats, speed control, electronically-controlled AM/FM radio with cassette player and clock and styled road wheels ($207). Preferred equipment package for 5.0-liter LX sedan and hatchback including power-operated dual remote-control electric mirrors, power side windows, power lock group, cargo tie-down net, front floor mats, speed control, electronically-controlled AM/FM radio with cassette player and clock, premium sound system, custom equipment group, manual-control air conditioning and dual illuminated visor mirrors visor mirrors ($1,314). Preferred equipment package for 5.0-liter LX convertible including power-operated dual remote-control electric mirrors, power side windows, power lock group, cargo tie-down

1991 Ford Mustang GT 5.0-Liter Convertible (OCW)

net, front floor mats, speed control, electronically-controlled AM/FM radio with cassette player and clock, premium sound system, custom equipment group, manual-control air conditioning and dual illuminated visor mirrors visor mirrors ($749). Preferred equipment package for 5.0-liter GT hatchback including power-operated dual remote-control electric mirrors, power side windows, power lock group, cargo tie-down net, front floor mats, speed control, electronically-controlled AM/FM radio with cassette player and clock, premium sound system, custom equipment group, manual-control air conditioning and dual illuminated visor mirrors visor mirrors ($1,314). Preferred equipment package for 5.0-liter GT convertible including power-operated dual remote-control electric mirrors, power side windows, power lock group, cargo tie-down net, front floor mats, speed control, electronically-controlled AM/FM radio with cassette player and clock, premium sound system, custom equipment group, manual-control air conditioning and dual illuminated visor mirrors visor mirrors ($749). California emissions system ($100). Vinyl low-back seats for LX ($37). LX 5.0L and GT articulated sport seats with leather seating surfaces ($489). Cargo tie-down net ($66). Custom equip group for LX sedan and hatchback ($917). Rear window defroster, except convertible ($160). Front floor mats ($33). Graphic equalizer and premium sound system ($139). Clear coat paint ($91). Power equipment group ($565, but standard on convertibles). Premium sound system ($168). Electronic AM/FM stereo radio with cassette ($155). Flip-up open-air roof for hatchback ($355). Speed control ($210). Titanium lower body side accent treatment for GT ($159). Wire wheel covers for LX only (NC). Wire wheel covers for other models ($193). Cast-aluminum wheels with up-sized P205/65R15 black sidewall tires for LX only ($167). Cast-aluminum wheels with up-sized P205/65R15 black sidewall tires for other models ($360). Styled roads wheels for LX ($193). Engine block heater ($20).

History:

U.S. model-year Mustang production totaled 98,737. U.S. calendar-year Mustang production totaled 81,558. In 1991, Ford's new engineering offshoot, called the Special Vehicle Team, began work on the Mustang Cobra — a higher performance version of the Mustang GT — tentatively

1992 Mustang

Mustang LX — (Four and V-8): The 1992 Mustang received several body enhancements including color-keyed body side moldings, bumper strips, a four-way power driver's seat option and two new colors: Bimini blue and Calypso green. Power train availability again included a 2.3-liter four-cylinder engine with electronic fuel injection and a 5.0-liter HO (High Output) V-8 engine. Both were available with either five-speed manual (standard) or four-speed automatic overdrive (optional) transmissions. Standard equipment for Mustang included a driver's side airbag, power front disc brakes, front- and rear-passenger shoulder seat belts, a modified MacPherson-strut rear suspension, rear spoiler, low-back reclining bucket seats with headrests and an electronic AM/FM stereo radio with four speakers.

Mustang GT — (V-8): The GT again came standard with the V-8 engine, aero body components, spoilers, air dams and articulated sport seats. It also had a heavier-duty suspension. GT models used 16-inch five-spoke aluminum wheels.

VIN:

The VIN was stamped on an aluminum tab riveted to the instrument panel and was viewable through the windshield. The first symbol indicated the country of origin: 1=U.S.A. The second symbol identified the manufacturer: F=Ford. The third symbol indicated the vehicle type: A=passenger car. The fourth symbol revealed the restraint system: C=air bags with active belts. The fifth symbol indicated the division: P=Ford passenger car. The sixth and seventh symbols indicated the body style: 40=LX Coupe, 41=LX Hatchback, 42=GT Hatchback, 44=LX Convertible and 45=GT Convertible. The eighth symbol was the engine: S=140-cid (2.3-liter) SOHC four-cylinder with electronic fuel injection and E=302-cid (5.0-liter) V-8 with electronic fuel injection. The ninth symbol was a check digit. The 10th symbol indicated the model year:

N=1992. The 11th symbol indicated the assembly plant: F=Dearborn, Michigan. The last six digits were the unit production numbers beginning at 100001 and going up.

Mustang LX (Four)

Model No.	Body/ Style No.	Body Type and Seating	Factory Price	Shipping Weight	Production Total
40	66B	2-dr. Coupe-4P	$10,215	2,759 lbs.	Note 1
41	61B	3-dr. Hatchback-4P	$10,721	2,824 lbs.	Note 1
44	66B	2-dr. Convertible-4P	$16,899	2,960 lbs.	Note 1

Mustang LX (V-8)

40	66B	2-dr. Coupe-4P	$13,422	3,010 lbs.	Note 1
41	61B	3-dr. Hatchback-4P	$14,207	3,069 lbs.	Note 1
44	66B	2-dr. Convertible-4P	$19,644	3,231 lbs.	Note 1

Mustang GT (V-8)

42	61B	3-dr. Hatchback-4P	$15,243	3,144 lbs.	Note 1
45	66B	2-dr. Convertible-4P	$20,199	3,365 lbs.	Note 1

Note 1: Ford reported total production 15,717 coupes, 40,093 hatchbacks, and 23,470 convertibles.

Engines:

Four: Inline, overhead cam. Cast-iron block and head. Displacement: 140-cid (2.3 liters). B & S: 3.78 x 3.12 in. Compression ratio: 9.5:1 Brake hp: 105 at 4600 rpm Torque: 135 lbs.-ft. at 2600 rpm Five main bearings. Hydraulic valve lifters. Induction: Port fuel injection. Code: S.
5.0-Liter HO V-8: 90-degree, overhead valve. Cast-iron block and head. Displacement: 302-cid (5.0 liters). B & S: 4.00 x 3.00 in. Compression ratio: 9.0:1. Brake hp: 225 at 4200 rpm Torque: 300 lbs.-ft. at 3200 rpm. Five main bearings. Hydraulic valve lifters. Induction: Sequential fuel injection. Code: E.

Chassis:

Wheelbase: 100.5 in. Overall length: 179.6 in. Height: 52.1 in. Width: 68.3 in. Front tread: 56.6 in. Rear tread: 57.0 in. Tires: P195/75R14 steel-belted radial with black sidewall and P225/55ZR16, GT and LX with V-8.

Technical:

Five-speed manual (floor shift) standard. Four-speed overdrive automatic available. Rack and pinion, power-assisted steering. Modified MacPherson struts front suspension with lower control arms and stabilizer bar (gas shocks on GT). Rigid rear axle with four-bar link (upper, leading and lower, arm) and unique Quadra-shock on LX 5.0L and GT). Front disc, rear drum (power-assisted) brakes. Unibody. 15.4 gallon fuel tank.

Options:

Four-speed automatic overdrive transmission ($595). Preferred equipment package for LX sedan and hatchback including power-operated dual remote-control electric mirrors, power side windows, power lock group, cargo tie-down net, front floor mats, speed control, electronically-controlled AM/FM radio with cassette player and clock and styled road wheels ($276). Preferred equipment package for LX convertible, including power-operated dual remote-control electric mirrors, power side windows, power lock group, cargo tie-down net, front floor mats, speed control, electronically-controlled AM/FM radio with cassette player and clock and styled road wheels ($122). Preferred equipment package for 5.0-liter LX sedan and hatchback including power-operated dual remote-control electric mirrors, power side windows, power lock group, cargo tie-down net, front floor mats, speed control, electronically-controlled AM/FM radio with cassette player and clock, premium sound system, custom equipment group, manual-control air conditioning and dual illuminated visor mirrors visor mirrors ($551). Preferred equipment package for 5.0-liter LX convertible including power-operated dual remote-control electric mirrors, power side windows, power lock group, cargo tie-down net, front floor mats, speed control, electronically-controlled AM/FM radio with cassette player and clock, premium sound system, custom equipment group, manual-control air conditioning and dual illuminated

1992 Ford Mustang LX 5.0-Liter Convertible (OCW)

1992 Ford Mustang GT 5.0-Liter Hatchback (OCW)

1993 Ford Mustang LX 5.0-Liter Convertible (OCW)

visor mirrors visor mirrors ($1,367). Preferred equipment package for 5.0-liter GT hatchback including power-operated dual remote-control electric mirrors, power side windows, power lock group, cargo tie-down net, front floor mats, speed control, electronically-controlled AM/FM radio with cassette player and clock, premium sound system, custom equipment group, manual-control air conditioning and dual illuminated visor mirrors visor mirrors ($1,314). Preferred equipment package for 5.0-liter GT convertible including power-operated dual remote-control electric mirrors, power side windows, power lock group, cargo tie-down net, front floor mats, speed control, electronically-controlled AM/FM radio with cassette player and clock, premium sound system, custom equipment group, manual-control air conditioning and dual illuminated visor mirrors visor mirrors ($763). California emissions system ($100). Vinyl low-back seats for LX ($76). LX 5.0L and GT articulated sport seats with leather seating surfaces ($523). Cargo tie-down net ($99). Rear window defroster, except convertible ($170). Clearcoat paint ($91). Power equipment group ($565, but standard on convertibles). Premium sound system ($307). Electronic AM/FM stereo radio with cassette ($155). Flip-up open-air roof for hatchback ($355). Speed control ($224). Titanium lower body side accent treatment for GT ($159). Wire wheel covers for LX only (NC). Wire wheel covers for other models ($193). Cast-aluminum wheels with up-sized P205/65R15 black sidewall tires for LX only ($167). Cast-aluminum wheels with up-sized P205/65R15 black sidewall tires for other models ($360). Styled roads wheels for LX ($193). Engine block heater ($20).

History:

U.S. model year Mustang production totaled 79,280. U.S. calendar year

1993 Mustang

Mustang LX — (Four and V-8): The Mustang LX lineup was again comprised of coupe, hatchback and convertible body style. The LX again used the 2.3-liter four-cylinder engine with electronic fuel injection, while the LX 5.0 models used a High Output 5.0-liter V-8 with sequential electronic fuel injection (SEFI). All models included a higher wattage radio with an easy-to-read display. The convertible had a new headliner. There were seven new exterior colors. New options included a compact disc player and an electronic premium cassette radio.

Mustang GT — (V-8): The GT again came standard with aero body components, spoilers, air dams and articulated sport seats. It also had a heavier-duty suspension. GT models used 16-inch five-spoke aluminum wheels. The GT was also powered by the 5.0-liter SEFI V-8 engine and had 16-inch cast-aluminum wheels and high-performance tires.

Mustang Cobra — (V-8): The aging Mustang lineup received a limited-edition Cobra model in 1993 to go along with its LX and GT series. This specialty model featured a "tweaked" 230-hp version of the GT's 5.0-liter V-8, five-speed manual transmission, 17-inch aluminum wheels, rear spoiler and ground-effects trim.

VIN:

The VIN was stamped on an aluminum tab riveted to the instrument panel and was viewable through the windshield. The first symbol indicated the country of origin: 1=U.S.A. The second symbol identified the manufacturer: F=Ford. The third symbol indicated the vehicle type: A=passenger car. The fourth symbol showed the restraint system: C=air bags with active belts. The fifth symbol indicated the division: P=Ford passenger car. The sixth and seventh symbols showed the body style: 40=LX Coupe, 41=LX Hatchback, 42=GT Hatchback, 44=LX Convertible and 45=GT Convertible. The eighth symbol indicated the engine: S=140-cid (2.3-liter) SOHC four-cylinder with electronic fuel injection, E=302-cid (5.0-liter) V-8 with electronic fuel injection and D=302-cid (5.0-liter) Cobra V-8. The ninth symbol was a check digit. The 10th symbol indicated the model year: P=1993. The 11th symbol revealed the assembly plant: F=Dearborn, Michigan. The last six digits were the sequential production numbers.

Mustang LX (Four)

Model No.	Body/Style No.	Body Type and Seating	Factory Price	Shipping Weight	Production Total
40	66B	2-dr. Coupe-4P	$10,719	2,751 lbs.	Note 1
41	61B	3-dr. Hatchback-4P	$11,224	2,812 lbs.	Note 1
44	66B	2-dr. Convertible-4P	$17,548	2,973 lbs.	Note 1

Mustang LX (V-8)

40	66B	2-dr. Coupe-4P	$13,926	3,035 lbs.	Note 1
41	61B	3-dr. Hatchback-4P	$14,710	3,096 lbs.	Note 1
44	66B	2-dr. Convertible-4P	$20,293	3,259 lbs.	Note 1

Mustang GT (V-8)

42	61B	3-dr. Hatchback-4P	$15,747	3,144 lbs.	Note 1
45	66B	2-dr. Convertible-4P	$20,848	3,365 lbs.	Note 1

Mustang Cobra (V-8)

42	61C	3-dr. Hatchback-4P	$18,247	3,200 lbs.	4,993

Note 1: Ford reported total production of 24,851 coupes, 57,084 non-Cobra hatchbacks, and 27,300 convertibles. Ford reported total production of 22,902 Mustang LX models and 26,101 GT models.

Engines:

Four: Inline, overhead cam. Cast-iron block and head. Displacement: 140-cid (2.3 liters). B & S: 3.78 x 3.12 in. Compression ratio: 9.5:1 Brake hp: 105 at 4600 rpm Torque: 135 lbs.-ft. at 2600 rpm Five main bearings. Hydraulic valve lifters. Induction: Port fuel injection. Code: S.

5.0-Liter HO V-8: 90-degree, overhead valve. Cast-iron block and head. Displacement: 302-cid (5.0 liters). B & S: 4.00 x 3.00 in. Compression ratio: 9.0:1. Brake hp: 205 at 4200 rpm Torque: 275 lbs.-ft. at 3200 rpm. Five main bearings. Hydraulic valve lifters. Induction: Sequential fuel injection. Code E.

5.0-Liter Cobra V-8: 90-degree, overhead valve. Cast-iron block and head. Displacement: 302-cid (5.0 liters). B & S: 4.00 x 3.00 in. Compression ratio: 9.0:1. Brake hp: 230 at 4200 rpm Torque: NA. Five main bearings. Hydraulic valve lifters. Induction: Sequential fuel injection. Code E.

Chassis:

Wheelbase: 100.5 in. Overall length: 179.6 in. Height: 52.1 in. Width: 68.3 in. Front tread: 56.6 in. Rear tread: 57.0 in. Standard Tires: P195/75R14 steel-belted radial with black sidewall and P225/55ZR16, GT and LX.

Technical:

Five-speed manual (floor shift) standard. Four-speed overdrive automatic available. Rack and pinion, power-assisted steering. Modified MacPherson struts front suspension with lower control arms and stabilizer bar (gas shocks on GT). Rigid rear axle with four-bar link (upper, leading and lower, arm) and unique Quadra-shock on LX 5.0L and GT. Front disc, rear drum (power-assisted) brakes. Unibody. 15.4 gallon fuel tank.

Options:

Four-speed automatic overdrive transmission ($595). Power equipment group including dual electric remote control mirrors, power side windows, power lock group, cargo tie-down net, front floor mats, speed control, AM/FM radio with cassette player and clock, styled road wheels for LX coupe and hatchback ($276). Power equipment group including dual electric remote control mirrors, power side windows, power lock group, cargo tie-down net, front floor mats, speed control, AM/FM radio with cassette player and clock, styled road wheels for LX coupe and hatchback for LX convertible ($306). Power equipment group including dual electric remote control mirrors, power side windows, power lock group, cargo tie-down net, front floor mats, speed control, AM/FM radio with cassette player and clock and premium sound system, custom equipment group, manual control air conditioning, dual illuminated visor mirrors for LX 5.0-

1993 Ford Mustang GT 5.0-Liter Hatchback (OCW)

liter coupe and hatchback ($567). Power equipment group including dual electric remote control mirrors, power side windows, power lock group, cargo tie-down net, front floor mats, speed control, AM/FM radio with cassette player and clock and premium sound system, custom equipment group, manual control air conditioning, dual illuminated visor mirrors for LX 5.0-liter convertible (no charge). Power equipment group including dual electric remote control mirrors, power side windows, power lock group, cargo tie-down net, front floor mats, speed control, AM/FM radio with cassette player and clock and premium sound system, custom equipment group, manual control air conditioning, dual illuminated visor mirrors for GT hatchback ($1,383). Power equipment group including dual electric remote control mirrors, power side windows, power lock group, cargo tie-down net, front floor mats, speed control, AM/FM radio with cassette player and clock and premium sound system, custom equipment group, manual control air conditioning, dual illuminated visor mirrors for GT convertible ($779). California emission system ($100). Leather seating surfaces articulated sport seats for LX 5.0L and GT ($523). Manual air conditioning ($817). Convenience group including cargo tie-down net, front floor mats ($99). Rear window defroster ($170 and not available on convertible). Engine block heater ($20). Dual illuminated visor mirrors ($100). Clearcoat paint ($91). Titanium lower body side accent treatment for GT only ($159). Power equipment group including dual electric remote control mirrors and power side windows ($604). Flip-up open-air roof for fastback only ($355). 4-way power driver's seat ($183). Speed control ($224). Cast aluminum wheels w/P205/65R-15 steel-belted radial black sidewall tires for LX convertible ($208). Cast aluminum wheels w/P205/65R-15 steel-belted radial black sidewall tires for LX coupe and hatchback ($401). Styled road wheels for LX only ($193). AM/FM stereo radio with CD player ($629). AM/FM stereo radio with cassette, auto reverse and premium sound ($339).

History:

U.S. model year Mustang production totaled 114,412. U.S. calendar year Mustang production totaled 106,238. The Special Vehicle Team

1994 Mustang

Base Mustang — (V-6): In its 30th Anniversary year, the Mustang was unveiled in two body styles — coupe and convertible. Gone was the three-door hatchback previously offered. Also gone was the LX series and the four-cylinder engine. Buyers of base Mustang models got a 3.8-liter V-6. Standard equipment included front and rear body-colored fascias with Mustang nomenclature, Mustang emblem fender badges, aerodynamic halogen headlights, wraparound taillights featuring three horizontal elements, dual electric, remote-control mirrors (convex mirror on right-hand side), color-keyed rocker panel moldings, driver and passenger air bags, a front ashtray, three-point "active" seat belts, 16-ounce carpeting, a cigarette lighter, a digital quartz clock, a stand-alone console with armrest, storage bin, cup-holder and CD/cassette storage, a driver's side foot rest, a glove box, full-instrumentation

(including tachometer and low-fluid lamp), an extensive light group assortment, dual visor mirrors with covers, reclining cloth bucket seats with cloth head restraints and four-way power driver's seat, split-back fold-down rear seat (not in convertibles), a leather-wrapped shift knob and parking brake lever with automatic transmission, stalk-mounted controls, a tilt steering wheel with center horn-blow, soft flow-through vinyl door trim panels with full armrests and cloth or vinyl inserts, a color-keyed headliner (including convertibles), color-keyed cloth sun visors, heavy-duty electrical components, power side window de-misters, an electronic engine control (EEC-V) system, stainless steel exhaust system, 15.4-gallon fuel tank with tethered cap, full tinted glass, a Power Vent ventilation system, a dual-note horn, a power lock group, a tunnel-mounted parking brake, an ETR stereo sound system with four 24-watt speakers, constant-ratio power rack-and-pinion steering, a modified MacPherson front suspension with stabilizer bar, links and coil springs, gas-pressurized front struts and rear shock absorbers, a mini-spare and interval-type windshield wipers. Convertibles also had a power retractable soft top with a hard convertible top boot, illuminated visor mirrors, a power deck lid release, power door locks and power side windows. The 1994 convertible was Ford's first post-1973 Mustang ragtop to be built as a topless car on the factory assembly line. Earlier ragtops started life as coupes and had their roofs removed. A glass backlight was standard and a built-in defroster cost extra. Convertible tops came in black, white, or saddle. The automotive trend toward bright, vibrant colors was not lost on Ford product planners. The 1994 Mustang could be ordered in one of 11 eye-catching hues, including Canary Yellow (GT only), Vibrant Red (GT only), Rio Red, Laser Red, Iris, Bright Blue, Deep Forest Green, Teal, Black, Opal Frost, and Crystal White. Interiors were available in five colors: Bright Red, Saddle, Opal Grey, Black, and White (convertible only).

Mustang GT — (V-8): In addition to (or in place of) standard equipment, the GT coupe and convertible had front and rear fascias with GT nomenclature and black finish on the lower rear end, Mustang GT fender badges, fog lamps, a single-wing rear spoiler, 16 x 7.5-inch wide five-spoke cast-aluminum wheels with locks, a 150-mph speedometer, GT bucket seats with cloth trim, cloth head restraints, adjustable cushions, power lumbar support, a four-way power driver's seat, a leather-wrapped steering wheel, a Traction-Lok rear axle, a handling brace to stiffen the engine compartment (similar to those utilized by Ford NASCAR teams), a stainless steel dual exhaust system, a GT suspension package with variable-rate coil springs, unique-calibrated gas struts and shocks, a Quadra-shock rear suspension with strut lever brace and illuminated visor mirrors with hard covers.

Mustang SVT Cobra — (V-8): The SVT (special vehicle team) again released a midyear Cobra for muscle enthusiasts. Its engine used the cast-iron GT-40 heads, a revised intake setup, a special camshaft and rockers, fuel injection, big valves and a low-restriction exhaust system for a gain of 25 hp. Other features of the Cobra included 13-in. Kelsey-Hayes disc wheels up front, 11.65-in. discs in the rear and a Bosch antilock braking system. Polished 17 x 8-inch five-spoke alloy wheels sported fat Goodyear GS-C tires. The suspension was revised from the GT with slightly softer springing that increased suspension travel and improved road holding. The Cobra's new front end treatment included crystal headlight lenses, a different grille and fog lamps. At the rear was a new curved deck lid spoiler. Badging was conservative, with snakes on the fenders and a Cobra plate on the deck lid. A peak inside revealed white-faced instruments and a 160-mph speedometer. Cobra floor mats and an airbag cover were subtle touches. Coming only in Rio Red was a Cobra convertible designed for Indy Pace Car duties. Plans called for making just 1,000 of them, compared to 5,000 coupes. Small badges were the main difference. A set of pace car decals came packaged in the trunk of each pace car.

VIN:

The VIN was stamped on an aluminum tab riveted to the instrument panel and was viewable through the windshield. The first symbol

1994 Ford Mustang convertible (PH)

1994 Ford Mustang 5.0-Liter GT coupe (PH)

1994 Ford Mustang 5.0-Liter GT convertible (PH)

1994 Ford Mustang 5.0-Liter Cobra coupe (OCW)

indicated the country of origin: 1=U.S.A. The second symbol identified the manufacturer: F=Ford. The third symbol indicated the vehicle type: A=passenger car. The fourth symbol revealed the restraint system: L=air bags with active belts. The fifth symbol indicated the division: P=Ford passenger car. The sixth and seventh symbols indicated the body style: 40=Coupe, 42=GT or Cobra Coupe, 44=Convertible and 45=GT or Cobra Convertible. The eighth symbol revealed the engine: 4=232-cid (3.8-liter) V-6 with electronic fuel injection, E=302-cid (5.0-liter) V-8 with electronic fuel injection and D=302-cid (5.0-liter) Cobra V-8 with electronic fuel injection. The ninth symbol was a check digit. The 10th symbol indicated the model year: R=1994. The 11th symbol indicated the assembly plant: F=Dearborn, Michigan. The last six digits were the sequential production numbers.

Mustang (V-6)

Model No.	Body/ Style No.	Body Type and Seating	Factory Price	Shipping Weight	Production Total
P	40	2-dr. Coupe-4P	$13,355	3,055 lbs.	42,883
P	44	2-dr. Convertible-4P	$20,150	3,193 lbs.	18,333

Mustang (V-6)

P	42	2-dr. Coupe-4P	$17,270	3,258 lbs.	30,592
P	45	2-dr. Convertible-4P	$21,960	3,414 lbs.	25,381

Mustang SVT Cobra (V-8)

P	42	2-dr. Coupe-4P	$20,765	-----	5,009
P	45	2-dr. Convertible-4P	$23,535	-----	1,000

Engines:

Mustang Base V-6: Overhead valve. Cast-iron block and head. Displacement: 232 cu. in. (3.8 liters). B & S: 3.80 x 3.40 in. Compression ratio: 9.0:1. Brake hp: 145 at 4000 RPM. Torque: 215 lbs.-ft. at 2500 RPM. Sequential fuel injection.

Mustang GT Base V-8: 90-degree, overhead valve. Cast-iron block and head. Displacement: 302 cu. in. (5.0 liters). Bore & stroke: 4.00 x 3.00 in. Compression ratio: 9.0:1. Brake hp: 215 at 4200 RPM. Torque: 285 lbs.-ft. at 3400 RPM. Sequential fuel injection.

Mustang SVT Cobra Base V-8: 90-degree, overhead valve. Cast-iron block and head. Displacement: 302 cu. in. (5.0 liters). B & S: 4.00 x 3.00 in. Compression ratio: 9.0:1. Brake hp: 240 at 4800 RPM. Torque: 285 lbs.-ft. at 4000 RPM. Sequential fuel injection.

Chassis:

Wheelbase: 101.3 in. Overall length: 181.5 in. Height: (Convertible) 52.8 in., (Coupe) 52.9 in. Width: 71.8 in. Front tread: 60.6 in. Rear tread: 59.1 in. Tires: P205/65R15 steel-belted radial with black sidewall, P225/55ZR16 steel-belted radial with black sidewall, GT and P255/45ZR17 steel-belted radial with black sidewall, SVT Cobra.

Technical:

Five-speed manual (floor shift) standard. Four-speed overdrive automatic available, except SVT Cobra. Rack and pinion, power-assisted steering. Modified MacPherson gas-pressurized struts and stabilizer bar. Rigid rear axle with four links and coil springs. Four-wheel disc brakes (antilock standard on SVT Cobra). Unibody construction. 15.4 gallon fuel tank.

Options:

Four-speed automatic overdrive transmission, except Cobra ($790). Mustang 241A preferred equipment package including air conditioning and electronically-tuned AM/FM stereo radio with cassette ($565). Mustang coupe 243A preferred equipment including air conditioning, power side windows, power door locks, power deck lid release, speed control, dual illuminated visor mirrors, 15-inch aluminum wheels, electronically-tuned AM/FM stereo with cassette and premium sound, remote keyless

illuminated entry and cargo net ($1,825). Mustang convertible preferred equipment including air conditioning, power side windows, power door locks, power deck lid release, speed control, dual illuminated visor mirrors, 15-inch aluminum wheels, electronically-tuned AM/FM stereo with cassette and premium sound, remote keyless illuminated entry and cargo net ($1,415). Mustang GT preferred equipment including air conditioning, speed control, dual illuminated visor mirrors, 15-inch aluminum wheels, electronically-tuned AM/FM stereo with cassette and premium sound ($1,405). Mustang GT convertible preferred equipment including air conditioning, speed control, dual illuminated visor mirrors, 15-inch aluminum wheels, electronically-tuned AM/FM stereo with cassette and premium sound ($1,405). Mustang Cobra coupe preferred equipment 250A including air conditioning, speed control, rear window defroster and front floor mats ($1,185). Mustang Cobra convertible preferred equipment package 250P including air conditioning, rear window defroster, front floor mats, speed control, remote keyless illuminated entry, CD player and Mach 460 stereo system ($2,835). California emission system ($95). 15-inch aluminum wheels, except GT or Cobra ($265). 17-inch aluminum wheels on GT only ($380). Leather sport bucket seats for Mustang convertible only ($500). Leather sport bucket seats for Mustang GT only ($500). Leather sport bucket seats for Cobra coupe only ($500). Manual air conditioning ($780). Antilock braking system ($565, but standard on Cobra). Anti-theft system ($235). Convertible hardtop ($1,545). Rear window defroster ($160). Front floor mats ($30). Engine block heater, except Cobra ($20). Body side moldings ($50). Electronically-tuned AM/FM stereo radio with cassette and premium sound ($165, but standard in Cobra and not available in base Mustang coupe). Mach 460 AM/FM stereo radio with cassette, seek-and-scan, 60-watt equalizer, upgraded speakers and amplifiers and CD changer ($375). CD player ($475, but not available with Mustang coupe).

History:

In Mustang's 30th Anniversary year, a Ford Mustang Cobra convertible paced the Indianapolis 500. The 1994 Mustang also had the distinction of being named *Motor Trend* magazine's "Car of the Year." U.S. model-year Mustang production totaled 137,074. U.S. calendar-year Mustang

1995 Mustang

Base Mustang — (V-6): Standard equipment on the base Mustang included a 3.8-liter V-6, front and rear body-colored fascias with Mustang lettering, Mustang emblem fender badges, aerodynamic halogen headlights, wraparound taillights featuring three horizontal elements, dual electric, remote-control mirrors (convex mirror on right-hand side), color-keyed rocker panel moldings, driver and passenger air bags, a front ashtray, three-point "active" seat belts, 16-ounce carpeting, a cigarette lighter, a digital quartz clock, a stand-alone console with armrest, storage bin, cup-holder and CD/cassette storage, a driver's side foot rest, a glove box, full-instrumentation (including tachometer and low-fluid lamp), an extensive light group assortment, dual visor mirrors, reclining cloth bucket seats with cloth head restraints and four-way power driver's seat, split-back fold-down rear seat (not in convertibles), a leather-wrapped shift knob and parking brake lever with automatic transmission, stalk-mounted controls, a tilt steering wheel with center horn-blow, soft flow-through vinyl door trim panels with full armrests and cloth or vinyl inserts, a color-keyed headliner (including convertibles), color-keyed cloth sun visors, heavy-duty electrical components, power side window de-misters, an electronic engine control (EEC-V) system, stainless steel exhaust system, 15.4-gallon fuel tank with tethered cap, full tinted glass, a Power Vent ventilation system, a dual-note horn, a power lock group, a tunnel-mounted parking brake, an ETR stereo sound system with four 24-watt speakers, constant-ratio power rack-and-pinion steering, a modified MacPherson front suspension with stabilizer bar, links and coil springs, gas-pressurized front struts and rear shock absorbers, a mini-spare and interval-type windshield wipers. Convertibles also had a power retractable soft top with a hard convertible top boot, illuminated visor mirrors, a power deck lid release, power door locks and power

1995 Ford Mustang convertible (OCW)

1995 Ford Mustang 5.0-Liter GT coupe (OCW)

shown above.

side windows. A glass backlight was standard in the convertible. Buyers of Mustang convertibles again could order the removable hardtop that was introduced midyear in 1994.

Mustang GTS — (V-8): The big change for Mustang in 1995 was the addition of a GTS coupe positioned between the base Mustang and Mustang GT. The GTS coupe was powered by the 5.0-liter HO (High Output) V-8 and featured 16-inch/five-spoke cast aluminum wheels and stainless steel dual exhaust. while GTS, GT and Cobra models all used a version of the 5.0-liter V-8. The five-speed manual transmission was the standard unit and all but the Cobra series offered an AX4N electronically controlled automatic overdrive transmission as optional equipment.

Mustang GT — (V-8): In addition to (or in place of) standard equipment, the Mustang GT coupe and convertible had front and rear fascias with GT nomenclature and black finish on the lower rear end, Mustang GT fender badges, fog lamps, a single-wing rear spoiler, 16 x 7.5-inch wide five-spoke cast-aluminum wheels with locks, a 150-mph speedometer, GT bucket seats with cloth trim, cloth head restraints, adjustable cushions, power lumbar support, a four-way power driver's seat, a leather-wrapped steering wheel, a Traction-Lok rear axle, a handling brace to stiffen the engine compartment, a stainless steel dual exhaust system, a GT suspension package with variable-rate coil springs, unique-calibrated gas struts and shocks, a Quadra-shock rear suspension with strut lever brace and illuminated visor mirrors with hard covers.

Mustang SVT Cobra — (V-8): The SVT Cobra had a 5.0-liter engine with cast-iron GT-40 heads, a revised intake setup, a special camshaft and rockers, fuel injection, big valves, a low-restriction exhaust system, 13-in. Kelsey-Hayes disc wheels up front, 11.65-in. discs in the rear, a Bosch antilock braking system, polished 17 x 8-inch five-spoke alloy wheels, Goodyear GS-C tires, a special suspension, crystal headlight lenses, a different grille, fog lamps and a curved deck lid spoiler.

VIN:

The VIN was stamped on an aluminum tab riveted to the instrument panel and was viewable through the windshield. The first symbol indicated the country of origin: 1=U.S.A. The second symbol identified the manufacturer: F=Ford. The third symbol indicated the vehicle type: A=passenger car. The fourth symbol revealed the restraint system: L=air bags with active belts. The fifth symbol indicated the division: P=Ford passenger car. The sixth and seventh symbols indicated the body style: 40=Coupe, 42=GT or Cobra Coupe, 44=Convertible and 45=GT or Cobra Convertible. The eighth symbol was the engine: 4=232-cid (3.8-liter) V-6 with electronic fuel injection, E=302-cid (5.0-liter) V-8 with electronic fuel injection and D=302-cid (5.0-liter) Cobra V-8 with electronic fuel injection. The ninth symbol was a check digit. The 10th symbol indicated the model year: S=1995. The 11th symbol indicated the assembly plant: F=Dearborn, Michigan. The last six digits were the sequential production numbers.

Mustang (V-6)

Model No.	Body/ Style No.	Body Type and Seating	Factory Price	Shipping Weight	Production Total
P	40	2-dr. Coupe-4P	$14,330	3,077 lbs.	Note 1
P	44	2-dr. Convertible-4P	$20,795	3,257 lbs.	Note 1

Mustang GTS (V-8)

P	42	2-dr. Coupe-4P	$16,910	3,246 lbs.	Note 1

Mustang GT (V-8)

P	42	2-dr. Coupe-4P	$17,905	3,280 lbs.	Note 1
P	45	2-dr. Convertible-4P	$22,595	3,451 lbs.	Note 1

Mustang SVT Cobra (V-8)

P	42	2-dr. Coupe-4P	$21,300	3,354 lbs.	4,005
P	45	2-dr. Convertible-4P	$24,070	3,524 lbs.	1,003
P	42	2-dr. R Coupe-4P	$34,499	3,280 lbs.	250

Note 1: Not including SVT Cobras, Ford reported total production of 137,722 coupes and 48,264 convertibles. These totals include the Cobra production total

Engines:

Mustang Base V-6: Overhead valve. Cast-iron block and head Displacement: 232 cu. in. (3.8 liters). B & S: 3.80 x 3.40 in. Compressio ratio: 9.0:1. Brake horsepower: 145 at 4000 RPM. Torque: 215 lb.-ft. a 2500 RPM. Sequential fuel injection.

Mustang GTS Base V-8: 90-degree, overhead valve. Cast-iron bloc and head. Displacement: 302 cu. in. (5.0 liters). B & S: 4.00 x 3.00 in Compression ratio: 9.0:1. Brake hp: 215 at 4200 RPM. Torque: 28 lbs.-ft. at 3400 RPM. Sequential fuel injection.

Mustang GTS Base V-8: 90-degree, overhead valve. Cast-iron bloc and head. Displacement: 302 cu. in. (5.0 liters). B & S: 4.00 x 3.00 in Compression ratio: 9.0:1. Brake hp: 215 at 4200 RPM. Torque: 28 lbs.-ft. at 3400 RPM. Sequential fuel injection.

Mustang SVT Cobra Base V-8: 90-degree, overhead valve V-8. Cast iron block and head. Displacement: 302 cu. in. (5.0 liters). B & S: 4.00 3.00 in. Compression ratio: 9.0:1. Brake hp: 240 at 4800 RPM. Torque 285 lbs.-ft. at 4000 RPM. Sequential fuel injection.

Chassis:

Wheelbase: 101.3 in. Overall length: 181.5 in. Height: (Convertible 53.2 in., (Coupe) 53.0 in. Width: 71.8 in. Front tread: 60.6 in. Rea tread: 59.1 in. Tires: P205/65R15 steel-belted radial with black sidewal P225/55ZR16 steel-belted radial with black sidewall, GTS and GT an P255/45ZR17 steel-belted radial with black sidewall, SVT Cobra.

Technical:

Five-speed manual (floor shift) standard. Four-speed overdriv automatic available, except SVT Cobra. Rack and pinion, power assisted steering. Modified MacPherson gas-pressurized struts an stabilizer bar. Rigid rear axle with four links and coil springs. Four-whee disc brakes (antilock standard on SVT Cobra). Unibody construction 15.4 gallon fuel tank.

Options:

Four-speed automatic overdrive transmission, except Cobra ($815) Mustang 214A preferred equipment package including air conditionin and electronically-tuned AM/FM stereo radio with cassette ($565) Mustang coupe 243A preferred equipment package including manua air conditioning, power side windows, power door locks, power deck li release, speed control, dual illuminated visor mirrors, 15-inch aluminun wheels, electronically-tuned AM/FM stereo with cassette and premiun sound, remote keyless illuminated entry and cargo net ($2,030) Mustang convertible 243C preferred equipment package including a conditioning, power side windows, power door locks, power deck li release, speed control, dual illuminated visor mirrors, 15-inch aluminun wheels, electronically-tuned AM/FM stereo with cassette and premiun sound, remote keyless illuminated entry and cargo net ($1,625) Mustang GTS preferred equipment package 248A including manua air conditioning and electronically-tuned AM/FM stereo with cassett ($640). Mustang GT preferred equipment package including manual a conditioning, power driver's seat, dual illuminated visor mirrors, spee control, 15-inch aluminum wheels, electronically-tuned AM/FM stereo with cassette and premium sound ($1,615). Mustang Cobra coup preferred equipment package 250A including air conditioning, spee control, rear window defroster and front floor mats ($1,260). Mustang Cobra convertible preferred equipment package 250C including manua air conditioning, rear window defroster, front floor mats, speed contro remote keyless illuminated entry, CD player, Mach 460 stereo system and sport leather seats ($2,755). California emission system ($95). 15 inch aluminum wheels, base Mustang only ($265). 17-inch aluminun wheels on GT only ($380). Leather sport bucket seats for Mustan convertible only ($500). Power driver's seat, except Cobra ($175) Manual air conditioning ($855). Antilock braking system ($565, bu standard on Cobra). Anti-theft system ($145). Optional axle ratio fo GTS and GT ($45). Convertible hardtop ($1,825). Electric rear windo defroster ($160). Front floor mats ($30). Body side moldings for bas Mustang and Mustang GT ($50). Speed control ($215). CD playe except GTS ($215). Electronically-tuned AM/FM stereo radio wit cassette and premium sound ($165, but standard in Cobra and no available in base Mustang coupe. Mach 460 AM/FM stereo radio with cassette, seek-and-scan, 60-watt equalizer, upgraded speakers and amplifiers and CD changer ($375 in Cobra and $670 in base Mustang and Mustang GT). Engine block heater, except Cobra ($20).

History:

U.S. model-year Mustang production totaled 174,924. U.S. calendar-year Mustang production totaled 143,947. Ford's Special Vehicle Team

1996 Mustang

Base Mustang — (V-6): The base, GT and Cobra Mustang series all returned for 1996, but after only one year of availability in 1995 the GTS coupe was discontinued. Standard equipment on the base Mustang included Dual front air bags, Mustang-unique badging, four-wheel power disc brakes, full 13-ounce carpeting, a stand-alone digital clock, a console with an armrest, integral storage bin, cup holder and CD storage provisions, side window demisters, full soft flow-through door trim panels with full-length armrests and cloth or vinyl inserts, a 3.8-liter EFI V-6, a stainless steel exhaust system, body-color front and rear fascias, a driver's footrest, a 15.5-gallon fuel tank, tinted glass, aerodynamic halogen headlights, a color-keyed cloth headliner, a tachometer, a trip odometer, a voltmeter, a temperature gauge, a fuel gauge, and oil pressure gauge, an overdrive-off indicator, a 120-mph speedometer, a license plate bracket molded into the front bumper, a light group package, a dome light with front-door switches, an engine compartment light, an under-hood light, a glove box light, a luggage compartment light, a headlights-on alert chime, a power lock group package with power deck lid release, dual covered and illuminated visor mirrors, dual electric remote-control outside rearview mirrors, a passenger-restraint system with 3-point active safety belts, color-keyed rocker moldings, rear-wheel drive, split and folding rear seatbacks (in coupes), reclining cloth front bucket seats with head restraints, an ETR AM/FM stereo with seek function and four speakers, power rack-and-pinion steering, a tilt steering wheel with center horn, color-keyed cloth sun visors, a modified MacPherson strut 4-link front suspension with coil springs and stabilizer bars, gas-pressurized front struts, gas-pressurized rear shock absorbers with unique calibrations, wraparound taillights, P205/65R15 All-Season black sidewall tires, a five-speed manual transmission and interval windshield wipers. Convertibles also have a 10.9 cu. ft. luggage capacity, a power retractable cloth top, a semi-hard top boot and standard power side windows.

Mustang GT — (V-8): The 5.0-liter V-8 offered previously in the GT and Cobra Mustangs was discontinued and replaced by a 4.6-liter modular V-8. In addition to (or in place of) standard equipment included on the base Mustangs, the Mustang GT models included an anti-theft system, a 4.6-liter single overhead-cam engine, a dual stainless-steel exhaust system, GT front bucket seats with cloth trim, a 150-mph speedometer, a GT suspension package with Quadra shocks and variable-rate springs, P225/55ZR16 black sidewall all-season tires, a Traction-Lok axle and 16 x 7.5-inch cast-aluminum wheels with locking lug nuts. The GT convertible also had fog lamps, 4-way lumbar-support front power bucket seats, a single rear deck lid "wing" type spoiler and a leather-wrapped steering wheel.

Mustang Cobra — (V-8): The Cobra had a number of standard features in addition to (or in place of) base Mustang equipment. The list included anti-lock braking (ABS) system, manual air conditioning, a limited-slip axle, a rear window defroster, a double-overhead-cam version of the 4.6-liter Modular V-8, illuminated remote keyless entry, front floor mats, a power lock group package, specific upgraded front bucket seats, speed control, a 180-mph speedometer, a spoiler, a single rear deck

wing spoiler with integral LED stop lamp, variable-rate coil springs, P245/45ZR17 blackwall performance tires, a mini spare tire and wheel and 17 x 8-inch polished aluminum wheels. Ford's Special Vehicle Team's Cobra convertible was not put into production until the spring of 1996, while the coupe was available at the beginning of the model year. The Cobra also used a new T45 five-speed manual transmission, which replaced its predecessor T5 unit. Also new in the Cobra was a 3.27:1 rear axle ratio.

VIN:

The VIN was stamped on an aluminum tab riveted to the instrument panel and was viewable through the windshield. The first symbol indicated the country of origin: 1=U.S.A. The second symbol identified the manufacturer: F=Ford. The third symbol indicated the vehicle type: A=passenger car. The fourth symbol revealed the restraint system: L=air bags with active belts. The fifth symbol indicated the division: P=Ford passenger car. The sixth and seventh symbols identified the body style: 40=Coupe, 42=GT or Cobra Coupe, 44=Convertible, 45=GT Convertible, 46=Cobra convertible and 47=Cobra R coupe. The eighth symbol indicated the engine: 4=232-cid (3.8-liter) V-6 with electronic fuel injection, V=281-cid (4.6-liter) double overhead cam V-8 with electronic fuel injection, X=single overhead cam 281-cid (4.6-liter) V-8 with electronic fuel injection built at Romeo, Michigan, plant. The ninth symbol was a check digit. The 10th symbol indicated the model year: T=1996. The 11th symbol was the assembly plant: F=Dearborn, Michigan. The last six digits were the sequential production numbers.

Mustang (V-6)

Model No.	Body/ Style No.	Body Type and Seating	Factory Price	Shipping Weight	Production Total
P	40	2-dr. Coupe-4P	$15,180	3,057 lbs.	61,187
P	44	2-dr. Convertible-4P	$21,060	3,269 lbs.	15,246

Mustang GT (SOHC V-8)

P	42	2-dr. Coupe-4P	$17,610	3,279 lbs.	31,624
P	45	2-dr. Convertible-4P	$23,495	3,468 lbs.	17,917

Mustang Cobra (DOHC V-8)

P	47	2-dr. Coupe-4P	$24,810	3,401 lbs.	7,496
P	46	2-dr. Convertible-4P	$27,580	3,566 lbs.	2,510

Engines:

Mustang Base V-6: Overhead valve. Cast-iron block and head. Displacement: 232 cu. in. (3.8 liters). B & S: 3.80 x 3.40 in. Compression ratio: 9.0:1. Brake hp: 145 at 4000 RPM. Torque: 215 lbs.-ft. at 2500 RPM. Sequential fuel injection.

Mustang GTS Base V-8: 90-degree, overhead valve, SOHC. Cast-iron block and head. Displacement: 281 cu. in. (4.6 liters). B & S: 3.60 x 3.60 in. Compression ratio: 9.0:1. Brake hp: 215 at 4400 RPM. Torque: 285 lbs.-ft. at 4800 RPM. Sequential fuel injection.

Mustang SVT Cobra Base V-8: 90-degree, overhead valve, DOHC. Cast-iron block and head. Displacement: 281 cu. in. (4.6 liters). B & S: 4.00 x 3.00 in. Compression ratio: 9.85:1. Brake hp: 305 at 5800 RPM. Torque: 300 lbs.-ft. at 4800 RPM. Sequential fuel injection.

Chassis:

Wheelbase: 101.3 in. Overall length: (Mustang/Mustang GT) 181.5 in., (Cobra) 182.5 in. Height: (Convertible) 53.4 in., (Coupe) 53.2 in. Width: 71.8 in. Front tread: 60.6 in. Rear tread: 59.1 in. Tires: P205/65R15 steel-belted radial with black sidewall, Mustang, P225/55ZR16 steel-belted radial with black sidewall, GTS and GT and P245/45ZR17 steel-belted radial with black sidewall, SVT Cobra.

Technical:

Five-speed manual (floor shift) standard. Four-speed overdrive automatic available, except Cobra. Rack and pinion, power-assisted steering.

1996 Ford Mustang Cobra coupe (OCW)

1996 Ford Mustang Cobra coupe (OCW)

1996 Ford Mustang Cobra convertible (OCW)

1997 Ford Mustang GT coupe (OCW)

Modified MacPherson gas-pressurized struts and stabilizer bar. Rigid rear axle with four links and coil springs. Four-wheel disc brakes (antilock standard on SVT Cobra). Unibody construction. 15.4 gallon fuel tank.

Options:

Four-speed automatic overdrive transmission, except Cobra ($815). Mustang 214A preferred equipment package including air conditioning and electronically-tuned AM/FM stereo radio with cassette ($670). Mustang coupe 243A preferred equipment package including manual air conditioning, power side windows, power door locks, power deck lid release, speed control, dual illuminated visor mirrors, 15-inch aluminum wheels, electronically-tuned AM/FM stereo with cassette and premium sound, remote keyless illuminated entry and cargo net ($2,020). Mustang convertible 243C preferred equipment package including air conditioning, power side windows, power door locks, power deck lid release, speed control, dual illuminated visor mirrors, 15-inch aluminum wheels, electronically-tuned AM/FM stereo with cassette and premium sound, remote keyless illuminated entry and cargo net ($1,590). Mustang GT 249A preferred equipment package including manual air conditioning, power driver's seat, dual illuminated visor mirrors, speed control, 15-inch aluminum wheels, electronically-tuned AM/FM stereo with cassette and premium sound ($2,845). Mustang Cobra coupe preferred equipment package 250A including air conditioning, speed control, rear window defroster and front floor mats ($1,260). Mustang Cobra convertible preferred equipment package 250C including manual air conditioning, rear window defroster, front floor mats, speed control, remote keyless illuminated entry, CD player, Mach 460 stereo system and sport leather seats ($2,755). California emission system ($95). 15-inch aluminum wheels, base Mustang only ($265). 17-inch aluminum wheels on GT only ($400). Leather sport bucket seats for Mustang convertible only ($500). Power driver's seat, except Cobra ($175). Manual air conditioning ($855). Antilock braking system ($565, but standard on Cobra). Anti-theft system ($145). Optional axle ratio for GTS and GT ($45). Convertible hardtop ($1,825). Electric rear window defroster ($160). Front floor mats ($30). Body side moldings for base Mustang and Mustang GT ($50). Speed control ($215). CD player, except GTS ($215). Electronically-tuned AM/FM stereo radio with cassette and premium sound ($165, but standard in Cobra and not available in base Mustang coupe. Mach 460 AM/FM stereo radio with cassette, seek-and-scan, 60-watt equalizer, upgraded speakers and amplifiers and CD changer ($375 in Cobra and $670 in base Mustang and Mustang GT). Engine block heater, except Cobra ($20).

History:

U.S. model-year Mustang production totaled 124,698. U.S. calendar-year Mustang production totaled 130,488. 2,000 of the 5,496 1996 Cobra coupes produced were finished in light-refracting Mystic Clearcoat paint, which changed hue based on light intensity and from what angle it was viewed. The Mystic finish was an $815 option available only in 1996 and only on the Cobra coupe.

1997 Mustang

Base Mustang — (V-6): The Mustang series offered for 1997 remained the base, GT and limited-production Cobra from Ford's Special Vehicle Team. Each series again was comprised of coupe and convertible. The Mustang's 3.8-liter V-6 delivered 150-hp performance. Standard equipment on the base Mustang included dual front air bags, power four-wheel disc brakes, side window demisters, a 3.8-liter V-6 engine, a stainless steel exhaust system, complete tinted glass, a power ventilation system with four dashboard registers with positive shut offs,, full instrumentation including overdrive-off indicator, dual electric remote-control outside rearview mirrors (right-hand convex), passive anti-theft system, electronically-tuned AM/FM stereo with seek and four

speakers, reclining cloth bucket seats with head restraints, split and fold-down rear seat backs (in coupe only), a tilt steering wheel with center horn, P205/65TR15 black sidewall all-season tires, a five-speed manual overdrive transmission, interval windshield wipers, 15-inch full wheel covers and power side windows. Convertibles also featured a power retractable top, a semi-hard convertible top boot, power door locks and power side windows as standard equipment. The Mustang convertible had new gray leather seating surfaces instead of white. A thicker, firmer and more ergonomic shift handle with an overdrive button on the knob was included with the four-speed automatic transmission, which was optional on all Mustangs except the Cobra (NA). Mustang's instrument panel retained its two-tone appearance. Installation of Passive Anti-Theft System (PATS) was made standard on all models. PATS used an encoded ignition key with a transponder to electronically disable the engine if the transponder code did not match a preset code in the Electronic Engine Control System.

Mustang GT — (V-8): In addition to or in place of base Mustang features, the GT models included the 4.6-liter single overhead cam Modular V-8, a dual exhaust system, GT front bucket seats with cloth trim, a 150-mph speedometer, P225/55ZR16 black sidewall all-season tires, and 16 x 7.5-inch cast-aluminum five-spoke wheels with locking lug nuts. The GT featured a new flecked seat fabric pattern. New diamond-cut, brightly machined 17-inch cast-aluminum wheels with a dark gray metallic center were available on the GT.

Mustang Cobra — (V-8): In addition to or in place of base Mustang features, the Cobra models featured a 4.6-liter DOHC Modular V-8, P245/45ZR17 performance tires and a five-speed manual transmission. The Cobra's engine was hand-assembled and signed by its builders. Pacific Green clear coat metallic was a new color available on the Cobra.

VIN:

The VIN was stamped on an aluminum tab riveted to the instrument panel and was viewable through the windshield. The first symbol indicated the country of origin: 1=U.S.A. The second symbol identified the manufacturer: F=Ford. The third symbol indicated the vehicle type: A=passenger car. The fourth symbol revealed the restraint system: L=air bags with active belts. The fifth symbol indicated the division: P=Ford passenger car. The sixth and seventh symbols identified the body style: 40=Coupe, 42=GT or Cobra Coupe, 44=Convertible and 45=GT Convertible, 46=Cobra convertible and 47=Cobra R coupe. The eighth symbol indicated the engine: 4=232-cid (3.8-liter) V-6 with electronic fuel injection, V=281-cid (4.6-liter) double overhead cam V-8 with electronic fuel injection, X=single overhead cam 281-cid (4.6-liter) V-8 with electronic fuel injection built at Romeo, Michigan, plant. The ninth symbol was a check digit. The 10th symbol indicated the model year: V=1997. The 11th symbol was the assembly plant: F=Dearborn, Michigan. The last six digits were the sequential production numbers.

1997 Ford Mustang Cobra coupe (OCW)

1997 Ford Mustang convertible (OCW)

Mustang (V-6)

Model No.	Body/ Style No.	Body Type and Seating	Factory Price	Shipping Weight	Production Total
P	40	2-dr. Coupe-4P	$15,880	3,084 lbs.	56,812
P	44	2-dr. Convertible-4P	$21,280	3,264 lbs.	11,606

Mustang GT SOHC (V-8)

P	42	2-dr. Coupe-4P	$18,525	3,288 lbs.	18,464
P	45	2-dr. Convertible-4P	$24,510	3,422 lbs.	11,464

Mustang Cobra DOHC (V-8)

P	47	2-dr. Coupe-4P	$25,335	3,404 lbs.	6,961
P	46	2-dr. Convertible-4P	$28,135	3,540 lbs.	3,088

Engines:

Mustang Base V-6: Overhead valve Cast-iron block and head. Displacement: 232 cu. in. (3.8 liters). B & S: 3.80 x 3.40 in. Compression ratio: 9.0:1. Brake hp: 150 at 4000 RPM. Torque: 215 lbs.-ft. at 2750 RPM. Sequential fuel injection.

Mustang GT Base V-8: 90-degree, overhead valve, SOHC. Cast-iron block and head. Displacement: 281 cu. in. (4.6 liters). B & S: 3.60 x 3.60 in. Compression ratio: 9.0:1. Brake hp: 215 at 5000 RPM. Torque: 285 lbs.-ft. at 4800 RPM. Sequential fuel injection.

Mustang Cobra Base V-8: 90-degree, overhead valve, DOHC. Cast-iron block and head. Displacement: 281 cu. in. (4.6 liters). B & S: 3.60 x 3.60 in. Compression ratio: 9.85:1. Brake hp: 305 at 5800 RPM. Torque: 300 lbs.-ft. at 4800 RPM. Sequential fuel injection.

Chassis:

Wheelbase: 101.3 in. Overall length: 181.5 in., Mustang and Mustang GT, 182.5 in., Cobra. Height: 53.4 in., convertible and 53.2 in., coupe. Width: 71.8 in. Front tread: 60.6 in. Rear tread: 59.1 in. Tires: P205/65TR15 steel-belted radial with black sidewall, Mustang, P225/55ZR16 steel-belted radial with black sidewall, GT and P245/45ZR17 steel-belted radial with black sidewall, Cobra.

Technical:

Five-speed manual (floor shift) standard. Four-speed overdrive automatic available, except Cobra. Rack and pinion, power-assisted steering. Modified MacPherson gas-pressurized struts and stabilizer bar. Rigid rear axle with four links and coil springs. Four-wheel disc brakes (antilock standard on GT convertible and Cobras). Unibody construction. 15.4 gallon fuel tank.

Options:

Four-speed automatic overdrive transmission, except Cobra ($815). Mustang 241A preferred equipment package including manual air conditioning and electronically-tuned AM/FM stereo radio with cassette ($615). Mustang 243A preferred equipment package with manual air conditioning, dual illuminated visor mirrors, remote keyless entry, power driver's seat, power side windows, power door locks and power deck lid release, speed control, electronically-tuned AM/FM stereo radio with cassette, premium sound and 15-inch aluminum wheels in coupe ($2,115). Mustang 243A preferred equipment package with manual air conditioning, dual illuminated visor mirrors, remote keyless entry, power driver's seat, power side windows, power door locks and power deck lid release, speed control, electronically-tuned AM/FM stereo radio with cassette, premium sound and 15-inch aluminum wheels in convertible ($1,615). Mustang GT 248A preferred equipment package including manual air conditioning and electronically-tuned AM/FM stereo radio with cassette ($670). Mustang GT coupe 249A preferred equipment package with manual air conditioning, power driver's seat, power side windows, power door locks and power deck lid release, electronically-tuned AM/FM stereo radio with cassette, premium sound

1997 Ford Mustang Cobra convertible (OCW)

and 15-inch aluminum wheels ($2,940). Mustang GT convertible 249A preferred equipment package with manual air conditioning, power driver's seat, power side windows, power door locks and power deck lid release, electronically-tuned AM/FM stereo radio with cassette, premium sound and 15-inch aluminum wheels ($1,685). Cobra 250A preferred equipment package includes CD player, Mach 460 radio, anti-theft system and leather seats ($1,335). California emission system ($170). Cast-aluminum with P205/65TR15 BSW tires on base Mustang only ($265). Polished aluminum wheels with P245/45ZR17 BSW tires ($500). Leather Sport bucket seats in base Mustang ($500). Leather Sport bucket seats in Mustang GT ($500). Power driver's seat ($210). Manual air conditioning ($895). Sport appearance group including rear deck lid spoiler, 15-inch aluminum wheels, leather-wrapped steering wheel and lower body side accent stripe ($345). Anti-lock braking system in base Mustang ($570). Anti-theft system ($145). Optional rear axle ratio for base Mustang ($200). Electric rear window defroster ($190). Dual illuminated visor mirrors ($95). Front floor mats ($30). Rear deck lid spoiler ($195, but standard on GT convertible). Remote keyless illuminated entry system for Mustang GT only ($270). Speed control for Mustang GT only ($215). CD player ($295). Electronically-tuned AM/FM stereo radio with cassette ($165). Electronically-tuned AM/FM stereo radio with cassette and premium sound ($295). MACH 460 AM/FM stereo radio with cassette ($690). Engine block heater ($20).

History:

Tommy Kendall, driving a Ford Mustang Cobra in the Trans-Am series, set a record for consecutive race victories (11) en route to winning the

1998 Mustang

Mustang — (V-6): Improvements to the Mustang for 1998 included polished aluminum wheels and a premium sound system with cassette and CD play capability added as standard equipment on the base coupe and convertible. Standard equipment was comprised of dual front air bags, power disc brakes all around, side window demisters, a 3.8-liter V-6 engine, a stainless steel exhaust system, complete tinted glass, a power ventilation system with four dashboard registers with positive shut offs,, full instrumentation including overdrive-off indicator, dual electric remote-control outside rearview mirrors (right-hand convex), passive anti-theft system, electronically-tuned AM/FM stereo with seek and four speakers, reclining cloth bucket seats with head restraints, split and fold-down rear seat backs (in coupe only), a tilt steering wheel with center horn, P205/65TR15 black sidewall all-season tires, a five-speed manual overdrive transmission, interval windshield wipers, 15-inch full wheel covers, air conditioning, power windows, power door locks, a power deck lid release, remote keyless illuminated entry and

1998 Ford Mustang GT convertible (OCW)

Ford's Passive Anti-Theft System (PATS). Convertibles also featured a power retractable top and a semi-hard convertible top boot. Mustangs equipped with the four-speed automatic transmission qualified as Low Emission Vehicles (LEV) in four states that posted tighter emissions standards: California, New York, Massachusetts and Connecticut.

Mustang GT — (V-8): In addition to or in place of base Mustang features, the GT models included the 4.6-liter single overhead cam Modular V-8, a dual exhaust system, GT sport front bucket seats with cloth trim, a 150-mph speedometer, P225/55ZR16 black sidewall all-season tires, a sound system upgrade, a spoiler and 16 x 7.5-inch cast-aluminum five-spoke wheels with locking lug nuts. The power receptacle was relocated inside the console storage box. Ford's SecuriLock anti-theft system was standard on the Mustang.

Mustang SVT Cobra — (V-8): In addition to or in place of base Mustang features, the limited-production SVT Cobra models featured a 4.6-liter DOHC Modular V-8, P245/45ZR17 performance tires and a five-speed manual transmission. The Cobra's engine was hand-assembled and signed by its builders. Pacific Green clear coat metallic was a new color available on the Cobra. New five-spoke alloy wheels were added to the list.

VIN:

The VIN was stamped on an aluminum tab riveted to the instrument panel and was viewable through the windshield. The first symbol indicated the country of origin: 1=U.S.A. The second symbol identified the manufacturer: F=Ford. The third symbol indicated the vehicle type: A=passenger car. The fourth symbol identified the restraint system: L=air bags with active belts. The fifth symbol indicated the division: P=Ford passenger car. The sixth and seventh symbols indicated the body style: 40=Coupe, 42=GT or Cobra Coupe, 44=Convertible and 45=GT Convertible, 46=Cobra convertible and 47=Cobra R coupe. The eighth symbol indicated the engine: 4=232-cid (3.8-liter) V-6 with electronic fuel injection, V=281-cid (4.6-liter) double overhead cam V-8 with electronic fuel injection and X=single overhead cam 281-cid (4.6-liter) V-8 with electronic fuel injection built at Romeo, Michigan, plant. The ninth symbol was a check digit. The 10th symbol indicated the model year: W=1998. The 11th symbol was the assembly plant: F=Dearborn, Michigan. The last six digits were the sequential production numbers.

Mustang (V-6)

Model No.	Body/Style No.	Body Type and Seating	Factory Price	Shipping Weight	Production Total
P	40	2-dr. Coupe-4P	$15,970	3,065 lbs.	99,801
P	44	2-dr. Convertible-4P	$20,470	3,210 lbs.	21,254

Mustang GT SOHC (V-8)

P	42	2-dr. Coupe-4P	$19,970	3,227 lbs.	28,789
P	45	2-dr. Convertible-4P	$23,970	3,400 lbs.	17,024

Mustang Cobra DOHC (V-8)

P	47	2-dr. R Coupe-4P	$26,400	3,344 lbs.	5,174
P	46	2-dr. Convertible-4P	$30,200	3,506 lbs.	3,480

Engines:

Mustang Base V-6: Overhead valve. Cast-iron block and head. Displacement: 232 cu. in. (3.8 liters). B & S: 3.80 x 3.40 in. Compression ratio: 9.0:1. Brake hp: 150 at 4000 RPM. Torque: 215 lbs.-ft. at 2750 RPM. Sequential fuel injection.

Mustang GT Base V-8: 90-degree, overhead valve, SOHC. Cast-iron block and head. Displacement: 281 cu. in. (4.6 liters). B & S: 3.60 x 3.60 in. Compression ratio: 9.0:1. Brake hp: 225 at 4750 RPM. Torque: 290 lbs.-ft. at 3500 RPM. Sequential fuel injection.

Mustang Cobra Base V-8: 90-degree, overhead valve, DOHC. Cast-iron block and head. Displacement: 281 cu. in. (4.6 liters). B & S: 3.60 x 3.60 in. Compression ratio: 9.85:1. Brake hp: 305 at 5800 RPM. Torque: 300 lbs.-ft. at 4800 RPM. Sequential fuel injection.

Chassis:

Wheelbase: 101.3 in. Overall length: 181.5 in., Mustang and Mustang GT and 182.5 in., Cobra. Height: (Convertible) 53.4 in., (Coupe) 53.2 in. Width: 71.8 in. Front tread: 60.6 in. Rear tread: 59.2 in. Tires: P205/65TR15 steel-belted radial with black sidewall, Mustang, P225/55HR16 steel-belted radial with black sidewall, GT and P245/45ZR17 steel-belted radial with black sidewall, Cobra.

Technical:

Five-speed manual (floor shift) standard. Four-speed overdrive automatic available, except Cobra. Rack and pinion, power-assisted steering. Modified MacPherson gas-pressurized struts and stabilizer bar. Rigid rear axle with four links and coil springs. Four-wheel disc brakes (antilock standard on GT convertible and Cobras). Unibody

1997 Ford Mustang GT coupe (BB)

1998 Ford Mustang SVT Cobra coupe (BB)

construction. 15.7 gallon fuel tank.

Options:

Four-speed automatic overdrive transmission, except Cobra ($815). Anti-theft system ($145). Optional axle ratio on GT only ($200). Antilock braking system ($500). Convenience group including front floor mats, rear window defroster, speed control and power driver's seat on base Mustang ($495). Convenience group including front floor mats, rear window defroster, speed control and power driver's seat on Mustang GT ($295). Electric rear window defroster ($190). Dual illuminated visor mirrors ($95, but standard in convertible). Engine block heater ($20). Color-keyed body side moldings ($60). MACH 460 AM/FM stereo radio with cassette and CD changer compatibility ($395). California emissions system ($170). Leather bucket seats for base and GT only ($500). Rear deck lid spoiler ($195, but standard on GT). 17-inch aluminum wheels

1999 Mustang

Mustang — (V-6): Remembering how badly it had been criticized in the press for "forgetting" the Mustang's 25th anniversary, Ford gave fans of the marque a year-long surprise party in 1999. All Mustangs (whether powered by the V-6 or V-8) wore beautiful wreath design emblems on their front fenders that featured a solid ring encircling the classic running horse and tricolor bar. Not content to merely spruce up a six-year-old design with fender jewelry, Ford's designers went on to give the line a much-appreciated facelift and tummy tuck, while prescribing some steroid therapy. The smooth, mostly feminine, curves of the 1994-1998 Mustang were replaced with strong creases and straight lines. The sides of the car took on a more vertical angle and the tallest scoop ever to grace a Mustang was installed just behind the door. This "pumping up" of the previous design reminded many Mustang fans of the changes that had given the original 1965 a "body builder" look in 1967. Up front, the Mustang's headlights took on a sinister appearance. Taillights received the same treatment as the rest of the car, going from soft and rounded to hard and harsh. Looking for ways to lose weight at every turn, designers created a new deck lid made from a sheet molded compound. While the exterior improvements were enough to bring new customers, there were refinements in areas that couldn't be seen so easily, such as the revised floor pan sealing and foam-packed rocker panels — both of which reduced road noise. Engineers reduced a troublesome "mid-car shake" on the convertible models through the use of sub-frame connectors and gained a tiny bit of rear suspension travel on all models by raising the drive tunnel 1.5 inches. As the Mustang drew nearer to the end of the century, it received new technology provided in the form of an optional all-speed traction control system (TCS), a $230 option that worked in harmony with the also-optional (on base models) ABS to reduce tire spin in slippery conditions. Taller *Mustangers* no doubt appreciated the extra inch of travel built into the driver's seat for 1999.

1999 Mustang GT two-door coupe (FMC)

1999 Mustang GT two-door coupe (FMC)

Thanks to a higher-lift camshaft, coil-on-plug ignition, bigger valves and a revised intake manifold, the V-8 Mustang received its biggest power increase since 1987. Standard equipment included dual second-generation airbags, manual control air conditioning, the SecuriLock™ passive anti-theft system, power four-wheel disc brakes with new front calipers, a CD player, a clock integrated into the radio, side window demisters, power door locks, a 3.8-liter EFI V-6 engine, a stainless steel exhaust system, Solar-Tinted glass, a power ventilation system with four instrument panel registers with positive shutoffs, an analog instrument cluster (with tachometer, trip odometer, voltmeter, temperature gauge, fuel gauge, oil pressure gauge and overdrive-off indicator with automatic transmission), remote keyless entry, dual electric remote-control outside rearview mirrors (right-hand convex), dual visor-vanity mirrors with covers (and illumination on convertible), ETR AM/FM stereo with cassette tape player, premium sound system with premium speakers and 80-watt amplifier, reclining cloth bucket seats with cloth head restraints, a bench rear seat with split-folding seatback, a tilt steering wheel with center horn, power rack-and-pinion steering, P205/65R15 black sidewall all-season tires, a five-speed manual overdrive transmission, interval windshield wipers, 15-in. six-spoke cast aluminum wheels with ornaments and power side windows with driver's side "express down" feature. The convertible also had a power folding top and power rear quarter windows.

Mustang GT — (V-8): On GT models the hood grew a simulated recessed scoop that recalled the air-grabber that the 1968 sported when it received its first 428-cid V-8. GT exhaust tips also were enlarged slightly, from 2.75 inches to three inches. The GT's 4.6-liter was boosted to 260 hp and the base 3.8-liter V-6 jumped to 190 hp. Standard GT equipment included dual second-generation airbags, manual control air conditioning, the SecuriLock™ passive anti-theft system, power four-wheel disc antilock brakes with new front calipers, a CD player, a clock integrated into the radio, side window demisters, power door locks, a 4.6-liter SOHC V-8 engine, a stainless steel dual exhaust system, Solar-Tinted glass, a power ventilation system with four instrument panel registers with positive shutoffs, an analog instrument cluster (with tachometer, trip odometer, voltmeter, temperature gauge, fuel gauge, oil pressure gauge and overdrive-off indicator with automatic transmission), remote keyless entry, dual electric remote-control outside rearview mirrors (right-hand convex), dual visor-vanity mirrors with covers (and illumination on convertible), ETR AM/FM stereo with cassette tape player, premium sound system with premium speakers and 80-watt amplifier, GT Sport two-tone cloth trim bucket seats, a 150-mph speedometer, a bench rear seat with split-folding seatback, a leather-wrapped tilt steering wheel with center horn (two-toned when combined with Medium Graphite and Medium Parchment interior), power rack-and-pinion steering, P225/55R16 black sidewall all-season tires, a five-speed manual overdrive transmission, interval windshield wipers, 16-in. six-spoke forged aluminum wheels with carryover ornaments and power side windows with driver's side "express down" feature. The convertible also had a power folding top and power rear quarter windows.

35th Anniversary Mustang GT — (V-8): To commemorate the Mustang's 35th anniversary in grand style, Ford produced a special run of Limited Edition models that stickered for $2,695 above the cost of a GT. Originally, it was announced that 5,000 of these cars were scheduled to be built, but actual production came to 4,628 units. Features included a special, raised hood scoop (at the end of a wide black stripe), a rear deck wing, stand-out side scoops, a black honeycomb deck lid appliqué, body color rocker moldings, a Midnight Black GT leather interior with silver leather inserts, special floor mats with a 35th Anniversary script and a special aluminum shift knob (in cars with the five-speed transmission only). Exterior colors were limited to Black, Silver, Crystal White and Performance Red. Mustangers did not realize it at the time, but the Limited Edition model incorporated many of the cosmetic upgrades that would become standard with the 2001 model. Standard 35th Anniversary equipment included: Aerodynamic

halogen headlamps, front fog lamps, a hood scoop, a black appliqué on the hood, body side scoops, rocker panel moldings, dual electric control outside rearview mirrors, a power retractable convertible top with semi-hard boot (on convertibles only, of course), a rear deck lid spoiler, a black deck lid appliqué between the taillights, 17 x 8-in. bright machined five-spoke aluminum wheels, Midnight Black leather-and-vinyl seats with silver leather inserts and a pony logo, a split/fold-down rear seat (coupe only), air conditioning, a console with an armrest and integral storage bin and dual cupholders, an auxiliary 12-volt power point, an 80-watt premium sound system with cassette and CD players, a leather-wrapped tilt steering wheel, a driver's footrest, an instrument cluster with gray mask and 35th Anniversary script (with speedometer, tachometer, voltmeter, engine temperature gauge, fuel gauge and oil pressure gauge), stalk-mounted controls (for turn signals, wiper-washer, high beams and flash-to-pass feature), courtesy lamps, a dome with side-door-ajar switches, a luggage compartment lamp, power door locks, one touch power windows, a deck lid release, Midnight Black carpeted floor mats with the 35th Anniversary logo, silver leather door trim inserts, an aluminum shift knob (manual transmission), second-generation driver and front passenger airbags, three-point lap/shoulder safety belts, high-strength side door intrusion beams, interval windshield wipers, the SecuriLock™ passive anti-theft system, remote keyless entry system and antilock brakes.

Mustang SVT Cobra — (V-6): The SVT Cobra was based on the GT. Standard SVT Cobra equipment included dual second-generation airbags, manual control air conditioning, the SecuriLock™ passive anti-theft system, power four-wheel disc antilock brakes with new front calipers, a CD player, a clock integrated into the radio, side window demisters, rear window defroster, power door locks, a 4.6-liter DOHC V-8 engine, a stainless steel dual exhaust system, Solar-Tinted glass, a power ventilation system with four instrument panel registers with positive shutoffs, an analog instrument cluster (with tachometer, trip odometer, voltmeter, temperature gauge, fuel gauge, oil pressure gauge and overdrive-off indicator with automatic transmission), remote keyless entry, dual electric remote-control outside rearview mirrors (right-hand convex), dual illuminated visor-vanity mirrors, ETR AM/FM stereo with cassette tape player, premium sound system with premium speakers and 80-watt amplifier, sport bucket seats with leather trim and six-way power on driver's seat, color-keyed sun visors, a 150-mph speedometer, speed control, a bench rear seat with split-folding seatback, a leather-wrapped tilt steering wheel with center horn (two-toned when combined with Medium Graphite and Medium Parchment interior), power rack-and-pinion steering, P245/45ZR17 black sidewall performance tires, a five-speed manual overdrive transmission, interval windshield wipers, 17-in. five-spoke forged aluminum wheels, power side windows with driver's side "express down" feature, power door locks and a power deck lid release. The convertible also had a power folding top and power rear quarter windows.

VIN:

A 17-character Vehicle Identification Number was stamped on an aluminum tab on the instrument panel and was viewable through the windshield. The vehicle certification label was found on the body side of the driver's door. The first symbol indicated the national origin: 1=United States of America. The second symbol indicated the manufacturer: F=Ford Motor Co. The third symbol identified the vehicle type: A=passenger car. The fourth symbol was the type of restraint system: L= driver and front passenger airbags with passive front belts and active rear belts. The fifth symbol was the designation: P=passenger car. The sixth and seventh symbols indicated the car line and body type: 40=two-door coupe, 42=two-door GT coupe, 44=two-door convertible, 45=two-door GT convertible, 46=two-door Cobra convertible and 47=two-door Cobra or Cobra R coupe. The eighth symbol indicated the engine type: 4=232-cid (3.8-liter) EFI V-6, X=281-cid (4.6-liter) EFI SOHC V-8 and V=281-cid (4.6-liter) EFI DOHC V-8. The ninth symbol was a check digit. The 10th symbol indicated the model year: X=1999. The

11th symbol identified the assembly plant: F=Dearborn, Michigan. The last six symbols were the consecutive unit production numbers staring at 100001 at each factory. Paint Codes were: BZ=Chrome Yellow, ES=Performance Red, E8=Rio Red, E9=Laser Red, FU=Dark Green Satin, K6=Atlantic Blue, K7=Bright Atlantic Blue, SW=Electric Green, UA=Black, YN=Silver and ZR=Crystal White.

Mustang (V-6)

Model No.	Body/ Style No.	Body Type and Seating	Factory Price	Shipping Weight	Production Total
P	40	2-dr. Coupe-4P	$15,880	3,084 lbs.	56,812
P	44	2-dr. Convertible-4P	$21,280	3,264 lbs.	11,606

Mustang GT SOHC (V-8)

P	42	2-dr. Coupe-4P	$18,525	3,288 lbs.	18,464
P	45	2-dr. Convertible-4P	$24,510	3,422 lbs.	11,464

Mustang Cobra DOHC (V-8)

P	47	2-dr. Coupe-4P	$25,335	3,404 lbs.	6,961
P	46	2-dr. Convertible-4P	$28,135	3,540 lbs.	3,088

Base Mustang (V-6)

P	40	2-dr. Coupe-4P	$16,470	3,069 lbs.	73,180
P	44	2-dr. Convertible-4P	$21,070	3,211 lbs.	19,299

Mustang GT (V-8)

P	42	2-dr. Coupe-4P	$20,870	3,242 lbs.	17,316
P	45	2-dr. Convertible-4P	$24,870	3,386 lbs.	11,383

35th Anniversary Mustang GT (V-8)

P	42	2-dr. Coupe-4P	$21,395	3,069 lbs.	2,318
P	45	2-dr. Convertible-4P	$25,395	3,211 lbs.	2,310

Mustang SVT Cobra (V-8)

P	47	2-dr. Coupe-4P	$27,995	3,240 lbs.	4,040
P	46	2-dr. Convertible-4P	$31,995	3,384 lbs.	4,055

Notes: Prices included dealer destination charges. The 35th Anniversary production included 1,555 red cars, 1,299 black cars, 1,259 silver cars and 515 white cars. SVT Cobra coupe production by color was: (Black) 1,619, (Red) 1,219, (White) 794 and (Green) 408. The SVT Cobra convertible production by color was: (Black) 1,755, (Red) 1,251, (White) 731 and (Green) 318.

Engines:

Base Mustang V-6: Overhead valve. Cast-iron block. Hydraulic valve lifters. Four main bearings. Displacement: 232 cid (3.8 liters). B & S: 3.80 x 3.40 in. Compression ratio: 9.36:1. Brake hp: 190 at 5250 rpm. Torque: 220 lbs.-ft. at 2750 rpm. Sequential electronic fuel injection. Code 4.

Mustang GT V-8: Single overhead camshaft. Cast-iron block. Hydraulic valve lifters. Displacement: 281 cid (4.6 liters). B & S: 3.60 x 3.60 in. Compression ratio: 9.0:1. Brake hp: 260 at 5250 rpm. Torque: 302 lbs.-ft. at 4000 rpm. Sequential electronic fuel injection. Code W.

SVT Cobra DOHC V-8: Double-overhead camshaft. Aluminum block. Hydraulic valve lifters. Displacement: 281 cid (4.6 liters). B & S: 3.60 x 3.60 in. Compression ratio: 9.85:1. Brake hp: 320 at 6000 rpm. Torque: 315 lbs.-ft. at 4000 rpm. Sequential electronic fuel injection. Code V.

Chassis:

Wheelbase: 101.3 in. Overall length: 183.5 in. Height 53.2 in. Width 73.1 in. Front tread: 59.9 in. Rear tread: 59.9 in.

Technical:

Standard transmission: five-speed manual overdrive. Drive axle: rear. Steering: Power assisted rack-and-pinion. Front suspension: modified MacPherson gas-pressurized shock struts with coil springs and stabilizer bar. Rear suspension: four-bar link and coil spring system, gas shocks. Front brakes: power assisted discs. Rear brakes: power assisted discs. Ignition: electronic. Body construction: unibody with front isolated mini-frame. Fuel tank: 15.4 gallons.

Options:

44U four-speed automatic overdrive transmission, not available on Cobra ($815). 552 antilock braking system ($500). 60C convenience group including front floor mats, rear window defroster, speed control and power driver's seat ($550). GT Sport group includes 17-in. five-spoke aluminum wheels, hood stripe and wraparound fender stripes, leather-wrapped shift knob and engine oil cooler ($595). V6 Sport Appearance group includes 15-in. cast aluminum wheels, rear spoiler, leather-wrapped steering wheel, lower body side accent stripe, base model only ($310). 35th Anniversary Limited Edition package, includes 17-in. five-spoke aluminum wheels, black appliqué on hood,

side scoops, rocker panel moldings, rear spoiler, taillight appliqué, black and silver leather seats, silver door trim inserts, silver and black floor mats with 35th Anniversary logo and aluminum shifter knob, GT only ($2,695). 57Q Electric rear window defroster ($190). 677 dual illuminated visor mirrors, standard on convertible ($95). Color-keyed body side moldings ($60). 588 Mach 460 AM/FM stereo radio with cassette and CD changer compatibility ($395). 13K single wing rear spoiler, standard on GT ($195). 422 California emissions system (no cost). 428 high altitude emissions (no cost). T leather front bucket seats with vinyl trim, base and GT only ($500). X leather front sport bucket seats, GT only ($500). 41H engine block immersion heater ($20). 63B smoker's package including ashtray and lighter ($15). 553 all-speed traction control, requires antilock brakes, standard on Cobra ($230). 64X 17-in. forged aluminum wheels with P245/45ZR17 black sidewall tires and locking lug nuts, GT only ($500).

History:

The heavily face-lifted 1999 model, despite positive reviews from the motor press, saw a decline in sales from the previous year, at 133,637 total. Model year production included 91,847 coupes and 34,220 convertibles for a grand total of 126,067 Mustangs. The four-speed automatic transmission was used in 61.8 percent of production. The five-speed manual transmission was used in 38.2 percent. Four-wheel power disc brakes were installed on 52.5 percent and 48.3 percent had ABS braking. Leather seats were installed in 29.8 percent. The V-6 was used in 70.2 percent of all 1999 Mustangs, 23.6 percent had the SOHC V-8 and 6.2 percent had the DOHC V-8. The Ford Racing Technology Group built two Mustang FR500 prototypes. These awesome cars had a 415-hp engine attached to a six-speed manual transmission. They could go from 0-60 mph in 4.5 seconds. For additional facts about 35th Anniversary

1999 Mustang GT two-door convertible (FMC)

1999 Mustang SVT Cobra two-door coupe (BB)

1999 Mustang SVT Cobra two-door convertible (FMC)

2000 Mustang

Mustang — (V-6): Three new Mustang colors called Sunburst Gold, Performance Red and Amazon Gold, replaced Chrome Yellow, Rio Red and Dark Green Satin. That was about it for the obvious changes to the 2000 model. Two new safety features were added. First, child seat tether anchor brackets were added to the rear seating areas of all Mustangs. Second, an inside-the-trunk deck lid release with glow-in-the-dark illumination became standard equipment after news reports of carjacking victims being locked in the trunks of their cars. Standard equipment included dual second-generation airbags, manual control air conditioning, the SecuriLock™ passive anti-theft system, power four-wheel disc brakes with new front calipers, a CD player, a clock integrated into the radio, side window demisters, power door locks, a 3.8-liter EFI V-6 engine, a stainless steel exhaust system, Solar-Tinted glass, a power ventilation system with four instrument panel registers with positive shutoffs, an analog instrument cluster (with tachometer, trip odometer, voltmeter, temperature gauge, fuel gauge, oil pressure gauge and overdrive-off indicator with automatic transmission), remote keyless entry, dual electric remote-control outside rearview mirrors (right-hand convex), dual visor-vanity mirrors with covers (and illumination on convertible), ETR AM/FM stereo with cassette tape player, premium sound system with premium speakers and 80-watt amplifier, reclining cloth bucket seats with cloth head restraints, a bench rear seat with split-folding seatback, child seat tether anchors, a tilt steering wheel with center horn, power rack-and-pinion steering, P205/65R15 black sidewall all-season tires, a five-speed manual overdrive transmission, interval windshield wipers, 15-in. six-spoke cast aluminum wheels with ornaments, an inside-the-trunk deck lid release and power side windows with driver's side "express down" feature. The convertible also had a power folding top and power rear quarter windows.

Mustang GT — (V-8): On GT models the hood grew a simulated recessed scoop that recalled the air-grabber that the 1968 sported when it received its first 428-cid V-8. GT exhaust tips also were enlarged slightly, from 2.75 inches to three inches. The GT's 4.6-liter engine was boosted to 260 hp and the base 3.8-liter V-6 jumped to 190 hp. Standard GT equipment included dual second-generation airbags, manual control air conditioning, the SecuriLock™ passive anti-theft system, power four-wheel disc antilock brakes with new front calipers, a CD player, a clock integrated into the radio, side window demisters, power door locks, a 4.6-liter SOHC V-8 engine, a stainless steel dual exhaust system, Solar-Tinted glass, a power ventilation system with four instrument panel registers with positive shutoffs, an analog instrument cluster (with tachometer, trip odometer, voltmeter, temperature gauge, fuel gauge, oil pressure gauge and overdrive-off indicator with automatic transmission), remote keyless entry, dual electric remote-control outside rearview mirrors (right-hand convex), dual visor-vanity mirrors with covers (and illumination on convertible), ETR AM/FM stereo with cassette tape player, premium sound system with premium speakers and 80-watt amplifier, GT Sport two-tone cloth trim bucket seats, a 150-mph speedometer, a bench rear seat with split-folding seatback, child seat tether anchors, a leather-wrapped tilt steering wheel with center horn (two-toned when combined with Medium Graphite and Medium Parchment interior), power rack-and-pinion steering, P225/55R16 black sidewall all-season tires, a five-speed manual overdrive transmission, interval windshield wipers, 16-in. six-spoke forged aluminum wheels with carryover ornaments, an inside-the-trunk deck lid release and power side windows with driver's side "express down" feature. The convertible also had a power folding top and power rear quarter windows.

Mustang SVT Cobra R – (V-8): Ford called the 2000 SVT Cobra R the "fastest and best-handling Mustang ever." A total of 300 Mustang Cobra R models rolled off the Dearborn, Mich. production line in May 2000.

2000 Mustang two-door convertible (BB)

2000 Mustang GT two-door coupe (BB)

These cars were offered by certified SVT dealers. The Cobra R was a limited production street legal race-prepped version of the Mustang. Built with the racetrack in mind, it featured a 5.4L DOHC modular V-8 that produced 385 hp and 385 ft.-lbs. of torque. The new Cobra R also featured exterior enhancements including a front air-splitter and tall rear deck spoiler (designed to create a down force that promoted increased stability at track speeds). Other distinctions of the Cobra R included a "power dome" hood with a rear air extractor for improved engine cooling, 18-in. wheels, BF Goodrich g-Force KD tires and a lowered suspension for enhanced handling. Interior enhancements included Recaro sport bucket seats and the deletion of a radio, air-conditioner and back seat to save weight. A number of approved aftermarket performance parts suppliers worked with Ford's Special Vehicles Team (SVT) to develop the Cobra R. They contributed the Brembo brake rotors and calipers, Tremec transmission, Eibach and Bilstein suspension components and Borla exhaust system. In the spring, a new 2000 model became the third in a series of Cobra R models. This new, limited-edition racing car followed the tradition of the 1993 and 1995 Cobra R Mustangs.

VIN:

A 17-character Vehicle Identification Number was stamped on an aluminum tab on the instrument panel and was viewable through the windshield. A vehicle certification label was found on the body side of the driver's door. The first symbol indicated the nation of origin: 1=United States of America. The second symbol indicated the manufacturer: F=Ford Motor Co. The third symbol identified the vehicle type: A=passenger car. The fourth symbol indicated the type of restraint system: L= driver and front passenger airbags with passive front belts and active rear belts. The fifth symbol was the designation number: P=passenger car. The sixth and seventh symbols indicated the car line and body type: 40=two-door coupe, 42=two-door GT coupe, 44=two-door convertible, 45=two-door GT convertible, 46=two-door Cobra convertible and 47=two-door Cobra/Cobra R coupe. The eighth symbol indicated the engine type: 4=232-cid (3.8-liter) EFI V-6 and X=281-cid (4.6-liter) EFI SOHC V-8. The ninth symbol was a check digit. The 10th symbol indicated the model year: Y=2000. The 11th symbol indicated the assembly plant: F=Dearborn, Michigan. The last six symbols were the consecutive unit production numbers starting at 100001 at each factory. The 2000 paint codes were: BP=Sunburst Gold, ES=Performance Red, E9=Laser Red, K6=Atlantic Blue, K7=Bright Atlantic Blue, SU=Amazon Green, SW=Electric Green, UA=Black, YN=Silver and ZR=Crystal White

Base Mustang (V-6)

Model No.	Body/Style No.	Body Type and Seating	Factory Price	Shipping Weight	Production Total
P	40	2-dr. Coupe-4P	$17,070	3,069 lbs.	Note 2
P	44	2-dr. Convertible-4P	$21,920	3,111 lbs.	Note 2

Mustang GT (V-8)

Model No.	Body/Style No.	Body Type and Seating	Factory Price	Shipping Weight	Production Total
P	42	2-dr. Coupe-4P	$21,565	3,242 lbs.	Note 2
P	45	2-dr. Convertible-4P	$25,820	3,386 lbs.	Note 2

Mustang SVT Cobra (V-8)

Model No.	Body/Style No.	Body Type and Seating	Factory Price	Shipping Weight	Production Total
P	47	2-dr. Coupe-4P	$54,995	3,590 lbs.	300

Note: Prices include dealer destination charges.
Note 2: Total production of all models was 218,525. This included the base V-6 and Mustang GTs. About 30 percent were GTs.

Engines:

Base V-6: Overhead valve. Cast-iron block. Hydraulic valve lifters. Four main bearings. Displacement: 232 cid (3.8 liters). B & S: 3.80 x 3.40 in. Compression ratio: 9.36:1. Brake hp: 190 at 5250 rpm. Torque: 220 lbs.-ft. at 2750 rpm. Sequential electronic fuel injection. Code 4.

GT V-8: Single overhead camshaft. Cast-iron block. Hydraulic valve lifters. Displacement: 281 cid (4.6 liters). B & S: 3.60 x 3.60 in. Compression ratio: 9.0:1. Brake hp: 260 at 5250 rpm. Torque: 302 lbs.-ft. at 4000 rpm. Sequential electronic fuel injection. Code W.

2000 Mustang Cobra R two-door coupe (FMC)

Cobra R V-8: Double overhead camshaft. Cast-iron block. Aluminum heads. Hydraulic valve lifters. Displacement: 330 cid (5.4 liters). B & S: 3.55 x 4.15 in. Compression ratio: 9.6:1. Brake hp: 385 at 6250 rpm. Torque: 385 lbs.-ft. at 4250 rpm. Sequential electronic fuel injection. Code H.

Chassis:

Wheelbase: 101.3 in. Overall length: 183.2 in. Height: 52.2 in., Cobra R coupe and 53.3 in., other Mustang modelsl. Width 73.1 in. Front tread: 60.4 in. Rear tread: 60.6 in.

Technical:

Base V-6 and GT: Standard transmission: five-speed manual overdrive. Drive axle: rear. Steering: Power assisted rack-and-pinion. Front suspension: modified MacPherson gas-pressurized shock struts with coil springs and stabilizer bar. Rear suspension: four-bar link and coil spring system, gas shocks. Front brakes: power assisted discs. Rear brakes: power assisted discs. Ignition: electronic. Body construction: unibody with front isolated mini-frame. Fuel tank: 15.4 gallons.

Cobra R: five-speed manual overdrive. Drive axle: rear. Steering: Power assisted rack-and-pinion. Front suspension: modified MacPherson gas-pressurized shock struts with coil springs and stabilizer bar, lowered for enhanced handling. Rear suspension: four-bar link and coil spring system, gas shocks, lowered for enhanced handling. Brakes: power assisted four-wheel disc brakes with Brembo rotors and calipers. Ignition: electronic. Body construction: unibody with front isolated mini-frame. Fuel tank: 15.4 gallons.

Options:

44U four-speed automatic overdrive transmission ($815). 552 antilock braking system ($500). 553 all-speed traction control, requires antilock brakes ($230). 60C convenience group including front floor mats, rear window defroster, speed control and power driver's seat ($550). GT Sport group includes 17-in. five-spoke aluminum wheels, hood stripe and wraparound fender stripes, leather-wrapped shift knob and engine oil cooler ($595). V6 Sport Appearance group includes 15-in. cast aluminum wheels, rear spoiler, leather-wrapped steering wheel, lower body side accent stripe, base model only ($310). 57Q Electric rear window defroster ($190). 677 dual illuminated visor mirrors, standard on convertible ($95). Color-keyed body side moldings ($60). 588 Mach 460 AM/FM stereo radio with cassette and CD changer compatibility ($395). 13K single wing rear spoiler, standard on GT ($195). 422 California emissions system (no cost). T Leather front bucket seats with vinyl trim, base and GT only ($500). X Leather front sport bucket seats, GT only ($500). 41H engine block immersion heater ($20). 63B smoker's package including ashtray and lighter ($15). 64X 17-in. forged aluminum wheels with P245/45ZR17 black sidewall tires and locking lug nuts, GT only ($500).

History:

Mustang production climbed more than 70 percent from 1999. The total included 39,791 Black cars, 37,617 Silver cars, 33,804 Laser Red cars, 32,606 Crystal White cars, 17,764 Performance Red cars, 13,262 Amazon Tropic Green cars, 11,873 Atlantic Blue cars, 5,206 Electric Green cars, 5,171 Sunburst Gold cars, 4,979 Bright Atlantic Blue cars and 917 Zinc Yellow spring feature cars. For more information about yellow Mustangs visit www.2stylin.stangenet.com. Ford had planned to market a 2000 SVT Cobra coupe and convertible with a single overhead cam (SOHC) V-8 with introductory prices of $28,155 for the coupe and $32,155 for the convertible. The National Insurance Crime Bureau's *2000 Passenger Vehicle Identification Manual* showed body code numbers for these models. However, due to heavy recalls on 1999 models with the 4.6-liter DOHC V-8, the 2000 SVT Cobra was not produced. Instead the Cobra R bowed in the spring with a bigger DOHC V-8 based on a heavily-modified 5.4-liter Ford truck engine. Ford's newest concept car — the 2000 Bullitt Mustang GT — made its world debut at the 2000 Los Angeles Auto Show. The car was designed with all the excitement of its namesake classic Hollywood film in mind and paid homage to the 1968 fastback Mustang GT featured in the edge-of-your-seat police thriller, the 1968 Warner Brothers film "Bullitt" with Steve McQueen. Many of the 2000 Bullitt Mustang's styling cues are based on the

original Mustang featured in one of cinema history's most memorable car chases, which depicted Det. Frank Bullitt (Steve McQueen) in hot pursuit of bad guys through the challenging streets of San Francisco. "With the Bullitt concept, we have visually and emotionally recreated the excitement of one of the greatest movie car chase scenes," said J. Mays, Ford Motor Co. vice president of design. "Still as popular today as it was when it was introduced in 1964, the Mustang and the Bullitt concept show the possibilities for customizing this car and keeping the excitement alive as ever." The Bullitt concept was a 2000 Mustang GT that had been modified to resemble the Mustang used in the film. It featured new front and rear fascias, a new hood, front and rear lamps, five-spoke 18-in. aluminum wheels reminiscent of the originals, unique gauges on the instrument panel and racing-inspired seats. The exterior body panels were finished in pursuit green.

2001 Mustang

Mustang — (V-6): The 2001 Mustang still retained some of the original styling cues that first turned heads more than three decades ago, but remained a highly contemporary looking automobile befitting its performance image. The exterior profile reinforced its sports car heritage with an overall ground-hugging appearance that emphasized an agile, aggressive stance. The hood scoop, side scoop and pony emblem in chrome "corral" brand incorporated classic Mustang design elements. All models had new blacked out headlights and spoilers. Inside, the dual cockpit shape was reminiscent of the original Mustang, yet, its wraparound design was modern and user-friendly. The headliner, rear package tray and A- and C-pillar moldings were color-keyed to the rest of the interior. The Mustang convertible provided a fun-to-drive experience, but had a practical and easy-to-use design. The power retractable convertible top came with a semi-hard boot that protected the top from dust when lowered and enhanced the exterior appearance. A hydraulic system allowed quick raising and lowering of the top. The rear window was made of scratch-resistant glass. A new "value leader" V-6 coupe was made available in the 2001 Mustang lineup. This year's base Mustang got a new console with a larger rear cupholder, a repositioned front cupholder, a 12-volt power point, a tissue holder and a parking brake boot. A rear-window defroster became standard on all models. A new six-disc in-dash CD player was available with the Mach® 460 Sound System. New colors for the year were Mineral Grey Clearcoat Metallic, True Blue Clearcoat Metallic, Zinc Yellow Clearcoat and Oxford White Clearcoat.

Coupe: Standard equipment for the base Mustang Coupe included included body color front and rear fascias with Mustang nomenclature, a composite hood with scoop, complex reflector halogen headlights with integral turn/park lamps, three-tiered taillights, dual electric remote-control outside rearview mirrors (right-hand with convex glass), clear coat paint, color-keyed rocker panel moldings, 15 x 7-in six-spoke cast-aluminum wheels, a steel mini spare and 15-in. temporary tire, second generation driver and front passenger airbags, a three-point active restraint system, deluxe carpets, child seat tether anchor brackets on the package tray, a cigarette lighter port and auxiliary power point, a clock integrated with the radio, a console (with armrest, integral storage bin, tissue holder, dual cupholders and parking brake boot), a power-operated inside-the-trunk deck lid release with glow-in-the-dark handle, a driver's footrest, a locking glove box, an analog instrument cluster (including a tachometer, a trip odometer, a voltmeter, a temperature gauge, a fuel gauge, an oil pressure gauge and an "overdrive-off" indicator with automatic transmission), a light group (with lamps in dome, front "door ajar" switches and a "headlamps on" chime), luggage compartment trim and carpeting, dual visor-vanity mirrors, reclining cloth bucket seats with cloth head restraints, a split-folding rear seat, stalk-mounted controls, a tilt steering wheel with center horn, monochromatic full wrap over door trim, soft flow-through door panels with full-length armrests and vinyl inserts, color-keyed upper instrument panel finish, a color keyed headliner, color-keyed safety belts, a color-keyed shifter bezel, color-keyed A and C pillar appliqués,

2001 Mustang two-door convertible (FMC)

color-keyed instrument cluster finish, manual control air conditioning, a heavy-duty 130-amp alternator, a 58-amp/hr heavy-duty maintenance-free battery, four-wheel power disc brakes, side window demisters, power door locks, an electro drive cooling fan, EEC-V electronic engine controls, a 3.8-liter SEFI V-6, a stainless steel exhaust system, a fuel pump inertia shutoff switch, a 15.5-gal. fuel tank with tethered cap, complete Solar-Tinted glass, power ventilation with four instrument panel registers and positive shutoff, a dual note horn, a tunnel mounted parking brake with integral boot, an electronic AM/FM stereo cassette tape player with single disc CD and premium speakers and 80-watt integrated amplifier, the SecuriLock™ passive anti-theft system, remote keyless entry, power rack-and-pinion steering, a modified MacPherson strut front suspension with front stabilizer bar, a rear coil spring four-bar-link suspension with increased travel for smoother ride, gas pressurized front struts and rear shock absorbers, P205/65R15 all-season black sidewall tires, a rear window defroster, a five-speed manual overdrive transmission, interval windshield wipers and one touch power windows.

Convertible: Standard equipment for the base Mustang convertible included body color front and rear fascias with Mustang nomenclature, a power retractable convertible top with semi-hard boot, a composite hood with scoop, complex reflector halogen headlights with integral turn/park lamps, three-tiered taillights, dual electric remote-control outside rearview mirrors (right-hand with convex glass), clear coat paint, color-keyed rocker panel moldings, 16 x 7-in cast-aluminum wheels, a steel mini spare and 15-in. temporary tire, second generation driver and front passenger airbags, a three-point active restraint system, deluxe carpets, child seat tether anchor brackets on the seatbacks, a cigarette lighter port and auxiliary power point, a clock integrated with the radio, a console (with armrest, integral storage bin, tissue holder, dual cupholders and parking brake boot), a power-operated inside-the-trunk deck lid release with glow-in-the-dark handle, a driver's footrest, a locking glove box, an analog instrument cluster (including a tachometer, a trip odometer, a voltmeter, a temperature gauge, a fuel gauge, an oil pressure gauge and an "overdrive-off" indicator with automatic transmission), a light group (with dome lamps integrated in mirror, front "door ajar" switches and a "headlamps on" chime), luggage compartment trim and carpeting, dual illuminated visor-vanity mirrors, reclining cloth bucket seats with cloth head restraints, a split-folding rear seat, stalk-mounted controls, a tilt steering wheel with center horn, monochromatic full wrap over door trim, soft flow-through door panels with full-length armrests and vinyl inserts, color-keyed upper instrument panel finish, a color keyed headliner, color-keyed safety belts, a color-keyed shifter bezel, color-keyed A and C pillar appliqués, color-keyed instrument cluster finish, manual control air conditioning, a heavy-duty 130-amp alternator, a 58-amp/hr heavy-duty maintenance-free battery, four-wheel power disc brakes, side window demisters, power door locks, an electro drive cooling fan, EEC-V electronic engine controls, a 3.8-liter SEFI V-6, a stainless steel exhaust system, a fuel pump inertia shutoff switch, a 15.5-gal. fuel tank with tethered cap, complete Solar-Tinted glass, power ventilation with four instrument panel registers and positive shutoff, a dual note horn, a tunnel mounted parking brake with integral boot, an electronic AM/FM stereo cassette tape player with single disc CD and premium speakers and 80-watt integrated amplifier, the SecuriLock™ passive anti-theft system, remote keyless entry, power rack-and-pinion steering, a modified MacPherson strut front suspension with front stabilizer bar, a rear coil spring four-bar-link suspension with increased travel for smoother ride, gas pressurized front struts and rear shock absorbers, P205/65R16 all-season black sidewall tires, a five-speed manual overdrive transmission, a rear window defroster, interval windshield wipers, one touch power windows and power rear quarter windows.

Mustang GT — (V-8): The Mustang became even more of a 1960s muscle car throwback with the 2001 GT model with the pumped-up body gained a tall (though non-functional) hood scoop and side scoops that were designed to set it more apart from the V-6 series. New 17-in. premium aluminum heavier spoke wheels with bright flanges were available with the GT Premium option group.

GT Coupe: Standard equipment included body color front and rear fascias with Mustang nomenclature and dual tailpipe outlets at rear, a GT hood and side scoop, complex reflector halogen headlights with integral turn/park lamps, front fog lamps, three-tiered taillights, dual electric remote-control outside rearview mirrors (right-hand with convex glass), a single-wing rear deck lid spoiler, clear coat paint, color-keyed rocker panel moldings, 17 x 8-in six-spoke forged aluminum wheels with carryover ornaments, an aluminum spare wheel and 15-in. mini spare tire, second generation driver and front passenger airbags, a three-point active restraint system, deluxe carpets, child seat tether anchor brackets on the package tray, a cigarette lighter port and auxiliary power point, a clock integrated with the radio, a console (with armrest, integral storage bin, tissue holder, dual cupholders and parking brake boot), a power-operated inside-the-trunk deck lid release with glow-in-the-dark handle, a driver's footrest, a locking glove box, an analog instrument cluster including a tachometer, a trip odometer, a voltmeter, a temperature gauge, a fuel gauge, an oil pressure gauge and an "overdrive-off"

2001 Mustang GT two-door coupe (FMC)

indicator with automatic transmission), a 150-mph speedometer, a light group (with lamps in dome, front "door ajar" switches and a "headlamps on" chime), luggage compartment trim and carpeting, dual visor-vanity mirrors, reclining two-tone cloth GT sport seats with cloth head restraints, a split-folding rear seat, stalk-mounted controls, a leather-wrapped tilt steering wheel with center horn (two-tone in combination with Medium Graphite and Medium Parchment interior), monochromatic full wrap over door trim, soft flow-through door panels with full-length armrests and vinyl inserts, color-keyed upper instrument panel finish, a color keyed headliner, color-keyed safety belts, a color-keyed shifter bezel, color-keyed A and C pillar appliqués, color-keyed instrument cluster finish, manual control air conditioning, a heavy-duty 130-amp alternator, a Traction-Loc rear axle, a 58-amp/hr heavy-duty maintenance-free battery, four-wheel power ABS disc brakes, side window demisters, power door locks, an electro drive cooling fan, EEC-V electronic engine controls, a 4.6-liter SOHC two-valve V-8, a dual stainless steel exhaust system, a fuel pump inertia shutoff switch, a 15.5-gal. fuel tank with tethered cap, complete Solar-Tinted glass, power ventilation with four instrument panel registers and positive shutoff, a dual note horn, a tunnel mounted parking brake with integral boot, an electronic AM/FM stereo cassette tape player with single disc CD and premium speakers and 80-watt integrated amplifier, the SecuriLock™ passive anti-theft system, remote keyless entry, power rack-and-pinion steering, a modified MacPherson strut front suspension with front stabilizer bar, a rear coil spring four-bar-link suspension with increased travel for smoother ride, gas pressurized front struts and rear shock absorbers with unique GT calibrations, a GT suspension package with variable rate coil springs and a quadra-link-shock rear suspension, P245/45ZR17 sidewall performance tires, a rear window defroster, a five-speed manual overdrive transmission, interval windshield wipers and one touch power windows.

GT Convertible: Standard equipment included body color front and rear fascias with Mustang nomenclature and dual tailpipe outlets at rear, a power retractable convertible top with semi-hard boot, a GT hood and side scoop, complex reflector halogen headlights with integral turn/park lamps, front fog lamps, three-tiered taillights, dual electric remote-control outside rearview mirrors (right-hand with convex glass), a single-wing rear deck lid spoiler, clear coat paint, color-keyed rocker panel moldings, 16 x 7-in cast-aluminum wheels, a steel mini spare and 15-in. temporary tire, second generation driver and front passenger airbags, a three-point active restraint system, deluxe carpets, child seat tether anchor brackets on the seatbacks, a cigarette lighter port and auxiliary power point, a clock integrated with the radio, a console (with armrest, integral storage bin, tissue holder, dual cupholders and parking brake boot), a power-operated inside-the-trunk deck lid release with glow-in-the-dark handle, a driver's footrest, a locking glove box, an analog instrument cluster (including a tachometer, a trip odometer, a voltmeter, a temperature gauge, a fuel gauge, an oil pressure gauge and an "overdrive-off" indicator with automatic transmission), a 150-mph speedometer, a light group (with dome lamps integrated in mirror, front "door ajar" switches and a "headlamps on" chime), luggage compartment trim and carpeting, dual illuminated visor-vanity mirrors, reclining two-tone cloth GT sport seats with cloth head restraints, a split-folding rear seat, stalk-mounted controls, a leather-wrapped tilt steering wheel with center horn (two-tone in combination with Medium Graphite and Medium Parchment interior), monochromatic full wrap over door trim, soft flow-through door panels with full-length armrests and vinyl inserts, color-keyed upper instrument panel finish, a color keyed headliner, color-keyed safety belts, a color-keyed shifter bezel, color-keyed A and C pillar appliqués, color-keyed instrument cluster finish, manual control air conditioning, a Traction-Loc rear axle, a heavy-duty 130-amp alternator, a 58-amp/hr heavy-duty maintenance-free battery, four-wheel power ABS disc brakes,, side window demisters, power door locks, an electro drive cooling fan, EEC-V electronic engine controls, a 4.6-liter SOHC two-valve V-8, a dual stainless steel exhaust system, a fuel pump inertia shutoff switch, a 15.5-gal. fuel tank with tethered cap, complete Solar-Tinted glass, power ventilation with four instrument panel registers and positive shutoff, a dual note horn, a tunnel mounted parking brake with integral boot, an electronic AM/FM stereo cassette tape player with single disc CD and premium speakers and 80-watt integrated amplifier, the SecuriLock™ passive anti-theft system, remote keyless entry, power rack-and-pinion steering, a modified MacPherson strut front suspension with front stabilizer bar, a rear coil spring four-bar-link suspension with increased travel for smoother ride, gas pressurized front struts and rear shock absorbers with unique GT calibrations, a GT suspension package with variable rate coil springs and a quadra-link shock rear suspension, P245/45ZR17 black sidewall performance tires, a five-speed manual overdrive transmission, a rear window defroster, interval windshield wipers, one touch power windows and power rear quarter windows.

Mustang GT Bullitt Coupe — (V-8): Never one to shy away from a limited-production "special" model, Ford brought to showrooms in 2001 a version of its 2000 Bullitt show car. Some sources say that production of the Bullitt Mustang was set at 5,000 units and some say 6,000 units. The actual production fell between the two numbers at 5,532. Based on the 1968 fastback driven by Steve McQueen in the gritty detective drama *Bullitt*, this coupe-only model featured exterior enhancements that visually and emotionally connected it to the classic film's famous chase scene. Modifications to the Bullitt Mustang included unique side scoops, a set of 17-in. American Racing aluminum wheels, a lowered suspension, modified *C* pillars and a quarter panel molding that set the car apart from a stock GT. Rocker panel moldings enhanced the car's lowered appearance. A bold, brushed aluminum fuel filler door was prominently placed on the quarter panel. Special Bullitt badging and polished-rolled tailpipe tips further distinguished the car. The Bullitt Mustang was available in Dark Highland Green, True Blue and Black. Providing 270 hp was a mildly modified 4.6-liter V-8 with a twin 57mm diameter throttle body, a cast aluminum intake manifold and high-flow mufflers. Re-valved Tokico™ struts and shocks, unique stabilizer bars (at the front and rear), frame rail connectors, 13-in. Brembo™ front brake rotors and Brembo™ performance brake calipers made up a unique suspension for this special Mustang model. Other standard Bullitt Mustang features included unique leather-surfaced seat trim, a "Heritage" instrument cluster, underhood clear coat paint (in UA Black or PY Green), a charcoal interior and serialized special edition identification.

Mustang SVT – (V-8): As always, the SVT Cobra was distinguished from other Mustangs by a number of visual signatures. They included a unique hood design, a front fascia incorporating round driving lights and a deep intake that forced air through the cooling system. Cobra badges decorated the front fenders. At the rear, tri-color taillights, polished three-inch diameter exhaust tips, an SVT badge, the word "Cobra" across the rear fascia and an optional low-drag spoiler set the SVT Cobra apart. Both the hood and the rear deck were constructed of lightweight composite materials. The 2001 model was scheduled for release in May of the year, with deliveries starting in the summer. When it arrived it had minor exterior and interior changes. External revisions included the use of five of the year's new exterior colors on the Cobra. They were True Blue, Zinc Yellow, Mineral Gray, Performance Red and Laser Red. The Cobra interior received all-new seats with added support and a six-disc in-dash CD player. The engine used was the 4.6-liter 90-degree 32-vale DOHC V-8 rated for 320 hp at 6000 rpm and 317 ft.-lbs. of torque at 4750 rpm.

SVT Cobra Coupe: Standard coupe equipment included the 4.6-liter DOHC V-8, a five-speed manual transmission, rear-wheel drive, a rear limited-slip differential, a modified MacPherson strut front suspension with stabilizer bar and 500 lb./in. coil springs, an independent rear suspension with steel upper and aluminum lower control arms and 470 lb./in. coil springs, front ABS brakes with 13-in. vented Brembo™ discs and PBR™ twin-piston caliper, rear ABS brakes with 11.65-in. vented discs and single-piston calipers, 17 x 8-in. five-spoke cast aluminum alloy wheel rims with painted surfaces, P245/45ZR17 black sidewall performance tires, an alloy spare wheel with mini spare tire, variable intermittent windshield wipers, all-speed traction control, a rear defogger, a tachometer, a clock, a rear deck lid spoiler, the SecuriLock™ anti-theft system with engine immobilizer, an inside-the-trunk emergency deck lid release, remote power door locks, one touch power windows, dual power outside rearview mirrors, cruise control, a leather-wrapped tilt-adjustable steering wheel, power steering, front door pockets, a front console with storage provisions, sport front bucket seats with six-way power driver's seat and front seat adjustable lumbar support, a remote trunk release, a rear split-folding bench seat, air conditioning, dual illuminated visor-vanity mirrors, a leather-trimmed gearshift knob, front and rear floor mats, an AM/FM stereo cassette with six-disc in-dash multi-CD player and 460-watts speakers.

SVT Cobra Convertible: Standard convertible equipment included the 4.6-liter DOHC V-8, included a five-speed manual transmission, rear-wheel drive, a rear limited-slip differential, a modified MacPherson strut front suspension with stabilizer bar and 500 lb./in. coil springs, an independent rear suspension with steel upper and aluminum lower control arms and 470 lb./in. coil springs, front ABS brakes with 13-in. vented Brembo™ discs and PBR™ twin-piston caliper, rear ABS brakes with 11.65-in. vented discs and single-piston calipers, 17 x 8-in. five-spoke cast aluminum alloy wheel rims with painted surfaces, P245/45ZR17 black sidewall performance tires, an alloy spare wheel with mini spare tire,

2001 Mustang SVT Cobra two-door coupe (FMC)

variable intermittent windshield wipers, a power convertible roof, a glass rear window, all-speed traction control, a rear defogger, a tachometer, a clock, a rear deck lid spoiler, the SecuriLock™ anti-theft system with engine immobilizer, an inside-the-trunk emergency deck lid release, remote power door locks, one touch power windows, dual power outside rearview mirrors, cruise control, a leather-wrapped tilt-adjustable steering wheel, power steering, front door pockets, a front console with storage provisions, sport front bucket seats with six-way power driver's seat and front seat adjustable lumbar support, a remote trunk release, a rear bench seat, air conditioning, dual illuminated visor-vanity mirrors, a leather-trimmed gearshift knob, front and rear floor mats, an AM/FM stereo cassette with six-disc in-dash multi-CD player and 460-watts speakers.

VIN:

A 17-character Vehicle Identification Number was stamped on an aluminum tab on the instrument panel and was viewable through the windshield. A vehicle certification label was found on the body side of the driver's door. The first symbol indicated the national origin: 1=United States of America. The second symbol indicated the manufacturer: F=Ford Motor Co. The third symbol identified the vehicle type: A=passenger car. The fourth symbol indicated the type of restraint system: L= driver and front passenger airbags with passive front belts and active rear belts. The fifth symbol was the designation: P=passenger car. The sixth and seventh symbols indicated the car line and body type: 40=two-door coupe, 42=two-door GT coupe, 44=two-door convertible, 45=two-door GT convertible, 46=two-door SVT Cobra convertible and 47=two-door SVT Cobra coupe. The eighth symbol indicated the engine type: 4=232-cid (3.8-liter) EFI V-6, X=281-cid (4.6-liter) EFI SOHC V-8, W=281-cid (4.6-liter) EFI SOHC "Bullitt" V-8 and V=281-cid (4.6-liter) EFI DOHC V-8. The ninth symbol was a check digit. The 10th symbol indicated the model year: 1=2001. The 11th symbol identified the assembly plant: F=Dearborn, Mich. The last six symbols were the consecutive unit production numbers starting at 100001 at each factory. The paint codes were: B7=Zinc Yellow, ES=Performance Red, E9=Laser Red, L2=True Blue, PY=Bullitt Green, SU=Amazon Green, SW=Electric Green, TK=Mineral Gray, YN=Silver and Z1=Oxford White

Mustang Value Leader (V-6)

Model No.	Body/Style No.	Body Type and Seating	Factory Price	Shipping Weight	Production Total
P	40	2-dr. Coupe-4P	$17,695	3,069 lbs.	Note 1

Mustang Deluxe (V-6)

Model No.	Body/Style No.	Body Type and Seating	Factory Price	Shipping Weight	Production Total
P	40	2-dr. Coupe-4P	$18,260	3,069 lbs.	Note 1
P	44	2-dr. Convertible-4P	$23,110	3,111 lbs.	Note 1

Mustang Premium (V-6)

Model No.	Body/Style No.	Body Type and Seating	Factory Price	Shipping Weight	Production Total
P	40	2-dr. Coupe-4P	$19,490	3,069 lbs.	Note 1
P	44	2-dr. Convertible-4P	$25,675	3,111 lbs.	Note 1

Mustang GT Deluxe (V-8)

Model No.	Body/Style No.	Body Type and Seating	Factory Price	Shipping Weight	Production Total
P	42	2-dr. Coupe-4P	$23,330	3,242 lbs.	Note 1
P	45	2-dr. Convertible-4P	$27,585	3,386 lbs.	Note 1

Mustang Premium (V-8)

Model No.	Body/Style No.	Body Type and Seating	Factory Price	Shipping Weight	Production Total
P	42	2-dr. Coupe-4P	$24,480	3,242 lbs.	Note 1
P	45	2-dr. Convertible-4P	$28,735	3,386 lbs.	Note 1

Mustang GT Bullitt (V-8)

Model No.	Body/Style No.	Body Type and Seating	Factory Price	Shipping Weight	Production Total
P	42	2-dr. Coupe-4P	$26,830	3,242 lbs.	Note 1

Mustang SVT Cobra (V-8)

Model No.	Body/Style No.	Body Type and Seating	Factory Price	Shipping Weight	Production Total
P	47	2-dr. Coupe-4P	$29,205	3,242 lbs.	Note 1
P	46	2-dr. Convertible-4P	$33,205	3,386 lbs.	Note 1

Note 1: Total production was 155,162 units. That total included 3,867 SVT Cobra coupes and 3,384 SVT Cobra convertibles. There were 5,582 Bullitt coupes produced.

2001 Mustang "Bullit" GT two-door coupe (FMC)

Engines:

Base Mustang V-6: Overhead valve. Cast-iron block. Hydraulic valve lifters. Four main bearings. Displacement: 232 cid (3.8 liters). B & S: 3.80 x 3.40 in. Compression ratio: 9.36:1. Brake hp: 190 at 5250 rpm. Torque: 220 lbs.-ft. at 2750 rpm. Sequential electronic fuel injection. Code 4.

Mustang GT V-8: Single overhead camshaft. Cast-iron block. Hydraulic valve lifters. Displacement: 281 cid (4.6 liters). B & S: 3.60 x 3.60 in. Compression ratio: 9.0:1. Brake hp: 260 at 5250 rpm. Torque: 302 lbs.-ft. at 4000 rpm. Sequential electronic fuel injection. Code W.

Bullitt Mustang GT V-8: Single overhead camshaft. Cast-iron block. Hydraulic valve lifters. Displacement: 281 cid (4.6 liters). B & S: 3.60 x 3.60 in. Compression ratio: 9.0:1. Brake hp: 265 at 5250 rpm. Torque: 305 lbs.-ft. at 4000 rpm. Sequential electronic fuel injection. Code X.

SVT Cobra V-8: Double overhead camshaft. Aluminum block and heads. Hydraulic valve lifters. Displacement: 330 cid (5.4 liters). B & S: 3.55 x 4.15 in. Compression ratio: 9.85:1. Brake hp: 320 at 6000 rpm. Torque: 317 lbs.-ft. at 4750 rpm. Sequential electronic fuel injection. Code V.

Chassis:

Wheelbase: 101.3 in. Overall length: 183.2 in. Height: 53.1 in., coupe and 53.2 in., convertible. Width 73.1 in. Front tread: 60.2 in. Rear tread: 60.6 in.

Technical:

Base V-6: Standard transmission: five-speed manual overdrive. Drive axle: rear. Steering: Power assisted rack-and-pinion. Front suspension: modified MacPherson gas-pressurized shock struts with coil springs and stabilizer bar. Rear suspension: four-bar link and coil spring system, gas shocks. Front brakes: power assisted discs. Rear brakes: power assisted discs. Ignition: electronic. Body construction: unibody with front isolated mini-frame. Fuel tank: 15.5 gallons.

GT V-8: Standard transmission: five-speed manual overdrive. Drive axle: rear. Steering: Power assisted rack-and-pinion. Front suspension: modified MacPherson gas-pressurized shock struts with unique GT calibrations and coil springs and stabilizer bar. Rear suspension: four-bar link and GT-specific variable-rate coil springs, and quadra-link shocks. Front brakes: power assisted discs. Rear brakes: power assisted discs. Ignition: electronic. Body construction: unibody with front isolated mini-frame. Fuel tank: 15.7 gallons.

Bullitt GT V-8: Standard transmission: five-speed manual overdrive. Drive axle: rear. Steering: Power assisted rack-and-pinion. Front suspension: modified MacPherson strut with Tokico™ struts, coil springs and a unique stabilizer bar. Rear suspension: four-bar link and coil spring system, with Tokico™ shocks, unique stabilizer bar and frame rail connectors. Front brakes: power assisted discs with 13-in. Brembo™ front brake rotors and Brembo™ performance brake calipers. Rear brakes: power assisted discs with Brembo™ front brake rotors and Brembo™ performance brake calipers. Ignition: electronic. Body construction: unibody with front isolated mini-frame. Fuel tank: 15.5 gallons.

Cobra SVT V-8: Standard transmission: five-speed manual overdrive. Drive axle: rear. Steering: Power assisted rack-and-pinion. Front suspension: modified MacPherson gas-pressurized shock struts with coil springs and stabilizer bar, lowered for enhanced handling. Rear suspension: four-bar link and coil spring system, gas shocks, lowered for enhanced handling. Brakes: power assisted four-wheel disc brakes with Brembo™ rotors and calipers. Ignition: electronic. Body construction: unibody with front isolated mini-frame. Fuel tank: 15.5 gallons.

Options:

V-6 Value Leader Coupe: 422 California emissions system (no cost). 44U four-speed automatic overdrive transmission ($815). 428 high-altitude emissions (no cost). 93N non-California emissions (no cost). V-6 Deluxe Coupe: 552 antilock braking system with all-speed traction control ($730). 422 California emissions system (no cost). 44U four-speed

automatic overdrive transmission ($815). 428 high-altitude emissions (no cost). 58M Mach 460 stereo system ($550). 93N non-California emissions (no cost). 54V Sport Appearance package ($250). V-6 Deluxe Convertible: 552 antilock braking system with all-speed traction control ($730). 422 California emissions system (no cost). 44U four-speed automatic overdrive transmission ($815). 428 high-altitude emissions (no cost). T Leather front bucket seats ($500). 58M Mach 460 stereo system ($550). 93N non-California emissions (no cost). V-6 Premium Coupe: 422 California emissions system (no cost). 44U four-speed automatic overdrive transmission ($815). 428 high-altitude emissions (no cost). T Leather front bucket seats ($500). 93N non-California emissions (no cost). V-6 Premium Convertible: 422 California emissions system (no cost). 428 high-altitude emissions (no cost). 93N non-California emissions (no cost). V-6 GT Deluxe Coupe: 422 California emissions system (no cost). 44U four-speed automatic overdrive transmission ($815). 428 high-altitude emissions (no cost). X Leather front sport bucket seats ($500). 58M Mach 460 stereo system ($550). 93N non-California emissions (no cost). GT Deluxe Convertible: 422 California emissions system (no cost). 44U four-speed automatic overdrive transmission ($815). 428 high-altitude emissions (no cost). X Leather front sport bucket seats ($500). 58M Mach 460 stereo system ($550). 93N non-California emissions (no cost). GT Premium Coupe: 422 California emissions system (no cost). 44U four-speed automatic overdrive transmission ($815). 428 high-altitude emissions (no cost). 93N non-California emissions (no cost). GT Premium Convertible: 422 California emissions system (no cost). 44U four-speed automatic overdrive transmission ($815). 428 high-altitude emissions (no cost). 93N non-California emissions (no cost). GT Bullitt Coupe: 422 California emissions system (no cost). 428 high-altitude emissions (no cost). 58M Mach 460 stereo system ($550). 93N non-California emissions (no cost). SVT Cobra Coupe: 64W 17 x 8 polished forged aluminum wheels ($395) 422 California emissions system (no cost). 12H front floor mats ($30). 428 high-altitude emissions (no cost). 93N non-California emissions (no cost). 13K rear spoiler ($195). SVT Cobra Convertible: 64W 17 x 8 polished forged aluminum wheels ($395) 422 California emissions system (no cost). 12H front floor mats ($30). 428 high-altitude emissions (no cost). 93N non-California emissions (no cost). 13K rear spoiler ($195).

History:

The Ford Special Vehicle Team and the 623 Ford dealers in North America who sell and service SVT's compelling line of high-performance vehicles proudly announced a SVT Premium Service plan during 2001. Every 2001 SVT vehicle was part of this enhancement to SVT ownership. SVT Premium Service provided SVT Mustang Cobra owners with subtle touches that gave them a special ownership experience. It provided a 2001 loaner vehicle while their Cobra was at a certified SVT dealer's service department. The loaner was available from the time the vehicle was dropped off until it was picked up and the cost was covered. In addition, the customer's 2001 Cobra was returned washed and vacuumed as a part of the program. Every SVT dealer was required to participate in special training courses designed to teach each dealership employee the expectations and demands of SVT vehicle owners. "They are given the training and tools to not only meet these needs, but exceed them," said Ford.

2002 Mustang

Mustang — (V-6): For 2002, Ford refreshed the exterior and interior of the base V-6 models and added new audio options. Two new colors, Satin Silver Clearcoat and Torch Red Clearcoat replaced Silver Metallic and Performance Red. A new tape stripe was included in the V-6 Sport Appearance group. Sixteen-inch wheels and tires were standard on base and deluxe V-6 coupes. A new speed-sensitive radio was now part of the Mach 1000 and Mach 460 audio systems. Also new was a four-piece two-tone leather steering wheel, a new storage net in coupes and optional Nudo leather-trimmed seats. Option program changes included a new MP3/CD radio for standard and deluxe configurations and a new Mach 1000 audio option for premium configurations.

2002 Mustang SVT Cobra two-door convertible

Coupe: Standard equipment for the base Mustang coupe included body color front and rear fascias with Mustang nomenclature, a composite hood with scoop, complex reflector halogen headlights with integral turn/park lamps, three-tiered taillights, dual electric remote-control outside rearview mirrors (right-hand with convex glass), clear coat paint, color-keyed rocker panel moldings, 16 x 7-in five-spoke cast-aluminum wheels, a steel spare rim 15-in. mini spare tire, second generation driver and front passenger airbags, a three-point active restraint system, deluxe carpets, child seat tether anchor brackets on the package tray, a cigarette lighter port and auxiliary power point, a clock integrated with the radio, a console (with armrest, integral storage bin, tissue holder, dual cupholders and parking brake boot), a power-operated inside-the-trunk deck lid release with glow-in-the-dark handle, a driver's footrest, a locking glove box, an analog instrument cluster (including a tachometer, a trip odometer, a voltmeter, a temperature gauge, a fuel gauge, an oil pressure gauge and an "overdrive off" indicator with automatic transmission), a light group (with lamps in dome, front "door ajar" switches and a "headlamps on" chime), luggage compartment trim and carpeting, dual visor-vanity mirrors, reclining cloth bucket seats with cloth two-way head restraints, a split-folding rear seat, stalk-mounted controls (turn signals, wiper/washer, high-beam and flash-to-pass), a storage net between visors on the headliner, a tilt steering wheel with center horn, monochromatic full wrap over door trim, soft flow-through door trim panels with full-length armrests and vinyl inserts, color-keyed upper instrument panel finish, a color keyed headliner, color-keyed safety belts, a color-keyed shifter bezel, color-keyed A and C pillar appliqués, color-keyed instrument cluster finish, manual control air conditioning, a heavy-duty 130-amp alternator, a 58-amp/hr heavy-duty maintenance-free battery, four-wheel power disc brakes, side window demisters, power door locks, an electro-drive cooling fan, EEC-V electronic engine controls, a 3.8-liter SEFI V-6, a stainless steel exhaust system, a fuel pump inertia shutoff switch, a 15.5-gal. fuel tank with tethered cap, complete Solar-Tinted glass, power ventilation with four instrument panel registers and positive shutoff, a dual note horn, a tunnel mounted parking brake with integral boot, an electronic AM/FM stereo cassette tape player with single disc CD and premium speakers and 80-watt integrated amplifier, the SecuriLock™ passive anti-theft system, remote keyless entry, power rack-and-pinion steering, a modified MacPherson strut front suspension with front stabilizer bar, a rear coil spring four-bar-link suspension with increased travel for smoother ride, gas pressurized front struts and rear shock absorbers, P225/55R16 all-season black sidewall tires, a rear window defroster, a five-speed manual overdrive transmission, one touch power windows and interval windshield wipers.

Convertible: Standard equipment for the base Mustang convertible included body color front and rear fascias with Mustang nomenclature, a power retractable convertible top with semi-hard top boot, a composite hood with scoop, complex reflector halogen headlights with integral turn/park lamps, three-tiered taillights, dual electric remote-control outside rearview mirrors (right-hand with convex glass), clear coat paint, color-keyed rocker panel moldings, 16 x 7-in five-spoke cast-aluminum wheels, a steel spare rim 15-in. mini spare tire, second generation driver and front passenger airbags, a three-point active restraint system, deluxe carpets, child seat tether anchor brackets on the seatback, a cigarette lighter port and auxiliary power point, a clock integrated with the radio, a console (with armrest, integral storage bin, tissue holder, dual cupholders and parking brake boot), a power-operated inside-the-trunk deck lid release with glow-in-the-dark handle, a driver's footrest, a locking glove box, an analog instrument cluster (including a tachometer, a trip odometer, a voltmeter, a temperature gauge, a fuel gauge, an oil pressure gauge and an "overdrive off" indicator with automatic transmission), a light group (with lamps in dome, front "door ajar" switches and a "headlamps on" chime), luggage compartment trim and carpeting, dual visor-vanity mirrors, reclining cloth bucket seats with cloth two-way head restraints, a bench rear seat, stalk-mounted controls (turn signals, wiper/washer, high-beam and flash-to-pass), a storage net between visors on the headliner, a tilt steering wheel with center horn, monochromatic full wrap over door trim, soft flow-through door trim panels with full-length armrests and vinyl inserts, color-keyed upper instrument panel finish, a color keyed headliner, color-keyed safety belts, a color-keyed shifter bezel, color-keyed A and C pillar appliqués, color-keyed instrument cluster finish, manual control air conditioning, a heavy-duty 130-amp alternator, a 58-amp/hr heavy-duty maintenance-free battery, four-wheel power disc brakes, side window demisters, power door locks, an electro-drive cooling fan, EEC-V electronic engine controls, a 3.8-liter SEFI V-6, a stainless steel exhaust system, a fuel pump inertia shutoff switch, a 15.5-gal. fuel tank with tethered cap, complete Solar-Tinted glass, power ventilation with four instrument panel registers and positive shutoff, a dual note horn, a tunnel mounted parking brake with integral boot, an electronic AM/FM stereo cassette tape player with single disc CD and premium speakers and 80-watt integrated amplifier, the SecuriLock™ passive anti-theft system, remote keyless entry, power rack-and-pinion steering, a modified MacPherson strut front suspension with front stabilizer bar, a rear coil spring four-bar-link suspension with increased

travel for smoother ride, gas pressurized front struts and rear shock absorbers, P225/55R16 all-season black sidewall tires, a rear window defroster, a five-speed manual overdrive transmission, one touch power windows, power quarter windows and interval windshield wipers.

Mustang GT — (V-8): The 2002 Mustang GT was a carryover of the 2001 model with the tall, non-functional hood scoop and side scoops that set it more apart from the V-6 models.

GT Coupe: Standard equipment on the Mustang GT coupe included body color front and rear fascias with Mustang nomenclature and dual tailpipe outlets at rear, a GT hood and side scoop, complex reflector halogen headlights with integral turn/park lamps, front fog lamps, three-tiered taillights, dual electric remote-control outside rearview mirrors (right-hand with convex glass), a single-wing rear deck lid spoiler, clear coat paint, color-keyed rocker panel moldings, 17 x 8-in five-spoke forged aluminum wheels with carryover ornaments, an aluminum spare wheel and 15-in. mini spare tire, second generation driver and front passenger airbags, a three-point active restraint system, deluxe carpets, child seat tether anchor brackets on the package tray, a cigarette lighter port and auxiliary power point, a clock integrated with the radio, a console (with armrest, integral storage bin, tissue holder, dual cupholders and parking brake boot), a power-operated inside-the-trunk deck lid release with glow-in-the-dark handle, a driver's footrest, a locking glove box, an analog instrument cluster (including a tachometer, a trip odometer, a voltmeter, a temperature gauge, a fuel gauge, an oil pressure gauge and an "overdrive off" indicator with automatic transmission), a 150-mph speedometer, a light group (with lamps in dome, front "door ajar" switches and a "headlamps on" chime), luggage compartment trim and carpeting, dual visor-vanity mirrors, reclining two-tone cloth GT sport seats with two-way cloth head restraints, a split-folding rear seat, stalk-mounted controls, a leather-wrapped tilt steering wheel with center horn (two-tone in combination with Medium Graphite and Medium Parchment interior), a storage net between sun visors on headliner, monochromatic full wrap over door trim, soft flow-through door panels with full-length armrests and vinyl inserts, color-keyed upper instrument panel finish, a color keyed headliner, color-keyed safety belts, a color-keyed shifter bezel, color-keyed A and C pillar appliqués, color-keyed instrument cluster finish, manual control air conditioning, a heavy-duty 130-amp alternator, a Traction-Loc rear axle, a 58-amp/hr heavy-duty maintenance-free battery, four-wheel ABS disc brakes, side window demisters, power door locks, an electro-drive cooling fan, EEC-V electronic engine controls, a 4.6-liter SOHC two-valve V-8, a dual stainless steel exhaust system, a fuel pump inertia shutoff switch, a 15.5-gal. fuel tank with tethered cap, complete Solar-Tinted glass, power ventilation with four instrument panel registers and positive shutoff, a dual note horn, a tunnel mounted parking brake with integral boot, an electronic AM/FM stereo cassette tape player with single disc CD and premium speakers and 80-watt integrated amplifier, the SecuriLock™ passive anti-theft system, remote keyless entry, power rack-and-pinion steering, a modified MacPherson strut front suspension with front stabilizer bar, a rear coil spring four-bar-link suspension with increased travel for smoother ride, gas pressurized front struts and rear shock absorbers with unique GT calibrations, a GT suspension package with variable rate coil springs and a quadra-shock rear suspension, P245/45ZR17 sidewall performance tires, a rear window defroster, a five-speed manual overdrive transmission, interval windshield wipers and one touch power windows.

GT Convertible: Standard equipment on the Mustang GT convertible included body color front and rear fascias with Mustang nomenclature and dual tailpipe outlets at rear, a power retractable convertible top with semi-hard boot, a GT hood and side scoop, complex reflector halogen headlights with integral turn/park lamps, front fog lamps, three-tiered taillights, dual electric remote-control outside rearview mirrors (right-hand with convex glass), a single-wing rear deck lid spoiler, clear coat paint, color-keyed rocker panel moldings, 16 x 7-in cast-aluminum wheels, a steel mini spare and 15-in. temporary tire, 17 x 8-in five-spoke forged aluminum wheels with carryover ornaments, an aluminum spare wheel and 15-in. mini spare tire, second generation driver and front passenger airbags, a three-point active restraint system, deluxe carpets, child seat tether anchor brackets on the seatbacks, a cigarette lighter port and auxiliary power point, a clock integrated with the radio, a console (with armrest, integral storage bin, tissue holder, dual cupholders and parking brake boot), a power-operated inside-the-trunk deck lid release with glow-in-the-dark handle, a driver's footrest, a locking glove box, an analog instrument cluster (including a tachometer, a trip odometer, a voltmeter, a temperature gauge, a fuel gauge, an oil pressure gauge and an "overdrive off" indicator with automatic transmission), a 150-mph speedometer, a light group (with dome lamps integrated in mirror, front "door ajar" switches and a "headlamps on" chime), luggage compartment trim and carpeting, dual illuminated visor-vanity mirrors, reclining two-tone cloth GT sport seats with cloth two-way head restraints, a bench rear seat, stalk-mounted controls, a leather-wrapped tilt steering wheel with center horn (two-tone in combination with Medium Graphite and Medium Parchment interior), a storage net between sun visors on headliner, monochromatic full wrap over door trim, soft flow-through door panels with full-length armrests and vinyl inserts, color-keyed upper instrument panel finish, a color keyed headliner, color-keyed safety belts, a color-keyed shifter bezel, color-keyed A and C pillar appliqués, color-keyed instrument cluster finish, manual control air conditioning, a Traction-Loc rear axle, a heavy-duty 130-amp alternator, a 58-amp/hr heavy-duty maintenance-free battery, four-wheel ABS disc brakes, side window demisters, power door locks, an electro-drive cooling fan, EEC-V electronic engine controls, a 4.6-liter SOHC two-valve V-8, a dual stainless steel exhaust system, a fuel pump inertia shutoff switch, a 15.5-gal. fuel tank with tethered cap, complete Solar-Tinted glass, power ventilation with four instrument panel registers and positive shutoff, a dual note horn, a tunnel mounted parking brake with integral boot, an electronic AM/FM stereo cassette tape player with single disc CD and premium speakers and 80-watt integrated amplifier, the SecuriLock™ passive anti-theft system, remote keyless entry, power rack-and-pinion steering, a modified MacPherson strut front suspension with front stabilizer bar, a rear coil spring four-bar-link suspension with increased travel for smoother ride, gas pressurized front struts and rear shock absorbers with unique GT calibrations, a GT suspension package with variable rate coil springs and a quadra-shock rear suspension, P245/45ZR17 black sidewall performance tires, a five-speed manual overdrive transmission, a rear window defroster, interval windshield wipers, one touch power windows and power rear quarter windows.

VIN:

A 17-character Vehicle Identification Number was stamped on an aluminum tab on the instrument panel and was viewable through the windshield. A vehicle certification label was found on the body side of the driver's door. The first symbol indicated the national origin: 1=United States of America. The second symbol indicated the manufacturer: F=Ford Motor Co. The third symbol identified the vehicle type: A=passenger car. The fourth symbol indicated the type of restraint system: F=driver and front passenger airbags with active rear belts. The fifth symbol was the designation number: P=passenger car. The sixth and seventh symbols indicated the car line and body type: 40=two-door coupe, 42=two-door GT coupe, 44=two-door convertible and 45=two-door GT convertible. The eighth symbol was the engine type: 4=232-cid (3.8-liter) EFI V-6 and X=281-cid (4.6-liter) EFI SOHC V-8. The ninth symbol was a check digit. The 10th symbol indicated the model year: 2=2002. The 11th symbol indicated the assembly plant: F=Dearborn, Michigan. The last six symbols are the consecutive unit production numbers staring at 100001 at each factory. The 2002 paint codes for Mustang were: B7=Zinc Yellow, D3 Torch Red Clearcoat, E9=Laser Red, L2=True Blue, PY=Bullitt Green, SU=Amazon Green, SW=Electric Green, TK=Mineral Gray, TL=Satin Silver Clearcoat and Z1=Oxford White.

Mustang (Six)

Model No.	Body/ Style No.	Body Type and Seating	Factory Price	Shipping Weight	Production Total
07	65A	2-dr. Hardtop-4P	$2,321	2,465 lbs.	167,025
08	63A	2-dr. 2 + 2 Hardtop-4P	$2,533	2,515 lbs.	12,271
08	76A	2-dr. Convertible-4P	$2,558	2,650 lbs.	19,595

Mustang Value Leader (V-6)

P	40	2-dr. Coupe-4P	$17,820	3,069 lbs.	Note 1

Mustang Deluxe (V-6)

P	40	2-dr. Coupe-4P	$18,425	3,069 lbs.	Note 1
P	44	2-dr. Convertible-4P	$23,140	3,111 lbs.	Note 1

Mustang Premium (V-6)

P	40	2-dr. Coupe-4P	$19,540	3,069 lbs.	Note 1
P	44	2-dr. Convertible-4P	$25,725	3,111 lbs.	Note 1

Mustang GT Deluxe (V-8)

P	42	2-dr. Coupe-4P	$23,360	3,242 lbs.	Note 1
P	45	2-dr. Convertible-4P	$27,615	3,386 lbs.	Note 1

Mustang GT Premium (V-8)

P	42	2-dr. Coupe-4P	$24,530	3,242 lbs.	Note 1
P	45	2-dr. Convertible-4P	$28,785	3,386 lbs.	Note 1

Note 1: Total production was 142,404.

Engines:

Base Mustang V-6: Overhead valve. Cast-iron block. Hydraulic valve lifters. Four main bearings. Displacement: 232 cid (3.8 liters). B & S: 3.80 x 3.40 in. Compression ratio: 9.36:1. Brake hp: 190 at 5250 rpm. Torque: 220 lbs.-ft. at 2750 rpm. Sequential electronic fuel injection. Code 4.

Mustang GT V-8: Single overhead camshaft. Cast-iron block. Hydraulic valve lifters. Displacement: 281 cid (4.6 liters). B & S: 3.60 x 3.60 in. Compression ratio: 9.0:1. Brake hp: 260 at 5250 rpm. Torque: 302 lbs.-ft. at 4000 rpm. Sequential electronic fuel injection. Code W.

2002 Mustang two-door coupe (BB)

Chassis:

Wheelbase: 101.3 in. Overall length: 183.2 in. Height: 53.1 in., coupe and 53.2 in., convertible. Width 73.1 in. Front tread: 60.2 in. Rear tread: 60.6 in.

Technical:

Base Mustang: Standard transmission: five-speed manual overdrive. Drive axle: rear. Steering: Power assisted rack-and-pinion. Front suspension: modified MacPherson gas-pressurized shock struts with coil springs and stabilizer bar. Rear suspension: four-bar link and coil spring system, gas shocks. Front brakes: power assisted discs. Rear brakes: power assisted discs. Ignition: electronic. Body construction: unibody with front isolated mini-frame. Fuel tank: 15.7 gallons.

Mustang GT: Standard transmission: five-speed manual overdrive. Drive axle: rear. Steering: Power assisted rack-and-pinion. Front suspension: modified MacPherson gas-pressurized shock struts with unique GT calibrations and coil springs and stabilizer bar. Rear suspension: four-bar link and GT-specific variable-rate coil springs, and quadra shocks. Front brakes: power assisted discs. Rear brakes: power assisted discs. Ignition: electronic. Body construction: unibody with front isolated mini-frame. Fuel tank: 15.7 gallons.

Options:

V-6 Value Leader Coupe: 58Z AM/FM stereo with MP3 CD player (no cost). 422 California emissions system (no cost). 423 California emissions system not required (no cost). 44U four-speed automatic overdrive transmission ($815). 93N non-California emissions (no cost). V-6 Deluxe Coupe: 58Z AM/FM stereo with MP3 CD player (no cost). 552 antilock braking system with all-speed traction control ($730). 422 California emissions system (no cost). 423 California emissions system not required (no cost). 44U four-speed automatic overdrive transmission ($815). 589 Mach 460 stereo system ($550). 93N non-California emissions (no cost). 54V Sport Appearance package ($125). V-6 Deluxe Convertible: 58Z AM/FM stereo with MP3 CD player (no cost). 552 antilock braking system with all-speed traction control ($730). 422 California emissions system (no cost). 423 California emissions system not required (no cost). 44U four-speed automatic overdrive transmission ($815). 88T leather bucket seats ($525). 589 Mach 460 stereo system ($550). 93N non-California emissions (no cost). V-6 Premium Coupe: 422 California emissions system (no cost). 423 California emissions system not required (no cost). 44U four-speed automatic overdrive transmission ($815). 88T leather bucket seats ($525). 918 Mach 1000 stereo ($1,295). 93N non-California emissions (no cost). V-6 Premium Convertible: 422 California emissions system (no cost). 423 California emissions system not required (no cost). 918 Mach 1000 stereo ($1,295). 93N non-California emissions (no cost). 54V Sport Appearance package ($125). V-6 GT Deluxe Coupe: 58Z AM/FM stereo with MP3 CD player (no cost). 422 California emissions system (no cost). 423 California emissions system not required (no cost). 44U four-speed automatic overdrive transmission ($815). 88X leather sport bucket seats ($525). 589 Mach 460 stereo system ($550). 93N non-California emissions (no cost). GT Deluxe Convertible: 58Z AM/FM stereo with MP3 CD player (no cost). 422 California emissions system (no cost). 423 California emissions system not required (no cost). 44U four-speed automatic overdrive transmission ($815). 88X leather sport bucket seats ($500). 58M Mach 460 stereo system ($550). 93N non-California emissions (no cost). GT Premium Coupe: 422 California emissions system (no cost). 423 California emissions system not required (no cost). 44U four-speed automatic overdrive transmission ($815). 918 Mach 1000 stereo ($1,295). 93N non-California emissions (no cost). GT Premium Convertible: 422 California emissions system (no cost). 423 California emissions system not required (no cost). 44U four-speed automatic overdrive transmission ($815). 918 Mach 1000 stereo ($1,295). 93N non-California emissions (no cost).

History:

Robert "Bob" Penninger, a dedicated SVT Mustang Cobra enthusiast and secretary-treasurer of the SVT Owner's Association (www.svtoa. com) was a passenger on the American Airlines flight that terrorists flew into the Pentagon, in Washington, DC, on September 11, 2001. The SVTOA noted his contribution's to getting the San Diego Chapter started and mourned his passing. Only 100 SVT Cobra were manufactured in 2002 and all of them were sent to Australia.

How to Use the Price Guide

The worth of an old car is a "ballpark" estimate at best. Our prices come from compilations of national/regional data by the editors of our weekly publication, *Old Cars Weekly News & Marketplace*. (Sample copies of *Old Cars* are available for $1.95 each from Krause Publications, 700 E. State St., Iola, WI 54990).

These data include prices from collector-car auctions, verified reports of private sales, and input from experts.

We list values for cars in six different states of condition as explained below. Prices are for complete vehicles; not parts cars, except as noted. Modified-car values are not included, but can be estimated by figuring the cost of restoring to original and deducting from the figures shown here.

Old Cars Price Guide condition codes fit the following descriptions:

2) FINE: Well-restored, or a combination of superior restoration and excellent original. Also, an *extremely* well-maintained original showing very minimal wear.

Except for the very closest inspection, a No. 2 vehicle may appear as a No. 1. The No. 2 vehicle will take the top award in many judged shows, except when squared off against a No. 1 example in its own class. It may also be driven 800-1,000 miles each year to shows, on tours, and simply for pleasure.

3) VERY GOOD: Completely operable original or "older restoration" showing wear. Also, a good amateur restoration, all presentable and serviceable inside and out. Plus, combinations of well-done restoration and good operable components; or a partially restored car with all parts necessary to complete it and/or valuable NOS parts.

This is a "20-footer." That is, from 20 feet away it may look perfect. But as we approach it, we begin to notice that the paint may be getting a little thin in spots from frequent washing and polishing. Looking inside we might detect some wear on the driver's seat, foot pedals, and carpeting. The chrome trim, while still quite presentable, may have lost the sharp, mirror-like reflective quality it had when new. All systems and equipment on the car are in good operating order. In general, most of the vehicles seen at car shows are No. 3s.

4) GOOD: A driveable vehicle needing no, or only minor, work to be functional. Also, a deteriorated restoration or a very poor amateur restoration. All components may need restoration to be "excellent," but the car is mostly useable "as is."

This is a driver. It may be in the process of restoration or its owner may have big plans, but even from 20 feet away, there is no doubt that it needs a lot of help.

5) RESTORABLE: Needs *complete* restoration of body, chassis and interior. May or may not be running, but isn't weathered, wrecked, and/or stripped to the point of being useful only for parts.

This car needs everything. It may not be operable, but it is essentially all there and has only minor surface rust, if any rust at all. While presenting a real challenge to the restorer, it won't have him doing a lot of chasing for missing parts.

1) EXCELLENT: Restored to current maximum professional standards of quality in every area, or perfect original with components operating and appearing as new. A 95-plus point show car that is not driven.

In national show judging, a car in No. 1 condition is likely to win top honors in its class. In a sense, it has ceased to be an automobile and has become an object of art. It is transported to shows in an enclosed trailer, and, when not being shown, it is stored in a climate-controlled facility. It is not driven. There are very few No. 1 cars.

6) PARTS CAR: May or may not be running, but *is* weathered, wrecked, and/or stripped to the point of being useful primarily for parts.

This is an incomplete or greatly deteriorated, perhaps rusty, vehicle that has value only as a parts donor for other restoration projects.

FORD

1908 Model T, 4-cyl., 2 levers, 2 foot pedals (1,000 produced)

Tr	1,860	5,580	9,300	20,930	32,550	46,500

1909 Model T, 4-cyl.

Rbt	1,260	3,780	6,300	14,180	22,050	31,500
Tr	1,220	3,660	6,100	13,730	21,350	30,500
Trbt	1,140	3,420	5,700	12,830	19,950	28,500
Cpe	1,060	3,180	5,300	11,930	18,550	26,500
Twn Car	1,260	3,780	6,300	14,180	22,050	31,500
Lan'let	1,140	3,420	5,700	12,830	19,950	28,500

1910 Model T, 4-cyl.

Rbt	1,220	3,660	6,100	13,730	21,350	30,500
Tr	1,180	3,540	5,900	13,280	20,650	29,500
Cpe	1,020	3,060	5,100	11,480	17,850	25,500
Twn Car	1,060	3,180	5,300	11,930	18,550	26,500
C'ml Rds	1,020	3,060	5,100	11,480	17,850	25,500

1911 Model T, 4-cyl.

Rbt	1,180	3,540	5,900	13,280	20,650	29,500
Tor Rds	1,140	3,420	5,700	12,830	19,950	28,500
Tr	1,140	3,420	5,700	12,830	19,950	28,500
Trbt	1,100	3,300	5,500	12,380	19,250	27,500
Cpe	940	2,820	4,700	10,580	16,450	23,500
Twn Car	1,100	3,300	5,500	12,380	19,250	27,500
C'ml Rds	980	2,940	4,900	11,030	17,150	24,500
Dely Van	900	2,700	4,500	10,130	15,750	22,500

1912 Model T, 4-cyl.

Rds	1,100	3,300	5,500	12,380	19,250	27,500
Tor Rds	1,140	3,420	5,700	12,830	19,950	28,500
Tr	1,140	3,420	5,700	12,830	19,950	28,500
Twn Car	1,100	3,300	5,500	12,380	19,250	27,500
Dely Van	940	2,820	4,700	10,580	16,450	23,500
C'ml Rds	1,020	3,060	5,100	11,480	17,850	25,500

1913 Model T, 4-cyl.

Rds	1,100	3,300	5,500	12,380	19,250	27,500
Tr	1,140	3,420	5,700	12,830	19,950	28,500
Twn Car	1,020	3,060	5,100	11,480	17,850	25,500

1914 Model T, 4-cyl.

Rds	1,100	3,300	5,500	12,380	19,250	27,500
Tr	1,140	3,420	5,700	12,830	19,950	28,500
Twn Car	1,060	3,180	5,300	11,930	18,550	26,500
Cpe	820	2,460	4,100	9,230	14,350	20,500

1915 & early 1916 Model T, 4-cyl., (brass rad.)

Rds	1,100	3,300	5,500	12,380	19,250	27,500
Tr	1,100	3,300	5,500	12,380	19,250	27,500
Conv Cpe	1,140	3,420	5,700	12,830	19,950	28,500
Ctr dr Sed	860	2,580	4,300	9,680	15,050	21,500
Twn Car	1,020	3,060	5,100	11,480	17,850	25,500

1916 Model T, 4-cyl., (steel rad.)

Rds	900	2,700	4,500	10,130	15,750	22,500
Tr	860	2,580	4,300	9,680	15,050	21,500
Conv Cpe	900	2,700	4,500	10,130	15,750	22,500
Ctr dr Sed	660	1,980	3,300	7,430	11,550	16,500
Twn Car	740	2,220	3,700	8,330	12,950	18,500

1917 Model T, 4-cyl.

Rds	880	2,640	4,400	9,900	15,400	22,000
Tr	820	2,460	4,100	9,230	14,350	20,500
Conv Cpe	700	2,100	3,500	7,880	12,250	17,500
Twn Car	620	1,860	3,100	6,980	10,850	15,500
Ctr dr Sed	540	1,620	2,700	6,080	9,450	13,500
Cpe	580	1,740	2,900	6,530	10,150	14,500

1918 Model T, 4-cyl.

Rds	880	2,640	4,400	9,900	15,400	22,000
Tr	820	2,460	4,100	9,230	14,350	20,500
Cpe	580	1,740	2,900	6,530	10,150	14,500
Ctr dr Sed	540	1,620	2,700	6,080	9,450	13,500

1919 Model T, 4-cyl.

Rds	880	2,640	4,400	9,900	15,400	22,000
Tr	860	2,580	4,300	9,680	15,050	21,500
Cpe	580	1,740	2,900	6,530	10,150	14,500
Ctr dr Sed	580	1,740	2,900	6,530	10,150	14,500

1920-21 Model T, 4-cyl.

Rds	820	2,460	4,100	9,230	14,350	20,500
Tr	860	2,580	4,300	9,680	15,050	21,500
Cpe	540	1,620	2,700	6,080	9,450	13,500
Ctr dr Sed	540	1,620	2,700	6,080	9,450	13,500

1922-23 Model T, 4-cyl.

Rds	740	2,220	3,700	8,330	12,950	18,500
'22 Tr	780	2,340	3,900	8,780	13,650	19,500
'23 Tr	800	2,400	4,000	9,000	14,000	20,000
Cpe	540	1,620	2,700	6,080	9,450	13,500
4d Sed	480	1,440	2,400	5,400	8,400	12,000
2d Sed	500	1,500	2,500	5,630	8,750	12,500
Ctr dr Sed	560	1,680	2,800	6,300	9,800	14,000

1924 Model T, 4-cyl.

Rds	740	2,220	3,700	8,330	12,950	18,500
Tr	800	2,400	4,000	9,000	14,000	20,000
Cpe	580	1,740	2,900	6,530	10,150	14,500
4d Sed	480	1,440	2,400	5,400	8,400	12,000
2d Sed	500	1,500	2,500	5,630	8,750	12,500
Rds PU	620	1,860	3,100	6,980	10,850	15,500

1925 Model T, 4-cyl.

Rds	740	2,220	3,700	8,330	12,950	18,500
Tr	780	2,340	3,900	8,780	13,650	19,500
Cpe	580	1,740	2,900	6,530	10,150	14,500
2d	480	1,440	2,400	5,400	8,400	12,000
4d	500	1,500	2,500	5,630	8,750	12,500

1926 Model T, 4-cyl.

Rds	780	2,340	3,900	8,780	13,650	19,500
Tr	820	2,460	4,100	9,230	14,350	20,500
Cpe	580	1,740	2,900	6,530	10,150	14,500
2d	500	1,500	2,500	5,630	8,750	12,500
4d	500	1,510	2,520	5,670	8,820	12,600

1927 Model T, 4-cyl.

Rds	820	2,460	4,100	9,230	14,350	20,500
Tr	860	2,580	4,300	9,680	15,050	21,500
Cpe	600	1,800	3,000	6,750	10,500	15,000
2d	520	1,560	2,600	5,850	9,100	13,000
4d	500	1,500	2,500	5,630	8,750	12,500

1928 Model A, 4-cyl.

NOTE: Add 20 percent average for early "AR" features.

2d Rds	1,320	3,960	6,600	14,850	23,100	33,000
4d Phae	1,400	4,200	7,000	15,750	24,500	35,000
2d Cpe	600	1,800	3,000	6,750	10,500	15,000
2d Spl Cpe	620	1,860	3,100	6,980	10,850	15,500
2d Bus Cpe	560	1,680	2,800	6,300	9,800	14,000
2d Spt Cpe	640	1,920	3,200	7,200	11,200	16,000
2d Sed	520	1,560	2,600	5,850	9,100	13,000
4d Sed	520	1,570	2,620	5,900	9,170	13,100

1929 Model A, 4-cyl.

2d Rds	1,360	4,080	6,800	15,300	23,800	34,000
4d Phae	1,440	4,320	7,200	16,200	25,200	36,000
2d Cabr	1,280	3,840	6,400	14,400	22,400	32,000
2d Cpe	640	1,920	3,200	7,200	11,200	16,000
2d Bus Cpe	600	1,800	3,000	6,750	10,500	15,000
2d Spl Cpe	660	1,980	3,300	7,430	11,550	16,500
2d Spt Cpe	680	2,040	3,400	7,650	11,900	17,000
2d Sed	520	1,560	2,600	5,850	9,100	13,000
4d 3W Sed	540	1,620	2,700	6,080	9,450	13,500
4d 5W Sed	560	1,680	2,800	6,300	9,800	14,000
4d DeL Sed	640	1,920	3,200	7,200	11,200	16,000
4d Twn Sed	680	2,040	3,400	7,650	11,900	17,000
4d Taxi	1,800	5,400	9,000	20,250	31,500	45,000
4d Twn Car	920	2,760	4,600	10,350	16,100	23,000
4d Sta Wag	1,840	5,520	9,200	20,700	32,200	46,000

1930 Model A, 4-cyl.

2d Rds	1,400	4,200	7,000	15,750	24,500	35,000
2d DeL Rds	1,440	4,320	7,200	16,200	25,200	36,000
4d Phae	1,480	4,440	7,400	16,650	25,900	37,000
2d DeL Phae	1,520	4,560	7,600	17,100	26,600	38,000
2d Cabr	1,320	3,960	6,600	14,850	23,100	33,000
2d Cpe	680	2,040	3,400	7,650	11,900	17,000
2d DeL Cpe	720	2,160	3,600	8,100	12,600	18,000
2d Spt Cpe	700	2,100	3,500	7,880	12,250	17,500
2d Std Sed	560	1,680	2,800	6,300	9,800	14,000
2d DeL Sed	720	2,160	3,600	8,100	12,600	18,000
2d 3W Cpe	680	2,040	3,400	7,650	11,900	17,000
2d 5W Cpe	700	2,100	3,500	7,880	12,250	17,500
4d DeL Sed	680	2,040	3,400	7,650	11,900	17,000
4d Twn Sed	720	2,160	3,600	8,100	12,600	18,000
2d Vic	880	2,640	4,400	9,900	15,400	22,000
4d Sta Wag	1,880	5,640	9,400	21,150	32,900	47,000

1931 Model A, 4-cyl.

2d Rds	1,400	4,200	7,000	15,750	24,500	35,000
2d DeL Rds	1,440	4,320	7,200	16,200	25,200	36,000
4d Phae	1,480	4,440	7,400	16,650	25,900	37,000
2d DeL Phae	1,520	4,560	7,600	17,100	26,600	38,000
2d Cabr	1,320	3,960	6,600	14,850	23,100	33,000
2d Conv Sed	1,600	4,800	8,000	18,000	28,000	40,000
2d Cpe	680	2,040	3,400	7,650	11,900	17,000
2d DeL Cpe	720	2,160	3,600	8,100	12,600	18,000
2d Spt Cpe	700	2,100	3,500	7,880	12,250	17,500
2d Sed	560	1,680	2,800	6,300	9,800	14,000
2d DeL Sed	720	2,160	3,600	8,100	12,600	18,000
4d Sed	600	1,800	3,000	6,750	10,500	15,000
4d DeL Sed	640	1,920	3,200	7,200	11,200	16,000
4d Twn Sed	720	2,160	3,600	8,100	12,600	18,000
2d Vic	880	2,640	4,400	9,900	15,400	22,000
4d Sta Wag	1,880	5,640	9,400	21,150	32,900	47,000

1932 Model B, 4-cyl.

2d Rds	2,600	7,800	13,000	29,250	45,500	65,000
4d Phae	2,280	6,840	11,400	25,650	39,900	57,000
2d Cabr	2,680	8,040	13,400	30,150	46,900	67,000
4d Conv Sed	2,160	6,480	10,800	24,300	37,800	54,000
2d Cpe	2,400	7,200	12,000	27,000	42,000	60,000
2d Spt Cpe	2,440	7,320	12,200	27,450	42,700	61,000
2d Sed	1,280	3,840	6,400	14,400	22,400	32,000
4d Sed	880	2,640	4,400	9,900	15,400	22,000
2d Vic	1,720	5,160	8,600	19,350	30,100	43,000
4d Sta Wag	3,200	9,600	16,000	36,000	56,000	80,000

1932 Model 18, V-8

2d Rds	2,800	8,400	14,000	31,500	49,000	70,000
2d DeL Rds	2,680	8,040	13,400	30,150	46,900	67,000
4d Phae	2,320	6,960	11,600	26,100	40,600	58,000
4d DeL Phae	2,680	8,040	13,400	30,150	46,900	67,000
2d Cabr	2,720	8,160	13,600	30,600	47,600	68,000
4d Conv Sed	2,200	6,600	11,000	24,750	38,500	55,000
2d Cpe	2,400	7,200	12,000	27,000	42,000	60,000
2d DeL Cpe	2,500	7,500	12,500	28,130	43,750	62,500
2d Spt Cpe	2,540	7,620	12,700	28,580	44,450	63,500
2d Sed	1,400	4,200	7,000	15,750	24,500	35,000
2d DeL Sed	1,500	4,500	7,500	16,880	26,250	37,500
4d Sed	1,000	3,000	5,000	11,250	17,500	25,000
4d DeL Sed	1,100	3,300	5,500	12,380	19,250	27,500
2d Vic	1,760	5,280	8,800	19,800	30,800	44,000
4d Sta Wag	3,480	10,440	17,400	39,150	60,900	87,000

1933 Model 40, V-8

4d Phae	2,240	6,720	11,200	25,200	39,200	56,000
4d DeL Phae	2,280	6,840	11,400	25,650	39,900	57,000
2d Rds	2,720	8,160	13,600	30,600	47,600	68,000
2d DeL Rds	2,800	8,400	14,000	31,500	49,000	70,000
2d 3W Cpe	2,420	7,260	12,100	27,230	42,350	60,500
2d 3W DeL Cpe	2,540	7,620	12,700	28,580	44,450	63,500
2d 5W Cpe	2,340	7,020	11,700	26,330	40,950	58,500
2d 5W DeL Cpe	2,380	7,140	11,900	26,780	41,650	59,500
2d Cabr	2,640	7,920	13,200	29,700	46,200	66,000
2d Sed	1,320	3,960	6,600	14,850	23,100	33,000
2d DeL Sed	1,420	4,260	7,100	15,980	24,850	35,500
4d Sed	920	2,760	4,600	10,350	16,100	23,000
4d DeL Sed	1,020	3,060	5,100	11,480	17,850	25,500
2d Vic	2,280	6,840	11,400	25,650	39,900	57,000
4d Sta Wag	3,620	10,860	18,100	40,730	63,350	90,500

1933 Model 40, 4-cyl.

NOTE: All models deduct 20 percent average from V-8 models.

1934 Model 40, V-8

2d Rds	2,760	8,280	13,800	31,050	48,300	69,000
4d Phae	2,320	6,960	11,600	26,100	40,600	58,000
2d Cabr	2,680	8,040	13,400	30,150	46,900	67,000
5W Cpe	2,360	7,080	11,800	26,550	41,300	59,000
2d 3W DeL Cpe	2,560	7,680	12,800	28,800	44,800	64,000
2d 5W DeL Cpe	2,400	7,200	12,000	27,000	42,000	60,000
2d Sed	1,360	4,080	6,800	15,300	23,800	34,000
2d DeL Sed	1,460	4,380	7,300	16,430	25,550	36,500
4d Sed	960	2,880	4,800	10,800	16,800	24,000
4d DeL Sed	1,060	3,180	5,300	11,930	18,550	26,500
2d Vic	2,320	6,960	11,600	26,100	40,600	58,000
4d Sta Wag	3,640	10,920	18,200	40,950	63,700	91,000

1935 Model 48, V-8

4d Phae	2,240	6,720	11,200	25,200	39,200	56,000
2d Rds	2,520	7,560	12,600	28,350	44,100	63,000
2d Cabr	2,360	7,080	11,800	26,550	41,300	59,000
4d Conv Sed	2,440	7,320	12,200	27,450	42,700	61,000
2d 3W DeL Cpe	1,680	5,040	8,400	18,900	29,400	42,000
2d 5W Cpe	1,520	4,560	7,600	17,100	26,600	38,000
2d 5W DeL Cpe	1,560	4,680	7,800	17,550	27,300	39,000
2d Sed	960	2,880	4,800	10,800	16,800	24,000
2d DeL Sed	1,000	3,000	5,000	11,250	17,500	25,000
4d Sed	920	2,760	4,600	10,350	16,100	23,000
4d DeL Sed	940	2,820	4,700	10,580	16,450	23,500
4d Sta Wag	3,320	9,960	16,600	37,350	58,100	83,000
4d C'ham Twn Car	3,000	9,000	15,000	33,750	52,500	75,000

1936 Model 68, V-8

2d Rds	2,560	7,680	12,800	28,800	44,800	64,000
4d Phae	2,280	6,840	11,400	25,650	39,900	57,000
2d Cabr	2,400	7,200	12,000	27,000	42,000	60,000
2d Clb Cabr	2,440	7,320	12,200	27,450	42,700	61,000
4d Conv Trk Sed	2,520	7,560	12,600	28,350	44,100	63,000
4d Conv Sed	2,480	7,440	12,400	27,900	43,400	62,000
2d 3W Cpe	1,640	4,920	8,200	18,450	28,700	41,000
2d 5W Cpe	1,600	4,800	8,000	18,000	28,000	40,000
2d 5W DeL Cpe	1,640	4,920	8,200	18,450	28,700	41,000
2d Sed	1,000	3,000	5,000	11,250	17,500	25,000
2d Tr Sed	1,020	3,060	5,100	11,480	17,850	25,500
2d DeL Sed	1,040	3,120	5,200	11,700	18,200	26,000
4d Sed	960	2,880	4,800	10,800	16,800	24,000
4d Tr Sed	980	2,940	4,900	11,030	17,150	24,500
4d DeL Sed	1,000	3,000	5,000	11,250	17,500	25,000
4d DeL Tr Sed	1,020	3,060	5,100	11,480	17,850	25,500
4d Sta Wag	3,400	10,200	17,000	38,250	59,500	85,000

1937 Model 74, V-8, 60 hp

2d Sed	720	2,170	3,620	8,150	12,670	18,100
2d Tr Sed	740	2,230	3,720	8,370	13,020	18,600
4d Sed	720	2,160	3,600	8,100	12,600	18,000
4d Tr Sed	740	2,220	3,700	8,330	12,950	18,500
2d Cpe	1,320	3,960	6,600	14,850	23,100	33,000
2d Cpe PU	1,360	4,080	6,800	15,300	23,800	34,000
4d Sta Wag	2,920	8,760	14,600	32,850	51,100	73,000

1937 Model 78, V-8, 85 hp

2d Rds	2,760	8,280	13,800	31,050	48,300	69,000
4d Phae	2,400	7,200	12,000	27,000	42,000	60,000
2d Cabr	2,480	7,440	12,400	27,900	43,400	62,000
2d Clb Cabr	2,520	7,560	12,600	28,350	44,100	63,000
4d Conv Sed	2,560	7,680	12,800	28,800	44,800	64,000
2d Cpe	1,400	4,200	7,000	15,750	24,500	35,000
2d Clb Cpe	1,440	4,320	7,200	16,200	25,200	36,000
2d Sed	780	2,350	3,920	8,820	13,720	19,600
2d Tr Sed	800	2,410	4,020	9,050	14,070	20,100
4d Sed	780	2,340	3,900	8,780	13,650	19,500
4d Tr Sed	800	2,400	4,000	9,000	14,000	20,000
4d Sta Wag	3,560	10,680	17,800	40,050	62,300	89,000

1938 Model 81A Standard, V-8

2d Cpe	1,260	3,780	6,300	14,180	22,050	31,500
2d Sed	720	2,170	3,620	8,150	12,670	18,100
4d Sed	720	2,160	3,600	8,100	12,600	18,000

1938 Model 81A DeLuxe, V-8

4d Phae	2,360	7,080	11,800	26,550	41,300	59,000
2d Conv	2,400	7,200	12,000	27,000	42,000	60,000
2d Clb Conv	2,440	7,320	12,200	27,450	42,700	61,000
4d Conv Sed	2,520	7,560	12,600	28,350	44,100	63,000
2d Cpe	1,360	4,080	6,800	15,300	23,800	34,000
2d Clb Cpe	1,400	4,200	7,000	15,750	24,500	35,000
2d Sed	760	2,290	3,820	8,600	13,370	19,100
4d Sed	760	2,280	3,800	8,550	13,300	19,000
4d Sta Wag	3,520	10,560	17,600	39,600	61,600	88,000

NOTE: Deduct 10 percent average for 60 hp 82A Ford.

1939 Standard, V-8

2d Cpe	1,360	4,080	6,800	15,300	23,800	34,000
2d Sed	740	2,230	3,720	8,370	13,020	18,600
4d Sed	740	2,220	3,700	8,330	12,950	18,500
4d Sta Wag	3,560	10,680	17,800	40,050	62,300	89,000

1939 DeLuxe, V-8

2d Conv	3,120	9,360	15,600	35,100	54,600	78,000
4d Conv Sed	3,240	9,720	16,200	36,450	56,700	81,000
2d Cpe	1,400	4,200	7,000	15,750	24,500	35,000
2d Sed	800	2,410	4,020	9,050	14,070	20,100
4d Sed	800	2,400	4,000	9,000	14,000	20,000
4d Sta Wag	4,220	12,660	21,100	47,480	73,850	105,500

NOTE: Deduct 10 percent average for V-8, 60 hp models.

1940 Standard & DeLuxe, V-8

2d Conv	3,160	9,480	15,800	35,550	55,300	79,000
2d Cpe	1,440	4,320	7,200	16,200	25,200	36,000
2d DeL Cpe	1,520	4,560	7,600	17,100	26,600	38,000
2d Sed	840	2,530	4,220	9,500	14,770	21,100
2d DeL Sed	860	2,590	4,320	9,720	15,120	21,600
4d Sed	840	2,520	4,200	9,450	14,700	21,000
4d DeL Sed	860	2,580	4,300	9,680	15,050	21,500
4d Sta Wag	4,260	12,780	21,300	47,930	74,550	106,500

NOTE: Deduct 10 percent average for V-8, 60 hp models.

1941 Model 11A Special, V-8

2d Cpe	1,360	4,080	6,800	15,300	23,800	34,000
2d Sed	700	2,100	3,500	7,920	12,300	17,600
4d Sed	700	2,100	3,500	7,880	12,300	17,500

1941 DeLuxe

3P Cpe	1,480	4,440	7,400	16,650	25,900	37,000
5P Cpe	1,440	4,320	7,200	16,200	25,200	36,000
2d Sed	750	2,300	3,800	8,600	13,400	19,100
4d Sed	750	2,300	3,800	8,550	13,300	19,000
4d Sta Wag	3,120	9,360	15,600	35,100	54,600	78,000

1941 Super DeLuxe

2d Conv	2,360	7,080	11,800	26,550	41,300	59,000
3P Cpe	1,520	4,560	7,600	17,100	26,600	38,000
5P Cpe	1,560	4,680	7,800	17,550	27,300	39,000
2d Sed	800	2,350	3,900	8,820	13,700	19,600
4d Sed	800	2,350	3,900	8,780	13,700	19,500
4d Sta Wag	3,520	10,560	17,600	39,600	61,600	88,000

NOTE: Deduct 10 percent average for 6-cyl.

1942 Model 2GA Special, 6-cyl.

3P Cpe	1,240	3,720	6,200	13,950	21,700	31,000
2d Sed	700	2,050	3,400	7,700	12,000	17,100
4d Sed	700	2,050	3,400	7,650	11,900	17,000

1942 Model 21A DeLuxe, V-8

2d Cpe	1,280	3,840	6,400	14,400	22,400	32,000
5P Cpe	1,320	3,960	6,600	14,850	23,100	33,000
2d Sed	700	2,100	3,500	7,920	12,300	17,600
4d Sed	700	2,100	3,500	7,880	12,300	17,500
4d Sta Wag	3,160	9,480	15,800	35,550	55,300	79,000

1942 Super DeLuxe

2d Conv	2,400	7,200	12,000	27,000	42,000	60,000
3P Cpe	1,400	4,200	7,000	15,750	24,500	35,000
5P Cpe	1,360	4,080	6,800	15,300	23,800	34,000
2d Sed	700	2,100	3,500	7,880	12,300	17,500
4d Sed	700	2,050	3,450	7,740	12,000	17,200
4d Sta Wag	3,560	10,680	17,800	40,050	62,300	89,000

NOTE: Deduct 10 percent average for 6-cyl.

1946-48 Model 89A DeLuxe, V-8

3P Cpe	1,240	3,720	6,200	13,950	21,700	31,000
2d Sed	684	2,052	3,420	7,700	11,970	17,100
4d Sed	680	2,040	3,400	7,650	11,900	17,000

1946-48 Model 89A Super DeLuxe, V-8

2d Conv	2,080	6,240	10,400	23,400	36,400	52,000
2d Sptman Conv	8,380	25,140	41,900	94,280	146,650	209,500
2d 3P Cpe	1,280	3,840	6,400	14,400	22,400	32,000
2d 5P Cpe	1,320	3,960	6,600	14,850	23,100	33,000
2d Sed	704	2,112	3,520	7,920	12,320	17,600
4d Sed	700	2,100	3,500	7,880	12,250	17,500
4d Sta Wag	3,720	11,160	18,600	41,850	65,100	93,000

NOTE: Deduct 5 percent average for 6-cyl.

1949-50 DeLuxe, V-8, 114" wb

2d Bus Cpe	1,040	3,120	5,200	11,700	18,200	26,000
2d Sed	880	2,640	4,400	9,900	15,400	22,000
4d Sed	800	2,400	4,000	9,000	14,000	20,000

1949-50 Custom DeLuxe, V-8, 114" wb

2d Clb Cpe	1,080	3,240	5,400	12,150	18,900	27,000
2d Sed	920	2,760	4,600	10,350	16,100	23,000
4d Sed	840	2,520	4,200	9,450	14,700	21,000
2d Crest (1950 only)	1,120	3,360	5,600	12,600	19,600	28,000
2d Conv	1,880	5,640	9,400	21,150	32,900	47,000
2d Sta Wag	2,600	7,800	13,000	29,250	45,500	65,000

NOTE: Deduct 5 percent average for 6-cyl.

1951 DeLuxe, V-8, 114" wb

2d Bus Cpe	1,080	3,240	5,400	12,150	18,900	27,000
2d Sed	920	2,760	4,600	10,350	16,100	23,000
4d Sed	840	2,520	4,200	9,450	14,700	21,000

1951 Custom DeLuxe, V-8, 114" wb

2d Clb Cpe	1,120	3,360	5,600	12,600	19,600	28,000
2d Sed	960	2,880	4,800	10,800	16,800	24,000
4d Sed	880	2,640	4,400	9,900	15,400	22,000
2d Crest	1,160	3,480	5,800	13,050	20,300	29,000
2d HT	1,200	3,600	6,000	13,500	21,000	30,000
2d Conv	1,720	5,160	8,600	19,350	30,100	43,000
2d Ctry Sq Sta Wag	2,840	8,520	14,200	31,950	49,700	71,000

NOTE: Deduct 5 percent average for 6-cyl.

1952-53 Mainline, V-8, 115" wb

2d Bus Cpe	760	2,280	3,800	8,550	13,300	19,000
2d Sed	684	2,052	3,420	7,700	11,970	17,100
4d Sed	680	2,040	3,400	7,650	11,900	17,000
2d Sta Wag	760	2,280	3,800	8,550	13,300	19,000

1952-53 Customline, V-8, 115" wb

2d Clb Cpe	840	2,520	4,200	9,450	14,700	21,000
2d Sed	780	2,340	3,900	8,780	13,650	19,500
4d Sed	776	2,328	3,880	8,730	13,580	19,400
4d Sta Wag	840	2,520	4,200	9,450	14,700	21,000

1952-53 Crestline, 8-cyl., 115" wb

2d HT	980	2,940	4,900	11,030	17,150	24,500
2d Conv	1,200	3,600	6,000	13,500	21,000	30,000
4d Ctry Sq Sta Wag	1,060	3,180	5,300	11,930	18,550	26,500

NOTE: Deduct 5 percent average for 6-cyl. Add 50 percent for 1953 Indy Pace Car replica convertible.

1954 Mainline, 8-cyl., 115.5" wb

2d Bus Cpe	720	2,160	3,600	8,100	12,600	18,000
2d Sed	684	2,052	3,420	7,700	11,970	17,100
4d Sed	680	2,040	3,400	7,650	11,900	17,000
2d Sta Wag	760	2,280	3,800	8,550	13,300	19,000

1954 Customline, V-8, 115.5" wb

2d Clb Cpe	860	2,580	4,300	9,680	15,050	21,500
2d Sed	820	2,460	4,100	9,230	14,350	20,500
4d Sed	816	2,448	4,080	9,180	14,280	20,400
2/4d Sta Wag	880	2,640	4,400	9,900	15,400	22,000

1954 Crestline, V-8, 115.5" wb

4d Sed	820	2,460	4,100	9,230	14,350	20,500
2d HT	1,040	3,120	5,200	11,700	18,200	26,000
2d Sky Cpe	1,280	3,840	6,400	14,400	22,400	32,000
2d Conv	1,360	4,080	6,800	15,300	23,800	34,000
4d Ctry Sq Sta Wag	1,100	3,300	5,500	12,380	19,250	27,500

NOTE: Deduct 5 percent average for 6-cyl.

1955 Mainline, V-8, 115.5" wb

2d Bus Sed	664	1,992	3,320	7,470	11,620	16,600
2d Sed	672	2,016	3,360	7,560	11,760	16,800
4d Sed	668	2,004	3,340	7,520	11,690	16,700

1955 Customline, V-8, 115.5" wb

2d Sed	696	2,088	3,480	7,830	12,180	17,400
4d Sed	692	2,076	3,460	7,790	12,110	17,300

1955 Fairlane, V-8, 115.5" wb

2d Sed	752	2,256	3,760	8,460	13,160	18,800
4d Sed	748	2,244	3,740	8,420	13,090	18,700
2d HT Vic	1,000	3,000	5,000	11,250	17,500	25,000
2d Crn Vic	1,560	4,680	7,800	17,550	27,300	39,000
2d Crn Vic Plexi-top	2,320	6,960	11,600	26,100	40,600	58,000
2d Conv	2,140	6,420	10,700	24,080	37,450	53,500

1955 Station Wagon, V-8, 115.5" wb

2d Custom Ran Wag	800	2,400	4,000	9,000	14,000	20,000
2d Ran Wag	780	2,340	3,900	8,780	13,650	19,500
4d Ctry Sed Customline	800	2,400	4,000	9,000	14,000	20,000
4d Ctry Sed Fairlane	840	2,520	4,200	9,450	14,700	21,000
4d Ctry Sq	880	2,640	4,400	9,900	15,400	22,000

NOTE: Deduct 5 percent average for 6-cyl.

1956 Mainline, V-8, 115.5" wb

2d Bus Sed	668	2,004	3,340	7,520	11,690	16,700
2d Sed	676	2,028	3,380	7,610	11,830	16,900
4d Sed	672	2,016	3,360	7,560	11,760	16,800

1956 Customline, V-8, 115.5" wb

2d Sed	700	2,100	3,500	7,880	12,250	17,500
4d Sed	696	2,088	3,480	7,830	12,180	17,400
2d HT Vic	920	2,760	4,600	10,350	16,100	23,000

1956 Fairlane, V-8, 115.5" wb

2d Sed	752	2,256	3,760	8,460	13,160	18,800
4d Sed	748	2,244	3,740	8,420	13,090	18,700
4d HT Vic	1,000	3,000	5,000	11,250	17,500	25,000
2d HT Vic	1,200	3,600	6,000	13,500	21,000	30,000
2d Crn Vic	1,740	5,220	8,700	19,580	30,450	43,500
2d Crn Vic Plexi-top	2,360	7,080	11,800	26,550	41,300	59,000
2d Conv	2,180	6,540	10,900	24,530	38,150	54,500

1956 Station Wagons, V-8, 115.5" wb

2d Ran Wag	760	2,280	3,800	8,550	13,300	19,000
2d Parklane	1,540	4,620	7,700	17,330	26,950	38,500
4d Ctry Sed Customline	800	2,400	4,000	9,000	14,000	20,000
4d Ctry Sed Fairlane	840	2,520	4,200	9,450	14,700	21,000
4d Ctry Sq	880	2,640	4,400	9,900	15,400	22,000

NOTE: Deduct 5 percent average for 6-cyl. Add 10 percent for "T-Bird Special" V-8. Add 30 percent for 312-cid with dual four-barrel carbs.

1957 Custom, V-8, 116" wb

2d Bus Cpe	524	1,572	2,620	5,900	9,170	13,100
2d Sed	536	1,608	2,680	6,030	9,380	13,400
4d Sed	532	1,596	2,660	5,990	9,310	13,300

1957 Custom 300, V-8, 116" wb

2d Sed	640	1,920	3,200	7,200	11,200	16,000
4d Sed	544	1,632	2,720	6,120	9,520	13,600

1957 Fairlane, V-8, 118" wb

2d Sed	644	1,932	3,220	7,250	11,270	16,100
4d Sed	640	1,920	3,200	7,200	11,200	16,000
4d HT Vic	880	2,640	4,400	9,900	15,400	22,000
2d Vic HT	960	2,880	4,800	10,800	16,800	24,000

1957 Fairlane 500, V-8, 118" wb

2d Sed	652	1,956	3,260	7,340	11,410	16,300
4d Sed	648	1,944	3,240	7,290	11,340	16,200
4d HT Vic	880	2,640	4,400	9,900	15,400	22,000
2d HT Vic	1,040	3,120	5,200	11,700	18,200	26,000
2d Sun Conv	1,880	5,640	9,400	21,150	32,900	47,000
2d Sky HT Conv	2,240	6,720	11,200	25,200	39,200	56,000

1957 Station Wagons, 8-cyl., 116" wb

2d Ran Wag	680	2,040	3,400	7,650	11,900	17,000
2d DeL Rio Ran	1,100	3,300	5,500	12,380	19,250	27,500
4d Ctry Sed	800	2,400	4,000	9,000	14,000	20,000
4d Ctry Sq	760	2,280	3,800	8,550	13,300	19,000

NOTE: Deduct 5 percent average for 6-cyl. Add 20 percent for "T-Bird Special" V-8 (Code E). Add 30 percent for Supercharged V-8 (Code F).

1958 Custom 300, V-8, 116.03" wb

2d Bus Cpe	388	1,164	1,940	4,370	6,790	9,700
2d Sed	520	1,560	2,600	5,850	9,100	13,000
4d Sed	492	1,476	2,460	5,540	8,610	12,300

1958 Fairlane, V-8, 116.03" wb

2d Sed	500	1,500	2,500	5,630	8,750	12,500
4d Sed	496	1,488	2,480	5,580	8,680	12,400
4d HT	800	2,400	4,000	9,000	14,000	20,000
2d HT	840	2,520	4,200	9,450	14,700	21,000

1958 Fairlane 500, V-8, 118.04" wb

2d Sed	532	1,596	2,660	5,990	9,310	13,300
4d Sed	528	1,584	2,640	5,940	9,240	13,200
4d HT	840	2,520	4,200	9,450	14,700	21,000
2d HT	920	2,760	4,600	10,350	16,100	23,000
2d Sun Conv	1,800	5,400	9,000	20,250	31,500	45,000
2d Sky HT Conv	2,160	6,480	10,800	24,300	37,800	54,000

1958 Station Wagons, V-8, 116.03" wb

2d Ran	668	2,004	3,340	7,520	11,690	16,700
4d Ran	660	1,980	3,300	7,430	11,550	16,500
4d Ctry Sed	700	2,100	3,500	7,880	12,250	17,500
2d DeL Rio Ran	1,120	3,360	5,600	12,600	19,600	28,000
4d Ctry Sq	740	2,220	3,700	8,330	12,950	18,500

NOTE: Deduct 5 percent average for 6-cyl.

1959 Custom 300, V-8, 118" wb

2d Bus Cpe	500	1,500	2,500	5,630	8,750	12,500
2d Sed	504	1,512	2,520	5,670	8,820	12,600
4d Sed	496	1,488	2,480	5,580	8,680	12,400

1959 Fairlane, V-8, 118" wb

2d Sed	396	1,188	1,980	4,460	6,930	9,900
4d Sed	392	1,176	1,960	4,410	6,860	9,800

1959 Fairlane 500, V-8, 118" wb

2d Sed	484	1,452	2,420	5,450	8,470	12,100
4d Sed	480	1,440	2,400	5,400	8,400	12,000
4d HT	780	2,340	3,900	8,780	13,650	19,500
2d HT	900	2,700	4,500	10,130	15,750	22,500
2d Sun Conv	1,840	5,520	9,200	20,700	32,200	46,000
2d Sky HT Conv	2,200	6,600	11,000	24,750	38,500	55,000

1959 Galaxie, V-8, 118" wb

2d Sed	492	1,476	2,460	5,540	8,610	12,300
4d Sed	488	1,464	2,440	5,490	8,540	12,200
4d HT	820	2,460	4,100	9,230	14,350	20,500
2d HT	940	2,820	4,700	10,580	16,450	23,500
2d Sun Conv	1,840	5,520	9,200	20,700	32,200	46,000
2d Sky HT Conv	2,200	6,600	11,000	24,750	38,500	55,000

1959 Station Wagons, V-8, 118" wb

2d Ran	540	1,620	2,700	6,080	9,450	13,500
4d Ran	680	2,040	3,400	7,650	11,900	17,000
2d Ctry Sed	720	2,160	3,600	8,100	12,600	18,000
4d Ctry Sed	700	2,100	3,500	7,880	12,250	17,500
4d Ctry Sq	720	2,160	3,600	8,100	12,600	18,000

NOTE: Deduct 5 percent average for 6-cyl.

1960 Falcon, 6-cyl., 109.5" wb

2d Sed	368	1,104	1,840	4,140	6,440	9,200
4d Sed	364	1,092	1,820	4,100	6,370	9,100
2d Sta Wag	372	1,116	1,860	4,190	6,510	9,300
4d Sta Wag	368	1,104	1,840	4,140	6,440	9,200

1960 Fairlane, V-8, 119" wb

2d Bus Cpe	372	1,116	1,860	4,190	6,510	9,300
2d Sed	384	1,152	1,920	4,320	6,720	9,600
4d Sed	380	1,140	1,900	4,280	6,650	9,500

1960 Fairlane 500, V-8, 119" wb

2d Sed	388	1,164	1,940	4,370	6,790	9,700
4d Sed	384	1,152	1,920	4,320	6,720	9,600

1960 Galaxie, V-8, 119" wb

2d Sed	500	1,500	2,500	5,630	8,750	12,500
4d Sed	496	1,488	2,480	5,580	8,680	12,400
4d HT	720	2,160	3,600	8,100	12,600	18,000
2d HT	880	2,640	4,400	9,900	15,400	22,000

1960 Galaxie Special, V-8, 119" wb

2d Starliner HT	1,280	3,840	6,400	14,400	22,400	32,000
2d Sun Conv	1,480	4,440	7,400	16,650	25,900	37,000

1960 Station Wagons, V-8, 119" wb

2d Ran	652	1,956	3,260	7,340	11,410	16,300
4d Ran	640	1,920	3,200	7,200	11,200	16,000
4d Ctry Sed	660	1,980	3,300	7,430	11,550	16,500
4d Ctry Sq	680	2,040	3,400	7,650	11,900	17,000

NOTE: Deduct 5 percent average for 6-cyl. Add 100 percent for 352-cid, 360-hp.

1961 Falcon, 6-cyl., 109.5" wb

2d Sed	392	1,176	1,960	4,410	6,860	9,800
4d Sed	388	1,164	1,940	4,370	6,790	9,700
2d Futura Sed	640	1,920	3,200	7,200	11,200	16,000
2d Sta Wag	396	1,188	1,980	4,460	6,930	9,900
4d Sta Wag	392	1,176	1,960	4,410	6,860	9,800

1961 Fairlane, V-8, 119" wb

2d Sed	396	1,188	1,980	4,460	6,930	9,900
4d Sed	392	1,176	1,960	4,410	6,860	9,800

1961 Galaxie, V-8, 119" wb

2d Sed	500	1,500	2,500	5,630	8,750	12,500
4d Sed	496	1,488	2,480	5,580	8,680	12,400
4d Vic HT	680	2,040	3,400	7,650	11,900	17,000
2d Vic HT	760	2,280	3,800	8,550	13,300	19,000
2d Star HT	1,360	4,080	6,800	15,300	23,800	34,000
2d Sun Conv	1,560	4,680	7,800	17,550	27,300	39,000

1961 Station Wagons, V-8, 119" wb

4d Ran	620	1,860	3,100	6,980	10,850	15,500
2d Ran	628	1,884	3,140	7,070	10,990	15,700
4d 6P Ctry Sed	720	2,160	3,600	8,100	12,600	18,000
4d Ctry Sq	740	2,220	3,700	8,330	12,950	18,500

NOTE: Deduct 5 percent average for 6-cyl. Add 30 percent for 390 cid, 401 hp. Add 25 percent for 390 cid, 375 hp. Add 50 percent for 4-Speed on either 390-cid, 375-hp or 390-cid, 401-hp.

1962 Falcon, 6-cyl., 109.5" wb

4d Sed	336	1,008	1,680	3,780	5,880	8,400
2d Sed	340	1,020	1,700	3,830	5,950	8,500
2d Fut Spt Cpe	680	2,040	3,400	7,650	11,900	17,000
4d Sq Wag	392	1,176	1,960	4,410	6,860	9,800

1962 Falcon Station Bus, 6-cyl., 109.5" wb

Sta Bus	332	996	1,660	3,740	5,810	8,300
Clb Wag	336	1,008	1,680	3,780	5,880	8,400
DeL Wag	340	1,020	1,700	3,830	5,950	8,500

1962 Fairlane, V-8, 115.5" wb

4d Sed	332	996	1,660	3,740	5,810	8,300
2d Sed	336	1,008	1,680	3,780	5,880	8,400
2d Spt Cpe	352	1,056	1,760	3,960	6,160	8,800

1962 Galaxie 500, V-8, 119" wb

4d Sed	348	1,044	1,740	3,920	6,090	8,700
4d HT	640	1,920	3,200	7,200	11,200	16,000
2d Sed	392	1,176	1,960	4,410	6,860	9,800
2d HT	720	2,160	3,600	8,100	12,600	18,000
2d Sun Conv	1,080	3,240	5,400	12,150	18,900	27,000

1962 Galaxie 500 XL, V-8, 119" wb

2d HT	800	2,400	4,000	9,000	14,000	20,000
2d Sun Conv	1,200	3,600	6,000	13,500	21,000	30,000

1962 Station Wagons, V-8, 119" wb

4d Ranch	580	1,740	2,900	6,530	10,150	14,500
4d Ctry Sed	600	1,800	3,000	6,750	10,500	15,000
4d Ctry Sq	620	1,860	3,100	6,980	10,850	15,500

NOTE: Deduct 5 percent for 6-cyl. Add 30 percent for 406 V-8. Add 20 percent for 390 cid, 330 hp. Add 20 percent for 390 cid, 300 hp.

1963 Falcon/Falcon Futura, 6-cyl., 109.5" wb

4d Sed	344	1,032	1,720	3,870	6,020	8,600
2d Sed	348	1,044	1,740	3,920	6,090	8,700
2d Spt Sed	360	1,080	1,800	4,050	6,300	9,000
2d HT	640	1,920	3,200	7,200	11,200	16,000
2d Spt HT	680	2,040	3,400	7,650	11,900	17,000
2d Conv	800	2,400	4,000	9,000	14,000	20,000
2d Spt Conv	840	2,520	4,200	9,450	14,700	21,000
4d Sq Wag	420	1,260	2,100	4,730	7,350	10,500
4d Sta Wag	400	1,200	2,000	4,500	7,000	10,000
2d Sta Wag	404	1,212	2,020	4,550	7,070	10,100

NOTE: Add 10 percent for V-8 models.

1963 Station Buses, 6-cyl., 90" wb

Sta Bus	372	1,116	1,860	4,190	6,510	9,300
Clb Wag	376	1,128	1,880	4,230	6,580	9,400
DeL Clb Wag	384	1,152	1,920	4,320	6,720	9,600

1963 Sprint, V-8, 109.5" wb

2d HT	760	2,280	3,800	8,550	13,300	19,000
2d Conv	880	2,640	4,400	9,900	15,400	22,000

1963 Fairlane, V-8, 115.5" wb

4d Sed	332	996	1,660	3,740	5,810	8,300
2d Sed	336	1,008	1,680	3,780	5,880	8,400
2d HT	420	1,260	2,100	4,730	7,350	10,500
2d Spt Cpe	440	1,320	2,200	4,950	7,700	11,000
4d Sq Wag	580	1,740	2,900	6,530	10,150	14,500
4d Cus Ran	576	1,728	2,880	6,480	10,080	14,400

NOTE: Add 20 percent for 271 hp V-8.

1963 Ford 300, V-8, 119" wb

4d Sed	336	1,008	1,680	3,780	5,880	8,400
2d Sed	340	1,020	1,700	3,830	5,950	8,500

1963 Galaxie 500, V-8, 119" wb

4d Sed	340	1,020	1,700	3,830	5,950	8,500
4d HT	720	2,160	3,600	8,100	12,600	18,000
2d Sed	344	1,032	1,720	3,870	6,020	8,600
2d HT	800	2,400	4,000	9,000	14,000	20,000
2d FBk	880	2,640	4,400	9,900	15,400	22,000
2d Sun Conv	1,120	3,360	5,600	12,600	19,600	28,000

1963 Galaxie 500 XL, V-8, 119" wb

4d HT	760	2,280	3,800	8,550	13,300	19,000
2d HT	840	2,520	4,200	9,450	14,700	21,000
2d FBk	920	2,760	4,600	10,350	16,100	23,000
2d Sun Conv	1,240	3,720	6,200	13,950	21,700	31,000

1963 Station Wagons, V-8, 119" wb

4d Ctry Sed	600	1,800	3,000	6,750	10,500	15,000
4d Ctry Sq	620	1,860	3,100	6,980	10,850	15,500

NOTE: Deduct 5 percent average for 6-cyl. Add 30 percent for 406 & add 40 percent for 427. Add 5 percent for V-8 except Sprint. Add 20 percent for 390 cid, 330 hp. Add 20 percent for 390 cid, 300 hp.

1964 Falcon/Falcon Futura, 6-cyl., 109.5" wb

4d Sed	340	1,020	1,700	3,830	5,950	8,500
2d Sed	344	1,032	1,720	3,870	6,020	8,600
2d HT	540	1,620	2,700	6,080	9,450	13,500
2d Spt HT	700	2,100	3,500	7,880	12,250	17,500
2d Conv	720	2,160	3,600	8,100	12,600	18,000
2d Spt Conv	760	2,280	3,800	8,550	13,300	19,000
4d Sq Wag	420	1,260	2,100	4,730	7,350	10,500
4d DeL Wag	400	1,200	2,000	4,500	7,000	10,000
4d Sta	400	1,200	2,000	4,500	7,000	10,000
2d Sta	404	1,212	2,020	4,550	7,070	10,100

NOTE: Add 10 percent for V-8 models.

1964 Station Bus, 6-cyl., 90" wb

Sta Bus	360	1,080	1,800	4,050	6,300	9,000
Clb Wag	364	1,092	1,820	4,100	6,370	9,100
DeL Clb	372	1,116	1,860	4,190	6,510	9,300

1964 Sprint, V-8, 109.5" wb

2d HT	740	2,220	3,700	8,330	12,950	18,500
2d Conv	800	2,400	4,000	9,000	14,000	20,000

1964 Fairlane, V-8, 115.5" wb

4d Sed	324	972	1,620	3,650	5,670	8,100
2d Sed	328	984	1,640	3,690	5,740	8,200
2d HT	660	1,980	3,300	7,430	11,550	16,500
2d Spt HT	700	2,100	3,500	7,880	12,250	17,500
4d Sta Wag	524	1,572	2,620	5,900	9,170	13,100

NOTE: Add 20 percent for 271 hp V-8.

1964 Fairlane Thunderbolt

1964 Custom, V-8, 119" wb

4d Sed	324	972	1,620	3,650	5,670	8,100
2d Sed	328	984	1,640	3,690	5,740	8,200

1964 Custom 500, V-8, 119" wb

4d Sed	328	984	1,640	3,690	5,740	8,200
2d Sed	332	996	1,660	3,740	5,810	8,300

1964 Galaxie 500, V-8, 119" wb

4d Sed	376	1,128	1,880	4,230	6,580	9,400
4d HT	800	2,400	4,000	9,000	14,000	20,000
2d Sed	380	1,140	1,900	4,280	6,650	9,500
2d HT	880	2,640	4,400	9,900	15,400	22,000
2d Sun Conv	1,080	3,240	5,400	12,150	18,900	27,000

1964 Galaxie 500XL, V-8, 119" wb

4d HT	840	2,520	4,200	9,450	14,700	21,000
2d HT	920	2,760	4,600	10,350	16,100	23,000
2d Sun Conv	1,200	3,600	6,000	13,500	21,000	30,000

1964 Station Wagons, V-8, 119" wb

4d Ctry Sed	720	2,160	3,600	8,100	12,600	18,000
4d Ctry Sq	740	2,220	3,700	8,330	12,950	18,500

NOTE: Add 40 percent for 427 V-8. Add 20 percent for 390 cid, 330 hp. Add 20 percent for 390 cid, 300 hp. Add 10 percent for 390 cid, 275 hp.

1965 Falcon/Falcon Futura, 6-cyl., 109.5" wb

4d Sed	316	948	1,580	3,560	5,530	7,900
2d Sed	320	960	1,600	3,600	5,600	8,000
2d HT	480	1,440	2,400	5,400	8,400	12,000
2d Conv	760	2,280	3,800	8,550	13,300	19,000
4d Sq Wag	400	1,200	2,000	4,500	7,000	10,000
4d DeL Wag	380	1,140	1,900	4,280	6,650	9,500
4d Sta	360	1,080	1,800	4,050	6,300	9,000
2d Sta	368	1,104	1,840	4,140	6,440	9,200

NOTE: Add 10 percent for V-8 models.

1965 Sprint, V-8, 109.5" wb

2d HT	720	2,160	3,600	8,100	12,600	18,000
2d Conv	800	2,400	4,000	9,000	14,000	20,000

1965 Falcon Station Buses, 6-cyl., 90" wb

Sta Bus	324	972	1,620	3,650	5,670	8,100
Clb Wag	332	996	1,660	3,740	5,810	8,300
DeL Wag	340	1,020	1,700	3,830	5,950	8,500

1965 Fairlane, V-8, 116" wb

4d Sed	328	984	1,640	3,690	5,740	8,200
2d Sed	332	996	1,660	3,740	5,810	8,300
2d HT	480	1,440	2,400	5,400	8,400	12,000
2d Spt HT	660	1,980	3,300	7,430	11,550	16,500
4d Sta Wag	340	1,020	1,700	3,830	5,950	8,500

NOTE: Add 10 percent for 271 hp V-8.

1965 Custom, V-8, 119" wb

4d Sed	316	948	1,580	3,560	5,530	7,900
2d Sed	320	960	1,600	3,600	5,600	8,000

1965 Custom 500, V-8, 119" wb

4d Sed	320	960	1,600	3,600	5,600	8,000
2d Sed	324	972	1,620	3,650	5,670	8,100

1965 Galaxie 500, V-8, 119" wb

4d Sed	360	1,080	1,800	4,050	6,300	9,000
4d HT	600	1,800	3,000	6,750	10,500	15,000
2d HT	680	2,040	3,400	7,650	11,900	17,000
2d Conv	760	2,280	3,800	8,550	13,300	19,000

1965 Galaxie 500 XL, V-8, 119" wb

2d HT	720	2,160	3,600	8,100	12,600	18,000
2d Conv	800	2,400	4,000	9,000	14,000	20,000

1965 Galaxie 500 LTD, V-8, 119" wb

4d HT	700	2,100	3,500	7,880	12,250	17,500
2d HT	780	2,340	3,900	8,780	13,650	19,500

1965 Station Wagons, V-8, 119" wb

4d Ran	560	1,680	2,800	6,300	9,800	14,000
4d 9P Ctry Sed	580	1,740	2,900	6,530	10,150	14,500
4d 9P Ctry Sq	600	1,800	3,000	6,750	10,500	15,000

NOTE: Add 40 percent for 427 V-8. Add 20 percent for 390 cid, 330 hp. Add 20 percent for 390 cid, 300 hp.

1966 Falcon/Falcon Futura, 6-cyl., 110.9" wb

4d Sed	320	960	1,600	3,600	5,600	8,000
2d Clb Cpe	320	970	1,620	3,650	5,670	8,100
2d Spt Cpe	330	1,000	1,660	3,740	5,810	8,300
4d 6P Wag	400	1,190	1,980	4,460	6,930	9,900
4d Sq Wag	400	1,200	2,000	4,500	7,000	10,000

1966 Falcon Station Bus, 6-cyl., 90" wb

Clb Wag	312	936	1,560	3,510	5,460	7,800
Cus Clb Wag	316	948	1,580	3,560	5,530	7,900
DeL Clb Wag	320	960	1,600	3,600	5,600	8,000

1966 Fairlane, V-8, 116" wb

4d Sed	320	960	1,600	3,600	5,600	8,000
2d Clb Cpe	324	972	1,620	3,650	5,670	8,100

1966 Fairlane 500, V-8

4d Sed	350	1,060	1,760	3,960	6,160	8,800
2d Cpe	380	1,140	1,900	4,280	6,650	9,500
2d HT	580	1,740	2,900	6,530	10,150	14,500
2d Conv	880	2,640	4,400	9,900	15,400	22,000

1966 Fairlane 500 XL, V-8, 116" wb

2d HT	660	1,980	3,300	7,430	11,550	16,500
2d Conv	960	2,880	4,800	10,800	16,800	24,000

1966 Fairlane 500 GT, V-8, 116" wb

2d HT	800	2,400	4,000	9,000	14,000	20,000
2d Conv	1,000	3,000	5,000	11,250	17,500	25,000

1966 Station Wagons, V-8, 113" wb

6P DeL	320	960	1,600	3,600	5,600	8,000
2d Sq Wag	368	1,104	1,840	4,140	6,440	9,200

1966 Custom, V-8, 119" wb

4d Sed	324	972	1,620	3,650	5,670	8,100
2d Sed	328	984	1,640	3,690	5,740	8,200

1966 Galaxie 500, V-8, 119" wb

4d Sed	360	1,080	1,800	4,050	6,300	9,000
4d HT	500	1,500	2,500	5,630	8,750	12,500
2d HT	540	1,620	2,700	6,080	9,450	13,500
2d Conv	760	2,280	3,800	8,550	13,300	19,000

1966 Galaxie 500 XL, V-8, 119" wb

2d HT	660	1,980	3,300	7,430	11,550	16,500
2d Conv	800	2,400	4,000	9,000	14,000	20,000

1966 LTD, V-8, 119" wb

4d HT	600	1,800	3,000	6,750	10,500	15,000
2d HT	680	2,040	3,400	7,650	11,900	17,000

1966 Galaxie 500, 7-litre V-8, 119" wb

2d HT	920	2,760	4,600	10,350	16,100	23,000
2d Conv	1,320	3,960	6,600	14,850	23,100	33,000

NOTE: Add 50 percent for 427 engine option on 7-litre models.

1966 Station Wagons, V-8, 119" wb

4d Ran Wag	580	1,740	2,900	6,530	10,150	14,500
4d Ctry Sed	600	1,800	3,000	6,750	10,500	15,000
4d Ctry Sq	620	1,860	3,100	6,980	10,850	15,500

NOTE: Add 40 percent for 427 or 30 percent for 428 engine option.

1967 Falcon, 6-cyl., 111" wb

4d Sed	316	948	1,580	3,560	5,530	7,900
2d Sed	320	960	1,600	3,600	5,600	8,000
4d Sta Wag	360	1,080	1,800	4,050	6,300	9,000

1967 Futura

4d Sed	320	960	1,600	3,600	5,600	8,000
2d Clb Cpe	324	972	1,620	3,650	5,670	8,100
2d HT	380	1,140	1,900	4,280	6,650	9,500

1967 Fairlane

4d Sed	316	948	1,580	3,560	5,530	7,900
2d Cpe	320	960	1,600	3,600	5,600	8,000

1967 Fairlane 500, V-8, 116" wb

4d Sed	320	960	1,600	3,600	5,600	8,000
2d Cpe	324	972	1,620	3,650	5,670	8,100
2d HT	500	1,500	2,500	5,630	8,750	12,500
2d Conv	880	2,640	4,400	9,900	15,400	22,000
4d Wag	380	1,140	1,900	4,280	6,650	9,500

1967 Fairlane 500 XL, V-8

2d HT	660	1,980	3,300	7,430	11,550	16,500
2d Conv	960	2,880	4,800	10,800	16,800	24,000
2d HT GT	800	2,400	4,000	9,000	14,000	20,000
2d Conv GT	1,000	3,000	5,000	11,250	17,500	25,000

NOTE: When fitted with automatic transmission, the GT was named GTA.

1967 Fairlane Wagons

4d Sta Wag	360	1,080	1,800	4,050	6,300	9,000
4d 500 Wag	364	1,092	1,820	4,100	6,370	9,100
4d Sq Wag	372	1,116	1,860	4,190	6,510	9,300

1967 Ford Custom

4d Sed	316	948	1,580	3,560	5,530	7,900
2d Sed	320	960	1,600	3,600	5,600	8,000

1967 Ford Custom 500

4d Sed	320	960	1,600	3,600	5,600	8,000
2d Sed	324	972	1,620	3,650	5,670	8,100

1967 Galaxie 500, V-8, 119" wb

4d Sed	332	996	1,660	3,740	5,810	8,300
4d HT	580	1,740	2,900	6,530	10,150	14,500
2d HT	660	1,980	3,300	7,430	11,550	16,500
2d Conv	800	2,400	4,000	9,000	14,000	20,000

1967 Galaxie 500 XL

2d HT	700	2,100	3,500	7,880	12,250	17,500
2d Conv	840	2,520	4,200	9,450	14,700	21,000

1967 LTD, V-8, 119" wb

4d HT	640	1,920	3,200	7,200	11,200	16,000
2d HT	720	2,160	3,600	8,100	12,600	18,000

1967 Station Wagons

4d Ranch	560	1,680	2,800	6,300	9,800	14,000
4d Ctry Sed	580	1,740	2,900	6,530	10,150	14,500
4d Ctry Sq	600	1,800	3,000	6,750	10,500	15,000

NOTE: Add 5 percent for V-8. Add 40 percent for 427 or 428 engine option.

1968 Standard Falcon

4d Sed	296	888	1,480	3,330	5,180	7,400
2d Sed	300	900	1,500	3,380	5,250	7,500
4d Sta Wag	340	1,020	1,700	3,830	5,950	8,500

1968 Falcon Futura, 6-cyl., 110.0" wb

4d Sed	300	900	1,500	3,380	5,250	7,500
2d Sed	304	912	1,520	3,420	5,320	7,600
2d Spt Cpe	312	936	1,560	3,510	5,460	7,800
4d Sta Wag	344	1,032	1,720	3,870	6,020	8,600

1968 Fairlane

4d Sed	304	912	1,520	3,420	5,320	7,600
2d HT	380	1,140	1,900	4,280	6,650	9,500
4d Sta Wag	352	1,056	1,760	3,960	6,160	8,800

1968 Fairlane 500, V-8, 116" wb

4d Sed	308	924	1,540	3,470	5,390	7,700
2d HT	440	1,320	2,200	4,950	7,700	11,000
2d FBk	560	1,680	2,800	6,300	9,800	14,000
2d Conv	720	2,160	3,600	8,100	12,600	18,000
4d Sta Wag	356	1,068	1,780	4,010	6,230	8,900

1968 Torino, V-8, 116" wb

4d Sed	292	876	1,460	3,290	5,110	7,300
2d HT	500	1,500	2,500	5,630	8,750	12,500
4d Wag	360	1,080	1,800	4,050	6,300	9,000

1968 Torino GT, V-8

2d HT	880	2,640	4,400	9,900	15,400	22,000
2d FBk	960	2,880	4,800	10,800	16,800	24,000
2d Conv	1,120	3,360	5,600	12,600	19,600	28,000

1968 Custom

4d Sed	296	888	1,480	3,330	5,180	7,400
2d Sed	300	900	1,500	3,380	5,250	7,500

1968 Custom 500

4d Sed	300	900	1,500	3,380	5,250	7,500
2d Sed	304	912	1,520	3,420	5,320	7,600

1968 Galaxie 500, V-8, 119" wb

4d Sed	308	924	1,540	3,470	5,390	7,700
4d HT	440	1,320	2,200	4,950	7,700	11,000
2d HT	520	1,560	2,600	5,850	9,100	13,000
2d FBk	680	2,040	3,400	7,650	11,900	17,000
2d Conv	760	2,280	3,800	8,550	13,300	19,000

1968 XL

2d FBk	720	2,160	3,600	8,100	12,600	18,000
2d Conv	800	2,400	4,000	9,000	14,000	20,000

1968 LTD

4d Sed	320	960	1,600	3,600	5,600	8,000
4d HT	460	1,380	2,300	5,180	8,050	11,500
2d HT	540	1,620	2,700	6,080	9,450	13,500

1968 Ranch Wagon

4d Std Wag	520	1,560	2,600	5,850	9,100	13,000
4d 500 Wag	528	1,584	2,640	5,940	9,240	13,200
4d DeL 500 Wag	532	1,596	2,660	5,990	9,310	13,300

1968 Country Sedan

4d Std Wag	560	1,680	2,800	6,300	9,800	14,000
DeL Wag	568	1,704	2,840	6,390	9,940	14,200

1968 Country Squire

4d Sta Wag	600	1,800	3,000	6,750	10,500	15,000
4d DeL Wag	616	1,848	3,080	6,930	10,780	15,400

NOTE: Add 50 percent for 429 engine option. Add 40 percent for 427 or 428 engine option.

1969 Falcon Futura, 6-cyl., 111" wb

2d Spt Cpe	284	852	1,420	3,200	4,970	7,100
2d Sed	268	804	1,340	3,020	4,690	6,700

1969 Fairlane 500, V-8, 116" wb

4d Sed	264	792	1,320	2,970	4,620	6,600
2d HT	360	1,080	1,800	4,050	6,300	9,000
2d FBk	380	1,140	1,900	4,280	6,650	9,500
2d Conv	640	1,920	3,200	7,200	11,200	16,000

1969 Torino, V-8, 116" wb

4d Sed	280	840	1,400	3,150	4,900	7,000
2d HT	480	1,440	2,400	5,400	8,400	12,000

1969 Torino GT, V-8

2d HT	880	2,640	4,400	9,900	15,400	22,000
2d FBk	960	2,880	4,800	10,800	16,800	24,000
2d Conv	1,120	3,360	5,600	12,600	19,600	28,000

1969 Cobra

2d HT	1,440	4,320	7,200	16,200	25,200	36,000
2d FBk	1,680	5,040	8,400	18,900	29,400	42,000

1969 Galaxie 500, V-8, 121" wb

4d HT	340	1,020	1,700	3,830	5,950	8,500
2d HT	380	1,140	1,900	4,280	6,650	9,500
2d FBk	520	1,560	2,600	5,850	9,100	13,000
2d Conv	720	2,160	3,600	8,100	12,600	18,000

1969 XL

2d FBk	660	1,980	3,300	7,430	11,550	16,500
2d Conv	760	2,280	3,800	8,550	13,300	19,000

NOTE: Add 10 percent for GT option.

1969 LTD

4d HT	360	1,080	1,800	4,050	6,300	9,000
2d HT	460	1,380	2,300	5,180	8,050	11,500

1969 Falcon Wagon, 6-cyl.

4d Wag	280	840	1,400	3,150	4,900	7,000
4d Futura Sta Wag	324	972	1,620	3,650	5,670	8,100

1969 Fairlane, 6-cyl.

4d Wag	364	1,092	1,820	4,100	6,370	9,100
4d 500 Sta Wag	388	1,164	1,940	4,370	6,790	9,700
4d Torino Sta Wag	372	1,116	1,860	4,190	6,510	9,300

NOTE: Add 30 percent for V-8 where available.

1969 Custom Ranch Wagon, V-8

4d Wag	440	1,320	2,200	4,950	7,700	11,000
4d 500 Sta Wag 2S	444	1,332	2,220	5,000	7,770	11,100
4d 500 Sta Wag 4S	448	1,344	2,240	5,040	7,840	11,200

NOTE: Deduct 30 percent for 6-cyl.

1969 Galaxie 500 Country Sedan, V-8

4d Wag 2S	448	1,344	2,240	5,040	7,840	11,200
4d Wag 4S	452	1,356	2,260	5,090	7,910	11,300

1969 LTD Country Squire, V-8

4d Wag 2S	500	1,500	2,500	5,630	8,750	12,500
4d Wag 4S	504	1,512	2,520	5,670	8,820	12,600

NOTE: Add 40 percent for 428 engine option. Add 50 percent for 429 engine option.

1970 Falcon, 6-cyl., 110" wb

4d Sed	292	876	1,460	3,290	5,110	7,300
2d Sed	296	888	1,480	3,330	5,180	7,400
4d Sta Wag	332	996	1,660	3,740	5,810	8,300

1970 Futura, 6-cyl., 110" wb

4d Sed	300	900	1,500	3,380	5,250	7,500
2d Sed	304	912	1,520	3,420	5,320	7,600
4d Sta Wag	340	1,020	1,700	3,830	5,950	8,500

NOTE: Add 10 percent for V-8.

1970 Maverick

2d Sed	288	864	1,440	3,240	5,040	7,200

1970 Fairlane 500, V-8, 117" wb

4d Sed	312	936	1,560	3,510	5,460	7,800
2d HT	360	1,080	1,800	4,050	6,300	9,000
4d Sta Wag	348	1,044	1,740	3,920	6,090	8,700

1970 Torino, V-8, 117" wb

4d Sed	316	948	1,580	3,560	5,530	7,900
4d HT	360	1,080	1,800	4,050	6,300	9,000
2d HT	420	1,260	2,100	4,730	7,350	10,500
2d Sports Roof HT	540	1,620	2,700	6,080	9,450	13,500
4d Sta Wag	360	1,080	1,800	4,050	6,300	9,000

1970 Torino Brougham, V-8, 117" wb

4d HT	380	1,140	1,900	4,280	6,650	9,500
2d HT	500	1,500	2,500	5,630	8,750	12,500
4d Sta Wag	352	1,056	1,760	3,960	6,160	8,800

1970 Torino GT, V-8, 117" wb

2d HT	800	2,400	4,000	9,000	14,000	20,000
2d Conv	1,040	3,120	5,200	11,700	18,200	26,000

1970 Cobra, V-8, 117" wb

2d HT	1,440	4,320	7,200	16,200	25,200	36,000

1970 Custom, V-8, 121" wb

4d Sed	280	840	1,400	3,150	4,900	7,000
4d Sta Wag	348	1,044	1,740	3,920	6,090	8,700

1970 Custom 500, V-8, 121" wb

4d Sed	284	852	1,420	3,200	4,970	7,100
4d Sta Wag	352	1,056	1,760	3,960	6,160	8,800

1970 Galaxie 500, V-8, 121" wb

4d Sed	288	864	1,440	3,240	5,040	7,200
4d HT	340	1,020	1,700	3,830	5,950	8,500
2d HT	380	1,140	1,900	4,280	6,650	9,500
4d Sta Wag	356	1,068	1,780	4,010	6,230	8,900
2d FBk	520	1,560	2,600	5,850	9,100	13,000

1970 XL, V-8, 121" wb

2d FBk	540	1,620	2,700	6,080	9,450	13,500
2d Conv	700	2,100	3,500	7,880	12,250	17,500

1970 LTD, V-8, 121" wb

4d Sed	292	876	1,460	3,290	5,110	7,300
4d HT	308	924	1,540	3,470	5,390	7,700
2d HT	340	1,020	1,700	3,830	5,950	8,500
4d Sta Wag	360	1,080	1,800	4,050	6,300	9,000

1970 LTD Brougham, V-8, 121" wb

4d Sed	296	888	1,480	3,330	5,180	7,400
4d HT	320	960	1,600	3,600	5,600	8,000
2d HT	360	1,080	1,800	4,050	6,300	9,000

NOTE: Add 40 percent for 428 engine option. Add 50 percent for 429 engine option.

1970-1/2 Falcon, 6-cyl., 117" wb

4d Sed	296	888	1,480	3,330	5,180	7,400
2d Sed	300	900	1,500	3,380	5,250	7,500
4d Sta Wag	340	1,020	1,700	3,830	5,950	8,500

1971 Pinto

2d Rbt	288	864	1,440	3,240	5,040	7,200

1971 Maverick, 6-cyl.

2d Sed	310	940	1,560	3,510	5,460	7,800
4d Sed	310	920	1,540	3,470	5,390	7,700
2d Grabber Sed	390	1,170	1,950	4,390	6,830	9,750

NOTE: Add 20 percent for V-8.

1971 Torino, V-8, 114" wb, Sta Wag 117" wb

4d Sed	316	948	1,580	3,560	5,530	7,900
2d HT	380	1,140	1,900	4,280	6,650	9,500
4d Sta Wag	356	1,068	1,780	4,010	6,230	8,900

1971 Torino 500, V-8, 114" wb, Sta Wag 117" wb

4d Sed	320	960	1,600	3,600	5,600	8,000
4d HT	364	1,092	1,820	4,100	6,370	9,100
2d Formal HT	640	1,920	3,200	7,200	11,200	16,000
2d Sports Roof HT	660	1,980	3,300	7,430	11,550	16,500
4d Sta Wag	320	960	1,600	3,600	5,600	8,000
4d HT Brougham	364	1,092	1,820	4,100	6,370	9,100
2d HT Brougham	500	1,500	2,500	5,630	8,750	12,500
4d Sq Sta Wag	404	1,212	2,020	4,550	7,070	10,100
2d HT Cobra	1,320	3,960	6,600	14,850	23,100	33,000
2d HT GT	760	2,280	3,800	8,550	13,300	19,000
2d GT Conv	1,000	3,000	5,000	11,250	17,500	25,000

1971 Custom, V-8, 121" wb

4d Sed	304	912	1,520	3,420	5,320	7,600
4d Sta Wag	400	1,200	2,000	4,500	7,000	10,000

1971 Custom 500, V-8, 121" wb

4d Sed	308	924	1,540	3,470	5,390	7,700
4d Sta Wag	404	1,212	2,020	4,550	7,070	10,100

1971 Galaxie 500, V-8, 121" wb

4d Sed	316	948	1,580	3,560	5,530	7,900
4d HT	320	960	1,600	3,600	5,600	8,000
2d HT	340	1,020	1,700	3,830	5,950	8,500
4d Sta Wag	416	1,248	2,080	4,680	7,280	10,400

1971 LTD

4d Sed	320	960	1,600	3,600	5,600	8,000
4d HT	324	972	1,620	3,650	5,670	8,100
2d HT	344	1,032	1,720	3,870	6,020	8,600
2d Conv	660	1,980	3,300	7,430	11,550	16,500
4d Ctry Sq Sta Wag	560	1,680	2,800	6,300	9,800	14,000

1971 LTD Brougham, V-8, 121" wb

4d Sed	324	972	1,620	3,650	5,670	8,100
4d HT	340	1,020	1,700	3,830	5,950	8,500
2d HT	380	1,140	1,900	4,280	6,650	9,500

NOTE: Add 40 percent for 429 engine option.

1972 Pinto

2d Sed	296	888	1,480	3,330	5,180	7,400
3d HBk	300	900	1,500	3,380	5,250	7,500
2d Sta Wag	304	912	1,520	3,420	5,320	7,600

1972 Maverick

4d Sed	296	888	1,480	3,330	5,180	7,400
2d Sed	300	900	1,500	3,380	5,250	7,500
2d Grabber Sed	390	1,170	1,950	4,390	6,830	9,750

NOTE: Deduct 20 percent for 6-cyl. Add 20 percent for Sprint pkg.

1972 Torino, V-8, 118" wb, 2d 114" wb

4d Sed	296	888	1,480	3,330	5,180	7,400
2d HT	380	1,140	1,900	4,280	6,650	9,500
4d Sta Wag	348	1,044	1,740	3,920	6,090	8,700

1972 Gran Torino

4d Pillared HT	300	900	1,500	3,380	5,250	7,500
2d HT	440	1,320	2,200	4,950	7,700	11,000

1972 Gran Torino Sport, V-8

2d Formal HT	480	1,440	2,400	5,400	8,400	12,000
2d Sports Roof HT	620	1,860	3,100	6,980	10,850	15,500
4d Sta Wag	340	1,020	1,700	3,830	5,950	8,500

1972 Custom, V-8, 121" wb

4d Sed	304	912	1,520	3,420	5,320	7,600
4d Sta Wag	360	1,080	1,800	4,050	6,300	9,000

1972 Custom 500, V-8, 121" wb

4d Sed	308	924	1,540	3,470	5,390	7,700
4d Sta Wag	380	1,140	1,900	4,280	6,650	9,500

1972 Galaxie 500, V-8, 121" wb

4d Sed	312	936	1,560	3,510	5,460	7,800
4d HT	360	1,080	1,800	4,050	6,300	9,000
2d HT	440	1,320	2,200	4,950	7,700	11,000
4d Sta Wag	400	1,200	2,000	4,500	7,000	10,000

1972 LTD, V-8, 121" wb

4d Sed	330	980	1,640	3,690	5,740	8,200
4d HT	330	1,000	1,660	3,740	5,810	8,300
2d HT	350	1,060	1,760	3,960	6,160	8,800
2d Conv	670	2,000	3,340	7,520	11,690	16,700
4d Sta Wag	570	1,700	2,840	6,390	9,940	14,200

1972 LTD Brougham, V-8, 121" wb

4d Sed	330	1,000	1,660	3,740	5,810	8,300
4d HT	350	1,040	1,740	3,920	6,090	8,700
2d HT	390	1,160	1,940	4,370	6,790	9,700

NOTE: Add 40 percent for 429 engine option. Add 30 percent for 460 engine option.

1973 Pinto, 4-cyl.

2d Sed	212	636	1,060	2,390	3,710	5,300
2d Rbt	216	648	1,080	2,430	3,780	5,400
2d Sta Wag	220	660	1,100	2,480	3,850	5,500

1973 Maverick, V-8

2d Sed	224	672	1,120	2,520	3,920	5,600
4d Sed	228	684	1,140	2,570	3,990	5,700
2d Grabber Sed	300	900	1,500	3,380	5,250	7,500

1973 Torino, V-8

4d Sed	216	648	1,080	2,430	3,780	5,400
2d HT	300	900	1,500	3,380	5,250	7,500
4d Sta Wag	224	672	1,120	2,520	3,920	5,600

1973 Gran Torino, V-8

4d Pillared HT	220	660	1,100	2,480	3,850	5,500
2d HT	320	960	1,600	3,600	5,600	8,000
4d Sta Wag	268	804	1,340	3,020	4,690	6,700

1973 Gran Torino Sport, V-8

2d Sports Roof HT	560	1,680	2,800	6,300	9,800	14,000
2d Formal HT	480	1,440	2,400	5,400	8,400	12,000
4d Sq Sta Wag	320	960	1,600	3,600	5,600	8,000

1973 Gran Torino Brgm, V-8

4d Pillared HT	224	672	1,120	2,520	3,920	5,600
2d HT	460	1,380	2,300	5,180	8,050	11,500

1973 Custom 500, V-8

4d Pillared HT	224	672	1,120	2,520	3,920	5,600
4d Sta Wag	300	900	1,500	3,380	5,250	7,500

1973 Galaxie 500, V-8

4d Pillared HT	228	684	1,140	2,570	3,990	5,700
2d HT	288	864	1,440	3,240	5,040	7,200
4d HT	232	696	1,160	2,610	4,060	5,800
4d Sta Wag	320	960	1,600	3,600	5,600	8,000

1973 LTD, V-8

4d Sed	232	696	1,160	2,610	4,060	5,800
2d HT	300	900	1,500	3,380	5,250	7,500
4d HT	240	720	1,200	2,700	4,200	6,000
4d Sta Wag	340	1,020	1,700	3,830	5,950	8,500

1973 LTD Brgm, V-8

4d Sed	236	708	1,180	2,660	4,130	5,900
2d HT	320	960	1,600	3,600	5,600	8,000
4d HT	280	840	1,400	3,150	4,900	7,000

NOTE: Add 30 percent for 429 engine option. Add 30 percent for 460 engine option.

1974 Pinto

2d Sed	212	636	1,060	2,390	3,710	5,300
3d HBk	216	648	1,080	2,430	3,780	5,400
2d Sta Wag	220	660	1,100	2,480	3,850	5,500

1974 Maverick, V-8

2d Sed	224	672	1,120	2,520	3,920	5,600
4d Sed	228	684	1,140	2,570	3,990	5,700
2d Grabber Sed	300	900	1,500	3,380	5,250	7,500

1974 Torino, V-8

4d Sed	224	672	1,120	2,520	3,920	5,600
2d HT	288	864	1,440	3,240	5,040	7,200
4d Sta Wag	260	780	1,300	2,930	4,550	6,500

1974 Gran Torino, V-8

4d Sed	228	684	1,140	2,570	3,990	5,700
2d HT	304	912	1,520	3,420	5,320	7,600
4d Sta Wag	264	792	1,320	2,970	4,620	6,600

1974 Gran Torino Sport, V-8

2d HT	360	1,080	1,800	4,050	6,300	9,000

1974 Gran Torino Brgm, V-8

4d Sed	232	696	1,160	2,610	4,060	5,800
2d HT	300	900	1,500	3,380	5,250	7,500

1974 Gran Torino Elite, V-8

2d HT	320	960	1,600	3,600	5,600	8,000

1974 Gran Torino Squire, V-8

4d Sta Wag	284	852	1,420	3,200	4,970	7,100

1974 Custom 500

4d Sed	220	660	1,100	2,480	3,850	5,500
4d Sta Wag	280	840	1,400	3,150	4,900	7,000

1974 Galaxie 500, V-8

4d Sed	224	672	1,120	2,520	3,920	5,600
2d HT	248	744	1,240	2,790	4,340	6,200
4d HT	236	708	1,180	2,660	4,130	5,900
4d Sta Wag	284	852	1,420	3,200	4,970	7,100

1974 LTD, V-8

2d HT	260	780	1,300	2,930	4,550	6,500
4d Sed	228	684	1,140	2,570	3,990	5,700
4d HT	240	720	1,200	2,700	4,200	6,000
4d Sta Wag	320	960	1,600	3,600	5,600	8,000

1974 LTD Brgm, V-8

4d Sed	228	684	1,140	2,570	3,990	5,700
2d HT	280	840	1,400	3,150	4,900	7,000
4d HT	260	780	1,300	2,930	4,550	6,500

NOTE: Add 30 percent for 460 engine option.

1975 Pinto

2d Sed	220	660	1,100	2,480	3,850	5,500
3d HBk	224	672	1,120	2,520	3,920	5,600
2d Sta Wag	240	720	1,200	2,700	4,200	6,000

1975 Maverick

2d Sed	240	720	1,200	2,700	4,200	6,000
4d Sed	236	708	1,180	2,660	4,130	5,900
2d Grabber Sed	300	900	1,500	3,380	5,250	7,500

1975 Torino

2d Cpe	240	720	1,200	2,700	4,200	6,000
4d Sed	220	660	1,100	2,480	3,850	5,500
4d Sta Wag	224	672	1,120	2,520	3,920	5,600

1975 Gran Torino

2d Cpe	244	732	1,220	2,750	4,270	6,100
4d Sed	228	684	1,140	2,570	3,990	5,700
4d Sta Wag	232	696	1,160	2,610	4,060	5,800

1975 Gran Torino Brougham

2d Cpe	252	756	1,260	2,840	4,410	6,300
4d Sed	248	744	1,240	2,790	4,340	6,200

1975 Gran Torino Sport

2d HT	280	830	1,380	3,110	4,830	6,900

1975 Torino Squire

4d Sta Wag	280	840	1,400	3,150	4,900	7,000

1975 Elite

2d HT	280	840	1,400	3,150	4,900	7,000

1975 Granada

2d Cpe	212	636	1,060	2,390	3,710	5,300
4d Sed	188	564	940	2,120	3,290	4,700
2d Ghia Cpe	224	672	1,120	2,520	3,920	5,600
4d Ghia Sed	220	660	1,100	2,480	3,850	5,500

1975 Custom 500

4d Sed	224	672	1,120	2,520	3,920	5,600
4d Sta Wag	228	684	1,140	2,570	3,990	5,700

1975 LTD

2d Cpe	236	708	1,180	2,660	4,130	5,900
4d Sed	228	684	1,140	2,570	3,990	5,700

1975 LTD Brougham

2d Cpe	240	720	1,200	2,700	4,200	6,000
4d Sed	232	696	1,160	2,610	4,060	5,800

1975 LTD Landau

2d Cpe	248	744	1,240	2,790	4,340	6,200
4d Sed	236	708	1,180	2,660	4,130	5,900

1975 LTD Station Wagon

4d Sta Wag	268	804	1,340	3,020	4,690	6,700
4d Ctry Sq	288	864	1,440	3,240	5,040	7,200

NOTE: Add 30 percent for 460 engine option.

1976 Pinto, 4-cyl.

2d Sed	200	600	1,000	2,250	3,500	5,000
2d Rbt	204	612	1,020	2,300	3,570	5,100
2d Sta Wag	208	624	1,040	2,340	3,640	5,200
2d Sq Wag	212	636	1,060	2,390	3,710	5,300

NOTE: Add 10 percent for V-6.

1976 Maverick, V-8

4d Sed	192	576	960	2,160	3,360	4,800
2d Sed	196	588	980	2,210	3,430	4,900

NOTE: Deduct 5 percent for 6-cyl.

1976 Torino, V-8

4d Sed	200	600	1,000	2,250	3,500	5,000
2d HT	204	612	1,020	2,300	3,570	5,100

1976 Gran Torino, V-8

4d Sed	204	612	1,020	2,300	3,570	5,100
2d HT	208	624	1,040	2,340	3,640	5,200

NOTE: Add 20 percent for "Starsky & Hutch" Ed.

1976 Gran Torino Brougham, V-8

4d Sed	208	624	1,040	2,340	3,640	5,200
2d HT	212	636	1,060	2,390	3,710	5,300

1976 Station Wagons, V-8

4d 2S Torino	240	720	1,200	2,700	4,200	6,000
4d 2S Gran Torino	244	732	1,220	2,750	4,270	6,100
4d 2S Gran Torino Sq	250	740	1,240	2,790	4,340	6,200

1976 Granada, V-8

4d Sed	188	564	940	2,120	3,290	4,700
2d Sed	212	636	1,060	2,390	3,710	5,300

1976 Granada Ghia, V-8

4d Sed	220	660	1,100	2,480	3,850	5,500
2d Sed	224	672	1,120	2,520	3,920	5,600

1976 Elite, V-8

2d HT	208	624	1,040	2,340	3,640	5,200

1976 Custom, V-8

4d Sed	196	588	980	2,210	3,430	4,900

1976 LTD, V-8

4d Sed	204	612	1,020	2,300	3,570	5,100
2d Sed	212	636	1,060	2,390	3,710	5,300

1976 LTD Brougham, V-8

4d Sed	212	636	1,060	2,390	3,710	5,300
2d Sed	220	660	1,100	2,480	3,850	5,500

1976 LTD Landau, V-8

4d Sed	220	660	1,100	2,480	3,850	5,500
2d Sed	228	684	1,140	2,570	3,990	5,700

1976 Station Wagons, V-8

4d Ranch Wag	256	768	1,280	2,880	4,480	6,400
4d LTD Wag	268	804	1,340	3,020	4,690	6,700
4d Ctry Sq Wag	288	864	1,440	3,240	5,040	7,200

1977 Pinto, 4-cyl.

2d Sed	204	612	1,020	2,300	3,570	5,100
2d Rbt	208	624	1,040	2,340	3,640	5,200
2d Sta Wag	228	684	1,140	2,570	3,990	5,700
2d Sq Wag	232	696	1,160	2,610	4,060	5,800

NOTE: Add 5 percent for V-6.

1977 Maverick, V-8

4d Sed	196	588	980	2,210	3,430	4,900
2d Sed	200	600	1,000	2,250	3,500	5,000

NOTE: Deduct 5 percent for 6-cyl.

1977 Granada, V-8

4d Sed	188	564	940	2,120	3,290	4,700
2d Sed	212	636	1,060	2,390	3,710	5,300

1977 Granada Ghia, V-8

4d Sed	220	660	1,100	2,480	3,850	5,500
2d Sed	224	672	1,120	2,520	3,920	5,600

1977 LTD II "S", V-8

4d Sed	132	396	660	1,490	2,310	3,300
2d Sed	136	408	680	1,530	2,380	3,400

1977 LTD II, V-8

4d Sed	136	408	680	1,530	2,380	3,400
2d Sed	140	420	700	1,580	2,450	3,500

1977 LTD II Brougham, V-8

4d Sed	144	432	720	1,620	2,520	3,600
2d Sed	148	444	740	1,670	2,590	3,700

1977 Station Wagons, V-8

4d 2S LTD II	200	550	900	2,030	3,150	4,500
4d 3S LTD II	200	550	900	2,070	3,200	4,600
4d 3S LTD II Sq	200	600	950	2,160	3,350	4,800

1977 LTD, V-8

4d Sed	208	624	1,040	2,340	3,640	5,200
2d Sed	212	636	1,060	2,390	3,710	5,300

1977 LTD Landau, V-8

4d Sed	216	648	1,080	2,430	3,780	5,400
2d Sed	220	660	1,100	2,480	3,850	5,500

1977 Station Wagons, V-8

4d 2S LTD	292	876	1,460	3,290	5,110	7,300
4d 3S LTD	296	888	1,480	3,330	5,180	7,400
4d 3S Ctry Sq	300	900	1,500	3,380	5,250	7,500

1978 Fiesta

2d HBk	112	336	560	1,260	1,960	2,800

1978 Pinto

2d Sed	200	600	1,000	2,250	3,500	5,000
3d Rbt	204	612	1,020	2,300	3,570	5,100
2d Sta Wag	224	672	1,120	2,520	3,920	5,600
2d Sq Wag	228	684	1,140	2,570	3,990	5,700

1978 Fairmont

4d Sed	124	372	620	1,400	2,170	3,100
2d Sed	120	360	600	1,350	2,100	3,000
2d Cpe Futura	150	450	700	1,620	2,500	3,600
4d Sta Wag	150	400	700	1,580	2,450	3,500

1978 Granada

4d Sed	188	564	940	2,120	3,290	4,700
2d Sed	212	636	1,060	2,390	3,710	5,300

1978 LTD II "S"

4d Sed	100	350	600	1,400	2,150	3,100
2d Cpe	100	350	600	1,350	2,100	3,000

1978 LTD II

4d Sed	128	384	640	1,440	2,240	3,200
2d Cpe	124	372	620	1,400	2,170	3,100

1978 LTD II Brougham

4d Sed	132	396	660	1,490	2,310	3,300
2d Cpe	128	384	640	1,440	2,240	3,200

1978 LTD

4d Sed	208	624	1,040	2,340	3,640	5,200
2d Cpe	212	636	1,060	2,390	3,710	5,300
4d 2S Sta Wag	292	876	1,460	3,290	5,110	7,300

1978 LTD Landau

4d Sed	216	648	1,080	2,430	3,780	5,400
2d Cpe	220	660	1,100	2,480	3,850	5,500

1979 Fiesta, 4-cyl.

3d HBk	116	348	580	1,310	2,030	2,900

1979 Pinto, V-6

2d Sed	150	450	800	1,760	2,750	3,900
2d Rbt	150	500	800	1,800	2,800	4,000
2d Sta Wag	200	550	900	2,030	3,150	4,500
2d Sq Wag	200	550	900	2,070	3,200	4,600

NOTE: Deduct 5 percent for 4-cyl.

1979 Fairmont, 6-cyl.

4d Sed	128	384	640	1,440	2,240	3,200
2d Sed	124	372	620	1,400	2,170	3,100
2d Cpe	144	432	720	1,620	2,520	3,600
4d Sta Wag	132	396	660	1,490	2,310	3,300
4d Sq Wag	136	408	680	1,530	2,380	3,400

NOTE: Deduct 5 percent for 4-cyl. Add 5 percent for V-8.

1979 Granada, V-8

4d Sed	150	500	850	1,940	3,000	4,300
2d Sed	150	450	750	1,670	2,600	3,700

NOTE: Deduct 5 percent for 6-cyl.

1979 LTD II, V-8

4d Sed	128	384	640	1,440	2,240	3,200
2d Sed	124	372	620	1,400	2,170	3,100

1979 LTD II Brougham, V-8

4d Sed	132	396	660	1,490	2,310	3,300
2d Sed	128	384	640	1,440	2,240	3,200

1979 LTD, V-8

4d Sed	144	432	720	1,620	2,520	3,600
2d Sed	136	408	680	1,530	2,380	3,400
4d 2S Sta Wag	140	420	700	1,580	2,450	3,500
4d 3S Sta Wag	144	432	720	1,620	2,520	3,600
4d 2S Sq Wag	148	444	740	1,670	2,590	3,700
4d 3S Sq Wag	152	456	760	1,710	2,660	3,800

1979 LTD Landau

4d Sed	152	456	760	1,710	2,660	3,800
2d Sed	144	432	720	1,620	2,520	3,600

1980 Fiesta, 4-cyl.

2d HBk	124	372	620	1,400	2,170	3,100

1980 Pinto, 4-cyl.

2d Cpe Pony	150	450	750	1,670	2,600	3,700
2d Sta Wag Pony	150	450	800	1,760	2,750	3,900
2d Cpe	150	450	750	1,710	2,650	3,800
2d HBk	150	450	750	1,710	2,650	3,800
2d Sta Wag	200	550	900	1,980	3,100	4,400
2d Sta Wag Sq	200	550	900	2,030	3,150	4,500

1980 Fairmont, 6-cyl.

4d Sed	136	408	680	1,530	2,380	3,400
2d Sed	132	396	660	1,490	2,310	3,300
4d Sed Futura	144	432	720	1,620	2,520	3,600
2d Cpe Futura	164	492	820	1,850	2,870	4,100
4d Sta Wag	152	456	760	1,710	2,660	3,800

NOTE: Deduct 10 percent for 4-cyl. Add 12 percent for V-8.

1980 Granada, V-8

4d Sed	156	468	780	1,760	2,730	3,900
2d Sed	152	456	760	1,710	2,660	3,800
4d Sed Ghia	164	492	820	1,850	2,870	4,100
2d Sed Ghia	160	480	800	1,800	2,800	4,000
4d Sed ESS	168	504	840	1,890	2,940	4,200
2d Sed ESS	164	492	820	1,850	2,870	4,100

NOTE: Deduct 10 percent for 6-cyl.

1980 LTD, V-8

4d Sed S	168	504	840	1,890	2,940	4,200
4d Sta Wag	176	528	880	1,980	3,080	4,400
4d Sed	172	516	860	1,940	3,010	4,300
2d Sed	168	504	840	1,890	2,940	4,200
4d Sta Wag	180	540	900	2,030	3,150	4,500
4d Sta Wag CS	188	564	940	2,120	3,290	4,700

1980 LTD Crown Victoria, V-8

4d Sed	184	552	920	2,070	3,220	4,600
2d Sed	180	540	900	2,030	3,150	4,500

1981 Escort, 4-cyl.

2d HBk SS	144	432	720	1,620	2,520	3,600
4d HBk SS	148	444	740	1,670	2,590	3,700

NOTE: Deduct 5 percent for lesser models.

1981 Fairmont, 6-cyl.

2d Sed S	136	408	680	1,530	2,380	3,400
4d Sed	140	420	700	1,580	2,450	3,500
2d Sed	140	420	700	1,580	2,450	3,500
4d Futura	144	432	720	1,620	2,520	3,600
2d Cpe Futura	168	504	840	1,890	2,940	4,200
4d Sta Wag	156	468	780	1,760	2,730	3,900
4d Sta Wag Futura	160	480	800	1,800	2,800	4,000

NOTE: Deduct 10 percent for 4-cyl. Add 12 percent for V-8.

1981 Granada, 6-cyl.

4d Sed GLX	160	480	800	1,800	2,800	4,000
2d Sed GLX	156	468	780	1,760	2,730	3,900

NOTE: Deduct 5 percent for lesser models. Deduct 10 percent for 4-cyl. Add 12 percent for V-8.

1981 LTD, V-8

4d Sed S	172	516	860	1,940	3,010	4,300
4d Sta Wag S	180	540	900	2,030	3,150	4,500
4d Sed	176	528	880	1,980	3,080	4,400
2d Sed	172	516	860	1,940	3,010	4,300
4d Sta Wag	184	552	920	2,070	3,220	4,600
4d Sta Wag CS	192	576	960	2,160	3,360	4,800

1981 LTD Crown Victoria, V-8

4d Sed	192	576	960	2,160	3,360	4,800
2d Sed	188	564	940	2,120	3,290	4,700

NOTE: Deduct 15 percent for 6-cyl.

1982 Escort, 4-cyl.

2d HBk GLX	144	432	720	1,620	2,520	3,600
4d HBk GLX	148	444	740	1,670	2,590	3,700
4d Sta Wag GLX	152	456	760	1,710	2,660	3,800
2d HBk GT	156	468	780	1,760	2,730	3,900

NOTE: Deduct 5 percent for lesser models.

1982 EXP, 4-cyl.

2d Cpe	180	540	900	2,030	3,150	4,500

1982 Fairmont Futura, 4-cyl.

4d Sed	120	360	600	1,350	2,100	3,000
2d Sed	116	348	580	1,310	2,030	2,900
2d Cpe Futura	132	396	660	1,490	2,310	3,300

1982 Fairmont Futura, 6-cyl.

4d Sed	148	444	740	1,670	2,590	3,700
2d Cpe Futura	172	516	860	1,940	3,010	4,300

1982 Granada, 6-cyl.

4d Sed GLX	164	492	820	1,850	2,870	4,100
2d Sed GLX	160	480	800	1,800	2,800	4,000

NOTE: Deduct 10 percent for 4-cyl. Deduct 5 percent for lesser models.

1982 Granada Wagon, 6-cyl.

4d Sta Wag GL	172	516	860	1,940	3,010	4,300

1982 LTD, V-8

4d Sed S	176	528	880	1,980	3,080	4,400
4d Sed	180	540	900	2,030	3,150	4,500
2d Sed	176	528	880	1,980	3,080	4,400

1982 LTD Crown Victoria, V-8

4d Sed	196	588	980	2,210	3,430	4,900
2d Sed	192	576	960	2,160	3,360	4,800

1982 LTD Station Wagon, V-8

4d Sta Wag S	184	552	920	2,070	3,220	4,600
4d Sta Wag	188	564	940	2,120	3,290	4,700
4d Sta Wag CS	196	588	980	2,210	3,430	4,900

NOTE: Deduct 15 percent for V-6.

1983 Escort, 4-cyl.

2d HBk GLX	144	432	720	1,620	2,520	3,600
4d HBk GLX	148	444	740	1,670	2,590	3,700
4d Sta Wag GLX	152	456	760	1,710	2,660	3,800
2d HBk GT	148	444	740	1,670	2,590	3,700

NOTE: Deduct 5 percent for lesser models.

1983 EXP, 4-cyl.

2d Cpe	180	540	900	2,030	3,150	4,500

1983 Fairmont Futura, 6-cyl.

4d Sed	148	444	740	1,670	2,590	3,700
2d Sed	144	432	720	1,620	2,520	3,600
2d Cpe	172	516	860	1,940	3,010	4,300

NOTE: Deduct 5 percent for 4-cyl.

1983 LTD, 6-cyl.

4d Sed	168	504	840	1,890	2,940	4,200
4d Sed Brgm	176	528	880	1,980	3,080	4,400
4d Sta Wag	184	552	920	2,070	3,220	4,600

NOTE: Deduct 10 percent for 4-cyl.

1983 LTD Crown Victoria, V-8

4d Sed	200	600	1,000	2,250	3,500	5,000
2d Sed	196	588	980	2,210	3,430	4,900
4d Sta Wag	204	612	1,020	2,300	3,570	5,100

1984 Escort, 4-cyl.

4d HBk LX	140	420	700	1,580	2,450	3,500
2d HBk LX	140	420	700	1,580	2,450	3,500
4d Sta Wag LX	144	432	720	1,620	2,520	3,600
2d HBk GT	144	432	720	1,620	2,520	3,600
2d HBk Turbo GT	152	456	760	1,710	2,660	3,800

NOTE: Deduct 5 percent for lesser models.

1984 EXP, 4-cyl.

2d Cpe	160	480	800	1,800	2,800	4,000
2d Cpe L	168	504	840	1,890	2,940	4,200
2d Cpe Turbo	184	552	920	2,070	3,220	4,600

1984 Tempo, 4-cyl.

2d Sed GLX	140	420	700	1,580	2,450	3,500
4d Sed GLX	140	420	700	1,580	2,450	3,500

NOTE: Deduct 5 percent for lesser models.

1984 LTD, V-6

4d Sed	168	504	840	1,890	2,940	4,200
4d Sed Brgm	172	516	860	1,940	3,010	4,300
4d Sta Wag	172	516	860	1,940	3,010	4,300
4d Sed LX, (V-8)	184	552	920	2,070	3,220	4,600

NOTE: Deduct 8 percent for 4-cyl.

1984 LTD Crown Victoria, V-8

4d Sed S	188	564	940	2,120	3,290	4,700
4d Sed	196	588	980	2,210	3,430	4,900
2d Sed	196	588	980	2,210	3,430	4,900
4d Sta Wag S	200	600	1,000	2,250	3,500	5,000
4d Sta Wag	204	612	1,020	2,300	3,570	5,100
4d Sta Wag Sq	208	624	1,040	2,340	3,640	5,200

1985 Escort, 4-cyl.

4d HBk LX	144	432	720	1,620	2,520	3,600
4d Sta Wag LX	144	432	720	1,620	2,520	3,600
2d HBk GT	148	444	740	1,670	2,590	3,700
2d HBk Turbo GT	156	468	780	1,760	2,730	3,900

NOTE: Deduct 5 percent for lesser models.

1985 EXP, 4-cyl.

2d Cpe HBk	164	492	820	1,850	2,870	4,100
2d Cpe HBk Luxury	172	516	860	1,940	3,010	4,300
2d Cpe HBk Turbo	188	564	940	2,120	3,290	4,700

NOTE: Deduct 20 percent for diesel.

1985 Tempo, 4-cyl.

2d Sed GLX	140	420	700	1,580	2,450	3,500
4d Sed GLX	140	420	700	1,580	2,450	3,500

NOTE: Deduct 5 percent for lesser models. Deduct 20 percent for diesel.

1985 LTD

4d V-6 Sed	172	516	860	1,940	3,010	4,300
4d V-6 Sed Brgm	176	528	880	1,980	3,080	4,400
4d V-6 Sta Wag	176	528	880	1,980	3,080	4,400
4d V-8 Sed LX	188	564	940	2,120	3,290	4,700

NOTE: Deduct 20 percent for 4-cyl. where available.

1985 LTD Crown Victoria, V-8

4d Sed S	192	576	960	2,160	3,360	4,800
4d Sed	200	600	1,000	2,250	3,500	5,000
2d Sed	196	588	980	2,210	3,430	4,900
4d Sta Wag S	204	612	1,020	2,300	3,570	5,100
4d Sta Wag	208	624	1,040	2,340	3,640	5,200
4d Sta Wag Ctry Sq	216	648	1,080	2,430	3,780	5,400

1986 Escort

2d HBk	144	432	720	1,620	2,520	3,600
4d HBk	140	420	700	1,580	2,450	3,500
4d Sta Wag	148	444	740	1,670	2,590	3,700
2d GT HBk	160	480	800	1,800	2,800	4,000

1986 EXP

2d Cpe	184	552	920	2,070	3,220	4,600

1986 Tempo

2d Sed	144	432	720	1,620	2,520	3,600
4d Sed	144	432	720	1,620	2,520	3,600

1986 Taurus

4d Sed	188	564	940	2,120	3,290	4,700
4d Sta Wag	192	576	960	2,160	3,360	4,800

1986 LTD

4d Sed	208	624	1,040	2,340	3,640	5,200
4d Brgm Sed	208	624	1,040	2,340	3,640	5,200
4d Sta Wag	216	648	1,080	2,430	3,780	5,400

1986 LTD Crown Victoria

2d Sed	216	648	1,080	2,430	3,780	5,400
4d Sed	216	648	1,080	2,430	3,780	5,400
4d Sta Wag	220	660	1,100	2,480	3,850	5,500

NOTE: Add 10 percent for deluxe models. Deduct 5 percent for smaller engines.

1987 Escort, 4-cyl.

2d HBk Pony	148	444	740	1,670	2,590	3,700
2d HBk GL	152	456	760	1,710	2,660	3,800
4d HBk GL	156	468	780	1,760	2,730	3,900
4d Sta Wag GL	156	468	780	1,760	2,730	3,900
2d HBk GT	160	480	800	1,800	2,800	4,000

1987 EXP, 4-cyl.

2d HBk LX	188	564	940	2,120	3,290	4,700
2d HBk Spt	192	576	960	2,160	3,360	4,800

1987 Tempo

2d Sed GL	148	444	740	1,670	2,590	3,700
4d Sed GL	152	456	760	1,710	2,660	3,800
2d Sed GL Spt	152	456	760	1,710	2,660	3,800
4d Sed GL Spt	156	468	780	1,760	2,730	3,900
2d Sed LX	156	468	780	1,760	2,730	3,900
4d Sed LX	160	480	800	1,800	2,800	4,000
2d Sed 4WD	180	540	900	2,030	3,150	4,500
4d Sed 4WD	184	552	920	2,070	3,220	4,600

1987 Taurus, 4-cyl.

4d Sed	192	576	960	2,160	3,360	4,800
4d Sta Wag	196	588	980	2,210	3,430	4,900

1987 Taurus, V-6

4d Sed L	196	588	980	2,210	3,430	4,900
4d Sta Wag L	200	600	1,000	2,250	3,500	5,000
4d Sed GL	200	600	1,000	2,250	3,500	5,000
4d Sta Wag GL	204	612	1,020	2,300	3,570	5,100
4d Sed LX	204	612	1,020	2,300	3,570	5,100
4d Sta Wag LX	208	624	1,040	2,340	3,640	5,200

1987 LTD Crown Victoria, V-8

4d Sed S	220	660	1,100	2,480	3,850	5,500
4d Sta Wag S	224	672	1,120	2,520	3,920	5,600
4d Sed	224	672	1,120	2,520	3,920	5,600
2d Cpe	220	660	1,100	2,480	3,850	5,500
4d Sta Wag	224	672	1,120	2,520	3,920	5,600
4d Sta Wag Ctry Sq	230	700	1,160	2,610	4,060	5,800
4d Sed LX	228	684	1,140	2,570	3,990	5,700
2d Cpe LX	224	672	1,120	2,520	3,920	5,600
4d Sta Wag LX	228	684	1,140	2,570	3,990	5,700
4d Sta Wag Ctry Sq LX	240	710	1,180	2,660	4,130	5,900

1988 Festiva, 4-cyl.

2d HBk L	92	276	460	1,040	1,610	2,300
2d HBk L Plus	100	300	500	1,130	1,750	2,500
2d HBk LX	116	348	580	1,310	2,030	2,900

1988 Escort, 4-cyl.

2d HBk Pony	88	264	440	990	1,540	2,200
2d HBk GL	100	300	500	1,130	1,750	2,500
4d HBk GL	104	312	520	1,170	1,820	2,600
4d Sta Wag GL	116	348	580	1,310	2,030	2,900
2d HBk GT	140	420	700	1,580	2,450	3,500
2d HBk LX	112	336	560	1,260	1,960	2,800
4d HBk LX	116	348	580	1,310	2,030	2,900
4d Sta Wag LX	124	372	620	1,400	2,170	3,100

1988 EXP, 4-cyl.

2d HBk	120	360	600	1,350	2,100	3,000

1988 Tempo, 4-cyl.

2d Sed GL	132	396	660	1,490	2,310	3,300
4d Sed GL	140	420	700	1,580	2,450	3,500
2d Sed GLS	140	420	700	1,580	2,450	3,500
4d Sed GLS	144	432	720	1,620	2,520	3,600
4d Sed LX	148	444	740	1,670	2,590	3,700
4d Sed 4x4	180	540	900	2,030	3,150	4,500

1988 Taurus, 4-cyl., V-6

4d Sed	168	504	840	1,890	2,940	4,200
4d Sed L	176	528	880	1,980	3,080	4,400
4d Sta Wag L	184	552	920	2,070	3,220	4,600
4d Sed GL	180	540	900	2,030	3,150	4,500
4d Sta Wag GL	200	600	1,000	2,250	3,500	5,000
4d Sed LX	220	660	1,100	2,480	3,850	5,500
4d Sta Wag LX	228	684	1,140	2,570	3,990	5,700

1988 LTD Crown Victoria, V-8

4d Sed	204	612	1,020	2,300	3,570	5,100
4d Sta Wag	212	636	1,060	2,390	3,710	5,300
4d Ctry Sq Sta Wag	230	700	1,160	2,610	4,060	5,800
4d Sed S	212	636	1,060	2,390	3,710	5,300
4d Sed LX	216	648	1,080	2,430	3,780	5,400
4d Sta Wag LX	220	660	1,100	2,480	3,850	5,500
4d Ctry Sq Sta Wag	240	720	1,200	2,700	4,200	6,000

1989 Festiva, 4-cyl.

2d HBk L	128	384	640	1,440	2,240	3,200
2d HBk L Plus	132	396	660	1,490	2,310	3,300
2d HBk LX	136	408	680	1,530	2,380	3,400

1989 Escort, 4-cyl.

2d HBk Pony	132	396	660	1,490	2,310	3,300
2d HBk LX	136	408	680	1,530	2,380	3,400
2d HBk GT	152	456	760	1,710	2,660	3,800
4d HBk LX	140	420	700	1,580	2,450	3,500
4d Sta Wag LX	144	432	720	1,620	2,520	3,600

1989 Tempo, 4-cyl.

2d Sed GL	140	420	700	1,580	2,450	3,500
4d Sed GL	144	432	720	1,620	2,520	3,600
2d Sed GLS	152	456	760	1,710	2,660	3,800
4d Sed GLS	156	468	780	1,760	2,730	3,900
4d Sed LX	168	504	840	1,890	2,940	4,200
4d Sed 4x4	192	576	960	2,160	3,360	4,800

1989 Probe, 4-cyl.

2d GL HBk	200	600	1,000	2,250	3,500	5,000
2d LX HBk	220	660	1,100	2,480	3,850	5,500
2d GT Turbo HBk	240	720	1,200	2,700	4,200	6,000

1989 Taurus, 4-cyl.

4d Sed L	184	552	920	2,070	3,220	4,600
4d Sed GL	188	564	940	2,120	3,290	4,700

1989 Taurus, V-6

4d Sed L	190	580	960	2,160	3,360	4,800
4d Sta Wag L	200	600	1,000	2,250	3,500	5,000
4d Sed GL	200	610	1,020	2,300	3,570	5,100
4d Sta Wag GL	240	720	1,200	2,700	4,200	6,000
4d Sed LX	230	700	1,160	2,610	4,060	5,800
4d Sta Wag LX	360	1,080	1,800	4,050	6,300	9,000
4d Sed SHO	400	1,200	2,000	4,500	7,000	10,000

1989 LTD Crown Victoria, V-8

Model						
4d Sed S	220	660	1,100	2,480	3,850	5,500
4d Sed	228	684	1,140	2,570	3,990	5,700
4d Sed LX	252	756	1,260	2,840	4,410	6,300
4d Sta Wag	256	768	1,280	2,880	4,480	6,400
4d Sta Wag LX	260	780	1,300	2,930	4,550	6,500
4d Ctry Sq Sta Wag	260	790	1,320	2,970	4,620	6,600
4d Ctry Sq LX Sta Wag	270	800	1,340	3,020	4,690	6,700

1990 Festiva, 4-cyl.

Model						
2d	112	336	560	1,260	1,960	2,800
2d L	120	360	600	1,350	2,100	3,000
2d LX	140	420	700	1,580	2,450	3,500

1990 Escort, 4-cyl.

Model						
2d Pony HBk	120	360	600	1,350	2,100	3,000
2d LX HBk	140	420	700	1,580	2,450	3,500
4d LX HBk	144	432	720	1,620	2,520	3,600
4d LX Sta Wag	152	456	760	1,710	2,660	3,800
2d GT HBk	164	492	820	1,850	2,870	4,100

1990 Tempo, 4-cyl.

Model						
2d GL Sed	144	432	720	1,620	2,520	3,600
4d GL Sed	148	444	740	1,670	2,590	3,700
2d GLS Sed	160	480	800	1,800	2,800	4,000
4d GLS Sed	164	492	820	1,850	2,870	4,100
4d LX Sed	168	504	840	1,890	2,940	4,200
4d Sed 4x4	220	660	1,100	2,480	3,850	5,500

1990 Probe

Model						
2d GL HBk, 4-cyl.	220	660	1,100	2,480	3,850	5,500
2d LX HBk, V-6	260	780	1,300	2,930	4,550	6,500
2d GT HBk, Turbo	360	1,080	1,800	4,050	6,300	9,000

1990 Taurus, 4-cyl.

Model						
4d L Sed	160	480	800	1,800	2,800	4,000
4d GL Sed	168	504	840	1,890	2,940	4,200

1990 Taurus, V-6

Model						
4d L Sed	190	560	940	2,120	3,290	4,700
4d L Sta Wag	200	600	1,000	2,250	3,500	5,000
4d GL Sed	200	590	980	2,210	3,430	4,900
4d GL Sta Wag	210	620	1,040	2,340	3,640	5,200
4d LX Sed	230	700	1,160	2,610	4,060	5,800
4d LX Sta Wag	260	770	1,280	2,880	4,480	6,400
4d SHO Sed	360	1,080	1,800	4,050	6,300	9,000

1990 LTD Crown Victoria, V-8

Model						
4d S Sed	220	660	1,100	2,480	3,850	5,500
4d Sed	240	720	1,200	2,700	4,200	6,000
4d LX Sed	260	780	1,300	2,930	4,550	6,500
4d Sta Wag	232	696	1,160	2,610	4,060	5,800
4d LX Sta Wag	248	744	1,240	2,790	4,340	6,200
4d Ctry Sq Sta Wag	260	780	1,300	2,930	4,550	6,500
4d LX Ctry Sq Sta Wag	270	820	1,360	3,060	4,760	6,800

1991 Festiva, 4-cyl.

Model						
2d HBk	124	372	620	1,400	2,170	3,100
2d GL HBk	132	396	660	1,490	2,310	3,300

1991 Escort, 4-cyl.

Model						
2d Pony HBk	140	420	700	1,580	2,450	3,500
2d LX HBk	148	444	740	1,670	2,590	3,700
4d LX HBk	148	444	740	1,670	2,590	3,700
4d LX Sta Wag	156	468	780	1,760	2,730	3,900
2d GT HBk	164	492	820	1,850	2,870	4,100

1991 Tempo, 4-cyl.

Model						
2d L Sed	144	432	720	1,620	2,520	3,600
4d L Sed	144	432	720	1,620	2,520	3,600
2d GL Sed	152	456	760	1,710	2,660	3,800
4d GL Sed	152	456	760	1,710	2,660	3,800
2d GLS Sed	160	480	800	1,800	2,800	4,000
4d GLS Sed	160	480	800	1,800	2,800	4,000
4d LX Sed	168	504	840	1,890	2,940	4,200
4d Sed 4x4	200	600	1,000	2,250	3,500	5,000

1991 Probe, 4-cyl.

Model						
2d GL HBk	188	564	940	2,120	3,290	4,700
2d LX HBk	220	660	1,100	2,480	3,850	5,500
2d GT HBk Turbo	240	720	1,200	2,700	4,200	6,000

1991 Taurus, 4-cyl.

Model						
4d L Sed	144	432	720	1,620	2,520	3,600
4d GL Sed	152	456	760	1,710	2,660	3,800

1991 Taurus, V-6

Model						
4d L Sed	152	456	760	1,710	2,660	3,800
4d L Sta Wag	180	540	900	2,030	3,150	4,500
4d GL Sed	168	504	840	1,890	2,940	4,200
4d GL Sta Wag	220	660	1,100	2,480	3,850	5,500
4d LX Sed	208	624	1,040	2,340	3,640	5,200
4d LX Sta Wag	260	780	1,300	2,930	4,550	6,500
4d SHO Sed	380	1,140	1,900	4,280	6,650	9,500

1991 LTD Crown Victoria, V-8

Model						
4d S Sed	180	540	900	2,030	3,150	4,500
4d Sed	220	660	1,100	2,480	3,850	5,500
4d LX Sed	240	720	1,200	2,700	4,200	6,000
4d 3S Sta Wag	196	588	980	2,210	3,430	4,900
4d 2S Sta Wag	236	708	1,180	2,660	4,130	5,900
4d LX 3S Sta Wag	256	768	1,280	2,880	4,480	6,400
4d Ctry Sq 3S Sta Wag	210	620	1,040	2,340	3,640	5,200
4d Ctry Sq 2S Sta Wag	250	740	1,240	2,790	4,340	6,200
4d Ctry Sq LX 3S Sta Wag	250	800	1,350	3,020	4,700	6,700

1992 Festiva, 4-cyl.

Model						
2d L HBk	140	420	700	1,580	2,450	3,500
2d GL HBk	152	456	760	1,710	2,660	3,800

1992 Escort, 4-cyl.

Model						
2d HBk	168	504	840	1,890	2,940	4,200
2d LX HBk	168	504	840	1,890	2,940	4,200
4d LX HBk	168	504	840	1,890	2,940	4,200
4d LX Sed	160	480	800	1,800	2,800	4,000
4d LX Sta Wag	176	528	880	1,980	3,080	4,400
4d LX-E Sta Wag	180	540	900	2,030	3,150	4,500
2d GT HBk	200	600	1,000	2,250	3,500	5,000

1992 Tempo, 4-cyl.

2d GL Cpe	152	456	760	1,710	2,660	3,800
4d GL Sed	156	468	780	1,760	2,730	3,900
4d LX Sed	160	480	800	1,800	2,800	4,000
2d GLS Sed V-6	220	660	1,100	2,480	3,850	5,500
4d GLS Sed V-6	220	660	1,100	2,480	3,850	5,500

1992 Probe, 4-cyl.

2d GL HBk	220	660	1,100	2,480	3,850	5,500
2d LX HBk V-6	256	768	1,280	2,880	4,480	6,400
2d GT HBk Turbo	260	780	1,300	2,930	4,550	6,500

1992 Taurus, V-6

4d L Sed	200	600	1,000	2,250	3,500	5,000
4d L Sta Wag	200	600	1,000	2,250	3,500	5,000
4d GL Sed	220	660	1,100	2,480	3,850	5,500
4d GL Sta Wag	220	660	1,100	2,480	3,850	5,500
4d LX Sed	240	720	1,200	2,700	4,200	6,000
4d LX Sta Wag	240	720	1,200	2,700	4,200	6,000
4d SHO Sed	420	1,260	2,100	4,730	7,350	10,500

1992 Crown Victoria, V-8

4d S Sed	240	720	1,200	2,700	4,200	6,000
4d Sed	260	780	1,300	2,930	4,550	6,500
4d LX Sed	380	1,140	1,900	4,280	6,650	9,500
4d Trg Sed	320	960	1,600	3,600	5,600	8,000

1993 Festiva, 4-cyl.

2d Sed	144	432	720	1,620	2,520	3,600

1993 Escort, 4-cyl.

2d HBk	172	516	860	1,940	3,010	4,300
2d LX HBk	176	528	880	1,980	3,080	4,400
2d GT HBk	180	540	900	2,030	3,150	4,500
4d HBk	176	528	880	1,980	3,080	4,400
4d LX Sed	180	540	900	2,030	3,150	4,500
4d LXE Sed	184	552	920	2,070	3,220	4,600
4d LX Sta Wag	188	564	940	2,120	3,290	4,700

1993 Tempo, 4-cyl.

2d GL Sed	168	504	840	1,890	2,940	4,200
4d GL Sed	172	516	860	1,940	3,010	4,300
4d LX Sed	180	540	900	2,030	3,150	4,500

1993 Probe

2d HBk, 4-cyl.	244	732	1,220	2,750	4,270	6,100
2d GT HBk, V-6	256	768	1,280	2,880	4,480	6,400

1993 Taurus, V-6

4d GL Sed	248	744	1,240	2,790	4,340	6,200
4d LX Sed	252	756	1,260	2,840	4,410	6,300
4d GL Sta Wag	264	792	1,320	2,970	4,620	6,600
4d LX Sta Wag	268	804	1,340	3,020	4,690	6,700
4d SHO Sed	380	1,140	1,900	4,280	6,650	9,500

1993 Crown Victoria, V-8

4d Sed S	284	852	1,420	3,200	4,970	7,100
4d Sed	292	876	1,460	3,290	5,110	7,300
4d LX Sed	296	888	1,480	3,330	5,180	7,400

1994 Aspire, 4-cyl.

2d HBk	128	384	640	1,440	2,240	3,200
2d SE HBk	140	420	700	1,580	2,450	3,500
4d HBk	136	408	680	1,530	2,380	3,400

1994 Escort, 4-cyl.

2d HBk	156	468	780	1,760	2,730	3,900
2d LX HBk	180	540	900	2,030	3,150	4,500
4d LX HBk	180	540	900	2,030	3,150	4,500
2d GT HBk	200	600	1,000	2,250	3,500	5,000
4d LX Sed	188	564	940	2,120	3,290	4,700
4d LX Sta Wag	192	576	960	2,160	3,360	4,800

1994 Tempo, 4-cyl.

2d GL Sed	168	504	840	1,890	2,940	4,200
4d GL Sed	172	516	860	1,940	3,010	4,300
4d LX Sed	180	540	900	2,030	3,150	4,500

1994 Probe

2d HbK, 4-cyl.	250	750	1,200	2,750	4,250	6,100
2d GT HBk, V-6	250	750	1,300	2,880	4,500	6,400

1994 Taurus, V-6

4d GL Sed	250	750	1,250	2,790	4,350	6,200
4d LX Sed	250	750	1,250	2,840	4,400	6,300
4d GL Sta Wag	250	800	1,300	2,970	4,600	6,600
4d LX Sta Wag	250	800	1,350	3,020	4,700	6,700
4d SHO Sed	400	1,150	1,900	4,280	6,650	9,500

1994 Crown Victoria, V-8

4d Sed S	288	864	1,440	3,240	5,040	7,200
4d Sed	300	900	1,500	3,380	5,250	7,500
4d LX Sed	320	960	1,600	3,600	5,600	8,000

1995 Aspire, 4-cyl.

2d HBk	150	400	650	1,440	2,250	3,200
2d SE HBk	150	400	700	1,580	2,450	3,500
4d HBk	150	400	700	1,530	2,400	3,400

1995 Escort, 4-cyl.

2d HBk	150	450	800	1,760	2,750	3,900
2d LX HBk	200	550	900	2,030	3,150	4,500
4d LX HBk	200	550	900	2,030	3,150	4,500
4d LX Sed	200	550	950	2,120	3,300	4,700
4d LX Sta Wag	200	600	950	2,160	3,350	4,800
2d GT HBk	200	600	1,000	2,250	3,500	5,000

1995 Contour, 4-cyl. & V-6

4d GL Sed	200	600	1,050	2,340	3,650	5,200
4d LX Sed	200	650	1,050	2,390	3,700	5,300
4d SE Sed (V-6 only)	220	670	1,120	2,520	3,920	5,600

1995 Probe, 4-cyl. & V-6

2d HBk, 4-cyl.	250	750	1,200	2,750	4,250	6,100
2d GT HBk, V-6	250	750	1,300	2,880	4,500	6,400

1995 Taurus, V-6

4d GL Sed	250	750	1,250	2,790	4,350	6,200
4d GL Sta Wag	250	800	1,300	2,970	4,600	6,600
4d LX Sed	250	750	1,250	2,840	4,400	6,300
4d LX Sta Wag	250	800	1,350	3,020	4,700	6,700
4d SE Sed	250	750	1,300	2,880	4,500	6,400
4d SHO Sed	400	1,150	1,900	4,280	6,650	9,500

1995 Crown Victoria, V-8

4d S Sed	300	850	1,450	3,240	5,050	7,200
4d Sed	300	900	1,500	3,380	5,250	7,500
4d LX Sed	300	950	1,600	3,600	5,600	8,000

1996 Aspire, 4-cyl.

2d HBk	150	400	650	1,440	2,250	3,200
4d HBk	150	400	700	1,530	2,400	3,400

1996 Escort, 4-cyl.

2d HBk	150	450	800	1,760	2,750	3,900
2d LX HBk	200	550	900	2,030	3,150	4,500
4d LX HBk	200	550	900	2,030	3,150	4,500
4d LX Sed	200	550	950	2,120	3,300	4,700
4d LX Sta Wag	200	600	950	2,160	3,350	4,800
2d GT HBk	200	600	1,000	2,250	3,500	5,000

1996 Contour, 4-cyl. & V-6

4d GL Sed	200	600	1,050	2,340	3,650	5,200
4d LX Sed	200	650	1,050	2,390	3,700	5,300
4d SE Sed (V-6 only)	220	670	1,120	2,520	3,920	5,600

1996 Probe, 4-cyl. & V-6

2d HBk, 4-cyl.	250	750	1,200	2,750	4,250	6,100
2d GT HBk, V-6	250	750	1,300	2,880	4,500	6,400

1996 Taurus, V-6

4d G Sed	250	700	1,200	2,700	4,200	6,000
4d GL Sed	250	750	1,250	2,790	4,350	6,200
4d GL Sta Wag	250	800	1,300	2,970	4,600	6,600
4d LX Sed	250	750	1,250	2,840	4,400	6,300
4d LX Sta Wag	250	800	1,350	3,020	4,700	6,700

1996 Crown Victoria, V-8

4d S Sed	300	850	1,450	3,240	5,050	7,200
4d Sed	300	900	1,500	3,380	5,250	7,500
4d LX Sed	300	950	1,600	3,600	5,600	8,000

1997 Aspire, 4-cyl.

2d HBk	128	384	640	1,440	2,240	3,200
4d HBk	136	408	680	1,530	2,380	3,400

1997 Escort, 4-cyl.

4d Sed	180	540	900	2,030	3,150	4,500
4d LX Sed	188	564	940	2,120	3,290	4,700
4d LX Sta Wag	192	576	960	2,160	3,360	4,800

1997 Contour, 4-cyl. & V-6

4d Sed (4-cyl. only)	200	600	1,000	2,250	3,500	5,000
4d GL Sed	208	624	1,040	2,340	3,640	5,200
4d LX Sed	212	636	1,060	2,390	3,710	5,300
4d SE Sed (V-6 only)	220	670	1,120	2,520	3,920	5,600

NOTE: Add 5 percent for Sport Pkg on GL or LX models.

1997 Probe, 4-cyl. & V-6

2d HBK, 4-cyl.	244	732	1,220	2,750	4,270	6,100
2d GT HBk, V-6	256	768	1,280	2,880	4,480	6,400

NOTE: Add 5 percent for GTS Sport Pkg on GT model.

1997 Taurus, V-6

4d G Sed	240	720	1,200	2,700	4,200	6,000
4d GL Sed	248	744	1,240	2,790	4,340	6,200
4d GL Sta Wag	264	792	1,320	2,970	4,620	6,600
4d LX Sed	252	756	1,260	2,840	4,410	6,300
4d LX Sta Wag	268	804	1,340	3,020	4,690	6,700

1997 Taurus, V-8

4d SHO Sed	420	1,260	2,100	4,730	7,350	10,500

1997 Crown Victoria, V-8

4d S Sed	288	864	1,440	3,240	5,040	7,200
4d Sed	300	900	1,500	3,380	5,250	7,500
4d LX Sed	320	960	1,600	3,600	5,600	8,000

1998 Escort, 4-cyl.

4d LX Sed	180	550	920	2,070	3,220	4,600
4d SE Sed	190	580	960	2,160	3,360	4,800
4d SE Sta Wag	200	590	980	2,210	3,430	4,900
2d ZX2 "Cool" Cpe	200	610	1,020	2,300	3,570	5,100
2d ZX2 "Hot" Cpe	210	620	1,040	2,340	3,640	5,200

NOTE: Add 5 percent for ZX2 Spt Pkg.

1998 Contour, 4-cyl. & V-6

4d LX Sed	210	640	1,060	2,390	3,710	5,300
4d SE Sed	220	670	1,120	2,520	3,920	5,600
4d SVT Spt Sed (V-6 only)	420	1,260	2,100	4,730	7,350	10,500

1998 Taurus, V-6

4d LX Sed	250	760	1,260	2,840	4,410	6,300
4d SE Sed	260	780	1,300	2,930	4,550	6,500
4d SE Sta Wag	270	800	1,340	3,020	4,690	6,700

1998 Taurus, V-8

4d SHO Sed	420	1,260	2,100	4,730	7,350	10,500

NOTE: Add 10 percent for Spt Pkg on SE Sed.

1998 Crown Victoria, V-8

4d S Sed	290	860	1,440	3,240	5,040	7,200
4d Sed	300	900	1,500	3,380	5,250	7,500
4d LX Sed	320	960	1,600	3,600	5,600	8,000

NOTE: Add 5 percent for 41G Handling & Performance Pkg.

1999 Escort, 4-cyl.

4d LX Sed	180	550	920	2,070	3,220	4,600
4d SE Sed	190	580	960	2,160	3,360	4,800
4d SE Sta Wag	200	590	980	2,210	3,430	4,900
2d ZX2 "Cool" Cpe	200	610	1,020	2,300	3,570	5,100
2d ZX2 "Hot" Cpe	210	620	1,040	2,340	3,640	5,200

NOTE: Add 5 percent for ZX2 Spt Pkg.

1999 Contour, 4-cyl. & V-6

4d LX Sed	210	640	1,060	2,390	3,710	5,300
4d SE Sed	220	670	1,120	2,520	3,920	5,600
4d SVT Spt Sed (V-6 only)	420	1,260	2,100	4,730	7,350	10,500

1999 Taurus, V-6

4d LX Sed	250	760	1,260	2,840	4,410	6,300
4d SE Sed	260	780	1,300	2,930	4,550	6,500
4d SE Sta Wag	270	800	1,340	3,020	4,690	6,700

NOTE: Add 10 percent for Sport Pkg on SE Sed.

1999 Taurus, V-8

4d SHO Sed	440	1,320	2,200	4,950	7,700	11,000

1999 Crown Victoria, V-8

4d S Sed	290	860	1,440	3,240	5,040	7,200
4d Sed	300	900	1,500	3,380	5,250	7,500
4d LX Sed	320	960	1,600	3,600	5,600	8,000

NOTE: Add 5 percent for 41G Handling & Performance Pkg. Add 5 percent for natural gas-fueled Sed.

2000 Focus, 4-cyl.

4d LX Sed	190	560	940	2,120	3,290	4,700
4d SE Sed	200	590	980	2,210	3,430	4,900
4d ZTS Sed	210	640	1,060	2,390	3,710	5,300
4d SE Sta Wag	210	620	1,040	2,340	3,640	5,200
2d ZX3 HBk	200	610	1,020	2,300	3,570	5,100

2000 Escort, 4-cyl.

4d SE Sed	190	580	960	2,160	3,360	4,800
2d ZX2 Cpe	200	610	1,020	2,300	3,570	5,100

NOTE: Add 5 percent for ZX2 S/R pkg.

2000 Contour, 4-cyl. & V-6

4d SE Sed	220	670	1,120	2,520	3,920	5,600
4d Spt Sed (V-6 only)	250	740	1,240	2,790	4,340	6,200
4d SVT Sed (V-6 only)	420	1,260	2,100	4,730	7,350	10,500

2000 Taurus, V-6

4d LX Sed	250	760	1,260	2,840	4,410	6,300
4d SE Sed	260	780	1,300	2,930	4,550	6,500
4d SES Sed	260	790	1,320	2,970	4,620	6,600
4d SEL Sed	270	800	1,340	3,020	4,690	6,700
4d SE Sta Wag	270	800	1,340	3,020	4,690	6,700
4d SES Sta Wag	270	820	1,360	3,060	4,760	6,800

NOTE: Add 5 percent for flex-fuel SE Sed.

2000 Crown Victoria, V-8

4d S Sed	290	860	1,440	3,240	5,040	7,200
4d Sed	300	900	1,500	3,380	5,250	7,500
4d LX Sed	320	960	1,600	3,600	5,600	8,000

NOTE: Add 5 percent for 41G Handling & Performance Pkg. Add 5 percent for natural gas-fueled Sed.

2001 Focus, 4-cyl.

4d LX Sed	190	560	940	2,350	3,290	4,700
4d SE Sed	200	590	980	2,450	3,430	4,900
4d ZTS Sed	210	640	1,060	2,650	3,710	5,300
4d SE Sta Wag	210	620	1,040	2,600	3,640	5,200
2d ZX3 HBk	200	610	1,020	2,550	3,570	5,100

NOTE: Add 5 percent for Sony or Kona pkgs.

2001 Escort, 4-cyl.

2d ZX2 Cpe	200	610	1,020	2,550	3,570	5,100

NOTE: The 4d SE Sed was now available only to fleet service.

2001 Taurus, V-6

4d LX Sed	250	760	1,260	3,150	4,410	6,300
4d SE Sed	260	780	1,300	3,250	4,550	6,500
4d SES Sed	260	790	1,320	3,300	4,620	6,600
4d SEL Sed	270	800	1,340	3,350	4,690	6,700
4d SE Sta Wag	270	800	1,340	3,350	4,690	6,700

NOTE: Add 5 percent for flex-fuel SE Sed.

2001 Crown Victoria, V-8

4d S Sed	290	860	1,440	3,600	5,040	7,200
4d Sed	300	910	1,520	3,800	5,320	7,600
4d LX Sed	320	970	1,620	4,050	5,670	8,100

NOTE: Add 5 percent for 41G Handling & Performance Pkg. Add 5 percent for natural gas-fueled Sed.

2002 Focus, 4-cyl.

4d LX Sed	190	560	940	2,350	3,290	4,700
4d SE Sed	200	590	980	2,450	3,430	4,900
4d ZTS Sed	210	640	1,060	2,650	3,710	5,300
4d SE Sta Wag	210	620	1,040	2,600	3,640	5,200
4d ZTW Sta Wag	220	670	1,120	2,800	3,920	5,600
2d ZX3 HBk	200	610	1,020	2,550	3,570	5,100
4d ZX5 HBk	230	700	1,160	2,900	4,060	5,800
2d SVT HBk	270	820	1,360	3,400	4,760	6,800

NOTE: Add 5 percent for AdvanceTrac on all Z models.

2002 Escort, 4-cyl.

2d ZX2 Cpe	200	610	1,020	2,550	3,570	5,100
4d Sed	180	550	920	2,300	3,220	4,600

2002 Taurus, V-6

4d LX Sed	250	760	1,260	3,150	4,410	6,300
4d SE Sed	260	780	1,300	3,250	4,550	6,500
4d SES Sed	260	790	1,320	3,300	4,620	6,600
4d SEL Sed	270	800	1,340	3,350	4,690	6,700
4d SE Sta Wag	270	800	1,340	3,350	4,690	6,700
4d SEL Sta Wag	300	900	1,500	3,750	5,250	7,500

NOTE: Add 5 percent for Duratec V-6 (except SEL Sed).

2002 Crown Victoria, V-8

4d S Sed	290	860	1,440	3,600	5,040	7,200
4d S Ext Sed	300	900	1,500	3,750	5,250	7,500
4d Sed	300	910	1,520	3,800	5,320	7,600
4d LX Sed	320	970	1,620	4,050	5,670	8,100
4d LX Sport Sed	360	1,080	1,800	4,500	6,300	9,000

NOTE: Add 5 percent for 41G Handling & Performance Pkg.

THUNDERBIRD

1955 102" wb

Conv	2,360	7,080	11,800	26,550	41,300	59,000

NOTE: Add $1,800 for hardtop.

1956 102" wb

Conv	2,520	7,560	12,600	28,350	44,100	63,000

NOTE: Add $1,800 for hardtop. Add 10 percent for 312 engine.

1957 102" wb

Conv	2,600	7,800	13,000	29,250	45,500	65,000

NOTE: Add $1,800 for hardtop. Add 100 percent for supercharged V-8 (Code F). Add 25 percent for "T-Bird Special" V-8 (Code E).

1958 113" wb

2d HT	1,240	3,720	6,200	13,950	21,700	31,000
Conv	2,040	6,120	10,200	22,950	35,700	51,000

1959 113" wb

2d HT	1,200	3,600	6,000	13,500	21,000	30,000
Conv	2,000	6,000	10,000	22,500	35,000	50,000

NOTE: Add 30 percent for 430 engine option.

1960 113" wb

SR HT	1,360	4,080	6,800	15,300	23,800	34,000
2d HT	1,200	3,600	6,000	13,500	21,000	30,000
Conv	2,000	6,000	10,000	22,500	35,000	50,000

NOTE: Add 30 percent for 430 engine option Code J.

1961 113" wb

2d HT	1,000	3,000	5,000	11,250	17,500	25,000
Conv	1,440	4,320	7,200	16,200	25,200	36,000

NOTE: Add 25 percent for Indy Pace Car.

1962 113" wb

2d HT	1,000	3,000	5,000	11,250	17,500	25,000
2d Lan HT	1,040	3,120	5,200	11,700	18,200	26,000
Conv	1,400	4,200	7,000	15,750	24,500	35,000
Spt Rds	2,780	8,340	13,900	31,280	48,650	69,500

NOTE: Add 40 percent for M Series option.

1963 113" wb

2d HT	1,000	3,000	5,000	11,250	17,500	25,000
2d Lan HT	1,040	3,120	5,200	11,700	18,200	26,000
Conv	1,400	4,200	7,000	15,750	24,500	35,000
Spt Rds	2,820	8,460	14,100	31,730	49,350	70,500

NOTE: Add 12 percent for Monaco option. Add 40 percent for M Series option. Add 10 percent for 390-330 hp engine.

1964 113" wb

2d HT	840	2,520	4,200	9,450	14,700	21,000
2d Lan HT	880	2,640	4,400	9,900	15,400	22,000
Conv	1,320	3,960	6,600	14,850	23,100	33,000

NOTE: Add 10 percent for Tonneau convertible option. Add 30 percent for tonneau option and wire wheels.

1965 113" wb

2d HT	840	2,520	4,200	9,450	14,700	21,000
2d Lan HT	880	2,640	4,400	9,900	15,400	22,000
Conv	1,360	4,080	6,800	15,300	23,800	34,000

NOTE: Add 5 percent for Special Landau option.

1966 113" wb

2d HT Cpe	880	2,640	4,400	9,900	15,400	22,000
2d Twn Lan	960	2,880	4,800	10,800	16,800	24,000
2d HT Twn	920	2,760	4,600	10,350	16,100	23,000
Conv	1,400	4,200	7,000	15,750	24,500	35,000

NOTE: Add 20 percent for 428 engine.

1967 117" wb

4d Lan	600	1,800	3,000	6,750	10,500	15,000

1967 115" wb

2d Lan	640	1,920	3,200	7,200	11,200	16,000
2d HT	648	1,944	3,240	7,290	11,340	16,200

NOTE: Add 30 percent for 428 engine option.

1968 117" wb

4d Lan Sed	600	1,800	3,000	6,750	10,500	15,000

1968 115" wb

2d HT	620	1,860	3,100	6,980	10,850	15,500
2d Lan HT	628	1,884	3,140	7,070	10,990	15,700

NOTE: Add 30 percent for 429 engine option, Code K or 428 engine.

1969 117" wb

4d Lan	600	1,800	3,000	6,750	10,500	15,000

1969 115" wb

2d HT	620	1,860	3,100	6,980	10,850	15,500
2d Lan HT	630	1,880	3,140	7,070	10,990	15,700

1970 117" wb

4d Lan	600	1,800	3,000	6,750	10,500	15,000

1970 115" wb

2d HT	620	1,860	3,100	6,980	10,850	15,500
2d Lan HT	630	1,880	3,140	7,070	10,990	15,700

1971 117" wb

4d HT	600	1,800	3,000	6,750	10,500	15,000

1971 115" wb

2d HT	620	1,860	3,100	6,980	10,850	15,500
2d Lan HT	628	1,884	3,140	7,070	10,990	15,700

1972 120" wb

2d HT	580	1,740	2,900	6,530	10,150	14,500

NOTE: Add 20 percent for 460 engine option.

1973 120" wb

2d HT	560	1,680	2,800	6,300	9,800	14,000

1974 120" wb

2d HT	560	1,680	2,800	6,300	9,800	14,000

1975 120" wb

2d HT	472	1,416	2,360	5,310	8,260	11,800

1976 120" wb

2d HT	452	1,356	2,260	5,090	7,910	11,300

1977 114" wb

2d HT	364	1,092	1,820	4,100	6,370	9,100
2d Lan	368	1,104	1,840	4,140	6,440	9,200

1978 114" wb

2d HT	380	1,140	1,900	4,280	6,650	9,500
2d Twn Lan	420	1,260	2,100	4,730	7,350	10,500
2d Diamond Jubilee	520	1,560	2,600	5,850	9,100	13,000

NOTE: Add 5 percent for T-tops.

1979 V-8, 114" wb

2d HT	360	1,080	1,800	4,050	6,300	9,000
2d HT Lan	380	1,140	1,900	4,280	6,650	9,500
2d HT Heritage	400	1,200	2,000	4,500	7,000	10,000

NOTE: Add 5 percent for T-tops.

1980 V-8, 108" wb

2d Cpe	240	720	1,200	2,700	4,200	6,000
2d Twn Lan Cpe	252	756	1,260	2,840	4,410	6,300
2d Silver Anniv. Cpe	260	780	1,300	2,930	4,550	6,500

1981 V-8, 108" wb

2d Cpe	224	672	1,120	2,520	3,920	5,600
2d Twn Lan Cpe	232	696	1,160	2,610	4,060	5,800
2d Heritage Cpe	236	708	1,180	2,660	4,130	5,900

NOTE: Deduct 15 percent for 6-cyl.

1982 V-8, 108" wb

2d Cpe	232	696	1,160	2,610	4,060	5,800
2d Twn Lan Cpe	240	720	1,200	2,700	4,200	6,000
2d Heritage Cpe	248	744	1,240	2,790	4,340	6,200

NOTE: Deduct 15 percent for V-6.

1983 V-6

2d Cpe	364	1,092	1,820	4,100	6,370	9,100
2d Cpe Heritage	376	1,128	1,880	4,230	6,580	9,400

1983 V-8

2d Cpe	376	1,128	1,880	4,230	6,580	9,400
2d Cpe Heritage	392	1,176	1,960	4,410	6,860	9,800

1983 4-cyl.

2d Cpe Turbo	380	1,140	1,900	4,280	6,650	9,500

1984 V-6

2d Cpe	276	828	1,380	3,110	4,830	6,900
2d Cpe Elan	368	1,104	1,840	4,140	6,440	9,200
2d Cpe Fila	372	1,116	1,860	4,190	6,510	9,300

1984 V-8

2d Cpe	376	1,128	1,880	4,230	6,580	9,400
2d Cpe Elan	384	1,152	1,920	4,320	6,720	9,600
2d Cpe Fila	388	1,164	1,940	4,370	6,790	9,700

NOTE: Deduct 10 percent for V-6 non turbo.

1984 4-cyl.

2d Cpe Turbo	376	1,128	1,880	4,230	6,580	9,400

1985 V-8, 104" wb

2d Cpe	256	768	1,280	2,880	4,480	6,400
2d Elan Cpe	272	816	1,360	3,060	4,760	6,800
2d Fila Cpe	276	828	1,380	3,110	4,830	6,900

1985 4-cyl. Turbo

2d Cpe	360	1,080	1,800	4,050	6,300	9,000

NOTE: Deduct 10 percent for V-6 non-turbo. Add 5 percent for 30th Anv. Ed.

1986 104" wb

2d Cpe	256	768	1,280	2,880	4,480	6,400
2d Elan Cpe	264	792	1,320	2,970	4,620	6,600
2d Turbo Cpe	368	1,104	1,840	4,140	6,440	9,200

1987 V-6, 104" wb

2d Cpe	260	780	1,300	2,930	4,550	6,500
2d LX Cpe	264	792	1,320	2,970	4,620	6,600

1987 V-8, 104" wb

2d Cpe	360	1,080	1,800	4,050	6,300	9,000
2d Spt Cpe	368	1,104	1,840	4,140	6,440	9,200
2d LX Cpe	372	1,116	1,860	4,190	6,510	9,300

1987 4-cyl. Turbo

2d Cpe	368	1,104	1,840	4,140	6,440	9,200

1988 V-6

2d Cpe	180	540	900	2,030	3,150	4,500
2d LX Cpe	200	600	1,000	2,250	3,500	5,000

1988 V-8

2d Spt Cpe	220	660	1,100	2,480	3,850	5,500

1988 4-cyl. Turbo

2d Cpe	350	1,100	1,850	4,140	6,450	9,200

NOTE: Add 20 percent for V-8 where available.

1989 V-6

2d Cpe	272	816	1,360	3,060	4,760	6,800
2d LX Cpe	360	1,080	1,800	4,050	6,300	9,000
2d Sup Cpe	520	1,560	2,600	5,850	9,100	13,000

1990 V-6

2d Cpe	260	780	1,300	2,930	4,550	6,500
2d LX Cpe	360	1,080	1,800	4,050	6,300	9,000
2d Sup Cpe	520	1,560	2,600	5,850	9,100	13,000

NOTE: Add 10 percent for Anniversary model.

1991 V-6

2d Cpe	240	720	1,200	2,700	4,200	6,000
2d LX Cpe	260	780	1,300	2,930	4,550	6,500
2d Sup Cpe	340	1,020	1,700	3,830	5,950	8,500

1991 V-8

2d Cpe	360	1,080	1,800	4,050	6,300	9,000
2d LX Cpe	380	1,140	1,900	4,280	6,650	9,500

1992 V-6

2d Cpe	360	1,080	1,800	4,050	6,300	9,000
2d LX Cpe	368	1,104	1,840	4,140	6,440	9,200
2d Sup Cpe	380	1,140	1,900	4,280	6,650	9,500

1992 V-8

2d Cpe	364	1,092	1,820	4,100	6,370	9,100
2d Spt Cpe	392	1,176	1,960	4,410	6,860	9,800
2d LX Cpe	380	1,140	1,900	4,280	6,650	9,500

1993 V-6

2d LX Cpe	372	1,116	1,860	4,190	6,510	9,300
2d Sup Cpe	380	1,140	1,900	4,280	6,650	9,500

1993 V-8

2d LX Cpe	404	1,212	2,020	4,550	7,070	10,100

1994 V-6

2d LX Cpe	300	900	1,500	3,380	5,250	7,500
2d Sup Cpe	360	1,080	1,800	4,050	6,300	9,000

1994 V-8

2d LX Cpe	320	960	1,600	3,600	5,600	8,000

1995 V-6

2d LX Cpe	300	900	1,500	3,380	5,250	7,500
2d Sup Cpe	350	1,100	1,800	4,050	6,300	9,000

1995 V-8

2d LX Cpe	300	950	1,600	3,600	5,600	8,000

1996 V-6

2d LX Cpe	300	900	1,500	3,380	5,250	7,500

NOTE: Add 10 percent for V-8.

1997 V-6

2d LX Cpe	300	900	1,500	3,380	5,250	7,500

NOTE: Add 10 percent for V-8. Add 5 percent for Sport Pkg. Thunderbird production ceased until 2002.

2002 V-8

2d Conv	860	2,580	4,300	10,750	15,050	21,500

NOTE: Add $500 for removable HT. Add 10 percent for Nieman Marcus Ed.

MUSTANG

1964

| 2d HT | 1,020 | 3,060 | 5,100 | 11,480 | 17,850 | 25,500 |
| Conv | 1,520 | 4,560 | 7,600 | 17,100 | 26,600 | 38,000 |

NOTE: Deduct 20 percent for 6-cyl. Add 20 percent for Challenger Code "K" V-8. First Mustang introduced April 17, 1964 at N.Y. World's Fair. Add 20 percent for Indianapolis 500 pace car edition.

1965

2d HT	1,020	3,060	5,100	11,480	17,850	25,500
Conv	1,520	4,560	7,600	17,100	26,600	38,000
FBk	1,560	4,680	7,800	17,550	27,300	39,000

NOTE: Add 30 percent for 271 hp Hi-perf engine. Add 20 percent for "GT" Package. Add 10 percent for "original pony interior". Deduct 20 percent for 6-cyl.

1965 Shelby GT

| 350 FBk | 10,000 | 30,000 | 50,000 | 112,500 | 175,000 | 250,000 |

1966

2d HT	1,020	3,060	5,100	11,480	17,850	25,500
Conv	1,560	4,680	7,800	17,550	27,300	39,000
FBk	1,600	4,800	8,000	18,000	28,000	40,000

NOTE: Same as 1965.

1966 Shelby GT

| 350 FBk | 6,320 | 18,960 | 31,600 | 71,100 | 110,600 | 158,000 |
| 350H FBk | 6,620 | 19,860 | 33,100 | 74,480 | 115,850 | 165,500 |

1967

2d HT	940	2,820	4,700	10,580	16,450	23,500
Conv	1,600	4,800	8,000	18,000	28,000	40,000
FBk	1,640	4,920	8,200	18,450	28,700	41,000

NOTE: Same as 1964-65 plus. Add 10 percent for 390 cid V-8 (code "S"). Deduct 15 percent for 6-cyl.

1967 Shelby GT

| 350 FBk | 5,680 | 17,040 | 28,400 | 63,900 | 99,400 | 142,000 |
| 500 FBk | 6,600 | 19,800 | 33,000 | 74,250 | 115,500 | 165,000 |

1968

2d HT	940	2,820	4,700	10,580	16,450	23,500
Conv	1,400	4,200	7,000	15,750	24,500	35,000
FBk	1,360	4,080	6,800	15,300	23,800	34,000

NOTE: Same as 1964-67 plus. Add 10 percent for GT-390. Add 30 percent for 428 cid V-8 (code "R"). Add 15 percent for "California Special" trim. Add 200 percent for 135 Series.

1968 Shelby GT

350 Conv	5,520	16,560	27,600	62,100	96,600	138,000
350 FBk	4,200	12,600	21,000	47,250	73,500	105,000
500 Conv	6,880	20,640	34,400	77,400	120,400	172,000
500 FBk	5,520	16,560	27,600	62,100	96,600	138,000

NOTE: Add 35 percent for KR models.

1969

2d HT	900	2,700	4,500	10,130	15,750	22,500
Conv	1,300	3,900	6,500	14,630	22,750	32,500
FBk	1,240	3,720	6,200	13,950	21,700	31,000

NOTE: Deduct 20 percent for 6-cyl.

Mach 1	2,440	7,320	12,200	27,450	42,700	61,000
Boss 302	3,520	10,560	17,600	39,600	61,600	88,000
Boss 429	8,400	25,200	42,000	94,500	147,000	210,000
Grande	940	2,820	4,700	10,580	16,450	23,500

NOTE: Same as 1968; plus. Add 30 percent for Cobra Jet V-8. Add 40 percent for "Super Cobra Jet" engine.

1969 Shelby GT

350 Conv	5,240	15,720	26,200	58,950	91,700	131,000
350 FBk	3,920	11,760	19,600	44,100	68,600	98,000
500 Conv	6,600	19,800	33,000	74,250	115,500	165,000
500 FBk	5,240	15,720	26,200	58,950	91,700	131,000

1970

2d HT	820	2,460	4,100	9,230	14,350	20,500
Conv	1,220	3,660	6,100	13,730	21,350	30,500
FBk	1,160	3,480	5,800	13,050	20,300	29,000
Mach 1	2,240	6,720	11,200	25,200	39,200	56,000
Boss 302	3,320	9,960	16,600	37,350	58,100	83,000
Boss 429	8,200	24,600	41,000	92,250	143,500	205,000
Grande	940	2,820	4,700	10,580	16,450	23,500

NOTE: Add 30 percent for Cobra Jet V-8. Add 40 percent for "Super Cobra Jet". Deduct 20 percent for 6-cyl.

1970 Shelby GT

350 Conv	5,240	15,720	26,200	58,950	91,700	131,000
350 FBk	3,920	11,760	19,600	44,100	68,600	98,000
500 Conv	6,600	19,800	33,000	74,250	115,500	165,000
500 FBk	5,240	15,720	26,200	58,950	91,700	131,000

1971

2d HT	680	2,040	3,400	7,650	11,900	17,000
Grande	700	2,100	3,500	7,880	12,250	17,500
Conv	1,080	3,240	5,400	12,150	18,900	27,000
FBk	1,000	3,000	5,000	11,250	17,500	25,000
Mach 1	1,420	4,260	7,100	15,980	24,850	35,500
Boss 351	2,420	7,260	12,100	27,230	42,350	60,500

NOTE: Same as 1970. Deduct 20 percent for 6-cyl. Add 20 percent for HO option where available.

1972

2d HT	680	2,040	3,400	7,650	11,900	17,000
Grande	700	2,100	3,500	7,880	12,250	17,500
FBk	880	2,640	4,400	9,900	15,400	22,000
Mach 1	1,280	3,840	6,400	14,400	22,400	32,000
Conv	1,040	3,120	5,200	11,700	18,200	26,000

NOTE: Deduct 20 percent for 6-cyl. Add 20 percent for HO option where available.

1973

2d HT	660	1,980	3,300	7,430	11,550	16,500
Grande	680	2,040	3,400	7,650	11,900	17,000
FBk	840	2,520	4,200	9,450	14,700	21,000
Mach 1	1,240	3,720	6,200	13,950	21,700	31,000
Conv	1,000	3,000	5,000	11,250	17,500	25,000

1974 Mustang II, Mustang Four

HT Cpe	240	720	1,200	2,700	4,200	6,000
FBk	252	756	1,260	2,840	4,410	6,300
Ghia	252	756	1,260	2,840	4,410	6,300

1974 Mustang II, Six

HT Cpe	250	700	1,200	2,700	4,200	6,000
FBk	250	750	1,300	2,880	4,500	6,400
Ghia	250	750	1,300	2,880	4,500	6,400

1974 Mach 1, Six

FBk	400	1,150	1,900	4,280	6,650	9,500

1975 Mustang II

HT Cpe	250	700	1,200	2,700	4,200	6,000
FBk	250	750	1,250	2,840	4,400	6,300
Ghia	250	750	1,250	2,840	4,400	6,300

1975 Mustang II, Six

HT Cpe	250	750	1,200	2,750	4,250	6,100
FBk	250	750	1,300	2,880	4,500	6,400
Ghia	250	750	1,300	2,880	4,500	6,400
Mach 1	400	1,150	1,900	4,280	6,650	9,500

1975 Mustang II, V-8

HT Cpe	350	1,100	1,800	4,100	6,350	9,100
FBk Cpe	350	1,100	1,850	4,140	6,450	9,200
Ghia	400	1,150	1,900	4,280	6,650	9,500
Mach 1	400	1,250	2,100	4,730	7,350	10,500

1976 Mustang II, V-6

2d	252	756	1,260	2,840	4,410	6,300
3d 2 plus 2	256	768	1,280	2,880	4,480	6,400
2d Ghia	268	804	1,340	3,020	4,690	6,700

NOTE: Deduct 20 percent for 4-cyl. Add 20 percent for V-8. Add 20 percent for Cobra II.

1976 Mach 1, V-6

3d	360	1,080	1,800	4,050	6,300	9,000

1977 Mustang II, V-6

2d	260	780	1,300	2,930	4,550	6,500
3d 2 plus 2	268	804	1,340	3,020	4,690	6,700
2d Ghia	276	828	1,380	3,110	4,830	6,900

NOTE: Deduct 20 percent for 4-cyl. Add 30 percent for Cobra II option. Add 20 percent for V-8.

1977 Mach 1, V-6

2d	368	1,104	1,840	4,140	6,440	9,200

1978 Mustang II

Cpe	244	732	1,220	2,750	4,270	6,100
3d 2 plus 2	252	756	1,260	2,840	4,410	6,300
Ghia Cpe	256	768	1,280	2,880	4,480	6,400

1978 Mach 1, V-6

Cpe	360	1,080	1,800	4,050	6,300	9,000

NOTE: Add 20 percent for V-8. Add 30 percent for Cobra II option. Add 50 percent for King Cobra option. Deduct 20 percent for 4-cyl.

1979 V-6

2d Cpe	248	744	1,240	2,790	4,340	6,200
3d Cpe	252	756	1,260	2,840	4,410	6,300
2d Ghia Cpe	260	780	1,300	2,930	4,550	6,500
3d Ghia Cpe	264	792	1,320	2,970	4,620	6,600

NOTE: Add 30 percent for Pace Car package. Add 30 percent for Cobra option. Add 20 percent for V-8.

1980 6-cyl.

2d Cpe	212	636	1,060	2,390	3,710	5,300
2d HBk	216	648	1,080	2,430	3,780	5,400
2d Ghia Cpe	224	672	1,120	2,520	3,920	5,600
2d Ghia HBk	228	684	1,140	2,570	3,990	5,700

NOTE: Deduct 20 percent for 4-cyl. Add 30 percent for V-8.

1981 6-cyl.

2d S Cpe	196	588	980	2,210	3,430	4,900
2d Cpe	204	612	1,020	2,300	3,570	5,100
2d HBk	208	624	1,040	2,340	3,640	5,200
2d Ghia Cpe	208	624	1,040	2,340	3,640	5,200
2d Ghia HBk	212	636	1,060	2,390	3,710	5,300

NOTE: Deduct 20 percent for 4-cyl. Add 35 percent for V-8.

1982 4-cyl.

2d L Cpe	180	540	900	2,030	3,150	4,500
2d GL Cpe	184	552	920	2,070	3,220	4,600
2d GL HBk	188	564	940	2,120	3,290	4,700
2d GLX Cpe	196	588	980	2,210	3,430	4,900
2d GLX HBk	200	600	1,000	2,250	3,500	5,000

1982 6-cyl.

2d L Cpe	196	588	980	2,210	3,430	4,900
2d GL Cpe	200	600	1,000	2,250	3,500	5,000
2d GL HBk	204	612	1,020	2,300	3,570	5,100
2d GLX Cpe	212	636	1,060	2,390	3,710	5,300
2d GLX HBk	216	648	1,080	2,430	3,780	5,400

1982 V-8

2d GT HBk	390	1,170	1,950	4,390	6,830	9,750

1983 4-cyl.

2d L Cpe	184	552	920	2,070	3,220	4,600
2d GL Cpe	188	564	940	2,120	3,290	4,700
2d GL HBk	196	588	980	2,210	3,430	4,900
2d GLX Cpe	200	600	1,000	2,250	3,500	5,000
2d GLX HBk	204	612	1,020	2,300	3,570	5,100

1983 6-cyl.

2d GL Cpe	204	612	1,020	2,300	3,570	5,100
2d GL HBk	208	624	1,040	2,340	3,640	5,200
2d GLX Cpe	216	648	1,080	2,430	3,780	5,400
2d GLX HBk	220	660	1,100	2,480	3,850	5,500
2d GLX Conv	300	900	1,500	3,380	5,250	7,500

NOTE: Add 30 percent for V-8.

1983 V-8

2d GT HBk	390	1,170	1,950	4,390	6,830	9,750
2d GT Conv	440	1,330	2,220	5,000	7,770	11,100

1984 4-cyl.

2d L Cpe	188	564	940	2,120	3,290	4,700
2d L HBk	192	576	960	2,160	3,360	4,800
2d LX Cpe	192	576	960	2,160	3,360	4,800
2d LX HBk	196	588	980	2,210	3,430	4,900
2d GT Turbo HBk	250	760	1,260	2,840	4,410	6,300
2d GT Turbo Conv	290	880	1,460	3,290	5,110	7,300

1984 V-6

2d L Cpe	192	576	960	2,160	3,360	4,800
2d L HBk	196	588	980	2,210	3,430	4,900
2d LX Cpe	196	588	980	2,210	3,430	4,900
2d LX HBk	200	600	1,000	2,250	3,500	5,000
LX 2d Conv	300	900	1,500	3,380	5,250	7,500

1984 V-8

2d L HBk	200	600	1,000	2,250	3,500	5,000
2d LX Cpe	204	612	1,020	2,300	3,570	5,100
2d LX HBk	204	612	1,020	2,300	3,570	5,100
2d LX Conv	340	1,020	1,700	3,830	5,950	8,500
2d GT HBk	390	1,170	1,950	4,390	6,830	9,750
2d GT Conv	440	1,330	2,220	5,000	7,770	11,100

NOTE: Add 20 percent for 20th Anniversary Edition. Add 40 percent for SVO Model.

1985 4-cyl.

2d LX	196	588	980	2,210	3,430	4,900
2d LX HBk	200	600	1,000	2,250	3,500	5,000
2d SVO Turbo	280	840	1,400	3,150	4,900	7,000

1985 V-6

2d LX	204	612	1,020	2,300	3,570	5,100
2d LX HBk	208	624	1,040	2,340	3,640	5,200
2d LX Conv	396	1,188	1,980	4,460	6,930	9,900

1985 V-8

2d LX	220	660	1,100	2,480	3,850	5,500
2d LX HBk	224	672	1,120	2,520	3,920	5,600
2d LX Conv	420	1,260	2,100	4,730	7,350	10,500
2d GT HBk	400	1,200	2,000	4,500	7,000	10,000
2d GT Conv	560	1,680	2,800	6,300	9,800	14,000

NOTE: Add 40 percent for SVO Model.

1986 Mustang, 4-cyl.

2d Cpe	200	600	1,000	2,250	3,500	5,000
2d HBk	200	600	1,000	2,250	3,500	5,000
2d Conv	380	1,140	1,900	4,280	6,650	9,500
2d Turbo HBk	280	840	1,400	3,150	4,900	7,000

1986 V-8

2d HBk	240	720	1,200	2,700	4,200	6,000
2d Conv	420	1,260	2,100	4,730	7,350	10,500
2d GT HBk	400	1,200	2,000	4,500	7,000	10,000
2d GT Conv	560	1,680	2,800	6,300	9,800	14,000

NOTE: Add 40 percent for SVO Model.

1987 4-cyl.

2d LX Sed	200	600	1,000	2,250	3,500	5,000
2d LX HBk	204	612	1,020	2,300	3,570	5,100
2d LX Conv	360	1,080	1,800	4,050	6,300	9,000

1987 V-8

2d LX Sed	200	600	1,000	2,250	3,500	5,000
2d LX HBk	204	612	1,020	2,300	3,570	5,100
2d LX Conv	424	1,272	2,120	4,770	7,420	10,600
2d GT HBk	390	1,160	1,940	4,370	6,790	9,700
2d GT Conv	560	1,680	2,800	6,300	9,800	14,000

1988 V-6

2d LX Sed	160	480	800	1,800	2,800	4,000
2d LX HBk	168	504	840	1,890	2,940	4,200
2d LX Conv	360	1,080	1,800	4,050	6,300	9,000

1988 V-8

2d LX Sed	200	600	1,000	2,250	3,500	5,000
2d LX HBk	220	660	1,100	2,480	3,850	5,500
2d LX Conv	400	1,200	2,000	4,500	7,000	10,000
2d GT HBk	380	1,140	1,900	4,280	6,650	9,500
2d GT Conv	560	1,680	2,800	6,300	9,800	14,000

1989 4-cyl.

2d LX Cpe	180	540	900	2,030	3,150	4,500
2d LX HBk	188	564	940	2,120	3,290	4,700
2d LX Conv	420	1,260	2,100	4,730	7,350	10,500

1989 V-8

2d LX Spt Cpe	236	708	1,180	2,660	4,130	5,900
2d LX Spt HBk	240	720	1,200	2,700	4,200	6,000
2d LX Spt Conv	560	1,680	2,800	6,300	9,800	14,000
2d GT HBk	388	1,164	1,940	4,370	6,790	9,700
2d GT Conv	680	2,040	3,400	7,650	11,900	17,000

1990 4-cyl.

2d LX	184	552	920	2,070	3,220	4,600
2d LX HBk	192	576	960	2,160	3,360	4,800
2d LX Conv	380	1,140	1,900	4,280	6,650	9,500

1990 V-8

2d LX Spt	240	720	1,200	2,700	4,200	6,000
2d LX HBk Spt	248	744	1,240	2,790	4,340	6,200
2d LX Conv Spt	520	1,560	2,600	5,850	9,100	13,000
2d GT HBk	400	1,200	2,000	4,500	7,000	10,000
2d GT Conv	560	1,680	2,800	6,300	9,800	14,000

1991 4-cyl.

2d LX Cpe	180	540	900	2,030	3,150	4,500
2d LX HBk	200	600	1,000	2,250	3,500	5,000
2d LX Conv	360	1,080	1,800	4,050	6,300	9,000

1991 V-8

2d LX Cpe	220	660	1,100	2,480	3,850	5,500
2d LX HBk	240	720	1,200	2,700	4,200	6,000
2d LX Conv	400	1,200	2,000	4,500	7,000	10,000
2d GT HBk	380	1,140	1,900	4,280	6,650	9,500
2d GT Conv	540	1,620	2,700	6,080	9,450	13,500

1992 4-cyl.

2d LX Cpe	200	600	1,000	2,250	3,500	5,000
2d LX HBk	220	660	1,100	2,480	3,850	5,500
2d LX Conv	400	1,200	2,000	4,500	7,000	10,000

1992 V-8

2d LX Sed	360	1,080	1,800	4,050	6,300	9,000
2d LX HBk	380	1,140	1,900	4,280	6,650	9,500
2d LX Conv	520	1,560	2,600	5,850	9,100	13,000
2d GT HBk	420	1,260	2,100	4,730	7,350	10,500
2d GT Conv	600	1,800	3,000	6,750	10,500	15,000

NOTE: Add 5 percent for LX convertible Summer Special edition released mid model year.

1993 4-cyl.

2d LX Cpe	220	660	1,100	2,480	3,850	5,500
2d LX HBk	224	672	1,120	2,520	3,920	5,600
2d LX Conv	408	1,224	2,040	4,590	7,140	10,200

1993 V-8

2d LX Cpe	360	1,080	1,800	4,050	6,300	9,000
2d LX HBk	368	1,104	1,840	4,140	6,440	9,200
2d LX Conv	552	1,656	2,760	6,210	9,660	13,800
2d GT HBk	400	1,200	2,000	4,500	7,000	10,000
2d GT Conv	620	1,860	3,100	6,980	10,850	15,500

1993 Cobra

2d HBk	700	2,100	3,500	7,880	12,250	17,500

NOTE: Add 40 percent for Code R.

1994 V-6

2d Cpe	320	960	1,600	3,600	5,600	8,000
2d Conv	440	1,320	2,200	4,950	7,700	11,000

1994 GT, V-8

2d GT Cpe	420	1,260	2,100	4,730	7,350	10,500
2d GT Conv	480	1,440	2,400	5,400	8,400	12,000

1994 Cobra, V-8

2d Cpe	560	1,680	2,800	6,300	9,800	14,000
2d Conv	640	1,920	3,200	7,200	11,200	16,000

1995 V-6

2d Cpe	300	950	1,600	3,600	5,600	8,000
2d Conv	450	1,300	2,200	4,950	7,700	11,000

1995 V-8

2d GTS Cpe	400	1,200	2,000	4,500	7,000	10,000
2d GT Cpe	400	1,250	2,100	4,730	7,350	10,500
2d GT Conv	500	1,450	2,400	5,400	8,400	12,000
2d Cobra Cpe	550	1,700	2,800	6,300	9,800	14,000
2d Cobra Conv	650	1,900	3,200	7,200	11,200	16,000

1996 V-6

2d Cpe	300	950	1,600	3,600	5,600	8,000
2d Conv	450	1,300	2,200	4,950	7,700	11,000

1996 V-8

2d GT Cpe	400	1,250	2,100	4,730	7,350	10,500
2d GT Conv	500	1,450	2,400	5,400	8,400	12,000
2d Cobra Cpe	550	1,700	2,800	6,300	9,800	14,000
2d Cobra Conv	650	1,900	3,200	7,200	11,200	16,000

1997 V-6

2d Cpe	320	960	1,600	3,600	5,600	8,000
2d Conv	440	1,320	2,200	4,950	7,700	11,000

1997 V-8

2d GT Cpe	420	1,260	2,100	4,730	7,350	10,500
2d GT Conv	480	1,440	2,400	5,400	8,400	12,000
2d Cobra Cpe	560	1,680	2,800	6,300	9,800	14,000
2d Cobra Conv	640	1,920	3,200	7,200	11,200	16,000

1998 V-6

2d Cpe	320	960	1,600	3,600	5,600	8,000
2d Conv	440	1,320	2,200	4,950	7,700	11,000

1998 V-8

2d GT Cpe	420	1,260	2,100	4,730	7,350	10,500
2d GT Conv	480	1,440	2,400	5,400	8,400	12,000
2d Cobra Cpe	560	1,680	2,800	6,300	9,800	14,000
2d Cobra Conv	640	1,920	3,200	7,200	11,200	16,000

NOTE: Add 10 percent for SVT Pkg.

1999 V-6

2d Cpe	320	960	1,600	3,600	5,600	8,000
2d Conv	440	1,320	2,200	4,950	7,700	11,000

1999 V-8

2d GT Cpe	420	1,260	2,100	4,730	7,350	10,500
2d GT Conv	480	1,440	2,400	5,400	8,400	12,000
2d SVT Cobra Cpe	580	1,740	2,900	6,530	10,150	14,500
2d SVT Cobra Conv	660	1,980	3,300	7,430	11,550	16,500

NOTE: Add 10 percent for 35th Anv Pkg on GT models.

2000 V-6

2d Cpe	320	970	1,620	3,650	5,670	8,100
2d Conv	440	1,330	2,220	5,000	7,770	11,100

2000 V-8

2d GT Cpe	430	1,280	2,140	4,820	7,490	10,700
2d GT Conv	490	1,460	2,440	5,490	8,540	12,200
2d SVT Cobra R Cpe (300 built)	2,400	7,200	12,000	27,000	42,000	60,000

NOTE: Cobra SVT coupe and convertible not available as 2000 models.

2001 V-6

2d Cpe	320	970	1,620	4,050	5,670	8,100
2d Conv	440	1,330	2,220	5,550	7,770	11,100

2001 V-8

2d GT Cpe	430	1,280	2,140	5,350	7,490	10,700
2d GT Conv	490	1,460	2,440	6,100	8,540	12,200
2d Cobra Cpe	660	1,980	3,300	8,250	11,550	16,500
2d Cobra Conv	700	2,100	3,500	8,750	12,250	17,500
2d GT Bullitt Cpe	960	2,880	4,800	10,800	16,800	24,000

2002 V-6

2d Cpe	320	970	1,620	4,050	5,670	8,100
2d Conv	440	1,330	2,220	5,550	7,770	11,100

NOTE: Add 5 percent for Sport Appearance pkg.

2002 V-8

2d GT Cpe	430	1,280	2,140	5,350	7,490	10,700
2d GT Conv	490	1,460	2,440	6,100	8,540	12,200

NOTE: A revised Cobra was introduced mid-model year as a 2003 model.

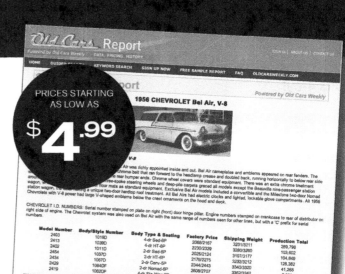